A Richard Wright Bibliography

Fifty Years of Criticism and Commentary, 1933–1982

Compiled by
Keneth Kinnamon
*with the help of Joseph Benson,
Michel Fabre, and Craig W~~~er*

Bibliographies and Indexes in Afro-American and African Studies, Number 19

GREENWOOD PRESS
New York • Westport, Connecticut • London

Library of Congress Cataloging-in-Publication Data

Kinnamon, Keneth.
  A Richard Wright bibliography.

  (Bibliographies and indexes in Afro-American and
African studies, ISSN 0742-6925 ; no. 19)
    1. Wright, Richard, 1908-1960—Bibliography.
I. Title. II. Series.
Z8986.323.K56 1988 [PS3545.R815] 016.813'52 87-27831
ISBN 0-313-25411-7 (lib. bdg. : alk. paper)

British Library Cataloguing in Publication Data is available.

Library of Congress Catalog Card Number: 87-27831
ISBN: 0-313-25411-7
ISSN: 0742-6925

First published in 1988

Greenwood Press, Inc.
88 Post Road West, Westport, Connecticut 06881

Printed in the United States of America

The paper used in this book complies with the
Permanent Paper Standard issued by the National
Information Standards Organization (Z39.48-1984).

10 9 8 7 6 5 4 3 2 1

A
Richard Wright
Bibliography

Recent Titles in
Bibliographies and Indexes in Afro-American and African Studies

Wole Soyinka: A Bibliography of Primary and Secondary Sources
James Gibbs, Ketu H. Katrak, and Henry Louis Gates, Jr., compilers

Afro-American Demography and Urban Issues: A Bibliography
R. A. Obudho and Jeannine B. Scott, compilers

Afro-American Reference: An Annotated Bibliography of Selected Resources
Nathaniel Davis, compiler and editor

The Afro-American Short Story: A Comprehensive, Annotated Index
with Selected Commentaries
Preston M. Yancy, compiler

Black Labor in America, 1865-1983: A Selected Annotated Bibliography
Joseph Wilson, compiler and editor

Martin Luther King, Jr.: An Annotated Bibliography
Sherman E. Pyatt, compiler

Blacks in the Humanities, 1750-1984: A Selected Annotated Bibliography
Donald Franklin Joyce, compiler

The Black Family in the United States: A Revised, Updated, Selectively
Annotated Bibliography
Lenwood G. Davis, compiler

Black American Families, 1965-1984: A Classified, Selectively Annotated
Bibliography
Walter R. Allen, editor

Index to Poetry by Black American Women
Dorothy Hilton Chapman, compiler

Black American Health: An Annotated Bibliography
Mitchell F. Rice and Woodrow Jones, Jr., compilers

Ann Allen Shockley: An Annotated Primary and Secondary Bibliography
Rita B. Dandridge, compiler

Index to Afro-American Reference Resources
Rosemary M. Stevenson, compiler

To the Memory of

Lucile Kinnamon

Contents

Preface

This book is a bibliography of 13,117 annotated items published from 1933 to 1982 pertaining to Richard Wright. The most comprehensive such list ever compiled for any American writer, it is the result of thirteen years of effort, during which I had substantial help at various stages from Joseph Benson, Michel Fabre, and Craig Werner. What was originally projected as a manuscript of moderate length to be completed late in 1975 has grown twelvefold to reach its present size.

In its earlier years the project was a relatively modest joint venture by Benson, Fabre, and me. When the Beinecke Rare Book and Manuscript Library at Yale University acquired Wright's papers from his widow early in 1976, the task took on much larger dimensions. The Richard Wright Archive at the Beinecke includes massive collections of clippings of reviews and news items about Wright, often without indication of dates or even sources and almost always without page numbers. The process of identifying, locating, and securing full bibliographical information for the thousands of items at Yale proved to be lengthy, as did the continuing search for the thousands of items not there collected. By this time Craig Werner was serving as my research assistant. As the project continued through the seventies, Benson and Fabre yielded more and more of the work to me, assisted by Werner. I have performed almost all of the work during the last five years: adding entries, editing all annotations, assembling and typing the manuscript, compiling the index, and proofreading the whole more than once. In my card file of items, containing many duplicates, 73.4% of the

annotations are by me, 13.1% by Benson, 10.2% by Werner, 2.7% by Fabre, and .6% by Yoshinobu Hakutani and Toru Kiuchi, who have generously permitted the inclusion here of the items in their previously published lists of Japanese scholarship on Wright.

I hope that this book will expand current notions of what constitutes a total literary reputation, foreign as well as domestic, provincial as well as metropolitan. A truly comprehensive record must include all books, articles, reviews, notes, news items, publishers' catalogs and promotional materials, dissertations, theses, encyclopedias and biographical dictionaries, handbooks and study guides, headnotes and endnotes in anthologies, bibliographies, library reports, best seller charts, the Index Translationum, playbills, advertisements, editorials, dust jackets, radio transcripts, published letters, interviews--in short, all published mentions of the author or his work in all the languages in which those mentions appear. In this bibliography the literary researcher will find items from the Bad Axe, Michigan, Huron Daily Tribune and the Bulletin of the Kyushu Dental College as well as The New York Times and PMLA. And since Wright's career, more than that of most major authors, engaged race, history, politics, sociology, and psychology as well as belles-lettres in a thoroughly international context, scholars in those fields can also encounter much of interest between these covers.

Problems of size and bibliographic control have prevented inclusion of items from the last five years, but

Wright continues to be the subject of much scholarly and popular interest. In 1984 appeared Richard Macksey and Frank E. Moorer's compilation, Richard Wright: A Collection of Critical Essays, which includes a substantial introduction and reprints of fourteen classic studies as well as new articles by Horace Porter and Maria K. Mootry. In the following year Michel Fabre published one of the half-dozen indispensable books in the field, The World of Richard Wright, consisting of an even dozen of his essays from two decades, a four-part appendix, and a fascinating introduction tracing changes in Fabre's critical approach as well as Wright's career. Among recent books on more general subjects that include important treatments of Wright are Houston Baker's Blues, Ideology, and Afro-American Literature, Michael Cooke's Afro-American Literature in the Twentieth Century, Melvin Dixon's Ride Out the Wilderness, and Trudier Harris's Exorcising Blackness. Periodical articles and dissertations continue to appear at a brisk pace (the former including work by Robert Butler, Ralph Ellison, Keneth Kinnamon, John McCluskey, and Janice Thaddeus), but the great event in Wright studies in recent years was undoubtedly the symposium on "Mississippi's Native Son" organized by Maryemma Graham and held at the University of Mississippi on 21-23 November 1985, fourteen years after the historic Iowa conference. The first published result of this highly successful enterprise was the special Wright issue of Callaloo, edited by Graham, appearing in the summer of 1986. In December of the same year the Hollywood film version of Native Son was released with considerable fanfare. Looking to the future, I can mention my collection of new essays on Native Son with contributions by Houston Baker, Henry Louis Gates, Trudier Harris, John Reilly, and Craig Werner, to be submitted for publication before the end of 1987. Also, Michel Fabre and I plan to collect interviews with Wright for publication. Other Wright scholars, old and new, are busy with various other projects. Much remains to be done, especially in textual studies. The bibliographer of the second half century of commentary on Wright, 1983 to 2032, will have a considerable task to perform.

The user of A Richard Wright Bibliography should keep in mind the following points.

Scope

Although the original goal was to include every mention of Wright in print, some practical compromises had to be made. It seemed pointless to list all newspaper advertisements of the stage and film versions of Native Son for each performance or showing. In general, advertisements for books, plays, the film, and lectures by Wright have been included when they have been encountered in the Yale collection or while searching newspapers and periodicals for reviews and news items, but no systematic effort was made to locate all of them. Many hundreds of brief mentions of Wright in treatments of other authors have been caught in the wide net I have cast, but surely many others have slipped through its meshes. Domestic and foreign newspaper files listed in Newspapers in Microform and available through interlibrary loan have been searched for relevant material, but it was seldom feasible to consult newsprint collections outside the major research libraries in the United States.

Otherwise, I think that we have come close to being comprehensive. Items are included from Algeria, Argentina, Austria, Belgium, Brazil, Bulgaria, Canada, Chile, China, Costa Rica, Colombia, Cuba, Czechoslovakia, Denmark, Egypt, Ecuador, England, Finland, France, Germany, Ghana, Haiti, Hungary, India, Indonesia, Ireland, Israel, Italy, Jamaica, Japan, Lebanon, Martinique, Mexico, Morocco, Nigeria, Norway, Poland, Portugal, Puerto Rico, Scotland, Senegal, South Africa, the Soviet Union, Spain, Sweden, Switzerland, Syria, Trinidad, Turkey, the United States, Uruguay, Venezuela, Yugoslavia, and Zaire. During the first half century of its development Wright's reputation acquired global dimensions.

Arrangement

The arrangement of entries is chronological by year. Within each year items are numbered and alphabetized by author. When the author is unknown, an entry is alphabetized under "Anon." Alphabetization in both the entries and the index follows the letter-by-letter system. Cross references cite the year and item number. Thus 1951.186 refers to the entry numbered 186 in the year 1951.

Entries

Each entry consists of bibliographical information followed by annotation provided by Kinnamon, Benson, Werner, Fabre, or, in the case of most Japanese items, Hakutani and Kiuchi. All reprintings, partial or full, are indicated in or immediately following the annotation.

Items in Germanic and Romance languages have been annotated from the originals by me or one of my three collaborators. The procedure for items beyond our linguistic competence was to annotate from written or tape-recorded translations, but in each case one of us saw the original (except for the Hakutani and Kiuchi items). The few items appearing in other lists but eluding our search have been omitted. This method should assure that no ghost items appear in A Richard Wright Bibliography.

Index

The index is uncommonly full. In addition to titles of books and names of real and fictional persons, I have included titles of Wright's short stories, poems, and essays, places significant in Wright's career, organizations, newspapers and periodicals, important literary terminology (e.g., characterization, naturalism, style, symbolism), and a few miscellaneous categories (e.g., bibliographies, communism and communists, interviews with Wright, photographs of Wright). For the sake of users interested in a particular book by Wright, an asterisk preceding an item number in the index indicates special importance.

Many scholarly debts are incurred in a project of this nature and magnitude. Like most bibliographies, this one builds on earlier compilations. Together with other "Wrightians" over the years, we have benefited from the labor of such scholars as Jackson Bryer (1960.126), Donald Gibson (1969.107), and, especially, John Reilly (1971.260; 1978.208, 209). One should also mention dissertations by Moylan C. Mills (1974.131), Jerry Ward (1979.274), Catherine Daniels Hurst (1980.128), and Kandi Baba Kumasi (1981.78). Stefania Piccinato's exemplary bibliography of Afro-American literature in Italy (1979. 198) contains well over one hundred items on Wright.

We are grateful for institutional support received from the University of Illinois, the University of Arkansas, North Carolina Agricultural and Technical State University, the University of Mississippi, the University of Wisconsin, and the University of Paris III. Scores of librarians have provided cheerful and expert help at many libraries, both in person and through interlibrary loan. Without access to the great collections of the University of Illinois Library and the Yale University Library, a work of this scope would have been impossible.

Many individuals brought items to our attention, provided translations, answered queries, helped with proofreading and indexing, or offered encouragement: Masayuki Akiyama, Trudy Atkins, Richard K. Barksdale, Faith Berry, Curtis Blaylock, Rosa Bobia, Margaret Bolsterli, Paula Brickey, Isaac Brumfield, Robert Cochran, Howard Cole, Larry Danielson, the late Richard Beale Davis, Rasio Dunatov, John Dussinger, Harry Finestone, Benjamin Franklin Fisher IV, Ralph Fisher, Chester Fontenot, Maurice Friedman, Paul Gaeng, Samuel Garren, Ronald Gottesman, Yoshinobu Hakutani, Robert Halsband, Anna Hantz, Jeff Hendricks, Steve P. Hill, Jan Hillegas, Emina Huang, Geoff King, Toru Kiuchi, Joan Klein, Yuji Kobayashi, Missy Dehn Kubitschek, Phyllis Lang, Robert T. Levine, Moylan C. Mills, Satya Mohanty, Robert G. O'Meally, June Pachuta, Bob Patel, Ruth Prigozy, Terri Randall, David Ransel, Willi Real, John Reilly, Yang Renjing, David Rogers, Marjorie Rudolph, Amritjit Singh, Werner Sollors, Olivia Sordo, Stuart M. Sperry, Karen Stauffacher, Rosemary Stevenson, Jack Stillinger, Ethel Taylor, Johnny E. Tolliver, Benjamin Uroff, Leo Van Scyoc, Leon Waldoff, Janasdan M. Waghmare, Paul Weichsel, Charles Weir, Joe Weixlmann, J. L. Williams, Xing Xiao-ming, Chunjian Xue, Alene Young, and Qin Zhou.

Like all who worked on Afro-American topics at Yale in the seventies, my collaborators and I cherished the hospitality, encouragement, and good cheer dispensed by the late Charles T. Davis. As Master of Calhoun College, he made its gracious guest suite available to us on several occasions. I must also single out for special mention my research assistant David Strain, whose skill with word processors and sustained application of it were invaluable in preparing camera-ready copy of this book, and my colleague Claude Faulkner, who devoted three weeks to the tedious task of helping me to proofread the index. Finally, I wish to acknowledge gratefully the help of my sons and wife. Ted worked with me for several days on Wright's scrapbooks at Yale, Louis checked some items in the Newspaper Collection of the New York Public Library, and John mowed the yard. Paquita Kinnamon has not only lived with my intense interest in Wright since it began in 1962, but she has also traveled to New Haven twice and worked by my side in the Beinecke. I owe more to her than to anyone.

Abbreviations

W	Richard Wright
AH	American Hunger
BB	Black Boy
BP	Black Power
CC	The Color Curtain
EM	Eight Men
LD	The Long Dream
LT	Lawd Today
NS	Native Son
O	The Outsider
PS	Pagan Spain
SH	Savage Holiday
TMBV	12 Million Black Voices
UTC	Uncle Tom's Children
WML	White Man, Listen!

BIBLIOGRAPHY

1933

1. Anon. "Open Forum."
   Mimeographed announcement of a lecture by W on "The Literature of the Negro" sponsored by the Chicago John Reed Club on 7 September at 312 State Street.

1934

1. Anon. "'Langston Hughes' a Lecture by Richard Wright Negro Poet of Chicago." Mimeographed announcement of a lecture by W on 23 November sponsored by the John Reed Club of Indianapolis.

2. Anon. "Midwest Club News." Left Front, 1 (May-June), 21.
   Cites W's talk on "Revolutionary Negro Poetry" to the John Reed Club of Indianapolis.

3. Anon. "Our Contributors." Left Front, 1 (January-February), 20.
   Identifies W as "a young Negro whose first published work appears here."

4. Johns, Orrick. "The John Reed Clubs Meet." New Masses, 13 (30 October), 25-26.
   Reports on the second national conference of the clubs and mentions W as a "Negro poet, impressive for his quiet gravity, a day-to-day worker for the John Reed Club of Chicago, who nevertheless finds time to write and to serve as an editor on Left Front" (p. 25).

5. Tell, Waldo. "Left Front . . . The Anvil . . . Blast . . . Dynamo." Partisan Review, 1 (February-March), 60-63.
   Reviews four little magazines on the left, noting W's "Rest for the Weary" and "A Red Love Note" as revealing "genuine feeling and potential power." But "they are not poetry" (p. 61).

1935

1. Anon. "Call for an American Writers' Congress." New Masses, 14 (22 January), 20.
   Lists W as one of the sixty-four early signers.

2. Anon. Untitled note. The New Talent, No. 10 (October-December), p. 29.
   Reports that W was awarded second prize in an essay contest conducted by The New Talent and James Neill Northe.

3. Anon. "Writers' Group."
   Leaflet announcement of an appearance by W on 21 December to "recite and

. . . give a short talk on certain interesting aspects of poetry."

4. Bulliet, C. J. "Bulliet's Artless Comment." The Chicago Daily News (26 January), p. 19.
   Contains a letter by W protesting the treatment of the Chicago John Reed Club by Bulliet, an art critic. Bulliet comments briefly on the matter.

5. Calmer, Alan. "A New Period in American Leftwing Literature." International Literature, No. 7 (July), pp. 73-78.
   Reports on the American Writers' Congress and the formation of the League of American Writers, mentioning W's presence and participation.

6. Clay, Eugene. "The Negro and American Literature." International Literature, No. 6 (June), pp. 77-89.
   Revised and expanded version of 1935.7. Includes a section on "Richard Wright, Young Negro Poet" analyzing "Everywhere Burning Waters Rise" and praising "I Have Seen Black Hands." "Rest for the Weary" and "A Red Love Note" derive too directly from Langston Hughes, but generally W is a good poet who "has quickly achieved a surer mastery of technique and image association" (p. 85).

7. _____. "The Negro in Recent American Literature," in American Writers Congress. Ed. by Henry Hart. New York: International Publishers, pp. 145-153.
   Contains a brief discussion of W's poetry praising its simplicity and lack of racialism. "I Have Seen Black Hands is admittedly one of the finest poems that has appeared in the New Masses" (p. 151).

8. Hart, Henry, ed. American Writers Congress. New York: International Publishers, pp. 12, 178-179, 188.
   Lists W as one of the callers of the Congress, quotes his remarks in "Discussion and Proceedings," and lists him as a member of the National Council.
   Partially reprinted: 1971.158.

9. Hicks, Granville, Michael Gold, Isidor Schneider, Joseph North, Paul Peters, and Alan Calmer. "Contributors," in their Proletarian Literature in the United States: An Anthology. New York: International Publishers, pp. 381-384.
   Identifies W as "a young Negro poet of Chicago's South Side."

1936

1. Anon. "Delegates at Negro Parley to

Speak Here." Champaign-Urbana (Ill.) News-Gazette (11 March), p. 12.
Announces that W, "colored," is to speak at the Salem Baptist Church on the National Negro Congress.

2. Anon. "Expect Next Literary Renaissance to Come from Chicago Group." Unidentified Associated Negro Press clipping.
Article on the Southside Writers' Group stating that W is revising a novel.

3. Anon. "Mass Meeting."
Mimeographed announcement of a speech by W on "What Prospects National Negro Congress?" at the Salem Baptist Church in Champaign, Illinois, on 15 March.

4. Anon. "Negro Meeting Sunday 3 P. M." The Urbana (Ill.) Evening Courier (14 March), p. 3.
Announces a meeting to report on the National Negro Congress and to organize a local council. W, identified as a "Chicago Negro attorney," will appear.

5. Anon. "Negroes Will Hold Mass Meeting Today." The University of Illinois Daily Illini (15 March), p. 3.
Announces a meeting on the National Negro Congress at the Salem Baptist Church in Champaign with W, "prominent Negro writer," as a speaker.

6. Anon. "Nesbitt Elected President of Negro Council in Meeting." The Urbana (Ill.) Evening Courier (17 March), p. 7.
Reports that W was the main speaker at this meeting to establish a local council of the National Negro Congress.

7. Anon. "Young Writer Claims Attention by Story." New York Amsterdam News.
Praises "Big Boy Leaves Home" as a high point of The New Caravan. Reprinted: 1936.8.

8. _____. "Young Writer Wins Acclaim for His Work." Unidentified clipping.
Reprint of 1936.7.

9. Arvin, Newton. "A Letter on Proletarian Literature." Partisan Review and Anvil, 3 (February), 12-14.
Notes approvingly that "Between the World and Me" is a poem which avoids both "prosaic literalness" and "excessive indirectness" (p. 13).

10. Coates, Robert M. "New Faces." The New Republic, 89 (16 December), 222-223.
In a somewhat unfavorable review of The New Caravan, Coates praises "Big

Boy Leaves Home" for the genuinely personal quality--the "defiant leanness"--of its style.

11. Munson, Gorham. "Caravan Veering Left." The Saturday Review of Literature, 15 (19 December), 15.
Reviews The New Caravan citing W as one of the three "discoveries" of the anthology and praising "Big Boy Leaves Home" for its power.

12. N.[orth], S.[terling]. "Book of the Week (No. 8, New Series)." The Chicago Daily News (2 December), p. 26.
Reviews The New Caravan praising "Big Boy Leaves Home" as exemplary proletarian prose comparing favorably to the Dadaism of the twenties.

13. Phillips, William. "Marking Time?" New Masses, 21 (22 December), 23-24.
In a generally unfavorable review of The New Caravan, Phillips praises "Big Boy Leaves Home" as "one of the first realistic sketches of Negro life" (p. 23).

13a. Quinn, Kerker. "Remarks on Some Young American Poets." Life and Letters To-Day, 14 (Spring), 28-39.
Contains a favorable reference to W (p. 37).

14. Seaver, Edwin. "Books of the Day." Daily Worker (18 November), p. 7.
Contains a review of The New Caravan noting favorably "Big Boy Leaves Home," a "great story" by a "twenty-seven-year-old writer" who "is going places."

15. Selby, John. "Reading and Writing." The Bristol (Conn.) Press (22 December), p. 19.
Half of this review of The New Caravan concerns "Big Boy Leaves Home," which Selby calls "the best thing in the book." After summarizing the plot, he comments on the story's emotional impact. W "can write magnificently."

16. Van Gelder, Robert. "Books of the Times." The New York Times (2 November), p. 19.
Reviews The New Caravan noting W's "unusual dramatic talent."

1937

1. Anon. "Between Ourselves." New Masses, 24 (24 August), 2.
Identifies W, whose short story "Silt" appears in this issue, as "a young Negro author and poet."

2. Anon. "Between Ourselves." New Mas-

ses, 25 (5 October), 2.
　Identifies W, whose poem "Between Laughter and Tears" appears in this issue, as "a frequent contributor to the New Masses and associate editor of the forthcoming New Challenge, a magazine of Negro literature."

3. Anon. "Dick Wright Noted Author Off to N. Y." The Chicago View, p. 1.
　Apparently a prank special printing, for there is no record of this newspaper. Only the banner headline of this "extra" appears.

4. Anon. "George C. Hall Library Notes." Unidentified clipping (April).
　Announces a review by Russell Marshall of The New Caravan on 21 April and states that W will be present.

5. Anon. "Headlines Bulletin."
　Broadside published by The Constitutional Educational League of New Haven, Connecticut, attacking American Stuff and the Federal Writers Project for Communist leanings. W is singled out for special attention.

6. Anon. "Malcolm Cowley." Unidentified clipping.
　Comments on the possibility of a new Midwestern magazine and mentions W.

7. Anon. "'New Challenge' Quarterly Appears." Unidentified Associated Negro Press clipping.
　Mentions W as a contributor.
　Reprinted: 1937.11

8. Anon. "The Second American Writers' Congress," in The Writer in a Changing World. Ed. Henry Hart. New York: Equinox Cooperative Press, pp. 195-256.
　Quotes W's warning at one of the sessions about "the tendency of writers going into labor work and trying to escape their writer's personality. There is no backwardness on the part of trade unionists in accepting the writer as a writer. They realize his function, if the writer realizes it" (pp. 226-27). W chaired a later session at which he introduced Henry Alsberg of the Federal Writers Project, which W called "one of the most interesting experiments in the history of America."

9. Anon. Untitled clipping. Daily Worker.
　Announces a projected "caravan of American writing" edited by W, Ben Field, and two others for fall publication.

10. Anon. "Young Writer Scores in Caravan Revival." The Philadelphia Tribune

(28 January), p. 20.
　Announces the publication of "Big Boy Leaves Home" in The New Caravan.

11. Anon. "Young Writers Launch Literary Quarterly." San Antonio Register (10 July), p. 4.
　Reprint of 1937.7.

12. Armfield, Eugene. "W. P. A. Workers in Mufti." The Saturday Review of Literature, 16 (4 September), 10.
　Review of American Stuff citing "The Ethics of Living Jim Crow" as one of the best prose pieces in the collection.

13. Bain, Wilfred E. "WPA Writers Rap Jim-Crow Reports in N. Y." The Philadelphia Tribune (14 January), p. 11.
　Does not mention W by name, but praises the work of black writers on the Federal Writers Project in New York.

14. Benét, Stephen Vincent. "A Vigorous Anthology of Mixed Americana." New York Herald Tribune Books (5 September), p. 1.
　Review of American Stuff praising "Richard Wright's bitter, factual and quite unforgettable 'The Ethics of Living Jim Crow.'"

15. Brawley, Benjamin. The Negro Genius. New York: Dodd, Mead, p. 266.
　Comments on "the vigorous and lusty verse of Willard [sic] Wright," but thinks that it "could be more articulate."

16. Brown, Sterling A. "The Negro Genius. By Benjamin Brawley." Opportunity, 15 (September), 280-281.
　Review correcting factual errors about W.

17. _____. The Negro in American Fiction. Washington, D. C.: Associates in Negro Folk Education, pp. 186-187.
　Contains a laudatory paragraph on "Big Boy Leaves Home," which Brown calls "well informed realism, rendered with power and originality." Reprinted: 1969.44.

18. _____. Negro Poetry and Drama. Washington, D. C.: Associates in Negro Folk Education, p. 78.
　Comments on W's poetry and quotes from "I Have Seen Black Hands." Reprinted: 1969.44.

19. C.[happell], J.[ohn] O. "No Answer." The Cincinnati Enquirer (23 January), p. 5.
　In a generally unfavorable review of The New Caravan, Chappell notes that

the "magnificent 'Big Boy Leaves Home' is powerful nerve-shaking drama ... a masterpiece, an authentically American story whose tragic implications do more to reveal one's kinship to his suffering fellow man than all the sociological novels ever written."

20. Conroy, Jack. "Review and Comment." New Masses, 24 (14 September), 24-25.
In a review of American Stuff, Conroy singles out "The Ethics of Living Jim Crow" as one of the best contributions.
Reprinted: 1969.58a.

21. Drury, John. "The Surprising Success of the Federal Writers." Unidentified clipping.
In a review of American Stuff, Drury mentions W's success.

22. Dugan, James. "New Negro Quarterly." Daily Worker (25 October), p. 7.
Discusses New Challenge and comments favorably on W's "Blueprint for Negro Writing."

23. Gold, Mike. "Change the World." Daily Worker (2 November), p. 9.
Notes with approval plans by Harlem writers, including W, for a new literary magazine dedicated to realism in the depiction of black life instead of pandering "to the bourgeois white dilettantes."

24. Holmes, Eugene C. "Problems Facing the Negro Writer Today." New Challenge, 2 (Fall), 69-75.
Contains brief, favorable comments on W's verse.

25. _____. "A Writer's Social Obligations," in The Writer in a Changing World. Ed. Henry Hart. New York: Equinox Cooperative Press, pp. 172-179.
Contains brief mention of W as poet.

26. Jack, Peter Monro. "The New Caravan's Wide Diversity." The New York Times Book Review (17 January), pp. 2, 16.
Praises "Big Boy Leaves Home" and gives biographical details about W.

27. Kees, Weldon. "Fifth Caravan." Midwest: A Review, 1 (January), 31.
In a review of The New Caravan, Kees expresses admiration for "Big Boy Leaves Home," noting especially W's gift for dialogue.

28. Kelly, Paul. "New Writing." New Frontier, 1 (February), 30.
In an unfavorable review of The New Caravan, Kelly praises "Big Boy

Leaves Home" as "the best thing in the collection." Stylistically "clean, lean, muscular," the story is comparable to the best of Bierce and Crane in its evocation of horror. "We may expect big things from this young Negro novelist and poet."

29. Locke, Alain. "God Save Reality! Part I. Retrospective Review of the Literature of the Negro: 1936." Opportunity, 15 (January), 8-13.
Comments favorably on W's poetry, which signifies "a new strain in Negro poetry and a slow maturing of one of our really vital poetic talents. Willard [sic] Wright faces crude reality and dares to try to render it poetically, which is the contemporary poet's real job; in time it will ring more clearly and artistically" (p. 11).

30. _____. "God Save Reality! Part II. Retrospective Review of the Literature of the Negro: 1936." Opportunity, 15 (February), 40-44.
Corrects the mistake in Wright's first name in 1937.29.

31. Moon, Henry Lee. "New Song of America." New Challenge, 2 (Fall), 88-89.
In a review of American Stuff, Moon gives special praise to "The Ethics of Living Jim Crow." The bitter terror experienced by W is conveyed in this sketch as "an unforgettable picture of life in the Deep South" (p. 89).

32. Schuyler, George S. "Writers on Relief." Opportunity, 15 (December), 377-378.
In a review of American Stuff, Schuyler ranks "The Ethics of Living Jim Crow" as "certainly the most outstanding piece in the collection" (p. 378), notable especially for its portrayal of "the more savage side of jim crow life in a stark and unforgettable manner" (p. 378).

33. Seaver, Edwin. "Books and Authors." Sunday Worker (22 August), Sec. 2, p. 9.
In a review of American Stuff, Seaver singles out "The Ethics of Living Jim Crow" for praise.

34. Seldes, George, "American Writers Choose Sides." Sunday Worker.
Mentions a paper read to the League of American Writers by W, "a brilliant young Negro novelist."

35. Spingarn, Arthur B. "Books by Negro Authors in 1936." The Crisis, 44 (February), 47-48.
Contains a notice of The New Caravan

calling "Big Boy Leaves Home" a "remarkable story . . . in poetic prose" (p. 48).

36. Walton, Eda Lou. "A Federal Writers' Anthology." The New York Times Book Review (29 August), p. 2.
  In a review of American Stuff, Walton praises "The Ethics of Living Jim Crow" as "one of the most impersonal and shocking accounts of a youngster learning to be a Negro in the South."

37. Whitcomb, Robert. "American Stuff." Unidentified clipping (October).
  Reviews the anthology noting that "The Ethics of Living Jim Crow" is one of the best exposures of segregation.

1938

1. Agar, Herbert. "Time and Tide." The Louisville Courier-Journal (29 March), p. 6.
  In a favorable review of UTC, Agar emphasizes W's corrective to the white notion of contented, submissive blacks. The work should refocus national attention on domestic social injustice instead of totalitarianism abroad. Agar would like more variety instead of the uniformly tragic tone, however.
  Reprinted: 1938.2; 1978.209.

2. _____. "'Uncle Tom's Children.'" Chicago Times (29 March), p. 13.
  Reprint of 1938.1.

3. Anon. "Among the Publishers." The Publishers' Weekly, 133 (19 March), 1279.
  Announces that Harper will publish the Story magazine contest winner UTC on 24 March.

4. Anon. "Between Ourselves." New Masses, 27 (19 April), 2.
  Announces that UTC is the Book Union selection for April.

5. Anon. "Between Ourselves." New Masses, 27 (3 May), 2.
  Announces the forthcoming publication of "Bright and Morning Star" in New Masses.

6. Anon. "Between Ourselves." New Masses, 27 (7 June), 2.
  Announces a cocktail party and dance in W's honor on 4 June at the I. W. O. Community Center in Harlem.

7. Anon. "Between Ourselves." New Masses, 27 (14 June), 2.
  Announces the replacement of Horace

Gregory by W on the editorial board of the literary section of New Masses.

8. Anon. "Between Ourselves." New Masses, 28 (28 June), 2.
  Announces the forthcoming publication in New Masses of W's article on the Louis-Schmeling fight.

9. Anon. "Between Ourselves." New Masses, 29 (15 November), 2.
  Announces a talk by W on "Negro Culture in America" on 22 November in Philadelphia "under the auspices of the New World Bookshop Forum, in association with the National Negro Congress."

10. Anon. "Between Ourselves: Who's Who." New Masses, 28 (5 July), 2.
  Mentions that W, a contributor to this issue, recently joined the editorial board of the literary section of the magazine.

11. Anon. "Book Marks for Today." New York World-Telegram (10 March), p. 23.
  Contains an announcement of UTC.

12. Anon. "Book Marks for Today." New York World-Telegram (16 March), p. 23.
  Mentions the award of the Story magazine prize to W.

13. Anon. "Book Marks for Today." New York World-Telegram (23 March), p. 23.
  Mentions a cocktail party for W given by Whit Burnett and Martha Foley.

14. Anon. "Book Marks for Today." New York World-Telegram (6 April), p. 23.
  Mentions a talk by W to the Columbia University Writers' Club.

15. Anon. "Book Notes." New York Herald-Tribune (4 November), p. 23.
  Announces the award to W of the $200 second prize for "Fire and Cloud" in the O. Henry Memorial Award Prize Stories of 1938.

16. Anon. "Book Notes." The New York Times (11 April), p. 13.
  Notes that UTC is the selection of the Book Union for April.

17. Anon. "Book Notes." The New York Times (23 July), p. 11.
  UTC is being translated into Russian, and W has made arrangements with Langston Hughes to dramatize one of the stories.

18. Anon. "Book Published." Norfolk Journal and Guide (9 April), Home Edition, p. 5.
  Reprint of 1938.82.

19. Anon. "Book Reviews by City Librarian: 'Uncle Tom's Children' by Richard Wright." Burley (Idaho) Bulletin (26 May).
  Comments on the Story magazine prize, quotes from W's autobiographical statement, compares the work's style to Steinbeck's "lean and strong" prose, and calls the collection "a forceful, unsparing" one which "brings home with stunning impact the essential tragedy of the Negro in a white man's civilization." Part of this review relies on Harper's promotional material.

20. Anon. "Book Reviews: Uncle Tom's Children, by Richard Wright." National Educational Outlook Among Negroes, 2 (June), 66.
  Favorable review praising the work's literary qualities and social message. "It should help to broaden the altogether too narrow perspective both races have of the status of the Negro in his struggle for freedom."

21. Anon. "Book Reviews: Uncle Tom's Children--By Richard Wright." The Indianapolis Recorder (21 May), p. 10.
  A black reviewer complains that the characters are not of "the elevating type" and that "the dialect is not only terrible but it seems unfair and unreal."

22. Anon. "Books." Work (23 April), p. 11.
  Favorable review of UTC summarizing briefly each story and commenting on the work's emotional and persuasive power. It "should be read in every Alliance Local in the country. It will answer more questions than a dozen pamphlets."

23. Anon. "Books and Authors." Chester (Pa.) Times (24 March), p. 5.
  Mentions the award of the Story prize to W and gives biographical details.

24. Anon. "Books and Authors." The New York Times Book Review (13 November), p. 18.
  Notes that W won the second prize award of $200 for "Fire and Cloud" in the O. Henry Memorial Award Prize Stories of 1938.

25. Anon. "Books and Authors." The New Orleans Sunday Item-Tribune (27 March), Society Fashions Sec., p. 6.
  Notes that UTC won the Federal Writers Project contest.

26. Anon. "Books Out Today." Unidentified clipping (c. March).
  Lists UTC under "New Fiction."

27. Anon. "Books Published Today." The New York Times (24 March), p. 19.
  Contains a brief notice of UTC.

28. Anon. "Bound to Be Read." The Westfield (Mass.) Valley Herald (10 March), p. 3.
  Notes that UTC won the Federal Writers Project fiction contest.

29. Anon. "Briefly Noted." Unidentified clipping (5 November).
  Brief notice of O. Henry Memorial Award Prize Stories of 1938 mentioning "Fire and Cloud" as the second prize winner.

30. Anon. "Comments on New Books at Library." Stamford (Conn.) Advocate (8 June), p. 2.
  Contains a notice of UTC, W's "graphic prose present[s] glimpses of the 'darkey' in all his moods and modes of living."

31. Anon. "Communism's Antiseptic Squad,'" in Investigation of Un-American Propaganda Activities in the United States. Vol. 1. Washington: United States Government Printing Office, pp. 374-375.
  Lists W among the signatories of a statement supporting the Moscow purge trials.

32. Anon. "Communist Literature Distributors Decide on a Big Job--15,000,000 Copies of Tracts." Daily Worker (17 June), p. 5.
  Mentions briefly a talk by W at a Communist conference.

33. Anon. "Davis to Review Novel by Wright." The Chicago Defender (9 April), p. 7.
  Announces a lecture on UTC by Frank Marshall Davis for the South Side Forum on 13 April.

34. Anon. Dust jacket of Uncle Tom's Children. London: Gollancz.
  Mentions the foreword by Paul Robeson, who calls W "a great artist."

35. Anon. Dust jacket of Uncle Tom's Children. New York: Harper.
  The front inside flap, "Uncle Tom's Children by Richard Wright," is Harper's promotional release. The back inside flap, "Richard Wright," is W's autobiographical letter.

36. Anon. "Embittered Negro Tells Race Story." U. C. L. A. California Daily Bruin (9 May), p. 4.
  Highly favorable review of UTC praising W as both racial spokesman and

literary artist. The reviewer emphasizes the guilt and shame that white readers of the stories will feel.

37. Anon. "Emergency Meeting for New Masses." New Masses, 29 (11 October), 25.
Advertisement listing W as one of seven speakers.

38. Anon. "Fiction." The Portland Sunday Oregonian (24 April), Sec. 6, p. 4.
Contains a favorable review of UTC, with emphasis on "Big Boy Leaves Home" and "Down By the Riverside." W's view of the South is bitter but valid, at least from the black perspective. Some biographical details are given.
Reprinted: 1978.209.

39. Anon. "First Prize Winner." Story, 12 (March), 1.
Congratulates W for winning the contest for Federal Writers Project writers, sketches his life, and praises UTC for its "brilliance, clarity and sincerity" and "dramatic quality."

40. Anon. "$500 Brief Respite from Poverty to Winner in National WPA Short Novel Prize Contest." New York Amsterdam News (26 February), p. 5.
Emphasizes, along with biographical details, the wise use to which W will put his prize money: clothes, rent, and food. Quotes W on the black worker as "the real symbol of the struggle of the working class in America" and in defense of the Federal Writers Project.

41. Anon. "A Garbage Can Book." Jackson (Miss.) Daily News (26 April), p. 6.
This editorial denunciation of UTC calls it "nothing more or less than a squawk against lynching and obviously written as propaganda for the National Association for the Advancement of Colored People," complains that W ignores the "peace and harmony" of race relations in the South, and chides Harper's for publishing "such slush, slop and drivel."

42. Anon. "Granville Hicks to Speak on Literature." Daily Worker (17 May), p. 7.
Notes that W serves as chairman of a meeting scheduled for 18 May at Steinway Hall in New York under the sponsorship of New Masses.

43. Anon. "Great Variety of Books About the South and Its Problems." Worcester Sunday Telegram (17 July), Sec. 4, p. 8.

Includes a favorable notice of UTC, "written to make the blood boil." W "has a masterful pen indeed in depicting the sufferings of his own downtrodden race."

44. Anon. "Harlem Author Wins 1st Prize of $500 for Book." The Chicago Sunday Bee (26 February).
Reprint of 1938.104.

45. Anon. "Harlem Author Writes Best Book Wins First Prize." Chicago World (26 February).
Reprint of 1938.104.

46. Anon. "Honored." New York Amsterdam News (30 July), Sec. 2, p. 3.
Photograph of W with caption noting the Russian translation of UTC to be published in the Soviet Union and announcing arrangements with Langston Hughes to dramatize some of the stories in the collection.

47. Anon. "In the News Columns--Richard Wright." Opportunity, 16 (March), 70.
Along with the information about the impending publication of UTC and other current activities, this article-interview quotes W on his desire to visit Mexico and on his childhood and youth.

48. Anon. "James W. Ford Accorded Huge Applause Here." New York Amsterdam News (4 June), p. 2.
Ford praises W in a speech at a Communist Party convention.

49. Anon. "Jim-Crowing Writers." New Masses, 29 (18 October), 12.
Mentions W in support of Nelson Antrim Crawford's attack on the Kansas Authors Club for excluding black writers from a literary contest.

50. Anon. "Just Out." The New York Times Book Review (27 March), p. 12.
Advertisement for UTC.

51. Anon. "Leading Artists, Educators Support Soviet Trial Verdict." Daily Worker (28 April), p. 4.
Lists W as one of 123 signatories of a statement supporting "the verdicts of the recent Moscow trials of the Trotskyite-Buckharinite traitors."
Reprinted: 1940.209.

52. Anon. "League of American Writers and the John Reed Club," in Investigation of Un-American Propaganda Activities in the United States. Vol. 1. Washington: United States Government Printing Office, pp. 557-563.
Mentions W's connection with the League of American Writers.

53. Anon. Letter to Mike Gold. Daily Worker (30 May), p. 9.
In Mike Gold's "Change the World" column, a correspondent signing himself "Harvard Square" and identifying himself as a black who has lived in the Deep South refers to Corbin's letter to Gold and refutes Calmer's complaint about a contrived quality in UTC. Asserting the verisimilitude of W's presentation of Southern social conditions, the correspondent states that "there is nothing forced or false about these tales; they are life itself. "Bright and Morning Star," comparable to Gorky's Mother, is "the best story of its kind ever written in the United States."

54. Anon. "Literary Party in Honor of Richard Wright." Sunday Worker (29 May), p. 12.
"Prominent citizens of Harlem, together with well known leaders in the literary world," will honor W at the I. W. O. Center on 125th Street in New York on 4 June.

55. Anon. "Literature Overtakes Life in Dealing with the South." Buffalo Evening News (11 June), Saturday Magazine Sec., p. 7.
Includes a rather favorable review of UTC. The reviewer emphasizes the relevance of W's "starkly written" stories to debate in Congress on anti-lynching legislation.

56. Anon. "Louis Wins by K. O. in the 1st Round." Daily Worker (23 June), p. 1.
Mentions that W's story on the fight will appear "in tomorrow's Daily Worker."

57. Anon. "Makes You Want to Fight." The Crisis, 46 (October), 340.
Advertisement for UTC.

58. Anon. "Maltz and Wright Among O. Henry Prize Winners." Daily Worker.
Announces the award to W of the $200 second prize for "Fire and Cloud."

59. Anon. "Negro Author to Speak on Radio Friday." Sunday Worker (19 June), p. 12.
Announces W's talk on "The Author and His People" on 24 June for the Public Use of Arts Committee in a series sponsored by the Federal Theatre Radio Division. Contains a brief sketch of Wright's literary career.

60. Anon. "Negro in Literature Discussed." New York Amsterdam News (19 November), p. 11.
Mentions W's attendance at a forum

sponsored by the League of American Writers.

61. Anon. "Negro W. P. A. Writer Sees Prize Winning Book Placed on Sale." The New Age (14 May), p. 3.
Reprint of 1938.90.

62. Anon. "Negro Who Schooled Himself Wins National Fiction Award." New York World-Telegram (15 February), p. 3.
Article-interview on the occasion of the Story magazine award. W acknowledges the influence of Mencken.

63. Anon. "Negro Writer Wins Story Contest." The New York Times (15 February), p. 14.
Announces the award to W for UTC.

64. Anon. "Negro Writer Wins WPA Fiction Contest." The Huntington Herald-Advertiser (20 March), Magazine Sec., p. 1.
Announces that UTC won the Federal Writers Project contest.

65. Anon. "New Books at Library." Beaumont Journal (2 April), p. 5.
Includes brief comment on "The Ethics of Living Jim Crow" and quotes the first paragraph, noting its "poignancy and subconscious racial pain."

66. Anon. "New Books of Interest to New Masses' Readers." New Masses, 27 (12 April), 18.
Advertisement for UTC with two blurbs.

67. Anon. "New Books Today: Public Library Presents--." Indianapolis Times (28 May), Sec. 2, p. 9.
Favorable notice of UTC pointing out the forceful narrative and the lack of sympathy. The reviewer believes that all blacks in the book are Uncle Toms except Rev. Taylor.

68. Anon. "New Theatre Night." Daily Worker (10 June), p. 7.
States that W will be present at the Bayes Theater to see plays by Langston Hughes and Alice Holdship Ware.

69. Anon. "The New World Bookshop Forum."
Announces a lecture by W on "Negro Culture in America" sponsored by the National Negro Congress to be held at the O. V. Catto Lodge Auditorium on 22 November.

70. Anon. "New Year's Eve Ball for Refugees from Nazi Terror." Daily Worker (21 December), p. 7.
Lists W among the sponsors.
Reprinted: 1941.362.

71. Anon. "New York Committee Honors Paul Robeson." New York Amsterdam News.
Notes that W and Langston Hughes are being sought as screen writers by Pioneer Films.

72. Anon. "New Yorker Winner of National Novel Contest." Norfolk Journal and Guide (26 February), p. 3.
Reprint of 1938.104.

73. Anon. "Note." New York Post (5 April), p. 20.
Note identifying W appended to his letter to the editor protesting Jim Crow in baseball.

74. Anon. "Notes on Books and Authors." The Times-Picayune and New Orleans States (6 March), Sec. 2, p. 9.
Announces the award of the Story magazine prize to UTC.

75. Anon. "Novelist Inspects Exhibits." The Indianapolis Recorder (1 January), p. 7.
Photograph of Zora Neale Hurston perusing a copy of American Stuff with caption mentioning that W is a contributor.

76. Anon. "O. Henry Awards Made for Best Short Stories." The New York Times (4 November), p. 25.
Announces the award to W of the second prize of $200 for "Fire and Cloud."

77. Anon. "O. Henry Memorial Award." The Atlanta Journal (25 December), Sunday Magazine, p. 10.
States that the "magnificent" story "Fire and Cloud" is the best in the collection.

78. Anon. "The O. Henry Prize Stories." The Philadelphia Inquirer (24 December), p. 30.
Notes that "Fire and Cloud" won second prize.

79. Anon. "One Hundred Notable Books: 1938." The New Republic, 97 (7 December), p. 140.
Lists UTC as one of seventeen titles in the fiction category.

80. Anon. "Plus & Minus: A Survey of Reviews." Story, 12 (June), 99-104.
Quotes from ten reviews of UTC and evaluates them as plus, 75/25, or 50/50 (pp. 99-100).

81. Anon. "Portrait of Harlem Made Part of 'New York Panorama.'" New York Amsterdam News (3 September), p. 7.
Advance notice summarizing W's chapter on Harlem without mentioning his name.

82. Anon. "Prize Book Published." The Buffalo Star (March).
Associated Negro Press photograph of W with caption announcing the publication of UTC.
Reprinted: 1938.18, 83, 84, 142.

83. Anon. "Prize Book Published." The Carolina Times (March).
Reprint of 1938.82.

84. Anon. "Prize Book Published." Unidentified clippings (March).
Five reprints of 1938.82.

85. Anon. "Prize Short Stories." New Haven Register (c. 30 October).
Review of O. Henry Memorial Award Prize Stories of 1938 mentioning "Fire and Cloud."

86. Anon. "Prize Stories of 1938." The Christian Science Monitor (28 December), Weekly Magazine Sec., p. 10.
Cites "Fire and Cloud" as representative of the American quality of the stories in O. Henry Memorial Award Prize Stories of 1938.

87. Anon. "Prize Winning Book By Negro WPA Writer Published." Columbia (S. C.) Palmetto Leader (2 April), pp. 4, 7.
Reprint of 1938.90.

88. Anon. "Prize Winning Book by Negro WPA Writer Published." Unidentified clipping from an Indianapolis newspaper.
Reprint of 1938.90.

89. Anon. "Prize Winning Book by Negro WPA Writer Published." Unidentified clipping from a Tampa newspaper (2 April).
Reprint of 1938.90.

90. Anon. "Prize Winning Book by Negro WPA Writer Published." Waco Messenger (1 April).
Reviews UTC and sketches W's life and career, emphasizing his WPA experience. Quotes from W's autobiographical letter.
Reprinted: 1938.61, 87, 88, 89, 91, 92, 95, 108.

91. Anon. "Prize Winning Book by WPA Writer Is Put on Sale." Philadelphia Independent (3 April), p. 8.
Reprint of 1938.90.

92. Anon. "Prize-Winning Book by WPA Writer Published." The Crisis, 45 (April), 123.
Reprint of 1938.90.

93. Anon. "Project Prattle." Red Pen (1

May).
   Notes that Granville Hicks believes
   that "Bright and Morning Star" is W's
   best work.

94. Anon. "Promise in the Ranks of the
Younger Poets." Washington Afro-American
(28 May), p. 11.
   Langston Hughes includes W among
   three promising younger poets.

95. Anon. "Publish Richard Wright's
Novel." The Chicago Defender (2 April),
p. 5.
   Reprint of 1938.90.

96. Anon. "Rambles in Bookland." The
American News Trade Journal, 20 (April),
20-21.
   Contains a brief notice of the award
   of the Federal Writers Project prize
   to UTC.

97. Anon. "Readers OK Fite Predix, Campaign." Daily Worker (28 June), p. 8.
   Includes a letter from "Jimmy" praising W's article on the Louis-Schmeling fight.

98. Anon. "Reception Dinner for Theodore
Dreiser." New Masses, 28 (13 September),
30.
   Lists W as one of the sponsors of a
   dinner to raise funds for an American
   relief ship for Loyalist Spain.

99. Anon. "Richard Wright." The Chicago
Daily News (23 March), p. 21.
   Photograph of W with a caption mentioning his $500 prize and the publi-
   cation of UTC on 24 March.

100. Anon. "Richard Wright Given Literary Post for Work." The New York Amsterdam News (25 June), p. 6.
   Announces W's appointment to the
   editorial board of New Masses and
   describes a reception in his honor.
   Speakers included Samuel Sillen
   (quoted), Ben Davis, Jr., Charles
   Alexander, Mike Gold, Louise Thompson, Eugene Gordon, Alta Douglass,
   and Melva Price.

101. Anon. "Richard Wright Speaks at
Camp Unity Sunday." Daily Worker (16
July), p. 3.
   The topic is "the Negro and Literature today," with readings from UTC
   and comments on "what prompted him to
   write it."

102. Anon. "Richard Wright Will Get
Honor." New York Amsterdam News (4
June), p. 9.
   Announces the cocktail party at the
   I. W. O. Community Center in Harlem,
   at which a large attendance is expec-

ted. Discusses briefly UTC.

103. Anon. "Richard Wright Wins First
Prize." Houston Defender (12 March).
   Reprint of 1938.104.

104. Anon. "Richard Wright's Novel Wins
$500 First Prize." The Kansas City Call
(25 February), p. 10.
   Associated Negro Press article on the
   award of the Federal Writers Project
   first prize to UTC. Mentions also his
   poetry, his move from Chicago to New
   York, his publication of "The Ethics
   of Living Jim Crow," and his associate editorship of New Challenge.
   Reprinted: 1938.44, 45, 72, 103, 105,
   131, 141, 147, 153.

105. Anon. "Richard Wright's Novel Wins
$500 First Prize." Unidentified clip-
ping.
   Reprint of one paragraph of 1938.104.

106. Anon. "A Selected List of Important
Spring Books." New York Herald Tribune
Books (3 April), pp. 7-11.
   Contains a brief notice of UTC, a
   book showing the position of "the
   Negro in a white man's civilization"
   (p. 10).

107. Anon. "The Spice of Life." The
Argonaut (2 December), p. 23.
   Reviews the O. Henry Memorial Award
   Prize Stories of 1938, noting that
   "Fire and Cloud" received second
   prize.

108. Anon. "Stories in the Prize-Winning
Book 'Burn Like House Afire.'" The
Pittsburgh Courier (2 April), p. 7.
   Reprint of 1938.90.

109. Anon. "'Terror . . .'" The Nation,
146 (30 April), 509.
   Half-page advertisement for UTC with
   excerpts from reviews in New York
   Herald Tribune, New York World Tele-
   gram, Los Angeles Times, New York
   Times Book Review, New York Post, and
   The New York Times.

110. Anon. "'These Stories Burn Like a
House Afire.'"
   Broadside advertisement for UTC and
   You Have Seen Their Faces, as well as
   Modern Age Publications, from Affi-
   lated [sic] Distributors, 543 East
   47th Street.

111. Anon. "Tragic Picture of Far South
Negro Life." Los Angeles Times (27
March), Part 3, p. 6.
   Highly favorable review of UTC praising the simplicity and power of the
   stories, which "create those effects
   which, according to Aristotle, are

the aim of tragedy." As a Southerner, the reviewer is forced to recognize the truth of W's themes.
Reprinted: 1978.209.

112. Anon. "2 Magazines in 1." Daily Worker (5 May), p. 5.
Advertisement for 10 May issue of New Masses containing "a complete novelette by Richard Wright."

113. Anon. "Uncle Tom's Children." Springfield (Mass.) Sunday Union and Republican (13 March).
Notes that UTC won the Federal Writers Project contest.

114. Anon. "Uncle Tom's Children," in Victor Gollancz Catalogue. London: Gollancz, p. 61.
Publisher's advertisement for "one of the most important pieces of literature we have published."

115. Anon. "Uncle Tom's Children, by Richard Wright." Charleston News and Courier (27 March), Sec. III, p. 3.
Mixed review noting W's promise but claiming that except for "Fire and Cloud," he "is still a little too close to his subject emotionally."

116. Anon. "Uncle Tom's Children by Richard Wright." Harper's Magazine, 176 (April), [xxxviii].
Advertisement with a blurb by Lewis Gannett.

117. Anon. "Uncle Tom's Children. By Richard Wright." Newsweek, 11 (28 March), 30.
Brief notice of "four short stories full of honest anger and beautiful prose."

118. Anon. "Uncle Tom's Children by Richard Wright." Story, 12 (April), inside front cover-1.
Advertisement.

119. Anon. "Uncle Tom's Children by Richard Wright." Story, 12 (May), inside front cover.
Advertisement.

120. Anon. "Uncle Tom's Children by Richard Wright." Story, 12 (June), 8.
Advertisement.

121. Anon. "Uncle Tom's Children--By Richard Wright." The Augusta Chronicle (27 March), p. 16.
Favorable brief notice calling the stories "frank, raw . . . nevertheless a sincere and forceful exposition of the Negro point of view. And after all the Negro does have a point of view."

122. Anon. "Uncle Tom's Children, by Richard Wright." The Lynchburg Daily Advance (29 April).
Favorable review calling the work "highly colored propaganda" but admitting its essential truth. The writing is violent and explosive. Summarizes briefly "Big Boy Leaves Home" and "Down by the Riverside."

123. Anon. "Uncle Tom's Children. By Richard Wright." The Modern Quarterly, 10 (June), 14.
Favorable notice placing the book in the context of black literature since the twenties. Praises W's treatment of black psychology and calls "Big Boy Leaves Home" a "little masterpiece."
Reprinted: 1978.209.

124. Anon. "Uncle Tom's Children, by Richard Wright." The New Yorker, 14 (26 March), 69.
Favorable brief notice of "these bitter, fast-moving tales of oppression and injustice in the Deep South."

125. Anon. "Uncle Tom's Children--Four Novellas, by Richard Wright." Bangor Daily Commercial (14 September), p. 2.
Brief notice including some biographical details.

126. Anon. Untitled clipping. Buffalo Times (6 May).
Notes that UTC, which shows "the tragedy of the Negro in a white man's civilization," is the Book Union's April selection.

127. Anon. Untitled clipping. Burlington Free Press (12 March), p. 7.
Notes that UTC won first prize in the Federal Writers Project contest.

128. Anon. Untitled clipping. Contest Magazine, 10 (May).
Notes that UTC won first prize in the Federal Writers Project contest.

129. Anon. Untitled clipping. Greenwich Press (9 June).
Favorable notice of UTC praising its literary qualities and pointing out its theme of racial injustice.

130. Anon. Untitled clipping. New York Daily Telegraph (26 March).
Favorable notice of UTC.

131. Anon. Untitled clipping. Unidentified Washington newspaper.
Reprint of 1938.104.

132. Anon. Untitled clipping. United Automobile Workers (13 August).
Highly favorable review of UTC stres-

sing the importance of solidarity between white and black workers. W "has strong passion, keen dramatic sense, and the power to tell a stirring tale in simple language." Reprinted: 1978.209.

133. Anon. Untitled photograph of Wright. The Chicago Daily News (c. 25 March).
Caption notes that UTC won the Federal Writers Project contest.

134. Anon. Untitled photograph of Wright. Tops.
Long caption discusses UTC, a volume of harsh, realistic stories.

135. Anon. "Vigorous Stories Portray Tragedy of Southern Negro." The Dallas Morning News (27 March), Sec. 3, p. 10.
Mixed review of UTC praising its style and construction but finding its characterization one-sided and oversimplified. The reviewer compares W to Steinbeck and Bierce. He has "the makings of a major writer." Reprinted: 1978.209.

136. Anon. "Vocational Guidance and Training for Negroes." Pueblo Star Journal (c. 1 May).
Mentions W as winner of the Federal Writers Project contest.

137. Anon. "What's On: Coming!" Sunday Worker (15 May), p. 9.
Notes that W will be program chairman for a lecture by Granville Hicks.

138. Anon. "'White Fog.'" Time, 31 (28 March), 63-64.
Favorable review of UTC judging W, unlike other black writers, "neither subjective nor sentimental." In rendering racial conflict in its psychological dimensions, the stories achieve power, intensity, "and a kind of impersonal eloquence in voicing the tragedy of his people" (p. 64). W resembles Stephen Crane more than John Steinbeck.
Reprinted: 1978.209.

139. Anon. "Winner of Story Magazine's National Prize Contest for WPA Writers." New Masses, 27 (10 May), 125.
Full-page advertisement for UTC with a photograph of W and quotations from five reviews.

140. "Wins $500 Award." El Paso Herald Post (12 March), p. 5.
Notice of the award to W of first prize for UTC in the Federal Writers Project contest.

141. Anon. "Wins $500; Buys Steak." The Baltimore Afro-American (26 February), pp. 1-2.
Reprint of 1938.104.

142. Anon. "Wins Prize." The Kansas City Call (25 March), p. 1.
Reprint of 1938.82.

143. Anon. "With the Makers of Books." The Jacksonville (Fla.) Sunday Times-Union (27 March), Sec. 3, p. 11.
Brief notice of the award of the Story magazine prize to UTC.

144. Anon. "Wright, Richard." The Publisher's Weekly, 133 (26 March), 1389.
Brief notice of the publication of UTC, which relates "the tragedy of the Negro in a white man's civilization."

145. Anon. "Wright, Richard. Uncle Tom's children; four novellas." The Booklist, 34 (1 May), 318.
Favorable brief notice pointing out the "unusual dramatic intensity" of the "bitter and violent" stories. W's "Negro characters are not whitewashed."

146. Anon. "Wright Wins a New Prize." New York Amsterdam News (12 November), p. 15.
Notes the award to W of second prize in the O. Henry short story contest. Mentions that W is living in Brooklyn.

147. Anon. "Writer Wins Novel Award." Detroit Tribune (26 February), p. 1.
Reprint of 1938.104.

148. Anon. "Writers League Lauds Services of Dr. Johnson." New York Amsterdam News (16 July), p. 5.
Mentions W as an officer of the League of American Writers.

149. Anon. "Writers Mourn J. W. Johnson." The Baltimore Afro-American (16 July), p. 3.
Mentions W (identified as a playwright) as an officer of the League of American Writers, which expresses its condolences on the death of James Weldon Johnson.

150. Anon. "The Year's Prize Winners." New York Sunday News (4 December), p. 29C.
Notes that "Fire and Cloud" is included in the O. Henry Memorial Award Prize Stories of 1938, which demonstrates an "exceptionally good" year for stories.

151. Anon. "You are cordially invited to a cocktail party and literary evening in

honor of Richard Wright author of 'Uncle Tom's Children.'"
Printed invitation to the event at the Harlem I. W. O. Center on 4 June listing a sponsoring committee of twenty-eight, including Samuel Sillen, Mike Gold, Roy Wilkins, James W. Ford, Ralph Ellison, Langston Hughes, and Ben Davis, Jr.
Partially reprinted: 1938.152.

152. Anon. "You are cordially invited to a Cocktail Party and Literary Evening in honor of Richard Wright author of 'Uncle Tom's Children.'"
Reprint of 1938.151 without the list of sponsors.

153. Anon. "Young Author Wins First Prize." California Voice (c. 25 February).
Reprint of 1938.104.

154. Appleby, John T. "A Gifted Negro." The Washington Post (24 April), Sec. III, p. 10.
Highly favorable review of UTC giving special praise to the construction, style ("luminous in its clarity, its simplicity and its directness"), and sense of tragedy in the first three stories. "Fire and Cloud" is too propagandistic, but the other stories place W "close to the front rank of American short story writers."

155. B., H. "Protest Against Racial Injustice." Philadelphia Record (26 March), p. 9.
Highly favorable review of UTC. Although the author is a black Communist, the first three stories "are striking examples of blazing passion under the control of a notable degree of artistic skill."

156. Banta, Edwin P. and Joe Starnes. "Testimony of Edwin P. Banta, Manhattan," in Investigation of Un-American Propaganda Activities in the United States. Vol. 2. Washington: United States Government Printing Office, pp. 981-1017.
Banta testifies to W's leadership in the Workers Alliance of the Federal Writers Project (pp. 106, 108). Representative Starnes introduces excerpts from "The Ethics of Living Jim Crow," calling it "so vile that it is unfit for youth to read" (p. 1010).

157. Barsov, V. "Deti diadi Toma." Literaturnyi kritik, No. 11 (November), pp. 196-198.
Favorable review of the Russian translation of UTC. Instead of addressing white readers or black readers, W addresses, with literary skill, the proletariat. Barzov analyzes "Big Boy Leaves Home" and "Bright and Morning Star" to show W's understanding of different kinds of whites. Stark, tragic, artistic, the stories in the collection are truly memorable.

158. Beals, Helen. "Fortnightly Fiction Review." Worcester Sunday Telegram (18 December), Sec. Four, p. 8.
Contains a notice of the O. Henry Memorial Award Prize Stories of 1938 with favorable comment on "Fire and Cloud."

159. Beilin, I. "Deti diadi Toma." Internatsional'naia literatura, No. 7 (July), pp. 42-46.
Favorable review of the Russian translation of UTC. Placing W in the geographical-social context of Chicago and the literary context of Stowe, McKay, Walter White, and George Spivak, Beilin notes that W rejects the bourgeois hope of changing the hearts of racists and embraces the concept of revolutionary struggle. Discussion of the stories focuses on "Fire and Cloud" and "Bright and Morning Star," emphasizing their ideological thrust. The unifying thematic principle of the stories is noted. Beilin also praises W's honest realism and dramatic intensity.

160. Bower, Ruth. "O. Henry Memorial Award Prize Stories of 1938. Edited by Harry Hansen." New York Herald Tribune Books (6 November), p. 14.
Contains high praise for "Fire and Cloud": "a very moving drama in three acts, the old story of pain and deliverance, with unfamiliar characters, beautifully told here, with homely simplicity and realism and a keen sense of drama."

161. Bradley, Hugh. "Hugh Bradley Says: Notebook Reveals Wall Street Lads Plan 'Gimme' Game." New York Post (16 March), p. 28.
UTC serves as a point of departure for a discussion of racial discrimination in sports.

162. Brickell, Herschel. "Books on Our Table: A Look Backward Over the First Quarter of the Year." New York Post (31 March), p. 19.
UTC "showed very distinct talent and power." W is "an obviously gifted young Negro writer."

163. _____. "Books on Our Table: Story Magazine's Prize-Winning Book in the WPA Contest." New York Post (25 March), p. 17.

In this favorable review of UTC,
Brickell praises the impact, style,
and artistic control of the stories
and concedes their authenticity of
subject matter but claims the picture
is not whole or just. "Wright's talent is individual and unmistakable."
Reprinted: 1978.209.

164. Brown, Sterling A. "From the Inside." The Nation, 146 (16 April), 448.
Favorable review of UTC praising W
for his "power and originality" in
treating with dignity black Southern
life and its violent struggles. His
work surpasses that of white writers
like Julia Peterkin and Roark Bradford. Perhaps W relies too much on
coincidence in his stories, but in
general they are vigorous and authentic.
Reprinted: 1960.198; 1961.214; 1963.
146; 1978.209.

165. _____. "The Literary Scene." Opportunity, 16 (April), 120-121.
Favorable review of UTC comparing W
to Toomer, Faulkner, Erskine Caldwell, T. S. Stribling, and Paul
Green. W relies too much on coincidence and "Long Black Song" is
sketchy in characterization, but the
other three stories receive high
praise for their literary quality and
for their depiction of the South.
Reprinted: 1978.209.

166. Burley, Dan. "Lists Recognition
Negroes Received During Year 1938." New
York Amsterdam News (31 December), p. 5.
Mentions W's "prize-winning novellas"
and his appointment to the editorial
board of New Masses.

167. C., H. "Answers to Inquiries."
Harper's Magazine, 177 (June), an unnumbered front advertising page.
Mentions W among the literary prize
winners.

168. C., M. "Handout Highlights." The
Louisville Courier-Journal (13 March),
Magazine Sec., p. 7.
Announces the Story magazine award to
W for UTC and sketches briefly his
previous life and career.

169. Calmer, Alan. "Books of the Day."
Daily Worker (4 April), p. 7.
Mixed review of UTC praising W's
storytelling ability, his emphasis on
action, his sense of coherence, and
his hard, clean prose. Yet Calmer
fears that W's method is "too simple
and surfacy and narrow," so that "it
rarely reaches upward toward an intensity of perception and imagery."
Reprinted: 1978.209.

170. Cameron, May. "Author! Author!:
Prize-Winning Novelist Talks of Communism and Importance of 'Felt Life.'" New
York Post (12 March), p. 7.
Based on an interview, this biographical article discusses W's allegiance to Communism, his Southern
background, his migration north, his
early reading, and his literary purposes. The Bible, H. L. Mencken, and
naturalism influenced W.

171. _____. "Books on Our Table." New
York Post (4 November), p. 19.
Contains a notice of the O. Henry
Memorial Award Prize Stories of 1938
mentioning that "Fire and Cloud"
received second prize.

172. Carmon, Walt. "About Books." Daily
Worker (12 December), p. 7.
Notes that a Russian translation of
UTC has been published in Moscow by
the State Publishing House in a much
larger edition than the original.

173. _____. "What'll We Do? Let's
See--." Daily Worker (4 June), p. 7.
Mentions the party for W at the I. W.
O. Center in Harlem.

174. Casson, R. Habenicht. "Today's
Book." Macon Telegraph (15 November), p.
4.
Review of the O. Henry Memorial Award
Prize Stories of 1938 with brief,
rather unfavorable mention of "Fire
and Cloud."

175. Cheny, Meyer. "Book Reviews: Writer
Focuses on Negro Persecution." Hollywood
Now (20 May).
Favorable review of UTC from an anti-
Fascist perspective. Commenting on
all four stories, Cheny praises W's
social message and literary artistry.
"From problem to solution here is the
best integrated story of the negro
people that has ever appeared."

176. C.[hilders], J.[ames] S.[axon].
"This Kind of Book Does Little Good and
Much Harm." Birmingham News-Age-Herald
(1 May), Magazine Sec., p. 7.
Unfavorable review of UTC objecting
to W's bitterness and one-sided view
of race relations. Overlooking efforts at amelioration by whites of
good will, W exacerbates the problem
by his shrill overstatement.
Reprinted: 1978.209.

177. Conroy, Jack. "O. Henry Memorial
Award Prize Stories of 1938. Edited by
Harry Hansen." Sunday Worker (27 Novem-
ber), Progressive Weekly Sec., p. 10.
Review praising "Fire and Cloud." W's
talent is richly inventive.

178. ____ . "Son of the South." Sunday
Worker (10 April), Sec. 2, pp. 6, 9.
    Favorable review of UTC with a dis-
    cussion of the social and biographi-
    cal background of the work. By em-
    bracing Marxism, W overcame unreason-
    ing hatred of all whites and produced
    "a real contribution to American
    literature."

179. Cooke, Marvel. "Prize Novellas,
Brave Stories." New York Amsterdam News
(9 April), p. 16.
    Highly favorable review of UTC plac-
    ing W "in the vanguard of American
    literature." Cooke praises his use of
    dialect, which he finds even better
    than Zora Neale Hurston's, and his
    use of "underwriting." These "start-
    ling, tragic stories" are "quite the
    most exciting proletarian literature
    produced during the past twelve
    months."
    Reprinted: 1978.209.

180. Corbin, Phil. Letter to Mike Gold.
Daily Worker (9 May), p. 7.
    In Gold's "Change the World" column,
    Corbin disputes Alan Calmer's Daily
    Worker review of UTC and praises the
    work highly.

181. Cowley, Malcolm. "Long Black Song."
The New Republic, 94 (6 April), 280.
    Favorable review of UTC, which Cowley
    finds "both heartening, as evidence
    of a vigorous new talent, and terri-
    fying as the expression of a racial
    hatred that has never ceased to grow
    and gets no chance to die." The plots
    of the first three stories are simi-
    lar. Cowley likes "Big Boy Leaves
    Home" best and "Long Black Song"
    least. "Fire and Cloud" tries to
    transform race conflict into class
    conflict. Cowley finds the first
    three "headlong narratives" lacking
    in "technical devices . . . and with-
    out psychological subtlety," but
    effective nevertheless.
    Reprinted: 1960.198;1961.214; 1963.
    146; 1978.209.

182. Cullen, Countee. "Uncle Tom's Cabin
[sic], by Richard Wright." The African,
1 (July-August), 139.
    Favorable review of UTC calling W "an
    important and impressive addition to
    American writers." He is angry, but
    keeps his anger under strict artistic
    control. Cullen singles out "Fire and
    Cloud" and "Big Boy Leaves Home" for
    special praise. Let "those in high
    places . . . not deplore the anger,
    the terror, the sickening horror of
    these stories. Let them remove the
    causes."
    Reprinted: 1978.209.

183. Davis, Alfred. "The Story of a
Winner--." Daily Worker (25 February),
p. 7.
    Not wholly accurate biographical
    sketch of W as the Story contest
    winner. Quotes W on his working class
    and Communist allegiances, and quotes
    "The Ethics of Living Jim Crow" at
    length. Includes a large photograph
    of W.

184. Davis, Bennett. "Books of the Week
in Review." Buffalo Courier Express (13
March), Sec. V, p. 4.
    Contains an announcement of the award
    of the Story prize to W. Includes
    brief biographical details.

185. Davis, Elrick B. "Colored Author
Emerges From Writers' Project." The
Cleveland Press (28 September), p. 13.
    Favorable notice of UTC comparing W
    to Hughes and Steinbeck, praising the
    dramatic quality of the stories, and
    explaining the title.

186. Davis, Frank Marshall. "ANP Review-
er Says Richard Wright's Prize-Winning
Volume, 'Uncle Tom's Children' Vividly
Portrays South." San Antonio Register.
    Favorable review of UTC with sum-
    maries of the four stories. Davis
    compares W to Hemingway as a "master
    of rugged realism." Rejecting the
    stereotype of the contented Southern
    black, W presents the truth about
    race relations in the South with
    artistry and power.
    Reprinted: 1938.187, 188, 189, 190,
    191, 192.

187. ____ . "Book Review." Chicago Bee
(2 April).
    Reprint of 1938.186.

188. ____ . "Book Review." The Kansas
City Call (1 April), p. [20].
    Reprint of 1938.186.

189. ____ . "Cover to Cover: Richard
Wright's Prize Volume 'Uncle Tom's Children,' Is Strong and Brilliant." Columbus (Ohio) Advocate.
    Reprint of 1938.186.

190. ____ . "A Review of 'Uncle Tom's
Children.'" Unidentified Houston (?)
newspaper.
    Reprint of 1938.186.

191. ____ . "Richard Wright's Prize Volume 'Uncle Tom's Children,' Brilliant."
Atlanta Daily World (1 April), p. 2.
    Reprint of 1938.186.

192. ____ . "Richard Wright's Prize Volume 'Uncle Tom's Children,' Brilliant."
Orlando Morning Sentinel (2 April).

Reprint of 1938.186.

193. Deshler, David. "Uncle Tom's Children by Richard Wright." Book-of-the-
Month Club News (May), p. 5.
    Favorable notice mentioning the Story
prize and commenting on the theme of
injustice: "Here is Negro experience,
profoundly felt and incisively set
down, bitterly set down." Deshler
praises W's writing ability, especially his "rare skill at dramatic
narrative."

194. Elistratova, A. "Deti diadi Toma."
Moscow Pravda (21 October), p. 4.
    Favorable review of the Russian
translation of UTC. Noting the transition from Harriet Beecher Stowe's
submissive sufferer and quoting Lenin
on the conditions of black life in
America, Elistratova expresses admiration for W's revolutionary spirit.
Despite the gloom of the situations
depicted, the work as a whole offers
hope for a new South of free workers.
Elistratova praises W's theme of the
rise of black revolutionary class
consciousness and his realistic
style. "In its political and literary
significance Richard Wright's Uncle
Tom's Children belongs among the best
works of contemporary literature."

195. F., I. K. "Reading and Writing."
Philadelphia Record (26 February), p.
11.
    Mentions the award of the Story prize
to W.

196. ____. "Reading and Writing." Philadelphia Record (12 March), p. 11.
    Mentions the award of first prize in
the Federal Writers Project contest
to UTC.

197. F., J. "Literary Achievement by
Young Negro Brings Picture of Race's
Plight." The San Diego Sunday Sun (29
May), p. 13.
    Favorable review of UTC comparing W
to Hemingway and Steinbeck. Rev.
Taylor's message at the end is the
book's message. The reviewer considers W's style "as typically musical
as the Negro race itself." The
stories are "the greatest literary
achievement from the Negro race . . .
stark, searing, sensitive."
Reprinted: 1978.209.

198. Farrell, James T. "Lynch Patterns."
Partisan Review, 4 (May), 57-58.
    Favorable review of UTC, a work of
coherence, authenticity, and power.
Farrell prefers W's direct realism to
the "tortured allegories" of other
writers. W's use of coincidence is
not a contrivance but a means of
emphasizing the operation of lynch
law. Farrell praises W's use of the
vernacular, but complains of certain
stylistic mannerisms. On the whole
UTC is "a true and powerful work
. . . a genuine literary achievement."
Reprinted: 1978.209.

199. Ford, James W. "The Negro People
March." Sunday Worker (14 August), Magazine Sec., pp. 5, 9.
    Calls W "our new comet" in litera-
ture. A photograph of W appears on p.
5.

200. Frazier, C. L. "Book Reviews."
Washington Tribune (26 February).
    Brief biographical sketch of W.

201. Gannett, Lewis. "Books and Things."
New York Herald Tribune (25 March), p.
17.
    Favorable review of UTC by a judge of
the Federal Writers Project contest.
Gannett expresses the hope that W's
life will "bring him happier experiences" to write about in the future.
But Gannett is deeply impressed by
the "power . . . brutal reality and
. . . occasional high-singing note of
black manhood" in the stories.
Reprinted: 1978.209.

202. ____. "Books and Things." New York
Herald Tribune (13 July), p. 17.
    Includes favorable mention of UTC.

203. ____. "Books and Things." New York
Herald Tribune (10 December), p. 11.
    Devotes two paragraphs to a "Footnote
on Filth," rebutting the claim of
U. S. Representative Joe Starnes of
Alabama that "The Ethics of Living
Jim Crow" was "the filthiest thing
that he had ever read." Gannett calls
it "a distinguished piece of writing,
clean as growing grass in its implicit philosophy, and written with
restraint as well as power."

204. ____. "Books and Things." New York
Herald Tribune (19 December), p. 13.
    Notes that UTC has been included in
the selections of the best books of
1938 by The Nation, The New Republic,
and Time.

205. ____. "Uncle Tom's Children by
Richard Wright." Book Union Bulletin
(April), pp. 1-2.
    Highly favorable review stressing the
theme of resistance. Gannett summarizes the four stories with special
attention to "Fire and Cloud," which
he considers "a beautifully told
story" that lifts the book "out of

the ruts of anger and despair" (p. 2). W is "the voice of a new generation of black America . . . not merely a prize-winner but a new American writer" (p. 2).

206. Gold, Mike. "Change the World: Give Us More Songs Like 'Casey Jones.'" Daily Worker (26 January), p. 7.
Column on Leadbelly referring to W's Daily Worker article on the singer.

207. Goldstein, Albert. "Literature and Less." New Orleans Times-Picayune (10 April), Sec. 2, p. 7.
Includes a brief notice of UTC praising W's craftsmanship, but complaining that "probably because he is so emotionally absorbed in his material, he fails to create characters that are anything but idealistic lay figures expressing his personal views."

208. Gordon, Eugene. "She Dramatized Slavery Before the World." Daily Worker (20 June), p. 7.
Concludes an article on Stowe and Uncle Tom's Cabin by referring to Uncle Tom's successor in UTC: "the Negro who knows how to distinguish between those whites who are his friends and those who are his enemies with that most effective of all modern weapons--correct organization."

209. G.[ovan], G.[ilbert] E. "Writers' Project Product." Chattanooga Sunday Times (17 April), Magazine Sec., p. 11.
Favorable review of UTC placing it in a developing tradition of black literature. The major themes of the stories are the fear and misunderstanding which lead to racial violence.
Reprinted: 1978.209.

210. Graham, M. "Change the World." Daily Worker (13 June), p. 7.
Letter in Mike Gold's column correcting an error made by "Harvard Square" in an earlier letter concerning Alan Calmer's review of UTC.

211. Grigor'ev, V. "Rasskazy o negritianskom proletariate. (Dedi diadi Toma)." Kniga i proletarskaia revoliutsiia, No. 12 (December), pp. 125-127.
Favorable review of the Russian translation of UTC. In contrast to the meek acquiescence of Stowe's Uncle Tom, W promotes resistance and revolution as means of confronting oppression. Grigor'ev praises the political dimension of W's stories, especially "Fire and Cloud" and "Bright and Morning Star," but he also comments favorably on W's presentation of character through drama-

tic action, his use of landscape, and his socially committed and committing realism.

212. H., H. H. "Books on Review: Uncle Tom's Children--By Richard Wright." Durham Sunday Herald-Sun (15 May), p. 7.
Favorable review noting the Federal Writers Project contest won by W and praising all the stories, especially "Big Boy Leaves Home." "Richard Wright is a writer with a sure-fire social sense and a talent that is alive and distinguished."

213. Hansen, Harry. "The First Reader." New York World-Telegram (26 March), p. 23.
Favorable review of UTC praising W as a racial spokesman and as a powerful and dramatic prose stylist. "Only after we have thought of the stories as social documents do we recognize the powerful impact of straightshooting prose." Hansen also provides some biographical details.
Reprinted: 1978.209.

214. _____. "The First Reader." New York World-Telegram (4 November), p. 27.
Favorable review of the O. Henry Memorial Award Prize Stories of 1938 with a paragraph on "Fire and Cloud" commenting on its length, power, and theme.

215. _____. "The First Reader." New York World-Telegram (7 December), p. 30.
Includes UTC on a list of recommended Christmas gift books.

216. _____. "Introduction," in his O. Henry Memorial Award Prize Stories of 1938. New York: Doubleday, Doran, pp. vii-xii.
Contains a discussion of "Fire and Cloud" emphasizing W's "vitality and power" (p. ix). Refers to "Blueprint for Negro Writing" for an understanding of W's literary theory (pp. ix-x).

217. _____. "Richard Wright," in his O. Henry Memorial Award Prize Stories of 1938. New York: Doubleday, Doran, p. 18.
Biographical headnote to "Fire and Cloud."

218. Hart, Scott. "The Federal Diary." The Washington Post (24 February), p. 6.
Mentions W's Story magazine award and gives a brief sketch of his background.

219. Hendry, Marion. "Prize Stories." The Jacksonville (Fla.) Sunday Times-Union (3 July), Sec. 3, p. 7.
Favorable review of UTC with summa-

ries of "Big Boy Leaves Home" and
"Fire and Cloud." "These accounts of
negro life sing with a plaintive
melody, haunting our souls, in telling of the few simple things necessary for the happiness of the negro;
they shout the protests of the black
man against the misunderstandings and
mistreatment by brutes who have no
code of discipline save the lash;
they plead for sympathetic understanding and a chance to be left
alone."
Reprinted: 1978.209.

220. Herndon, Angelo. "Uncle Tom's Children. By Richard Wright." Young Communist Review, 3 (June), 28.
    In this favorable review, Herndon
takes pride in W's achievement as a
black man and as a Communist. His
treatment of black life is realistic,
both in its depiction of Southern
injustice and its assertion of hopeful struggle. "Fire and Cloud" receives special praise.

221. Hetlage, Doris Talbot. "From the
Negro Viewpoint." St. Louis Post-Dispatch (3 April), p. 4-I.
    Favorable review of UTC praising W's
emotional power and "terse prose."
Each story is briefly summarized.
Despite the excellent characterization of Rev. Taylor, "Fire and Cloud"
conveys "the only slightly false note
of the entire book."
Reprinted: 1978.209.

222. Hicks, Granville. "Richard Wright's
Prize Novellas." New Masses, 27 (29
March), 23-24.
    Favorable review of UTC, a book show-
ing that "the revolutionary movement
has given birth to another first-rate
writer" (p. 23). W not only shows the
deep resentment of the Southern black
but expresses hope for a better way,
as in "Fire and Cloud." Hicks praises
W's intensity, straightforward narrative, dialogue, and emotional complexity. "Down by the Riverside" and
"Fire and Cloud" have some structural
problems, but for the most part UTC
"is not only a fine piece of writing;
it is the beginning of a distinguished career" (p. 24).
Reprinted: 1974.81; 1978.209.

223. Holmes, Eugene C. "New Stories of
the Negro People." American Teacher, 22
(May-June), 34.
    Highly favorable review of UTC, an
"unforgettable landmark in American
fiction." The stories are powerful
enough to inspire a determination to
rectify the conditions they portray.
Reprinted: 1978.209.

224. H.[orton], P.[hilip]. "A Bracket of
Newer Novels." The Providence Sunday
Journal (10 April), Sec. VI, p. 6.
    Contains an unfavorable review of UTC
expressing the hope that "the race
hatred that animates these tales will
be softened somewhat in the author's
future work." Admitting that W does
not exaggerate the "community hysteria" of white racism, the reviewer
argues that some humane whites do
exist and their recognition would
make for contrast and balance.
Reprinted: 1978.209.

225. Hurston, Zora Neale. "Stories of
Conflict." The Saturday Review of Literature, 17 (2 April), 32.
    Unfavorable review of UTC conceding
W's "facility" and "beautiful writing," but complaining that his violence and sensationalism do not touch
"the broader and more fundamental
phases of Negro life." W's characters
are too "elemental and brutish," and
his ideology is too Communist.
Reprinted: 1978.209.

226. Jackson, Joseph Henry. "A Bookman's
Notebook." San Francisco Chronicle (19
April), p. 11.
    Favorable review of UTC deeming the
stories "a brutal, horrifying fictional record" of Southern black
life, but an utterly authentic one.
"Big Boy Leaves Home," "Down by the
Riverside," and "Fire and Cloud"
receive specific discussion.

227. Jewett, Philip. "Short Stories of
Early 1938." The Philadelphia Inquirer
(18 June), p. 12.
    Includes a highly favorable notice of
UTC, than which "no better short
stories have been written in our
time." Realistic, powerful, and un-
sentimental, they have great literary
quality "regardless of the intentions
with which they were written." Jewett
finds in them "hope and humor" as
well as "terror and despair."

228. Keith, Allen. "Books: Uncle Tom's
Children Richard Wright." Bags and Bag-
gage (April).
    Favorable review finding the stories
"structurally unrelated but in theme
and mood forming an impressive unity." Keith comments on the ideological implications of religion and the
class struggle in the work. He
praises W's literary artistry.

229. Kolstad, Freddie. "Have You Read
. . ." The Shreveport Times (3 April),
Sec. A, p. 3.
    Mixed review of UTC with emphasis on
the social theme. "Although Wright

has developed a technique that is clear and swift, although his structure is sound and logical, he is weak in character portrayal, subverting character to his thesis."

230. L., M. "Books." Workers Age (7 May), p. 5.
Favorable review in a Trotskyist newspaper of UTC noting the movement of the stories from individualism to collectivism and from caste consciousness to class consciousness. Describes each story briefly.

231. Lanman, Richard, "'Uncle Tom's Children' by Richard Wright." The Atlanta Journal (17 April), Sunday magazine, p. 12.
Favorable review emphasizing the black point of view and W's mastery of technique. The stories are "poignant, lusty tales" which "hold more of sorrow than joy, but more of hope than defeatism."
Reprinted: 1978.209.

232. Locke, Alain. "Jingo, Counter-Jingo and Us--Part 1. Retrospective Review of the Literature of the Negro: 1937." Opportunity, 16 (January), 7-11, 27.
Praises both "The Ethics of Living Jim Crow" and "Big Boy Leaves Home," calling the latter "the strongest note yet struck by one of our own writers in the staccato protest realism of the rising school of 'proletarian fiction.'" W's debut is as auspicious as Jean Toomer's in Cane.

233. Lyons, Leonard. "Lyons Den." New York Post (3 May), p. 13.
States that New Masses will publish "Bright and Morning Star" because Harper's Magazine rejected it.

234. M., G. E. Untitled clipping. Detroit Michigan Chronicle.
Favorable review of UTC, a book written without exaggeration for effect that counters popular beliefs about the South. Despite the fact that W provides an "overdose of tragedy" and could have included some "pleasant details," the book's focus on the present adds "dramatic force and intensity."
Reprinted: 1978.209.

235. Manngreen. "Left on Broadway." Daily Worker (9 April), p. 7.
Contains words of support for Eleanor Roosevelt's praise of UTC.

236. _____. "Left on Broadway." Daily Worker (16 May), p. 7.
Notes that W will chair a New Masses meeting on 18 May.

237. _____. "Left on Broadway." Daily Worker (6 June), p. 7.
Mentions that Lou Levenson is dramatizing "Bright and Morning Star" for the New York stage.

238. _____. "Left on Broadway." Daily Worker (c. 8 June).
Mentions W's novel in progress about juvenile delinquency based on an actual murder case.

239. _____. "Left on Broadway." Daily Worker (20 June), p. 7.
Mentions W's assignment to cover the Louis-Schmeling fight for New Masses.

240. Mar'ianov, M. "Pokolenie boz'by." Khar'kovskii Rabochii (14 October).
Favorable review of the Russian translation of UTC. In contrast to the submission of Stowe's Uncle Tom, W's characters find the meaning of their lives in militant struggle. Mar'ianov praises W's compressed, realistic style. The only defect of the book is the lack of white Communists, but W, a black Communist, is "undoubtedly a major literary figure."

241. Marsh, Fred T. "Hope, Despair and Terror." New York Herald Tribune Books (8 May), p. 3.
Highly favorable review of UTC calling the stories "one-act plays, poetic dramas, translated into a narrative prose that is nothing short of magnificent. The novellas are compounded of music and passion; and three of them (I except 'Down by the Riverside') are as fine long short stories as any of modern times." Marsh nominates W for the Pulitzer Prize.
Reprinted: 1978.209.

242. Martin, Lawrence. "Esquire's Five-Minute Shelf." Esquire, 10 (August), 86, 89.
Contains a brief, enthusiastic review of UTC. W's stories "carry a wallop" and evince "sheer writing power," causing the reviewer to "look for Richard Wright to go places."

243. Max, Alan. "Negroes March Against Reaction, Says Ford in Report to Communist Party Convention." Daily Worker (30 May), pp. 1, 4.
Reports that the delegates "applauded vigorously" James W. Ford's praise of W.

244. Maxwell, Allen. "Uncle Tom's Children by Richard Wright." Southwest Review, 23 (April), 362-365.
Favorable review calling W one of

"the most promising young writers in America today" (p. 362). Maxwell praises W's style--"in the favorite Steinbeck tradition of meaty terseness" (p. 364)--his use of dialogue, his narrative technique, and his avoidance of overt propaganda. Reprinted: 1978.209.

245. Mendez, Edith. "Crossroads of a New World." Daily Worker (9 August), p. 7.
    States that "regularly of an evening Richard Wright, Ben Field, Albert Maltz and the young poet Ben Funaroff get together" at the Workers Bookshop in New York.

246. Minor Marcia. "An Author Discusses His Craft." Daily Worker (13 December), p. 7.
    Interview with W accompanied by a photograph of the author. W describes his method of studying other writers, mentioning Dostoevsky, Chekhov, Conrad, and Turgenev. He explains that the dialect in UTC resulted largely from eliminating apostrophes for the sake of convenience and time. He also discusses his purpose in writing UTC and comments on the gestation of his work in progress (NS).

247. Moon, Henry Lee. "Uncle Tom's Children by Richard Wright." Cleveland Eagle (8 April).
    Highly favorable review confirming the validity of W's depiction of Southern race relations and praising his literary artistry. Summarizes briefly each of the four stories. Moon has special praise for the message of hope in "Fire and Cloud."

248. M.[orrow], E. F.[rederic]. "Uncle Tom's Children by Richard Wright." The Crisis, 45 (May), 155.
    Favorable review praising the "dramatic and graphic fashion" with which W depicts white violence. Unlike other writers, he makes the lynchers rather than their victims the villains of the stories.

249. Murphy, Beatrice M. "The Book Worm." Washington Afro-American (7 May), p. 14.
    Although objecting strongly to obscene language in "Big Boy Leaves Home," Murphy reviews UTC favorably, praising the work's emotional power, characterization, and realism. She advises black readers to read the book despite its lapses of good taste.

250. Oak, V. V. "Uncle Tom's Children, by Richard Wright." The Quarterly Review of Higher Education Among Negroes, 6 (October), 309-310.
    Highly favorable review summarizing the plots of the four stories, emphasizing the theme of injustice and inhumanity, and praising W's simple but vivid style. Oak calls the work a "masterpiece" and "a book of the year," comparing its potential effect to that of Uncle Tom's Cabin.

251. O'Brien, Edward J., ed. The best Short Stories 1938 and the Yearbook of the American Short Story. Boston: Houghton Mifflin, p. 401.
    Lists "Silt" with an asterisk in the "Index of Distinctive Short Stories in American Magazines." "One, two or three asterisks are used to indicate relative distinction" (p. 393).

252. P., I. M. "Turns with a Bookworm." New York Herald Tribune Books (27 March), p. 14.
    Mentions a party to be given for W by Martha Foley and Whit Burnett.

253. ____. "Turns with a Bookworm." New York Herald Tribune Books (10 April), p. 18.
    Mentions a party given for W by Martha Foley and Whit Burnett.

254. Parker, Helen B. "Negro Prize-Winner." Nashville Banner (2 April), Magazine Sec., p. 2.
    Favorable review of UTC emphasizing the powerful social protest and praising W's language, dialect, humor, style, and characterization. Parker compares W to Faulkner. Of the four stories, "Big Boy Leaves Home" is the most artistic and "Fire and Cloud" the most socially articulate.

255. Pollack, Herman. Untitled article. Memphis Hebrew Watchman (26 May).
    Favorable review of UTC noting its special importance to Jewish readers because every type of racial prejudice breeds fascism. In his stories W proves that "in order for art to attain fulfillment, life must be portrayed as it is, not as it is wished for." Reprinted: 1978.209.

256. Poore, Charles. "Books of the Times." The New York Times (2 April), p. 13.
    Favorable review of UTC. Poore objects to W's use of phonetic dialogue and his implausibly villainous white characters, but he praises the author's descriptive power and his treatment of the theme of racial violence. Reprinted: 1978.209.

257. _____. "Books of the Times." The New York Times (8 July), p. 15.
Cites UTC as one of several recent books Poore has liked.

258. _____. "Books of the Times." The New York Times (15 December), p. 33.
Notes that UTC presents graphic and realistic pictures of black life.

259. Purcell, Malcolm, Jr. "Today's Book: Uncle Tom's Children, by Richard Wright." Macon Telegraph (15 April).
Mixed review praising W's style, description, dialogue, and narrative skill, but complaining that his presentation of Southern race relations is unfair and one-sided. Summarizes briefly each of the four stories. Reprinted: 1978.209.

260. Reeve, Agnes M. "Far Cry from Uncle Tom." Dayton Journal (12 June), Spotlight Sec., p. 9.
Unfavorable review of UTC. Conceding W's literary talent, Reeve objects to the violence and tragedy of the book. Readers of both races will dislike it, "For Negro and white man of these stories are equally cruel, lustful and bloodthirsty."
Reprinted: 1978.209.

261. Roberts, Carl. "Young Negro Writes Tales of Own Race." Dayton Daily News (3 April), Society Sec., p. 7.
Favorable review of UTC summarizing each of the four stories and calling "Wright's technique . . . powerful and realistic, and the conversations and thoughts of his characters . . . convincing." W may become "an outstanding writer" if he retains his power while broadening his scope.

262. Roberts, Mary-Carter. "Uncle Tom's Children. By Richard Wright." The Washington Sunday Star (27 March), p. F-4.
Unfavorable review attacking proletarian literature in general and W's book in particular. Inspired by hatred of whites, W has oversimplified his characters ("innocent and noble black men and women . . . and unrelievedly wicked whites") and resorted to sensationalism. UTC is "lacking in essential vitality."

263. Roosevelt, Eleanor. "My Day." New York World-Telegram (1 April), p. 25.
Includes a brief comment on the "beautifully written" UTC. Mrs. Roosevelt is most impressed by "the tragedy of fear portrayed."
Reprinted: 1938.264.

264. _____. "My Day." The Atlanta Constitution (2 April), p. 12.

Reprint of 1938.263.

265. Russell, Caro Green. "The Literary Lantern." Greensboro Daily News (13 March), Sec. 3, p. 5.
Mentions the award of the Story prize to W.

266. S., G. M. "Erskine's Novel of Whitman and Other Recent Fiction." New Haven Register (30 October), Sec. 4, p. 4.
Contains a notice of O. Henry Memorial Award Prize Stories of 1938 mentioning "Fire and Cloud."

267. Selby, John. "The Literary Guidepost." The Bridgeport Telegram (2 April), p. 16.
Favorable notice of UTC. The "stories are real, ablaze with emotion, compact, economical." W presents only one side of the racial issue, however.
Reprinted: 1938.268, 269, 270, 271, 272, 273.

268. _____. "Literary Guidepost." The Bristol (Va.-Tenn.) News Bulletin (2 April), p. 4.
Reprint of 1938.267.

269. _____. "The Literary Guidepost." Charlotte News (15 May), p. 5.
Reprint of 1938.267.

270. _____. "The Literary Guidepost." Lodi (Cal.) Times (4 April).
Reprint of 1938.267.

271. _____. "Literary Guidepost." The San Bernardino Daily Sun (3 April), p. 20.
Reprint of 1938.267.

272. _____. "The Literary Guidepost." Tampa Sunday Tribune (3 April), Part Three, p. 12.
Reprint of 1938.267.

273. _____. "A Novel a Day." Gastonia Daily Gazette (9 April), p. 12.
Reprint of 1938.267.

274. Shapiro, Irvin T. "On Proletarian Stories." New Masses, 27 (24 May), 21.
In a letter to the editor, Shapiro complains about the general quality of proletarian literature but praises highly "Bright and Morning Star" for its careful construction and dramatic quality.

275. Shneider, A. "Richard Rait." Internatsional'naia literatura, No. 7 (July), pp. 175-177.
Favorable review of the Russian translation of UTC. After placing the work in its full historical, social,

and political context, Shneider reviews W's career showing the relation of his poetry to his prose. Among his outstanding literary qualities are his use of poetic folk materials, his ability to show character through dramatic action, and his empathy with black workers.
Reprinted in abridged form: 1939.103.

276. Sillen, Samuel. "Books of the Season." New Masses, 29 (4 October), 22-23.
Refers favorably to UTC.

277. _____. "Review and Comment: The Funeral Is Off Again." New Masses, 29 (8 November), 23-24.
Claims that O. Henry Award prizes to W, Steinbeck, and Albert Maltz demonstrate the vitality of proletarian literature. Quotes W on the greater importance of social relevance compared to literary technique.

278. Smiley, Nixon. "The Right to a Hearing." The Miami Herald (25 December), Magazine-Editorial Sec., p. 5.
Favorable review of UTC appearing in Pauline Corley's column "Heralding New Books." Smiley praises highly W's use of dialect and gives an extensive summary of "Fire and Cloud," which he considers the best of the four stories.
Reprinted: 1978.209.

279. Smith, Lillian E. "Dope with Lime." The North Georgia Review, 3 (Spring), 2, 31-32.
States that UTC "is receiving much favorable notice."

280. Thomas, Aubrey L. Untitled clipping. Philadelphia Evening Public Ledger (29 March).
Favorable review of UTC stressing the theme of lynching and focusing on "Big Boy Leaves Home" and "Fire and Cloud."

281. Thomas, Jesse O. "Urban League." The Atlanta Constitution (24 April), p. 3-C.
Discusses the discovery of W through the Federal Writers Project contest. Quotes from the opinions of the judges and from W's autobiographical letter.

282. Tobias, Rowena Wilson. "Southern Fiction." The Charleston (S. C.) News and Courier (27 March), Sec. III, p. 3.
Includes an unfavorable notice of UTC complaining of propaganda and subjectivity. "Fire and Cloud" is the best story of the four.

283. Tolson, M.[elvin] B. "Caviar and Cabbage: The Biggest Event of 1938 in Black America." Washington Tribune (19 March), p. 4.
Celebrates W's success in winning the Federal Writers Project contest and chastises the black press for failing to take adequate notice of this event. Tolson admires W's genius in "Fire and Cloud" and the poetry.
Reprinted: 1982.136a.

284. Tooill, Kenneth D. "Books." Columbus Ohio State Journal (6 April), p. 5.
Contains a favorable review of UTC stressing W's role as a militant racial spokesman. But he is also a powerful "literary genius" with an "exquisite talent for dramatic narrative."

285. Tourtellot, Arthur Bernon. "A Voice for the Negro." Boston Evening Transcript (9 April), Sec. 3, p. 1.
Generally favorable review of UTC praising W's talent and powerful style. He will be a distinguished voice for his race. But the stories are "a little too impassioned," lacking "that necessary minimum of restraint that makes an eloquent appeal a permanently forceful one."

286. Tyus, William H. L. "'Uncle Tom's Children' Are Stories about Negroes, Written by a Negro." Memphis Commercial Appeal (1 May), Sec. IV, p. 9.
Mixed review calling W's depiction of Southern race relations "grossly fictionalized," one-sided, and potentially inflammatory. But Tyus praises highly the work's literary qualities, the "colorfully written, dramatics-filled, soul-stirring presentation." Because of the dialect, obscenities, and sexual candor, however, the book is not suitable for young readers.
Reprinted: 1978.209.

287. Van Doren, Carl. "Carl Van Doren Discusses Two Books Dealing with Share-Croppers." The Boston Herald (2 April), p. 7.
Most of this review concerns Land Without Moses by Charles Curtis Munz, but UTC is also noticed. Van Doren calls it "less discouraging" than Land Without Moses because W's blacks, unlike Munz's whites, move toward resistance.

288. Van Gelder, Robert. "Four Tragic Tales." The New York Times Book Review (3 April), pp. 7, 16.
Favorable review of UTC comparing W to Hemingway and emphasizing the literary skill of the stories, especially "Down by the Riverside." "For all the load of hate and bitterness

they carry, his stories come alive as art." Van Gelder takes consolation in the notion that the literary recognition that W is receiving is "illustrative of the freedom that minorities enjoy in this country." Reprinted: 1978.209.

289. Vostokova, S. "Richard Rait. 'Dedi Diadi Toma.'" Novy mir (November), pp. 281-283.
    Favorable review of the Russian translation of UTC appearing in International Literature. In contrast to the submissive meekness of Stowe's Uncle Tom, W's protagonists are strong and assertive, resisting white oppression. Vostokova summarizes and comments on each of the four stories included: "Big Boy Leaves Home," "Down by the Riverside," "Fire and Cloud," and "Bright and Morning Star." He compares Aunt Sue of the last story to the heroine of Gorky's Mother. Departing from the alienated, individual heroes of the writers of the Harlem Renaissance, the Wrightian hero identifies with his people. Vostokova praises W's ideology and all aspects of his literary art.

290. Wallace, Henry. "Young Negro Tells of Trials of His Race." The Lexington (Ky.) Sunday Herald-Leader (10 April), p. 5.
    Favorable review of UTC commenting on each of the four stories. Wallace emphasizes their coherence, their validity as social documents, and their emotional power, a power achieved "through the medium of detached objectivity."

291. Walton, Edith H. "O. Henry Prizes." The New York Times Book Review (13 November), pp. 6-7.
    Favorable review of O. Henry Memorial Award Prize Stories of 1938 with two laudatory paragraphs on "Fire and Cloud," judged "a long, fine, and very moving story."

292. Webster, Harvey Curtis. "Story's Prize W. P. A. Winner." The Louisville Courier-Journal (3 April), Sunday Magazine Sec., p. 7.
    Favorable review of UTC praising W's literary excellence but stressing "the controversial nature of his subject matter." The theme of the four stories is racial antagonism that can erupt in violence.

293. Wells, Simon. "Current Magazines: New Masses Supplements Feature Outstanding Work." Daily Worker (17 June), p. 7.
    Praises highly "Bright and Morning

Star" for its style and ideas. The story is not tragic but prophetic in depicting the heroism of the oppressed that will lead to eventual triumph.

1939

1. Anon. "Alain Locke Criticizes 1938 Negro Literature." Washington Tribune (21 January), p. 9.
    Mentions briefly UTC.

1a. Anon. "America Must Belong to Citizens, Hughes Tells 500 Writers." Washington Tribune (17 June), p. 4.
    Mentions briefly W's attendance at the American Writers Congress.

1b. Anon. "Among the Signers of Peace Appeal to All Americans." Daily Worker (14 August), p. 2.
    W is one of four hundred signers of a letter supporting peace in cooperation with the Soviet Union.

2. Anon. "Anthology of New Negro Writing Is to Be Published." Norfolk Journal and Guide (1 April), p. 9.
    Announces preparation of "a little anthology of NEW NEGRO WRITING, edited by Richard Wright and Alan Calmer," to be issued by International Publishers.

3. Anon. "Between Ourselves." New Masses, 30 (7 February), 2.
    W is one of "the sponsors of the Pink Slip Cabaret being held by the Writers Division of the Committee for the Arts Projects on . . . February 5" in New York.

4. Anon. "Between Ourselves." New Masses, 31 (4 April), 2.
    Mentions the award of a Guggenheim Fellowship to W.

5. Anon. "Between Ourselves." New Masses, 31 (13 June), 2.
    Mentions a New Masses party which W attended.

6. Anon. "Between Ourselves." New Masses, 32 (15 August), 2.
    Announces that Theodore Ward will read his dramatization of "Bright and Morning Star" at the 135th Street Branch of the New York Public Library under the sponsorship of the Harlem Suitcase Theater.

7. Anon. "Book Marks for Today." New York World-Telegram (2 February), p. 19.
    Notes that on 5 February W will attend a fund-raising affair for writers dismissed from the Federal Writers Project.

8. Anon. "Book Notes." New York Herald Tribune (29 April), p. 13.
Mentions that W "will receive a token of esteem from federal Arts Council members" at a dance and exhibition on 12 May.

9. Anon. "Book Notes." New York Herald Tribune (5 August), p. 9.
Contains an announcement that NS will be published in September.

10. Anon. "Book Notes." New York Herald Tribune (8 December), p. 24.
Announces the forthcoming publication of NS and notes W's talk in Edwin Seaver's course at the New School for Social Research on 8 December.

11. Anon. "Books and Authors." New Masses, 30 (14 February), 27.
Mentions the inclusion of "Bright and Morning Star" in Edward J. O'Brien's forthcoming Best Short Stories for 1939.

11a. Anon. "Books on the Negro in America Being Compiled by Federal Writers." Washington Tribune (11 March), p. 5.
Mentions briefly W's affiliation with the Writers Project.

12. Anon. "Brief Notices." New Masses, 34 (26 December), 27.
Compares the O. Henry Memorial Award Prize Stories of 1939 unfavorably to the collection of the preceding year, which included "Fire and Cloud."

13. Anon. "Chicagoans Create Best Race Literature of 1938." The Chicago Defender (21 January), p. 5.
Cites Alain Locke's annual review mentioning W. See 1939.91.

13a. Anon. "Civic Affairs Committee Presents Richard Wright."
Flyer announcing a lecture by W as part of "An Evening of Negro Culture."

14. Anon. "Cultural Conference to Sponsor Meeting." New York Amsterdam News (3 June), p. 6.
Lists W as a member of a committee sponsoring protest of the dismissal of workers from the WPA arts project.

15. Anon. "Ford, Wright, Hughes to Speak at Savoy Sept. 2." The Chicago Defender (2 September), p. 5.
Announces a talk by W at the Festival of Negro Culture. Mentions W's work in progress.

16. Anon. "Former Jackson Youth Awarded $2,500 Scholarship." Unidentified clipping.

Praises W's literary work and announces his Guggenheim fellowship.

16a. Anon. "Former Laborer Gets Guggenheim Award to Write." Washington Tribune (8 April), p. 9.
Announces the fellowship, mentions UTC, and sketches briefly W's background.

17. Anon. "Forthcoming Books." The New York Times Book Review (31 December), p. 11.
Announces NS for February publication.

17a. Anon. "Graphic Picture of Harlem in N. Y. Guide." Washington Tribune (17 June), p. 5.
Describes and quotes from the chapter on Harlem without mentioning W's authorship.

18. Anon. "Guggenheim Award to WPA Worker for His Brilliant Creative Writings." The Chicago Defender (8 April), p. 4.
Announces the award and states that the success of UTC inspired W to continue work on his novel.

19. Anon. "Guggenheim Fund Names 69 Fellows." The New York Times (27 March), p. 21.
Lists W.

20. Anon. "Guggenheim Prize to Richard Wright." New York Amsterdam News (1 April), pp. 1, 15.
Quotes liberally from an interview with W. The Guggenheim book will deal with urban women. W comments on his youth and his affiliation with the Communist Party, which began in 1933. A photograph of W appears.

21. Anon. "Harlem Suitcase Theatre."
Printed announcement of Theodore Ward's premiere reading of his adaptation of "Bright and Morning Star" on 11 August 1939 at the West 135th Street Library.

22. Anon. "Harlem to Hold Cultural Parley This Week-End." Daily Worker (3 May), p. 7.
Lists W as a sponsor of the Harlem Cultural Convention.

23. Anon. "Mr. O'Brien Chooses--In Two Volumes." Book-of-the-Month Club News (July), p. [10].
Review of Edward J. O'Brien's Fifty Best American Short Stories and Best Short Stories, 1939 mentioning W briefly.

24. Anon. "Native Son," in Harper's Catalogue. New York: Harper Brothers.

Compares the novel to Crime and Punishment as a gripping tale of murder,
pursuit, and punishment.

25. Anon. "Negro Art." Sunday Worker (12
February), p. 4.
Photograph with caption of UTC and
other works displayed by a WPA art
project in Harlem.

26. Anon. "Negro Culture Conference
Opens Here." Daily Worker (6 May), p. 4.
Announces that W will be present.

27. Anon. "Negro Leader to Speak on
Anti-Lynch Bill." Daily Worker (2 May),
p. 3.
Announces that W will speak at a
future forum sponsored by the Abraham
Lincoln Club.

28. Anon. "Negro Writers Make Fine Contribution to Literature." New York Amsterdam News (17 June), p. 5.
Mentions W's talk on "The Short Novel" at the American Writers Congress.

29. Anon. "New Wright Book Due in Sep-
tember." New York Amsterdam News (26
August), p. 3.
Favorable review of NS stressing its
social import and mentioning the
Nixon case.

30. Anon. "Noted Figures in World of
Letters at Third American Writers' Congress." Daily Worker (2 June), p. 7.
W, whose photograph appears, will
participate in a session on the
writing of fiction.

31. Anon. "Noted Negro Writers Urge
Congress to Back Art Projects." Daily
Worker (17 May), p. 9.
W, Countee Cullen, and Alain Locke
support the Federal Arts Projects.

32. Anon. "Noted Writers Back Fight for
Art Projects." Daily Worker (25 April),
p. 5.
W is one of the signers of a letter
to Congress supporting the Federal
Arts Projects.

33. Anon. "The O'Brien Short Stories and
Other Recent Works of Fiction." The New
York Times Book Review (4 June), p. 6.
Singles out "Bright and Morning Star"
as one of the best stories in the
O'Brien collection. The dramatic
quality with which the protest theme
is rendered and the "fine, glowing
imagery" make it "a tragic story, yet
a strangely beautiful one."

34. Anon. "O'Brien's Short Story
Annual." New York Herald Tribune (c.
March).

Mentions "Bright and Morning Star."

35. Anon. "Portrait of John Reed Is
Presented to New Masses." Daily Worker
(6 June), p. 7.
Notes that W was present at a New
Masses reception.

36. Anon. "Recital."
Printed announcement of W's lecture
"The Cultural Contributions of the
Negro to America" to be given, together with two other events, at the
Central YMCA in Brooklyn on 12 May
1939 under the sponsorship of Gwendolyn Bennett, Helen Taschner Tas,
and Benjamin F. Butler, Jr.

37. Anon. "Reprints, New Editions." New
York Herald Tribune Books (9 July), p.
14.
Review of Edward J. O'Brien's anthology of the Fifty Best American Short
Stories 1915-1939 mentioning "Bright
and Morning Star."

38. Anon. "Richard Wright Awarded Guggenheim Fellowship to Complete Book."
Opportunity, 17 (May), 151.
News item with some biographical
details.

39. Anon. "Richard Wright, Negro Prize-
Winning Author, Is Awarded Guggenheim
Honor." Daily Worker (29 March), p. 2.
News announcement accompanied by a
photograph of W. His "life story [is]
as interesting as that of Joe Louis."

40. Anon. "Richard Wright on Central Y
Program." Daily Worker.
Announces W's lecture on "The Cul-
tural Contributions of the Negro to
America."

41. Anon. "Richard Wright to Be Honored." Daily Worker (8 May), p. 7.
Announces a dance honoring W to be
held by members of the Federal Arts
Council.

42. Anon. "Richard Wright's Work in
Collection of Fifty Best Short Stories."
Daily Worker (13 May), p. 7.
Refers to the Edward J. O'Brien
volume.

43. Anon. "69 Fellowships of Guggenheim
Fund Awarded." New York Herald Tribune
(27 March), p. 11.
Lists W as a winner.

44. Anon. "Soviet Critics Praise Books
by Sinclair, Wright and Hemingway."
Daily Worker (27 March), p. 7.
All three writers, whose photographs
appear, are viewed as anti-fascists.
The concluding installment is "Soviet

Critics, Readers Laud Books by Sinclair, Wright and Angelo Herndon."

45. ____. "Soviet Critics, Readers Laud Books by Sinclair, Wright and Angelo Herndon." Daily Worker (28 March), p. 7.
    Comments on the favorable reception of the Russian translation of UTC and quotes from A. Elistratova's review in Pravda. The first installment is "Soviet Critics Praise Books by Sinclair, Wright and Hemingway."

46. Anon. "Soviet Views of Some American Books." International Literature, No. 2, pp. 101-104.
    Contains an account of the favorable Soviet reception of the Russian translation of UTC and quotes from reviews by A. Elistratova and M. Mar'ianov (pp. 103-104).

47. Anon. "Symposium on Negro Culture Today." Daily Worker (11 February), p. 7.
    Announces a talk by W on "Negro Culture in New York" at the Harlem Community Center under the sponsorship of the Federal Arts Project.

48. Anon. "To Adapt Wright's Book." Daily Worker.
    Announces Theodore Ward's dramatic version of "Bright and Morning Star."

49. Anon. "To Honor Ford at Harlem Dinner Friday." Daily Worker (12 April), p. 5.
    W is one of the sponsors of a testimonial for James W. Ford.

49a. Anon. "Tribune Columnist Gets Omega Award." Washington Tribune (4 November), p. 3.
    Mentions W briefly.

50. Anon. "Uncle Tom's Children by Richard Wright." The London Times Literary Supplement (8 April), p. 205.
    Mixed review taking issue with Paul Robeson's characterization of W in the preface to the British edition as "a great artist." The reviewer applauds "the starkness, the economy, the clarity" of W's treatment of his subject, but argues that the author's portrayal of whites is lacking "even the rudiments of decency and fair play" and is deficient in the balance--the "broad sane appreciation of human nature"--essential to great art.

51. Anon. Unidentified clipping.
    Photograph of W with a caption on his biographical and literary background.

52. Anon. Untitled clipping. The New York Sun.
    Announces that W will speak in Edwin Seaver's course on "These United States" at the New School for Social Research.

53. Anon. "W. E. B. Du Bois' New Book at Hall Library." The Chicago Defender (8 July), p. 23.
    Mentions "Bright and Morning Star."

54. Anon. "Wright, Richard," in Harper Brothers Trade List. New York: Harper Brothers, p. 71.
    Lists UTC and NS, the latter still in press.

55. Anon. "Wright Speaks Tonight on Negro Culture." Daily Worker (12 May), p. 3.
    Other participants in the program "An Evening of Negro Culture" at the Brooklyn YMCA are Juanita Lewis and Leonard Franklin.

56. Anon. "Wright to Talk at Negro Arts Meeting Friday." Daily Worker (9 May), p. 5.
    Announces W's talk on "The Cultural Contributions of the Negro to America" at the Brooklyn YMCA.

57. Anon. "Writers Congress." New Masses, 31 (16 May), 17.
    Lists W as one of many signers of a call of the League of American Writers to its third congress.

58. Aswell, Edward C. "Don't Burn the Books!" New Masses, 30 (24 January), 15.
    Praises W as an example of the importance of the support given to young writers by the Federal Writers Project. Predicts that W's "will be one of the distinguished careers in American letters."

59. Benét, Stephen Vincent. "O'Brien's Choice." The Saturday Review of Literature, 20 (8 July), 5.
    Reviewing Fifty Best American Short Stories, 1914 to 1939, Benét praises O'Brien for including "Bright and Morning Star," in which "Wright displays gifts that ought to take him a long, long way."

60. Brown, Sterling A. "The American Race Problem as Reflected in American Literature." The Journal of Negro Education, 8 (July), 275-290.
    Contains a brief, favorable discussion of UTC (p. 289).

61. Bruegel, Pete. "A Reviewer Takes a Critical Look at the Best Books Written in '38." People's Daily World (10 January), p. 5.

Mentions UTC and includes a photograph of W with caption.

62. Burnett, Whit. "Don't Burn the
Books!" New Masses, 30 (24 January), 16.
   Cites W as an example of the impor-
   tance of the Federal Writers Project.

63. Cameron, May. "Books on Our Table:
Old Home Week for Story Fans." New York
Post (28 June), p. 15.
   Mentions favorably "Bright and Morn-
   ing Star," included in Edward J.
   O'Brien's Fifty Best American Short
   Stories, 1915-1939.

64. Chase, Bill. "All Ears." New York
Amsterdam News (1 April), p. 20.
   Social column containing a congratu-
   latory note on the award of a Guggenheim Fellowship to W.

65. Conroy, Jack. "A Novel of Negro
Migration from the South to the North."
Sunday Worker (23 July), Progressive
Weekly Sec., p. 10.
   Somewhat unfavorable review of Waters
   E. Turpin's O Canaan! concluding that
   W could have done a better job with
   Turpin's theme of the Great Migra-
   tion.

66. _____. "O'Brien's 'Best Short
Stories' Fail to Mirror American Life."
Sunday Worker (11 June), Progressive
Weekly Sec., p. 10.
   Includes praise of "Bright and Morning Star" for its narrative skill,
   emotional power, and political relevance. But Conroy would also like to
   see stories about successful labor
   struggles.

67. _____. "Outstanding Books of 1938."
Sunday Worker (1 January), Progressive
Weekly Sec., p. 10.
   Praises UTC, especially "Fire and
   CLoud," as proletarian literature
   showing "skillful . . . fusion of
   competent literary technique with
   accurate social analysis."

68. _____. "The Pulitzer Prize Novel."
People's Daily World (13 May), Progressive Weekly Sec., p. 10.
   Objects to the selection of The Year-
   ling and argues for the superior
   merit of UTC.
   Reprinted: 1939.69.

69. _____. "The Pulitzer Prize Novel."
Sunday Worker (14 May), Progressive
Weekly Sec., p. 10.
   Reprint of 1939.68.

70. _____. "Young Writers Need Elbow
Room; Do Little Magazines Solve Problem?" Sunday Worker (25 June), Progres-

sive Weekly Sec., p. 10.
   Stresses the importance of proletarian little magazines in fostering
   new talent, citing W as an example.

71. Crawford, Charlotte E. "'Bright and
Morning Star,' by Richard Wright." The
Arts Quarterly (Dillard University), 2
(September), 33.
   Highly favorable review of the story.
   Crawford views faith--in Christianity
   and in communism--as the central
   theme. She praises W's power and
   narrative skill.

72. Day, Daniel E. and Sherman Briscoe.
"Is the South Side Doomed? A Comprehen-
sive Study of Chicago's Great South
Side: Installment XIX: Many Famous
Authors Live on South Side." The Chicago
Defender (4 November), Sec. Two, p. 15.
   Mentions the past residence of W,
   "one of the most dynamic writers of
   the age."

73. Fletcher, Stuart. "Negro Fact and
Fiction." London Daily Herald (2 March),
p. 8.
   Favorable review of UTC. Rejecting
   stereotypes, W presents his black
   characters "as human beings, capable
   of dishonesty and cowardice as well
   as heroism, determination, and tenderness." Thus the reader sympathizes
   with them. The writing is "tense and
   vivid and convincing."

73a. Frazier, C. Leslie. "Book Comment."
Washington Tribune (4 February), p. 4.
   Lists UTC as "recommended reading."

74. Gannett, Lewis. "The Books You May
Be Reading This Fall." New York Herald
Tribune Books (17 September), pp. 1-2,
16, 19.
   Mentions W's work on a new novel (p.
   2).

75. Gitlow, Benjamin, Joseph E. Casey,
Joe Starnes, Martin Dies, Noah M. Mason,
Jerry Voorhis, Rhea Whitley, J. Parnell
Thomas, and J. B. Matthews. "Testimony
of Benjamin Gitlow--Resumed," in Inves-
tigation of Un-American Activities in
the United States. Vol. 7. Washington:
United States Government Printing
Office, pp. 4578-4603.
   In response to a question from Repre-
   sentative Starnes, Gitlow states that
   he does not know W (p. 4595).

76. Gold, Mike. "Change the World:
Readers and Writers Need a Magazine Like
Conroy's 'New Anvil.'" Daily Worker (14
June), p. 7.
   Stresses the role of little magazines
   in fostering new talent, citing W as
   an example.

77. Gordon, Donald. Untitled clipping. American News of Books (September).
    Comments on NS stressing its psychological insight.

78. Gordon, Eugene. "Negro Arts to Keynote 2-Day Talks." Daily Worker (25 April), p. 5.
    Lists W as a sponsor of the Harlem Community Cultural Conference.

79. _____. "Negro Genius Exhibits Work at Harlem Fair." Daily Worker (3 July), p. 4.
    Suggests that the books and manuscripts of W and other black writers should also have been included in the exhibits of the Negro Industrial Fair.

80. _____. "Negroes Contribute Great Cultural Wealth to U. S. on WPA Art Projects." Sunday Worker (25 June), p. 3.
    Quotes Roi Ottley on the benefits to W of the Federal Writers Project and the resulting enrichment of black and American culture.

81. _____. "A People's Theatre in Harlem." Daily Worker (7 August), p. 7.
    Mentions the planned production of Theodore Ward's dramatization of "Bright and Morning Star" by the Harlem Suitcase Theatre.

82. Gruliow, Leo. "The Russian Edition of 'International Literature.'" International Literature, No. 1 (January), pp. 123-124.
    Mentions the Russian translation of UTC and the Pravda review.

83. Hansen, Harry. "Short Stories Chosen for O. Henry Awards Are Collected in Book." The Pittsburgh Press (26 November), Society Sec., p. 8.
    A judge of the competition, Hansen expects W to write more "fine short stories."

84. Hayes, Sibyl C. "The Best Short Stories--1939. Edited by Edward J. O'Brien." San Jose Mercury Herald (16 July), p. 10.
    Favorable review including a summary of "Bright and Morning Star."

85. Ha.[ynes], G.[eorge] E.[dward]. "Negroes (American)," in 1939 Britannica Book of the Year. Ed. Walter Yust. Chicago: Encyclopaedia Britannica, pp. 470-471.
    Lists UTC.

86. Hughes, Langston. "'We Want America to Really Be America for Everybody,' Says Langston Hughes." Daily Worker (5 June), p. 7.
    Mentions W as an "excellent . . . craftsman."
    Reprinted: 1973.174.

87. Jack, Peter Monro. "Fiction," in The American Year Book. Ed. William M. Schuyler. New York: Thomas Nelson & Sons, pp. 799-805.
    Mentions briefly UTC and the inclusion of "Fire and Cloud" in the O. Henry Prize collection (p. 803).

88. [Jensen, Arthur E.]. "Literature, English and American," in The New International Year Book. Ed. Frank H. Vizetelly and Charles Earle Funk. New York: Funk & Wagnalls, pp. 413-418.
    Mentions briefly UTC (p. 416).

89. Kauffman, George. "Wright's 'Native Son' Is High on Fall List." Daily Worker (26 October), p. 7.
    Despite the general reluctance of publishers to release social protest, Harper's will publish NS in the fall.

90. Keys, Ulysses S. "Today's Talk: Richard Wright: 'Imprisoned Splendor': Opportunity and Ability." Chicago Bee (2 April).
    Laudatory column on W's achievements. Mentions his Guggenheim Fellowship and Story prize. Keys also quotes from W's autobiographical statement and moralizes on his success.

91. Locke, Alain. "The Negro: 'New' or Newer--A Retrospective Review of the Literature of the Negro for 1938. Part I." Opportunity, 17 (January), 4-10.
    Forecasts "a major literary career" for W because in UTC he "uses the novella with the sweep and power of epic tragedy" (p. 8). "Big Boy Leaves Home" and "Long Black Song" are preferable "for their poignant beauty" (p. 8) to "Down by the Riverside" and "Fire and Cloud," but the latter are powerful social indictments. "The force of Wright's versions of Negro tragedy in the South lies in the correct reading of the trivialities that in that hate-charged atmosphere precipitate these frightful climaxes of death and violence" (p. 8).

92. _____. "The Negro: 'New' or Newer--A Retrospective Review of the Literature of the Negro for 1938. Part II." Opportunity, 17 (February), 36-42.
    Finds the sections (by W) on black people in New York Panorama unsatisfactory because the treatment of Harlem "vacillates between superficial flippancy and hectic propagandistic expose" (p. 39).

93. _____. "The Negro's Contribution to American Culture." The Journal of Negro Education, 8 (July), 521-529.
Mentions W's work as an outstanding example of black protest fiction.

94. Lovell, John, Jr. "Negro-True." The Journal of Negro Education, 8 (January), 71-73.
Favorable review of UTC praising its refusal to perpetuate the plantation-tradition stereotypes which have dominated both black and white writing on the Southern black. While he believes that W's narrative power and thematic strength should guarantee the book a reading, Lovell asks whether the real drama of black life lies in the threat of lynching rather than its relatively rare fulfillment. Reprinted: 1978.209.

95. Manngreen. "Left on Broadway." Daily Worker.
Notes that W's work in progress required him to seek expert advice on the representation of legal matters.

96. McHenry, Beth. "Thomas Mann Elected Honorary President of Writers Congress; Fight on Fascism Stressed." Daily Worker (6 June), p. 5.
Notes that W participated actively in the organization and was elected to its national board.

97. Meltzer, Milton. "William Attaway, Negro Novelist." Daily Worker (26 June), p. 7.
Mentions a meeting at the University of Illinois between Attaway, a student, and W, who was addressing a meeting of a literary society.

98. Morgan, Henry. "Wright's Story Is Tops in 50 Best Short Stories." Daily Worker (17 July), p. 7.
Favorable review of the O'Brien collection praising "Bright and Morning Star" for its attack on racism and its emotional profundity. W's talent "burns with the fierceness of right and conviction."

99. Nevel'skii, V. "Deti diadi Toma." Oktiabr', Nos. 10-11 (October-November), pp. 326-328.
Favorable review of the Russian translation of UTC placing it in the context of Stowe's novel and cultural symbol. Nevel'skii notes the arrangement and structure of the stories leading toward revolutionary class consciousness. He analyses the four stories--"Big Boy Leaves Home," "Down by the Riverside," "Fire and Cloud," and "Bright and Morning Star"--to show the growth of the protagonist.

Aunt Sue is compared to the title character in Gorky's Mother.

100. R., H. "50 Best Stories." Sunday Worker (2 July), Progressive Weekly Sec., p. 10.
Praises O'Brien's inclusion of "Bright and Morning Star."

101. Randall, Richard. "Frederick Douglass Would Be Proud of Them." Sunday Worker (27 August), Progressive Weekly Sec., p. 3.
Notes that W will attend the Chicago Festival of Negro Culture and praises his anti-fascism, progressivism, and protest.

102. Robeson, Paul. "Foreword," in Uncle Tom's Children: Four Novellas. By Richard Wright. London: Gollancz, pp. 7-8.
Praises the stories for their truthful picture of life in the Deep South and for their literary artistry. "Would that everyone who has read Gone With the Wind would read Uncle Tom's Children!! [sic]" (p. 8).

103. Shneider, A. "Richard Rait," in Deti diadi Toma. By Richard Wright. Moscow: Goslitzdat, pp. 5-9.
Abridged reprint of 1938.275.

104. Shukotoff, Arnold. "Proletarian Short Stories." New Masses, 30 (3 January), 22-23.
Praises "Fire and Cloud" and "Bright and Morning Star" as excellent examples of the genre. W's melodrama and optimism are realistic, reflecting the social advances being made by black people.

105. Sillen, Samuel. "American Writers: 1935-1939." New Masses, 31 (20 June), 22-24.
Mentions W twice in a "survey of the growth and maturity of the American Writers Congresses."

106. _____. "In Defense of Optimism." New Masses, 31 (9 May), 23-24.
Cites W as an example of a writer who recognizes the facts of racist oppression without yielding to despair.

107. _____. "Book Notes." New Masses, 33 (10 October), 28.
Announces the scheduled publication of NS on 1 November as a highlight of the fall season.

108. Smith, Lillian E. "Dope with Lime." The North Georgia Review, 4 (Winter), 4-6.
Announces the scheduled publication of NS in March and calls W "probably

the most talented of the younger Negro novelists."

109. Spingarn, Arthur B. "Books by Negro Authors in 1938." The Crisis, 46 (February), 45-46, 62.
Lists UTC (p. 62) and includes a photograph of W (p. 46).

110. Strazov, Konst.[antin]. "Deti diadi Toma." Rabochaia penza (26 January).
Favorable review of the Russian translation of UTC appearing in International Literature. Stresses W's Chicago background. Unlike previous writers on racial themes such as Harriet Beecher Stowe, W advocates active class struggle, not prayers and appeals.

111. Swinnerton, Frank. "New Novels: American Mosaic." The London Observer (5 March), p. 6.
Of the five works of American fiction reviewed, Swinnerton is most impressed by UTC. W's "staccato manner and the negro idioms he uses throughout help to create a very dramatic effect of reality. And the emotion from which all four stories gather their power is as genuine as it is impressive."

111a. Tolson, M. B. "Caviar and Cabbage: Claude McKay: Black Ulysses." Washington Tribune (3 June), p. 4.
Quotes from "Blueprint for Negro Writing" and contrasts W's "dramatic Marxist vision" and McKay's "black chauvinism."

111b. _____. "Caviar and Cabbage: Found in the Mail-Bag of a Columnist." Washington Tribune (10 June), p. 4.
Mentions W briefly.

111c. _____. "Caviar and Cabbage: I Am Thankful for the Great Depression." Washington Tribune (7 October), p. 4.
Contains a paragraph on W, "our most powerful Negro writer."
Reprinted: 1982.136c.

111d. _____. "Caviar and Cabbage: The Biggest Question in the World: When Is a Man Dead?" Washington Tribune (23 December), p. 8.
Mentions W briefly and favorably.

111e. _____. "Caviar and Cabbage: The Negro and Radicalism." Washington Tribune (12 August), p. 4.
Mentions W briefly.
Reprinted: 1982.136d.

112. W.[alker], M.[ary] A. "Literary Prizes," in 1939 Britannica Book of the Year. Ed. Walter Yust. Chicago: En-

cyclopaedia Britannica, pp. 396-397.
Lists W's second prize in the O. Henry Memorial Awards contest.

1940

1. Aaron, Abe. "Off Project Activities." In a mimeographed magazine of the Federal Writers Project, Aaron comments favorably on How 'Bigger' Was Born and the enlarged edition of UTC. The inclusion of "Bright and Morning Star" gives the collection a wholeness W originally intended.

2. Abramov, Al. "Syn diadi Toma." Literaturnaia gazeta (8 September), p. 5.
Favorable review of the Russian translation of NS with extensive analysis. Rejecting the three traditions of writing about racial themes--Stowe's sentimental humanitarianism, Du Bois's black "Zionism," and the primitivism of the Harlem Renaissance--W treats the resistance, not the acquiescence, of the black working class from which he comes. Both Bigger and the earlier Big Boy are rebellious, "bad" blacks, not "good" blacks adhering to bourgeois values. NS, combining skillfully a gripping adventure story and acute psychological analysis, proves W to be "one of the most important and truly progressive masters of contemporary American prose."

2a. Adams, Franklin P. "Books I Have Liked." Unidentified clipping.
Lists NS.

3. _____. "The Conning Tower." Boston Evening Transcript (2 March), Part Two, p. 3.
Reprint of 1940.4.

4. _____. "The Conning Tower." New York Post (2 March), p. 12.
Contains Pepysian diary entries for the preceding week, including one for 25 February about NS. Comparing W to Steinbeck and Stowe, Adams emphasizes the novel's social implications.
Reprinted: 1940.3.

5. _____. "The Conning Tower." New York Post (4 March), p. 14.
Contains the following couplet entitled "Book Review": "All the prizes should be won / By Richard Wright's 'Native Son.'"

6. Allan, William. "75 Years of Negro Progress Features Ten-day Exposition in Detroit." Daily Worker (13 May), p. 5.
Notes good sales of NS and UTC at a communist bookstore in Michigan.

7. Allen, Cleveland G. "Dr. Charlotte Brown Scores 'Native Son' in Address at Church." The New York Age (5 October), p. 6.
     In a speech at the Mother AME Zion Church on 29 September, Brown, president of the Palmer Memorial Institute of Sedalia, North Carolina, attacked the novel as "mere propaganda" while admitting that she "refused to read through the book because of its language." She attributes its success among black readers to the prior approval it received from whites.

8. Anon. "Adler Asks Readers to Group." Buffalo Evening News (18 May), Magazine Sec., p. 7.
     Contains a report on best-sellers noting that NS is in second place in Chicago and saying that the book may win the Pulitzer Prize.

9. Anon. ("A Reader"). "Afro Readers Write About 'Native Son.'" The Baltimore Afro-American (1 June), p. 13.
     As a member of the black middle class, the writer of this letter attests from her own experience to the point she derives from W--the need for something "to shock our sensibilities and cause us to think and face truth lest we revert to the ape."

10. Anon. "Among Books Reviewed in March Boston Evening Transcript Especially Recommends." Boston Evening Transcript (6 April), Part Five, p. 1; (13 April), Part Five, p. 1.
     Lists NS "because it carries a tremendous wallop."

11. Anon. "Among New Books at Greenwich Library." Greenwich Press (4 April), p. 22.
     Contains a favorable notice of NS praising the work's literary power and social analysis.

12. Anon. "Among the Publishers." The Publishers' Weekly, 138 (12 October), 1504-1506.
     Includes announcement of the new edition of UTC, noting the addition of a fifth story.

13. Anon. "Announcement Extraordinary!" The Coolidge Corner Theatre in Brookline, Massachusetts, will present a live book review of NS by Charles Lee, literary editor of The Boston Herald, on 10 April at 2 p. m.

14. Anon. "Another Book Soon by Richard Wright." New York Amsterdam News (8 June), p. 17.
     Notes that W "is busy working on a new novel dealing with the status of Negro women in modern American society."

15. Anon. "At Chi Expo." Unidentified clipping.
     Notes that W will appear at the literature exhibit of the American Negro Exposition on 5 July.

16. Anon. "At Last--An Entire Race Has Found Its Spokesman!" New York Herald Tribune Books (17 March), p. 21.
     Half-page advertisement for NS with quotations from six reviews.

17. Anon. "At Last--An Entire Race Has Found Spokesman." Chicago Daily Tribune (13 March), p. 18.
     Advertisement for NS with quotations from reviews by Fanny Butcher and Sterling North.

18. Anon. "At Last an Entire Race Has Found Spokesman." The New York Times (7 March), p. 21.
     Advertisement for NS.

19. Anon. "At the American Negro Exposition." Sunday Worker (14 July), Sec. 2, p. 2.
     Photograph with caption of W, Horace Cayton, Claude Barnett, Arna Bontemps, Langston Hughes, and two others in the Chicago Coliseum.

20. Anon. "Authors and Their Work." Chicago Daily Tribune (13 March), p. 18.
     Notes that W has visited Chicago and bought his mother a home.

21. Anon. "Authors and Their Work." Chicago Daily Tribune (3 July), p. 13.
     Notes that W will be an honored guest and autograph copies of NS at the American Negro Exposition.

22. Anon. "'Bad Nigger.'" Time, 35 (4 March), 72.
     Favorable review of NS emphasizing its black perspective in revealing "the murderous potentialities of the whole U. S. Negro problem." Along with a plot summary and a comparison to Crime and Punishment, the review contains a tribute to "one of the most devastating accounts yet printed of that tragicomic, Negrophilous bohemianism which passes among Communists as a solution of the Negro Problem."
     Reprinted: 1978.209.

23. Anon. "Banning Books Indirectly." The Birmingham News (5 April), p. 16.
     Lead editorial protesting the refusal of the Birmingham Public Library to purchase NS.

24. Anon. "Ben Davis Talks on 'Native Son' This Saturday." Daily Worker (8 May), p. 6.
Announces a talk at the Workers School in New York on 11 May.

25. Anon. "Ben Davis to Lead Discussion on 'Native Son.'" Sunday Worker (5 May), p. 5.
Announces a talk at the Workers School in New York on 11 May.

26. Anon. "Benét Tops in the List in Latest O. Henry Memorial." Wilmington (N. C.) News (3 December).
Review of O. Henry Memorial Award Prize Stories of 1940 mentioning "Almos' a Man."

27. Anon. "Benét Wins O. Henry Story Prize." The Publishers' Weekly, 138 (9 November), 1844.
Lists W as a contributor to the O. Henry Memorial Award Prize Stories of 1940.

28. Anon. "Best Seller Book List." The Memphis Commercial Appeal (31 March), Sec. IV, p. 10.
Lists NS in sixth place in the fiction category.

29. Anon. "Best Sellers." The Boston Sunday Globe (5 May), Editorial and News Feature Sec., p. 5.
Lists NS in third place in the fiction category.

30. Anon. "Best Sellers." The Boston Sunday Globe (12 May), Editorial and News Feature Sec., p. 5.
Lists NS in fourth place in the fiction category.

31. Anon. "Best Sellers." The Boston Sunday Globe (16 June), Editorial and News Feature Sec., p. 45.
Lists NS in fifth place in the fiction category.

32. Anon. "Best Sellers." The Boston Sunday Globe (21 July), Editorial and News Feature Sec., p. 5.
Lists NS in sixth place in the fiction category.

33. Anon. "Best Sellers." Chicago Daily Tribune (13 March), p. 19.
Lists NS in fifth place in the fiction category.

34. Anon. "Best Sellers." Chicago Daily Tribune (20 March), p. 23.
Lists NS in third place in the fiction category.

35. Anon. "Best Sellers." Chicago Daily Tribune (27 March), p. 15.

Lists NS in first place in the fiction category.

36. Anon. "Best Sellers." Chicago Daily Tribune (3 April), p. 14.
Lists NS in first place in the fiction category.

37. Anon. "Best Sellers." Chicago Daily Tribune (10 April), p. 23.
Lists NS in third place in the fiction category.

38. Anon. "Best Sellers." Chicago Daily Tribune (17 April), p. 17.
Lists NS in first place in the fiction category.

39. Anon. "Best Sellers." Chicago Daily Tribune (24 April), p. 13.
Lists NS in second place in the fiction category.

40. Anon. "Best Sellers." Chicago Daily Tribune (1 May), p. 22.
Lists NS in second place in the fiction category.

41. Anon. "Best Sellers." Chicago Daily Tribune (8 May), p. 23.
Lists NS in first place in the fiction category.

42. Anon. "Best Sellers." Chicago Daily Tribune (15 May), p. 17.
Lists NS in first place in the fiction category.

43. Anon. "Best Sellers." Chicago Daily Tribune (22 May), p. 17.
Lists NS in second place in the fiction category.

44. Anon. "Best Sellers." Chicago Daily Tribune (29 May), p. 12.
Lists NS in second place in the fiction category.

45. Anon. "Best Sellers." Chicago Daily Tribune (5 June), p. 20.
Lists NS in sixth place in the fiction category.

46. Anon. "Best Sellers." Chicago Daily Tribune (12 June), p. 22.
Lists NS in fifth place in the fiction category.

47. Anon. "Best Sellers." The Louisville Courier-Journal (16 June), Sunday Magazine Sec., p. [7].
Lists NS in third place in the fiction category in Chicago.

48. Anon. "Best Sellers." New York Daily News (31 March).
Lists NS in fourth place in the fiction category.

49. Anon. "Best Sellers." New York Journal and American (c. 31 March).
Lists NS in first place in the fiction category.

50. Anon. "Best Sellers." St. Louis Globe-Democrat (6 April), p. 1B.
Lists NS in third place in the fiction category.

51. Anon. "Best Sellers." St. Louis Globe-Democrat (13 April), p. 1B.
Lists NS in third place in the fiction category.

52. Anon. "Best Sellers." St. Louis Globe-Democrat (20 April), p. 1B.
Lists NS in third place in the fiction category.

53. Anon. "Best Sellers." St. Louis Globe-Democrat (27 April), p. 1B.
Lists NS in second place in the fiction category.

54. Anon. "Best Sellers." St. Louis Globe-Democrat (4 May), p. 1B.
Lists NS in second place in the fiction category.

55. Anon. "Best Sellers." St. Louis Globe-Democrat (11 May), p. 1B.
Lists NS in third place in the fiction category.

56. Anon. "Best Sellers." St. Louis Globe-Democrat (18 May), p. 1B.
Lists NS in third place in the fiction category.

57. Anon. "Best Sellers." St. Louis Globe-Democrat (25 May), p. 1B.
Lists NS in first place in the fiction category.

58. Anon. "Best Sellers." St. Louis Globe-Democrat (1 June), p. 1B.
Lists NS in sixth place in the fiction category.

59. Anon. "Best Sellers." St. Louis Globe-Democrat (8 June), p. 1B.
Lists NS in fourth place in the fiction category.

60. Anon. "Best Sellers." St. Louis Globe-Democrat (15 June), p. 1B.
Lists NS in sixth place in the fiction category.

61. Anon. "Best Sellers East and West." The Louisville Courier-Journal (14 April), Sunday Magazine Sec., p. [7].
Lists NS in fourth place in the fiction category in Boston and in second place in San Francisco.

62. Anon. "Best Sellers East and West."

The Louisville Courier-Journal (12 May), Sunday Magazine Sec., p. [7].
Lists NS in second place in the fiction category in Chicago, in fifth place in New York, and in seventh place in San Francisco.

63. Anon. "Best Sellers East and West." The Louisville Courier-Journal (26 May), Sunday Magazine Sec., p. [5].
Lists NS in second place in the fiction category in Chicago and in fifth place in New York.

64. Anon. "Best Sellers East and West." The Louisville Courier-Journal (2 June), Sunday Magazine Sec., p. [7].
Lists NS in fifth place in the fiction category in San Francisco.

65. Anon. "Best Sellers in Boston." The Boston Sunday Globe (7 April), Editorial and News Feature Sec., p. 5.
Lists NS in fourth place in the fiction category.

66. Anon. "Best Sellers in Boston." The Boston Sunday Globe (2 June), Editorial and News Feature Sec., p. 5.
Lists NS in fifth place in the fiction category.

67. Anon. "Best Sellers in New Orleans." The Times-Picayune New Orleans States (21 April), Sec. Two, p. 11.
Lists NS in fifth place.

68. Anon. "Best Sellers of the Week. The New York Times (1 April), p. 17.
Lists NS in second place in the fiction category in New York, fourth in Boston, second in Philadelphia, third in Washington, first in Chicago, second in San Francisco, and third in Los Angeles.

69. Anon. "The Best Sellers of the Week." The New York Times (8 April), p. 17.
Lists NS in second place in the fiction category in New York, fourth in Boston, third in Philadelphia, second in Washington, second in Atlanta, second in Chicago, third in St. Louis, third in New Orleans, second in San Francisco, and third in Los Angeles.

70. Anon. "Best Sellers of the Week." The New York Times (22 April), p. 15.
Lists NS in fourth place in the fiction category in New York, third in Philadelphia, sixth in Washington, sixth in Atlanta, second in Chicago, third in St. Louis, fourth in San Francisco, and third in Los Angeles.

71. Anon. "Best Sellers of the Week."

The New York Times (29 April), p. 13.
Lists NS in fifth place in the fiction category in New York, sixth in Philadelphia, sixth in Washington, third in Atlanta, second in Chicago, second in St. Louis, second in New Orleans, fifth in San Francisco, and second in Los Angeles.

72. Anon. "Best Sellers of the Week." The New York Times (20 May), p. 15.
Lists NS in fourth place in the fiction category in Philadelphia, fifth in Atlanta, second in Chicago, third in St. Louis, fifth in San Francisco, and fifth in Los Angeles.

73. Anon. "Best Sellers of the Week." The New York Times (3 June), p. 13.
Lists NS in third place in the fiction category in Chicago, sixth in St. Louis, sixth in San Francisco, and fifth in Los Angeles.

74. Anon. "Best Sellers of the Week." The New York Times (24 June), p. 13.
Lists NS in fifth place in the fiction category in Atlanta and in sixth place in San Francisco.

75. Anon. "Best Sellers of the Week." The New York Times (8 July), p. 15.
Lists NS in sixth place in the fiction category in Los Angeles.

76. Anon. "Best Sellers of the Week." The New York Times (22 July), p. 14.
Lists NS in fourth place in the fiction category in Los Angeles.

77. Anon. "Best Sellers of the Week." The Publishers' Weekly, 137 (23 March), 1236.
Lists NS in fifth place.

78. Anon. "Best Sellers of the Week." The Publishers' Weekly, 137 (30 March), 1318.
Lists NS in fourth place.

79. Anon. "Best Sellers of the Week." The Publishers' Weekly, 137 (6 April), 1410.
Lists NS in third place.

80. Anon. "Best Sellers of the Week." The Publishers' Weekly, 137 (20 April), 1596.
Lists NS in second place.

81. Anon. "Best Sellers of the Week." The Publishers' Weekly, 137 (27 April), 1666.
Lists NS in third place.

82. Anon. "Best Sellers of the Week." The Publishers' Weekly, 137 (4 May), 1747.

Lists NS in second place.

83. Anon. "Best Sellers of the Week." The Publishers' Weekly, 137 (18 May), 1918.
Lists NS in third place.

84. Anon. "Best Sellers of the Week." The Publishers' Weekly, 137 (25 May), 2009.
Lists NS in third place.

85. Anon. "Best Sellers of the Week." The Publishers' Weekly, 137 (1 June), 2146.
Lists NS in fourth place.

86. Anon. "Best Sellers of the Week." San Francisco Chronicle (11 August), This World Sec., p. 16.
Lists NS in fifth place in the fiction category.

87. Anon. "Best Sellers of the Week Here and Elsewhere." The New York Times (11 March), p. 13.
Lists NS in fourth place in the fiction category in New York, first in Philadelphia, fifth in Atlanta, and fifth in Los Angeles.

88. Anon. "Best Sellers of the Week Here and Elsewhere." The New York Times (18 March), p. 15.
Lists NS in first place in the fiction category in New York, second in Philadelphia, fourth in Washington, third in Atlanta, first in San Francisco, and fourth in Los Angeles.

89. Anon. "Best Sellers of the Week Here and Elsewhere." The New York Times (25 March), p. 13.
Lists NS in second place in the fiction category in New York, sixth in Boston, first in Philadelphia, fourth in Washington, first in Chicago, second in San Francisco, and third in Los Angeles.

90. Anon. "Best Sellers of the Week Here and Elsewhere." The New York Times (15 April), p. 15.
Lists NS in second place in the fiction category in New York, fourth in Boston, fourth in Philadelphia, second in Washington, second in Atlanta, second in Chicago, third in San Francisco, and second in Los Angeles.

91. Anon. "Best Sellers of the Week Here and Elsewhere." The New York Times (13 May), p. 15.
Lists NS in fifth place in the fiction category in New York, sixth in Boston, sixth in Philadelphia, fifth in Washington, third in Atlanta,

second in Chicago, third in St. Louis, and second in New Orleans.

92. Anon. "Best Sellers of the Week Here and Elsewhere." The New York Times (27 May), p. 17.
    Lists NS in seventh place in the fiction category in New York, second in Atlanta, second in Chicago, first in St. Louis, fourth in San Francisco, and fourth in Los Angeles.

93. Anon. "Best Sellers of the Week Here and Elsewhere." The New York Times (10 June), p. 15.
    Lists NS in sixth place in the fiction category in Washington, fifth in Chicago, third in St. Louis, and second in Los Angeles.

94. Anon. "Best Sellers of the Week Here and Elsewhere." The New York Times (17 June), p. 13.
    Lists NS in fourth place in the fiction category in Atlanta, sixth in Chicago, sixth in St. Louis, and fourth in Los Angeles.

95. Anon. "Best Sellers of the Week Here and Elsewhere." The New York Times (1 July), p. 17.
    Lists NS in sixth place in the fiction category in San Francisco and in fourth place in Los Angeles.

96. Anon. "Best Sellers of the Week Here and Elsewhere." The New York Times (12 August), p. 13.
    Lists NS in fifth place in the fiction category in San Francisco.

97. Anon. "Best Sellers of the Week Here and Elsewhere." The New York Times (2 September), p. 13.
    Lists NS in sixth place in the fiction category in Los Angeles.

98. Anon. "The Best Sellers of the Week in New York and Elsewhere." The New York Times (6 May), p. 15.
    Lists NS in fifth place in the fiction category in New York, fourth in Philadelphia, fourth in Baltimore, fifth in Atlanta, second in Chicago, second in St. Louis, and second in Los Angeles.

99. Anon. "Best Sellers of the Week in San Francisco." San Francisco Chronicle (14 April), This World Sec., p. 20.
    Lists NS in third place in the fiction category.

100. Anon. "Best Sellers of the Week in San Francisco." San Francisco Chronicle (21 April), This World Sec., p. 20.
    Lists NS in fourth place in the fiction category.

101. Anon. "Best Sellers of the Week in San Francisco." San Francisco Chronicle (28 April), This World Sec., p. 21.
    Lists NS in fifth place in the fiction category.

102. Anon. "Best Sellers of the Week in San Francisco." San Francisco Chronicle (19 May), This World Sec., p. 21.
    Lists NS in fifth place in the fiction category.

103. Anon. "Best Sellers of the Week in San Francisco." San Francisco Chronicle (26 May), This World Sec., p. 19.
    Lists NS in fourth place in the fiction category.

104. Anon. "Best Sellers of the Week in San Francisco." San Francisco Chronicle (2 June), This World Sec., p. 16.
    Lists NS in sixth place in the fiction category.

105. Anon. "Best Sellers of the Week in San Francisco." San Francisco Chronicle (9 June), This World Sec., p. 19.
    Lists NS in seventh place in the fiction category.

106. Anon. "Best Sellers of the Week in San Francisco." San Francisco Chronicle (16 June), This World Sec., p. 19.
    Lists NS in eighth place in the fiction category.

107. Anon. "Best Sellers This Week." The Houston Post (28 April), Sec. 4, p. 2.
    Lists NS in third place.

108. Anon. "Best Sellers This Week." PM's Weekly (30 June), p. 41.
    Lists NS in second place in the fiction category under the heading "At the Public Library."

109. Anon. "Best Sellers This Week." PM's Weekly (7 July), p. 41.
    Lists NS in second place in the fiction category under the heading "At the Public Library."

110. Anon. "Best Sellers This Week." PM's Weekly (14 July), p. 41.
    Lists NS in second place in the fiction category under the heading "At the Public Library."

111. Anon. "Best Sellers This Week." PM's Weekly (21 July), p. 41.
    Lists NS in second place in the fiction category under the heading "At the Public Library."

112. Anon. "Best Sellers This Week." PM's Weekly (28 July), p. 41.
    Lists NS in second place in the fiction category under the heading "At

the Public Library."

113. Anon. "Between Ourselves." New Masses, 34 (30 January), 2.
Mentions the Harlem Cabaret scheduled for 3 February, a musical and theatrical event sponsored by the Theater Arts Committee with W as one of the honored guests.

114. Anon. "Between Ourselves." New Masses, 34 (20 February), 2.
Mentions W's scheduled participation in a rally to defend New Masses from government suppression.

115. Anon. "Between Ourselves." New Masses, 34 (27 February), 2.
Discusses a meeting of writers, including W, who support New Masses against political interference.

116. Anon. "Between Ourselves." New Masses, 34 (19 March), 2.
Announces an auction of manuscripts by W and others on 7 April to raise money for New Masses.

117. Anon. "Between the Leaves." The New York Sun (25 March), p. 16.
Notes that NS was the best-seller in fiction in Brentano's bookstore for the week ending 20 March.

117a. Anon. "Bigger Thomas' Role May Go to Canada Lee." Washington Tribune (31 August), p. 15.
Emphasizes Lee's eagerness to be cast in the role.

118. Anon. "Book Babble." Baltimore Evening Sun (c. 5 March).
Unfavorable review of NS. Objecting to W's theme, the reviewer would prefer a decent, intelligent story about people with good minds.

119. Anon. "Book Club Selections." New York Daily Mirror (20 February), p. 15.
Lists NS.

120. Anon. "Book Clubs." The Oklahoma City Daily Oklahoman (3 March), p. D-3.
Notes that NS is a Book-of-the-Month Club selection for March.

121. Anon. "Book Marks." New York World-Telegram (6 March), p. 27.
Notes that W has returned to Chicago to buy a home for his mother with his first earnings from NS.

122. Anon. "Book Marks." New York World-Telegram (18 March), p. 17.
Notes that NS has displaced Kitty Foyle as the leading best-seller.

123. Anon. "Book Marks." Unidentified clipping (4 March).
Mentions an interview of W by Edwin Seaver at the New School for Social Research on 4 March.

124. Anon. "Book Marks for Today." New York World-Telegram (12 March), p. 17.
Announces a lecture by W on "How 'Bigger' Was Born" at Columbia University and notes that first-week sales, advance sales, and Book-of-the-Month Club distribution of the novel total 215,000 copies.

125. Anon. "Book Marks for Today." New York World-Telegram (25 March), p. 17.
Mentions that NS "still leads best-selling fiction."

126. Anon. "Book Marks for Today." New York World-Telegram (1 April), p. 13.
Notes that NS is the leading best-seller of the week.

127. Anon. "Book Marks for Today." New York World-Telegram (5 April), p. 27.
Announces a lecture on NS by Sender Garlin at the Progressive Forum.

128. Anon. "Book Marks for Today." New York World-Telegram (29 April).
Notes that NS is in fifth place on the best-seller list.

129. Anon. "Book Marks for Today." New York World-Telegram (3 June), p. 17.
Notes that NS is in third place on a best-seller list compiled by the American News Company.

130. Anon. "Book Marks for Today." New York World-Telegram (4 September), p. 31.
Notes that W has returned from Chapel Hill, where he worked with Paul Green on the play NS. Also announces W's talk at the Golden Gate Ballroom on 6 September.

131. Anon. "Book Notes." Allentown Sunday Call-Chronicle (17 March), p. 10.
Mentions the printing of more than 215,000 copies of NS within one week of publication.

132. Anon. "Book Notes." Daily Worker (4 April), p. 7.
Announces a talk by Sender Garlin on NS at the Progressive Forum on 5 April.

133. Anon. "Book Notes." Daily Worker (17 September), p. 7.
Lists W as one of the sponsors of the 1940 Book Ball, a costume dance to be given at the Manhattan Center on 8 November.

134. Anon. "Book Notes." New York Herald Tribune (12 March), p. 23.
    Announces a lecture by W at Columbia University on 12 March and notes the large sale of NS.

135. Anon. "Book Notes." New York Herald Tribune (6 May), p. 15.
    Notes that the total sales of NS are more than 250,000.

136. Anon. "Book Notes." New York Herald Tribune (3 June), p. 13.
    Mentions W's novel in progress on the status of women in America. He is drawing on his childhood experiences for material.

137. Anon. "Book Notes." New York Herald Tribune (5 August), p. 11.
    Mentions that W was one of three vice-presidents elected by the League of American Writers.

138. Anon. "Book Notes." New York Herald Tribune (4 September), p. 23.
    Mentions W's return from Chapel Hill, where he worked with Paul Green on the dramatic version of NS.

139. Anon. "Book Notes." New York Herald Tribune (10 October), p. 21.
    Mentions the forthcoming revised and expanded edition of UTC and the pamphlet version of How "Bigger" Was Born.

140. Anon. "Book-of-the-Month Club Novelist Now Writing His Third Volume." The Pittsburgh Courier (2 March), p. 24.
    Associated Negro Press article sketching W's life, literary career, work in progress, working habits, recreational interests, personal characteristics, and plans for a trip to Mexico.

141. Anon. "Book-of-the-Month." The Chicago Defender (30 March), p. 6.
    Advertisement for NS, available by mail order from the newspaper.

142. Anon. "Book Review." The Blue Pencil (June).
    Review of NS emphasizing its melodrama, sex, and sensationalism. It shows compassion for a racial minority, but its handling of psychology is weak.

143. Anon. "The Book Shelf." Saratoga Springs Saratogian (30 March), p. 4.
    Favorable review of NS praising its realism and narrative momentum. Includes a plot summary.

144. Anon. "Book Stores' Best Sellers." St. Louis Post-Dispatch (24 March), p. 3D.
    Lists NS in sixth place in the fiction category.

145. Anon. "Book Stores' Best Sellers." St. Louis Post-Dispatch (31 March), p. 3C.
    Lists NS in fourth place in the fiction category.

146. Anon. "Book Stores' Best Sellers." St. Louis Post-Dispatch (7 April), p. 4C.
    Lists NS in fourth place in the fiction category.

147. Anon. "Book Stores' Best Sellers." St. Louis Post-Dispatch (14 April), p. 3C.
    Lists NS in fourth place in the fiction category.

148. Anon. "Book Stores' Best Sellers." St. Louis Post-Dispatch (21 April), p. 3C.
    Lists NS in third place in the fiction category.

149. Anon. "Book Stores' Best Sellers." St. Louis Post-Dispatch (28 April), p. 3C.
    Lists NS in fourth place in the fiction category.

150. Anon. "Book Stores' Best Sellers." St. Louis Post-Dispatch (5 May), p. 3C.
    Lists NS in sixth place in the fiction category.

151. Anon. "Book Stores' Best Sellers." St. Louis Post-Dispatch (12 May), p. 3C.
    Lists NS in fifth place in the fiction category.

152. Anon. "Book Stores' Best Sellers." St. Louis Post-Dispatch (19 May), p. 3C.
    Lists NS in sixth place in the fiction category.

153. Anon. "Book Stores' Best Sellers." St. Louis Post-Dispatch (26 May), p. 3C.
    Lists NS in sixth place in the fiction category.

154. Anon. "Books and Authors." Buffalo Evening News (23 March), Magazine Sec., p. 7.
    Mixed notice of NS. The reviewer comments on the popularity of the novel and concedes W's knowledge of black problems and an element of universality in the work, but complains of too much sociology and propaganda.

155. Anon. "Books and Bookfolk." Portland (Maine) Press Herald (9 March), p. 13.

Contains a brief notice of NS stressing its power as a story "of a mean Negro who might have been a solid asset in another environment."

156. Anon. "Books and Writers." South-bridge Evening News (5 March), p. 4.
United Press review of NS stressing Bigger's representativeness as an urban black man. "Here is a story that throbs from the opening line, with a wallop propelled to the end." Reprinted: 1940.165, 169, 279, 413, 421, 446, 531.

157. Anon. "Books--Authors." The New York Times (8 July), p. 15.
Mentions W's return from a trip to Mexico and Chicago during which he worked on a new novel.

158. Anon. "Books--Authors." The New York Times (24 August), p. 11.
Mentions W's talk on "How 'Bigger' Was Born" at the fund raiser for the Negro Playwrights Company.

159. Anon. "Books--Authors." The New York Times (19 October), p. 15.
Announces the publication on 19 October of How "Bigger" Was Born and of the enlarged version of UTC.

160. Anon. "Books of the Year." Time, 36 (23 December), 62-64.
Mentions NS briefly and includes a photograph of W.

161. Anon. "Books Published Today." The New York Times (19 October), p. 15.
Brief notice of the publication of the enlarged version of UTC.

162. Anon. "Books Received." New York Herald Tribune Books (20 October), p. 20.
Contains a brief notice of the enlarged edition of UTC.

163. Anon. "Bookshop Notes." The Publishers' Weekly, 137 (30 March), 1312-1314.
Photograph with caption of W at an autographing party at the Columbia University Bookstore (p. 1313).

164. Anon. "Bookstores Reordered 13,719 Copies in the First Week!"
Postcard advertisement for NS from Harper's.

165. Anon. "Bound to Be Read." Greenwich Time (8 March), p. 4.
Reprint of 1940.156.

166. Anon. "Boys and Girls!! Win a Prize Writing the Biographies of Famous Negroes." The Pittsburgh Courier (9 March), p. 19.
W is one of the five subjects announced in this contest. Reprinted in issues of 16 March, p. 19; 23 March, p. 19; 30 March, p. 19; and 6 April, p. 19.

167. Anon. "Brentano's Best Sellers." The Louisville Courier-Journal (17 March), Sunday Magazine Sec., p. [7].
Lists NS in second place in the fiction category.

168. Anon. "Brentano's Best Sellers." The Louisville Courier-Journal (21 April), Sunday Magazine Sec., p. [7].
Lists NS in fourth place in the fiction category.

169. Anon. "Brief Reviews of New Books." New Orleans Item (10 March), Sec. 2, p. 8.
Reprint of 1940.156.

170. Anon. "Brooklyn Library Denies Ban Against Native Son." The New York Age (20 April), p. 4.
Refutes a rumor that the National Association for the Advancement of Colored People requested the ban.

171. Anon. "The Bulletin Board." The Chicago Defender (16 March), p. 5.
Mentions a lecture on NS by Robert Davis on 20 March. "So much favorable comment about this outstanding piece of work has been printed that everyone by this time is well aware of its excellence and reputation." The novel is available at the Hall Branch of the Chicago Public Library.

172. Anon. "The Bulletin Board." The Chicago Defender (20 April), p. 3.
Announces a review of NS by Langston Hughes sponsored by the Chicago Public Library Employees Union.

173. Anon. "The Bulletin Board." The Chicago Defender (18 May), p. 8.
Announces a symposium on NS on 17 May sponsored by the North American Spanish Aid Committee. "Speakers will be William Patterson, representing the Negro; Harvey O'Connor, who will speak for labor, and Joseph Carroll, who will voice the sentiments of the literary world."

174. Anon. "Chicago is Reading." The Chicago Daily News (13 March), p. 15.
Lists NS in fourth place in the fiction category.

175. Anon. "Chicago is Reading." The Chicago Daily News (20 March), p. 18.
Lists NS in first place in the fiction category.

176. Anon. "Chicago is Reading." The Chicago Daily News (27 March), p. 17.
Lists NS in first place in the fiction category.

177. Anon. "Chicago is Reading." The Chicago Daily News (3 April), p. 17.
Lists NS in first place in the fiction category.

178. Anon. "Chicago is Reading." The Chicago Daily News (10 April), p. 20.
Lists NS in first place in the fiction category.

179. Anon. "Chicago is Reading." The Chicago Daily News (17 April), p. 15.
Lists NS in first place in the fiction category.

180. Anon. "Chicago is Reading." The Chicago Daily News (24 April), p. 17.
Lists NS in first place in the fiction category.

181. Anon. "Chicago is Reading." The Chicago Daily News (1 May), p. 21.
Lists NS in first place in the fiction category.

182. Anon. "Chicago is Reading." The Chicago Daily News (15 May), p. 21.
Lists NS in first place in the fiction category.

183. Anon. "Chicago is Reading." The Chicago Daily News (22 May), p. 17.
Lists NS in second place in the fiction category.

184. Anon. "Chicago is Reading." The Chicago Daily News (5 June), p. 21.
Lists NS in fourth place in the fiction category.

185. Anon. "The Chicago Pan-Hellenic Council Presents Mr. Richard Wright."
Printed postcard invitation to a lecture by W on "Why [sic] Bigger Was Born" at the Church of the Good Shepherd on the South Side of Chicago on 7 July. The postcard is dated 2 July.

186. Anon. "Chicago Slum Shown in Negro Writer's Novel." Public Housing Weekly News, 1 (9 April), 2.
Emphasizes poor housing as an important factor in the development of Bigger's criminality.

187. Anon. "Chicago's Renaissance in Literature." The Chicago Daily News (27 March), p. 16.
Places W in the realistic tradition and compares him favorably to Dreiser. Includes a photograph with caption of W and other Chicago writers.

188. Anon. "Class to Make Study of Negro Literature." Santa Barbara News-Press (20 February), p. 5.
Beatrice Greene, who will conduct the evening class, cites NS as an example of the trend in modern black literature.

189. Anon. "Clearing the Desk." The El Paso Times (26 May), p. 6.
Mentions's Harper's success with NS, The Return of the Native, and Louis Adamic's The Native's Return.

190. Anon. "Columbia, N. Y. U. Men Indorsed Stalin's Purge." New York Journal and American (4 December), p. 12.
Lists W among many others.

191. Anon. "The Column." The Atlantic Monthly, 165 (June), [4] of front matter.
Contains a biographical sketch of W commenting on "I Bite the Hand That Feeds Me," which appears in this issue.

192. Anon. "Community Library Announces New Books Available." Norfolk Journal and Guide (31 August), p. 12.
NS is one of the titles newly acquired by the Portsmouth Community Library.

193. Anon. "Conditions Breed 'Bigger Thomases'; Bring Terror and Violence to Community." New York Amsterdam News (14 September), p. 1.
Photograph of bleeding victims of a street brawl with caption comparing them to Bigger.

194. Anon. "Contest Winner." The Pittsburgh Courier (13 April), p. 19.
Myrtle Senior of Nashville won the juvenile contest for a biographical essay on W. See 1940.166.

195. Anon. "Una conversación con Richard Wright autor de 'Native Son.'" Romance (Mexico), 1 (15 June), 2.
W comments on his novel, the political concern of his literary generation, his literary antecedents, his work in progress, his concept of the writer's role, and the need for unity among blacks and among writers throughout the hemisphere.

196. Anon. "Criminal or Victim?" The London Times Literary Supplement (27 April), p. 205.
Mixed review of NS. The reviewer is impressed by "the overwhelming sincerity with which the social and moral implications of Bigger's guilt are brought home" and the narrative power of the book, but considers the

Communist thesis irrelevant and the Gothic elements spurious. Also W's "rationalization of negro disabilities" causes him to "flounder at times between the conventions of a shocker, a sociological treatise and a Dostoevskian fabrication on the subject of the soul."

196a. Anon. "Crisis Editor Talks on 'Native Son.'" Washington Tribune (20 July), p. 5.
Announces a New York radio interview with Roy Wilkins on "Negro Response to Native Son," 13 July 1940.

197. Anon. "Crowd Hears Noted Author." New York Amsterdam News (16 March), p. 3.
Reports W's speech on "How 'Bigger' Was Born" as delivered to an audience at the Schomburg Collection on 14 March. Includes a photograph of W autographing NS.

198. Anon. "Defend Your Magazine!" New Masses, 34 (27 February), 24.
Lists W as one of the sponsors of a rally on behalf of New Masses.

199. Anon. "Dixie Library Bans 'Native Son': Alabama Library Won't Place 'Native Son' on Its Shelves." The Pittsburgh Courier (20 April), pp. 1, 4.
Banner-headline Associated Negro Press article on the refusal of the Birmingham public libraries to buy W's novel. Quotes from letters to the editors of Birmingham newspapers by Clara Hall and Eddie Burke.

200. Anon. "Dr. R. M. [sic] Moton." Christian Advocate (Nashville), 101 (14 June), 740.
Contrasts Moton's career favorably with that of Bigger Thomas.

201. Anon. Dust jacket of Native Son. London: Gollancz.
Quotes from Henry Seidel Canby's Book-of-the-Month Club review.

202. Anon. Dust jacket of Native Son. New York: Grosset & Dunlap.
Front cover contains blurbs from reviews. Front inside flap quotes from Henry Seidel Canby.

203. Anon. Dust jacket of Native Son. New York: Harper.
Quotes from Henry Seidel Canby's Book-of-the-Month Club review and from Edward A. Weeks's prepublication comment.

204. Anon. Dust jacket of Native Son (book club edition). New York: Harper.

Front cover contains blurbs. Flaps include a quotation from Henry Seidel Canby and a biographical sketch.

205. Dust jacket of Uncle Tom's Children: Five Long Stories. New York: Harper.
Quotes several blurbs from reviews of the 1938 edition and explains that the success of NS prompted publication of this enlarged edition.

206. Anon. "The Editor's Choice of Books About the South." The North Georgia Review, 5 (Summer), 38-40.
Lists ten basic books, then fifty-one others. NS is among the fifty-one. None of the first ten is a novel.

207. Anon. "The Editor's Guest Book." Harper's Bazaar, 74 (January), 9.
Biographical note with a photograph of W.

208. Anon. "Events Scheduled Today." The New York Times (12 March), p. 21.
Richardson [sic] Wright will attend a literary luncheon.

209. Anon. "Exhibit No. 114," in Investigation of Un-American Propaganda Activities in the United States. Appendix--Part I. Washington: United States Government Printing Office, pp. 808-809.
Reprint of 1938.51.

210. Anon. "Exploring the Book World." Newark Sunday Call (3 March), Part III, p. 5.
Contains a notice of NS comparing it unfavorably to UTC. The reviewer objects strongly to the Communist message of the novel.

211. Anon. "Fifteen of the New Fall Books." Des Moines Sunday Register (27 October), Sec. Eight, p. 7.
Contains a brief notice of the enlarged edition of UTC.

212. Anon. "Fifty-one Books Added to Library." Hoboken Jersey Observer (13 March), p. 5.
NS is among the new books.

213. Anon. "Former Negro Errand Boy's Book Called Powerful American Novel." Memphis Press-Scimitar (5 March), p. 13.
Brief article on NS quoting from reviews by Clifton Fadiman and Henry Seidel Canby.

214. Anon. "Former Negro Laborer Wins $2,500 Guggenheim Scholarship." The Negro History Bulletin, 3 (February), 79.
Partial reprint of 1939.18.

215. Anon. "From Relief Job to Author's Fame." The Madison (Wis.) Capital Times (17 March), p. 22.
Reprint of 1940.372.

216. Anon. "Give Book Review at Woman's Club." Perth Amboy Evening News (12 March), p. 2.
Helen Burrows, an English teacher at the Tottenville, New Jersey, high school, reviewed NS.

217. Anon. "Golden Gate Ballroom."
Program of the benefit event in Harlem for The Negro Playwrights Company, Inc. W, listed as an associate member of the Company, lectured on "How 'Bigger' Was Born."

218. Anon. "Harlem."
Mimeographed one-page commercial for Look and its article on NS broadcast from 7 to 20 May on the following stations: WOR New York, WJR Detroit, WMAQ Chicago, KSO Des Moines, WMT Cedar Rapids, and WNAX Yankton.
Reprinted: 1940.288.

219. Anon. "Harper & Brothers." The Publishers' Weekly, 137 (27 January), 386-388.
Notes the forthcoming publication of NS, which "Harper will give . . . a first-rate start and . . . follow up vigorously any signs of encouraging sales" (p. 387).

220. Anon. "Highlights from Latest Books." Ordersberg (N. Y.) Journal (18 November).
Lists W as a contributor to the O. Henry Memorial Award Prize Stories of 1940.

221. Anon. "Highlights in New Books." The Bakersfield Californian (26 March), p. 18.
Favorable review of NS praising its "power and drama and truth," its rapid narrative pace, and its depiction of Jan, who fills Bigger "with empty phrases of an equality he knows does not exist." The novel is sordid but realistic.

222. Anon. "Highlights of New Books." Ithaca Journal (2 November), p. 6.
Notes that the success of NS prompts the enlarged edition of UTC, which will include an autobiographical essay.

223. Anon. "The House of Harper." New York: Harper.
Brochure announcing publication of the enlarged edition of UTC.

224. Anon. "In Distinguished Company."
New Bedford Sunday Standard-Times (28 April), p. 19.
Notes that W won second prize in the 1938 O. Henry Memorial Award Competition.

225. Anon. "In Harlem Tonite." Daily Worker (6 September), p. 7.
Photograph of Paul Robeson with caption mentioning W's lecture at the Golden Gate Ballroom.

226. Anon. "In the Cause of Midwestern Literacy." The Chicago Daily News (24 July), p. 8.
Includes a photograph with caption of W presenting an inscribed copy of NS to Curtis D. MacDougall, director of the Illinois Writers' Project.

227. Anon. "In the Wind." The Nation, 150 (18 May), 627.
Comments on the debate among Communists over NS and notes that most reviews ignored W's membership in the Party.

228. Anon. "In the World of Books." Buffalo Evening News (20 April), Magazine Sec., p. 7.
Notes that readers have "returned to more literary fare" after a "flurry of excitement" caused by the "sociological" NS.

229. Anon. "Is Peace Criminal?" New Masses, 34 (20 February), 25.
Advertisement for a rally scheduled for 26 February protesting government suppression of New Masses. Lists W among the "sponsors and speakers."

230. Anon. "'Jobs' and 'Native Son' Discussed by New Yorker." The Chicago Defender (20 April), p. 17.
Reports a speech by George S. Schuyler in Memphis at the Centenary M. E. Church in which he "took time out to 'pan' 'Native Son,'" calling it "a good detective tale, but its psychology of the young Negro is far-fetched and too lacking in humor."

231. Anon. "Just Out!" Unidentified clipping.
Announces the publication of "How 'Bigger' Was Born" in The Saturday Review of Literature.

232. Anon. "Latest Books." Salinas Index-Journal (7 December), p. 6.
Mentions W as a contributor to the O. Henry Memorial Award Prize Stories of 1940.

233. Anon. "League Members Now Read These." The Memphis Commercial Appeal (17 March), Sec. IV, p. 10.

One member is reading NS.

234. Anon. "Lectures." The Chicago Daily
News (24 April), p. 17.
  Notes Langston Hughes's review of NS
  for the Chicago Public Library Employees Union.

235. Anon. "Lectures." The Chicago Daily
News (1 May), p. 20.
  "Dr. Preston Bradley will discuss
  Richard Wright's 'Native Son' at the
  Peoples Church tonight."

236. Anon. "Lectures." The Chicago Daily
News (15 May), p. 20.
  Announces a symposium on NS scheduled
  for 17 May to benefit the North American Spanish Aid Committee. Participants are Harvey O'Connor, William
  Patterson, and Joseph Carroll.

237. Anon. "Library Books Ready for
Circulation." York Gazette and Daily (8
March), p. 5.
  Notice of NS referring to "society's
  double accusation" for Bigger's life.

238. Anon. "Library Notes." Gastonia
Daily Gazette (7 December), p. 10.
  Mentions the inclusion of W in the O.
  Henry Memorial Award Prize Stories of
  1940.

239. Anon. "Literature and Art," in
Cavalcade of the American Negro. Ed.
Arna Bontemps. Chicago: Diamond Jubilee
Exposition Authority, pp. 41-46.
  Mentions the success of NS (p. 44).

240. Anon. "Local College Group Reviews
'Native Son.'" The Chicago Defender (11
May), p. 8.
  Reports that the Tougaloo College
  Alumni, led by Mattie Purgerson,
  reviewed NS on 10 May.

241. Anon. "Look Into the Future with
Us!" The New Anvil, 1 (May-June), back
cover-inside back cover.
  Cites W's connection with the magazine in pleading for support.

242. Anon. "Look Magazine Recording
#12."
  Typescript of a commercial for Look
  and its article on NS. Three speakers
  participate: Lady Customer, Bookseller, and Announcer.
  See 1940.218.

243. Anon. "Marian Anderson, WABC; 'Native Son' Talk, 11:30 PM." Sunday Worker
(14 April), p. 7.
  Lists a radio program on WBNX New
  York.

244. Anon. "El mejor libro del mes."

Romance (Mexico), 1 (1 June), 20.
  Brief note on the popularity and
  importance of NS.

245. Anon. "Memphis Proud of 'Native
Son' Author." The Pittsburgh Courier (9
March), p. 9.
  States that black and white Memphis
  friends "by the score" have communicated their congratulations to W,
  whose connection with Memphis is then
  sketched briefly.

246. Anon. Messenger (West End Syna-
gogue, New York), 13 (December).
  One-page sheet announcing a book
  review of NS to be given by Mrs.
  Mayme P. Vogel at an open meeting of
  the Shaaray Tefila Sisterhood on 2
  December.

247. Anon. "Mrs. Paul Henry is Guest in
City." The Lincoln (Neb.) Star (6
March), p. 3.
  Rabbi J. J. Ogle reviewed NS.

248. Anon. "Mrs. Roosevelt Leads List of
Those Aiding Race Relations in '39." The
Washington Evening Star (14 February),
p. A-3.
  Associated Press report listing W as
  one of eleven blacks and five whites
  selected by a poll taken by the
  Schomburg Collection and the Associa-
  tion for the Study of Negro Life and
  History.

249. Anon. "Music Notes." The New York
Times (6 September), p. 24.
  Announces that W will appear at a
  benefit for the Negro Playwrights
  Company.

250. Anon. "National Best Sellers--
April." The Publishers' Weekly, 137 (11
May), 1854.
  Lists NS in third place in the fic-
  tion category.

251. Anon. "National Best Sellers--
March." The Publishers' Weekly, 137 (13
April), 1502.
  Lists NS in fifth place in the fic-
  tion category.

252. Anon. "National Best Sellers--May."
The Publishers' Weekly, 137 (8 June),
2226.
  Lists NS in fourth place in the fiction category.

253. Anon. "Nation's Best Sellers
Through the Month." Brooklyn Eagle (21
April), Sec. E, p. 9.
  Lists NS in fourth place in the fic-
  tion category.

254. Anon. "Nation's Best Sellers

Through the Month." Brooklyn Eagle (19
May), Trend Sec., p. 9.
   Lists NS in third place in the fic-
tion category.

255. Anon. "Nation's Best Sellers
Through the Week." Brooklyn Eagle (31
March), Trend Sec., p. 9.
   Lists NS in fifth place in the fic-
tion category.

256. Anon. "Nation's Best Sellers
Through the Week." Brooklyn Eagle (7
April), Sec. E, p. 9.
   Lists NS in fourth place in the fic-
tion category.

257. Anon. "Nation's Best Sellers
Through the Week." Brooklyn Eagle (28
April), Sec. E, p. 9.
   Lists NS in second place in the fic-
tion category.

258. Anon. "Nation's Best Sellers
Through the Week." Brooklyn Eagle (5
May), Trend Sec., p. 9.
   Lists NS in third place in the fic-
tion category.

259. Anon. "Nation's Best Sellers
Through the Week." Brooklyn Eagle (26
May), Trend Sec., p. 9.
   Lists NS in third place in the fic-
tion category.

260. Anon. "Native Son," in Harper's
Catalogue. New York: Harper.
   Publisher's notice comparing the
novel to Crime and Punishment.

261. Anon. "Native Son." Story, 16 (May-
June), 100-101.
   Brief excerpts from reviews by Joseph
Daniels, James Gray, Samuel Sillen,
Lewis Gannett, Malcolm Cowley, the
Newsweek reviewer, Sterling North,
Margaret Wallace, Milton Rugoff,
Peter Monro Jack,Margaret Marshall,
and Howard Mumford Jones.

262. Anon. "Native Son." The London
Observer (12 May), p. 5.
   Advertisement citing Rosamond Leh-
mann's review in the Spectator.

263. Anon. "'Native Son.'" The New York
Age (16 March), p. 12.
   Favorable editorial noting the
acclaim which W's novel, "a book of
deep compassion," has received and
comparing it to An American Tragedy.
"Richard Wright has through this book
placed himself in the vanguard of
young authors and won recognition for
himself and race undreamed of a generation ago."

264. Anon. "Native Son." The New York

Times Book Review (28 April), p. 17.
   Large advertisement.

265. Anon. "Native Son, A Novel. By
Richard Wright." The Christian Century,
57 (24 April), 546.
   Favorable notice emphasizing the
novel's element of shock and its
universality and de-emphasizing its
racial message. "The author is not
concerned to vindicate Bigger and
throw the blame on 'society.' . . .
The meaning of the novel goes far
beyond the color line."
   Reprinted: 1978.209.

266. Anon. "'Native Son'--A Sensational
Novel by a Young Negro Author." The
Galveston News (10 March), p. 14.
   Favorable review praising W's literary skill and calling the story "exciting, lurid, sensational, absorbingly interesting." The reviewer is
less impressed by W's theme, which is
"likely to be scorned by negrophobes
and overpraised by negrophiles."

267. Anon. "'Native Son' Adapted for
Screen by Wright." Daily Worker (30
July), p. 7.
   Despite the title, this article con-
cerns the stage version of the novel.
"There is a possibility . . . that
Paul Robeson may play the part of
Bigger Thomas."

268. Anon. "'Native Son' Author Admits
He's Member of Communist Party." The
Pittsburgh Courier (14 September), p. 3.
   W mentioned his membership during his
speech at the Golden Gate Ballroom.

269. Anon. "'Native Son' Author Backs
Ford, Browder." Daily Worker (30 Septem-
ber), p. 1.
   Notes that the National Election
Campaign Committee of the Communist
Party has announced W's declaration
of support. Includes excerpts from
W's statement emphasizing the appeal
of the ticket to black voters.

270. Anon. "'Native Son' Author Has Book
Reissued." The Baltimore Afro-American
(26 October), p. 13.
   Announces the enlarged edition of
UTC.
   Reprinted: 1940.271.

271. Anon. "'Native Son' Author Has Book
Reissued." Washington Afro-American (26
October), p. 19.
   Reprint of 1940.270.

272. Anon. "'Native Son' Author Says
Slump Wrecked Illusions." Durham Morning
Herald (29 July), p. 3.
   Reports W's talk on "How 'Bigger' Was

Born" at the White Rock Baptist Church in Durham. Includes a report on an interview with W in which he tells of the impact of the Depression, compares his fiction to Steinbeck's, speaks of his collaboration with Paul Green, comments on his work in progress, and discusses the economic situation of blacks.

273. Anon. "'Native Son' Author to Relate Birth of 'Bigger.'" The Chicago Defender (6 July), p. 6.
Announces W's lecture on "How 'Bigger' Was Born."

274. Anon. "'Native Son' by Former Memphis Boy, Is Praised." Unidentified clipping.
Quotes extensively from Clifton Fadiman's review in The New Yorker. W is remembered as an errand boy for the American Optical Company.

275. Anon. "Native Son by Richard Wright." Reader's Observer, 3 (April), 5.
Favorable notice of "one of those rare books that introduce the reader to an entirely new world."

276. Anon. "Native Son by Richard Wright." The New York Times Book Review (14 April), p. 15.
Advertisement.

277. Anon. "Native Son--by Richard Wright." Unidentified clipping.
Favorable notice of the "colored man's Grapes of Wrath."

278. Anon. "Native Son by Richard Wright," in Victor Gollancz Ltd. Second Supplementary List. London: Gollancz, pp. 2-3.
Favorable review summarizing the plot and praising W's psychological subtlety. NS is comparable to Joyce Cary's The African Witch, but is of even finer quality.

279. Anon. "'Native Son' Delves Into Race Problem." The Bloomington (Ill.) Sunday Pantagraph (10 March), p. 9.
Reprint of 1940.156.

280. Anon. "Native Son Fades." Unidentified clipping.
Unfavorable analysis of the novel in a black magazine. W's effort to make Bigger typical overlooks racial progress in the face of segregation.

281. Anon. "'Native Son' Is Due to Be Dramatized." The New York Times (17 July), p. 25.
Comments on the W-Green collaboration in progress and mentions the interest

of John Houseman and Orson Welles in a production.

282. Anon. "'Native Son' May Be Dramatized . . . Robeson as Bigger." The Pittsburgh Courier (25 May), p. 20.
Robeson "is said to be the ideal type for the leading character."

283. Anon. "Native Son. Richard Wright." The Carmel Pine Cone (28 June), p. 4.
Favorable notice quoting from reviews by Lewis Gannett and Sterling North. "It is genuine because it is such a book as only a Negro could write."

284. Anon. "'Native Son' Sales Near Quarter Million Within Two Weeks!" The New York Times Book Review (24 March), p. 15.
Full-page advertisement with a biographical sketch and excerpts from fifteen reviews.

285. Anon. "'Native Son' Sells Rapidly." The Publishers' Weekly, 137 (16 March), 1161.
Notes rates of reorders and Harper's advertising campaign.

286. Anon. "'Native Son' to Be Dramatized." The Pittsburgh Courier (27 July), p. 20.
Associated Negro Press news release noting the W-Green collaboration and the interest of John Houseman and Orson Welles in producing the play.

287. Anon. "'Native Son' Used to Halt an Eviction." The Chicago Defender (11 May), National edition, pp. 1-2.
Relates an anecdote of a lawyer's use of the novel to prevent the eviction of a black man.

288. Anon. "Native Sons."
Reprint of 1940.218.

289. Anon. "Native Sons." Japanese American News (22 May).
Favorable notice of NS comparing it to The Good Earth and remarking that an analogous book is needed dealing with the life of Japanese.

290. Anon. "Need of Negro Education Proved by Experience of Richard Wright." The Louisville Times (5 March), p. 6.
Editorial arguing for improved educational opportunities for black people, citing W's recognition by the Book-of-the-Month Club and his use of a white man's library card in Memphis among other examples of black potential.

291. Anon. "Negro Hailed as New Writer." The New York Sun (4 March), p. 3.

Detailed biographical article based on an interview with W. Explains the background of NS, mentioning the Nixon case. Compares W to Dostoevsky, Dreiser, Steinbeck, and Gertrude Stein.

292. Anon. "Negro Leaders Protest Attacks Against Communist Candidates." Daily Worker (16 September), p. 1.
Lists W as one of seventeen signers of a protest against efforts to curb the electoral rights of the Communist Party. See 1940.359.

293. Anon. "Negro Playwright Co. Will Reopen Lincoln." New York Amsterdam News (10 August), p. 17.
Mentions W's appearance at the Golden Gate Ballroom.

294. Anon. "Negro Playwrights Company in Debut." New York Amsterdam News (20 July), p. 21.
Announces W's talk on "How 'Bigger' Was Born" at the Golden Gate Ballroom.

295. Anon. "Negro Playwright's Company Is Formed." The Pittsburgh Courier (3 August), p. 10.
Mentions W's talk in the Golden Gate Ballroom on "How 'Bigger' Was Born" and states that Bigger "has been the bone for more discussion than any Negro character ever created in American fiction."

296. Anon. "Negro Playwrights Make Debut, Pack the Golden Gate." The New York Age (14 September), p. 4.
Reports that the length of W's talk on "How 'Bigger' Was Born" bored the audience, especially in contrast to the singing of Paul Robeson.

297. Anon. "Negro Writes on Lynch Bill." Memphis Press-Scimitar (1 April), p. 13.
Reports a speech by George Schuyler in which he expresses dislike for NS.

298. Anon. "Negroes Condemn Effort to Deny Communists Place on Ballot; Say It Endangers Minorities Rights." The New York Age (28 September), p. 2.
Lists W as one of seventeen signers of the statement, the text of which is included.

299. Anon. "Negro's Answer." Newsweek, 15 (4 March), 40-41.
Favorable review calling NS "at once a flaming pamphlet on the race question in the United States and a novel of tremendous power and beauty." After a brief plot summary, the review points out W's message of white responsibility for Bigger. But

the reviewer takes solace in the fact that in "our system of government" such a book "can be openly printed, discussed, and answered."

300. Anon. "Negro's Novel Is Overwhelming, Bitter, Profound." The Houston Press (22 March), p. 27.
Favorable review of NS comparing it to The Grapes of Wrath and Crime and Punishment. The impact of the story is brutal, overpowering. Southerners will object to the novel's theme, but "Wright makes a masterful, unrelenting appeal" for racial understanding.

301. "A Negro's Tragedy in Eloquent Tale." Springfield (Mass.) Republican (10 March), Sec. E, p. 7.
Favorable review of NS praising its narrative pace, characterization, and use of dialogue. Without sentimentality, W shows how Bigger's social condition of bondage to white society results in his criminality. Compares W favorably to Dreiser, Steinbeck, and Farrell.

302. Anon. "New Anvil Reception for Richard Wright."
Mimeographed announcement of the event on 5 July at Swiss Hall, 637 West Webster, Chicago.

303. Anon. "New Book Check List." Oakland Post-Enquirer (30 March), p. 12.
Contains a favorable notice of NS, a novel with an impressive "intensity and a quality of inherent truth."

304. Anon. "The New Books." The Indianapolis News (14 March), p. 6.
Favorable review of NS stressing W's environmental determinism. Bigger's problems result from the conflict between the slums of his experience and the Dalton world, which is strange and frightening. The novel succeeds both as narrative and as social analysis.

305. Anon. "New Books." Washington Times-Herald (5 April), p. 20.
Lists five novels including NS.

306. Anon. "New Books Received During Week." Boston Evening Transcript (19 October), Part Four, p. 4.
Brief notice of the enlarged edition of UTC.

307. Anon. "New Edition." The New York Sun (10 October), p. 40.
Announces the scheduled publication on 19 October of the enlarged edition of UTC and the pamphlet How "Bigger" Was Born.

308. Anon. "New Englanders Charter Bus to Hear Paul Robeson and Wright." Norfolk Journal and Guide (7 September), p. 17.
Reports that a group led by Rev. R. H. Gross will attend the benefit.

309. Anon. "News and Gossip of the Rialto." The New York Times (11 August), Sec. 9, p. 1.
Recounts the theatrical plans of John Houseman, including a production of NS in California.

310. Anon. "News and Views of the New Books." Syracuse Herald-Journal (17 November), Sec. 2, p. 19.
Includes a very brief notice of the enlarged edition of UTC.

311. Anon. "News of Books and Authors." Daily Worker (15 July), p. 7.
Notes the continued popularity of NS in the New York Public Library.

312. Anon. "News of the Stage." The New York Times (13 April), p. 20.
Reports that Eddie Dowling, Marc Connelly, and Paul Robeson are seeking rights to dramatize NS.

313. Anon. "Notes on Books and Authors." The New York Times (12 October), p. 15.
Announces the enlarged edition of UTC.

314. Anon. "Notes on Books and Authors." The Times-Picayune New Orleans States (17 March), Sec. Two, p. 11.
Mentions the large printing of NS.

315. Anon. "Novel by Young Negro Is Book-of-the-Month Choice." The Bristol (Conn.) Press (2 March), p. 5.
Biographical article with emphasis on NS. Quotes W several times.

316. Anon. "A Novel to Trouble Midnight and the Noon's Repose and to Haunt the Imagination." The New York Times Book Review (28 April), p. 17.
Half-page advertisement for NS.

317. Anon. "O. Henry Memorial Award Prize Stories for 1940, Selected and Edited by Harry Hansen." Birmingham News-Age-Herald (15 December), p. 7.
Lists W as a contributor.

318. Anon. "Officers of the American Peace Mobilization." Daily Worker (3 September), p. 4.
Reports W's election on 2 September to the National Council of American Peace Mobilization.

318a. Anon. "On Radio." Washington Tribune (13 July). p. 14.
Photograph of W announcing his appearance on "We the People," 16 July.

319. Anon. "Origin of an Idea." The New York Sun (31 May), p. 25.
Announces the publication of "How 'Bigger' Was Born" in the Saturday Review of Literature.

320. Anon. "Orson Welles Buys 'Native Son' for the Stage." The Pittsburgh Courier (10 August), p. 21.
States that Welles intends to produce the play first on the West Coast and then in New York.

321. Anon. "Orson Welles May Produce 'Native Son.'" Washington Afro-American (27 July), p. 15.
Reports from Chapel Hill that Welles intends to confer with W and Green in August.

322. Anon. "Our Best Sellers." The Philadelphia Inquirer (13 March), p. 15.
Lists NS in first place in the fiction category in Philadelphia book stores.

323. Anon. "Our Best Sellers." The Philadelphia Inquirer (20 March), p. 17.
Lists NS in second place in the fiction category in Philadelphia book stores.

324. Anon. "Our Best Sellers." The Philadelphia Inquirer (27 March), p. 24.
Lists NS in second place in the fiction category in Philadelphia book stores.

325. Anon. "Our Best Sellers." The Philadelphia Inquirer (3 April), p. 14.
Lists NS in second place in the fiction category in Philadelphia book stores.

326. Anon. "Our Best Sellers." The Philadelphia Inquirer (10 April), p. 28.
Lists NS in second place in the fiction category in Philadelphia book stores.

327. Anon. "Our Best Sellers." The Philadelphia Inquirer (17 April), p. 12.
Lists NS in fourth place in the fiction category in Philadelphia book stores.

328. Anon. "Our Best Sellers." The Philadelphia Inquirer (24 April), p. 21.
Lists NS in fifth place in the fiction category in Philadelphia book stores.

329. Anon. "Our Best Sellers." The Philadelphia Inquirer (1 May), p. 16.

Lists NS in sixth place in the fiction category in Philadelphia book stores.

330. Anon. "Our Best Sellers." The Philadelphia Inquirer (8 May), p. 12.
Lists NS in fourth place in the fiction category in Philadelphia book stores.

331. Anon. "Our Best Sellers." The Philadelphia Inquirer (15 May), p. 18.
Lists NS in sixth place in the fiction category in Philadelphia book stores.

332. Anon. "Our Best Sellers." The Philadelphia Inquirer (22 May), p. 15.
Lists NS in fourth place in the fiction category in Philadelphia book stores.

333. Anon. "Our Contributors." Negro World Digest, 1 (September), 96.
Includes a brief note on W, whose "How 'Bigger' Was Born" is excerpted on pp. 24-28 as "The Birth of Bigger Thomas."

334. Anon. "Outstanding Books of the Year Named by Time Magazine." The Atlanta Constitution (29 December), Magazine Sec., p. [6].
Includes NS among the works of fiction.

335. Anon. "Outstanding in Fiction." The Baltimore Sunday Sun (10 March), Magazine Sec. 1, p. 8.
Favorable review of NS comparing it to The Grapes of Wrath. W's social message is powerful. Rough and raw, "the most important novel ever to flow from the pen of an American Negro," NS is especially effective in developing emotional force.

336. Anon. "Outstanding Negroes and Whites of 1939 Selected in Nationwide Poll, Named Over Station WEVD." The New York Age (17 February), p. 3.
W is one of twelve distinguished blacks selected by a poll sponsored by the Schomburg Collection and the New York branch of the Association for the Study of Negro Life and History.

337. Anon. "Paul Robeson." New York Amsterdam News (7 September), p. 17.
Advertisement, mentioning W, for the Negro Playwrights Company benefit at the Golden Gate Ballroom in Harlem.

338. Anon. "Paul Robeson May Produce 'Native Son.'" Norfolk Journal and Guide (20 April), p. 18.
Reports Robeson's intense interest in producing and perhaps acting in a dramatic version of "the greatest Negro novel of all time." W is considering that possibility in Mexico, where "he is studying the collectivist program outlined by President Cardenas . . . and . . . may adapt his findings to the theme of another novel."

339. Anon. "Paul Robeson, Richard Wright on Program to Aid New Negro Theatre." Daily Worker (2 September), p. 7.
Article on the benefit evening at the Golden Gate Ballroom for the Negro Playwrights Company.

340. Anon. "Perry Watkins Joins Playwrights Group." New York Amsterdam News (24 August), p. 17.
Mentions W's appearance at the Golden Gate Ballroom.

341. Anon. "Photo Contest Prizes Offered Youths." Unidentified clipping (5 September).
Reprint of 1940.389.

342. Anon. "Playwrights Ready for Inaugural." New York Amsterdam News (31 August), p. 17.
Mentions W's talk on "How 'Bigger' Was Born" at the Golden Gate Ballroom.

343. Anon. "Playwrights to Hear Robeson." The Baltimore Afro-American (3 August), p. 14.
Mentions W's forthcoming appearance at the Golden Gate Ballroom in New York.
Reprinted: 1940.344.

344. Anon. "Playwrights to Hear Robeson." Washington Afro-American (3 August), p. 15.
Reprint of 1940.343.

345. Anon. "Plus & Minus." Story, 16 (May-June), 100-104.
Includes excerpts from twelve reviews of NS.

346. Anon. "Popular in Kansas City." The Kansas City Star (23 March), p. F [16].
Lists NS in fifth place in the fiction category.

347. Anon. "Popular in Kansas City." The Kansas City Star (30 March), p. 14.
Lists NS in fifth place in the fiction category.

348. Anon. "Popular in Kansas City." The Kansas City Star (6 April), p. 14.
Lists NS in fourth place in the fiction category.

349. Anon. "Popular in Kansas City." The Kansas City Star (13 April), p. F [14].
   Lists NS in third place in the fiction category.

350. Anon. "Popular in Kansas City." The Kansas City Star (20 April), p. F [14].
   Lists NS in fourth place in the fiction category.

351. Anon. "Popular in Kansas City." The Kansas City Star (27 April), p. 14.
   Lists NS in first place in the fiction category.

352. Anon. "Popular in Kansas City." The Kansas City Star (4 May), p. [14].
   Lists NS in third place in the fiction category.

353. Anon. "Popular in Kansas City." The Kansas City Star (18 May), p. G [14].
   Lists NS in fifth place in the fiction category.

354. Anon. "Popular in Kansas City." The Kansas City Star (25 May), p. 14.
   Lists NS in sixth place in the fiction category.

355. Anon. "Popular in Kansas City." The Kansas City Star (1 June), p. 14.
   Lists NS in fifth place in the fiction category.

356. Anon. "Powerful Plea for Negro Race." Akron Beacon Journal (10 March), p. 8-D.
   Favorable review of NS. The plot summary emphasizes that the efforts of Jan and Mary to achieve friendship with Bigger precipitate his nightmare. The third book is artistically weaker than the first two, "but the picture of the Negro, against the white world, as presented by Wright, is the most illuminating, the most stirring I have ever read."

357. Anon. "Powerful Story of Negro's Plight in 'Native Son.'" Friday.
   Favorable review. The novel is sordid but powerfully realistic. The story of a "bad nigger," its impact and suspense are noteworthy.

358. Anon. "Prepare to Dramatize 'Native Son.'" Norfolk Journal and Guide (3 August), p. 11.
   Photograph with caption of W and Paul Green working on the play.

358a. Anon. "Problems Beset Efforts of Richard Wright, Paul Green to Turn 'Native Son' Into Play." Washington Tribune (10 August), p. 14.
   Describes the collaboration of W and Green, noting difficulty with the

final scene.

359. Anon. "Prominent Negroes Urge Ballot Rights for Communists." Daily Worker (23 September), p. 4.
   Gives the full text of the statement signed by W and others. See 1940.292.

360. Anon. "Public Library Corner." Newport News Daily Press (24 March), pp. 6-A, 3-C.
   Contains a favorable review of NS with quotations from Henry Seidel Canby. Superficially an exciting crime story, the novel is remarkable for its characterization and theme.

361. Anon. "Public Stampedes Bookstores for 'Native Son.'"
   Broadside advertisement quoting from several reviews and including a photograph of W.

362. Anon. "Public Stampedes Bookstores for 'Native Son.'" The Publishers' Weekly, 137 (9 March), [1060].
   Full-page advertisement with quotations from a dozen reviews.

363. Anon. "Public Stampedes for 'Native Son.'" New York Amsterdam News (9 March), p. 2.
   Advertisement with an order blank and excerpts from reviews.

364. Anon. "Public Stampedes for 'Native Son.'" The New York Age (16 March), p. 2.
   Advertisement for sale of the novel by the newspaper. Includes quotations from several reviews and a photograph of W. States that "every Negro should read 'Native Son.'"

365. Anon. "Public Stampedes for 'Native Son.'" The Pittsburgh Courier (23 March), p. 4; (30 March), p. 15; (6 April), p. 14; (13 April), p. 15; (20 April), p. 15; (11 May), p. 2.
   Advertisement with quotations from reviews.

365a. Anon. "Public Stampedes for 'Native Son.'" Washington Tribune (16 March), p. 16.
   Advertisement quoting from various favorable reviews. Also contains a coupon for purchase of the novel and subscription to the Washington Tribune.

365b. Anon. "Public Stampedes for 'Native Son.'" Washington Tribune (23 March), p. 16; (6 April), p. 16; (13 April), p. 16; (20 April), p. 16; (27 April), p. 16; (4 May), p. 16; (11 May), p. 5; (18 May), p. 5; (25 May), p. 5; (1 June), p. 5; (22 June), p. 16; (29

June), p. 16.
Advertisement containing blurbs from reviews and a photograph of W.

366. Anon. "Pulitzer Awards." New Masses, 35 (14 May), 26.
"Nobody can doubt that Richard Wright's Native Son is as inevitable a choice for next year as The Grapes of Wrath was for this."

367. Anon. "R. Wright, The Author, Backs Photo Contest." Unidentified clipping.
Reprint of 1940.389.

368. Anon. "Readers Discuss 'Native Son.'" Daily Worker (26 April), p. 7.
Letters to two reviewers of NS, Benjamin Davis, Jr., and Mike Gold, from Herbert Newton, E. G., Herbert Aptheker, Bruno I., B. T., and "Sister Carrie."

369. Anon. ("Sister Carrie"). "Readers Discuss 'Native Son.'" Daily Worker (26 April), p. 7.
A black Communist writes to Mike Gold disputing his review and supporting that of Benjamin Davis, Jr., on the issue of the characterization of blacks. W fails in this regard because all his black characters are "thoroughly beaten and backward."

370. Anon. "Real 'Native Son' Family in Harlem Fights Conditions Through Organization." Sunday Worker (13 October), p. 4.
Reports on a deprived black family living under conditions similar to those experienced by Bigger Thomas.

371. Anon. "A Remarkable Book by Negro." The Hartford Courant (3 March), Magazine Sec., p. 6.
Favorable review of NS stressing its psychological rather than sociological theme. "It is a terrible story, a horrible story, but, as a study of the inner workings of the feelings and emotions of a human being, it is masterly." Bigger's evening with Jan and Mary is especially well rendered.

372. Anon. "Remarkable 5-Year Rise." The Marion (Ohio) Star (29 February), p. 6.
Book-of-the-Month Club press release summarizing W's career and the plot of NS. "One of the leading authors of his generation," W has written a novel comparable to The Grapes of Wrath. Reprinted: 1940.215, 395, 398, 540, 541.

373. Anon. "Renaissance?" The Chicago Daily News (21 February), p. 18.
Photograph with caption of W and two other Chicago writers.

374. Anon. "Reprints, New Editions." New York Herald Tribune Books (27 October), p. 30.
Contains reviews and comparisons of the enlarged edition of UTC and Eneas Africanus by Harry Stillwell Edwards. W's book is "the best account in fiction of their [black people's] changing attitude and status."

375. Anon. "Rev. Austin Preaches on Wright's 'Native Son.'" The Chicago Defender (15 June), p. 9.
Detailed report of a sermon on the novel. Rev. Austin praises God for W's talent, but deplores the sexual theme of the novel, which may confirm white stereotypes about the attraction of black men to white women.

376. Anon. "Reviews Book." Unidentified clipping from a New York newspaper (9 June).
Announces a lecture on NS by John Haynes Holmes on 9 June at the Harlem Unitarian Church.

377. Anon. "Richard Wright." The Hartford Courant (24 March), Magazine Sec., p. 7.
Sketch of W by Hartford artist James Britton II with caption.

378. Anon. "Richard Wright." Trenton Sunday Times Advertiser (3 March), Part Four, p. 3.
Photograph with caption.

379. Anon. "Richard Wright Answers a Lynch Apologist." Sunday Worker (9 June), Sec. 2, p. 5.
Comments on and quotes from the exchange between W and David L. Cohn in The Atlantic Monthly.

380. Anon. "Richard Wright, Author of March Book-of-the-Month 'Native Son.'" Washington Afro-American (9 March), p. 16.
Partial reprint of 1940.381.

381. Anon. "Richard Wright, Author of March Book-of-the-Month 'Native Son' Writing New Novel, Never Went Past Eighth Grade." The Baltimore Afro-American (9 March), p. 13.
Associated Negro Press biographical article with brief description of his work in progress, "a study of the role and position of the colored woman in American society."
Partially reprinted: 1940.380.

382. Anon. "Richard Wright Explains." The New York Age (8 June), p. 12.
Editorial showing how the essay "How 'Bigger' Was Born" answers the questions of middle-class blacks

about the racial representativeness
of Bigger Thomas. The editorialist
agrees with W's case for the responsibility of society for criminal
types.

383. Anon. "Richard Wright Heard in New
York." The Baltimore Afro-American (23
March), p. 2.
   Reports W's talk at the Schomburg
   Collection.
   Reprinted: 1940.384.

384. Anon. "Richard Wright Heard in New
York." Washington Afro-American (23
March), p. 2.
   Reprint of 1940.383.

385. Anon. "Richard Wright Is Guest
Speaker at Writers School." Daily Worker
(25 January), p. 7.
   Announces that W and other leftist
   writers will speak on 26 January.

386. Anon. "Richard Wright Novel Book of
Month Choice." Sunday Worker (14 Jan-
uary), p. 7.
   Announces that W will speak at the
   Writers' School on 26 January.

387. Anon. "Richard Wright Rates as One
of Country's Foremost Contemporary
Novelists." The Kansas City Call (1
March), p. 4.
   Associated Negro Press biographical
   article based on an interview in
   Chicago. Reviews W's life and literary apprenticeship, concluding with
   comments on work in progress, work
   habits, and personal details.

388. Anon. "Richard Wright Sponsors
$1550 Youth Photo Contest." St. Louis
Argus (6 September), p. 8.
   Reprint of 1940.389.

389. _____. "Richard Wright Sponsors
Youth Photo Contest." Daily Worker (24
August), p. 7.
   Announces that W is one of ten spon-
   sors of the "Youth in Focus" contest.
   Reprinted: 1940.341, 367, 388, 389a.

389a. _____. "Richard Wright Sponsors
Youth Photo Contest." Washington Tribune
(31 August), p. 14.
   Reprint of 1940.389.

390. Anon. "Richard Wright Tells Library
Forum How He Wrote 'Native Son.'" The
New York Age (16 March), p. 2.
   Reports W's talk on "How 'Bigger' Was
   Born" on 14 March at the 135th Street
   Branch of the New York Public Libra-
   ry. Henry Seidel Canby introduced the
   speaker, and L. D. Reddick presided
   over the question period. W expressed
   support of the left.

391. Anon. "Richard Wright to Be Guest
on Negro Day at 'Lost Colony.'" Norfolk
Journal and Guide (17 August), p. 4.
   Reports that W will accompany Paul
   Green to view his historical pageant
   The Lost Colony in Manteo, North
   Carolina, on 16 August.

392. Anon. "Richard Wright to Speak."
The New York Age (24 February), p. 2.
   Announces a Talk by W at the 135th
   Street Branch of the New York Public
   Library on 7 March.

393. Anon. "Richard Wright to Speak at
Library." The New York Amsterdam News (2
March), p. 11.
   Announces W's talk on "How 'Bigger'
   Was Born" at the 135th Street Branch
   of the New York Public Library sched-
   uled for 7 March 1940.

394. Anon. "Richard Wright to Speak at
White Rock Sunday." The Durham Carolina
Times (27 July), p. 1.
   Announces a lecture on "How 'Bigger'
   Was Born" to be given on 28 July at
   the White Rock Baptist Church under
   the sponsorship of the Durham Negro
   Youth Council. Includes a brief
   account of W's literary career with
   comparisons to Dostoevsky and Tolstoy.

395. Anon. "Richard Wright Wins Third
Literary Honor." Bridgeport Post (4
March), p. 9.
   Reprint of 1940.372.

396. Anon. "Richard Wright's Native
Son." The Chicago Defender (16 March),
p. 14.
   Favorable editorial review comparing
   W to Alexandre Dumas and emphasizing
   the social theme of the novel. The
   editorialist hopes that NS will focus
   attention on black problems and "by
   the very urgency of its message,
   transform a rotten social, economic
   system into a living democracy for
   all."
   Reprinted: 1970.5; 1978.209.

397. Anon. "Richard Wright's New Novel
'Book of Month' Selection." Plaindealer
(2 February).
   Also mentions W's Story and Guggenheim awards.

398. Anon. "Rise of Negro Author." Journal and Courier (29 February).
   Reprint of 1940.372.

399. Anon. "Robeson in Harlem." The
Baltimore Afro-American (14 September),
p. 3.
   Mentions W's appearance at the Golden
   Gate Ballroom.

Reprinted: 1940.400.

400. _____. "Robeson in Harlem." Washington Afro-American (14 September), p.
5.
    Reprint of 1940.399.

401. Anon. "Robeson Seeks 'Native Son.'"
The Baltimore Afro-American (20 April),
p. 14.
    Reports that Paul Robeson, Eddie
    Dowling, and Marc Connelly are seek-
    ing dramatic rights to W's novel.
    Racial groups will protest putting
    the novel on the stage, however,
    because it would be "detrimental to
    the colored race." Provides a plot
    summary.

402. Anon. "Robeson, Wright to Be in
Playwright Co. Debut." The Baltimore
Afro-American (20 July), p. 14.
    Announces W's appearance at the Gol-
    den Gate Ballroom in New York.
    Reprinted: 1940.403.

403. _____. "Robeson, Wright to Be in
Playwright Co. Debut." Washington Afro-
American (20 July), p. 17.
    Reprint of 1940.402.

404. Anon. "San Francisco Best Sellers."
San Francisco Chronicle (17 March), This
World Sec., p. 21.
    Lists NS in first place in the fic-
    tion category.

405. Anon. "San Francisco Best Sellers."
San Francisco Chronicle (24 March), This
World Sec., p. 18.
    Lists NS in second place in the fic-
    tion category.

406. Anon. "San Francisco Best Sellers."
San Francisco Chronicle (31 March), This
World Sec., p. 14.
    Lists NS in second place in the fic-
    tion category.

407. Anon. "San Francisco Best Sellers."
San Francisco Chronicle (7 April), This
World Sec., p. 17.
    Lists NS in second place in the fic-
    tion category.

408. Anon. "San Francisco Best Sellers."
San Francisco Chronicle (23 June), This
World Sec., p. 14.
    Lists NS in sixth place in the fic-
    tion category.

409. Anon. "San Francisco Best Sellers."
San Francisco Chronicle (30 June), This
World Sec., p. 17.
    Lists NS in sixth place in the fic-
    tion category.

410. Anon. "San Francisco Best Sellers."

San Francisco Chronicle (14 July), This
World Sec., p. 19.
    Lists NS in eighth place in the fic-
    tion category.

411. Anon. "Says 'Native Son'" Fails Its
Purpose." The Chicago Defender (25 May),
p. 7.
    Summarizes an interview with George
    R. Dorsey, a sociologist who had read
    and analyzed NS. Recognizing the
    literary merit of the novel, Dorsey
    believes that it fails sociologically
    because it has no sympathetically
    rendered characters.

412. Anon. "Search for Stage 'Bigger'
Gets Drama Fans' Fancy." New York Amsterdam News (17 August), p. 17.
    Canada Lee is receiving more support
    than anyone else.

413. Anon. "Sinewy Novel Chronicles Rise
and Fall of a Negro." Milwaukee Evening
Post (9 March), p. 5.
    Reprint of 1940.156.

414. Anon. "Some Harper Books Scheduled
for Spring." The Publishers' Weekly, 137
(27 January), 314.
    Lists NS for March publication.

415. Anon. "Some Interesting Notes About
Books and Authors." Savannah Morning
News (2 June), p. 34.
    Mentions the good sales of NS.
    Reprinted: 1940.449.

416. Anon. "Sorority Unit Plans Dinner,
Bridge Party." Wilmington (Del.) Journal-Every Evening (13 March), p. 14.
    Notes that Mrs. Preston Cox reviewed
    NS at a Beta Sigma Phi meeting.

417. Anon. "Sorors Hear Book Review."
The Chicago Defender (6 April), p. 22.
    Account of a lecture on NS by John
    Davis, "a local poet," at a meeting
    of the Theta Sigma chapter of Delta
    Sigma Theta sorority.

418. Anon. "Special Performance." Brooklyn Citizen (27 March).
    Announces that Ethel Waters will
    perform at a book fair for W.

419. Anon. "The Spring Isn't So Bad."
The Publishers' Weekly, 137 (30 March),
1296-1297.
    Reports continued good sales of NS,
    especially in Chicago and the South.

420. Anon. ". . . A Star for Notable
Success." The Publishers' Weekly, 137 (3
February), 567.
    Full-page advertisement for NS.

421. Anon. "The Star's Book Corner." The

Muncie Sunday Star (10 March), Sec. 2, p. 6.
  Reprint of 1940.156.

422. Anon. "State College Gets Many Rare Books for 3-Day Exhibit." Charleston (W. Va.) Daily Mail (3 March), p. 4.
  In a book exhibit at West Virginia State College, "possibly the highlight of contemporary books . . . will be 'The Native Son.'"

423. Anon. "Still for 'Peace.'" New York Daily Mirror.
  Photograph with caption of a student demonstration in New York. One placard refers to "Native Sons."

424. Anon. "Success Story." The Publishers' Weekly, 137 (6 April), 1387-1388.
  Based on an interview with Cass Canfield of Harper's, this is an account of W's discovery by the Story magazine contest, the success of NS, and W's current activities.

425. Anon. "Talent of Race Recognized in Inscriptions on Wall of Honor at N. Y. World Fair." The Pittsburgh Courier (20 July), p. 4.
  W is one of forty-one blacks and four black writers included.

426. Anon. "Theater: Notes." PM (5 September), p. 12.
  W and Paul Robeson will appear at the Golden Gate Ballroom for the benefit of the Negro Playwrights Guild.

427. Anon. "13,719 Copies Sold in First Week." New York World-Telegram (c. 28 March).
  Advertisement for NS.

428. Anon. "32 Year Old Unschooled Negro Who Lives at Mohegan Colony Highly Praised By Critics for Fast-Selling Novel 'Native Son.'" Peekskill Democrat (7 March), pp. 1, 8.
  Notes the success of NS and mentions W's residence at Crompond, New York. Includes extensive quotation from a biographical sketch of W in The New York Sun.

429. Anon. "300 Writers Warn Civil Liberties Are in Danger." Daily Worker (13 June), pp. 1, 4.
  W is one of the signers of a League of American Writers statement expressing hatred of fascism but opposing American involvement in the war.

430. Anon. "Throwing No Stone." The Raleigh News and Observer (1 April), p. 4.
  Editorial protesting the banning of

NS from the Birmingham Public Library.

431. Anon. "Tragic Story of a Negro Boy." The Knoxville News-Sentinel (31 March), p. C-9.
  Favorable review of NS summarizing the plot and commending W's emotional power, realism, brisk narrative pace, and characterization of Mary and Jan.

432. Anon. "Two New Novels by Authors Whose Work Has Appeared in Story Magazine." Story, 16 (May-June), 1.
  Includes advertisement for NS with quotations from reviews by Clifton Fadiman and Sterling North.

433. Anon. "Uncle Tom's Children, by Richard Wright." Washington Afro-American (16 November).
  Favorable review of the revised, enlarged edition with special praise for the additions--"The Ethics of Living Jim Crow" and "Bright and Morning Star."

434. Anon. Unidentified clipping.
  Favorable comment on the magazine version of "How 'Bigger' Was Born." It is "must" reading.

435. Anon. Unidentified clipping.
  Favorable review of NS commending the novel's power, pointing out the theme of environmental determinism, and briefly summarizing the plot.

436. Anon. Unidentified clipping.
  Photograph of Paul Robeson with a long caption mentioning W's appearance at the Golden Gate Ballroom in Harlem.

437. Anon. Unidentified clipping (c. November).
  Review of O. Henry Memorial Award Prize Stories of 1940 calling "Almos' a Man" a "moving study."

438. Unidentified clipping (Boston newspaper?).
  Advertisement for Charles Lee's review of NS at the Coolidge Corner Theatre in Brookline, Massachusetts, on 10 April.

439. Anon. Untitled article. Oakland Tribune (15 December), p. 6-B.
  Brief notice of NS quoting Sidney Meller's favorable review. See 1940.795.

440. Anon. Untitled article. The New York Sun (13 March), p. 27.
  NS was the week's fiction best seller in Doubleday bookstores.

441. Anon. Untitled article. The New York Sun (27 March), p. 25.
NS was the week's fiction best seller in Doubleday bookstores.

442. Anon. Untitled article. The New York Sun (19 October), p. 33.
Brief notice of the publication of the enlarged edition of UTC and the pamphlet How "Bigger" Was Born.

443. Anon. Untitled article. The New York Times Book Review (26 May), p. 12.
Includes an excerpt from a letter by W complaining of various living and working problems in Cuernavaca.

444. Anon. Untitled clipping. Chicago Daily Tribune.
Corrects an error by W on p. 188 of NS concerning the correct price of a copy of the Chicago Daily Tribune.

445. Anon. Untitled clipping. Cincinnati Times-Star (15 March).
Favorable review of NS stressing its power and violence. The entire racial tragedy is implicit in Bigger's story.

446. Anon. Untitled clipping. Corry Evening Journal (9 March).
Partial reprint of 1940.156.

447. Anon. Untitled clipping. New York Journal and American (c. May).
Favorable review of NS commenting on its power and comparing it to The Grapes of Wrath.

448. Anon. Untitled clipping. New York World-Telegram (1 April).
Notes that NS was the leading best seller for the preceding week.

449. Anon. Untitled clipping. The El Paso Times (26 May).
Reprint of 1940.415.

450. Anon. Untitled clipping. The Pittsburgh Courier.
Photograph of W at a speaker's platform. The year is conjectural.

451. Anon. Untitled clipping. The New York Sun (25 March).
NS was the fiction best seller at Brentano's during the week ending 20 March.

452. Anon. Untitled clipping. Sydney Sunday Telegraph (21 April).
Generally favorable review of NS. Bigger seems too articulate to be plausible, however.

453. Anon. Untitled clipping. Tribune and Register (2 August).
Favorable notice of NS pointing out the theme of environmental determinism and praising the narrative pace.

454. Anon. Untitled clipping. Wilmington (N. C.) News (13 November).
Notice of the enlarged edition of UTC.

455. Anon. Untitled photograph. People's Daily World (2 May), p. 5.
Photograph of W with caption praising NS and calling its author "one of the most searching and brilliant American writers."

456. Anon. "Wall of Fame of the American Common World's Fair of 1940 in New York."
W is included in this mimeographed list of "the Names of American Citizens of Foreign Birth, American Indians and Negroes who have made Notable Contributions to our Living, Ever-Growing Democracy Devoted to Peace and Freedom."

457. Anon. "War and Peace Is Subject of Authors' Talks." Daily Worker (17 February), p. 7.
Article on forums sponsored by the League of American Writers begins with a quotation from W's talk on the writer and society.

458. Anon. "Week's Best Sellers." Charlotte Sunday Observer (10 March), Sec. Three, p. 5.
Lists NS in second place in the fiction category.

459. Anon. "The Week's Best Sellers." Chicago Sunday Herald-American (31 March), Part V, p. 6.
Lists NS in fifth place in the fiction category.

460. Anon. "The Week's Best Sellers." Chicago Sunday Herald-American (7 April), Part V, p. 6.
Lists NS in second place in the fiction category.

461. Anon. "The Week's Best Sellers." Chicago Sunday Herald-American (14 April), Part V, p. 7.
Lists NS in third place in the fiction category.

462. Anon. "The Week's Best Sellers." Chicago Sunday Herald-American (21 April), Part V, p. 9.
Lists NS in second place in the fiction category.

463. Anon. "The Week's Best Sellers."

Chicago Sunday Herald-American (28
April), Part V, p. 8.
    Lists NS in second place in the fic-
    tion category.

464. Anon. "The Week's Best Sellers."
Chicago Sunday Herald-American (5 May),
Part V, p. 7.
    Lists NS in second place in the fic-
    tion category.

465. Anon. "The Week's Best Sellers."
Chicago Sunday Herald-American (12 May),
Part V, p. 7.
    Lists NS in second place in the fic-
    tion category.

466. Anon. "The Week's Best Sellers."
Chicago Sunday Herald-American (19 May),
Part V, p. 6.
    Lists NS in fourth place in the fic-
    tion category.

467. Anon. "The Week's Best Sellers."
Chicago Sunday Herald-American (26 May),
Part V, p. 6.
    Lists NS in fourth place in the fic-
    tion category.

468. Anon. "The Week's Best Sellers."
Chicago Sunday Herald-American (2 June),
Part III, p. 8.
    Lists NS in fourth place in the fic-
    tion category.

469. Anon. "The Week's Best Sellers."
Chicago Sunday Herald-American (9 June),
Part IV, p. 8.
    Lists NS in tenth place in the fic-
    tion category.

470. Anon. "The Week's Best Sellers."
Chicago Sunday Herald-American (16
June), Part III, p. 8.
    Lists NS in ninth place in the fic-
    tion category.

471. Anon. "Week's Best Sellers Through
the Nation." Brooklyn Eagle (14 April),
Sec. E, p. 9.
    Lists NS in third place in the fic-
    tion category.

472. Anon. "Week's Best Sellers Through
the Nation." Brooklyn Eagle (12 May),
Trend Sec., p. 9.
    Lists NS in second place in the fic-
    tion category.

473. Anon. "What America Is Reading."
New York Herald Tribune Books (24
March), p. 23.
    Lists NS in sixth place in the fic-
    tion category.

474. Anon. "What America Is Reading."
New York Herald Tribune Books (31
March), p. 27.

Lists NS in fourth place in the fiction category.

475. Anon. "What America Is Reading."
New York Herald Tribune Books (7 April),
p. 23.
    Lists NS in fourth place in the fic-
    tion category.

476. Anon. "What America Is Reading."
New York Herald Tribune Books (14
April), p. 27.
    Lists NS in fourth place in the fic-
    tion category.

477. Anon. "What America Is Reading."
New York Herald Tribune Books (21
April), p. 23.
    Lists NS in third place in the fic-
    tion category.

478. Anon. "What America Is Reading."
New York Herald Tribune Books (28
April), p. 23.
    Lists NS in fourth place in the fic-
    tion category.

479. Anon. "What America Is Reading."
New York Herald Tribune Books (5 May),
p. 27.
    Lists NS in sixth place in the fic-
    tion category.

480. Anon. "What America Is Reading."
New York Herald Tribune Books (12 May),
p. 23.
    Lists NS in fifth place in the fic-
    tion category.

481. Anon. "What America Is Reading."
New York Herald Tribune Books (19 May),
p. 19.
    Lists NS in sixth place in the fic-
    tion category.

482. Anon. "What America Is Reading."
New York Herald Tribune Books (26 May),
p. 19.
    Lists NS in sixth place in the fic-
    tion category.

483. Anon. "What America Is Reading."
New York Herald Tribune Books (2 June),
p. 15.
    Lists NS in seventh place in the
    fiction category.

484. Anon. "What America Is Reading."
New York Herald Tribune Books (9 June),
p. 15.
    Lists NS in eighth place in the fic-
    tion category.

485. Anon. "What America Is Reading."
New York Herald Tribune Books (16 June),
p. 19.
    Lists NS in tenth place in the fic-
    tion category.

486. Anon. "What America Is Reading."
New York Herald Tribune Books (23 June),
p. 15.
    Lists NS in eleventh place in the
    fiction category.

487. Anon. "What America Is Reading."
New York Herald Tribune Books (30 June),
p. 19.
    Lists NS in eleventh place in the
    fiction category.

488. Anon. "What America Is Reading."
New York Herald Tribune Books (7 July),
p. 15.
    Lists NS in thirteenth place in the
    fiction category.

489. Anon. "What America Is Reading."
New York Herald Tribune Books (14 July),
p. 15.
    Lists NS in fourteenth place in the
    fiction category.

490. Anon. "What America Is Reading."
New York Herald Tribune Books (21 July),
p. 15.
    Lists NS in twenty-second place in
    the fiction category.

491. Anon. "What Atlanta Is Reading
Now." The Atlanta Constitution (31
March), Magazine Sec., p. 6.
    Lists NS in fifth place in the fic-
    tion category.

492. Anon. "What Atlanta Is Reading
Now." The Atlanta Constitution (28
April), Magazine Sec., p. 6.
    Lists NS in second place in the fic-
    tion category.

493. Anon. "What Atlanta Is Reading
Now." The Atlanta Constitution (5 May),
Magazine Sec., p. 6.
    Lists NS in second place in the fic-
    tion category.

494. Anon. "What Atlanta Is Reading
Now." The Atlanta Constitution (12 May),
Magazine Sec., p. 6.
    Lists NS in fifth place in the fic-
    tion category.

495. Anon. "What Atlanta Is Reading
Now." The Atlanta Constitution (19 May),
Magazine Sec., p. 6.
    Lists NS in third place in the fic-
    tion category.

496. Anon. "What Atlanta Is Reading
Now." The Atlanta Constitution (26 May),
Magazine Sec., p. 6.
    Lists NS in fifth place in the fic-
    tion category.

497. Anon. "What Atlanta Is Reading
Now." The Atlanta Constitution (2 June),

Magazine Sec., p. 6.
    Lists NS in third place in the fic-
    tion category.

498. Anon. "What Atlanta Is Reading
Now." The Atlanta Constitution (9 June),
Magazine Sec., p. 6.
    Lists NS in fifth place in the fic-
    tion category.

499. Anon. "What Atlanta Is Reading
Now." The Atlanta Constitution (16
June), Magazine Sec., p. 6.
    Lists NS in second place in the fic-
    tion category.

500. Anon. "What Atlanta Is Reading
Now." The Atlanta Constitution (23
June), Magazine Sec., p. 6.
    Lists NS in fourth place in the fic-
    tion category.

501. Anon. "What Atlanta Is Reading
Now." The Atlanta Constitution (7 July),
Magazine Sec., p. 6.
    Lists NS in fourth place in the fic-
    tion category.

502. Anon. "What Atlanta Is Reading
Now." The Atlanta Constitution (14
July), Magazine Sec., p. 6.
    Lists NS in fifth place in the fic-
    tion category.

503. Anon. "What Atlanta Is Reading
Now." The Atlanta Constitution (4
August), Magazine Sec., p. 6.
    Lists NS in ninth place in the fic-
    tion category.

504. Anon. "What Readers Are Reading."
PM's Weekly (4 August), p. 41.
    Lists NS in second place in the fic-
    tion category under "From the Public
    Library."

505. Anon. "What Readers Are Reading."
PM's Weekly (11 August), p. 41.
    Lists NS in third place in the fic-
    tion category under "From the Public
    Library."

506. Anon. "What Readers Are Reading."
PM's Weekly (18 August), p. 51.
    Lists NS in third place in the fic-
    tion category under "From the Public
    Library."

507. Anon. "What Readers Are Reading."
PM's Weekly (25 August), p. 41.
    Lists NS in fourth place in the fic-
    tion category under "From the Public
    Library."

508. Anon. "What Readers Are Reading."
PM's Weekly (1 September), p. 41.
    Lists NS in third place in the fic-
    tion category under "From the Public

Library."

509. Anon. "What Readers Are Reading." PM's Weekly (8 September), p. 41.
Lists NS in third place in the fiction category under "From the Public Library."

510. Anon. "What Readers Are Reading." PM's Weekly (15 September), p. 41.
Lists NS in third place in the fiction category under "From the Public Library."

511. Anon. "What Readers Are Reading." PM's Weekly (22 September), p. 41.
Lists NS in third place in the fiction category under "From the Public Library of New York City."

512. Anon. "What Readers Are Reading." PM's Weekly (29 September), p. 43.
Lists NS in third place in the fiction category under "From the Public Library of New York City."

513. Anon. "Will Review Book." Freeport (N. Y.) Nassau Review and Star (14 March).
Announces a lecture on NS by Rabbi Edward T. Sandrow at the South Shore meeting of the women's league of the American Jewish Congress.

514. Anon. "William Allen White Doesn't Like Current Books." Lewiston (Maine) Saturday Journal (27 July), Illustrated Magazine Sec., p. A-8.
Derived from 1940.981.

515. Anon. "Womrath Recommends." The New York Times (9 May), p. 21.
Bookstore advertisement mentioning NS.

516. Anon. "Wordstorm." The Argonaut (5 April), p. 32.
Favorable notice of NS emphasizing its social message.

517. Anon. "A Work of Genius." New York Amsterdam News (23 March), p. 14.
Lead editorial praising the artistic quality and thematic importance of NS. The novel is most important because it reveals the economic and social consequences of racism. It is a document to which whites must react positively.

518. Anon. "Wright Backs Red Candidates." The Pittsburgh Courier (12 October), p. 2.
Asociated Negro Press news item about W's support of Earl Browder and James W. Ford.

519. Anon. "Wright Describes Bigger Thomas' [sic] as 'Cowardly Bully.'" The Pittsburgh Courier (16 March), p. 4.
Account of W's speech on "How 'Bigger' Was Born" delivered at the 135th Street Branch of the New York Public Library.

520. Anon. "Wright, Richard." Current Biography, 1 (March), 61-62.
Biographical and critical sketch dealing at some length with NS, which is compared to An American Tragedy. W's habits, views of Hollywood, and current literary activities receive mention.
Reprinted: 1940.521.

521. Anon. "Wright, Richard," in Current Biography, 1940. Ed. Maxine Block. New York: The H. W. Wilson Company, pp. 885-887.
Reprint of 1940.520.

522. Anon. "Wright, Richard." The Publishers' Weekly, 138 (19 October), 1614.
Brief notice of How "Bigger" Was Born referring to NS as "one of the most significant novels of our time."

523. Anon. "Wright, Richard." The Publishers' Weekly, 138 (19 October), 1615.
Brief notice of the enlarged edition of UTC pointing out the new material.

524. Anon. "Wright, Richard. Native son." Pratt Institute Library Quarterly Booklist, 6 (October), 24.
Brief notice stressing the work's power and its theme of environmental determinism.

525. Anon. "Wright, Richard. Native son." The Booklist, 36 (1 April), 307.
Favorable brief notice praising the power, realism, "understanding of Negro psychology," and compassion of the novel, but warning that "its frank brutalities" and the menace of black resentment "will horrify many readers."

526. Anon. "Wright, Richard. Native son." The Open Shelf, Nos. 5-6 (May-June), p. 12.
Very brief notice emphasizing the novel's power and theme.

527. Anon. "Wright, Richard. Native son." The Publishers' Weekly, 137 (2 March), 1031.
Brief notice of a "powerful story" of a crime made inevitable by social and psychological causes.

528. Anon. "Wright, Richard. Native son." Wilson Library Bulletin, 14 (April), 603.
Brief notice consisting of two quota-

tions from Book-of-the-Month Club News and Saturday Review of Literature.

529. Anon. "Wright, Richard. Native son." Wisconsin Library Bulletin, 36 (May), 101.
Brief, somewhat favorable notice comparing the novel to The Grapes of Wrath and An American Tragedy and deeming it "relentlessly hard and brutal" but "powerful and impressive."

530. Anon. "Wright, Robeson to Speak in Aid of Negro Theatre." Daily Worker (18 August), p. 7.
Announces W's speech on "How 'Bigger' Was Born" at the Golden Gate Ballroom on 6 September.

531. Anon. "Wright Sees Negro Problem." The San Francisco News (16 March), p. 15.
Reprint of 1940.156.

532. Anon. "Wright Shows New Book." The Chicago Defender (24 February), p. 22.
Photograph of W and Ulysses S. Keys with caption on W's talks at Woodlawn A. M. E. Church and at the home of Keys.

533. Anon. "Wright's 'Native Son' Topic of Lecture at Forum Tonight." Daily Worker (5 April), p. 7.
Announces Sender Garlin's lecture on "Wright's development as a writer and the significance of his emergence as an outstanding American novelist. The speaker will analyze 'Native Son' and comment on the reviews that have appeared, particularly in the Southern press."

533a. Anon. "Wright's New Novel Is 'Book of Month' Choice." Washington Tribune (3 February), p. 16.
Mentions NS, UTC, and W's talk at the Writers School on 26 January.

534. Anon. "Wright's Tragedy of Young Chicago Negro Reflects Bitter Irony." The Columbia Missourian (11 May), p. 4.
Favorable review of NS praising its dramatic quality, rapid narrative tempo, and skillful characterization. The reviewer finds the passages conveying W's social message dull, even though Bigger's alienation from his environment is a theme the novel develops. NS is compared to The Grapes of Wrath and Macbeth.

535. Anon. "Writers League Elects Outstanding Authors as Vice-Presidents." Daily Worker (5 August), p. 7.
W is one of the three elected.

536. Anon. "The Year's Most Amazing Offer!" Negro World Digest, 1 (September), inside back cover.
Advertisement for subscription to the magazine combined with the purchase of NS.

537. Anon. "You Are Cordially Invited to Come to the Regular Reunion of the Writers' School."
Printed invitation to a lecture by W on "The Problems of the Fiction Writer Today," 26 January 1940, at the Dalcroze School of Music, New York, under the auspices of the League of American Writers.

538. Anon. "You Are Cordially Invited to Hear Richard Wright."
Printed invitation to a lecture on "How 'Bigger' Was Born" at the White Rock Baptist Church in Durham, North Carolina, on 28 July 1940, under the auspices of the Southern Negro Youth Council.

539. Anon. "Young Negro Author Writes Great American Book." Friday, 1 (22 March), 22.
Notes the popular success of NS, "the Negro American Tragedy." Contains a brief biographical paragraph and six photographs of W.

540. Anon. "Young Negro's Novel Book-of-the-Month Selection for March." Gastonia Daily Gazette (2 March), p. 12.
Reprint of 1940.372.

541. Anon. "Young Negro's Novel Choice of Book-of-the-Month Club." The Marquette Daily Mining Journal (2 March), p. [14].
Reprint of 1940.372.

542. Aptheker, Herbert. "Readers Discuss 'Native Son.'" Daily Worker (26 April), p. 7.
Letter praising Michael Gold's review of NS, agreeing that Bigger is not intended to symbolize all black people, and calling the novel "a stroke of genius."

543. A.[tkins], B.[en] E. "You May Wish You'd Not Read This Book." Gastonia Daily Gazette (16 March), p. 10.
Highly favorable review of NS stressing its powerful, disturbing emotional impact on the reader. Compares W to George Lee as a black novelist.

544. B., B. "Readers' Forum." New Masses, 37 (17 December), 21.
Letter to the editor mentioning NS and The Grapes of Wrath as books "that make one fighting mad at the injustices of capitalism."

545. ____. "Readers Write Choices in Fiction." Daily Worker (29 April), p. 6.
Letter to the editor suggesting the serialization of NS.

546. Bagnall, Rev. Robert W. "Taken in Stride: Native Son--The Novel and Its Social Implications." The Philadelphia Tribune (9 May), pp. 4, 15.
Analyzes Bigger as a psychopath with fear his overwhelming motive. Though defending W's novelistic privilege of choosing such a villain for his protagonist, Bagnall fears adverse social reaction to the novel--more repression than reform. W's communism and the characters Jan and Max are sharply criticized.

547. Ball, Barbara. "The Vicarious World." Berkeley Daily Californian (26 March), p. 4.
Favorable review of NS. Though not a masterpiece of literary art or psychological insight, it is extremely important as a revelation of social injustice and a demand for change.

548. Banks, John W. "Woodlawn News." The Chicago Defender (24 February), p. 22.
Mentions W's speech on the preceding Sunday.

549. Barnes, Margaret Ayer. "Margaret Ayer Barnes Praises Two Good Collections of Short Stories." The Chicago Daily News (4 December), Christmas Book Sec., p. 47.
Contains a review of O. Henry Memorial Award Prize Stories of 1940 praising "Almos' a Man."

550. Beals, Helen. "Fortnightly Fiction Review." Worcester Sunday Telegram (27 October), Sec. Four, p. 8.
Contains a notice of the enlarged edition of UTC. Beal admits the social need of the book with its "horrible ring of truth," but she is pained by the cruelty and rage depicted.

551. Bell, Muriel. "Looking Through the Magazines." Savannah Morning News (9 June), p. 34.
Includes a detailed summary of "How 'Bigger' Was Born."

552. Belloli, Joseph A. "Book Angles." Pacific Grove Tide (8 March), p. 8.
Contains a favorable notice of NS emphasizing its psychological insight and emotional power.

553. ____. "Book Angles." Pacific Grove Tide (12 April), p. 8.
Contains a favorable notice of NS, "a true interpretation how [sic] a Negro feels and reacts in a white man's world."

554. Bernard, George. "More GWTW Version of the Negro People." Daily Worker (9 September), p. 7.
Review of Edward Harris Heth's Light Over Ruby Street comparing it briefly and unfavorably to NS.

555. Berry, Lee. "This World of Books." Pittsburgh Post-Gazette (9 March), p. 7.
Column containing a highly favorable review of NS, which Berry calls "a brilliant and daring dramatization of the greatest of American tragedies: The unresolved Negro problem." More than a shocking novel, NS is "a revelatory and unforgettable experience" for the reader. W's "dialogue is electric, his prose is as firm as steel, his characterizations are ruthless." Bigger is a pathological case, but the responsibility for him rests on white society.
Reprinted: 1940.556.

556. ____. "This World of Books." Toledo Blade (9 March), p. 5.
Reprint of 1940.555.

557. ____. "The World of Books." Toledo Blade (23 November), p. 5.
Lists W as a contributor to the O. Henry Memorial Award Prize Stories.

558. Bessie, Alvah. "New Negro Theater." New Masses, 37 (24 September), 23.
Mentions W's speech on "How 'Bigger' Was Born" at the Golden Gate Ballroom on 6 September.

559. ____. "Sights & Sounds." New Masses, 36 (10 September), 22-23.
Notice of W's speech on "How 'Bigger' Was Born" at the Golden Gate Ballroom on 6 September.

560. Bond, Alice Dixon. "Host of Memorable Novels Found in Review of '40 Fiction." The Boston Herald (28 December), p. 5.
Includes mention of NS, not a likable novel but a brilliant and powerful one.

561. Bonnoitt, Murray du Q. "Under the Covers." The Columbia (S. C.) State (18 August), p. 5-B.
Contains a mainly unfavorable notice of NS. Some parts are well done, but "at times Wright achieves easily the worst writing of the year." Though worth reading, the novel has much "that carries a strong odor of Communist and Negro propaganda."

562. Bourne, St. Clair. "Role of 'Bigger

Thomas' Continues to Excite Thespians; Canada Lee Latest." New York Amsterdam News (31 August), p. 17.

Canada Lee is the leading candidate. He has an intense desire to play the part.

563. _____. "Who Should Portray the Role of 'Bigger' Thomas." New York Amsterdam News (10 August), pp. 1, 17.

Speculates on the casting of Bigger, mentioning Paul Robeson, Rex Ingram, P. J. Sidney, Alvin Childress, Theodore Ward, Earl Jones, and Canada Lee. Bourne prefers Lee for the role, an especially difficult one because of the audience's familiarity with the fictional character.

564. Bradley, Preston. "Native Son by Richard Wright." 16 pp.

Mimeographed lecture delivered on 1 May 1940 at the Peoples Church of Chicago. Bradley discusses and speculates, not always accurately, on W's life, emphasizing the role of Professor Lawrence Martin of Chicago. Bradley praises the novel's plot and style. Most of the lecture is an extensive summary of the story with running interpretive commentary on the racial and social implications.

565. Brenneman, Johnson. "Chat About Books." The Canonsburg Daily Notes (15 March), p. 4.

Favorable review of NS praising the novel for its technical proficiency and its thematic importance. In its understanding of criminal psychology, especially the sense of liberation stimulated by murder, NS is comparable to Crime and Punishment. W's warning of social disaster unless racism is eliminated is also impressive.

566. Brevard, Elizabeth W. "Afro Readers Write About 'Native Son.'" The Baltimore Afro-American (11 May), p. 13.

Letter supporting Lillian Johnson's position. Brevard finds the novel immoral, irreligious, and unduly critical of the race. Impressed by W's talents, she hopes that he will write more elevating books.
Reprinted: 1940.567.

567. _____. "Afro Readers Write About 'Native Son.'" Washington Afro-American (11 May), p. 18.

Reprint of 1940.566.

568. Breyer, F. A. "How 'Bigger' Was Born. By Richard Wright." The Cincinnati Enquirer (23 November), p. 5.

Review summarizing the pamphlet, which shows how W wrote the novel and

"how his own philosophy became articulate through the book."

569. _____. "Young Black Man's Nemesis." The Cincinnati Enquirer (2 March), p. 5.

Favorable review of NS. After summarizing the plot, Breyer praises W's artistry, power, and satire on young radicals.

570. Brooks, Alvin G. "Because Their Skin Is Black." The American Mercury, 50 (August), 503.

Brooks refutes Burton Rascoe's remark that "I can't see that Bigger Thomas had anything more to contend with in childhood than I or dozens of my friends had" by citing racial discrimination in education and employment.

571. Brooks, Samuel I. "World This Week." The Pittsburgh Courier (6 April), p. 1.

Column citing W as an example of the possibility of literary success despite racial and economic obstacles.

572. Brown, Sterling A. "Insight, Courage, and Craftsmanship." Opportunity, 18 (June), 185-186.

Favorable review of NS noting the great interest in the book among blacks. Admiring the social realism, the symbolic compression of the narrative (while admitting the implausibility of some details), and above all the characterization of Bigger, Brown thinks that NS will stir the national conscience if any book can.
Reprinted: 1970.5; 1978.209.

573. Buchalter, Helen. "Books of the Week." Washington Sunday Star (3 March).

Favorable review of NS emphasizing its candor, power, and literary skill. Buchalter compares NS favorably to The Grapes of Wrath, which is more didactic.
Partially reprinted: 1940.574.

574. _____. "Some Notable Comment on Native Son," in Native Son. "Seventh Edition." New York: Harper, pp. 365-366.

Partial reprint of 1940.573.

575. Burke, Eddie. "Fact Remains--Those Books Are Popular." The Birmingham Post (2 April), p. 4.

Reprint of 1940.576.

576. _____. "The Library's Choice of Books." The Birmingham News (30 March), p. 4.

Letter to the editor protesting the banning of NS from the Birmingham Public Library.
Reprinted: 1940.575.

576a. Burke, Kenneth. "Surrealism," in New Directions in Prose & Poetry 1940. Ed. James Laughlin. Norfolk, Conn.: New Directions, pp. 563-579.

Shows the relation between the killing of the rat by Bigger ("the plot in germ") and Max's speech (the "argument"). "Bigger's actions make narratively explicit what is implicit in the killing of the rat--and Max's advocacy makes conceptually explicit what is implicit in Bigger's actions" (p. 564).

577. Burley, Dan. "Playwrights Draw 4,200 to Program." New York Amsterdam News (14 September), p. 17.

Includes a review of W's speech on "How 'Bigger' Was Born" at the Golden Gate Ballroom. Burley and much of the audience considered it too long, especially since W delivered it in a "monotonous drone."

578. B.[urnett], W.[hit]. "End Pages." Story, 16 (May-June), 2, 4-6.

Includes comments on the success of NS, on W's "charming and quiet-spoken" personality, on his trip to Mexico, and on the radio dramatization of "Fire and Cloud."

579. Burns, Ben. "Book Marks." People's Daily World (18 July), p. 5.

Mentions W's visit to the American Negro Exposition in Chicago.

580. _____. "Book Marks." People's Daily World (25 July), p. 5.

Provides details about plans for producing the dramatic version of NS. Burns praises Paul Green's liberalism.

581. _____. "Book Notes: Richard Wright Answers Some Questions That Have Arisen From the Controversy Over 'Native Son.'" People's Daily World (14 June), p. 5.

Notes dispute over W's treatment of the relation between the Communist Party and black people in the novel. W's "I Bite the Hand That Feeds Me" confirms his solidarity with the proletariat and the Party.

582. _____. "Book Review: A Path Through Darkness." People's Daily World (2 April), p. 5.

Highly favorable review of NS stressing W's background in the Communist Party. The novel breaks out of the formalism of journalism to achieve an intense and vivid sense of life. W's theme applies to white workers as well as to blacks. NS "is an event in American literature."

583. Butcher, Fanny. "Fanny Butcher Se-

lects 10 Best Novels of 1940." Chicago Daily Tribune (4 December), Sec. Two, pp. 1-2.

NS is the "best psychological novel," suspenseful and powerful. Photographs of W and the other nine novelists appear on p. 2.

584. _____. "N. Y. Is Abuzz Over 2 Books by Chicagoans." Chicago Daily Tribune (27 March), p. 15.

The popularity of NS induced W to sail for Mexico in quest of privacy.

585. _____. "Negro Writes Brilliant Novel, Remarkable Both as Thriller and as Psychological Record." Chicago Daily Tribune (6 March), p. 19.

Favorable review of NS praising W's narrative skill and development of suspense: "for the first two-thirds of the book no tale of pursuit and capture has rivaled it." The characterization of Bigger is complete and psychologically convincing. But Butcher says nothing about W's social theme.

586. C., H. "Native Son by Richard Wright." Unidentified article (March).

Mixed review noting the work's power but complaining that it is overwritten and exaggerated. It is not a book for the fastidious.

587. Cabey, C. W. "Afro Readers Write About 'Native Son.'" The Baltimore Afro-American (1 June), p. 13.

Letter to the editor disparaging Lillian Johnson's critical capacity and imputing her disapproval of NS to her jealousy of W's success.

588. Calverton, V. F. "Land of Literary Plenty." The Saturday Review of Literature, 22 (11 May), 3-4, 16-17.

Discusses W as one of the best examples of proletarian literature, comparing him to Steinbeck. In both UTC and NS W underlines his social demands with the threat of violence.

589. _____. "The Negro and American Culture." The Saturday Review of Literature, 22 (21 September), 3-4, 17-18.

States that W "has written the best fiction of any Negro writer in the United States" (p. 18).

590. Cameron, May. "Prize-Winner Pens Novel: Richard Wright Tells a Fury Packed Story." New York Post (1 March), p. 19.

Favorable review of NS with a lengthy plot summary. Cameron praises the power and speed of W's narrative and the insight of Bigger's characterization ("With consummate psychological skill Mr. Wright analyzes the dim compulsion of this spiritually sick young man"), but she says little about the novel's social message. Reprinted: 1978.209.

591. Campbell, Ouida. "Bigger Is Reborn." The Carolina Magazine (October), pp. 21-23.
  The story of the W-Green collaboration on the stage version of NS is related by their secretary, who emphasizes their contrasting personalities. In the first draft of the play the characterization of Bigger is divided: "one half Mr. Green's Bigger--sensitive, misguided, puzzled about life in general; and the other half Wright's Bigger--full of hate and fear, cunning, but at the same time looking for an answer to the questions that rise in his mind."

592. Canby, Henry Seidel. "Native Son by Richard Wright." Book-of-the-Month Club News (February), pp. 2-3.
  Favorable review praising W's style, dialogue, and development of suspense. Canby emphasizes the psychological dimension of the novel more than the social, calling it a book "which only a Negro could have written." A plot summary is provided. Reprinted: 1970.5; 1978.209.

593. _____. "The Right Questions." The Saturday Review of Literature, 21 (23 March), 8.
  Laudatory article on W and Steinbeck. By raising the right questions, Steinbeck in The Grapes of Wrath and W in NS perform a valuable service. Their refusal to give pat, easy, Marxist answers raises them above the level of most proletarian fiction. W's book is even better than Steinbeck's, especially in its construction. NS reveals "a creative mind of unusual power, discipline, and grasp of large ideas," but the story unfolds in "an intensely human context."
  Partially reprinted: 1960.198; 1961.214; 1963.146.

594. [Carter, Elmer Anderson]. "Richard Wright." Opportunity, 18 (April), 99.
  Editorial praising W's success against heavy odds. Endowed with literary genius, W "belongs to the Negro but in a larger sense he belongs to America and to the world of art and literature."

595. Carter, Michael. "244,000 Native Sons." Look, 4 (21 May), 8-13.
  Amply illustrated article on living conditions in Harlem showing the social environment against which W protests in his "intelligent and profoundly moving" NS.

596. Casto, John W. "The Book Review." Rock Island, Moline, and Davenport Tri-Cities Labor Review (29 March), p. 10.
  Highly favorable review of NS praising W for eschewing propaganda yet showing the responsibility of society for Bigger's plight. Casto provides a very detailed summary of the plot and concludes with a plea for social action to ameliorate the conditions the novel reveals.

597. Castrence, Pura Santillán. "Book Review: Native Son by Richard Wright." Manila Daily Bulletin (19 September), p. 12.
  Favorable review quoting from Dorothy Canfield Fisher and praising W's "masterly, strong language" and his psychological insight into both blacks and whites. Castrence notes the theme of self-realization through violence.

598. Cayton, Horace R. "Negro Housing in Chicago." Social Action, 6 (15 April), 4-38.
  Quotes two passages from NS to illustrate points.

599. Chamberlin, Jo Hubbard. "The Forum Quiz." The Forum and Century, 103 (May), 250-251.
  The tenth question quotes the opening sentences of NS and gives four possible sources.

600. Chase, Bill. "All Ears." Unidentified article (16 November).
  Note about W's plans and his first publication in Abbott's Monthly, for which he was not paid.

601. Clark, Mary. "Book Barometer." Boston Evening Transcript (23 March), Part Five, p. 8.
  Lists NS in fifth place in sales in the fiction category in New England.

602. _____. "Book Barometer." Boston Evening Transcript (30 March), Part Five, p. 2.
  Lists NS in fourth place in sales in the fiction category in New England.

603. _____. "Book Barometer." Boston Evening Transcript (6 April), Part Five, p. 3.
  Lists NS in eighth place in sales in the fiction category in New England.

604. _____. "Book Barometer." Boston Evening Transcript (13 April), Part Five, p. 2.

Lists NS in fifth place in sales in the fiction category in New England.

605. _____. "Book Barometer." Boston Evening Transcript (20 April), Part Five, p. 1.

Lists NS in fifth place in sales in the fiction category in New England.

606. _____. "Book Barometer." Boston Evening Transcript (27 April), Part Five, p. 1.

Lists NS in fifth place in sales in the fiction category in New England.

607. Clubbs, Abram A. "Afro Readers Write About 'Native Son.'" The Baltimore Afro-American (29 June), p. 13.

Letter to the editor praising highly Lillian Johnson's review, though Clubbs admits that he has not read W's novel.

608. Cohn, David L. "The Negro Novel: Richard Wright." The Atlantic Monthly, 165 (May), 659-661.

Unfavorable review of NS. Cohn, a white Mississippian, calls the novel "a blinding and corrosive study in hate." Only gradualism will improve racial relations, Cohn believes, not W's demand for immediate social justice. Blacks should follow the Jewish example in learning to wait.
Reprinted: 1970.5; 1978.209.
Partially reprinted: 1971.72a.

609. C.[ooke], M.[arvel] J. "Dick Wright's 'Native Son' Praised Highly." New York Amsterdam News (2 March), p. 3.

Highly favorable review praising the novel's shocking power, but asserting that in addition to being a crime thriller, it "is a scientific, psychological study of the effects of poor housing, unemployment, discrimination and segregation in the formation of the character of Bigger Thomas." Cooke notes the satire in the depiction of white radicals and ends by comparing NS to The Grapes of Wrath.

609a. Cooper, Anna J. "Writer Flays 'Native Son'; Would Like Story on Victor Hugo Theme." Washington Tribune (17 August), p. 7.

Criticizes W's divisive propaganda at a time when national unity is needed. Cooper, whose racial identity is not clear, admits that she has not read NS.

610. Cornell, Robert. "Plea for More Liberal Library Board." The Birmingham Post (10 April), p. 6.

Letter to the editor protesting censorship but not mentioning NS by name.

611. Cosgrove, Gerald. "The Reading Lamp." The South Bend Tribune (10 March), Sec. Two, p. 6.

Includes comment on NS as a Book-of-the-Month Club choice, comparing it to The Grapes of Wrath in its frankness.

612. Cosulich, Bernice. "The Literary Lantern." The Tucson Arizona Daily Star (3 March), Sec. 2, p. 4.

Biographical article occasioned by the publication of NS. Quotes Canby on the novel and W on his early reading.

613. Couch, W. T. "Native Son: Pro and Con." The Atlantic Monthly, 165 (June), [7 of front matter].

Letter to the editor endorsing David L. Cohn's review because "his ideals are founded in a working knowledge of Negro-white relationships in this country" instead of "on a slushy sentimentality."

614. Cowley, Malcolm. "The Case of Bigger Thomas." The New Republic, 102 (18 March), 382-383.

Favorable review of NS comparing W to Steinbeck. The work is an improvement over UTC mainly because the author has better control of his racial anger. For Cowley the third part of the novel is the best. Bigger emerges as both a symbol and a human being.
Reprinted: 1967.24; 1970.5; 1978.209.

615. Crawford, Nelson Antrim. "The Editor Looks On: Negro Contribution." The Household Magazine, 40 (September), 2-3.

Notes that W was among those honored at the American Negro Exposition in Chicago.

616. D., G. I. "Black and White Problem." Minneapolis Star-Journal (14 April), p. 13.

Favorable review of NS praising it both as exciting narrative and as a penetrating study of the psychological dimension of the racial problem. Although W is a Communist, the novel is not excessively didactic.

617. Daiches, David. "The American Scene." Partisan Review, 7 (May-June), 244-247.

Review of NS and five other works of fiction. Daiches praises W's honesty, power, and significance, but objects to the novel's melodrama and excessive violence. "Mr. Wright is trying to prove a normal thesis by an abnormal case . . . The gap between the fable and the moral may weaken the

book as a novel, but the separate parts are well done."
Reprinted: 1978.209.

618. Dalton. "First Novel Wins Acclaim for Young Negro Writer." The Stanford Daily (10 April), p. 4.
    Favorable review of NS praising the novel's presentation of a social problem and ranking W with Steinbeck (who is more sentimental), Dos Passos, Farrell, and Caldwell. W understands black psychology, but parts of the novel are awkward, and except for Bigger, the characterization tends to be somewhat vague.

619. Daniels, Jonathan. "Jonathan Daniels Praises Wright's 'Native Son.'" Richmond Times-Dispatch (31 March), Magazine Sec., p. 13.
    Reprint of 1940.620.

620. _____. "Man Against the World." The Saturday Review of Literature, 21 (2 March), 5.
    Favorable review of NS with special praise for W's narrative skill. Admitting the particular problems imposed by racism,Daniels argues that Bigger's story is essentially that of any environmentally conditioned criminal. The first two books of the novel are superior to the last.
    Reprinted: 1940.619; 1970.5; 1978. 209.

621. _____. "A Native at Large." The Nation, 151 (10 August), 114.
    Using NS--both the novel and the play in progress--as a point of departure, Daniels discusses the problems of Southern poverty and emigration.

622. Daugherty, James E. "Powerful Novel of Negro Life." St. Louis Globe-Democrat (9 March), p. 1B.
    Mixed review of NS praising its literary quality and emphasizing the theme of social conditioning, but complaining of "special pleading on behalf of Communism and the Jewish question." W's technique is almost too facile--"the parts click into place almost too smoothly."

623. Davis, Almena. "Book Notes." Los Angeles California Eagle (21 March), p. 2-B.
    Without having read NS, Davis summarizes the plot, contrasts it to the work of other black writers, quotes from several reviews, sketches W's life, and notes that Paul Robeson plans to play Bigger in a stage version.

624. Davis, Benjamin J., Jr. "A New Negro Theatre Is Born." Sunday Worker (15 September), p. 7.
    Account of the benefit event for the Negro Playwrights Company at which W lectured on "How 'Bigger' Was Born." Received warmly by the audience, W related his novel to the tradition of Lenin and Gorky and to nascent American proletarian literature.

625. _____. "Richard Wright's 'Native Son' a Notable Achievement." Sunday Worker (14 April),Sec. 2, pp. 4, 6.
    Generally favorable review praising the novel for its literary merit and general social significance. But Davis has a number of objections: Bigger should not be made "a symbol of the whole Negro people"; Bigger's introspection "is sometimes baffling and mystical"; W omits progressive forces, black and white; the Communists presented in the novel are not typical.
    Reprinted: 1970.5; 1978.209.

626. _____. "Wright's 'Native Son,' Gorky and Dostoevsky." Sunday Worker (23 June), Sec. 2, pp. 4, 6.
    Considers W much closer to Gorky than to Dostoevsky and predicts even greater works than NS in W's future. Like Gorky, W rejects Dostoevskyan mysticism, choosing instead a brutal realism looking to communism as a solution to social problems.

627. Davis, Bennett. "Books of the Week in Review." Buffalo Courier-Express (3 March), Sec. 6, p. 2.
    Favorable review of NS with comparisons to Humphrey Cobb, Steinbeck, Dreiser, Dickens, and Dostoevsky. Davis attests to the extraordinary impact of the novel: it "is a book which takes you by the ears and gives you a good shaking, whirls you on your toes and slaps you dizzy against the wall."

628. Davis, Frank Marshall. "Book Review, Synopsis and Criticism. 'Native Son' Greatest Novel Yet by an American Negro." The Kansas City Call (8 March), National Edition, p. 22.
    Highly favorable review with a plot summary. Davis draws the parallel to the Nixon case, praises the social validity and literary skill of the novel, and predicts the controversy of its reception. Predicts that W will become the first black novelist to win a Pulitzer Prize.
    Reprinted: 1940.629, 630.

629. _____. "'Native Son' Greatest Novel Yet by American Negro." Nashville Defender (9 March).

Reprint of 1940.628.

630. _____. "'Native Son' Greatest Novel Yet by American Negro." Tampa Bulletin (9 March), p. 13.
Reprint of 1940.628.

631. Dean, Mary Scott. "Indictment." El Paso Herald-Post (16 March), p. 7.
Highly favorable review of NS praising W's incisive social protest, narrative skill, psychological insight, and superb characterization of Bigger. "If this book does not eat at the quick of the social conscience of every white reader, then we are indeed in a state of moral atrophy."

632. Derleth, August. "Book of the Week." Madison (Wis.) East Side News (7 November), p. 7.
Contains a favorable review of the enlarged edition of UTC, "a moving, dramatic performance, sometimes bitter, sometimes angry and fiery, but always tellingly written." W has no peers in presenting racial issues, and UTC is better than NS in some ways.

633. Douglas, James W., Jr. "Aeronautics." Washington Tribune (c. 30 March).
Criticizing blacks for failure to capitalize on opportunities in aviation, Douglas uses a scene from NS as an introduction.

634. Du Bois, W. E. B. "As the Crow Flies." New York Amsterdam News (9 March), pp. 1, 14.
Contains an account of a luncheon in Chicago with W, Langston Hughes, and Arna Bontemps. W represents racial hope for the future.

635. Dunphy, Margaret. "Great Books Are Found Rarely." The Cincinnati Post (23 April), Woman's City Club Edition, p. 38.
Discusses NS, The Grapes of Wrath, and How Green Was My Valley as novels raising grave social questions. Dunphy believes that W "seems to agree with the group of thinks [sic] who hold that superior cultural and economic groups inevitably degenerate if they come in close association with the under-privileged, exploited, and culturally backward groups upon which they are dependent." Dunphy also quotes without acknowledgement from Milton Rugoff's review of NS.

636. Eddy, Sherwood. "Some Notable Comment on Native Son," in Native Son. "Seventh Edition." New York: Harper, p. 368.
Brief but enthusiastic remarks comparing W to Dostoevsky and praising the novel's social message.

637. Edwards, Doris. "We Native Sons." Unidentified poem.
In praise of W and NS.

638. Eldridge, Paul. "Men, Like Rats Will Kill When They're Afraid." The Oklahoma City Daily Oklahoman (14 April), Sec. D, p. 5.
Favorable review of NS emphasizing the analogy between the rat and Bigger. Praises W's "insight into the mind of a certain kind of Negro, his distorted views of the dominant white race, his vague, objectless hostilities, his hopelessness." Although not stylistically comparable to Jean Toomer, W is "worth watching."

639. Ellison, Ralph. "Book Reviews." TAC, 2 (April), 8.
Review of NS stressing Bigger as symbolic of both oppressed blacks and the oppressed in general. His violence, a reaction to his oppressive environment, is not to be explained away as neurotic. Its implications for American society must be faced.

640. Essary, Helen. "Dear Washington: How Not to Fight a Cold: Mix 'Native Son' with Confucius." Washington Times Herald (April).
Favorable review of NS, a book that is "powerful medicine." The power of its theme of racism makes it better than The Grapes of Wrath.

641. F., A. M., "A Powerful Novel of Negro's Struggle in a White World." Milwaukee Journal (3 March), Part V, p. 3.
Review of NS noting its frankness and power, but focusing on its social implications. The reviewer is somewhat reluctant to accept W's environmental determinism.

642. F., L. R. "Native Son." Lubec (Maine) Herald (29 June).
Favorable review praising the novel's literary quality. Compares it to The Grapes of Wrath.

643. F., R. "War Influences Demand for Books." PM's Weekly (23 June), p. 41.
Mentions NS as a best-selling book in a depressed market.

644. Fadiman, Clifton. "A Black 'American Tragedy.'" The New Yorker, 16 (2 March), 52-53.
Favorable review of NS specifying several literary defects--redundancy, thin characterization of wealthy whites, excessive melodrama--but stating that W has "the two absolute

necessities of the first-rate novelist--passion and intelligence." Fadiman compares the novel to The Grapes of Wrath, to the fiction of Dostoevsky, and especially to An American Tragedy.
Reprinted: 1970.5; 1978.209.
Partially reprinted: 1940.646.

645. _____. "Books: A Certain Disarming Charm." The New Yorker, 16 (21 December), 85-86.
Fadiman still admires NS, but he is becoming more aware of its faults, which include "its length, the woodenness of the white characters, the garrulity of all the characters, the genteelism of the expository style."

646. _____. "Some Notable Comment on Native Son," in Native Son. "Seventh Edition." New York: Harper, pp. 361-362.
Partial reprint of 1940.644.

647. Fairall, Helen K. "An Engrossing, Terrible Story Is This Novel About a Negro by a Negro." Des Moines Sunday Register (3 March), p. 9.
Review of NS calling the first two books "high drama, swift in its pace, strong in suspense." But the third book is too propagandistic, for Bigger becomes "too clear a thinker" and the thesis of social responsibility is unconvincing. Fairall also objects to W's communism.

648. Farrell, James T. "Farrell Throws Brickbats at Saroyan, Fante, Wright, Maltz, di danto [sic], Weidman, and Brand--Merry Xmas." The Chicago Daily News (4 December), p. 39.
Farrell attacks W's Stalinism, especially in the "Fate" section of NS, a "stylistically and psychologically immature" book that is also defective in structure.

649. Fauset, Arthur Huff. "I Write as I See: A Negro Renaissance?" The Philadelphia Tribune (4 April), p. 4.
Contains a paragraph on W predicting an eventual Nobel Prize.

650. _____. "I Write as I See: More About 'Native Son.'" The Philadelphia Tribune (16 May), pp. 4-5.
Defends NS against Rev. Bagnall's critique in the preceding issue (9 May) of The Philadelphia Tribune. Fauset sharply attacks Bagnall for calling W a Communist, for complaining that he does not present the black middle class, and for pontificating that "Native Son is not a great novel."

651. Fisher, Dorothy Canfield. "Introduction," in Native Son. New York: Harper, pp. ix-xi.
NS is the first report in fiction of the consequences of racism in America, which leads black youth to neuroses and psychopathic problems that are common knowledge in research psychology. Black people have no chance to live up to the ideals of the nation. W, comparable in form and impact to Dostoevsky, explores "a human soul in hell because it is sick with a deadly spiritual sickness." Fisher also distinguishes between the acquiescent and rebellious black types that W creates. NS is realistic, concrete, and powerful as an indictment against our closed society.
Reprinted: 1940.652; 1970.5.

652. _____. "Introduction," in Native Son. New York: Grosset & Dunlap, pp. ix-xi.
Reprint of 1940.651.

653. Fletcher, Thomas Fortune. "The New Negro Comes of Age." Chicago Metropolitan Post (16 March), p. 7.
Highly laudatory review of NS comparing it favorably to the Harlem Renaissance novel. It is the best of all black novels and "one of the finest novels America has produced." After a plot summary noting the symbolic nature of the rat episode in "Fear," Fletcher calls NS "a savage indictment of the hypocrisy of so-called American civilization in its treatment of the Negro." But it "is not a moral tract; it is a work of art."

654. Floyd, Mrs. T. M. "The Book of the Week." The Alabama Baptist (11 April), p. 7.
Includes favorable comments on NS by a "young college professor" and by one Thelma Brown. Mrs. Floyd suggests that "all preachers will do well to read this book" and that women's clubs will review it.

655. Frederick, John T. "Of Men and Books." The Columbia Broadcasting System: Script No. 26 (2 April), 4 pp.
Mimeographed script from a series sponsored by CBS and Northwestern University. Frederick reviews NS and, at lesser length, three other novels. He considers W's narrative technique excellent and his theme of black resentment valid, but finds the characterization weaker, particularly with respect to the discrepancy between Bigger's instinctive actions and his extensive reflections on them. NS is "an important and valuable book," but not "a great novel."

656. Freeman, Melvin R. "Negro Author's Second Yarn Thoughtful and Thrilling." The Boston Herald (9 March), p. 9.
   Highly favorable review of NS pointing out its importance both as a social document and as a literary work. Freeman emphasizes the responsibility of white society for black hatred. He "could not find a single flaw in either the story or its presentation."

656a. Friede, Donald. "Of Books and Writers." The Hollywood Reporter (29 March), p. 4.
   Mentions NS as "the top book of the month." It "must be read, but unfortunately it cannot be put on the screen."

657. G., A. R. "O. Henry Memorial Award Prize Stories of 1940." Cincinnati Enquirer (23 November), p. 5.
   Lists W as a contributor.

658. G., E. "Readers Discuss 'Native Son.'" Daily Worker (26 April), p. 7.
   Letter to Benjamin Davis, Jr., congratulating him for his constructive review of NS. "I am prouder than ever of being a Communist--of being a member of a Party which is capable of producing people with ability both to do a 'Native Son' and to write so masterful a criticism."

659. G., H. "Readers Write Choices in Fiction." Daily Worker (29 April), p. 6.
   Letter to the editor suggesting the serialization of NS.

660. G., V. G. "In the Bookshops." The London Observer (12 May), p. 3.
   Mentions the popularity of NS in libraries.

661. Gannett, Lewis. "Books and Things." New York Herald Tribune (1 March), p. 17.
   Favorable review of NS, published on this date, providing biographical information on the author and summarizing the plot. "It is a super-shocker; it is also a deeply compassionate and understanding novel. As nearly as anything can be, it is the 'Grapes of Wrath' of 1940."
   Reprinted: 1940.662, 663; 1978.209.

662. _____. "Books and Things." The Washington Post (5 March), p. 13.
   Partial reprint of 1940.661.

663. _____. "Some Notable Comment on Native Son," in Native Son. "Seventh Edition." New York: Harper, pp. 366-368.
   Partial reprint of 1940.661.

664. Garside, E. B. "Father and Son. By

James T. Farrell; Uncle Tom's Children. By Richard Wright; A Man's Place. By Ramon Sender." Boston Evening Transcript (9 November), Part Five, p. 2.
   Favorable review of the enlarged edition, with emphasis on "Big Boy Leaves Home." W is "a genuine artist."

665. Gay, Eustace. "Facts and Fancies: Native Son." The Philadelphia Tribune (11 April), p. 4.
   Conceding that W's novel is well written, Gay fears that white readers, missing the point of environmental determinism and ignorant of black life, will take Bigger as typical. The outcome would harm race relations.

666. Geraghty, June R. "Club Activities." St. Louis Star-Times (14 March), p. 21.
   Announces a book review of NS to be presented at a woman's club in a St. Louis suburb.

667. Gilbert, Leonard B. "Bigger Thomas." The Chicago Defender (17 August), p. 16.
   Letter to the editor using Bigger Thomas metaphorically in commenting on intraracial prejudice.

668. Gillespie, M. J. "Afro Readers Write About 'Native Son.'" The Baltimore Afro-American (18 May), p. 13.
   Objects to Lillian Johnson's bourgeois attitudes. Bigger is a typical native son, Gillespie argues. He also praises W's style and characterization and justifies his use of sex in NS.
   Reprinted: 1940.669.

669. _____. "Afro Readers Write About 'Native Son.'" Washington Afro-American (18 May), p. 13.
   Reprint of 1940.668.

670. Gillis, Rev. James M., C. S. P. "Sursum-Corda . . . What's Right With the World: A Reviewer Rebukes the Reviewers." New World (17 May), p. 4.
   Rev. Gillis supports Burton Rascoe's point that in NS Bigger's slum environment does not justify murder, but he refutes Rascoe's belief that blacks do not suffer more than whites from social oppression and racial discrimination.

671. Gilroy, William E. "What Will Be Its Effect?" Advance, 132 (1 June), pp. 242, 274.
   Review of NS comparing it favorably to The Grapes of Wrath. Gilroy reviews criticism of the novel, summa-

rizes the plot, and speculates on its possible social effects. Examples of black achievement such as W's improve race relations, according to Gilroy, but this novel about a black criminal may damage them.

672. Glenn, Charles. "Hollywood Vine." People's Daily World (2 April), p. 5.
Suggests that NS be filmed, for it has "action, thrills, suspense, mystery, character development, conflict." But it will not be put on the screen because of racism and anti-Communism in Hollywood.

673. Gold, Michael. "Change the World." Daily Worker (15 April), p. 7.
Mentions NS as a "great novel."

674. _____. "Change the World: Dick Wright Gives America a Significant Picture in 'Native Son.'" Sunday Worker (31 March), Sec. 2, p. 7.
Favorable review recalling Gold's acquaintance with W at the Chicago John Reed Club and on the staff of the Daily Worker. Gold attributes to Communism the formative influence on W's development and defends from Canby's attack the novel's portrayal of white Communists. As a classic of proletarian literature, NS ranks with The Grapes of Wrath.

675. _____. "Change the World: Open Letters to a Fighting Dentist and to a Famous Author." Sunday Worker (29 September), Sec. 2, p. 5.
Rejects W's argument in "How 'Bigger' Was Born" that Bigger is representative of black people. Instead, he is a lumpen-proletarier, not suitable revolutionary material as are the oppressed but not degraded black masses.

676. _____. "Change the World: Some Reflections on Richard Wright's Novel, 'Native Son.'" Daily Worker (17 April), p. 7.
Defends the novel against those Communist readers who fear that bourgeois reviewers will misuse it. NS is a masterly study of a complex human situation, based on Communist truth, but it is not an agitational tract.

677. _____. "Change the World: Still More Reflections on Richard Wright's Novel, 'Native Son.'" Daily Worker (29 April), p. 7.
Responding to letters concerning NS, Gold praises the novel for stimulating discussion of the racial issue. Its value as a social document depends, however, on its artistic quality. W achieved an "aesthetic mastery

of form" in his intense focus on Bigger.

678. _____. "Change the World: The Great Tradition: Can the Literary Renegades Destroy It?" Daily Worker (15 November), p. 7.
Includes comments comparing NS to The Grapes of Wrath and stressing the debt of both to the Communist movement.
Reprinted: 1941.742.

679. _____. "Change the World: The Great Tradition: Can the Literary Renegades Destroy It?" Daily Worker (16 November), p. 7.
Relates Steinbeck and W to the tradition of proletarian literature. W "is himself the native son of the Communist movement, born and brought up in its bosom."
Reprinted: 1941.742.

680. _____. "Change the World: The Great Tradition: Can the Literary Renegades Destroy It?" Sunday Worker (17 November), Sec. 2, pp. 5-6.
Cites W and his poetry to show the break of the thirties from the mood of the Harlem Renaissance.
Reprinted: 1941.742.

681. _____. "Change the World: The Representation of the Negro People in American Literature." Sunday Worker (8 September), Sec. 2, p. 5.
Mentions W briefly.

682. Goldstein, Albert. "Literature and Less." The Times-Picayune and New Orleans States (3 March), Sec. 2, p. 9.
Contains an unfavorable review of NS. Goldstein concedes that W "is a writer with purpose and spirit and a sure sense of craftsmanship," but disagrees with his analysis of the racial situation.

683. _____. "Literature and Less." The Times-Picayune and New Orleans States (13 October), Sec. Two, p. 9.
Mentions NS as one of the "best-lenders" in twenty-four large public libraries.

684. Govan, Gilbert E. "Roaming Through the Realm of Books." Chattanooga Sunday Times (31 March), Magazine Sec., p. 5.
Mixed review of NS. Govan discounts some of the praise received by the novel, arguing that it is too topical. W is too close to Bigger for the novel to qualify as great literature. Max's arguments, too, are unconvincing, for race relations can be ameliorated only gradually through increased understanding. Still, "we can

admire the author's construction of his novel, the vividness of his writing, the sense of excitement he conveys."

685. _____. "Uncle Tom's Children." Chattanooga Sunday Times.
Views the collection of stories as a stepping stone for NS. W is a vivid, exciting, and powerful writer.

686. Gray, James. "A Disturbing View of Our Unsolved Race Problem." St. Paul Dispatch (8 March), p. 10.
Favorable review of NS stressing the disturbing, powerful impact of the novel on the white reader. Bigger is not presented as typical or pitiable, but his characterization has important social implications. "My literary experience . . . offers nothing so effective in its grim and frightening way as this picture of man against society, his teeth bared like an animal in desperate protest at its threat."

687. Griffin, Tom F. "'Filth' in Books." The Birmingham News (5 April), p. 16.
Letter to the editor admitting the brilliance of NS but defending the banning of the work from the Birmingham Public Library because of its "rape, murder, mutilation and filth of minute emotional reaction to sexual and other experiences of Bigger Thomas, Wright's principal moronic character."

688. Gunsky, Frederic R. "Uncle Tom's Children (new edition, enlarged). By Richard Wright." San Francisco Chronicle (8 December), This World Sec., p. 25.
Favorable notice identifying W's subject as "the brutal oppression of Negro Americans by white Americans" and praising the "psychological insight and sheer color and shock" which place the stories "among the first-rate achievements of American fiction."

689. H., B. K. "The Sideshow." The Providence Journal (1 March), p. 12.
Favorable review of NS noting its stark sincerity and the memorable characterization of Bigger. The reviewer considers the racial problem insoluble, but W forces readers to consider it.

690. Hall, Clara. "Library Censorship." The Birmingham News (17 March), p. 12.
Reprint of 1940.691.

691. _____. "Objects to Banning of Book from Library." The Birmingham Post (16 March), p. 4.

Letter to the editor protesting the failure of the fiction librarian of the Birmingham Public Library to recommend purchase of NS.
Reprinted: 1940.690.

692. Hansen, Harry. "The First Reader." The New Bedford Morning Mercury (5 March), p. 4.
Reprint of 1940.694.

693. _____. "The First Reader." The New Bedford Morning Mercury (16 March), p. 4.
Reprint of 1940.695.

694. _____. "The First Reader." New York World-Telegram (2 March), p. 17.
Favorable review of NS commenting on the widespread attention being given to the work, summarizing the plot, and providing brief biographical details about W. Hansen praises the book's power and social message, but complains than "in places Bigger seems to understand more than he should."
Reprinted: 1940.692, 703, 704; 1978. 209.

695. _____. "The First Reader." New York World-Telegram (14 March), p. 25.
Mentions attending a cocktail party given for W by Gene Saxton.
Reprinted: 1940.693.

696. _____. "The First Reader." New York World-Telegram (29 April), p. 15.
Reviews the critical controversy on NS, especially the issue of environmental determinism as discussed by Burton Rascoe and David L. Cohn. Hansen refutes Rascoe and Cohn, but then discusses some of the difficulties in W's dual role as writer and radical. If the problems of black people are not alleviated, Communist influence among them will grow.

697. _____. "The First Reader." New York World-Telegram (29 May), p. 13.
Includes discussion of the W-Cohn controversy, with quotations from W's rebuttal of Cohn.

698. _____. "The First Reader." New York World-Telegram (10 July), p. 23.
Claims that although many believe that the popularity of NS demonstrates the interest of the general reader in social themes, many readers see the book as a murder thriller and fail to see the social implications.

699. _____. "The First Reader." New York World-Telegram (9 September), p. 17.
Includes an account of W's lecture on "How 'Bigger' Was Born" at the Golden

Gate Ballroom. "I have never heard such an eloquent, as well as precise, analysis of a book by its author."

700. _____. "The First Reader." New York World-Telegram (2 October), p. 23.
Discussing political alignments of authors, Hansen notes that W is going to vote for Browder and Ford.

701. _____. "The First Reader." New York World-Telegram (15 November), p. 27.
Contains a review of O. Henry Memorial Award Prize Stories of 1940 with brief mention of "Almos' a Man."

702. _____. "The First Reader." New York World-Telegram (30 December), p. 15.
Reviewing the year's literary production, Hansen finds NS to be "the best novel of social significance," although he considers the writing in UTC to be better.

703. _____. "The First Reader." Norfolk Virginian-Pilot (8 March), p. 6.
Reprint of 1940.694.

704. _____. "The First Reader." The Pittsburgh Press (6 March), p. 33.
Reprint of 1940.694.

705. Hard, Ruth. "Books in Town: Some of God's Chillen Ain't Got Wings." The Brattleboro Daily Reformer (15 July), p. 4.
From a self-professed naive white liberal perspective, Hard reviews NS favorably, noting its skill in creating sympathy for an unattractive protagonist. The social message of the novel is emphasized.

706. Hardwicke, Hallie Read. "A Plea in Avoidance." Fort Worth Star-Telegram (3 March), Sec. 2, p. 5.
Favorable review of NS praising the power of its presentation of the theme of hate. W's social message is dubious, for whites will not yet tolerate social equality. Bigger's portrait may be a tacit admission of "an inherent savagery" in blacks. Biographical details and a plot summary are included.

707. Harkness, Samuel. "Some Notable Comment on Native Son," in Native Son. "Seventh Edition." New York: Harper, pp. 363-364.
The minister of the Winnetka Congregational Church, which has conducted a study of living conditions on the South Side of Chicago, confirms the accuracy of the novel's background. NS is important for revealing the black mind and for showing "that the 'Negro Problem' is not only Negro, but White."

708. Harper, Lucius C. "Dustin' off the News: We Dwell Amid Acres of Diamonds But Know It Not." The Chicago Defender (9 March), pp. 1-2.
Favorable review of NS. W knows his subject and his characters. The reference to acres of diamonds concerns black awareness of black culture. Mentions W's story "Superstition."

709. Harrison, William. "Book Review: The Five Best Books of 1940." Boston Chronicle (21 December), p. 18.
NS leads this list of books by black authors. W's novel, "very nearly the book of a generation," is especially valuable for its acute and imaginative social analysis.

710. Hart, Bret. "Hart Recommends 'Native Son,' Others." Providence Herald [?] (4 March?).
Calls NS the most important book of the year. It will promote racial tolerance.

711. Hart, Henry. "Books." Direction, 3 (April), 21.
Contains a favorable review of NS. Hart is impressed by W's technique and his psychological insight, but he thinks that the author "has distorted where he has not avoided the truths which explain why such things happen and how they can be erased from the earth."

712. Hayes, Frank L. "Murder Motive in Book Traced to Housing Evil." The Chicago Daily News (6 May), p. 11.
Reviews the controversy stirred by NS and emphasizes the generally overlooked theme of poor housing conditions.

713. Haywood, Clara Helen. "Native Son: Pro and Con." The Atlantic Monthly, 165 (June), [6 of the front matter].
Letter to the editor objecting sharply to David L. Cohn's review, especially to its racist overtones.

714. Helfling, Dorothy. "Book Reviews." Sterling (Kansas) Bulletin (23 May).
Mixed review of NS, a moving novel. Its horror and fascination are not for the fastidious, however.

715. Hermanson, Mrs. C. A. "Choice of Library Books." The Birmingham News (14 April), p. 10.
Letter to the editor applauding the editorial "Banning Books Indirectly," praising W, and denouncing library censorship.

716. Herndon, Angelo. "Books Read at Harlem Library Show People Seek a Way Out of Poverty." Sunday Worker (7 April), p. 5.
Notes that the eight copies of NS at the 135th Street Branch of the New York Public Library do not meet the demand.

717. _____. "Negroes Have No Stake in This War, Wright Says." Sunday Worker (11 February), p. 7.
In this interview, W supports the Nazi-Soviet pact and opposes aid to Finland. He also comments briefly on NS, saying "it is not a sentimental picture" but "accounts for human behavior and personality in terms of environmental factors." Herndon praises W's "intellectual tenacity," his lucid literary style," and his struggle against racism.

718. Hicks, Granville. "The Failure of Left Criticism." The New Republic, 103 (9 September), 345-347.
Mentions NS briefly.

719. Hochstein, Irma. "Wright Puts Foot Through Screens." The Madison (Wis.) Capital Times (19 May), p. 23.
Favorable review of NS. Hochstein sees in the novel the fulfillment of a desire expressed in The Living Torch by A. E. for a novelist who would portray unflinchingly the grim reality of urban squalor. "Terrible in its truth, its human sympathy, its understanding, irony, and sadness," NS should stimulate its readers to work to change the environment it portrays.

720. Holt, Arthur E. "The Wrath of the Native Son." The Christian Century, 57 (1 May), 570-572.
Discussion of the social and political problems raised by NS and The Grapes of Wrath, especially those concerning migration, housing restrictions, and religion. Holt's point of view is that of a Protestant and a democrat who rejects both fascism and communism.

721. Hood, Sam. "Full Knowledge of 'Bigger' Led Author to 'Native Son.'" Norfolk Journal and Guide (c. 5 August).
Interview following W's talk at the White Rock Baptist Church in Durham, North Carolina. If W had known only one Bigger, he could not have written his novel.

722. Horan, Kenneth. "Native Son by Richard Wright." The Evanston Review (14 March).
Favorable review, but Horan thinks

that the book should "be judged more by legislative than by literary standards," for it convinces the reader that something should "be done about helpless, desperate people." Bigger is bad, doomed by both heritage and environment.

723. Howry, Erle. "Tale of Young Writer's Life Affords Quiet, Refreshing Reading." The Memphis Commercial Appeal (16 June), Sec. IV, p. 10.
Review of James Gould Cozzens's Ask Me Tomorrow contrasting him with W, Faulkner, Hemingway, and other "dynamic" writers.

724. Hyman, Roslyn. "Author of 'Native Son' Speaks of Negroes' Place in America." The Abraham Lincoln High School (New York) Lincoln Log (11 October).
Interview with W including comments on Jim Crow and its consequences, the development of black literature, his work in progress on the labor conditions of black women, and the presentation of black people in books and films.

725. I., Bruno. "Readers Discuss 'Native Son.'" Daily Worker (26 April), p. 7.
Brief letter praising Michael Gold for his review of NS. "Long live your proletarian pen!"

726. Imes, William Lloyd. "Native Son, by Richard Wright." Social Progress, 30 (May), 21.
As a reviewer in a Christian magazine, Imes objects to the novel's politics and its "needless display of vulgarity and profanity," but he is deeply impressed by its message on racism and its literary artistry.

727. Ivy, James W. "'Whipped Before You Born.'" The Crisis, 47 (April), 122.
Extremely favorable review of NS comparing it to Greek tragedy and to the novels of Dostoevsky. Ivy emphasizes the novel's penetrating analysis of the psychological consequences of social injustice. The review concludes: "Native Son is undoubtedly the greatest novel written by an American Negro. In fact, it is one of the best American novels, and Mr. Wright is one of the great novelists of this generation."
Reprinted: 1970.5; 1978.209.

728. Jack, Peter Monro. "Some Notable Comment on Native Son," in Native Son. "Seventh Edition." New York: Harper, pp. 362-363.
Partial reprint of 1940.729.

729. _____. "A Tragic Novel of Negro

Life in America." The New York Times Book Review (3 March), pp. 2, 20.

Favorable review of NS comparing it to An American Tragedy with respect to the theme of environmental determinism. But the racial issue makes the case of Bigger Thomas more difficult than that of Clyde Griffiths. W transforms sociology and psychology into vivid characterization and dramatic action. Bigger is too articulate and W insists too much on his representativeness, but these are minor flaws in "an American author as distinctive as any of those now writing."
Reprinted: 1940.728; 1978.209.

730. Jackson, Joseph Henry. "The Bookman's Daily Notebook: Notes on the Margin." San Francisco Chronicle (1 August), p. 17.

Notes the collaboration of W and Green in Chapel Hill. Hints that a musical element will be used in the dramatization of NS.

731. _____ . "A Bookman's Notebook: A Powerful Story by a Great Negro Writer." San Francisco Chronicle (11 March), p. 15.

Favorable review of NS sketching W's life and stressing the credibility of the story despite its shocking violence. Jackson praises W's handling of the psychology of both blacks and whites conditioned by white racism. Naive radicals are also criticized. W offers no specific program of action to resolve the social problems the novel reveals, but the shock effect he produces should at least jolt readers into serious thought.

732. [James, C. L. R.] ("J. R. Johnson"). "Native Son and Revolution." The New International, 6 (May), 92-93.

Favorable review of NS stressing Bigger's self-realization through revolutionary struggle. "To scheme, to plan, to fight--this is to be free. In this bold stroke, the central theme of his book, W has distilled the very essence of what is in the Negro's future." James also praises Bigger's experiential sense of solidarity with white Communists. As a Trotskyist, James ends by warning W against the Stalinists. See 1940.737.

733. James, Mertice M. and Dorothy Brown, eds. "Wright, Richard. Native son." The Book Review Digest, 36 (April).

Excerpts or lists some early reviews.

734. Jeanes, Charlotte. "Native Son by Richard Wright." Unidentified clipping.

Review stressing the story's sensationalism, but admitting that W's message had to be conveyed.

735. Jenkins, Joseph H., Jr. "'Saucy Doubts and Fears.'" Phylon, 1 (Second Quarter), 195-197.

Highly favorable review emphasizing the responsibility of society for Bigger's personality and behavior. "Mr. Wright has such keen insight, such sound judgment, such a great spirit as enabled him to produce what is perhaps the best book on the race problem so far written." Jenkins also praises W's literary ability to "marshal incidents of compelling verisimilitude into a clear, swift, steady narrative and work those incidents into a tissue of symbols charged with extended meaning."
Reprinted: 1970.5

736. Jerome, J. D. "Native Son. By Richard Wright." The Journal of Negro History, 25 (April), 251-252.

Favorable review stressing W's primacy in presenting an effective portrait "of the underprivileged Negro constituting the main problem in the American social order." As an historian Jerome agrees with W that race prejudice has created the problem.
Reprinted: 1970.5.

737. Johnson, J. R. See C. L. R. James.

738. Johnson, Janice. "Native Son: A Tribute to Richard Wright's Book." The Crisis, 47 (November), 357.

Poem on the present alienation of black people from white society and their future integration into it.

739. Johnson, Lillian. "Light and Shadow." The Baltimore Afro-American (27 April), p. 13.

Responding to Pericles McDuffie's criticism of her review of NS, Johnson stresses her own concern about the unfavorable social consequences of the novel. It is a best seller "because it tells the people who buy it that they have been right in their opinions of the colored man all the time. It tells the white race that the native colored son is a mean, ornary [sic] baboon-appearing individual, who will rape and kill their daughters as soon as they are let into the house."

740. _____ . "'Native Son' Is Personal Triumph, But No Value to a Nation." The Baltimore Afro-American (13 April), p. 13.

Review praising W's literary technique--"his power of imagination, his

ability to write graphically, and his knack for beautiful phrasing." Nevertheless, NS could harm race relations, especially if it is made into a movie. Johnson considers Bigger atypical in his hatred, objects to gratuitous sex and racial epithets, and complains that the third part of the novel is weak. "We need writers like Mr. Wright. We don't need books like 'Native Son.'"
Reprinted: 1940.741.

741. ____. "'Native Son' Is Personal Triumph, But No Value to a Nation." Washington Afro-American (13 April), p. 16.
Reprint of 1940.740.

742. Johnson, Oakley. "Pioneers of Modern Literature." Sunday Worker (15 December), Sec. 2, p. 5.
Mentions W briefly as one of the "brilliant young writers" of contemporary American literature.

743. Jones, Gardner. "Afro Readers Write About 'Native Son.'" The Baltimore Afro-American (25 May), p. 13.
Rebuts several of Lillian Johnson's complaints about the novel: W's unprejudiced mind cannot be compared to that of Margaret Mitchell or D. W. Griffith; the title of the novel is ironic; Bigger's reactions to the murders of Mary and Bessie are valid; the novel's use of sex is both realistic and meaningful.

744. Jones, Howard Mumford. "Uneven Effect." Boston Evening Transcript (2 March), Part Five, p. 1.
Unfavorable review of NS. Jones concedes the excellence of the early scenes, but complains of dialogue unrelated to the narrative and weak characterization, except for Bigger, who "wavers between being a poor colored boy and a monster of amorality." The theme of the novel confuses "humanitarianism and determinism."
Reprinted: 1978.209.

745. Kapustka, Bruce. "We Review Native Son By Richard Wright." The Kapustkan, 1 (September), 23.
Hyperbolically favorable review comparing W to Samson, Jesus, and Lincoln as a champion of the underdog and to Stowe and Upton Sinclair as a writer. Kaputska calls the novel a "TNT Testament of Truth, a Cataclysmic, Catastrophic, Cosmic, yet Creative Cry for Justice, a Realistic yet Radiant Rhapsody for Rights and Recognition," as well as "one of the Mightiest Masterpieces of this Age or Any Age."

746. ____. "Wright is Might." The Kapustkan, 1 (August), 26.
Highly laudatory brief account of an interview with W at the American Negro Exposition in Chicago. Mentions influence of Hemingway on W.

747. Kaufman, Kenneth C. "A Word for the Pink Ear of a Totally Irresponsible Cherub: 1941 Books Need More Cheer." The Oklahoma City Daily Oklahoman (29 December), Sec. D, p. 3.
Contains a brief complaint about W's "hard and bitter 'Native Son.'"

748. K.[hinoy], A.[ndrew]. "An American Tragedy, Negro Version." The Philadelphia Inquirer (6 March), p. 15.
Favorable review of NS comparing it to Crime and Punishment and An American Tragedy, but arguing that its author could only have been black. The plot is melodramatic, but it serves as a vehicle of W's "passion for social justice." NS signals "the arrival of a major talent in American literature."

749. Kilgallen, Dorothy. "The Voice of Broadway." New Orleans States (7 March), p. 2.
Claims that NS "hits harder than Babe Ruth in his prime."

750. Kirnon, Hodge. "Guest Editorial: Why No Criticism of 'Native Son'?" New York Amsterdam News (11 May), p. 16.
Noting that The Birth of a Nation, Nigger Heaven, and other controversial films and books are strongly criticized by the black press, Kirnon wonders why NS has been exempt from criticism. Perhaps the critics are indifferent.

751. Kohan, Jackie. "Turning Pages." The Abraham Lincoln High School Lincoln Log (12 April).
Favorable review of NS drawing on the Associated Press news release. Notes the novel's power and social relevance. It is "a crime thriller and a psychological study" which "burns down to the roots of Negro discrimination."

752. Kubly, Herb. "Books and Authors: 'Native Son' Richard Wright." Pittsburgh Sun-Telegraph (7 March), p. 18.
Favorable review emphasizing the shocking, disturbing power of the novel. Melodramatic at times, the work excels in "fine writing," such as Max's courtroom speeches. Max and Jan offer some hope in an otherwise gloomy book.

753. L., W. "Another 'American Trag-

edy.'" The Raleigh News and Observer (24 March), Sec. M, p. 5.
Highly favorable review of NS calling it "at once one of the most powerful novels of all time, and a flaming tract on the race question." Summarizes the plot, noting the prophetic symbolism of the opening rat scene. The review concludes by comparing NS to Crime and Punishment, The Grapes of Wrath, and An American Tragedy.

754. Lacy, Sam. "Wright's Novel Comes True: Washington's 'Native Son' Blames Poverty for Life of Crime." Washington Afro-American (1 June), p. 5.
Compares Ralph Waldo Green, arrested for armed robbery, to Bigger Thomas as a victim of unemployment and poor housing. A photograph of W is included.

755. Lane, Layle. "'Land of the Noble Free.'" The New York Age (11 May), pp. 12, 10.
Unfavorable review of NS admitting the effectiveness of W's prose, especially his "marvelous descriptive power," but complaining of implausible details in the plot. Bigger's characterization will reinforce white racism. Langston Hughes's Not Without Laughter is both more honest and more effective as a novel.
Reprinted: 1940.756.

756. _____. "A Review of 'Native Son.'" The Call (25 May), p. 2.
Reprint of 1940.755. Lane is identified as a "member of the Socialist Party's Negro Committee."

757. Lawson, Victor. "Afro Readers Write About 'Native Son.'" The Baltimore Afro-American (11 May), p. 13.
Objects to Lillian Johnson's failure to analyze W's attack on private property and his depiction of Bigger's effort to find a place in a hostile world.
Reprinted: 1940.758.

758. _____. "Afro Readers Write About 'Native Son.'" Washington Afro-American (11 May), p. 18.
Reprint of 1940.757.

759. Lee, Annie. "Pen Feathers." Winston-Salem Twin City Sentinel (21 April), p. 12.
Objects to critics who have compared W to Dostoevsky, Steinbeck, and Dreiser. W is American and himself.

760. Lee, Charles. "New Names Stand Out on 1940's Books." Philadelphia Record (1 December), Christmas Books Supplement, pp. 1, 11.
Lists W as a contributor to a "brilliant" literary year. Includes a photograph of W.

761. Lehman, Milton. "O. Henry Memorial Award Prize Stories of 1940." New York Herald Tribune Books (17 November), p. 16.
Criticizes "Almos' a Man" as "indistinct" in effect, largely because W fails to make its hero "vital."

762. Lehmann, Rosamond. "New Novels." The Spectator, 164 (19 April), 574.
Review of NS and three other novels. Lehmann praises W highly, calling the novel a masterpiece and comparing it favorably to An American Tragedy. She stresses the social meaning of NS. Bigger is "a figure of sublime dimensions; one who inspires the kind of love and pity we bestow upon the tragic hero."

763. Leishman, Archibald. "Public Best Judge of Library Books." The Birmingham Post (20 March), p. 6.
Letter to the editor favoring a wide selection of books by the Birmingham Public Library but not mentioning NS by name.

764. Lemmon, C. E. "Book Chat." World Call, 22 (May), 23, 46.
Favorable review of NS in the organ of the Disciples of Christ. Compares its potential social effect to that of The Grapes of Wrath. Not for the squeamish, "it would be a good book for all judges, police officers, and prosecutors who have to do with the Negro to read."

765. Lemon, W. P. "The Book Parade." The Presbyterian Tribune, 56 (November), 29-30.
Contains a brief comparison of the effect of Anna Louise Strong's My Native Land to that of NS.

766. L.[ewis], R. J., [Jr.]. "Between the Book Covers." Albany Times-Union (3 March), p. 10A.
Highly favorable review of NS praising the power of W's social indictment and the literary quality of his writing. "He has proven with this vigorous novel that for psychological imagination, for power of dramatic construction, for the convincingness and reality of his characters, he has few equals."

767. _____. "Between the Book Covers." Albany Times-Union (15 March), p. 24.
Quarterly review of books read since 1 January 1940 giving first place in the novel category to NS.

768. _____. "Between the Book Covers."
Albany Times-Union (5 July), p. 8.
    Mentions NS as one of the year's best
    sellers.

769. L.[ewis], T.[heophilus]. "Books."
Interracial Review, 13 (April), 64-65.
    Rather favorable review of NS includ-
    ing a detailed plot summary. Lewis
    admires what he considers W's jour-
    nalistic technique. Less impressed
    with the novel's theme, he thinks
    that the novelist exaggerates the
    power of racism.
    Reprinted: 1970.5; 1978.209.

770. Lindauer, Sydney. "Book Chatter."
Red Bluff (Cal.) Daily News (23 March),
p. 4.
    Includes a brief comment on the ex-
    cessive frankness of NS.

771. Littell, Robert. "Outstanding Novels." The Yale Review, 29 (Summer), vi,
viii, x, xii.
    Contains a review of NS (p. x) admit-
    ting its power and "effective but
    bludgeoning realism," but complaining
    about the lack of suspense and the
    obtrusive social message of the third
    part.
    Reprinted: 1978.209.

772. Lobenthal, Martin. "Murder as Salvation." New York University Washington
Square Review (March-April).
    Mixed review of NS. W lets his char-
    acters explain themselves too much,
    but the novel does convey an essen-
    tial if disturbing truth.

773. Locke, Alain. "Dry Fields and Green
Pastures." Opportunity, 18 (January), 4-
10, 28.
    Includes a notice of "Bright and
    Morning Star." Locke considers it the
    best story in the O'Brien collection,
    but argues that the Marxist theme is
    too insistent and the influence of
    Erskine Caldwell is too apparent.

774. Lockhart, Jack. "Young Negro Writes
Novel Full of Force and Depth." The
Memphis Commercial Appeal (10 March),
Sec. IV, p. 10.
    Favorable review of NS, a "brutal,
    bloody, battering" book. After summa-
    rizing the plot, Lockhart opines that
    the South will comprehend the book
    better than other regions. W has
    revealed a "cancer in our civiliza-
    tion."

775. Logan, Rayford W. "Negro Youth and
the Influence of the Press, Radio, and
Cinema." The Journal of Negro Education,
9 (July), 425-434.
    Notes that a faithful film version of

NS would be an effective weapon
against racism.

776. Lovell, James F. "Afro Readers
Write About 'Native Son.'" The Baltimore
Afro-American (8 June), p. 13.
    Defends W from criticism by Lillian
    Johnson and other middle-class re-
    viewers. W's environmental determin-
    ism is sociologically valid; middle-
    class black readers should confront
    the truth NS presents.
    Reprinted: 1940.777.

777. _____. "Afro Readers Write About
'Native Son.'" Washington Afro-American
(8 June), p. 18.
    Reprint of 1940.776.

778. Lunin, D. "Gants Amerike kokht itst
mit a neger velkher iz iber nakht gevorn
barimt." Der New York Tog (9 March).
    Article noting W's sudden fame after
    the publication of NS and praising
    the novel's narrative tension, human-
    istic insight, and depiction of
    racial tragedy. The meaning of the
    title is explained and the relation
    of the novel to the Nixon case is
    noted. After commenting on the possi-
    bility of filming the novel, W's work
    in progress, and his writing habits,
    Lunin provides a rather full bio-
    graphical sketch.

779. Lyons, Leonard. "Broadway Medley."
Bridgeport Post (13 March), p. 3.
    Reports that W, who is finishing a
    new novel, will go to Mexico when it
    is completed.

780. M., A. S. "The Watchtower: Books."
The Augusta (Ga.) Chronicle (10 March),
p. 4.
    Review of NS emphasizing its impor-
    tance, especially for Southern read-
    ers, and its reception, as exempli-
    fied by quotations from several re-
    views.

781. Maltz, Albert. "The Meaning of
Native Son." Equality, 2 (June), 35.
    Highly favorable review of NS calling
    it "the most important novel of the
    year . . . a fine and noble book."
    Maltz's main emphasis is on environ-
    mental determinism, by which Bigger
    was victimized. But W himself must
    have enjoyed "favorable circumstan-
    ces, to a minimum degree at least,"
    in order to become a writer instead
    of a criminal.

782. Maraniss, Elliott. "Perspectives:
'Native Son.'" Unidentified clipping.
    Favorable review placing W in the
    context of the social fiction of
    Steinbeck, Di Donato, Faulkner, Dos

Passos, Caldwell, Farrell, and Millen Brand. Bigger is engaged in a "search for self-realization" that sounds great psychological depths. "It is a courageous theme, expertly and courageously handled."

783. Marriott, Charles. "New Novels." The Manchester Guardian (16 April), p. 3.
Column containing a review of NS denying the importance of the racial theme. A white chauffeur might have acted in the same way that Bigger did. The novel is merely a "good thriller."

784. Marshall, Margaret. "Black Native Son." The Nation, 150 (16 March), 367-368.
Favorable review of NS praising W's honesty and passion in treating his theme of racial prejudice. Marshall cites as defects inadequate characterization and a bookish style, but these fade before W's "talent and seriousness . . . maturity of thought and feeling."
Reprinted: 1960.198; 1961.214; 1963. 146; 1970.5; 1978.209.

785. Martin, Lawrence. "Native Son's 'Native Son' a Great Book." Chicago Sunday Times (14 April), Magazine Sec., p. 4.
Favorable review stressing W's narrative skill, comparable to that of Alexandre Dumas. Martin recalls meeting W in Chicago, reading "Big Boy Leaves Home," and recommending W for a Guggenheim Fellowship.

786. M.[axwell], A.[llen]. "Troubles of Negro in America Probed in Courageous Novel." The Dallas Morning News (3 March), Sec. III, p. 14.
Highly favorable review of NS placing W near "the very top rank of American novelists" and at the top among black writers. "His command of language, his understanding of what goes on in the Negro mind, his deep-probing insight into the problem of the Negro in America, place his work in a category by itself." A plot summary of the novel is included.

787. McC., R. "Native Son. Richard Wright." The Intercollegian, 57 (May), 179.
Favorable notice emphasizing the value of facing domestic racial problems during a period of international political concerns.

788. McDowell, Doris. "Black Joads." The Louisville Courier-Journal (10 March), Sunday Magazine Sec., p. [7].

Favorable review of NS comparing W to Steinbeck especially but also to Hugo, Zola, Tolstoy, Dostoevsky, and Gorky, all of whom "through the medium of the novel have cried out against injustice and oppression." McDowell predicts that NS will interest both the sociologist and the psychologist, and stir the conscience of all who read it.

789. McDuffie, Pericles. "Afro Readers Write About 'Native Son.'" The Baltimore Afro-American (27 April), p. 13.
Charges Lillian Johnson with stifling creativity in her unfavorable review of W's novel. McDuffie thinks that the social consequences of NS will be beneficial, awakening influential whites to racial injustice. He also defends W's fiction against specific charges brought by Johnson.

790. McGraw, Ed. "The Library and 'Native Son.'" The Birmingham News (31 March), p. 12.
Letter to the editor protesting the banning of NS from the Birmingham Public Library.

791. McHenry, Beth. "Books in the Deep South." Sunday Worker (9 June), p. 7.
Notes the popularity of NS at a communist bookstore in Birmingham, Alabama.

792. McKelway, St. Clair. "Gossip Writer." The New Yorker, 16 (13 July), 21-26.
Reports that W's literary agent has dismissed Walter Winchell's claim that W is seeing Ethel Waters.

793. McManis, John. "Negro Bad Man Delineated in an Intense Social Novel." The Detroit News (24 March), Home and Society Sec., p. 14.
Favorable review of NS with special praise for W's blend of social protest with literary values. "Only a few times in contemporary fiction has this great depth of feeling, scope of action and clarity of interpretation been equaled." The novel has universal significance.

794. McS.[orley], J.[oseph]. "Native Son. By Richard Wright." The Catholic World, 151 (May), 243-244.
Somewhat unfavorable review. McSorley agrees with W's thesis that white racism is responsible for Bigger's personality and situation, but fears that his portrait of this "bestial, treacherous, utterly unlovable" black man will only stimulate more white repression. McSorley also thinks NS too wordy.

Reprinted: 1970.5; 1978.209.

795. Meller, Sidney, "Race Plight Is Theme of Novel." Oakland Tribune (7 April), p. 4-B.
Favorable review of NS noting the tripartite structure and relating it to Bigger's psychology. Max's plea to the judge is too long, the characterization of the reporters is stereotyped, and at times Bigger's thinking is the author's, but otherwise W's craft is impressive.

796. Meyer, Lewis. "Urgent Sociological Thesis Presented in Strong Novel." Tulsa Sunday World (21 April), Sec. Five, p. 5.
Mixed review of NS. Conceding that it is a good book, Meyer argues that it is not a great one because of an excessive use of horror and faulty integration of the social theme and literary craft. He compares W unfavorably to Dostoevsky and, especially, to Steinbeck.

797. Mifflin, B. "'Uncle Tom's Children,' by Richard Wright." Austin Tribune (c. 21 November).
Favorable review of the revised, enlarged edition of UTC noting "The Ethics of Living Jim Crow" and stating that the stories "are told with a poignant supplication for understanding and charity."

798. Miller, Carrie G. "Afro Readers Write About 'Native Son.'" The Baltimore Afro-American (15 June), p. 13.
Miller offers a strong defense of the novel and a point-by-point rebuttal of Lillian Johnson's review. NS "is wonderful because it's real; beautiful because it's ugly, and overwhelming because it's true. . . . More power to the book of the century." Reprinted: 1940.799.

799. _____. "Afro Readers Write About 'Native Son.'" Washington Afro-American (15 June), p. 18.
Reprint of 1940.798.

800. Miller, Ruby King and Cistelle Allen. "Native Son Is Evaluated by Two Native Daughters." Knoxville News-Sentinel (14 April).
W's novel is a challenge to the democratic principles Americans profess. It is realistic, but a fuller treatment of Bigger's background is needed.

801. Morse, Edrie Ann. "Book Review." Altoona Tribune (5 April), p. 14.
Favorable review of NS along with some biographical information. The novel, the best written by a black American, "is a fully realized story of unfortunates, realistic, and quite as human as it is Negro." Bigger is portrayed unsentimentally.

802. Moulin, Charles. "De la littérature américaine." Tribune des Nations (16 September).
Mentions W in a list of prominent American writers.

803. Muir, Edwin. "New Novels." The Listener, 23 (18 April), 806.
Favorable review of NS praising W's handling of social forces issuing in Bigger's violence. Here his "political theories and his imagination work admirably together." But in not permitting Bigger to repent, W lets his theories distort his sense of life. Still, he evokes horror superbly, and "at his best Mr. Wright is better than either Mr. Dreiser or Mr. Steinbeck," though inferior to Dostoevsky.

804. Mulder, Arnold. "Library Adventures." The Chicago Daily News (c. 1 May).
Although NS is brutal, violent, and obscene, its power is remarkable, especially in the characterization of Bigger.

805. _____. "'Native Son' Strong Book." Green Bay Press-Gazette (30 March), p. 17.
Highly favorable review emphasizing the novel's immense emotional power. Brutal, obscene, profoundly disturbing, it is nevertheless "bathed . . . without sentimentality, in a pity that can come only from largeness of soul in the author." NS conveys a social message, but it also induces "that catharsis of terror and pity" characteristic of great literature.

806. Mullaney, Bernard J. "Approving Mr. Rascoe." The American Mercury, 50 (July), 377.
Letter to the editor endorsing Burton Rascoe's attack on NS and criticizing other "conspicuous faults": the newspaper references, Bigger's lack of white friends except Communists, Bigger's abandonment by his own race.

807. Murphy, Beatrice M. "The Book Worm." The Baltimore Afro-American (30 March), p. 8.
Reprint of 1940.810.

808. _____. "The Book Worm." The Baltimore Afro-American (2 November), p. 15.
Reprint of 1940.812.

809. _____. "The Book Worm." The Balti-

more Afro-American (14 December), p. 9.
Mentions NS as one of the most significant books of the year.

810. ____. "The Book Worm." Washington Afro-American (9 March), p. 7.
Urges black readers to read W, "the Erskine Caldwell or John Steinbeck of his race." Murphy mentions the painful experiences of his life as an explanation of the bitterness of his writing.
Reprinted: 1940.807.

811. ____. "The Book Worm." Washington Afro-American (29 June), p. 10.
Contains a brief, favorable opinion of NS.

812. ____. "The Book Worm." Washington Afro-American (26 October), p. 20.
Praises W's genius but contests his claim in How "Bigger" Was Born that Bigger is representative of the race. W is "the most talented and promising writer in the race today," but not its "prophet and interpreter."
Reprinted: 1940.808.

813. ____. "The Book Worm." Washington Afro-American (16 November), p. 20.
Contains a favorable review of the enlarged edition of UTC. Murphy gives special praise to "The Ethics of Living Jim Crow" and "Bright and Morning Star."

814. Myers, J. S. "Book Reviews and News." The Middletown (Ohio) Sunday News Journal (31 March), Second Sec., p. 4.
Contains a favorable review of NS praising the characterization of Bigger, the handling of the efforts of Jan and Mary to fraternize with Bigger, and the narrative pace. A plot summary is provided.

815. Needham, Wilbur. "Negro Author Pens Story of Racial Relationships." Los Angeles Times (10 March), Part III, p. 7.
Mixed review of NS admitting the novel's gripping power but criticizing W's characterization of Bigger, who "represents the sort of Negro who has absorbed all white vices and retained none of the Negro virtues." The work may harm rather than help race relations.

816. Newton, Herbert. "Readers Discuss 'Native Son.'" Daily Worker (26 April), p. 7.
Brief letter congratulating Benjamin Davis, Jr., for his review of NS.

817. Nicholas, Louis. "The Book Shelf." Philadelphia Record (3 March), Metropolitan Sec., p. 15.
Highly favorable review of NS calling it "one of the finest novels by anyone regardless of color or creed." Nicholas praises both theme and craftsmanship, including the third book. Indebted to Crime and Punishment and An American Tragedy, NS is nevertheless an original work about black life, vastly superior to Nigger Heaven. The review concludes with a sketch of W's life emphasizing parallels with Bigger Thomas.

818. Norris, Hoke. "'Native Son' to Become a Drama." The Washington Sunday Star (4 August), Sec. F, p. 1.
Account of the W-Green collaboration stressing the role of Green.

819. North, Sterling. "Book of the Week." The Chicago Daily News (28 February), p. 15.
Highly favorable review of NS comparing it to Crime and Punishment and The Grapes of Wrath. Its extraordinary power and perception will cause it to be widely read and controversial, North predicts. He demurs at the notion that Bigger is completely innocent and society completely guilty, but he urges the improvement of living conditions for black people.
Partially reprinted: 1940.820.

820. ____. "Some Notable Comment on Native Son," in Native Son "Seventh Edition." New York: Harper, pp. 364-365.
Partial reprint of 1940.819.

821. Oak, Eleanor Hill. "Native Son--An Appraisal." Wilberforce University Quarterly, 1 (July), 14-15.
Reprint of 1940.822.

822. ____. "Now I Think--Richard Wright's Native Son." The Philadelphia Tribune (16 May), p. 4.
Favorable review finding Bigger "alarming, convincing, and challenging." W uses symbolic realism, Bigger being a "symbol of the suppressed human impulses of the Negro masses under their oppressive sense of being excluded from the rights and privileges of other Americans."
Reprinted: 1940.821.

823. Oliver, María Rosa. "Dos novelas norteamericanas." Buenos Aires La Nación (3 November), Sec. 2, p. 2.
Essay-review of NS and Erskine Caldwell's Trouble in July. W idealizes his white characters; Caldwell idealizes his black characters. Both represent the American struggle against racism and social injustice, though Caldwell is more artistic. Oliver

sketches W's life and analyzes Bigger in psychological and social terms, comparing him to Kafka's Gregor Samsa and Emily Bronte's Heathcliff.

824. O'N., H. "Native Son, by Richard Wright." The Albany Knickerbocker News (8 March), p. A-17.
Favorable review stressing the novel's power and lack of moralizing. W excels at developing tension and narrative momentum. NS is "genuine, moving and unforgettable."

825. P., B. "History of Labor Movement His Choice for Next Serial in 'Daily.'" Daily Worker (3 May), p. 6.
Letter to the editor suggesting also NS for serialization.

826. P., J. "News of the Theater." New York Herald Tribune (3 September), p. 16.
Announces that W will speak on "How 'Bigger' Was Born" at a benefit for the Negro Playwrights Company.

827. P., M. "Life Ruled by Hate and Fear." Worcester Sunday Telegram (3 March).
Review of NS arguing for an autobiographical element in the characterization of Bigger. W's characterization and narration are excellent, but he utilizes too much propaganda.

828. Parker, Adele. "Books." Washington New Dealer (16 May).
Favorable review of NS stressing the universality of its theme of class rather than caste prejudice. Its examination of thwarted youth should provide a warning to society.

829. Parry, Florence Fisher. "I Dare Say." The Pittsburgh Press (6 March), p. 2.
Claims that the cover blurb "spoiled" NS.

830. Patterson, Alicia. "The Book of the Week." New York Sunday News (3 March), p. C24.
Favorable review of NS quoting extensively from Dorothy Canfield Fisher's introduction and summarizing the plot. Patterson comments on Bigger as a social victim who has been so brutalized as to become "no more responsible for his actions than a trapped and tortured animal."
Reprinted: 1940.832.

831. ____. "Book Teams of 1940." New York Sunday News (15 December), p. 90.
Warns that NS is "not for the tender minded."

832. ____. "Books: Smash Hit." Washington Times-Herald (3 March), p. C-13.
Reprint of 1940.830.

833. Peters, Richard. "Finds 'Native Son' Strong Medicine, Highly Significant." Cleveland Press (5 March), p. 13.
Favorable review comparing NS to The Grapes of Wrath for power and social importance. The story is sensational, lurid, and melodramatic, but these qualities are subordinate to the central theme: "Bigger's fight against a society he can't understand."

834. Peterson, Ed. "'Native Son' Good But--." The Baltimore Afro-American (22 June), p. 4.
Letter to the editor conceding W's ability to tell a story but charging NS with failure "to create warm sympathy for its characters." Peterson would prefer heroic tales of success against odds.
Reprinted: 1940.835.

835. ____. "'Native Son' Good But--." Washington Afro-American (22 June), p. 4.
Reprint of 1940.834.

836. Pettey, Tom. "What Hollywood Is Reading Now." PM's Weekly (8 September), p. 41.
Rita Hayworth is reading NS.

837. Pihodna, Joseph. "The Playbill: George Abbott Lines Up Four Productions." New York Herald Tribune (29 September), Sec. VI, p. 1.
Mentions that John Houseman will begin work on NS with W and Paul Green.

838. Pike, Alberta. "'Native Son' Novel by Negro Showing How Chicago Black Becomes Murderer." Denver Rocky Mountain News (10 March), Second Sec., p. 8.
Favorable review including biographical information and comparing NS with The Grapes of Wrath and Crime and Punishment. "Wright's tools are galloping vivid narrative, staccato dialogue, brilliant satire and something to say. He has used them well, to produce a powerful and disturbing novel."

839. Pinckard, H. R. "A Powerful Novel on Race Problems." The Huntington (W. Va.) Herald Advertiser (31 March), Sec. 4, p. 2.
Mixed review of NS insisting on the powerful social impact of the novel but criticizing its verboseness, brutality, and "extremely tenuous" characterization. Pinckard refutes the

comparison of NS to An American Tragedy. Contains a detailed plot summary through Mary's death.

840. Pinkowski, Edward. "Book Review." Hazleton News [?] (16 August).
Review of Albert Maltz's The Underground Stream in comparison to NS and The Grapes of Wrath. NS is "an absorbing story," but the plot has implausible elements and it fails in its social purpose.

841. Pío, Claudio. "Native Son." Caracas Venezuelan Herald.
Favorable review emphasizing the social message of the novel. A story of human shame and disgrace, it presents undeniable facts in its drama of a black man trapped by American society.

842. Poore, Charles. "Books of the Times." The New York Times (1 March), p. 19.
Favorable review of NS noting prepublication praise of the novel. Bigger is too articulate, but otherwise W's literary technique is excellent: his "method is generally Dreiserian; but he has written his American tragedy in a notably firm prose. He knows how to tell a story. He knows how to develop a character. . . Reflection blends into action. Accents and intonations are caught. Ideas are dramatized with concrete and inescapable images. And dialogue goes crackling down the page." Poore also compares W to Dickens and Steinbeck.
Reprinted: 1970.5; 1978.209.

843. _____. "Books of the Times." The New York Times (2 March), p. 11.
Review of Conrad Richter's The Trees with a brief comparison to NS.

844. _____. "Books of the Times." The New York Times (25 October), p. 19.
Contains a brief notice of the enlarged edition of UTC, "a book of searing and unforgettable stories."

845. Porteous, Clark. "What Is This Book by an Ex-Memphis Negro That Has Become Best Seller? A Press-Scimitar Reporter Explains." Memphis Press-Scimitar (19 March), p. 5.
Review of NS with favorable quotations from other reviews and a full plot summary. Porteous takes satisfaction in the novel's revelation of racism in the North and W's satiric treatment of Mary and Jan. The work is eloquent but brutal.

846. Postgate, Raymond. "New Thrillers."

Time and Tide, 21 (25 May), 562.
Contains a favorable notice of NS calling it "a long, important and extremely moving novel."

847. Powell, Adam, Jr. "Soap Box." New York Amsterdam News (16 March), p. 13.
Favorable review of NS emphasizing the work's realism and social message. W speaks fearlessly and tells the truth. Powell expresses satisfaction that Red baiters have not attacked W.

848. Preece, Harold. "Chicago's Exposition--A Monument to the Struggles and Progress of the Negro People." Sunday Worker (14 July), Sec. 2, p. 2.
Photograph with caption of W, Horace Cayton, Arna Bontemps, Claude Barnett, Langston Hughes, and others.

849. Provine, June. "Front Views and Profiles." Unidentified clipping.
Notes that collectors are buying first editions of NS.

850. Provost, Clarence. "Bouquet Dep't." The Saturday Review of Literature, 22 (6 July), 9.
Letter to the editor praising the magazine's attention to black culture and mentioning briefly NS.

851. Quercus, P. E. G. "Trade Winds." The Saturday Review of Literature, 22 (29 June), 24.
Points out a mistake in an English notice of NS by Raymond Postgate.

852. Quillen, Robert. "Any Social Problem Is Half Solved When People Deserve One Another's Respect." Unidentified clipping.
Rebuts W's notion expressed in NS that blacks hate whites. In the South, good feeling prevails between the races because subordination is a way of life. The year is conjectural.

852a. [Quinn, Kerker]. "Accent."
Flyer mentioning a forthcoming contribution by W.

853. R., B. "Wrath in Black and White." The Kansas City Star (2 March), p. 14.
Highly favorable review of NS calling it "far and away the finest novel ever written by an American Negro, and . . . also the finest novel ever written about an American Negro." It is comparable to The Grapes of Wrath in revealing to the majority the oppression suffered by a minority. Conceding that the third part of the novel is somewhat weak, the reviewer praises the power, suspense, and style of the work.

854. R., E. J. "Native Son. By Richard
Wright." Christian Advocate (9 August),
p. 1010.
Somewhat unfavorable review. The work
is "one of the season's most powerful
novels," but the picture W presents
is distorted. After quoting David L.
Cohn's article, the reviewer concludes: "Wright's picture of the
Negro is too black."

855. R., E. S. "Bookly Chatter." Jacksonville Florida Times-Union (21 July),
p. 14.
Includes comments on NS and Bigger as
a type. W's literary gifts are recognized, but his theme is questioned.

856. Rascoe, Burton. "Do Critics Help?"
The American Mercury, 50 (August), 502-
503.
Responds to W's "Rascoe-Baiting,"
accusing W as a Communist of inciting
racial hatred.

857. _____. "The Library: Neglected
Books." The American Mercury, 50
(August), 495-498.
Contains a review of O Canaan! comparing it favorably to the "febrile
hate . . . sensational melodramatic
devices . . . communist propaganda"
of NS.

858. _____. "Negro Novel and White Reviewers." The American Mercury, 50
(May), 113-116.
Extremely unfavorable review of NS
comparing it to pulp fiction. "Sanely
considered, it is impossible for me
to conceive of a novel's being worse,
in the most important respects, than
Native Son." The social message is
both obtrusive and erroneous, and the
characterization is faulty. Furthermore W's own success disproves his
thesis. W replied to this review in
"Rascoe-Baiting."
Reprinted: 1970.5; 1978.209.

859. Rhodes, Arthur. "New Books in Review: Native Son: Negro Pursued by
Society and Dread." Brooklyn Eagle (4
March), p. 20.
Favorable review comparing Bigger to
his author and providing biographical
details about W's youth. Rhodes notes
the symbolic quality both of the
opening episode and of Bigger's entire character and situation. He
praises W's narrative skill, characterization, and dialogue. His only
complaints concern "an occasional
lack of reserve" and the implausibility of some of Bigger's more advanced reflections.

860. _____. "Realism in Fiction Retains

Lofty Peak." Brooklyn Eagle (28 March),
p. 24.
Relates the intense interest in NS to
its "social awareness . . . [and]
preoccupation with violence." Comparing W to Steinbeck and Hemingway,
Rhodes considers NS to epitomize an
important trend in American fiction.

861. Rhodes, E. Washington. "Under the
Microscope." The Philadelphia Tribune (2
May), p. 4.
Contains disparaging remarks about
NS. According to Rhodes, "the only
type of book dealing with Negro life
must be filled with slime and filth
or it will not be published." His
comments on NS are based on hearsay,
not on his reading the novel.

862. Richardson, Irving. "Afro Readers
Write About 'Native Son.'" The Baltimore
Afro-American (22 June), p. 13.
Richardson believes that W was not
concerned with either helping or
harming the race. "He merely wrote a
story that he wanted to sell."

863. Riddell, Hugh J. "New Negro Playwrights Group Formed in Harlem." Daily
Worker (27 July), p. 7.
Announces W's lecture on "How 'Bigger' Was Born" and lists W as an
associate member of the Negro Playwrights Company. Includes a photograph of W.

864. Rivera, A. M., Jr. "'Native Son' to
Be Drama." The Baltimore Afro-American
(3 August), p. 14.
Essay-interview with W in Chapel
Hill, where he was working with Paul
Green on the play. W comments on the
fidelity of the book to the play, on
the school of writers emphasizing
environmental determinism to which he
belongs, and on his work in progress.

865. Roberts, Mary-Carter. "Native Son.
By Richard Wright." The Washington Sunday Star (3 March), p. F-6.
Favorable review endorsing the realistic characterization. Unlike black
characters in UTC, Bigger is not vir-
tuous or saintly. But W does not
convince Roberts that Bigger's criminality is the result of environmental
determinism. Nevertheless, she
praises the gripping suspense and
horrible fascination of the narrative. A plot summary is included.
Reprinted: 1978.209.

866. Robinson, Ted. "Native Son. By
Richard Wright." Cleveland Plain Dealer
(10 March), All Feature Sec., p. 3.
Mixed review calling the novel
"absorbingly written" and "a fine

achievement" but noting "many crudities." Robinson finds significant the satire on negrophiles, especially the Communist variety.

867. Rodman, Selden. "The Meaning of a Murder." Common Sense, 9 (April), 26-27.
Favorable review of NS finding it both "the most penetrating psychological study and the most terrible social protest the Negro problem has yet evoked." Bigger's understanding of his fate transcends that of Boris Max, a fact that attests to W's literary genius.

868. Rogof, Halel. "A starker roman fun dem neger-kvartal in Shikago." New York Forverts (17 March), Sec. 2.
Favorable review of NS. Not as good as Dreiser, W is nevertheless a powerful writer. The characterization of the brutalized Bigger may not convince whites to eliminate racial injustice, however, for he is consumed by hatred and fear. Rogof includes a detailed plot summary.

869. Romanova, E. "Amerikanskaia pressa o novom romane Richarda Raita." Internatsional'naia literatura, Nos. 7-8 (July-August), pp. 314-315.
Reports the American response to the novel NS in three categories: the black press, the bourgeois press, and the left press. Discusses and quotes from The Chicago Defender, The Crisis, and Frank Marshall Davis in the Associated Negro Press; from The New York Times, The Washington Star, Texas (Houston?) Chronicle, San Francisco Chronicle, and the Worcester Telegram; and from Michael Gold, Ben Davis, and Samuel Sillen.

870. Rosenblum, William F. "Some Notable Comment on Native Son," in Native Son. "Seventh Edition." New York: Harper, p. 368.
The Rabbi of Temple Israel, New York, expresses satisfaction with the success of NS "because it evidences the fact that here in our democracy we do not study a man's blood cells to evaluate genius but merely his creative ability."

871. Rouzeau, Edgar T. "Star Dust: Harlem Has Its Theatrical Epidemic." Norfolk Journal and Guide (14 September), p. 16.
Discusses the Negro Playwrights Company and lists W as an associate member. Includes a photograph of W.

872. Rowe, Billy. "Moe Gale Planning All-Colored Radio Show: Band Booker-Manager Confers with Langston Hughes About Big Unit." The Pittsburgh Courier (21 September), p. 20.
Gale also conferred with W about "writing a full length charter radio revue for an all-colored cast."

873. Rugoff, Milton. "A Feverish Dramatic Intensity." New York Herald Tribune Books (3 March), p. 5.
Favorable review of NS stressing the narrative excitement and the element of dignity beneath Bigger's confused and violent behavior. The book's "revelatory intellectual experience" consists in W's emphasis on environmental determinism in showing in "one individual's pathology . . . the whole tragedy of the Negro spirit in a white world."
Reprinted: 1970.5; 1978.209.

874. Russel[1], Cara Green. "Earlier Work of Richard Wright Now Reprinted." The Columbia (S. C.) State (27 October), p. 7-D.
Favorable review of the enlarged edition of UTC concentrating on "The Ethics of Living Jim Crow." W is a gifted spokesman for his people. Through his work white readers can understand the tragic black experience.
Reprinted: 1940.875, 876, 877.

875. _____. "The Literary Lantern." The Charlotte Observer (27 October), Sec. 3, p. 5.
Reprint of 1940.874.

876. _____. "The Literary Lantern." Greensboro (N. C.) Daily News (27 October), p. D-5.
Reprint of 1940.874.

877. _____. "The Literary Lantern: Richard Wright, Negro Author, Dramatizes Plight of Race." Durham Herald-Sun (27 October), Sec. 2, p. 2.
Reprint of 1940.874.

878. S., N. "Readers' Forum." New Masses, 37 (17 December), 21.
Letter to the editor from an eighteen-year-old citing NS as one of the books having a profound effect on him.

879. Schuyler, George S. "Looks at Books." The Pittsburgh Courier (30 March), p. 7.
Somewhat favorable review of NS. Schuyler praises W's exciting narrative and his racial protest, which is somewhat exaggerated, however. As a psychological study, the work is weaker. It is not as great a novel as those of Dreiser, Malraux, and Dostoevsky, but it is "a good one" and

"a milestone in American literature."

880. _____. "Looks at Books." The Pittsburgh Courier (28 December), p. 11.
    Contains a review of Len Zinberg's
    novel Walk Hard--Talk Loud, which
    Schuyler compares very favorably to
    NS. W's novel fails to arouse sympa-
    thy in the reader and depicts carica-
    tures rather than realistic charac-
    ters. Also contains an unfavorable
    review of How "Bigger" Was Born cal-
    ling W "very confused and bewil-
    dered."

881. _____. "Views and Reviews." The
Pittsburgh Courier (17 August), p. 6.
    In response to queries from white
    friends about NS, Schuyler argues
    that it will not help to ameliorate
    the racial situation because Bigger
    is an unsympathetic character. The
    novel also has structural defects. W
    lacks "the artistry of Arna Bontemps
    or Jessie Fauset."

882. Seaver, Edwin. "Books." Direction,
3 (December), 18-19.
    Contains a highly favorable review of
    How "Bigger" Was Born and a brief
    notice of the enlarged edition of
    UTC. Seaver praises W's recognition
    of Bigger as a universal type as well
    as an individual black. Therein is
    the revolutionary dimension of NS.
    "Wright is a master and . . . the
    contribution he has it in him to make
    to our American literature is im-
    mense."

883. _____. "Richard Wright." Book-of-
the-Month Club News (February), p. 6.
    Seaver narrates the anecdote of W's
    borowing books from the library in
    Memphis, sketches W's earlier life,
    mentions his reading in Chicago and
    the beginning of his literary career,
    and cites some of the materials that
    went into NS. Several quotations from
    an interview with W are included.

884. Selby, John. "Among New Books."
Fitchburg Daily Sentinel (2 March), p.
6.
    Reprint of 1940.901.

885. _____. "Among New Books: Negro
Writer Shows Literary Talent." East
Liverpool (Ohio) Review (6 March), p.
12.
    Reprint of 1940.901.

886. _____. "Bigger Thomas." Durham
Herald (3 March), Part II, p. 2.
    Reprint of 1940.901.

887. _____. "Book a Day." Rockford Morning Star (8 March), p. 8.

Reprint of 1940.901.

888. _____. "Book Review." Malone Evening Telegram (2 March).
    Reprint of 1940.901.

889. _____. "Books." The Eureka Humboldt
Times (5 March), p. 4.
    Reprint of 1940.901.

890. _____. "Fine Writing Doesn't Excuse
Muddled Ideas." New Bedford Sunday Standard-Times (3 March), p. 19.
    Reprint of 1940.901.

891. _____. "Good Writing But Muddled
Theme." The Rock Island Argus (2 March),
p. 7.
    Reprint of 1940.901.

892. _____. "The Literary Guidepost."
Annapolis Evening Capital (2 March).
    Reprint of 1940.901.

893. _____. "The Literary Guidepost."
Ashland Daily Independent (3 March), p.
4.
    Reprint of 1940.901.

894. _____. "The Literary Guidepost."
The Bridgeport (Conn.) Telegram (7
March), p. 12.
    Reprint of 1940.901.

895. _____. "The Literary Guidepost."
The Danbury News-Times (2 March), p. 7.
    Reprint of 1940.901.

896. _____. "The Literary Guidepost."
Hazleton Standard-Sentinel (2 March), p.
10.
    Reprint of 1940.901.

897. _____. "The Literary Guidepost."
Lancaster (Pa.) Daily Intelligencer-
Journal (2 March), p. 4.
    Reprint of 1940.901.

898. _____. "The Literary Guidepost."
Madisonville Daily Messenger (2 March).
    Reprint of 1940.901.

899. _____. "The Literary Guidepost."
The Muncie Morning Star (2 March), p. 3.
    Reprint of 1940.901.

900. _____. "The Literary Guidepost."
Niagara Falls Gazette (2 March), p. 17.
    Reprint of 1940.901.

901. _____. "The Literary Guidepost."
Oshkosh Daily Northwestern (1 March),
p. 8.
    Mixed review of NS praising W's li-
    terary skill but condeming his "warp-
    ed ideology" of communism. "Less
    affecting" than UTC, NS is as good as
    the Chicago fiction of James T. Far-

rell.
Reprinted: 1940.884, 885, 886, 887,
888, 889, 890, 891, 892, 893, 894,
895, 896, 897, 898, 899, 900, 902,
903, 904, 905, 906, 907, 908, 909,
910, 911.

902. _____. "Literary Guidepost." Ottawa
(Ill.) Daily Republican-Times (2 March),
p. 4.
Reprint of 1940.901.

903. _____. "The Literary Guidepost."
Poughkeepsie Eagle-News (2 March), p. 6.
Reprint of 1940.901.

904. _____. "The Literary Guidepost."
The Rocky Mount Telegram (2 March), p.
4.
Reprint of 1940.901.

905. _____. "The Literary Guidepost."
The Sandusky Register (3 March), p. 4.
Reprint of 1940.901.

906. _____. "The Literary Guidepost."
Sayre Evening Times (2 March), p. 4.
Reprint of 1940.901.

907. _____. "The New Books." The Morgan-
town Post (2 March), p. 6.
Reprint of 1940.901.

908. _____. "Reading and Writing." The
Ansonia Evening Sentinel (2 March), pp.
4, 8.
Reprint of 1940.901.

909. _____. "Warped Ideology." The Knoxville Journal (3 March), Sec. 5, p. 8.
Reprint of 1940.901.

910. _____. "Well-Written and Idealistic." The Columbus (Ohio) Sunday Dispatch (3 March), First Magazine Sec., p.
[8].
Abridged reprint of 1940.901.

911. _____. "Wright Shows Ability in
'Native Son.'" Youngstown Vindicator and
the Youngstown Telegram (3 March), p. B-
8.
Reprint of 1940.901.

912. Sellers, T. J., Jr. "Book Critic
Gets a Rose." The Baltimore Afro-American (4 May), p. 13.
Praises Lillian Johnson's review of
NS. Too many white readers will regard Bigger the criminal as typical
of young black men, thus supporting
racist views. Sellers thinks that W's
aesthetic and propagandistic intentions are confused.

913. Senior, Myrtle. "Prize Winning Biography." The Pittsburgh Courier (13
April), p. 19.

Brief biographical essay on W--the
winning entry in a contest for juve-
niles.

914. Shackford, John B. "Atlantic Repartee." The Atlantic Monthly, 166 (July),
[4 of front matter].
Letter to the editor attacking David
L. Cohn's "The Negro Novel: Richard
Wright" for emotionalism and misunderstanding. Shackford praises W for
appealing to the conscience of America.

915. Shneider, Isidor. "Novosti litera-
turny i iskusstva v S Sh A." Internatsional'naia literatura, Nos. 7-8 (July-
August), pp. 302-303.
Includes discussion of the critical
response to NS, especially the question of Bigger as a bad black. Unlike
the genteel and the exotic writers of
Afro-American literary tradition, W
does not appeal for sympathy. Instead, he addresses a wide audience,
black and white, and he makes his
protagonist representative of the
masses.

916. Sillen, Samuel. "The Meaning of
Bigger Thomas." New Masses, 35 (30
April), 26-28.
Corrects previous critics and gives
Sillen's own views on Bigger's characterization, on Bigger as a symbol
of black people, on Jan, and on Max's
courtroom speech. Sillen sees Bigger
as a creative rebel struggling
against social injustice, but also
"tender and warm beneath his hard-
boiled exterior." He does not represent all black people, but to ask
for black progressives is to ask for
a novel different from the one W
wrote. Like Bigger, Jan grows, but
his initial awkward and discomforting
kindness to Bigger lingers in the
memory. Max's speech is unsuccess-
ful--redundant, rhetorical, unclear.
Reprinted: 1971.147; 1978.209.

917. _____. "'Native Son': Pros and
Cons." New Masses, 35 (21 May), 23-26.
Long excerpts from five letters to
Sillen about the novel. Eugene Holmes
mostly agrees with Sillen's "The
Meaning of Bigger Thomas," especially
the appraisal of Bigger's creativity,
but he also likes Max. Chester Himes
uses the scene in which Bigger sees
the airplane skywriting as an index
of his humanity--his sense of the
mystery of life--which the social
system crushes. Joseph H. Cole attacks the novel because its action
does not fulfill its author's progressive intentions. Millicent Lang
defends Sillen's interpretation and

comments on Bigger as "a total human figure . . . passionate and sensitive, desirous of the fullness of life's measure, and denied." Joel Shaw denies Bigger's revolutionary potentiality, calling his characterization "as esthetically false as it is politically confused." Reprinted: 1971.147.

918. _____. "The Response to 'Native Son.'" New Masses, 35 (23 April), 25-27.
Having read more than two hundred reviews of NS, Sillen presents his findings: "There is fairly universal agreement that Richard Wright, who was virtually unheard of a year or two ago, is one of the leading American novelists. Most readers and critics are agreed that Native Son is a novel of tremendous dramatic impact. On the social meaning of the novel there is a division of opinion. The Negro press regards Native Son as a smashing challenge to inequality. A section of the nation's press uses the book as a confirmation of anti-Communist prejudice. Another treats it as a propaganda tract for Communism. The press reaction indicates that there is a correlation between the degree of a reviewer's progressivism and the degree of his enthusiasm for the book." Reprinted: 1971.147; 1978.209.

919. _____. "Richard Wright's 'Native Son.'" New Masses, 34 (5 March), 24-25.
Highly favorable review attributing "the tremendous power of Native Son" to "its ultimate source in a revolutionary vision of life." Though artistic not propagandistic, the novel will convey its social message to its readers. Sillen takes issue with Canby's remarks on the novel, for Bigger does affirm solidarity with Jan and Max. W's most impressive achievement is what Sillen calls his "dramatic realism," his fusion of "the valid elements in the naturalistic and psychological traditions," earning him a place "in the first ranks of American literature in our time." Reprinted: 1970.5; 1978.209.

920. Sims, Jay. "Saturday Chatter with Jay Sims." WBBM Radio-Script (16 March), 2 pp.
Highly favorable "minute review" of NS praising especially W's success in establishing the reader's empathy with Bigger. Sims is also impressed by narrative technique and characterization, including that of Boris Max. He concludes by predicting that "'Native Son' will be the most talked

about, the most widely read and the best all-around book of fiction in 1940."

921. Skillin, Edward, Jr. "Native Son. Richard Wright." The Commonweal, 31 (8 March), 438.
Favorable review comparing it advantageously to An American Tragedy, especially with respect to style and narrative pace. NS "is brutal, frank, sordid. . . . But this brutality is skillfully subordinated to a wider purpose," that of convincing the reader of the injustice of racial discrimination. Reprinted: 1970.5; 1978.209.

922. Skolsky, Sidney. "Peggy Joyce Sought for Paramount Role." New York Post (25 March), p. 8.
Reports that "Paul Robeson is said to have bought the stage rights to . . . 'Native Son.'"

923. Smith, Blanche Hixson. "Have You Read--'Native Son.'" Meriden Record (12 April), p. 7.
Highly favorable review praising plot construction and characterization, especially Bigger's and Max's. Smith compares NS to The Grapes of Wrath as a social novel. Concludes with a brief biographical sketch of W.

924. Smith, Iola E. "Afro Readers Write About 'Native Son.'" The Baltimore Afro-American (29 June), p. 13.
Agrees with Lillian Johnson's review.

925. Smith, Isadora. "Harlem Playwrights Take First Step Toward Local Legit Production Uptown." The Pittsburgh Courier (24 August), p. 20.
Mentions W's speech in the Golden Gate Ballroom on "How 'Bigger' Was Born."

926. Smith, Lillian E. "Dope with Lime." The North Georgia Review, 5 (Spring), 4-6, 26, 42.
Rebuts David Cohn's attack on W and reprimands his racism, but also rejects, less strenuously, W's response to Cohn.

927. _____. "Dope with Lime." The North Georgia Review, mimeographed letter (Spring), p. 1.
Discussing social and racial conditions in the South, Smith reports that "we read Native Son though the public library in the South's largest city banned it for a few days and then quite inexplicably changed its mind and now you may put your name on the waiting list if you like though the waiting list is long. . . Yes,

we southerners are reading <u>Native Son</u> with grim satisfaction in our knowledge that those yankees in Chicago made a terrible mess of their handling of the race problem."

928. _____ and Paula Snelling. "Editors' Choice of 1940 Southern Books." <u>The North Georgia Review</u>, 5 (Winter), inside back cover.
NS is one of four novels listed.

929. Smith, Stevie. "<u>Native Son</u>. Richard Wright." <u>Life and Letters To-Day</u>, 26 (August), 185-186.
Mixed review finding the novel "naive and vigorous." Smith praises the first part, but criticizes the second and third parts for a textbook understanding of psychology. "When he [Wright] is tough he is good, when he is good he is mediocre."

930. Snelling, Paula. "Three Native Sons." <u>The North Georgia Review</u>, 5 (Spring), 7-12.
Review of NS, <u>Trouble in July</u>, and <u>The Hamlet</u>. Snelling admires W's power, talent, and understanding, but criticizes his sensationalism and his emphasis on sociological over psychological determinism.
Reprinted: 1972.181.

931. Snow, Carmel. "The Editor's Guest Book." <u>Harper's Bazaar</u>, 74 (January), 9.
Contains a brief biographical note on W, whose "Almos' a Man" appears in this issue of the magazine.

932. Spearman, Walter. "Best in Movies and Books in Looking Back Over 1940." <u>The Columbia</u> (S. C.) <u>State</u> (29 December), p. 9-B.
Calls NS a "disturbing, exciting, moving" book, one of the five best novels of the year.

933. Spicehandler, Miriam. "On the Book Front: Native Son." <u>Justice</u> (15 May), p. 11.
Favorable review in the newspaper of the International Ladies' Garment Workers' Union emphasizing the social message of the novel. W's view of black life refutes the sentimental stereotypes. Spicehandler praises the author's emotional intensity, his ear for black speech, and his intellectual honesty.

934. Spingarn, Arthur B. "Books by Negro Authors in 1939." <u>The Crisis</u>, 47 (February), 46, 50.
Contains a notice of "Bright and Morning Star" as published in <u>Fifty Best American Short Stories 1915-1939</u>, edited by Edward J. O'Brien.

935. Squire, Sir John. "Three Panoramic and Dashing U. S. Novels." <u>The Illustrated London News</u> (27 April), p. 570.
Contains a favorable review of NS, "a remarkable <u>tour de force</u> as narrative and exposition." Squire is impressed both by W's intense feeling and by his avoidance of sentimentality. Bigger is brutish, but so clearly conditioned by his environment as to elicit some sympathy from the reader. Mrs. Dalton and her cat are called "Poë-esque."

936. Stanley, Lee. "A New Voice in the Theatre." <u>Sunday Worker</u> (27 October), p. 7.
Article on the Negro Playwrights Company quoting a favorable comment by W, a member of the group's board.

937. Startsev, A. "Amerikanskaia tragediia." <u>Internatsional'naia literatura</u>, Nos. 9-10 (September-October), pp. 207-212.
Favorable review of NS with a detailed plot summary. Relating W's novel to its social background, especially lynching, Startsev argues that its great achievement lies in its protest, which prepares the way for militant black revolutionaries.

938. Steele, Margaret. "The World of Books: Native Son by Richard Wright." <u>The Arroyo Grande</u> (Cal.) <u>Herald-Recorder</u> (29 March), p. 5.
Favorable review comparing the novel to <u>The Grapes of Wrath</u> and praising its realism and narrative excitement. "No reader, however harrowed by this book's frank brutalities, will be able to stop in its engrossing story."

939. Stegner, Wallace. "The New Novels." <u>The Virginia Quarterly Review</u>, 16 (Summer), 459-465.
Contains a review of NS (p. 462) along with twenty-five other novels. Stegner views unfavorably W's melodrama, his projection of Bigger as a symbol, and his plea through Max for understanding of Bigger's behavior. "A pitiable and warped figure, he is hardly tragic."
Reprinted: 1978.209.

940. Stevens, Mrs. Arthur K. "Atlantic Repartee." <u>The Atlantic Monthly</u>, 166 (July), [4 of the front matter].
Letter to the editor supporting David L. Cohn's "The Negro Novel: Richard Wright" and claiming that blacks have advanced and should not strive for social equality. "Let us hope that Mr. Wright will use his undenied talents for the betterment of his

race rather than preaching hatred of the white race through the medium of a novel."

941. Stewart, Donald Ogden. Fighting Words. New York: Harcourt, Brace, p. 60.
Quotes Langston Hughes calling W an "excellent craftsman."

942. Stone, I. F. "The Rat and Res Judicata." The Nation, 151 (23 November), 495-496.
Using NS as a point of departure, Stone discusses a Chicago court case involving restrictive covenants responsible for crowded black housing.

943. Sturdevant, Robert. "Critics Praise Newest Novel." Birmingham Age-Herald (5 March), p. 6.
Associated Press article, mainly biographical, with several quotations from W. NS "is a study of Negro psychology, a fact which lifts it above the usual murder story."
Reprinted: 1940.944, 945, 946, 947, 948, 949, 950, 951, 952, 953, 954, 955, 956.

944. _____. "Negro Acclaimed by Critics for Graphic Novel." Norman Oklahoma Daily (6 March).
Reprint of 1940.943.

945. _____. "Negro Author Is Widely Acclaimed for New Volume." Northampton (Mass.) Daily Hampshire Gazette (8 March), p. 5.
Reprint of 1940.943.

946. _____. "Negro Author Wins Acclaim." Montgomery Alabama Journal and the Times (6 March), p. 3.
Reprint of 1940.943.

947. _____. "Negro Climbs from Poverty to Book Fame." Oklahoma City Times (c. 8 March).
Reprint of 1940.943.

948. _____. "Negro 'Destined for Bad End,' Writes Moving Novel." Rochester (N. Y.) Democrat-Chronicle (17 March).
Reprint of 1940.943.

949. _____. "Negro 'Destined' for Gallows Writes Book Praised by Critics." The Louisville Courier-Journal (5 March), p. 8.
Reprint of 1940.943.

950. _____. "Negro Who Battled Way Up Hailed for Tale About Killer." The Detroit Free Press (5 March), p. 12.
Abridged reprint of 1940.943.

951. _____. "Negro Whose Grandma Predicted He'd End on Gallows Wins Ac-

claim." Springfield (Mass.) Weekly Republican (7 March), p. 7.
Reprint of 1940.943.

952. _____. "Negro Wins Fame by Novel of Race." Chattanooga Daily Times (8 March), p. 11.
Reprint of 1940.943.

953. _____. "Negro Youth Who Beat Poverty Hailed as Author of Novel." The Cleveland News (c. March).
Reprint of 1940.943.

954. _____. "Some Brighter in the South." The Raleigh News and Observer (10 March), Sec. M, p. 5.
Reprint of 1940.943.

955. _____. "Southern Negro's Novel Is Book-of-Month Club Choice." Charlotte Sunday Observer (10 March), Sec. Three, p. 5.
Reprint of 1940.943.

956. _____. "Young Negro Acclaimed for Book of Month." Utica Observer-Dispatch (5 March).
Reprint of 1940.943.

957. Swan, Addie May. "Tragedy of Race Gives Theme for Harrowing Novel." Davenport Times (27 April), p. 3.
Favorable review of NS consisting mainly of an extensive plot summary. Probably "the greatest American novel of the year," it is also an eloquent plea for justice for blacks. Includes a photograph of W with caption.

958. Swan, Maurice. "Book Reviews: An Eye on the New." Santa Barbara News Press (25 February), p. 17.
Favorable review of NS, which fulfills the promise of W's poems and short stories. Swan notes W's literary power in spite of--or because of--his lack of formal education.

959. T., B. "Readers Discuss 'Native Son.'" Daily Worker (26 April), p. 7.
Letter to Michael Gold taking issue with him on the effect of the novel. NS gives a distorted picture of Communists to the reading public.

960. T., S. A. "Brought to Book." New Haven Journal-Courier and New Haven Times (7 March), p. 6.
Favorable review of NS comparing its power to that of The Grapes of Wrath. Notes the metaphor of walls to represent the constricting forces of Bigger's circumstances. The reviewer concludes that NS "is more than a picture of the Negro's mind; the book contains the soul of the persecuted everywhere."

961. Tarry, Ellen. "Native Daughter."
The Commonweal, 31 (12 April), 524-526.
Tarry writes as a black Catholic
defending W. If he is a communist, he
has been made one by social, economic, and political racism, for
which white Catholics must share the
blame.
Reprinted: 1940.962.

962. ____. "Native Daughter." The Baltimore Afro-American (25 May), p. 12.
Reprint of 1940.961.

963. Taylor, D.[ora]. "Banning Books."
The Birmingham News (12 April), p. 12.
Letter to the editor applauding the
editorial "Banning Books Indirectly."

964. ____. "A Book Banned from the
Library." The Birmingham News (22
March), p. 6.
Letter to the editor protesting the
banning of NS from the Birmingham
Public Library.

965. Thomas, Aubrey L. "Book of the
Day." Philadelphia Evening Public Ledger
(1 March), p. 20.
Favorable review of NS emphasizing
its emotional power and suspense.
Bigger is depicted as "a mean, lying
thief and coward," but the responsibility for his character rests with
white society. The novel is "a vital
document dealing boldly and frankly"
with a major American social problem.

966. Thomas, H. H. "Says Columnists Have
Wrong Slant on Book." The Philadelphia
Tribune (23 May), p. 4.
Letter to the editor taking issue
with Eustace Gay and E. Washington
Rhodes, who think that NS is a dis-
service to black people. Thomas ad-
mires W's emphasis on social deter-
minism and his belief that racism is
deep-rooted. He compares NS to The
Grapes of Wrath and Langston Hughes's
Mulatto.

967. Thomas, Jessie O. "Urban League
Bulletin." The Atlanta Constitution (3
March), p. 11A.
Biographical sketch of W on the occasion of his being honored by the poll
conducted by the Schomburg Collection
and the New York branch of the Association for the Study of Negro Life
and History. Quotes W on his early
life and his Writers Project job in
Chicago.

968. Thompson, John H. "Robeson, Wright
Win Praise on N. Y. Appearance." The
Baltimore Afro-American (21 September),
p. 14.
Reviews favorably W's speech on "How

'Bigger' Was Born" given at the Golden Gate Ballroom in Harlem.
Reprinted: 1940.969.

969. ____. "Robeson, Wright Win Praise
on N. Y. Appearance." Washington Afro-
American (21 September), p. 16.
Reprint of 1940.968.

970. Timmons, Marsha L. "Afro Readers
Write About 'Native Son.'" The Baltimore
Afro-American (11 May), p. 13.
Letter to Lillian Johnson reporting
that Langston Hughes praised her
review and expressed similar opinions
about NS in a lecture in Chicago.
Reprinted: 1940.971.

971. ____. "Afro Readers Write About
'Native Son.'" Washington Afro-American
(11 May), p. 18.
Reprint of 1940.970.

972. Tobias, Rowena W. "Race Problem in
Novel." The Charleston (S. C.) News and
Courier (24 March), Sec. III, p. 3.
Highly favorable review of NS praising it as both literature and sociology. Avoiding sentimentality and
special pleading, W develops his
story with relentless force amounting
to a sense of fate. His prose style
is grippingly effective. Max's courtroom speech is "the most eloquent and
clear-sighted investigation of the
racial problem ever written."

973. Toliver, Clarence. "The Point in
This." Washington Afro-American (23
March), p. 3.
Reports that NS sold 13,000 copies in
Atlanta in the first week after pub-
lication.

973a. Tolson, M. B. "Caviar and Cabbage:
Does Human Nature Change?" Washington
Tribune (31 August), p. 4.
Mentions briefly Bigger Thomas.

973b. ____. "Caviar and Cabbage: My
Apologies to the Graduates of 1940."
Washington Tribune (1 June), p. 4.
Mentions W briefly.

973c. ____. "Caviar and Cabbage: What
Richard Wright Said to America in 'Native Son.'" Washington Tribune (12 October), p. 4.
Discusses the public impact and theme
of the novel. Read by blacks of all
social classes, it is misunderstood
by many educated blacks. W's theme is
Marxist social determinism. Rejecting
the charge of vulgarity, Tolson
praises W's realism.

974. ____. "Richard Wright: Native
Son." The Modern Quarterly, 11 (Winter),

19-24.
Favorable review comparing W to the Greek tragedians, Steinbeck, Dostoevsky, and Dreiser, and contrasting him to Faulkner and Hemingway. "Hemingway's characters are exteriorized; Wright's interiorized" (p. 23). But Tolson also emphasizes W's social sense and racial militancy, predicting that black people in America will regard him as the literary spokesman of their pain and hope.

975. Tooill, Kenneth D. "Books." Columbus Ohio State Journal (4 March), p. 6.
Favorable review of NS noting the development of W's career and including a detailed plot summary. The novel "is the frankest and boldest book ever written by a Negro . . . a document of vast importance," but W's artistic control falters at times, resulting in emotionalism and exaggeration. Book Three is too propagandistic.

976. Townend, Marion. "1940 Was Important Year in World of Books." Charlotte Sunday Observer (29 December), Sec. Three, p. 5.
Among novels of the year NS stands "alone, not perhaps in surpassing literary excellence, but as powerful, intense, and inspired writing."

977. Tuck, William A. "Wright Attacks Leaders." The Durham Carolina Times (3 August), pp. 1, 8.
Reports W's lecture on "How 'Bigger' Was Born" given at the White Rock Baptist Church in Durham on 28 July 1940. Tuck's emphasis is on W's criticism of the black bourgeoise.

978. Tupas, Peter. "Book Reviews: Native Son by Richard Wright." Lihue (Hawaii) Garden Island (25 June).
Highly favorable review praising W's "clear, vivid, unemotional prose, which gives his stories their brilliant intensity." W builds suspense masterfully in the first two books, and Bigger's rebirth in the third is deeply moving. NS is shocking with its "intimate and gory details," but it is comparable in psychological insight and "inventive genius" to Crime and Punishment.

979. Upmal, Marjorie. "Book Reviews." Montpelier Evening Argus (6 April), p. 4.
Favorable review of NS predicting a variety of responses to the novel and widespread controversy concerning it. Some white readers will have their racism reinforced by the portrayal of Bigger, but they will have missed W's

purpose. The book could have been written only by a black writer able to convey a black reality without the use of dialect.

980. Van Doren, Carl. The American Novel: 1789-1939. New York: Macmillan, p. 359.
Mentions UTC, "four fiery stories of Negroes who defy and resist white injustice."

981. Van Gelder, Robert. "William Allen White Talks of Writing and Reading." The New York Times Book Review (14 July), p. 2.
Includes favorable comments on NS despite its communism. See 1940.514.

982. Vincennes, Gilbert de. "Louis Mariano nous répond." Cinévogue (31 August).
Contains a brief reference to W. The date is uncertain.

983. W., P. "Black American Epic." The Canadian Tribune (20 April), p. 7.
Highly favorable review of NS summarizing the plot and quoting from Dorothy Canfield Fisher's introduction before rendering this judgment: "Not often does a reviewer come across a work of fiction so tremendous in its conception, so perfect in its execution and so strong in its impact that he realizes he is face to face with genius. Native Son is such a work." Thus it ranks with The Grapes of Wrath.

984. W., P. "Richard Wright's 'Native Son' Is a Superb Plea for the American Negro; Faulkner Book Typical, Not His Best." Lincoln Nebraska State Journal (30 April).
Contains a favorable review of NS. It is a powerful story of the outcast, as moving as The Grapes of Wrath but more informative and authentic.

985. Wagner, Charles A. "Books." New York Sunday Mirror (c. 3 March).
Reports that W will teach fiction at the Writers School.

986. _____. "Books." New York Daily Mirror (7 March), p. 23.
Favorable review of NS stressing its sympathy for the underdog and comparing W to Stowe, Steinbeck, Di Donato, and Maltz. "The beat of passionate truth hovers over his work, like unremitting wings of conscience and vision."

987. Wakefield, Eleanor. "Study of Negro Problem Praised as Best Book Ever Produced by Race." The Houston Chronicle

(10 March), Fourth Sec., p. 10.
Favorable review of NS comparing W to Steinbeck and Dreiser. The novel "is a dramatic masterpiece, a literary achievement written with a driving, intense sincerity, crusading fervor, a burning desire to state the case so that a wrong might be understood, but with sanity and reason." On the other hand, Wakefield thinks that W exaggerates the racial aspects of his theme, and she finds Bigger repulsive and considers Jan and Mary "idiotic, idealistic Communists."

988. Walcutt, Charles C. "Story of Negroes Is Bitter Exposé." The Oklahoma City Daily Oklahoman (15 December), Sec. D, p. 3.
Review of the enlarged edition of UTC emphasizing W's bitterness and violence.

989. Walker, Danton. "Broadway." New York Daily News (7 October), p. 32.
Reports that W and Langston Hughes are collaborating on a radio variety show.

990. Walker, Viola White. "Books and Authors." The Lawrence (Mass.) Evening Tribune (15 March), p. 16.
Contains a notice of NS, "a violent story which goes into emotional and social causes."

991. Wallace, Margaret. "The Book of the Day: A Powerful Novel About a Boy from Chicago's Black Belt." The New York Sun (5 March), p. 34.
Highly favorable review of NS emphasizing its powerful impact and providing a detailed plot summary. Bigger is unattractive but plausible. His story "comes through heaped-up horror to an emotion not far removed from those Aristotle described as pity and terror." The book is "an amazingly expert performance" and "the finest novel yet written by an American Negro."
Reprinted: 1978.209.

992. Ware, Lewis W. "Atlantic Repartee." The Atlantic Monthly, 166 (July), [4 of front matter.]
Letter to the editor from a black reader who attacks W's Marxism, admonishes the race to be patient, and deplores the lack of racial unity and sound leadership.

993. Warner, Ralph. "'Stay Out!' Say U. S. Writers." Daily Worker (22 June), p. 7.
W is one of the signers of the League of American Writers statement opposing American involvement in the war.

994. Warwick, Ray. "'Native Son' by Richard Wright." The Atlanta Journal (24 March), Sunday Magazine Sec., p. 10.
Mixed review conceding the justice of the book's anger but deeming the idea of achieving freedom through murder "a rather romantic metaphysics." Warwick finds the writing to have a "forced quality" typical of thesis novels.

995. Weaver, Janet. "Red Army Men Are Masters of All the World's Best and Finest Culture." Daily Worker (23 February), p. 5.
Reports that a Soviet librarian referred to UTC as a "very fine book."

996. Webb, Elizabeth M. "Native Son: Pro and Con." The Atlantic Monthly, 165 (June), [7 of front matter].
Letter to the editor objecting sharply to David L. Cohn's review, especially his claim that the novel preaches hatred and his belief that the racial question is insoluble.

997. Weigle, Edith. "Year's Literary Spotlight Focuses on Chicagoans." Chicago Daily Tribune (4 December), Sec. Two, p. 1.
Notes that W recently purchased a house on the South Side of Chicago.

998. Weintroub, Benjamin. "Negro Life." Chicago Jewish Chronicle (26 April).
Favorable review of NS placing it in the tradition of Turgenev, Hugo, Upton Sinclair, Dickens, and Stowe-- writers who have yearned for justice. After summarizing the plot, Weintroub calls the book "a passionate and yet cooly deliberate exposition" of the racial oppression and economic exploitation suffered by black people.

999. Werkman, Ed. "Negro Tells Moving Tale of Race Woe." Pittsburgh Press (31 March), Society Sec., p. 9.
Favorable review of NS with a detailed plot summary. Like Steinbeck, W is a social realist. He handles suspense well, but the novel's "frank brutalities are distressing." Nevertheless, it "should increase sympathy for the problems of the Negro."

1000. West, Anthony. "New Novels." The New Statesman and Nation, 19 (20 April), 542-543.
Contains an extremely unfavorable review of NS objecting sharply to "the poisonous guff of Behaviourism." Bigger is a "dumb ox with a habit of not using his brains" who, West implies, should be contented with his position at the Dalton house. The novel is "unimpressive and silly, not

even as much fun as a thriller."

1001. Williamson, Simon. "Guest Editorial." New York Amsterdam News (25 May), p. 8.
    Compares Claude McKay's Jake in Home to Harlem favorably to Bigger Thomas, who is "representative of the savage ape-like idea of the Negro as conceived by the reactionary Negrophobist." With such a portrayal W is comparable to Thomas Dixon.

1002. Winchell, Walter. "On Broadway." New York Daily Mirror (1 April), p. 10.
    Calls W "a leader of the intelligentsia in the Mahogany-skinned set."

1003. _____. "On Broadway." New York Sunday Mirror (5 May), p. 10.
    Suggests that the award of the Pulitzer Prize to W would be "another stab at the Kluxers."

1004. Wright, J. Wesley. "Letters to the Editor: 'Native Son.'" The New York Age (25 May), p. 12.
    Argues that white praise of the novel is based on inadequate understanding of black psychology. Bigger is not representative of black people. The novelist has substituted "artificially constructed sensationalism for the tragic realities of Negro experiences and existence."

1005. Wyke, Marguerite. "South Side Negro." The Canadian Forum, 20 (May), 60.
    Favorable review of NS stressing the social dimension of the novel and comparing W to Caldwell, Faulkner, and Steinbeck. "Mr. Wright is a realist who goes below the surface to root causes and the tragic climax of the book shows clearly that the violence and racial strife have become accepted modes of life and are the inevitable consequences of our social system."

1941

1. Adams, James Truslow. "The Democratic Fashion." The Saturday Review of Literature, 24 (27 September), 3-4, 18-20.
    Unfavorable essay-review of Bernard Smith's anthology The Democratic Spirit objecting to the inclusion of W and other radical writers.

2. Albert, John. "Watching the Stars: Radio, Stage, Screen." The Philadelphia Tribune (13 September), p. 15.
    Mentions the success of the play NS.

3. Allen. Kelcey. "Amusements: Additions to 'Native Son' Cast." Women's Wear Daily (c. February).

Lists four actors who have joined the cast of the play.

4. _____. "Amusements: Ann [sic] Burr to Address Two Groups." Women's Wear Daily (25 April), p. 31.
    Announces a speech by the actress who plays Mary Dalton in NS.

5. _____. "Amusements: Ann [sic] Burr to Discuss 'Native Son' Today." Women's Wear Daily (5 May), p. 17.
    Announces a speech at the New School for Social Research by the actress who plays Mary Dalton.

6. _____. "Amusements: Canada Lee to Be Honored Monday Evening." Women's Wear Daily (6 June), p. 41.
    Announces that a radio program will honor the actor who plays Bigger. W, Robeson, Duke Ellington, and Bill Robinson will participate.

7. _____. "Amusements: Collins Returns to 'Native Son.'" Women's Wear Daily (28 April), p. 21.
    Reports that Ray Collins will return to play Max after an illness. John Berry has been his understudy.

8. _____. "Amusements: Designs Scenery for 'Native Son.'" Women's Wear Daily (7 March), p. 36.
    Notes that James Morcom is the designer.

9. _____. "Amusements: Join Cast of 'Native Son.'" Women's Wear Daily (12 March), p. 28.
    Lists the five actors who complete the cast.

10. _____. "Amusements: 'Man Who Came to Dinner' at Maplewood Theatre." Women's Wear Daily (31 July), p. 31.
    Reports that NS did well financially the preceding week.

11. _____. "Amusements: 'Native Son' at Flatbush Theatre." Women's Wear Daily (2 September), p. 24.
    Announces a return engagement of the play in Brooklyn.

12. _____. "Amusements: 'Native Son' at Maplewood, N. J." Women's Wear Daily (28 July), p. 20.
    Announces the opening of the play "tonight."

13. _____. "Amusements: 'Native Son' at Windsor, Bronx." Women's Wear Daily (4 August), p. 16.
    Announces an opening of the play.

14. _____. "Amusements: 'Native Son' at Windsor Theatre Again." Women's Wear

Daily (25 August).
    Announces a revival of the play in the Bronx.

15. _____. "Amusements: 'Native Son' Booked for Windsor Next Week." Women's Wear Daily (30 July), p. 24.
    Announces an opening of the play in the Bronx on 5 August.

16. _____. "Amusements: 'Native Son' Complete Sell-Out at Flatbush." Women's Wear Daily (20 August), p. 24.
    Reports that the play is breaking attendance records in Brooklyn.

17. _____. "Amusements: 'Native Son' Producers Returning to Hollywood." Women's Wear Daily (26 March), p. 24.
    Reports that Orson Welles and John Houseman left for Hollywood on 25 March.

18. _____. "Amusements: 'Native Son' to Omit Wednesday Matinees." Women's Wear Daily (6 May), p. 22.
    Reports that the omission will begin "this week."

19. _____. "Amusements: 100 Times of 'Native Son.'" Women's Wear Daily (16 June), p. 20.
    Notes the hundredth performance of the play at the St. James Theater.

20. _____. "Amusements: Preview Tonight for 'Native Son.'" Women's Wear Daily (21 March), p. 32.
    Notes that the preview performance is "for the benefit of the Robert Louis Stevenson School."

21. _____. "Amusements: Prices for 'Native Son.'" Women's Wear Daily (18 March), p. 31.
    Explains pricing of tickets for the play and notes postponement of the opening.

22. _____. "Amusements: Seats Ready for 'Native Son.'" Women's Wear Daily (3 March), p. 20.
    Announces that the seats for the play go on sale "today" at the St. James Theater.

23. _____. "Amusements: Signed for 'Native Son.'" Women's Wear Daily (26 February), p. 27.
    Lists five actors who have joined the cast of the play.

24. _____. "Amusements: St. James Theatre to Get 'Native Son.'" Women's Wear Daily (20 February), p. 32.
    Announces the opening of the play and mentions the previews.

25. _____. "Amusements: To Appear in 'Native Son.'" Women's Wear Daily (5 March), p. 32.
    Mentions the addition of six actors to the cast of the play.

26. _____. "Amusements: To Be in 'Native Son.'" Women's Wear Daily (24 February), p. 21.
    Lists the leading members of the cast of the play.

27. _____. "Amusements: To Give Previews of 'Native Son.'" Women's Wear Daily (13 March), p. 28.
    Mentions the benefit performance of the play for the NAACP.

28. _____. "Amusements: Trade Attends 'Native Son' Benefit Performance." Women's Wear Daily (2 April), p. 27.
    The garment trade attended a benefit performance of the play for the East Side Hebrew Institute.

29. _____. "Amusements: Votes for Best Performances." Women's Wear Daily (5 June), p. 37.
    Canada Lee of NS came in second to Paul Lukas of Watch on the Rhine for the best acting performance of the season.

30. _____. "Amusements: Welles and Houseman Offer 'Native Son.'" Women's Wear Daily (17 February), p. 19.
    Mentions Canada Lee as well as the producers.

31. _____. "'Native Son.'" Women's Wear Daily (25 March), pp. 31-32.
    Favorable review of the play describing at length the leading characters and praising their performances. The work "is high melodrama and . . . stark realism. Yet it sacrifices nothing of good theatre to attain these ends."

32. A.[ltman], I.[rving] B. "A Folk History of the Negro." Dynamic America, 13 (December), 28.
    Favorable review of TMBV summarizing the contents and praising both W's factual objectivity and his pity. Solution to the problems W reveals is necessary to the endurance of American democracy.

33. Anderson, John. "Dean of Critics May Have Clairvoyant Gift." New York Journal and American (1 April), p. 10.
    Chides fellow critic Burns Mantle for comparing the play NS to the novel without having read the latter.

34. _____. "List of 10 Best Plays Reflects Lean Season." New York Journal

and American (4 November), p. 8.
    Mentions NS briefly.

35. _____. "'Native Son' Links Red,
Racial Themes." New York Journal and
American (25 March), p. 12.
    Extremely unfavorable review of the
    play complaining vehemently about the
    element of Communist propaganda "that
    seems nearer Moscow than Harlem."
    Some of the scenes are forceful, and
    Lee's performance is good, but for
    the most part "the play seemed over-
    wrought with a sort of monotonous
    hysteria, phony in its argument and
    finally tiresome."
    Reprinted: 1941.36.

36. _____. "'Native Son' Links Red,
Racial Themes." Critics' Theatre Reviews, 2 (20 April), 352.
    Reprint of 1941.35.

37. _____. "Plays and Players: Critics
of Critics Distort Reviews." New York
Sunday Journal and American (30 March).
    Summarizes the critical response to
    the play NS. Anderson dislikes the
    Communist orientation of the work.

38. _____. "'Watch on the Rhine' Wins
Critics' Award." New York Journal and
American (23 April), p. 10.
    Notes that Burns Mantle "maintained a
    lonely but staunch support for 'Na-
    tive Son.'"

39. Anon. "A. Quade's Outdoor Tour: New
Summer Show Plans." New York Sunday News
(30 March).
    Notes that the sled Rosebud from
    Citizen Kane is used as a prop in NS.
    Mentions Canada Lee's pay.

40. Anon. "About Books." Unidentified
clipping.
    Contains a favorable notice of TMBV,
    "a moving story of protest in behalf
    of the disinherited of the nation."

41. Anon. "About Books and Authors."
Newark Evening News (8 February), p. 4.
    Contains a brief, nonevaluative no-
    tice of How "Bigger" Was Born.

42. Anon. "About Some Awards." The
Philadelphia Inquirer (c. 16 February).
    Reports that NS was fifth in a poll
    conducted by the Book-of-the-Month
    Club to select the outstanding book
    of 1940.

43. Anon. "Actor's Guild Stages Annual
Ball." The Chicago Defender (3 May),
National edition, p. 21.
    Photograph of Canada Lee and others
    with caption mentioning NS.

44. Anon. "Actresses Spurn Star Role in
'Native Son.'" Norfolk Journal and Guide
(8 March), p. 12.
    Discusses the withdrawal of Doris
    Dudley, who was to play Mary Dalton,
    from the cast of NS to avoid teasing
    by her friends. The situation was
    intensified by an actual trial of a
    Connecticut black man for the rape of
    his white employer.

45. Anon. "After Working Hours." PM (31
August), p. 56.
    Photograph with caption of Anne Burr,
    "leading lady of Native Son," and
    other theatrical people in a New York
    bar.

46. Anon. "Aides of Benefit Will Meet at
Tea." The New York Times (29 April), p.
22.
    Announces that Mrs. Walter Poor, Jr.,
    will sponsor a benefit performance of
    NS for the Colored Orphans' Asylum
    and other philanthropic causes.

47. Anon. "Amer. Negro Theatre Gives
'Natural Man.'" Daily Worker (2 April),
p. 7.
    Notes that two members of the group
    are playing in NS.

48. Anon. "American Authors Select Leading Books for Today." Savannah Morning
News (6 July), p. 30.
    NS is one of seventy-seven books on a
    list of "Books for Today" compiled by
    the Committee on College Reading and
    the National Council of Teachers of
    English.

49. Anon. "American Writers Pledge Full
Aid to Britain and the Soviet Union."
Daily Worker (24 July), p. 7.
    Mentions W, whose photograph appears,
    as one of the vice-presidents of the
    League of American Writers.

50. Anon. "Among the New Books." San
Francisco Chronicle (4 May), This World
Sec., p. 21.
    Contains a review of the published
    version of the play NS comparing it
    unfavorably to the novel. Oversimpli-
    fied and melodramatic, the play lacks
    the continuity, profundity, and
    social understanding of the book,
    which is "probably one of the finest
    realistic novels by an American."

51. Anon. "Anne Burr." Brooklyn Eagle
(29 May), p. 5.
    Photograph of Burr and Canada Lee in
    a scene from the play NS.

52. Anon. "Anne Burr Clicks After 3
Years Effort." Brooklyn Eagle (10
August), Sec. E, p. 7.

Biographical article on the actress who plays Mary Dalton.

53. Anon. "Another of the Literati Awarded the Spingarn Medal." The Baltimore Afro-American (15 February), p. 4.
Editorial praising W and NS, "a revolutionary book" compared to Uncle Tom's Cabin. Bigger is in the tradition of Nat Turner and Denmark Vesey.

54. Anon. "Arna Bontemps Aids Prof. in New Book." The Philadelphia Tribune (15 November), p. 15.
Mentions TMBV.

55. Anon. "Author, Author!" The Saturday Review of Literature, 23 (19 April), 17-18.
Includes an anecdote concerning producer Lee Shubert's shock at the opening of NS to learn that the play had Communist characters.

56. Anon. "B. Bernard, MCA Agent, Others Backing Welles' Prod. of 'Native Son.'" Variety (19 February), p. 49.
Gives details concerning financial supporters of the play.

57. Anon. "Back to Nixon." The Pittsburgh Courier (18 October), p. 20.
Photograph of Canada Lee with caption stating that NS will play a week's return engagement at the Nixon Theater in Pittsburgh beginning 20 October.

58. Anon. "Barbara Everest to Appear Here." The New York Times (19 August), p. 24.
Announces that the play NS will return to the Windsor Theater "next Tuesday."

59. Anon. "Basement Melodrama in 'Native Son.'" New York Post (19 June), p. 8.
Picture with caption of the second furnace scene in the play.

60. Anon. "Basie's Band and Robeson Wax Joe Louis Blues." The Pittsburgh Courier (11 October), p. 21.
Mentions W.

61. Anon. "The Bell Rings Critical Poll." The New York Sun (10 February), p. 10.
NS ranked fifth among the outstanding books of 1940 according to a poll of 159 critics.

62. Anon. "Benefit." Daily Worker (5 March), p. 7.
Advertisement for the benefit performance of the play NS for New Masses and the Veterans of the Abraham Lincoln Brigade on 14 March.

63. Anon. "Benefit Performance of 'Native Son' to Aid Colored Orphans." The New York Age (26 April), p. 4.
The performance is scheduled for 22 May.

64. Anon. "'Berlin Diary' in England and Elsewhere." Chelsea (Mass.) Evening Record (25 October), p. 4.
Mentions a lecture on "Contemporary American Literature" (including NS) by the Soviet critic Startsev. The title of this item should be "U. S. Literature in the U. S. S. R.," transposed to another article.

65. Anon. "Best Books of 1940." The Dallas Morning News (23 February), Sec. Three, p. 15.
Mentions the Book-of-the-Month Club poll, in which NS placed fifth.

66. Anon. "Best Books of 1940 Chosen in a Poll." The New York Times (10 February), p. 15.
With fifty-seven votes, NS ranked fifth in a Book-of-the-Month Club poll of 159 literary critics to select the outstanding books of 1940.

67. Anon. "Between Ourselves." New Masses, 38 (11 February), 2.
Congratulates W on the Spingarn Award, recalls his publications in New Masses, and comments on his work in progress.

68. Anon. "Between Ourselves." New Masses, 38 (4 March), 2.
Announces a special New Masses performance of the play NS scheduled for 14 March (later cancelled). Also mentions that W is a speaker at a celebration of Michael Gold's twenty-fifth annniversary of literary activity in the labor movement.

69. Anon. "Between Ourselves." New Masses, 38 (11 March), 2.
Mentions W as a speaker at the celebration for Michael Gold and the New Masses performance of the play NS (later cancelled).

70. Anon. "Bigger Than Ever." Pic, 10 (5 August), 28-29.
Article on Canada Lee with mention of the play NS and a photograph of the bedroom scene with Bigger and Mary.

71. Anon. "Bigger Thomas Comes to Life in 'Native Son,' at the St. James Theater." New York Herald Tribune (30 March), Sec. VI, p. 5.
Sketch of the bedroom scene.

72. Anon. "Bigger Thomas' Lawyer Visits Him in Prison." New York Post.

Photograph with caption from the play NS.

73. Anon. "'Bilateral Economy of the South Is All So Silly'--Paul Green." Norfolk Journal and Guide (1 March), p. 4.
Report on Green's attack on segregation at the North Carolina Interracial Commission. Praising the novel NS, Green states that he will interpret Bigger in the play more in terms of free will than W's preferred environmental determinism.

74. Anon. "Bontemps, Hughes Write CBS Skit for Actor Canada Lee." The Pittsburgh Courier (13 December), p. 20.
Mentions Lee's role as Bigger Thomas.

75. Anon. "Book Marks." New York World-Telegram (11 February), p. 31.
Notes that in the branches of the New York Public Library "there are 1199 requests on file for Native Son and only 294 copies."

76. Anon. "Book Marks." New York World-Telegram (14 February), p. 23.
Mentions that W is scheduled to speak at a Writers School forum.

77. Anon. "Book Marks." New York World-Telegram (4 June), p. 23.
Announces that W will speak at the fourth congress of the League of American Writers.

78. Anon. "Book Marks." People's Daily World (16 April), p. 5.
Suggests reading the published play for a "racy rendition" of NS.

79. Anon. "Book News: Honor: Negro Novelist Gets Coveted Award." People's Daily World (5 February), p. 5.
Announces the Spingarn Award to W, quotes the citation and W's acceptance statement, and reviews W's career. A photograph with caption of W appears above the article.

80. Anon. "Book Notes." New York Herald-Tribune (27 February), p. 15.
Announces that the book version of the play NS will be published by Harper's on 17 March.

81. Anon. "Book Notes." New York Herald Tribune (24 April), p. 19.
Notes that W contributed to William Kozlenko's American Scenes.

82. Anon. "Book Notes." Sunday Worker (6 July), p. 4.
Contains an announcement of TMBV.

83. Anon. "Book Review." The New York

Age (5 April), p. 6.
Favorable notice of the published version of the play NS emphasizing reader enjoyment to complement the novel and the stage version.

84. Anon. "Book Review: Native Son--Richard Wright." Las Vegas (Nev.) Evening Review-Journal (23 October), p. 8.
Consists almost entirely of a quotation from Canby's review.

85. Anon. "Book Talk." The Hamilton (N. Y.) Republican (16 January).
Reports that NS was ranked seventh by reviewers, twentieth by librarians, twenty-fifth by booksellers, and eighth by the general public in a poll on the "Outstanding Books of 1940."

86. Anon. "Books and Authors." The New York Times Book Review (4 May), p. 16.
Contains an announcement of William Kozlenko's American Scenes mentioning W.

87. Anon. "Books--Authors." The New York Times (4 February), p. 17.
Announces the W-Rosskam collaboration in progress.

88. Anon. "Books--Authors." The New York Times (4 March), p. 21.
Contains an announcement of the scheduled publication of the book version of the play NS.

89. Anon. "Books--Authors." The New York Times (6 November), p. 21.
Contains a brief notice of TMBV, for which W dropped work on a new novel.

90. Anon. "Books--Authors." The New York Times (13 December), p. 19.
Notes that W's new novel will be about black domestic workers.

91. Anon. "Books by American Authors Popular with Soviet Readers." Daily Worker (25 June), p. 7.
Comments on the popularity of NS in the Soviet Union. Includes a photograph of W.

92. Anon. "Books for Christmas Among the Recent Publications." The New York Times Book Review (7 December), pp. 3, 34, 36, 46, 48, 49-50, 52, 61.
Contains a brief notice of TMBV, the "bitter saga of the Negro" (p. 61).

93. Anon. "Books Make Best Xmas Gifts." Daily Worker (24 December), p. 3.
Advertisement of Workers Book Shop listing TMBV.

94. Anon. "Books, Pamphlets on War on 1942 Publishing List." Sunday Worker (28 December), Sec. 2, p. 4.
Mentions TMBV.

95. Anon. "Books Published Today." The New York Times (28 March), p. 21.
Lists the published version of the play NS.

96. Anon. "Books Received." New York Herald-Tribune Books (6 April), p. 28.
Contains a brief notice of the published version of the play NS.

97. Anon. "Books: Richard Wright, Book of the Month Club Novelist Writing Third Volume." Unidentified clipping.
Associated Negro Press article indicating that W has completed the first writing of a novel which will study the position of the black woman from the "feudal" South to the "Fascist" North.

98. Anon. "Books to Be Published This Fall." The New York Times Book Review (21 September), p. 31.
Lists TMBV and includes a photograph of W.

99. Anon. "The Bookshelf." Atlanta Daily World (21 December), p. 4.
Favorable review of TMBV praising both text and photographs. The reviewer has reservations about W's Marxism and his exclusion of the talented tenth, but he is impressed by the work's social message and superb prose.

100. Anon. "Bourne Award Planned by U. S. Writers." Sunday Worker (4 May), Sec. 2, p. 4.
Mentions W as one of the vice-presidents of the League of American Writers.

101. Anon. The Brandts Present Canada Lee in Orson Welles' "Native Son." New York.
Playbill for the road show. Includes newspaper articles on W, Canada Lee, and Anne Burr; photographs from the play; Burns Mantle's review; and other information.

102. Anon. "Brief Reviews." The Washington Sunday Star (16 November), p. E-7.
Contains a brief notice of TMBV calling it "very effective."

103. Anon. "The Bright Lights." PM's Weekly (15 June), p. 40.
Includes a photograph of Orson Welles, who "panics his staff with his direction of the Broadway hit, Native Son."

104. Anon. "Bring 'Native Son' to South, Texans Urge." Daily Worker (28 July), p. 4.
From Houston the writer urges that the play be produced in the South. W spoke to a packed house in Houston at the N. A. A. C. P. Convention, but the novel NS "is refused to Negro readers by Negro librarians in the South."

105. Anon. "Brisk Ticket Sale for 'Native Son' Benefit." The Pittsburgh Courier (15 March), p. 20.
Concerns the benefit performance of the play for the N. A. A. C. P.

106. Anon. "Broadway Job Hunting." New York Post (24 April), p. 10.
Concerns Anne Burr, who plays Mary Dalton in NS.

107. Anon. "Broadway Reaches Ebb Tide; Even 'Rhine' Dips, $17,500; 'Hattie' $23,500." Variety (2 July), p. 50.
Mentions the closing of the play NS after fourteen weeks.

108. Anon. "Broadway Report." PM (23 February), p. 52.
Notes that NS has gone into rehearsal.

109. Anon. "Broadway to Get View of 'Native Son.'" Norfolk Journal and Guide (1 March), Home Edition, p. 16.
Notes that "Bigger Thomas . . . has been responsible for more drawing room debates than any other character in recent American fiction history." Gives details about the stage production, including planned deletion of "the Communist tinge."

110. Anon. "Bronx to See 'Native Son.'" New York Daily Mirror (2 August), p. 17.
Announces the opening of the play at the Windsor Theater.

111. Anon. "Browder Speaks Today at Rally to Honor Mike Gold." Sunday Worker (2 March), p. 2.
W is one of the speakers.

112. Anon. "Browder to Speak at Mike Gold Celebration." Sunday Worker (23 February), p. 3.
W will be one of the speakers on 2 March.

113. Anon. "Bulletin!" New York Amsterdam Star-News (22 March), p. 20.
Announces the second postponement of the opening of the play NS until 25 March.

114. Anon. Bulletin White Mountain Writers Conference, p. 9.

Lists W as one of the lecturers at a conference sponsored by the League of American Writers at Jefferson, New Hampshire, 18 August-2 September.

115. Anon. "Burr Production Here on April 10." The New York Times (3 March), p. 11.
Mentions that "tickets go on sale today" for the play NS.

116. Anon. "B'way Dearth Progressive." Variety (4 June), p. 47.
Calls the play NS a "moderate success" at the box office.

117. Anon. "B'way Dips Again, But 'Rhine,' $19,300, 'Arsenic,' $16,600, 'Lady,' $31,700, Still SRO; 'People,' Some Profit, 7G." Variety (7 May), p. 75.
Weekly gross for NS was about $14,000.

118. Anon. "B'way Dips as Lent Takes Its Toll, But 'Rhine,' 16G, 'Dilemma,' 22G Big; Ditto 'Lady' 32G, 'Hattie,' $31,500." Variety (9 April), p. 43.
In its second week the play NS "is not as big as expected but quite lively around $14,000."

119. Anon. "B'way Fadeaway Continues; 'Native,' $11,500, 'Corn,' 14 G, Among Those Off, 'Lady,' 31½G, 'Rhine,' 19½G, Still SRO." Variety (14 May), p. 51.
Weekly gross for NS of $11,500 "is claimed to better even break."

120. Anon. "B'way Legit Spurts: 'Corn,' $19,000, 'Eileen,' $16,500, 'Heat,' $13,000, 'La.,' $28,000, All in Upswing." Variety (26 March), p. 51.
First appearance of NS, which opened on 24 March, in regular weekly report.

121. Anon. "B'way List Shorter, But Biz Better; 'Claudia,' 'Eileen,' 11½G, 'Son' Slips." Variety (18 June), p. 51.
Weekly gross for the twelfth week of NS is under $8,500.

122. Anon. "B'way Off Another 10%; 'Snookie,' a Dud, $3,000, 'Ice,' 14G, Will Fold." Variety (11 June), p. 42.
Weekly gross for NS slips to $8,500, a new low.

123. Anon. "B'way Settling Into Summer Groove; 'Days' $5,000, Doubtful, 'Rhine' 19G, 'Arsenic' 16½G, 'Claudia' 12G, All OK." Variety (21 May), p. 51.
Weekly gross for NS is $11,500.

124. Anon. "B'way Still on Upbeat; 'Native Son' Strong Draw at $15,000 in 1st Week, 'Lady,' $31,900, SRO, 'Joey' Big

22G." Variety (2 April), p. 44.
Includes the following report on the first week's performance of NS: "Attracting plenty of attention; starting pace approached $15,000; way house is scaled and several parties at concession the count is very strong."

125. Anon. "B'way Still Tapering Off: Saroyan Moderate 7G, 'Lady' 31½G, 'Hattie,' 30G, Hold Up, 'Rhine' Solid Hit." Variety (30 April), p. 67.
Weekly gross for NS is estimated at $14,500.

126. Anon. "C. Lee in a Trap; Dancers Wanted." New York Daily News (3 August).
Reports the failure of the producers of the play NS to pay for a car given to Canada Lee when the play "first opened and looked like a sure hit."

127. Anon. "Canada Lee." Brooklyn Eagle (25 May), Sec. E, p. 6.
Sketch of Lee as Bigger with caption.

128. Anon. "Canada Lee." Brooklyn Eagle (15 June), Sec. E, p. 6.
Sketch with caption of Lee, Wardell Saunders, Rochester Timmons, and J. Flashe Riley in a scene from NS.

129. Anon. "Canada Lee." Brooklyn Eagle (22 June), Sec. E, p. 7.
Photograph with caption of Lee as Bigger behind bars in the final scene of NS.

130. Anon. "Canada Lee." Brooklyn Eagle (10 August), Sec. E, p. 6.
Photograph with caption of Lee and Anne Burr in a scene from NS.

131. Anon. "Canada Lee." The Chicago Sun (11 December), p. 18.
Photograph with caption of Lee and Evelyn Ellis in a scene from NS.

132. Anon. "Canada Lee and Bigger." The New York Times (30 March), Sec. 9, p. 1.
Biographical sketch of Lee comparing him to Bigger in his energy and violence, but contrasting him with respect to background, talent, and luck.

133. Anon. "Canada Lee and J. Livert Kelly Feted in The Loop." The Chicago Defender (13 December), p. 14.
Describes a party for Lee at the Covenant Club in Chicago.

134. Anon. "Canada Lee and Renya Mitchell." New York Sunday News (16 March).
Photograph with caption of the two actors in a scene from the play NS.

135. Anon. "Canada Lee 'Feels Punchy' as

Stage Star." Brooklyn Eagle (27 March),
p. 15.
   Lee discusses his quick rise to fame.

136. Anon. "Canada Lee Fetes Other Stars
in 'Native Son.'" The Chicago Defender
(29 November), p. 13.
   Describes a cast party given by Lee
   at the Du Sable Hotel.

137. Anon. "Canada Lee Forms Radio
Troupe: Seeks Suitable Air Scripts."
Writers' Journal, 3 (August), 2.
   Announces that Canada Lee will work
   on radio. Mentions his role in NS.

138. Anon. "Canada Lee Gets an Award."
The Indianapolis Recorder (13 December),
p. 13.
   Mentions Lee's role in NS.

139. Anon. "Canada Lee Gets Out of Tight
Spot." The New York Sun (c. 15 August).
   Reports Lee's favorable decision in a
   court case over the automobile given
   to him by the producers of NS. Notes
   that Lee "was getting only $75 a week
   at the height of the successful run
   of the show."

140. Anon. "Canada Lee Gets Tribute."
Norfolk Journal and Guide (21 June), p.
14.
   Account of a radio tribute to Lee on
   which W appeared.

141. Anon. "Canada Lee Gets Two Pages in
'Pic.'" Norfolk Journal and Guide (2
August), p. 14.
   Mentions Lee's role in NS.

142. Anon. "Canada Lee Is Trouping in
Harlem." New York Sunday News (8 July).
   Lee is playing the second scene of NS
   as part of a variety show at the
   Apollo Theater in Harlem.

143. Anon. "Canada Lee Launches Ambitious Radio Drive for Negro Talent." The
New York Age (5 July), p. 10.
   Mentions that "a month ago, over the
   same station [WABC], he played the
   final scene from 'Native Son' in a
   broadcast sponsored by a group of
   Negro celebrities in tribute to his
   great acting in that play."

144. Anon. "Canada Lee Seeks to Boost
Negro Radio Talent." The Philadelphia
Tribune (10 July), p. 11.
   Mentions Lee's success in NS.

145. Anon. "Canada Lee Sees Preview."
The Indianapolis Recorder (16 August),
p. 12.
   Photograph with caption mentioning
   Lee's role in NS and the tour of the
   play.

146. Anon. "Canada Lee Started Out as a
Violinist--Became Jockey, Boxer, Now
He's an Actor." The Indianapolis Record-
er (15 February), pp. 11, 14.
   Reprint of 1941.147.

147. Anon. "Canada Lee Started Out as a
Violinist, Became Jockey, Boxer, Now
He's an Actor." The Philadelphia Tribune
(23 January), p. 14.
   Mentions Lee's desire to play the
   role of Bigger Thomas.
   Reprinted: 1941.146.

148. Anon. "Canada Lee Takes on a New
Job." Brooklyn Eagle (16 March), Sec. E,
p. 6.
   Article on Lee emphasizing his role
   in NS. A sketch of a scene in the
   Thomas flat appears on the same page.

148a. Anon. "Canada Lee to Play 'Othello' Soon; Gets Two Screen Offers." Washington Tribune (14 June), p. 11.
   Mentions the play NS.

149. Anon. "Canada Lee Will Play Role of
'Bigger Thomas' in Stage Version of
Native Son." The Pittsburgh Courier (1
March), p. 20.
   Gives details about Lee and other
   black members of the cast. Notes that
   the novel's Communist message will be
   softened in the play.

150. Anon. "Canada Lee's 4-Starred Car
Backfired." The Philadelphia Tribune (14
August), p. 11.
   Mentions Lee's role in NS and the
   success of the play in Maplewood, New
   Jersey.

151. Anon. "Cast of 'Native Son' Give
Scholarship." The Pittsburgh Courier (14
June), p. 21.
   The scholarship is designated for
   black students at the New Theatre
   school in New York.

152. Anon. "Cast of 'Native Son' Give
Scholarship to New Theatre School."
Sunday Worker (13 July), p. 7.
   The scholarship is designated for
   black students.

153. Anon. "Cast of 'Native Son' Grooms
for Big Opening on Broadway." The Pittsburgh Courier (8 March), p. 5.
   Three photographs with caption.

154. Anon. "Chi B. O. Bounces from Xmas
Slump; 'Purchase' $22,000, 'Papa'
$9,000." Variety (31 December), p. 52.
   Gross for the seventh week of the
   Chicago production of NS is $5,500.

155. Anon. "Chi Legiters in Deep Dip;
'Claudia' Down to $10,000, 'Native Son,'

$4,500." Variety (24 December), p. 51.
    Weekly gross of $4,500 for NS in Chicago creates pressure for closing.

156. Anon. "Chi Looks to New Year's for Full Legit Skid; 'Purchase' $26,500, Tops B. O.s." Variety (10 December), p. 51.
    Weekly gross for NS in Chicago is $7,000.

157. Anon. "Closing Tonight." New York Post (28 June), p. 4.
    Accounces the closing of the play NS after 115 performances.

158. Anon. "A Colored Man's Case History." Cue, 10 (29 March), 30.
    Favorable review of the play NS with special praise for the production by Welles and the acting by Canada Lee. The stage version effectively telescopes the novel, making for "a deeply moving, highly exciting evening."

159. Anon. "Critics Praise Staging of 'Native Son.'" The Chicago Sunday Bee.
    Reprint of 1941.223.

160. Anon. "Critics' Prize Goes to 'Watch on the Rhine.'" The New York Times (23 April), p. 24.
    Notes that Burns Mantle votes for NS. Reprinted: 1972.6.

161. Anon. "Critics Weigh 'Native Son' for Pulitzer Prize." The Baltimore Afro-American (12 April), p. 14.
    Reprint of 1941.223.

162. Anon. "The Daily Worker Celebrates Mike Gold's 25th Anniversary of Literary Activity in the Labor Movement." Daily Worker (1 March), p. 5.
    Advertisement listing W as one of the speakers.

163. Anon. "Danny Kaye Signs for 'Let's Face It.'" The New York Times (27 June), p. 14.
    Notes that the play NS is attempting a tour after closing.

164. Anon. "Designing Settings." Brooklyn Citizen (7 March).
    Notes that James Marcom is the stage designer for NS.

165. Anon. "Dime a Dozen Awards." The Pittsburgh Courier (15 February), pp. 1, 4.
    Questions the social utility of NS and the award of the Spingarn Medal to W. More whites were frightened by Bigger than sympathetic to him.

166. Anon. "Direct Hits on Broadway." New York World-Telegram (12 April), p.

5.
    An artist's sketch of Broadway stars including Canada Lee.

167. Anon. "Distinguished Writers Will Greet Dreiser at Testimonial." Daily Worker (28 February), p. 7.
    W is included.

168. Anon. "Doings of the Race." The Cleveland Gazette (15 February), p. [2].
    Mentions the award of the Spingarn Medal to W.

169. Anon. "Doings of the Race." The Cleveland Gazette (1 March), p. 1.
    Announces the play NS.

170. Anon. "Doings of the Race." The Cleveland Gazette (2 August), p. [2].
    Reports that W is an officer of the American Writers Congress, "said to be Communistic."

171. Anon. "Doings of the Race." The Cleveland Gazette (20 September), p. [3].
    Reports a raise in Canada Lee's wages in the play NS.

172. Anon. "Doings of the Race." The Cleveland Gazette (8 November), p. 1.
    Mentions Canada Lee in the play NS and W as the author of the novel.

172a. Anon. "Doris Dudley Sought for Lead." The New York Times (14 February), p. 14.
    Reports that Dudley is sought to play Mary Dalton in NS.

173. Anon. "Dowling as O'Neill's Star; Sundgaard's 2nd Farm Play; 'Playwright!'" New York Daily News (27 April).
    Notes that NS cost $47,000 to produce, but the ticket sales are good.

174. Anon. "Down in Maplewood." Brooklyn Citizen (28 July).
    Announces the opening of the play NS in Maplewood, New Jersey.

175. Anon. "Drama Book Shelf." The New York Times (30 March), Sec. 9, p. 1.
    Contains a brief notice of the book form of the play NS.

176. Anon. "Drama Books." Unidentified clipping.
    Brief notice of William Kozlenko's anthology American Scenes listing W as a contributor.

177. Anon. "Drama Critics Lavish with Praise of Play." The Houston Defender (5 April).
    Reprint of 1941.223.

178. Anon. "Drama Critics Rave Over Native Son." The Forum [?].
  Reprint of 1941.223.

179. Anon. "Drama Critics Rave Over 'Native Son.'" Unidentified clipping.
  Reprint of 1941.223.

180. Anon. "Drama Dept." The Argonaut, 120 (12 December).
  Review of Burns Mantle's The Best Plays, 1940-1941 mentioning NS.

181. Anon. "Drama in Sensational Colors on Broadway." The Pittsburgh Courier (5 April), p. 21.
  Photographs with captions of two scenes from NS.

182. Anon. "Drama Prizes May Come to 'Native Son.'" The Indianapolis Recorder (12 April), p. 9.
  Reprint of 1941.223.

183. Anon. "Dudley's Unusual Role in 'Native Son'; Zorina to Dance for Britain." New York Daily News (7 February).
  Announces the casting of Doris Dudley as Mary Dalton.

184. Anon. Dust jacket of Native Son: A Play. By Paul Green and Richard Wright. New York: Harper.
  Blurbs and favorable excerpts from reviews on front cover and front inside flap. Biographical sketches of W and Green on back inside flap.

185. Anon. Dust jacket of Sohn dieses Landes. By Richard Wright. Trans. by Klaus Lambrecht. Zurich: Humanitas Verlag.
  Includes an extended quotation from a highly favorable review in the Basel National-Zeitung. Mentions also the impact of the American publication of the novel (NS) and compares W to Dostoevsky.

186. Anon. Dust jacket of 12 Million Black Voices. Photo-Direction by Edwin Rosskam. New York: Viking.
  Blurb on front inside flap and excerpt from Current Biography sketch on back inside flap.

187. Anon. "Eat, Drink, Dance, Be Entertained by 'Cafe Society' 'Porgy and Bess.'"
  Printed invitation to a party on 31 January [1941?] at 6 East 12th Street, New York, sponsored by W and the Council on Negro Culture.

188. Anon. "Editing Book of Short Plays by Living Americans." Charlotte Sunday Observer (27 April), Sec. Three, p. 5.
  Notes that a selection by W will be included in American Scenes, an anthology edited by William Kozlenko.

188a. Anon. "Elmer Carter to Present Spingarn Medal to Richard Wright." Washington Tribune (14 June), p. 9.
  Announces the presentation at the annual convention of the NAACP in Houston on 27 June.

189. Anon. "Ernie Henderson, Chicago's Wealthy Fried Chicken King, Dies in Hospital." The Pittsburgh Courier (26 July), p. 3.
  Reprint 1941.190.

190. _____. "Ernie Henderson, 'Chicken King,' 44, Dies in Chicago." The Philadelphia Tribune (17 July), p. 15.
  Associated Negro Press article mentioning W's use of Henderson's restaurant in NS.
  Reprinted: 1941.189.

191. Anon. "Evelyn Ellis Praised in 'Native Son.'" The Pittsburgh Courier (7 June), p. 21.
  Brief article on the actress playing Bigger's mother.

192. Anon. "Fellow Negro Artists Salute Canada Lee, the Bigger Thomas of Broadway's Native Son, (MBS, Mon., 9:30 p. m.)." PM (c. 8 June).
  Photograph of Lee as Bigger. The caption is the title of this entry.

193. Anon. "Fetes Canada Lee." The Chicago Defender (6 December), p. 14.
  Photograph with caption of Rudy Henderson of The Chicken Shack, who will host the cast of NS on 8 December.

194. Anon. "Film Committee Active in Planning Writers Congress." Daily Worker (15 May), p. 7.
  Mentions W as one of the original signers of the call to the Fourth American Writers Congress.

195. Anon. "First Night." PM (24 March), p. 22.
  Announces the opening of the play NS.

196. Anon. "First Nighters' Guide." Brooklyn Citizen (22 March).
  Announces the opening of the play NS.

197. Anon. "The First Nights." Women's Wear Daily (17 March), p. 21.
  Announces the opening of the play NS.

198. Anon. "The First Nights." Women's Wear Daily (24 March), p. 19.
  Announces the opening of the play NS.

199. Anon. "The First Time on Any Stage!" The New York Age (8 March), p.

10.
Advertisement for the premiere preview of the play NS, a benefit performance for the NAACP.
Reprinted 1941.200.

200. _____. "The First Time on Any
Stage!" New York Amsterdam Star-News (8
March), p. 21.
Reprint of 1941.199.

201. Anon. "Flood of Books, Pamphlets
Aid Fight on Hitlerism." Unidentified
clipping.
TMBV is "one of the most important
books of the year."

202. Anon. "For Native Son." Brooklyn
Citizen (24 February).
Announces the final cast for NS.

203. Anon. "Fourth Writers' Congress
Held." The Publishers' Weekly, 139 (14
June), 2371.
Reports that W was elected a vice-
president of the League of American
Writers and that NS was selected as
the best work of fiction of the past
two years.

204. Anon. "Friends of Soviet Meet." The
New York Times (2 March), p. 37.
W attended a luncheon sponsored by
the American Council on Soviet Relations.

205. Anon "'Gift' Auto Backfires, Canada
Lee Almost Gets Into Real Jail." New
York Daily News (16 August).
Relates the narrow escape of Lee in
the case of the automobile given to
him by the producers of NS.

206. Anon. "Give Us Pat on Back; Canada
Lee Is 'Bigger.'" New York Amsterdam
Star-News (22 February), p. 20.
Claims credit for supporting Lee for
the lead role and notes other details
about the casting of the play.

207. "Gossip of the Rialto." The New
York Times (14 September), Sec. 9, p.
1.
Reports that Bern Bernard and Lionel
Stander, part owners of NS, will
begin another dramatic production.

208. Anon. "The Gossip of Times Square."
The New York Times (2 March), Sec. 9, p.
1.
Announces that NS will open at the
St. James Theatre on 17 March.

209. Anon. "Gotham Critics Rave Over
'Native Son': Critics Praise, Pan 'Native Son.'" The Baltimore Afro-American
(5 April), p. 14.
Reprint 1941.223.

210. Anon. "The Great Chaplin Congratulates Canada Lee." The Pittsburgh Courier (19 April), p. 20.
Photograph with caption of Chaplin,
Lee, and Lionel Stander backstage.

211. Anon. "A Guide to the Outstanding
Fall Books." New York Herald Tribune
Books (7 December), pp. 7-10, 12, 16.
Lists TMBV in the category "The Amer-
ican Scene."

212. Anon. "Guild Selects Lawyer; Cheap
Seats for 'Son.'" Unidentified clipping.
Contains information about the price
of seats at the play NS.

213. Anon. "Harlem Has Its Own Way in
Lead for 'Native Son.'" PM (17 February), p. 22.
Announces the beginning of rehearsals
and mentions Canada Lee.

214. Anon. "Harlem Readies Itself for
'Native Son' Opening." New York Amsterdam Star-News (15 March), p. 20.
Provides biographical sketches of W,
Green, Welles, and Lee, as well as
information about the production and
its cast.

215. Anon. "The Hearsters Gang Up on
Welles' 'Native Son.'" PM (26 March), p.
22.
Hearst's anti-Communist and anti-
Welles bias is reflected in his New
York newspapers' reviews of the play.

216. Anon. "Heat Wilts B'way B. O.s;
'Hattie' $25,000, 'Joey' $17,000,
'Eileen' $12,000, 'Corn' 13G, All Ease
Off." Variety (28 May), p. 51.
Weekly gross for NS is $10,500, the
lowest to date.

217. Anon. "Hellman Play Wins Critic's
Circle Award." New York Daily News (23
April).
Reports the final vote, including one
ballot for NS.

218. Anon. "Hits and Flops of 1940-41."
Variety (4 June), p. 47.
Of three categories--Hits (twelve),
Moderates (four), and Failures
(forty-seven)--NS is placed in the
second.

219. Anon. "Holdovers and New Arrivals."
Sunday Worker (20 April), p. 7.
Contains a photograph with caption of
Charlie Chaplin, Canada Lee, and
Lional Stander backstage after a
performance of NS.

220. Anon. "Holiday Influx Matches Out-
go, But B'way Still Slips Off; 'Rhine'
19G, 'Corn,' $12,000, 'Claudia,'

$11,000." Variety (4 June), p. 50.
  With another weekly gross of
  $10,500, NS is "figured to stick
  indefinitely."

220a. Anon. "Hollywood in Bronze." Washington Tribune (19 April), p. 12.
  Mentions briefly the play NS.

221. Anon. "Houston Awaits Conference." The Crisis, 48 (June), 194-195.
  Mentions the award of the Spingarn Medal to W.

222. Anon. "How Other Critics Felt About 'Native Son.'" PM (25 March), p. 21.
  Quotes from reviews of the play by Brooks Atkinson, Richard Watts, Jr., and Burns Mantle.

223. Anon. "Hurrah for 'Native Son' Say All the Critics--Except Hearst Paper Men Who See 'Red.'" The Philadelphia Tribune (3 April), p. 14.
  Associated Negro Press article on the mainly favorable critical response to the play. It is in the running for the Pulitzer Prize and awards from the New York Drama Critics' Circle and the Playwrights' Company.
  Reprinted: 1941.159, 161, 177, 178, 179, 182, 209, 309, 363, 390, 602, 603, 624.

224. Anon. "If Bigger Wasn't Black and If He Had Money and If They'd Let Him Go to Aviation School, He Could Fly." PM (7 May), p. 12.
  Reprints the conversation between Bigger and Gus in Book One of NS. A headnote uses the excerpt to protest discrimination against blacks in the military services and in defense industries.

225. Anon. "In the Name of Justice." New Masses, 41 (4 November), 22.
  Notes that W endorses a conference in New York to free Earl Browder from prison.

226. Anon. "Individual Nominations of the Nation's Book Reviewers." The Saturday Review of Literature, 24 (26 April), 6-7.
  Reports that NS was nominated for the Pulitzer Prize in fiction by Robert Barlow of Paul Black Papers.

227. Anon. "Inside Stuff--Legit." Variety (19 March), p. 50.
  Includes discussion of the postponed opening of NS and comment on ticket and seating problems.

228. Anon. "Inside Stuff--Legit." Variety (2 April), p. 42.
  Includes discussion of the reception of NS, especially its biased treatment by the Hearst newspapers, and of ticket pricing policy for the play.

229. Anon. "Inside Stuff--Legit." Variety (16 April), p. 50.
  Notes that Welles decided not to distribute programs for NS until after the performance so that the audience would not light matches and thus spoil the blackouts at the end of each scene.

230. Anon. Investigation of Un-American Propaganda Activities in the United States. Appendix--Part V: Transport Workers Union. Washington: United States Government Printing Office, p. 1625.
  Mentions W as a sponsor in December 1938 of a New Year's Eve Ball of the Non-Sectarian Committee for Political Refugees and as a signer of a statement supporting the Moscow purge trials.

231. Anon. "Japs' Blitz, Xmas Shopping Nick Chi; 'Purchase,' $22,000, 'Claudia,' 11G Dip." Variety (17 December), p. 60.
  Weekly gross for the Chicago production of NS slipped to $6,000, but black patronage was good.

232. Anon. "'Jim Crow Blues' Record Album Tells of Trials of Negro People." Norfolk Journal and Guide (13 September), p. 12.
  Mentions W's "vivid and moving foreword" to the Josh White album.

233. Anon. "Join 'Native Son' Cast." Brooklyn Citizen (26 February).
  Lists five actors who have joined the cast.

234. Anon. "Just Before 'Bigger's Crime Bares.'" Norfolk Journal and Guide (19 April), p. 14.
  Photograph with caption of a scene from the play NS.

235. Anon. "'King Joe' by Richard Wright." Unidentified clipping.
  Prefatory note to the poem states that it was written after the Louis-Nova fight.

236. Anon. "'Lady Exit Speeds 'Hattie' to 26½G as B'way Topper; 'Rhine' Fine 19G." Variety (25 June), p. 42.
  Weekly gross for NS was just over $8,000.

237. Anon. "Largest Representation at Houston Conference." The Crisis, 48 (August), 263-264.
  Mentions the presentation of the Spingarn Medal to W by Elmer Anderson

Carter at the Good Hope Baptist Church. "Wright told the story of his life and urged his hearers to live adventurously."

238. Anon. "Latest Books Received." The New York Times Book Review (6 April), p. 27.
Contains a brief notice of the book version of the play NS.

239. Anon. "Leaders in Labor and Art to Honor Gold." Daily Worker (28 February), pp. 1-2.
W, "America's greatest Negro author," will be one of the speakers honoring Mike Gold on 2 March.

240. Anon. "Lee May Act 'Othello.'" Unidentified clipping.
Also mentions Welles's "plans to organize this season a Chicago company for 'Native Son.'"

241. Anon. "'Let's Free Browder Now.'" New Masses, 40 (16 September), 20.
Mentions W as a signer of a petition sponsored by Citizens Committee to Free Earl Browder.

242. Anon. "Lillian Hellman Play Is Critics' Choice for 1941." New York Herald Tribune (23 April), p. 18.
Notes that NS received one vote, that of Burns Mantle.

243. Anon. "Lionel Stander." PM (9 June), p. 22.
Photograph with caption of the angel for NS.

244. Anon. "Lionel Stander, Impresario." PM (2 April), p. 22.
Notes Stander's major financial investment in the play NS.

245. Anon. "Little Theater's Opening Play Among Year's 10 Best." The Charlotte Observer (30 November), p. 24.
Review of Burns Mantle's The Best Plays of 1940-1941 mentioning NS.

246. Anon. "Looking Over Defender's Files Democratic Confab . . . Richard Wright." The Chicago Defender (4 January), p. 7.
Includes a photograph of W, who is mentioned in the caption.

247. Anon. "Louisville Editor Sounds Call for Real Democracy in U. S. A." The Pittsburgh Courier (28 June), pp. 1, 4.
Article on the NAACP convention in Houston mentioning the award of the Spingarn Medal to W.

248. Anon. "'Mamba's Daughter,' 'Native Son' Revived." Norfolk Journal and Guide

(9 August), p. 15.
Announces the revival of NS at the Windsor Theatre in the Bronx and comments on the presentation of the second act in the Apollo Theatre in Harlem.

249. Anon. "March Openings on Broadway Stages." New York Post (1 March), p. 4.
Includes mention of NS.

250. Anon. "Martha Foley Picks Up the Torch of Literature for Edward J. O'Brien." New York Post (11 March), p. 3.
Lists W as a writer first published in Story.

251. Anon. "May Get Part in 'Native Son.'" The Pittsburgh Courier (8 March), p. 3.
Photograph with caption of the actress Alma Forrest.

252. Anon. "MGM May Produce Revised 'Native Son.'" The Baltimore Afro-American (12 April), p. 13.
Associated Negro Press article on plans for a film version. "The story would be changed somewhat to replace the racial theme with an indictment of slum conditions and their result."

253. Anon. "Micheaux Writes New Novel But Doubts Viewpoint of the Whites." The Chicago Defender (6 September), p. 14.
In this interview, Oscar Micheaux argues that the novel NS would not be feasible for filming because "its vile horror; its sordid and distorted preamble of hatred" would elicit censorship. Its sensational elements account for its popularity.

254. Anon. "Mike Gold Celebration Keeps 'Daily' Staff Busy." Daily Worker (27 February), p. 1.
W will be one of the speakers at the event on Sunday, 2 March.

255. Anon. "More Notes About the Broadway Plays and Playhouses." The New York Times (27 April), Sec. 9, p. 3.
Includes a photograph with caption of the scene from NS with Bigger and the reporter in the furnace room.

256. Anon. "More U. S. Writers Answer Soviet Plea." People's World (15 October), p. 5.
Reports that W has issued a statement supporting the Soviet people in response to an appeal from Alexander Fadeyev.

257. Anon. "Mother and Son." Sunday Worker (23 November), Sec. 2, p. 6.
Photograph with caption from TMBV to

accompany Ben Davis, Jr.'s review of E. Franklin Frazier's The Negro Family in the United States.

258. Anon. "Mrs. Walter S. Poor Jr. Is Hostess at Tea Today." New York Herald Tribune (29 April), p. 21.
    The event is "for a group of young women who are forming a junior committee to assist in a benefit performance of the play 'Native Son' on 22 May for the Colored Orphan Asylum and Association for the Benefit of Colored Children in the City of New York."

259. Anon. "NAACP Sponsors First Broadway Showing of 'Native Son' March 13." The New York Age (1 March), p. 10.
    Mentions the names of black actors in the cast.
    Reprinted: 1941.260, 261.

260. Anon. "NAACP Sponsors 'Native Son' in B'way Showing." New York Amsterdam Star-News (8 March), p. 21.
    Reprint of 1941.259.

261. Anon. "N. A. A. C. P. to Sponsor First Showing of Wright's 'Native Son.'" The Pittsburgh Courier (1 March), p. 21.
    Reprint of 1941.259.

262. Anon. "Nation Pays Tribute to 'Bigger Thomas' of the Stage." The Chicago Defender (21 June), National edition, p. 20.
    Account of the radio tribute to Canada Lee. W was one of the participants.

263. Anon. "Native Son." Brooklyn Citizen (26 July).
    Announces the opening of the play in Maplewood, New Jersey.

264. Anon. "Native Son." Life, 10 (7 April), 94-96.
    Amply illustrated notice of the play. "As a play, Native Son is less a story of race prejudice, more the bare melodrama of a Negro, Bigger Thomas, who unwittingly murders a white girl. But as such, it is reported in highly imaginative theatrical terms." Canada Lee's performance is praised.

265. Anon. "Native Son." New York Post (31 May), p. 4.
    Advertisement for the play with quotations from four reviews.

266. Anon. Native Son. New York: The New York Theatre Program Corporation, 16 pp.
    Playbill for the original production at the St. James Theatre.

267. Anon. "Native Son." The New York Sun (26 March), p. 27.
    Large advertisement for the play with quotations from six reviews.

268. Anon. "Native Son." The New York Times (26 March), p. 21.
    Harper's advertisement for the book version of the play and for the novel, with seven favorable statements by reviewers of the play.

269. Anon. "Native Son." New York World-Telegram (15 March), p. 7.
    Photograph with caption of a scene from the play in which Bigger is lighting Mary's cigarette.

270. Anon. "Native Son Adds Five." New York World-Telegram (26 February), p. 21.
    Reports that five actors have been added to the cast.

271. Anon. "'Native Son' and Others Are Listed to Open This Week." The New York Times (23 March), Sec. 9, p. 1.
    Announcement including four photographs of scenes from the play.

272. Anon. "'Native Son' as Drama Is Real Broadway Theatre." The Chicago Defender (22 March), p. 11.
    Favorable review noting some unevenness but generally praising Canada Lee's performance. W's character embodies "the dejection and desperation, the stunted expression of a considerable part of the Negro race."

273. Anon. "'Native Son' as Play to Begin Rehearsals." The Chicago Defender (22 February), National edition, p. 21.
    Mentions the producers, Canada Lee, and the offer of a role to Doris Dudley.

274. Anon. "Native Son Attracts Many Out of Towners." Unidentified clipping (1 May).
    Reports that NS is a favored entertainment by visitors to New York.

275. Anon. "'Native Son' Author Is New Spingarn Medalist." The Chicago Defender (8 February), National edition, pp. 1-2.
    Quotes from citation for the award and W's response, names the award committee, and reviews W's career with emphasis on NS.

276. Anon. "'Native Son' Author Wins High Award." The Philadelphia Tribune (6 February), p. 19.
    On the award of the Spingarn Medal. Includes citation and W's statement of acceptance.

277. Anon. "'Native Son' Author Writes on Negro Life." Unidentified clipping.
Reports that W and Edwin Rosskam are at work on a thirty-thousand-word commentary on black life in America.

278. Anon. "'Native Son' Back at the Flatbush." Brooklyn Eagle (3 September), p. 8.
Announces the opening on 2 September and mentions the success of the earlier engagement at the Flatbush Theater. A photograph of Anne Burr also appears on this page.

279. Anon. "'Native Son' Benefit Show to Aid Orphans." The Indianapolis Recorder (17 May), p. 3.
Associated Negro Press article on the benefit to aid the Colored Orphan Asylum at Riverdale, New York.

280. Anon. "'Native Son' Boasts Several Good Actors." The Chicago Defender (22 November), p. 9.
Urges attendance at the play and praises the acting of Evelyn Ellis.

281. Anon. "Native Son Booked." New York World-Telegram (28 July), p. 10.
Announces openings of the play in the Bronx and Brooklyn.

282. Anon. "Native Son by Paul Green and Richard Wright." The Argonaut (29 May?).
Favorable notice of the book version of the play.

283. Anon. "'Native Son' by Richard Wright and Paul Green." New Masses, 38 (18 March), 29.
Advertisement for the play.

284. Anon. "'Native Son' Canada Lee at A. C. Pier." Philadelphia Public Ledger (16 August).
Favorable review with plot summary of a performance in Atlantic City.

285. Anon. "'Native Son' Cast Is Given Honor Party." Unidentified clipping.
Associated Negro Press report of a party at the Mimo Club given by the American Negro Theatre.

286. Anon. "'Native Son' Cast Lives the American Way." The Pittsburgh Courier (11 October), p. 21.
Photograph with caption of the cast before departing for Detroit. While in Pittsburgh, the interracial cast stayed at a black-owned hotel.

287. Anon. "'Native Son' Clicks in St. Louis But Segregation Remains Intact." The Pittsburgh Courier (8 November), p. 22.
Reports that black members of the

audience were segregated in the balcony of the American Theater, and Canada Lee could not find a place to eat in downtown St. Louis.

288. Anon. "Native Son Clicks on Road Tour." The Philadelphia Tribune (28 August), p. 11.
Notes success of the play in Maplewood, New Jersey, the Bronx, and Brooklyn.

289. Anon. "'Native Son' Closes After 114 Performances." The Pittsburgh Courier (5 July), p. 21.
Points out the success of the play in conveying a social message, making Canada Lee famous, and increasing the fame of Orson Welles. Mentions the scheduled fall tour, indicating cast changes. A photograph of Lee and Hattie McDaniel also appears on this page.

290. Anon. "'Native Son' Closes Run." The Chicago Defender (12 July), p. 11.
Announces the closing of the play and Canada Lee's plans and activities.

291. Anon. "'Native Son' Closes, $30,000 in the Red." The Philadelphia Tribune (10 July), p. 11.
Notes that sex and radicalism offended some. "Colored playgoers, expected to offer much help, could not meet the prices for the show and only about 15 per cent of the total attendance consisted of Negroes."

292. Anon. "Native Son Closes, $36,000 in the Red." Unidentified clipping.
Praises the theatrical genius of Orson Welles. The critics can break a play, but they cannot make one.

293. Anon. "'Native Son' Closing." PM (26 June), p. 22.
Announces the closing of the play on Saturday after 115 performances.

294. Anon. "'Native Son' Comes to Chicago's Loop Soon." The Chicago Defender (1 November), p. 11.
Announces the opening of the play at the Studebaker Theater on 10 November. "The play is one of the best ever to hit the legit stage."

295. Anon. "'Native Son' Comes to Flatbush Stage." Brooklyn Eagle (12 August), p. 4.
Announces the opening of the play on 12 August. Advance ticket sales have been large.

296. Anon. "'Native Son' Comes to the Stage." The New York Times (16 March), Sec. 9, p. 3.

Photograph with caption of Orson Welles, Canada Lee, and Anne Burr at rehearsal.

297. Anon. "'Native Son' Excites Broadway: Robeson or Ingram to Play Leading Role." The Philadelphia Tribune (20 February), p. 14.
    Mainly concerns the casting and production of the play. Mentions talk of filming the novel, "but the obstacles seem to [sic] great to overcome."

298. Anon. "'Native Son' for Flatbush Starring Canada Lee." Brooklyn Eagle (7 August), p. 6.
    Announces the opening of the play in Brooklyn.

299. Anon. "'Native Son' Gets Put Over Again." Brooklyn Eagle (19 March), p. 10.
    Announces postponement of the opening of NS, now rescheduled for 24 March.

300. Anon. "'Native Son' Grosses $9,000 in Atlantic City." Norfolk Journal and Guide (6 September), p. 15.
    The play had a very successful week's run, including five matinees.

300a. Anon. "'Native Son' Had Deficit of $36,000 When It Closed." Washington Tribune (12 July), p. 11.
    Reviews briefly the financial history of the play.

301. Anon. "'Native Son' Has No Intermissions." New York Post (15 March), p. 4.
    Mainly a biographical sketch of W and an account of his career, with quotations. A drawing of a scene from the play also appears.

302. Anon. "'Native Son' Here March 17." Unidentified clipping.
    Announces the opening of the play.

303. Anon. "'Native Son' Hits Broadway in Premiere on March 13th." Norfolk Journal and Guide (8 March), p. 12.
    Announces the benefit performance for the NAACP, giving some details about the production and the cast.

304. Anon. "'Native Son' in Braille So Blind Can Read It." The Philadelphia Tribune (27 March), p. 10.
    The work is available for blind readers at the Free Public Library of Philadelphia and the Parkway (Department for the Blind).

305. Anon. "'Native Son' in Drama on Broadway March 13." The Chicago Defender (1 March), National edition, p. 20.
    Reports the production of the play.

306. Anon. "'Native Son' in Jersey." The Pittsburgh Courier (2 August), p. 20.
    Announces the opening of the summer tour of the play in Maplewood.

307. Anon. "'Native Son,' in Red for 36G, Closes." Variety (2 July), p. 48.
    Analyses reasons for the production's loss of money despite "moderate success" at the box office and critical acclaim. Some readers of the novel, especially women, could not tolerate on stage interracial episodes involving Mary Dalton and Bigger. Other people stayed away because of the work's radicalism.

308. Anon. "'Native Son' in the Bronx Next Week." New York Post (2 August), p. 7.
    Announces the opening of the play at the Windsor Theatre.

309. Anon. "'Native Son' Is Studied for Drama Award." The Chicago Defender (c. 12 April).
    Reprint of 1941.223.

310. Anon. "'Native Son' Lures Gotham Visitors." Norfolk Journal and Guide (3 May), p. 3.
    Notes the demand of persons outside of New York for tickets to the play.

311. Anon. "'Native Son' Maplewood's Biggest Drama." New York Daily News (4 August).
    Notes that the Maplewood Theatre production of NS outdrew a production of Twelfth Night.

312. Anon. "'Native Son' May End Its Stay Early." The Chicago Defender (19 April), p. 13.
    Notes prediction of critics that the run of the play will be short.

313. Anon. "'Native Son' Misses Out in N. Y. Critics' Balloting." The Philadelphia Tribune (1 May), p. 14.
    Announces the results and analyzes the balloting for the New York Drama Critics Circle Award.

314. Anon. "'Native Son' Notes." New York Amsterdam Star-News (22 March), p. 20.
    Points out how rapidly the play went into rehearsal.

315. Anon. "'Native Son' Notes." New York Amsterdam Star-News (29 March), p. 20.
    Miscellaneous notes on the production and its premiere. A photograph from the play also appears on this page.

316. Anon. "'Native Son' Opening Delayed

for Third Time." Norfolk _Journal_ _and_ _Guide_ (29 March), p. 15.
> Notes that "in theatrical circles, the play has been facetiously retitled 'Native Grandson' because of the delay."

317. Anon. "'Native Son' Opening Is Postponed." _The_ _Pittsburgh_ _Courier_ (22 March), p. 21.
> Announces that the opening is set for 22 March "after two benefit previews and several changes."

318. Anon. "'Native Son' Opening Next Monday Evening." _New_ _York_ _Post_ (18 March), p. 6.
> Announces a postponement.

319. Anon. "Native Son Opening Off Till Wednesday." _PM_ (16 March), p. 15.
> Orson Welles decided that the play needed more polishing.

320. Anon. "Native Son Panel Topic." _The_ _Indianapolis_ _Recorder_ (26 April), p. 4.
> The novel will be discussed at the Mt. Zion Baptist Church on 29 April, with one speaker defending and another attacking it.

321. Anon. "'Native Son' Plan Benefit Performance in Chicago Nov. 10." _The_ _Chicago_ _Defender_ (25 October), p. 26.
> Announces a performance of the play at the Good Shepherd Community Center arranged by Horace Cayton. Notes that "when in Chicago recently, Richard Wright stayed at the center two weeks while gathering material for a new book."

322. Anon. "'Native Son,' Play Set 'Before April.'" _The_ Baltimore _Afro-American_ (15 February), p. 14.
> Announces the production.

323. Anon. "'Native Son' Play Shows Signs of a Broadway Sellout." _The_ _Chicago_ _Defender_ (15 March), National edition, p. 20.
> The inference is drawn from the good sale of tickets for the NAACP benefit performance.

324. Anon. "'Native Son' Premiere to Be Church Benefit." _The_ _Chicago_ _Defender_ (8 November), p. 11.
> The Church of the Good Shepherd will handle the advance ticket sales and receive the proceeds.

325. Anon. "'Native Son' Returns for 2d Flatbush Week." _Brooklyn_ _Eagle_ (27 August), p. 9.
> Notes the excellent attendance.

326. Anon. "'Native Son' Smashes Record

in Bronx Run." Norfolk _Journal_ _and_ _Guide_ (23 August), p. 15.
> Comments on the popularity of the revival of the play and analyzes the reasons for it.

327. Anon. "'Native Son' Sold?" New York _Daily_ _News_ (2 July).
> Reports a rumor that Jules Leventhal has bought the play.

328. Anon. "'Native Son' Soon to Reach the Broadway Stage." _New_ _York_ _Post_ (15 March), p. 4.
> Sketch of a scene from the play with caption noting that it will open at the St. James Theatre on Wednesday.

329. Anon. "'Native Son' Stands Chance of Winning Drama Critics' Award." _Philadelphia_ _Tribune_ (10 April), p. 14.
> Speculates on the play's chances to win the New York Drama Critics Circle Award, the Sidney Howard Memorial Prize, and the Pulitzer Prize.

330. Anon. "'Native Son' Star to Help Kiddies." _The_ _Chicago_ _Defender_ (6 December), p. 14.
> Photograph with caption of Canada Lee and Thomas Anderson visiting a day nursery in Chicago for black children.

331. Anon. "'Native Son' Starts Run Soon on Broadway; Cast Is Completed." _New_ _York_ _Amsterdam_ _Star-News_ (1 March), p. 21.
> Lists the leading members of the cast and announces the opening for 17 March.

332. Anon. "'Native Son' Subject of Ben Davis Lecture at Forum Tomorrow." _Daily_ _Worker_ (1 April), p. 7.
> Announces his lecture on both the novel and the play at the University Heights Book and Play Club.

333. Anon. "Native Son Takes with the Patrons." _The_ _Chicago_ _Defender_ (3 May), National edition, p. 20.
> Cites the success of the play: "scores of persons outside of New York have been writing in to the management of Harlem's Hotel Theresa requesting tickets for the play along with room reservations."

334. Anon. "'Native Son' $10,000, Stronger in Chi.; 'Claudia' $13,000, Still Holding Pace." _Variety_ (3 December), p. 60.
> Gross for the third week of _NS_ in Chicago makes it look "capable of staying around."

335. Anon. _Native_ _Son:_ _The_ _Playbill_. New

York: The New York Theatre Program Corporation, 20 pp.

Includes comments by W disclaiming special pleading. The play depicts actual social forces at work. W thanks Orson Welles and Bern Bernard for their help in the production. The pamphlet also contains scenes from the play, the dramatis personae, synopsis of scenes, and other information.

336. Anon. "'Native Son' to Appear in Mound City." The Pittsburgh Courier (25 October), p. 21.

Announces the opening of the play in St. Louis for a week's run beginning 27 October.

337. Anon. "Native Son to Be Shown on Sunday." The Pittsburgh Courier (12 April), p. 20.

Comments on the intense interest in the play and mentions Orson Welles's aborted plan to record a production. Reprinted: 1941.525.

338. Anon. "'Native Son' to Close Saturday." New York Post (26 June), p. 8.

Announces the closing of the play after 115 performances.

338a. Anon. "'Native Son' to Have First Showing on Broadway Stage Mar. 13, NAACP to Sponsor." Washington Tribune (1 March), p. 11.

Lists the cast and gives information about authorship, production, and tickets.

339. Anon. "'Native Son' to Open Monday." New York Daily Mirror (11 March).

Lists the four actors who complete the cast of the play.

340. Anon. "'Native Son' to Play Return Run at Windsor." New York Post (18 August), p. 9.

Announces the opening of NS for a week's run at a theater in the Bronx.

341. Anon. "'Native Son' to Show in Chicago Center." The Philadelphia Tribune (25 October), p. 15.

Concerns the benefit performance on 10 November at Horace Cayton's Good Shepherd Community Center.

342. Anon. "'Native Son' Was $36,000 'In Red' When It Closed." The Pittsburgh Courier (12 July), p. 20.

Discusses the play's financial problems and comments on its reception, claiming that Harlemites objected to the unfavorable presentation of the race and to the flaunting of white resentment of interracial stage productions. Mentions also a Harlem per-

formance at the Apollo Theater of two scenes from the play. A photograph of Canada Lee appears on this page.

343. Anon. "'Native Son' Will Tour Tank Towns." The Pittsburgh Courier (19 July), p. 21.

Notes summer tour beginning on 28 July in Maplewood, New Jersey, and predicts trouble with censors for scheduled performances in Boston and Chicago.

344. Anon. "'Native Son' Wins Award for Novel." The New York Times (8 June), p. 46.

Announces that NS was chosen by the fourth American Writers Congress as the outstanding American novel of the year. W was a speaker at the Congress.

345. Anon. "'Native Son' Wins Praise from Fighter in Red Army." Sunday Worker (9 November), Sec. 2, p. 6.

Notes interest in the Russian translation of NS conveyed in a letter to W from Rokotov, editor of International Literature. In addition to mention of reviews, the article contains a letter to W from a Soviet soldier named Grigory Narizhory.

346. Anon. "'Native Son' Wins Spingarn Medal for Richard Wright." New York Amsterdam Star-News (8 February), p. 3.

Reports that W's acceptance speech was an exceptional statement.

347. Anon. "'Native Son' Writes an Editorial." The Indianapolis Recorder (21 June), pp. 9, 16.

Reprint of 1941.347a.

347a. Anon. "'Native Son' Writes an Editorial." Washington Tribune (14 June), p. 6.

Prefatory note to excerpts from "What We Think of Their War," W's speech at the Fourth American Writers' Congress.

Reprinted: 1941.347.

348. Anon. "Negro Native Son on His Own Race." The Philadelphia Inquirer (12 November), p. 25.

Favorable notice of TMBV, a "beautifully and passionately written book." W's message is "Let my people go."

349. Anon. "Negro Theatre Fetes 'Native Son' Player." The Philadelphia Tribune (3 April), p. 14.

Cocktail party was given for Rena Mitchell, who plays Clara and is a member of the American Negro Theater.

350. Anon. "Negroes Speak Out!" The

Pittsburgh Courier (31 May), p. 3.
W is one of twenty-seven members of
the "initiating group" of this statement denouncing racism and economic,
political, and social discrimination.

351. Anon. "New Books on American History Published for Soviet Readers."
People's Daily World (25 June), p. 5.
Mentions translation and favorable
reception of NS and an abridged version of "How 'Bigger' Was Born."

352. Anon. "New Hits from Harper." The
New York Times Book Review (23 February), p. 18.
Advertisement for Henrietta Buckmaster's Let My People Go quoting W's
blurb.

353. Anon. "New Masses and the Veterans
of the Abraham Lincoln Brigade Offer
'Native Son' by Richard Wright and Paul
Green." New Masses, 38 (4 March), 27.
Advertisement for the play.

354. Anon. "New Masses and Vets Sponsor
'Native Son' Tonight at St. James."
Daily Worker (14 March), p. 7.
Announces a benefit performance.

355. Anon. "New Masses Presents 'Native
Son' by Richard Wright and Paul Green."
New Masses, 38 (11 March), 26.
Advertisement for the play.

356. Anon. "New Photo Book by Richard
Wright and Edwin Rosskam, Nov. 7." Sun-
day Worker (2 November), Sec. 2, p. 4.
Announcement of TMBV.

357. Anon. "New Plays in Manhattan."
Time, 37 (7 April), 76-77.
Includes a favorable review of NS
calling it "by all odds the strongest
drama of the season." The reviewer
claims that "in the lawyer's speech
the play shifts from art to propaganda," but admits that the propaganda is effective. A biographical
sketch of Canada Lee is provided.

358. Anon. "New Show for Song Team; Big
Advance Sale for 'Son.'" New York Daily
News (2 March).
Notes the success of the novel NS as
a factor in creating interest in the
play.

359. Anon. "A New Spingarn Medalist."
The Pittsburgh Courier (8 February), p.
6.
Expresses editorial disapproval of
the selection of W, whose "portrayal
of Negro life and character leaves a
great deal to be desired by Negroes,
regardless of what white people may
think."

360. Anon. "New Wright Pamphlet Hits
Jailing of Browder." Daily Worker (21
April), pp. 1, 3.
Announces the pamphlet Bright and
Morning Star and reprints Ford's
introduction and W's letter to
International Publishers.

361. Anon. "New Wright-Rosskam Book Off
Press Soon." The Pittsburgh Courier (25
October), p. 21.
Associated Negro Press announcement
of TMBV, "fashioned after the famous
book of photographs by Margaret
Bourke-White."

362. Anon. "New Year's Eve Ball for
Refugees from Nazi Terror," in Investi-
gation of Un-American Propaganda Acti-
vities in the United States. Appendix--
Part V: Transport Workers Union.
Washington: United States Government
Printing Office, p. 1657.
Reprint of 1938.70.

363. Anon. "New York Drama Critics Rave
Over Play 'Native Son.'" The Kansas City
Call.
Reprint of 1941.223.

364. Anon. "News and Gossip of the Rialto." The New York Times (6 July), Sec.
9, p. 2.
Notes that the play NS will have a
road tour in the fall sponsored by
Wee and Leventhal. Censorship problems are anticipated in Boston and
Chicago.

365. Anon. "News in the World of Stage
and Screen." Sunday Worker (16 March),
p. 7.
Notes that the Hearst newspapers have
not mentioned the play NS because of
Welles and Citizen Kane.

366. Anon. "News of the Stage." The New
York Times (17 February), p. 10.
Mentions the production of NS, "which
enters rehearsal today."

367. Anon. "News of the Stage." The New
York Times (20 February), p. 24.
Announces the opening date of the
play NS. Anne Burr, not Doris Dudley,
will play the role of Mary Dalton.

368. Anon. "News of the Stage." The New
York Times (5 March), p. 16.
Mentions the presence in the cast of
NS of Ray Collins, Nell Harrison,
Everett Sloan, Paul Stewart, Frances
Bavier, and Helen Martin.

369. Anon. "News of the Stage." The New
York Times (18 March), p. 27.
Announces the second postponement of
the opening of NS.

370. Anon. "News of the Stage." The New York Times (24 March), p. 13.
Announces the opening of NS after two postponements.

371. Anon. "News of the Stage." The New York Times (6 May), p. 25.
Announces that NS will eliminate Wednesday afternoon performances. Matinees will be given on Saturday and Sunday.

372. Anon. "News of the Stage." The New York Times (28 June), p. 11.
Mentions the closing of the play.

373. Anon. "News of the Stage." The New York Times (2 July), p. 18.
Mentions that O. E. Wee and Jules Leventhal are negotiating for the road show rights to NS.

374. Anon. "News of the Stage." The New York Times (8 July), p. 14.
Announces that NS will play in Maplewood, New Jersey, the week of 28 July.

375. Anon. "News of the Studios." The New York Sun (17 February), p. 14.
Mentions Welles's plans for a film in Mexico after the completion of the play NS.

376. Anon. "News of the Theater." New York Herald Tribune (24 February), p. 8.
Announces the final cast of NS.

377. Anon. "News of the Theater." New York Herald Tribune (28 February), p. 12.
Notes the arrival of Paul Green to attend rehearsals of NS.

378. Anon. "News of the Theater." New York Herald Tribune (3 March), p. 8.
Announces the sale of tickets for NS.

379. Anon. "News of the Theater." New York Herald Tribune (7 March), p. 14.
Notes that James Morcom designed the sets for NS.

380. Anon. "News of the Theater." New York Herald Tribune (13 March), p. 16.
Mentions the benefit performance of NS for the NAACP.

381. Anon. "News of the Theater." New York Herald Tribune (15 March), p. 6.
Announces the postponement of the opening of NS.

382. Anon. "News of the Theater." New York Herald Tribune (4 April), p. 17.
Announces that NS will present Sunday matinee and evening performances beginning on 13 April.

383. Anon. "News of the Theater." New York Herald Tribune (10 July), p. 12.
Notes that Canada Lee will perform the second scene of NS in Washington and then in Baltimore.

384. Anon. "News of the Theater." New York Herald Tribune (26 July), p. 6.
Announces the opening of NS in Maplewood, New Jersey.

385. Anon. "News of the Theater." New York Herald Tribune (28 July), p. 6.
Announces the opening of NS in Maplewood, New Jersey, "tonight."

386. Anon. "News of the Theater." New York Herald Tribune (5 August), p. 12.
Announces the opening of NS at the Windsor Theatre in the Bronx.

387. Anon. "News of the Theater." New York Herald Tribune (20 August), p. 12.
Announces that NS will play return engagements in Brooklyn and the Bronx.

388. Anon. "News of the Theater." New York Herald Tribune (26 August), p. 10.
Announces the opening "tonight" of NS at the Windsor Theatre in the Bronx.

389. Anon. "News of the Theaters." New York Herald Tribune (17 February), p. 8.
Announces that Canada Lee will play Bigger Thomas in NS.

390. Anon. "News of the Theaters: New York Critics Rave Over Canada Lee in Native Son." Knoxville East Tennessee News (3 April), p. 7.
Reprint of 1941.223.

391. Anon. "Next Week." The Pittsburgh Courier (c. 15 March).
Advertisement for the article "Harlem Is Raging Over 'Native Son'" by Edgar T. Rouzeau.

392. Anon. "Next Week's Openings." The New York Sun (15 March), p. 26.
Announces the opening of the play NS on Wednesday and lists the cast.

393. Anon. "Next Week's Openings." The New York Sun (22 March), p. 24.
Announces the opening of the play NS on Monday and lists the cast.

394. Anon. "1940 News Names." The Chicago Defender (4 January), p. 8.
Mentions W as the author of a best seller.

395. Anon. "1941's Coming Dramatic Smash." Daily Worker (20 February), p. 7.

Advertisement of ticket sales for the play NS to benefit the Veterans of the Abraham Lincoln Brigade and New Masses.

396. Anon. "No Battered Hat, No Gin Bottle Mark Modern Stage Reporter." New York Herald Tribune (13 April), Sec. VI, p. 2.
Detailed examination of Paul Stewart's performance in the role of the reporter in NS.

397. Anon. "No Drama Award for 'Native Son.'" Norfolk Journal and Guide (3 May), pp. 1-2.
Discusses the balloting for the New York Drama Critics Circle Award.

398. Anon. "Non Fiction at City Library." The Sacramento Bee (29 November), p. 19.
Contains a brief notice of Burns Mantle's play collection mentioning NS.

399. Anon. "'North' Good $9,500, 'Native Son' Fairish $6,000 in 1st Chi Wks." Variety (19 November), p. 59.
In its first week at the Studebaker Theater in Chicago, NS "drew mixed comment and, after strong start on plenty of colored patronage, fell off to finish with $6,000."

400. Anon. "Noted American Writers Denounce Oklahoma Criminal Syndicalism Trials and Book Burnings." Daily Worker (23 June), p. 5.
W is one of the signers of the protest. UTC is one of the books confiscated from an Oklahoma City bookshop.

401. Anon. "Noted Authors Add Names to Writers Congress Call." Sunday Worker (11 May), p. 7.
Mentions W as one of the original signers of the call to the Fourth American Writers Congress.

402. Anon. "Noted Authors Plan Congress Drama Sessions." Daily Worker (14 May), p. 7.
Mentions W as one of the original signers of the call to the Fourth American Writers Congress.

403. Anon. "Noted Writers Talk on Books." The Pittsburgh Courier (22 November), p. 3.
Arna Bontemps and John T. Frederick discussed TMBV and other books on the radio program "Of Men and Books" on 18 November.

404. Anon. "Notes of the Stage." The New York Sun (27 June), p. 14.
Mentions the closing of NS "tomorrow."

405. Anon. "Now a Mercury Production by Orson Welles."
Flyer advertising the opening of the play NS.

406. Anon. "O. Henry Award Stories." The Christian Science Monitor (1 February), Weekly Magazine Sec., p. 10.
Lists W as a contributor.

407. Anon. "Off Again." Brooklyn Citizen (18 March).
Announces the postponement of the opening of the play NS because of scenery changes.

408. Anon. "159 Literary Editors Throughout the Country Vote Eleven Book-of-the-Month Club Selections Among the Twenty Outstanding Books of 1940." New York Herald Tribune Books (9 March), p. 24.
NS is among the books highlighted in this advertisement.
Reprinted: 1941.409.

409. Anon. "159 Literary Editors Throughout the Country Vote Eleven Book-of-the-Month Club Selections Among the Twenty Outstanding Books of 1940!" The New York Times Book Review (9 March), p. 38.
Reprint of 1941.408.

410. Anon. "One of the 12,000,000." Philadelphia Record (9 November), Metropolitan Sec., p. 13.
Photograph from TMBV. The caption is a favorable notice of the book.

411. Anon. "Only 'Lady,' $31,500, 'Rhine,' $18,000, Hold Up in Holy Week on B'way; 'Hattie,' 28G, 'Corn' 14G, Off." Variety (16 April), p. 51.
Weekly report lists proceeds of NS as more than $13,500, "good business for heavy drama."

412. Anon. "Opening Nights." New York Daily Mirror (16 March).
Lists the play NS.

413. Anon. "Opening This Week." PM's Weekly (16 March), p. 46.
Announces the opening of the play NS.

414. Anon. "The Openings." New York Post (15 March), p. 4.
Mentions the opening of the play NS and lists the important members of the cast.

415. Anon. "The Openings." New York Post (22 March), p. 4.
Announces the rescheduling of NS for 24 March. Mentions the producers and the leading members of the cast.

416. Anon. "Openings." The New York Times (16 March), Sec. 10, p. 1.
Announces the opening of the play NS. A large sketch of Canada Lee as Bigger also appears on this page.

417. Anon. "The Openings." The New York Times (23 March), Sec. 9, p. 1.
Announces the opening of the play NS and includes four photographs.

418. Anon. "Opinion and Discussion." PM (8 April), p. 30.
Announces a radio appearance by W at 3:30 p. m. on station WNYC speaking "about the problems of Native Son: From Novel to Play." Includes a photograph of W.

419. Anon. "Orson Welles." Life, 10 (26 May), 108-116.
Includes a photograph of Welles in front of the St. James Theater, where NS is playing.

420. Anon. "Orson Welles Is Sued." The New York Times (25 April), p. 16.
The suit is brought by the Federated Theatre Party Service in a dispute over ticket sales to the play NS.

421. Anon. "Orson Welles to Produce 'Native Son' on Stage." The Chicago Defender (c. 22 February).
Associated Negro press news release noting that rehearsals have begun.

422. Anon. "Orson Welles' 12G in Bag for Stagehands; Everybody's Pretty Blah." Variety (26 March), p. 50.
Discusses production details of the play NS, especially Welles's relentless pace, and other activities of Welles and John Houseman.

422a. Anon. "Panorama of New Books." Book-of-the-Month Club News (January), pp. 13-18.
Contains a notice of O. Henry Memorial Award Prize Stories of 1940 mentioning W (p. 13).

423. Anon. "Paul Stewart." Brooklyn Eagle (22 May), p. 12.
Photograph of Stewart and Canada Lee in a scene from the play NS.

424. Anon. Photograph. Friday.
Photograph of W with caption pointing out that he is one of many excellent black writers.

425. Anon. Photograph. The New York Times (27 April), Sec. 9, p. 3.
Photograph with caption of a basement scene from the play NS.

426. Anon. "Pioneer Lounge Shows Off Entertaining Lee." The Chicago Defender (27 December), p. 11.
Describes a party for the cast of NS on 22 December.

427. Anon. "Pioneer to Honor Cast of Loop's 'Native Son.'" The Chicago Defender (20 December), p. 15.
Mentions a cast party at the Pioneer Lounge in Chicago on 22 December.

428. Anon. "Plan Showing of Play 'Native Son.'" The Chicago Defender (18 October), p. 11.
Horace Cayton has arranged for a benefit performance at the Good Shepherd Community Center on 10 November.

429. Anon. "Plantation Cafe Fetes Players of 'Native Son.'" The Chicago Defender (6 December), p. 12.
Mentions a party given on 1 December for the cast of NS.

430. Anon. "Plays of the Week." New York Herald Tribune (16 March), Sec. VI, p. 1.
Announces the opening of the play NS and includes a sketch of a scene from the play.

431. Anon. "Plays of the Week." New York Herald Tribune (23 March), Sec. VI, p. 1.
Announces the opening of NS on 24 March.

432. Anon. "PM's Calendar of Theater, Art and Music." PM (26 March), p. 21.
Lists NS, calling it "vivid theater," but "less impressive than the book." The listing is repeated in subsequent issues of the newspaper until the play's closing.

433. Anon. "PM's Directory: Plays." PM's Weekly (6 April), p. 43.
Includes a note on NS, which "makes vivid theatre" because of Welles's stagecraft and Lee's performance.

434. Anon. "Poetry Society to Hear Paul Green Thursday." Charleston (S. C.) News and Courier (13 April), Sec. III, p. 2.
Points out that Green wrote the dramatic version of NS.

435. Anon. "Policing Is Not Enough." New York Herald Tribune (11 November), p. 24.
Editorial calling for greater economic opportunity for Harlemites ends with a quotation from W.

436. Anon. "Postponed." New York Daily News (19 March).
Announces the postponement of the opening of the play NS.

437. Anon. "Postponed." New York World-Telegram (18 March), p. 12.
Announces the postponement of the opening of the play NS.

438. Anon. "The Pulitzer Prizes." New Masses, 39 (13 May), 21.
Criticizes the selection committee for not awarding a Pulitzer Prize to W for NS.

439. Anon. "R. Wright Gets Medal." New York World-Telegram (c. 1 February).
Brief notice of the Spingarn award.

440. Anon. "Race Leaders Urge Roosevelt to Free Communist Leader." The Pittsburgh Courier (15 November), p. 5.
W is one of the signers of a letter to the President urging the release of Earl Browder.

441. Anon. "Radio Portrays Lives of Great Negro Figures." Daily Worker (28 April), p. 7.
Mentions an appearance by W as a commentator on a program honoring black singers for 26 July.

442. Anon. "Radio Work Keeps Canada Lee Busy During the Summer Months." The New York Age (2 August), p. 10.
Includes praise of Lee's performance in NS.

443. Anon. "Ray Collins." New York Herald Tribune (27 April), Sec. VI, p. 1.
Sketch of Collins in the role of Boris Max visiting Bigger's cell in the play NS.

444. Anon. "Ray Collins Rejoins Cast of 'Native Son.'" Daily Worker (8 May), p. 7.
Collins returns after an illness.

445. Anon. "Ray Collins That Son of a Critic." Brooklyn Eagle (1 June), Sec. E, p. 6.
Biographical article on the actor who plays Boris Max in the play NS.

446. Anon. "'Rhine' for Fund; Anne Burr to RKO." New York Daily News (17 June).
Concerns the actress who plays Mary Dalton in the play NS.

447. Anon. "'Rhine' $19,000, 'Arsenic' $16,600, 'Corn' 17½G, 'Eileen' 16½G, All Big Despite B'way's Easter W'k Dip." Variety (23 April), p. 51.
Reports that an additional matinee raises the weekly proceeds of the play NS to $15,500.

448. Anon. "Rialto Rambling." Brooklyn Citizen (24 March).

Announces the opening of the play NS.

449. Anon. "Richard Wright."
Mimeographed announcement of a reading by W on 1 April at the Parkway Community House in Chicago.

450. Anon. "Richard Wright." PM (7 May), p. 18.
Photograph with caption.

451. Anon. "Richard Wright." Unidentified clipping.
Favorable review in Spanish of the Spanish translation of NS emphasizing its social import. It will appeal to the casual reader as a detective story, to the more intelligent reader as a social novel, and to the most intelligent as a psychological novel.

452. Anon. "Richard Wright, Author of 'Native Son,' Is 26th Winner of the Spingarn Medal." The New York Age (8 February), p. 1.
Provides the texts of the citation and W's acceptance statement.

453. Anon. "Richard Wright Awarded Spingarn Medal." Opportunity, 19 (July), 216.
Also notes that the Fourth American Writers Congress selected NS as "the most distinguished American novel published since 1939."

453a. Anon. "Richard Wright Awarded Spingarn Medal." Washington Tribune (8 February), p. 9.
News article containing a photograph of W.

454. Anon. "Richard Wright Busy on New Novel About Domestic Workers." The New York Age (24 May), p. 3.
Reports that W conducted interviews with social workers, city officials, and judges, all arranged by his attorney Allan Taub. Relates W's first meeting with Taub in Detroit in 1934.

455. Anon. "Richard Wright Calls Upon Writers to Aid Peace Fight." Daily Worker (11 February), p. 7.
Prefatory note to W's greeting to New Masses. A photograph of W is included.

456. Anon. "Richard Wright Misses Mark in Book on Negroes." New Haven Sunday Register (28 December), Sec. 4, p. 4.
Unfavorable review of TMBV complaining of W's "sin" of oversimplification and his neglect of the talented tenth.

457. Anon. "Richard Wright Receives Medal." The New York Sun (1 February),

p. 25.
Reports the award of the Spingarn Medal.

458. Anon. "Richard Wright Receives Spingarn Medal." The Publishers' Weekly, 139 (8 February), 736.
Gives details about the award itself, the citation, and W's literary career.

459. Anon. "Richard Wright Salutes Foster, Hails Peace Fight." Daily Worker (19 March), p. 5.
Contains a prefatory note and the full text of W's birthday greeting and tribute to William Z. Foster.

460. Anon. "Richard Wright Speaks." Daily Worker (28 February), p. 7.
Announces a lecture on "experimental writing techniques at the Find Yourself in Writing Form [sic] Friday, February 28th."

461. Anon. "Richard Wright Speaks on 'Native Son' WNYC 3:30." Daily Worker (8 April), p. 7.
The announced topic of the radio broadcast is "Native Son, from Novel to Stage Play."

462. Anon. "Richard Wright Speaks on Writing Techniques on Friday, February 28." Daily Worker (18 February), p. 7.
Announces a lecture on experimental techniques in a series sponsored by the League of American Writers.

463. Anon. "Richard Wright Tells the Story of His People." The New York Times (13 November), p. 31.
Advertisement for TMBV.

464. Anon. "Richard Wright the Author Backs Photo Contest." Unidentified clipping.
Reprint of 1940.341. Date uncertain. Perhaps identical to 1940.367.

465. Anon. "Richard Wright to Aid in Writing Negro Book." The Philadelphia Tribune (20 February), p. 4.
Announces the W-Rosskam collaboration.

466. Anon. "Richard Wright to Lecture on Writing at Writer's School." The New York Age (11 January), p. 4.
Announces that W is scheduled to lecture on "How to Find Yourself in Writing" during the school term beginning 20 January.

467. Anon. "Richard Wright to Serve on May Day Committee." Daily Worker (22 March), p. 5.
Announces that W and Ruth McKenney will serve with Rockwell Kent as honorary chairmen. Contains the texts of statements accepting the post by W and McKenney.

468. Anon. "Richard Wright to Speak at Meeting to Honor Mike Gold at Manhattan Center." Daily Worker (14 February), p. 1.
Sketches W's career and mentions the Spingarn Medal. The meeting is scheduled for 2 March.

469. Anon. "Richard Wright Winner of the Spingarn Medal." New York Herald Tribune (1 February), p. 13.
Brief article quoting from the award citation.

470. Anon. "Richard Wright Wins 1940 Spingarn Medal." The Pittsburgh Courier (8 February), p. 2.
Reprint of 1941.501

471. Anon. "Richard Wright Wins the Spingarn Award." Daily Worker (1 February), pp. 1-2.
Quotes the citation and W's statement of acceptance, reviews W's career, comments on sales and background of NS, discusses work in progress, and lists previously published work.

472. Anon. "Richard Wright Working on New Documentary Book." The Philadelphia Tribune (8 November), p. 20.
Favorable announcement of TMBV.

473. Anon. "Richard Wright Writes New Epic on Negro." The Philadelphia Tribune (14 August), p. 11.
Favorable announcement of TMBV, a book "written with fire and passion."

474. Anon. "Richard Wright Writing Another." Brooklyn Eagle (25 May), Sec. E, p. 7.
Mentions W's work-in-progress on domestics and discusses his friendship with his attorney Allan Taub.

475. Anon. "Richard Wright's Story of His People." The Publishers' Weekly, 140 (13 September), 880.
Full-page advertisement for TMBV, scheduled for publication on 27 October.

476. Anon. "Robeson Has 'Blues' Debut." The Pittsburgh Courier (11 October), p. 20.
Photograph with caption of W, Robeson, and Count Basie during the recording of "Joe Louis Blues."

477. Anon. "Robeson Sings 'Louis Blues.'" Unidentified clipping.
Photograph with caption of W and

Robeson recording "Joe Louis Blues."

478. Anon. "<u>Sangre Negra</u>." Unidentified clipping.
Advertisement in a Cuban newspaper for the Spanish translation of <u>NS</u>.

479. Anon. "Saroyan, an Exit and Two Setbacks." <u>PM</u> (19 March), p. 22.
Announces the postponement of the opening of the play <u>NS</u>.

480. Anon. "Saroyan Casting in Own Fashion; Loving, Blair Sign." New York <u>Daily News</u> (27 March).
Notes Metro-Goldwyn-Mayer's interest in the film rights to <u>NS</u>, from which it wishes to eliminate the racial theme.

481. Anon. "The Season of 1940-41 Goes Into the Books." <u>The New York Times</u> (1 June), Sec. 9, pp. 1-2.
Lists the play <u>NS</u> as having eighty-two performances.
Reprinted: 1972.13.

482. Anon. "Series of Readings by Writers Begun." <u>Writers' Journal</u>, 4 (December), 5.
Announces readings of works in progress by W and others sponsored by the League of American Writers.

483. Anon. "Seven Prominent Americans Give Their Point of View." <u>New Masses</u>, 39 (6 May), 15.
Includes the following statement by W: "During these days of war, NEW MASSES gives unique voice and utterance to the aspirations of peace-loving men."

484. Anon. "Shake Down the Stars." <u>Defender</u> (1 March).
Mentions rehearsals and scheduled opening of <u>NS</u>.

485. Anon. "Shop Wise." <u>PM</u> (23 April), p. 26.
Notes that <u>NS</u> is on sale for $1.69 at the 44th Street Book Fair.

486. Anon. "Signs Anne Burr, 'Native Son' Player, for RKO Pictures." <u>Brooklyn Eagle</u> (13 June), p. 13.
Reports that the actress who plays Mary Dalton is going to Hollywood.

487. Anon. "Six Legiters Now Open in Chicago; 'Purchase' $26,500, 'Claudia' 14G, Big." <u>Variety</u> (26 November), p. 59.
The second week's gross for <u>NS</u> in Chicago was $10,000, with the less expensive seats selling out.

488. Anon. "Six Scholarships Offered Negro Writers by Authors' Organization." <u>Daily Worker</u> (30 September), p. 7.
W is one of the sponsors of a project of the Writers' School, which is "hoping to discover new Langston Hughes' [sic] and Richard Wrights."

489. Anon. "The Skies Are High." <u>The San Francisco Chronicle</u> (30 November), This World Sec., p. 18.
Reprints, with caption, a photograph from <u>TMBV</u>.

490. Anon. "Socialites at 'Native Son.'" Unidentified clipping.
Black newspaper lists distinguished members of the audience at the NAACP benefit performance of the play.

491. Anon. "Socialites Preview Latest Broadway Show with NAACP." <u>The Pittsburgh Courier</u> (22 March), p. 10.
Five photographs of notables, including W, who attended the NAACP benefit preview of <u>NS</u>.

492. Anon. "Some Interesting Notes About Books and Authors." <u>Savannah Morning News</u> (4 May), p. 34.
Reports that W contributed a play to William Kozlenko's anthology <u>American Scenes</u>.

493. Anon. "Some Notes on Books and Authors." <u>Buffalo Evening News</u> (15 February), Magazine Sec., p. 7.
Includes results of a "poll of critics conducted by the Book-of-the-Month Club" listing <u>NS</u> fifth after <u>For Whom the Bell Tolls</u>, <u>New England: Indian Summer</u>, <u>Oliver Wiswell</u>, and <u>How Green Was My Valley</u>.

494. Anon. "Some of America's Outstanding Literary Figures." <u>Daily Worker</u> (c. 9 June).
Photograph with caption from Fourth American Writers Congress. W and Dashiel Hammett are featured.

495. Anon. "'Son' Fails." <u>The Chicago Defender</u> (3 May), National edition, p. 20.
Associated Negro Press announcement that <u>NS</u> did not win the New York Drama Critics Circle Award.

496. Anon. "'Son' Next Week in Maplewood: Barn Theatres." New York <u>Daily News</u> (24 July).
Announces the opening of the play <u>NS</u> in Maplewood, New Jersey.

497. Anon. "'Son' Off Till Wed. Evening: Cantor Show." New York <u>Daily News</u> (15 March).
Announces the postponement of the opening of the play <u>NS</u>.

498. Anon. "Soviet Public Welcomes New Books on U. S. History." Daily Worker (17 June), p. 2.
    Reports that the Soviet press has carried favorable reviews of NS.

499. Anon. "Special Events." New York Daily News (13 April).
    Mentions a special matinee of NS.

500. Anon. "'Special Laughter' at Social Evils in Clever Verse." The Hartford Times (28 June), p. 11.
    Review of Howard Nutt's Special Laughter noting W's appreciative introduction.

501. Anon. "Spingarn Award Given Author of 'Native Son.'" Norfolk Journal and Guide (8 February), Home Edition, pp. 1, 10.
    Includes excerpts from the award citation and from W's acceptance statement. Details are given concerning the novel's popularity, the Nixon case, W's career, and the Spingarn award.
    Reprinted: 1941.470, 503.

502. Anon. "Spingarn Award to Richard Wright." The New York Times (1 February), p. 18.
    Quotes from the award citation, explains the background of the award, reviews W's literary career, quotes in full his statement of acceptance, and lists the members of the selection committee. Includes a photograph of W.

503. Anon. "Spingarn Medal Goes to Wright." The Baltimore Afro-American (8 February), pp. 1-2.
    Reprint of 1941.501.

504. Anon. "Spingarn Medalist." The Indianapolis Recorder (22 February), p. 2.
    Photograph of W by Ernest Brooks with caption.

505. Anon. "Spingarn Medalist." The Philadelphia Tribune (6 February), p. 1.
    Photograph of W with caption.

506. Anon. "The Spot News." Soviet Russia Today, 10 (July), 30.
    Mentions a lecture by the critic Startsev, "Soviet authority on contemporary American literature," on NS, Trouble in July, and The Grapes of Wrath.

507. Anon. "St. James Theatre." New York, 1 p.
    Flyer with seating chart and notice that ushers will distribute playbills at the end of the performance.

508. Anon. "St. James Theatre." New York, 1 p.
    Short playbill for NS, "beginning Monday, March 24, 1941."

509. Anon. "St. James Theatre." New York: The New York Theatre Program Corporation, 2 pp.
    Short playbill for NS, "beginning Monday, March 17, 1941."

510. Anon. "Stage Notes." Daily Worker (5 March), p. 7.
    Announces the benefit performance for New Masses and the Veterans of the Abraham Lincoln Brigade on 14 March.

511. Anon. "Stage Notes." Daily Worker (19 April), p. 7.
    Mentions a party honoring the cast of NS at which guests will wear costumes of characters in the play.

512. Anon. "Stage Notes." Daily Worker (10 June), p. 7.
    Reports that "the Cast and Director of the current Broadway hit, 'Native Son,' have presented a scholarship for Negro students to the Scholarship fund of the New Theatre School."

513. Anon. "Stage Notes." Daily Worker (11 June), p. 7.
    Reports that the company of NS took a night off to play softball.

514. Anon. "Stage Notes." New York Amsterdam Star-News (22 March), p. 20.
    Includes critical comment on another New York columnist who claimed that the play NS paralleled "the Strubing-Spell case in Connecticut."

515. Anon. "Stage Notes." The New York Sun (14 June), p. 14.
    Points out that NS will play its one-hundredth performance on 15 June at the St. James Theatre.

515a. Anon. "Stage Verson of 'Native Son' Draws Unanimous Praise of N. Y. Critics." Washington Tribune (5 April), p. 11.
    Quotes from reviews, describes the first scene, and mentions Metro-Goldwyn-Mayer's interest in filming the work.

516. Anon. "Staging Native Son." New York World-Telegram (17 February), p. 11.
    Announces that the play NS will go into rehearsal "this morning."

517. Anon. "Star of 'Son' in Mix-Up Over New Auto Purchase." Norfolk Journal and Guide (23 August), p. 15.
    Reports Canada Lee's legal diffi-

culties in an automobile deal.

518. Anon. "Stars Honor Canada Lee Via Radio." The Pittsburgh Courier (21 June), p. 21.
    Reports that several celebrities honor Lee in a radio tribute. W does so with "down to earth literacy."

519. Anon. "Stars of 'Native Son.'" Daily Worker (27 August), p. 7.
    Photographs with caption of Anne Burr and Canada Lee.

520. Anon. "A Stout Anthology of the Literature of Democracy Announced for Publication." The Galveston Daily News (7 September), p. 21.
    Lists W as a contributor to Bernard Smith's The Democratic Spirit.

521. Anon. "Studebaker--Starts Mon., Nov. 10." The Chicago Defender (1 November), p. 9.
    Advertisement for the play NS. Reprinted 8 November, p. 11.

522. Anon. "Subway Circuit Plays." New York Post (30 August), p. 4.
    Mentions return engagement of NS at the Flatbush Theatre in Brooklyn.

523. Anon. "Subway Circuit Plays." The New York Sun (c. 23 August).
    Mentions the return engagement of NS in the Bronx.

524. Anon. "The Summer Playhouses Present." Brooklyn Eagle (27 July), Sec. E, p. 5.
    Mentions the opening of the play NS in Maplewood, New Jersey.

525. Anon. "Sun. Showing Scheduled for 'Native Son'; Guild Nips Check-Up Disc Plan." The Pittsburgh Courier (19 April), p. 20.
    Reprint of 1941.337.

526. Anon. "Sunday Matinees for 'Native Son'; Theatre Notes." New York Daily News (4 April).
    Announces that Sunday matinees will replace Wednesday matinees.

527. Anon. "Sweetheart in 'Native Son.'" Norfolk Journal and Guide (19 April), p. 14.
    Photograph with caption of Rene [sic] Mitchell, who played Clara in NS.

528. Anon. "Test Your Broadway Learning in This End-of-Season Quiz." PM's Weekly (27 April), pp. 43, 59.
    Includes a question on the play NS.

529. Anon. "Testimonial Dinner and reception for the Hon. Vito Marcantonio." New Masses, 39 (1 April), 29.
    Advertisement listing W as a guest of honor.

530. Anon. "The Theater." New York World-Telegram (15 March), p. 7.
    Brief notice of the opening of the play NS.

531. Anon. "Theater." Newsweek, 17 (5 May), 67.
    Notes that one vote was cast for NS in the annual New York Drama Critics Circle Award contest.

532. Anon. "The Theater: Monday." New York World-Telegram (22 March), p. 6.
    Announces the opening of the play NS and lists the cast.

533. Anon. "Theatre Night." Brooklyn Citizen (29 March).
    Notes that members of the casts of NS and other plays "will be guests at a 'Theatre Night for Peace.'"

534. Anon. "Theatre Party Service Sues Welles-Houseman for 50G on 'Native Son.'" Variety (30 April), p. 65.
    Two promoters bring suit for breach of agreement on block ticket sales.

535. Anon. "Theodore Dreiser Gets Peace Award." The New York Times (7 June), p. 5.
    Mentions W as a speaker at the opening session of the Fourth American Writers Congress.

536. Anon. "They Support the Soviet Union." Unidentified clipping (September).
    Excerpts a cable sent by W to International Literature supporting the Red Army after the Nazi invasion.

537. Anon. "This Week, as Britain Fights to Hold Off Hitler, the U. S. Theater Offers the Following." PM's Weekly (27 April), p. 44.
    Includes a photograph with caption of Canada Lee as Bigger behind bars.

538. Anon. "Three Papers Given at English Session." Greensboro Daily News (6 April), p. A-7.
    Nick Aaron Ford and Sterling Brown mention W in papers delivered at the annual meeting of the black Association of Teachers of English at Bennett College.

539. Anon. "Three Shows Quit Broadway Tonight." The New York Times (15 March), p. 13.
    Contains an explanation that some adjustments after the preview of NS required postponing the opening.

540. Anon. "3,500 Here Pay Rousing Tribute to Mike Gold, Browder Hails Him as Courageous People's Poet." Daily Worker (3 March), pp. 1, 5.
Notes that W was one of the speakers.

541. Anon. "To Honor Canada Lee." The Pittsburgh Courier (14 June), p. 21.
Announces that W and others will participate in a radio broadcast honoring Lee. Comments on the success of the play NS.

542. Anon. "To Publish Mike Gold's New Book on His 25th Anniversary Celebration." Daily Worker (26 February), p. 1.
W will be one of the speakers at the celebration honoring Gold on 2 March.

543. Anon. "Today's the Day The Daily Worker Celebrates Mike Gold's 25th Anniversary of Literary Activity in the Labor Movement." Sunday Worker (2 March), p. 4.
Advertisement listing W as one of the speakers.

544. Anon. ("Bibliotaph"). "Tomes and Titles." The Providence Sunday Journal (16 February), Sec. VI, p. 6.
Notes the award of the Spingarn Medal to W and reviews briefly his career.

545. _____. "Tomes and Titles." The Providence Sunday Journal (15 June), Sec. VI, p. 5.
Brief notice of the issue of Theatre Arts containing Jean Rosenthal's comments on the staging of NS.

546. Anon. "Tomorrow Is 'The Day' for Mike Gold & Friends." Daily Worker (1 March), pp. 1, 5.
Notes that W will be one of the speakers.

547. Anon. "Tour Trouble Looms for 'Native Son.'" The Philadelphia Tribune (17 July), p. 11.
Associated Negro Press article mentioning fear of censorship of the play in Chicago and Boston.

548. Anon. "Trade Notes and Price Changes." The Retail Bookseller, 44 (April), 93-96.
Contains a notice of the dramatization of NS and the version published on 17 March.

549. Anon. "Trade Winds." The Saturday Review of Literature, 24 (10 May), 21.
Three of nine staff members of the magazine favor NS for the Pulitzer Prize.

550. Anon. "'Twelfth Night' Closes March

8." The New York Times (8 February), p. 19.
Includes discussion of the dramatization and production of NS.

551. Anon. "12 Million Black Voices." Philadelphia Public Ledger (12 November).
Brief notice.

552. Anon. "12 Million Black Voices," in Viking Press List. New York: Viking Press.
Favorable publisher's notice of a book that "tells the all important history of the hidden nation within a nation."

553. Anon. "Twelve Million Black Voices, by Richard Wright." Hamilton (Ont.) Spectator (13 December), p. 85.
Brief notice calling the book "a modern Uncle Tom's Cabin" whose poignancy is increased by the photographs.

554. Anon. "12 Million Black Voices. By Richard Wright." The New York Times Book Review (9 November), p. 45.
Brief notice.

555. Anon. "Twelve Million Black Voices by Richard Wright." The Retail Bookseller, 44 (October), 96.
Brief notice stating that W "has written this book as a special project."

556. Anon. "12 Million Black Voices, by Richard Wright and Edwin Rosskam." The New Yorker, 17 (15 November), 110.
Favorable notice calling the book a "burning commentary on three centuries of slavery, persecution, and want. Somewhat oversimplified, perhaps, but a moving and powerful work."

557. Anon. "Twelve Million Black Voices: 'We Want to Share in the March of American Life.'" U. S. Week, 1 (20 December), 17.
Favorable review with special praise for the photographs. Reading this book, the white reader must feel his complicity in the oppression of blacks.

558. Anon. "24 Scholarships Offered in Writers School Contest." Sunday Worker (30 November), Sec. 2, p. 4.
Lists W as one of the judges.

559. Anon. "Two Plays Open Here Next Week." The New York Times (14 March), p. 17.
One of the two is NS.

560. Anon. "Two Premieres Here Next Week." The New York Times (17 March), p. 21.
   Notes the postponement of the opening of NS and explains procedure for exchange of tickets.

561. Anon. "'U. S. Negroes Greet You,' Wright Cables to USSR." Daily Worker (1 September), p. 7.
   Includes the complete text of W's cable and a photograph of the author.

562. Anon. "U. S. Writers Send Greetings to Soviet." Daily Worker (8 October), p. 7.
   W is one greeter.

563. Anon. Unidentified clipping.
   Advertisement for "King Joe."

564. Anon. Unidentified clipping.
   O. Pagani advertisement for "King Joe."

565. Anon. Unidentified clipping (14 March).
   Advertisement of the benefit performance of the play NS on 15 March for the United American Spanish Aid Committee.

566. Anon. Unidentified clipping.
   Announces the publication of TMBV.

567. Anon. Unidentified clipping.
   Favorable notice of TMBV. W tells "with passion and fire the story of his people."

568. Anon. Unidentified clipping.
   Photograph with caption of W and Donald Ogden Stewart on a picket line protesting The Day, a Yiddish newspaper.

569. Anon. Untitled article. Greenwich Press (2 July).
   Lists W as a contributor to O'Brien's The Best Short Stories of 1941.

570. Anon. Untitled article. The New York Times Book Review (4 May), p. 11.
   Notes that W will address the White Mountain Writers Conference of the League of American Writers.

571. Anon. Untitled clipping. Brooklyn Citizen (3 March).
   Announces that tickets are on sale for the play NS.

572. Anon. Untitled clipping. Brooklyn Citizen (12 March).
   Reports the completion of casting for the play NS.

573. Anon. Untitled clipping. Brooklyn Citizen (7 April).
   Announces matinee performances of NS.

574. Anon. Untitled clipping. Brooklyn Citizen (31 October).
   Prepublication notice of TMBV.

575. Anon. Untitled clipping. Durham Morning Herald (c. 29 June).
   Favorable notice of the play NS, which is for inarticulate blacks what An American Tragedy is for inarticulate whites.

576. Anon. Untitled clipping. Lawrence (Mass.) Daily Eagle (28 February).
   Concerns the National Book Award selections. Notes that W spoke to Richard Llewellyn in London by radio.

577. Anon. Untitled clipping. New York Daily Mirror (c. February).
   Mentions the alliance of Thelma Schnee with William Hertz, co-producer of the play NS.

578. Anon. Untitled clipping. New York Daily News (17 February).
   Notes that the play NS has gone into rehearsal and will open the week of 17 March.

579. Anon. Untitled clipping. New York Daily News (20 February).
   Notes that Anne Burr will have the female lead in the play NS.

580. Anon. Untitled clipping. New York Daily News (24 February).
   Notes that one of the backers of the play NS has gone to the theater department of the Music Corporation of America.

581. Anon. Untitled clipping. New York Daily News (12 March).
   Lists the eight actors who complete the cast of NS.

582. Anon. Untitled clipping. New York Daily News (13 March).
   Announces the first of three benefit performances of the play NS.

583. Anon. Untitled clipping. New York Daily News (7 April), p. 37M.
   Notes that Canada Lee has been given an automobile for his performance in NS.

584. Anon. Untitled clipping. New York Daily News (8 April).
   Notes that twenty-one standees attended the Sunday night performance of NS.

585. Anon. Untitled clipping. New York Daily News (16 April).

Notes that Orson Welles wants NS and Citizen Kane to run simultaneously on the same block in New York.

586. Anon. Untitled clipping. New York Daily News (22 April).
Announces Wednesday matinee performances of NS beginning 23 April.

587. Anon. Untitled clipping. New York Daily News (23 April).
After praising NS, New York critics vote for Lillian Hellman's Watch on the Rhine.

588. Anon. Untitled clipping. New York Daily News (3 August).
Photograph of Canada Lee and Anne Burr in a performance of NS at the Windsor Theatre in the Bronx.

589. Anon. Untitled clipping. New York Daily News (11 August).
Announces the opening of NS at the Flatbush Theatre in Brooklyn with the largest advance sale of the summer.

590. Anon. Untitled clipping. New York Daily News (13 August).
Notes that NS broke all attendance records at the Windsor Theatre in the Bronx. There were many standees.

591. Anon. Untitled clipping. New York Daily News (1 September).
Announces matinee and evening performances of NS at the Windsor Theater in the Bronx.

592. Anon. Untitled clipping. New York Daily News (7 September).
Indicates that NS may earn back its $36,000 losses on Broadway from the success of the road show. Canada Lee will earn $400 a week plus percentage.

593. Anon. Untitled clipping. New York Journal-American (c. September).
Announces that TMBV is scheduled for publication in October.

594. Anon. Untitled clipping. Philadelphia Record (c. 10 August).
Brief notice of TMBV.

595. Anon. Untitled clipping. PM (c. 11 February).
Relates an anecdote about an article to be written by W for The New York Times on the dramatization of NS.

596. Anon. Untitled clipping. Sunday Worker (c. March).
Comments on Argentinian reactions to NS and Trouble in July.

597. Anon. Untitled clipping. The Rock-land (Maine) Courier-Gazette (c. 22 March).
Notes the opening of the play NS on Broadway and its publication by Harper's.

598. Anon. "Viking Plans Promotion for a Big Fall List." The Publishers' Weekly, 139 (31 May), 2135-2136.
Notes that W wrote close to 50,000 words in TMBV instead of the 20,000 originally intended.

599. Anon. "Viking Press Announces Forthcoming Book by Richard Wright." Opportunity, 19 (September), 280.
Announces TMBV.

599a. Anon. "'We Are Not Fighting for Enough'--Wright." Washington Tribune (12 July), p. 7.
Quotes from W's speech in Houston accepting the Spingarn Medal.

600. Anon. "The Week Will See Two More Plays Added to the List." The New York Times (16 March), Sec. 10, p. 1.
Announces the opening of NS and includes a sketch of Canada Lee in a scene from the play.

601. Anon. "The Weekly Record." The Publishers' Weekly, 139 (5 April), 1493-1503.
Contains a notice of the published version of the play NS (p. 1496).

602. Anon. "Weigh 'Native Son' for Drama Pries [sic]." Oklahoma City Black Dispatch.
Reprint of 1941.223.

603. _____. "Weigh 'Native Son' for Drama Prizes." Nashville Defender.
Reprint of 1941.223.

604. Anon. "Welles Denies Citizen Kane Depicts Hearst; Threatens to Sue If Movie Isn't Released." New York World-Telegram (12 March), p. 13.
Mentions briefly Welles's direction of NS.

605. Anon. "Welles' Disks of His 'Native Son' Cast Not OK for Sound with Equity." Variety (2 April), p. 1.
Welles rejects his plan to record performances of the play in his absence because of pressure from Actors' Equity.

606. Anon. "Welles Quick with 'Native Son.'" The New York Sun (9 May), p. 30.
Describes the strenuous production style of Orson Welles.

607. Anon. "Welles Will Produce Wright's

'Native Son.'" Norfolk _Journal_ _and_ _Guide_ (1 March), p. 4.
   Brief news item.

608. Anon. "What Canada Lee Thinks of Bigger Thomas." _The_ Baltimore _Afro-American_ (29 March), p. 14.
   In an exclusive interview, Lee states that he wants his audience to pity Bigger as a social victim of unemployment and crowded living conditions.

609. Anon. "When 'Bigger' Thomas Gets Job as Butler." Norfolk _Journal_ _and_ _Guide_ (19 April), p. 14.
   Photograph with caption of a scene from the play _NS_.

610. Anon. "White Mountain Writers Conference."
   Flyer noting that W will be a special lecturer at a conference in Jefferson, New Hampshire, to be held from 18 August to 2 September.

611. Anon. "Wide Range of Books on Fall List." _Sunday_ _Worker_ (28 September), Sec. 2, p. 4.
   Contains an announcement of _TMBV_.

612. Anon. "Will Bigger Thomas Turn Canada Lee?" _The_ Baltimore _Afro-American_ (12 April), p. 14.
   Concerns the remarkable success achieved by the actor.

613. Anon. "Willkie, Hutchins: Call Act 'Outrageous' NAACP Protest Sharp." _The_ _Indianapolis_ _Recorder_ (21 June), pp. 1, 8.
   Mentions the Award of the Spingarn Medal to W.

614. Anon. "Win Chicago's Loop." _The_ _Chicago_ _Defender_ (13 December), p. 15.
   Photograph with caption of Canada Lee and Rena Mitchell in a scene from the play _NS_.

615. Anon. "Worth Saving." _The_ _Christian_ _Science_ _Monitor_ (19 July), Weekly Magazine Sec., p. 10.
   Lists W as a writer recognized by Edward J. O'Brien.

616. Anon. "Wright Aids Writer." _The_ Baltimore _Afro-American_ (15 February), p. 14.
   Reports the W-Rosskam collaboration. The projected length of the commentary is 30,000 words.
   Reprinted: 1941.617, 620, 623.

617. Anon. "Wright Collaborates in Book on Negro Life." Unidentified clipping.
   Reprint of 1941.616.

618. Anon. "Wright, Richard." _The_ _Publishers'_ _Weekly_, 140 (8 November), 1864.
   Brief notice of _TMBV_, which emphasizes current conditions among "submerged" groups.

619. Anon. "Wright, Richard and Green, Paul. Native son (the biography of a young American): a play in ten scenes . . . from the novel by Richard Wright." _The Booklist_, 37 (15 May), 435.
   Brief notice calling the play "full of suspense, excitement, and tragedy," but finding it "less moving" than the novel.

620. Anon. "Wright Will Collaborate on New Book." _The_ _Pittsburgh_ _Courier_ (15 February), p. 13.
   Reprint of 1941.616.

621. Anon. "Wright Wins Award of Spingarn Medal." _The Christian_ _Century_, 58 (12 February), 238.
   Notes that on the same day that W won the award, Joseph Spell, a black butler, was acquitted of rape and Joe Louis won a championship prizefight.

622. Anon. "Wright Wins '40 Spingarn Award." _The_ _Chicago_ _Bee_ (9 February), p. 1.
   News article.

623. Anon. "Wright Works on Non-Fiction Book." Unidentified clipping (c. 15 February).
   Reprint of 1941.616.

624. Anon. "Writer Says 'Native Son' Is in Running for Drama Prize." _The_ Kansas City _Call_ (11 April).
   Reprint of 1941.223.

625. Anon. "Writers and Books: Wright Gets Award." _Pasadena_ _Star-News_ (5 April), p. 6.
   Announcement of the award of the Spingarn medal.

626. Anon. "Writers and the War." _New_ _Masses_, 40 (5 August), 23.
   W is one of 130 signers of this "expression of solidarity in the fight against fascism" by the League of American Writers.

627. Anon. "Writers Congress Adopts Firm Anti-War Program." _Daily_ _Worker_ (9 June), pp. 1-2.
   Notes that W has been elected one of seven vice-presidents of the League of American Writers and that _NS_ has been chosen "as the best novel since the last Congress."

628. Anon. "Writers Congress Holds Peace Rally Friday." _Daily_ _Worker_ (4 June), p.

4.

Announces that W will speak at the Fourth American Writers Congress on 6 June.

629. Anon. "Writers League Plans Summer Conference." Daily Worker (14 March), p. 7.

Announces W's scheduled appearance at the White Mountain Writers Conference in New Hampshire.

630. Anon. "Writers Offer Talents in War Against Axis." Daily Worker (10 December), p. 7.

Mentions W as one of the vice-presidents of the League of American Writers.

631. Anon. "Writers Open Congress with Peace Rally." Daily Worker (7 June), pp. 1-2.

Includes extensive quotations from W's speech against war.

632. Anon. "Writers Rally to Feature Peace Pageant." Daily Worker (3 June), p. 1.

Announces that W will give a brief speech at the Fourth American Writers Congress on 6 June.

633. Anon. "Youths Invited to Study Fate of 'Bigger Thomas.'" Norfolk Journal and Guide (23 August), p. 15.

Photograph with caption of Canada Lee meeting with "some fifty underprivileged youngsters" from Harlem who had seen the play NS.

634. Arnold, Aerol. "The Social Novel as a Best Seller." The University Review, 8 (October), 59-64.

Contains a paragraph from NS (p. 64) arguing that its popularity derives from its "management of plot and suspense," not from its social message.

635. Atkinson, Brooks. "Critics' Prize Plays." The New York Times (27 April), Sec. 9, p. 1.

Reports on the balloting on the New York Drama Critics Circle Award in which NS placed third after Watch on the Rhine and The Beautiful People.

636. _____. "'Native Son.'" The New York Times (6 April), Sec. 9, p. 1.

Favorable review of the play. Welles's direction is theatrically effective and exciting if somewhat superficial. The play itself is "realism with psychological overtones," uncompromising in its honesty. Bigger is monstrous, but he is shown to be a product of society. The acting is good, especially that of Canada Lee and Anne Burr. Reprinted: 1971.27.

637. _____. "'Native Son,' by Paul Green and Richard Wright, Put on by Orson Welles and John Houseman." Critics' Theatre Reviews, 2 (20 April), 349.

Reprint of 1941.638.

638. _____. "The Play." The New York Times (25 March), p. 26.

Favorable review of NS. The change from the subjectivity of the novel to the objectivity of the play diminishes the effectiveness and enlightenment of the trial scene, but Atkinson otherwise endorses enthusiastically the stage version--"the biggest American drama of the season." Except for the device of the rumbling furnace, Welles's "bravura style" is very effective, and Canada Lee gives "a clean, honest, driving performance of remarkable versatility."

Reprinted: 1941.637; 1971.28.

639. Barron, Mark. "'Native Son' Scores Hit in Gotham." The Baltimore Sunday Sun (30 March), Magazine Sec. 1, p. 9.

Favorable review of the play praising all aspects of the production, especially the direct involvement of the audience and the acting of Canada Lee and Ray Collins. The play is "an eloquent plea for racial tolerance" and "a successful theatrical approach to a fine literary work."

Reprinted: 1941.640.

640. _____. "'Native Son' Is Pinnacle of Season." The Philadelphia Inquirer (30 March), Sec. SO, p. 9.

Reprint of 1941.639.

641. Barry, Sue. "Christmas Sale Brings Rush of Customers to Progressive Bookshops." People's World (10 December), p. 5.

Notes that TMBV is selling well.

642. Becker, May Lamberton. "The Reader's Guide: Books Across the Sea." New York Herald Tribune Books (13 July), p. 12.

Argues that despite opposition, NS should be called to the attention of international readers even though it reveals American mistakes.

643. Beebe, Lucius. "This New York." New York Herald Tribune (1 March), p. 14.

Mentions the direction of NS by Orson Welles.

644. _____. "This New York." New York Herald Tribune (19 April), p. 7.

Mentions the dispute between New York drama critics John Anderson and Burns

Mantle over the merits of NS.

645. Belloli, Joseph. "Book Angles." Pacific Grove (Cal.) Tide (28 November), p. 7.

Contains a favorable notice of TMBV, "a sensitive, vigorous story of the large under-privileged minority which lives in America."

646. Benchley, Nathaniel. "Orson Welles's Patented System of Direction." New York Herald Tribune (16 March), Sec. VI, p. 1.

Discusses Welles's work habits as a director with special reference to NS. Of W's work Welles comments: "You've heard of people wanting to get away from it all--well, this is what they want to get away from." Includes a sketch of the opening scene in the Thomas flat.

647. Bessie, Alvah. "End of a Season." New Masses, 39 (20 May), 28-30.

Reviewing the theatrical season, Bessie notes an encouraging trend toward a progressive view of human life. This is best exemplified in NS, though the play has serious shortcomings. Its exposition of black life in white society should allow for a sympathetic view of the issue.

648. Bolden, Frank E. "'Native Son' Stinging Plea for Brown America." The Pittsburgh Courier (11 October), p. 21.

Very favorable review of the play as staged at the Nixon Theater in Pittsburgh. Praises the acting, production, and theme. Welles has substituted symbolism for realism.

649. Bond, Alice Dixon. "Mrs. Bond Recommends for Christmas Gifts." The Boston Herald (1 December), Christmas Book Sec., pp. 3, 6, 26.

Lists TMBV among many other books.

650. Bower, Helen. "The Book Rack." The Detroit Free Press (9 November), Part Five, p. 7.

Contains a favorable review of TMBV, in which W tells the story of cruelty to black people from slavery to the present "in moving, restrained and objective prose."

651. Bradford, David H. "A Book Which Tells of Negro's Struggling Hope." The Louisville Courier-Journal (18 November), p. 7.

Favorable review of TMBV calling it "a brilliant and deeply stirring commentary on the effect of urban life on the Negro in the United States." It is "much better sociology than history," however. Bradford objects to W's exclusion of the talented tenth. After summarizing the contents, the reviewer concludes by emphasizing the work's social message.

652. Brand, Millen. "Books." Sunday Worker (12 January), Sec. Two, p. 4.

In a favorable review of the first issue of American Writing, Brand praises a story by Ellison in which the conclusion moves "in the cadence of the same revolt as Dick Wright's Bigger."
Reprinted: 1941.653.

653. _____. "'Writing' First-Rate Poetry, Progressive Prose." People's World (22 January), p. 5.
Reprint of 1941.652.

654. B.[rickell], H.[erschel]. "American Literature," in 1941 Britannica Book of the Year. Ed. Walter Yust. Chicago: Encyclopaedia Britannica, pp. 43-46.

Comments on the novel NS: "A melodramatic theme, which was handled with a good deal of skill, helped to put the book over, although it was hardly so successful an artistic achievement as Mr. Wright's long short story volume, Uncle Tom's Children" (p. 44).

655. Bright, John. "What Will Hollywood Do with 'Native Son'?" New York Amsterdam Star-News (5 April), p. 21.

Despite the resounding success of the stage version and the potential profits of a film version, Bright believes that Hollywood will not produce the work because of the frankness of its social criticism.

656. Britton, Beverley. "Balancing the Books." Richmond Times-Dispatch (9 February), Sec. IV, p. 9.

Lists NS ninth of the ten outstanding books of 1940.

657. _____. "Balancing the Books." Richmond Times-Dispatch (23 February), Sec. IV, p. 8.

Britton voted for NS in the Book-of-the-Month Club poll on outstanding books of 1940.

658. _____. "Balancing the Books." Richmond Times-Dispatch (29 June), Sec. IV, p. 8.

Includes NS on a list of seventy-seven "Books for Today."

659. Bromberg, Lester. "Broadway Success Leaves Canada Lee Unchanged." New York World-Telegram (26 March), p. 33.

Emphasizes that Lee's life experiences had prepared him for the role of Bigger Thomas.

660. Brooks, Samuel L. "The World This Week." The Pittsburgh Courier (1 March), p. 6.
Announces that the play NS will open on Broadway, but expresses the hope that "the play does not follow too closely the action of the novel."

661. Brousch, Michael. "Young Negro Girl Writes Fine Novel." Daily Worker (8 November), p. 7.
Uses W as a point of departure in a review of House of Fury by Felice Swados.

662. Brown, John Mason. "Christmas Gift Books About the Theater." New York World-Telegram (18 December), p. 28.
Mentions NS in Burns Mantle's The Best Plays of 1940-1941.

663. _____. "'Native Son' as a Novel and a Play." New York Post (29 March), p. 4.
Brown considers the theoretical problems of the adaptation of a novel to the stage before turning to the case of NS. Though he admires the theatrical effectiveness of the play, he much prefers the novel. "In spite of the weakness of its last section and the childish simplification of its Communist solution, it is a novel of tremendous power. Its force is galvanic, its tension almost unbearable, its psychological truth irrefutable."

664. _____. "Orson Welles Presents Mr. Wright's 'Native Son.'" New York Post (25 March), p. 12.
Favorable review. The stage version succeeds as well as one could possibly expect, especially in the scene of Mary's murder and the scene of Bigger and the reporters by the furnace. Canada Lee is excellent as Bigger. But the great qualities of the novel--"the sledge-hammer impact and nerve-wracking excitement of the story; the insistent and terrible swiftness of its action; the full devastation of its exposure of the wounding truth"--have not been and cannot be transferred to a stage version.
Reprinted: 1941.665.

665. _____. "Orson Welles Presents Mr. Wright's 'Native Son.'" Critics' Theatre Reviews, 2 (20 April), 350.
Reprint of 1941.664.

666. _____. "Prizes, Prophecies, and a Certain Prediction." New York Post (1 April), p. 6.
Mentions NS as a competitor for the best play of the season.

667. Brown, Sterling A. "The Negro Author and His Publisher." The Quarterly Review of Higher Education Among Negroes, 9 (July), 140-146.
Includes brief mention of NS and Uncle Tom's Children.
Reprinted: 1942.210.

668. _____, Arthur P. Davis, and Ulysses Lee. "Richard Wright (1909 [sic]-   )," in their The Negro Caravan. New York: The Dryden Press, pp. 105-106, 401, 1050.
Biographical headnotes to "Bright and Morning Star," "I Have Seen Black Hands," and "The Ethics of Living Jim Crow."
Reprinted: 1970.73.

669. _____. "The Short Story," in their The Negro Caravan. New York: The Dryden Press, pp. 10-17.
Contains a short analysis of Uncle Tom's Children as a new type of exploration of black life.
Reprinted: 1970.74.

670. Bryan, A. P. "O. Henry Memorial Stories Not Up to Usual Standard." Lexington (Ky.) Herald (5 January), p. 29.
Review mentioning "Almos' a Man" as a high point in an otherwise disappointing collection.

671. Burcher, Dorothy G. "From My Book Shelf." Chowchilla (Cal.) News (10 April).
Contains a notice of the novel NS occasioned by its dramatization. The story it tells is one of horror.

672. Burley, Dan. "Back Door Stuff." New York Amsterdam Star-News (22 March), p. 13.
Quotes a remark by Eslanda Robeson that her husband could not have excelled Canada Lee's performance as Bigger Thomas.

673. _____. "Back Door Stuff." New York Amsterdam Star-News (18 October), p. 14.
Mentions briefly Bigger Thomas.

674. _____. "Dick Wright's Bigger Thomas Comes to Life in Clinton Brewer." New York Amsterdam Star-News (11 October), pp. 1, 28.
Extended comparison of Bigger and Clinton Brewer, the murderer-musician befriended by W.

675. Burns, Ben. "Book Marks." People's Daily World (12 March), p. 5.
Contains an announcement of the published version of the play NS.

676. C., J. A. "Best Short Stories."
Durham Herald (15 June), Part II, p. 2.
   Lists W as an established writer who
   helps "guarantee" the high quality of
   Edward O'Brien's anthology of The
   Best Short Stories 1941.

677. Cabot, Jane. "Youth Makes Good Use
of Time in Prison; Ready for Musical
Career." Norfolk Journal and Guide (2
August), p. 14.
   Discusses the Clinton Brewer case,
   mentioning W's interest in him. Includes a photograph of W.

678. Calvin, Bernice and Dolores Calvin.
"Canada Lee to Star in 'Othello' After
'Native Son' Closes." The Indianapolis
Recorder (14 June), p. 12.
   Praises Lee's acting and tells of a
   backstage interview with him after
   the eighty-first performance of NS.

679. Canfield, Cass. "The House of Harper." The Saturday Review of Literature,
23 (19 April), 11.
   Letter crediting Edward C. Aswell
   with successfully editing W's work.

680. Cayton, Horace R. "Black Voices:
Wright's New Book More Than a Study of
Social Status." The Pittsburgh Courier
(15 November), p. 13.
   After a prefatory paragraph on the
   sociological validity of NS, Cayton
   reviews enthusiastically TMBV, a work
   "magnificent in its simplicity, directness and force." It is both a
   description of "the social matrix
   from which warped social personalities such as Bigger Thomas arise" and
   "a philosophy of the history of the
   Negro in America." Cayton considers W
   "a great writer; not a great negro
   writer, but the real McCoy."
   Reprinted: 1942.216; 1978.209.

681. ____. "Negro Morale." Opportunity,
19 (December), 371-375.
   Mentions W.

682. Chapman, John. "Hollywood." New
York Daily News (18 February).
   Mentions Welles's plan to stage NS
   before making his next film.

683. ____. "Hollywood." New York Daily
News (3 May).
   Reports that H. Mankiewicz owns one-
   third of the play NS.

684. ____. "Hollywood." New York Daily
News (17 November).
   Mentions favorable prospects for the
   financial backers of the play NS when
   it opens in Chicago.

685. Clark, Annemarie. "Von einem Neger

geschreiben." Die Zurich Weltwoche.
   Favorable review of Sohn dieses
   Landes (NS). The true greatness of
   the novel is in its tolerance. While
   it indicates the problems with the
   Daltons, Jan, and Bigger, it does not
   condemn them. W provides no easy
   cures for the pervasive blindness the
   work depicts. The only bright spot
   lies in the fact that the conditions
   which produced Bigger also produced
   W.

686. Clark, William E. "Broadway Production of 'Native Son' Is Faithful to
Novel." The New York Age (22 March), p.
10.
   Mixed review admiring the acting, the
   fidelity to the novel and the staging. Clark objects, however, to the
   leftist propaganda of the play. He
   also argues that Bigger is not a
   typical black man.

687. Cohn, Herbert. "The Sound Track."
Brooklyn Eagle (6 April), Sec. E, p. 10.
   Mentions possible purchase by Holly-
   wood of the screen rights to NS.

688. Coleman, Robert. "'Native Son'
Carries Heavy Load of Propaganda." New
York Daily Mirror (26 March), p. 30.
   Unfavorable review of the play objecting to its radicalism. Some
   scenes are melodramatically effective
   and Lee's acting is excellent, but
   otherwise the play is weak as well as
   wrongheaded.

689. Coles, L. F. "'Native Son' Medal
Award Protested." The Baltimore Afro-
American (15 February), p. 14.
   Letter to the editor disparaging W's
   contribution to the race and pro-
   posing William Pickens as a more
   suitable recipient of the Spingarn
   Medal.

690. Collins, Howard. "Your Literary
I. Q." The Saturday Review of Litera-
ture, 24 (26 July), 17.
   One question on this quiz concerning
   blacks in literature is on "Bigger
   Thompson" [sic] in NS.

691. Conrad, Harold. "Gotham Grapevine."
Brooklyn Eagle (14 April), p. 4.
   Mentions the controversy ensuing from
   the effort of the management of
   Sardi's to prevent "Canada Lee, Negro
   star of 'Native Son'" from being
   interviewed on the premises.

692. C.[ooke], M.[arvel]. "Max Pleads
for Bigger." New York Amsterdam Star-
News (5 April), p. 21.
   Favorable review of the published
   version of the play NS. Cooke quotes

from the National Youth Commission Report quoted in the foreword and, at length, from Max's speech to the court.

693. _____. "Mercury's 'Native Son' Makes Theatrical History." New York Amsterdam Star-News (29 March), p. 20.
Highly favorable review of the play finding it in some respects "a more authentic commentary on American life" than the novel. It avoids sensationalism while revealing the destructive influence of the environment. Cooke praises the production and the acting. A comment by W at the curtain call is quoted.

694. _____. "New Play Revolutionary Experience." New York Amsterdam Star-News (22 March), p. 20.
Notes that even though NS presents for the first time on the Broadway stage a black mother instead of a mammy and depicts friendly relations between a white woman and a black man, the writing and direction "have been done so subtly and with such authenticity that there should be no reverberations from anyone." W is quoted on his faith in Welles.

695. _____. "Orson Welles Conducts 'Native Son' Rehearsal." New York Amsterdam Star-News (22 March), pp. 20-21.
Concerned mainly with Welles, who reports that, in addition to Canada Lee, Raymond Massey, Robert Montgomery, and Welles himself had all been mentioned for the role of Bigger. Welles also comments on the desire of an RKO executive to film NS with an all-white cast. W is said to trust implicitly the theatrical judgment of Welles. Includes three photographs and several sketches from the play.

696. Cotter, Jerry. "Stage and Screen." The Sign, 20 (May), 625.
Contains an unfavorable review of the play NS, which Cotter treats as Communist propaganda. Bigger is implausible as a racial symbol, and his criminality cannot be ignored, for "to absolve the malefactor because of the sins of his oppressors is not Christian logic." The production by Welles and the acting by Lee are excellent, but "in addition to the political implications, the play contains an abundance of blasphemy, sensuality, and general sordidness of a nature to make it generally unacceptable."

697. Crandell, Richard F. "Dark Thoughts on Dark Citizens." New York Herald Tribune Books (23 November), p. 8.
Favorable review of TMBV calling it "the black 'J'Accuse.'" W's mood is angry and bitter, and he sees little hope for improvement. The book will make both whites and successful blacks uncomfortable.

698. Creekmore, Hubert. "Social Factors in Native Son." The University of Kansas City Review, 8 (Winter), 136-143.
Presents a general analysis of the critical reception of NS. The novel combines two types of romance: the thriller, in "Fear" and "Flight"; and the proletarian, in "Fate." W does expose the hypocrisy of the white North in dealing with the racial question, but he is guilty of exaggeration.

699. Cummiskey, Joe. "Sports Ticker Talk." PM (30 March), p. 21.
Discusses Canada Lee's boxing career and, more briefly, his theatrical career.

700. Dancer, Maurice. "Tan Manhattan." The Chicago Defender (5 April), National edition, p. 21.
Claims that Orson Welles had Canada Lee in mind for the role of Bigger from the beginning.

701. _____. "Tan Manhattan." The Chicago Defender (21 June), National edition, p. 20.
Mentions the RKO contract of Anne Burr, "Canada Lee's ofay leading lady" in NS.

702. Davis, Benjamin J., Jr. "Twelve Million Black Voices." Sunday Worker (9 November), Sec. 3, p. 6.
Favorable review praising the book for its class-conscious perspective and its literary skill. Davis thinks, however, that W could have given more attention to black achievement to balance the story of white oppression of blacks.
Reprinted: 1978.209.

703. DeCasseres, Benjamin. "The March of Events." New York Journal-American (27 August), p. 16.
Quoting a letter from a black hotel maid in Los Angeles that Bigger "was mean and low from choice," not from poverty, the columnist praises her as "an aristocrat of the mind and a Negress who cannot be bamboozled by such rubbishy stuff as 'Native Son.'"

704. Dodson, Nell. "Around Harlemtown." The Chicago Defender (12 April), National edition, p. 20.
Criticizes the New York Daily Mirror

for suppressing a favorable review of the play NS and printing an unfavorable one.

705. _____. "Can Canada Lee Take Success as Bigger?" The Indianapolis Recorder (12 April), p. 13.
Praises Lee's performance as Bigger Thomas.

706. _____. "Success Hasn't Gone to Canada Lee's Head Despite Fine Notices." The Philadelphia Tribune (10 April), p. 14.
Discusses Lee's success in his role as Bigger Thomas.

707. Drewry, John E. "New Book News." The Atlanta Constitution (27 April), Sec. E, p. 6.
Contains a review of the play NS. Drewry admires the skillful production but dislikes the work: "it is a kind of modern 'Uncle Tom's Cabin,' with a lot of cursing, Communism, and other unsavory items introduced."

708. Du Bois, W. E. B. "Wright, Richard. 12 Million Black Voices; a folk history of the Negro in the United States." The United States 1865-1900, 1 (September), 26.
Favorable review recommending the work to "those who dare listen to the voice of the stricken Negro masses," though most of "the American public is not yet used to hearing Negroes complain."
Reprinted: 1977.100.

709. Duckett, Alfred A. "Uncensored." The New York Age (2 August), p. 7.
At a bathing beauty contest on 21 July at the Sonia Ballroom, "we will never forget the crowd's approbation and admiration which greeted the introduction of Dick Wright's 'Bigger Thomas' who came to life . . . in the person of the one and only Canada Lee."

710. Eaton, William Prichard. "Plays and Playwrights." New York Herald Tribune Books (19 October), p. 24.
Lists W as a contributor to William Kozlenko's American Scenes.

711. _____. "Theater of Melodrama." New York Herald Tribune Books (28 December), p. 13.
Notes the inclusion of NS in Burns Mantle's The Best Plays of 1940-1941.

712. Elliott, Mabel A and Francis E. Merrill. Social Disorganization. Revised edition. New York: Harper, p. 709.
Footnote to a discussion of the desertion of black women by black men

cites the example of Mrs. Thomas in NS.
Reprinted in revised form: 1950.135.

713. Ellison, Ralph. "Recent Negro Fiction." New Masses, 40 (5 August), 22-26.
Claims that W's achievement, supreme among black writers of fiction, was made possible by his association with "advanced white writers." UTC is a successful delineation of "the universals embodied in Negro experience," and NS is a "philosophical novel" that "possesses an artistry, penetration of thought, and sheer emotional power that places [sic] it into the front rank of American fiction."

714. _____. "Richard Wright and Recent Negro Fiction." Direction, 4 (Summer), 12-13.
Praises NS as marking the highest point of contrast between black fiction of the thirties and twenties since it points out the effect of political and cultural segregation on black intellectual life. W is an artist to be emulated by other black writers. Waters Turpin and William Attaway show promise, but they do not yet meet W's standard.

715. Estcourt, Charles J. R. "The Way It Is with Orson Welles, The Boy Wonder of Hollywood." The Baltimore Sunday Sun (16 March), Magazine Sec., p. 5.
Includes a detailed description of the Welles directorial style and technique in NS.

716. Ettinghausen, Ruth. "Above the Crowd." The Richmond Hill High School Domino (8 May).
Interview with W discussing the Nixon case and its relation to NS among other topics.

717. F., D. M. "Darkest America." The Hartford Courant (30 November), Magazine Sec., p. 11.
Favorable review of TMBV emphasizing W's racial perspective. At times the white man is dealt with unfairly, but W's assertive voice carries authority.

718. Farrell, Frank. "Caviar & Beans." New York World-Telegram (25 March), p. 15.
Having attended the premiere of the play NS, Farrell remarks that Orson Welles "has done something with this one."

719. Fenwick, James M. "The Voice of Richard Wright." The New International, 7 (November), 287-288.

Ostensibly a review of the pamphlet edition of Bright and Morning Star, this essay treats the general significance of W's fiction. Fenwick praises W's use of the theme of racial struggle, the heroism of his black characters, his uncompromisingly realistic presentation of racism, and his lean style and accurate dialect. "Wright's stories are an excellent refutation of the scholasticism of bourgeois critics who pose the conception of art and propaganda as mutually exclusive opposites."

720. Field, Rowland. "Broadway: 'Native Son' Vigorous, Exciting." Newark Evening News (25 March), p. 30.
Favorable review praising the adaptation from the novel, the production and the acting. The stage version emphasizes action and melodrama more than the social message.

721. Fishback, J. M. "'Native Son' Programs." The New York Times (25 May), Sec. IX, p. 2.
Letter to the editor praising Orson Welles's practice of distributing programs for the play after rather than before the performance.

722. Flexner, Eleanor. "'Native Son' and Dramatists Session at Writers Congress." Sunday Worker (15 June), p. 7.
Corrects alleged distortions in Ralph Warner's "In Their Plays, The Aspirations of the People Will Find Voice," insisting that Bigger's reaction, not his plight, is exceptional.

723. Ford, James W. "Foreword," in Bright and Morning Star. By Richard Wright. New York: International Publishers, p. [5].
Expresses deep appreciation of W's achievements. He is an example of black cultural genius. In presenting the plight of the blacks to the American people, W has performed a great service. Black and white Americans rejoice that W identifies with his people's aspirations.

724. Ford, Nick Aaron. "I Teach Negro Literature." College English, 2 (March), 530-541.
Cites W as a protest novelist with real social impact (p. 534).

725. _____. "The Negro Novel as a Vehicle of Propaganda." The Quarterly Review of Higher Education Among Negroes, 9 (July), 135-139.
Contains a brief discussion of NS, which attempts favorable propaganda for the improvement of the racial situation, but which will have the opposite effect on many white readers. Bigger will frighten rather than win over potential employers or philanthropists.

726. Francis, Robert. "Candid Close-ups: Anne Burr, Three Years Broadway Bound, Gets Her Opportunity in 'Native Son.'" Brooklyn Eagle (8 June), Sec. E, p. 6.
Biographical sketch of the actress who plays Mary Dalton.

727. _____. "'Native Son' Comes to the Flatbush." Brooklyn Eagle (13 August), p. 4.
Favorable review of the play emphasizing the successful transition from the novel to the stage. The theme of the "utter futility and lack of understanding between black and white" is presented with moving power. The production and the acting are excellent.

728. Frederick, John T. and Arna Bontemps. "Negro Writers." Northwestern University on the Air, 1 (18 November), 2-8.
Transcript of the radio program "Of Men and Books" including a review by Frederick, with comments by Bontemps, of TMBV. Frederick has some reservations about historical oversimplification, but otherwise praises the book both as literature and as social document. Bontemps admires the poetic quality of W's prose.

729. Freidin, Seymour. "Boxer, Jockey, Band Leader, Canada Lee Becomes Star Actor." New York Herald Tribune (30 March), Sec. VI, p. 5.
Essay-interview with a drawing of the bedroom scene in the play NS. Quotes Lee at length on his knowledge of the Bigger type and on the importance of the play.

730. Gannett, Lewis. "Books and Things." New York Herald Tribune (10 November), p. 13.
Contains a favorable notice of TMBV calling it a "cinematic prose poem." Gannett is impressed by the range of rhythms in W's prose, which is "somber but singing."

731. Gardner, Jennie B. "Book Ends." The Memphis Commercial Appeal (16 February), Sec. IV, p. 10.
Gives the results of a poll of critics by the Book-of-the-Month Club listing NS in fifth place.

732. Garlin, Sender. "Constant Reader." Daily Worker (11 June), p. 7.
Mentions W in a report on the Writers Congress.

733. Garlington, S. Wycliffe. "'Fit to Print'?" Opportunity, 19 (May), 148-150, 158.

Mentions coverage of the news story of the award of the Spingarn Medal to W in The New York Times and PM.

734. Gassner, John W. "Stage." Direction, 4 (Summer), 42-43.

Writing on the highlights of the New York theatrical season, Gassner reviews NS favorably. In the play Bigger is not developed as a social victim, but the dramatic form--"another approach to analytical 'epic' style"--is interesting, and the production and acting are excellent.

735. Gaver, Jack. "Up and Down Broadway." Roanoke Times (1 June), p. 7.

Mentions the closing of the play NS.

736. Gibbons, John. "In Peace and War, U. S. Authors Popular with Soviet Readers." Daily Worker (26 December), p. 7.

Discusses an exhibition of American authors, including W, at the Library of Foreign Literature in Moscow. W's photograph accompanies this article.

737. Gibbs, Wolcott. "Black Boy." The New Yorker, 17 (5 April), 33-34.

Review of the play NS arguing that it is inferior to the novel because it is "a much too drastic oversimplification of Mr. Wright's story as well as a considerable garbling of his message." Still, it is good melodrama, "one of the few satisfactory dramas of this unfortunate season." Gibbs praises highly Canada Lee's performance and Orson Welles's direction.

738. Gilbert, Douglas. "Word from Miss Cornell Helped Put a Girl on Her Feet-- Now She Has Broadway Part." New York World-Telegram (26 April), p. 3.

Biographical sketch with photograph of Anne Burr, who plays Mary Dalton in NS.

739. Gilder, Rosamond. "Glamour and Purpose." Theatre Arts, 25 (May), 327-335.

Contains a mixed review of the play NS (pp. 329-332) comparing Bigger's flight to that in The Emperor Jones. Except for what is restored by Canada Lee's excellent performance, the play loses much of the subjective element of the novel, but it is nevertheless "violently exciting, absorbing, not a little lurid."

740. _____. "Prizes That Bloom in the Spring: The Broadway Season in Review." Theatre Arts, 25 (June), 409-418.

Comments briefly on NS (p. 418)

praising the production by Welles and the acting by the black members of the cast.

741. Gloster, Hugh M. "Richard Wright: Interpreter of Racial and Economic Maladjustments." Opportunity, 19 (December), 361-365, 383.

As a successful and influential writer, W calls attention to the negative effects of discrimination and economic oppression of blacks. "The Ethics of Living Jim Crow" is one of his better efforts. Gloster analyzes at length the stories in UTC, especially "Bright and Morning Star." NS is treated in terms of its critique of a prejudiced and capitalistic social order.

Reprinted: 1948.167; 1960.198; 1961.214; 1963.146.

742. Gold, Michael. The Hollow Men. New York: International Publishers, pp. 9, 26, 27-28, 29, 44, 48.

Reprint of 1940.678, 679, 680.

743. Goldstein, Albert. "Literature and Less." The Times-Picayune New Orleans States (16 February), Sec. Two, p. 9.

Mentions that NS took fifth place in the Book-of-the-Month Club's poll of critics for the ten best books of 1940.

744. Govan, Gilbert E. "Roaming Through the Realm of Books." Chattanooga Sunday Times (2 March), Sec. Four, p. 5.

Reports that W has been awarded the Spingarn Medal.

745. Grattan, C. Hartley. "The Literary Scene in Australia." The New York Times Book Review (2 February), pp. 8, 14.

Reports that an Australian publishing house is advertising NS.

746. Gray, Sara. "From the Left." PM (4 April), p. 2.

Letter to the editor stressing the importance of the People's Meeting on 5-6 April. Gray writes "for the initiating Co.": W, Dreiser, Marc Blitzstein, Professor W. Rautenstrauch, Earl Robinson, and Herbert Biberman.

747. Greenwall, June. "Richard Wright," in Mercury Theatre. 3 pp.

Comments on the play NS and reproduces W's summary of his career similar to that he sent to Story in 1937.

748. Gross, Ben. "Listening In." New York Daily News (7 April).

Gross joins Orson Welles in praising NS.

749. Grossman, Sid. "'12,000,000 Black

Voices.'" Photo Notes (December).
Favorable review praising the "profound, personal emotion" of W's text,
which indicates his total identification with his people. The text and
the excellent photographs complement
each other well.

750. Gunsky, Frederic R. "Some Documents
of Democracy." San Francisco Chronicle
(28 September), This World Sec., p. 20.
Lists W as a contributor to Bernard
Smith's The Democratic Spirit.

751. H., R. F. "Wright Stirs Emotions,
Fails to Solve Problems." Springfield
(Mass.) Daily News (1 December), p. 9.
Mixed review of TMBV deeming W's
fiction to be stylistically superior
to his nonfiction. In both "he is
inclined to be wordy . . . given to
overwriting, and . . . appeals to the
heart rather than to the mind."
Nevertheless, his "deadly sincerity"
is extremely effective.

752. Hackett, Alice. "P. W. Forecast for
Buyers." The Publishers' Weekly, 140 (4
October), 1392-1394.
Includes a prepublication notice of
TMBV stressing the "good advertis-
ing."

753. Haden, Allen. "South America Is
Reading Gone with the Wind, Rebecca,
Native Son, Tobacco Road." The Chicago
Daily News (3 December), p. 17B.
Reports good sales of Sangre Negra
(NS) at "highbrow bookstalls" in
Buenos Aires.

754. Hall, Florencia. Letras contempor-
áneas en los Estados Unidos. San José,
Costa Rica: Imprenta Nacional.
Four lectures, the first of which, on
the novel, treats NS, "an epic of
fear worthy of Poe, Maupassant, Dostoevsky" (p. 16). The two-page commentary consists mainly of plot summary.

755. Hamshar, Walter. "The Playbill."
New York Herald Tribune (30 March), Sec.
VI, p. 1.
Reports that Orson Welles will organ-
ize a Chicago company for NS.

756. _____. "The Playbill: Theater
Guild's Road Season." New York Herald
Tribune (6 April), Sec. VI, p. 1.
Mentions the possibility of a Chicago
company of NS.

757. Hansen, Harry. "The First Reader."
Greensboro Daily News (3 January), p. 6.
In an annual review of important
books, NS is judged "the best novel
of social significance" of 1940, but

Hansen believes that "Wright has
written better in short stories."

758. _____. "The First Reader." Norfolk
Virginian-Pilot (3 December), p. 6.
Reprint of 1941.759.

759. _____. "The First Reader: The March
of the Negro." New York World-Telegram
(11 November), p. 13.
Favorable review of TMBV emphasizing
the book's message to affluent
whites. Hansen praises W's sincerity,
vitality, and power, comparing the
work to Erskine Caldwell's You Have
Seen Their Faces.
Reprinted: 1941.758; 1978.209.

759a. Hardwick, Leon. "Is America Chang-
ing Its Views Concerning Negroes and
Defense?" Washington Tribune (17 May),
p. 7.
Mentions the excerpt from the novel
NS in the 7 May issue of PM.

759b. _____. "The Theatrical Broadcast:
'Native Son' as a Play Is Courageous
Work, Well Acted and Extremely Timely."
Washington Tribune (19 April), p. 12.
Favorable review praising the acting,
production, and theme. Hardwick is
impressed by the play's frankness,
especially in the bedroom and courtroom scenes. He also approves of W's
portrayal of Bigger, despite the
preference of other blacks for a more
"acceptable" protagonist.

760. Hart, James D. "Wright, Richard,"
in his The Oxford Companion to American
Literature. London: Oxford University
Press, p. 851.
Brief biographical-critical sketch
emphasizing NS.
Reprinted in revised form: 1944.103;
1948.174; 1956.198; 1965.74.

761. Hayes, Frank L. "Songs and Suffer-
ings of the Great People Lincoln Set
Free." The Chicago Daily News (3 Decem-
ber), p. 14B.
Reviews favorably Arna Bontemps's
Golden Slippers and less favorably
TMBV. W emphasizes the negative and
is sometimes inaccurate.

762. Hobart, John. "A Critic Squares the
Critics' Circle." San Francisco Chronicle (26 April), This World Sec., p. 18.
Compares the play NS unfavorably to
Watch on the Rhine, which conveys its
social message more deftly. With
excellent direction and acting, NS is
"electrifying theater," but not "a
play of stature."

762a. Holmes, John. "Poems and Things."
Boston Evening Transcript (7 April), p.

9.
Contains a review of Howard Nutt's
Special Laughter mentioning W's pre-
face.

763. Houghton, Norris. Advance from
Broadway: 19,000 Miles of American Theatre. New York: Harcourt, Brace, pp. 103,
297.
Mentions favorably the play NS.

764. Hughes, Elinor. "Burns Mantle Picks
Plays." Boston Herald (1 December), p.
23.
Review of The Best Plays of 1940-1941
mentioning NS.

765. Hughes, Langston. "The Need for
Heroes." The Crisis, 48 (June), 184-185,
206.
Calling for black writers to cease
concentrating on defeat and death,
Hughes cites Bigger Thomas as an
example of the anti-hero. Good writers such as W should now turn their
attention to heroic black figures.

766. Ibee. "Plays on Broadway: Native
Son." Variety (26 March), p. 52.
Review providing many details about
the production--sound effects, lighting, sets, etc. Praises the acting
and staging, but predicts that the
grim theme makes a long run doubtful.
The reviewer notes the element of
protest, which makes the play more
than mere melodrama.

767. Isaacs, Edith J. R. "Paul Green: A
Case in Point." Theatre Arts, 25 (July),
489-498.
Article on Paul Green mentioning his
collaboration with W on the dramatization of NS.

768. Ivy, James W. "Dramatic Version of
Native Son." The Crisis, 48 (December),
396.
Favorable review admitting that "the
play often reads like straight melodrama or badly disguised pro-Negro
propaganda with a leftist twist," but
asserting that "the Bigger of the
play is a much more human and a much
more plausible Bigger than the Bigger
of the novel."

769. Jack, Peter Monro. "Fiction," in
The American Year Book. Ed. William M.
Schuyler. New York: Thomas Nelson &
Sons, pp. 880-887.
Contains favorable comments on the
novel NS.

770. Jackson, Joseph Henry. "The Book-
man's Daily Notebook: A Photographic
Story of the Negro in the United
States." San Francisco Chronicle (25

November), p. 15.
Contains a favorable review of TMBV
emphasizing W's omission of the talented tenth.

771. James, Mertice M. and Dorothy
Brown, eds. "Wright, Richard. Native
son," in their The Book Review Digest.
New York: H. W. Wilson Company, pp.
1014-1015.
Contains excerpts and listings of
twenty-three reviews of the novel.

772. Johnson, Ernest. "Best Seller Comes
to Life: Lee's 'Bigger' Goes Over Big."
The Philadelphia Tribune (20 March), p.
14.
Favorable review of the play NS with
special praise for Canada Lee's performance. Johnson discusses some of
the problems in adapting the novel to
the stage.
Reprinted: 1941.773.

773. _____. "Canada Lee Praised for
'Bigger' Portrayal." Norfolk Journal and
Guide (22 March), p. 14.
Reprint of 1941.772.

774. Johnson, Oakley. "Negro Poet Sponsor of Scholarships." Daily Worker (4
October), p. 7.
Mentions W as one of the sponsors of
scholarships offered by the League of
American Writers to young black writers.

775. Jordan, Elizabeth. "Theatre." America, 65 (12 April), 26.
Review of the play NS from a Catholic
perspective. Jordan interprets the
social message to be "that there is
no hope for Negroes such as Canada
Lee until they have been educated in
Christian principles." Bigger is
"crawlingly vicious" and Mary is
"loathsome." The reviewer also summarizes the plot and praises the acting
and the production. At the end of the
review the editor warns against W's
Communist propaganda.

776. Keller, Allen. "Bigger Finds a
Judge Who Understands." New York World-
Telegram (3 April), p. 37.
Reports Lee's problems with his establishment, the Chicken Coop, which
was judged not a cabaret but a restaurant.

777. Korman, Seymour M. "Books of Plays
Bring Stage to Your Armchair." Chicago
Daily Tribune (28 May), p. 16.
Contains a favorable notice of the
published form of the play NS.
"It is in simple, earthy idiom
with powerful movements toward its
climaxes."

778. Kreymborg, Alfred. "The Old South." The Crisis, 48 (January), 29.
    A poem dedicated to W.

779. Kronenberger, Louis. "Critic Sums Up Season--It Might Have Been Worse." PM (25 May), p. 56.
    Although it fell short of the novel, the play NS had its merits.

780. _____. "Critics Vote 'Watch on the Rhine' Season's Best." PM (23 April), p. 21.
    Notes that NS received one vote, that of Burns Mantle.

781. _____. "A Fascist American Stage Couldn't Even Be Amusing." PM (4 May), p. 43.
    Points out that such a play as NS would not be possible without freedom of the stage.

782. _____. "The Tragic Saga of Bigger Thomas Makes Vivid Theater." Critics' Theatre Reviews, 2 (20 April), 350.
    Reprint of 1941.783.

783. _____. "The Tragic Saga of Bigger Thomas Makes Vivid Theater." PM (25 March), p. 21.
    Mixed review of the play NS. It is effective theater--"tense, dramatic and frequently compelling"--but it "lacks the richness and subterraneous power of the book, as well as the essential meaning." Bigger's psychology is drastically oversimplified and the social indictment is toned down. Kronenberger provides quotations from three other reviews of the play.
    Reprinted: 1941.782.

784. Krutch, Joseph Wood. "Minority Report." The Nation, 152 (5 April), 417-418.
    Unfavorable review of the play NS. Krutch finds it less satisfactory than the novel, which is comparable to An American Tragedy in its plodding sincerity. The play separates further "the two elements of the novel--crude melodrama and social preachment." Most of the review criticizes "the new stagecraft" of Orson Welles as exemplified in the production of NS.

785. L., D. "Negro 'Folk History.'" PM's Weekly (2 November), pp. 56-58.
    Favorable notice of TMBV emphasizing the photographs, two of which are reproduced on pp. 57-58.

786. Lachatañere, Rómulo. "Crónica de teatro: Hijo nativo ('Native Son')." Norte: Revista Continental (August), pp.

26-27.
    Favorable illustrated review of the play with a detailed plot summary. Praises Welles's "new, audacious" theatrical technique.

786a. Lamont, William H. F. "Novels of 1922 to 1941," in Good Reading. Ed. Atwood H. Townsend. Chicago: The National Council of Teachers of English, pp. 29-32.
    Lists and comments briefly on NS.
    Reprinted: 1946.223a; 1960.259a.
    Reprinted in revised form: 1947.221a; 1948.184a, 184b; 1951.192a; 1952.61a; 1954.164b.

787. Laycock, Edward A. "Notes and Comment" The Boston Daily Globe (14 February), p. 21.
    Reports that NS placed fifth among the ten best books of 1940 in a Book-of-the-Month Club poll.

788. Layne, Lou. "Theatres." Tatler.
    Notes the difficulty of finding a suitable actor to play the role of Bigger Thomas in NS.

789. League of American Writers. Writers Teach Writing. New York.
    Pamphlet listing W as one who has "taught or lectured" for The Writers School of New York between 1937-1940.

789a. Lechlitner, Ruth. "Brave Verse of Today." New York Herald Tribune Books (2 February), p. 12.
    Review of Howard Nutt's Special Laughter praising W's introduction.

790. Lee, Annie. "Pen Feathers." Winston-Salem Journal & Sentinel (4 May), Sec. 2, p. 14.
    Presents John Mason Brown's comment that the correct medium of NS was the novel rather than the stage.

791. Lee, Charles. "Did the Pulitzer Prize Board Read Their Books?" Philadelphia Record (11 May), Sec. M, p. 7.
    Criticizes the Pulitzer committee's decision not to award a fiction prize for 1940. Mentions NS as one of six novels deserving the honor.

792. Lewis, Lloyd. "'Native Son,' Blend of Horror Pathos and Stump Speeches." The Chicago Daily News (11 November), p. 12.
    Mixed review of the play. Lewis praises the acting and dramatic action, but considers the overt plea for social justice in Max's speech ineffective. Notes in passing the Othello parallel.

793. Lewis, R. J., Jr. "Speaking of

Books." Albany Times-Union (24 November), p. 12.
    Favorable review of TMBV summarizing the book, commending its candor and force, and calling it "an eloquent statement and an effective work of propaganda for racial equality and anti-discrimination." Nevertheless, Lewis prefers "the more subtle" NS both as literature and as protest.

794. Lewis, Theophilus. "Plays and a Point of View: Native Son." Interracial Review, 14 (April), 62.
    Unfavorable review finding that the play misrepresents black life and misfires as racial protest. The production by Welles, moreover, is mediocre and sensationalistic. Only the acting, especially Canada Lee's, is well done. Lewis takes white reviewers to task for liking the play.

795. ____. "The Saga of Bigger Thomas." The Catholic World, 153 (May), 201-206.
    After a detailed summary of the plot of NS, Lewis denounces it as "technically defective, aesthetically delinquent and misrepresentative of normal Negro character." Bigger is "a thoroughly worthless creature," utterly devoid of tragic stature.

796. Locke, Alain. "Broadway and the Negro Drama." Theatre Arts, 25 (October), 745-752.
    Includes remarks on NS, "incontestably one of the deepest and most unconventional of Negro tragedies" (p. 746).

797. ____. "Negroes (American)," in 1941 Britannica Book of the Year. Ed. Walter Yust. Chicago: Encyclopaedia Britannica, pp. 486-487.
    Mentions W briefly.

798. ____. "Of Native Sons: Real and Otherwise." Opportunity, 19 (January), 4-9.
    Singles out NS as the major work of black literature of 1940. A novel of the stark realistic school, it is a timely and perceptive analysis of central dilemmas of the American racial situation. Its Zolaesque denunciation should put America on the defensive.

799. Lockridge, Richard. "The New Play: Richard Wright's 'Native Son' Is Offered at the St. James Theater." The New York Sun (25 March), p. 16.
    Mildly favorable review arguing that the honesty of conception and characterization of Bigger and the melodramatic qualities of the story of his life are successfully trans-

ferred from the novel to the play, though certain other qualities are lost. Lockridge objects to the implausible eloquence of Bigger's self-examination and to excessive physical violence, but he praises the vitality of the play as a whole and especially Canada Lee's performance. Reprinted: 1941.800.

800. ____. "Richard Wright's 'Native Son' Is Offered at the St. James Theater." Critics' Theatre Reviews, 2 (20 April), 349.
    Reprint of 1941.799.

801. L.[oveman], A.[my]. "Literature," in The World Book Encyclopedia Annual for 1940. Ed. J. Morris Jones. Chicago: The Quarrie Corporation, pp. 109-112.
    Contains favorable comments on NS (p. 110).

802. Luccock, Halford E. American Mirror: Social, Ethical, and Religious Aspects of American Literature 1930-1940. New York: Macmillan, pp. 79-84, 135, 246.
    Favorable discussion of NS emphasizing its social meaning. Includes briefer comments on UTC (pp. 83, 135).

803. Lyons, Eugene. The Red Decade. Indianapolis: Bobbs-Merrill, pp. 147, 249, 349, 350, 387, 390.
    Unfavorable references to W in a fiercely anti-Communist book. Lyons cites W's support of Communist causes and interests.

804. Lyons, Leonard. "The Lyons Den." New York Post (8 February), p. 9.
    Reports a rumor that Kenneth Spencer will play the role of Bigger in the play NS.

805. ____. "The Lyons Den." New York Post (12 February), p. 9.
    Mentions the play NS, noting that Orson Welles will direct it and that Canada Lee will probably play Bigger.

806. ____. "The Lyons Den." New York Post (3 March), p. 11.
    Reports that Everett Sloane and Paul Stewart have been cast in the play NS.

807. ____. "The Lyons Den." New York Post (4 March), p. 11.
    Mentions the scheduled opening of the play NS.

808. ____. "The Lyons Den." New York Post (12 March), p. 13.
    Relates an anecdote about Orson

Welles during a rehearsal of NS.

809. _____. "The Lyons Den." New York
Post (15 March), p. 9.
    Mentions Canada Lee in the role of
    Bigger.

810. _____. "The Lyons Den." New York
Post (c. 20 March).
    Relates that Orson Welles did not
    allow the cast of NS to bow after a
    poor performance.

811. _____. "The Lyons Den." New York
Post (c. 24 March).
    Notes an unexpected substitution in
    the cast of one performance of the
    play NS.

812. _____. "The Lyons Den." New York
Post (25 March), p. 9.
    Mentions the enthusiastic critical
    response to the opening of the play
    NS.

813. _____. "The Lyons Den." New York
Post (26 March), p. 13.
    Mentions the departure of Orson
    Welles for Mexico City and his plan
    to audit performances of NS by re-
    cordings.

814. _____. "The Lyons Den." New York
Post (31 March), p. 9.
    Remarks that charity benefit perfor-
    mances have cost NS $7,000.

815. _____. "The Lyons Den." New York
Post (4 April), p. 17.
    Reports that Canada Lee has received
    a draft deferment because of his
    impaired vision.

816. _____. "The Lyons Den." New York
Post (7 April), p. 11.
    Reports that producers of NS have
    given Canada Lee a new automobile
    together with a plaque stating that
    "Canada Lee is superb."

817. _____. "The Lyons Den." New York
Post (11 April), p. 13.
    Reports that Canada Lee has been
    trying to succeed with his restaurant
    in Harlem named The Chicken Coop.

818. _____. "The Lyons Den." New York
Post (3 May), p. 9.
    Mentions critical acclaim for the
    acting of Paul Stewart and Everett
    Sloane in NS.

819. _____. "The Lyons Den." New York
Post (9 May), p. 17.
    Reports that Canada Lee's son has
    been missing for several days.

820. _____. "The Lyons Den." New York
Post (30 May), p. 7.
    Mentions the actor Everett Sloane in
    NS.

821. _____. "The Lyons Den." New York
Post (18 June), p. 13.
    Reports that Paul Stewart, who plays
    a reporter in NS, is campaigning for
    independent candidates.

822. _____. "The Lyons Den." New York
Post (25 June), p. 13.
    Mentions the musical activity of
    Canada Lee, "now star of 'Native
    Son.'"

823. _____. "The Lyons Den." New York
Post (23 September), p. 9.
    Announces the forthcoming publication
    of TMBV. Lyons states that after
    viewing the photographs, "Wright de-
    cided to write a novel about the
    conditions he saw portrayed." The
    result was NS.

824. _____. "The Lyons Den." New York
Post (30 September), p. 9.
    Mentions the recording of "Joe Louis
    Blues" on the afternoon of 1 Octo-
    ber.

825. _____. "The Lyons Den." New York
Post (c. October).
    Announces that TMBV will be published
    "next month."

826. M., J. "Best Short Stories." Oakland Tribune (5 January), p. 6-B.
    Notes that the O. Henry Memorial
    Award Prize Stories of 1940 contains
    "Almos' a Man," which "explores deli-
    cately a difficult problem in Negro
    psychology."

826a. Maas, Willard. "Considerably Heal-
thy." Poetry, 58 (June), 162-164.
    Review of Howard Nutt's Special
    Laughter mentioning W's introduction.

827. Manson, Richard. "Going Out Tonight?" New York Post (24 March), p. 16.
    Announces the opening of NS and lists
    the producers and leading members of
    the cast.

828. Mantle, Burns. "Appears There Were
a Couple of Other Fellows in on This."
New York Daily News (c. March).
    Corrects an earlier article (7 March)
    on the advance ticket sales for the
    play NS.

829. _____. The Best Plays of 1940-1941
and The Year Book of the Drama in America. New York: Dodd, Mead, pp. viii-ix,
11-12, 29-63, 369, 421, 436.
    In the introduction Mantle praises NS
    for its social message. Reviewing

the New York theatrical season, he describes the production of the play and its effect on the audience. On pp. 29-63 he provides a full narrative version of the play, with extensive quotations and descriptions of the settings and action. Other information includes a biographical sketch of W, the cast, and a note on the Drama Critics Circle Award, for which NS received some votes.

830. ____. "Here Are a Couple of Native Sons." New York Daily News (6 April).
Dramatic and biographical descriptions of NS and Canada Lee. Mantle emphasizes the play's emotional impact.

831. ____. "Lillian Hellman's 'Watch on the Rhine' Enters Season's Best Play Contest." New York Daily News (13 April).
Reports that NS competes closely with the Hellman play for the Drama Critics Circle Award.

832. ____. "Lukas and Lawrence Named the Season's Outstanding Actors." New York Daily News (6 June).
Commends also Canada Lee, Anne Burr, Evelyn Ellis and Ray Collins from the cast of NS.

833. ____. "'Native Son' Is Praised by Drama Critic." New York Daily News.
Highly favorable review praising the play's power. Notes that each of the ten scenes is played in a dim light. Mantle discusses several scenes at length, with special attention to the furnace scene.

834. ____. "'Native Son' Stirs Audience to Emotional Pitch at the St. James." Critics' Theatre Reviews, 2 (20 April), 351.
Reprint of 1941.835.

835. ____. "'Native Son' Stirs Audience to Emotional Pitch at the St. James." New York Daily News (25 March).
Highly favorable review of the play. Mantle believes that the essence of the novel is faithfully transferred to the stage version. The excellence of the production, which receives a four-star rating, is mainly owing to the theatrical genius of Orson Welles. Mantle also notes the theme of social guilt for Bigger's plight. Reprinted: 1941.834.

836. ____. "Predicts Tour Troubles for Two N. Y. Plays." New York Daily News.
Censorship problems await NS and Robert Sherwood's There Shall Be No Night.

837. ____. "Prize Play Debate Still On; 'Flight to West' Is Expanding." New York Daily News (1 April).
Notes that Lester Judson wrote to say that NS and Lady in the Dark do not deserve any awards.

838. ____. "Pulitzer Awards to be Made at 4 Today; Actors' Fund Elects." New York Daily News (5 May).
Mentions the play NS as a possible candidate.

839. ____. "Selling 26,000 Seats for Unknown Drama; 'Native Son' Guarantee." New York Daily News (7 March).
Explains details of advance ticket sales which assure a run of at least three weeks for the play.

840. ____. "Theatre Season's 10 Best Plays." New York Sunday News (1 June), p. 72.
NS leads the list.

841. ____. "Who, For Just Once, Would You Say Is the Greatest Actress You Ever Saw?" New York Daily News (25 May).
Includes photographs of Paul Stewart and Canada Lee in scenes from the play NS.

842. Margolin, Leo. "Paroled Musician Enjoys the World After 19 Years in New Jersey Prison." PM (22 August), p. 12.
Reports that paroled musician Clinton Brewer visited W, one of his sponsors.

843. Maun, Emmett V. "Record of a New York Day." PM (4 April), p. 13.
Relates anecdote about Charles Chaplin congratulating Canada Lee for his portrayal of Bigger.

844. McHenry, Beth. "Negro Leaders Hit Police Terror." Sunday Worker (9 November), p. 3.
Quotes W on police brutality in Harlem.

845. McManus, John T. "'Citizen Kane' Will be Shown in Spite of Hearst." PM's Weekly (13 April), p. 55.
Points out that resentment of Citizen Kane caused Hearst newspapers to roast the play NS as Communist propaganda.

846. Meacham, William Shands. "The Bitter Saga of the Negro." The New York Times Book Review (23 November), p. 11.
Favorable review of TMBV calling W's prose "astringent" and his point of view that of the folk. The book concludes hopefully, but W does not take account of the great progress achieved for black people by the New

Deal.
Reprinted: 1978.209.

847. Meltzer, Milton. "Robeson, Richard Wright, Basie Join in Tribute to Joe Louis." Daily Worker (3 October), p. 7.
    Provides an account of the recording session. Two photographs appear, with W in one. Includes the text of "Joe Louis Blues" in twelve stanzas.

848. Mendel'son, M.[oris Osipovich]. "Chernokozii pasynok." Novy mir, No. 6, pp. 238-241.
    Favorable review of the Russian translation of NS. After providing historical background on the black situation in America and a plot summary of the stories in UTC, Mendel'son summarizes the plot of NS. Despite such defects as faulty characterization of Communists, Max's streak of liberalism, and excessive didacticism in the third part, the novel is a bold and truthful work of art which is a powerful indictment of capitalist society.

849. Meredith, J. Mercer. "Canada Lee Stems from a Sturdy Flock at St. Croix." Norfolk Journal and Guide (26 April), p. 15.
    Relates the family background of the star of the play NS.

850. M.[erlin], M.[ilton]. "Story of Negroes in America Reflected in Life's Mirror." Los Angeles Times (7 December), Part III-A, p. 7.
    Favorable review of the "powerfully and beautifully written" TMBV. Quoting W on black life as a mirror of white life, Merlin concludes: "Anyone who loves and wants to know his America will be wise to look into this mirror and study it well."

851. Mitchell, Billie Kyle. "Chicago's Mayfair." The Pittsburgh Courier (c. 19 April).
    Summarizes W's lecture about Bigger at a dinner party given by Horace Cayton. Arna Bontemps and Edward Embree were among those present.

852. Monroe, Al. "Bigger Thomas in 'Native Son' Is Big 'Theatre' Scribe Says." The Chicago Defender (15 November), pp. 12, 15.
    Favorable review of the Chicago production of the play. Monroe emphasizes societal responsibility for Bigger's plight and compares NS favorably to The Green Pastures.

853. Morehouse, Ward. "Broadway After Dark." The New York Sun (3 March), p. 10.

Contains an announcement of the opening of the play NS.

854. _____. "Broadway After Dark." The New York Sun (21 March), p. 25.
    Announces the opening of the play NS and lists the producers and the leading actors.

855. _____. "Broadway After Dark." The New York Sun (24 March), p. 13.
    Notes the opening of the play NS.

856. _____. "Broadway After Dark." The New York Sun (1 April), p. 24.
    Mentions several persons attending the play NS, including Paul Muni, Oscar Levant, Fred Allen, and Robert Benchley.

857. _____. "Broadway After Dark." The New York Sun (22 July), p. 22.
    Announces the opening of a revival of the play NS in Maplewood, New Jersey.

858. _____. "Broadway After Dark." The New York Sun (4 August), p. 14.
    Announces the beginning of a week's engagement of the play NS at the Windsor Theatre in the Bronx.

859. _____. "Broadway After Dark." The New York Sun (5 August), p. 12.
    Notes that Canada Lee and Anne Burr will play in NS at the Windsor Theatre in the Bronx.

860. _____. "Broadway After Dark." The New York Sun (13 August), p. 26.
    Producer Jules Leventhal reports that the revival of NS is doing well at the box office.

861. _____. "Broadway After Dark: What's the News in Theatertown?" The New York Sun (31 July), p. 12.
    Announces the opening of the play NS at the Windsor Theatre in the Bronx.

862. _____. "Broadway Beacon." The New York Sun (7 April), p. 15.
    "The Beacon Recommends" Canada Lee in the play NS.

863. Munz, Charles Curtis. "The New Negro." The Nation, 153 (13 December), 620.
    Mixed review of TMBV. Munz maintains that while the work is superficial as folk or political history, it is effective as "an appeal, sometimes a defense, and again a defiance, a demand, and a promise—and possibly even a threat." He defends W's militant tone.
    Reprinted: 1978.209.

864. Murphy, Beatrice M. "Wright's New

Book Biased, Depressing." The Baltimore Afro-American (22 November), p. 9.
Mixed review of TMBV. Murphy concedes W's literary skill and the accuracy of his treatment of the black lower class, but she complains at length about the unfairness of omitting the black middle class and thereby distorting the whole picture.

865. Muse, Clarence. "What's Going on in Hollywood." The Chicago Defender (22 February), National edition, p. 21.
Mentions the intense interest in NS in Hollywood.

866. _____. "What's Going on in Hollywood." The Chicago Defender (12 April), National edition, p. 20.
States that the film version of NS will have a new title and an all-white cast. The play is considered a sensation in Hollywood.

867. Myers, J. S. "Book Reviews and News." Middletown (Ohio) Sunday News Journal (3 August), p. 4.
Lists W as a contributor to Edward J. O'Brien's anthology The Best Short Stories of 1941.

868. N., R. J. "Between the Lines." The Calgary Herald (27 December), p. 12.
Favorable review of TMBV, which extends the theme of NS. The only hope for ameliorating the racial situation, the reviewer believes, is for white Americans to change their attitudes. Includes an illustration from TMBV.

869. Narizhny, Grigory. "'Native Son' Wins Praise from Fighter in Red Army." Sunday Worker (9 November), Sec. 2, p. 6.
Note on the Soviet reception of the novel and a letter of appreciation to W which attests its popularity in the Red Army.

870. Nathan, George Jean. "The Theatre: Laurels and Raspberries." The American Mercury, 53 (July), 104-108.
Canada Lee was runner-up for best actor of the 1940-1941 season; Orson Welles was runner-up for best director.

871. Nichols, Lewis. "Seven Recent Plays." The New York Times Book Review (20 April), p. 16.
Includes a brief notice of NS, which Nichols finds "faithful to the original" and "much more than just a good melodrama, although it is that, too."

872. Nikulin, L. "Prestuplenie i nakazanie Tomas Biggera." Internatsional'-
naia literatura, No. 5 (May), pp. 182-185.
Favorable analysis of NS. W complicates his task by making his protagonist a "bad nigger," by using the form of the crime novel, and by risking sensationalism in his use of grisly naturalistic detail. His triumph is to create sympathy for the brutal Bigger despite these complications. Nikulin discusses the plot, stressing the tripartite structure and Bigger's awakening consciousness. The third book is repetitious and the Communist characters are not typical, but overall NS is highly successful. Nikulin compares W to Balzac, Poe, and Dostoevsky.

873. _____. "Syn Ameriki." Pravda (13 April), p. 4.
Favorable review of the Russian translation of NS. The theme is the desire for self-assertion of a persecuted minority. Nikulin contrasts W to Stowe, comments on his use of the genre of the crime novel, summarizes the plot, criticizes the portrayal of Jan and Max, and praises the work's literary quality.

874. North, Gladys and Sterling North. "Being a Literary Map of These United States." New York Post (3 December), p. 20.
W appears on the Mississippi map along with Faulkner and Stark Young.

875. North, Sterling. "Sterling North Reviews the Chicago Scene." Philadelphia Record (7 December), Sec. B, p. 4.
Mentions briefly W's success with TMBV and the play NS.

876. O'Hara, John. "The Coast is Clear." Newsweek, 17 (31 March), 67.
Expresses disappointment at not being able to see the opening performance of the play NS.

877. _____. "Prize Collection." Newsweek, 17 (28 April), 64.
Comments on the competition for the New York Drama Critics Circle Award, praising Burns Mantle for voting for NS.

878. Parsons, Margaret. "Book Chat." The Worcester Evening Gazette (23 May), p. 18.
Mentions that W will deliver a lecture to the White Mountain Writers Conference in Jefferson, New Hampshire.

879. Peterson, Ed. "Novels on Colored Life 'Ephemeral.'" The Philadelphia Tribune (8 November), p. 4.

Letter to the editor claiming that NS lacks tragic stature.

880. _____. "Public Sentiment: In the Editor's Mail." The Indianapolis Record-er (15 March), p. 10.
Letter to the editor urging the film-ing of NS as a way of combating ra-cism.

881. Pihodna, Joseph. "The Playbill: O'Neill and the Guild." New York Herald Tribune (16 February), Sec. VI, p. 1.
Mentions a turntable to be used in the play NS.

882. _____. "The Playbill: Seven Entries in March." New York Herald Tribune (23 February), Sec. VI, p. 1.
Mentions the play NS, scheduled to open 17 March.

883. Pippett, Roger. "Book Ends." PM's Weekly (1 June), p. 43.
Announces that W will address the Fourth American Writers Congress.

884. _____. "There's War on the List, Good Americana and Anthologies." PM's Weekly (7 December), p. 57.
Contains a brief notice of the "splendidly illustrated" TMBV.

885. Pittman, John. "Richard Wright's New Book: The Voice of U. S. Negroes Is Heard." People's World (19 November), p. 5.
Favorable review of TMBV emphasizing its importance in the struggle against "Hitlerism" at home as well as abroad. W's task is that of the social scientist, but he writes "the impassioned intimate language of an abolitionist."

886. Pollak, Robert. "Native Son Comes Home." Chicago Daily Times (11 November), p. 35.
Favorable review of the Chicago pro-duction of the play NS. Pollak praises the direction and outstanding performances of the cast.

887. Pollock, Arthur. "'Native Son' Keeps All the Promises of a Fine Novel." Brooklyn Eagle (25 March), p. 7.
Highly favorable review of "a beauti-ful, stark and fluent drama." Pollock praises the adaptation, the produc-tion, and the acting. "This is to-day's theater at its finest."

888. _____. "Playthings." Brooklyn Eagle (22 June), Sec. E, p. 6.
Contains favorable comments about NS, "one of the most compelling plays of the last few seasons," well acted and produced.

889. _____. "Playthings." Brooklyn Eagle (29 June), Sec. E, p. 5.
Notes with regret the closing of NS, too serious a play for the frivolous taste of summer theater audiences.

890. _____. "Playthings: Messrs. Wright, Green and Welles Make 'Native Son' a Little Epochal." Brooklyn Eagle (30 March), Sec. E, p. 6.
Highly favorable review of the play NS. Not having read the novel, Pol-lock can respond with unrestrained enthusiasm to the stage version. He summarizes the plot, focusing on the sympathetic depiction of Bigger. All aspects of the play are excellent: "There is beauty in the play and force and vividness and a rich reali-ty that few plays can boast."

891. _____. "'Watch on the Rhine' Wins Critics' Award." Brooklyn Eagle (23 April), p. 11.
Pollock notes that he first voted for NS, but when he saw it had no chance switched his vote to Watch on the Rhine.

892. Pressey, Benfield. "Literature, English and American," in The New Inter-national Year Book. Ed. Charles Earle Funk. New York: Funk & Wagnalls, pp. 411-415.
Mentions briefly the novel NS (p. 413).

893. Price, Edgar. "The Premiere." Brooklyn Citizen (25 March), p. 12.
Highly favorable review of the play NS praising all aspects of the pro-duction. Price provides a summary of the action and predicts a Pulitzer Prize and a New York Drama Critics Circle Prize for the play.

894. Putnam, Samuel. "Steinbeck, Wright, Caldwell Favorites in Latin-America." Daily Worker (19 August), p. 7.
Reports that NS "is creating what can only be described as a 'sensation.'" Includes a photograph of W.

895. Randolph, John. "'Negro People Will Join Fight Against Axis,' Says Richard Wright Revising 'Native Son.'" Daily Worker (13 December), p. 7.
Discusses the efforts of the company of NS to fight fascism and racism. Includes W's revisions of the play telegraphed to Chicago, where it was playing, after the outbreak of the war.

896. Rhodes, Arthur. "Passed in Review: 'Native Son' Glorified as 1940's Best Novel; Other Choices of Outstanding Literature." Brooklyn Eagle (5 January),

Sec. E, p. 7.
Contains a favorable notice of NS comparing it to The Grapes of Wrath and praising its imaginative power, brutal expression, and "vivid characterization." W "is one of the greats of our lush era of fiction."

897. Rice, Robert. "Broadway Report." PM (6 March), p. 22.
Based on an interview with W. Discusses his collaboration with Paul Green, his lack of knowledge about theatrical technique, his personal appearance, his background, and his work in progress, the source of which is identified.

898. _____. "Broadway Report." PM (11 March), p. 22.
Reports a conversation between W and his press agent, who reminded the author that a thousand-word piece for The New York Times about the dramatization of NS was overdue.

899. _____. "Broadway Report." PM's Weekly (23 March), p. 50.
Mentions the postponement of the opening of NS.

900. _____. "Broadway Report." PM's Weekly (30 March), p. 44.
Mentions the opening of NS and its generally favorable reception (the Hearst newspapers excepted).

901. _____. "Broadway Report." PM (3 April), p. 20.
Reports that Orson Welles refuses to sell screen rights to NS unless W "is in the contract as a technical adviser at least."

902. _____. "Broadway Report." PM's Weekly (6 April), p. 42.
Mentions the critical dispute over the play NS involving John Anderson, Burns Mantle, Arthur Pollock, and John Mason Brown.

903. _____. "Broadway Report." PM's Weekly (27 April), p. 43.
Mentions the third-place finish of NS in the competition for the New York Drama Critics Circle Award.

904. _____. "Theater: 'Native Son,' Directed by Orson Welles, Opens Monday." PM's Weekly (16 March), pp. 44-45.
Illustrated article on Welles's methods as a director.

905. _____. "'Watch on Rhine' Is Odds-On to Cop Critics' Prize." PM's Weekly (13 April), p. 43.
Full-page listing of the competition for the New York Drama Critics Circle

Award. Only Burns Mantle is listed as supporting NS.

906. Robinson, Major. "'Native Son' Is Real Broadway Material, Scribe Says." The Chicago Defender (5 April), National edition, p. 21.
Favorable review emphasizing the excellent acting and Welles's superb stagecraft.

907. Rogers, J. A. "Rogers Says: I Found Nothing in 'Native Son' That I Could Object To." The Pittsburgh Courier (3 May), p. 13.
Unlike the novel, which was too sensationalistic, the play NS is both "powerful drama" and a competent presentation of a valid racial message. In the play Bigger is not a monster, mainly because the murder of Bessie (Clara) is omitted. The acting and production are skillful.

908. _____. "Rogers Says: Picking Leaders, Negroes or Anybody, Always Calls for Omniscience." The Pittsburgh Courier (22 February), p. 24.
Consists mainly of sharp criticism of NS for its characterization of Bigger as a beast. Not typical of blacks, Bigger will frighten whites, especially white employers. W writes well, but his social effect is deleterious.

909. Rokotov, T. "Tvorcheskii rost Richarda Raita." Internatsional'naia literatura, No. 2 (February), pp. 154-157.
The critical success of NS has invoked comparisons of W to Dostoevsky, Dickens, Dreiser, and others. The popular success of the work derives from W's use of the popular form of the crime novel to develop serious progressive ideas. Drawing from "How 'Bigger' Was Born," Rokotov analyzes and defends the characterization of Bigger. His savage individualism derives from the capitalist system and leads to his downfall. Neither Bigger nor the Communists in NS are typical, but W remains loyal to Communism.

910. Rollins, Charlemae. We Build Together: A Reader's Guide to Negro Life and Literature for Elementary and High School Use. Pamphlet Publication of the National Council of Teachers of English, No. 2. Chicago: The National Council of Teachers of English, p. 15.
Argues that the "mighty sociological novel" NS is important but dangerous unless handled with care. Otherwise, "it may kindle the bitterest hatred in the mind of an otherwise unbiased person." See also the revised edi-

tion, 1948.224. The third edition
(1967) contains nothing on W.

911. Romero, Emanuel A. "Twelve Million
Black Voices." The Commonweal, 35 (26
December), 247.
     Letter to the editor praising W's
     book for stimulating discussion.
     Mainly, Romero stresses the need for
     the unity of black people regardless
     of complexion.

912. Rose, Ernestine. "Wright, Richard.
Twelve Million Black Voices." Library
Journal, 66 (15 November), 999.
     Favorable notice emphasizing the
     book's documentary quality and call-
     ing it "fair, honest, and very mov-
     ing."
     Reprinted: 1978.209.

913. Rosen, Norman. "Surveying." Bronx
High School of Science Science Survey, 5
(2 April).
     Mixed review of the play NS. Rosen
     praises its dramatic qualities but
     considers the social message less
     successfully realized than in the
     novel. "In the book, Bigger Thomas
     . . . is a symbol of the oppressed
     Negro. In the play, he emerges only
     as an individual who is a victim of
     circumstance."

914. _____. "Wright's Life Indicates
Background of Novels." Bronx High School
of Science Science Survey, 5 (2 April).
     Interview with W concerned mostly
     with his youth, but also treating
     briefly his literary career and his
     ideas about current racial condi-
     tions.

915. Rosenberger, Coleman. "Schulberg's
Study in Psycho-Dynamics." The Washington Post (13 April), Sec. VI, p. 10.
     Review of Budd Schulberg's What Makes
     Sammy Run? comparing its protagonist
     to Bigger Thomas.

916. Rosenthal, Jean. "Native Son--Back-
stage." Theatre Arts, 25 (June), 467-
470.
     Detailed account of scenery move-
     ments, sets, etc. by the man who
     "supervised the entire intricate and
     smooth-running production." Includes
     drawings by James Marcom. Two photo-
     graphs of the production showing
     Canada Lee, Evelyn Ellis, Eileen
     Burns, Flashe Riley, and Wardell
     Saunders appear on p. 415 of this
     issue.

917. Ross, George. "So This Is Broadway." New York World-Telegram (19 February), p. 19.
     Notes that Native Son Inc. could not

be used as a corporation name for the
producers of the play because of pre-
emption by other groups. Instead,
Orsonjohn, Inc. was used.

918. _____. "So This Is Broadway." New
York World-Telegram (21 February), p. 6.
     Notes that the Music Corporation of
     America is among the backers of the
     play NS.

919. _____. "So This Is Broadway." New
York World-Telegram (7 March), p. 18.
     Notes that Orson Welles uses the
     revolving stages from an earlier
     production for NS.

920. _____. "So This Is Broadway." New
York World-Telegram (17 March), p. 13.
     Notes that Welles produced NS in only
     five weeks after first reading the
     script.

921. _____. "So This Is Broadway." New
York World-Telegram (18 March), p. 12.
     Mentions an accident suffered by
     Orson Welles during rehearsal of NS
     that may be considered a "good omen."
     Also notes the postponement of the
     opening of the play.

922. _____. "So This Is Broadway." New
York World-Telegram (25 March), p. 15.
     Reports that a couple watching a
     preview of NS "protested aloud from
     their front pews, stalked up the
     aisle and threatened to take the
     matter to City Hall. (P. S. They
     didn't.)."

923. _____. "So This Is Broadway." New
York World-Telegram (26 March), p. 27.
     Mentions the excellent acting of Anne
     Burr in NS.

924. _____. "So This Is Broadway." New
York World-Telegram (31 March), p. 10.
     Notes that Orson Welles used the
     sleigh named Rosebud from Citizen
     Kane as a prop in the first scene of
     NS.

925. _____. "So This Is Broadway." New
York World-Telegram (1 April), p. 12.
     Notes that Canada Lee's performance
     in NS has improved business at his
     Harlem restaurant.

926. _____. "So This Is Broadway." New
York World-Telegram (2 April), p. 31.
     Includes discussion of W's interest
     in the Clinton Brewer Case.

927. Ross, Paul. "Broadway Report."
PM's Weekly (8 June), p. 56.
     Mentions W's participation in a radio
     program honoring Canada Lee on 9
     June.

928. Rouzeau, Edgar T. "Broadway to Witness Rare Scene in 'Native Son.'" The Pittsburgh Courier (8 March), p. 21.
    The rare scene is that of a white woman and a black man together on the stage. After several other actresses rejected the part, Anne Burr was cast as Mary Dalton.

929. _____. "Give-and-Take Philosophy Rules Opinions on Broadway's Controversial 'Native Son.'" The Pittsburgh Courier (19 April), p. 13.
    Extensive quotations on the effect of the play from various black spokesmen and from a white sociologist. Sixty percent of the blacks interviewed believe that the social effects of the play will benefit the race. Rouzeau himself compares the play to Uncle Tom's Cabin.

930. _____. "Harlem is Raging Over 'Native Son.'" The Pittsburgh Courier (22 March), pp. 1, 4.
    Discusses the controversy in Harlem over the play after its NAACP benefit performance. Some support it; others attack it for presenting in Bigger an image harmful to the race. Some believe that the casting of a light-skinned black woman as Mary Dalton might have forestalled unfavorable white reaction.

931. _____. "'Native Son' Ends Short Run on Broadway." Norfolk Journal and Guide (5 July), p. 14.
    Reports lack of financial success in New York and announces plans for a road show. Comments also on the relation of the play to the novel, the divided opinion of theatrical critics, and the risque nature of some scenes.

932. _____. "'Native Son' Swell for Indian or Mongolian--But Being a Negro, It's Hard to Decide." The Pittsburgh Courier (5 April), pp. 1, 4.
    Ambivalent review of the play. Rouzeau admires its acting and production, but has misgivings about the sense of shame it induces in blacks. The Bigger Thomas type does exist, but he is not representative.

933. _____. "Star Dust." Norfolk Journal and Guide (22 March), p. 14.
    Speculates at length on the possible white reaction to the Dalton bedroom scene in NS. Relates the situation to the Spell-Strubing case in Connecticut.

934. _____. "Star Dust." Norfolk Journal and Guide (5 April), p. 15.
    Discusses various aspects of the play

NS: white and black reactions, W's earnings, the racial-sexual tension.

935. _____. "Star Dust." Norfolk Journal and Guide (12 April), p. 14.
    Discusses Anne Burr's performance as Mary Dalton in NS, emphasizing the interest of white women in the audience (who outnumber men) in her bedroom scene with Bigger. Rouzeau also quotes from white reviews of the play.

936. _____. "Stardust." Norfolk Journal and Guide (19 April), p. 15.
    Praises Canada Lee's performance in NS, but argues that it is not better than Richard Harrison's in Green Pastures or Charles Gilpin's in The Emperor Jones.

937. _____. "Stardust." Norfolk Journal and Guide (26 April), p. 15.
    Compares Theodore Ward's play Big White Fog and W's NS. The former is addressed to a black audience; the latter to a white audience.

938. _____. "Stardust." Norfolk Journal and Guide (10 May), p. 15.
    Discusses the critical reception of the play NS and the balloting for the New York Drama Critics Circle Award.

939. _____. "Stardust." Norfolk Journal and Guide (12 July), p. 14.
    Concerns Canada Lee's plans for a radio series. Mentions his role in NS.

940. _____. "Stardust." Norfolk Journal and Guide (13 September), p. 12.
    Contrasts the financial success of NS as a road show with its mediocre financial record on Broadway.

941. _____. "Star Dust: 'Native Son' Should Take Well." Norfolk Journal and Guide (1 March), Home Edition, p. 17.
    Despite the failure of Theodore Ward's play Big White Fog, the stage version of NS should do well because of advance publicity, the theatrical talent of Orson Welles, and the acting ability of Canada Lee.

942. _____. "White Press Loud in Praise for 'Native Son.'" Norfolk Journal and Guide (5 April), p. 14.
    Favorable review of the play with analysis of Bigger as a social phenomenon. Like many blacks, Rouzeau despises the Bigger type, but he understands that the type is a product of white society. Praises the acting and the production.

943. Rowe, Billy. "First Night Audience

Cheers 'Native Son.'" The Pittsburgh Courier (5 April), p. 21.
Unfavorable review of the play admitting the excellence of its acting and staging but deploring the falsity of its presentation of Bigger as a representative black person.

944. _____. "Interest Around Broadway Production of Richard Wright's Famed 'Native Son.'" The Pittsburgh Courier (15 February), p. 20.
Discusses the problems of casting. Paul Robeson and Rex Ingram are said to be the leading candidates for the role of Bigger.

945. _____. "Orson Welles Plans to Break Broadway Ban with Race Star." The Pittsburgh Courier (19 April), p. 20.
Concerns the possible production of Othello with Canada Lee in the title role, Welles as Iago, and a white actress as Desdemona. Such a production is feasible after the precedent of NS.

946. Russell, Cara Green. "The Literary Lantern." The Charlotte Observer (16 November), Sec. 3, p. 5.
Reprint of 1941.949.

947. _____. "The Literary Lantern." Greensboro Daily News (6 April), p. D-5.
Favorable review of the published version of the play NS. "It is hard, fateful, and fast." The theme of environmental determinism is dubious, however. Though generally favorable to NS, Russell believes that Green's other plays, written alone, are better.
Reprinted: 1941.948, 950, 951.

948. _____. "The Literary Lantern." Norfolk Virginian-Pilot (6 April), p. 8.
Reprint of 1941.947.

949. _____. "The Literary Lantern." Norfolk Virginian-Pilot (9 November), p. 10.
Contains a highly favorable review of TMBV emphasizing the emotional intensity of the work, greater even than that of NS. "This is one of the most emotional books it has ever been our experience to read, but it is naked emotion rigidly controlled and never veering from its purpose--which is to burn into the reader's consciousness an awareness of the injustices suffered by the American Negro with the pledge that something must be done about it."
Reprinted: 1941.946.

950. _____. "P. Green and Book's Author Collaborate on Stage Hit." The Charlotte Observer (6 April), Sec. 3, p. 5.
Reprint of 1941.947.

951. _____. "Paul Green's and Richard Wright's Dramatization of 'Native Son' Makes Women Scream, Strong Men Mutter." The Columbia (S. C.) State (6 April), p. 9-B.
Reprint of 1941.947.

952. _____. "13 Years Make a Difference! Traces Renaissance to Koch's Playmakers." Charlotte Sunday Observer (7 December), Sec. Three, p. 5.
Includes W in a list of Southerners represented in the O. Henry Memorial Award Prize Stories of 1941.

953. S., E. J. "News of the Theater." New York Herald Tribune (24 March), p. 8.
Announces the opening of NS at the St. James Theatre and gives ticket prices.

954. Saroyan, William. "William Saroyan Speaks Up for His Latest Drama." New York Herald Tribune (27 April), Sec. VI, p. 1.
Includes a brief expression of admiration for the play NS.

955. Schneider, Isidor. "The Fellowship of Laughter." New Masses, 38 (11 February), 23.
Review of Howard Nutt's Special Laughter quoting from W's introduction.

956. S.[elby], J.[ohn]. "Books [sic] on Slavery Is Anachronism." Asheville Citizen (2 March), Sec. B, p. 3.
Unfavorable review of Henrietta Buckmaster's Let My People Go criticizing W's blurb as "inexact, at best."
Reprinted: 1941.958.

957. _____. "Negro's Case Poorly Stated." Youngstown Vindicator (30 November), p. B-6.
Reprint of 1941.960.

958. _____. "Reviews in Brief of Recent Worthwhile Books." Savannah Morning News (20 April), p. 30.
Reprint of 1941.956.

959. _____. "Richard Wright Commits Cardinal Literary Sin." Toldeo Times (30 November), p. 4A.
Reprint of 1941.960.

960. _____. "Richard Wright Does Negro Cause Little Good in His New Book." The Gastonia Daily Gazette (29 November), p. 12.
Unfavorable review of TMBV complaining of oversimplification, faulty

logic, and impatience. W ignores black achievement and forgets that "the solution of the problem of minorities is frequently a matter of centuries, and that sometimes there may be no solution."
Reprinted: 1941.957, 959, 961, 962.

961. ____. "Too-Simple Story Weakens Position." The Knoxville Journal (30 November), Sec. Four, p. 11.
Reprint of 1941.960.

962. ____. "Wright Does Poor Job with Negroes." Asheville Citizen-Times (30 November), Sec. B, p. 5.
Reprint of 1941.960.

963. Sergeev, N. "Syn Ameriki." Internatsional molodezhi, No. 6, pp. 48-49.
Favorable review of the Russian translation of NS noting Bigger's fear-shame-hatred syndrome and stressing his "purification" through his development of a revolutionary consciousness. NS is a masterful novel showing the racism of a corrupt capitalist society.

963a. Sewall, Joe. "Your Stars and Mine." Washington Tribune (3 May), p. 10.
Mentions briefly the play NS.

963b. ____. "Your Stars and Mine." Washington Tribune (10 May), p. 10.
Mentions briefly Canada Lee and the play NS.

964. Shalit, Sid. "Listening In." New York Daily News (9 April).
Reports that W discussed the play NS with Professor Warren Bower on radio station WNYC at 3:30 p. m. on 8 April.

965. Shields, Art. "History Week Exhibition Shows Creative Genius of Negro People." Sunday Worker (9 February), Sec. 2, p. 5.
Reports that an exhibit at the Schomburg Collection includes W material. "The unexpurgated galley proofs" of NS reveal censorship by W's publisher.
See 1965.89.

966. ____. "Writers Congress Scores War Drive; Theodore Dreiser Gets Peace Award." Sunday Worker (8 June), p. 3.
Mentions W's participation in picketing of The Day newspaper on 7 June.

967. Sillen, Samuel. "Bigger Thomas on the Boards." New Masses, 39 (8 April), 27-28.
Highly favorable review of the play NS. It is successful in achieving

"fidelity to the essential spirit of the original and independent vitality in the new medium." Sillen praises the production and acting, but emphasizes the social message, which not even the projected Hollywood "whitewash" version would cancel.

968. ____. "The 'Masses' Fights for the American Dream." Daily Worker (21 February), p. 7.
Mentions NS as one of the works growing out of the movement for proletarian literature led by New Masses.

969. ____. "Sharpen Up the Arrows." New Masses, 40 (1 July), 23-25.
Discussion of proletarian literature citing W as a prime example. Mentions his work in progress on domestic workers.

970. ____. "12 Million Black Voices." New Masses, 41 (25 November), 22-24.
Highly favorable review lauding the presentation of history, the use of the collective voice, the emotional impact, and the underlying ideology of the work. In it "Wright has demonstrated again and with new intensity that he is one of the great, one of the truly great American artists of our time."
Reprinted: 1978.209.

971. S--m, H. "En Amerikansk Tragedi." Unidentified clipping (7 January).
Lengthy Swedish review of NS stressing its pessimism, honesty, and intensity. Although it is not very original, drawing heavily on Dreiser, it effectively portrays the effect of social pressures on black psychology. The reviewer notes the danger that Bigger's violence may reinforce white stereotypes.

972. Smith, Bernard. "The Democratic Spirit." The Saturday Review of Literature, 24 (11 October), 11-12.
In a letter to the editor Smith defends his decision to include radical writers such as W in his anthology The Democratic Spirit.
See 1941.973.

973. ____. "Richard Wright," in his The Democratic Spirit: A Collection of American Writings from the Earliest Times to the Present Day. New York: Knopf, p. 819.
Biographical headnote to an excerpt from NS.

974. Smith, Cecil. "Canada Lee's Acting Superb in 'Native Son.'" Chicago Daily Tribune (11 November), p. 20.
Favorable review of the play with

special emphasis on the excellent
acting. Terse and exciting, NS "possesses the unmistakable aspect of
greatness." The play's concentration
is so great, however, that motivation
and secondary characterization are
somewhat weak.

975. Smith, Isodora, "Canada Lee to
Appear in Radio Series When 'Native Son'
Closes." The Pittsburgh Courier (5
July), p. 21.
    Mentions also the fall road tour of
    the play.

976. _____. "Producer's Present Backfires on Canada Lee in Court Tiff." The
Pittsburgh Courier (23 August), p. 20.
    Mainly concerns Lee's legal difficul-
    ties, but also includes information
    on plans for future performances of
    NS. A photograph with caption of Lee
    and admirers also appears on this
    page.

977. [Smith, Lillian E. and Paula Snel-
ling]. "Novelists." The North Georgia
Review, 6 (Winter), 55.
    Contains a paragraph on W calling his
    work "strong and powerful and excit-
    ing." He must learn artistic control
    of his hatred, however.

978. Smith, Theodore. "Of the Making of
Books." The San Francisco News (13
November), p. 16.
    Contains a favorable review of TMBV.
    Its "pulsating prose" conveys effec-
    tively "the tragic bitterness of 300
    years of a subjected race."

979. Stanford, Don. "The Beloved Returns
and Other Recent Fiction." The Southern
Review, 6 (Winter), 610-628.
    NS (pp. 618-619) is one of thirty
    novels reviewed. Stanford complains
    about excessive violence, but sees
    merit in the novel's "fine psycho-
    logical study of race hatred." He
    notes "all the earmarks of the natur-
    alistic technique--sordid atmosphere
    of violence and terror, a crude,
    repetitious prose, and a central
    character who is not a free agent but
    who is completely at the mercy of his
    environment and of his ungoverned
    passions."

980. Stanford, Theodore. "Book Review."
The Philadelphia Tribune (6 December),
p. 11.
    Highly favorable review of TMBV
    praising W's literary genius. He
    is "in the foremost ranks of the
    really great American artists of our
    day."

980a. Starr, Ernest. "Should Races Col-

laborate? Asks Starr." Winston-Salem
Journal and Sentinel (27 April), Second
Sec., p. 15.
    Defends the W-Green collaboration in
    dramatizing NS. Summarizes the plot
    of the novel with emphasis on its
    social significance.

981. Steinbarger, Helen T. "Library Sug-
gests Books Pertaining to Negroes." The
Washington Sunday Star (26 January), p.
F7.
    Contains a brief review of Waters E.
    Turpin's O Canaan! comparing its
    realism with W's.

982. Streator, George. "Contemporary
Social Problems." The Commonweal, 35 (28
November), 147-148.
    Mixed review of TMBV calling it "good
    propaganda" but deploring W's Marxism
    and the effort of W and others to
    turn dark-skinned blacks against
    light-skinned blacks (such as Strea-
    tor himself).
    Reprinted: 1978.209.

983. Sullivan, Ed. "Little Old New
York." New York Daily News (17 March).
    Notes that the play NS "is a shocker,
    paralleling the Strubing-Spell case
    in Connecticut."

984. _____. "Little Old New York." New
York Daily News (26 March).
    Contains a favorable notice of the
    play NS with special praise for the
    acting of Canada Lee.

985. _____. "Little Old New York." New
York Daily News (27 March).
    Claims that NS fails as a novel
    because Bigger is not typical of his
    race. W should have made his hero a
    college graduate.

986. _____. "Little Old New York." New
York Daily News (3 April).
    Mentions Paul Muni's telegram to
    Canada Lee congratulating him on his
    performance in NS.

987. _____. "Little Old New York." New
York Daily News (28 April).
    Mentions that Jerry Lavan is one of
    the financial backers of the play NS.

988. _____. "Little Old New York." New
York Daily News (3 May).
    Notes similarities in technique be-
    tween the film Citizen Kane and the
    play NS.

989. _____. "Little Old New York." New
York Daily News (11 August).
    Mentions the Hollywood activites and
    the engagement of Anne Burr of the
    cast of NS.

990. Swan, Maurice. "An Eye on the New."
Santa Barbara News-Press (2 March), p.
15.
    Review of Howard Nutt's Special
    Laughter noting W's introduction and
    comparing Nutt and W as "rebel writ-
    ers."

991. Sylvester, Robert. "Hollywood
Teaches Orson Welles Some New Theater
Tricks." New York Daily News (25 Febru-
ary).
    Discusses the work of Welles as di-
    rector of NS.

992. Taubman, Howard. "Records: China at
War." The New York Times (30 November),
Sec. 9, p. 6.
    Contains a favorable notice of the
    Robeson recording of W's "King Joe."

993. Taylor, Harold. "Death, Terror, and
Aesthetics." The University Review, 8
(October), 3-10.
    Compares the use of violence, espe-
    cially rape, in NS and Studs Lonigan.

994. Taylor, Sylvia. "Canada Lee Has
Many Trades--Master of All." Daily Worker (21 August), p. 7.
    Includes discussion of Lee's work in
    NS.

995. _____. "Thorny Path to Fame for
'Native Son' Star." Daily Worker (26
August), p. 7.
    Biographical article on Anne Burr,
    who plays Mary Dalton.

996. Thompson, Ralph. "Books of the
Times." The New York Times (18 November), p. 29.
    Favorable review of TMBV, praising
    both the photographs and the prose.
    "A more eloquent and belligerent
    statement of its kind could hardly
    have been devised." Admittedly one-
    sided, it is very effective protest.
    Reprinted: 1978.209.

997. Tighe, Dixie. "Going Places." New
York Post (22 April), p. 15.
    Notes the use of a live rat onstage
    in NS.

997a. Tolson, M. B. "Caviar and Cabbage:
Fighting Preachers in the District of
Columbia." Washington Tribune (12
April), p. 8.
    Mentions recommending "Fire and
    Cloud" before W became famous.
    Reprinted: 1982.136b.

997b. _____. "Caviar and Cabbage: Frank-
enstein Monsters and 'Native Sons' in D.
C. Educational System." Washington Tribune (15 February), p. 6.
    Mentions W briefly.

997c. _____. "Caviar and Cabbage:
Richard Wright, the Negro Emancipator:
His Tribute to the Washington Tribune."
Washington Tribune (6 April), p. 4.
    Noting white acclaim for NS, Tolson
    urges blacks to read the work, which
    correctly identifies the economic
    source of racism. Tolson notes his
    support of W two years earlier and
    W's letter expressing appreciation.

998. T.[ooill], K.[enneth] D. "12 Million Black Voices by Richard Wright with
photographs by Edwin Rosskam." Columbus
Ohio State Journal (1 December), p. 10.
    Unfavorable review complaining of
    emotionalism and distortion. By ig-
    noring black progress, W presents a
    one-sided picture.

999. Van Pelt, Nicholas. "In Theatres
Along Broadway." The Raleigh News and
Observer (1 June), Sec. M, p. 5.
    Reports weekly proceeds of $11,500
    for NS, an "overrated play."

1000. Van Vechten, Carl. "Books I Have
Liked." New York Herald Tribune Books (7
December), p. 10.
    TMBV is one of three fall books
    listed.

1001. Verbitsky, Bernardo. "'Sangre Negra' de Richard Wright." Noticias Gráfi-
cas (20 May).
    Highly favorable review of the Span-
    ish translation of NS. Verbitsky
    especially admires W's synthesis of
    Marxism and psychoanalysis. Bigger
    will become a lasting literary arche-
    type.

1001a. Verissimo, Erico. Gato Preto em
Campo de Neve. Puerto Allegre: Edicão da
Livraria do Globo, pp. 52, 71, 72, 178.
    Mentions W and comments briefly on
    NS, both the novel and the play.

1002. Vernon, Grenville. "Native Son."
The Commonweal, 33 (11 April), 622.
    Mixed review of the play. While
    praising the production and acting,
    Vernon considers it "a rather crude
    melodrama with an interesting psycho-
    logical study in its leading pro-
    tagonist." Bigger is "a moral imbe-
    cile," and W's idea of his regenera-
    tion through murder is "the apotheo-
    sis of sadism."

1003. Waldorf, Wilella. "Billy Rose and
The Group Producing New Odets Play." New
York Post (20 February), p. 8.
    Notes that NS will open in New York
    without tryouts elsewhere.

1004. _____. "Canada Lee's Future Plans;
Soft Pedal on 'Othello.'" New York Post

(23 June), p. 9.
Reports that Lee will perform in NS for at least a year.

1005. _____. "Guild's New Play Laid in Pre-Vichy France." New York Post (13 March), p. 6.
Mentions the play NS.

1006. _____. "'Native Son' and 'My Fair Ladies' Both Postponed." New York Post (19 March), p. 16.
Announces postponement of the opening of the play and notes Welles's decision concerning intermissions.

1007. _____. "Spring Prize-Giving Under Way on Broadway." New York Post (15 March), p. 4.
Mentions the play NS as one of those "still to come."

1008. _____. "Spring Producing in the Broadway District." New York Post (10 March), p. 10.
Mentions the play NS.

1009. _____. "Theatre Clubs Awarding Shower of Spring Prizes." New York Post (4 April), p. 14.
Mentions the beginning of Sunday matinees of NS on 12 April.

1010. _____. "Too Many Angels in the Theater District." New York Post (7 May), p. 14.
Mentions investments in the play NS.

1011. _____. "Two Openings Next Week in Broadway Playhouses." New York Post (18 February), p. 6.
Mentions the dramatization of NS.

1012. _____. "Two Shumlin Shows Win Critics' Circle Prizes." New York Post (23 April), p. 20.
NS figured in the balloting for the prize, but Watch on the Rhine won.

1013. Walker, Danton. "Broadway." New York Daily News (19 February).
Notes that "the Theatre Guild, which finds Left Wing sentiments no longer fashionable, has asked Orson Welles to tone down the Communistic angle in the stage version of 'Native Son.'"

1014. _____. "Broadway." New York Daily News (19 March).
Predicts the drama awards for the year. NS is a dark horse.

1015. _____. "Broadway." New York Daily News (26 March).
Includes laudatory comments on NS, "as forceful and brilliant a piece of theatre as we're likely to see for many a season." It deserves consider-

ation for a Pulitzer Prize.

1016. _____. "Broadway." New York Daily News (2 April), p. 58.
Notes W's determination not to sell film rights to NS unless his theme is retained.

1017. _____. "Broadway." New York Daily News (29 April).
Notes that Canada Lee will spend time at the Savoy Ballroom as well as on the stage performing in NS.

1018. Walker, Viola White. "Books and Authors." Lawrence (Mass.) Evening Tribune (21 February), p. 8.
Reports that W chaired the Book and Authors Luncheon in New York on 11 February. National Book Award winners were announced on this occasion.

1019. Ward, Frank T. "Generous Backers of Hit Play Donate Auto to Canada Lee." Washington Tribune (19 April), p. 11.
Mentions also W's appearance on a New York radio program and his visit to Detroit to interview black workers.

1019a. _____. "Seein' Stars." The Indianapolis Recorder (22 February), p. 11.
Mentions the difficulty in casting the role of Mary Dalton in NS.

1019b. _____. "Seein' Stars." Washington Tribune (26 April), p. 11.
Mentions the gift of an automobile to Canada Lee by the financial backers of NS.

1020. Warner, Ralph. "'Blood on the Forge' Is Story of Negro Brothers." Daily Worker (8 November), p. 7.
Compares Big Mat of William Attaway's novel to Bigger Thomas.

1021. _____. "Broadway Gets Those Summer Doldrum Blues." Sunday Worker (13 July), p. 7.
Analyzes the reasons for the closing of NS. The social message was too strong for many playgoers, and even some misguided progressives failed to understand its import.

1022. _____. "Broadway Highlights: Some Brighter Spots on Broadway Today." Sunday Worker (9 March), p. 7.
Mentions the play NS.

1023. _____. "The Critics Have Their Say About 'Native Son.'" Sunday Worker (13 April), p. 7.
Corrects distortions in reviews of the play in the capitalist press and emphasizes its Communist point of view. Artistically successful and ideologically correct, the play "has

made it easier for other dramatists to write serious plays about Negroes."

1024. _____. "Fall Crop of Plays on Broadway Soon." Daily Worker (23 August), p. 7.

Announces the opening of NS at the Windsor Theatre in the Bronx.

1025. _____. "Hearst Attempts to Sabotage 'Native Son.'" Sunday Worker (30 March), p. 7.

After a sharp attack on the Hearst newspaper drama critics John Anderson and Robert Coleman for anti-Communist bias, Warner himself discusses NS. He praises the work highly, finding it superior to the novel in characterization, especially Bigger's, and in the precision of its ideas.

1026. _____. "In Their Plays, the Aspirations of the People Will Find Voice." Daily Worker (9 June), p. 7.

Report on the drama session of the Fourth American Writers Congress. Speaking on the play NS, Eleanor Flexner criticized W for confirming racist stereotypes by presenting Bigger as typical instead of exceptional. Warner disagrees.

1027. _____. "Mass Appeal of 'Native Son' Brings It to Many Theatres." Daily Worker (5 September), p. 7.

Announces the road tour of the play, including engagements in the Bronx, Brooklyn, Boston, Hartford, Pittsburgh, Detroit, Cleveland, Cincinnati, Columbus, and Akron. Censorship problems are anticipated in Boston.

1028. _____. "'Native Son' Scheduled for Road Tour--Orson Welles Aids Chaplin." Sunday Worker (10 August), p. 7.

Reports on the Maplewood, New Jersey, summer engagement and announces the fall road tour. Includes discussion of the play's financial problems.

1029. _____. "Season's Best Plays Beat No War Drums." Sunday Worker (6 April), p. 7.

Contains laudatory comments on the progressive stance of the play NS.

1030. _____. "Stage Version of 'Native Son' a Compelling Social Document." Daily Worker (27 March), p. 7.

Lengthy, favorable review detailing many aspects of the play's production. Warner praises the acting. W's message is clearer in the play than in the novel, although the final prison scene is politically incomplete. "From the theatrical point of view, it is a technical masterpiece.

As a brilliant political document, it lives with the fire of an angry message. This is America today."

1031. _____. "They Have Not Retreated." Sunday Worker (8 June), p. 7.

Reports that in an American Writers Congress session on "Cities in the Modern Novel" W spoke briefly from the floor.

1032. _____. "25 Years of Theatre in Pictorial Review." Daily Worker (16 August), p. 7.

Reviews favorably a special issue of Theatre Arts, but regrets the omission of NS.

1033. Watkins, Tommy. "Escapading in Brooklyn." New York Amsterdam Star-News (22 March), p. 11.

Gossip column including this item: "The boys in the Stuyvesant sector are anxious to learn the moniker of the nifty-looking chick who is jaunting about with R. W."

1034. Watts, Richard, Jr. "Killer at Large." Critics' Theatre Reviews, 2 (20 April), 351.

Reprint of 1941.1035.

1035. _____. "Killer at Large." New York Herald Tribune (25 March), p. 14.

Favorable review of the play NS commending especially the direction by Orson Welles and the performance by Canada Lee. The play strives to be faithful to the novel, but with its focus on external events the dramatic medium cannot convey the full import of the original work.

Reprinted: 1941.1034.

1036. _____. "The Theater." New York Herald Tribune (6 April), Sec. VI, p. 1.

In opposition to other reviewers of the play NS, Watts argues that it is legitimate to compare play and novel. Doing so, he finds the play, "a stirring and highly effective melodrama," faithful to the novel but lacking something of its "emotional impact . . . largeness of conception . . . sociological insight." Watts de-emphasizes the Communist theme. He praises Lee's acting and Welles's direction. A sketch of a scene from the play appears on the following page.

1037. _____. "The Theater." New York Herald Tribune (27 April), Sec. VI, pp. 1-2.

In a review of Watch on the Rhine, Watts remarks that the novel NS is superior to the dramatic version.

Reprinted: 1941.1040.

1038. _____. "The Theater." New York
Herald Tribune (11 May), Sec. VI, p. 1.
Compares NS and Watch on the Rhine as
plays of topical and social importance. The racism W and Green reveal
is a national failure, but the success of the play is a hopeful sign.

1039. _____. "The Theater." New York
Herald Tribune (1 June), Sec. VI, p. 1.
Praises Anne Burr for her performance
as Mary Dalton in NS.

1040. _____. "'Watch on Rhine' Is Watts'
Choice for Season's Top Play." The Wash-
ington Post (27 April), Sec. VI, p. 3.
Reprint of 1941.1037.

1041. Webber, Harry B. "Richard Wright
Tells How He Wrote Native Son; Lauds
Lee." New Jersey Herald News (5 April).
Interview with W, who comments on the
elements of NS, the power of the
press, writers, his new novel, and
Harlem.

1042. Wedemar, Lou. "Swing Tune by Negro
Convict May Send Him Into This World."
PM (20 June), p. 13.
Reports that W contacted Count Basie
on behalf of the convict-songwriter
Clinton Brewer.

1043. Werner, Ludlow W. "Across the
Desk." The New York Age (22 March), p.
6.
Contains a review of the NAACP benefit performance of NS. Despite de-
lays, Werner enjoyed the play, but he
fears that Broadway may not be ready
for so serious a social message.

1044. West, Josephine. "Powerful Tale of
Revolt Told in 'House of Fury.'"
People's World (12 November), p. 5.
Review of Felice Swados's House of
Fury comparing the novel's material
with that of NS.

1045. Whipple, Sidney B. "Native Son
Stark Drama Stamped with Genius." Crit-
ics' Theatre Reviews, 2 (20 April), 352.
Reprint of 1941.1046.

1046. _____. "Native Son Stark Drama
Stamped with Genius." New York World-
Telegram (25 March), p. 14.
Highly favorable review calling the
play "a stark melodrama, touched by
the hand of genius." All aspects of
the production are praised, especially Welles's direction, Lee's performance, and James Morcom's settings.
Whipple concedes that the sociological significance of the novel is
muted in the play, but he argues that
there is a corresponding gain in dramatic values.

Reprinted: 1941.1045.

1047. _____. "Theater." New York World-
Telegram (21 April), p. 10.
Selects NS as the best melodramatic
play of the year "because of its
miraculous staging, directing and
acting."

1048. _____. "Welles Strives Only for
Effects." New York World-Telegram (29
March), p. 7.
In the play NS the sociological import of the novel is sacrificed for
theatrical effect. In this way character and action become more important than "social causes and results." Whipple considers Wellesian
stagecraft to be superb, even in the
case of the rumbling furnace to which
some critics objected.

1049. Whitney, Norman J. "The Short
Story," in Good Reading. Ed. Atwood H.
Townsend. Chicago: The National Council
of Teachers of English, pp. 39-40.
Contains an annotated listing of UTC
under its subtitle, Five Long
Stories.

1050. Wilder, Roy. "Wright, Negro Ex-
Field Hand, Looks Ahead to New
Triumphs." New York Herald Tribune (17
August), Sec. VI, p. 4.
Interview with W including comments
on past, present, and future activi-
ties. W mentions work on a novel
about black domestics.

1051. Wilson, Earl. "Canada Lee: 'Crazy
Guy' and Swell Actor." New York Post (31
March), p. 3.
Interview with Lee and some addition-
al biographical information. Includes
a photograph of W and Lee backstage.

1052. Winchell, Walter. "On Broadway."
New York Daily Mirror (17 February), p.
10.
Mentions William Hertz, co-producer
of the play NS.

1053. _____. "On Broadway." New York
Daily Mirror (23 March), p. 10.
Announces the postponement of the
opening of NS.

1054. _____. "On Broadway." New York
Sunday Mirror (30 March), p. 10.
Notes briefly the reviews of the play
NS appearing in New York newspapers.

1055. _____. "On Broadway." New York
Daily Mirror (9 April), p. 10.
Mentions that Dick Maney is press
agent for the play NS.

1056. _____. "On Broadway." New York

Sunday Mirror (11 May), p. 10.
    Lists NS as a potentially prize-winning drama.

1057. Wolfert, Ira. "Dramatized 'Native Son' Becomes a Melodrama." The Washington Sunday Star (30 March), pp. F-1, F-3.
    Compares the play unfavorably to the novel. "As a novel, Richard Wright's 'Native Son' was an extraordinary dramatization of squalid life. It created intense excitement in its pages and left agony in its wake," but as a play "it is not a work of art, but it is a flamboyant and malignant drama, played at scorching heat and packed full of about as many heart-squeezing tricks as even Orson Welles could think up." In the novel the intense concentration on Bigger made the characterization of whites pallid. This problem becomes more serious in the play. Wolfert provides a detailed plot summary.

1058. Wyatt, Euphemia Van Rensselaer. "Native Son." The Catholic World, 153 (May), 217-218.
    Extremely unfavorable review of the play. Wyatt considers the production sensationalistic and all the characters except Mrs. Thomas repugnant. "The producers have no regard to niceties--the realism is vicious, the blasphemy continuous, the brutality of compound increase."

1059. Young, Stark. "Book Basis." The New Republic, 104 (7 April), 468-469.
    Mixed review of the play NS discussing differences between it and the novel. Young praises the production but argues that the treatment of the race problem in the play has been weakened and diluted.

1942

1. A., R. "Reviewing the Play: Canada Lee Is Outstanding in 'Native Son.'" Syracuse Herald-Journal (11 February), p. 20.
    Favorable review of the road show praising the direction and acting. Welles brings to the play "a flare for arresting realism and flashy dramatics, a violent use of chiaroscuro lighting, an arresting blackout technique and a feeling for swift pacing." Compares NS to An American Tragedy in its sociological approach, but the play presents Bigger more unsympathetically than the novel.

1a. Addison, Jr. "Book Ends and Odds." Philadelphia Record (8 March), Metropolitan Sec., p. 11.

Announces the forthgoming publication of the Modern Library edition of NS.

2. Allen, Kelcey. "Amusements: 'Native Son' Again at the Flatbush." Women's Wear Daily (28 April), p. 19.
    Announces that the play will make its fourth appearance in Brooklyn.

3. _____. "Amusements: 'Native Son' Is Restored." Women's Wear Daily (8 December).
    Reports that Lee Shubert, owner of the Majestic Theater, has decided not to submit to pressure to close NS.

4. _____. "Amusements: 'Native Son' Opens at Flatbush Tonight." Women's Wear Daily (14 April), p. 26.
    Announces the third engagement of the play in Brooklyn and lists the cast.

5. _____. "Amusements: 'Native Son' Returns to Windsor Tonight." Women's Wear Daily (5 May), p. 24.
    Announces the fourth engagement of the play in the Bronx.

6. _____. "Amusements: 'Native Son' to Open at Windsor Theatre." Women's Wear Daily (20 April), p. 15.
    Announces a return engagement of the play in the Bronx.

7. _____. "Amusements: 'Native Son' to Open Flatbush." Women's Wear Daily (7 April), p. 24.
    Announces that NS will inaugurate the new season on 14 April at the Brooklyn theater.

8. Anon. "Algren, Nelson." The Publishers' Weekly, 141 (18 April), 1510.
    Brief notice of Never Come Morning mentioning W's introduction.

9. Anon. "All Trades: Lee, 'Native Son' Actor, 'Happened' to Get Stage Job." Minneapolis Sunday Tribune and Star Journal (11 January), Society Sec., p. 10.
    Biographical article on Canada Lee with two paragraphs on W and NS.

9a. Anon. "Along the Rialto: 'Native Son' Opens Tonight at the Empire." Syracuse Herald-Journal (10 February), p. 18.
    Contains an announcement of the road show version of the play.

10. Anon. "Among the Publishers." The Publishers' Weekly, 141 (28 February), 946-948.
    Notes that Grosset & Dunlap will reprint NS in a one-dollar edition on 15 March.

11. Anon. "Announcing Postcard Poll." The People's Voice (4 April), p. 30.
Asks readers to decide the question of whether the serialization of NS should continue. The newspaper had already received many requests for discontinuation.

12. Anon. "Archbishop Voices Vigorous Protest on Stage Indecency." The Catholic News (7 November), pp. 1-2.
Does not mention NS, but notes that "four other shows listed as 'wholly objectionable' by the Catholic Theater Movement were placed under police scrutiny." NS was one of the plays so listed.

13. Anon. "Are George M. Cohan's Standards 'Fascist'?" The Catholic Citizen-Herald (c. December).
Editorial in the newspaper of the archdiocese of Milwaukee rebuking Canada Lee for calling stage censorship efforts "fascist-minded." Instead of playing in NS, Lee should concentrate on more wholesome plays such as Green Pastures.
Reprinted: 1942.14.

14. Anon. "Are George M. Cohan's Standards 'Fascist'?" The Catholic News (26 December), p. 3.
Reprint of 1942.13.

15. Anon. "Artists, Writers, Actors, Musicians Say SECOND FRONT NOW." The Worker (26 July), p. 7.
Includes W in a list of supporters of two military fronts against the Nazis.

16. Anon. "Authors Between Books." Book-of-the-Month Club News (February), pp. 17-18.
Contains a note on W, whose TMBV "is really the outline for a whole series of historical novels he hopes to write, telescoping Negro history in terms of the urbanization of feudal folk." According to W, this black experience "parallels the development of all people everywhere."

17. Anon. "Backers Decide Not to Halt Run of 'Native Son.'" New York Herald Tribune (8 December), p. 23.
Lee Shubert, William Brandt, and others rescind a decision to close the play for financial reasons in order to protest the attack on the play by The Catholic News.

18. Anon. "A Bad Example." Variety (9 December), p. 49.
Editorial criticizing Lee Shubert for not closing Wine, Women and Song, a dirty play, thus invoking the censor-

ship of NS, a legitimate drama.

19. Anon. "The Best Plays of 1940-1941, edited by Burns Mantle." Better English, 7 (February), 12.
Mentions the inclusion of NS.

20. Anon. "Between Ourselves." New Masses, 42 (24 February), 2.
Notes that W has been named to the 1941 Honor Roll of Race Relations in a poll conducted by the Schomburg Collection for three achievements: TMBV, the play NS, and "King Joe."

21. Anon. "Book Burning Exhibit at Library Launches December War Bond Drive." PM Daily (30 November), p. 20.
NS is on a list of books banned by Nazi Germany.

22. Anon. "Book Marks." New York World-Telegram (5 March), p. 19.
Announces the Modern Library edition of NS.

23. Anon. "Book Notes: 'Mission to Moscow' Is Leading Best-Seller." People's Daily World (18 March), p. 5.
Announces the Modern Library edition of NS.

24. Anon. "Book Reviews." The Troy (N. Y.) Observer-Budget (26 April), Sec. C, p. 4.
Contains a brief review of Nelson Algren's Never Come Morning considering W's introduction appropriate because Bruno Bicek is the "Polish counterpart of the misfit" Bigger Thomas.

25. Anon. "The Book That Rocked a Nation." Weekly Review, 7 (19 May), 14.
Advertisement offering NS and a six-month subscription to Weekly Review for $1.50.

26. Anon. "Books Published Today." The New York Times (1 October), p. 20.
Quotes W's prediction that Saunders Redding's No Day of Triumph will antagonize the black bourgeoisie.

27. Anon. "Books to Own." Hillsville (Va.) Carroll News (26 February), p. 3.
Review of William Kozlenko's American Scenes mentioning the radio play version of "Fire and Cloud."

28. Anon. "The Bookworm." The San Francisco Call-Bulletin (21 March), p. 12.
Contains a favorable notice of the Modern Library edition of NS, a "harsh, profoundly moving story" essential to an understanding of the race problem.

29. Anon. ("The Bookie.") "Bound to Be

Read." San Mateo Times (11 May), p. 8.
   Contains a notice of Never Come Morning mentioning W and relates anecdote
   of the refusal of a Washington restaurant to serve him during the planning of the stage version of NS.
   See 1971.169.

30. Anon. The Brandts Present Canada Lee
in Native Son by Paul Green and Richard
Wright. New York.
   Playbill for the second season of the
   road show.

31. Anon. "Broadway, Labor Fight Closing
of 'Native Son': Halting of 'Native Son'
Thwarted by Protests of People." The New
York Age (12 December), pp. 1, 10.
   Discusses pressure by Catholic groups
   to close the play and pressure by
   other groups to keep it open. Quotes
   Canada Lee on the importance of the
   play as racial protest.

32. Anon. "Broadway Report." PM Daily (8
December), p. 22.
   Notes that NS will remain at the
   Majestic Theater.

33. Anon. "The Bulletin Board." The
Chicago Defender (14 February), p. 7.
   Announces a book review of TMBV by
   Arna Bontemps at the Hall Branch
   Library in Chicago on 18 February.

34. Anon. "Canada Lee." New York Herald
Tribune (21 July), p. 12.
   Photograph with caption of Lee as
   Bigger.

35. Anon. "Canada Lee and Ann [sic] Burr
of the Returning 'Native Son.'" The New
York Times (18 October), Sec. 8, p. 2.
   Photograph of a scene from NS. The
   caption is the title of the entry.

36. Anon. "Canada Lee, Fighter Turned
Actor." Daily Worker (22 October), p. 7.
   Discusses Lee's career, including his
   role in the play NS.

37. Anon. "Canada Lee Fights Closing."
New York Post (7 December), p. 33.
   Lee protests the threatened closing
   of NS by producer Shubert because of
   objections to the play by Catholics.

38. Anon. "Canada Lee Gets Spot in New
Play." Norfolk Journal and Guide (1
August), p. 16.
   Mentions Lee's role in NS.

39. Anon. "Canada Lee Has Title Role in
'Native Son.'" New York Herald Tribune
(6 December), Sec. VI, p. 2.
   Cartoon with caption.

39a. Anon. "Canada Lee in Leading Radio

Role." Washington Tribune (10 October),
p. 21.
   Mentions briefly the play NS.

39b. Anon. "Canada Lee Launches Own
Radio Agency." Washington Tribune (12
July), p. 12.
   Mentions Lee's radio broadcast of the
   final scene in the play.

39c. Anon. "Canada Lee Narrator for
First Government Film." Washington Trib-
une (24 October), p. 10.
   Mentions briefly the play NS.

40. Anon. "Canada Lee Quick on Changes."
New York Amsterdam Star-News (7 Novem-
ber), p. 16.
   Explains the quick costume changes of
   Lee in NS.

41. Anon. "Chi Legit Toboggans with
Temp.; 'Purchase,' $22,000, 'Claudia,' 7
½G." Variety (14 January), p. 50.
   NS grosses $6,000 in its ninth and
   last week in Chicago.

42. Anon. "Clifton Lamb Directs, Acts in
'Native Son.'" Norfolk Journal and Guide
(28 March), p. 14.
   Favorable review of a performance of
   the play at Prairie View A. and M.
   College in Texas.

43. Anon. "Closing of 'Native Son' Disturbs Leaders Here." The Chicago Daily
News (c. 7 December).
   Reports that Horace Cayton protests
   the threatened censorship of the
   play.

44. Anon. "Contributors." Accent, 2
(Spring), [130].
   Mentions W's three books.

45. Anon. "Current Plays." The Catholic
News (24 October), p. 22; (31 October), p. 26; (14 November), p. 26; (21
November), p. 26; (5 December), p. 26;
(12 December), p. 30; (19 December), p.
26; (26 December), p. 22.
   The Catholic Theater Movement lists
   NS in the category of "wholly objectionable."

46. Anon. "Current Road Shows." Variety
(14 January), p. 50.
   NS is scheduled for production in
   Minneapolis on the 14th, in St. Paul
   on the 15th, in Madison on the 16th-
   17th, and in Milwaukee on the 19-24th
   January.

47. Anon. "Current Road Shows." Variety
(21 January), p. 51.
   NS is scheduled for 21-24 January in
   Milwaukee and 26-31 January in Detroit.

48. Anon. "Current Road Shows." Variety (28 January), p. 51.
NS is scheduled for 28-31 January in Detroit and 2-7 February in Toronto.

49. Anon. "Current Road Shows." Variety (4 February), p. 50.
NS is scheduled for 4-7 February in Toronto, 9 February in Rochester, 10-11 February in Syracuse, and 12-14 February in Buffalo.

50. Anon. "Current Road Shows." Variety (11 February), p. 45.
NS is scheduled for 11 February in Syracuse and 12-14 February in Buffalo.

51. Anon. "Current Road Shows." Variety (18 February), p. 43.
NS is scheduled for 18-21 February in Baltimore and 23-28 February in Philadelphia.

52. Anon. "Current Road Shows." Variety (25 February), p. 44.
NS is scheduled for 25-27 February in Philadelphia, not 23-28 February as previously announced.

53. Anon. "Current Road Shows." Variety (4 March), p. 51.
Performances of NS in Philadelphia are scheduled to continue through 14 March.

54. Anon. "Did You Know That . . ." Chelsea (Mass.) Evening Record (25 July), p. 2.
Mentions NS first in a list of the six best selling Modern Library books during the preceding six months.

55. Anon. "Dies Gives List of Alleged Reds in U. S. Service." New York Herald Tribune (26 September), p. 7.
Representative Martin Dies charges (erroneously) that a "Communist film 'Native Land'" was based on NS. He also charges that W was a member of the national committee of the American Peace Mobilization.

56. Anon. "Duncan, W. C. Handy, Richard Wright Donate to War Relief Art Show." Daily Worker (28 March), p. 7.
Notes that W "has loaned a modern abstract work 'Composition on a String.'"

57. Anon. Dust jacket of Native Son. New York: Modern Library.
Blurb on inside front flap. "It is the story of a hunted human being doomed by the tensions within and without himself to be what he is until his very last breath."

58. Anon. "500 Distinguished Writers Back President for Immediate Opening of a Second Front." Daily Worker (14 September), p. 7.
Lists W as a vice-president of the League of American Writers.

59. Anon. "Flatbush Opening with 'Native Son.'" Brooklyn Eagle (12 April), Sec. E, p. 6.
Announces the opening of the play on 14 April. Most of the article concerns Canada Lee, who appears with Patricia Palmer in a photograph of a scene from the play on this page.

59a. Anon. "Footlight Favorites." Washington Tribune (20 June), p. 20.
Notes that NS is playing in Asbury Park, New Jersey.

60. Anon. "For Saroyan." New York Amsterdam Star-News (25 July), p. 15.
Photograph of Canada Lee with caption mentioning his performance in NS.

61. Anon. "Ford's, Beginning Tomorrow Night, 8.30." The Baltimore Sunday Sun (15 February), Sec. 1 (Magazine Sec.), p. 6.
Advertisement for NS with "2nd balcony reserved exclusively for Negro patrons."

61a. Anon. "Freedom's People Program Hits Grand High Over NBC." Washington Tribune (21 March), p. 23.
Notes mention of W in a radio broadcast about black creative achievement.

62. Anon. "Friday Night." Women's Wear Daily (19 October), p. 17.
Announces the return engagement of NS on Broadway.

63. Anon. "Hammett Enlists; Writers Climax 2nd Front Campaign, in Letter to President Roosevelt." Daily Worker (22 September), p. 7.
W's name and photograph appear.

64. Anon. "How 'Native Son' Was Born and Staged." The Worker (15 November), p. 7.
Provides details, including locations, of the actual Chicago counterparts of the buildings in NS. Includes a detailed account of the play's staging and a photograph of Canada Lee and Anne Burr in a scene.

65. Anon. "In Native Son Role." New York World-Telegram (15 December), p. 19.
Patricia Palmer replaces Anne Burr in the role of Mary Dalton.

66. Anon. "Indecency Fuss May Strike 'Son.'" Norfolk Journal and Guide (14

November), p. 17.
  Notes the threat of censorship of the play, which has been attacked by Archbishop Francis J. Spellman.

67. Anon. "Jean Rosenthal." PM (30 June), p. 23.
  Photograph with caption of a lighting technician who worked on NS.

68. Anon. "Joe Louis, Dr. Just, Pearl Buck on 1941 Honor Roll." New York Amsterdam Star-News (14 February), p. 7.
  W is one of twelve blacks and six whites named in a nationwide poll to select contributors to good race relations.

69. Anon. "Latest Books." The New York Times Book Review (15 March), p. 22.
  Lists the Modern Library reprint of NS.

70. Anon. "Lee Shubert to Close 'Native Son,' Negro Drama Attacked by Church." The New York Times (7 December), pp. 1, 16.
  "Rather than face possible court action and the subsequent closing of another theatre," Shubert closed NS because of Catholic objections to the play. Canada Lee sharply protested the closing.

71. Anon. "Library Notes." The St. John's Daily News (17 January), p. 4.
  Contains a favorable notice of TMBV, a startling account of the minority problem in America.

72. Anon. "Lists for Fall Offer Relief to War Weary." Buffalo Evening News (27 June), Magazine Sec., p. 7.
  Mentions a novel by W on the fall Harper list.

73. Anon. "Lyceum." Minneapolis Morning Tribune (12 January), p. 11.
  Advertisement for NS. Reprinted 13 January, p. 7; 14 January, p. 7.

74. Anon. "Lyceum." Minneapolis Star Journal (12 January), p. 15.
  Advertisement for NS. Reprinted 13 January, p. 14; 14 January, p. 17.

75. Anon. "Lyceum--3 Days, Jan. 12-13-14." Minneapolis Sunday Tribune and Star Journal (11 January), p. 11.
  Advertisement for the play NS.

76. Anon. "Lytell and Mayor Confer on Play-Jury Proposal." New York Herald Tribune (10 December), p. 22.
  Reports controversy over the threatened closing of NS.

77. Anon. "The Markets for Serious Fic-

tion." Writers Journal, 5 (May), 12.
  Lists W as a writer first published in little magazines.

78. Anon. "Matinee to Open 'Native Son' Run." The Philadelphia Inquirer (18 February), p. 21.
  Announces the opening of the play in Philadelphia on 23 February.

79. Anon. ("Emcee"). "Memo." Daily Worker (8 May), p. 7.
  Announces the final, benefit performance of the play NS for the Harlem Open Door Canteen.

80. _____. "Memo." Daily Worker (19 May), p. 7.
  Suggests that W write a biography of Joe Louis.

81. _____. "Memo." Daily Worker (10 May), p. 7.
  Mentions W's introduction to Nelson Algren's Never Come Morning.

82. Anon. "Modern Library." Honolulu Star-Bulletin (9 May), p. 20.
  Lists NS as a new title in the series.

83. Anon. "Modern Library Announces 'Native Son' Reprint." The Publishers' Weekly, 141 (31 January), 465-466.
  Predicts a large sale in the 95¢ Modern Library edition. Publication date is 16 March.

84. Anon. "Moving Story of a Race." The Baltimore Sunday Sun (1 February), Magazine Sec., p. 12.
  Favorable review of TMBV praising W's "passionate sympathy" and understanding in telling his race's story.

85. Anon. "N. Y. Library Poll Results Announced." The Chicago Defender (14 February), p. 14.
  W is included among twelve blacks and six whites making significant contributions to race relations.

86. Anon. "'Native,' $8,800, Not Very Strong in Balto." Variety (25 February), p. 44.
  Called a "daring booking" for a city so far south, the road show of NS had a "fairish" week's gross of $8,800, mainly on black balcony patrons at 75¢ a seat.

87. Anon. "'Native' $5,000 in Buff." Variety (18 February), p. 43.
  The road show gross of $5,000 for four performances of the play NS in Buffalo is considered good.

88. Anon. "'Native' 6 1/2 in Toronto."

Variety (11 February), p. 45.
The week's gross for NS was a disappointing $6,500, mainly on "balcony
trade."

89. Anon. "Native Son." The Indianapolis
Recorder (10 January), p. 1.
Directs the reader to the current
installment of the serialized novel.

90. Anon. Native Son. New York: Playbill
Incorporated, 12 pp.
Playbill for the booking at the Ma-
jestic Theatre the "week beginning
October 25, 1942."

91. Anon. "Native Son." The Raleigh News
and Observer (27 December), Sec. M, p.
5.
Announces the reopening of NS at the
Majestic Theatre on Broadway.

91a. Anon. "Native Son at Erlanger, With
Canada Lee." Buffalo Courier-Express (12
February), p. 11.
Announces the opening of a four-per-
formance run of the road show of NS.

92. Anon. "'Native Son' Back Again Tuesday." Brooklyn Eagle (25 April), p. 14.
Announces the return of the play to
the Flatbush Theater on 28 April.

93. Anon. "'Native Son' Benefit Will Aid
Canteen." New York Amsterdam Star-News
(9 May), p. 11.
Announces the benefit performance of
the play on 9 May to aid the Harlem
Open Door Canteen.

94. Anon. "'Native Son' Closes in Chicago January 10." The Chicago Defender
(10 January), p. 11.
From Chicago the road show will move
to Minneapolis.

95. Anon. "'Native Son' Closes Its Run
This Week." Brooklyn Eagle (7 December),
p. 5.
Explains Lee Shubert's decision to
close the play under pressure from
Catholics.

96. Anon. "'Native Son' Comes Again."
Brooklyn Eagle (27 September), Sec. E,
p. 4.
Announces the revival of the play for
a week's run beginning 29 September
at the Flatbush Theater.

97. Anon. "'Native Son' Comes Back to
Broadway." Daily Worker (19 October), p.
7.
Announces the opening of the play at
the Majestic Theatre on 23 October.

98. Anon. "'Native Son' Does Fair in
Baltimore." The Pittsburgh Courier (7

March), p. 21.
Attendance at the play in Baltimore
was mainly black, segregated in the
top balcony. Few whites attended.

99. Anon. "'Native Son' Free to Service
Men." New York Journal-American (2 November), p. 15.
Free tickets to NS are available "to
a limited number of service men."

100. Anon. "'Native Son' Here Again;
Carey Play." Unidentified clipping (7
April).
Announces the reopening of the play
at the Flatbush Theater.

101. Anon. "'Native Son' Is Done by
Texas School Prof." The Chicago Defender
(4 April), p. 17.
Reports a production of the play at
Prairie View A. and M. College.

101a. Anon. "'Native Son' May Be Hit by
Indecency Stuff." Washington Tribune (21
November), p. 2.
Reports the threat of censorship of
the play instigated by Catholics.

102. Anon. "'Native Son' May Extend
Stay." The Philadelphia Inquirer (19
February), p. 16.
Notes that the military "draft is
calling many members of the cast and
production staff" of the play.

103. Anon. "'Native Son' Next to Close
in Clean Show Drive." New York Journal-
American (7 December), p. 3.
Announces that Lee Shubert has decided to close the play under pressure from "Mayor LaGuardia's and
License Commissioner Moss' theatre
cleanup campaign."

104. Anon. "'Native Son' on Subway Circuit for a Fifth Engagement." New York
Post (22 September), p. 32.
The play breaks "its own record for
the most times any one attraction has
been offered on the Subway Circuit"
in New York.

105. Anon. "'Native Son' Opens at Majestic Tonight." Brooklyn Eagle (c. 23
October).
Announces a return engagement of the
play on Broadway.

106. Anon. "'Native Son' Opens Mosque."
Newark Evening News (22 July), p. 12.
Favorable review of the road show of
the play, which opened on 21 July to
a capacity crowd of nearly 3,000. The
"dynamic drama" and Canada Lee's
acting combine with excellent effect
in "a grim story told with relentless
realism."

107. Anon. "'Native Son' Opens Passaic Play Season." Newark Evening News (20 May), p. 12.
    Reports that a capacity crowd of 3,000 attended the opening of NS.

108. Anon. "'Native Son' Opens Tonight at Passaic." New York Post (19 May), p. 30.
    Announces the opening of the play at the Passaic Central Theatre.

109. Anon. "Native Son Painting." New York World-Telegram (c. 30 October).
    Notes that "Problem Case" by Anne Beadenkopf is on display at the Majestic Theatre.

110. Anon. "'Native Son' Published Serially by Oklahoma Black Dispatch." Daily Worker (21 January), p. 7.
    Reports that the newspaper is serializing the novel.

111. Anon. "'Native Son' Re-Played in Brooklyn." Daily Worker (15 April), p. 7.
    Lists members of the cast, comments on the plot, and notes that the play "holds the box-office record for last season."

112. Anon. "Native Son Returns at Popular Prices." New York World-Telegram (23 October), p. 27.
    Announces the opening of the play at the Majestic Theatre.

113. Anon. "'Native Son' Returns to Flatbush Tonight." New York Post (29 September), p. 32.
    Announces the "fifth engagement in two seasons" in Brooklyn.

114. Anon. "'Native Son' Returns to Gotham." Norfolk Journal and Guide (25 April), p. 15.
    Reviews briefly the stage history of the play and future plans for it.

115. Anon. "'Native Son' Returns to New York." The Pittsburgh Courier (18 April), p. 21.
    After a third run in Pittsburgh, NS returns to Brooklyn and the Bronx.

116. Anon. "The 'Native Son' Returns Tonight." The New York Times (23 October), p. 24.
    Announces the revival of the play at popular prices "under the auspices of Louis and George W. Brandt."

117. Anon. "'Native Son' Still Road Hit; Plays Pittsburgh Third Time." Norfolk Journal and Guide (28 March), p. 15.
    Emphasizes the controversial nature of the play.

118. Anon. "'Native Son' to Broadway." The Pittsburgh Courier (24 October), p. 21.
    Announces the play's return to Broadway for a run at the Majestic Theatre.

119. Anon. "'Native Son' to Close Saturday; On Church 'Objectionable' List." New York Herald Tribune (7 December), p. 16.
    Reports that the play will close abruptly because of pressure from the Catholic Theater Movement.

120. Anon. "'Native Son' to Continue." New York Post (8 December), p. 27.
    Responding to protests against censorship, Lee Shubert decides against closing NS.

121. Anon. "'Native Son' to Continue." PM Daily (8 December), p. 23.
    Reports that the order to close the play because of the "cleanup" campaign has been rescinded under pressure from liberal groups.

122. Anon. "'Native Son' to Open Flatbush." Brooklyn Eagle (7 April), p. 5.
    Announces the return of NS on 14 April and notes that it "established the box office record at a dollar top last season at the Flatbush Theater."

123. Anon. "'Native Son' to Return." New York Herald Tribune (14 October), p. 17.
    Announces the revival of NS and gives details about past performances.

124. Anon. "'Native Son' Too Serious for M'w'kee, Does $7,000." Variety (28 January), p. 52.
    Despite good reviews, the road show production of NS grossed only $7,000 in six evening performances and two matinees in Milwaukee.

125. Anon. "Native Son 'Weak' in Minneapolis." The Pittsburgh Courier (31 January), p. 21.
    Poor attendance at the three-night stand of the play in Minneapolis is attributed to inadequate publicity.

126. Anon. "'Native Son' Won't Close." New Masses, 45 (15 December), 22.
    Reports that Lee Shubert has rescinded his decision to close the play NS.

127. Anon. "'Native Son's' Closing Order Is Cancelled." Norfolk Journal and Guide (19 December), p. 17.
    Associated Negro press article on the controversy over the threatened censorship of the play by Catholic pres-

sure groups.

128. Anon. "'Native' 3G in Mpls." Variety (21 January), p. 51.
Despite good reviews, the gross of $3,000 was weak for three night performances and a matinee.

129. Anon. "'Negro Caravan' Reveals Race's Cultural Life." The Dallas Daily Times Herald (12 April), Third Sec., p. 10.
Mentions W briefly.

130. Anon. "The Negro Quarterly Is Out." Daily Worker (4 August), p. 7.
Mentions W's contribution.

131. Anon. "Negroes and the War." Unidentified clipping.
Photograph of W with caption announcing his support of the war effort. The year is conjectural.

132. Anon. "Negroes in Picture and Text." The New Sign (February).
Favorable review of TMBV with praise for both photographs and W's "magnificent prose."

133. Anon. "Negro's Record in American Theatre." Daily Worker (16 July), p. 7.
Review of The Negro in the American Theatre mentioning Canada Lee and NS.

134. Anon. "New Book Bargains." Daily Worker (16 March), p. 3.
Workers Bookshop advertisement listing TMBV and the Modern Library edition of NS.

135. Anon. "A New 'Native Son'?" New York Post (23 November), p. 32.
Discusses W's work in progress, a novel about female domestic workers in New York. W comments on his work habits and the reaction to the play NS.

136. Anon. "News and Gossip of the Rialto." The New York Times (4 October), Sec. 8, p. 1.
Reports that NS is the fifth most popular play in the Bronx and the sixth most popular in Brooklyn.

137. Anon. "News of the Theater." New York Herald Tribune (14 July), p. 12.
Reports that NS will be the first production for the summer in the Mosque Theater.

138. Anon. "News of the Theater." New York Herald Tribune (22 September), p. 18.
Notes that NS appears at Brooklyn's Flatbush Theater for the fifth time.

139. Anon. "News of the Theater." New York Herald Tribune (21 October), p. 16.
Notes that Frances Bavier resumes the role of Peggy in NS.

140. Anon. "1941 News Names." The Chicago Defender (10 January), p. 6.
Includes W as winner of the Spingarn Medal.

141. Anon. "Non Fiction at City Library." The Sacramento Bee (28 February), p. 15.
Contains a favorable brief notice of TMBV.

142. Anon. "Notes of the Stage." The New York Sun (7 December), p. 29.
Announces the closing of NS at the Majestic Theater on 12 December.

143. Anon. "Opening at Mosque." Newark Evening News (20 July), p. 12.
Photograph of Canada Lee and Evelyn Ellis in a scene from NS.

144. Anon. "Opening Tonight of 'Moon Is Down.'" The New York Times (7 April), p. 27.
Announces the engagement of NS at the Flatbush Theater in Brooklyn on 14-19 April.

145. Anon. "Outstanding News Stories of 1941." The Chicago Defender (10 January), p. 5.
Mentions W's Spingarn medal and the dramatization of NS.

146. Anon. "Passaic to See 'Native Son.'" The New York Times (15 May), p. 25.
Announces the opening of the play at the Central Theater in Passaic on 19 May.

147. Anon. "Plan Party for 'Native Son' Company Which Never Came Off." Norfolk Journal and Guide (11 April), p. 15.
Explains the "mysterious" circumstances of the aborted party.

148. Anon. "Plans Revue." Norfolk Journal and Guide (13 June), p. 17.
Photograph of W with caption announcing his plans to produce a "tropical revue" on Broadway.

149. Anon. "Play by Lillian Hellman, 'Native Son' Open Today." The Philadelphia Inquirer (23 February), p. 13.
Announces the opening of W's play at the Walnut Theater and compares it to Watch on the Rhine as "a plea for freedom and equality everywhere."

150. Anon. "A Poignant Novel." Chicago Daily Tribune (29 April), p. 17.

Review of Nelson Algren's <u>Never Come</u>
<u>Morning</u> citing W's introduction and
arguing that, like <u>NS,</u> the novel is a
warning of conditions which breed
future problems.

151. Anon. "Premiere Tonight of 'Beat
the Band.'" <u>The</u> <u>New</u> <u>York</u> <u>Times</u> (14 October), p. 28.
    Announces the return of <u>NS</u> to the
    Majestic Theatre on 23 October.

152. Anon. "Protest Closing of 'Native
Son.'" <u>PM</u> (c. 8 December).
    Discusses Canada Lee's efforts to
    rescind Lee Shubert's decision to
    close the play in response to objec-
    tions published in <u>The</u> <u>Catholic</u> <u>News</u>
    on 5 December.

153. Anon. "Protests Restore 'Native
Son' Drama." <u>The</u> <u>New</u> <u>York</u> <u>Times</u> (8 December), pp. 27, 34.
    Detailed account of the decision to
    rescind the closing of the play.
    Quotes protests from various sources
    concerning censorship of the theater.

154. Anon. "A Public Service." New York
<u>Sunday</u> <u>News</u> (15 November).
    Reports that Brooks Atkinson has
    publicly acknowledged the service
    provided to the public by the low
    ticket prices of <u>NS</u> ($1.65 the most
    expensive).

155. Anon. "'R. U. R.'Is Closed After
Brief Stay." <u>The</u> <u>New</u> <u>York</u> <u>Times</u> (7 December), p. 23.
    Reports that Lee Shubert has ordered
    the closing of the play <u>NS.</u>

156. Anon. "A Reader's List." <u>The</u> <u>New</u>
<u>Republic,</u> 106 (5 January), 29.
    Contains a favorable notice of <u>TMBV</u>
    calling it "a forthright, often angry
    account . . . told . . . with vivid
    economy."

157. Anon. "Recent Outstanding Fiction
and Non-Fiction Are Listed." <u>Dayton</u>
<u>Daily</u> <u>News</u> (15 February), Society Sec.,
p. 9.
    Contains a favorable brief notice of
    <u>TMBV.</u>

158. Anon. "Reprints, New Editions." <u>New</u>
<u>York</u> <u>Herald</u> <u>Tribune</u> <u>Books</u> (15 March), p.
14.
    Notes the Modern Library edition of
    <u>NS</u> and quotes from Dorothy Canfield
    Fisher's introduction.

159. Anon. "Revival of 'Native Son'
Opens at Majestic Theater." <u>New</u> <u>York</u>
<u>Herald</u> <u>Tribune</u> (24 October), p. 6.
    Announces the return of the play with
    many members of the original cast.

160. Anon. "'Rhine' Strong $20,000,
Philly." <u>Variety</u> (4 March), p. 51.
    Reports that the road show of <u>NS</u> had
    a delayed opening on 2 March. "No-
    tices okay and biz regarded as fair
    with just under $8,000."

161. Anon. "Rialto Ramblings." <u>Brooklyn</u>
<u>Eagle</u> (23 October).
    Announces the return engagement of <u>NS</u>
    in Brooklyn.

162. Anon. "Richard Wright Lauds Book on
Modern Negro." <u>The</u> <u>Pittsburgh</u> <u>Courier</u>
(10 October), p. 3.
    Quotes at length from W's introduc-
    tion to Saunders Redding's <u>No</u> <u>Day</u> <u>of</u>
    <u>Triumph.</u>

163. Anon. "Richard Wright Lauds Controversy on Music." <u>Daily</u> <u>Worker</u> (13 February), p. 7.
    Prefatory editorial note to a letter
    from W.

164. Anon. "Richard Wright (1908-   ):
A Note on the Author of <u>Native Son,</u>" in
<u>Native</u> <u>Son.</u> New York: Modern Library, p.
[vii].
    Biographical note.

164a. Anon. "RKO Empire." Syracuse <u>Post-</u>
<u>Standard</u> (11 February), p. 16.
    Advertisement for the play <u>NS.</u>

164b. Anon. "RKO Schine Empire." <u>Syra-</u>
<u>cuse</u> <u>Herald-Journal</u> (10 February), p.
18.
    Advertisement for the play <u>NS.</u>
    Reprinted: 1942.164c.

164c. _____. "RKO Schine Empire." <u>Syra-</u>
<u>cuse</u> <u>Herald-Journal</u> (11 February), p.
20.
    Reprint of 1942.164b.

165. Anon. "Roundup." White Plains <u>News</u>
(17 April).
    Mentions W's contribution to <u>The</u>
    <u>Negro</u> <u>Caravan.</u>

166. Anon. "Russian War Play Will Open
Tonight." <u>The</u> <u>New</u> <u>York</u> <u>Times</u> (29 December), p. 26.
    Includes announcement of the closing
    of the return engagement of <u>NS</u> after
    eighty-three performances.

167. Anon. "Schomburg Collection." <u>The</u>
<u>Crisis,</u> 49 (October), 328.
    Mentions "the uncut galleys of <u>Native</u>
    <u>Son</u>" among the holdings.

168. Anon. "Shubert Changes Mind, 'Na-
tive Son' to Run On." <u>New</u> <u>York</u> <u>Amsterdam</u>
<u>Star-News</u> (12 December), p. 17.
    Reports that protests have persuaded
    Lee Shubert to rescind the closing of

the play.

169. Anon. "Shubert Rescinds 'Native Son' Fold After Closing Notice Causes Furore." Variety (9 December), pp. 49, 52.
Relates the protest over the threatened closing of the play and the subsequent reversal of the decision.

170. Anon. "'Son' in Brooklyn." New York Daily News (14 April).
Announces that NS will begin a week's run at the Flatbush Theater.

171. Anon. "Stage Cleanup Indicated as Show Is Closed." The Catholic News (12 December), p. 2.
Mentions Lee Shubert's announcement that he would close NS and his reversal of that decision.

172. Anon. "Stage News." New York Post (7 April), p. 26.
Announces that NS will open at the Flatbush Theater in Brooklyn on 14 April.

173. Anon. "Stage Notes." New York Post (4 December), p. 50.
Notes that NS will reach the fiftieth performance of its present run on 5 December.

174. Anon. "Star-News Suggests Wallace as 'Bigger' No. 2." New York Amsterdam Star-News (24 October), p. 10.
Proposes Emmett Wallace as Canada Lee's understudy in the role of Bigger Thomas in NS.

175. Anon. "Text of the National Call to Browder Congress." Sunday Worker (15 February), p. 3.
W is one of the signers.

176. Anon. "Thirteen Matinees for Election Day." The New York Times (3 November), p. 19.
Reports that the first full week's proceeds for the revival of NS were $8,200.

177. Anon. "Three Openings Here Next Week." New York Post (14 October), p. 37.
Announces the opening of NS at the Majestic Theater on 23 October.

178. Anon. "3 Plays Close." New York Daily News (7 December).
NS is one of the three.

179. Anon. "3 Plays to Close." New York Daily News (3 December).
NS is one of the three.

180. Anon. "Tolerance by Request." PM's Weekly (22 February), p. 12.
Reports that some white and black soldiers have defied Jim Crow by insisting on sitting together in the orchestra section of the Ford Theater in Baltimore at a performance of NS.

181. Anon. "Tonight's First Night." The New York Sun (23 October), p. 24.
Announces the opening of NS at the Majestic Theater.

182. Anon. "12 Million Black Voices." The Vancouver Sun (c. 31 January).
Favorable notice emphasizing W's sincerity and dignity in presenting the moving story of his race.

183. Anon. Unidentified clipping.
Reports that "Jules Leventhal has decided to keep 'Native Son' at the Majestic indefinitely" despite Mayor LaGuardia's objections to the play.

184. Anon. Unidentified clipping.
Enumerates the scenes in the play NS found objectionable despite their artistic merit by the Catholic Theater Movement.

185. Anon. Untitled article. Detroit Free Press (19 April), Part 5, p. 7.
Review of Nelson Algren's Never Come Morning mentioning W's introduction.

186. Anon. Untitled clipping. Brooklyn Citizen (c. 15 October).
Announces a return engagement of NS at the Majestic Theater.

187. Anon. Untitled clipping. New York Daily News (5 May).
Announces a performance of NS in the Bronx to benefit the Open Door Canteen of Harlem.

188. Anon. Untitled clipping. Newark Evening News (c. April).
Notes that NS is held over for a third week at the Flatbush Theater in Brooklyn.

189. Anon. "War Work Specialty of Writers School." Daily Worker (6 June), p. 7.
Lists W as a sponsor of the Writers School.

190. Anon. "'Watch on the Rhine,' 'Native Son' Bow Here." The Philadelphia Inquirer (22 February), Society Sec., p. 11.
Announces the opening of NS on 23 February and discusses the cast and production.

191. Anon. "The Weekly Record." The Publishers' Weekly, 141 (14 March),

1122-1131.
     Lists the Grosset & Dunlap and Modern
     Library reprints of NS (p. 1131).

192. Anon. "Welles in Special Phone
Hookup from Rio as Part of 'Son' Celebration in Pitt." Unidentified clipping.
     Describes the celebration of the
     first anniversary of the play at the
     Nixon Theatre in Pittsburgh.

193. Anon. "Welles Solved Scenic Problem." Brooklyn Eagle (26 April), Sec. E,
p. 6.
     Explains the staging of the ten
     scenes of NS with three levels and a
     "jigsaw" arrangement on casters rath-
     er than a revolving stage.

194. Anon. "Wright, Richard," in Who's
Who in America. Ed. Albert Nelson Marquis. Vol. 22. Chicago: The A. N. Marquis Company, p. 2408.
     Biographical sketch. This entry, re-
     vised periodically, continues through
     Vol. 31 for 1960-61.

195. Anon. "Wright, Richard. 12 million
black voices; a folk history of the
Negro in the United States; photo-direction by Edwin Rosskam." The Booklist,
38 (1 January), 152.
     Favorable notice praising W's "suc-
     cinct, moving prose" and Rosskam's
     photography.

196. Anon. "Wright Wrote His 'Native
Son' Because He Couldn't Help It."
Brooklyn Eagle (27 December), p. B7.
     Relates how W and Horace Cayton
     searched the South Side of Chicago
     for specific buildings that were to
     serve as models for buildings in
     the novel, thus achieving great veri-
     similitude. The same buildings were
     later visited by W, Orson Welles, and
     designer James Morcum in order to
     make the stage settings authentic.

197. Anon. "Writers and Artists." Unidentified clipping.
     Announcement mentioning W's presence
     at an anti-war meeting sponsored by
     the Fourth American Writers Congress.

198. Anon. "Writers School Aiding in War
Effort of U. S." Writers' Journal, 5
(July), 3.
     Lists W as a sponsor of a school for
     propaganda agencies.

199. Anon. "Writer's Slur on Efforts for
Stage Decency Answered." The Catholic
News (26 December), p. 3.
     Reprint of 1942.200.

200. Anon. "Writer's Slur on Efforts for
Stage Decency Answered." The Tablet (c.

December).
     Editorial rebutting Howard Barnes's
     attack in the New York Herald Tribune
     on stage censorship. Mentions NS.
     Reprinted: 1942.199.

201. Atkinson, Brooks. "Native Son." The
New York Times (1 November), Sec. 8, p.
1.
     Discusses the economics of the thea-
     ter and praises the Brandts for
     charging a maximum of $1.65 for tick-
     ets to the revival of the play. At-
     kinson complains that scene shifting
     at times tends to destroy the mood,
     but praises other aspects of the
     play, including sets, acting, and
     social significance.

202. _____. "The Play: Canada Lee Giving
a Superb Performance in a Revival of
'Native Son,' Put on at the Majestic at
Popular Prices." The New York Times (24
October), p. 10.
     Claims that Lee's acting is even
     better in the revival than in the
     original production. The play itself
     is "virtuoso theatre, a social docu-
     ment written with bitterness and
     passion." There are some minor stag-
     ing and lighting flaws in the reviv-
     al. Topical references to lynchings
     and the war bring the play up to
     date.

203 Balfour, David. "'Twelve Million
Black Voices.'" Atlanta Daily World (1
March), p. 4.
     Highly favorable review emphasizing
     W's protest against racism written in
     "distinctly poetical and non-socio-
     logical" prose. "No white American,
     unless he has a heart of steel, can
     read this book without being greatly
     chastened by its brutal indictment.
     No Negro can read it without being
     made to realize that the great masses
     of Negroes, both urban and rural,
     live at the bottom of the economic
     ladder."

204. Barnes, Howard. "Interference with
Theater by Moralists a War-Time Cer-
tainty." New York Herald Tribune (13
December), Sec. VI, pp. 1, 4.
     Strong attack on stage censorship
     mentioning the threatened closing of
     NS.

205. Barron, Mark. "'Fight Is On' as
Show Censors Come to Life." The Washington Sunday Star (13 December), p. E-2.
     Mentions the censorship problems of
     the play NS.

206. Bradford, Ben. "The Theatre," in
The American Year Book. Ed. William M.
Schuyler. New York: Thomas Nelson &

Sons, pp. 946-953.
    Contains a favorable review of the
    play NS, "one of the most important
    events of the season."

207. Brewster, Dorothy. "From Phillis
Wheatley to Richard Wright." The Negro
Quarterly, 1 (Spring), 80-83.
    Review of The Negro Caravan referring
    to "Bright and Morning Star" as "that
    magnificent short story."

208. Brookhauser, Frank. "Lower Depths
in a Powerful Chicago Novel." The Philadelphia Inquirer (6 May), p. 20.
    Favorable review of Nelson Algren's
    Never Come Morning calling it the
    most significant social novel since
    NS and praising Algren for avoiding
    W's occasional melodramatic touches.

209. Br.[own], I.[vor]. "Theatre," in
1942 Britannica Book of the Year. Ed.
Walter Yust. Chicago: Encyclopaedia Britannica, pp. 654-655.
    Mentions the play NS, which "missed
    most of the novel's vitality."

210. Brown, Sterling A. "The Negro Auth-
or and His Publisher." The Negro Quarterly, 1 (Spring), 9-20.
    Reprint of 1941.667.

211. Burnett, Whit. "Biographies and
Bibliographies," in his This Is My Best.
New York: The Dial Press, pp. 1119-1169.
    The W entry appears on pp. 1168-1169.
    Burnett states that the entries "have
    been checked personally by each auth-
    or." The selection from W included in
    this anthology is "How 'Bigger' Was
    Born."
    Reprinted: 1945.814.

212. Carey, Ralph W. "Theater," in The
New International Year Book. Ed. Charles
Earle Funk. New York: Funk & Wagnalls,
pp. 652-655.
    Comments favorably on the play NS.

213. Carmon, Walt. "Books." The Worker
(17 May), Sec. 2, p. 6.
    Review of Nelson Algren's Never Come
    Morning quoting from W's introduc-
    tion and comparing the social message
    of the two authors.

214. Chamberlain, John. "Books of the
Times." The New York Times (25 April),
p. 11.
    Review of Nelson Algren's Never Come
    Morning mentioning W's praise of
    Algren's vernacular style.

215. Charles, Charles V., M. D. "Opti-
mism and Frustration in the American
Negro." The Psychoanalytic Review, 29
(July), 270-299.

Psychological study of the "idea-
tional life" of Bigger Thomas.
Charles concludes that Bigger is
"basically a neurotic individual" and
that his "being a Negro is only inci-
dental." Essentially an optimistic
personality type, Bigger reacts to
thwarted desires with narcissism,
ambivalence, and finally violence as
a release of psychic tensions.

216. Clayton [sic], Horace R. "Negro
History: Black Voices." The Echo (25
February), pp. 5-6.
    Reprint of 1941.680. The Echo is the
    organ of the Maywood, Illinois,
    Branch of the NAACP.

217. Clayton, Robert. "Violent Novel."
Chattanooga Sunday Times (31 May), p. M-
5.
    Review of Nelson Algren's Never Come
    Morning disagreeing with W's belief
    that it will "awaken some readers."

218. Cournos, John. "New Books in Review." New Haven Register (3 May), p. 4.
    Contains a notice of Nelson Algren's
    Never Come Morning mentioning W's
    introduction.

219. Daniels, Jonathan. "12 Million
Black Voices Text by Richard Wright."
Book-of-the-Month Club News (January),
p. 11.
    Favorable review concentrating on the
    text but also praising the photo-
    graphs. Considering the burden of
    racial griefs W bears, Daniels finds
    it remarkable that W is not more
    bitter.

220. Davis, Benjamin, Jr. "Jim-Crow Censorship." Daily Worker (8 December), p.
7.
    Relates the effort to censor the play
    NS to "powerful, defeatist forces"
    which are impeding the war effort
    against fascism.

221. Davis, Frank Marshall. "Books of
Interest." Norfolk Journal and Guide (30
May), p. 10.
    Review of Nelson Algren's Never Come
    Morning noting W's preface and com-
    paring Bigger Thomas and Algren's
    protagonist.

222. Davis, Harry E. "Richard Wright,
'Native Son' Author, Traces History of
Negro in U. S." Cleveland News (21 Jan-
uary), p. 20.
    Favorable review of TMBV summarizing
    its contents and agreeing with its
    analysis and conclusions.

223. Du Bois, W. E. B. "Wright, Richard. 12 Million Black Voices: A Folk

History of the Negro in the United States." The United States 1865-1900, 1 (September 1941-August 1942), 26.
Favorable review noting the reluctance of Americans to face the tragic side of black experience. Same as 1941.708.
Reprinted: 1977.115.

224. E., U. E. "Prose, Photos Tell U. S. Racial History." Columbus (Ohio) Citizen (4 January), Feature Magazine Sec., p. 4.
Favorable review of TMBV praising W's poetic prose and his challenge to white prejudice and indifference. The reviewer summarizes the four parts of the book.

225. E.[aton], W.[alter] P.[richard]. "Theater," in The World Book Encyclopedia Annual for 1941. Ed. J. Morris Jones. Chicago: The Quarrie Corporation, pp. 174-175.
Mentions briefly NS.

226. Embree, Edwin R. American Negroes: A Handbook. New York: John Day, pp. 53-63, 70, 71.
Contains brief references to W, including his subterfuge to borrow library books in Memphis.

227. _____. "Negroes Lift Their Voices in Poetry and Protest--A Tribute from Edwin R. Embree." The Chicago Daily News (2 December), p. 46.
Contains a favorable notice of TMBV. Also comments that W and other black novelists "are beginning to see Negroes as figures in the total American scene, rather than as separate beings in a world apart."

228. Fadiman, Clifton. "Books: An Over-All View, and Some Others." The New Yorker, 18 (18 April), 74-75.
Notes that Nelson Algren's Never Come Morning is "in the same vein" as NS and shares some of its "powerful, unwelcome wallop."

229. Field, Rowland. "Broadway." Newark Evening News (24 October), p. 20.
Announces the beginning of a limited return engagement of NS at the Majestic Theatre in New York.

230. Ford, James W. "New Masses Special Issue on 'Negro and the War.'" Daily Worker (17 October), p. 7.
Includes "Bright and Morning Star" in a list attesting to the interest of New Masses in the black struggle.

231. Frazier, George. "Something to Talk About: Records." Mademoiselle, 14 (March), 145, 184.

Article on Count Basie containing very favorable comments on "King Joe." The lyric "is a simple and decent tribute" to Louis.

232. Gannett, Lewis. "Books and Things." New York Herald Tribune (23 April), p. 17.
Contains a review of Nelson Algren's Never Come Morning stating that W was the "proper person" to introduce the novel because of its parallels with NS.

233. _____. "New Books Selected for Flavor." New York Herald Tribune (4 October), Sec. VII, p. 7.
Notes that W has selected the title Black Hope for his new novel.

234. Geismar, Maxwell. Writers in Crisis: The American Novel Between Two Wars. Boston: Houghton Mifflin, p. 288.
Mentions W.

235. Gibbs, Wolcott. "The Theatre: Out of the Mothballs." The New Yorker, 18 (31 October), 30, 32.
Includes a favorable but qualified review of the revival of NS, "a tragic and eloquent play." Gibbs notes some updating of details in this version, a "partial rewrite."

236. Gilder, Rosamond. "Matter for Thanksgiving." Theatre Arts, 26 (December), 735-744.
Includes a review of NS admitting some deficiencies in the production of the revival but praising Lee's performance. "Canada Lee has added a figure of heroic dimensions and tremendous implication to the theatre's gallery of great portraits" (p. 744).

237. _____. "Who's Who in the Tributary Theatre." Theatre Arts, 26 (July), 460-463.
Sketch of Paul Green mentioning his collaboration with W in the play NS.

238. Gilhagen, Evelyn. "The Curtain Rises." Independent Woman, 21 (December), 367-368, 378-379.
Favorable review of NS calling it "one of the best offerings of the theatrical season." Praises the performance of Canada Lee. However, Gilhagen notes that "the play, great as is its impact on the audience, does not achieve, except in two episodes, the dynamic quality of the book."

239. Gold, Michael. "Change the World: To Richard Wright, the Pen Is a Sacred Weapon in the Liberation War of Humanity." Daily Worker (9 December), p. 7.
Protests vigorously the effort to

censor the play NS, exonerating W from the charge of obscenity. Comparing W to Dostoevsky and others, Gold asserts that social justice is W's central theme.

240. Gordon, Eugene. "'Native Son' Goes On; Public Protest Saves It." Daily Worker (8 December), pp. 1, 7.
Reports that Lee Shubert has rescinded his decision to close the play. Gordon gives details of the meeting which saved the play from censorship pressure brought by the Catholic Theater League. Mentions some of the people protesting the closing. A cartoon on the matter appears on p. 1.

241. _____. "'Native Son Is Great Message, Says Brandt." Daily Worker (14 December), p. 7.
Interview with William Brandt, producer of the revival of the play, who defends it staunchly from its reactionary critics and praises highly its social message.

242. _____. "Paul Laurence Dunbar: Poet of the Negro People." Sunday Worker (15 February), Sec. 2, p. 4.
Mentions W.

243. _____. "A Valuable Book by a New and Promising Young Negro Writer." The Worker (25 October), Magazine Sec., p. 13.
Review of Saunders Redding's No Day of Triumph quoting from W's introduction.

244. Govan, Gilbert E. "Roaming Through the Realm of Books." Chattanooga Sunday Times (19 April), Sec. Four, p. 5.
Announces the Modern Library edition of NS.

245. Graver, Otto C. "Back of Books." Buffalo Courier-Express (26 April), Sec. 7, p. 2.
Notes that W, who is "no Louisa May Alcott when it comes to reporting the more violent aspects of life," praises the literary realism of Nelson Algren's Never Come Morning.

246. Grennard, Elliott, "New Blues." New Masses, 42 (20 January), 30-31.
Favorable review of the recording of "King Joe." Grennard has special praise for the collaboration of W, Robeson, and Count Basie.

247. Guernsey, Otis L., Jr. "The Playbill: Censorship Condemned by Producers and Actors." New York Herald Tribune (13 December), Sec. VI, pp. 1-2.
Consists mainly of quotations from various well-known theatrical figures on the issue of censorship occasioned by the closing of Wine, Women and Song and the threatened closing of NS.

248. Hansen, Harry. "The First Reader." Norfolk Virginian-Pilot (21 April), p. 6.
Review of Nelson Algren's Never Come Morning noting W's claim that there is "a social responsibility" for the novel's "misguided youths."

249. Hays, H. R. "A Bitter Indictment." Common Sense, 11 (February), 66.
Review of TMBV placing it in the genre of photo-documentaries. As such its photographs are excellent, but W's text is neither "frankly statistical" nor written "in a sustained poetic mood." Instead, it either blunts of overinterprets the photographs.

250. Herndon, Angelo. "Voice of Freedom." The Negro Quarterly, 1 (Spring), 85-87.
Favorable review of TMBV summarizing in some detail W's narrative, verifying its accuracy, and praising its skill and emotional impact.

250a. Hinners, Marjorie. "'Native Son' Is Spellbinder with Most Effective Staging." Syracuse Post-Standard (11 February), p. 16.
Favorable review of the road show praising the staging and acting. The play retains the power of the novel.

251. Isaacs, Edith J. R. "The Negro in the American Theatre: A Record of Achievement." Theatre Arts, 26 (August), 494-543.
Contains a large picture of Canada Lee as Bigger and favorable comments on the play NS (pp. 526-527).

252. Jackson, Joseph Henry. "The Bookman's Daily Notebook." San Francisco Chronicle (20 February), p. 12.
Review of Chalmers S. Murray's Here Comes Joe Mungin claiming that it presents the positive aspects of black life which W omits.

253. Jackson, Katherine Gauss. "12 Million Black Voices, by Richard Wright." Harper's Magazine, 184 (January), [xii].
Favorable notice stressing that wretched social conditions produce criminals.

254. Kazin, Alfred. On Native Grounds. New York: Harcourt, Brace, pp. 386-387.
Comments rather unfavorably on W in a section entitled "The Revival of

Naturalism." Points out the influence on W of left-wing thought. Reprinted: 1944.114; 1956.220.

255. Kirkley, Donald. "'Native Son.'" The Baltimore Sun (17 February), p. 10.
Reviews the play rather favorably, but points out differences which make it inferior to the original New York production: softened dialogue, shabby sets, weaker acting. Still, the play attests to Welles's theatrical genius and Lee's brilliance as an actor, and its attack on racism "can scarcely be ignored at the present time." Summarizes the plot.

256. _____. "The Theater." The Baltimore Sunday Sun (8 February), Sec. 1 (Magazine Sec.), p. 9.
Announces the opening of the road show NS in Baltimore on 16 February.

257. _____. "The Theater." The Baltimore Sunday Sun (15 February), Sec. 1 (Magazine Sec.), p. 6.
Recounts the stage history of NS, which is scheduled to open in Baltimore on 16 February. Summarizes the plot, "a powerful story told with vast theatrical skill."

258. _____. "The Theater." The Baltimore Sunday Sun (22 February), Sec. 1 (Magazine Sec.), p. 5.
Mentions "the grim business set forth in 'Native Son.'"

259. Kristensen, Sven Møller. Amerikansk Literatur 1920-1940. Copenhagen: Athenaeum, pp. 174-177, 220, 223, 225.
Includes a segment on W comparing NS to works by Dostoevsky and Faulkner. Notes that the book has "justly been seen as a black American Tragedy," attesting to the dominance of Dreiserian naturalism in this literary period.

260. Kronenberger, Louis. "An Editorial." PM (c. 8 December).
Protests the fear of censorship which induced Lee Shubert to announce the closing of the play NS.

261. _____. "Going to Theater." PM (13 April), p. 23.
States that no play of the 1942 season matches NS or Watch on the Rhine.

262. _____. "Going to Theater." PM (27 October), p. 22.
Favorable review of the revival of NS. Kronenberger points out that though the play is good theater, it loses some of the richness of the novel. The theme of social guilt is clear, however. Canada Lee's performance is even better in the revival, though otherwise the original production is preferable.

263. _____. "Going to Theater." PM (6 November), p. 22.
Includes a favorable reference to the revival of NS.

264. Kunitz, Stanley J. and Howard Haycraft. "Wright, Richard," in their Twentieth Century Authors. New York: H. W. Wilson, pp. 1553-1554.
Biographical sketch.

265. L., D. "Negro 'Folk History.'" PM's Weekly (2 November), pp. 56-58.
Favorable notice of TMBV. Conveying a personal, experienced quality, "it is a study of Negro life from the inside." Full-page photographs from the book appear on pp. 57 and 58.

266. LaFarge, John. "The Negro Diaspora." America, 66 (28 February), 580-581.
Review of TMBV and five other books on racial matters. W's work is concerned with the "proletarianizing" of black people. "Deliberately, Wright paints a picture of uprooted masses, not persons; of futility, not achievement; of frustration, not triumphs. But certain things had to be said, and Wright and Rosskam have said them powerfully."

267. Le Sueur, Meridel. "An Individual Case?" Minneapolis Morning Tribune (17 January), p. 4.
Letter to the editor criticizing William J. McNalley's review of the play NS, especially for its lack of compassion, and supporting W's thesis of environmental determinism.

268. Lewis, Theophilus. "The Frustration of Negro Art." The Catholic World, 155 (April), 51-57.
Mentions Evelyn Ellis, who plays Mrs. Thomas in NS.

269. L.[ocke], A.[lain] LeR.[oy]. "Negroes (American)," in 1942 Britannica Book of the Year. Ed. Walter Yust. Chicago: Encyclopaedia Britannica, p. 472.
Mentions the play NS, TMBV, and W's receipt of the Spingarn Medal.

270. _____. "Who and What Is 'Negro'?" Opportunity, 20 (February), 36-41.
As a point of departure, Locke takes issue with W's exclusion of the talented tenth in TMBV, claiming that this proletarian class approach ignores the racial factor. Contains also a notice of the play NS, which

Locke admires, pointing out, however, the diminution of dramatic
power at the end of both the play
and the novel.

271. _____. "Who and What Is 'Negro'?--
Part II." Opportunity, 20 (March), 83-
87.
     Contains a notice of TMBV finding
     its economic analysis important. The
     work as a whole, Locke believes, is
     polemical rather than objective.

272. Lomax, Louis. "The New Movies." Los
Angeles Tribune.
     Reports that Canada Lee is consider-
     ing bringing a new production of NS
     to the west coast. The date of this
     item is conjectural.

273. Lyons, Leonard. "The Lyons Den."
New York Post (5 January), p. 13.
     Mentions that W "has just completed a
     new novel--a combination of allegory
     and realism, called, 'The Man Who
     Lived Underground.'"

274. _____. "The Lyons Den." New York
Post (6 April), p. 38.
     Mentions W's completion of two nov-
     els, a long one and a short one.

275. _____. "The Lyons Den." New York
Post (10 April), p. 30.
     Mentions W's impending arrival in New
     York and relates a Jim Crow incident
     involving him in Washington, D.C.,
     in 1940.

276. _____. "The Lyons Den." New York
Post (28 May), p. 26.
     Mentions that W "has written the book
     and lyric for a Negro musical. He and
     Barney Josephson, proprietor of Cafe
     Society, will co-produce it. Duke
     Ellington will compose the music for
     it."

277. _____. "The Lyons Den." New York
Post (24 August).
     Reports that W volunteered for army
     service. He wants only to finish
     Black Hope and The Man Who Lived
     Underground.

278. _____. "The Lyons Den." New York
Post (17 December), p. 38.
     Notes that despite his dependents, W
     has received a selective service
     classification of 1-A.

279. M., A. M. W. "About Books." New
York Amsterdam Star-News (7 February),
p. 7.
     Review of The Negro Caravan mention-
     ing W.

280. M., H. "Book Review." Laurel

(Miss.) Leader Call (18 March), p. 3.
     Review of Burns Mantle's The Best
     Plays of 1940-1941 mentioning NS as a
     "darker psychological tragedy."

280a. M., W. E. J. "Reviews of the Theaters: Erlanger." Buffalo Courier-Express
(13 February), p. 8.
     Favorable review of the road show
     version of NS praising the acting
     (especially Canada Lee's), direction,
     and settings. Includes a plot summary
     of the "somewhat staccato story."

281. Mantle, Burns. The Best Plays of
1941-42 and The Year Book of the Drama
in America. New York: Dodd, Mead, pp.
20, 462.
     Mentions the Chicago production of NS
     and gives statistics on the original
     New York production.

282. _____. "Couple of Stripteasers to
Cheer China." New York Sunday News (15
November), p. 90.
     Notes that the play NS is being scru-
     tinized by a morals committee.

283. _____. "The Good Old Days Were Bad,
Too." New York Daily News (26 July).
     Mentions the popularity of the play
     NS, a "four-star attraction."

284. _____. "The Theatre's Holiday
Gifts." New York Daily News (27 December).
     Mentions the play NS as an important
     and much discussed social drama.

285. _____. "There Were Bank Panics the
Year That 'The Merry Widow' Was Glamor-
ous Success." New York Daily News (26
July).
     Mentions the play NS as a "four-star
     attraction."

286. _____. "Vaudeville, It Seems, Only
Half-Way Back; Colored Actors Gain." New
York Daily News (21 July).
     Mentions Canada Lee and his role in
     NS.

287. Martin, Linton. "'Native Son' on
Stage at Walnut, Canada Lee Stars." The
Philadelphia Inquirer (24 February), p.
14.
     Favorable review emphasizing the
     play's grimness. Martin praises Lee's
     acting and Welles's staging. Martin
     calls Mary Dalton "a trouble-making,
     cockeyed Communist."

288. Maslin, Marsh. "The Browser." Lawrence (Mass.) Eagle (28 March).
     Mentions the Modern Library edition
     of NS.

289. McNally, William J. "'Native Son'

Is So-So as Play, But Acting's Great, McNally Says." Minneapolis Morning Tribune (13 January), p. 7.
Review objecting strenuously to W's environmental determinism, a "phony and windbag social philosophy." Bigger is simply a born criminal. McNally finds Canada Lee's performance superb.

290. Meacham, William Shands. "Negro Writers Speak for Themselves." The New York Times Book Review (29 March), pp. 3, 20.
Review of The Negro Caravan mentioning W as a "powerful protest" writer.

291. Mulholland, John Field. "'For We Are You.'" The Presbyterian Tribune, 57 (January), 28-29.
Favorable review of TMBV praising both the "rich, tense, earnest prose" and the photography. "If racial problems were more often presented in this fashion, its problems would demand solution."

292. _____. "Negroes in Pictures and Text." The Christian Century, 59 (18 February), 219.
Highly favorable review of TMBV praising both pictures and text--and their integration. Mulholland considers the social accusation forcefully presented.
Reprinted: 1978.209.

293. Murray, Florence. The Negro Handbook. New York: Wendell Malliet, pp. 7, 250, 251, 252, 256.
Mentions the play NS and honors given to W.

294. Nixon, H. C. "Richard Wright Author of Negro Folk History." Nashville Banner (28 January), Sec. X, p. 4.
Favorable review of TMBV comparing W to Du Bois and praising the style and powerful protest of the book. But Nixon believes that W errs by ignoring both the black and white middle class while concentrating on the black lower class and the white upper class.

295. Norton, W. W. "Wartime Trends in Reading and Publishing." The Retail Bookseller, 45 (June), 37-42.
Uses NS as an example of prewar taste in fiction.

296. O., G. "Richard Wright Conquered Poverty to Become Playwright." The Philadelphia Inquirer (22 February), Society Sec., p. 14.
Sketches W's life and literary career on the occasion of the opening of a revival of the play NS. Quotes W on

the novel NS, including comments on his use of the Nixon case. Includes a photograph of William Challee as a reporter in the play (p. 13).

297. O'Neil, Will. "'12 Million Black Voices' Speaks for a Blighted Race." The Chicago Sun (3 January), p. 15.
Favorable review calling W a "noble champion" of his people. Unhappily, his plea for racial justice will probably not be answered.

298. Peterson, Ed. "Give Us Credit, Too!" The Indianapolis Recorder (3 January), Second Sec., p. 2.
Letter to the editor mentioning TMBV.

299. Pihodna, Joseph. "A Theatrical Guide for the Holidays." New York Herald Tribune (20 December), Sec. VI, p. 1.
Lauds NS as one of the finest plays on the Broadway stage.

300. Pollock, Arthur. "Canada Lee Climbs to the Top of the Pile." Brooklyn Eagle (26 October), p. 7.
Highly favorable analysis of Canada Lee's acting, with special reference to the role of Bigger Thomas.

301. _____. "'Native Son' Is Back with All Its Power." Brooklyn Eagle (24 October), p. 14.
Highly favorable review of the play. "Nothing now visible in the theaters takes hold of its audience as this does, nothing has its depth, its wisdom, its feeling and its consistency." The script now contains references to the war. Lee's acting is better than ever.

302. _____. "Negro Actors Are Getting Somewhere." Brooklyn Eagle (1 August), p. 14.
Notes that Canada Lee and W made hits with NS.

303. _____. "Playthings." Brooklyn Eagle (25 October), p. B7.
Comments favorably on the revival of the play NS.

304. _____. "Playthings: More Plays Arrive to Swell the List for Christmas Shoppers." Brooklyn Eagle (20 December), p. B7.
Mentions NS, "probably the thrill of your lifetime."

305. Prescott, Orville. "Books of the Times." The New York Times (6 May), p. 17.
Refers to NS as a "murderous melodrama" illuminating the "tragic" conditions of Chicago's slums.

306. Price, Edgar. "The Premiere." Brooklyn Citizen (24 October).
Announces the revival of the play NS produced by the Brandt Brothers at the Majestic Theatre.

307. Puckett, Rev. J. Niles. "Racial Problems." The Quarterly Review, 2 (July, August, September), 273.
Favorable review of TMBV by a Southern Baptist minister from Mississippi. Urges prejudiced whites to read this book to understand the black perspective on the racial problem.

307a. [Quinn, Kerker]. "Accent."
Flyer mentioning W as a contributor.

307b. _____. "Accent Opens Volume Three with the Autumn 1942 Issue."
Flyer listing W and "The Man Who Lived Underground."

307c. _____. "Answering Three Questions About Accent."
Flyer mentioning a forthcoming contribution by W.

308. R., E. G. "12 Million Black Voices, by Richard Wright and Edwin Rosskam." Social Progress, 32 (February), 26-27.
Favorable review of "an important but a most disturbing book." In treating social and racial injustice, W writes "with devastating skill, the detachment of cold anger, and the deep passion of understanding."

309. Randolph, John. "'Native Son' Down Below." New Masses, 42 (10 March), 21.
The actor who plays Jan Erlone in the road show of the play describes a performance in Baltimore under Jim Crow conditions.

310. Ransom, Llewelyn. "Kent Cleaner Employees Charge Firm with Labor Violations." The People's Voice (26 March), p. 6.
Notes that W reported on unsafe working conditions.

311. Reddick, L. D. "Negro and Jew." The Jewish Survey, 1 (January), 25.
Review of TMBV urging Jewish-black alliance to combat prejudice against both groups. W's book "is the most poetic prose statement of the folk history of the Negro in this land yet produced." W's "poetry is not romantic, but brilliant, flint-like . . . stark, finely imaginative and yet restrained. The whole suggests America's epic."
Reprinted: 1978.209.

312. Rokotov, T. "Soviet Magazine Prints Many Foreign Writers." Daily Worker (18 March), p. 7.
Notes that International Literature has serialized NS.

313. R.[omero], E.[manuel] A. "Books." Interracial Review, 15 (January), 17.
Favorable review of TMBV praising W's musical prose. He should not have omitted the black middle class from treatment, however.
Reprinted: 1978.209.

314. Rouzeau, Edgar T. "Sepia Artists Achieved Notably during 1941." Norfolk Journal and Guide (3 January), p. 14.
Mentions Canada Lee in NS.

315. _____. "Stardust." Norfolk Journal and Guide (16 May), p. 15.
Contrasts the responses to Porgy and Bess and NS, more favorable to the former and less favorable to the latter than they should have been.

316. Schubart, Mark. "An Editorial." PM Daily (8 December), p. 23.
Argues that the importance of the particular circumstances of the dispute over the threatened closing of the play NS has been exaggerated, but the censorship danger is a real one.

317. Schuyler, George. "Looks at Books." The Pittsburgh Courier (14 February), p. 7.
Mentions W in a review of The Negro Caravan.

318. Schwartzstein, Rose. "News Book Review Missed Big Point." Office and Professional News (15 February), p. 4.
Letter to the editor protesting that Vera Solomon's review in the preceding issue missed W's point that black-white unity, especially in the labor movement, is the key to solving the racial problem.

319. Sherman, John K. "Drama: 'Native Son' Opens at the Lyceum." Minneapolis Star Journal (13 January), p. 14.
Favorable review of the play, a "painful, uncomfortable, searing" story of racial maladjustment. Praises the production and the acting.

320. Slochower, Harry. "In the Fascist Styx." The Negro Quarterly, 1 (Fall), 227-240.
Analyzes NS treating Bigger Thomas and his creator as disinherited exiles in their own land. Bigger is a "black Jew" of the new world, but in contrast to the victims of European fascism, he reacts violently. His killings are creative acts of daring. Slochower provides a lengthy discus-

sion of the fire imagery in the novel.
Reprinted: 1945.1135.

320a. Smith, Ardis. "Welles' Touch Plainly Evident in Swift-Moving 'Native Son.'" Buffalo Evening News (13 February), p. 30.
Favorable review of the road show of the play with special praise for the direction, often melodramatic but effective, and the acting. Paul Green's script and Orson Welles's sense of theater complement each other.

321. Smith, Lillian E. "Addressed to Intelligent White Southerners: 'These Are Things to Do.'" South Today, 7 (Autumn-Winter), 34-43.
Includes TMBV in a suggested reading list.

322. _____. "Dope with Lime." South Today, 7 (Spring), 4, 68-70.
Contains a brief notice of TMBV (p. 69). Smith is favorable, but she prefers the pictures to the words.

323. S.[olomon], V.[era]. "Books: The Negro's Tragic History." Office and Professional News (1 February), p. 7.
Favorable review of TMBV praising both the writing and the social message. Notes W's acute analysis of the economic basis of white racism. W reminds whites that the nation must struggle to end slavery at home as well as abroad.

324. Sullivan, Ed. "Little Old New York." New York Daily News (8 April), p. 28.
Notes that W is about to become a father.

325. Suskind, Peter. "Stardust." Norfolk Journal and Guide (31 October), p. 17.
Announces the return of NS to Broadway and analyzes the reasons for the poor original reception and the success of the play on the road.

326. Sylvester, Robert. "Native Son Stop, Fights." New York Daily News (8 December).
Notes that the play NS will not be closed despite efforts to purge the theater.

327. Van Vechten, Carl. "The J. W. Johnson Collection at Yale." The Crisis, 49 (July), 222-223, 226.
Mentions the inclusion of W material and the Van Vechten photographs of W.

328. Walker, Jean. "On the Dial: Quip-Wit, History Talks, Music, Langston

Hughes." Daily Worker (3 March), p. 7.
Mentions W as one of the writers included in The Negro Caravan.

329. Warner, Ralph. "'Native Son' Revived at Majestic Theatre." Daily Worker (29 October), p. 7.
Favorable review examining the play in the light of the changed world conditions since the first production. It is an effective "weapon against discrimination."

330. _____. "Saroyan's New Plays Dangerously Muddled." Daily Worker (20 August), p. 7.
Mentions the play NS and includes a photograph of Canada Lee as Bigger.

331. _____. "Tribute to Negro in American Theatre." Daily Worker (4 August), p. 7.
Review of The Negro in the American Theatre mentioning NS and including a photograph of Canada Lee as Bigger.

332. _____. "Victory Over Censorship: 'Native Son' Will Stay On." Daily Worker (8 December), p. 7.
Written before the decision to close the play was rescinded, this article is preceded by a note on the new development. Warner reviews the message and reception of the play and protests its closing. "The suppression of 'Native Son' is good news to Hitler." A photograph of Canada Lee as Bigger appears with the article.

333. Wilson, David. "Treasury of Negro Literature." Sunday Worker (8 March), Sec. 2, p. 6.
Favorable review of The Negro Caravan mentioning W and relating him to the militant Douglass tradition.

334. Winchell, Walter. "On Broadway." New York Daily Mirror (20 April), p. 10.
Mentions the birth of Julia Wright.

335. _____. "On Broadway." New York Daily Mirror (15 June), p. 10.
Reports that Gypsy Rose Lee "just rented her Brooklyn shack to Richard Wright."

336. Wingfield, Marshall. Literary Memphis: A Survey of Its Writers and Writings. Memphis: The West Tennessee Historical Society, p. 62.
Paragraph on W noting his Memphis connection and citing praise accorded to NS.

337. Young, Harriet. "The Plight of the Negro Masses." Opportunity, 20 (January), 26-27.

Favorable review of TMBV. W does not present new facts or analysis, but he does state racial problems clearly and graphically to make them comprehensible to all Americans.

1943

1. Anon. "About Canada Lee: Role in 'Lifeboat' Best for Race." Norfolk Journal and Guide (11 September), p. 14.
    Mentions Lee's role in NS.

1a. Anon. "'Accent,' Literary Magazine, Edited by Staffmen, Wins Fame." Illinois Alumni News (2 June), p. 6.
    Mentions briefly W and NS.

2. Anon. "Canada Lee in Radio Drama." The Worker (17 January), p. 7.
    Mentions Lee's role in the play NS.

3. Anon. "Canada Lee Is Back." The Chicago Defender (27 February), p. 13.
    Mentions Lee's role as Bigger Thomas.

4. Anon. "Canada Lee Signed for Role in Movie Version of 'Lifeboat.'" New York Amsterdam News (24 July), p. 17.
    Mentions Lee's performance as Bigger in NS.

5. Anon. "Canada Lee to Speak." The Pittsburgh Courier (6 February), p. 21.
    Mentions Lee's performance in NS.

6. Anon. Dust jacket of Uncle Tom's Children. Cleveland: World.
    This is a cheap reprint of the enlarged edition. Six blurbs on front inside flap.

7. Anon. "Five Shows to End Runs Tomorrow." Unidentified clipping (1 January).
    Notes the closing of NS after eighty-three performances.

7a. Anon. "Footlight Favorites." Washington Tribune (13 February), p. 13.
    Reports that W is completing his second play.

8. Anon. "Harlemites Make Showing in Negro History Quiz." New York Amsterdam News (8 May), p. 11.
    Six of a random sampling of ten named W as the author of NS.

8a. Anon. "Hugh Morris Gloster Receives Doctorate." Washington Tribune (13 March), p. 2.
    Reports that his New York University dissertation is "American Negro Fiction from Charles W. Chesnutt to Richard Wright."

9. Anon. "Looking Backward at the 1942-43 Season." The New York Times (30 May), Sec. II, p. 1.
    Notes that the revival of NS had eighty-three performances. Reprinted: 1972.14.

10. Anon. "'Native Son' Author Has a New Show." The Chicago Defender (6 February), p. 12.
    Mentions that W "is finishing his second play."

11. Anon. "News of the Stage." The New York Times (1 January), p. 26.
    Mentions the closing of NS after eighty-three performances.

12. Anon. "News of the Theater." New York Herald Tribune (1 January), p. 19.
    Mentions the closing of NS.

13. Anon. "100,000,000 Have Learned to Read and Write." Life, 14 (29 March), 80.
    Includes a photograph of a sidewalk bookstall in Moscow. The caption mentions W as one of six favorite United States authors in the Soviet Union.

14. Anon. "Orson Welles Gave Race Actors 'Shot in the Arm.'" The Pittsburgh Courier (23 October), p. 19.
    Discusses the Welles productions of Macbeth and NS.

15. Anon. "Program, Fisk University Chapel, Friday, April 9, 1943, 7:30 p. m." Nashville: Fisk University.
    Program for a speech by W on the topic "What I've Been Thinking."

16. Anon. "See For Yourself: Native Son." Theatre Arts, 27 (January), unnumbered page immediately preceding p. 1.
    Favorable notice of the play praising Lee's performance.

17. Anon. "U. S. Observes Book-Burning Anniversary." Daily Worker (10 May), p. 7.
    Lists TMBV among the books banned by the Nazis.

18. Anon. Untitled article. The Clarion (Fisk University), 7 (9 April), 1.
    Announces that W will address the Fisk Sociology Club.

19. Anon. "Voices for Victory: 'Masses' Continues Traditional Search for People's Poets." Daily Worker (12 March), p. 7.
    Names W, Sandburg, and Langston Hughes as three great people's poets published by New Masses.

20. Anon. "Who's Who." Negro Digest, 1 (September), 14.
    Contains a photograph of W and a question about him.

21. Brewer, W. M. "No Day of Triumph. By J. Saunders Redding." The Journal of Negro History, 28 (January), 107-110.
    Condemns Redding and W for presenting unfavorable images of blacks to white readers.

22. Brown, Ross. Afro-American World Almanac. Chicago: The Author, p. 98.
    Lists W among famous black men who have married white women.

23. Burgum, Edwin Berry. "The Promise of Democracy and the Fiction of Richard Wright." Science and Society, 7 (Fall), 338-352.
    Marxist analysis of NS. Because Bigger is unaware of his circumstantial limitations, serious problems arise. W portrays realistically the economic and political forces at work in the society. He focuses the reader's attention upon their effects, especially their consequences on the individual.
    Reprinted: 1947.156; 1963.63; 1970.5; 1971.147.

24. Burke, W. J. and Will D. Howe. "Native Son," in their American Authors and Books 1640-1940. New York: Gramercy Publishing Company, p. 515.
    Note identifying author and theme.
    Reprinted: 1962.44a; 1972.42a.

24a.   . "Wright, Richard," in their American Authors and Books 1640-1940. New York: Gramercy Publishing Company, p. 849.
    Brief biographical note.
    Reprinted in revised form: 1962.44b; 1972.42b.

25. Burns, Ben. "Books." The Chicago Defender (31 July), p. 17.
    Review of Carl R. Offord's The White Face comparing the author to W, the leader of the school of protest fiction. W's view of racial problems is too despairing.

26.   . "Books." The Chicago Defender (14 August), p. 17.
    Review of Roi Ottley's 'New World A-Coming' mentioning W and "his grim and ghastly study of Bigger Thomas."

27.   . "Books." The Chicago Defender (21 August), p. 17.
    Mentions the publisher's comparison of Bucklin Moon's The Darker Brother to NS.

28.   . "Books." The Chicago Defender (18 September), p. 15.
    Review of Bucklin Moon's The Darker Brother comparing it unfavorably to NS.

29.   . "Books." The Chicago Defender (25 September), p. 17.
    Complains of W's silence since NS and TMBV.

30. Carmon, Walt. "Writers of the World Meet in the Pages of a Soviet Magazine." Daily Worker (18 January), p. 7.
    Mentions the letter to W from a Soviet soldier (see 1941.869) and includes a drawing of W.

31. Cayton, Horace R. "Exhibitionism." The Pittsburgh Courier (26 June), p. 13.
    Commenting on the riot in Los Angeles, Cayton writes that zoot suiters have a "Bigger Thomas mentality."

32. Cooke, Marvel. "Herndon, Ellison Win Success as Negro-Life Book Publishers." New York Amsterdam News (10 April), p. 24.
    Mentions W as a contributor to Negro Quarterly.

33. Curtis, Constance M. "About Books." New York Amsterdam News (25 September), p. 13-A.
    Review of Bucklin Moon's The Darker Brother comparing its prose to W's.

34. Embree, Edwin R. Brown Americans: The Story of a Tenth of a Nation. New York: The Viking Press, pp. 180, 194, 218.
    Mentions W briefly.

35. Fields, Sidney. "Only Human." New York Daily Mirror (1 January), p. 18.
    Biographical sketch of Canada Lee discussing his performance in NS.

36. Franken, Jerry. "Negroes Protest CBS Radio Script." PM (4 June), p. 26.
    Reports that Richard Campbell, a black actor in the cast of NS, refused to read a part in a radio script demeaning to blacks.

37. Garlin, Sender. "Constant Reader." Daily Worker (24 April), p. 7.
    Mentions the selection of NS by the Book-of-the-Month Club.

38. Geismar, Maxwell. "Nomads and Adventures on the Australian Frontiers." The New York Times Book Review (25 April), p. 3.
    Review of Xavier Herbert's Capricornia mentioning W as another writer concerned with race relations.

39. Hayakawa, S. I. "Happy Birthday." Negro Digest, 2 (November), back cover-inside back cover.
Partial reprint of 1943.40.

40. _____. "Second Thoughts." The Chicago Defender (16 October), p. 17.
Mentions W as a contributor to Negro Digest.
Reprinted: 1943.39.

41. Hopper, Hedda. "Hollywood." New York Daily News (3 October).
Reports that Canada Lee wants to play Bigger in the film version of NS.

42. Howard, Donald S. The WPA and Federal Relief Policy. New York: Russell Sage Foundation, p. 237.
Cites W's transfer from manual labor to the Writers Project as an example of WPA success in screening for competence.

43. Hughes, Langston. "The Future of Black America." Negro Digest, 2 (November), 3-6.
Partial reprint of 1943.44.

44. _____. "The Future of Black America." New World.
Mentions W.
Reprinted: 1943.43.

45. _____. "Here to Yonder." The Chicago Defender (4 December), p. [14].
Points out that "three of the leading colored writers"--W, Schuyler, and Ottley--"are married to white women."
Reprinted: 1944.107.

46. Lewis, Elsie Graves. "The Week in Richmond." Norfolk Journal and Guide (3 April), p. 15.
Mentions a lecture at Virginia Union University on "The Negro in the American Theatre" by Richard Campbell, who played in NS.

47. Locke, Alain. Le Role du nègre dans la culture des Amériques. Port-au-Prince: Imprimerie de l'état, pp. 70, 101, 102.
Favorable comments on NS and UTC.

48. Lyons, Leonard. "The Lyons Den." New York Post (23 January), p. 18.
Mentions that W "is finishing his second play."

49. _____. "The Lyons Den." New York Post (14 June), p. 22.
Mentions that W "is completing a new play."

50. Mantle, Burns. The Best Plays of 1942-43 and The Yearbook of the Drama in America. New York: Dodd, Mead, pp. 6,

439-440, 481.
Comments on the revival of NS. Mantle finds it "noticeably cheapened in staging and direction."

51. Nathan, George Jean. The Theatre Book of the Year, 1942-1943: A Record and an Interpretation. New York: Knopf, pp. 113-115.
Unfavorable review of the play NS. Although it contains some powerful scenes, the characterization is weak. Important elements of the novel are objectified unsatisfactorily in the play. Some of the rhetoric is confusing. The greatest defect, Nathan believes, is the play's appeal to sympathy for merely being black.

52. Neville, Marion. "The Spectator." The Chicago Sun (c. 15 August).
Lists NS as a good Chicago ethnic novel.

53. Ottley, Roi. 'New World A-Coming'. Boston: Houghton Mifflin, p. 240.
Mentions W's articulation of black aspirations.

54. Perry, Edward G. "Welles to Help with Race Theatre." Norfolk Journal and Guide (23 October), p. 14.
Mentions NS in a discussion of the longstanding interest of Orson Welles in black theater.

55. Putnam, Samuel. "Good Neighbor: Calls Offord Novel 'Thrilling Experience.'" Daily Worker (16 July), p. 7.
Favorable review of The White Face comparing Offord to W.

55a. [Quinn, Kerker]. "Accent Announces the Spring 1943 Issue."
Flyer listing W and "The Man Who Lived Underground."

55b. _____. "Accent Announces the Summer 1943 Issue."
Mentions W as a contributor.

55c. _____. "Accent Announces the Winter 1943 Issue."
Flyer listing "The Man Who Lived Underground" as a "highlight."

56. Schubart, Mark. "Richard Wright Feels Grip of Harlem Tension." PM Daily (3 August), p. 8.
Interview with W on the Harlem riot, which he attributes to economic causes. W points to the tension and continuing danger.

57. Sobol, Louis. "New York Cavalcade." New York Journal-American (24 September), p. 21.
Mentions that the actor Philip Bour-

neuf played in NS.

57a. Tolson, M. B. "Caviar & Cabbage: Our Good White Friends Get Cold Feet." Washington Tribune (23 January), p. 7.
Mentions W briefly.

58. Torrey, Volta. "Campus 1943." PM's Sunday Picture News (31 October), pp. 2-5.
Reports that NS is among the favorite novels at Eastern colleges.

1944

1. Adams, J. Donald. The Shape of Books to Come. New York: Viking, pp. 79, 83.
Reprint of 1944.2

2. _____. "Speaking of Books." The New York Times Book Review (28 May), p. 2.
Compares Strange Fruit favorably to NS. W's novel was "scarred with hatred," Bigger was a repulsive character, and W failed to understand the white viewpoint. "In spite of its melodramatic force, 'Native Son' was basically illogical, confused and unsound."
Reprinted: 1944.1; 1945.2; 1948.1.

3. Anon. "American Books in Russia." The Dallas Daily Times Herald (c. 4 June).
Reports that Hemingway, Steinbeck, and W are among the best selling authors in the Soviet Union.

4. Anon. "American Hunger. By Richard Wright," in Harper's Spring Catalog. New York: Harper, p. 25.
Highly favorable review of BB summarizing W's "story of fear, struggle, eternal hunger of body and spirit, and final emergence into some sort of livable world." The narrative is thus an American success story despite racism. The book is "powerful, terrible and magnificent."

5. Anon. "Autobiography Chosen." Columbus (Ohio) Dispatch (c. 24 September).
Announces that BB will be offered by the Book-of-the-Month Club.

6. Anon. "Autobiography Picked by Club." The Columbus (Ohio) Citizen (31 December).
Reports the selection of BB by the Book-of-the-Month Club.

7. Anon. "Black Boy's Story." Pasadena Star-News (16 September), p. 8.
Announcement of BB and its selection by the Book-of-the-Month Club.

8. Anon. "Book Notes." New York Herald Tribune (20 September), p. 19.
Mentions that BB is one of the "re-serve selections" of the Book-of-the-Month Club.

9. Anon. "Books and Authors." Keene Evening Sentinel (15 September), p. 12.
Notes that BB will be offered by the Book-of-the-Month Club.

10. Anon. "Books and Authors." The New York Times Book Review (17 September), p. 14.
Announces that W's autobiography is forthcoming and mentions his work in progress on "a Negro serving girl."

11. Anon. "Books and Authors." The New York Times Book Review (22 October), p. 16.
Mentions BB as a forthcoming Book-of-the-Month Club selection.

12. Anon. "Books--Authors." The New York Times (20 September), p. 21.
Notes that BB will be offered by the Book-of-the-Month Club.

13. Anon. "Books--Authors." The New York Times (23 December), p. 16.
Announces that BB will be part of a dual March selection of the Book-of-the-Month Club.

14. Anon. "Bookstall Gossip." Boston Sunday Post (31 December), p. A-2.
Notes that BB promises to be a "powerful" autobiography.

15. Anon. "Canada Lee Earned $75,000 as a Boxer, But It Went Fast; Now He's Stage Star." New York Amsterdam News (1 January), p. 11-A.
Notes Lee's role in NS.

16. Anon. "Citizens' Committee Lists 24 Books for Race Study." New York Herald Tribune (28 May), Sec. II, p. 2.
NS is included in this list "recommended by outstanding Americans."

17. Anon. "'Cross-Section,' Edited by Edwin Seaver." Lawrence (Mass.) Evening Tribune (2 June), p. 6.
Review mentioning W.
Reprinted: 1944.43.

18. Anon. "Cross-Section Edited by Edwin Seaver." The Retail Bookseller, 47 (April), 63A.
Mentions "Wright's first story since 'Native Son.'"

19. Anon. "'Cross-Section' Reveals New Writing Trend." Detroit Free Press (4 June), Part 4, p. 6.
Includes favorable comments on "The Man Who Lived Underground."

20. Anon. "December Book Choice." The

Springfield (Mass.) Sunday Union and Republican (1 October), p. 4D.
    Notes that BB will be offered by the Book-of-the-Month Club.

21. Anon. "Did You Know That . . ." Chelsea (Mass.) Evening Record (2 October).
    Notes that BB will be offered by the Book-of-the-Month Club.

22. Anon. Dust jacket of American Hunger. New York: Harper.
    Proposed jacket of W's autobiography before the title was changed to BB.

23. Anon. "Exodus from the Left Wing." Los Angeles Tribune (7 August), p. 10.
    Editorial endorsing W's withdrawal from the Communist Party. As W, A. Philip Randolph, Angelo Herndon, and Langston Hughes have recognized, the Party treats black problems as a matter of expediency, not with real conviction.

24. Anon. "Gromyko Praises U. S.-Russian Ties." The New York Times (20 October), p. 7.
    In a speech delivered at a banquet of the American Russian Institute in New York, the Soviet Ambassador mentioned the popularity of several American writers, including W, in the Soviet Union.

25. Anon. "Guild Gossip." Wings, 18 (October), inside front cover.
    Mentions the popularity of NS in Sweden.

26. Anon. "Harper." The Publishers' Weekly, 145 (29 January), 387.
    Announces that AH will be published on 14 June.

27. Anon. "His Eyes Were Opened." Church of St. John (New York) Parish Monthly (September), p. 9.
    Applauds W's rejection of Communism as recorded in "I Tried to Be a Communist." Instead of Communism, blacks in America should turn to Catholicism.

28. Anon. "Library Notes." West Bend (Wis.) News (28 September), Sec. 2, p. 1.
    Mentions "I Tried to Be a Communist" as an outstanding magazine article.

29. Anon. "Magazine Digest: Air Power for Policing the World." New York Post (2 August), p. 36.
    Contains a favorable notice with summary of the first installment of "I Tried to Be a Communist."

30. Anon. "Magazine Digest: Does Dewey Differ from Harding?" New York Post (18 September), p. 28.
    Refers to and quotes from "I Tried to Be a Communist."

31. Anon. "Negro Author Criticizes Reds as Intolerant." New York Herald Tribune (28 July), p. 11.
    Reports W's formal break with the Communist Party. According to W, the organization is no longer an effective instrument of social change.

32. Anon. "Notes of the Stage." The New York Sun (2 June), p. 26.
    Announces the opening of the play NS at the Queensboro Theater for a week's run beginning 6 June.

33. Anon. "News of the Theater." New York Herald Tribune (2 June), p. 12.
    Announces the revival of NS at the Queensboro Theater.

34. Anon. "P. R. Reynolds Dies; Literary Agent, 80." The New York Times (20 August), p. 34.
    Mentions W as one of his clients.

35. Anon. "Party Saturday Fetes Canada Lee." New York Amsterdam News (8 January), p. 11-A.
    Mentions the play NS.

36. Anon. "Paul Reynolds Dead; Long Literary Agent." Unidentified clipping (20 August).
    Mentions W as one of his clients.

37. Anon. "Paul Reynolds Is Dead; Pioneer Literary Agent." New York Herald Tribune (20 August), p. 36.
    Mentions W as one of his clients.

38. Anon. "People." Time, 44 (7 August), 42.
    Quotes from W's New York Herald Tribune interview on his attitude toward Communists.

39. Anon. "Pyle's New One." Nashville Banner (27 September), p. 12.
    Notes that BB will be offered by the Book-of-the-Month Club.

40. Anon. "Racial Hatred Among Communists Revealed." Los Angeles Examiner (30 July), p. 11.
    Favorable commentary on "I Tried to Be a Communist."

41. Anon. "Richard Wright Breaks with Communist Party." The Chicago Defender (5 August), p. 7.
    Quotes W on his relation to the Party and refers to "I Tried to be a Communist." W states that he left in 1940.

42. Anon. "Richard Wright Describes the Birth of 'Black Boy'--An Autobiography Destined to Disturb White Egotism." New York Post (30 November), p. B6.
Headnote to an article by W on the genesis of his autobiography in a speech he delivered at Fisk University.

43. Anon. "Seaver Salvages Wide Array of Shelved Writing." New Haven Register (4 June), Sec. III, p. 10.
Reprint of 1944.17.

44. Anon. "Selection." The Charleston (S. C.) News and Courier (31 December), p. 9.
Notes that BB will be part of a dual selection of the Book-of-the-Month Club for March.

45. Anon. "Speaking of Books." Life, 17 (14 August), 12-14.
Includes NS in a list of the one hundred outstanding books of the past twenty years.

46. Anon. "'Strange Play' Off After One Showing." The New York Times (3 June), p. 10.
Mentions the revival of NS scheduled to open at the Queensboro Theater on 6 June.

47. Anon. "Success." The New York Times Book Review (22 October), p. 16.
Announces that BB will be a Book-of-the-Month Club selection.

48. Anon. "Summer Items." The New York Times (3 June), p. 10.
Notes that Canada Lee will play Bigger Thomas in the revival of NS at the Queensboro Theater.

49. Anon. "Sundry Notes on Books and Authors." The New York Times Book Review (31 December), p. 10.
Mentions BB as a Book-of-the-Month Club selection for March.

50. Anon. "Trade Notes and Price Changes." The Retail Bookseller, 47 (April), 80-83.
Announces that AH, "the manuscript of which was recently delivered to Harper and Brothers," is scheduled for publication in June.

51. Anon. "Trade Notes and Price Changes." The Retail Bookseller, 47 (October), 104-107.
Notes that the title of W's autobiography has been changed from AH to BB.

52. Anon. "29 Have Received Spingarn Medals." The Baltimore Afro-American (8 April), p. 3.
Lists W.

53. Anon. Untitled article. Chelsea (Mass.) Evening Record (30 September), p. 2.
Notes that BB will be offered by the Book-of-the-Month Club.

54. Anon. Untitled article. The New York Times (7 September), p. 21.
Notes that BB will be the title of W's autobiography.

55. Anon. "Wright, Richard. American Hunger. Harper." Bulletin from Virginia Kirkus' Bookshop Service, 12 (15 June), 271.
Favorable review emphasizing the grimness of W's story: "The whole tragedy of a race seems dramatized in this record; it is virtually unrelieved by any vestige of human tenderness, or humor; there are no bright spots." Yet its authenticity should compel attention to minority problems.

56. Babcock, Frederic. "Among the Authors." Chicago Sunday Tribune (17 September), Part 6, p. 17.
Notes that the title of W's autobiography has been changed from AH to BB.

57. Boutell, Clip. "Authors Are Like People." The Chicago Sun Book Week (5 March), p. 11.
Mentions AH, scheduled for publication in June, and a novelette in progress.

58. _____. "Authors Are Like People." New York Post (1 June), p. 21.
Predicts that AH, to be published in the summer, will be unpopular "among the poll tax politicians as well as the American communists."

59. _____. "Authors Are Like People." New York Post (24 August), p. 24.
Contains a favorable advance notice of Sylvestre C. Watkins's An Anthology of American Negro Literature, with emphasis on "The Ethics of Living Jim Crow." Mentions also W's forthcoming autobiography.

60. _____. "A Ghost Talks Shop." New York Post (20 June), Magazine Sec., p. 29.
Essay-interview with Edwin Seaver, who mentions W and "The Man Who Lived Underground."

61. Bower, Helen. "The Book Rack." The Detroit Free Press (4 June), Part Four, p. 6.

Contains a favorable review of Cross-Section with a laudatory reference to W.

62. [Browning, Alice C.]. "Current Town Talk." Negro Story, 1 (July-August), 62.
Announces the publication of AH "this month."

63. [_____ and Fern Gayden]. "Our Contributors." Negro Story, 1 (May-June), 2.
Identifies W as "the most important of Negro fiction writers."

64. Burgum, Edwin Berry. "The Art of Richard Wright's Short Stories." Quarterly Review of Literature, 1 (Spring), 198-211.
Analyzes all the stories in UTC. The analysis treats theme, symbols, technique, characterization, point of view, and evaluation. Compares W's method to Hemingway's and Sherwood Anderson's. W's heroic theme takes dramatic form in physical conflict. Reprinted: 1947.156; 1963.62; 1970.75; 1971.147.

65. Burns, Ben. "Books." The Chicago Defender (1 January), p. 15.
Contains an announcement of "The Man Who Lived Underground," to be published in Cross-Section, and speaks of a new completed novel "on his publisher's desk."

66. _____. "Books." The Chicago Defender (24 June), p. 15.
Mentions the forthcoming publication of W's autobiography.

67. _____. "Books." The Chicago Defender (1 July), p. 15.
Review of Cross-Section with an ambivalent discussion of "The Man Who Lived Underground." Admiring W's prose, Burns considers the story incredible and gloomy. Comparable to NS in theme and mood, it is less successful.

68. _____. "Books." The Chicago Defender (8 July), p. 15.
Announces 23 August as the publication date of AH and quotes a favorable comment by Dorothy Canfield.

69. _____. "Books." The Chicago Defender (19 August), p. 15.
Enthusiastic review of Howard Fast's Freedom Road. In comparison, "'Strange Fruit' and 'Native Son' fade into obscurity."

70. _____. "Books." The Chicago Defender (9 September), p. 15.

Announces postponement of the publication of W's autobiography.

71. _____. "Books." The Chicago Defender (9 December), p. 15.
Announces the postponement of the publication of W's autobiography until spring.

72. C., N. R. "Contemporary Writing in America." Richmond Times-Dispatch (11 June), p. D-6.
Review of Cross-Section mentioning "The Man Who Lived Underground."

73. Canfield, Dorothy. "13 Against the Odds By Edwin R. Embree." Book-of-the-Month Club News (March), p. 16.
Favorable review mentioning W.

74. Carter, Michael. "Miss Pearl Harbor." Negro Digest, 2 (April), 64.
Reprint of 1944.75.

75. _____. "The Week." The Baltimore Afro-American (12 February), pp. 1, 14.
Contains an anecdote told by W concerning a misunderstanding among black people in a Southern town who thought that Pearl Harbor was the name of a white woman. Reprinted: 1944.74.

76. Cayton, Horace R. "The Communists: War Relationship with Negroes Is Not Creditable." The Pittsburgh Courier (26 August), p. 7.
Notes the silence of the Communists after W's break with the Party and points out the decline of Communist militancy on black issues.

77. Cerf, Bennett. "Trade Winds." The Saturday Review of Literature, 27 (15 July), 16-17.
Contains a laudatory announcement of AH scheduled for publication in the fall.

78. _____. "Trade Winds." The Saturday Review of Literature, 27 (14 October), p. 39.
Notes that BB will be offered by the Book-of-the-Month Club.

79. Clough, Ben C. "New Writing in Many Fields." The Providence Sunday Journal (18 June), Sec. VI, p. 6.
Review of Cross-Section mentioning "The Man Who Lived Underground" and objecting to its symbolism.

80. Collins, Thomas Lyle. "New American Writing." New York Herald Tribune Weekly Book Review (28 May), p. 4.
Review of Cross-Section pointing out that "The Man Who Lived Underground" symbolically depicts "the way in

which white suppression forces the Negro psyche 'underground.'"

81. Conroy, Jack. "Writers of Today." New Masses, 52 (26 September), 25-26.
Review of Cross-Section. Conroy admires the "sheer literary versatility and vivid imagery" of "The Man Who Lived Underground," but deplores its lack of realism.

82. Curtis, Constance H. "About Books." New York Amsterdam News (29 April), p. 10-A.
Mentions NS as a book which legitimately uses obscenity for verisimilitude.

83. Davis, Benjamin J., Jr. "New Times: A Few Words on Richard Wright and 'New Ideas.'" The Worker (6 August), p. 9.
Defends the Communists against W's attack on them for intolerance, distrust of new ideas, and neglect of the cause of black rights.

84. _____. "New Times: What Makes Mr. Cayton Tick." The Worker (3 September), p. 11.
Rebuts Cayton's (actually W's) defense of W against Davis' attack resulting from W's defection and criticism of the Party. Davis accuses Cayton of Trotskyism.

85. Embree, Edwin R. "Native Son," in his 13 Against the Odds. New York: Viking, pp. 25-46.
Biographical essay with many details previously unavailable. Includes excerpts from "The Ethics of Living Jim Crow," "How 'Bigger' Was Born," and BB. Embree emphasizes W's fascination with fear as an emotion.
Reprinted: 1944.86.

86. _____. "Native Son." Negro Digest, 2 (March), 53-60.
Partial reprint of 1944.85.

87. Engle, Paul. "Writing Collection Shows Much Variety and Strength." Chicago Sunday Tribune (4 June), Part 6, p. 10.
Review of Cross-Section mentioning "The Man Who Lived Underground" as a story of "curious intent."

88. Farber, Marjorie. "The Younger Writers." The New York Times Book Review (28 May), p. 4.
Review of Cross-Section mentioning W.

89. Ford, James W. "The Case of Richard Wright: A Disservice to the Negro People." Daily Worker (5 September), p. 6.
Attacks W for his defection from the Communist Party. Ford stresses W's distaste for writing assignments given to him by the Party. He contends that W could make a significant contribution toward social change by writing about the problems of black people.

90. Gannett, Lewis. "Books and Things." New York Herald Tribune (1 June), p. 19.
Review of Cross-Section mentioning W.

91. Garlington, S. W. "Popular Negro Magazies Offer Broad Opportunities in Reading." New York Amsterdam News (15 July), p. 7-A.
Mentions unfavorably W's contribution to Negro Story.

92. Glicksberg, Charles I. "The Negro Cult of the Primitive." The Antioch Review, 4 (Spring), 47-55.
Stresses W's objectivity, realism, and detachment, qualities lacking in earlier black writers. NS is intrinsically an indictment of white America. W's fiction is important because his revolutionary consciousness neutralizes the traditional glorification of black people as primitive and barbaric.

93. Goss, Margaret T. "Write Artists Views on Efforts." Norfolk Journal and Guide (30 September), p. 11.
Suggests writing letters to such figures as Canada Lee and W. "Richard Wright should know that we think he is quite young to be bringing out a story of his life when there is so much dramatic material around us in the part that the Negro is playing in this war."

94. Granger, Lester B. "13 Against the Odds, by Edwin R. Embree." Survey Graphic, 33 (April), 224.
Mentions W.

95. Guilfoil, Kelsey. "Present Day Negro Writings Collected." Chicago Tribune (c. 17 September).
Review of Sylvestre C. Watkins's An Anthology of American Negro Literature mentioning W's fame.

96. Haddon, Bruce. "On Books." Erie Dispatch-Herald (31 December), Sec. Two, p. 6.
Mentions that BB will be part of a dual March selection for the Book-of-the-Month Club.

97. Handley, Catherine. "New Year Will Bring Books by Steinbeck, Ferber, Hilton." Chicago Daily News (13 December), p. 19.
Contains an announcement of BB.

98. Hansen, Harry. "Autobiography of Richard Wright Is a Forceful Book." Chicago Sunday Tribune (21 May), Part 6, p. 10.
    Relates favorable reports on the advance sheets of AH. W excels James Weldon Johnson and Langston Hughes in "expressing indignation and resentment in prose."

99. _____. "Book Themes of Permanent Interest Are Being Sought." Chicago Sunday Tribune (13 August), Part 6, p. 9.
    Predicts that AH will be an important fall book on the racial issue.

100. _____. "The First Reader." New York World-Telegram (31 May), p. 27.
    Review of "The Man Who Lived Underground" in Cross-Section praising W's narrative skill and his ability to describe the tense feeling, the indecision, and the desperation of the hunted. Although Hansen recognizes a symbolic dimension in the story, he insists that "Wright is not a symbolist and his story stands or falls on the narrative, not on the suspected implications."

101. _____. "The First Reader." New York World-Telegram (11 August), p. 15.
    Mentions W's forthcoming autobiography and the essay "I Tried to Be a Communist."

102. _____. "James T. Farrell Attacks Views of Van Wyck Brooks." Chicago Sunday Tribune (17 December), Part 6, p. 10.
    Mentions W's lectures "The American Negro Discovers Himself" and "The American Negro's Contribution to Literature."

103. Hart, James D. "Wright, Richard," in his The Oxford Companion to American Literature. London: Oxford University Press, p. 851.
    Reprint of 1941.760.

104. Hill, Abe. "Lillian Hellman Rates Small Weight on Negro." New York Amsterdam News (8 July), p. 5-A.
    Quotes Hellman mentioning W as a playwright.

105. _____. "Reader Denounces 52nd St. Write-Ups." New York Amsterdam News (5 August), p. 10-A.
    Praises Lee's pantomime in a scene in NS.

106. H.[illyer], D.[orothy]. "Over the Fence." The Boston Daily Globe (14 September), p. 15.
    Includes a favorable advance notice of BB.

107. Hughes, Langston. "Color Combination." Negro Digest, 2 (January), 98.
    Reprint of 1943.45.

108. _____. "Here to Yonder." The Chicago Defender (4 March), p. 14.
    Notes that W "sublimated his Jim Crow shocks into a mighty novel, 'Native Son.'"

109. _____. "Here to Yonder." The Chicago Defender (16 December), p. 16.
    Points out that W is one of Edwin R. Embree's subjects in 13 Against the Odds.

110. Jackson, Joseph Henry. "Bookman's Notebook." San Francisco Chronicle (28 December), p. 10.
    Notes that BB will be offered by the Book-of-the-Month Club.

111. [James, C. L. R.] ("J. R. Johnson"). "Laski, St. Paul and Stalin." The New International, 10 (June), 182-186.
    Mentions W briefly (p. 185). See 1944.112.
    Reprinted: 1977.180.

112. Johnson, J. R. See James, C. L. R.

113. Kaempffert, Waldemar. "Science in Review: An Author's Mind Plumbed for the Unconscious Factor in the Creation of a Novel." The New York Times (24 September), Sec. 4, p. 11.
    Account of Frederic Wertham's psychological profile of W. Wertham and W discussed the latter's childhood, NS, and various fantasies. Out of this discussion some of the sources of the novel became apparent, thus indicating that the unconscious is important in the creative process.

114. Kazin, Alfred. On Native Grounds. New York: Overseas Edition, pp. 319-320.
    Reprint of 1942.254.

115. Knight, Elizabeth Buell. "Beauty Is Found in Season's Second Novel on Negro Theme." The Dallas Daily Times Herald (16 April), Sec. Three, p. 13.
    Review of Edith Pope's Colcarton discussing NS briefly and inaccurately. W is said to be "the head of the Society for the Advancement of the Negro Race," and the setting of the novel is said to be Detroit. Indicting "the sloppy sentimentalizing indulged in by the white Negrophile," NS stands for black racial dignity, which together with time will eventually evoke white understanding and thus solve the racial problem.

116. Lambright, E. D. "Books and Bookmen." Tampa Sunday Tribune (31 December), p. 8.
      Notes that BB will be offered by the Book-of-the-Month Club in March.

117. Loveman, Amy. "Almanac for Summer Reading." The Saturday Review of Literature, 27 (24 June), 9, 37-39.
      Notes that AH is scheduled for publication on 23 August. It is a "powerful and terrible book" (p.38) which gives further proof of W's great abilities.

118. Lyons, Leonard. "The Lyons Den." New York Post (2 May), p. 18.
      Mentions the possibility of arbitration by the Dramatists Guild to resolve a dispute between W and Paul Green, who fears that production of the play NS in Argentina and Europe after the war "might reflect upon America's Good Neighbor policy."

119. _____. "The Lyons Den." New York Post (18 September), p. 18.
      Announces that W "will have a second volume to his autobiography."

120. _____. "The Lyons Den." New York Post (19 December), p. 18.
      Claims that on the insistence of the Book-of-the-Month Club the chapters "describing his experience with the Communists" will not appear in "Black Hunger" [sic].

121. _____. "The Lyons Den." New York Post (20 December), p. 20.
      Notes that W omitted the Communist episodes from BB because he is using them in the sequel to his autobiography.

122. M'Carter, Pete Klye. "Collection Stars New Writers." The Memphis Commercial Appeal (18 June), Sec. IV, p. 10.
      Review of Cross-Section mentioning W's predilection for the theme of the black fugitive.

123. McCarthy, Dorsey. "Midwest Book Briefs." The Chicago Sun Book Week (19 March), p. 10.
      Contains an announcement of AH, scheduled for publication in June. The manuscript was "recently delivered" to the publisher.

124. McLean, Helen V., M. D. "Racial Prejudice." American Journal of Orthopsychiatry, 14 (October), 706-713.
      Mentions W's talk in the winter of 1943 at the Chicago Institute for Psychoanalysis stressing fear and hostility, exemplified by Bigger Thomas and his mother, as central to black psychology.

125. Minor, Robert. "To Tell the Truth: Mr. Wright Didn't Discover It." Daily Worker (15 August), p. 6.
      Attacks W vigorously for his defection from the Communist Party, accusing him of being anti-black and anti-Semitic. Believing W guilty of distortion, Minor argues that he should no longer be considered a minority spokesman or a leading writer.

126. Murray, Florence. The Negro Handbook 1944. New York: Current Reference Publications, pp. 69, 252.
      Mentions the award of the Spingarn Medal to W and the appearance of NS as a Modern Library book.

127. Myrdal, Gunnar. An American Dilemma: The Negro Problem and Modern Democracy. 2 vols. New York: Harper, pp. 656, 734, 735, 936, 989, 992.
      Cites W several times and quotes him once on the role of the black church (p. 936).
      Reprinted: 1962.86; 1964.86; 1969.179.

128. North, Sterling. "New Talent." New York Post (1 June), p. 20.
      Review of Cross-Section with emphasis on "The Man Who Lived Underground." "As an enthusiastic Wright fan," North fears that the author's themes are too repetitive and his characters too "subhuman" for his works to ameliorate racial relations.
      Reprinted: 1944.129, 130.

129. _____. "The Post's Books of the Week: Cross-Section: A Collection of New American Writing. Edited by Edwin Seaver." The Washington Post (4 June), Sec. IV, p. 10.
      Reprint of 1944.128.

130. _____. "Seaver and Huxley." The Chicago Sun Book Week (4 June), p. 2.
      Reprint of 1944.128.

131. Overstreet, Harry A. "Images and the Negro: Do Our Writers Really Know and Understand This American?" The Saturday Review of Literature, 27 (26 August), 5-6.
      Mentions W's "psychological approach" in NS.

132. _____. "The Negro as Spokesman." The Saturday Review of Literature, 27 (2 September), 5-6, 26-27.
      Contains a paragraph on Bigger Thomas as a victim of an environment made by whites.

133. Peat, Harold R. "Peat Presents Two

New Platform Sensations," in his Program Year Book.

    Contains a photograph of W and the titles of two of his lectures, "The American Negro Discovers Himself" and "The American Negro's Contribution to Literature and the Arts."

134. Piller, E. A. "Books in Review." Liberty, 21 (19 August), 46.

    Contains a review of Cross-Section identifying "The Man Who Lived Underground" as a highlight of the anthology.

135. Prattis, P. L. "The Horizon." The Pittsburgh Courier (14 October), p. 7.

    Mentions W in a column on Harry Overstreet's article "The Negro Writer as Spokesman."

136. Putnam, Samuel. "Literary Lookout." Daily Worker (22 August), p. 11.

    Attacks W for his defection from the Communist Party. "I Tried to Be a Communist" is so shoddy, cheap, and poorly written as to make it difficult to believe that it was written by the author of NS. Cites Robert Minor's point about anti-Semitic overtones in W's essay.

136a. [Quinn, Kerker]. "Accent Announces for Summer 1944."

    Flyer listing "The Man Who Lived Underground."

137. Quinn, Susan. "Off the Bookshelves." Richmond Times-Dispatch (1 October), p. 6-D.

    Notes that BB will be offered by the Book-of-the-Month Club.

138. R., B. P. "Regarding Richard Wright." Daily Worker (18 August), p. 7.

    Letter to the editor following publication of "I Tried to Be a Communist." The writer believes that W lies about his relations with the Party. He was never a true believer, as NS proves. The editor refers the writer of the letter to articles by Ben Davis and Robert Minor.

139. Robeson, Paul. "Préface." L'Arbalète, 9 (Autumn), 237-238.

    Preface to the French translation of "Big Boy Leaves Home." Robeson praises W's social realism in depicting black life in the South. He places W in the tradition of Nat Turner, Denmark Vesey, Sojourner Truth, and Frederick Douglass.

140. S., B. K. "Authors Between Books." Book-of-the-Month Club News (September), pp. 25-27.

    Mentions the popularity of NS in Sweden.

141. Schuyler, George S. "Views and Reviews." The Pittsburgh Courier (12 August), Sec. 2, p. 7.

    Refers favorably to W's denunciation of Communism.

142. Schwartz, Delmore. "New Writing in Wartime." The Nation, 159 (12 August), 190-191.

    Unfavorable review of Edwin Seaver's Cross-Section with the following comment on "The Man Who Lived Underground": "Richard Wright's ambitious story fails because of melodrama of several kinds, and because of the usual failing of allegory, the oversimplified correspondence between particular detail and theme."

143. Selby, John. "Successful Anthology." Durham Morning Herald (4 June), Sec. 2, p. 5.

    Review of Cross-Section calling "The Man Who Lived Underground" one of "the two most striking of the long pieces" in the anthology. Selby complains of W's overstated argument, however.

144. Sillen, Samuel. "Richard Wright in Retreat." New Masses, 52 (29 August), 25-26.

    Criticizes sharply W's rejection of Communism as expressed in "I Tried to Be a Communist," contrasting it with his views in "Blueprint for Negro Writing." He has estranged himself from the masses and from progressivism. "The Man Who Lived Underground" exemplifies the result in its cloacal pessimism and its sense of futility.

145. Spectorsky, A. C. "Deep Into the Mind and Soul of a Small Southern Town." The Chicago Sun Book Week (5 March), p. 3.

    Favorable review of Lillian Smith's Strange Fruit noting the dissimilarity of Nonnie to W's characters.

146. Stern, Philip Van Doren. "Cross-Section Edited by Edwin Seaver." Book-of-the-Month Club News (May), p. 13.

    Favorable review citing "The Man Who Lived Underground" as one of "at least two distinguished novelettes" in the collection.

147. T.[aylor], H.[oward]. "New Work by Mr. Wright, Mr. Wolfert and 38 Others." The Philadelphia Inquirer (28 May), Society Sec., p. 11.

    Favorable review of Cross-Section praising "The Man Who Lived Under-

ground," a story "powerfully written
and full of eerie suspense."

148. Thompson, Lovell. "Books, Business
and Finance." The Publishers' Weekly,
146 (11 November), 1916-1918.
    Lists NS as an example of recent
successful books on racial issues.

149. Townend, Marion. "Odds & Book
Ends." Charlotte Sunday Observer (2
July), Sec. Four, p. 2.
    Announces AH and notes general inter-
est in black topics.

150. Tripp, Thomas Alfred. "Our Leading
Negroes." Advance, 136 (May), 29.
    Review of 13 Against the Odds men-
tioning W in the journal of the Congregational Christian Churches.

151. Van Deusen, John G. The Black Man
in White America. Washington, D. C.:
Associated Publishers, p. 280.
    Treats W briefly in a chapter on "The
Negro's Contribution to American Literature."

152. Van Vechten, Carl. "How the Theatre
Is Represented in the Negro Collection
at Yale," in The Theatre Annual 1943.
New York: Theatre Library Association,
pp. 32-38.
    Mentions the play NS.
    Reprinted: 1979.270.

153. Walker, Danton. "Broadway." New
York Daily News (22 April).
    Notes that AH is forthcoming in June.

154. Watkins, Sylvestre C. "Biographical
Notes," in his Anthology of American
Negro Literature. New York: Modern Library, pp. 459-481.
    Includes a biographical sketch of W
(p. 479).

155. _____. "Preface," in his Anthology
of American Negro Literature. New York:
Modern Library, pp. xi-xiii.
    Recommends NS.

156. Wertham, Frederic. "An Unconscious
Determinant in Native Son." Journal of
Clinical Psychopathology and Psychotherapy, 6 (July), 111-115.
    Through psychoanalysis of W, Wertham
recovers the submerged memories which
became characters and situations in
the novel, especially "the key scene
. . . when Bigger Thomas uninten-
tionally kills Mary Dalton in the
presence of her blind mother." Wertham concludes that psychoanalytic
criticism of a literary work is possible only when the living author is
psychoanalyzed.
    Reprinted: 1964.113.

1945

1. A., R. "Books." Charm, 3 (September),
208.
    Contains a favorable notice of BB.
Although W has written "a powerful
indictment of racial prejudice in the
United States," he is not didactic.
He shows a determination to succeed.
    Reprinted: 1978.209.

2. Adams, J. Donald. The Shape of Books
to Come. New York: Viking, pp. 82-83.
    Reprint of 1944.2.

3. Allen, S. Eugene. "Interesting Books:
'Black Boy.'" Portland Oregon Labor
Press (18 May), p. 2.
    Favorable review praising W's objec-
tivity and lack of emotionalism. W
was the kind of questioning boy who
would have encountered trouble even
if he had been white. The book's
realism does not spare blacks themselves. "This is a book that ought to
be read by every American."

4. Anderson, LaVere. "Under the Reading
Lamp." Tulsa Daily World (11 March), p.
3.
    Favorable review of BB with extensive
summary and a sketch of W's literary
career. W tells the shocking and
terrible truth of one segment of life
in America. The book will provoke
controversy.

5. Anderson, Stanley. "Story of a Childhood Traces a Challenge in Flaming Letters." Cleveland Press (27 February).
    Favorable review of BB emphasizing
its social message. The autobiography
explains the bitterness of NS.

6. Anon. "About Books." Newark Evening
News (16 March), p. 14.
    Favorable review of BB as an artistic
expression of extreme misanthropy.
Seemingly a work of racial protest,
it displays hatred of blacks as well
as whites.

7. Anon. "About the Authors in 'Cross
Section 1945.'" The Book Find News, 11
(December), 7.
    Mentions W and "Early Days in Chi-
cago."

8. Anon. "Album de Grabados de Ant. R.
Frasconi." El Montevideo Plata (29 January).
    Favorable review of Frasconi's en-
gravings with mention of W's letter.

9. Anon. "All Hits--All Harper's." New
York Herald Tribune Weekly Book Review
(1 April), p. 9.
    Contains an advertisement for BB with

a photograph of W.

10. Anon. "American Writer Arrives in Quebec." Quebec Chronicle-Telegraph (28 June), p. 3.
Reports that before moving to Ste. Petronille, W was the guest of Professor Jean-Charles Falardeau of Laval University.

11. Anon. "America's Best-Selling, [sic] Fiction, Non-Fiction Listed." The Seattle Sunday Times (14 October), p. 27.
Lists BB in fourth place in the nonfiction category.

12. Anon. "Amusement Notes." Women's Wear Daily (20 June), p. 23.
Notes the possibility of a drama based on BB.

13. Anon. "Anthology for Thoughtful Americans, White and Black." Book-of-the-Month Club News (November), p. 27.
Lists W as a contributor to Bucklin Moon's Primer for White Folks.

14. Anon. "Appointed Director." Worcester Sunday Telegram (8 April), Feature Parade Sec., p. [13].
Announces W's appointment to the board of the American Council on Race Relations.

15. Anon. "Appraisal of Richard Wright's Black Boy." Pulse, 3 (May), 22.
Explanatory note to accompany commentaries by eight people on BB.

16. Anon. "Approves Court Ban of 'Strange Fruit': Bilbo Goes Literary, Attacks Lillian Smith, Richard Wright." The Pittsburgh Courier (29 September), p. 3.
Reports that Senator Bilbo considers BB even worse than Strange Fruit.

17. Anon. "Asserts Negro's Fight for Equality Benefit to Nation." The Des Moines Register (15 November), p. 7.
Account of W's evening lecture at the Negro Community Center in Des Moines on 14 November. He argues that although America is technologically advanced, it is backward in its social and racial attitudes. With the encouragement provided by Russia and other European countries, blacks must struggle for their rights against the resistance of Bilbo, Rankin, and other selfish and racist politicians. W's afternoon lecture on black literature is also discussed briefly.

18. Anon. "L'auteur américain Richard Wright, à Québec." Québec L'Evénement-Journal (28 June), p. 1.

Announces W's arrival in Quebec for the summer and reviews his literary career. He was invited to Quebec by Profesor Jean-Charles Falardeau.

19. Anon. "Author." Chicago Sunday Bee (18 March), Sec. Two, p. 15.
Photograph with caption mentioning Homer Jack's review on the same page.

20. Anon. "Author Meets the Critics." Unidentified clipping (c. March).
Announces that W will defend BB on a radio program on WHN.

21. Anon. "The Author of Native Son Writes the Passionate Story of His Own Youth." Chicago Sunday Tribune (11 March), Part 6, p. 15.
Advertisement for BB.

22. Anon. "The Author of Native Son Writes the Passionate Story of His Own Youth." The New York Times Book Review (4 March), p. 9.
Advertisement for BB.

23. Anon. "The Author of Native Son Writes the Passionate Story of His Own Youth." Opportunity, 23 (Spring), 115.
Advertisement for BB.

24. Anon. "The Author of Native Son Writes the Passionate Story of His Own Youth." The Saturday Review of Literature, 28 (10 March), 27.
Large advertisement for BB with laudatory quotations from Dorothy Canfield, Bennett Cerf, David Appel, and Charles Lee.

25. Anon. "Authors in the News!" Unidentified clipping.
Book-of-the-Month Club advertisement with a laudatory paragraph on W and BB together with a photograph of the author. W "is one of the most powerful of modern American writers."

26. Anon. "Authors of Prize Winning Books." Sunday Chicago Bee (30 December), Sec. Two, p. 16.
Photograph with caption of W and Spencer Logan.

27. Anon. "Begin Your Subscription with Any One of These Nation-Wide Best-Sellers." Unidentified clipping.
Book-of-the-Month Club advertisement mentioning BB.

28. Anon. "Best Books of 1945." Chicago Tribune (2 December), Sec. 4, p. 4.
Several critics selected BB.

29. Anon. "Best Sellers." The Atlanta Constitution (21 October), p. 6-B.
Lists BB in fifth place in the non-

fiction category.

30. Anon. "Best Sellers." The Boston Daily Globe (31 May), p. 9.
Lists BB in third place in the non-fiction category.

31. Anon. "Best Sellers." Boston Evening Globe (14 March), p. 15.
Lists BB in third place in the non-fiction category.

32. Anon. "Best Sellers." Boston Evening Globe (21 March), p. 21.
Lists BB in fifth place in the non-fiction category.

33. Anon. "Best Sellers." Boston Evening Globe (28 March), p. 17.
Lists BB in fifth place in the non-fiction category.

34. Anon. "Best Sellers." Boston Evening Globe (4 April), p. 15.
Lists BB in fourth place in the non-fiction category.

35. Anon. "Best Sellers." Boston Evening Globe (11 April), p. 17.
Lists BB in fourth place in the non-fiction category.

36. Anon. "Best Sellers." Boston Evening Globe (18 April), p. 19.
Lists BB in fourth place in the non-fiction category.

37. Anon. "Best Sellers." Boston Evening Globe (25 April), p. 17.
Lists BB in third place in the non-fiction category.

38. Anon. "Best Sellers." Boston Evening Globe (2 May), p. 15.
Lists BB in third place in the non-fiction category.

39. Anon. "Best Sellers." Boston Evening Globe (9 May), p. 17.
Lists BB in second place in the non-fiction category.

40. Anon. "Best Sellers." Boston Evening Globe (16 May), p. 17.
Lists BB in fourth place in the non-fiction category.

41. Anon. "Best Sellers." Boston Evening Globe (23 May), p. 13.
Lists BB in second place in the non-fiction category.

42. Anon. "Best Sellers." Boston Evening Globe (6 June), p. 9.
Lists BB in third place in the non-fiction category.

43. Anon. "Best Sellers." Boston Evening Globe (13 June), p. 15.
Lists BB in second place in the non-fiction category.

44. Anon. "Best Sellers." Boston Evening Globe (20 June), p. 15.
Lists BB in second place in the non-fiction category.

45. Anon. "Best Sellers." Boston Evening Globe (27 June), p. 15.
Lists BB in fifth place in the non-fiction category.

46. Anon. "Best Sellers." Boston Evening Globe (5 July), p. 7.
Lists BB in fifth place in the non-fiction category.

47. Anon. "Best Sellers." Boston Evening Globe (11 July), p. 15.
Lists BB in third place in the non-fiction category.

48. Anon. "Best Sellers." Boston Evening Globe (18 July), p. 15.
Lists BB in fourth place in the non-fiction category.

49. Anon. "Best Sellers." Boston Evening Globe (8 August), p. 15.
Lists BB in fifth place in the non-fiction category.

50. Anon. "The Best Sellers." Los Angeles Times (22 July), Part III, p. 1.
Lists BB in second place in the non-fiction category in the nation and in first place in Los Angeles.

51. Anon. "The Best Sellers." Los Angeles Times (30 September), Part III, p. 1.
Lists BB in third place in the non-fiction category.

52. Anon. "The Best Sellers." Los Angeles Times (28 October), Part III, p. 1.
Lists BB in third place in the non-fiction category.

53. Anon. "The Best Sellers." Los Angeles Times (11 November), Part III, p. 1.
Lists BB in fourth place in the non-fiction category.

54. Anon. "Best Sellers." The Louisville Courier-Journal (1 April), Sec. 3, p. 9.
Lists BB in fifth place in the non-fiction category.

55. Anon. "Best Sellers." The Louisville Courier-Journal (15 April), Sec. 3, p. 8.
Lists BB in third place in the non-fiction category.

56. Anon. "Best Sellers." The Louisville

Courier-Journal (29 April), Sec. 3, p. 8.
Lists BB in first place in the non-fiction category.

57. Anon. "Best Sellers." The Louisville Courier-Journal (6 May), Sec. 3, p. 9.
Lists BB in second place in the non-fiction category.

58. Anon. "Best Sellers." The Louisville Courier-Journal (13 May), Sec. 3, p. 8.
Lists BB in second place in the non-fiction category.

59. Anon. "Best Sellers." The Louisville Courier-Journal (20 May), Sec. 3, p. 10.
Lists BB in second place in the non-fiction category.

60. Anon. "Best Sellers." The Louisville Courier-Journal (27 May), Sec. 3, p. 10.
Lists BB in second place in the non-fiction category.

61. Anon. "Best Sellers." The Louisville Courier-Journal (3 June), Sec. 3, p. 10.
Lists BB in second place in the non-fiction category.

62. Anon. "Best Sellers." The Louisville Courier-Journal (10 June), Sec. 3, p. 8.
Lists BB in second place in the non-fiction category.

63. Anon. "Best Sellers." The Louisville Courier-Journal (17 June), Sec. 3, p. 7.
Lists BB in second place in the non-fiction category.

64. Anon. "Best Sellers." The Louisville Courier-Journal (24 June), Sec. 3, p. 7.
Lists BB in second place in the non-fiction category.

65. Anon. "Best Sellers." The Louisville Courier-Journal (1 July), Sec. 3, p. 7.
Lists BB in second place in the non-fiction category.

66. Anon. "Best Sellers." The Louisville Courier-Journal (15 July), Sec. 3, p. 9.
Lists BB in third place in the non-fiction category.

67. Anon. "Best Sellers." The Louisville Courier-Journal (22 July), Sec. 3, p. 7.
Lists BB in fifth place in the non-fiction category.

68. Anon. "Best Sellers." The Louisville Courier-Journal (29 July), Sec. 3, p. 7.
Lists BB in third place in the non-fiction category.

69. Anon. "Best Sellers." The Louisville Courier-Journal (5 August), Sec. 3, p. 7.
Lists BB in fourth place in the non-fiction category.

70. Anon. "Best Sellers." The Louisville Courier-Journal (16 September), Sec. 3, p. 8.
Lists BB in third place in the non-fiction category.

71. Anon. "Best Sellers." The Louisville Courier-Journal (7 October), Sec. 3, p. 15.
Lists BB in fifth place in the non-fiction category.

72. Anon. "Best Sellers." The Louisville Courier-Journal (14 October), Sec. 3, p. 15.
Lists BB in fourth place in the non-fiction category.

73. Anon. "Best Sellers." The Louisville Courier-Journal (28 October), Sec. 3, p. 12.
Lists BB in fifth place in the non-fiction category.

74. Anon. "The Best Sellers." The New York Times Book Review (9 September), p. 8.
Lists BB in fifth place in the general category.

75. Anon. "The Best Sellers." The New York Times Book Review (16 September), p. 14.
Lists BB in fourth place in the general category.

76. Anon. "The Best Sellers." The New York Times Book Review (23 September), p. 10.
Lists BB in fourth place in the general category.

77. Anon. "The Best Sellers." The New York Times Book Review (30 September), p. 34.
Lists BB in fourth place in the general category.

78. Anon. "The Best Sellers." The New York Times Book Review (7 October), p. 34.
Lists BB in fifth place in the general category.

79. Anon. "The Best Sellers." The New York Times Book Review (14 October), p. 28.
Lists BB in fifth place in the general category.

80. Anon. "The Best Sellers." The New York Times Book Review (21 October), p. 18.
Lists BB in fourth place in the general category.

81. Anon. "The Best Sellers." The New York Times Book Review (28 October), p. 24.
Lists BB in fifth place in the general category.

82. Anon. "The Best Sellers." The New York Times Book Review (4 November), p. 32.
Lists BB in eighth place in the general category.

83. Anon. "The Best Sellers." The New York Times Book Review (11 November), p. 34.
Lists BB in sixth place in the general category.

84. Anon. "The Best Sellers." The New York Times Book Review (18 November), p. 29.
Lists BB in ninth place in the general category.

85. Anon. "The Best Sellers." The New York Times Book Review (25 November), p. 28.
Lists BB in seventh place in the general category.

86. Anon. "The Best Sellers." The Retail Bookseller, 48 (April), 60-61.
Lists BB in third place in the nonfiction category and calls it "a much more impressive plea for social justice than the author's 'Native Son.'"

87. Anon. "The Best Sellers." The Retail Bookseller, 48 (May), 56-58.
Lists BB in fourth place in the nonfiction category.

88. Anon. "The Best Sellers." The Retail Bookseller, 48 (June), 48-49.
Lists BB in third place in the nonfiction category.

89. Anon. "The Best Sellers." The Retail Bookseller, 48 (July), 52-53.
Lists BB in fifth place in the nonfiction category.

90. Anon. "The Best Sellers." The Retail Bookseller, 48 (August), 96-97.
Lists BB in fourth place in the nonfiction category.

91. Anon. "The Best Sellers." The Retail Bookseller, 48 (September), 132-133.
Lists BB in seventh place in the nonfiction category.

92. Anon. "The Best Sellers." The Retail Bookseller, 48 (October), 72-73.
Lists BB in eighth place in the nonfiction category.

93. Anon. "The Best Sellers." The Retail Bookseller, 48 (November), 46-47.
Lists BB in fourteenth place in the nonfiction category.

94. Anon. "Best Sellers Among Books." New York Sunday News (11 March).
Lists BB in second place in the nonfiction category.

95. Anon. "Best Sellers Among Books." New York Sunday News (25 March).
Lists BB in second place in the nonfiction category.

96. Anon. "Best Sellers Among Books." New York Sunday News (1 April).
Lists BB in second place in the nonfiction category.

97. Anon. "Best Sellers Among Books." New York Sunday News (8 April).
Lists BB in second place in the nonfiction category.

98. Anon. "Best Sellers Among Books." New York Sunday News (15 [?] April).
Lists BB in first place in the nonfiction category.

99. Anon. "Best Sellers Among Books." New York Sunday News [?] (c. April or May).
Lists BB in first place in the nonfiction category.

100. Anon. "Best Sellers Among Books." New York Sunday News (2 September).
Lists BB in third place in the nonfiction category.

101. Anon. "Best Sellers: Fiction and Non-Fiction." The Seattle Sunday Times (6 May), Part 2, p. 8.
Lists BB in second place in the nonfiction category.

102. Anon. "Best Sellers in Fiction, Non-Fiction." The Seattle Sunday Times (12 August), Part 2, p. 7.
Lists BB in third place in the nonfiction category.

103. Anon. "Best Sellers in Midwest." Chicago Sunday Tribune (11 March), Part 6, p. 10.
Lists BB in first place in the nonfiction category in Milwaukee.

104. Anon. "Best Sellers in Midwest." Chicago Sunday Tribune (18 March), Part 6, p. 10.
Lists BB in third place in the nonfiction category in Indianapolis and in fifth place in Chicago.

105. Anon. "Best Sellers in Midwest." Chicago Sunday Tribune (22 April), Part 6, p. 15.

Lists BB in first place in the non-fiction category in Chicago and Milwaukee.

106. Anon. "Best Sellers in Midwest." Chicago Sunday Tribune (29 April), Part 6, p. 11.
    Lists BB in second place in the non-fiction category in Chicago.

107. Anon. "Best Sellers in Midwest." Chicago Sunday Tribune (13 May), Part 6, p. 14.
    Lists BB in third place in the non-fiction category in Chicago and Milwaukee.

108. Anon. "Best Sellers in Midwest." Chicago Sunday Tribune (20 May), Part 6, p. 10.
    Lists BB in second place in the non-fiction category in Chicago and in fourth place in Milwaukee.

109. Anon. "Best Sellers in Midwest." Chicago Sunday Tribune (27 May), Part 6, p. 10.
    Lists BB in first place in the non-fiction category in Milwaukee, in second place in Peoria, and in third place in Chicago.

110. Anon. "Best Sellers in Midwest." Chicago Sunday Tribune (17 June), Part 6, p. 14.
    Lists BB in third place in the non-fiction category in Milwaukee and Peoria, and in fourth place in Chicago and the Tri-Cities (Davenport, Moline, and Rock Island).

111. Anon. "Best Sellers in Midwest." Chicago Sunday Tribune (24 June), Part 6, p. 10.
    Lists BB in first place in the non-fiction category in Peoria, in third place in Chicago, and in fourth place in Milwaukee.

112. Anon. "Best Sellers in Midwest." Chicago Sunday Tribune (1 July), Part 6, p. 9.
    Lists BB in first place in the non-fiction category in Peoria.

113. Anon. "Best Sellers in Midwest." Chicago Sunday Tribune (22 July), Part 6, p. 12.
    Lists BB in third place in the non-fiction category in Peoria and in fourth place in Milwaukee.

114. Anon. "Best Sellers in Midwest." Chicago Sunday Tribune (29 July), Part 6, p. 10.
    Lists BB in first place in the non-fiction category in the Tri-Cities (Davenport, Moline, and Rock Island),

and in fourth place in Peoria.

115. Anon. "Best Sellers in Midwest." Chicago Sunday Tribune (5 August), Part 6, p. 11.
    Lists BB in third place in the non-fiction category in Milwaukee, Peoria, and the Tri-Cities (Davenport, Moline, and Rock Island).

116. Anon. "Best Sellers in Midwest." Chicago Sunday Tribune (19 August), Part 6, p. 15.
    Lists BB in second place in the non-fiction category in Milwaukee, in third place in Peoria, and in fourth place in the Tri-Cities (Davenport, Moline, and Rock Island).

117. Anon. "Best Sellers in Midwest." Chicago Sunday Tribune (26 August), Part 6, p. 17.
    Lists BB in third place in the non-fiction category in Milwaukee, and in fourth place in the Tri-Cities (Davenport, Moline, and Rock Island).

118. Anon. "Best Sellers in Midwest." Chicago Sunday Tribune (9 September), Part 6, p. 14.
    Lists BB in fourth place in the non-fiction category in Milwaukee.

119. Anon. "Best Sellers in Midwest." Chicago Sunday Tribune (7 October), Part 6, p. 17.
    Lists BB in third place in the non-fiction category in Milwaukee and in fourth place in Peoria and the Tri-Cities (Davenport, Moline, and Rock Island).

120. Anon. "Best Sellers in Midwest." Chicago Sunday Tribune (4 November), Part 6, p. 10.
    Lists BB in third place in the non-fiction category in the Tri-Cities (Davenport, Moline, and Rock Island).

121. Anon. "Best Sellers in Midwest." Chicago Sunday Tribune (11 November), Part 6, p. 21.
    Lists BB in fourth place in the non-fiction category in the Tri-Cities (Davenport, Moline, and Rock Island).

122. Anon. "Best Sellers in Midwest." Chicago Sunday Tribune (30 December), Part 6, p. 10.
    Lists BB in fourth place in the non-fiction category in the Tri-Cities (Davenport, Moline, and Rock Island).

123. Anon. "Best Sellers in New Orleans." The Times Picayune New Orleans States (27 May), Sec. 2, p. 7.
    Lists BB in ninth place in the non-fiction category.

124. Anon. "Best Sellers in New Orleans." The Times Picayune New Orleans States (3 June), Sec. 2, p. 9.
     Lists BB in fourth place in the non-fiction category.

125. Anon. "Best Sellers in the Midwest." Chicago Sunday Tribune (1 April), Part 6, p. 10.
     Lists BB in second place in the non-fiction category in Peoria and in fourth place in Chicago.

126. Anon. "Best Sellers in the Midwest." Chicago Sunday Tribune (8 April), Part 6, p. 13.
     Lists BB in second place in the non-fiction category in Peoria.

127. Anon. "Best Sellers in the Midwest." Chicago Sunday Tribune (15 April), Part 6, p. 12.
     Lists BB in second place in the non-fiction category in Chicago and in fourth place in Milwaukee.

128. Anon. "Best Sellers in the Midwest." Chicago Sunday Tribune (6 May), Part 6, p. 14.
     Lists BB in third place in the non-fiction category in Chicago and Milwaukee.

129. Anon. "Best Sellers in the Midwest." Chicago Sunday Tribune (3 June), Part 6, p. 12.
     Lists BB in first place in the non-fiction category in Chicago and Milwaukee, and in second place in Peoria.

130. Anon. "Best Sellers in the Midwest." Chicago Sunday Tribune (10 June), Part 6, p. 10.
     Lists BB in first place in the non-fiction category in Milwaukee, in second place in Peoria, and in fourth place in Chicago.

131. Anon. "Best Sellers in the Midwest." Chicago Sunday Tribune (8 July), Part 6, p. 13.
     Lists BB in third place in the non-fiction category in Peoria.

132. Anon. "Best Sellers in the Midwest." Chicago Sunday Tribune (15 July), Part 6, p. 15.
     Lists BB in third place in the non-fiction category in Peoria.

133. Anon. "Best Sellers in the Midwest." Chicago Sunday Tribune (12 August), Part 6, p. 10.
     Lists BB in second place in the non-fiction category in Peoria and in third place in Milwaukee.

134. Anon. "Best Sellers in the Midwest." Chicago Sunday Tribune (2 September), Part 6, p. 11.
     Lists BB in second place in the non-fiction category in Milwaukee.

135. Anon. "Best Sellers in the Midwest." Chicago Sunday Tribune (16 September), Part 6, p. 14.
     Lists BB in third place in the non-fiction category in Milwaukee.

136. Anon. "Best Sellers in the Midwest." Chicago Sunday Tribune (23 September), Part 6, p. 16.
     Lists BB in second place in the non-fiction category in the Tri-Cities (Davenport, Moline, and Rock Island), in third place in Peoria, and in fourth place in Milwaukee.

137. Anon. "Best Sellers in the Midwest." Chicago Sunday Tribune (30 September), Part 6, p. 14.
     Lists BB in third place in the non-fiction category in Milwaukee and the Tri-Cities (Davenport, Moline, and Rock Island).

138. Anon. "Best Sellers in the Midwest." Chicago Sunday Tribune (14 October), Part 6, p. 14.
     Lists BB in third place in the non-fiction category in the Tri-Cities (Davenport, Moline, and Rock Island).

139. Anon. "Best Sellers in the Midwest." Chicago Sunday Tribune (21 October), Part 6, p. 19.
     Lists BB in third place in the non-fiction category in the Tri-Cities (Davenport, Moline, and Rock Island).

140. Anon. "Best Sellers in the Midwest." Chicago Sunday Tribune (18 November), Part 6, p. 21.
     Lists BB in fourth place in the non-fiction category in the Tri-Cities (Davenport, Moline, and Rock Island).

141. Anon. "The Best Sellers Mid-March to Mid-April, 1945." The Retail Bookseller, 48 (May), 56-57.
     Lists BB in fourth place in the non-fiction category.

142. Anon. "Best Sellers, Nationally, As of Last Monday." The Seattle Sunday Times (8 July), p. 6.
     Lists BB in third place in the non-fiction category.

143. Anon. "Best Sellers of the Week." The Louisville Courier-Journal (12 August), Sec. 3, p. 7.
     Lists BB in third place in the non-fiction category.

144. Anon. "Best Sellers of the Week."
The Louisville Courier-Journal (30 September), Sec. 3, p. 6.
    Lists BB in fourth place in the non-
    fiction category.

145. Anon. "Best Sellers of the Week."
The Publishers' Weekly, 147 (31 March),
1383.
    Lists BB in fifth place in the non-
    fiction category.

146. Anon. "Best Sellers of the Week."
The Publishers' Weekly, 147 (14 April),
1579.
    Lists BB in third place in the non-
    fiction category.

147. Anon. "Best Sellers of the Week."
The Publishers' Weekly, 147 (21 April),
1667.
    Lists BB in second place in the non-
    fiction category.

148. Anon. "Best Sellers of the Week."
The Publishers' Weekly, 147 (28 April),
1768.
    Lists BB in first place in the non-
    fiction category.

149. Anon. "Best Sellers of the Week."
The Publishers' Weekly, 147 (5 May),
1844.
    Lists BB in second place in the non-
    fiction category.

150. Anon. "Best Sellers of the Week."
The Publishers' Weekly, 147 (19 May),
2013.
    Lists BB in second place in the non-
    fiction category.

151. Anon. "Best Sellers of the Week."
The Publishers' Weekly, 147 (26 May),
2089.
    Lists BB in second place in the non-
    fiction category.

152. Anon. "Best Sellers of the Week."
The Publishers' Weekly, 147 (2 June),
2207.
    Lists BB in second place in the non-
    fiction category.

153. Anon. "Best Sellers of the Week."
The Publishers' Weekly, 147 (9 June),
2307.
    Lists BB in second place in the non-
    fiction category.

154. Anon. "Best Sellers of the Week."
The Publishers' Weekly, 147 (23 June),
2455.
    Lists BB in second place in the non-
    fiction category.

155. Anon. "Best Sellers of the Week."
The Publishers' Weekly, 147 (30 June),
2527.
    Lists BB in second place in the non-
    fiction category.

156. Anon. "Best Sellers of the Week."
The Publishers' Weekly, 148 (7 July),
48.
    Lists BB in third place in the non-
    fiction category. Notes that "World
    will take over publication on August
    6 with a first printing of 50,000
    copies."

157. Anon. "Best Sellers of the Week."
The Publishers' Weekly, 148 (21 July),
241.
    Lists BB in fifth place in the non-
    fiction category.

158. Anon. "Best Sellers of the Week."
The Publishers' Weekly, 148 (28 July),
335.
    Lists BB in third place in the non-
    fiction category.

159. Anon. "Best Sellers of the Week."
The Publishers' Weekly, 148 (4 August),
419.
    Lists BB in third place in the non-
    fiction category.

160. Anon. "Best Sellers of the Week."
The Publishers' Weekly, 148 (18 August),
613.
    Lists BB in fourth place in the non-
    fiction category.

161. Anon. "Best Sellers of the Week."
The Publishers' Weekly, 148 (1 September), 879.
    Lists BB in fifth place in the non-
    fiction category.

162. Anon. "Best Sellers of the Week."
The Publishers' Weekly, 148 (8 September), 984.
    Lists BB in fifth place in the non-
    fiction category.

163. Anon. "Best Sellers of the Week."
The Publishers' Weekly, 148 (29 September), 1569.
    Lists BB in fourth place in the non-
    fiction category.

164. Anon. "Best Sellers of the Week."
The Publishers' Weekly, 148 (6 October),
1682.
    Lists BB in fifth place in the non-
    fiction category.

165. Anon. "Best Sellers of the Week."
The Publishers' Weekly, 148 (13 October), 1781.
    Lists BB in fourth place in the non-
    fiction category.

166. Anon. "Best Sellers of the Week."

The Publishers' Weekly, 148 (27 October), 1984.
   Lists BB in fifth place in the nonfiction category.

167. Anon. "Best Sellers of the Week." San Francisco Chronicle (11 March), This World Sec., p. 14.
   Lists BB in first place in the nonfiction category.

168. Anon. "Best Sellers of the Week." San Francisco Chronicle (18 March), This World Sec., p. 8.
   Lists BB in second place in the nonfiction category.

169. Anon. "Best Sellers of the Week." San Francisco Chronicle (25 March), This World Sec., p. 14.
   Lists BB in first place in the nonfiction category.

170. Anon. "Best Sellers of the Week." San Francisco Chronicle (1 April), This World Sec., p. 8.
   Lists BB in first place in the nonfiction category.

171. Anon. "Best Sellers of the Week." San Francisco Chronicle (8 April), This World Sec., p. 10.
   Lists BB in first place in the nonfiction category.

172. Anon. "Best Sellers of the Week." San Francisco Chronicle (15 April), This World Sec., p. 8.
   Lists BB in first place in the nonfiction category.

173. Anon. "Best Sellers of the Week." San Francisco Chronicle (22 April), This World Sec., p. 1.
   Lists BB in first place in the nonfiction category.

174. Anon. "Best Sellers of the Week." San Francisco Chronicle (29 April), This World Sec., p. 8.
   Lists BB in second place in the nonfiction category.

175. Anon. "Best Sellers of the Week." San Francisco Chronicle (6 May), This World Sec., p. 8.
   Lists BB in fourth place in the nonfiction category.

176. Anon. "Best Sellers of the Week." San Francisco Chronicle (13 May), This World Sec., p. 14.
   Lists BB in fifth place in the nonfiction category.

177. Anon. "Best Sellers of the Week." San Francisco Chronicle (27 May), This World Sec., p. 10.

Lists BB in third place in the nonfiction category.

178. Anon. "Best Sellers of the Week." San Francisco Chronicle (3 June), This World Sec., p. 10.
   Lists BB in third place in the nonfiction category.

179.. Anon. "Best Sellers of the Week." San Francisco Chronicle (10 June), This World Sec., p. 10.
   Lists BB in second place in the nonfiction category.

180.. Anon. "Best Sellers of the Week." San Francisco Chronicle (17 June), This World Sec., p. 10.
   Lists BB in second place in the nonfiction category.

181.. Anon. "Best Sellers of the Week." San Francisco Chronicle (24 June), This World Sec., p. 14.
   Lists BB in fourth place in the nonfiction category.

182. Anon. "Best Sellers of Week Announced." The Seattle Sunday Times (19 August), Part 2, p. 7.
   Lists BB in fourth place in the nonfiction category.

183. Anon. "Best Selling Books." The Atlanta Constitution (5 August), p. 8-B.
   Lists BB in fourth place in the nonfiction category.

184. Anon. "Best Selling Books." The Atlanta Constitution (12 August), p. 8-B.
   Lists BB in third place in the nonfiction category.

185. Anon. "Best Selling Books." The Atlanta Constitution (9 September), p. 11-C.
   Lists BB in fifth place in the nonfiction category.

186. Anon. "Best-Selling Books." St. Louis Post Dispatch (1 April), p. 2B.
   Lists BB in fifth place in the nonfiction category.

187. Anon. "Best-Selling Books." St. Louis Post Dispatch (8 April), p. 2D.
   Lists BB in fifth place in the nonfiction category.

188. Anon. "Best-Selling Books." St. Louis Post Dispatch (15 April), p. 2B.
   Lists BB in second place in the nonfiction category.

189. Anon. "Best-Selling Books." St. Louis Post Dispatch (22 April), p. 2D.
   Lists BB in first place in the non-

fiction category.

190. Anon. "Best-Selling Books." St. Louis Post Dispatch (29 April), p. 2D.
Lists BB in third place in the non-fiction category.

191. Anon. "Best-Selling Books." St. Louis Post Dispatch (13 May), p. 3D.
Lists BB in second place in the non-fiction category.

192. Anon. "Best-Selling Books." St. Louis Post Dispatch (20 May), p. 2D.
Lists BB in second place in the non-fiction category.

193. Anon. "Best-Selling Books." St. Louis Post Dispatch (27 May), p. 2D.
Lists BB in second place in the non-fiction category.

194. Anon. "Best-Selling Books." St. Louis Post Dispatch (3 June), p. 2D.
Lists BB in second place in the non-fiction category.

195. Anon. "Best-Selling Books." St. Louis Post Dispatch (10 June), p. 2B.
Lists BB in second place in the non-fiction category.

196. Anon. "Best-Selling Books." St. Louis Post Dispatch (17 June), p. 2B.
Lists BB in second place in the non-fiction category.

197. Anon. "Best-Selling Books." St. Louis Post Dispatch (24 June), p. 2B.
Lists BB in second place in the non-fiction category.

198. Anon. "Best-Selling Books." St. Louis Post Dispatch (1 July), p. 2B.
Lists BB in second place in the non-fiction category.

199. Anon. "Best-Selling Books." St. Louis Post Dispatch (8 July), p. 2B.
Lists BB in second place in the non-fiction category.

200. Anon. "Best-Selling Books." St. Louis Post Dispatch (15 July), p. 2B.
Lists BB in fourth place in the non-fiction category.

201. Anon. "Best-Selling Books." St. Louis Post Dispatch (22 July), p. 2D.
Lists BB in third place in the non-fiction category.

202. Anon. "Best-Selling Books." St. Louis Post Dispatch (29 July), p. 2B.
Lists BB in fourth place in the non-fiction category.

203. Anon. "Best-Selling Books." St. Louis Post Dispatch (5 August), p. 2B.
Lists BB in sixth place in the non-fiction category.

204. Anon. "Best-Selling Books." St. Louis Post Dispatch (9 September), p. 2D.
Lists BB in third place in the non-fiction category.

205. Anon. "Best-Selling Books." St. Louis Post Dispatch (16 September), p. 2D.
Lists BB in fourth place in the non-fiction category.

206. Anon. "Best-Selling Books." St. Louis Post Dispatch (23 September), p. 2D.
Lists BB in fifth place in the non-fiction category.

207. Anon. "Best-Selling Books." St. Louis Post Dispatch (30 September), p. 2D.
Lists BB in fourth place in the non-fiction category.

208. Anon. "Best-Selling Books." St. Louis Post Dispatch (7 October), p. 2D.
Lists BB in third place in the non-fiction category.

209. Anon. "Best-Selling Books." St. Louis Post Dispatch (14 October), p. 2F.
Lists BB in fifth place in the non-fiction category.

210. Anon. "Best-Selling Books." St. Louis Post Dispatch (21 October), p. 2D.
Lists BB in fifth place in the non-fiction category.

211. Anon. "Best-Selling Books." St. Louis Post Dispatch (28 October), p. 2D.
Lists BB in fifth place in the non-fiction category.

212. Anon. "The Best Selling Books, Here and Elsewhere." The New York Times Book Review (25 March), p. 27.
Lists BB in sixth place in the general category.

213. Anon. "The Best Selling Books, Here and Elsewhere." The New York Times Book Review (1 April), p. 29.
Lists BB in fourth place in the general category.

214. Anon. "The Best Selling Books, Here and Elsewhere." The New York Times Book Review (8 April), p. 25.
Lists BB in fourth place in the general category.

215. Anon. "The Best Selling Books, Here and Elsewhere." The New York Times Book

Review (15 April), p. 27.
Lists BB in second place in the general category.

216. Anon. "The Best Selling Books, Here and Elsewhere." The New York Times Book Review (22 April), p. 27.
Lists BB in second place in the general category.

217. Anon. "The Best Selling Books, Here and Elsewhere." The New York Times Book Review (29 April), p. 29.
Lists BB in first place in the general category.

218. Anon. "The Best Selling Books, Here and Elsewhere." The New York Times Book Review (6 May), p. 19.
Lists BB in second place in the general category.

219. Anon. "The Best Selling Books, Here and Elsewhere." The New York Times Book Review (13 May), p. 19.
Lists BB in second place in the general category.

220. Anon. "The Best Selling Books, Here and Elsewhere." The New York Times Book Review (20 May), p. 21.
Lists BB in second place in the general category.

221. Anon. "The Best Selling Books, Here and Elsewhere." The New York Times Book Review (27 May), p. 18.
Lists BB in second place in the general category.

222. Anon. "The Best Selling Books, Here and Elsewhere." The New York Times Book Review (3 June), p. 21.
Lists BB in second place in the general category.

223. Anon. "The Best Selling Books, Here and Elsewhere." The New York Times Book Review (10 June), p. 19.
Lists BB in second place in the general category.

224. Anon. "The Best Selling Books, Here and Elsewhere." The New York Times Book Review (17 June), p. 19.
Lists BB in second place in the general category.

225. Anon. "The Best Selling Books, Here and Elsewhere." The New York Times Book Review (24 June), p. 20.
Lists BB in second place in the general category.

226. Anon. "The Best Selling Books, Here and Elsewhere." The New York Times Book Review (1 July), p. 19.
Lists BB in second place in the general category.

227. Anon. "The Best Selling Books, Here and Elsewhere." The New York Times Book Review (8 July), p. 21.
Lists BB in fourth place in the general category.

228. Anon. "The Best Selling Books, Here and Elsewhere." The New York Times Book Review (15 July), p. 23.
Lists BB in third place in the general category.

229. Anon. "The Best Selling Books, Here and Elsewhere." The New York Times Book Review (22 July), p. 19.
Lists BB in third place in the general category.

230. Anon. "The Best Selling Books, Here and Elsewhere." The New York Times Book Review (29 July), p. 23.
Lists BB in third place in the general category.

231. Anon. "The Best Selling Books, Here and Elsewhere." The New York Times Book Review (5 August), p. 29.
Lists BB in third place in the general category.

232. Anon. "The Best Selling Books, Here and Elsewhere." The New York Times Book Review (12 August), p. 27.
Lists BB in fifth place in the general category.

233. Anon. "The Best Selling Books, Here and Elsewhere." The New York Times Book Review (19 August), p. 29.
Lists BB in fourth place in the general category.

234. Anon. "The Best Selling Books, Here and Elsewhere." The New York Times Book Review (26 August), p. 29.
Lists BB in third place in the general category.

235. Anon. "The Best Selling Books, Here and Elsewhere." The New York Times Book Review (2 September), p. 17.
Lists BB in seventh place in the general category.

236. Anon. "Best Selling Books in Philadelphia." The Philadelphia Inquirer (11 March), Society Sec., p. 10.
Lists BB in second place in the nonfiction category.

237. Anon. "Best Selling Books in Philadelphia." The Philadelphia Inquirer (18 March), Society Sec., p. 11.
Lists BB in first place in the nonfiction category.

238. Anon. "Best Selling Books in Philadelphia." The Philadelphia Inquirer (25
March), Society Sec., p. 11.
    Lists BB in first place in the non-
    fiction category.

239. Anon. "Best Selling Books in Philadelphia." The Philadelphia Inquirer (1
April), Society Sec., p. 10.
    Lists BB in second place in the non-
    fiction category.

240. Anon. "Best Selling Books in Philadelphia." The Philadelphia Inquirer (8
April), Society Sec., p. 10.
    Lists BB in second place in the non-
    fiction category.

241. Anon. "Best Selling Books in Philadelphia." The Philadelphia Inquirer (15
April), Society Sec., p. 6.
    Lists BB in second place in the non-
    fiction category.

242. Anon. "Best Selling Books in Philadelphia." The Philadelphia Inquirer (22
April), Society Sec., p. 12.
    Lists BB in second place in the non-
    fiction category.

243. Anon. "Best Selling Books in Philadelphia." The Philadelphia Inquirer (29
April), Society Sec., p. 12.
    Lists BB in third place in the non-
    fiction category. An advertisement
    for the book also appears on this
    page.

244. Anon. "Best Selling Books in Philadelphia." The Philadelphia Inquirer (6
May), Society Sec., p. 10.
    Lists BB in third place in the non-
    fiction category.

245. Anon. "Best Selling Books in Philadelphia." The Philadelphia Inquirer (13
May), Society Sec., p. 10.
    Lists BB in third place in the non-
    fiction category.

246. Anon. "Best Selling Books in Philadelphia." The Philadelphia Inquirer (20
May), Society Sec., p. 10.
    Lists BB in fourth place in the non-
    fiction category.

247. Anon. "Best Selling Books in Philadelphia." The Philadelphia Inquirer (27
May), Society Sec., p. 10.
    Lists BB in fifth place in the non-
    fiction category.

248. Anon. "Best Selling Books in Philadelphia." The Philadelphia Inquirer (3
June), Society Sec., p. 10.
    Two book stores report good sales of
    BB, but it is not listed among the
    top ten in the nonfiction category.

249. Anon. "Best Selling Books in Philadelphia." The Philadelphia Inquirer (10
June), Society Sec., p. 10.
    Lists BB in eighth place in the non-
    fiction category.

250. Anon. "Best Selling Books in Philadelphia." The Philadelphia Inquirer (17
June), Society Sec., p. 10.
    Lists BB in sixth place in the non-
    fiction category.

251. Anon. "Best Selling Books in Philadelphia." The Philadelphia Inquirer (24
June), Society Sec., p. 10.
    Lists BB in fifth place in the non-
    fiction category.

252. Anon. "Best Selling Books in Philadelphia." The Philadelphia Inquirer (1
July), Society Sec., p. 11.
    Lists BB in sixth place in the non-
    fiction category.

253. Anon. "Best Selling Books in Philadelphia." The Philadelphia Inquirer (8
July), Society Sec., p. 8.
    Lists BB in fifth place in the non-
    fiction category.

254. Anon. "Best Selling Books in Philadelphia." The Philadelphia Inquirer (15
July), Society Sec., p. 11.
    Lists BB in fifth place in the non-
    fiction category.

255. Anon. "Best Selling Books in Philadelphia." The Philadelphia Inquirer (22
July), Society Sec., p. 8.
    Lists BB in fifth place in the non-
    fiction category.

256. Anon. "Best Selling Books in Philadelphia." The Philadelphia Inquirer (29
July), Society Sec., p. 11.
    Lists BB in sixth place in the non-
    fiction category.

257. Anon. "Best Selling Books in Philadelphia." The Philadelphia Inquirer (5
August), Society Sec., p. 11.
    Lists BB in ninth place in the non-
    fiction category.

258. Anon. "Best Selling Books in Philadelphia." The Philadelphia Inquirer (12
August), Society Sec., p. 10.
    One book store reports good sales of
    BB, but it is not listed among the
    top ten in the nonfiction category.

259. Anon. "Best Selling Books in Philadelphia." The Philadelphia Inquirer (19
August), Society Sec., p. 10.
    One book store reports good sales of
    BB, but it is not listed among the
    top ten in the nonfiction cate-
    gory.

260. Anon. "Best Selling Books in Philadelphia." The Philadelphia Inquirer (26
August), Society Sec., p. 11.
    Lists BB in ninth place in the non-
    fiction category.

261. Anon. "Best Selling Books in Philadelphia." The Philadelphia Inquirer (2
September), Society Sec., p. 11.
    Two book stores report good sales of
    BB, but it is not listed among the
    top ten in the nonfiction category.

262. Anon. "Best Selling Books in Philadelphia." The Philadelphia Inquirer (9
September), Society Sec., p. 13.
    Two book stores report good sales of
    BB, but it is not listed among the
    top ten in the nonfiction category.

263. Anon. "Best Selling Books in Philadelphia." The Philadelphia Inquirer (16
September), Society Sec., p. 10.
    Lists BB in ninth place in the non-
    fiction category.

264. Anon. "Best Selling Books in Philadelphia." The Philadelphia Inquirer (23
September), Society Sec., p. 10.
    Lists BB in tenth place in the non-
    fiction category.

265. Anon. "Best Selling Books in Philadelphia." The Philadelphia Inquirer (30
September), Society Sec., p. 11.
    Three book stores report good sales
    of BB, but it is not listed among the
    top ten in the nonfiction category.

266. Anon. "Best Selling Books in Philadelphia." The Philadelphia Inquirer (7
October), Society Sec., p. 10.
    One book store reports good sales of
    BB, but it is not listed among the
    top ten in the nonfiction category.

267. Anon. "Best Selling Books in Philadelphia." The Philadelphia Inquirer (14
October), Society Sec., p. 13.
    One book store reports good sales of
    BB, but it is not listed among the
    top ten in the nonfiction category.

268. Anon. "Best-Selling Books in U. S.
Listed." The Seattle Sunday Times (5
August), p. 15.
    Lists BB in fourth place in the non-
    fiction category.

269. Anon. "Best-Selling Fiction, Non-
Fiction Listed." The Seattle Sunday
Times (1 April), Part 2, p. 5.
    Lists BB in fifth place in the non-
    fiction category.

270. Anon. "Best-Selling Fiction, Non-
Fiction Listed." The Seattle Sunday
Times (8 April), p. 13.

Lists BB in fourth place in the non-
fiction category.

271. Anon. "Best-Selling Fiction, Non-
Fiction Listed." The Seattle Sunday
Times (20 May), p. 13.
    Lists BB in second place in the non-
    fiction category.

272. Anon. "Best-Selling Fiction, Non-
Fiction Listed." The Seattle Sunday
Times (10 June), p. 6.
    Lists BB in second place in the non-
    fiction category.

273. Anon. "Best-Selling Fiction, Non-
Fiction Listed." The Seattle Sunday
Times (17 June), p. 22.
    Lists BB in second place in the non-
    fiction category.

274. Anon. "Best-Selling Fiction, Non-
Fiction Listed." The Seattle Sunday
Times (15 July), p. 6.
    Lists BB in third place in the non-
    fiction category.

275. Anon. "Best-Selling Novels, Non-
Fiction Listed." The Seattle Sunday
Times (9 September), p. 33.
    Lists BB in fifth place in the non-
    fiction category.

276. Anon. "Best Writings on the Negro."
The Philadelphia Inquirer (29 July),
Society Sec., p. 11.
    Review of Bucklin Moon's anthology
    Primer for White Folks mentioning W's
    contributions.

277. Anon. "'Bilbo a Disgrace'--White
Mississippian: Senator Retorts in Usual
Manner." The Pittsburgh Courier (29
December), p. 9.
    Quotes a letter from Guy H. Raver,
    Jr., a white Mississippian, including
    praise of "the sincere and deeply
    moving" BB. Bilbo's reply attacks W
    and intermarriage.

278. Anon. "Black Boy." The Atlanta
Journal (8 April), p. 8-C.
    Advertisement.

279. Anon. "Black Boy." Chicago Daily
News (25 April), p. 24.
    Advertisement.

280. Anon. "Black Boy." The Chicago Sun
Book Week (1 July), p. 5.
    Large advertisement with a photograph
    of W and nine quotations from re-
    views.

281. Anon. "'Black Boy.'" The Iola (Kansas) Register (3 April), p. 4.
    Favorable editorial review of "an
    utterly engrossing book." Contrary to

preconceptions, the work is not didactic and W is not a typical black.
His "dramatic and tragic experiences"
result mainly from "influences entirely apart from race or color."

282. Anon. "Black Boy." Life, 18 (4
June), 87-93.
    Prefatory note calls W's book "not
    only a brilliant autobiography but a
    powerful indictment of a caste system
    which is one of America's biggest
    problems." The article itself is a
    lavishly illustrated "picture-drama-
    tization" summarizing episodes and
    quoting from BB. The photographs are
    by George Karger.

283. Anon. "Black Boy." Los Angeles Herald Examiner (11 March), Sec. VI, p. 5.
    Favorable notice praising the power-
    ful emotional quality of the work and
    predicting that it will become a
    classic.

284. Anon. "Black Boy." The Nation, 160
(24 March), 337.
    Advertisement.

285. Anon. "Black Boy." The Negro
(July), p. [xviii].
    Book-of-the-Month Club advertisement.

286. Anon. "Black Boy." The New Republic, 112 (26 March), 427.
    Advertisement.

287. Anon. "Black Boy." The New York
Times (12 March), p. 32.
    Large advertisement with eleven quo-
    tations from reviews.

288. Anon. "Black Boy." The New York
Times (26 March), p. 32.
    Large advertisement with ten quota-
    tions from reviews.

289. Anon. "Black Boy." The Pittsburgh
Courier (17 March), p. 5.
    Advertisement.

290. Anon. "'Black Boy' and Bond Buying." Unidentified clipping (c. March or
April).
    Editorial pointing out the inconsis-
    tency of W's denunciation of the
    United States in BB and his dust
    jacket plea to buy war bonds.

291. Anon. "'Black Boy' Author Foresees
Racial Trouble Following War." Unidentified clipping.
    Associated Negro Press interview with
    W quoting his comments predicting an
    accelerated struggle for black
    rights, describing the plight of
    black juvenile delinquents, and stat-
    ing that money is not his motive for

writing. The interviewer provides
some background information.

292. Anon. "Black Boy, by Richard
Wright." The American Mercury, 60
(April), 389.
    Favorable review stressing W's "pro-
    found sincerity and restraint" in
    relating his "honest story of heart-
    break." The effect of BB will be even
    greater than that of NS.

293. Anon. "Black Boy. By Richard
Wright." Cleveland Plain Dealer (4
March), Pictorial Magazine Sec., p. 12.
    Objecting to lapses of taste, this
    otherwise favorable review admires
    W's courage and persuasiveness. Mov-
    ing and effective, BB promises "per-
    manence for itself and a high place
    in American letters for its author."

294. Anon. "Black Boy, by Richard
Wright." Companion (October).
    Favorable review stressing the shock-
    ing impact of the work, "a valuable
    and useful commentary on present-day
    race relations."

295. Anon. "Black Boy by Richard
Wright." The Framingham Evening News (28
April), p. 8.
    Favorable notice praising the work's
    vividness, starkness, and simplicity
    of style. W is "the most gifted liv-
    ing American Negro writer."

295a. Anon. "Black Boy by Richard
Wright." Liberty, 22 (29 September), 39.
    Brief headnote to an illustrated
    condensation of the book.

296. Anon. "Black Boy. By Richard
Wright." Negro College Quarterly, 3
(June), 96.
    Review noting W's emphasis on the
    hardships and bleakness of his youth.

297. Anon. "Black Boy by Richard
Wright." Negro Story, 1 (May-June), back
cover; 2 (August-September), back cover.
    Advertisement.

298. Anon. "Black Boy by Richard
Wright." New York Sunday News (22
April).
    Advertisement.

299. Anon. "Black Boy by Richard
Wright." The Retail Bookseller, 48 (February), 119B.
    Favorable notice of "revealing and
    absorbing reading" which will prove
    "a sure best seller."

300. Anon. "Black Boy by Richard
Wright." San Luis Obispo Golden West (23
March).

Favorable notice of a "document of simple sincerity and tremendous power."

301. Anon. "Black Boy by Richard Wright." The Saturday Review of Literature, 28 (13 October), 61.
Large advertisement with five quotations from reviews.

302. Anon. "Black Boy by Richard Wright." Sunday Chicago Bee (27 May), Sec. Two, p. 15; (8 July), Sec. Two, p. 15.
Advertisement.

303. Anon. "Black Boy, by Richard Wright." Theatre Arts, 29 (June), 382.
Favorable review emphasizing W's use of dramatic conflict. As in his other works, dramatic conflict stimulates his creativity. "To read Black Boy cannot help but sharpen the perceptions that the reader turns back upon the problem of race, as well as on the tortures of the artist who struggles through darkness into light."
Reprinted: 1978.209.

304. Anon. "Black Boy by Richard Wright." Unidentified clipping.
Advertisement for the Paramount Book Company in Newark emphasizing the sensational and inspirational aspects of the work.

305. Anon. "Black Boy by Richard Wright." Unidentified clipping.
Advertisement.

306. Anon. "Black Boy in Brooklyn." Ebony, 1 (November), 26-27.
Fully illustrated biographical article on W living in Brooklyn. Gives attention to BB and points out W's contribution to the struggle for fair and adequate housing.

307. Anon. "'Black Boy Is Unusual Negro Autobiography." Lewiston (Maine) Evening Journal (31 March), Magazine Sec., p. A-8.
Favorable review stressing the work's powerful impact and its seriousness. Summarizes and quotes from the book, concluding that it is required reading "for the student of social and economic problems."

308. Anon. "'Black Boy' Leading Non-Fiction Volume." The Seattle Sunday Times (29 April), Part 2, p. 6.
Lists BB in first place in the non-fiction category.

309. Anon. "'Black Boy' to World." Chicago Sunday Tribune (9 September), Part 6, p. 12.

Notes that World Publishing Company has acquired rights to BB.

310. Anon. "Black Boyhood." Time, 45 (5 March), 94, 96, 98.
Favorable review of BB recounting the narrative and quoting several passages. The story is one of a man set apart from other members of his race by his sensitivity and his intellect, the reviewer believes. Praises W's style, which is simple and direct but not flat.
Reprinted: 1978.209.

311. Anon. "Black Metropolis, by St. Clair Drake and Horace R. Cayton." The New Yorker, 21 (27 October), 99-100.
Review concluding with this sentence: "Richard Wright, somewhat less angry than usual, contributes an introduction that is one of the best things he has ever done."

312. Anon. "'The Black Rose' Leads Best-Selling Novels." The Seattle Sunday Times (7 October), p. 16.
Lists BB in fifth place in the nonfiction category.

313. Anon. "Book Barometer." Cleveland News (15 March), p. 12.
Lists BB in tenth place in the nonfiction category.

314. Anon. "Book Boom for Negro Authors." Ebony, 1 (November), 24-25.
Comments on the popularity of W's books.

315. Anon. "Book Circle Disbands for the Summer." Sunday Chicago Bee (1 July), Sec. Two, p. 15.
Discusses an oral review of BB by Clara Green, who disapproved of W's obscenity. Other members of the black book club praised the work.

316. Anon. "Book Club Choices." San Jose News (c. 13 March).
Notice giving more attention to Glenway Wescott's Apartment in Athens than to BB.

317. Anon. "Book News." The Atlanta Journal (4 February), p. 12-C.
Notes that BB will be part of a dual Book-of-the-Month Club selection for March.

318. Anon. "Book Notes." New York Herald Tribune (31 January), p. 17.
Announces W's lecture on "The American Negro Discovers Himself" in the McMillin Theater at Columbia University on 6 February.

319. Anon. "Book Notes." New York Herald

Tribune (2 March), p. 17.
  Notes that W will defend BB on a WHN
  radio review.

320. Anon. "Book Notes." New York Herald
Tribune (14 March), p. 23.
  Reports that W has been appointed to
  the board of directors of the American Council on Race Relations. He
  will serve in an advisory capacity.

321. Anon. "Book Notes." New York Herald
Tribune (27 March), p. 17.
  Discusses the sale of foreign rights
  to BB and the play NS.

322. Anon. "Book Notes." New York Herald
Tribune (18 July), p. 29.
  Reports that paper shortages have
  caused Harper's to sell the rights to
  BB to World Publishing Company.

323. Anon. "Book Notes." New York Herald
Tribune (5 November), p. 17.
  Announces that W and Lewis Gannett
  will discuss Black Metropolis on "The
  Author Meets the Critics," a radio
  program to be broadcast on 5 November
  over WHN.

324. Anon. "Book-of-Month Announces New
Dual Selection." The Columbia (S. C.)
Record (4 January), p. 8.
  Reports that Blank [sic] Boy will be
  a March selection.

325. Anon. "Book-of-the-Month Club Ad-
vertisement." Harper's Magazine, 190
(July), [xviii].
  Notes that the controversial BB is
  available from the Book-of-the-Month
  Club.

326. Anon. "Book-of-the-Month Club Selection." Chelsea (Mass.) Evening Record
(9 April), p. 6.
  Cartoons with captions on W's life.

327. Anon. "The Book-of-the-Month Club
Suggests That You Begin Your Subscrip-
tion With These Two Best-Sellers." New
York Herald Tribune Weekly Book Review
(1 April), p. 24.
  Advertises BB.

328. Anon. "Bookmarks of New Books." The
Beloit Daily News (11 January), p. 12.
  Announces that BB is a Book-of-the-
  Month Club selection.

329. Anon. "Book of the Week: Black Boy
by Richard Wright." The Cleveland Gazette (20 May), p. 11.
  Favorable review of "a document of
  simple sincerity and tremendous
  power," emphasizing the American
  character of W's experience. Includes
  a sketch of W's career after he left

the South.

330. Anon. "Book Reveals Lone Picture of
Negro Life." The Ogden Standard-Examiner
(4 March), p. 12B.
  Favorable review of BB consisting
  mainly of quotation from the publisher's statement about the work.

331. Anon. "Book Review: Black Boy by
Richard Wright." The Painesville Telegraph (9 March), p. 4.
  Favorable review emphasizing W's
  early hardships and his present
  status as "one of America's most
  distinguished authors."

332. Anon. "Book Reviews." Middletown
(Ohio) Sunday News Journal (18 Febru-
ary), p. 4.
  Notes that BB is a Book-of-the-Month
  Club selection for March.

333. Anon. "Book Savings for Book-
stores." New York Herald Tribune (19
March), p. 4.
  Bloomingdale's advertisement listing
  BB.

334. Anon. "Book Section: Black Boy by
Richard Wright." Negro Digest, 3 (June),
71-72.
  Headnote and footnote to an excerpt
  from BB, which "scorches with the
  white heat of bitterness and anger
  America's race relations."

335. Anon. "Books and Art: 'Black Boy.'"
Headlines and Pictures (April), pp. 36-
37.
  Mixed review claiming that W's "David
  Copperfieldian youth" is more individual than representative. He tele-
  scopes chronology at times, and the
  second part of the book is better
  than the first. Includes quotations
  from five other reviews.

336. Anon. "Books and Authors." The New
York Times (16 April), p. 21.
  Notes that W is included in Bucklin
  Moon's forthcoming anthology Primer
  for White Folks.

337. Anon. "Books--Authors." The New
York Times (14 March), p. 17.
  Announces W's appointment to the
  board of directors of the American
  Council on Race Relations.

338. Anon. "Books--Authors." The New
York Times (27 March), p. 17.
  Includes information on BB and NS
  concerning domestic sales, foreign
  rights, and stage presentations
  abroad.

339. Anon. "Books--Authors." The New

York _Times_ (4 April), p. 19.
Notes that BB is one of the three books currently recommended by the Writers' War Board.

340. Anon. "Books--Authors." _The New York Times_ (2 October), p. 21.
Mentions W's introduction to Black Metropolis.

341. Anon. "Books in Review: Black Boy, by Richard Wright." _The Charleston (S. C.)News and Courier_ (6 May),p. 7.
Unfavorable review minimizing W's indictment of white racism and emphasizing his maladjustment to his own family and race. Though well written, the book is one-sided in its presentation of black life as "unutterably dreary."

342. Anon. "Books, Music and Authors." _The_ Columbia (S. C.) _State_ (1 April), Sec. B, p. 4.
Mentions sale of foreign rights to BB, of which "a total of 410,000 copies . . . are in print" in the United States.

343. Anon. "The Bookseller's Almanac." _The_ Retail _Bookseller_, 48 (February), 105-107.
Contains a favorable notice of BB praising its candor and preferring it to NS.

344. Anon. "Born and Bred in Boston." Brooklyn _Citizen_ (3 January).
Mentions that Anne Burr won praise for her performance in NS.

345. Anon. "_The Brick Foxhole_." _The_ Retail _Bookseller_, 48 (May).
Advertisement for the novel quoting W's favorable comment: "I feel that the author of this slashing, shocking novel is serving his country well. _The Brick Foxhole_ is a call to realism, to seeing honestly again."

346. Anon. "The Brighter Side." _Time_, 46 (1 October), 58, 60.
Article on the new magazine _Ebony_ mentioning W as an example of a successful black man.

347. Anon. "Burton's." _The_ Montreal _Gazette_ (5 May), p. 7.
Book store advertisement for BB and other titles.

348. Anon. "Canada Lee, Elton Warren to Open Woodlawn Forum." _Chicago Defender_ (20 October), p. 29.
Mentions briefly Lee's role in NS.

349. Anon. "Canada Lee Is the Newest Caliban." _Sunday Chicago Bee_ (30 September), p. 7.
Mentions briefly Lee's role in NS.

350. Anon. "Candidates for the Best Seller List." _The Publishers' Weekly_, 147 (17 March), 1214.
Lists BB, which "led sales at Brentano's in N. Y. during the past week."

351. Anon. "Candidates for the Best Seller List." _The Publishers' Weekly_, 147 (24 March), 1307.
Lists BB, which is the nonfiction leader in Philadelphia.

352. Anon. "'Captain from Castile' Tops Fiction List." _The_ Seattle _Sunday_ Times (13 May), p. 13.
Lists BB in second place in the nonfiction category.

353. Anon. "Una carta de Richard Wright." Montevideo _Marcha_ (2 February), p. 15.
Headnote to W's letter to Antonio R. Frasconi explaining its circumstances and praising its commitment to the black struggle and to democratic ideals.

354. Anon. "Catholics & Color." _Ebony_, 1 (November), 21-23.
Contains a caption to a photograph of the ordination of a black priest in Natchez, Mississippi, noting that the local newspaper refused to run advertising for BB.

355. Anon. "Cayton to Review New Wright Book." _Chicago Sunday Bee_ (8 April), Sec. Two, p. 10.
Announces a review at the Parkway Community Center on 8 April.

356. Anon. "Center Forum 1945-6." Unidentified clipping.
Announces W's lecture on "The American Negro Discovers Himself" at a Jewish community center on 19 November.

357. Anon. "Chicago Is Reading." _Chicago Daily News_ (14 March), p. 19.
Lists BB in third place in the nonfiction category.

358. Anon. "Chicago Is Reading." _Chicago Daily News_ (21 March), p. 23.
Lists BB in fourth place in the nonfiction category.

359. Anon. "Chicago Is Reading." _Chicago Daily News_ (28 March), p. 19.
Lists BB in first place in the nonfiction category.

360. Anon. "Chicago Is Reading." _Chicago_

Daily News (4 April), p. 19.
    Lists BB in first place in the non-
    fiction category.

361. Anon. "Chicago Is Reading." Chicago
Daily News (11 April), p. 18.
    Lists BB in third place in the non-
    fiction category.

362. Anon. "Chicago Is Reading." Chicago
Daily News (18 April), p. 18.
    Lists BB in first place in the non-
    fiction category.

363. Anon. "Chicago Is Reading." Chicago
Daily News (25 April), p. 23.
    Lists BB in first place in the non-
    fiction category.

364. Anon. "Chicago Is Reading." Chicago
Daily News (2 May), p. 18.
    Lists BB in first place in the non-
    fiction category.

365. Anon. "Chicago Is Reading." Chicago
Daily News (9 May), p. 19.
    Lists BB in first place in the non-
    fiction category.

366. Anon. "Chicago Is Reading." Chicago
Daily News (16 May), p. 17.
    Lists BB in first place in the non-
    fiction category.

367. Anon. "Chicago Is Reading." Chicago
Daily News (23 May), p. 23.
    Lists BB in first place in the non-
    fiction category.

368. Anon. "Chicago Is Reading." Chicago
Daily News (29 May), p. 12.
    Lists BB in first place in the non-
    fiction category.

369. Anon. "Chicago Is Reading." Chicago
Daily News (13 June), p. 20.
    Lists BB in first place in the non-
    fiction category.

370. Anon. "Chicago Is Reading." Chicago
Daily News (20 June), p. 16.
    Lists BB in second place in the non-
    fiction category.

371. Anon. "Chicago Is Reading." Chicago
Daily News (27 June), p. 17.
    Lists BB in third place in the non-
    fiction category.

372. Anon. "Chicago Is Reading." Chicago
Daily News (4 July), p. 13.
    Lists BB in third place in the non-
    fiction category.

373. Anon. "Chicago Is Reading." Chicago
Daily News (11 July), p. 14.
    Lists BB in fourth place in the non-
    fiction category.

374. Anon. "Chicago Is Reading." Chicago
Daily News (25 July), p. 17.
    Lists BB in fifth place in the non-
    fiction category.

375. Anon. "Chicago Is Reading." Chicago
Daily News (8 August), p. 20.
    Lists BB tied for fifth place in the
    nonfiction category.

376. Anon. "Las 100 de Sangre Negra."
Unidentified clipping (3 May).
    Amply illustrated article on the
    celebration occasioned by the hun-
    dredth performance of the play NS in
    Buenos Aires.

377. Anon. "City Life of the Negro." The
Kansas City Star (3 November), p. 12.
    Review of Black Metropolis mentioning
    W's "provocative introduction."

378. Anon. "The Colored Man's Problem."
The Saints' Herald, 92 (5 May), 12.
    Favorable review of BB noting its
    power, timeliness, and "stark real-
    ism." This "moving and disturbing
    book" is an important statement on
    the racial issue.

379. Anon. "Coming in the June Issue."
Negro Digest, 3 (May), [99].
    Includes an advertisement for the
    excerpt from BB to appear in the June
    issue. "Don't miss this thrilling
    dramatic blockbuster indictment of
    race relations in Dixie!"

380. Anon. "Controversial 'Black Boy'
Tome Subject for 'Author Meets Critics.'" New York: WHN, 26 February.
    Flyer announcing the radio program
    with W, Sterling North, and Lewis
    Gannett.

381. Anon. "Coronet Condenses Richard
Wright's Black Boy." Sunday Chicago Bee
(25 November), Sec. Two, p. 11.
    Announces and quotes from the maga-
    zine condensation.

382. Anon. "The Critics Approve O'Hara's
'Pipe Line.'" Unidentified clipping
(April).
    Serving as one of the critics on a
    radio program with O'Hara, W com-
    ments: "O'Hara's short stories are
    almost as good as short stories can
    be written."

383. Anon. "Cross-Section 1945: A Collection of New American Writing Edited
by Edwin Seaver." The Retail Bookseller,
48 (November), 718.
    Mentions W as a contributor.

384. Anon. "Current Bookshelf." Erie
Dispatch-Herald (4 March), Sec. 4, p. 8.

Contains a favorable notice of BB.
W's American heritage included both
despair and hope.

385. Anon. "De 'Sangre negra.'" Unidentified clipping.
    Photograph with caption of a scene
    from the Buenos Aires production of
    the play NS with Narciso Ibañez Menta
    as Bigger.

386. Anon. "Detroit Best Sellers." The
Detroit Free Press (25 March), Part Two,
p. 6.
    Lists BB in fifth place in the non-
    fiction category.

387. Anon. "Detroit Best Sellers." The
Detroit Free Press (1 April), Part Two,
p. 6.
    Lists BB in second place in the non-
    fiction category.

388. Anon. "Detroit Best Sellers." The
Detroit Free Press (8 April), Part Two,
p. 6.
    Lists BB in second place in the non-
    fiction category.

389. Anon. "Detroit Best Sellers." The
Detroit Free Press (22 April), Part Two,
p. 6.
    Lists BB in second place in the non-
    fiction category.

390. Anon. "Detroit Best Sellers." The
Detroit Free Press (29 April), Part Two,
p. 6.
    Lists BB in second place in the non-
    fiction category.

391. Anon. "Detroit Best Sellers." The
Detroit Free Press (6 May), Part Two, p.
6.
    Lists BB in second place in the non-
    fiction category.

392. Anon. "Detroit Best Sellers." The
Detroit Free Press (13 May), Part Two,
p. 6.
    Lists BB in second place in the non-
    fiction category.

393. Anon. "Detroit Best Sellers." The
Detroit Free Press (20 May), Part Two,
p. 6.
    Lists BB in second place in the non-
    fiction category.

394. Anon. "Detroit Best Sellers." The
Detroit Free Press (27 May), Part Two,
p. 6.
    Lists BB in second place in the non-
    fiction category.

395. Anon. "Detroit Best Sellers." The
Detroit Free Press (3 June), Part Two,
p. 6.
    Lists BB in second place in the non-
    fiction category.

396. Anon. "Detroit Best Sellers." The
Detroit Free Press (10 June), Part Two,
p. 6.
    Lists BB in second place in the non-
    fiction category.

397. Anon. "Detroit Best Sellers." The
Detroit Free Press (17 June), Part Two,
p. 6.
    Lists BB in second place in the non-
    fiction category.

398. Anon. "Detroit Best Sellers." The
Detroit Free Press (24 June), Part Two,
p. 6.
    Lists BB in second place in the non-
    fiction category.

399. Anon. "Detroit Best Sellers." The
Detroit Free Press (1 July), Part Two,
p. 6.
    Lists BB in fourth place in the non-
    fiction category.

400. Anon. "Detroit Best Sellers." The
Detroit Free Press (15 July), Part Two,
p. 6.
    Lists BB in third place in the non-
    fiction category.

401. Anon. "Detroit Best Sellers." The
Detroit Free Press (22 July), Part Two,
p. 6.
    Lists BB in third place in the non-
    fiction category.

402. Anon. "Detroit Best Sellers." The
Detroit Free Press (29 July), Part Two,
p. 6.
    Lists BB in fourth place in the non-
    fiction category.

403. Anon. "Detroit Best Sellers." The
Detroit Free Press (12 August), Part
Two, p. 6.
    Lists BB in third place in the non-
    fiction category.

404. Anon. "Detroit Best Sellers." The
Detroit Free Press (19 August), Part
Two, p. 6.
    Lists BB in third place in the non-
    fiction category.

405. Anon. "Detroit Best Sellers." The
Detroit Free Press (26 August), Part
Two, p. 6.
    Lists BB in third place in the non-
    fiction category.

406. Anon. "Detroit Best Sellers." The
Detroit Free Press (2 September), Part
Two, p. 6.
    Lists BB in fourth place in the non-
    fiction category.

407. Anon. "Detroit Best Sellers." The Detroit Free Press (9 September), Part Two, p. 6.
    Lists BB in fifth place in the non-fiction category.

408. Anon. "Detroit Best Sellers." The Detroit Free Press (16 September), Part Two, p. 6.
    Lists BB in fifth place in the non-fiction category.

409. Anon. "Detroit Best Sellers." The Detroit Free Press (23 September), Part Two, p. 6.
    Lists BB in fifth place in the non-fiction category.

410. Anon. "Detroit Best Sellers." The Detroit Free Press (30 September), Part Two, p. 6.
    Lists BB in third place in the non-fiction category.

411. Anon. "Detroit Best Sellers." The Detroit Free Press (7 October), Part Two, p. 6.
    Lists BB in third place in the non-fiction category.

412. Anon. "Detroit Best Sellers." The Detroit Free Press (14 October), Part Two, p. 6.
    Lists BB in second place in the non-fiction category.

413. Anon. "Detroit Best Sellers." The Detroit Free Press (28 October), Part Two, p. 6.
    Lists BB in fourth place in the non-fiction category.

414. Anon. "Detroit Best Sellers." The Detroit Free Press (4 November), Part Two, p. 6.
    Lists BB in fourth place in the non-fiction category.

415. Anon. "Detroit Best Sellers." The Detroit Free Press (11 November), Part Two, p. 6.
    Lists BB in fourth place in the non-fiction category.

416. Anon. "Detroit's Best Sellers." The Detroit Free Press (8 July), Part Two, p. 6.
    Lists BB in second place in the non-fiction category.

417. Anon. "Difference of Opinion." The New York Times Book Review (1 April), p. 27.
    Quotes from Southern reviews of BB by Jessie Rehder and Frank McCallister to illustrate divergent opinions.

418. Anon. "Doubleday, Doran Book Shops." New York Post (3 May), p. 17.
    Advertisement mentioning BB.

418a. Anon. "D'une lettre de Richard Wright." Labyrinthe, No. 15 (15 December), p. 7.
    Headnote to a translation of part of W's letters to Antonio R. Frasconi.

419. Anon. Dust jacket of BB. New York: Harper.
    Front cover contains a blurb and a quotation from Bennett Cerf; back cover contains a biographical sketch of W and a photograph by Gordon Parks. Front inside flap contains a publisher's blurb on the book and a quotation from Dorothy Canfield Fisher; back inside flap contains W's "Don't Wear Your 'Sunday Best' Every Day."

419a. Anon. Dust jacket of Cross Section 1945. Ed. Edwin Seaver. New York: L. B. Fischer.
    Mentions W and refers to "Early Days in Chicago" on the inside front flap.

420. Anon. "Eaton's Book Room." The Montreal Gazette (5 May), p. 7.
    Advertisement containing a paragraph on BB praising it as "a moving, thought-provoking book."

421. Anon. "Ernie Pyle Book Leads Non-Fiction Favorites." The Seattle Sunday Times (22 April), Part 2, p. 6.
    Lists BB in second place in the non-fiction category.

422. Anon. "Everybody's Reading." Minneapolis Sunday Tribune (18 March), p. 13.
    Lists BB in first place in the non-fiction category.

423. Anon. "Everybody's Reading." Minneapolis Sunday Tribune (25 March), p. 15.
    Lists BB in fourth place in the non-fiction category.

424. Anon. "Everybody's Reading." Minneapolis Sunday Tribune (1 April), p. 13.
    Lists BB in second place in the non-fiction category.

425. Anon. "Everybody's Reading." Minneapolis Sunday Tribune (8 April), p. 13.
    Lists BB in fourth place in the non-fiction category.

426. Anon. "Everybody's Reading." Minneapolis Sunday Tribune (22 April), p. 15.
    Lists BB in third place in the non-fiction category.

427. Anon. "Everybody's Reading." Min-

neapolis Sunday Tribune (20 May), p. 13.
Lists BB in fourth place in the non-
fiction category.

428. Anon. "Everybody's Reading." Minneapolis Sunday Tribune (3 June), p. 13.
Lists BB in fourth place in the non-
fiction category.

429. Anon. "Everybody's Reading." Minneapolis Sunday Tribune (17 June), p.
13.
Lists BB in second place in the non-
fiction category.

430. Anon. "Everybody's Reading." Minneapolis Sunday Tribune (24 June), p.
11.
Lists BB in fourth place in the non-
fiction category.

431. Anon. "Everybody's Reading." Minneapolis Sunday Tribune (1 July), p. 13.
Lists BB in second place in the non-
fiction category.

432. Anon. "Everybody's Reading." Minneapolis Sunday Tribune (15 July), p.
11.
Lists BB in third place in the non-
fiction category.

433. Anon. "Everybody's Reading." Minneapolis Sunday Tribune (22 July), p.
13.
Lists BB in second place in the non-
fiction category.

434. Anon. "Fiction." St. Louis Globe-
Democrat (1 July), p. [5E].
Lists W as a contributor to Charles
Grayson's Half a Hundred Tales.

435. Anon. "Fiction and Non-Fiction Best
Sellers Listed." The Seattle Sunday
Times (30 September), p. 15.
Lists BB in fourth place in the non-
fiction category.

436. Anon. "Fiction and Non-Fiction Best
Sellers Listed." The Seattle Sunday
Times (21 October), Part 2, p. 6.
Lists BB in fifth place in the non-
fiction category.

437. Anon. "A Fight Against Fear." Unidentified clipping (18 March).
Highly favorable review of BB, "a
brilliant literary achievement, one
that is in the mainstream of great
English literature." W's realism is
restrained and artful, not sensationalistic, and the work is a "masterpiece of modern prose."

438. Anon. "Former Books-of-the-Month."
Book-of-the-Month Club News (April), p.
31.

Lists BB.

439. Anon. "4 Famous Authors to Speak
Here April 9." Philadelphia Record (25
March), p. M7.
W is one of the four scheduled to
speak at the Famous Authors Luncheon.
A photograph with caption is in-
cluded.

440. Anon. "Future of Liberated Countries." Brooklyn News [?].
Reports that W, commenting on the
question of granting democracy to
liberated countries, points out American isolationism. The year is conjectural.

441. Anon. "Glass Block." Unidentified
clipping (c. May).
Book store advertisement noting
availability of autographed copies of
BB and the Modern Library edition of
NS.

442. Anon. "Great American Negroes by
Ben Richardson." The Retail Bookseller,
48 (May), 82A.
Mentions that the book treats W.

443. Anon. "'Half-a-Hundred. . . . .
[sic] Tales by Great American Writers,'
Edited, with Introduction, by Charles
Grayson." Asheville Citizen-Times (10
June), p. 6.
Favorable notice mentioning W.

443a. Anon. "Harcourt, Brace and Company." The American Scholar, 15 (Winter), [10].
Contains an advertisement for Black
Metropolis mentioning and quoting
from W's introduction.

444. Anon. "Harper Books for Spring."
The Retail Bookseller, 48 (February),
33-37.
Contains an announcement of BB,
scheduled for publication on 28 February.

445. Anon. "Harper's Monthly Double."
Newsweek, 25 (5 March), 93-94, 96.
Favorable review of BB calling it
"one of the most heart-breaking indictments of American society ever
written by an American" (p. 93).
Summarizing the book, the reviewer
praises W's intensity, skill in portraiture, and truthfulness.

446. Anon. "Have You Heard It?" Unidentified clipping.
Advertisement for the WHN radio program "Author Meets the Critics."
Notes that W will discuss BB.

447. Anon. "Henry A. Wallace Book on

Best-Seller List." The Seattle Sunday
Times (28 October), p. 28.
    Lists BB in fifth place in the non-
    fiction category.

448. Anon. "Here Is What Chicago Is
Reading." Chicago Daily News (6 June),
p. 25.
    Lists BB in first place in the non-
    fiction category.

449. Anon. "Highlights of Modern Books."
The Waltham News-Tribune (6 January), p.
7.
    Notes that BB will be a Book-of-the-
    Month Club selection for March.

449a. Anon. "Himes, Chester B. If He
Hollers, Let Him Go." Bulletin from
Virginia Kirkus' Bookshop Service, 13
(15 August), 378.
    Unfavorable review calling Himes "a
    poor man's Richard Wright."

450. Anon. "Historic Associations of
Quebec Lauded." Unidentified clipping.
    Quotes W praising Quebec's attachment
    to the past.

451. Anon. "How Richard Wright Looks at
'Black Boy.'" PM (15 April), Magazine
Sec., pp. 3-4.
    Account of a WHN radio program in
    "The Author Meets the Critics
    Series." The participants are W,
    Sterling North, Lewis Gannett, and
    John McCaffrey. W explains the source
    and inspiration of his autobiography.
    He considers it a catharsis of sorts.
    Reprinted in condensed form: 1945.
    729; 1982.50.

452. Anon. "Howard University Forum
1945-1946."
    Brochure advertisement for W's lec-
    ture on "Democracy's Unfinished Busi-
    ness" scheduled for 1 November 1945.
    Includes a photograph and biographi-
    cal sketch of W.

453. Anon. "Los infrahumanos." El Montevideo Día (9 February).
    Review of Antonio R. Frasconi's
    volume of engravings with mention of
    W's letter.

454. Anon. "Los infrahumanos." Unidentified clipping.
    Advertisement for Antonio R. Fras-
    coni's volume of engravings with
    mention of W's letter.

455. Anon. "Iowa Students Will Discuss
Minorities." The Cornellian (9 November), pp. 1-2.
    Article on a "Racial Minorities Con-
    ference" at Cornell College. Mentions
    W's lecture on 15 November.

456. Anon. "It's Katz for Books." The
Kansas City Star (7 April), p. 12.
    Book store advertisement listing BB.

457. Anon. "Just Between Ourselves:
Wright Looks Back." Liberty, 22 (29
September), 11.
    Biographical note to accompany the
    condensation of BB in this issue.

457a. Anon. "Just Out." Unidentified
clipping.
    Advertisement of the Frederick Doug-
    lass Book Center in Harlem for BB and
    Walter White's A Rising Wind.

458. Anon. "Know His Book." The Bulletin
[of the Des Moines Women's Club], 12
(November), 2.
    Announces W's lecture in Des Moines
    and advertises BB at Younkers depart-
    ment store.

459. Anon. "Leading Fiction and Non-
Fiction Listed." The Seattle Sunday
Times (27 May), p. 13.
    Lists BB in second place in the non-
    fiction category.

460. Anon. "Lee, Canada," in Current
Biography 1944. Ed. Anna Rothe. New
York: H. W. Wilson, pp. 394-396.
    Biographical sketch commenting on
    Lee's performance as Bigger and quot-
    ing Lee on the play.
    Reprinted: 1945.532.

461. Anon. "Lehmann Novel Leads Fiction
Best-Sellers." The Seattle Sunday Times
(3 June), p. 6.
    Lists BB in second place in the non-
    fiction category.

462. Anon. "Librarian's Notebook." The
Seattle Sunday Times (25 March), p. 13.
    Lists BB among the new acquisitions
    of the Seattle Public Library.

463. Anon. "Library Corner: Black Boy by
Richard Wright." Turon Press (c. 23
September).
    Favorable review of BB emphasizing
    the social message. The book "is a
    document of simple sincerity and
    tremendous power."

464. Anon. "Library Notes." Marinette
Eagle-Star (15 March), p. 10.
    Contains a favorable notice of BB, a
    work of "autobiographical fiction."
    Praises the book's power, sincerity,
    and social significance.

465. Anon. "Like to Read Something?"
Cleveland Plain Dealer (c. 19 March).
    Favorable notice of BB.

466. Anon. "'Lion in the Streets' Week's

Best Seller." The Seattle Sunday Times (1 July), Part 2, p. 4.
Lists BB in second place in the non-fiction category.

467. Anon "'Lion Is in the Streets' Leads in Popularity." The Seattle Sunday Times (24 June), Part 2, p. 4.
Lists BB in second place in the non-fiction category.

468. Anon. "A List of the Current Best Renters." The Reading Guide (July), p. 4.
Includes BB.

469. Anon. "Manuscripts Chosen for Cross Section." The Memphis Commercial Appeal (19 August), Sec. IV, p. 10.
Mentions W.

470. Anon. "March Book Club Choices." The Springfield (Mass.) Sunday Union and Republican (7 January), p. 4 D.
Notes that BB will be part of a dual Book-of-the-Month Club selection for March.

471. Anon. "Men's Club to Present Richard Wright Sunday." Temple News of Temple Emanuel (16 November).
Announces a dinner followed by a lecture by W on "The American Negro Discovers Himself" scheduled for 18 November in Duluth, Minnesota.

472. Anon. "Midwest Best Sellers." The Chicago Sun Book Week (8 April), p. 13.
Lists BB in first place in the non-fiction category in Kansas City, Minneapolis, and Omaha, and in second place in Chicago.

473. Anon. "Midwest Best Sellers." The Chicago Sun Book Week (15 April), p. 8.
Lists BB in first place in the non-fiction category in Kansas City and Minneapolis and in second place in Chicago.

474. Anon. "Midwest Best Sellers." The Chicago Sun Book Week (22 April), p. 6.
Lists BB in first place in the non-fiction category in Cincinnati and Minneapolis and in second place in Chicago.

475. Anon. "Midwest Best Sellers." The Chicago Sun Book Week (29 April), p. 11.
Lists BB in first place in the non-fiction category in Detroit and in second place in Chicago.

476. Anon. "Midwest Best Sellers." The Chicago Sun Book Week (6 May), p. 10.
Lists BB in first place in the non-fiction category in Cincinnati and in second place in Chicago.

477. Anon. "Midwest Best Sellers." The Chicago Sun Book Week (20 May), p. 11.
Lists BB in first place in the non-fiction category in Cleveland and Kansas City and in second place in Chicago.

478. Anon. "Midwest Best Sellers." The Chicago Sun Book Week (27 May), p. 8.
Lists BB in first place in the non-fiction category in Cincinnati and in second place in Chicago.

479. Anon. "Midwest Best Sellers." The Chicago Sun Book Week (3 June), p. 12.
Lists BB in first place in the non-fiction category in Chicago.

480. Anon. "Midwest Best Sellers." The Chicago Sun Book Week (10 June), p. 15.
Lists BB in third place in the non-fiction category in Chicago.

481. Anon. "Midwest Best Sellers." The Chicago Sun Book Week (17 June), p. 11.
Lists BB in second place in the non-fiction category in Chicago.

482. Anon. "Midwest Best Sellers." The Chicago Sun Book Week (24 June), p. 10.
Lists BB in third place in the non-fiction category in Chicago.

483. Anon. "Midwest Best Sellers." The Chicago Sun Book Week (15 July), p. 10.
Lists BB in third place in the non-fiction category in Chicago.

484. Anon. "Midwest Best Sellers." The Chicago Sun Book Week (22 July), p. 10.
Lists BB in first place in the non-fiction category in Omaha.

485. Anon. "Midwest Book Briefs." The Chicago Sun Book Week (9 December), p. 21.
Notes the cancellation of W's scheduled lecture at the Sinai Temple because of illness.

486. Anon. "Modern American Short Stories Edited by Bennett Cerf." San Diego Journal (10 September), p. 15.
Favorable notice with a brief mention of W.

487. Anon. "Mss. Chosen for 'Cross Section 1945.'" Unidentified clipping.
Lists W as a contributor.

488. Anon. "Narciso Ibañez Menta en Sangre Negra." Buenos Aires: Enrique J. Muscio.
Playbill for the Spanish version of NS at the Teatro El Nacional in Buenos Aires, 8 March 1945.

489. Anon. "Natchez Needs It." The De-

troi Michigan Chronicle (14 April), p. 7.
    Reprint of 1945.490.

490.   . "Natchez Needs It." The New Republic, 112 (2 April), 437.
    Reports the refusal of a Natchez newspaper to accept an advertisement for BB.
    Reprinted: 1945.489.

491. Anon. "National Best Sellers." The Chicago Sun Book Week (15 April), p. 8.
    Lists BB in first place in the non-fiction category in Philadelphia.

492. Anon. "National Best Sellers." The Chicago Sun Book Week (22 April), p. 6.
    Lists BB in first place in the non-fiction category in New York, Philadelphia, and San Francisco.

493. Anon. "National Best Sellers." The Chicago Sun Book Week (29 April), p. 11.
    Lists BB in first place in the non-fiction category in San Francisco.

494. Anon. "National Best Sellers." The Chicago Sun Book Week (6 May), p. 10.
    Lists BB in first place in the non-fiction category in Los Angeles, New York, and San Francisco.

495. Anon. "National Best Sellers." The Chicago Sun Book Week (20 May), p. 11.
    Lists BB in first place in the non-fiction category in New York and San Francisco.

496. Anon. "National Best Sellers." The Chicago Sun Book Week (3 June), p. 12.
    Lists BB in first place in the non-fiction category in Washington.

497. Anon. "National Best Sellers." The Chicago Sun Book Week (10 June), p. 15.
    Lists BB in first place in the non-fiction category in Washington.

498. Anon. "National Best Sellers." The Chicago Sun Book Week (24 June), p. 10.
    Lists BB in first place in the non-fiction category in New York.

499. Anon. "National Best Sellers." The Chicago Sun Book Week (8 July), p. 9.
    Lists BB in first place in the non-fiction category in Boston.

500. Anon. "National Best Sellers." The Chicago Sun Book Week (15 July), p. 10.
    Lists BB in first place in the non-fiction category in Los Angeles and New York.

501. Anon. "National Best Sellers." The Chicago Sun Book Week (19 August), p. 8.

Lists BB in first place in the non-fiction category in Los Angeles.

502. Anon. "National Best Sellers." The Chicago Sun Book Week (2 September), p. 6.
    Lists BB in first place in the non-fiction category in San Francisco.

503. Anon. "National Best Sellers." The Chicago Sun Book Week (9 September), p. 7.
    Lists BB in first place in the non-fiction category in Los Angeles.

504. Anon. "National Best Sellers." The Chicago Sun Book Week (7 October), p. 13.
    Lists BB in fourth place in the non-fiction category.

505. Anon. "National Best Sellers." The Chicago Sun Book Week (21 October), p. 18.
    Lists BB in fourth place in the non-fiction category.

506. Anon. "National Best Sellers." The Chicago Sun Book Week (28 October), p. 18.
    Lists BB in fifth place in the non-fiction category.

507. Anon. "National Best Sellers." The Chicago Sun Book Week (4 November), p. 10.
    Lists BB in fifth place in the non-fiction category.

508. Anon. "National Best Sellers." The Louisville Courier-Journal (8 April), Sec. 3, p. 8.
    Lists BB in fourth place in the non-fiction category.

509. Anon. "National Best Sellers-- April." The Publishers' Weekly, 147 (12 May), 1930.
    Lists BB in second place in the non-fiction category.

510. Anon. "National Best Sellers-- August." The Publishers' Weekly, 148 (15 September), 1105.
    Lists BB in third place in the non-fiction category.

511. Anon. "National Best Sellers-- July." The Publishers' Weekly, 148 (11 August), 519.
    Lists BB in third place in the non-fiction category.

512. Anon. "National Best Sellers-- June." The Publishers' Weekly, 148 (14 July), 147.
    Lists BB in third place in the non-fiction category.

513. Anon. "National Best Sellers--March." The Publishers' Weekly, 147 (7 April), 1471.
    Lists BB in fourth place in the non-fiction category.

514. Anon. "National Best Sellers--May." The Publishers' Weekly, 147 (16 June), 2380.
    Lists BB in second place in the non-fiction category.

515. Anon. "National Best Sellers--November." The Publishers' Weekly, 148 (15 December), 2640.
    Lists BB in seventh place in the non-fiction category.

516. Anon. "National Best Sellers--October." The Publishers' Weekly, 148 (10 November), 2157.
    Lists BB in sixth place in the non-fiction category.

517. Anon. "National Best Sellers--September." The Publishers' Weekly, 148 (20 October), 1863.
    Lists BB in fifth place in the non-fiction category.

518. Anon. "Nation's Best Sellers." The Seattle Sunday Times (29 July), Part 2, p. 7.
    Lists BB in third place in the non-fiction category.

519. Anon. "Nation's Best-Sellers in Fiction, Non-Fiction." The Seattle Sunday Times (22 July), Part 2, p. 7.
    Lists BB in fifth place in the non-fiction category.

520. Anon. "Negro Best-Sellers." Negro Digest, 3 (July), 2.
    Lists BB in first place in the non-fiction category.

521. Anon. "Negro Speaks Out." Cleveland News (15 March), p. 12.
    Favorable review of BB, "a blunt and forceful indictment" of racism. The reviewer emphasizes W's rebellion and calls the book "frank, beautifully written."

522. Anon. "Negro Strife Ever Here, Wright Says." The Hartford Times (27 October), p. 2.
    Summarizes W's lecture on "The Literature of the Negro in the United States" as delivered to the Connecticut State Teachers Association.

523. Anon. "Negro's Outlook Brighter--Wright." Unidentified clipping (15 November).
    Reports W's lecture in Des Moines, in which he derives hope from the black perception of the cause as more a class strugle than a race struggle. Notes that W is scheduled to lecture later at Cornell College in Mt. Vernon, Iowa.

524. Anon. "New Hilton Novel at Top of Fiction List." The Seattle Sunday Times (2 September), Part 2, p. 6.
    Lists BB in fifth place in the non-fiction category.

525. Anon. "New Hilton Novel Tops Best-Selling Fiction." The Seattle Sunday Times (16 September), p. 25.
    Lists BB in third place in the non-fiction category.

526. Anon. "New Non-Fiction at Public Library." The La Crosse Tribune (31 March), p. 7.
    Contains a favorable notice of BB, into which W "put all the power, passion, and honesty of Native Son."

527. Anon. "The New York Sponsors of National Sharecroppers Week Cordially Invite You to Attend a Dinner-Forum on the Subject What Will Peace Bring to the South?" 4 pp.
    Printed invitation to an event to be held at the Hotel Roosevelt in New York on 23 April 1945. W is one of the speakers.

528. Anon. "News and Gossip of the Rialto." The New York Times (24 June), Sec. 2, p. 1.
    Notes that BB may be dramatized.

529. Anon. "Next Famous Authors Luncheon April 9." The Publishers' Weekly, 147 (24 March), 1291.
    W is one of four writers scheduled to speak at this event in Philadelphia.

530. Anon. "1945 Spring Books." The Commonweal, 42 (20 April), 22-23.
    Includes a notice of BB, an "agonized story."

531. Anon. "Noted Negro Writer Will Lecture Nov. 15." Mount Vernon (Iowa) Hawkeye-Record and Lisbon Herald (8 November), p. 1.
    Announces W's lecture on "The American Negro Discovers Himself" at Cornell College as "one of the most highly anticipated events of the current college year." Includes a photograph of W.

532. Anon. "Nothing Too Big for 'Bigger.'" Negro Digest, 3 (February), 77-80.
    Condensed reprint of 1945.460.

533. Anon. "Of Time and the People."

Newsweek, 26 (31 December), 92-93.
   Review of Edwin Seaver's "gloomy"
   Cross Section 1945 referring to W as
   one of the contributors.

534. Anon. "Omnibook Foreword." Omnibook
Magazine, 7 (August), 1.
   Brief critical and biographical headnote to an abridgement of BB. W "has
   recalled a bitter story with illuminating insight and dramatic power."

535. Anon. "People Say." PM's Sunday
Picture News (1 April), p. m9.
   Quotes a comment by W from the Braggiotti interview: "I'd rather wash
   dishes than write just for money."

536. Anon. "People Who Read and Write."
The New York Times Book Review (18
March), p. 24.
   Notes, s. v. "Sequel," that BB as
   published omitted "Early Job-Hunting
   Days in Chicago," to be published in
   Cross Section.

537. Anon. "People Who Read and Write."
The New York Times Book Review (27 May),
p. 14.
   Quotes, s. v. "Curtain Going Up,"
   from Sinclair Lewis's review of BB in
   Esquire.

538. Anon. "People Who Read and Write."
The New York Times Book Review (15
July), p. 25.
   Lists W as a contributor to Edwin
   Seaver's Cross Section 1945.

539. Anon. "The Philadelphia Record."
   Printed invitation to a "Famous Authors Luncheon" at the Hotel Bellevue-
   Stratford in Philadelphia on 9 April
   1945. W is to appear.

540. Anon. "Popular in Kansas City." The
Kansas City Star (31 March), p. 12.
   Lists BB in third place in the non-
   fiction category.

541. Anon. "Popular in Kansas City." The
Kansas City Star (7 April), p. 12.
   Lists BB in second place in the non-
   fiction category.

542. Anon. "Popular in Kansas City." The
Kansas City Star (14 April), p. 12.
   Lists BB in second place in the non-
   fiction category.

543. Anon. "Popular in Kansas City." The
Kansas City Star (28 April), p. 12.
   Lists BB in first place in the non-
   fiction category.

544. Anon. "Popular in Kansas City." The
Kansas City Star (5 May), p. 12.
   Lists BB in third place in the non-

fiction category.

545. Anon. "Popular in Kansas City." The
Kansas City Star (12 May), p. 12.
   Lists BB in second place in the non-
   fiction category.

546. Anon. "Popular in Kansas City." The
Kansas City Star (2 June), p. 12.
   Lists BB in second place in the non-
   fiction category.

547. Anon. "Popular in Kansas City." The
Kansas City Star (9 June), p. 12.
   Lists BB in second place in the non-
   fiction category.

548. Anon. "Popular in Kansas City." The
Kansas City Star (16 June), p. 12.
   Lists BB in second place in the non-
   fiction category.

549. Anon. "Popular in Kansas City." The
Kansas City Star (23 June), p. 12.
   Lists BB in second place in the non-
   fiction category.

550. Anon. "Popular Titles." The Kansas
City Star (24 March), p. 12.
   Lists BB in fifth place in the non-
   fiction category.

551. Anon. "Popular Titles." The Kansas
City Star (21 April), p. 12.
   Lists BB in second place in the non-
   fiction category.

552. Anon. "Popular Titles." The Kansas
City Star (26 May), p. 12.
   Lists BB in second place in the non-
   fiction category.

553. Anon. "Popular Titles." The Kansas
City Star (30 June), p. 12.
   Lists BB in second place in the non-
   fiction category.

554. Anon. "Popular Titles." The Kansas
City Star (7 July), p. 12.
   Lists BB in second place in the non-
   fiction category.

555. Anon. "Popular Titles." The Kansas
City Star (14 July), p. 12.
   Lists BB in second place in the non-
   fiction category.

556. Anon. "Popular Titles." The Kansas
City Star (21 July), p. 12.
   Lists BB in second place in the non-
   fiction category.

557. Anon. "Popular Titles." The Kansas
City Star (28 July), p. 12.
   Lists BB in fifth place in the non-
   fiction category.

558. Anon. "Popular Titles." The Kansas

City Star (4 August), p. 12.
Lists BB in third place in the non-
fiction category.

559. Anon. "Popular Titles." The Kansas
City Star (18 August), p. 12.
Lists BB in fifth place in the non-
fiction category.

560. Anon. "Popular Titles." The Kansas
City Star (25 August), p. 12.
Lists BB in fourth place in the non-
fiction category.

561. Anon. "Popular Titles." The Kansas
City Star (1 September), p. 12.
Lists BB in third place in the non-
fiction category.

562. Anon. "Popular Titles." The Kansas
City Star (8 September), p. 12.
Lists BB in fourth place in the non-
fiction category.

563. Anon. "Popular Titles." The Kansas
City Star (15 September), p. 12.
Lists BB in sixth place in the non-
fiction category.

564. Anon. "Popular Titles." The Kansas
City Star (22 September), p. 12.
Lists BB in third place in the non-
fiction category.

565. Anon. "Popular Titles." The Kansas
City Star (6 October), p. 12.
Lists BB in fourth place in the non-
fiction category.

566. Anon. "Popular Titles." The Kansas
City Star (13 October), p. 12.
Lists BB in second place in the non-
fiction category.

567. Anon. "Popular Titles." The Kansas
City Star (3 November), p. 12.
Lists BB in fourth place in the non-
fiction category.

568. Anon. "The Preacher Ate the Chick-
en." Zion's Herald (16 May).
Brief review of BB emphasizing the
role of religion in warping the protagonist's outlook. The book warns
that "where religion is staged . . .
the spirit of Christ cannot get
through."
Reprinted: 1978.209.

569. Anon. "Primer for White Folks
Edited by Bucklin Moon." The Retail
Bookseller, 48 (July), 64A.
Mentions W as a contributor.

570. Anon. "Problem Children Lead Wright
to Forsee [sic] Post-War Racial
Clashes." The Daily Bulletin.
Associated Negro Press article summa-

rizing, with quotations, comments by
W on black problem children.

571. Anon. "Program Northwest Wisconsin
Teachers Association, Eau Claire, Wisconsin, Thursday and Friday, October 11
& 12, 1945."
The theme of the meeting is "Democracy in Human Relations." W is one
of the speakers. Beneath his photograph are three paragraphs by Harold
R. Peat from 1945.1071.

572. Anon. "Public Library Book Notes."
Green Bay Press-Gazette (21 April), p.
7.
Contains a notice of BB, "a terrify-
ingly tense and somber document,
unrelieved by humor."

573. Anon. "Public Library Reviews
Briefly 12 New Volumes." Tiffin Adver-
tiser-Tribune (9 April), p. 2.
Contains a notice of BB pointing out
its grimness, subjectivity, and possible "distorted emphasis."

574. Anon. "Publishers' Notes." The
Springfield (Mass.) Sunday Union and
Republican (19 August), p. 4D.
Lists W as a contributor to Edwin
Seaver's anthology Cross Section
1945.

575. Anon. "Publishers Plan Heavy Advertising for Leading Fall Titles." The
Publishers' Weekly, 148 (22 September),
1325-1346.
Mentions that Cross Section 1945
contains an unpublished chapter from
BB (p. 1333).

576. Anon. "Pyle's 'Brave Men' Continues
to Lead Nonfiction Book Sales." The
Atlanta Constitution (20 May), p. 6-B.
Lists BB in second place in the non-
fiction category.

577. Anon. "Quebec Culture Admired by
Noted U. S. Author." The Quebec Chronicle Telegraph (c. 28 August).
W praises Quebec's tranquil way of
life and its attachment to the past.

578. Anon. "Quotes Quebec Prices." Unidentified clipping (from a Brooklyn
newspaper?).
Quotes a letter W wrote from Quebec.

579. Anon. "Race Conference in Progress
on Hilltop This Week-end." The Cornellian (16 November), pp. 1, 4.
Article on a conference on race relations sponsored by the Cornell Christian Association in Mt. Vernon, Iowa.
W inaugurated the conference with his
lecture on "The American Negro Discovers Himself" on 15 November.

580. Anon. "Race Problem Exposed in Sordid Story." The Montreal Gazette (5 May), p. 7.
Unfavorable review of BB complaining of triviality, vulgarity, and imbalance. W is an unsympathetic protagonist.

581. Anon. "Race Relations Advisor." The Chicago Sun Book Week (15 April), p. 4.
Reports that W has been appointed to the board of directors of the American Council on Race Relations.

582. Anon. "Racial Minorities." New York Post (6 December), p. B10.
Includes a favorable mention of BB.

583. Anon. "Radio Narrator." Unidentified clipping (c. February).
Associated Negro Press photograph of W misidentified as Gordon Heath.

584. Anon. "Radio Roundup, Comment." New York Post (6 March), p. 24.
Quotes from W's remarks in his appearance on WHN, including the statement that his purpose was "to render judgment on my environment."

585. Anon. "Radio Roundup, Comment." New York Post (17 April), p. 24.
Appearing as a critic with John O'Hara on the "Author Meets the Critics" radio program, W commented: "O'Hara's short stories are almost as good as short stories can be written."

586. Anon. "Radio Roundup, Comment." New York Post (25 May), p. 36.
Reviews the Town Meeting of the Air Program on race problems. Notes that W opposes gradualism.

587. Anon. "Read 'Black Boy' Our Choice of the Best Sellers." Chicago Daily News (4 April), p. 19.
Advertisement for Utility Stationery Stores.

588. Anon. ("Jack"). "A Reader's Observations on Wright's 'Black Boy.'" Labor Action (28 May), p. 2.
Letter to the editor reviewing BB. The writer places the book in the naturalist tradition, arguing that this tradition exposes social problems but does not eradicate them. To do so more militance is needed.

589. Anon. ("Bookwright"). "Reprints, New Editions." New York Herald Tribune Weekly Book Review (9 September), p. 2.
Mentions the new edition (World) of BB.

590. Anon. "Review of Wright's Book by Psychologist Is Must for Readers." Cleveland Call and Post (4 August).
Announces a review of BB by Marie Miller, a white psychologist, in a program sponsored by the Educational Committee of the Cleveland Branch of the NAACP.

590a. Anon. "Une Revue américaine: Twice a Year." Labyrinthe, No. 15 (15 December), p. 10.
Includes translation of the passages from Horace Cayton's "Frightened Children of Frightened Parents." Partially reprinted: 1950.56.

590b. Anon. "Les Revues." Labyrinthe, No. 15 (15 December), p. 10.
Mentions briefly the translation of "Fire and Cloud" in Les Temps Modernes.

591. Anon. "Richard Wright." The Indianapolis Recorder (24 February), p. 3.
Associated Negro Press photograph of W with a caption announcing the publication of BB.

592. Anon. "Richard Wright." New York Post (17 April), p. 24.
Photograph with caption directing the reader to "Radio Roundup" on the same page.

593. Anon. "Richard Wright." The Philadelphia Record (25 March).
Photograph with caption praising BB.

594. Anon. "Richard Wright Black Boy." Unidentified clippings.
Advertisements.

595. Anon. "Richard Wright Coming Here Twice to Lecture." Detroit Tribune (24 November), p. 3.
Announces W's lectures on "The Negro in the Post War Era" on 29 November and "The American Negro Finds Himself" on 13 December. Includes brief biographical information.

596. Anon. "Richard Wright Honored." San Jose News (c. 10 April).
Announces W's appointment to the American Council on Race Relations and discusses the popularity of his work abroad.

597. Anon. "Richard Wright Is Speaker Here." Newark New Jersey Record (3 November).
Account of a speech by W on the racial problem delivered at the West Side High School auditorium.

598. Anon. "Richard Wright Opens Conference." The Cornellian (9 November), p. 1.

Announces W's lecture on "The American Negro Discovers Himself" opening a three-day "Racial Minorities Conference" at Cornell College in Mount Vernon, Iowa, on 15 November. Sketches W's life and career and includes a photograph.

599. Anon. "Richard Wright 'The American Negro Discovers Himself.'" Center Forum 1945-6.
Announcement of W's lecture in Duluth on 19 November 1945.

600. Anon. "Richard Wright's." Unidentified clipping.
Advertisement of BB.

601. Anon. "Richard Wright's Autobiography." Chicago Daily News (28 February), p. 19.
Favorable review of BB noting its bitterness and praising its honesty. Begining where Strange Fruit and Freedom Road end, it is an important statement on the racial situation in America.

602. Anon. "Richard Wright's 'Black Boy.'" Sunday Chicago Bee (11 March), Sec. Two, p. 24.
Favorable editorial review praising W's "craftsmanship--his poignant, moving, searching, bitter intensity." The change in title from American Hunger to Black Boy is unfortunate, however.

603. Anon. "Richard Wright's Black Boy." Unidentified clipping.
Advertisement.

604. Anon. "Richard Wright's 'Black Boy' to Be Reviewed." The Chicago Defender (10 March), p. 3.
Announces that Fern Gayden of Negro Story will review the work on 14 March at the Book Review and Lecture Forum of the Hall Branch Library.

605. Anon. "Richard Wright's Passionate Story of His Own Youth Black Boy." New York Herald Tribune Weekly Book Review (15 April), p. 18.
Advertisement.

606. Anon. "'A Rising Wind,' by Walter White (Doubleday, Doran); 'Black Boy,' by Richard Wright (Harper)." Toledo Sunday Times (11 March), p. 18.
Favorable review of the two books on racial prejudice by two of "our most competent observers, our most persuasive and stirring writers."

607. Anon. "A Savage Novel on Racial Issue." St. Louis Post-Dispatch (16 November), p. 2C.

Unfavorable review of If He Hollers Let Him Go attacking W as well as Himes for hatred of whites and inflammatory treatment of the racial issue.

608. Anon. "Says 'Black Boy' Banned at Army Post." Sunday Chicago Bee (6 May), p. 6.
Associated Negro Press item relating the removal and destruction of the book at the base library of Deming Air Field in New Mexico.

609. Anon. "Selection for January--Cross Section 1945 edited by Edwin Seaver." Unidentified clipping.
Mentions W and includes his photograph.

610. Anon. "Short Stories." Charlotte Sunday Observer (1 July), Sec. Two, p. 6.
Lists W as a contributor to Charles Grayson's Half a Hundred . . . Tales by Great American Writers.

611. Anon. "Snellenburgs." The Philadelphia Jewish Times (16 March), p. 13.
Department store advertisement for BB.

612. Anon. "A Sociological Study of Chicago's South Side." The Philadelphia Inquirer (28 October), Society Sec., p. 12.
Review of Black Metropolis mentioning W's introduction and his "bitterness."

613. Anon. "The Southern Press Reviews Richard Wright's 'Black Boy.'" Sunday Chicago Bee (6 May), Sec. Two, p. 15.
Excerpts reviews by Elizabeth W. Matthews in the Richmond Times-Dispatch, John B. Blalock in The Durham Herald-Sun, Bill Strawn in the Charlotte News, and E. T. Krueger in The Nashville Tennessean.

614. Anon. "The Speakers' Column." Town Meeting, 11 (24 May), 12.
Contains a biographical sketch of W to accompany "Are We Solving America's Race Problem?"

615. Anon. "Speaking of Authors . . . These Are in the News." New York Herald Tribune Weekly Book Review (25 February), p. 24.
Book-of-the-Month Club advertisement containing a photograph and biographical sketch of W.

616. Anon. "Stewart's." The Louisville Courier-Journal (1 April), Sec. 3, p. 9.
Includes an advertisement for BB.

617. Anon. "Stimulants for Tucumcari." _Time_, 45 (19 March), 74.
    Article on the radio program "Author Meets the Critics" mentioning W.

618. Anon. "Story of 'Black Boy' Grips Mind Like Bitter Experience." _Eastern Kansas Register_ (20 April), p. 4.
    Favorable review in a Catholic newspaper. W's literary skill is high, but he exaggerates Southern racism and overlooks whites who are favorably disposed toward blacks.

619. Anon. "Svart passionsdrama." _Göteborgs Posten_ (11 March).
    Review of the Swedish production of the play _NS_. Although the reviewer complains of the state theater's recent concentration on plays dealing with American social problems, he observes that Bigger's plight represents that of many of the oppressed. Bigger holds the audience's interest, but as a whole the play relies too much on spectacle.

620. Anon. "Teachers Hear Talk by Wright." _The Hartford Daily Courant_ (27 October), p. 4.
    Account of W's lecture on "The Literature of the Negro in the United States" delivered to the Connecticut State Teachers Convention.

621. Anon. ("El Duende"). "Teatro y cine." _Histonium_, 6 (March), 195-197.
    Contains an announcement of the opening of the play _Sangre Negra_ (_NS_) in Buenos Aires.

622. _____. "Teatro y cine." _Histonium_, 6 (April), 269-271.
    Contains a notice (p. 271) of _Sangre Negra_ (_NS_) emphasizing the exotic (from an Argentinian perspective) elements of the play and praising the acting and direction.

623. Anon. "Ten Christmas Lists of Ten 'Best.'" _The New York Times Book Review_ (2 December), p. 5.
    _BB_ is listed by Lewis Gannett, Harry Hansen, Joseph Henry Jackson, Joseph A. Margolies, A. C. Spectorsky, and Edward Weeks.

624. Anon. "Third Book on Sea War Is Started." _The Columbus_ (Ohio) _Citizen_ (14 January), Magazine Sec., p. 6.
    Mentions that _BB_ will be part of a dual Book-of-the-Month Club selection for March.

625. Anon. "Thrifty Cut Rate Drug Stores." _Los Angeles Times_ (28 October), p. 14.
    Includes an advertisement for _BB_.

626. Anon. "Thursday, November 1, 1945. Richard Wright--Democracy's Unfinished Business," in _Howard University Forum, 1945-1946_. Washington, D. C.: Howard University.
    Announces W's lecture and includes a photograph and a paragraph on his literary and biographical background. "Mentally keen and alert, he interprets social problems with skill, directness and understanding."

627. Anon. "Tidbits About Books and Authors." _Sunday Chicago Bee_ (27 May), Sec. Two, p. 15.
    Notes that _BB_ is second on the national best seller list in nonfiction.

628. Anon. "Tidbits About Books, Authors." _Sunday Chicago Bee_ (14 January), Sec. Two, pp. 12, 15.
    Announces _BB_ mentioning the changes of title and date of publication.

629. Anon. "Tips from the Publishers." _The Publishers' Weekly_, 147 (24 March), 1303.
    Includes details about Harper's advertising campaign for _BB_.

630. Anon. "Tips from the Publishers." _The Publishers' Weekly_, 147 (16 June), 2376-2377.
    Contains an account of the _Life_ magazine photo-article dramatizing _BB_. The photographer, George Karger, spent three weeks in Jackson and Memphis working on the project.

631. Anon. "Tips from the Publishers." _The Publishers' Weekly_, 147 (30 June), 2523-2525.
    Notes that World Publishing Company plans two printings of 50,000 copies each after securing the rights to _BB_ from Harper's.

632. Anon. "To Argue Race Problem." _New York Amsterdam News_ (26 May), Sec. B, p. 1.
    Announces the topic "Are We Solving America's Race Problem?" for America's Town Meeting on 24 May. Elmer Carter and Irving Ives take the affirmative side; W and Jerry Voorhis the negative.

633. Anon. "Today's Profile." _Brooklyn Eagle_ (11 January), p. 9.
    Interview with W concerning his work habits on his autobiography, his criticism of black musicians, his distrust of political parties and trust in the common man, and his prognosis concerning the postwar racial situation.

634. Anon. "Too Good to Be a Negro." The Chicago Defender (10 March), p. 10.
    Editorial criticism of the Time magazine review of BB for calling the work too good to be written by a black and for attempting to separate W from his race.

635. Anon. "Top Best Sellers." Los Angeles Times (18 March), Part III, p. 1.
    Lists BB in third place in the non-fiction category in Los Angeles.

636. Anon. "Top Best Sellers." Los Angeles Times (25 March), Part III, p. 1.
    Lists BB in third place in the non-fiction category in Los Angeles.

637. Anon. "Top Best Sellers." Los Angeles Times (8 April), Part III, p. 1.
    Lists BB in first place in the non-fiction category in Los Angeles.

638. Anon. "Top Best Sellers." Los Angeles Times (15 April), Part III, p. 1.
    Lists BB in first place in the non-fiction category in Los Angeles.

639. Anon. "Top Best Sellers." Los Angeles Times (22 April), Part III, p. 1.
    Lists BB in second place in the non-fiction category in Los Angeles.

640. Anon. "Top Best Sellers." Los Angeles Times (29 April), Part III, p. 1.
    Lists BB in second place in the non-fiction category in Los Angeles and in fourth place in the nation.

641. Anon. "Top Best Sellers." Los Angeles Times (6 May), Part III, p. 1.
    Lists BB in second place in the non-fiction category in Los Angeles and in fourth place in the nation.

642. Anon. "Top Best Sellers." Los Angeles Times (13 May), Part III, p. 1.
    Lists BB in second place in the non-fiction category in Los Angeles and in the nation.

643. Anon. "Top Best Sellers." Los Angeles Times (20 May), Part III, p. 1.
    Lists BB in third place in the non-fiction category in Los Angeles and in first place in the nation.

644. Anon. "Top Best Sellers." Los Angeles Times (27 May), Part III, p. 1.
    Lists BB in second place in the non-fiction category in Los Angeles and in third place in the nation.

645. Anon. "Top Best Sellers." Los Angeles Times (3 June), Part III, p. 1.
    Lists BB in first place in the non-fiction category in Los Angeles and in second place in the nation.

646. Anon. "Top Best Sellers." Los Angeles Times (10 June), Part III, p. 1.
    Lists BB in second place in the non-fiction category in Los Angeles and in the nation.

647. Anon. "Top Best Sellers." Los Angeles Times (17 June), Part III, p. 1.
    Lists BB in first place in the non-fiction category in Los Angeles and in second place in the nation.

648. Anon. "Top Best Sellers." Los Angeles Times (24 June), Part III, p. 1.
    Lists BB in first place in the non-fiction category in Los Angeles and in second place in the nation.

649. Anon. "Top Best Sellers." Los Angeles Times (1 July), Part III, p. 1.
    Lists BB in first place in the non-fiction category in Los Angeles and in second place in the nation.

650. Anon. "Top Best Sellers." Los Angeles Times (8 July), Part III, p. 1.
    Lists BB in second place in the non-fiction category in the nation and in third place in Los Angeles.

651. Anon. "Top Best Sellers." Los Angeles Times (15 July), Part III, p. 1.
    Lists BB in second place in the non-fiction category in the nation and in third place in Los Angeles.

652. Anon. "Top Best Sellers." Los Angeles Times (29 July), Part III, p. 1.
    Lists BB in second place in the non-fiction category in the nation and in fourth place in Los Angeles.

653. Anon. "Top Best Sellers." Los Angeles Times (5 August), Part III, p. 1.
    Lists BB in second place in the non-fiction category in the nation and in third place in Los Angeles.

654. Anon. "Top Best Sellers." Los Angeles Times (12 August), Part III, p. 1.
 Lists BB in first place in the non-fiction category in Los Angeles and in second place in the nation.

655. Anon. "Top Best Sellers." Los Angeles Times (19 August), Part III, p. 1.
 Lists BB in third place in the non-fiction category in Los Angeles and in the nation.

656. Anon. "Top Best Sellers." Los Angeles Times (26 August), Part III, p. 1.
 Lists BB in second place in the non-fiction category in Los Angeles.

657. Anon. "Top Best Sellers." Los Angeles Times (2 September), Part III, p. 1.
 Lists BB in third place in the non-fiction category in Los Angeles.

658. Anon. "Top Best Sellers." Los Angeles Times (9 September), Part III, p. 1.
 Lists BB in first place in the non-fiction category in Los Angeles.

659. Anon. "Top Best Sellers." Los Angeles Times (16 September), Part III, p. 1.
 Lists BB in third place in the non-fiction category in Los Angeles.

660. Anon. "Top Best Sellers." Los Angeles Times (23 September), Part III, p. 1.
 Lists BB in second place in the non-fiction category in Los Angeles.

661. Anon. "Top Best Sellers." Los Angeles Times (7 October), Part III, p. 1.
 Lists BB in third place in the non-fiction category in Los Angeles.

662. Anon. "Top Best Sellers." Los Angeles Times (14 October), Part III, p. 1.
 Lists BB in second place in the non-fiction category in Los Angeles and in fourth place in the nation.

663. Anon. "Top Best Sellers." Los Angeles Times (4 November), Part III, p. 1.
 Lists BB in third place in the non-fiction category in the nation and in fourth place in Los Angeles.

664. Anon. "Top Best Sellers." Los Angeles Times (18 November), Part III, p. 1.
 Lists BB in third place in the non-

fiction category in Los Angeles.

665. Anon. "Top Best Sellers." Los Angeles Times (25 November), Part III, p. 1.
 Lists BB in fourth place in the non-fiction category in Los Angeles.

666. Anon. Town Hall Lecture Division Annual Announcement Fifty-first Season 1945-1946. New York, pp. 4-5.
 Contains a photograph of W with caption. His lecture topic is "The Negro's Contribution to American Culture."

667. Anon. "The Town Hall Presents America's Town Meeting."
 Program of a radio panel discussion held 24 May 1945 on the topic "Are We Solving America's Race Problem?" The participants are W, Irving Ives, Elmer Carter, and Jerry Voorhis.

668. Anon. "Trade Notes and Price Changes." The Retail Bookseller, 48 (August), 125-128.
 Notes that World Publishing Company is taking over manufacture and distribution of BB.

669. Anon. "Two Reviews of 'Black Boy' Are in Negro Story." The Chicago Defender (26 May), p. 7.
 Refers to reviews by Richard Bentley and F. K. Richter. Also quotes from an article by W in Tomorrow.

670. Anon. Unidentified clipping (c. February).
 Associated Negro Press photograph of W with caption announcing the publication of BB.

671. Anon. Untitled clipping. The Austinite (28 March).
 Review of BB questioning the veracity of the unrelieved bleakness of W's portrayal of his childhood. The effect of the book, intended to shock the reader, is "disturbing and terrible."
 Reprinted: 1978.209.

672. Anon. Untitled clipping. The Columbus (Ga.) Ledger (c. 4 January).
 Announces that BB will be part of a dual Book-of-the-Month Club selection in March.

673. Anon. Untitled clipping. Dayton Daily News (8 April).
 Brief report on the good sales of BB. Asks whether W is buying several houses in Greenwich Village.

674. Anon. Untitled clipping. Headlines and Pictures (February).

Photograph of W with caption mentioning BB.

675. Anon. Untitled clipping. New York
Herald Tribune (c. 15 April).
 Announces John O'Hara's appearance on
the "Author Meets the Critics" radio
program. W will be one of the critics.

676. Anon. Untitled clipping. Ohio State
News (c. March).
 Associated Negro Press photograph of
W with caption announcing the publi-
cation of BB.

677. Anon. Untitled clipping. Puerto
Rico World Journal (2 April).
 Excerpt from a column summarizing
certain episodes in BB and comparing
American to Nazi racism.

678. Anon. Untitled note. The Springfield (Mass.) Sunday Union and Republican (3 June), p. 4D.
 Concerns the sale of foreign rights
to BB.

679. Anon. "Wednesday, November 7, 1945,
Richard Wright." Unidentified clipping.
 Brochure or magazine announcement of
W's lecture on "The American Negro's
Contribution to Literature." The pre-
siding officer is Albert P. Morwitz.

680. Anon. "The Week's Best Sellers."
The Louisville Courier-Journal (22
April), Sec. 3, p. 10.
 Lists BB in second place in the non-
fiction category.

681. Anon. "What America Is Reading."
New York Herald Tribune Weekly Book
Review (18 March), p. 23.
 Lists BB in eleventh place in the
nonfiction category.

682. Anon. "What America Is Reading."
New York Herald Tribune Weekly Book
Review (25 March), p. 23.
 Lists BB in eighth place in the non-
fiction category.

683. Anon. "What America Is Reading."
New York Herald Tribune Weekly Book
Review (1 April), p. 26.
 Lists BB in fifth place in the non-
fiction category.

684. Anon. "What America Is Reading."
New York Herald Tribune Weekly Book
Review (8 April), p. 23.
 Lists BB in fifth place in the non-
fiction category.

685. Anon. "What America Is Reading."
New York Herald Tribune Weekly Book
Review (15 April), p. 23.

Lists BB in second place in the non-
fiction category.

686. Anon. "What America Is Reading."
New York Herald Tribune Weekly Book
Review (22 April), p. 24.
 Lists BB in first place in the non-
fiction category.

687. Anon. "What America Is Reading."
New York Herald Tribune Weekly Book
Review (29 April), p. 24.
 Lists BB in third place in the non-
fiction category.

688. Anon. "What America Is Reading."
New York Herald Tribune Weekly Book
Review (6 May), p. 23.
 Lists BB in second place in the non-
fiction category.

689. Anon. "What America Is Reading."
New York Herald Tribune Weekly Book
Review (13 May), p. 23.
 Lists BB in second place in the non-
fiction category.

690. Anon. "What America Is Reading."
New York Herald Tribune Weekly Book
Review (20 May), p. 27.
 Lists BB in second place in the non-
fiction category.

691. Anon. "What America Is Reading."
New York Herald Tribune Weekly Book
Review (27 May), p. 23.
 Lists BB in second place in the non-
fiction category.

692. Anon. "What America Is Reading."
New York Herald Tribune Weekly Book
Review (3 June), p. 19.
 Lists BB in second place in the non-
fiction category.

693. Anon. "What America Is Reading."
New York Herald Tribune Weekly Book
Review (10 June), p. 23.
 Lists BB in second place in the non-
fiction category.

694. Anon. "What America Is Reading."
New York Herald Tribune Weekly Book
Review (17 June), p. 23.
 Lists BB in second place in the non-
fiction category.

695. Anon. "What America Is Reading."
New York Herald Tribune Weekly Book
Review (24 June), p. 19.
 Lists BB in second place in the non-
fiction category.

696. Anon. "What America Is Reading."
New York Herald Tribune Weekly Book
Review (1 July), p. 15.
 Lists BB in second place in the non-
fiction category.

697. Anon. "What America Is Reading."
New York Herald Tribune Weekly Book
Review (8 July), p. 19.
    Lists BB in second place in the non-
    fiction category.

698. Anon. "What America Is Reading."
New York Herald Tribune Weekly Book
Review (15 July), p. 15.
    Lists BB in fourth place in the non-
    fiction category.

699. Anon. "What America Is Reading."
New York Herald Tribune Weekly Book
Review (22 July), p. 15.
    Lists BB in third place in the non-
    fiction category.

700. Anon. "What America Is Reading."
New York Herald Tribune Weekly Book
Review (29 July), p. 27.
    Lists BB in fourth place in the non-
    fiction category.

701. Anon. "What America Is Reading."
New York Herald Tribune Weekly Book
Review (5 August), p. 31.
    Lists BB in sixth place in the non-
    fiction category.

702. Anon. "What America Is Reading."
New York Herald Tribune Weekly Book
Review (12 August), p. 19.
    Lists BB in fourth place in the non-
    fiction category.

703. Anon. "What America Is Reading."
New York Herald Tribune Weekly Book
Review (19 August), p. 23.
    Lists BB in sixth place in the non-
    fiction category.

704. Anon. "What America Is Reading."
New York Herald Tribune Weekly Book
Review (26 August), p. 31.
    Lists BB in third place in the non-
    fiction category.

705. Anon. "What America Is Reading."
New York Herald Tribune Weekly Book
Review (2 September), p. 11.
    Lists BB in fourth place in the non-
    fiction category.

706. Anon. "What America Is Reading."
New York Herald Tribune Weekly Book
Review (9 September), p. 23.
    Lists BB in third place in the non-
    fiction category.

707. Anon. "What America Is Reading."
New York Herald Tribune Weekly Book
Review (16 September), p. 27.
    Lists BB in fourth place in the non-
    fiction category.

708. Anon. "What America Is Reading."
New York Herald Tribune Weekly Book
Review (23 September), p. 31.
    Lists BB in fifth place in the non-
    fiction category.

709. Anon. "What America Is Reading."
New York Herald Tribune Weekly Book
Review (30 September), p. 31.
    Lists BB in fourth place in the non-
    fiction category.

710. Anon. "What America Is Reading."
New York Herald Tribune Weekly Book
Review (7 October), p. 27.
    Lists BB in third place in the non-
    fiction category.

711. Anon. "What America Is Reading."
New York Herald Tribune Weekly Book
Review (14 October), p. 31.
    Lists BB in fifth place in the non-
    fiction category.

712. Anon. "What America Is Reading."
New York Herald Tribune Weekly Book
Review (21 October), p. 27.
    Lists BB in fifth place in the non-
    fiction category.

713. Anon. "What America Is Reading."
New York Herald Tribune Weekly Book
Review (28 October), p. 27.
    Lists BB in fifth place in the non-
    fiction category.

714. Anon. "What America Is Reading."
New York Herald Tribune Weekly Book
Review (4 November), p. 27.
    Lists BB in ninth place in the non-
    fiction category.

715. Anon. "What America Is Reading."
New York Herald Tribune Weekly Book
Review (11 November), p. 47.
    Lists BB in tenth place in the non-
    fiction category.

716. Anon. "What America Is Reading."
New York Herald Tribune Weekly Book
Review (18 November), p. 31.
    Lists BB in eleventh place in the
    nonfiction category.

717. Anon. "What America Is Reading."
New York Herald Tribune Weekly Book
Review (25 November), p. 35.
    Lists BB in eighth place in the non-
    fiction category.

718. Anon. "What America Is Reading."
New York Herald Tribune Weekly Book
Review (2 December), p. 47.
    Lists BB in eleventh place in the
    nonfiction category.

719. Anon. "What America Is Reading."
New York Herald Tribune Weekly Book
Review (9 December), p. 31.
    Lists BB in seventeenth place in the

nonfiction category.

720. Anon. "What America Is Reading."
New York Herald Tribune Weekly Book
Review (16 December), p. 19.
  Lists BB in fourteenth place in the
  nonfiction category.

721. Anon. "What America Is Reading."
New York Herald Tribune Weekly Book
Review (23 December), p. 11.
  Lists BB in eighteenth place in the
  nonfiction category.

721a. Anon. "What Are Your Special Curi-
osities?" Book-of-the-Month Club News
(November), pp. 23-27.
  Contains a notice of Primer for White
  Folks mentioning W (p. 27).

722. Anon. "What Century?" Time, 45 (30
April), 8.
  Reports that the post commander at
  Deming Army Airfield banned BB from
  the base library and destroyed the
  copy.

723. Anon. "What Fear Can Do to a Boy."
The Detroit Free Press (4 March), Entertainment Sec., p. 10.
  Review of BB emphasizing W's bitterness. The book may harm race relations, but it is prophetic and reveals much about the racial problem.

724. Anon. "What SRL Reviewers Are Giv-
ing for Christmas: The Selections of 56
Contributors and Editors." The Saturday
Review of Literature, 28 (1 December),
20-21.
  BB is selected by Maurice Basseches,
  Robert Bierstadt, Alexander Laing,
  and Robert E. Spiller.

725. Anon. "What's Going on at Hall
Branch Library." Chicago Sunday Bee (11
March), Sec. Two, p. 15.
  Announces a lecture by Fern Gayden on
  BB.

726. Anon. "What's Your Literary I. Q.?"
Chicago Sunday Bee (22 April), Sec. Two,
pp. 15, 23.
  Includes a question on BB.

727. Anon. "White Folks Primer." Trenton
(N. J.) Sunday Times Advertiser (19
August), Part 4, p. 3.
  Favorable review of Bucklin Moon's
  anthology Primer for White Folks
  mentioning W.

728. Anon. "Why Richard Wright Wrote
Black Boy." The Negro, 3 (July), 49-50.
  Condensed reprint of 1945.451.

729. Anon. "Womrath Recommends." The New
York Times.
  Book store advertisement listing BB.

730. Anon. "Wonderful!" The New York
Times Book Review (1 April), p. 8.
  Advertisement for Gertrude Stein's
  Wars I Have Seen quoting W's PM re-
  view.

731. Anon. "Workshop in the Hills--Where
Writers and Would-Be's Hobnob with Ce-
lebrities: Taught by Writers and Poets."
The Christian Science Monitor (14 July),
p. 7.
  Notes that W is a member of the Bread
  Loaf Writers' Conference staff for
  1945.

732. Anon. "Wright (Ricardo)," in Diccionario enciclopédico abreviado. Second
edition. Ed. Julio Rey Pastor. Vol. 6.
Buenos Aires: Espasa-Calpe Argentina, p.
888.
  Brief biographical note.

733. Anon. "Wright, Richard." Book News
(December).
  Favorable notice of BB.

734. Anon. "Wright, Richard." The Publishers' Weekly, 147 (3 March), 1055.
  Brief notice of BB.

735. Anon. "Wright, Richard. Black Boy."
The Guide Post, 20 (June-July), 11.
  Rather unfavorable notice discounting
  racism as a factor in W's suffering.

736. Anon. "Wright, Richard. Black boy,
a record of childhood and youth." The
Booklist, 41 (1 April), 224.
  Brief, mixed notice complaining of a
  possibly "distorted emphasis" and
  calling the book "grim reading."

737. Anon. "Wright, Richard. Black Boy,
a record of childhood and youth." The
United States Quarterly Book List, 1
(June), 15-16.
  Favorable review of a "powerfully
  written, violent story" that is simultaneously a social document and an
  entwicklungsroman. BB compares favorably with W's fiction. "His psychological penetration is deeper, his
  style is sharper."
  Reprinted: 1978.209.

738. Anon. "Wright, Richard. BLACK BOY.
Harper." Bulletin from Virginia Kirkus
Bookshop Service, 13 (1 January), 9.
  Revised reprint of 1944.55. Claims
  that the work leaves a "bad taste in
  the mouth" of the reader.

739. Anon. "Wright to Return." The Chicago Sun Book Week (9 December), p. 21.
  Announces that W will return to Chicago to speak at the Temple Church.

He had cancelled a previous engagement because of a sudden illness.

740. Anon. "Wright's New Book Is 'Book of the Month.'" Unidentified clipping (c. March).
Reprint of 1945.741.

741. _____. "Wright's New Work Selected as 'Book of Month.'" Detroit Tribune (10 March), p. 6.
Associated Negro Press article on the selection of BB and early favorable reviews of the book.
Reprinted: 1945.740, 742.

742. _____. "Wright's New Work Selected by the 'Book of the Month' Club." Unidentified clipping (c. March).
Reprint of 1945.741.

743. Anon. "Writers' Conferences Convene During August." The Boston Herald (25 July), p. 7.
Announces W's participation in the Bread Loaf Writers' Conference.

744. Anon. "Writes New Book." Unidentified clipping.
Associated Negro Press photograph of W with caption mentioning BB.

745. Anon. "Yo ví 'Sangre Negra.'" Unidentified clipping.
Advertisement for the play NS in Buenos Aires with an endorsement by Ginger Rogers.

746. Anon. "You Can Begin Your Subscription with Any One of These Nation-Wide Best Sellers." Unidentified clipping.
Contains a brief comment on W and BB, which is "destined to become one of the most widely discussed books of our generation."

747. Anthony, Joseph. "Books in Review." Liberty, 22 (19 May), 54.
Favorable notice of BB, "a bitter and brilliant book of reminiscences," emphasizing W's dismissal of the notion that black people have a rich emotional life.

748. Apilado, Ruth. "'Black Boy,' Not Picture of Negro." The Chicago Defender (9 June), p. 14.
Letter to the editor denying the representativeness of W's self-portrait and criticizing his low opinion of black people. Despite W's opinion, black people do have deep emotions.

749. _____. "Browsing with Books." Sunday Chicago Bee (3 June), Sec. Two, p. 15.
Unfavorable review of BB arguing that W's childhood was atypical and rebut-

ting W's claim that black life is emotionally barren.

750. Appel, David. "Pared Down to Essentials: High Spots of the Spring Lists." The Publishers' Weekly, 147 (27 January), 425-428.
Includes a brief notice of BB, "potent stuff indeed" (p. 427).

751. _____. "Pre-Review of Black Boy," in Pre-Reviews of Black Boy. New York: Book-of-the-Month Club, March, p. 1.
Very favorable notice.

752. _____. "Richard Wright's Autobiography." Chicago Daily News (28 February), p. 19.
Favorable review of BB summarizing briefly the narrative. Appel calls the work "an intense and bitter treatment . . . a blunt and forceful indictment."

753. _____. "Turning a New Leaf." Chicago Daily News (17 January), p. 15.
Announces BB, "potent stuff."

754. B., M. "Books: 'Black Boy,' by Richard Wright." Fraternal Outlook (June-July), p. 12.
Mixed review emphasizing the universal implications of W's revelation of racial oppression but complaining of his subjectivity and pessimism. The book "is a forceful reminder to the progressive people of America that there is a big anti-fascist job yet to be done."

755. Babb, Stanley E. "Richard Wright's Autobiography, 'Black Boy,' a Grim Chronicle of Negro Life in the South." Galveston Daily News (8 April), p. 17.
Rather unfavorable review noting the work's shocking bluntness and vehemence. Babb believes that W's rebellious temperament causes him to exaggerate Southern racism. The story is personal, not representative.

756. Babcock, Frederic. "Among the Authors." Chicago Sunday Tribune (23 September), Part 6, p. 16.
Mentions meeting W at the Bread Loaf Writers' Conference.

757. _____. "Among the Authors." Chicago Sunday Tribune (30 December), Part 6, p. 10.
Notes that the Chicago Council Against Racial and Religious Discrimination has listed BB as one of the ten best books on intergroup relations for 1945.

758. _____. "10 Books Listed for Improving Race Relations." Chicago Sunday

Tribune (3 June), Part 6, p. 17.
Includes BB.

759. Baldwin, Mary. "Richard Wright and the Negro." Liberty, 22 (10 November), 10.
Letter to the editor responding to the magazine's condensation of BB by minimizing W's racial hardships, opposing social integration, and urging W and other successful blacks to do more for their own race.

760. Barish, Mildred. "Books: The American Negro." Opinion, 15 (April), 27-30.
Favorable review of BB and Walter White's A Rising Wind. Praises BB as "a terse, explosive yet deeply poignant story." Relates W's struggle for dignity to that of the oppressed everywhere.

761. Basso, Hamilton. "Thomas Jefferson and the Black Boy." The New Yorker, 21 (10 March), 86, 88-89.
Favorable review of BB stressing its truthfulness as a human document. The Dostoevskian underworld of black life which the book reveals will appall many readers, but it represents an American reality.

762. Bates, Graham. "Cross Section 1945." Book-of-the-Month Club News (December), p. 12.
Lists W as a "familiar" contributor to Seaver's anthology.

763. Bates, Ralph. "Mr. Seaver's Annual Potpourri." The New York Times Book Review (9 December), pp. 4, 20.
Mixed review of Cross Section 1945 calling "Early Days in Chicago" a "deeply moving" story.

764. Beach, Joseph Warren. "The Dilemma of the Black Man in a White World." The New York Times Book Review (2 December), p. 2.
Includes a review of If He Hollers Let Him Go comparing its protagonist to Bigger Thomas. Himes's novel does not have "the power and sweep, the subtlety and depth, of 'Native Son.'"

765. Beck, Clyde. "Pre-Review of Black Boy," in Pre-Reviews of Black Boy. New York: Book-of-the-Month Club, March, p. 2.
Favorable notice emphasizing the work's universality.

766. Becker, Charlotte. "Pre-Review of Black Boy," in Pre-Reviews of Black Boy. New York: Book-of-the-Month Club, March, p. 1.
Favorable notice.

767. Becker, May Lamberton. "The Reader's Guide." New York Herald Tribune Weekly Book Review (1 April), p. 21.
Contains a favorable notice of BB emphasizing its emotional power.

768. Bell, Agnes and Lillian Kinchloe. "Orchids to Richard Wright for Town Hall Broadcast." The Chicago Defender (23 June), p. 12.
Letter to the editor praising W's remarks at the Town Hall symposium on 24 May entitled "Are We Solving America's Race Problems?"

769. Bell, Mrs. A. L., Lillian I. Kinchloe, and Mrs. Bernice Morton. "Puzzled by Richard Wright's Marriage." The Chicago Defender (14 July), p. 14.
Letter to the editor criticizing W's marriage to a white woman, deemed inconsistent with his views toward whites expressed in BB.

770. Bentley, Richard. "Black Boy by Richard Wright." Negro Story, 1 (May-June), 91-92.
Favorable review emphasizing the sociological message of the book. All black people have likewise experienced racism. W's portrait of black degradation, brought about by the racist environment, is true. "Black Boy tells a much needed story and tells it in poetic prose, in meaningful word pictures."
Reprinted: 1978.209.

771. Bergman, A. Gunnar. "En ung amerikans levnadshistoria." Stockholm Afton Tidningen (11 March).
Highly favorable review of the Swedish production of the play NS. Emphasizes the ironies of Bigger's position as an outsider in his native land. The production improves on the treatment of similar issues in Tobacco Road, also produced by the state theater.

772. Beyer, Nils. "Märklig Negerpjäs i Göteborg." Stockholm Morgon Tidningen Social Demokraten (11 March), p. 4.
Review of the Swedish production of the play NS with a lengthy discussion of the psychological complexity and overt violence of the novel. Despite Paul Green's skillful dramatization, the production reduces the intensity and complexity of the novel, though the early scenes in the black slum are powerful.

773. Bilbo, Theodore G. Untitled speech. Congressional Record, 91, Part 5 (27 June), 6808.
During the course of a Senate filibuster, Bilbo denounces W and BB,

calling it "the dirtiest, filthiest, lousiest, most obscene piece of writing that I have ever seen in print." Reprinted: 1971.43; 1973.59, 60.

774. Birkins, R. Parker. "The Negro Problem." The American Mercury, 61 (December), 761.
Letter to the editor taking issue with Henry Steele Commager's remarks on BB in "The Negro Problem in Our Democracy." Birkins maintains that W did not learn of black subordination as a very small child, that he did not hate whites, and that he did not seek revenge.

775. Blalock, John V. "Notes and Reviews: The Case of a Scarred Body and Mind." The Durham Herald-Sun (4 March), Sec. II, p. 5.
Unfavorable review of BB. Blalock doubts the social utility of such extreme hatred and bitterness as W's. His suffering actually derived more from his family than from whites. Though well written, BB is "the confused thinking of a talented man."

776. Blodgett, Phil. "New Books." Astoria Evening Astorian-Budget (12 March), p. 4.
Contains a favorable notice of BB, an account that is "powerful, dramatic and unfortunately--true."

777. B---m, B. "Negerdrama pa Stadsteatern" Göteborgs Handels-och Sjöforts Tidningen (13 March).
Favorable review of the Swedish production of the play NS, which was enthusiastically received by the audience. Bertil Anderberg's successful empathy with the role of Bigger helps to overcome the problems which reduce Bigger to a less complex character than he was in the novel. Summarizing the novel, the reviewer notes that the play lacks its depth.

778. Boettcher, Miss. "It's a Funny World." Liberty, 22 (24 November), 8.
Letter to the editor applauding the magazine's condensation of BB. The nineteen-year-old, white Miss Boettcher finds corroboration of white racism in her own observation.

779. Bohn, William E. "The Home Front: The Black Boys." The New Leader, 28 (10 March), p. 7.
Favorable review of BB commenting on the issue of fact vs. fiction, the reluctant acceptance of the book by black reviewers, and W's theme of rebellion. Calling W "a black Erskine Caldwell," Bohn esteems him as "an authentic artist [who] demands the freedom which is necessary to artists."

780. Bond, Alice Dixon. "Pre-Review of Black Boy," in Pre-Reviews of Black Boy. New York: Book-of-the-Month Club, March, p. 1.
Very favorable notice.

781. Bontemps, Arna. "Negro Life in a Northern City." New York Herald Tribune Weekly Book Review (28 October), p. 4.
Review of Black Metropolis mentioning W's serious, subjective introduction. The study confirms the existence of the Bigger type.

782. _____. "The Two Harlems." The American Scholar, 14 (Spring), 167-173.
Notes that W no longer lives in Harlem.
Reprinted in condensed form: 1945.783.

783. _____. "The Two Harlems." Negro Digest, 3 (June), 57-61.
Condensed reprint of 1945.782.

784. Botkin, B. A. "Special Qualities of Midland Writing." The Chicago Sun Book Week (2 December), p. 5.
Lists W as a regionalist in an urban tradition.

785. Boutell, Clip. "Authors Are Like People." New York Post (8 March), p. 19.
Notes that Mrs. Harry Scherman reports that BB is a favorite topic of conversation at cocktail parties.

786. _____. "Authors Are Like People." New York Post (6 December), p. 15 B.
Extends Christmas greetings to W "for the courage and talent he poured into his partial autobiography, 'Black Boy.'"

787. _____. "Authors Are Like People: American Folklore--Mystery Hour." New York Post (5 April), p. 19.
Mentions that 415,000 copies of BB are in print. Conveys rumor that W is buying two houses in Greenwich Village.
Reprinted: 1945.791, 792.

788. _____. "Authors Are Like People: Richard Wright, Edgar Snow and Sinclair Lewis." New York Post (1 February), p. 18.
Includes a report on a luncheon-interview with W on postwar racial problems in the United States and abroad. Boutell also relates the story of W's first encounter with the writing of Mencken.
Reprinted: 1945.790.

789. _____. "Authors Are Like People: Tales of Two Cities--Writer from Columbus." New York Post (21 February), p. 13.
Mentions Paul Griffith's projected Life magazine article on the background of BB.

790. _____. "Books and Authors: Negro Advises an Indian on the 'Way to Freedom.'" Portland Oregon Daily Journal (18 February), p. 4.
Reprint of 1945.788.

791. _____. "'Dark of the Moon' Bodes Well for Theatre's Future." Portland Oregon Sunday Journal (22 April), Pacific Parade Magazine Sec., p. 13.
Reprint of 1945.787.

792. _____. "Henry Wallace Due for Publicity: 'Dark of Moon' C..lled Tolerance Play." The Washington Post (15 April), p. 12S.
Reprint of 1945.787.

793. _____. "Thursday Books." Unidentified clipping.
Quotes from a letter to W by the son of Uncle Hoskins of BB. The letter verifies W's account of Uncle Hoskins's death.

794. Bower, Helen. "The Book Rack: Wind Rises to Blow Us to World War III?" The Detroit Free Press (4 March), Part Two, p. 6.
Contains a favorable notice of BB and a photograph of W. The book is bitter and sordid, but it confronts important issues.

795. _____. "Pre-Review of Black Boy," in Pre-Reviews of Black Boy. New York: Book-of-the-Month Club, March, p. 2.
Mixed notice calling the work "sordid to a degree of sadism."

796. Bowman, Betty. "Wilma Jones Again Charms Her Big Audience of Woman's Club, Redondo Beach." Redondo Beach Daily Breeze (20 March), p. 5.
Account of BB, which made the reviewer "ashamed to be a member of the white race."

797. Bradford, David H. "Black Boy: A Record of Childhood and Youth. By Richard Wright." The Journal of Negro History, 30 (July), 337-339.
Reviewing W's autobiography in the light of his own experience as a black child in South Carolina, Bradford finds it frank but true. W emphasizes environment rather than personality. Bradford believes that materialism as well as Southern racism

is responsible for the tragedy depicted in BB.

798. Bragdon, Marshall. "Pre-Review of Black Boy," in Pre-Reviews of Black Boy. New York: Book-of-the-Month Club, March, p. 6.
Favorable notice contrasting BB to Anything Can Happen.

799. _____. "Thoughts on Reading 'Black Boy.'" The Springfield (Mass.) Sunday Union and Republican (4 March), p. 4D.
Favorable review emphasizing the blight of racism on W's sensibility. His case is not typical, but his indictment is needed. Bragdon contrasts Gordon Parks to W.
Reprinted: 1978.209.

800. Braggiotti, Mary. "Misery Begets Genius." New York Post (20 March), p. 21.
"Close-up" of W reviewing his life as described in BB and sketching his subsequent career. Braggiotti mentions his working habits and his family life and describes his physical appearance and speech habits. She quotes W on the emotional deprivation of black juvenile delinquents he observed in a Brooklyn courtroom, and on the probability of racial trouble as black expectations rise after the war.

801. Brandon, Mrs. Zack. Untitled clipping. Oklahoma City Star (6 April).
Favorable notice of BB pointing out that "great inner passion" went into its writing.
Reprinted: 1978.209.

802. Braude, Jo M. "Black Boy, by Richard Wright." Chicago Jewish Forum, 3 (Summer), 288-289.
Favorable review of a thought-provoking book which challenges white feelings of superiority. Braude finds especially intriguing W's explanation of petty thievery by blacks.
Reprinted: 1978.209.

803. Breit, Harvey. "Books." Mademoiselle, 20 (April), 177, 248-249.
Includes a favorable review of BB, which Breit calls not only "naked and bold and honest and plain and exciting" but "passionate, colorful, moving and, in spite of Wright, cheerful." He attributes W's survival and rise to his mother's courage.

804. Briscoe, Sherman. "You Ought to Know More About Black Boy." Pulse, 3 (May), 23.
Unfavorable review. Briscoe's own experiences growing up black in Mis-

sissippi verify W's depiction of racism, but the book suffers from hopelessness and obscenity.

805. Broaddus, Marian Howe. "Clearing the Desk." The El Paso Times (23 September), p. 6.
Cites an unnamed "authority" who includes BB in a list of ten books suitable for a memorial library in honor of Ernie Pyle.

806. Brodkin, Irving. "Black Boy: a Record of Childhood and Youth." New Mexico Quarterly, 15 (Fall), 369-371.
Favorable review of BB, which affords a glimpse of the raw material which ultimately developed into NS. BB reveals how interrelated the plight of the black man and that of the white man are. Its power cannot be conveniently compartmentalized. Rather than lamenting the limitations imposed on W's life, BB records his refusal to be claimed by external forces.

807. Brown, Earl. "Timely Topics." New York Amsterdam News (7 April), p. 6.
Highly favorable review of BB. Brown refutes the critics who think that W is dishonest in depicting racial problems. "Professionally, Black Boy is a perfect writing job: every sentence and every paragraph stand out as a work of art."

808. Brown, Lester. "Lester Brown Comments Briefly on 'Black Metropolis.'" Sunday Chicago Bee (11 November), Sec. Two, p. 16.
Calls W's introduction "brilliant."

809. [Browning, Alice C.]. "Just to Mention That . . ." Negro Story, 1 (March-April), 53-56.
Pleads for a story from W for the anniversary issue of the magazine and comments on Ben Burns's column on BB.

810. _____. "Just to Mention That--." Negro Story, 1 (May-June), 84-88.
Praises BB for confronting American problems. "Only intense love of country could impel a writer to so condemn it" (p. 85).

811. _____. "Just to Mention That--." Negro Story, 2 (August-September), 51-57.
Mentions BB as a best seller (p. 55) and notes that W "once turned down a post office clerkship to take his chance as a writer--We're glad he did" (p. 57).

812. _____. "Our Contributors." Negro Story, 1 (December 1944-January 1945), 2, 62.
Mentions Jack Conroy's relation to W.

813. Burke, Kenneth. A Grammar of Motives. New York: Prentice-Hall, p. 339.
Discusses NS to distinguish between "two kinds of epitomizing . . . one imagistic and the other conceptual."

814. Burnett, Whit. "Biographies and Bibliographies," in his This Is My Best. New York: The Dial Press, pp. 1119-1169.
Reprint of 1942.211.

815. Burns, Ben. "American Viewpoint: Double-Talk Prose; Common Sense Talk." The Chicago Defender, National Edition (27 October), p. 11.
Interview with Gertrude Stein including extensive quotation of her remarks on W, whom she regards as "the best American writer today. Only one or two creative writers like him come along in a generation. Wright follows in the tradition of creative writers like Twain, Henry James, Howells, Walt Whitman, and Gertrude Stein."

816. _____. "Off the Book Shelf." The Chicago Defender (6 October), p. 17.
Contains a notice of Era Bell Thompson's American Daughter contrasting it to NS.

817. _____. "Off the Book Shelf." The Chicago Defender (17 November), p. 17.
Contains a favorable review of Black Metropolis pointing out that it complements factually the fiction of NS.

818. _____. "Off the Book Shelf." The Chicago Defender (8 December), p. 15.
Contains an unfavorable review of "Early Days in Chicago." "It is banal and crude at moments, too talky and agitational in others."

819. _____. "Off the Book Shelf: Books A-Coming: Part II. " The Chicago Defender (3 February), p. 15.
Mentions W briefly.

820. _____. "Off the Book Shelf: Gunther Tries a Novel." The Chicago Defender (17 February), p. 15.
Announces that the publication date for BB is 28 February.

821. _____. "Off the Book Shelf: New Books A-Coming." The Chicago Defender (27 January), p. 15.
Announces BB as "the biggest book of the spring" and predicts a lively controversy. "Wright has already stated that he expects 'the race' to be mad about his frankness."

822. _____. "Off the Book Shelf: Return

of The Gadfly." The Chicago Defender (9 June), p. 14.
Contains favorable comparison of BB to the short stories about youth in Time to Be Young.

823. _____. "Off the Book Shelf: Richard Wright's 'Black Boy.'" The Chicago Defender (3 March), p. 11.
Unfavorable review attacking the work's sadism and negativism. It will have an unfortunate effect on the reading public. Burns wonders why W would so graphically emphasize the worst aspects of his childhood. Reprinted: 1945.824; 1978.209.

824. _____. "Off the Book Shelf: Richard Wright's 'Black Boy.'" The Chicago Defender (20 October), p. 19.
Reprint of 1945.823.

825. _____. "Off the Book Shelf: White Authors and Negro Books." The Chicago Defender (30 June), p. 15.
Compares NS and BB favorably to Miriam Monger's Tales from Toussaint and Lillian Smith's Strange Fruit.

826. _____. "Off the Book Shelf: Wright's 'Black Boy.'" The Chicago Defender (13 January), p. 15.
Explains the circumstances of the impending publication of the autobiography. Cites W's speech at Fisk University as its origin, quoting W himself on the matter.

827. Burns, Richard. "Color Craze." Negro Digest, 3 (June), 62.
Reports that the white newspaper in W's home town, Natchez, Mississippi, refused an advertisement for BB.

828. Butcher, Fanny. "'Black Boy' Travels Far." Chicago Sunday Tribune (3 June), p. 18.
Reports international interest in W's work. Rights to BB have been purchased by publishers in Sweden, Palestine, and Brazil, among others. The play NS premiered simultaneously in Argentina and Sweden in March.

829. _____. "Fanny Butcher Surveys Year's Memorable Books." Chicago Sunday Tribune (2 December), Part Four, p. 6.
Includes favorable comment on BB, "one of the greatest human documents of our day."

830. _____. "The Literary Spotlight." Chicago Sunday Tribune (4 March), Part 6, p. 14.
Contains a favorable review of BB, "one of the great human documents of our day." The power of the book derives more from the account of the

struggle for actual survival against poverty than from racial conflict. W does not explain how he emerged from Bigger-like savagery to literary achievement.

831. _____. "The Literary Spotlight." Chicago Sunday Tribune (3 June), Part 6, p. 18.
Cites the popularity of W's books abroad.

832. _____. "The Literary Spotlight." Chicago Sunday Tribune (22 July), Part 6, p. 13.
Notes that W will be on the staff of the Bread Loaf Writers' Conference in Middlebury, Vermont.

833. _____. "The Literary Spotlight." Chicago Sunday Tribune (23 December), Part 6, p. 10.
Includes BB in a list of books with colors in their titles.

834. _____. "Pre-Review of Black Boy," in Pre-Reviews of Black Boy. New York: Book-of-the-Month Club, March, p. 2.
Very favorable notice of "one of the greatest human documents of our day."

835. Cady, Ernest. "Reader's Note Book." The Columbus (Ohio) Sunday Dispatch (11 March), p. 4-A.
Favorable review of BB praising W's prose style as compared to that of other realists such as Dreiser, Anderson, and Farrell. One-sided "in that it gives only the darkest and most painful side of Negro life in the South," the book is nevertheless honest in its unfavorable depiction of both blacks and whites.

836. _____. "Reader's Note Book." The Columbus (Ohio) Sunday Dispatch (30 December), p. 4-A.
Names BB as the best serious book of personal experiences published in 1945.

837. Canby, Henry Seidel. "Radio Script on Black Boy, WQXR." 2 pp.
Highly favorable review comparing BB to autobiographies by Benjamin Franklin and Mary Antin. It is a genuine literary work, an imaginative presentation of a life. Though "objective, intensely, sometimes terribly, realistic," it is not mainly a work of protest. Despite the grimness of the story, the reader is left with hope by this example of individual achievement.

838. Canfield, Dorothy. "Black Boy by Richard Wright." Book-of-the-Month Club News (February), pp. 2-3.

Highly favorable review. W's "self-possession" and stylistic "restraint" make BB a great autobiography in additon to a valuable historical, psychological, and social document. The very fact that W seems unaware of the presence of well-intentioned whites indicates that their efforts have not been sufficient.
Reprinted: 1945.839.

839. _____. "A Slant on Books." The Elizabeth City Daily Advance (2 March), p. 6.
Reprint of 1945.838.

840. Carter, Elmer, George V. Denny, Jr., Irving Ives, Richard Wright, and Jerry Voorhis. "Are We Solving America's Race Problem?" Town Meeting, 11 (24 May), 3-22.
See 1945.875.

841. Carter, Michael. "Book-of-the-Month Author Talks for Afro: Richard Wright Believes Fear, Not Sex, Governs Race Relations." The Baltimore Afro-American (13 January), pp. 1, 19.
In this interview W comments on race relations, trade unions, BB and "The Man Who Lived Underground," black people and the war effort, foreign policy and race, black nationalism, and his readings in psychology. Carter provides descriptions of W's apartment, personal life, and habits of composition and conversation. "Wright is one of the few great novelists in America."

842. _____. "Richard Wright Talks to the AFRO." The Baltimore Afro-American (24 March), p. 5.
Favorable review of BB, but Carter considers W's case too exaggerated to be typical. After summarizing the autobiography, Carter cites unfavorable reviews by W. E. B. Du Bois and Samuel Sillen, together with W's responses in an interview. W also comments on the origin and expected social effects of BB.

843. Cayton, Horace R. "Black Boy: Negroes' Hatred of Whites and Fear of His Hate in Wright's Autobiography." The Pittsburgh Courier (10 March), p. 7.
Discusses the "fear-hate-fear" complex as a key to understanding BB and black life in America. W's book is "the most meaningful analysis of Negro personality that I have encountered." W triumphed over his own hate and fear by writing BB.

844. _____. "Fear and Hunger in Black America." The Chicago Sun Book Week (4 March), p. 3.

Favorable review of BB defending its accuracy and representativeness. Americans must face the fact of racism. W's book sets a high standard for its genre.

845. _____. "Frightened Children of Frightened Parents." Twice a Year, 12-13 (Spring-Summer, Fall-Winter), 262-269.
Favorable essay-review of BB, with attention also to NS and TMBV. W's constant subject "is how it feels to be a Negro in the United States" (p. 262). His treatment of this subject utilizes anthropological, sociological, and psychological concepts in a sophisticated way. "The central theme of Black Boy can be summed up in the fear-hate-fear complex of Negroes" (p. 264). The reality that W presents is bitter, but he "writes with the detachment of a surgeon, the objectivity of a scientist" (p. 268).
Reprinted: 1971.147; 1978.209.

846. _____. "'If He Hollers': Los Angeles Writer Has Produced Powerful Novel of American Life." The Pittsburgh Courier (3 November), p. 7.
Placing Himes in the W tradition, Cayton praises W's boldness and candor in treating racial matters.

847. Cerf, Bennett. "Trade Winds." The Saturday Review of Literature, 28 (14 April), 32-33.
Reports indignantly that the editor of a Natchez, Mississippi, newspaper refused to accept an advertisement for BB.

848. _____. "Trade Winds." The Saturday Review of Literature, 28 (19 May), 16-17.
Mentions that Lau Shaw's Rickshaw Boy is called a "worthy companion piece" to BB.

849. Chamberlain, John. "Pre-Review of Black Boy," in Pre-Reviews of Black Boy. New York: Book-of-the-Month Club, March, p. 2.
Rather favorable notice, but Chamberlain states that "Wright's rage . . . keeps him from making the most of his material."

850. Chapman, Esther. "Black Boy in the South." The Jamaica Daily Gleaner (c. 29 May).
Favorable review of BB addressed especially to Jamaicans. If the recollection of minute detail from early years is not plausible, the work as a whole has "an emotional integrity" and truth as well as literary distinction.

851. Coblentz, Stanton A. "Black Boy. By Richard Wright." Different, 1 (10 September), 20.
     Favorable review of a "vivid and arresting" but "bitter and terrible" autobiography. Coblentz emphasizes the struggle of the artist emerging from a hostile environment but de-emphasizes the theme of racism.

852. Coit, Betty Brooks. "News of Books and Authors." The Columbia (S. C.) Record (15 March), p. 10.
     Contains a favorable review of BB, "a probing light into the darkness of our ignorance of the mind of the Negro." Quotes from the work and sketches W's life. The autobiography is terrible but true.

853. Collier, Tarleton. "A Negro Voices a Racial Protest." The Louisville Courier-Journal (4 March), Sec. 3, p. 9.
     Favorable review of BB emphasizing W's description of black racial consciousness in the South as it determines behavior. The reviewer expresses the hope that W encountered a better life after leaving the South, which is itself not as bleak as W depicts it.

854. Collins, Thomas Lyle. "A Yearly Literary Event." New York Herald Tribune Weekly Book Review (16 December), p. 13.
     Review of Cross Section 1945 mentioning W.

855. Commager, Henry Steele. "The Negro Problem in Our Democracy." The American Mercury, 60 (June), 751-756.
     Essay-review of An American Dilemma and BB finding the latter to confirm the former. W may exaggerate somewhat, but essentially his story is an accurate depiction of black feelings. Commager urges amelioration of race relations in order to make American practice square with American democratic profession.

856. Conrad, Earl. "American Viewpoint: Blues School of Literature." The Chicago Defender (22 December), p. 11.
     Includes W, Ellison, and Himes in a "Blues School of Literature" specializing in the portrayal of tragic black figures oppressed by their racist environment. "Each of these writers is individually highly sensitized, nervous, jittery, ultra-critical, cynical."

857. Cottman, Catherine. "Blast at Richard Wright Called 'Unwarranted.'" The Chicago Defender (15 September), p. 14.
     Letter to the editor attacking Sonia Tomms for an earlier letter attacking W. Cottman surmises that Tomms must be a white man, not a black woman. BB is "cruel and ugly," but so is reality.

858. Cournos, John. "The Book Corner." The New York Sun (7 August), p. 16.
     Mentions the abridgement of BB appearing in Omnibook magazine.

859. _____. "The Book Corner." The New York Sun (14 December), p. 26.
     Mixed review of Cross Section 1945 praising "Early Days in Chicago" as "a nice piece of direct narrative prose with real meaning."

860. _____. "This Week's Book." The Philadelphia Evening Bulletin (3 March), p. 6.
     Favorable review of BB stressing W's case that the degradation of black people results from white racism. W is sensitive and truthful in his autobiography. "Now and again, it is pure Dostoevsky without the trimmings."
     Reprinted: 1978.209.

861. Crockett, Geo.[rge] W., Jr. "Black Boy, by Richard Wright." National Bar Journal, 3 (June), 172-174.
     Crockett, a black attorney and labor leader, urges other black professionals to read W's book in order to maintain contact and sympathy with the black masses.

862. Croughton, Amy H. "'Black Boy' Is Arresting Negro Yarn." Rochester (N. Y.) Times-Union (3 March), p. 7.
     Favorable review emphasizing both the racism W encountered and his own egocentric, anti-social personality. Croughton calls for a sequel to show how W became an accomplished author.
     Reprinted: 1978.209.

863. _____. "Pre-Review of Black Boy," in Pre-Reviews of Black Boy. New York: Book-of-the-Month Club, March, p. 5.
     Favorable notice.

864. Currier, Isabel. "Our Injustices to the Negroes." The Boston Herald (5 September), p. 6.
     Lists W as a "realistic" contributor to Bucklin Moon's anthology Primer for White Folks.

865. Curtis, Constance H. "About Books." New York Amsterdam News (3 March), p. 7.
     Favorable review of BB noting W's growing literary maturity. He "has never written more beautifully descriptive prose than in this work."

866. Daniel, Frank. "Pre-Review of Black Boy," in Pre-Reviews of Black Boy. New York: Book-of-the-Month Club, March, p. 1.
    Favorable notice.

867. Davis, Arthur P. "Black Boy." The Journal of Negro Education, 14 (Fall), 589-590.
    Favorable review praising W's literary artistry and stressing the theme of violence. W exaggerates for effect, but the basic pattern he traces of Southern race relations is true. Davis compares BB to Greek tragedy.

868. _____. "With a Grain of Salt: Reaction to 'Black Boy.'" The Norfolk Journal and Guide (14 April), p. 8.
    Favorable review noting the reservations black readers have expressed about the book. One-sided and overdrawn, W's social message is true in its essence. Its effects should be beneficial to both black and white readers.

869. Davis, Benjamin J., Jr. "New Times: Some Impressions of Black Boy." The Worker (1 April), p. 9.
    Mixed review applauding W's literary brilliance and BB's portrayal of racism in the South, but complaining of the author's excessive subjectivity and his estrangement from his people and from "the main progressive currents."

870. Davis, Frank Marshall. "Black Boy Richard Wright." Chicago Sunday Bee (4 March), Sec. Two, p. 15.
    Reprint of 1945.872.

871. _____. "People Are Talking About Black Boy by Richard Wright." Pulse, 3 (May), 20.
    Mixed notice praising the writing but deploring W's estrangement from black people.

872. _____. "Richard Wright's New Book Out of Step with War Torn World." Detroit Tribune (3 March), pp. 9, 13.
    Unfavorable Associated Negro Press review complaining that BB does not offer solutions or contribute to the struggle for democracy. Nevertheless, Davis says, "I still consider Richard Wright our greatest master of prose." Reprinted: 1945.870.

873. Davis, Robert Gorham. "Art and Anxiety." Partisan Review, 12 (Summer), 310-321.
    Includes a psychoanalytical analysis of NS (pp. 315-317). Bigger's murder of Mary represents W's own repressed impulses. Moreover, W "makes full

emotional and imaginative use of the deeper prejudices against Negroes and the part they play in dream fantasies, of women especially" (p. 316). Reprinted: 1957.168a; 1963.72a.

874. DeCasseres, Benjamin. "The Realm of Books." Los Angeles Examiner (11 March), Sec. VI, p. 5.
    Contains a favorable review of BB praising W's ability to overcome handicaps, his "vivid, poetic, realistic," and economical style, and his break with Communism. At times W indulges in self-pity, but this is a minor blemish.

875. Denny, George V, Jr., Irving Ives, Elmer Carter, Richard Wright, and Jerry Voorhis. "Are We Solving America's Race Problem?" Town Meeting, 11 (24 May), 3-22.
    Transcript of a radio program. After an initial statement by each participant, all question each other, followed by a question and answer session with the audience. W takes the negative side of the question.

876. Derby, John B. "Novel, The Modern," in The Encyclopedia Americana. Ed. A. H. McDannald. Vol. 20. New York: Americana Corporation, pp. 474-476.
    Mentions W briefly (p. 475h). Reprinted: 1946.186; 1951.155.

877. Derleth, August. "Books of Today." Madison (Wis.) Capital Times (20 March), p. [18].
    Favorable review of BB, "a social and human document of the first importance," comparable to Up from Slavery. Ironically, those whites who most need to grasp W's social message will not read the book or believe it if they do.

878. Dignan, Josef. "A Literary Platter Seasoned to Taste." The Louisville Courier-Journal (23 December), Sec. 3, p. 7.
    Review of Edwin Seaver's Cross Section 1945 mentioning W favorably.

879. Domingo, W. A. "Richard Wright--Author." Jamaica Public Opinion (March).
    Reviews the author's acquaintance with W and his work from the time he read "I Have Seen Black Hands." In New York in the late thirties Domingo saw W frequently. "A good raconteur, he was adept at telling slightly risqué jokes." Domingo comments on "I Have Seen Black Hands," "Bright and Morning Star," NS, and "How 'Bigger' Was Born" as well as on W's current literary activities.

880. Donahue, Elizabeth. "FEPC Support-

ers Firm in Face of Senate Filibuster."
PM (28 June), p. 5.
  Account of tirade by Senator Bilbo,
including an attack on W.

881. Drewry, John E. "The Book Corner."
Columbus (Ga.) Ledger (19 August), p. 5.
  Mentions sales of BB at "nearly half
a million."

882. ____. "New Book News." The Atlanta
Constitution (4 March), p. 9-C.
  Announces that BB is part of a dual
Book-of-the-Month Club selection for
March.

883. Du Bois, W. E. B. "Richard Wright
Looks Back." New York Herald Tribune
Weekly Book Review (4 March), p. 2.
  Unfavorable review of BB. More creative writing than the record of a
life, it raises doubts in the reader's mind about its veracity. When he
becomes commentator and prophet, W
sometimes forgets his artistic com-
mitments. The language of BB is
powerful and straightforward, but the
book fails because it is not convincing.
  Reprinted: 1977.114; 1978.209.

884. ____ and Guy B. Johnson. Encyclopedia of the Negro: Preparatory Volume
with Reference Lists and Reports. New
York: The Phelps-Stokes Fund, p. 161.
  Lists W in the "Alphabetical List
with Notes on Major Subjects and
Bibliographical Suggestions" as an
item to be included in the projected
encyclopedia.
  Reprinted: 1946.189.

885. Duffus, R. L. "Deep-South Memoir."
The New York Times Book Review (4
March), p. 3.
  Favorable review of BB, a "poignant
and disturbing" book. The reader
wonders how many other blacks suc-
cumbed to the system that W overcame.
Totally lacking in sentimentality, W
reveals the emotional shallowness of
black life, but he does not reveal
how his own literary power grew out
of such an oppressive social climate.
  Reprinted: 1978.209.

886. ____. "Negro Problems: A Sympo-
sium." The New York Times Book Review
(29 July), pp. 3, 23.
  Review of Bucklin Moon's Primer for
White Folks mentioning W's "Ethics of
Living Colored" [sic].

887. Dunlap, Mollie E. "A Selected Anno-
tated List of Books by or About the
Negro." The Negro College Quarterly, 3
(June), 94-96.
  Contains a notice of BB, "which dra-

matizes the whole tragedy of the
Negro race."

888. Dunne, George H. "The Sin of Segregation." The Commonweal, 42 (21 September), 542-548.
  Insists that reading BB should force
readers to sympathize with black
people (p. 544).

889. Ellison, Ralph. "Beating That Boy."
The New Republic, 113 (22 October), 535-
536.
  Review of Bucklin Moon's Primer for
White Folks mentioning W.
  Reprinted: 1964.43; 1970.112.

890. ____. "Richard Wright's Blues."
The Antioch Review, 5 (June), 198-211.
  Favorable review of BB. Ellison presents a detailed analysis of the
personal make-up of W's childhood and
his use of it as a representative
example of the black experience in
the South. As a writer, W always
envisioned a dual role for himself:
as a chronicler of black Southern
life and as a revealer of the emotional and psychological problems
which arise when blacks and whites
collide. Ellison compares W to Nehru,
Joyce, Dostoevsky, and others.
  Reprinted: 1953.121; 1964.48; 1969.
70; 1970.114; 1971.93, 94, 147; 1982.
43.
  Partially reprinted: 1978.87.

891. Embree, Edwin R. "The Problems of
Whites in a Democracy." The Chicago Sun
Book Week (5 August), p. 7.
  Review of Bucklin Moon's Primer for
White Folks mentioning W.

892. Engle, Paul. "'Black Boy' Is a
Powerful and Pathetic Life History."
Chicago Sunday Tribune (4 March), Part
6, p. 10.
  Favorable review citing the scenes of
setting the house on fire and fighting the other black youth for the
entertainment of whites as especially
good. At times W's dialogue is
strained, "a small blemish in a book
big with intense events." W's power
derives from his racial material and
emotions, but Engle hopes that he
will be able to transcend them in
subsequent books.

893. ____. "1945 Books Reveal U. S.
Humor Survived War." Chicago Sunday Tribune (2 December), Part Four, pp. 3, 40.
  Includes favorable comment on BB
noting that W had trouble with blacks
as well as whites.

894. English, Jack. "Book Review." The
Catholic Worker, 12 (June), 6.

Favorable review of BB comparing W to Dostoevsky and stressing the difficult questions of self-examination the work poses to the white reader.

895. Feikema, Maryanna. "Negro Problem Viewed as Largely 'White Problem.'" Minneapolis Sunday Tribune (30 December), p. 11.
Review of Bucklin Moon's Primer for White Folks noting that W's contribution is one of a number showing the lack of white "dignity and decency."

896. Ferguson, Dutton. "You Ought to Know More About Black Boy." Pulse, 3 (May), 22.
Mixed review praising W's literary genius but deploring his racial slander of black people.

897. Ferrell, Oneita. "Browsing with Books." Chicago Sunday Bee (18 March), Sec. Two, p. 15.
Notes heavy Bee reader response to BB.

898. _____. "Browsing with Books: Wright Discusses Function of the Writer in Interview." Sunday Chicago Bee (29 April), Sec. Two, p. 15.
Summarizes and quotes from the interview in Tomorrow.

899. Fisher, Dorothy Canfield. "Introductory Note," in Black Boy. New York: Harper, front matter.
Quotes Oliver Wendell Holmes and presents BB as "the honest, dreadful, heart-breaking story . . . by that rarely gifted American author, Richard Wright."

900. Flanagan, John T. "Compass Points of U. S. Literature." The Chicago Sun Book Week (25 November), p. 18.
Review of Charles Lee's anthology North, East, South, West mentioning W.

901. Flowers, Paul. "No Solution in 'Black Boy.'" The Memphis Commercial Appeal (1 April), Sec. IV, p. 10.
Unfavorable review accusing W of tendentiousness and bias. Dwelling melodramatically on the symptoms of the American racial situation, he does not offer a solution.
Reprinted: 1978.209.

902. F.[oote], R.[obert] O. "Marginal Memoranda." Pasadena Star-News (6 January), p. 10.
Announces that BB will be part of a dual Book-of-the-Month Club selection for March.

903. Frasconi, Antonio. "Frasconi to Wright." Twice a Year, Nos. 12-13, pp. 255-256.
Letter to W from a Uruguayan artist asking about publishing a book of engravings on the racial situation in America. W's reply follows.

904. Frazier, E. Franklin. "People Are Talking About Black Boy by Richard Wright." Pulse, 3 (May), 20.
Highly favorable notice praising the work as both sociology and literature.

905. Frederick, John T. "Pre-Review of Black Boy," in Pre-Reviews of Black Boy. New York: Book-of-the-Month Club, March, p. 5.
Rather favorable notice, but Frederick complains of "patches of self-conscious 'fine writing.'"

906. Friedrich, Patterson McLean. "Scarred Memories." The Cresset, 9 (April), 44-46.
Favorable review of BB emphasizing its protest against racial prejudice. Not pleasant reading, it "should cause every true American to feel heartily ashamed" (p. 44).

907. Furfey, Paul Hanly. "People Are Talking About Black Boy by Richard Wright." Pulse, 3 (May), 21.
Mixed review. The book is powerful and important, but it is difficult to identify with W because of "his fierce hatreds . . . , his abnormal fears, his peculiar sensitiveness, his utter lack of humor."

908. Gannett, Lewis. "'Black Boy' a Great Human Document." Jamaica Public Opinion (8 March).
Reprint of 1945.909.

909. _____. "Books and Things." New York Herald Tribune (28 February), p. 17.
Highly favorable review of BB, an unforgettable book which explains what made W compose NS. Gannett believes that BB may be one of America's great autobiographies.
Reprinted: 1945.908; 1978.209.

910. _____. "Books and Things." New York Herald Tribune (10 December), p. 19.
Recommends BB for Christmas giving as the most distinguished autobiography of the year.

911. _____. "Ten Christmas Lists of Ten 'Best.'" The New York Times Book Review (2 December), p. 5.
Lists BB.

912. Garfield, Frances O'Brien. "Richard Wright's." The Saturday Review of Liter-

ature, 28 (3 March), front cover.
  Wood engraving of W with caption.

913. Garlington, S. W. "An Ugly, Yet
Factual Portrait." The African: Journal
of African Affairs, 3 (April), 19-20.
  Favorable review of BB discussing the
  question of its genre. Garlington
  calls it "a masterpiece of romanced
  facts . . . a sort-of autobiography"
  representing the experience of many
  other blacks as well as W.
  Reprinted: 1978.209.

914. Gibbons, Ray. "Black Boy by Richard
Wright." Advance, 137 (April), 33.
  Favorable review praising W's liter-
  ary artistry and social message.
  Compares BB to Strange Fruit and
  Uncle Tom's Cabin.
  Reprinted: 1978.209.

915. Gm., S. af. "Negerdrama stor fram-
gang för Göteborgs stadsteater." Stockholm Dagens Nyheter (11 March).
  Favorable review of the Swedish production of the play NS. Despite the
  fact that the dramatization cannot
  capture the psychological complexity
  of the novel, it is a "magnificent
  social document." Notes the high
  level of tension established at the
  beginning and maintained throughout
  the play.

916. Gollomb, Joseph. "Richard Wright."
Book-of-the-Month Club News (February),
pp. 8-9.
  Biographical essay based partly on an
  interview with W. Gollomb is struck
  by the contrast between the degradation of W's youth and the "poised,
  objective . . . mellow" man he has
  become.
  Reprinted or partially reprinted:
  1945.917; 1978.209.

917. _____. "A Writer Defies the Psycho-
logists." Negro Digest, 3 (April), 65-
66.
  Partial reprint of 1945.916.

918. Goss, Margaret Taylor. "Charges
Richard Wright with 'Uncle Tomism.'" The
Chicago Defender (27 January), p. 14.
  Letter to the editor from a disillu-
  sioned admirer denouncing W for "I
  Tried to Be a Communist" and com-
  plaining that he does not write in-
  spirational books like Howard Fast's
  Freedom Road.

919. Gottlieb, Ferd. "Candid Book by
Negro Novelist Tells of Growing Up in
South." St. Louis Post Dispatch (28
February), p. 2B.
  Favorable review of BB showing the
  autobiographical sources of elements

in the characterization of Bigger
Thomas. BB is racial protest, but it
is also frank and sometimes unflattering self-portrayal.
Reprinted: 1978.209.

920. _____. "Pre-Review of Black Boy,"
in Pre-Reviews of Black Boy. New York:
Book-of-the-Month Club, March, p. 5.
  Mixed notice arguing that the theme
  of the growth of the artist dilutes
  the work's social protest.

921. Graham, Frank. "The Bookworm." The
San Francisco Call-Bulletin (22 December), p. 6.
  Favorable review of Cross Section
  1945 calling "Early Days in Chicago"
  "novelesque . . . but not novelette."

922. Graves, Patsy. "A Record of Childhood and Youth." Opportunity, 23 (Summer), 158-159.
  Favorable review of BB stressing W's
  interest in psychology and his
  "psycho-analytic technique" in treating his relation to his family and to
  society. Although some fictional elements may have been introduced into
  the autobiographical account, the
  brutal social treatment of Southern
  blacks depicted in BB is true to
  actuality.
  Reprinted: 1978.209.

923. Gray, James. "Dramatic Figure
Speaks in Duluth Sunday Night." Unidentified clipping (c. 18 November).
  General essay on W praising his
  treatment of racial matters. His
  success is due to his black perspective and his refusal to sentimen-
  talize.

924. _____. "Racial Prophet to Speak
Here Monday--Inequality's Dangers Bared
by Negro Scribe." St. Paul Pioneer-Press
(18 November), Magazine Sec., p. 6.
  Emphasizes W's importance as a racial
  spokesman. Comments on the experiential veracity of BB and the theme of
  white oppression and black rebellion
  in NS, comparing W to Harriet Beecher
  Stowe.

925. Grevenius, Herbert. "Göteborgstea-
ter." Stockholms Tidningen (c. 11
March).
  Mixed review of the Swedish production of the play NS. While discussing
  at length the development of Bigger's
  character from realistic victim-
  stereotype to symbolic stature, Grevenius regrets several of the changes
  in dramatization, singling out the
  sentimental final scene. Still, the
  work is one of the most important
  political works from America and

should bring important questions before the Swedish people.

926. Groth, John. "Artist John Groth." Chicago Daily News (5 December), p. 19A.
Sketch with caption of W, Groth, Ellery Queen, James T. Farrell, and David Appel.

927. Gruber, Ide. "Books in Review." Bronx Parkchester Press (22 March).
Favorable review of BB, "a hot, searing, passionate tale." Emphasizes W's racial suffering in his youth.

928. Guilfoil, Kelsey. "Guilfoil's 1945 Book Choice." Chicago Sunday Tribune (2 December), Part 4, p. 30.
Lists BB.

929. _____. "Second Book Compiled of New Writing." Chicago Sunday Tribune (30 December), Part 6, p. 13.
Review of Cross Section 1945 mentioning W.

930. Gwinn, Pat. "Negro Writes of Boyhood in Deep South." Ft. Worth Star-Telegram (1 April), Sec. 2, p. 5.
Favorable review of BB emphasizing W's corrective to the white Southern view of racial life. BB has "the same angry prose and clarity of style" as NS, but its themes are closer to those of UTC.
Reprinted: 1978.209.

931. H., R. F. "50 'Great American' Stories." The Springfield (Mass.) Sunday Union and Republican (1 July), p. 4D.
Lists W as a contributor to an anthology by Charles Grayson.

932. Hackett, Alice. "P. W. Forecast for Buyers." The Publishers' Weekly, 147 (3 February), 651.
Includes a note on the advertising campaign for BB.

933. Haddon, Bruce. "A Fight Against Fear." Erie Dispatch-Herald (18 March), Sec. 2, p. 7.
Highly favorable review of BB, a "masterpiece of modern prose" in the mode of restrained as opposed to lurid realism. Effective as social message, it is even more important as "a brilliant literary achievement, one that is in the mainstream of great English literature."
Reprinted: 1978.209.

934. H.[all], C.[ameron] P. "Black Boy, by Richard Wright." Social Progress, 35 (April), 31-32.
Favorable review of a book of "vivid realism, written in a gripping style." The message is a stern indictment of American racism, but Hall believes that awareness of this social problem is increasing.

935. Hamilton, W. B. "Black Boy." The South Atlantic Quarterly, 44 (July), 329-330.
Favorable review. Although as a "psychological autobiography" BB paints no clear picture of W's times or environment, it is a convincing work of art. Despite his politics, W is never doctrinaire; rather, he portrays a man struggling to understand his own mind and reactions. Ultimately, he escapes through books. In this way BB is an eloquent, if implicit, plea for education in the South.
Reprinted: 1978.209.

936. Hansen, Harry. "The First Reader: In Brief." New York World-Telegram (19 May), Sec. 2, p. 10.
Notes that BB was a best seller in April.

937. _____. "The First Reader: Negro Author's Boyhood." New York World-Telegram (28 February), p. 22.
Favorable review of BB. Hansen is particularly impressed by W's candor in revealing his own shortcomings as well as society's racism. After a summary of the book, the reviewer objects to "some inexcusably filthy matter" and remarks that W's "nature is not warm," though his mind is keenly analytical. He calls BB "an extraordinary work, a personal supplement to . . . An American Dilemma." Hansen announces W's forthcoming appearance on the "Author Meets the Critics" radio program.

938. _____. "The First Reader: Second Choice Tales." New York World-Telegram (5 June), p. 16.
Review of Charles Grayson's Half a Hundred Tales by Great American Writers noting that "Almos' a Man" was previously included in an O. Henry Award collection.

939. _____. "The First Reader: Youth and Its Books." New York World-Telegram (29 November), p. 18.
States that "Early Days in Chicago" is the best-written selection in Cross Section 1945.

940. _____. "Pre-Review of Black Boy," in Pre-Reviews of Black Boy. New York: Book-of-the-Month Club, March, p. 4.
Favorable notice emphasizing the work's frankness.

941. _____. "Tales of Sane Americans by Miss West Wins Favor." Chicago Sunday

Tribune (9 December), Part 6, p. 10.
  Notes that BB is one of the titles
  most frequently listed by critics in
  the East as the best nonfiction of
  the year.

942. _____. "Ten Christmas Lists of Ten
'Best.'" The New York Times Book Review
(2 December), p. 5.
  Lists BB.

943. _____. "To Be Young, Poor, and
Black." Survey Graphic, 34 (February),
68-69.
  Favorable review of BB praising W's
  complete candor. The social message
  of the book is important, but W's own
  rise "revives our democratic belief
  that brains may sprout in the hum-
  blest surroundings and that intellectual courage wins a way." Hansen
  compares BB to Rousseau's Confessions
  and to An American Dilemma.

944. Hardwick, Elizabeth. "Artist and
Spokesman." Partisan Review, 12 (Summer), 406-407.
  Favorable review of BB emphasizing
  its successful resolution of the
  artist-spokesman conflict that had
  damaged W's earlier work. The
  "pseudo-poetry" of benevolent nature
  linked to his degraded childhood
  strikes a false note, but for the
  most part BB is "an admirable and
  interesting achievement" because it
  does not explain and interpret excessively.

945. Harrison, William. Untitled
article. Boston Chronicle (8 December).
  Favorable review of BB praising W's
  mastery of his craft, which he uses
  to reveal the seriousness of the
  American racial problem. W's personal
  experiences are representative. His
  detailed recollection of early childhood may be difficult to believe,
  however.
  Reprinted: 1978.209.

946. Harshe, Florence. "Highlights of
New Books." The Lima (Ohio) News (30
April), p. 3.
  Contains a favorable notice of BB, a
  "simple, direct, poignant--and dis-
  turbing" book.

947. Hass, Victor P. "Pre-Review of
Black Boy," in Pre-Reviews of Black Boy.
New York: Book-of-the-Month Club, March,
p. 4.
  Very favorable notice of "a book with
  a splendid, shining soul."

948. _____. "20 Years of Misery." Omaha
Sunday World-Herald (25 February), Maga-

zine Sec., p. 17-C.
  Favorable review of BB emphasizing
  its social message. "Almost as an
  after-thought, I might add that
  'Black Boy' is something very close
  to being literature."
  Reprinted: 1978.209.

949. Havighurst, Walter. "The American
Short Story Boom." The Saturday Review
of Literature, 38 (13 October), 50.
  Lists W as a "stern" contributor to
  Bennett Cerf's anthology Modern Amer-
  ican Short Stories.

950. _____. "Best Books of 1945 as Selected by Tribune Critics." Chicago
Sunday Tribune (2 December), Part 4, p.
4.
  Lists BB.

951. Hendley, Coit, Jr. "Richard Wright
Stresses Realism in Dealing with Negro
Types." The Washington Sunday Star (11
November), pp. C-3, C-7.
  Interview in Washington with W, who
  discusses racial portrayal in Ameri-
  can literature. Black stereotypes
  from Washington Irving to Octavus Roy
  Cohen have been harmful, but Erskine
  Caldwell and Lillian Smith have moved
  toward realism. W also comments on
  his own work, especially NS.

952. Herring, Hubert. "Books I Have
Liked." New York Herald Tribune Weekly
Book Review (2 December), p. 6.
  Lists BB and two others.

953. Hindus, Maurice. "What They Read of
Ours in the U. S. S. R." New York Herald
Tribune Weekly Book Review (2 September), pp. 1, 2.
  Notes that despite his quarrels with
  the American Communist Party, W is
  one of the most popular American
  writers in Russia.

954. Horn, L. D. "Propaganda." Liberty,
22 (24 November), 8.
  Letter to the editor denouncing W as
  an anti-white propagandist fomenting
  racial hatred.

955. Horton, Peter, "'Cross Section
1945' Turns Up Unsuspected Treasure."
Buffalo Courier-Express (c. 29 Decem-
ber).
  Favorable review emphasizing "Early
  Days in Chicago" and, in the previous
  year's volume, "The Man Who Lived
  Underground."

956. Hughes, Langston. "Here to Yonder."
The Chicago Defender (1 September), p.
14.
  Mentions briefly W's interracial marriage.

957. I., W. "Books." St. Louis Star-Times (8 March), p. 16.
    Favorable review of BB emphasizing the racial terror of W's Southern environment. Some may accuse W of exaggeration, but "no one can say for certain unless he has lived as a Negro in the South. Few people would be willing to do so."
    Reprinted: 1978.209.

958. Ives, Irving, George V. Denny, Jr., Elmer Carter, Richard Wright, and Jerry Voorhis. "Are We Solving America's Race Problem?" Town Meeting, 11 (24 May), 3-22.
    See 1945.875.

959. Ivy, James W. "American Hunger." The Crisis, 52 (April), 117-118.
    Favorable review of BB stressing its frankness and refuting those who would deny its truth. Ivy summarizes the book in considerable detail and quotes freely.
    Reprinted: 1978.209.

960. Jack, Homer A. "Black Boy, by Richard Wright." Sunday Chicago Bee (18 March), Sec. Two, p. 15.
    Favorable review rebutting the censure of Frank Marshall Davis. The artist should force the reader to confront social problems; he need not offer solutions.

961. _____. "A Vivid Narrative." Unity, 131 (May), 46-47.
    Highly favorable review of BB emphasizing its social message. Whites must confront the racial problem if a solution is to be found. W's "vivid, biting narrative," the work of an artist, will induce white readers to make this necessary confrontation.

962. Jackson, Charles. "The Negro Struggle: 'Black Boy' Packs a Wallop." The Militant (7 April), p. 5.
    Mixed review praising W's blunt revelation of Southern racial injustice but criticizing his lack of economic analysis and his failure to point the way to social change.

963. Jackson, Joseph Henry. "Bookman's Notebook." San Francisco Chronicle (25 August), p. 10.
    Announces that BB will be abridged in the August Omnibook.

964. _____. "Bookman's Notebook." San Francisco Chronicle (4 December), p. 12.
    Lists W as a contributor to Edwin Seaver's anthology Cross Section 1945.

965. _____. "Pre-Review of Black Boy," in Pre-Reviews of Black Boy. New York: Book-of-the-Month Club, March, p. 5.
    Favorable notice.

966. _____. "Ten Christmas Lists of Ten 'Best.'" The New York Times Book Review (2 December), p. 5.
    Lists BB.

967. _____. "Wanted: An Answer to Fit Our Protestations of Democracy." San Francisco Chronicle (25 February), This World Sec., p. 14.
    Favorable review of BB and Walter White's A Rising Wind. In capsule form, W in his extraordinary book focuses on what will be postwar America's greatest internal problem--racism.

968. Jackson, Margot. "Wright Puts Into Words the Pain of Being Black." Akron Beacon Journal (4 March), p. 4-D.
    Favorable review of BB calling it "a hard, harsh, beautiful, frightening book. No one will ever say he 'enjoyed' it. But no one can fail to be impressed by it. And everyone should read it." Jackson's summary of the work stresses W's alienation from other blacks and white responsibility for black frustration.

969. J.[ohnson], C.[harles] S. "Review of the Month." A Monthly Summary of Events and Trends in Race Relations, 2 (February), 182-184.
    Contains a brief notice of BB calling it "a forceful and unforgettable autobiographical account of what it means to be poor, black and Southern."

970. Johnson, Fenton. "Trends in Negro Poetry." Sunday Chicago Bee (18 November), Sec. Two, p. 16.
    Calls Margaret Walker "a propagandist of the Richard Wright type."

971. Jones, Howard Mumford. "Up from Slavery: Richard Wright's Story." The Saturday Review of Literature, 28 (3 March), 9-10.
    Mixed review of BB deeming the work weak as literature but strong as protest. W fails to develop adequately the personality of his autobiographical protagonist, making him passive in contrast to the active forces oppressing him. The result is melodramatic. As "a deeply disturbing document in race relations," however, BB cannot be ignored. A drawing of W appears on the front cover of this issue.

972. Jones, John Hudson. "Richard Wright: Black Boy." Accent, 5 (Spring),

188-189.
 Favorable review praising W's technique and calling the work "the most
 serious indictment that any artist
 has ever leveled at American Society." But Jones warns W of an intense
 subjectivity that is dividing him
 from his people, from whom he has
 derived his strength.

973. Jordan-Smith, Paul. "Pre-Review of
Black Boy," in Pre-Reviews of Black Boy.
New York: Book-of-the-Month Club, March,
p. 3.
 Very favorable notice expressing surprise that W's "bitterness is not
 more intense."

974. ____. "Youth in Deep South Fights
Both Poverty and Prejudice." Los Angeles
Times (4 March), Part III, p. 4.
 Favorable review of BB emphasizing
 its emotive power in depicting W's
 struggle "to escape the taboos of the
 Deep South." The reviewer has "not
 read anywhere a more pitiful or brutal story of childhood experience."

975. Kantor, MacKinlay. "Books I Have
Liked." New York Herald Tribune Weekly
Book Review (2 December), p. 5.
 Lists BB and two others.

976. Kennedy, Raymond. "A Dramatic Autobiography." The Yale Review, 34 (Summer), 762-764.
 Favorable review of BB emphasizing
 its veracity as a social document.
 The book's great power derives from
 W's major talent as a writer, from
 the tragic pathos of his early life,
 and from its human theme of deep
 significance. Kennedy defends W
 against his critics by arguing that
 race relations in the South are in
 the starkly contrasting terms of
 black and white that W presents.
 Reprinted: 1978.209.

977. Kerr, Wilfred H. "Black Boy. By
Richard Wright." Politics, 2 (July),
210-211.
 Favorable review emphasizing W's "superb ego" which enabled him to survive such a hostile environment. Kerr
 is also impressed by the book's bitterness, which "ought to act as an
 antidote to shallow optimism in race
 relations and on America itself."

978. Knight, Elizabeth B. "Negro Writes
Telling Book About His Life." The Dallas
Daily Times Herald (15 April), p. 14.
 Favorable review of BB de-emphasizing
 the theme of racial conflict and
 stressing instead the universal theme
 of "searing poverty and the brutality
 which poverty so often engenders."

Knight attributes W's hatred of
whites to exposure to "white trash,"
from whom Jim Crow laws offer black
people some protection.

979. Krueger, E. T. "Disquieting Odyssey." The Nashville Tennessean (11
March), p. 13-B.
 Unfavorable review of BB conceding
 W's "dramatic storytelling ability,"
 but arguing that he relies too much
 on shock and sensationalism--"the
 extremes and distortions of lurid but
 inconsequential interracial immorali-
 ties and blighting antagonisms."
 Krueger quotes approvingly two passages in which W broods on "the cultural barrenness of black life."

980. Kuhnes, Daisy M. "Book Reviews:
Biography." The Educational Forum, 9
(May), 481-482.
 Favorable review of BB. The book is
 evidence that W is realizing his
 quest. It is above all an "honest
 book" which avoids cynicism.
 Reprinted: 1978.209.

981. La Torriente, Loló de. "Sangre
Negra, por Richard Wright." Afroamerica,
1 (January and July), 102-104.
 Very favorable review of the Spanish
 translation of NS with a plot summary. The review emphasizes the social theme and praises W's ideas and
 artistry. The third section is the
 strongest and deepest of the three.
 The reviewer also discusses W's current quarrel with the Communists.

982. Lane, Layle. "The American 'White':
At Home and Abroad." The Call (23
April), p. 4.
 Favorable review of BB in the organ
 of the Workmen's Circle. A "far more
 terrible and just" indictment of
 America than NS, BB tells the story
 not only of W but of millions of
 other blacks in America. Being poor
 and black and coming from a shattered
 family caused great bitterness in W
 toward white and black.
 Reprinted: 1978.209.

983. Langwin, Marjorie. "Roth's Weekly
Book Review: Black Boy by Richard
Wright." The Superior Evening Telegram
(c. 30 April), p. 5.
 Favorable review praising W's narrative style. BB "is a unique record; a
 story of a black boy's soul, as well
 as a record of discrimination against
 race."

984. Larrabee, Clark. "New American
Writing That Says Something." The Phila-
delphia Inquirer (23 December), Society
Sec., p. 9.

Review of Cross Section 1945 mentioning W and "Early Days in Chicago."

985. Lasker, Jack. "Shore Leave in Odes-
sa." New Masses, 56 (4 September), 6-8.
Relates a meeting with an English-
speaking Russian university student
who was enthusiastic about W.

986. Laws, Clifton. "Takes Issue with
Critic of 'Black Boy.'" The Chicago
Defender (22 September), p. 14.
Letter to the editor rebutting Sonia
Tomms. The race should attempt to
alleviate the conditions revealed by
NS and BB.

987. Laycock, Edward A. "An American
Boy." Boston Evening Globe (28 Febru-
ary), p. 15.
Favorable review of BB praising the
"remarkably restrained and quietly
beautiful" writing and emphasizing
W's rebellion against his family.
Laycock is also impressed by W's
psychological penetration.
Reprinted: 1978.209.

988. Lee, Charles. "Biographies," in his
North, East, South, West: A Regional
Anthology of American Writing. New York:
Howell, Soskin, pp. 534-555.
Includes a sketch of W (p. 555).

989. _____. "Black Boy." Philadelphia
Record (1 April), p. 7.
Favorable notice emphasizing the
work's candor. The study pays tribute
to the force of the human will. Its
impact is memorable.

990. _____. "Black Hunger." Philadelphia
Record (1 March), p. 8.
Highly favorable review of BB calling
it "one of the most memorable books
of our time, a kind of 20th century
'Uncle Tom's Cabin.'" Intimate and
candid, W's self-revelation is written in the cause of human dignity for
black people, which can be achieved
by the full implementation of democratic ideals.
Reprinted: 1978.209.

991. _____. "Books of the Future." Philadelphia Record (11 February), p. M 7.
Contains a very favorable announcement of BB, a book important for "its
ruthless honesty, its artistic realism, and its social significance."

992. _____. "Books of the Season." Philadelphia Record (1 April), p. M 7.
Includes a very favorable notice of
BB, "as candid and compelling an
autobiography as has ever been printed in America--or anywhere else, for
that matter."

993. _____. "May I Present--," in his
North, East, South, West: A Regional
Anthology of American Writing. New York:
Howell, Soskin, pp. 1-8.
Mentions "Richard Wright's sociology"
(p. 6).

994. _____. "Pre-Review of Black Boy,"
in Pre-Reviews of Black Boy. New York:
Book-of-the-Month Club, March, p. 4.
Very favorable notice comparing BB to
Uncle Tom's Cabin.

995. Levine, Philip. "Book Window." The
Philadelphia Jewish Times (16 March), p.
13.
Mixed review of BB. Memorable and
well-written, the book is too egocen-
tric yet at the same time lacking in
emotional involvement.

996. Lewis, Jasper R. "Reading: From
Left to Right." Forum and Column Review,
20 (May), 55-59.
Contains a highly favorable review of
BB, "a diamondcut piece of work."
Lewis is impressed by W's rigorous
evaluation both of white racism and
black shortcomings.

997. Lewis, Sinclair. "Gentlemen, This
Is Revolution." Esquire, 23 (June), 76.
Favorable review of BB rebutting the
charges of other reviewers that it is
too emotional and bitter. Fear is
the prevailing mood of the work.
Lewis also treats other current books
on the racial situation.
Reprinted: 1953.172; 1978.209; 1982.
50.

998. Lewis, Theophilus. "Black Boy."
Interracial Review, 18 (March), 48-49.
Unfavorable review by a black Catholic reviewer. Lewis considers the
book egotistical and dull.

999. _____. "Survival Through Flight."
America, 73 (14 April), 39.
Mixed review of BB by a black Catholic reviewer. The work has little
value as autobiography, for W takes
liberties with chronology and leaves
many matters unexplained. It is a
dull narrative. Nevertheless, the
book is valuable as a study of racism, especially for those unpersuaded
that color prejudice is unjust. Lewis
objects to the indelicacy of some
passages.
Reprinted: 1978.209.

1000. Lochard, Metz T. P. "Weapons for
Fight on Native Fascism." The Chicago
Sun Book Week (17 June), p. 2.
Refers to NS as a warning to whites.

1001. Logie, Iona R. Untitled clipping.

Books Across the Sea (6 September).
Favorable notice of BB.

1002. Lubinski, Kurt. "Literarische Welt: Von schwarzer Not." New York Aufbau (13 July), p. 10.
Review of BB noting the candor of its revelation of sordid episodes in the writer's life. Comments on black anti-Semitism.

1003. Ludington, Tracy. "Race Problems Exposed in Sordid Story." Unidentified clipping.
Unfavorable review of the Canadian edition of BB complaining of obscenity, a one-sided view of race relations, and an unsympathetic protagonist.

1003a. Lynch, William S. "Born Black." The Saturday Review of Literature, 28 (17 November), 53-54.
Review of If He Hollers Let Him Go contrasting its protagonist Bob Jones to Bigger Thomas.

1004. Lyons, Leonard. "The Lyons Den." New York Post (6 April), p. 22.
Mentions the Life magazine photo-essay on BB.

1005. M.[acGregor], M.[artha]. "Representative Short Stories by Americans Are Collected." The Washington Post (19 August), p. 11S.
Reprint of 1945.1006.

1006. _____. "Surfeit of Cerf? Certainly Not!" New York Post (14 August), p. 18.
Mentions W's "strong" story "Almos' a Man" in Bennett Cerf's anthology Modern American Short Stories. Reprinted: 1945.1005.

1007. Mahoney, W. J., Jr., "Wherein a Near-White Man Decides He Doesn't Care for a White South." The Montgomery Advertiser (4 March), p. 2-A.
Unfavorable review of BB emphasizing W's unpleasant personality and his poor relationships with other blacks. Despite some rave notices from Northerners quoted by Mahoney, he considers the work "mediocre," though "as a book written by an articulate negro, it might be termed excellent."

1008. Margolies, Joseph A. "Ten Christmas Lists of Ten 'Best.'" The New York Times Book Review (2 December), p. 5.
Lists BB.

1009. Martin, Gertrude Scott. "Book Notes." The Detroit Michigan Chronicle (3 March), p. 6.
Favorable review of BB stressing W's difficulty with familial hostility in the home and white racism outside it. The author's experiences are tellingly rendered, but they are not typical.

1010. _____. "Book Notes." The Detroit Michigan Chronicle (17 March), p. 6.
Mentions W's PM review of Gertrude Stein.

1011. _____. "Book Notes." The Detroit Michigan Chronicle (24 March), p. 6.
Notes W's appointment to the board of directors of the American Council on Race Relations and disputes points in the Time review of BB.

1012. _____. "Book Notes." The Detroit Michigan Chronicle (28 April), p. 6.
Mentions the inclusion of W in Primer for White Folks.

1013. _____. "Book Notes." The Detroit Michigan Chronicle (5 May), p. 6.
Mentions Charles J. Rolo's interview with W in Tomorrow.

1014. Martin, Suzanne. "Pre-Review of Black Boy," in Pre-Reviews of Black Boy. New York: Book-of-the-Month Club, March, p. 6.
Very favorable notice stressing W's incisive penetration of racial attitudes.

1015. Marty. "The Book Mark." Campbell (Cal.) Press (15 March), p. [3].
Favorable review of BB consisting mostly of summary. W succeeds in telling "the black truth" in a moving and informative way.

1016. Matthews, Elizabeth W. "The Race Issue in Dixie." Richmond Times-Dispatch (1 April), p. D-5.
Favorable review of BB focusing on the work's social and racial protest. Matthews admires W's "brilliant characterization of the failures, the lack of ambition, the narrow-mindedness, the cruelty and superficiality of members of his own race," but she recognizes the basic problems of white racism. W's case, she believes, is not typical.

1017. Mavity, Nancy Barr. "Books and Authors: Free Spirit Dominates New Autobiographies." Oakland Tribune (8 April), p. 2-C.
Contains a highly favorable review of BB. The work is a powerful social document indicting American racism, but it is also a moving story of the development of a genius necessarily at odds with his environment. A photograph of W appears adjacent to the column.

1018. Mayberry, George. "What Man Has Made of Man." The New Republic, 112 (12 March), 364-365.
Favorable review of BB, which Mayberry considers superior to UTC and NS. From the harsh experiences of his childhood, W has distilled painful truth and a literary triumph.

1019. Mayer, Milton. "Richard Wright: Unbreakable Negro." The Progressive, 9 (9 April), 8.
Somewhat unfavorable review of BB. Lacking the genius of a Proust, W fails to make his personal passion into great art. Nevertheless, the book is extremely important as history. But NS is far less naive and far more effective. BB remains the story of a single individual, lacking the representative dimension of NS.
Reprinted: 1978.209.

1020. McCallister, Frank. "Rejection, Rebellion, Agression." The Atlanta Journal (11 March), p. 10-C.
Somewhat favorable review of BB stressing the revelation of black feelings to those who "think they know the Negro." McCallister finds it remarkable that W managed to rise above the degradation of his youth. "The book is written with stark realism and bitterness," but W needs to outgrow this bitterness if he is to realize his considerable potential as a writer.
Reprinted: 1978.209.

1021. McCarthy, Augustine Patrick, C. P. "Black Boy." The Sign, 24 (April), 499-500.
Generally favorable review. McCarthy describes W as a distinguished black gentleman recording the personal tragedies of his early life. He offers no solution to the racial problem, the key to which is denied opportunity. The book is moving and truthful, but at times W violates good taste and decency.

1022. McCarthy, Mary. "Portrait of a Typical Negro?" The New Leader, 28 (23 June), 10.
Review of BB concentrating on the relation of the white reader to the book and the hostility it professes. W's problem is more one of psychology than sociology. He seems to have seized on the racial issue to rationalize his neurosis: "the disease of the system provides a dubious remedy for the sickness of the individual."

1023. [McCullough, Trudi]. "Author Richard Wright Champion of Negro Rights." New Haven Sunday Register (8 April), Sec. III, p. 10.
Associated Press article-interview. W comments on the American racial situation, especially in Chicago, predicting trouble if black demands are not met. He states that he broke with the Communist Party because it endorsed a film short on the status of blacks in the army despite Jim Crow. His present political position he calls "far left of left." BB resulted from a speech at Fisk University. McCullough notes the paradox of the determination of the successful W to help unsuccessful members of his race. She also comments on his physical appearance and his work in progress.
Reprinted: 1945.1024, 1025, 1026.

1024. _____. "Author Wright Is Militant Champ of Negro Rights." Erie Dispatch-Herald (22 April), Sec. 3, p. 11.
Reprint of 1945.1023.

1025. _____. "Author Wright's Life and His Works Pose a Paradox of Success and Failure." Buffalo Evening News (21 April), Magazine Sec., p. 5.
Reprint of 1945.1023.

1026. _____. "Negro Author Fights for Race He Left Behind." The Atlanta Journal (8 April), p. 8-D.
Reprint of 1945.1023.

1027. McGinnis, John H. "Pre-Review of Black Boy," in Pre-Reviews of Black Boy. New York: Book-of-the-Month Club, March, p. 2.
Favorable notice anticipating mixed responses in the South.

1028. McKenzie, Marjorie. "Pursuit of Democracy." The Pittsburgh Courier (30 June), p. 7.
Mentions W in a discussion of the Sinclair Lewis article on black literature in Esquire.

1029. _____. "Pursuit of Democracy: Paging Richard Wright: By What Methods Can Cultural Values Be Changed?" The Pittsburgh Courier (10 November), p. 6.
Reports at length a lecture by W in the Howard University Forum Series and the audience's lively response. Basing his analysis on the social sciences but having lost faith in revolutionary social change, W has taken the position of a Henry Wallace liberal. He is confident in his diagnosis but unsure of a prescription.

1030. McKinney, T. E. "Black Boy--By Richard Wright." The Quarterly Review of Higher Education Among Negroes, 13 (April), 172.

Favorable brief review. W "has called attention to certain aspects of the South that greatly affect the Negroes and are not generally known by the best citizens of our country, not even by many of those who live in the South."

1031. McLaughlin, Michael. "Black Boy. By Richard Wright." The Catholic World, 161 (April), 85-86.
Mixed review objecting to some passages and suggesting an expurgated edition. But W tells his story of racial injustice in a gripping fashion, thereby demonstrating black excellence in the expressive arts. McLaughlin notes with approval the decent behavior of W's Irish Catholic co-worker in Memphis.

1032. McLean, Helen V. "Racial Prejudice." Phylon, 6 (Second Quarter), 145-153.
Mentions a talk W gave in 1943 to the Chicago Institute for Psychoanalysis on fear as a dominant emotion of American blacks.

1033. Minot, George E. "'Black Boy, a Record of Childhood and Youth,' by Richard Wright." The Boston Herald (28 February), p. 12.
Highly favorable review emphasizing the cruelty young W suffered at the hands of both blacks and whites. "Deeply felt, sincerely honest, and bitterly realized, it cries out in appalling personalized frankness against the degradation of his race, laying bare in magnificent prose the suffering, the horror and the tragedy which were not only a part of his own fearful experiences but also in large measure those of his people."

1034. Molloy, Robert. "The Book of the Day." The New York Sun (2 March), p. 22.
Favorable review of BB and Walter White's A Rising Wind. W's book is bitter and uncompromising, but objective. "As writing, the style of 'Black Boy' lacks much of the power and brilliance of the novel, 'Native Son,' but the book is a tremendous document."
Reprinted: 1978.209.

1035. _____. "Pre-Review of Black Boy," in Pre-Reviews of Black Boy. New York: Book-of-the-Month Club, March, p. 4.
Favorable notice.

1036. Moon, Bucklin. "A Book for America to Read." People's Voice (3 March), p. 15.
Highly favorable review of BB finding it even better than W's fiction. The W of the autobiography and Bigger of the novel are similar in many ways, but the survival of W and many others makes BB hopeful as well as tragic. Even white racists will be moved by the book. Moon prefers the title AH to BB.

1037. _____. "Bronzeville, U. S. A." The Nation, 161 (17 November), 525-526.
Highly favorable review of Black Metropolis with special praise for W's introduction. The book as a whole provides the reader "everything there is to know about the background that molded Bigger Thomas."

1038. Moore, Harry Estill. "Racial Antagonisms." Southwest Review, 30 (Summer), 387-388.
Favorable review of BB from a sociological perspective. Emphasizes W's revelation of group transmission of racial antagonism on both sides of the color line. Moore looks forward to a sequel on W's life in the urban North.
Reprinted: 1978.209.

1039. Morgan-Powell, S. "The Black Man's Load." The Montreal Daily Star (14 April), p. 21.
Favorable review of BB placing it in the context of the struggle for democracy and the Atlantic Charter. Praises W for his sincerity and his devoted efforts to achieve black rights. BB tells an unpalatable but necessary truth.

1040. Morrow, Ora G. "Presenting Another Reaction to Richard Wright's Black Boy." Sunday Chicago Bee (8 April), Sec. Two, p. 15.
Favorable review emphasizing the book's power and message. It surpasses even NS.

1041. Moss, Howard. "Modern American Short Stories. Edited by Bennett Cerf." The New York Times Book Review (16 September), p. 34.
Notes that W is represented in Cerf's anthology with work that is typical, but not his best.

1042. Murphy, Beatrice M. "Black Boy by Richard Wright: a Review." Pulse, 3 (April), 32-33.
Extremely unfavorable review attacking W's character and behavior as "an obnoxious child" and his racial betrayal as an adult author. Includes factual discrepancies between BB and other biographical and autobiographical accounts.
Reprinted: 1978.209.

1043. Murphy, Carl. "New Richard Wright Book Draws Critics' Superlatives." The Baltimore Afro-American (17 March), pp. 1-2.

After quoting from eight favorable reviews of BB in white newspapers, Murphy relates some of the more sensational incidents in the book. He concludes by noting that "it is impossible for anybody who has had a happy childhood and loving care to imagine this childhood of Richard Wright in which the hand of every man, even his own father's, was against him."

1044. Murphy, Gertrude B. "Black Boy by Richard Wright." San Jose Mercury Herald and News (29 April), Social Sec., p. 13.

Favorable review praising the work's social message and its beautiful prose rhythm. Often crude and cruel, it "is not 'nice' reading," but it is essential.

1045. Neander-Nilsson, S. "Svart Shakespeare." Göteborgs Morgenpost (12 March).

Favorable review of the Swedish production of the play NS. The novel is extremely powerful and brutal; the stage version is necessarily less so, but still emotionally overwhelming even if it does not reach Shakespearean tragic dimensions. Bigger is crazed--half animalistic, half human. Neander-Nilsson praises the excellent acting, particularly that of Bertil Anderberg as Bigger. All in all, the play is the season's best production at the state theater.

1046. Newlin, Lyman W. "Books." Northwest Life (March), p. 31.

Favorable review of BB emphasizing the theme of racial protest and W's lack of didacticism in presenting it.

1047. Nishi, Setsuko Matsunaga. "New Book Is Scientific Analysis of Black Ghetto." Sunday Chicago Bee (11 November), Sec. Two, p. 16.

Associated Negro Press review of Black Metropolis quoting from W's introduction.

1048. Nomad, Max. "Treatment of Negroes the Shame of America." 338 News (June), pp. 43, 48.

Favorable review of BB placing it in an elaborate historical context and emphasizing episodes of white racism. Nomad deplores racial discrimination and praises black cultural contributions.

1049. Norman, Dorothy. "A World to Live In: Richard Wright's Book, 'Black Boy,'

Is News." New York Post (28 February), p. 30.

Highly favorable review stressing the potential social impact of the work, which "can most assuredly revolutionize our time." Norman also considers BB great art, especially in its universality and its development of the theme of human suffering.

1050. _____. "A World to Live In: Slavery Anywhere Is Slavery Everywhere." New York Post (4 May), p. 34.

Notes that BB leads the list of nonfiction best sellers.

1051. North, Joseph. "Culture of the War and Peace." New Masses, 54 (13 February), 15-16.

Mentions briefly the play NS.

1052. North, Sterling A. "Black Anger." Portland Oregon Sunday Journal (22 April), Pacific Parade Magazine Sec., p. 13.

Reprint of 1945.1058.

1053. _____. "Black Boy. By Richard Wright." The Washington Post (4 March), Sec. IV, p. 13.

Reprint of 1945.1058.

1054. _____. "Is This America's Cross Section?" The Chicago Sun Book Week (9 December), p. 2.

Favorable review of Cross Section 1945 with laudatory comments on "Early Days in Chicago." North notes, however, that the piece will "do little to make common ground between white and Negro readers."

Reprinted: 1945.1056, 1057, 1059.

1055. _____. "Pre-Review of Black Boy," in Pre-Reviews of Black Boy. New York: Book-of-the-Month Club, March, p. 3.

Favorable notice comparing BB to Agnes Smedley's Daughter of Earth and claiming progress for W since NS.

1056. _____. "Short Story Annual Fresh with Vital Young Realism, But Is Somber, North Says." The Cincinnati Enquirer (16 December), p. 14.

Reprint of 1945.1054.

1057. _____. "Sterling North Reviews: Young Realists." New York Post (13 December), pp. 22-24.

Reprint of 1945.1054.

1058. _____. "Today's Book: Boyhood of America's Black Rousseau." New York Post (2 March), p. 22.

Favorable review of BB emphasizing the social message and honesty of the book. North compares the work to Agnes Smedley's Daughter of Earth,

H. G. Wells's Experiment in Autobiography, and Rousseau's Confessions.
"Richard Wright has come an infinite
distance since the publication of
'Native Son.' From semi-articulate
and almost bestial protest he has
risen to self-criticism and intelligent social analysis."
Reprinted: 1945.1052, 1053.

1059. _____. "Young Realists." Columbus
(Ohio) Citizen (c. 30 December).
    Reprint of 1945.1054.

1060. Northe, James Neill. "Racial Problems Given New Angle in Black Boy."
Amarillo Times (11 March), Sec. 2, p.
8.
    Favorable review comparing W to Lil-
    lian Smith and Steinbeck. Northe
    points out similarities in the strug-
    gle for survival among blacks and
    poor whites. Praising W for the ho-
    nesty of his unfavorable depiction of
    blacks (including the "new angle" of
    black anti-Semitism), he nevertheless
    finds in the "deeply moving and
    touching story" the basis for a black
    nationalism.
    Reprinted: 1945.1061.

1061. _____. "With the Arts." The Terra
Bella (Cal.) News (23 March), p. 8.
    Reprint of 1945.1060.

1062. O., O. "Here Is a New Mississippi
Mark Twain Never Knew." Boston Sunday
Post (4 March), p. A-2.
    Favorable review of BB summarizing
    the narrative and admiring its extra-
    ordinary impact. "'Black Boy' is the
    'Uncle Tom's Cabin' of this century.
    But it is without sentimentality or
    dramatic distortion." The reviewer
    hopes that the book will be widely
    read and that W has found a better
    life in the North.

1063. O'Brian, Delos. "Black Boy." The
Wilmington (Del.) Sunday Morning Star
(15 April), p. 10.
    Favorable review. Reading W's auto-
    biography on the recommendation of
    Andrew Wyeth, O'Brian is greatly
    impressed by the truth and sincerity
    of the work. White guilt must be
    redeemed by changed attitudes and
    policies toward black people.

1064. P., A. "Two Able Negroes Discuss
Race Problems." High Point Enterprise
(c. 11 March).
    Favorable review of BB and Walter
    White's A Rising Wind. "While they
    have harsh things to say about their
    own people, they hardly leave the
    rest of us with a white leg to stand
    on."

1065. P., E. G. "Black Boy. By Richard
Wright." More Books, 20 (April), 178.
    Favorable review in a journal of the
    Boston Public Library. The reviewer
    stresses the hardships of W's youth.
    "The book tells a tragic story; it
    seems scarcely possible that the
    first few years of any one life could
    hold so much sorrow and frustration.
    Yet the writing is marked by a deep
    sincerity."

1066. Paige, Mary. "Books: New Book,
'Black Boy' Should Challenge the Thinking of a Nation." Wickenburg (Ariz.) Sun
(28 December).
    Favorable review drawn mainly from
    promotional materials.

1067. Parrot, Kenneth. "The Wright That
Failed." Brooklyn Branch N. A. A. C. P.
News (March).
    Unfavorable review of BB complaining
    of W's egocentricity and lack of
    literary skill. He does not portray
    black people favorably enough.

1068. Paulus, John D. "Negro Writes
Moving Life Story." The Pittsburgh Press
(18 February), p. 25.
    Highly favorable review of BB, "one
    of the best books in its class that
    you are ever likely to read," compa-
    rable to the autobiographies of Ben-
    jamin Franklin and Edward Bok. Paulus
    stresses W's sufferings and the so-
    cial indictment they imply, but notes
    his ability to transcend them.
    Praises the book's "narrative power"
    and "emotional tautness."
    Reprinted: 1978.209.

1069. _____. "Pre-Review of Black Boy,"
in Pre-Reviews of Black Boy. New York:
Book-of-the-Month Club, March, p. 4.
    Favorable notice emphasizing the
    work's candor.

1070. Payseur, Mrs. Pritchard. "Regular
Club Day Speakers." The Bulletin [of the
Des Moines Women's Club], 12 (November),
8.
    Describes W's background and announ-
    ces his lecture scheduled for 14
    November on "The Negro's Contribution
    to the Arts and Sciences."

1071. Peat, Harold R. "Harold R. Peat
Presents Richard Wright." 2 pp.
    Promotional brochure advertising W's
    lectures "The American Negro's
    Contribution to Literature" and
    "The American Negro Discovers
    Himself." Peat reviews W's life and
    quotes favorable comments on his
    lectures from PM and from Russell
    Potter of Columbia University.
    Partially reprinted: 1945.576.

1072. _____. "Peat Presents Two New Platform Sensations."

Flyer advertising W's lectures on "The American Negro Discovers Himself" and "The American Negro's Contributions to Literature and the Arts."

1073. Peters, Marjorie. "Poetess Brooks Calmly Greets Book's Success in Kitchenette." The Chicago Defender (25 August), p. 13.

Includes quotation from W's jacket comment on A Street in Bronzeville.

1074. Picon, Gaétan."Les Romans." Confluences (April), pp. 314-321.

Contains favorable mention of the French translation of "Big Boy Leaves Home" as published in the magazine L'Arbalète (p. 316).

1075. Pippett, Roger. "Pre-Review of Black Boy," in Pre-Reviews of Black Boy. New York: Book-of-the-Month Club, March, p. 5.

Favorable notice.

1076. _____. "Recommended." PM (11 March), Magazine Sec., p. m16; (18 March), Magazine Sec., p. m16; (25 March), Magazine Sec., p. m16; (1 April), Magazine Sec., p. m16; (8 April), Magazine Sec., p. m16; (15 April), Magazine Sec., p. m16; (22 April), Magazine Sec., p. m16; (29 April), Magazine Sec., p. m16.

Brief notice of BB.
Reprinted: 1945.1077.

1077. _____. "Recommended." St. Petersburg Times (29 April), p. 37.

Reprint of 1945.1076.

1078. Portuondo, José Antonio. "12 Million Black Voices." Afroamerica, 1 (January and July), 105-106.

Favorable review, in Spanish, describing the book with emphasis on its denunciation of the exploitation of the black proletariat. TMBV is even more effective as racial protest than NS. Portuondo concludes by expressing his surprise at W's recent attitude, which removes him from the ranks of black people demanding justice and liberty.

1079. Prattis, P. L. "The Horizon: Drake and Cayton Have Told It All in 'Black Metropolis,' Study of Black Chicago." The Pittsburgh Courier (29 December), p. 7.

Favorable review with praise for W's introduction.

1080. Prescott, Orville. "Books of the Times." The New York Times (28 February-

ary), p. 21.

Favorable review of BB emphasizing its emotional power. Offering no racial solutions, the work shows the cruelty of racism. Lacking restraint and subtlety because of the emotional scars its author still carries, BB "is powerful, moving and horrifying." Reprinted: 1978.209.

1081. Putzel, Henry, Jr. "You Ought to Know More About Black Boy." Pulse, 3 (May), 23.

Favorable review comparing the effect of the book to that of a grim etching by Goya. Putzel stresses W's conflicts first with his family and then with whites.

1082. Qualls, Youra. "Middletown of Negro Life in America." The Christian Science Monitor (6 November), p. 18.

Review of Black Metropolis contrasting the emotional tone of W's introduction with the restraint of the body of the work.

1082a. [Quinn, Kerker]. "Accent Announces for Winter 1945."

Flyer listing "The Man Who Lived Underground."

1083. Q.[uinn], S.[usan] A. "Fifty Stories by Americans." Richmond Times-Dispatch (22 July), p. D-5.

Lists W as a contributor to Charles Grayson's anthology Half a Hundred.

1084. _____. "Off the Bookshelves." Richmond Times-Dispatch (7 January), p. 6-D.

Announces that BB will be part of a dual Book-of-the-Month Club selection for March.

1085. _____. "Off the Bookshelves." Richmond Times-Dispatch (20 May), p. D-5.

Mentions Sinclair Lewis' column in Esquire on BB and other books on race.

1086. _____. "Off the Bookshelves." Richmond Times-Dispatch (5 August), p. D-5.

Lists W as a contributor to Edwin Seaver's anthology Cross Section 1945.

1087. _____. "Off the Bookshelves." Richmond Times-Dispatch (19 August), p. D-5.

Mentions the influence of Mencken on W. Also notes that BB has been published in abridged form in Omnibook.

1088. R., W. M. "A Negro Born to Be Free." The Kansas City Star (10 March),

p. 12.
Highly favorable review of BB, a work significant both as social protest and art. W "is a poet, a nonconformist, a fierce individualist who is seeking true independence and dignity for the human personality."

1089. Rabb, Miriam Glovier. "News of Books and Authors." The Columbia (S. C.) Record (22 February), p. 6B.
Contains a favorable notice of BB, s. v. "Book Club Selections," with quotations from two Southern reviewers.

1090. Reading, Samuel H. "Reading's Readings: Wright's Bad Boy." The Philadelphia Tribune (16 June), p. 5.
Highly favorable review of BB praising W for putting "into words--sometimes very profane, indecent and vulgar, the thoughts of every colored person, most of whom would not dare to use Wright's language, but most of whom have his same emotions and reactions." Reading claims a large black audience for BB.

1091. Rector, Beulah. "'Black Boy.'" Watertown Times (7 March).
Favorable review consisting mostly of summary. Rector emphasizes W's frankness in revealing the suffering of his childhood.

1092. Reddick, L. D. "Wright, Richard. Black Boy: a Record of Childhood and Youth." Library Journal, 70 (15 February), 163-164.
Favorable notice stressing W's self-confidence and the work's vivid grimness.

1093. Redding, J. Saunders. "The Negro Author: His Publisher, His Public and His Purse." The Publishers' Weekly, 147 (24 March), 1284-1288.
In an account of the special problems faced by black authors, Redding notes W's development of a common audience, both black and white.

1094. Redding, W. M. "Pre-Review of Black Boy," in Pre-Reviews of Black Boy. New York: Book-of-the-Month Club, March, p. 3.
Favorable notice of a book "as fascinating as it is disturbing."

1095. Reely, Katharine. "Wright, Richard. Black boy." Wisconsin Library Bulletin, 41 (April), 47.
Brief notice stating that here the reader will find the source of the brutality of NS. "Not pleasant reading and perhaps should not be taken as a typical experience."

1096. Rehder, Jessie. "Literary Lantern: Black Man's Burden." The Durham Herald-Sun (4 March), Sec. II, p. 5.
Review of Black Boy complaining of W's bias while conceding the existence of racism in the South. Whites too, Rehder argues, suffer from social oppression and dehumanization. Nevertheless, Rehder praises the literary merit of the work.

1097. Reid, Ira De A. "People Are Talking About Black Boy by Richard Wright." Pulse, 3 (May), 21.
Favorable review emphasizing W's candor in revealing the squalor of his childhood. Sociologically BB shows class stratification among blacks, exposes racism, and exemplifies black personality traits analyzed by social scientists.

1098. Renshaw, Charles C., Jr. "The New Books." Townsfolk, 33 (March), 28.
Contains a highly favorable review of BB, calling it equally admirable as "a passionate human document and an outstanding artistic success." W's objectivity enables him to view his experience as both individual and representative.

1099. Richardson, Ben. Great American Negroes. New York: Crowell, pp. 172-173.
Mentions W as an outstanding writer.

1100. Richter, F. K. "Black Boy by Richard Wright." Negro Story, 1 (May-June), 93-94.
Favorable review stressing the importance of W's appeal to the nation's conscience. The book's value is enhanced by its applicability to other minority groups. Richter is impressed by W's prose and his use of folklore. His sole misgiving is that in emphasizing his own growth W neglects external factors that must have aided it.
Reprinted: 1978.209.

1101. Rider, Ione. "Books: Black Boy by Richard Wright." Now, 2 (Second Half April), 11.
Favorable review emphasizing W's restraint in relating the disadvantages of his youth. His victory over them is "evidence of the strength and resilience of the human spirit."

1102. Roberts, Mary-Carter. "Pre-Review of Black Boy," in Pre-Reviews of Black Boy. New York: Book-of-the-Month Club, March, p. 6.
Very favorable notice. BB is "nobly sincere, the most convincing thing Richard Wright has done."

1103. _____. "Richard Wright Tells the Story of His Youth." The Washington Sunday Star (4 March), p. C-3.
Favorable review of BB praising W's presentation of his family problems, which Carter finds characteristic of any artist rebelling against the Philistines. Though the book does attack racism, it has greater breadth than UTC or NS, for the fact "that he can now present Negro society objectively indicates that his work is becoming free of his bitter personal emotion."
Reprinted: 1978.209.

1104. Robeson, Eslanda G. "American Tragedy." The Hartford Courant (8 April), Magazine Sec., p. 12.
Favorable review of BB praising W's presentation of appalling social and racial conditions in the South. But Robeson considers the W family atypical of black people in their lack of "sympathy, compassion and understanding."

1105. Robinson, Ted. "Black Boy. By Richard Wright." Cleveland Plain Dealer (4 March), Pictorial Magazine Sec., p. 12.
Favorable review complaining of lapses of taste in "certain unsavory passages," but praising the work as "new in its field, courageous in its candor, and tremendously effective for its purpose." After summarizing BB, Robinson concludes that it "is a work so moving as to promise permanence for itself and a high place in American letters for its author."

1106. Rogers, J. A. "Rogers Says: Exception Is Taken to Criticism of 'Black Boy,' Written by Theophilus Lewis." The Pittsburgh Courier (14 July), p. 7.
Defends BB against an unfavorable review. Rogers finds the autobiography factual and well written. It should have beneficial social effects. W is "one of America's greatest living writers."

1107. _____. "Rogers Says: Negro Writers Have Had to Depend Upon Approval of Whites to Win Status." The Pittsburgh Courier (31 March), p. 7.
Mentions W.

1108. _____. "Rogers Says: Writers Picked Up by White Publishers Fade Out Because Novelty of Product Wears Out." The Pittsburgh Courier (7 April), p. 7.
Argues that NS would have received much less attention if it had been published by a black publisher.

1109. Rogers, W. G. "The Literary Guide-

post." Redding Record-Searchlight (23 July), p. 6.
Reprint of 1945.1110.

1110. _____. "The Literary Guidepost." Wausau Daily Record-Herald (9 June), p. 8.
Lists W as a contributor to Charles Grayson's anthology Half a Hundred.
Reprinted: 1945.1109.

1111. _____. "Literary Guidepost." Zanesville Daily Signal (26 October), p. 30.
Review of Black Metropolis mentioning W's "provocative" introduction.

1112. _____. "Literary Guidepost." Zanesville Daily Signal (13 December), p. 4.
Lists W as a contributor to Edwin Seaver's Cross Section 1945.
Reprinted: 1945.1113.

1113. _____. "With Exceptions, 'Cross Section' Is Excellent One." New Haven Sunday Register (16 December), p. 19.
Reprint of 1945.1112.

1114. Rolo, Charles J. "This, Too, Is America." Tomorrow, 4 (May), 63-64.
Favorable review of BB with a summary of the narrative. The work is moving, memorable and graphic, but it does not explain how W the writer could have emerged from the environment of his youth. In any case, W's literary promise is very bright. Includes an interview with W, who comments on the relation of literature to politics, the urbanization of black people, racism, and white liberals.

1115. Rosenfeld, Isaac. "Autobiography of a Freedman." Jewish Frontier, 12 (June), 33-35.
Favorable review of BB, by critical consensus W's best book. Its theme is man's rise to artistic consciousness. Despite racist violence and inadequate schooling, W managed to transcend the barriers to a literary career.
Reprinted: 1962.96.

1116. Rovere, Richard H. "Books: Childhood in Occupied America." Common Sense, 14 (April), 32-33.
Very favorable review of BB comparing it to Adventures of Huckleberry Finn. W's story of growing up in a minority in America conveys great emotional power.

1117. Salpeter, Harry. "A Negro's Boyhood." Congress Weekly, 12 (17 August), 12.
Favorable review of BB emphasizing

its social and racial protest. Salpeter relates racism to anti-Semitism
and comments on W's revelation of
black anti-Semitism.
Reprinted: 1978.209.

1118. Sancton, Thomas. "Gone to Chicago." The New Republic, 113 (12 November), 647-648, 650.
Highly favorable review of Black
Metropolis calling "the brilliant
Wright introduction . . . the best
single essay in its field I have
read" (p. 650).

1119. Sandrof, Ivan. "Should Make Us
Blush." Worcester Sunday Telegram (18
March), Feature Parade Sec., p. [14].
Favorable review of BB comparing W's
prose to Whitman's poetry. "If Wright
had set out to make civilized humanity blush for its treatment of the
Negro, he has succeeded better than
he knows. Unfortunately, the people
who should read this book--won't."

1120. Schneider, Isidor. "One Apart."
New Masses, 55 (3 April), 23-24.
Rather unfavorable review of BB. "As
autobiography Black Boy has all the
faults of that riskiest form of writing; as a picture of the Negro people
it is a distortion; but as a document
of the psychological patterns of race
tension it is unique, powerful and of
considerable importance."
Reprinted: 1978.209.

1121. Schriftgiesser, Karl. "Books: A
Survey of American Letters in 1945."
Newsweek, 26 (17 December), 106.
Comments favorably on BB, the most
exciting autobiography of the year
and one of the five best works of
nonfiction.

1122. _____. "Pre-Review of Black Boy,"
in Pre-Reviews of Black Boy. New York:
Book-of-the-Month Club, March, p. 3.
Favorable notice of a "cruelly honest
story" which "kicks America's conscience in the face."

1123. Schuyler, Josephine. "Looks at
Books: Black Boy." The Pittsburgh Courier (9 June), p. 16.
Favorable review pointing out the
social oppression of the Southern
environment while stressing W's atypical qualities. The psychology of
fear revealed in BB helps the reader
to understand Bigger Thomas.

1124. Scoon, Anabelle. "Midwest Book
Briefs: Negro 'Middletown.'" The Chicago
Sun Book Week (15 July), p. 10.
Announcement of Black Metropolis men-
tioning W's introduction.

1125. _____. "Midwest Book Briefs: Panel
Discussion." The Chicago Sun Book Week
(29 April), p. 9.
Announces a discussion of BB at the
Abraham Lincoln School with Sylvestre
Watkins and Ben Burns.

1126. S.[cott], W. T. "Bookman's Galley." The Providence Sunday Journal (18
November), Sec. VI, p. 6.
Refers to BB in the course of an
argument against censorship.

1127. _____. "Richard Wright Tells Story
of Youth, 'Black Boy.'" The Providence
Sunday Journal (4 March), Sec. VI, p. 6.
Favorable review summarizing the narrative and remarking on the "extraordinary mystery" of his emergence as
a writer from his blighted background. Strong fare, BB will impress
its readers "with horror at the tale,
with profound admiration for the
writing."

1128. Seaver, Edwin. "Foreword," in his
Cross Section 1945. New York: L. B.
Fischer, pp. vii-xi.
Notes that "The Man Who Lived Under-
ground" now deserves publication
because it was written some time ago.

1129. _____. and Robin McKown. "Reading
& Writing." Charlotte Sunday Observer
(28 January), Sec. Four, p. 2.
Announces that BB will be part of a
dual Book-of-the-Month Club selection
for March.

1130. _____. "Reading & Writing." The
Summit (Miss.) Sun (3 May), p. 6.
Favorable review of BB. The reviewers
quote from Dorothy Canfield and recount W's life and literary career.

1131. Shapiro,, Karl. "Books I Have
Liked." New York Herald Tribune Weekly
Book Review (2 December), p. 8.
Lists BB and two others.

1132. S.[herman], J.[ohn] K. "Book of
the Week: A Searing Picture of Childhood
in the South." Minneapolis Tribune (4
March), Sec. G, p. 15.
Favorable review of BB, the work of
an artist, not a propagandist. Includes comments from an interview
with W in which he expressed concern
over the emphasis on bitterness in
the work.
Reprinted: 1978.209.

1133. _____. "Pre-Review of Black Boy,"
in Pre-Reviews of Black Boy. New York:
Book-of-the-Month Club, March, p. 3.
Favorable notice. The book is a
"black Studs Lonigan" which "tells
more about our race problem than a

dozen sociological studies."

1134. Sillen, Samuel. "Richard Wright's Book Marked by Rejection of His People." Daily Worker (9 March), p. 11.
    Highly unfavorable review of BB conceding W's narrative skill in some passages, but complaining of his excessive subjectivity, his estrangement from other black people, and his defection from Communist ranks. Sillen quotes approvingly from the review by W. E. B. Du Bois.

1135. Slochower, Harry. "In the Fascist Styx," in his No Voice Is Wholly Lost . . . . New York: Creative Age Press, pp. 75-92.
    Reprint of 1942.320.

1136. S.[loper], L.[eslie] A. "One Negro's Life Story." The Christian Science Monitor (9 March), p. 18.
    Rather favorable review of BB. W's case is exceptional and the viciousness of Southern whites is overdrawn, but the message that black rights should be respected is valid. W's literary success despite his sordid background is the most remarkable fact of his life history.
    Reprinted: 1978.209.

1137. _____. "Pre-Review of Black Boy," in Pre-Reviews of Black Boy. New York: Book-of-the-Month Club, March, p. 2.
    Very favorable notice. The book is "biting social comment and a moving human record."

1138. Smith, Blanche Hixson. "Have You Read Black Boy by Richard Wright?" Meriden Record (14 March), pp. 6, 10.
    Favorable review emphasizing the work's racial protest and the "miracle of survival by force of strong will" which made possible W's emergence from his Southern background to become a writer. BB contributes to racial understanding.

1139. Smith, Lillian. "Richard Wright Adds a Chapter to Our Bitter Chronicle." PM (4 March), Magazine Sec., p. 15.
    Favorable review of BB corroborating from a white Southern perspective W's indictment of Southern racism. The development of W's mature personality must derive from some unremembered love extended to him in childhood, but his childhood recollections are vague. His treatment of his youth is much better. Smith praises highly the literary quality of this part of the work and quotes from it extensively.
    Reprinted: 1978.209.

1140. S.[mith], P.[aul] J.[ordan].

"Youth in Deep South Fights Both Poverty and Prejudice." Los Angeles Times (4 March), Sec. III, p. 4.
    Highly favorable review of BB emphasizing its overwhelming power. W does exhibit some hope at the end.

1141. Smith, Theodore. "'Of Making Many Books There Is No End'--Ecclesiastes, 12-12: Reviews and News of Books." The San Francisco News (5 January), p. 12.
    Announces that BB will be part of a dual Book-of-the-Month Club selection for March.

1142. Spectorsky, A. C. "Authors, Atoms and Money." The Chicago Sun Book Week (2 December), p. 3.
    Lists W as an author whose integrity was rewarded by success.

1143. _____. "'The Ethics of Living Jim Crow' from 'Uncle Tom's Children' by Richard Wright," in North, East, South, West: A Regional Anthology of American Writing. Ed. Charles Lee. New York: Howell, Soskin, p. 399.
    Headnote to the essay.

1144. _____. "The Middle West," in North, East, South, West: A Regional Anthology of American Writing. Ed. Charles Lee. New York: Howell, Soskin, p. 376.
    Mentions W.

1145. _____. "Pre-Review of Black Boy," in Pre-Reviews of Black Boy. New York: Book-of-the-Month Club, March, p. 1.
    Very favorable notice emphasizing the work's value as a social document.

1146. _____. "Richard Wright," in North, East, South, West: A Regional Anthology of American Writing. Ed. Charles Lee. New York: Howell, Soskin, p. 555.
    Biographical note.

1147. _____. "Ten Christmas Lists of Ten 'Best.'" The New York Times Book Review (2 December), p. 5.
    Lists BB.

1148. Sprietsma, Lewis Roy. "Good Writing, Honest Presentations Make Best Seller of 'Black Boy.'" Chicago Daily Law Bulletin (June).
    Favorable review praising W's style--"unique in its simplicity and directness"--and his candor in presenting Southern race relations. Sprietsma provides a brief summary of the narrative.

1149. Stanard, Hugh. "What the Negro Wants. Edited by Rayford W. Logan." The Southern Packet, 1 (November), 2.
    Praising the optimism of the work

under review, Stanard remarks: "Altogether Chapel Hill has brought forth
a marvelous antidote for that dark
brown taste left in the mouth after
reading such current best sellers as
Black Boy."

1150. Stein, Gertrude. "The New Hope in
Our 'Sad Young Men.'" The New York Times
Magazine (3 June), pp. 5, 38.
    Contains a brief reference to W's
    literary ability.

1151. Stern, Philip Van Doren. "Cross
Section 1945." The Book Find News, II
(December), 4-5.
    Mentions the appearance of W in the
    previous volume of the collection. A
    photograph of W appears on p. 3.

1152. Strawn, Bill. "Book of the Month,
Humanities Children and Other Books
Here." Charlotte News (9 March), Sec. B,
p. 4.
    Contains a favorable review of BB.
    "Starkly realistic, passionately
    written, 'Black Boy' will give sober,
    honest Americans many questions over
    which to ponder."

1153. Streator, George. "More Books of
the Week: Black Boy. Richard Wright."
The Commonweal, 41 (23 March), 568-569.
    Favorable review emphasizing the so-
    cial implications, especially con-
    cerning other minority groups such as
    Jews and Irish Catholics. Notes the
    debate about W in the black middle
    class.
    Reprinted: 1978.209.

1154. Strindberg, Axel. "Svartas och
vitas värld." Stockholm Expressen (11
March).
    Favorable review of the Swedish pro-
    duction of the play NS. Praises the
    co-existence of stereotype and hu-
    manity in Bertil Anderberg's rendi-
    tion of Bigger. The crux of the drama
    lies in the inevitable outgrowth of
    violence when Bigger the person is
    turned into a thing.

1155. Strong, Augusta J. "Book Review."
Congress View, 3 (May), 8.
    Favorable review of BB in the organ
    of the National Negro Congress.
    Strong defends the representative
    truthfulness of the work. W is ab-
    sorbed with self, tending to overlook
    the depth of suffering of other
    blacks, but this preoccupation inten-
    sifies the effect of the narrative.
    Reprinted: 1945.1156; 1978.209.

1156. _____. "More Comments on 'Black
Boy.'" Sunday Chicago Bee (27 May), Sec.
Two, pp. 15, 23.

Reprint of 1945.1155.

1157. Sullivan, J. V. "What's New in
Book World: 'Black Boy' Is the Story of
a Negro Boy Who Could Not Accept His
'Place.'" The Stars and Stripes Magazine
(Marseilles edition) (10 June), p. VII.
    Favorable review summarizing the book
    and emphasizing W's objectivity and
    articulateness. The work itself is
    not controversial, but reactions to
    it may be.

1158. Sullivan, Richard. "Best Books of
1945 as Selected by Tribune Critics."
Chicago Sunday Tribune (2 December),
Part 4, p. 4.
    Lists BB.

1159. Taylor, Howard. "Pre-Review of
Black Boy," in Pre-Reviews of Black Boy.
New York: Book-of-the-Month Club, March,
p. 4.
    Favorable notice. The book is "dis-
    maying in its revelation of the
    depths of racial antagonism in Amer-
    ica."

1160. _____. "Rebellious 'Black Boy' in
the South." The Philadelphia Inquirer (4
March), Sec. SO, p. 11.
    Mixed review of BB. Taylor applauds
    W's literary skill, but shudders at
    his revelation of racial bitterness,
    which will not improve an already
    volatile racial situation. "Mr.
    Wright has a very great talent; he
    might well turn it to great purposes
    if only he would let time heal his
    scars."

1161. Terrell, Mary Church. "You Ought
to Know More About Black Boy." Pulse, 3
(May), 22.
    Unfavorable comment complaining about
    W's belief that blacks lack kindness.

1162. Thn., J. "Negerdrama pa Stadsteatern." Göteborgs Tidningen (11
March).
    Unfavorable review of the Swedish
    production of the play NS. Noting the
    high level of Swedish interest in
    Americal racial problems, the review-
    er remarks that the novel worked well
    as a standard mystery story. Debate
    centered on the question of whether W
    had overdone the sensationalism. The
    dramatization, however, brings prob-
    lems on itself because of excessively
    artificial earnestness.

1163. Thompson, E. Bruce. "Black Boy: A
Record of Childhood and Youth. By
Richard Wright." The Journal of Missis-
sippi History, 7 (July), 178-180.
    Favorable review stressing W's social
    indictment. Neither whites nor blacks

are spared, but the defects of the latter may be the result of white racism. BB refutes white racists and challenges whites of good will.
Reprinted: 1978.209.

1164. Tiempo, David. "Sangre negra: un exito firme de la temporada." Unidentified clipping.
Favorable review of the Buenos Aires production of the play NS contrasting its serious theme of liberation to the frivolous and superficial plays that dominate the Argentinian stage. The acting and production are excellent.

1165. T.[illman], N.[athaniel]. "As the Twig Is Bent." Phylon, 6 (Second Quarter), 185-186.
Favorable review of BB insisting that W's bitterness is authentic and typical, not exaggerated. Illustrative of the principles of psychology and sociology, BB "is the clearest exposition that has been written of the feelings of a sensitive Negro boy as he grows up under the domination of family ignorance and bigotry and the terror inspired by the practices of white supremacy."
Reprinted: 1978.209.

1166. Tomms, Sonia. "Southern Negro Rips Richard Wright." The Chicago Defender (1 September), p. 14.
Letter to the editor launching a vitriolic attack on W, "an addlepated black fool," for his unfavorable presentation of Southern blacks in BB.

1167. Tonnar, Bernard A., S. J. Untitled clipping. The Catholic Mirror (August), pp. 45-46.
Mixed review of BB. Despite the fact that W overemphasizes both "white domination and Negro discontent," the work stirs the reader's emotional depths. The reviewer suggests that a section on W's reaction to Chicago is necessary to test his theory that a black person can live only in the North.
Reprinted: 1978.209.

1168. Torrassa, A. E. "'Sangre negra' tiene interés." Unidentified clipping.
Highly favorable review of the Buenos Aires production of the play NS. Torrassa emphasizes the universality of the theme of the oppressed and the powerful. He praises Narciso Ibañez Menta for his direction and his acting of Bigger.

1169. Touhey, Eleanor. "Negro Writer Bares Race Problems in Newest Book." The

Portland Sunday Oregonian (18 March), Sec. Three, p. 7.
Favorable review of BB praising its social import and its literary artistry. W is "not only our most distinguished Negro writer of prose, but also the most convincing apologist the Negro race has yet had."

1170. Townend, Marion. "Odds & Book Ends." Charlotte Sunday Observer (18 March), Sec. Two, p. 10.
Includes comments and quotations from some of the reviews of BB.

1171. Tracy, Henry C. "The Bookshelf." Common Ground, 5 (Summer), 102-108.
Includes a favorable review of BB, a "painfully absorbing narrative." The first half emphasizes psychology; the second half, sociology.

1172. Trilling, Lionel. "A Tragic Situation." The Nation, 160 (7 April), 390, 392.
Favorable review of BB. More than a sociological document, it is a work of "moral and intellectual power" that does not permit the reader the vicarious suffering that substitutes for political or ethical action. W's objectivity toward his painful experience allows him to survive and to achieve liberation. "He is not an object; he is a subject; he is the same kind of person as his reader, as complex, as free." Trilling regrets that W does not continue his autobiography to treat the period after he left the South.
Reprinted: 1978.209.

1173. Van Gelder, Robert. "The World of Books at War's End." The New York Times Book Review (2 December), pp. 1, 16, 24, 26.
Notes that the attacks on BB published in 1945 were "tentative and inconclusive" (p. 16).

1174. Voorhis, Jerry, George V. Denny, Jr., Elmer Carter, and Richard Wright. "Are We Solving America's Race Problem?" Town Meeting, 11 (24 May), 3-22.
See 1945.875.

1175. W., E. "Ett negerdrama på Stadsteatern." Göteborg Ny Tid (12 March).
Favorable review of the Swedish production of NS. Although parts of the play are remote from Swedish experience, the power and importance of the work as a whole are still communicated. Bertil Anderberg's performance as Bigger receives praise, as does Sven Miliander's presentation of Max's speech, "the high point of the performance."

1176. W., J. C. "Black Boy, by Richard Wright." Social Progress (April), pp. 31-32.

Favorable review emphasizing W's veracity. "The book is vivid realism, written in a gripping style. Its message disturbs the complacency of any sincere reader." Reprinted: 1978.209.

1177. Wadsworth, Norman B. "Praises Wright's 'Black Boy.'" The Pittsburgh Courier (21 July), p. 6.

Letter to the editor expressing the belief that the work "will help to bring a great improvement to Negroes in the South."

1178. Walker, Danton. "Broadway." New York Daily News (31 December).

Notes that W "has purchased a Greenwich Village brownstone, but doesn't want to dispossess the tenants for fear of an uproar."

1179. Webster, Harvey C. "All Men Are Brothers, But." Louisville Defender (8 December).

Defends BB and Arna Bontemps's St. Louis Women from black critics who would have preferred a more respectable presentation of black life.

1180. Weeks, Edward. "The Peripatetic Reviewer." The Atlantic Monthly, 175 (March), 129, 131.

Favorable review of BB comparing it to Father Henson's Story. Notes W's detachment. Reprinted: 1978.209.

1181. _____. "Pre-Review of Black Boy," in Pre-Reviews of Black Boy. New York: Book-of-the-Month Club, March, p. 1.

Favorable notice with reservations about the "telling and tedious" dialogues.

1182. _____. "Ten Christmas Lists of Ten 'Best.'" The New York Times Book Review (2 December), p. 5.

Lists BB.

1183. Welles, Orson. "Orson Welles' Almanac." New York Post (2 March).

Contains a review of BB emphasizing its importance for those who think mistakenly that they "understand the Negro."

1184. Welters, Nona M. "Three Cheers for Richard Wright and 'Black Boy.'" The Chicago Defender (13 October), p. 14.

Letter to the editor rebutting Sonia Tomms's criticism of W. Welters verifies his depiction of Southern conditions and praises his protest.

1185. Werner, Hazen G. "Powerful Tale of Negro Life Told by Richard Wright." Dayton Daily Journal (8 April), Sec. 3, p. 6.

Highly favorable review of BB praising W's ability to use words. The two dominant forces in W's youth were fear of whites and the desire to learn. The revelation of white injustice to black people should arouse the reader's social conscience.

1186. Wertham, Frederic, M. D. "Black Boy, Richard Wright." Journal of Clinical Psychopathology and Psychotherapy, 6 (January-April), 643.

Favorable review. Drawing on his experience as a psychiatrist treating black patients, Wertham argues that W's autobiography is typical, especially in its patterns of family life. Moreover, these approximate "the experience of too many people all over the world."

1187. White, Walter. "A Hard-hitting-- And Entertaining--Study of a Black Metropolis." PM (11 November), Magazine Sec., p. m8.

Favorable review of Black Metropolis with high praise for W's introduction, "one of the most thoughtful analyses of the malady of race prejudice which this reviewer has read."

1188. Wiley, Paul I. "A Black Boy's Fight in World of White Men." The Milwaukee Journal (4 March), Sec. V, p. 3.

Favorable review of BB finding its chief significance that of a bildungsroman, not that of an attack on racism. W's home environment as well as white oppression conditioned his early life, creating bitter resentment. The style of the book is "hard, plain, and drab."

1189. _____. "Neglected Stories in This Anthology." The Milwaukee Journal (15 July), Sec. V, p. 3.

Lists W as a contributor to Charles Grayson's Half a Hundred.

1190. Williams, Ethel L. "About Books." The Baltimore Afro-American (24 March), p. 14.

Favorable review of BB summarizing the narrative and praising its frankness, which may be somewhat exaggerated at times, however. The work should increase the sympathy of white readers for the problems of black people.

1191. Williams, Mentor L. "'Richard Wright's Catharsis': Prof. Williams Reviews 'Black Boy.'" Ann Arbor Michigan Daily (8 April), p. 4.

Favorable review accepting the validity of W's indictment of the South.
After recounting several incidents
from the book illustrating racism,
Williams concludes that such purga-
tion of bitterness is necessary to
W's growth as a writer.

1192. Williams, Naomi. "'Modern Man Is
at War with Self': Wright." The Cornellian (16 November), pp. 1-2.
    Reports on W's lecture "The American
    Negro Discovers Himself" as delivered
    at Cornell College, Mount Vernon,
    Iowa, on 15 November.

1193. _____. "Richard Wright's 'Black
Boy' Is Vivid Story of Boyhood." The
Cornellian (2 November), p. 4.
    Favorable review of BB in the student
    newspaper of Cornell College. Wil-
    liams stresses W's sense of shame and
    the hope he found in books.

1194. Wilson, Dale. "Pre-Review of Black
Boy," in Pre-Reviews of Black Boy. New
York: Book-of-the-Month Club, March, p.
3.
    Very favorable notice. W has shown
    "proof of his genius."

1195. Wing, Joe. "Book World." Glendale
News-Press (10 August), p. 8A.
    Lists W as a contributor to Bucklin
    Moon's Primer for White Folks.

1196. Winston, W. T. "Wright, Richard.
Black Boy." Best Sellers, 4 (15 March),
219-220.
    Somewhat favorable review summarizing
    the narrative and praising W's vivid
    recollection of his youth. If well
    written, however, the book is im-
    mature in its "naive egoism," dis-
    regard of history, and fondness for
    vulgarity and obscenity.
    Reprinted: 1978.209.

1197. W.[interich], J.[ohn] T. "Playing
Ball." The Saturday Review of Literature, 28 (24 November), 12.
    Editorial on Jackie Robinson noting
    that very few baseball fans have read
    NS or BB.

1198. Wirth, Louis. "Negro Life in the
Urban North." The New York Times Book
Review (4 November), p. 5.
    Favorable review of Black Metropolis
    devoting two paragraphs of praise to
    W's "sensitive and penetrating" in-
    troduction.

1199. Woods, Mary Thomas. "Co-Book-of-
the-Month." The Argonaut, 124 (23
March), 21.
    Favorable review of BB consisting
    mainly of summary. Includes a sketch

of W's literary career.

1200. _____. "Easy Aces." The Argonaut,
124 (6 April), 19.
    Notes that W has been appointed to
    the board of directors of the Ameri-
    can Council on Race Relations.

1201. Zolotov, Sam. "Playwrights to
Meet." The New York Times (19 June), p.
15.
    Notes that BB may be dramatized.
    Canada Lee, Herbert Kline, and Mark
    Marvin own the rights.

1946

1. Adams, J. Donald. "Speaking of
Books." The New York Times Book Review
(2 June), p. 2.
    Notes that BB received some support
    in the Saturday Review poll of crit-
    ics.

2. Angleman, Margaret. "What Happened at
Home." Richmond Times-Dispatch (17 February), p. D-7.
    Mentions W as someone who would have
    provided a much different perspective
    on racial relations than that of
    While You Were Gone, a report on
    domestic life during the war.

3. Anon. "À tout hasard." Juin (16
July).
    Mentions French translations of works
    by W and Ann Petry.

4. Anon. "Action." Paris Libération (25
October), p. [4].
    Advertisement for Paris Action men-
    tioning interview with W in current
    issue.

5. Anon. "American Daughter." The Retail
Bookseller, 49 (April), 82-83.
    Brief notice of Era Bell Thompson's
    American Daughter referring to it as
    a "companion piece to Black Boy."

6. Anon. "Au fil de la plume." Paris
Carrefour (3 October), p. 6.
    Cites W's presence in Paris as evi-
    dence, among other signs, of the
    entrance of blacks into French intel-
    lectual and artistic life.

7. Anon. "Author's Guild Ordered to
Disclose Records to Members." The Publishers' Weekly, 150 (7 December), 3107.
    Notes that W is on the "official
    slate" for the Author's Guild coun-
    cil.

8. Anon. "Authors to Appeal." The New
York Sun (4 December), p. 27.
    Notes that W was elected to the coun-
    cil of the Author's Guild.

9. Anon. "Authors to Appeal on Opening Files." New York Herald Tribune (4 December), p. 23.
Notes that W was elected to the council of the Author's Guild.

10. Anon. "Authors to Appeal Open-Rolls Ruling." New York World-Telegram (c. 4 December).
Notes that W was elected to the council of the Author's Guild.

11. Anon. "Best Sellers? Capital Reads 'Em and Weeps." The Washington Post (15 September), p. 9B.
Reports that BB was named as "one of the best" books "I've ever read" by sixty percent of Washington, D. C., residents who had read it. It ranked fifteenth on the "most frequently read" list but second in positive response.

12. Anon. "Best Sellers in Harlem." New York Amsterdam News (21 September), p. 6.
Lists NS [sic] in seventh place in the fiction category.

13. Anon. "Best Sellers in Harlem." New York Amsterdam News (26 October), p. 16.
Lists BB in fifth place in the fiction [sic] category.

14. Anon. "Best Sellers in Midwest." Chicago Sunday Tribune (6 January), Part 6, p. 12.
Lists BB in third place in the nonfiction category in the Tri-Cities (Davenport, Moline, and Rock Island).

15. Anon. "Best Sellers in Midwest." Chicago Sunday Tribune (13 January), Part 6, p. 10.
Lists BB in third place in the nonfiction category in the Tri-Cities (Davenport, Moline, and Rock Island).

16. Anon. "Best Sellers in Midwest." Chicago Sunday Tribune (27 January), Part 6, p. 11.
Lists BB in fourth place in the nonfiction category in the Tri-Cities (Davenport, Moline, and Rock Island).

17. Anon. "Best Sellers in Midwest." Chicago Sunday Tribune (10 February), Part 4, p. 5.
Lists BB in fourth place in the nonfiction category in the Tri-Cities (Davenport, Moline, and Rock Island).

18. Anon. "Best Sellers in Midwest." Chicago Sunday Tribune (10 March), Part 4, p. 5.
Lists BB in third place in the nonfiction category in the Tri-Cities (Davenport, Moline, and Rock Island).

19. Anon. "Best Sellers in Midwest." Chicago Sunday Tribune (31 March), Part 4, p. 17.
Lists BB in third place in the nonfiction category in Peoria.

20. Anon. "Best Sellers in the Midwest." Chicago Sunday Tribune (20 January), Part 6, p. 12.
Lists BB in second place in the nonfiction category in the Tri-Cities (Davenport, Moline, and Rock Island).

21. Anon. "Best Sellers in the Midwest." Chicago Sunday Tribune (24 February), Part 4, p. 21.
Lists BB in fourth place in the nonfiction category in the Tri-Cities (Davenport, Moline, and Rock Island).

22. Anon. "The Best Sellers of 1945." The Publishers' Weekly, 149 (19 January), 297-299.
Reports that BB, the "leading autobiography of 1945," sold 195,000 trade copies and 351,000 book club copies for a total of 546,000, placing it fourth in the nonfiction category. A photograph of W is included.

23. Anon. "Black Boy av Richard Wright." Unidentified clipping.
Swedish newspaper advertisement.

24. Anon. "'Black Boy' Gets a Job." Ebony, 1 (May), 49.
Relates an anecdote concerning a request for a photograph of W from an employee of World Publishing Company, which had taken over distribution of BB from Harper.

25. Anon. "Book Notes." New York Herald Tribune (13 May), p. 15.
Mentions that W "has become co-editor . . . of 'Twice a Year' and will contribute an article to the forthcoming issue on the Wiltwyck School for Young Delinquents."

26. Anon. "Book Notes." New York Herald Tribune (20 May), p. 21.
Announces that W's books will be displayed in the New York Public Library branches as part of Harlem Week observations.

27. Anon. "Book Notes." New York Herald Tribune (21 June), p. 21.
Notice of new issue of TMBV.

28. Anon. "Bookman's Galley." The Providence Sunday Journal (2 June), Sec. VI, p. 2.
Notes that W is "profoundly concerned with morals" and does not, as some have claimed, present characters as

"slaves to animalistic souls."

29. Anon. "Books--Authors." The New York Times (6 April), p. 15.
    Notes that The Second Armchair Companion, edited by L. Furman, will include a biography of W along with sixteen others.

30. Anon. "The Bookseller's Almanac." The Retail Bookseller, 49 (April), 66-68.
    Briefly compares Era Bell Thompson's American Daughter with BB.

31. Anon. "Bookshelf of a Workingman: Candid, Authentic Profile of Life in a Negro Ghetto." Weekly People (20 April), p. 2.
    Favorable review of Black Metropolis commenting on and quoting from W's introduction. The true Marxist will disagree at times with W, "a disillusioned Stalinist who revolted against the Stalinists' opportunistic exploitation of the Negroes' tragedy."

32. Anon. "Canada Lee's Introduction to the Stage." New York Herald Tribune (18 August), Sec. V, p. 2.
    Includes NS in a list of Lee's performances.

33. Anon. "Le Carnaval des enfants." Les Nouvelles Littéraires (6 June), p. 4.
    Announces a reception for W and his family scheduled for 22 June and sponsored by La Societe des Gens des Lettres.

34. Anon. "Case History of an Ex-White Man." Ebony, 2 (December), 11-16.
    Article on the white jazz musician and Negrophile Milton "Mezz" Mezzrow. Notes that W suggested that he call his book The Autobiography of an Ex-White Man.

35. Anon. "Ce que vous lirez en 1947," in Almanach des Lettres 1947. Ed. Georges Duhamel. Paris: Les Editions de Flore and La Gazette des Lettres, pp. 241-244.
    Lists the French translations of NS and UTC to be published by Albin Michel.

36. Anon. "Ce vice impuni." Les Nouvelles Littéraires (17 October), p. 4.
    Mentions W's letter on the racial problem in Les Nouvelles Epitres.

37. Anon. "Chez les éditeurs." Bordeaux Courrier Français de Sud-Ouest (12 June).
    Mentions W's presence in France and announces plans to translate his works.

38. Anon. "Chez les éditeurs." Le Saint-Etienne Patriote (22 July).
    Mentions publication of the French translations of UTC and NS.

39. Anon. "Chez les traducteurs." Marseilles Midi-Soir (30 December).
    Mentions UTC as a work translated by Marcel Duhamel.

40. Anon. "La Chute des feuilles." La Buenos Aires France Nouvelle (c. 25 October).
    Mentions W's admiration for French literary weeklies.

41. Anon. "Combat." Paris Combat (25 June), p. 1.
    Advertisement for Combat listing W as a contributor.

42. Anon. "Courrier." Paris Résistance (30 July).
    Mentions publication of the French translation of UTC.

43. Anon. "Le Courrier." Paris Résistance (29 October).
    Mentions W's visit to Paris.

44. Anon. "Courrier Littéraire." Le Paris Monde (15 June), p. 4.
    Mentions the French translations by Marcel Duhamel of NS and UTC.

45. Anon. "Court Fight Is Due in Author's Guild." The New York Times (4 December), p. 33.
    Reports that W has been elected to the council of the Author's Guild on a slate opposed to an "insurgent faction."

46. Anon. "Current Literary Notes." The Columbia (S. C.) Record (9 May), p. 5-B.
    Mentions the popularity of W in the Moscow Central Library of Foreign Literature.

47. Anon. "Current Trends in the Trade: Negro Press Sees Steady Expansion of Book News." The Publishers' Weekly, 150 (16 November), 2801-2803.
    Reports that BB was advertised in thirty-two black newspapers over a four-week period.

48. Anon. "'Dans le monde entier je sais reconnaitre un nègre du Sud,' m'a dit le douanier du Texas qui ne pouvait pas croire que j'étais écrivain." Paris-Matin (27 June), p. 2.
    Headnote to a portion of the French translation of "How Jim Crow Feels" explaining the current racial situation in America and noting some hopeful signs.

49. Anon. "Dans le Sud, lorsqu'un noir parle a un blanc, sa voix grimpe de deux octaves." Paris-Matin (2 July).
Headnote to the third and last installment of Jacques de Montalais's translation of "How Jim Crow Feels."

50. Anon. "Dis-mois ce que tu lis." Les Nouvelles Litteraires (26 December), p. 4.
Reports that actress Josette Day named W her favorite writer.

51. Anon. "Un Ecrivain noir decouvre la France." Unidentified clipping (c. 1 June).
Sketches W's career and describes his experience in Paris.

52. Anon. "Facts of Cullen's Life Few, Direct and Simple." New York Amsterdam News (19 January), p. 2.
Lists W as an honorary pallbearer for Countee Cullen.

53. Anon. "Fifteen News Questions." The New York Times (13 January), Sec. 4, pp. 2, 6.
One question asks for a pairing of BB with W.

54. Anon. "First Guesses on the Pulitzer Awards." The Saturday Review of Literature, 29 (27 April), 14-15.
In a poll of twenty-nine book reviewers, BB received five votes in the biography category and one vote in the fiction category.

55. Anon. "First Novel." Ebony, 1 (April), 35-39.
Article on Ann Petry mentioning W, Dreiser, and Joyce as the authors she most admires.

56. Anon. "5 Greatest Books on Race Relations." Negro Digest, 5 (November), 47-51.
Nineteen experts chose An American Dilemma, Life and Times of Frederick Douglass, The Souls of Black Folk, Up From Slavery, and Black Metropolis. Books by Wright were chosen as follows: Arna Bontemps--BB, Horace Cayton--BB, Earl Conrad--UTC, Arthur P. Davis--BB and NS, Edwin R. Embree--NS, Howard Fast--UTC, Lewis Gannett--BB, Lester B. Granger--NS, Carey McWilliams--NS, Bucklin Moon--13 [sic] Million Black Voices, Sterling North--BB, J. Saunders Redding--NS.

57. Anon. "Friends Conduct Benefit for French Surrealist." New York Herald Tribune (Paris edition) (8 June), p. 3.
Reports that a manuscript by W is among the paintings and literary items to be auctioned to benefit Antonin Artaud.

58. Anon. "Harlem Pioneers with Mental Clinic." Headlines and Pictures (July), pp. 33-35.
Article on the Lafargue Clinic mentioning W.

59. Anon. "Harper Book Night with the Booksellers Association of Philadelphia."
Flyer advertising W's appearance at Kugler's Chestnutt Street Restaurant on 12 March. Contains a photograph and biographical sketch of W.

60. Anon. Have You Read 100 Great Books? New York: Jasper Lee Company, p. 44.
A list of 1000 great books includes NS.

61. Anon. "Los hijos del Tío Tom de Richard Wright." Ediciones (21 September).
Favorable review of the Spanish translation of UTC. Contrasting to BB, which reveals the pressure to conform to one's inferior status, the stories show blacks in revolt. Struggling toward freedom, they kill without being criminals.

62. Anon. "I Wish I'd Written That, Edited by Eugene J. Woods." The New Yorker, 22 (30 November), 143-144.
Lists W as a participant in the selection process.

63. Anon. "'Ich war ein Negerjunge' Von Richard Wright." Die Munich Neue Zeitung (14 January), p. [3].
Headnote to a German translation of a scene from BB involving W and Harrison. Also mentions NS.

64. Anon. "L'Imperial Sorcier du Ku Klux Klan." La Paris Presse (17 August).
Article on the Ku Klux Klan mentioning W's descriptions of racial outrages.

65. Anon. "Individual Nominations of Nation's Book Reviewers: The Saturday Review's Annual Pulitzer Prize Poll." The Saturday Review of Literature, 29 (27 April), 15.
BB is nominated by Fanny Butcher, Harry Hansen, Sterling North, and W. M. Redding.

66. Anon. "Josephine Pinckney Wins Southern Authors Award." The Publishers' Weekly, 149 (12 January), 167.
Notes that BB received honorable mention in the 1945 Southern Authors Award competition.

67. Anon. "Les Lettres." *Information Culturelle: Bulletin Hebdomadaire*, 2 (15 June), 1-2.
Mentions the reception for W given by the Société des Gens des Lettres.

68. Anon. "Les Lettres." *Une Semaine dans le monde* (9 November).
Mentions W's association with Sartre and his circle.

69. Anon. "Literary Life." *Time*, 47 (27 May), 43.
Notes W's arrival in Paris as the guest of the French government. Mentions Gertrude Stein's high opinion of W.

70. Anon. "Magazine Digest: What Southerners Don't Like." *New York Post* (30 October), p. 54.
Includes notice of "How Jim Crow Feels" in *True*.

71. Anon. "Magazine Digest: Why Segregate Negro Psychiatry?" *New York Post* (6 September), p. 54.
Summarizes and quotes from W's article on the Lafargue Clinic in *Free World*.

72. Anon. "Many Books Which Were Postponed or Out of Stock Are Available This Spring." *The Publishers' Weekly*, 149 (26 January), 585-588.
Mentions *TMBV*, the stock of which will be replenished, and *BB*, for which heavy advertising will continue.

73. Anon. "Marcel Duhamel nous écrit." Paris *Libération-Soir* (29-30 December).
Mentions W as a writer introduced to the French public through the translations of Duhamel.

74. Anon. "Midwest Book Briefs: Ten Best of 1945." *The Chicago Sun Book Week* (3 February), p. 9.
BB is included in a list drawn up by the Chicago Council Against Racial and Religious Discrimination.

75. Anon. "The N. Y. Press This Morning: Bringing the Food Crisis Home." *New York Post* (8 May), p. 51.
Notes that Danton Walker of the *Daily News* reports that W is moving with his family to Paris.

76. Anon. "Nouvelles de France." Le Paris *Figaro* (21 June), p. 2.
Mentions the reception for W sponsored by the Société des Gens des Lettres.

77. Anon. "Les Nouvelles Epitres." Paris *Libération-Soir* (14 August).
Reports that M. C. Claude-Max says that W will be among those published in *Les Nouvelles Epitres*.

78. Anon. "L'Opinion de la presse étrangère: La voix des 'sans droit.'" Paris *Tribune des Nations* (22 November).
Quotes from the Zurich *Weltwoche* interview with W, who comments on the racial situation in America.

79. Anon. "Papiers froissés." Paris *Gavroche* (20 June), p. 5.
Mentions the translations of *NS* and *UTC* by Marcel Duhamel.

80. Anon. "Papiers froissés." Paris *Gavroche* (19 December), p. 5.
Mentions Maurice Fleurent's interview with W in the December issue of *Paru*.

81. Anon. "Paris du soir au matin." *Paris-Matin* (6 July).
Relates anecdotes of W's standing in line to buy chocolate and finding an apartment.

82. Anon. "Pas de nègre au wagon-restaurant." *Paris-Matin* (1 July).
Headnote to second part of Jacques de Montalais's translation of "How Jim Crow Feels."

83. Anon. "Petit Dictionnaire des écrivains étrangers," in *Almanach des Lettres 1947*. Ed. Georges Duhamel. Paris: Les Éditions de Flore and La Gazette des Lettres, pp. 155-185.
A photograph of W appears between p. 162 and p. 163, but a biographical sketch is not included.

84. Anon. "Printer's Ink." *New York Amsterdam News* (4 May), p. 11.
Refers to the success of *NS*.

85. Anon. "Printer's Ink." *New York Amsterdam News* (27 July), p. 24.
Quotes a favorable comment by W on Jo Sinclair's novel *Wasteland*.

86. Anon. "Projets d'éditeurs." *La Gazette des Lettres*, 2 (8 June).
Notice of the French editions of *UTC* and *NS*.

87. Anon. "Projets d'éditeurs." *La Gazette des Lettres*, 2 (31 August).
Notice of the French editions of *UTC* and *NS*.

88. Anon. "Publishers' Notes." *The Springfield (Mass.) Sunday Union and Republican* (19 May), p. 4D.
States that "The Man Who Lived Underground" will soon appear in Swedish translation.

89. Anon. "Radio Roundup, Comment." New York Post (1 May), p. 50.
Includes a favorable review of the radio version of BB adapted by Ray Rosenthal and broadcast on 30 April.

90. Anon. "Rebels Win Fight in Authors Guild." The New York Times (27 November), p. 27.
Notes that W is on a slate of candidates for the council.

91. Anon. "Réception de Richard Wright à l'Hôtel de Massa." Le Paris Figaro (23 June), p. 2.
Notes the speakers' praise of W's work and his gracious response.

92. Anon. "Réception du Pen-Club." Le Parisien Libéré (3 July), p. 2.
Notice of a reception given for W by le Centre français du Pen-Club.

93. Anon. "Les Revues." Paris La France au Combat (19 December), p. 7.
Mentions the interview with W in the December issue of Paru.

94. Anon. "Richard Wright." Silhouettes.
Photograph of W with caption mentioning Sartre and Gide. The year 1946 is conjectural.

95. Anon. "Richard Wright." Paris Vérités (28 June).
Photograph with caption.

96. Anon. "Richard Wright à Paris." USA (c. 1 May).
United States Information Services press release sketching W's life and career and announcing his expected arrival in Paris on 8 or 9 May.

97. Anon. "Richard Wright apporte en France un scénario censuré aux Etats-Unis." Paris Images du Monde (4 June), pp. 10-11.
Includes photographs of W in Paris and a sketch of his career.

98. Anon. "Richard Wright nous parle du 'problème' noir." Paris-Matin (27 June), p. 1.
Advertisement for interview with W on p. 2. Includes a photograph with caption explaining W's background for writing "How Jim Crow Feels."

99. Anon. "Romancier noir." Paris L'Etoile du Soir (25 June).
Reports the reception for W by the Société des Gens des Lettres. Mentions his interest in France.

100. Anon. "La Saison du club 'Maintenant.'" Le Littéraire (2 November), p. 4.

Mentions that W will participate.

101. Anon. "Sommaire." Paris L'Ordre (9 December).
Mentions interview with W in the December issue of Paru.

102. Anon. "The Steps of Brooklyn." Time, 47 (18 February), 106-108.
Review of Jo Sinclair's Wasteland citing W's enthusiastic endorsement.

103. Anon. "Symphonie Magique." Cinévie (23 July).
Compares the "enthusiasm, resignation, and tenderness" of the black actors in Symphonie Magique to the same qualities in W's heroes.

104. Anon. "3,000 at Funeral of Countee Cullen." The New York Times (13 January), p. 44.
Notes that W was present.

105. Anon. "Trade Notes and Price Changes." The Retail Bookseller, 49 (February), 171-175.
Notes that W and BB received honorable mention for the 1945 Southern Authors Award given by the Southern Women's National Democratic Organization in New York for the "most distinguished book of the year by a Southern author on a Southern subject." The winner was Josephine Pinckney's Three O'Clock Dinner.

106. Anon. "Les Travaux des écrivains." Le Littéraire (7 December).
Mentions Marcel Duhamel's translations of W.

107. Anon. Unidentified and untitled clipping.
Announces that BB is back on the Harper list after being printed by World Publishing Company during the paper shortage.

108. Anon. Untitled article, in Los Hijos del Tío Tom. By Richard Wright. Trans. Floreal Mazía. Buenos Aires: Editorial Sudamericana, inside flap of front cover.
Biographical sketch of W and blurb emphasizing the necessity of violence, including killing, in reaction to white racism.

108a. Anon. Untitled article, in Mi Vida de Negro. By Richard Wright. Trans. Clara Diament. Buenos Aires: Editorial Sudamericana, inside flap front cover.
Biographical sketch and blurb.

109. Anon. Untitled article. Paris Carrefour (26 September), p. 7.
Describes briefly a meeting of writ-

ers and critics with W, whose French was "a little uncertain." W hopes to reside permanently in France.

110. Anon. Untitled article. The Springfield (Mass.) Sunday Union and Republican (7 July), p. 4D.
Notice of the reissue of TMBV.

111. Anon. Untitled clipping. The Argonaut (c. 24 June).
Mentions the Swedish translation of "The Man Who Lived Underground."

112. Anon. Untitled clipping. L'Argus des Industries du Livre, 1-2.
Mentions the French translations of UTC and NS.

113. Anon. Untitled clipping. Boston Herald (13 May).
Includes BB in a list of recommended autobiographies by blacks.

114. Anon. Untitled clipping. Le Brussels Phare (12 July).
Points out W's racial protest in the French translations of UTC and NS, wondering if it will have any practical effect.

115. Anon. Untitled clipping. Cavalcade (4 July).
Mentions W's presence in Paris and announces plans for translations of his works.

116. Anon. Untitled clipping. Columbus (Ohio) Citizen (19 May).
Notes that W is visiting Europe at the expense of the French government.

117. Anon. Untitled clipping. Dayton Daily News (12 May), p. 8.
Notes that W and his family have departed to Europe at the invitation of the French government.

118. Anon. Untitled clipping. Le Havre Libre (1 November).
Describes briefly the contents of the Paris Action interview with W.

119. Anon. Untitled clipping. Juin (17 December).
Mentions the Paru interview with W.

120. Anon. Untitled clipping. Lyon Libre (20 August).
Mentions W's visit to Paris and the publication of the French translations of UTC and NS.

121. Anon. Untitled clipping. Les Nouvelles Epitres (20 June).
Headnote to a letter by W identifying him and the "especially serious sub-

ject for the human problem" that his letter poses.

122. Anon. Untitled clipping. Paris Argus de la Presse (17 December).
Reports that W is Josette Day's favorite author.

123. Anon. Untitled clipping. Paris Aux Ecoutes (22 November).
Relates a conversation with W about learning French and seeing Paris. W states that he is learning Valéry by heart. He is impressed by the dignity of most Frenchmen, by existentialism, by the Eiffel Tower, and by Mme. Cecile Sorel.

124. Anon. Untitled clipping. Paris L'Echo de la Presse (15 July).
Announces W's presence in Paris and plans to translate his works.

125. Anon. Untitled clipping. Paris L'Ordre (11 June).
Announces the French editions of UTC and NS.

126. Anon. Untitled clipping. Spectateur (17 December).
Mentions the interview with W in the December issue of Paru.

127. Anon. Untitled clipping. La Vie Littéraire (November-December).
Mentions the French translations of UTC and NS.

128. Anon. "La Vie des lettres." Les Etoiles (20 August), p. 4.
Mentions the French translations of UTC and NS.

129. Anon. "La Vie des lettres." Paris Résistance (4 October).
Mentions W's presence in Paris.

130. Anon. "Vient de paraître."
Advertisement for a Paris concert by Marianne Oswald including a blurb by W. The year is conjectural.

131. Anon. "Wallace Stegner." Paris: Les Arts et les Lettres (12 July).
Notes that Stegner, like W, has been overlooked by French readers.

132. Anon. "What America Is Reading." New York Herald Tribune Weekly Book Review (6 January), p. 23.
Lists BB in twenty-second place in the nonfiction category.

133. Anon. "What America Is Reading." New York Herald Tribune Weekly Book Review (13 January), p. 27.
Lists BB in seventeenth place in the nonfiction category.

134. Anon. "What America Is Reading."
New York Herald Tribune Weekly Book
Review (27 January), p. 31.
   Lists BB in eighteenth place in the
   nonfiction category.

135. Anon. "What America Is Reading."
New York Herald Tribune Weekly Book
Review (10 February), p. 31.
   Lists BB in twentieth place in the
   nonfiction category.

136. Anon. "What America Is Reading."
New York Herald Tribune Weekly Book
Review (17 February), p. 31.
   Lists BB in nineteenth place in the
   nonfiction category.

137. Anon. "Wins Southern Award." The
New York Times (6 January), Sec. A, p.
34.
   Announces that BB won honorable mention in the Southern Authors Award
   competition. The winner was Josephine
   Pinckney for Three O'Clock Dinner.

138. Anon. "Wright Republished." The
Hartford Times (c. 11 August).
   Notice of the reissue of TMBV by the
   Viking Press.

139. A.[ppel], D.[avid]. "Literature,"
in The World Book Encyclopedia 1946
Annual Supplement. Chicago: The Quarrie
Corporation, pp. 123-126.
   Contains favorable mention of BB (p.
   125).

140. Aptheker, Herbert. "Black Metropolis, A Study of Negro Life in a Northern City, by St. Claire [sic] Drake and
Horace R. Cayton." Science and Society,
10 (Spring), 217-218.
   Review praising the research but
   criticizing the analysis, both in the
   work itself and in W's introduction.
   Instead of their moral defeatism
   concerning the racial problem, the
   authors and W should engage in a
   materialist analysis and submerge
   themselves "in the struggle of the
   people."

141. _____. "A Liberal Dilemma." New
Masses, 59 (14 May), 3-6.
   Attacks the W-Myrdal-Drake-Cayton
   school for considering the racial
   problem a moral rather than a "material" one. W to the contrary notwithstanding, oppressed blacks have an
   heroic, revolutionary tradition, not
   a submissive one.

141a. _____. The Negro People in America: A Critique of Gunnar Myrdal's 'An
American Dilemma'. New York: International Publishers, pp. 30, 63, 70, 80.
   Criticizes W for believing that the

racial question is a moral issue and
for denying the black tradition of
resistance to oppression.
Reprinted: 1977.49.

142. _____. "Reply to Mr. Cayton." New
Masses, 60 (23 July), 10, 12.
   Rebuttal of Horace Cayton's "Whose
   Dilemma?" (1946.173) accusing W of
   accepting Myrdal's argument.

143. Astre, Georges-Albert. "Un Grand
Romancier noir: Richard Wright." Paris
Fraternité (10 October), p. 3.
   Examines NS in the context of W's
   career and thought. W is an important
   spokesman, but he is also a brilliant
   literary artist at the height of his
   powers.

144. Babcock, Frederic. "Among the Auth-
ors." Chicago Sunday Tribune Magazine of
Books (30 June), p. 4.
   Mentions the reissue of TMBV.

145. Balakian, Nona. "The Best Short
Stories, 1945. Edited by Martha Foley.
Cross Section, 1945, A Collection of New
American Writing. Edited by Edwin
Seaver." Tomorrow, 5 (April), 76.
   Gives special praise to "Early Days
   in Chicago."

146. Balthazar, Albert. "L'Evolution de
l'âme nègre: Un grand romancier noir,
Richard Wright." Brussels L'Occident (c.
10-11 August).
   Places W in the American literary
   tradition as a major writer and analyses NS. W is a great artist, comparable to Dostoevsky, Tolstoy, and
   Dürer.

147. Bauer, Gérard. "Livres de femmes."
Paris-Presse, L'Intransigeant (21 June).
   Mentions the reception for W planned
   for 22 June by the Société des Gens
   des Lettres.

148. Becker, May Lamberton. "Fiction,"
in The American Year Book. Ed. William
M. Schuyler. New York: Thomas Nelson &
Sons, pp. 916-920.
   Contains favorable comments on BB (p.
   917).

149. _____. "Literature," in 1946 Col-
lier's Year Book Covering Events of the
Year 1945. Ed. Charles P. Barry. New
York: P. F. Collier & Son, pp. 293-300.
   Includes highly favorable comments on
   BB.

150. Beckett, Henry. "A Would-Be Fairy
Godmother." New York Post (22 January),
p. 25.
   Notes that Marianne Oswald, author of
   One Small Voice, says that it would

take a Richard W to tell the full truth about her grim experiences.

151. Benoist, J.-M. "Black Boy par Richard Wright." Paris Gavroche (12 September), p. 1.
Headnote to a translation of the excerpts published in Coronet. Benoist pleads for racial justice.

152. Bessie, Alvah. "What Is Freedom for Writers?" New Masses, 58 (12 March), 8-10.
Rebutting Albert Maltz's "What Shall We Ask of Our Writers?" Bessie makes unfavorable references to W as a political renegade. NS is superior to BB.

153. Bird, William. "'Forever Amber' $5; Hem, Dos, New Poets, Richard Wright Tops in Postwar Paris." The Bronx Home News (6 October).
Reprint of 1946.154.

154. _____. "'Forever Amber' $5; Hem, Dos, New Poets, Richard Wright Tops in Postwar Paris." New York Post (3 October), p. 9 B.
Notes that NS will be issued in Paris in an "enormous" first run of 25,000 copies.
Reprinted: 1946.153.

155. Blackman, Peter. "The Voice of the Coloured Man." Readers Union (June), pp. 2-5.
Treats James Weldon Johnson, Claude McKay, Langston Hughes, and W, considering the last the best of the four. Discusses NS. The Gollancz edition of BB is the July selection of the Readers Union, a book club.

156. Blake, Christopher. "Steinbeck, Wilder, Wright." Le Courrier de l'Etudiant (15 May), p. 1.
Blake, an American student in France, laments bitterly W's preoccupation with race. He must cure his paranoia and turn to other themes.

157. Boutell, Clip. "Authors Are Like People." New York Post (9 May), p. 34.
Mentions W's trip to France.

157a. [Bowman, Len]. "The Editor Speaking." True, 19 (November), 8, 10, 132.
Praises W's "How Jim Crow Feels," appearing in this issue, and denies that W is a Communist.

158. Breit, Harvey. "Books." Mademoiselle, 22 (February), 207, 298.
Contains an unfavorable review of Cross Section 1945 which excepts W from its indictment.

159. _____. "Louis Versus Conn--and 'Old Age.'" The New York Times Magazine (16 June), pp. 20, 47-48.
Article on Joe Louis quoting a stanza from "King Joe" to demonstrate Louis' status in the "John Henry tradition."

160. B.[rickell], H.[erschel]. "American Literature," in 1946 Britannica Book of the Year. Ed. Walter Yust. Chicago: Encyclopaedia Britannica, pp. 48-52.
Mentions briefly BB, "rated by many critics as among the year's best" (p. 51).

161. Broaddus, Marian Howe. "Clearing the Desk, Glancing Through the New Books." The El Paso Times (30 June), p. 6.
Contains a notice of the reissue of TMBV.

162. Brown, John L. "A Report from Paris." The New York Times Book Review (7 July), p. 20.
Reports that W was introduced to the French literary world by Gaston Gallimard, his publisher, at a lavish reception.

163. [Browning, Alice C.]. "Drama." Negro Story, 2 (April-May), [66].
George Anthony Moore reports that "the script of Richard Wright's Black Boy is being readied for a Broadway hearing."

164. _____. "Just to Mention That--." Negro Story, 2 (December 1945-January 1946), 2, 59-64.
Notes W's popularity in Russia (p. 61).

165. _____. "Off the Book Shelf." The Chicago Defender (18 May), p. 15.
Contrasts the frankness of such modern writers as W to the sexual reticence of Henry James.

166. Burdsal, Harriett C. "White Supremacy." The Saturday Review of Literature, 29 (22 June), 22.
Letter to the editor on the problem of racial stereotyping. Cites BB as an example of the kind of art which will help win the struggle without being obsessed by side issues.

167. Burns, Ben. "Off the Book Shelf." The Chicago Defender (9 February), p. 17.
Favorable review of Ann Petry's The Street with comparisons to NS.

168. Butcher, Fanny. "The Literary Spotlight." Chicago Sunday Tribune Magazine of Books (10 March), p. 10.
Notes that W is a member of a commit-

tee gathering books for Russia.

169. _____. "The Literary Spotlight." Chicago Sunday Tribune Magazine of Books (5 May), p. 8.
Mentions her vote for BB in The Saturday Review of Literature poll to determine the best books of 1945.

170. Cayton, Horace R. "Negro's Troubles: 'Black Boy' and 'If He Hollers Let Him Go' Reveal His Bitterness." The Pittsburgh Courier (2 March), p. 7.
Emphasizes the importance of BB as a revelation of the true inner feelings of black people and comments on the fear-hate syndrome.

171. _____. "A Psychological Approach to Race Relations." Reed College Bulletin, 25 (November), 1-27.
Contends that any useful discussion of the racial question must be within the context of the whole of American culture so as to isolate the contradictions and paradoxes involved. Cites W extensively, especially NS, TMBV, BB, and the introduction to Black Metropolis.
Reprinted: 1951.148; 1953.110; 1970.81.

172. _____. "Two Audiences: Negro Critics Can Better Evaluate Racial Novels; Are Closer to Problem." The Pittsburgh Courier (4 May), p. 7.
Mentions W.

173. _____. "Whose Dilemma?" New Masses, 60 (23 July), 8-10.
Defending Black Metropolis against Herbert Aptheker's "A Liberal Dilemma," Cayton makes several references to W.

174. _____. "Writing Schools: Mr. Cayton May Be Saying Reality Inhibits [sic] Only a Dark and Furtive Zone." The Pittsburgh Courier (15 June), p. 7.
Mentions W as a member of a "school of hard-boiled realism."

175. Chaulot, Paul. "Panorama des revues." La Gazette des Lettres, 2 (12 October).
Mentions W's contribution to Les Temps Modernes.

176. _____. "Les Revues et les hebdomadaires littéraires," in Almanach des Lettres 1947. Ed. Georges Duhamel. Paris: Les Éditions de Flore and La Gazette des Lettres, pp. 102-114.
Mentions the appearance of the French translation of "Fire and Cloud" in Les Temps Modernes.

177. Coindreau, Maurice-Edgard. Aperçus de littérature américaine. Paris: Gallimard, pp. 19, 102, 103.
Classifies NS as a good representative of the American novel of violence comparable to An American Tragedy. Also mentions UTC and BB.

178. Conroy, Jack. "Off the Book Shelf." The Chicago Defender (13 July), p. 17.
Notes that W's work first appeared in little magazines.

179. Curtis, Constance. "About Books and Authors." New York Amsterdam News (31 August), p. 6.
Cites W as an example of self-education through reading.

180. _____. "Negro Era in Books Dawns." New York Amsterdam News (8 June), p. 11.
Notes that the success of NS expanded publishing opportunities for black authors.

181. Dahl, Arthur. "Black Boy: Book Review." World Order, 11 (January), 309-310.
Favorable review praising W's style, emotional impact (especially on white readers), characterization, and expression of black feelings. Dahl concludes by arguing that only Baha'i teachings can solve the problems revealed in BB.

182. Davis, Arthur P. "Guide Book Shelf." The Norfolk Journal and Guide (8 June), p. 7.
Review of Era Bell Thompson's American Daughter contrasting its optimism to the pessimism of BB. Both attitudes are needed, Davis believes.

183. _____. "With a Grain of Salt." The Norfolk Journal and Guide (9 February), p. 8.
Favorable review of If He Hollers Let Him Go comparing it to BB.

184. Delpech, Jeanine. "Un Romancier noir a Paris." Les Nouvelles Littéraires (23 May), p. 6.
Interview with W centering on the melodramatic but not exaggerated realism of his books, the reactions of the American audience, his social and racial commitment, his favorite forms of recreation, and jive trends in jazz.

185. Dempsey, David. "Uncle Tom's Ghost and the Literary Abolitionists." The Antioch Review, 6 (September), 442-448.
Mentions Bigger Thomas and notes that Ann Petry's The Street lacks the "sense of the inevitable" (p. 445) found in NS.

186. Derby, John B. "Novel, The Modern," in The Encyclopedia Americana. Ed. A. H. McDannald. Vol. 20. New York: Americana Corporation, pp. 474-476.
Reprint of 1945.876.

187. Domkoehler, Esther. "The Wright Question." The Milwaukee Journal (4 August), Sec. V, p. 4.
Letter to the editor stating that BB asks the question "Will the racial problems be solved only theoretically, but not as it strikes us personally?"

188. Drewry, John E. "Books." The Macon Telegraph and News (24 February), p. 9.
Lists W as a past contributor to Cross Section.

189. Du Bois, W. E. B. and Guy B. Johnson. Encyclopedia of the Negro: Preparatory Volume with Reference Lists and Reports. Revised and enlarged edition. New York: The Phelps-Stokes Fund, p. 169.
Reprint of 1945.884.

190. Dumble, Wilson R. "A Footnote to Negro Literature." The Negro History Bulletin, 9 (January), 82-84, 94-95.
Quotes from NS and BB (p. 95).

191. Eibar, Eloi. "Littérature noire en Amérique du Sud." Paris Action (6 December), p. 10.
Article on Nicolás Guillén mentioning W as a well-known black writer.

192. Escoube, Lucienne. "'Aucun film n'a jamais dépeint la vie des noirs dans les villes américaines,' nous dit le romancier Richard Wright." L'Ecran Français (19 November), p. 12.
Interview with W, who talks about censorship in America, pointing out that it is to be felt in the movies more than on Broadway or in print. He describes Americans as the unhappiest people on earth because easy material life does not compensate for lack of balance and spiritual zest. Americans know what to do in a time of crisis, but they are depressed after victory.

193. F., E. "The Colour Question." The World's Children, 26 (December), 228.
Favorable review of BB and Peter Abrahams's Mine Boy. The comments on BB emphasize the misunderstanding as well as injustice the young W suffered. The reviewer also notes the strong psychological element. Books such as these should ameliorate race relations.

194. Farrell, James T. "Social Themes in American Realism." English Journal, 35 (June), 309-315.
Emphasizes the social problem of prejudice. UTC, NS, and BB are social tragedies with much violence. W approaches the problem correctly, and his account of life in America is truthful.
Reprinted: 1947.184.

195. _____. "Will the Commercialization of Publishing Destroy Good Writing? Some Observations on the Future of Books." New Directions 9. Ed. James Laughlin. Norfolk, Conn.: New Directions, pp. 6-37.
Mentions the good sales, "even in the South" (p. 15), of the paperback edition of UTC.

196. Farthouat, Denise. "A quoi s'intéressent les jeunes Américains?" Le Courrier de L'Etudiant (1 July).
Lists W as a novelist popular among American students.

197. Fast, Howard. "Art and Politics." New Masses, 58 (26 February), 6-8.
Rebutting Albert Maltz's essay "What Shall We Ask of Our Writers?" Fast makes unfavorable references to W.

198. Fleurent, Maurice. "Richard Wright à Paris." Paru, No. 25 (December), pp. 7-8.
Interview with W, who comments on his early career, the French publication of his short stories, and the coming translation of BB. W quotes Cullen, McKay, and Hughes, and lists Maupassant, Gide, and Malraux among his favorite French authors.
Reprinted: 1971.147.

199. Frederick, John T. "I've Been Reading: Sociological Short Stories." The Chicago Sun Book Week (13 October), p. 7.
Lists W as a contributor to Josephine Strode's Social Insight Through Short Stories.

200. Fyfe, Hamilton. "Black Boy. By Richard Wright." The Aryan Path, 17 (July), 274.
Unfavorable review complaining of exaggeration, morbid subjectivity, and excessive frankness. W is not like other black people, whose nature he misinterprets. While they live for the moment, he is filled with "brooding melancholy."

200a. Gannett, Lewis. "Books and Things." New York Herald Tribune (7 February), p. 21.
Review of Ann Petry's The Street mentioning briefly NS.

201. Geismar, Maxwell. "Books and Things." New York Herald Tribune (2 February), p. 14.
    Review of Cross Section 1945 mentioning "Early Days in Chicago" as one of the best selections in the volume. W "has solidified his position among the young writers today, and may even have picked up a little of the humanity and warmth that, for obvious reasons, have not hitherto marked his work."

202. Glicksberg, Charles I. "Negro Fiction in America." The South Atlantic Quarterly, 45 (October), 477-488.
    General treatment of black protest fiction giving considerable attention to W. Bigger is a crucial figure in the characterization of the complex, frustrated young black man filled with hate and aggression. NS is a story of the psychological consequences of his alienation. It presents the dangerous thesis that freedom can be achieved through violence, but its development is artistically successful. Also discusses BB in the context of protest literature.
    Reprinted: 1970.5; 1971.147.

203. _____. "Negro Poets and the American Tradition." The Antioch Review, 6 (June), 243-253.
    Mentions NS as an example of extremism in black writing.

204. Gordey, Michel. "L'Ecrivain Richard Wright nous parle des nègres d'Amérique." Les Etoiles (22 October).
    Interview with W dealing mostly with his experiences and opinions on the racial question in the United States, as treated in his own fiction and as a current issue.

205. _____. "Malheureuse à New-York où on l'a longtemps confondue avec une espionne, Marianne Oswald rêve de retrouver Paris." Paris-Matin (19 July).
    Reports that W was the only friend of Oswald who helped her during a period of extreme difficulty in New York.

206. Granger, Lester B. "Manhattan and Beyond." New York Amsterdam News (11 May), p. 10.
    Observes with approval that the play On Whitman Avenue "has little of the shock provided by 'Native Son.'"

207. Granier, Lucien. "Avec le père des fils de l'Oncle Tom." Paris Vérités (28 June).
    Detailed account of the reception for W given by the Société des Gens des Lettres attended by some fifty people.

208. Gray, James. On Second Thought. Minneapolis: University of Minnesota Press, p. 250.
    Notes that "Wright, the most distinguished Negro writer of our time, refuses to compromise with the desire of his people to be shown in star parts, displaying their cultivation and charm; he continues to force America to look at the tragedy of wastefulness and degradation wrought by keeping his people in a sordid environment."

209. Grippe-Soleil. "La Semaine d'un Parisien." Le Littéraire (21 September), p. 1.
    Notes that W visited the offices of Carrefour.

210. Guérin, Raymond. "Petites âmes mortes." Juin (17 December).
    Contrasts briefly W's mode of revolt with that of Ettore Settani.

211. Guth, Paul. "L'Interview de Paul Guth: Richard Wright." La Gazette des Lettres, No. 20 (14 September), pp. 1-2.
    W speaks mainly of his childhood and youth, with some comments on his work habits in Paris. Guth emphasizes W's difficulties in speaking French.
    Reprinted: 1947.207.

212. Hankin, Bernard. "More on the Literary Left." New Masses, 58 (12 March), 11, 21-22.
    Rebutting Albert Maltz's "What Shall We Ask of Our Writers?" Hankins claims that what is best in W's work derives from his "indignation with bourgeois morality" and "the direct inspiration of the working class struggle" (p. 21).

213. Hansen, Harry. "The First Reader: America's First Book." New York World-Telegram (7 January), p. 16.
    Notes that BB received honorable mention in the Southern Authors Award competition for 1945.

214. Havighurst, Walter. "Books Defy Boundary Lines of Nations." Cleveland News (30 November), Book Review Sec., p. 7.
    States that W shares with Franz Werfel and Thomas Wolfe the themes of "bewilderment and discovery, rebellion and aspiration."

215. Hayakawa, S. I. "Second Thoughts." The Chicago Defender (27 April), p. 17.
    Hayakawa predicts that Era Bell Thompson's American Daughter will influence white readers frightened by NS and BB, "which are definitely books for the tough-minded."

216. Hughes, Langston. "Here to Yonder." The Chicago Defender (6 April), p. 18.
Protesting Jim Crow, Hughes points out that even such artists as W and Marian Anderson are subjected to it.

217. _____. "Here to Yonder." The Chicago Defender (12 October), p. 16.
Mentions W as one of many celebrities who have visited the famous apartment house at 409 Edgecombe on Sugar Hill in Harlem.

218. _____. "Here to Yonder." The Chicago Defender (19 October), p. 18.
Notes W's departure from Greenwich Village for Paris.

219. Hutchens, John K. "Something About People Who Read and Write." The New York Times Book Review (3 February), p. 28.
Lists BB as a nonfiction best seller in 1945.

220. Jacno, S. "Lettres: Richard Wright." Bref, 2 (1 June), 20-21.
Account of the reception for W given by the Société des Gens des Lettres. Among those attending were Schlumberger, Paulhan, Queneau, Gertrude Stein, Merleau-Ponty, Michel Loris, Marcel Duhamel, and Roger Martin du Gard. Duhamel plans to translate W's books and to stage the play NS. The reaction to W at the reception was very favorable.

221. K., J. S. "'Cross Section 1945.'" The Springfield (Mass.) Sunday Union and Republican (13 January), Sec. D, p. 4.
Mentions W (calling him "Richard Hughes") and "Early Days in Chicago."

222. Katz, Sidney M. "Jim Crow Is Barred from Wertham's Clinic." Magazine Digest, 33 (September), 112-124.
Article on the Lafargue Clinic mentioning W.

223. Kielty, Bernardine. "Authors Between Books." Book-of-the-Month Club News (April), pp. 28-30.
Mentions that W's books are in demand in the Soviet Union.

223a. Lamont, William H. F. "Novels of 1922 to 1945," in Good Reading. Ed. Atwood H. Townsend. Chicago: The National Council of Teachers of English, pp. 29-32.
Reprint of 1941.786a.

224. Larreta, Carlos Toscano. "Mi vida de negro de Richard Wright." Ediciones, 1 (27 July), 1-2.
Favorable review of the Spanish translation of BB noting W's objectivity as narrator, the hereditary

cruelty that his childhood demonstrates, the racial injustices of his society, and the realism of his presentation.

225. Lash, John S. "The American Negro in American Literature: A Selected Bibliography of Critical Materials." The Journal of Negro Education, 15 (Fall), 722-730.
Lists one article on W.

226. _____. "The Study of Negro Literary Expression." The Negro History Bulletin, 9 (June), 207-211.
Notes that NS and BB have not yet led readers to further study of black writing, but Lash expects that W's popularity will enlarge the place of black writers in the curriculum.

227. Lawson, John Howard. "Art Is a Weapon." New Masses, 58 (19 March), 18-20.
Rebutting Albert Maltz's "What Shall We Ask of Our Writers?" Lawson makes unfavorable references to W as serving reaction.

228. Lyons, Leonard. "The Lyons Den." The Boston Herald (15 May), p. 33.
Reprint of 1946.231.

229. _____. "The Lyons Den." The New York Post (7 January), p. 22.
Mentions negotiations by Bryan Foy of 20th Century-Fox to secure W's services as a screenwriter.

230. _____. "The Lyons Den." New York Post (1 May), p. 30.
Mentions W's departure for France on the preceding day.

231. _____. "The Lyons Den." New York Post (13 May), p. 24.
Mentions W in connection with Dr. Frederic Wertham and the Lafargue Clinic.
Reprinted: 1946.228.

232. _____. "The Lyons Den." New York Post (14 October), p. 24.
Reports that W has changed his plans and is returning to the United States prior to the Paris publication of the French translations of NS and BB.

233. M., M. H. "Noteworthy Books, 1945." The Guide Post, 21 (January), 1-3.
Contains favorable comments on BB and Oliver LaFarge's Raw Material. W's book is commendable for its style as well as its sociological and psychological insight.

234. Maltz, Albert. "What Shall We Ask of Our Writers?" New Masses, 58 (12

February), 19-22.
> Arguing against the vulgarization of the doctrine that art is a weapon, Maltz comments that however dangerous W's political position may be, BB is a work of art.

235. Marceron, Jacques. "Richard Wright rencontre à Paris le premier metteur en scene qui s'intéresse à son oeuvre." Paris Libération (18 December), p. 2.
> Interview with W, whom Marceron considers both one of the best American writers and a spokesman for his race. W speaks of his literary beginnings, his influence in America, his warm reception by French writers, and Roberto Rossellini's interest in filming NS.

236. Martin, Ralph G. "Doctor's Dream in Harlem." The New Republic, 114 (3 June), 798-800.
> Mentions W's involvement in the founding of Dr. Frederic Wertham's psychiatric clinic in Harlem.

237. Matthews, Alice R. "Off the Bookshelves." Richmond Times-Dispatch (19 May), p. D-7.
> Reports that BB was second in the voting for best biography of 1945 in a critics' poll conducted by The Saturday Review of Literature.

238. McKenzie, Marjorie. "Pursuit of Democracy: Pleads for a Wright or a Petry to Help with a Problem That's Troubling Her." The Pittsburgh Courier (16 February), p. 6.
> Argues that in their concentration on the black lower class, novelists have ignored the racial problems of middle-class blacks.

239. McLean, Helen V. "Psychodynamic Factors in Racial Relations." The Annals of the American Academy of Political and Social Science, 244 (March), 159-166.
> Cites favorably NS and BB, and quotes from W's introduction to Black Metropolis.

240. McManus, Everett. "Black-and-White Culture." View, 5 (January), 19-20.
> Somewhat unfavorable review of BB praising its sociological value but finding it deficient as literature. W's "prose is pleasantly muscular, but it has no true style." In rebelling against white racism, W has adopted white culture and renounced the rich culture of black music, dance, and folklore.

241. McManus, John T. and Louis Kronenberger. "Motion Pictures, the Theater, and Race Relations." The Annals of the American Academy of Political and Social Science, 244 (March), 152-158.
> Notes the social impact of the play NS, but points out that the novel was a better, more complex work.

241a. Moody, J. N. "The Street. Ann Petry." The Commonweal, 43 (22 February), 486.
> Favorable review mentioning NS.

242. Moon, Bucklin. "Book Boom." Negro Digest, 4 (April), 79-81.
> Recalls a letter to the publishers of Chester Himes "from a Negro who felt that writers like Richard Wright and Chester Himes should be muzzled because they were setting race relations back fifty years!" (p. 79).

242a. ____. "Both Sides of the Street." The New Republic, 114 (11 February), 193-194.
> Favorable review of Ann Petry's The Street mentioning W briefly.

243. Moses, Earl R. "Drake, St. Clair, and Horace R. Cayton. Black Metropolis: A Study of Negro Life in a Northern City." The Annals of the American Academy of Political and Social Science, 244 (March), 186.
> Favorable review praising W's introduction.

244. Nadeau, Maurice. "Pas de problème noir aux U. S. A. mais un probleme blanc nous dit l'écrivain noir Richard Wright à son arrivée à Paris." Paris Combat (11 May), p. 1.
> Interview with W surveying his life and career. Nadeau is impressed by W's commitment to racial justice.

245. Norman, Dorothy. "Biographical Notes." Twice a Year, Nos. 14-15 (Fall-Winter 1946-1947), pp. 504-513.
> Includes an entry on W (p. 510).

246. ____. "Introductory Statement for Issue XIV-XV of Twice a Year." Twice a Year, Nos. 14-15 (Fall-Winter), pp. 11-18.
> Welcomes W as a new editor of the journal and comments on his letter from Europe.

247. ____. "A World to Live In: Help for the Troubled in Harlem." New York Post (10 March).
> Column on the Lafargue Clinic mentioning W.

248. ____. "A World to Live In: Operation: Richard Wright." New York Post (17 June), p. 34.
> Narrates W's difficulties in arranging his trip to France. Norman attri-

butes them mainly to the anti-communism of the State Department.

249. Oulmont, Charles. "La Vie étrangère en France: Un américain découvre l'Ancien Monde." Paris Spectateur (2 July).
Interview with W, who calls Europe, representing culture,the New World, and America, representing material civilization, the Old World.

250. Overlock, Ellen. "Public Library." The Washington Sunday Star (10 February), p. C-3.
Mentions BB as worthy of note during Negro History Week.

251. P., H. "Anthology." The Providence Sunday Journal (30 June), Sec. VI, p. 8.
States that "Early Days in Chicago" in Cross Section 1945 "continues in the same brilliant vein as Black Boy."

252. P., J. "Le Sang noir." Unidentified clipping.
Article from a French newspaper on the racial situation in the United States. Mentions W.

253. P., J. D. "Aid to Race Relations." The Pittsburgh Press (16 June), Sec. 3, p. 2.
Favorable review of Bucklin Moon's anthology Primer for White Folks mentioning W.

254. Perlman, Anne. "Richard Wright, Negro Author, Is Here to Make Home in Paris." New York Herald Tribune (Paris edition) (3 June), p. 2.
Interview with W and a description of his life style in Paris. W comments on life in New York, his first impressions of Paris, and the situation of blacks in America.

255. Petry, Ann. "Recommended Reading on the Race Problem." Boston Traveller (13 May), Spring Book Sec., p. 36.
Emphasizes the influence of W's portrayal of Bigger--"grim, humorless, completely frightening"--on subsequent writing about black people.

256. Phillips, Joseph B. "How the Russians Winnow American Culture." Newsweek, 27 (3 June), 44.
Reports that the "stock complaint" in Russian literary circles is that Hemingway, Steinbeck, and W are "out of date."

257. Poore, Charles. "Books of the Times." The New York Times (23 November), p. 13.
Reports that W chose Gertrude Stein's

"Early Days of a Woman" for Eugene J. Woods's anthology I Wish I'd Written That. W called this section from Melanctha "the first truly realistic treatment of Negro life" he had seen.

257a. Porzio, D.[omenico]. Untitled note. Il politecnico, 29 (May), 43-44.
To accompany an Italian translation of "I Have Seen Black Hands," Porzio identifies W as a playwright.

258. Prescott, Orville. "Books of the Times." The New York Times (1 January), p. 25.
Summarizing American books of 1945, Prescott describes BB as powerful and shocking.

259. Pressey, Benfield. "Literature, American and British," in The New International Year Book. Ed. Charles Earle Funk. New York: Funk & Wagnalls, pp. 336-339.
Mentions briefly BB (p. 336).

259a. [Quinn, Kerker]. "Accent Offers for Autumn 1946."
Lists "The Man Who Lived Underground" in Accent Anthology.

260. Quinn, Susan. "Off the Bookshelves." Richmond Times-Dispatch (10 February), p. D-7.
Mentions BB as a moving book that could be profitably read along with An American Dilemma.

261. Redman, Ben Ray. "Lots of Good Reading." The Saturday Review of Literature, 29 (9 February), 12-14.
Contains a review of Cross Section 1945 referring to Seaver's reprinting of "the most entertaining portion" of "Early Days in Chicago."

262. Robeson, Paul. "Préface," in Les Enfants de l'Oncle Tom. By Richard Wright. Trans. Marcel Duhamel. Paris: Editions Albin Michel, pp. 5-7.
Favorable comments emphasizing the courage and militance of the blacks W depicts.

263. Rogers, J. A. "Rogers Says: Drake and Cayton, in 'Black Metropolis,' Have Done Job He Wanted to Do." The Pittsburgh Courier (2 February), p. 7.
Favorable review praising W's "unusually fine introduction."

264. Rosenbluth, Robert. "Black Metropolis by St. Clair Drake and Horace R. Cayton." Public Aid in Illinois, 13 (May), 19.
Favorable review stating that W's "brilliantly written" introduction lends "perspective to the detailed

presentation" of the book.

265. S., H. L. "Reject Writing Given a
Break." Richmond Times-Dispatch (20 January), p. D-6.
Review of Cross Section 1945 mentioning W.

266. Sartre, Jean-Paul. Réflexions sur
la question juive. Paris: Paul Morihien,
pp. 196-197.
Cites W's comment that there is a
white problem, not a black problem,
in the United States.
Reprinted: 1947.274.

267. Schmid, Peter. "Die Stimme der
Entrechten." Die Zurich Weltwoche (15
November), p. 5.
Interview with W, who argues that
American racial relations are deteri-
orating despite black participation
in World War II and that the split
between the ideal and reality is
increasing. While black culture is
inherently rebellious, it can produce
only a limited acceptance of blacks
by whites. W believes that the tendency of modern American literature,
black and white, is toward an increasing sense of isolation.
Translated: 1947.276, 277.

268. Schuyler, Josephine. "Looks at
Books: A Hard-Hitting Novel." The Pitts-
burgh Courier (16 March), p. 7.
Unfavorable review of If He Hollers
Let Him Go pointing out that Himes
has less reason to be bitter than W.

269. Spears, Monroe. "Les Romanciers
américains devant le public et la critique." Cahiers des Langues Modernes,
pp. 287-313.
Contains a paragraph on NS comparing
it to An American Tragedy. W's novel
has a propagandistic power, but its
style is undistinguished and its
characterization weak (pp. 302-303).

270. Stane, Frédéric. "Avec Richard
Wright, romancier noir de la terreur
'sous-jacente.'" Paris Gavroche (20
June), p. 5.
Interview with W, who conveys his
negative reactions to postwar developments in race relations in the
United States. W also discusses the
state of French culture, particularly
as it parallels his own existential
position. He names André Gide's
Voyage to the Congo as his favorite
French book. He also speaks about NS.

271. Tardon, Raphaël. "Richard Wright
nous dit: Le problème blanc aux
U. S. A." Paris Action (24 October), pp.
10-11.

Lengthy interview ranging over W's
opinions on the political, psychological, economic, religious, and
social consequences of white racism
directed against blacks in America. W
also touches on racism in Europe.

272. Titus, Joseph H. "Primer for White
Folks. Edited by Bucklin Moon." The
Churchman, 160 (15 March), 15.
Mentions W.

273. Tjader, Marguerite. "Dreiser's Last
Visit to New York." Twice a Year, Nos.
14-15 (Fall-Winter), pp. 217-228.
Includes an account of a party for
Dreiser on 2 June 1944 attended by W
and others. W and Dreiser talked
about Chicago. Later W expressed his
admiration for Dreiser as a person
(p. 225).

274. Townend, Marion. "Odds & Book Ends:
Quality, Cid Rickett Sumner." The Char-
lotte Observer (22 September), Sec. D.,
p. 4.
Notes that W would probably consider
Quality a sentimental novel.

275. Tully, John C. "Books on Trial:
Black Metropolis by St. Clair Drake and
Horace R. Cayton." The Catholic Messenger (14 February), p. 7.
Favorable notice stating that
"Wright's essay, while not too accurate historically, is an impassioned
and moving plea for an intelligent
handling of the race question."

276. V., B. "Reviews: This Too is America." Common Sense, 6 (April), 136-137.
Favorable review of BB with some
veiled insinuations that W's case
against racism may also be applicable
to South Africa. The reviewer stresses W's sincerity and psychological
insight.

277. Vermandoy, Jean. "Littérature américaine." Formes et Couleurs, 8, No.
6.
Mentions W as an American novelist
not yet known in Europe.

278. Wagner, Philip M. "The Books Nobody
Reviews." The Atlantic Monthly, 177
(May), 117-119.
Claims that the presence of BB on
Margaret Marshall's list of important
books is indicative of its narrow
literary perspective.

279. Walcott, Lillian. "Looks at Books:
Chicago's Harlem." The Pittsburgh Courier (23 February), p. 7.
Favorable review of Black Metropolis
with specific praise for W's "eloquent and forceful introduction."

280. Webb, Constance. "Notes Preliminary to a Full Study of the Work of Richard Wright," in A Hitherto Unpublished Manuscript by Richard Wright Being a Continuation of Black Boy. New York: Privately printed and circulated, pp. 126-150.
Surveys W's writings and thought with numerous quotations. W has simultaneously "an overwhelming need for association and integration with humanity at large" and "a tragic, highly individualized loneliness." Webb discusses at length his relation to communism and existentialism. She concludes with an extended comparison of W to Sartre and Himes.
See 1949.156.

281. White, Walter. "People, Politics and Places." The Chicago Defender (5 January), p. 15.
Mentions W, Himes, and Petry as novelists who "have written powerfully of the seamy side of Negro life."

282. Whitford, Robert C. "Biography," in Good Reading. Ed. Atwood H. Townsend. Chicago: The National Council of Teachers of English, pp. 61-63.
Lists and comments briefly on BB.
Reprinted: 1947.300a; 1948.213a, 213b; 1951.211a.
Reprinted in revised form: 1952.55a; 1954.151a; 1960.206a.

283. Winebaum, B. V. "Second Armchair Companion. Edited by A. L. Furman." The New York Times Book Review (14 July), p. 16.
Mentions the inclusion of "Silt," a "saddening vignette."

284. Wolf, Leonard N. and Eugene P. Willging. "1945 Books Evaluated." The Catholic Messenger (14 February), p. 9.
Objects to "verbal vulgarities and obscenities" in BB which make it "unsuitable for general adult reading" despite the validity of its social message.

285. Woods, Eugene J. "Richard Wright: 'I wish I had written Early Days of a Woman from Melanctha by Gertrude Stein,'" in his I Wish I'd Written That. New York: Whittlesey House, p. 254.
Headnote identifying W and quoting from his letter on the Stein story.

286. Woods, Mary Thomas. "Easy Aces." The Argonaut, 125 (24 May), 18-19.
Notes that Edwin Seaver has stated that "The Man Who Lived Underground" will appear soon in Sweden.

1947

1. A., J. "Le Livre du jour: Un Enfant du pays par Richard Wright." Paris Ce Matin (1 August).
Favorable review of the French translation of NS. It is not only a crime story, but "an anguished drama, a psychological novel, an essay on the black soul, and an anti-racist document."

2. Adam, George. L'Amérique en liberté. Paris: Robert Laffont, pp. 184-187.
Adam relates the story of a meal he had with W at a Left Bank restaurant. W commented generally on the American racial situation and specifically on the discriminatory treatment he suffered upon returning from Mexico in 1940.

3. Adams, Franklin P. "The Diary of Our Own Samuel Pepys." New York Post (c. 19 November).
Mentions reading UTC, which shows "how little chance a Negro had, but for that matter how little he still has."

4. Altman, Georges. "A travers tous les barreaux." Paris Franc-Tireur (9 August), p. 2.
Contains a favorable review with plot summary of the French translation of NS. If W seems merciless or hopeless in his assessment of the American racial situation, the fault lies with those whites responsible for creating the problem.

5. Anon. "A travers les revues." Le Lyons Progrès (3 April), p. 3.
Mentions the translation of BB appearing in Les Temps Modernes.

6. Anon. "A travers les revues." Le Paris Populaire (26 June), p. 2.
Mentions the translation of BB appearing in Les Temps Modernes.

7. Anon. "About the Author Richard Wright," in Uncle Tom's Children. New York: Penguin Books, back cover.
Biographical sketch.

8. Anon. "About This Book," in Uncle Tom's Children. New York: Penguin Books, p. [i].
Emphasizes the black perspective of the book and contrasts W to such writers as Faulkner, Erskine Caldwell, Roark Bradford, Du Bose Heyward, and Julia Peterkin. Compares W to Swift and Kafka.

9. Anon. "Alinksy, Darrow and Debs." The Chicago Sun (4 May), p. 13.
Compares W to Saul Alinksy. Notes that W's books contain autobiographical material.

10. Anon. "Author's Guild to Appeal Ruling to Open Records; Draws Book Contract." Writers' Journal, 14 (January), 1.
    Announces that W is one of ten new members elected to the council of the Author's Guild.

11. Anon. "Bibliographie." Les Temps Modernes, 2 (October), 770.
    Lists Les Enfants de l'oncle Tom.

12. Anon. "Black Boy by Richard Wright." July to December 1947, p. 7.
    British book club pamphlet review. Highly laudatory of W's creativity and impartiality.

13. Anon. "Book Notes." New York Herald Tribune (13 June), p. 19.
    Mentions W as a contributor to Twice a Year.

14. Anon. "Book Shelf: 12 Million Black Voices." The Columbia (S. C.) State (12 January), p. 4-B.
    Brief notice of the reissue.

15. Anon. "La chanteuse de couleur Lena Horne débutera à Paris le 26 Novembre." Paris France Libre (8 November).
    Mentions W as a friend and "sometimes collaborator."

16. Anon. "Chez les éditeurs." La Paris Bataille (25 June), p. 7.
    Contains a brief notice of the French translation of NS.

17. Anon. "Le Cinéaste de jour." Paris Libération (1 July), p. 2.
    Notes that Roberto Rossellini plans to film NS.

18. Anon. "Une Déclaration inédite de Richard Wright: 'Je me sens plus chez moi en France que là où je suis né.'" Nuit et Jour, No. 139 (21 August), p. 6.
    Headnote to a statement by W comparing life in America unfavorably to life in France. Announces his return to Paris.

19. Anon. "Dernières publications." Les Temps Modernes, 3 (December), 1-6.
    Contains a favorable notice of the French translation of BB (p. 4) emphasizing the universal aspects of the black experience.

20. Anon. "Des textes de Christian Dedeyan, Jean Epstein, Giuseppe Galassi, Christian Murciaux, Richard Wright." L'Age Nouveau, No. 24, inside back cover.
    Advertisement.

21. Anon. "D'ici et . . ." Avenir de Cannes et du Sud-Est (18 January).
    Notes W's return to the United States and his highly favorable impression of France.

22. Anon. "Dis moi ce que tu lis." Courrier Français du Sud-Ouest (15 January).
    In a survey of French actors' favorite writers, Josette Day names W.

23. Anon. Dust jacket of Cerný Chlapec. By Richard Wright. Prague: V. Družtevní práce.
    Blurb on inside flaps for the Czech translation of BB.

24. Anon. Dust jacket of Ich Negerjunge. By Richard Wright. Trans. H. Rosbaud. Zurich: Steinberg Verlag.
    Biographical note on the front and back inside dust jacket of a German translation of BB claims that W is the first black to write what he felt rather than what whites demanded. The book's representative qualities are stressed; it pictures an America previously unknown to Europe.

25. Anon. Dust jacket of Ragazzo negro. By Richard Wright. Trans. Bruno Fonzi. Politecnico Biblioteca 9. Milan: Einaudi.
    Blurbs on inside front and back jacket of this Italian translation of BB.

26. Anon. Dust jacket of TMBV. London: Lindsay Drummond.
    Blurb on inside front jacket.

27. Anon. "Echos littéraires." Courrier Français du Sud-Ouest (18 June).
    Reprint of 1947.133.

28. Anon. "Les Editeurs annoncent." Le Paris Monde (24 October), p. 4.
    Announces the French translation of UTC.

29. Anon. "Editions Albin Michel." Bibliographie de la France, Nos. 43-44 (24-31 October), p. 3023.
    Publisher's advertisement for the French translation of NS as the choice of the Cercle Critique.

30. Anon. "Editions Albin Michel." La Nef (June).
    Advertisement for the French translation of NS.

31. Anon. "Editions Albin Michel." La Nef, No. 35 (October), p. III of advertising section following p. 176.
    Advertisement for the French translation of UTC.

32. Anon. "'Un Enfant du pays' (2), de

Richard Wright." Action Laïque.
Favorable review of the French translation of NS consisting mostly of plot summary. This novel gives W a prominent place in American literature.

33. Anon. "Un Enfant du pays (Native Son) Roman par Richard Wright." Unidentified clipping (28 June-5 July).
Favorable notice emphasizing the novel's psychological insight and its revelation of the racial situation.

34. Anon. "Un Enfant du pays par Richard Wright." Avenir de Cannes et du Sud-Est (22-23 June).
Favorable review of the French translation of NS stressing the novel's power and violence. It is both an exciting crime story and a penetrating analysis of racial psychology. As no other book has done, it reveals the racial situation in the cities of the United States.
Reprinted: 1947.37, 67.

35. Anon. "Un Enfant du pays par Richard Wright." Le Bourges Berry Républicain (25 July).
Favorable review of the French translation of NS by a European puzzled by American racism. Notes the novel's cinematic narrative technique and its power of analysis.

36. Anon. "Un Enfant du pays, par Richard Wright." Le Guide Protestant de l'Edition.
Favorable notice of the French translation of NS praising W's narrative talent and psychological insight. The novel is for adults.

37. Anon. "Un Enfant du pays, par Richard Wright." Rouen L'Echo de Normandie (22 July).
Reprint of 1947.34.

38. Anon. "Un Enfant du pays, par Richard Wright." Toulouse Victoire (6 November).
Notice of the French translation of NS stressing the novel's violence and its theme of the responsibility of society for Bigger's crimes.

39. Anon. "Un Enfant du pays, par Richard Wright, roman traduit de l'américain par Hélène Bokanowski et Marcel Duhamel.--Un Homme pareil aux autres, par René Maran." L'Afrique (October-November), pp. 46-48.
Favorable review of the French translation of NS and Maran's novel. Comparing the Afro-American and Afro-French experiences, the reviewer deems W's novel a masterpiece socially, artistically, and intellectually.

40. Anon. "Les Enfants de l'oncle Tom par Richard Wright." Le Bourges Berry Républicaine (18 November).
Favorable notice of the French translation of UTC emphasizing the theme of black resistance and citing the examples of Reverend Taylor and Silas.

41. Anon. "Les Enfants de l'oncle Tom, par Richard Wright." Le Guide de l'Edition (Christmas).
Brief notice of the French translation of UTC.

42. Anon. "Ex-Mississippi." The New York Times Book Review (10 August), p. 8.
Notes the admiration of Chester Himes for the work of W, particularly NS.

43. Anon. "Un Fabricant de dentifrice Lyonnais risque d'être censuré pars les vertueux." Paris Samedi-Soir (21 June).
Lists W as a controversial author.

43a. Anon. "Gen. Lee, They're at It Again." True, 20 (January), 3.
Letter to the editor from "Three White-trashers, Montgomery, Ala.": "Would you-all and Mister Wright care to drop down this way some day soon, together, and let us know what train you'll be on? We'll meet it."

44. Anon. "The Great Midwest Book Shelf." The Chicago Sun Book Week (4 May), p. 1.
Literary map of the Midwest with NS indicated.

45. Anon. "Gunther Program." New York Herald Tribune (23 May), p. 23.
Announces a radio discussion of John Gunther's U. S. A. W will serve on the panel.

46. Anon. "Harnett T. Kane." Cleveland News (31 December).
Relates an anecdote in which Kane outraged white matrons in Natchez by expressing admiration for W and calling him "Mister."

47. Anon. "Les Heures." Cols Bleus (8 August).
Contains a favorable brief notice of the French translation of NS.

48. Anon. "In Verbereitung: Richard Wright Ich Negerjunge."
Advertisement for the German translation of BB calling W America's greatest black author and quoting the Zurich Weltwoche review on the book's psychological subtlety.

49. Anon. "O inferno negro." Revisto do Globo (26 April), pp. 5, 65.
Translation of 1947.136.

50. Anon. "Jugez vous-même Un Enfant du pays par Richard Wright." La Gazette des Lettres (23 August), p. 15.
Headnote to Mary Dalton's death scene from the novel.

51. Anon. "Les Lettres." Information Culturelles, No. 29 (23 September), pp. 1-4.
Mentions the conclusion of BB to be published in Les Temps Modernes.

52. Anon. "Libri nelle immagini: Ragazzo negro." Il politecnico (c. 19 June).
Brief biographical article based on BB and amply illustrated with photographs from the Life article.

53. Anon. "Lire dans Une Semaine dans le Monde." Le Paris Monde (31 August-1 September), p. 1.
Advertisement for Claude-Edmonde Magny's article "Richard Wright ou l'univers n'est pas noir."

54. Anon. "Literary Whirl." The Philadelphia Sunday Bulletin (28 December), Book Review Sec., p. 2.
Relates an anecdote concerning Harriet Kane's admiration for W expressed to women's garden clubs in Natchez. The women were scandalized, especially because Kane used the title "Mister" in referring to W.

55. Anon. "Littérature." New York Herald Tribune (Paris edition) (6 July).
Contains a favorable notice, in French, of the French translation of NS.

56. Anon. "Les Livres." Rouen L'Echo de Normandie (18 November).
Contains a favorable notice of the French translation of UTC emphasizing its realism and the militance of its heroes.
Reprinted (last paragraph): 1947.101.

57. Anon. "Les Livres du mois." Bibliographie de la France (c. 7-14 November).
Lists the French translation of UTC.

58. Anon. "Les Livres nouveaux." Paris Samedi-Soir (2 August).
Review of the French translation of NS summarizing the plot, describing the racial problem in the United States, and alluding to other works by W.

59. Anon. "Livres reçus." Esprit, No. 140 (December), pp. 979-980.
Lists the French translation of NS.

60. Anon. "Livres: Un Enfant du pays, par R. Wright." Mercure de France, 301 (1 October), 346.
Favorable notice of the French translation of NS summarizing the plot and hailing the novel as a remarkable achievement on all counts.

61. Anon. "Mais ne lisez pas: Un Enfant du pays, de Richard Wright." La Vache Enragée (20 August).
Unfavorable notice of the French translation of NS calling it Communist propaganda, not a novel.

62. Anon. "Un Mot 'nature.'" Calais Nord-Littoral (23 October).
Reprint of 1947.63.

63. ____. "Un Mot 'nature.'" Les Nouvelles Littéraires (16 October), p. 4.
Relates a joke told by W about high prices.
Reprinted: 1947.62.

64. Anon. "'Native Son' in France." New York Herald Tribune (22 July), p. 19.
Notice of the publication of the French translation of the novel.

65. Anon. "Les Noirs." Paris L'Ordre (12 November).
Announcement of the French translation of UTC.

66. Anon. "Noirs et blancs aux Etats-Unis." La Paris Terre (4 September).
Favorable review, with a plot summary, of the French translation of NS. The third part is too propagandistic, but the novel nevertheless has great value both as a social document and as an artistic creation.

67. Anon. "Notes de lecture." Havre-Eclair (22 July).
Reprint of 1947.34.

68. Anon. "Nous allons mieux connaître Richard Wright." Paris Libération (1 July), p. 2.
Claims that W is a would-be white man who wishes to be accepted into fashionable circles.

69. Anon. "Nous avons lu pour vous Richard Wright.--Un Enfant du pays." Opéra (27 August).
Favorable review of the French translation of NS explaining the racial situation, summarizing the plot, and comparing the novel to Light in August.

70. Anon. "Nouvelles de l'édition." Le Monde Illustré, 91 (25 October), iii.
Announces the French translation of NS.

71. Anon. "Nowhere but in 'Twice a Year.'" Unidentified clipping.
Advertisement listing W as a contributor to the magazine. The year is conjectural.

72. Anon. "Nuova Orleans." Unidentified clipping.
Photograph with caption in Italian of W in his apartment in Paris, mistakenly thought to be in New Orleans. Mentions his work habits. The year is conjectural.

73. Anon. "On publie Un Enfant du pays." La Paris Presse (12 August).
Favorable notice of the French translation of NS, a "powerful and passionate" novel.

74. Anon. "People: Movers & Shakers." Time, 49 (20 January), 42.
Reports that W is coming back to America but later plans to return to France. Quotes W's comments on the Old and New World from the interview with Charles Oulmont.

75. Anon. "People Who Read and Write." The New York Times Book Review (20 April), p. 8.
Contains an anecdote relating that BB was displayed in a Columbus, Georgia, dime store under the heading "Animal Stories."

76. Anon. "People Who Read and Write: Bargain Shelf." The New York Times (12 January), p. 10.
Notes that World Publishing Company will issue an inexpensive edition of BB.

77. Anon. "Plumes et dents." La Paris Bataille (10 December).
Compares briefly Yves Malartic's Au pays du bon Dieu to W's work.

78. Anon. "Le Premier Roman traduit en France du grand écrivain noir." Le Figaro Littéraire (19 July), p. 2.
Reprint of 1947.80.

79. ____. "Le Premier Roman traduit en France du grand écrivain noir." Les Lettres Françaises (11 July), p. 5.
Reprint of 1947.80.

80. ____. "Le Premier Roman traduit en France du grand écrivain noir." Les Nouvelles Littéraires (3 July), p. 2.
Advertisement for the French translation of NS and announcement of the French translation of UTC.
Reprinted: 1947.78, 79, 81, 82, 83.

81. ____. "Le Premier Roman traduit en France du grand écrivain noir." Paris

Carrefour (9 July), p. 6.
Reprint of 1947.80.

82. ____. "Le Premier Roman traduit en France du grand écrivain noir." Paris Combat (4 July), p. 2.
Reprint of 1947.80.

83. ____. "Le Premier Roman traduit en France du grand écrivain noir." Le Paris Monde (10 July), p. 4.
Reprint of 1947.80.

84. Anon. "Les Premiers Prix littéraires." Paris L'Ordre (28 October).
Mentions the recognition of the French translation of NS by the Cercle Critique.

85. Anon. "1ers Prix littéraires de la saison." Paris Libération (25 October), p. 1.
Notes that the French translation of NS was one of two winners of the August-September award of the Cercle Critique.

86. Anon. "Présence Africaine." Le Figaro Littéraire (27 December), p. 2.
Advertisement listing W as a contributor.

87. Anon. "Présence Africaine." Poésie 47 (November).
Lists the table of contents of the first issue, including W's "Claire étoile du matin."

88. Anon. "Le Problème noir et la littérature aux Etats-Unis." Paris Aux Ecoutes (25 July).
Mentions W and other American writers dealing with the racial problem.

89. Anon. "Puissent tous les lecteurs." Flyer advertising the French translation of UTC.

90. Anon. "Qu'allons-nous lire?" Unidentified clipping (5-12 July).
Unfavorable review of the French translation of NS. Bigger is not representative, because blacks can be "grands enfants" capable of inconsiderate acts, but not of Bigger's extreme cruelty.

91. Anon. "Que tous les lecteurs d'autant en emport le vent lisent ces deux livres." Le Figaro Littéraire (25 October), p. 3.
Reprint of 1947.92.

92. Anon. "Que tous les lecteurs d'autant en emporte le vent lisent ces deux livres." Les Nouvelles Littéraires (23 October), p. 3.
Advertisement for the French transla-

tions of UTC and NS.
Reprinted: 1947.91.

93. Anon. "Quelques titres." Afrique
Magazine (28 August).
   Lists the French translation of NS.

94. Anon. "La Ressuscitée." Paris La
France au Combat (c. 22 May).
   Relates an anecdote concerning W's
   admiration for the singer Marianne
   Oswald.

95. Anon. "Richard Wright." Silhouettes
(2 July).
   Photograph with caption noting W's
   admiration for Sartre but not for his
   disciples.

96. Anon. "Richard Wright." The New
Leader, 30 (1 February), 12.
   Note praising W's "unusually sensitive and incisive mind" directed to
   "a ceaseless probing of Negro consciousness and of the effects of
   marginal living imposed on social and
   racial bodies en masse."

97. Anon. "Richard Wright and the
Coloured Writers." Pan-Africa, 1
(August), 35-36.
   Account of a lecture by W to the
   Coloured Writers' Association in Lon-
   don attended by Cedric Dover, Peter
   Abrahams, George Padmore, and others.
   W spoke of the need for contacts
   among Third-World intellectuals.

98. Anon. "Richard Wright Black Boy
(Jeunesse noire)." Bibliographie de la
France, Nos. 49-50 (5-12 December), p.
3617.
   Listing in a publisher's advertise-
   ment.

99. Anon. "Richard Wright Ich Neger-
junge." Unidentified clipping.
   Publisher's advertisement for the
   German translation of BB.

100. Anon. "Richard Wright Les Enfants
de l'oncle Tom." Bibliographie de la
France, Nos. 36-37 (5-12 September), p.
2351.
   Publisher's advertisement for the
   French translation of UTC.

101. Anon. "Richard Wright: Les Enfants
de l'oncle Tom." Gazette de Lausanne (5
December), p. 3.
   Favorable review of the French translation of UTC placing it in the great
   tradition of the American short
   story. The heroes of W's stories are
   in the militant vein of Nat Turner,
   Sojourner Truth, Denmark Vesey, and
   Frederick Douglass. The last paragraph of this review is reprinted

from 1947.56.

102. Anon. "Richard Wright Quits United
States." Unidentified clipping.
   Notes W's departure as a permanent
   expatriate.

103. Anon. "Richard Wright: Ragazzo
negro." Ausonia, Nos. 13-14 (June-July),
p. 32.
   Favorable notice of the Italian
   translation of BB. W's experience is
   symbolic of racial suffering, but he
   managed to rise above white prejudice
   and black misunderstanding. His prose
   is lucid and lively.

104. Anon. "Richard Wright: Ragazzo
negro." Letture, 2 (May), 161.
   Favorable review of the Italian
   translation of BB stressing its
   social indictment, religious as well
   as racial.

105. Anon. "Richard Wright Un Enfant du
pays." L'Activité Littéraire aux Editions Albin Michel, No. 23 (May), p. 1.
   Favorable notice of the French translation of NS.

106. Anon. "Richard Wright Un enfant du
pays." Bibliographie de la France, Nos.
21-22 (23-30 May), p. 1458.
   Publisher's advertisement for the
   French translation of NS.

107. Anon. "Richard Wright 'Zoon van
Amerika.'" Schakeling.
   Advertisement for the Dutch translation of NS containing quotations from
   reviews by Ben van Eysselsteyn in the
   Haagsche Courant, Nico Oosterbeck in
   Die Nieuwe Courant, J. W. Crom (at
   length) in Wereldknonick, and anonymous reviews in Nieuwe Haagsche Courant, Timotheus, Maasbode, Haagsche
   Post, and De Linie.

108. Anon. "Si vous aimez." L'Echo
d'Oran (19 July).
   Contains a brief notice of the French
   translation of NS.

109. Anon. "Something to Talk About."
Mademoiselle, 24 (March), 212-213, 351-
352.
   Notes that W is part of the spearhead
   of an "invasion" of France by American writers. His books are also popular in the Soviet Union.

110. Anon. "Les Temps Modernes." Biblio-
graphie de la France, Nos. 16-17 (18-25
April), p. 978.
   Reprint of 1947.115.

111. _____. "Les Temps Modernes." La
Gazette des Lettres (5 April), p. 3.

Reprint of 1947.115.

112. _____. "Les Temps Modernes." Les Lettres Françaises (28 March), p. 5.
Reprint of 1947.115.

113. _____. "Les Temps Modernes." Les Nouvelles Littéraires (27 March), p. 2.
Reprint of 1947.115.

114. _____. "Les Temps Modernes." Paris Action (4 April), p. 11.
Reprint of 1947.115.

115. _____. "Les Temps Modernes." Paris Carrefour (26 March), p. 7.
Advertisement for the magazine translation of BB.
Reprinted 1947.110, 111, 112, 113, 114, 116, 117.

116. _____. "Les Temps Modernes." Paris Combat (28 March), p. [2].
Reprint of 1947.115.

117. _____. "Les Temps Modernes." Le Paris Monde (2 April), p. 4.
Reprint of 1947.115.

118. Anon. "Les Temps Modernes." Les Temps Modernes, No. 21 (June), p. 18.
Advertisement listing W's "Le Feu dans la nuée" ("Fire and Cloud") and BB as works published by the magazine.

119. Anon. "Tout Paris le dit." Une Semaine dans le Monde (4 January).
Notes that W and Langston Hughes are the two writers most responsible for the increasing importance of black literature. They both concentrate on "satirizing" white attitudes and protesting abuses. W is more tragic in his approach.

120. Anon. "Twice a Year." Les Nouvelles Littéraires (13 November), p. 5.
Advertisement for the magazine listing W as one of the editors and as a contributor.

121. Anon. "Twice a Year." Paris Carrefour (2 January).
Advertisement for the magazine listing W as one of the editors.

122. Anon. Unidentified clipping (14 June).
Notes that W has sold his home in Greenwich Village and will return to France. He plans to film NS in Rome with the producers of The Open City.

123. Anon. Untitled article. The Dallas Daily Times Herald (9 November), Part 7, p. 10.
Notes arrangements for translation of

UTC and NS into Bengali.

124. Anon. Untitled article. The Dallas Daily Times Herald (7 December), Part 9, p. 2.
Notice of the Penguin edition of UTC.

125. Anon. Untitled clipping. Algiers L'Echo (31 July).
Brief notice of the French translation of NS.

126. Anon. Untitled clipping. Artistica (28 June).
Notice of the French translation of NS derived from the review in Avenir de Cannes et du Sud-Est. See 1947.34.

127. Anon. Untitled clipping. Chateauroux Centre-Eclair (22 October).
Favorable notice of the French translation of UTC.

128. Anon. Untitled clipping. L'Epoque (9 August).
Reprint of 1947.131.

129. Anon. Untitled clipping. Giornale di Trieste (5 June).
Notes that Henry Miller's Black Spring, unlike W's autobiography, has nothing to do with race.

130. Anon. Untitled clipping. La Montpellier Patrie (27 August).
Announcement of the French translation of UTC.

131. Anon. Untitled clipping. Paris L'Aube (8 August).
Notes that Billy Wilder plans to film NS.
Reprinted: 1947.128, 132.

132. Anon. Untitled clipping. Le Patriote (25 August).
Reprint of 1947.131.

133. Anon. Untitled clipping. Rouen L'Echo de Normandie (17 June).
Mentions the French translations of UTC and NS, "two great books [which] give a clear image of the colored man in the United States."
Reprinted: 1947.27.

134. Anon. Untitled clipping. Vogue (December 1947-January 1948).
Notes that BB won a "Prix des Critiques." Includes a photograph of W.

135. Anon. Untitled clipping. The Wading River Civic Association Bulletin, 1 (July).
Welcomes W to the village of Wading River, Long Island, for the summer. "The Village can well afford to have successful people around."

136. Anon. "Why Richard Wright Came Back from France." PM's Sunday Picture News (16 February), pp. m5-m6.
Interview with W, who comments on life in Paris and on American race relations in the context of world colonial problems.
Translated: 1947.49.

137. Aries, Philippe. "Sur l'histoire des Etats-Unis." La Revue Française de l'Elite, No. 1 (October), p. 52.
Cites W and Faulkner as examples of Southern contributors to American culture.

138. A.[stre], G.[eorges] - A.[lbert]. "Langston Hughes." Critique, 2 (March), 278.
Mentions W as a recently recognized black writer.

139. _____. "Sur le roman américain." Critique, 2 (April), 302-315.
Mentions W several times.

140. Babcock, Frederic. "Among the Authors." Chicago Sunday Tribune Magazine of Books (27 April), Part 4, p. 5.
Refers to Harry Hansen's article in Holiday mentioning W. See 1947.209.

141. Baroncelli, Jean de. "Crossfire." Une Semaine dans le Monde (25 October).
Lists W as a writer who has pictured American racism.

142. Bauer, Gérard. "Auteurs noirs: Richard Wright et René Maran." Paris-Presse (10-11 August).
Comments on W's fame and stature in American literature. Called a "black Dostoevsky," he ranks with Hemingway and Faulkner.

143. _____. "Une Littérature noire: Richard Wright et René Maran." La Brussels Lanterne (19 August).
General article on black literature, mainly in America. W is foremost, a genuinely talented writer though not quite a Dostoevsky. He has great power and intensity.

144. Bazelon, David T. "The Novel and the World's Dilemma. By Edwin Berry Burgum." Partisan Review, 14 (September-October), 540, 542.
Unfavorable review complaining that Burgum overrates W.
Reprinted: 1969.26.

145. Beauvoir, Simone de. "An American Renaissance in France." The New York Times Book Review (22 June), pp. 7, 29.
Contains a paragraph on W and Steinbeck as committed realists.

146. _____. "L'Amérique au jour le jour." Les Temps Modernes, 3 (December), 970-1003.
Includes an account of a visit to Harlem with W (pp. 978-980).
Reprinted: 1948.131.

147. _____. "Pour une morale de l'ambiguité." Les Temps Modernes, 2 (January), 638-664.
Refers to W as an author who refuses to allow a rhetorical patriotic hoax to reconcile him to the black situation in America (p. 648).

148. Bigiaretti, Libero. "'Ragazzo negro.'" La fiera letteraria (12 June), p. 9.
Favorable review of the Italian translation of BB emphasizing W's development of racial consciousness. Remarkable as a biographical document, the work is also impressive for its artistry.

149. Blanzat, Jean. "Un Enfant du pays de Richard Wright." Le Paris Figaro (5 July).
Mixed review of the French translation of NS with a plot summary and comments on racial problems in the United States. Blanzat finds a number of scenes in the novel unnecessarily melodramatic and lurid.

150. _____. "Les Romans de la semaine: Un Enfant du pays de Richard Wright." Le Figaro Littéraire (5 July), p. 5.
Somewhat favorable review of the French translation of NS. Blanzat objects to the melodramatic quality of certain episodes. Not the same as the preceding item.

151. Bokanowski, Hélène. "Carson MacCullers [sic] et le roman metaphysique." L'Arche, 27 (May), 155-158.
Discusses NS, claiming that the novel has some comic elements (p. 155).

152. Borel, Richard. "Paul Guth ou chacun son tour." Paris Gavroche (3 December).
Notes that W is among writers considered in Guth's Quarante contre un.

153. Boutell, Clip. "Authors Are Like People: Dream House or Nightmare?" New York Post (9 January), pp. 26-27.
Contains a review of Edwin Seaver's Cross-Section-1947 noting the lack of "any single high point like . . . 'The Man Who Lived Underground.'"
Reprinted: 1947.154.

154. _____. "Such Stuff as Dream House Is Made Of." Los Angeles Daily News (11 January), p. 4.

Reprint of 1947.153.

155. Brodin, Pierre. Ecrivains américains du vingtième siècle. Paris: Horizons de France, pp. 165-172.
 Chapter on W sketching his life and
 discussing his works in the American
 tradition of brutal realism. His
 style is direct and powerful. His
 message is an indictment of racism.

156. Brown, John S. "The Negro in the
Theatre, On the Radio and in Moving
Pictures," in Negro Year Book. Ed. Jes-
sie Parkhurst Guzman. Tuskegee, Ala.:
The Department of Records and Research,
Tuskegee Institute, pp. 439-455.
 Includes discussion of the reception,
 the plot, and the cast of the play
 NS. Mentions W's appearance on the
 WQXR radio program "Other People's
 Business" discussing Edwin Embree's
 13 Against the Odds.

157. Budry, Paul. "M. René Pallet."
Servir (10 July).
 Review of Pallet's autobiography men-
 tioning BB as a predecessor.

158. Burgum, Edwin Berry. "The Art of
Richard Wright's Short Stories," in his
The Novel and the World's Dilemma. New
York: Oxford University Press, pp. 241-
259.
 Reprint of 1944.64.

159. _____. "The Promise of Democracy in
Richard Wright's Native Son," in his The
Novel and the World's Dilemma. New York:
Oxford University Press, pp. 223-240.
 Reprint of 1943.23.
 Reprinted: 1970.5.

160. Buridan. Untitled clipping. Algiers
Fraternité (28 June).
 Quotes Paul Guth's description of W's
 physical appearance.

161. Butcher, Philip. "In Print, The
Literary Scene." Opportunity, 25 (Fall),
218-222.
 Contains a brief reference to W.

162. C., J. "Wright (Richard): Les
Enfants de l'oncle Tom." J'ai Lu, No. 11
(November), pp. 50-51.
 Favorable notice of the French translation of UTC commenting on W's ability to dramatize racial injustice in
 varied and striking images and plots.

163. C.[aliver], A.[mbrose]. "Negro," in
The World Book Encyclopedia. Ed. J.
Morris Jones. Vol 12. Chicago: The Quar-
rie Corporation, pp. 5486-5492.
 Mentions W briefly.
 Reprinted:1951.143; 1954.87; 1957.
 157.

164. _____. "Spingarn Medal," in The
World Book Encyclopedia. Ed. J. Morris
Jones. Vol. 15. Chicago: The Quarrie
Corporation, p. 7651.
 Lists W as a winner.
 Reprinted: 1951.144; 1954.88; 1957.
 158; 1959.69.

164a. Calmes, Dallas L. "James Crow,
Esq." True, 20 (February), 4-5.
 Letter to the editor from a white
 Texan praising W as "a great writer,
 intelligent and forceful" in "How Jim
 Crow Feels," but criticizing his
 impatient, radical approach to race
 relations.

165. Canby, Henry Seidel. American Memoir. Boston: Houghton Mifflin, p. 367.
 Mentions W among important authors
 promoted by the Book-of-the-Month
 Club.

166. _____. "How the Book-of-the-Month
Club Began." The Atlantic Monthly, 179
(May), 131-135.
 Lists W as a writer whom the Book-of-
 the-Month Club helped to elevate from
 obscurity to eminence.

166a. Cayton, Horace. "The Known City."
The New Republic, 116 (12 May), 30-31.
 Review of Knock On Any Door briefly
 comparing its protagonist to Bigger
 Thomas.

167. Crom, J. W. "Een praatje over 'Zoon
van Amerika' in de 'Wereldkronick.'"
Schakeling.
 Considers the Dutch translation of NS
 a powerful but gruesome book notable
 for its mixture of sympathy for Bigger and analysis of his problem. This
 excerpt is reprinted from a review in
 Wereldkronick.

168. Darnal, Albert. "Interdépendance au
sein d'une communauté française." Char-
leville L'Ardenne Nouvelle (17 April).
 Cites the fact that W can live in
 Paris freely as evidence of a dawning
 era of liberty.
 Reprinted: 1947.169.

169. _____. "Interdépendance au sein
d'une communauté française." Reims Concorde (17 April).
 Reprint of 1947.168.

170. Davis, Arthur P. "Negro American
Literature," in Negro Year Book. Ed.
Jessie Parkhurst Guzman. Tuskegee, Ala.:
The Department of Records and Research,
Tuskegee Institute, pp. 456-472.
 Discusses a "hard-boiled" school of
 protest writers led by W (p. 457), BB
 and "Early Days in Chicago" as bitter
 revelations of black personality (pp.

463-464), the radio version of "Fire and Cloud" and the Broadway success of the play NS, and the "passionate protest" of TMBV (p. 469).

171. D.[ebidour], V.-H. "Richard Wright. --Les Enfants de l'oncle Tom." Le Bulletin des Lettres, 9 (15 December), 285-286.
Favorable review of the French translation of UTC focusing on "Big Boy Leaves Home" but also exploring briefly other stories. Debidour emphasizes W's style--forceful, searching, but too lurid at times. The stories are seen in a more general context of growing into manhood and initiation.

172. ____. "Richard Wright.--Un Enfant du pays." Le Bulletin des Lettres, 9 (15 July), 139.
Favorable review of the French translation of NS comparing it to Crime and Punishment. It is remarkable for its psychological and social analysis. If it is as true as it seems, America should be ashamed and afraid. Debidour finds W's style somewhat faulty--wooden at times, too extreme, occasionally repetitious.

173. Debray, Pierre. "Les Livres: Le Romancier et ses personnages." Témoignage Chrétien (22 August), p. 5.
Contains a brief, favorable review of the French translation of NS emphasizing W's projection of his personal experience into fiction. The work is one of the best novels translated into French after the war.

174. Delasalle, J. "Black Boy (Jeunesse noire): Souvenirs d'enfance et de jeunesse." Lille Croix du Nord (25 July).
Favorable review with several quotations. Unlike the autobiographical writings of Rousseau and Proust, W's book reveals a youth that was hell, not a lost paradise. W managed to survive through reading and his vigorous personality, but he was exceptional. Most blacks must be prevented from realizing their humanity by Southern racism.

175. Descaves, Pierre. "Avec les classiques de l'univers." Paris Tel Quel (2 September).
Contains a favorable review of the French translation of NS. Impressed by W's talent and objectivity, Descaves considers the third book of the novel tendentious.

176. ____. "Mises en observation." Paris Tel Quel (23 December).
Notes that W is one of the writers considered in Paul Guth's Quarante contre un.

177. De Vries, Theuss. "Existentie op Revolutie." De Amsterdam Volkskrant (20 November, 5 December, and 31 December).
After a discussion of UTC, De Vries analyzes in some detail NS and BB.

178. Dover, Cedric. "Notes on Coloured Writing." Phylon, 8 (Third Quarter), 213-224.
Praises and quotes from "Blueprint for Negro Writing."

179. Doyelle, Henri. "La Condition noire." Lille Nord-Eclair (4 October).
Favorable review of the French translation of NS with references to UTC and BB. W's subject is one of great topical interest, but his literary merit is also evident.

180. D.[umay], R.[aymond]. "Wright (Richard): Un Enfant du pays traduit par Hélène Bokanovski [sic] et Marcel Duhamel." La Gazette des Lettres, 3 (23 August), 10.
Favorable review of the French translation of NS stressing the psychological reactions of Bigger to the fear instilled in him by the white power structure. Quotes from the novel, including a long extract from the death scene of Mary Dalton.

181. Du Passage, Henri. "Richard Wright. --Un Enfant du pays." Etudes, 255 (October), 140.
Review of the French translation of NS with a plot summary. Praises W's approach to the racial problem, but notes several flaws in technique and style: Bigger seems too articulate at the end; detail is sometimes excessive; the violence is overdone. Nevertheless, "the problem remains fully posed, with all its complex data whose cruel actuality and permanence are felt throughout the novel."

182. Durand, Léopold. "Des démocrates américains nous parlent." L'Humanité (31 October), p. 6.
Mentions W in conjunction with a humorous anecdote.

183. Dutoit, Ernest. "L'Adieu à l'enfance." Journal de Genève (23 November), p. 3.
Review of several autobiographies. Mentions the pathos of BB.

184. Farrell, James T. "Social Themes in American Realism," in his Literature and Morality. New York: Vanguard, pp. 15-25.
Reprint of 1946.194. Mentions the large sales of the paperback edition

of UTC (p. 48).

ly realized violence.

185. Fauchery, Pierre. "Comment peut-on être nègre?" Paris Action (25 July), p. 11.
  Favorable review of the French translation of NS comparing W to Dostoevsky in his ability to penetrate the consciousness of a killer. Fauchery considers Boris Max too theoretical and awkward in developing W's message. Nevertheless, W belongs with the great American writers.

186. Finkelstein, S.[idney]. "The Novel as Battleground." New Masses, 64 (26 August), 18-22.
  Essay-review of Edwin Berry Burgum's The Novel and the World's Dilemma including two paragraphs on his treatment of W (pp. 20-21). Burgum is too optimistic about racial problems, not understanding how W distorts the black situation.

187. Flanagan, John T. "Novels of the Midlands." The Chicago Sun Book Week (4 May), p. 4.
  Includes NS among the twenty-five best Midwestern novels, comparing W to Dreiser and Farrell.

188. Fontaine, Pierre. "Un Enfant du pays de Richard Wright." Paris L'Etendard (6 November).
  Favorable review of the French translation of NS concentrating on the work's racial message. W writes for blacks, but speaks as well to those white readers who can be redeemed from racism.

189. Francis, Don. "Popular Editions." Cleveland News (29 October), Books Sec., p. 8.
  Contains a notice of the Penguin edition of UTC.

190. Franklin, John Hope. From Slavery to Freedom: A History of American Negroes. New York: Knopf, pp. 506-507.
  Contains a paragraph on W's career. Reprinted: 1956.158.

191. G., B. D. "Peidooi voor de negers." De Tijd de Maasbode (c. 18 January).
  Favorable review of the Dutch translation of NS.

192. G., R. "Wright (Richard): Un Enfant du pays." J'ai Lu, Nos. 8-9 (August-September), pp. 71-72.
  Favorable review of the French translation of NS noting that Bigger's plight is symbolic of his people's. Perhaps the third book is too explicit and systematic, but the earlier narrative is gripping in its intense-

193. Gallois, Auguste. "Les Hommes et les livres." Le Paris Peuple (9 August), p. 5.
  Contains a favorable review of the French translation of NS comparing it to An American Tragedy but finding comparisons of W to Dostoevsky excessive. Notes the symbolic significance of killing the rat in the opening scene.

194. ____. "Les Hommes et les livres." Le Paris Peuple (18 October), p. 5.
  Contains a joint review of the French translations of UTC and Tobacco Road finding them very similar in deriving a certain poetry from Southern degradation and social injustice. W is a better artist than Caldwell, however.

195. Gautier, Madeleine. "Un Romancier de la race noire: Richard Wright." Présence Africaine, No. 1 (October-November), pp. 163-165.
  Favorable review of the French translation of NS. As a racial spokesman, W goes to the heart of the social problem of racism. He projects Bigger as a racial symbol in order to punish the whites. Whites in the novel are dehumanized and mechanized in contrast to the vital blacks. The scene in Mary Dalton's bedroom is crucial. Throughout, W's analysis of the frightening psychological dimension of the racial problem is a remarkable achievement. Gautier wonders how such a country as the United States is going to achieve unity.

196. Geismar, Maxwell. "Our Literary Inheritance." The Saturday Review of Literature, 30 (31 May), p. 21.
  Criticizes the omission of W from George Snell's The Shapers of American Fiction.

197. Gével, Claude. "Romans: Les Enfants de l'oncle Tom." Les Nouvelles Littéraires (23 October), p. 3.
  Favorable review of the French translation of UTC considering the work as a novel rather than as a collection of disparate tales. The stories all treat racial injustice and sexual taboo. Gével prefers "Long Black Song" to the other stories for its balance and treatment.

198. Glicksberg, Charles I. "For Negro Literature: The Catharsis of Laughter." Forum, 107 (May), 450-456.
  NS and the introduction to Black Metropolis are among several examples cited to support the thesis that Afro-American literature "is too

deadly serious in tone, too sombre, too violently tragic in content" (p. 454) and therefore needs more humor and irony.

199. _____. "Race and Revolution in Negro Literature." Forum, 108 (November), 300-308.
Points out that no revolutionary writers are black. Cites W as an example to show that ideology and philosophical searches do not long interest the black writer. Comments on "How 'Bigger' Was Born."

200. Gordey, Michel. "La Clinique des malheurs noirs." Les Lettres Françaises (1 August), pp. 1, 7.
Mentions W as a founder and supporter of Dr. Frederic Wertham's psychiatric clinic in Harlem.

201. _____. "Une Interview de l'écrivain Richard Wright: L'Amérique n'est pas le nouveau monde." Les Lettres Françaises (10 January), pp. 1, 7.
Interview with W in his Paris apartment shortly before his return to the United States. He comments on his favorable reception in France, compares the humanism of French life with the materialism of American life, expresses admiration for Sartre's The Respectful Prostitute, and discusses postwar life in France and French colonial problems. Gordey ranks W among the five or six greatest living American writers.
Excerpts reprinted: 1947.202.

202. _____. "La Vie culturelle dans l'Union française." Climats (23 January).
Reprint of excerpts of 1947.201.

203. Guérard, Albert-J. "Introduction," in his Prosateurs américains au xxᵉ siècle. Paris: Robert Laffont, pp. 7-34.
Mentions W as a radical writer and a naturalist (pp. 19, 30), and lists him along with nine others in a group of important American novelists in their thirties (p. 26).

204. Guilleminault, Gilbert. "Au pays de Jim le Corbeau." La Paris Bataille (31 December), p. 4.
Contains a favorable review of BB praising W's artistic achievement and his honest presentation of racial suffering in the South.

205. Guiselys. "Un Bilan des lettres françaises." La Gazette des Lettres (22 March), p. 5.
Whimsical piece mentioning W while playing with the word noir.

206. Gurko, Leo. The Angry Decade. New York: Dodd, Mead, pp. 270-271.
Discusses W in the context of his social commitment. NS and UTC awoke Americans to racial problems, but their effectiveness in promoting change is dubious.

207. Guth, Paul. "Richard Wright parle français," in his Quarante contre un. Paris: Corréa, pp. 297-302.
Reprint of 1946.211.

208. H., J.-J. "Hemingway Bikinise." Parallèle 50 (25 October).
Mentions W as a writer who handles racial problems more honestly than does the film Crossfire.

209. H.[ansen], H.[arry]. "Chicago Develops Realistic Writers." Holiday, 2 (May), 32-33.
Notes W's struggle against inequality in American society.

210. Hayakawa, S. I. "Second Thoughts." The Chicago Defender (4 January), p. 15; (11 January), p. 17.
Mentions and quotes W in a discussion of the Lafargue Clinic in Harlem.

211. Hermans, W. F. "Korte Besprekingen." Litterair Paspoort, 11 (September), 12-13.
Argues that BB demands reading whether or not it is a sociological novel like Steinbeck's speciality. Sartre's interest in W implies that W does more than Steinbeck, but the question of whom W is addressing poses serious problems of interpretation. W's concentration on his own awakening in BB and on Bigger's in NS indicates a real, though limited, affinity with Dostoevsky.

212. Hesse, Jean-Albert. "Les Livres et les hommes: L'Oncle Tom n'existe plus." Paris Franc-Tireur (25 November).
Favorable review of the French translation of UTC stressing the racial and social problems raised. W is acclaimed for the power and representativeness of his writing.

213. Hindus, Maurice. "Czechoslovakia Is Not Worried Over Next-Door Hungary Coup." New York Herald Tribune (20 June), p. 7.
Notes that BB is popular in Prague.

214. Hohenberg, John. "Harlem Clinic Now Official VA Agency." New York Post (24 February), p. 10.
Mentions and quotes W in an article on the Lafargue Clinic.

215. Humeau, Edmond. "L'Amérique dé-

grade-t-elle l'esprit?" Arts (31 October), p. 2.
Cites W as an exception to the general spiritual shallowness of America.

216. Isaacs, Edith J. R. The Negro in the American Theatre. New York: Theatre Arts, pp. 113-115.
Discusses the play NS, praising Canada Lee's performance and the work's power and realism.

217. J., E. "From Shakespeare to Saroyan." San Francisco Chronicle (5 January), This World Sec., p. 12.
Review of The Best American Short Stories 1946 crediting Martha Foley with discovering W.

218. Kanapa, Jean. "Petite anthologie des revues américaines." Poésie 47, No. 41 (November), pp. 115-133.
Examines W's relation to Les Temps Modernes, concluding that the magazine approves him because he is a despondent mystifier, Despite his talent, W no longer serves the cause of black people. Quotes frequently from Theodore Ward.
See 1947.297.

219. Keraly, Charlotte. "Dison tout haut." Journal de la Femme (2 October).
Includes W in a list of recommended writers.

220. Kielty, Bernardine. "Authors Between Books." Book-of-the-Month Club News (December), pp. 22-23.
Relates anecdote about W's arrival in Paris and a conversation with an official from the American Embassy.

220a. _____. "Richard Wright 1907-," in her A Treasury of Short Stories. New York: Simon and Schuster, p. 828.
Note on W's literary and personal honesty. "But for all the bitterness of [his] youth, he has an unflinching determination to see things straight: this young man's soul is not warped. He is kindly and open and friendly, his point of view objective, not personal."

221. Lalou, René. "Le Livre de la semaine: Un Enfant du Pays, par Richard Wright." Les Nouvelles Littéraires (17 July), p. 3.
Favorable review of the French translation of NS with a detailed analysis stressing the work's exemplariness.

221a. Lamont, William H. F. "Novels, 20th Century American," in Good Reading. Ed. Atwood H. Townsend. Pelican Books. New York: Penguin Books, pp. 126-131.
Revised reprint of 1941.786a.

222. Lanux, Pierre de. New York 1939-1945. Paris: Libraire Hachette, pp. 178, 207.
Mentions BB favorably.

223. Larnac, Jean. "La Littérature expression de la société." Unidentified clipping (August).
Compares NS to Graham Greene's Brighton Rock, relating them both to Gide and his concept of the gratuitous act.

224. Lash, John S. "What Is 'Negro Literature'?" College English, 9 (October), 37-42.
Contains two brief references to W.

225. Las Vergnas, Raymond. "Insurgence." Opéra (3 September).
Lists W as an American author with active social interests.

226. Le Hardouin, Maria. "Richard Wright parmi les siens." Paris Combat (11 July), p. 2.
Interview with W in New York discussing existentialism and the American character. W looks forward to returning to France.

227. Linscott, Roger Bourne. "On the Books." New York Herald Tribune Weekly Book Review (23 March), p. 28.
On his return from Paris, W reported that Faulkner was the most prestigious American writer in France, followed by Henry Miller and Steinbeck.

228. Litt, Iris and Marylou Buckley. "We Hitch Our Wagons." Mademoiselle, 25 (August), 250-253, 392-407.
Contains a photograph of W and Helen Lund, a would-be writer, with caption and other comments concerning his literary advice to her.

229. Locke, Alain. "Reason and Race: A Review of the Literature of the Negro for 1946." Phylon, 8 (First Quarter), 17-27.
Mentions NS and BB (p. 18).

230. Loewel, P.[ierre]. "La Vie des lettres: Du côté de chez l'oncle Sam." Paris L'Aurore (1 August), p. 2.
Mixed review of the French translation of NS with a plot summary. Loewel praises the novel for its power, but notes its lurid exaggeration. He admits the psychological effects of racism depicted by W, but resents their depiction.

231. Loisy, Jean. "Un Homme, un écrivain: Richard Wright." Ici France (17 October), p. 10.
Favorable review of the French trans-

lation of NS with a long description of the salient episodes and characters. W's achievement in this novel is remarkable.

232. Lovell, John, Jr. "Roundup: The Negro in the American Theatre (1940-1947)." The Crisis, 54 (July), 212-217.
Cites 114 Broadway performances of NS in 1941 and 84 of the revival in 1942. Notes the aid of Welles and Green in writing the play.

233. Lyons, Leonard. "The Lyons Den." New York Post (3 February), p. 18.
Mentions W's difficulties with his tenants on his return from France.

234. _____. "The Lyons Den." New York Post (23 June), p. 20.
Notes that W will live in Paris.

235. Magnan, Henry. "Les Spectacles." Le Paris Monde (26-27 October), p. 6.
Review of the film Crossfire asking why W's works have not been filmed.

236. Magny, Claude-Edmonde. "Richard Wright ou l'univers n'est pas noir." Une Semaine dans le monde (30 August), p. 8.
Discusses W's work, especially UTC, NS, and BB. More than documentaries on the racial problem, they are depictions of the condition of modern man as an innocent murderer. In W's fiction, violence and crime, however sensational they seem, assume a metaphoric value. The complex impartiality of W's vision leads him to see Bigger as an anti-hero, a distorted product of white society, but NS can be read as a palimpsest, with a black perspective under the white perspective. Magny compares NS to Kafka's The Castle and Graham Greene's Brighton Rock, other novels with innocent criminals as protagonists. W may be read in either a racial or a universal context. His power stems from his control of the "concrete universal."

237. _____. "Témoignages américains." Une Semaine dans le monde (17 May), p. 11.
Quotes from "Early Days in Chicago" and comments briefly on W's racial testimony.

238. Mallet, B. Untitled clipping. Le Bayonne Républicain du Sud-Ouest (19 November).
Favorable review of the French translation of UTC, which captures the poetic quality of the original.

239. Maulnier, Thierry. "Que pensez-vous de la littérature américaine? 'Gare au

danger d'une nouvelle convention.'" Paris Combat (13 February), p. 2.
Mentions W as a writer on racial themes.

240. Maynard, René. "L'Année littéraire 1947." Le Casablanca Petit Marocain (30 December).
Mentions W as an original writer.

241. McKean, Else. "Richard Wright," in her Up Hill. New York: Shady Hill Press, pp. 24-35.
Biographical essay for juvenile readers.

242. Morel, Henriette. "'Ce qui m'a amené à tuer, c'est ça que je suis.'" Paris Ce Matin (2 August).
Favorable review of the French translation of NS comparing it to Greek tragedy. Morel analyses at length the liberating effect of Bigger's killing of Mary.

243. Morpurgo, J. E. "The American Negro." The Fortnightly, 162 (July), 16-24.
Quotes from "Between the World and Me" without mentioning the title or author.

244. Mott, Frank Luther. Golden Multitudes: The Story of Best Sellers in the United States. New York: The Macmillan Company, p. 329.
Lists BB among the "Better Sellers."

245. Muray, Jean. "Littérature étrangère." Unidentified clipping.
Magazine article mentioning W briefly. Year conjectural.

246. Murray, Florence, ed. The Negro Handbook 1946-1947. New York: Current Books, A. A. Wyn, p. 233.
Favorable comment on BB.

247. N., G. "'Jag kande mig som fransman.'" Stockholm Expressen (c. March).
Interview with W on his return to New York from France. W comments favorably on the lack of racial prejudice of the French. He discusses the American racial issue in the larger context of such world problems as family vs. individual, hand work vs. mass production, individualism vs. collectivism, and East (colonial peoples) vs. West (white exploiters).

248. Nadeau, Maurice. "Un Enfant d'Amérique." Paris Combat (11 July), p. 2.
Highly favorable review of the French translation of NS. W treats the American racial situation, but his powerful genius transcends national and ethnic categories. He uses the ef-

fects of shock and horror to force the reader to confront truth, especially the truth of murder as a regenerative force for a social victim. Nadeau compares W to Kafka, Tolstoy, and, especially, Racine.

248a. Norton, Robert. "Gen. Lee, They're at It Again." True, (20 January), 3.
Letter to the editor praising "How Jim Crow Feels."

249. P., J. "Un Enfant du pays par Richard Wright." Bayonne Courrier (22-23 November).
Highly favorable review of the French translation of NS praising the novel for its important racial and social message and for its high literary art. It has the excitement of a crime story, the power of great art, and a deep knowledge of the human heart.

250. P., J. "Les Livres: Un Enfant du pays (Native son)." Paris Libération (7-8 September), p. 2.
Rather unfavorable review. W brings little that is new to the racial issue. The form of the novel often tends to the lurid and the melodramatic.

251. P., O. "Richard Wright: Un Enfant du pays." Paris Réforme (13 December), p. 4.
Favorable notice of the French translation of NS with a brief plot summary. Praises W's honesty and literary gifts.

252. P., P. M. "Au hasard des lettres: Un Enfant du pays de Richard Wright." Lyon Libre (12 August).
Review of the French translation of NS consisting mostly of plot summary.

253. Padmore, George. "World Views." The Chicago Defender (25 January), p. 19.
Editorial-report on W's brief visit to London, where he addressed the Coloured Writers' Association. Notes his endorsement of increased contact among black intellectuals throughout the world.

254. Palaiseul, Jean. "Sombre rossignol, Marian Anderson a changé l'opinion des blancs sur les noirs." Unidentified clipping (12 February).
Lists W as a celebrity whose achievement has helped to alter white American attitudes toward blacks.

255. Paz, Magdeleine. "Un Enfant du pays par Richard Wright." Paru, No. 34 (September), pp. 44-47.
Favorable review of the French translation of NS. Paz, a militant anti-

racist, focuses on the racial issue, but considers also the motives and fears of the protagonist, stresses the importance of W's indictment of American capitalism, and concludes with attention to technical and formal aspects of the novel.

256. Peyre, Henri. "American Literature Through French Eyes." The Virginia Quarterly Review, 23 (Summer), 421-438.
Notes the admiration for W in France (p. 428).

257. Potts, Paul. "A Very Short Story Indeed." Pan-Africa, 1 (June), 40.
Contains a brief reference to W.

258. Poulaille, Henry. "Littérature pour le cinéma." Paris Combat (13 February), p. 2.
Mentions W.

259. Prist, Paul. "La Vie Littéraire." La Louvière La Nouvelle Gazette (7 September).
Contains a highly favorable review of the French translation of NS attesting to its overwhelming emotional power. Reminiscent to a French reader of René Maran, W is one of the best writers of contemporary American literature.

259a. [Quinn, Kerker]. "Accent for Spring 1947."
Flyer listing "The Man Who Lived Underground" in Accent Anthology.

259b. ____. "Accent for Summer 1947."
Flyer listing W as a contributor to Accent Anthology.

259c. ____. "Accent for Winter 1947."
Flyer listing W as a contributor to Accent Anthology.

260. Rabaud, Jean. "Un Grand Ecrivain noir: Richard Wright." Le Populaire de Paris (16 July), p. 2.
Favorable review of the French translation of NS with biographical background. Although he has a tendency to explain too much, W demonstrates a narrative talent that makes this thesis novel an artistic success. W deserves his renown. Rabaud compares him to Cain and Faulkner.

261. Redding, J. Saunders. "What I Think of Richard Wright." The Baltimore Afro-American (1 March), Magazine Sec., p. 2.
Praises W for his powerful protest against racism in all its forms. He bridges the gap between black and white audiences.

261a. Rosati, Salvatore. "Tendenze della

prosa narrativa." Unidentified article. Mentions W briefly as a Southern writer.
Reprinted: 1958.234.

262. Rosmer, Alfred. "Que pensez-vous de la littérature américaine? 'Aux U. S. A. un ouvrage littéraire qui tire à 5.000 exemplaires est déjà un succès." Paris Combat (8 January), p. 2.
Mentions W.

263. Rousseaux, André. "Les Livres." Le Figaro Littéraire (6 September), p. 2.
Mentions W as one of the first-rate contemporary writers who have attracted Sartre's interest.

264. _____. "Les Livres." France Illustration, Nos. 104-106 (11 October), p. 321.
Generally favorable review of the French translation of NS. The scope of the novel is impressive, but the thesis is pressed too insistently. Rousseaux admires the depiction of fear and the rendering of the inferiority complex in Bigger, as well as the fundamental truth and rigorous accuracy in the delineation of the interracial attitudes in which fear prevails.

265. Roy, Claude. Clefs pour l'Amérique Geneva and Paris: Editions des Trois Collines, pp. 157, 282.
Mentions W.

266. _____. "La Peau noire." Europe, 25 (June), 17-34.
Article on American racism containing a brief reference to W (p. 26).

267. Rubin, Bernard. "Broadway Beat." Daily Worker (19 June), p. 12.
Notes that Canada Lee is recording BB for the American Foundation for the Blind.

268. S., C. "A travers les livres." Force Ouvrière (20 November), p. 4.
Recommends reading the French translations of NS and UTC for their attack on racial injustice.

269. S., G. "BRODIN (Pierre). Les Ecrivains américains du XXe siècle." La Gazette des Lettres (28 June), p. 12.
Lists W as a contributor to Pierre Brodin's anthology of modern American writing.

270. S., H. "Yesterday and Tomorrow." The Saturday Review of Literature, 30 (15 February), 24.
Article on the postwar literary scene pointing out that as racial antagonisms persist new writers such as W

will "suddenly appear as defenders of their race."

271. Saint-Hely, Marc. "Littérature étrangère: Peaux noires." Rolet (30 October).
Favorable review of the French translation of NS. Viewing it mainly as a statement against racism, Saint-Hely considers the last book of the three the most important. A work of exceptional power and wide distribution, it may, Saint-Hely hopes, help to ameliorate the racial situation.

271a. Sale, Robert. "Gen. Lee, They're at It Again." True, 20 (January), 3.
Letter to the editor from a black ex-soldier from Natchez who "cannot understand what Richard Wright is so bitter about."

272. Sans, Julien. "Qu'est-ce qui fait courir Sammy?" Climats (1 October).
Favorable notice of the French translation of NS, a beautiful work attacking racial oppression.

273. Sartre, Jean-Paul. "Qu'est-ce que la littérature?" Les Temps Modernes, 2 (March), 961-988.
Using BB as his primary example, Sartre argues that W addresses two audiences and employs two strategies simultaneously. For blacks he provides an emotional focus, for whites an intellectual argument (pp. 968-969).
Reprinted: 1948.241, 242.

274. _____. "Réflexions sur la question juive." Lille Croix du Nord (20 September).
Reprint of 1946.266.

275. _____. "'Vous nous embêtez avec Faulkner le Vieux' disent les Américains." Paris Combat (3 January), p. 2.
Mentions W as a great writer on racial themes.

276. Schmid, Peter. "An Interview with Richard Wright." Pan-Africa, 1 (August), 37-38; (September), 29-31.
Translation of 1946.267.

277. _____. "An Interview with Richard Wright." The New Leader, 30 (1 February), 12.
Translation of 1946.267.

278. Schneider, I. "Livres et portraits." Unidentified clipping.
Review of the French translation of UTC noting W's Communist affiliation. The characters in the story exercise some control, but they are victimized.

279. Sinclair, Upton. "If Writers Had a Magic Wand." The Saturday Review of Literature, 30 (11 January), 11-12.
Mentions W as a contributor to Eugene J. Woods's anthology I Wish I'd Written That.

280. Sorel, Jean-Jacques. "Richard Wright. Un Enfant du pays." La Nef, No. 33 (August), pp. 148-149.
Highly favorable review of the French translation of NS praising it as a social testament and as a literary work. Recognizing the centrality of violence in human life, W places American society on trial. Bigger is presented with completely authentic realism. Sorel compares W to Dostoevsky.

281. Soupault, Philippe. "Les Sept Jours de Paris." Les Lettres Françaises (3 January), p. 10.
Describes W's personality and his daily routine in Paris.

282. Stephen, S. "Un Enfant du pays, par Richard Wright." Noir et Blanc, 3 (6 August), 510.
Favorable review of the French translation of NS praising it for its literary skill and its social message. Few writers can excel W in depicting horror. Includes a plot summary.

283. ____. "Les Enfants de l'oncle Tom, par Richard Wright." Noir et Blanc (c. 12 November).
Favorable review of the French translation of UTC emphasizing the theme of revolt.

284. T., C. "Romans." Les Lettres Françaises (8 August), p. 5.
Favorable review of the French translation of NS stressing its social relevance. Bigger is essentially an antipathetic character, perhaps excessively so, but the novel has both poignance and grandeur.

285. Targ, William. "Exciting Discoveries in American Writing." Cleveland News (25 January), Book Review Sec., p. 4.
Reprint of 1947.287.

286. ____. "Manhattan Letter." Cleveland News (11 January), Book Review Sec., p. 6.
Notes that W will come home to New York for a few weeks after six months in France.

287. ____. "Young American Writers Blaze New Trails." The Philadelphia Inquirer (5 January), Books Sec., p. 3.
Review of Edwin Seaver's anthology Cross Section 1947 comparing Ann

Petry's short story "In Darkness and Confusion" to the stories in UTC.
Reprinted: 1947.285.

288. Tenney, Jack B., ed. Red Fascism Boring from Within . . . By the Subversive Forces of Communism. Los Angeles: Federal Printing Company, pp. 421, 424, 425.
Mentions W in relation to the American Writers Congress and the League of American Writers. Cites Eugene Clay's reference to and quotation from W's "I Have Seen Black Hands."

289. Theis, Edouard. "Un Grand Ecrivain noir américain Richard Wright." Christianisme Social, 55 (January-February), 57-63.
General estimate of W's work, particularly BB and NS. Notes W's rejection of the religion of the churches because it does not help blacks. Kierkegaardian religion is more appealing, however. As a man and as a writer, W is characterized by his sincerity and commitment to truth and justice.
Reprinted: 1950.230.

290. Thiébaut, Marcel. "Parmi les livres." Revue de Paris, 54 (October), 162-163.
Unfavorable review of the French translation of NS, a clumsy apology for crime and Communism. Thiebaut strongly criticizes W for attempting to present Bigger, who is a "downright bad boy," as "a kind of black Christ." Bigger's crimes can be explained neither by his psychological complexes nor by white oppression. The novel has some value as a detective story, however.

291. Thomas, Edith. "Un Enfant d'Amérique." La Marseillaise (23-29 July).
Review of the French translation of NS analyzing Bigger's plight and stressing its representative value.

292. T.[hompson], C.[harles] H. "Wright, Richard," in The World Book Encyclopedia. Ed. J. Morris Jones. Vol. 18. Chicago: The Quarrie Corporation, pp. 8932-8933.
Biographical sketch.
Reprinted: 1951.238; 1954.172; 1957.336; 1959.136.

293. Tindall, William York. "The Sociological Best Seller." College English, 9 (November), 55-62.
Includes favorable comments on BB. "Better as a work of art than most of the actual novels of this type and much more convincing, this crude, powerful book tells the story of an

exceptionally talented boy" (p. 57).

293a. Trigg, W. S. "Gen. Lee, They're at It Again." True, 20 (January), 3.
Letter to the editor condemning W as "disgusting" and praising Booker T. Washington and George Washington Carver.

294. Tuck, James L. "Here's Hope for Harlem." New York Herald Tribune (26 January), This Week Magazine Sec., pp. 9, 13, 20.
Mentions W's involvement in the Lafargue Clinic.

295. Turpin, Waters E. "Evaluating the Work of the Contemporary Negro Novelist." Negro History Bulletin, 11 (December), 59-60, 62-64.
Considers W and five other novelists. Treats NS as a protest novel in the tradition of Zola, Dostoevsky, and Dickens. W's "bitter honesty" is admirable, but his solution to racial and social problems is inadequate.

296. Waldorf, Wilella. "The Part Played by American Actors in American Theatre History." New York Post.
Review of Edith R.Isaacs's The Negro in the American Theatre mentioning Canada Lee and NS.

297. Ward, Theodore. "Five Negro Novelists: Revolt and Retreat." Mainstream, 1 (Winter), 100-110.
Examines W's influence on Carl Offord, Chester Himes, Ann Petry, and Frank Yerby, all of whom use their fiction as a weapon or as an expression of despair. Under W's sway, they have been unable to get at fundamental truths.

298. Weller, A. H. "New Audience." The New York Times (29 June), Sec. 2, p. 5.
Notes that Canada Lee is recording BB for the blind.

299. Wertham, Frederic, M. D. "Introduction: The Dreams That Heal," in The World Within: Fiction Illuminating Neuroses of Our Time. Ed. Mary Louise Aswell. New York: Whittlesey House, pp. xi-xxiv.
Uses W and NS to prove the Freudian thesis that dreams and the unconscious are important elements of literary creation. "How 'Bigger' Was Born" is a sincere account of the genesis of the novel, but Wertham's probing of W's unconscious revealed more.

300. White, Ralph K. "Black Boy: A Value-Analysis." The Journal of Abnormal and Social Psychology, 42 (October),

440-461.
A quantitative analysis of the social attitudes of W as revealed in his autobiography. White graphs and categorizes the various social types in the book, concluding that the primary adult values imposed on young W were obedience, purity, and religion.

300a. Whitford, Robert C. "Biography," in Good Reading. Ed. Atwood H. Townsend. New York: Penguin Books, pp. 150-153.
Reprint of 1946.282.

300b. Williams, Bill. "The Editor Speaking." True, 20 (February), 8, 10.
Notes that "our mail on . . . 'How Jim Crow Feels' . . . is at last thinning out. The record shows that the letters were approximately 60 per cent unfavorable and 40 per cent favorable. How do all you soreheads feel now, by the way?"

301. Witham, W. Tasker. Living American Literature. New York: Stephen Daye Press.
Includes a reprint of 1947.302, reprints Chapter XIII of BB, and provides a brief "chronological outline" of W's life (p. 931).

302. ____. Panorama of American Literature. New York: Stephen Daye Press, pp. 356-358.
Biographical-critical sketch of W with two photographs.
Reprinted: 1947.301.

303. Zevin, B. D. "Literary Box Score: Three Centuries of U. S. Best-Sellers." Cleveland News (17 December), Books Sec., p. 7.
Review of Frank Luther Mott's Golden Multitudes mentioning briefly BB.

1948

1. Adams, J. Donald. The Shape of Books to Come. New York: Viking, pp. 82-83.
Reprint of 1944.2.

2. Agàmben, A. "America, attenta a Richard Wright." Il Rome giornale della sera (19 February), p. 3.
Account of W's visit to Rome with flashbacks to his childhood and youth. Describes W's walking the streets, giving an interview to journalists, and having a drink with the author in a bar. Agàmben stresses racism with sexual overtones.

3. Algren, Nelson. "Du rire en bocaux: Reportage de Chicago." Les Temps Modernes, 3 (January), 1301-1307.
Contains a comparison of NS and Willard Motley's Knock on Any Door. W's

book is profound and creative; Motley's is superficial and journalistic (pp. 1303-1304).

4. Altman, Georges. "Nostalgie d'un monde plus libre." Paris Franc-Tireur (27 October).
Brief comparison of Ann Petry's The Street to W's work.

5. _____. "Nous étions cinq mille." La Gauche (20 December).
Names W as a supporter of the Rassemblement Démocratique Révolutionnaire.

6. Alude. "Une minute de détente . . . Les Enfants de l'oncle Tom." Rabat Maroc Matin (25 April).
Inspirational article praising France for its racial liberalism. Includes somewhat vague comments on the French translation of UTC.

7. Andry, Marc. "June Hennesey." Radio (27 June).
Reports that Hennesey names W as a favorite writer.

8. Anon. "A l'occasion de la parution de Black Boy."
Printed announcement of an autograph party in honor of the publication of the French translation.

9. Anon. "A l'occasion de la parution de Black Boy." Les Nouvelles Littéraires (22 January), p. 3.
Advertisement for an autograph party in honor of the publication of the French translation.

10. Anon. "A travers les revues." Paris L'Aube (24 July).
Mentions the appearance of the French translation of "How 'Bigger' Was Born" in the July issue of La Nef.

11. Anon. "L'Age Nouveau." Les Nouvelles Littéraires (1 April), p. 3.
Advertisement for the magazine listing the French translation of "Down By the Riverside."

12. Anon. "L'Age Nouveau." Paris Opéra (7 April).
Advertisement for the magazine listing the French translation of "Down by the Riverside."

13. Anon. "L'Age Nouveau." Paris Readers Digest (February).
Advertisement for the magazine listing the French translation of "Down by the Riverside."

14. Anon. "L'Arche." Cahiers de Monde Nouveau, 4 (February), [137].
Advertisement for the magazine men-

tioning a review of W.

15. Anon. "Art and Fiction."
Brochure advertising a special issue of Twice a Year. Lists W.

16. Anon. "L'Artiste ne peut être complice des ideologies contemporaines." L'Echo d'Oran (15 December).
Quotes W as telling a meeting in Paris that "my body was born in America; my heart was born in Russia." Reprinted: 1948.109.

17. Anon. "Aux yeux de M. Kanapa; Miller, Faulkner et . . . Rita Hayworth sont des 'gêneurs de l'action démocratique.'" Marseilles Dernière Heure (12 April).
Defends W against Kanapa's partisan Communist attack.

18. Anon. "La Bibliothèque municipale." Tours La Nouvelle République de Centre-Ouest (4 February).
Lists W among novelists whose books are circulating well at the Chateauroux Library.

19. Anon. "Black Boy, par Richard Wright." Paris Libération (25 February), p. 2.
Very favorable notice of the French translation.

20. Anon. "Boltons Theatre." The London Times (21 February), p. 6.
Favorable review of the London production of the play NS. It is well paced and highly effective. Robert Adams is weak as Bigger, but Irene Worth gives a good performance as Mary Dalton. The work is perhaps more suitable to the screen than to the stage.

21. Anon. "A Boycott of Maniac Roles Led Anne Burr to Society-Girl Part." New York Herald Tribune.
Relates the recent success of the actress who played Mary Dalton in NS.

22. Anon. "Cette manifestation d'aide aux etudiants sera organisée avec le concours de."
W is listed on this flyer. The year is conjectural.

23. Anon. "Les 'Citoyens du Monde' de Berlin ont tenu leur première réunion." Angoulême L'Essor du Centre-Ouest (30 December).
Lists W as an expatriate associated with "Citizens of the World."

24. Anon. "Les 'Citoyens du Monde' de Berlin tiennent leur première réunion." Le Paris Monde (30 December), p. 3.

Lists W as an expatriate associated with "Citizens of the World."

25. Anon. "Clinic Displays Work of Three Designers." The Publishers' Weekly, 153 (6 March), 1265-1269.
Contains a description of the printing of TMBV. The photographs were reproduced by gravure; the text was printed in Garamond bold.

26. Anon. "Club Maintenant." (11 March 1948).
Large flyer advertising W's lecture on "Black Poetry in the United States."

27. Anon. "Le Club Maintenant prie."
Printed invitation to W's lecture on "Black Poetry in the United States" to be delivered on 11 March.

28. Anon. "Coloured People." Une Semaine dans le Monde (c. 20 March).
Relates an anecdote anout W's surprise that Gaston Monnerville, a black man, could reach a high political position in France.

29. Anon. "Comme ça se trouve!" Le Canard Enchaîné (c. 24 March).
Relates an anecdote about W meeting Gaston Monnerville in the Palais du Luxembourg.

30. Anon. "Conférences." Paris Combat (16 January), p. 2.
Announces an autograph party on 24 January in honor of the publication of the French translation of BB.

31. Anon. "Conférences." Paris Opéra (10 March).
Announces W's lecture on "Black Poetry of the United States" scheduled for 11 March.

32. Anon. "Confidences." Paris Combat (17 December), p. 2.
Relates a false anecdote about W and Eleanor Roosevelt having breakfast together.

33. Anon. "D49 české kulturni středisko." Prague: Palasek a Kraus.
Playbill for the Prague production of the play NS with Gustav Heverle as Bigger and Stanislava Stroba as Mary. The opening was on 7 September 1948.

34. Anon. "Dangereux exemples." La Paris Bataille (11 February).
Interview with Elia Vittorini containing a brief mention of W.

35. Anon. "Den benhåller sitt grepp om svensk publik." Unidentified clipping.
Advertisement for the Swedish trans-

lation of BB.

36. Anon. "Divadlo: Premiéra u E. F. Buriana: Syn cerného nidu." Unidentified clipping (c. 8 September).
Favorable review of the Prague production of the play NS. The novel NS is compared to Steinbeck's novels. W's work emphasizes fear in black life. Omitting much from the novel, the play retains shock value. The review praises the direction, stage setting, and acting, all of which are in the mode of socialist realism.

37. Anon. "Un Don Juan vêtu de gris rose défend les gens de lettres en gérant la fortune des 'Bonnes Reproductrices.'" Paris Samedi-Soir (14 August).
Notes that W was received by the Société des Gens des Lettres.

38. Anon. "Duke Ellington arrive." Le Paris Populaire (17 July), p. 2.
Reports that W was among those greeting Ellington.

39. Anon. "D'un jour: Confidence pour confidence." Rodez Rouerque Républicain (19 December).
Relates a false ancedote about W and Eleanor Roosevelt having breakfast together.

40. Anon. Dust jacket of Paura. By Richard Wright. Milan: Bompiani.
Publisher's blurb on the front inside flap of the Italian translation of NS.

41. Anon. Dust jacket of Ragazzo negro. By Richard Wright. Turin: Einaudi.
Front inside flap of the dust jacket of the Italian translation of BB compares W to Faulkner and Saroyan and stresses his view of life as a painful struggle. A publisher's blurb appears on the back of the jacket.

42. Anon. "Les Enfants de l'oncle Tom, par R. Wright." Mercure de France, 302 (1 January), 151-152.
Notice of the French translation of UTC emphasizing the theme of black revolt. The book is powerful, but less important than NS.

43. Anon. "Les enfants de l'oncle Tom, par Richard Wright, traduit de l'américain par Marcel Duhamel." L'Afrique (January), pp. 31-32.
Favorable review of the French translation of UTC taking up some crucial episodes in the stories, especially in "Big Boy Leaves Home," and praising W's role of spokesman for oppressed blacks and his ability as a creator of vivid, quick-moving fiction.

44. Anon. "Les Existentialistes be-bop ont annexé Duke Ellington." Paris Lundi-Dimanche (20 July).
Reports that W attended a reception honoring Ellington at the Club St.-Germain-des-Prés.

45. Anon. "Idées et livres: Noirs et blancs par Richard Wright 'Black Boy.'" Quelques [?].
Favorable review of the French translation of BB stressing its revolutionary significance and its social commentary.

46. Anon. "Impérialisme et socialisme dans le même sac." L'Humanité Dimanche (19 December).
Mentions an article by W in Franc-Tireur.

47. Anon. "In nessuna letteratura." Giornale della libreria, 61 B, No. 1, p. 11.
Advertisement for Paura, the Italian translation of NS.

48. Anon. "Les Indiscrétions des les coulisses." Paris Samedi-Soir (4 February).
Mentions the friendship of Simone de Beauvoir with the Wrights. W does not want to return to the United States, but he is not convinced by existentialism and refuses to recognize that Sartre is a genius.

49. Anon. "Informations littéraires." Arts (8 October), p. 2.
Compares the enthusiasm concerning Camus's The Plague to that concerning W.

50. Anon. "J.-P. Sartre--André Breton." Paris Franc-Tireur (10 December), p. 1.
Advertisement for a political rally indicating W's support.

51. Anon. "Les Lettres." Vogue (September).
Notes that W is among the writers translated by Marcel Duhamel.

52. Anon. "Liste de soutien du cas Garry Davis." Paris Franc-Tireur (19 November).
Reports W among the signers of a group supporting Davis.

53. Anon. "La Littérature." Les Lettres (February).
Favorable review of the French translations of NS and UTC. Of the stories in the latter, the reviewer prefers "Long Black Song" for its evocation of black sexuality and jealousy.

54. Anon. "Littérature." Le Tunis Petit

Matin (29 February).
Disputes Jean Kanapa's partisan Communist attack on W.

55. Anon. "Les livres reçus." Arts (12 March), p. 2.
Questions the omission of W from A.-J. Guerard's anthology Prosateurs americains de xxᵉ siècle.

56. Anon. "London Lament." Paris Daily Mail (18 March).
A British journalist comments on W at a press club luncheon, relating an anecdote W told about a London taxi driver.

57. Anon. "Londoner's Diary: Last Night's First Night." London Evening Standard (21 February).
Favorable review of the London production of the play NS with Robert Adams as Bigger and Irene Worth as Mary.

58. Anon. "Lundi 13 decembre." Paris Franc-Tireur (c. 8 December).
Reports that W will attend a meeting with Sartre, Camus, and others on "The Internationalism of the Spirit."

59. Anon. "Mise au point." Marseilles Dernière Heure (27 December).
Relates a false anecdote about W and Eleanor Roosevelt having breakfast together.

60. Anon. "Le Monde devant la caméra." Paris Combat (18 October), p. 2.
Mentions a photograph of W pushing a wagon.

61. Anon. "Monnerville and Wright Guests of Press Today." New York Herald Tribune (Paris edition) (17 March), p. 3.
Notes their appearance as guests of honor at the Anglo-American Press Association luncheon.

62. Anon. "Native Son," in The Reader's Encyclopedia. Ed. William Rose Benét. New York: Crowell, p. 760.
Brief plot summary.
Reprinted: 1955.12.

63. Anon. "La Nef." La Nef, No. 40 (March), p. 178 (back cover).
Announces the forthcoming publication in the magazine of W's "Journal de l'enfant du pays."

64. Anon. "Nouvelles des lettres." Le Figaro Littéraire (6 March), p. 5.
Announces W's lecture on "Black Poetry in the United States" scheduled for 11 March.

65. Anon. "NRF." Bibliographie de la

France, 137 (2 July), 2162.
   Advertisement for Jean Cau's Maria-
   Nègre quoting W.

66. Anon. "Numéro spécial." Le Musée
Vivant.
   Advertisement for the exhibition on
   "La Culture Nègre" presented by W and
   Michel Leiris.

67. Anon. "Paul Guth: Quarante contre
un." La Paris Bataille (14 April).
   Lists W as a contemporary writer.

68. Anon. "Les Peuples ne se résignent
pas." L'Humanité Dimanche (19 December).
   Quotes disapprovingly a remark W made
   in Franc-Tireur about the Cold War.

69. Anon. "Poste parisien: 20 h. 50. Le
Feu dans la nuée." Radio Revue (25
March).
   Announces and quotes from Albert
   Vidalie's radio adaptation of "Fire
   and Cloud." Comments on American
   racism as revealed by W and Langston
   Hughes.

70. Anon. "Pour la liberté et la fraternité de tous les peuples." Paris Franc-
Tireur (13 December), pp. 1-2.
   Notes that W will attend a political
   rally at the Salle Pleyel.

71. Anon. "Présence Africaine." Dakar
L'A. O. F. (16 March).
   Advertisement for the magazine list-
   ing W.

72. Anon. "Présence Africaine." Les Nouvelles Littéraires (19 February), p. 3.
   Advertisement listing the concluding
   installment of the French translation
   of "Bright and Morning Star."

73. Anon. "Présence Africaine." Les Nouvelles Littéraires (25 March), p. 2.
   Advertisement for the second issue of
   the magazine listing W.

74. Anon. "Presenting New Plays." 20
February.
   Playbill for the London production of
   the play NS at Boltons Theatre, Ken-
   sington.

75. Anon. "4,000 Parisiens à la salle
Pleyel." Paris Franc-Tireur (14 December).
   Quotes W's remark that both Russia
   and the United States impose a form
   of slavery on writers and intellectuals.

76. Anon. "Quelques idées, quelques liv-
res: Noirs et blancs: Richard Wright:
'Black Boy.'" Lille La Voix du Nord (29
May).

Favorable review noting the relation
between BB and NS. W's psychological
insight in depicting black anxiety in
a world dominated by whites is worthy
of Kafka.

77. Anon. "Quelques livres choisis." Bon
Sens (March).
   Includes BB in a list of recommended
   books.

78. Anon. "Quelques publications ré-
centes." Les Temps Modernes, No. 28
(January), p. [1344e].
   Publisher's advertisement for the
   French translations of NS and UTC.

79. Anon. "Qu'en dites vous?" Orléans La
République du Centre (19 March).
   Reports a letter by Ella Vittorini
   commenting on the Italian Communist
   distrust of W's work.

80. Anon. "La Radio." Le Paris Pays (25
March).
   Radio schedule listing the adaptation
   in French of "Fire and Cloud."

81. Anon. "La Radio cette semaine."
Cette Semaine (24 March), p. 35.
   Notes that the radio adaptation of
   "Fire and Cloud" with Habib Benglia
   will be presented at 8:50 p. m. on 25
   March.

82. Anon. "La Radiodiffusion: Rappel des
principales émissions de la soirée (jeu-
di)." Le Paris Monde (26 March), p. 6.
   Announces the broadcast of the radio
   adaptation of "Fire and Cloud" by
   Albert Vidalie.

83. Anon. "Revue des revues." Toulon La
République Varoise (19 July).
   Mentions W's comments on American
   racism published in La Nef.

84. Anon. "Richard Wright." Paris Combat
(25-26 December), p. 6.
   Headnote to a statement by W on social conditions among American
   blacks.

85. Anon. "Richard Wright 'Un Enfant du
pays.'" Fiches Littéraires, No. 2
(March), fiche 22.
   After noting French interest in W and
   summarizing the plot of NS, this
   article reviews French criticism of
   the novel by G.-A. Astre, Jean-
   Jacques Sorel, André Rousseaux, Marcel Thiébaut, and Henri du Passage.
   The major categories concern the
   racial theme, the question of realism
   vs. propaganda, and fictional technique.

86. Anon. "Sélection des livres nouveaux

commentés par les grands critiques." Fiches Litteraires, No. 2 (March), fiche 23, p. [4].
　　Lists the French translations of BB and UTC.

87. Anon. "La Semaine littéraire." Paris Combat (3 January), p. 2.
　　Quotes from Jean Kanapa's attack on W in Poésie 47.

88. Anon. "La Semaine littéraire." Paris Combat (2 December), p. 4.
　　Notes that W will attend a meeting in support of the internationalism of the spirit.

89. Anon. "La Semaine littéraire: Un Grand Ecrivain américain." Le Paris Libertaire (8 January), p. 3.
　　Recommends reading the French translation of BB.

90. Anon. "Six millions de poings noirs." La Paris Presse (6 July).
　　Lists W as a supporter of Henry Wallace.

91. Anon. "Søn af de Sorte." Copenhagen Politiken.
　　Report of an interview with W in Paris including his condemnation of white-financed black institutions and his analysis of the link between fascist and American racist ideology. He also speaks on the context of the composition of "I Tried to Be a Communist."

92. Anon. "St. Germain-des-Prés fêtera Duke Ellington demain." Paris Libération (18 July), p. 2.
　　Reports that W will attend a reception for Ellington.

93. Anon. "Staline ne veut pas un Garry Davis à Moscou." Paris Inter (20 December).
　　Lists W as a supporter of Garry Davis.

94. Anon. "La Tournée du grand Duke Ellington fait suer tout Paris." Point de Vue (29 July).
　　Reports that W was seated at the head table at a reception for Ellington.

95. Anon. "A Treasury of Short Stories. By Bernardine Kielty." Newsweek, 31 (19 January), 95.
　　Review listing W as a contributor.

96. Anon. "Trois livres de Richard Wright." Paris Aux Ecoutes (30 January).
　　Mentions the three works available in French, citing their relevance to the racial problem and their Faulknerian and Kafkaesque qualities.

97. Anon. "U. S. Writer and French Statesman Meet." New York Herald Tribune (Paris edition) (18 March), p. 2.
　　Photograph with caption of W and Gaston Monnerville, the black French politician.

98. Anon. Unidentified clipping.
　　Photograph of W with caption in Italian announcing his talk on 18 February at the Teatro Carignano.

99. Anon. Unidentified clipping (c. September).
　　Photograph with caption of Gustav Heverle as Bigger in the Prague production of NS.

100. Anon. Unidentified clipping (c. September).
　　Photograph with caption of a scene from the Prague production of NS.

101. Anon. Untitled advertisement. Les Nouvelles Littéraires (15 April), p. 3.
　　Mentions a story by W in L'Age Nouveau, No. 27.

102. Anon. Untitled article. La Paris Bataille (21 January), p. 4.
　　Announces an autograph party for BB.

103. Anon. Untitled clipping. Bollettino di informazioni culturali (23 April).
　　Favorable notice of the Italian translation of BB. Stresses W's honesty and emotional power in recounting his suffering.

104. Anon. Untitled clipping. Bel Abbès Journal, No. 7 [?] (14 August).
　　Mentions the appearance of the French translation of "How 'Bigger' Was Born" in La Nef.

105. Anon. Untitled clipping. Cinémonde (1 June).
　　Suggests that Daryl Zanuck film a W novel.

106. Anon. Untitled clipping. Les Lettres Françaises (c. 23 December).
　　Report on the international literary scene noting that W is popular in Russia.

107. Anon. Untitled clipping. New York Herald Tribune (Paris edition) (c. 21 January).
　　Announces an autograph session with W in a Paris book store.

108. Anon. Untitled clipping. Paris Carrefour (10 March).
　　Announces W's lecture on "Black Poetry of the United States" scheduled for 11 March.

109. Anon. "Vers 'l'internationalisation des esprits.'" La Tangiers Dépêche Marocaine (15 December).
Reprint of 1948.16.

110. Anon. "La Vie des lettres." Les Nouvelles Littéraires (9 December), p. 6.
Notes that W will be one of the authors selling their books and autographs on 10 December for the benefit of student solidarity.

111. Anon. "Vient de paraître." Lille Nord Industriel et Commercial (1 May).
Lists W as a contributor to Pierre Brodin's Les Maîtres de la littérature américaine.

112. Anon. "Visite à la littérature américaine." Arts (6 February), p. 2.
Lists W as a well-known American writer.

113. Anon. "World Citizen Davis Indorsed by French Intellectual Group." New York Herald Tribune (Paris edition) (23 October), p. 1.
Notes that W joined in support of Garry Davis.

114. Anon. "Wright a Milano." Unidentified clipping.
Brief article on W's visit to Milan accompanied by two pages of photographs of W sightseeing and conversing with his Italian translators and publishers.

115. Anon. "Wright, Richard," in Gyldendals Nye Konversasjonsleksikon Ed. Leiv Amundsen. Oslo: Gyldenda Norsk Forlag, p. 4566.
Biographical note.

116. Anon. "Wright (Richard)." La Gazette des Lettres.
Bio-bibliographical sketch.

117. Anon. "Wright, Richard," in The Reader's Encyclopedia. Ed. William Rose Benêt. New York: Crowell, p. 1227.
Biographical note.
Reprinted: 1955.22.

118. Anon. "Wright, romanziere negro tra gli scrittori romani." Unidentified clipping (12 February).
Mentions meeting W in Rome and comments briefly on the Italian translations of NS and BB.

119. Anon. "Writers in Rome." The New York Times Magazine (7 March), p. 54.
Photograph with caption of W and Carlo Levi.

120. Antier, Maurice. "Aux cours munici-paux." Rennes Ouest-France (13 November).
Lists W among important recent American novelists.

121. Astruc, Alexandre. "Notes sur Orson Welles." La Table Ronde, No. 2 (February), pp. 330-335.
Quotes W's comment that one Orson Welles is enough (p. 332).

122. B., A. "Lettre de Paris." La Dijon Bourgogne Républicaine (20 December).
Reports that a group of writers, including W, is supporting Garry Davis.

123. B., J.-C. "Romans et nouvelles." La Gazette des Lettres (17 April).
Review of Mulk Raj Anand's Coolie using NS as a standard of novelistic success.

124. Balandier, Georges. "Erreurs noires." Présence Africaine, No. 3 (March-April), pp. 392-404.
Comments on W's explanation of black duplicity in a racist society.

125. Baldwin, James. "From the American Scene: The Harlem Ghetto: Winter 1948." Commentary, 5 (February), 165-170.
Refers briefly to W's point that blacks in America are "almost always acting" (p. 169).
Reprinted: 1955.25.

126. ____. "Previous Condition." Commentary, 6 (October), 334-342.
The protagonist of this short story, a black actor, mentions being offered the role of Bigger in a film version of NS (p. 339).
Reprinted: 1965.32.

127. Barkan, Raymond. "Les Procès." L'Ecran Français (30 November).
Briefly compares lynching, as W depicts it, with the atrocities of anti-Semitism.

128. Barry, Joseph A. "Americans in Paris--The More They Change . . ." The New York Times Magazine (15 August), pp. 18, 42-43.
Includes a photograph of W and his daughter Julia (p. 43).

129. Barton, Rebecca Chalmers. Witnesses for Freedom: Negro Americans in Autobiography. Foreword by Alain Locke. New York: Harper, pp. 254-268.
Discusses BB with comparisons to Angelo Herndon's Let Me Live. Analyzes the reasons for W's behavior as revealed in his autobiography. Notes W's influence on other writers, including Langston Hughes and Saunders

Redding.

130. Bataille. "Cinéma et acteurs noirs." *Présence Africaine*, No. 4, pp. 690-696.
   Mentions W's comment on the lack of great black films.

131. Beauvoir, Simone de. *L'Amérique au jour le jour*. Paris: Editions Paul Morihien, pp. 23, 33, 41-42, 58, 62, 103, 108, 246, 251, 276-280, 281, 317, 320, 328, 329, 339, 345, 346, 348, 350, 352, 353, 354.
   Reprint of 1947.146 along with many additional references to W in connection with de Beauvoir's American trip.
   Translated: 1952.23.

132. Belleville, Joseph de. "Point de vue du libraire: Le Cercle critique." *La Gazette des Lettres* (3 April).
   Contains a brief mention of W.

133. Bendiner, Robert. "Psychiatry for the Needy." *Tomorrow*, 7 (April), 22-26.
   Account of the Lafargue Clinic in Harlem mentioning W's role as one of the initiators of the project along with Dr. Frederic Wertham and Earl Brown.

134. Berys, Joseph de. "La Vie littéraire: Le Problème noir: 'Bagarre de Juillet.'" Marseilles *Midi-Soir* (24 March).
   Contrasting the treatment of lynching by Steinbeck, Caldwell, and W, de Berys points out the latter's emotion and poignant horror.

135. Blum, Léon. "Comme dirait Léon Blum." *L'Humanité Dimanche* (19 December).
   Quotes W's comments on Russia published in *Franc-Tireur*.

136. Boffino, G. D. "La letteratura di colore: la dignita in America puo avere la pelle nera." Rome *Avanti!* (29 January), p. 3.
   Discusses the Italian translations of BB and NS as well as works by Langston Hughes.

137. Bontemps, Arna. *Story of the Negro*. New York: Knopf, p. 203.
   Includes a paragraph on W's rise to fame, emphasizing the universal implications of his racial subject matter.
   Reprinted: 1955.26; 1958.88.

138. Brenner, Jacques. "Ecrit aux U. S. A." Rouen *Paris Normandie* (2 March).
   Laments the exclusion of W from A.-J. Guerard's anthology *Prosateurs améri-*

cains du xxe siècle.

139. Breton, André. "Un pour tous hormis quelques-uns." Paris *Combat* (20-21 November), pp. 1-3.
   Lists W as a supporter of Gary Davis.

140. Buenzod, Emmanuel. "Vues sur l'âme noire." *Gazette de Lausanne* (7 February), *La Gazette Littéraire* page.
   Contains reviews of Erskine Caldwell's *Trouble in July* and BB, giving more space and praise to W's book. Like Gorky's autobiography, BB compels the reader's confidence in its authenticity. W has literary gifts, intellectual insight, and humanity.

141. Butcher, Philip. "In Print . . . Our Raceless Writers." *Opportunity*, 26 (Summer), 113-115.
   Refers briefly to W.

142. Caillet, Gérard. "Nous avons lu pour vous romans: Richard Wright--*Black Boy* (*Jeunesse noire*)." Paris *Opéra* (4 February).
   Favorable review praising the book for its lucidity and the author for his courage.

143. Cayton, Horace R. "A Psychological Approach to Race Relations." *Présence Africaine*, No. 3 (Winter), pp. 418-431; No. 4 (Spring), pp. 549-563.
   Reprint of 1946.171.

144. Cecchi, Emilio. "L'angoscia di avere il pelle diversa." *L'Europeo* (7 March), p. 10.
   Comments on W's personality, his visit to Rome, and UTC and BB. Discusses NS with emphasis on its powerful social message, which contrasts with the gentler writings of earlier black writers.
   Reprinted: 1964.36.

145. Chandler, G. Lewis. "Coming of Age: A Note on American Negro Novelists." *Phylon*, 9 (First Quarter), 25-29.
   Discusses the importance of NS in the maturation of the black novelist. Bitter, propagandistic, and melodramatic, NS is nevertheless powerful and professional. Its theme has universal implications for oppressed people.

146. Chonez, Claudine. "De l'enfant noir à la libération de l'homme." *Présence Africaine*, No. 3 (March-April), pp. 515-518.
   Discusses BB, UTC, and NS. By analyzing in detail a number of episodes from W's youth, Chonez places his suffering in a perspective wider than race, concluding that his experience

has universal value.

147. Claris, Lise. "Ceux qui ne sont pas 'dans le champ': Un Scénariste et ses negres." Cinévogue (5 March).
Mentions W briefly.

148. C.[olombo], A.[chille]. "Wright Richard: Paura (trad. di Camillo Pellizzi)." Letture, 3 (January), 6.
Favorable review of the Italian translation of NS emphasizing the theme of racial protest. The description of Bigger's crimes is so vivid and the rendering of his fear is so intense that the novel is suitable only for mature readers.

149. Cornet, Edouard. "Les Américains." La Parisien Libéré (5 May).
Names W along with Hemingway and Henry Miller as one of the most prominent Americans to have lived in Paris.

150. Cowie, Alexander. The Rise of the American Novel. New York: American Book Company, p. 292.
Compares Richard Hildreth's The Slave with NS.

151. Cowley, Malcolm. "American Books Abroad," in Literary History of the United States. Ed. Robert E. Spiller, Willard Thorp, Thomas H. Johnson, and Henry Seidel Canby. Vol. 2. New York: Macmillan, pp. 1374-1391.
Mentions the popularity of NS in the Soviet Union (p. 1386).
Reprinted: 1953.113; 1963.71; 1974.52.

152. D., D. "Twelve Million Black Voices. A Folk History of the Negro in the United States. By Richard Wright. With photographs by Edwin Rosskam." Empire, 2 (September), 10.
Favorable review of the English edition. W "draws on the art of the cinema to aid him set forth his story by skillful interweaving of written word and photograph."

153. D'Aubras, Denis. "Le Problème nègre aux Etats-Unis." Unidentified clipping.
Favorable review of the French translations of NS and BB in the context of the American racial situation. Notes that in the last book of NS W "transforms the psychological and moral drama into an impeccable accusation against white American society."

154. D.[ebidour], V.-H. "John Steinbeck --Les Raisins de la colère." Le Bulletin des Lettres, 10 (15 April), 180-181.
Mentions W as a novelist of social protest along with Steinbeck and Erskine Caldwell.

155. Delasalle, J. Untitled clipping. Paris Ce Matin (26 February).
Includes favorable comments on the French translation of BB.

156. Delavignette, Robert. "Préface," in Karim. By Ousmane Socé. Paris: Nouvelles Editions Latines, pp. 7-15.
Delavignette concludes his preface to this Senegalese novel by comparing it to BB in order to show that French civilization is less repressive toward blacks.

157. Desternes, Jean. "Débat sur le réalisme." La Revue du Cinéma, 3 (October), 49-56.
Briefly compares the film Senza pietà with BB (p. 56).

158. Dickinson, Asa Don. The Best Books of the Decade 1936-1945. New York: H. W. Wilson, pp. 245-246, 249, 251-252, 255, 287.
Classifies NS and BB among the four hundred best books of the decade and provides a biographical sketch and excerpts from reviews. Ranks W as seventeenth among the twenty-five best authors of the period, BB as twenty-ninth and NS as forty-second among the fifty best books, NS as fifteenth among the forty best titles in American fiction, and UTC among the six hundred runners-up.

159. Douty, Esther. "Modern Approach to Writing." Writers Journal, 17 (March).
Notes that W is among the writers whom Martha Foley helped to develop.

160. Esteve, Anita. "Orson Welles, le révolutionnaire." Rabat L'Echo du Maroc (23 June).
Quotes W's statement that one Welles is enough.

161. F., E. "Indictment with a Weakness." London News Chronicle (21 February), p. 3.
Unfavorable review of the London production of the play NS. The acting is good, but it is difficult to view Bigger as a social victim because he has been presented as a "murderous thug."

162. F.-T. "'L'Humanité est plus grande que l'Amérique ou la Russie' par Richard Wright." Paris Franc-Tireur (16 December), p. 1.
Favorable headnote to W's essay.

163. Fauchery, Pierre. "Quelques américains: Erskine Caldwell, Howard Fast,

Henry Wallace." Paris _Action_ (6 January), p. 8.
    Contrasts the rural innocence of the lynch victim in Caldwell's _Trouble in July_ to the urban corruption of W's black characters.

164. Fontaine, Pierre. "Nous avons lu _Black Boy (Jeunesse noire)_ de Richard Wright." _L'Action Sociale_ (13 March), p. 4.
    Favorable notice summarizing some of the important episodes and praising the authenticity of the work.

165. Friedland, Jacques. "De sang royal." _France d'Abord_ (23 December).
    Review of Sinclair Lewis's _Kingsblood Royal_ finding its treatment of black psychology inferior to that of _NS_.

166. G., R. P. M. "'Native Son' at the Boltons." _The London Daily Telegraph and Morning Post_ (21 February), p. 3.
    Favorable notice of the London production of _NS_ starring Robert Adams and Irene Worth.

167. Gannett, Lewis. "Books and Things." _New York Herald Tribune_ (1 January), p. 24.
    Claims that W is an author whose reputation was established with the help of the "courage" of the Book-of-the-Month Club.

168. Geismar, Maxwell. "A Cycle of Fiction," in _Literary History of the United States_. Ed. Robert E. Spiller, Willard Thorp, Thomas H. Johnson, and Henry Seidel Canby. Vol. 2. New York: Macmillan, pp. 1296-1316.
    Discusses W, comparing him to James T. Farrell. Emphasizes W's power and integrity but deplores his bitterness (pp. 1314-1315).
    Reprinted: 1953.134; 1963.89; 1974.77.

169. _____. "The Negro Writer in America." _The New York Times Book Review_ (4 July), p. 4.
    Reviewing Hugh M. Gloster's _Negro Voices in American Fiction_, Geismar states that "Richard Wright reached down into the deepest levels of Negro consciousness to become, incidentally, one of the few new American literary voices of real promise today."

170. Gloster, Hugh M. _Negro Voices in American Fiction_. Chapel Hill: The University of North Carolina Press, pp. 227-234, et passim.
    Reprint of 1941.741. Contains numerous other references to W.

171. _____. "The Negro Writer and the

Southern Scene." _The Southern Packet_, 4 (January), 1-3.
    Refers to _UTC_ as "a graphic presentation of the hardships of the downtrodden masses of the Mississippi Delta."

172. Guyot, Charly. "Un Noir d'Amérique nous raconte sa jeunesse." Bâle _Coopération_ (17 April).
    Article on Langston Hughes mentioning W.

173. _____. _Les Romanciers américains d'aujourd'hui_. Paris: Editions Labergerie, pp. 109-112.
    Discusses W as a sincere writer of racial protest, lacking in art perhaps, but moving and just.

174. Hart, James D. "Wright, Richard," in his _The Oxford Companion to American Literature_. Second edition. New York: Oxford University Press, p. 852.
    Revised reprint of 1941.760.

174a. Hermlin, Stephan, ed. _Auch ich bin Amerika: Dichtungen amerikanischer Neger_. Berlin: Verlag Volk und Welt, pp. 7, 141.
    Mentions W briefly in the preface as a "newer talent" and provides a brief biographical note. Includes "I Have Seen Black Hands" with a German translation (pp. 98-103).

175. Hirsch, Nicole. "On ne vous a pas tout dit." Paris _France-Soir_ (25 October), Week-End Sec., p. 2.
    Reports that W considers the actions of Garry Davis "acts of supreme liberty."

176. Howlett, Jacques. "Notes sur Chester B. Himes et l'aliénation du noir." _Présence Africaine_, No. 4, pp. 697-704.
    Includes comparison of _If He Hollers Let Him Go_ and _NS_.

177. _____. "Les Revues." _Présence Africaine_, No. 2 (January), pp. 353-355.
    Discusses _Mainstream_ and its attacks on W. Notes that it prefers Johnny Boy and Sue to Bigger as representative black heroes.

178. Hrbas, Jiři. "Kulturni Hlidka: Americká hra v D 49." _Narodni osvobozeni_ (c. 8 September).
    Favorable review of the Prague production of _NS_, translated into Czech by H. Budinová and directed by E. F. Burian. Dramatically well constructed and sincere, the play nevertheless lacks the psychological depth of the novel, and the characterization of Mary is weak. Max's defense of Bigger is the high point of the

play. Hrbas praises the acting and the direction.

179. I. "Ecrivains noirs." Le Monde Illustré, 92 (11 September), 924.
Discusses African writers, contrasting briefly Ousmane Socé's Karim with BB.

179a. [James, C. L. R. ("J. Meyer")]. "The Revolutionary Answer to the Negro Problem in U. S." Fourth International (December), pp. 242-251.
Mentions briefly W, a member of "the Negro petty bourgeoisie, radical and concerned with communism" (p. 242), whose literary success exemplifies public interest in the racial question.
Reprinted: 1962.73a; 1977.180.

180. Jotterand, Franck. "Descente aux enfers." Gazette de Lausanne (8 May).
Review of J'irai cracher sur vos tombes comparing Boris Vian's black characters favorably with W's.

181. K., V. Ě. "Na puli cesty." Unidentified clipping (c. 8 September).
Unfavorable review of the Prague production of NS. The roles of Bigger and Mrs. Dalton are well played, but the work does not get to the root of the American racial problem and Burian's "realistic" staging is inadequate.

182. Kaiser, Ernest. "Racial Dialectics: The Aptheker-Myrdal School Controversy." Phylon, 9 (Fourth Quarter), 295-302.
Corrects Samuel Sillen in "Richard Wright in Retreat" by claiming that W was never totally pro-communist.

183. Kanapa, Jean. "Il y a deux littératures américaines." Les Lettres Françaises (5 February), p. 3.
Contains a paragraph of very adverse criticism of W as a saboteur of the struggle against racism. He promotes racial hatred.

184. La Madeleine, Ch. "On inaugurait une librairie." Climats (24 November).
Notes that W was present at the opening of an exhibition of African art.

184a. Lamont, William H. F. and Lisle A. Rose. "Novels, 20th Century American," in A Guide to Good Reading. Ed. Atwood H. Townsend. New York: Hendricks House, Farrar Straus, pp. 30-35, 127-131.
Revised reprint of 1941.786a and mention of W as a "vigorous new talent."
Reprinted: 1948.184b; 1951.192a; 1952.61a; 1954.164b.

184b. _____. "Novels, 20th Century American," in Good Reading. Mentor Books 19. New York: The New American Library, pp. 30-35, 127-131.
Reprint of 1948.184a; revised reprint of 1941.786a.

185. Le Brun-Keris, G. "Les Noirs seront les grands vainquers des élections américaines." Tours Le Courrier de la Loire (17 August).
Cites W as an accomplished black man.

186. Lemarchand, Jacques. "Othello au Théâtre Marigny." Paris Combat (18 September), p. 2.
Mentions W.

187. Lesdain, Pierre. "Richard Wright Black Boy." Volonté (10 April).
Highly favorable Belgian review with many quotations from the autobiography. BB is "a beautiful book, a great book, and . . . a necessary book." Its chief themes are fear and hunger.

188. _____. "Richard Wright Un Enfant du pays." Volonté (17 April).
Highly favorable Belgian review of the French translation of NS. After explaining how W's reading helped to elevate him from the circumstances of his youth, Lesdain compares W to Steinbeck and comments extensively on NS, giving a detailed plot summary. He notes the symbolic significance of the killing of the rat and of Mrs. Dalton's haunting presence.

188a. Lewis, Sinclair. "No Flight to Olympus," in The American People's Encyclopedia.
Mentions W briefly and favorably.
Reprinted: 1953.171, 173; 1967.70.

189. Liehm, A. J. "La Saison théâtrale." Parallèle 50 (19 November).
Comments on the success of the Prague production of NS.

190. Locke, Alain. "A Critical Retrospect of the Literature of the Negro for 1947." Phylon, 9 (First Quarter), 3-12.
Compares briefly Willard Motley to W.

191. M., H. "Coleman Hawkins et Errol Garner nous parlent à leur arrivée en France." Le Paris Populaire (11 May), p. 2.
Reports that a jazz musician named Charles Wright expresses admiration for Richard W's works.

192. Magnan, Henry. "Paris, cette semaine." Une Semaine dans le Monde (6 March).
Mentions a publisher's party at Gal-

limard with W, Louis Armstrong, Sartre, and de Beauvoir in attendance.

193. Marker, Chris. "Sauvages blancs seulement confondre." Esprit, 16 (July), 1-9.
    Includes a sardonic reference to W and Faulkner as "great friends" of the Ku Klux Klan.

194. Martens, Johannes Skancke. "Richard Wright bosetter seg i Paris." Oslo Morgenbladet (29 December), p. 3.
    Interview with W in Paris by a Norwegian journalist. W speaks of his fondness for the French capital, explains American political and racial conditions, expresses admiration for Sartre and Lillian Smith, discusses his work in progress, and cites Himes, Ellison, and Ann Petry as the best contemporary Afro-American writers.

195. Maurois, André. "Pour qui écrit-on?" Paris Opéra (20 October).
    Review of Sartre's Situations referring to W as a defender of blacks whose audience is composed largely of whites.

196. Maury, Jean. "Le Tout-Paris se bouscule à St. Germain-des-Prés." Paris Combat (c. 20 July).
    Notes that W was among those greeting Duke Ellington.

197. Maynard, René. "Bagarre de juillet." Le Casablanca Petit Marocain (18 February).
    Mentions W as a novelist who has handled the racial themes which also concern Erskine Caldwell.

198. _____. "Les Lettres et les arts: Un Enfant de son [sic] pays de Richard Wright." Le Casablanca Petit Marocain (14 April).
    Favorable review of the French translation of NS focusing on its statement against racism. Maynard notes that Communists as well as blacks suffer persecution from exploiters who resist efforts to create a humane society.

199. McIlwaine, Shields. Memphis Down in Dixie. New York: E. P. Dutton, p. 316.
    Denies the validity of W's account in BB of racial hostility in Memphis.

200. Mégret, Christian. "Les Livres: Black Boy, par Richard Wright." Radio 47 (29 February-6 March).
    After discussing the existence of racism in France, Mégret reviews BB favorably as a statement against

racism.

201. _____. "Les Livres étrangers: Noir sur noir." Paris Carrefour (28 April), p. 8.
    Favorable review of the French translations of BB, which analyzes American racism, and NS, which provides an example. In BB, the protagonist achieves heroic status in rejecting his racial role. In NS, W excels in depicting instinctive man.

202. Mendelson, M. Soviet Interpretation of Contemporary American Literature. Trans. Deming B. Brown and Rufus W. Mathewson. Washington: Public Affairs Press, p. 19.
    Brief discussion of W deploring his transition from proletarian to bourgeois writer. The case against American racial segregation is weaker in BB than in UTC.

203. Minne, P. "Langston Hughes ou 'Le Train de la liberté.'" Présence Africaine, No. 2 (January), pp. 340-342.
    Contains two brief references to W.

204. Monjou, Jacques. "Présence Africaine." Tunisie-France (16 August).
    Mentions W as a contributor to the magazine.

205. Morel, Henriette. "Un Témoignage sur la haine: Black Boy." Paris Ce Matin (26 February).
    Favorable review of the French translation. Morel praises W's efforts to recreate not only the stages of his early growth, but the conditions of black life in the South as well. Reprinted: 1948.206.

206. _____. Untitled clipping. La Lille Croix du Nord (26 February).
    Reprint of 1948.205.

207. Morgan, Claude. "Walt Whitman et Howard Fast." Parallèle 50 (15 October).
    Says that W's work presents a hopeless approach to the problems Fast treats in Freedom Road.

208. Morpurgo, J. E. "Harlem Test-Tube." The London Observer (11 July), p. 3.
    Review of TMBV and Roi Ottley's Inside Black America contrasting the approaches of a novelist and a journalist. Eschewing objectivity and moderation and overlooking faults of black behavior, W presents a bitter but "magnificent history of the Negro odyssey."

209. Murray, Jacques. "Henri Miller et ses imitateurs." Paris L'Etendard (1 January).

Rejecting the imitators of Henry Miller, Murray recommends instead the reading of W.

210. Nadeau, Maurice. "La Chronique littéraire de 'Gavroche': La Jeunesse d'un homme: Black Boy." Paris Gavroche (4 February).
Highly favorable review with extensive summary. Transcending racial and national categories, BB is a world masterpiece. Nadeau admires W's artistic restraint.

211. _____. "Richard Wright Black Boy." Sélection du Livre Français, No. 3.
Favorable review praising W's ability to engage the reader, to make him feel the suffering of the protagonist and desire to struggle against the forces of oppression.

212. Naville, Pierre. "Le Travail des noirs dans l'industrie aux Etats-Unis." Présence Africaine, No. 5, pp. 838-847.
Accuses W and Faulkner of vulgarizing the issues of racial discrimination for the French reading public.

213. Noble, Peter. The Negro in Films. London: S. Robinson, pp. 22, 45, 154.
Refers to W and the play NS. Reprinted: 1970.275.

213a. Nyland, Waino S. "Biography," in A Guide to Good Reading. Ed. Atwood H. Townsend. New York: Hendricks House, Farrar Straus, pp. 154-156.
Reprint of 1946.282.

213b. _____. "Biography," in Good Reading. Ed. Atwood H. Townsend. Mentor Books 19. New York: The New American Library, pp. 154-156.
Reprint of 1946.282.

214. Ottley, Roi. Black Odyssey: The Story of the Negro in America. New York: Scribner's, pp. 273, 275.
Mentions NS, the novel and the play, and discusses briefly BB, a seminal account of black life in the South.

215. P., H. "Quand l'intelligentzia parle à Pleyel." Le Paris Monde (15 December), p. 2.
Mentions briefly W's concern over the lack of intellectual freedom.

216. P., Louis. "Les Courriers de 'L'Epoque.'" L'Epoque (25 May).
Mentions W as a major American author.

217. Paccino, Dario. "Il teatro ad Harlem: non è più un mistero per la gente di colore." Rome Avanti! (29 January), p. 3.

Mentions W briefly.

218. Palante, Alain. "Les Lettres: Richard Wright, Les Enfants de l'oncle Tom--Un Enfant du pays." La France Catholique (13 February).
Favorable review of the French translations of UTC and NS noting how W has clarified the American racial situation for Frenchmen. He has the talents of a storyteller and a philosopher. Palante observes, somewhat disapprovingly, an existential element in NS. W to the contrary notwithstanding, only the theological virtue of charity, not revolt, will ameliorate racial problems.

219. Paz, Magdeleine. "Romans: La Caravan noir." Présence Africaine, No. 4, pp. 714-718.
Claims that W and Claude McKay are more closely related to Steinbeck, Hemingway and Waldo Frank than to many of their "racial brothers."

220. Peyrol, Pierre. "Radio." Présence Africaine, No. 4, pp. 710-711.
Mixed review of Albert Vidalie's radio adaptation of "Fire and Cloud." The radio version is serious and competent, but it is somewhat lacking in dramatic rhythm. Such a masterly writer as W deserves even better.

221. Pivano, Fernanda. "A Parigi con Wright." Rome Avanti! (28 May), p. 3.
Reprint of 1948.222.

222. _____. "A Parigi con Wright." Turin Avanti! (19 May).
Recounts a visit with W in Paris, describing his apartment and work habits and mentioning a party given in his honor by Peggy Guggenheim. W is the leader of a school of black American writers including Himes and Gwendolyn Brooks. His wide reading includes Heidegger and Jaspers. Reprinted: 1948.221.

223. _____. "Letteratura negro-americana." La rassegna d'Italia, 3 (November), 1142-1146.
Cites W's view in "The Literature of the Negro in the United States" that some black writers have written as whites and some as blacks.

224. Prist, Paul. Untitled clipping. La Nouvelle Gazette (February).
Discusses the French translations of NS and BB as statements against racism.

225. _____. "La Vie à Paris." La Nouvelle Gazette (24 October).
Lists W as an expatriate writer.

Reprinted: 1948.226.

226. _____. "La Vie à Paris." La Nouvelle Gazette de Bruxelles (24 October).
Reprint of 1948.225.

226a. [Quinn, Kerker]. "Accent . . . Summer 1948."
Flyer listing W as a contributor to Accent Anthology.

227. Rabaud, Jean. "'Présence Africaine' et montée des noirs d'Amérique et de l'Union française." La Populaire de Paris (6 January), p. 2.
Article on Présence Africaine discussing W and BB. Compares him to Hemingway, Dos Passos, and Steinbeck with respect to style and the use of violence. W is more American than African.

228. Radine, Serge. "Roman américain: 'Un Enfant du pays.'" Journal de Genève (17-18 January), pp. 3-4.
Favorable review of the French translation of NS placing it in the context of La Putain respecteuse, Strange Fruit, and Kingsblood Royal. Radine praises the realistic portrayal of Bigger. W indicts a racist society that produces criminals, but he also creates a novel with "a deep, durable, and universal significance."

228a. Roditi, Edouard. "Gibt es eine Neger-Lyrik? Bemerkungen über eine tendenziose Anthologie." Der Monat, 1, No. 2, pp. 102-107.
Mentions W briefly.
Partially reprinted: 1979.216.

229. Rollins, Charlemae. We Build Together: A Reader's Guide to Negro Life and Literature for Elementary and High School Use. Revised edition. Chicago: The National Council of Teachers of English, pp. 45, 51.
Reprint of 1941.910 with additional comments on BB, a "bitter, heartbreaking story."

230. Romani, Bruno. "I giovani disprezzano il patriottismo." Il messaggero di Roma (29 December).
Lists W among those attending a political rally in Paris.
Reprinted: 1949.143, 144.

231. Rosenthal, Gérard. "Le Caucase et l'Ethiopie." Droit de Vivre (October).
Review of Kingsblood Royal concluding with a reference to W's essay on black American literature and a quotation from TMBV.

232. Rougerie, R.-J. "Les Enfants de l'oncle Tom par Richard Wright." Présence Africaine, No. 3 (March-April), pp. 518-519.
Very favorable review of the French translation of UTC. Rougerie objects to W's use of black dialect, but otherwise his praise is high, especially for W's representation of black attitudes. The work is "more than a testimony--a prophetic cry."

233. _____. "Présence Africaine." Limoges Le Populaire du Centre (28 January).
Stresses the importance of W's works, and now the establishment of the magazine Présence Africaine, in shedding light on black reality.

234. Rousseaux, André. "Richard Wright et le terreur noire." Le Figaro Littéraire (17 January), p. 2.
Analyzes W's works in terms of white-inspired fear and anxiety. Rousseaux focuses on BB, placing it in the context of the American literature of the period.

235. Rousselot, Jeann. "Amérique-Russie-tradition." Oran L'Echo (13 November).
Briefly compares W to Ann Petry.

236. _____. Untitled clipping. Le Libre Poitou (21 January).
Favorable notice of the French translation of BB, calling it effective both as racial protest and as "a great and beautiful book, full of humanity and faith."

237. Roy, Claude. "Pourquoi me tuez-vous?" Europe, 31 (July), 99-105.
Contains a short review of the French translation of BB critical of Rouseaux's opinion in Le Figaro Littéraire that W's works overstep the limits of the racial problem.

238. S., E. A. "Kulturni Kronika: Misionářský realismus." Lidove noviny (c. 8 September).
Favorable review of the Prague production of NS comparing the play to The Merchant of Venice as a study of social outcasts persecuted because of their race. Director E. F. Burian stresses socialist realism as the dramatic mode of the production. The acting is good, especially that of Gustav Heverle as Bigger, and the translation by H. Budinová and the settings by J. Rabana are effective. The audience was responsive on opening night.

239. Salisbury, Harrison. "Russia Tightens the Iron Curtain on Ideas." The New York Times Magazine (26 December), pp. 9, 30-31.

Notes that W is among the writers attacked in the Soviet press.

240. Salomon, Michel. "D'un juif à des nègres." Présence Africaine, No. 5, pp. 774-779.
    Mentions W.

241. Sartre, Jean-Paul. "Qu-est-ce que la littérature?" in his Situations, II. Paris: Gallimard, pp. 55-330.
    Reprint of 1947.273.

242. _____. Qu'est-ce que la littérature? Paris: Gallimard, pp. 99-103.
    Reprint of 1947.273.

243. Schmidt, Albert-Marie. "Rentrée des noirs dans la littérature française." Paris Réforme (20 March), p. 7.
    Contains a favorable review of the French translation of BB praising its universal appeal and calling it "one of the most important works of our time."

244. Scotto-Lavina, E. "Ce siècle cherche en vain des raisons d'aimer qu'il a perdues." Paris Combat (14 December), pp. 1, 3.
    Quotes W's statement that both Russia and the United States impose forms of bondage on intellectuals.

245. Seaver, Edwin. "Today's Book: 'Twice a Year's' Tenth Anniversary Issue." New York Post (10 September), p. 42.
    Contains a disparaging remark on W's "subjective pessimism."

246. Sée, Edmond. "Des personnages qui vivent en petit malheur 'Tortilla Flat.'" Radio 48 (20 June).
    Compares W favorably to Steinbeck.

247. Sigaux, Gilbert. "Romans étrangers." Le Livre (c. May).
    Compares Erskine Caldwell's tragic vision of racial conflict with W's.

248. Smith, Bradford. "The Guggenheim Fellowships." Author's League Bulletin, 35 (February), 3-6.
    Lists W as a former Guggenheim fellow.

249. S.[mith], H.[arrison]. "American Literature and the Party Line." The Saturday Review of Literature, 31 (10 April), 20.
    Reports on Russian professor M. Mendelson's attack on W and others for representing their oppressed characters as incapable of effective protest.

250. Sorensen, Reginald, M. P. "Twelve Million Black Voices by Richard Wright." Unidentified clipping (April).
    Favorable review of the English edition, a "tragically beautiful volume." Sorensen emphasizes white guilt.

251. Spiller, Robert E., Willard Thorp, Thomas H. Johnson, and Henry Seidel Canby. "Richard Wright," in their Literary History of the United States. Vol. 3. New York: Macmillan, p. 789.
    Bibliography listing five primary and six secondary sources.
    Reprinted: 1963.172; 1974.165.

252. Tanous, Jean. "Saint-Germain-des-Prés lance l'art nègre." Paris Combat (19 November), p. 2.
    Notes that W met with several Africans, including the writer Peter Abrahams, at an exhibition of African art.

253. Tapiero, L.-J. "Les Ecrivains aux bras mous." Alger-Républicain (17 December), p. 1.
    Contains a brief reference to Sartre's comments on W.

254. Tavernier, René. "Livres." Le Progrès de Lyon (7 June).
    Contains a favorable review of the French translation of UTC. W denounces the plight of his race and calls for human dignity.

255. Thérive, André. "La Vie des livres." Paroles Françaises (16 January).
    Contains a mixed review of the French translation of BB expressing interest in the subject but objecting to some tediously pedantic passages.

256. Thimonier, Henry. "Pourquoi éditez-vous?" Les Lettres Françaises (c. 27 November).
    Mentions W as one author on the fall publication list of Robert Esmenard.

257. Villemagne, François. "Qui est responsable du crime 'noir' en Amérique." Syndicalisme (28 October).
    Favorable review of the French translation of NS along with a general account of the American racial situation. Villemagne emphasizes W's explanation that black fear induced by white racism leads to crime.

258. Watteau, Maurice. "Situations raciales et condition de l'homme dans l'oeuvre de J.-P. Sartre." Présence Africaine, No. 2 (January), pp. 209-229; No. 3 (March-April), pp. 405-417.
    Discusses briefly Sartre's use of W's

ideas on racial matters.

259. White, Walter. *A Man Called White: The Autobiography of Walter White.* New York: Viking, p. 174.
    Mentions W as a Spingarn Medalist. Reprinted: 1970.361.

260. Winchell, Walter. "In New York." New York *Daily Mirror* (20 September), p. 10.
    Reports that W "may add his name to the other 'citizens of the world'" (in the Rassemblement Démocratique Révolutionnaire).

261. Young, Stark. "Book Basis," in his *Immortal Shadows: A Book of Dramatic Criticism.* New York: Scribner's, pp. 223-226.
    Reprint of 1941.1058.

1949

1. Anon. "A Parigi contro-congresso di 'rivoluzionari' rosi." Unidentified clipping (22 April).
    Mentions W's support of the Rassemblement Démocratique Révolutionnaire.

2. Anon. "Amérique sans Hollywood." *Le Paris Populaire* (23 November), p. 2.
    Mme. Caro-Delavaille recounts a conversation with W in which he describes racist treatment of himself and his wife.

3. Anon. "El autor de 'Sangre negra.'" Unidentified clipping.
    Photograph with caption of W on board ship en route to Buenos Aires.

4. Anon. "Autres coincidences." *La Gazette de Lausanne* (23 October).
    Reports that NS is being filmed.

5. Anon. "Backstage." *Ebony*, 5 (December), 10.
    Reports that W will be the magazine's correspondent in France and that *Ebony* will soon publish his "Chicago: Ten Years After." Includes a photograph of W.

6. Anon. "Black Boy," in *Thesaurus of Book Digests.* Ed. Hiram Haydn and Edmund Fuller. New York: Crown Publishers, p. 91.
    Identifies the author and year of publication.

7. Anon. "Books--Authors." *The New York Times* (4 October), p. 25.
    Reports that W will play the lead in the film version of NS.

8. Anon. "Canada Lee in 'Native Son.'" 1 August.

Playbill for the Long Island production of the play.

9. Anon. "Cette semaine." *La Gazette de Lausanne* (27 September).
    Notes that W visited Lausanne.

10. Anon. "Les Citoyens du monde." Paris *Samedi-Soir* (30 July).
    Lists W as a famous expatriate.

11. Anon. "Coming--Next Week--An Interview with Richard Wright." *Labor Action* (23 May), p. 1.
    The interview concerns the Rassemblement Démocratique Révolutionnaire.

12. Anon. "'Comrade Strong: Don't You Remember . . .?'" *New York Herald Tribune* (Paris edition) (4 April), p. 4.
    Headnote to W's reply to Anna Louise Strong.

13. Anon. "Un critique modèle." *Liberté de l'Esprit* (March).
    Suggests that *Les Temps Modernes* publishes W's work not because it is interested in blacks but because W is a hoaxer.

14. Anon. "Crossman, Richard, M. P.--Ed. *The God That Failed.*" *Bulletin from Virginia Kirkus Bookshop Service*, 17 (1 November), 617.
    Mentions W briefly.

15. Anon. "La Défense de la paix." *La Toulon République Varoise* (2 May).
    Quotes a message condemning Russian and American political actions signed by W, Sartre, and Merleau-Ponty.

16. Anon. "D'innombrables organismes se préoccupent de la paix." *Témoignage Chrétien* (8 April), p. 3.
    Lists W as a supporter of Garry Davis.

17. Anon. "Diplomáticos, un escritor negro y un médico, llegaron en el 'Uruguay.'" *La Buenos Aires Epoca* (11 October).
    Reports the arrival of W in Buenos Aires to film NS.

18. Anon. "Dirigirá Pierre Chenal." *Radio-Film* (26 October).
    Reports briefly the plan to film NS.

19. Anon. "D'un congrès de la paix à un autre." *La France de Marseille et du Sud-Est* (2 May).
    Quotes the statement condemning the United States and the Soviet Union for lack of intellectual freedom signed by W, Sartre, and Merleau-Ponty.

20. Anon. "Editor's Corner: Our Cover."
The Baltimore Afro-American (18 January), Magazine Sec., p. 2.
    Mentions the drawing of W by Frank
    Yancey on the cover, the article by
    Nick Aaron Ford on W in the issue,
    and W's expatriation.

21. Anon. "Edouard Depreux et Marceau
Pivert." Le Gers Socialiste (7 May).
    Notes that a political message by W,
    Sartre, and Merleau-Ponty was read to
    a rally.

22. Anon. "Escritor." Unidentified clipping (12 October).
    Photograph with caption of W on his
    arrival in Buenos Aires for the film-
    ing of NS.

23. Anon. "El escritor Richard Wright."
Buenos Aires Laborista (12 October).
    Reports briefly W's arrival in Buenos
    Aires to film NS.

24. Anon. "Esprit noir." Paris Week End
(13 February).
    Relates an anecdote about W's comment
    on the "blackness" of Alexandre
    Dumas.

25. Anon. "Está en Buenos Aires el famoso escritor negro." La Buenos Aires
Razón (11 October).
    Reports the arrival of W in Buenos
    Aires to film NS and quotes his com-
    ments on the impossibility of doing a
    satisfactory version in the United
    States. W also comments on his liter-
    ary intentions with respect to the
    racial problem.

26. Anon. "Famous Negroes Married to
Whites." Ebony, 5 (December), 20-26, 28-
30.
    Includes a photograph with caption of
    W and Ellen Poplar.

27. Anon. "Filmase entre nosotros una
versión en Español de un film norteamer-
icano." La Película (30 October).
    Brief report on the filming of NS.

28. Anon. "Grand meeting." Paris Franc-
Tireur (26 April).
    Advertisement for a political rally
    listing W as a participant.

29. Anon. "Ideologies: The Little Man."
Time, 53 (10 January), 21-22.
    Article on Garry Davis mentioning and
    quoting from W. Supporting Davis'
    internationalism, W asks: "Can the
    people believe in the efforts of the
    U. S. for democracy and freedom when
    it is well known that the U. S. does
    not support her own democratic insti-
    tutions?"

30. Anon. "La Journée anticolonialiste
du 'Congrès des peuples.'" Paris Franc-
Tireur (3 May).
    Notes that W sent a message of sup-
    port to the Congress of Peoples.

31. Anon. "La Journée de résistance à la
dictature et à la guerre." La Tours
Nouvelle République du Centre-Ouest (2
May).
    Quotes from the message condemning
    lack of intellectual freedom in the
    United States and the Soviet Union
    signed by W, Sartre, and Merleau-
    Ponty.

32. Anon. "La 'Journée internationale':
contre la dictature et la guerre." Le
Paris Monde (3 May), p. 4.
    Mentions a letter of political pro-
    test from W, Sartre, and Merleau-
    Ponty.

33. Anon. "Katherine Durham." Le Patriote
de Nice et du Sud-Est (24 February).
    Includes W in a list of American
    blacks who have been refused service
    in the United States.

34. Anon. "Llega hoy el escritor negro
Richard Wright." Servicio Informativo de
Estados Unidos (11 October), pp. 1-2.
    Mimeographed bulletin from the United
    States Embassy in Buenos Aires
    sketching W's life and career. Empha-
    sizes the theme of success and ne-
    glects American racism.

35. Anon. "Llega hoy para filmar 'Sangre
negra,' su autor Richard Wright." Buenos
Aires Clarín (11 October).
    Announces the arrival of W in Buenos
    Aires to film NS and sketches his
    literary career, with comparisons to
    Langston Hughes.

36. Anon. "Llega mañana un vigoroso
escritor negro: R. Wright." Buenos Aires
Critica (10 October)
    Reports on plans for filming NS and
    sketches briefly W's literary career.

37. Anon. "Llegará esta mañana el escritor Richard Wright." La Buenos Aires
Prensa (11 October), p. 10.
    Announces W's arrival for the filming
    of NS and sketches briefly his life
    and literary career.

38. Anon. "Llegó el escritor Richard
Wright." La Buenos Aires Prensa (12
October), p. 9.
    Reports W's arrival in Buenos Aires
    to film NS and relates his opinions
    on the American influence on French
    literature.

39. Anon. "'Meet Your Author'--Nelson

Algren." Chicago Sun-Times (16 October),
p. 52.
    Mentions Jack Conroy, "who published
    the first work of Richard Wright,
    author of 'Native Son.'"

40. Anon. "Un Message de Jean-Paul
Sartre, Merleau-Ponty et Richard
Wright." Paris Franc-Tireur (3 May).
    Quotes the text of their message
    condemning the United States and the
    Soviet Union for lack of intellectual
    freedom.

41. Anon. "Native Son," in Masterplots.
Ed. Frank N. Magill. Vol. 2. New York:
Salem Press, pp. 643-645.
    Classifies the novel, summarizes the
    plot, lists the characters, and gives
    a brief critique.
    Reprinted: 1952.7; 1954.39; 1955.11;
    1957.41; 1976.16.

42. Anon. "'Native Son' Author to Play
in Film Version." Buenos Aires Herald
(12 October), p. 6.
    Article on W's arrival in Buenos
    Aires for the filming of the novel.
    Reviews W's career briefly and re-
    ports that he spoke of Gwendolyn
    Brooks and Chester Himes.

43. Anon. "Native Son (1940), by Richard
Wright," in Thesaurus of Book Digests.
Ed. Hiram Haydn and Edmund Fuller. New
York: Crown Publishers, pp. 511-512.
    Brief summary of the novel.

44. Anon. "Negro America's Most Exciting
Men." Ebony, 4 (June), 50-52.
    W is one of ten selected. The caption
    of his photograph states that he "is
    soft-spoken, easy-laughing . . .
    scholarly-looking" with "a tendency
    towards plumpness as he advances in
    years."

45. Anon. "New Paris Theatrical Group
Uses Taxicab for Rehearsal." New York
Herald Tribune (Paris edition) (6 July),
p. 2.
    Lists W among the supporters of the
    American Club Theatre, a repertory
    company in Paris.

46. Anon. "Nos visita un famoso escritor
negro para actuar en un film local."
Revista del Exhibidor (1 November).
    Brief report on the filming of NS.

47. Anon. "Nouvelles des Lettres." Paris
Combat (5 July), p. 2.
    Notes W's attendance at a reception
    for Henri Michaux given by Sylvia
    Beach.

48. Anon. "Opinion." Massalia (3 November).

Cites W's remark comparing the extent
of freedom in Paris and in the United
States. It is much greater in the
former for a black man.

49. Anon. "Pierre Chenal to Film in
Argentina." Buenos Aires Herald (1
October), p. 9.
    Reports the filming of NS. W, "one of
    the top figures in contemporary Amer-
    ican literature," will oversee the
    production.

50. Anon. "La Poétesse Lise Deharme qui
a eu trois maris assure. . . ." Paris
Samedi-Soir (5 November), p. 2.
    Lists W among the authors who have
    visited Deharme.

51. Anon. "Point du vue de Réforme."
Paris Réforme (21 May), p. 1.
    Relates a Jim-Crow anecdote concern-
    ing a party organized by Sinclair
    Lewis to honor W. Denied the use of
    the elevator, W did not attend be-
    cause he declined to climb fifteen
    flights of stairs.

52. Anon. "La Police américaine en
France." Paris Action (14 April), p. 2.
    Mentions W as an associate of Camus
    and Sartre.

53. Anon. "'Resistance Day' Crowd Boos
Compton's Speech on Bomb." New York
Herald Tribune (Paris edition) (2 May),
pp. 1-2.
    Contains a slighting reference to the
    political message signed by W,
    Sartre, and Merleau-Ponty.

54. Anon. "Richard Wright." Revue du
Jazz (April), p. 112.
    Full-page photograph.

55. Anon. "Richard Wright, autor de
'Sangre negra,' encarnará al protago-
nista en la pelicula." Unidentified
clipping (11 October).
    Reports W's arrival in Buenos Aires
    to film NS, sketches briefly his
    literary career, and relates his
    comments on recent black literature
    singling out Gwendolyn Brooks and
    Chester Himes.

56. Anon. "Richard Wright: 'Black boy.'"
Ecole Libératrice (9 July).
    Favorable review of the French trans-
    lation, half of which consists of
    quotations. W's sincerity is impres-
    sive.

57. Anon. "Richard Wright, écrivain
américain," in Les Archives Internationales (March), Sec. A, 2 pp.
    Detailed biographical-critical sketch
    with brief bibliography. W is an

impressive example of the engaged writer. BB is his best book.

58. Anon. "Richard Wright et Gloria Madison seront à l'écran les interprètes douloureux de leur race." Le Buenos Aires Quotidien (22 October).
    Interview with W on the filming of NS and the racial situation in the United States.

59. Anon. "Richard Wright, novelista negro, hará en Buenos Aires una pelicula basada en su propria vida: será actor por primera vez." Buenos Aires Clarín (12 October).
    Reports W's arrival in Buenos Aires to film NS and relates his comments on black writers.

60. Anon. "Richard Wright Turns Actor." Quick, 1 (3 October), 53.
    Reports that W was in Chicago filming background scenes for NS.

61. Anon. "Richard Wright va a Buenos Aires a filmar como actor su famosa novela 'Sangre negra.'" La Montevideo Plata (10 October).
    Reports a visit with W on board ship as he was bound for Buenos Aires to film NS. W comments on his role as Bigger and on race relations in the United States. Includes two photographs.

62. Anon. "La Rue." Rabat L'Echo du Maroc (27 January).
    Review of Ann Petry's The Street comparing her treatment of street life with W's.

63. Anon. "S. S. 'Uruguay' docks in B. A." The Buenos Aires Standard (12 October).
    Reports W's arrival in Buenos Aires for the filming of NS. He has lost twenty-two pounds in order to play the role of Bigger. Includes a photograph of W exercising on board ship.

64. Anon. "'Sangre negra.'" Buenos Aires Lider (14 October).
    Reports that the filming of NS has begun.

65. Anon. "Un 'Tapir' d'avenir." Paris Combat (c. 19 May).
    Notes that W is taking French lessons from a Belgian.

66. Anon. "Les Temps Modernes." Paris Carrefour (6 July), p. 9.
    Advertisement for number 45 of the magazine listing the French translation of "I Tried to Be a Communist."

67. Anon. "Toute la gauche démocratique mondiale à la journée du 30 avril." Paris Franc-Tireur (21 April).
    Lists W among the supporters of a political rally.

68. Anon. "U of C Student Named for Role in the Picture 'Native Son.'" Chicago Defender (1 October), p. 15.
    Reports on the production of NS noting differences between the film and the novel.

69. Anon. Unidentified clipping.
    Photograph with caption of a visit by the United States Ambassador to Argentina M. Stanton Griffis to the set of the film NS.

70. Anon. Untitled clipping. La Buenos Aires Epoca (14 October).
    Reports that W will play the lead role in the film NS.

71. Anon. Untitled clipping. Chicago Sun-Times.
    Reports on the filming of NS.

72. Anon. "El Uruguay trajo tambien a otras personalidades." Buenos Aires Critica (11 October).
    Reports W's arrival in Buenos Aires to film NS and sketches briefly his literary career. W notes an improvement in the American racial situation after the war owing to the activities of black soldiers.

73. Anon. "Vendrá Richard Wright, autor de 'Sangre negra.'" Unidentified clipping (October).
    Announces W's impending arrival in Buenos Aires to film NS and sketches his life and literary career.

74. Anon. "La Ville de Chelmsford." Neuilly-Seine Peuple du Monde (18 July).
    Notes that W attended a political rally in Chelmsford.

74a. Anon. "Wright, Richard," in Enciclopedia italiana di scienze, lettere ed arti 1938-1948. Ed. Mario Niccoli. Appendix 2. Vol. 2. Rome: Instituto della enciclopedia italiana, p. 1134.
    Biographical sketch.

75. Anon. "Wright, Richard," in Den Nye Salmonsen. Ed. Paula Strelitz, Gottlieb Japsen, and Mikal Rode. Copenhagen: J. H. Schultz Forlag, p. 4985.
    Brief biographical note.

76. Anon. "Wright (Richard)," in Nouveau Larousse universel. Ed. Paul Augé. Vol. 2. Paris: Librarie Larousse, p. 1074.
    Brief biographical note.

77. B., J. S. and E. S. "News of the

Screen: To Film 'Black Boy.'" New York Herald Tribune (6 July), p. 16.
    Announces a screen adaptation by Tony Petrina and plans for filming it.

78. Baldwin, James. "Everybody's Protest Novel." Partisan Review, 16 (June), 578-585.
    Reprint of 1949.79.

79. ____. "Everybody's Protest Novel." Zero, No. 1 (Spring), pp. 54-58.
    Discusses the genre of the protest novel beginning with Uncle Tom's Cabin. Like all such novels, NS fails because it employs stereotypes instead of complex characterization. Bigger is a "descendant" of Uncle Tom in Stowe's novel.
    Reprinted: 1949.78; 1953.77; 1955.25; 1970.50; 1972.29a.

80. Barry, Joseph A. "Americans in Paris." The New York Times Book Review (27 March), pp. 5, 18.
    Mentions W and expresses dislike for "The Man Who Killed a Shadow" in Zero.

81. Bau, Agnès. "L'Union française dans la vie de Paris." Europe, France Outre-Mer (February), pp. 63-64.
    Mentions W's interest in African art.

82. Baufrère, Marcel. "Un Fils de l'oncle Tom juge Richard Wright." Confrontation Internationale, No. 2 (May-June), pp. 54-55.
    Interview with an unnamed young African who praises W but considers him to belong to a transitional generation between Uncle Tom and Uncle Tom's children. NS is an excellent analysis of black-white relations, applicable to Africa as well as America.

83. Bercher, Marie-Louise. "Le Moi est haïssable." L'Alsace (Mulhouse) (21 November).
    Refers to Simone de Beauvoir's analogy between the position of French women and that of Bigger Thomas.

84. Bernard, Harry. Le Roman régionaliste aux Etats-Unis (1913-1940). Montreal: Fides, pp. 144, 152-153.
    Discusses NS and UTC.

85. Blanzat, Jean. "Fontamara." Paris Combat (8 July), p. 4.
    Review of the novel by Ignazio Silone mentioning W's concern with similar issues.

86. Blas, Alvaro. "'El cine yanqui necesita renovación." Aquí Está (October).
    Article-interview on Pierre Chenal,

with comments on the film NS.

87. Caro-Delavaille, Aline. L'Amérique sans Hollywood. Paris: Editions Emile-Paul Frères, pp. 49, 179-180.
    Mentions W briefly (p. 49) and recounts his experience with racism during his second transatlantic voyage.

88. Casey, Catherine. "At Home to the Arts." Paris Daily Mail (28 November).
    Mentions a visit by W to the salon of Marie-Louise Bosquet.

89. Castro, Ramiro Alberto. "Se hará en Buenos Aires la película que los negros aun esperan." Vea y Lea (October).
    Sketches W's life and literary career, quotes him on the racial problem and on contemporary American literature, and discusses the filming of NS, with quotations from Jaime Prades and Pierre Chenal.

90. Chonez, Claudine. "Chair à canon ou citoyens du monde?" Unidentified clipping.
    Lists W as a supporter of Garry Davis.

91. Colin, Pierre. "American Apologists Get Cold Reception from Crowd at Huge Rally: RDR Holds 'Anti-War Day' in Paris." Labor Action (23 May), pp. 1, 4.
    Mentions the declarations by W, Sartre, and Merleau-Ponty.

92. Crossman, Richard. "Introduction," in his The God That Failed. New York: Harper, pp. 1-11.
    Mentions W (pp. 4, 11), noting the effect on his personality of his experience with Communism.
    Reprinted: 1952.31; 1959.73.

93. Cunard, Nancy. Untitled clipping. Le Nouveau Cénacle (April).
    Contains favorable remarks about BB.

94. Darcyl, Léon. "Après Avoir tourné leurs extérieurs à Chicago, Pierre Chenal et Richard Wright vont finir à Buenos Aires le 'film le plus nègre du monde.'" Buenos Aires France-Journal (12 October).
    Plot summary of NS and an interview with Pierre Chenal on the filming of the novel.

95. Davis, Joe Lee, John T. Frederick, and Frank Luther Mott. "Richard Wright," in their American Literature: An Anthology and Critical Survey. Vol. 2. New York: Scribner's, p. 913.
    Brief biographical headnote to an excerpt from BB.

96. D.[ebidour], V.-H. "Sinclair Lewis. --De Sang royal." Le Bulletin des Lettres, XI (15 January), 31-32.
Review of the French translation of Kingsblood Royal calling W's work "stronger, more tragic, but less varied" than Lewis's.

97. Delile, Jacques. "Vifs incidents au Vélodrome d'Hiver." Le Amiens Courrier Picard (2 May).
Quotes from the message by W, Sartre, and Merleau-Ponty condemning both Russian and American political activity.

98. [Draper, Hal]. Rejoinder to "Farrell Objects on Wright Interview." Labor Action, 13 (27 June), 2.
Takes issue with Farrell's interpretation of the Salomon interview. See 1949.100.

99. Estol, Horacio. "Aquel muchacho negro que lavaba platos . . ." Aqui Está (November).
Biographical article on the hardships of W's childhood, which Estol considers racially typical in the United States. Quotes W's favorite saying, "Freedom belongs to the strong," and emphasizes his belief in the value of intelligence and anger.

100. Farrell, James T. "Farrell Objects on Wright Interview." Labor Action, 13 (27 June), 2.
Farrell comments on his meeting with W in Paris prior to the RDR conference, charging him with inaccuracy in the Salomon interview. This letter to the editor is followed by a rejoinder from editor Hal Draper. See 1949.98.

101. Ferran, André. "Poètes noirs aux U. S. A." La Toulouse Dépêche du Midi (31 March).
Survey of Afro-American poets beginning with a quotation from TMBV.

102. Foley, Martha and Abraham Rothberg. "Richard Wright," in their U. S. Stories: Regional Stories from the Forty-Eight States. New York: Hendricks-House--Farrar Strauss, pp. 682-683.
Biographical note.

103. Ford, Nick Aaron. "Juvenile Delinquent Becomes Famous Writer." The Baltimore Afro-American (22 January), Magazine Sec., p. 5.
Inspirational account of W's success in surmounting the obstacles of childhood and youth to become a famous author. His career gives hope to others in similar circumstances.

104. Frazier, E. Franklin. The Negro in the United States. New York: Macmillan, p. 517.
Brief evaluation of UTC, NS, and BB. Frazier considers UTC the best of the three.

105. Fréminville, Claude de. "Amérique sans Hollywood." Le Paris Populaire (23 November), p. 2.
Includes a quotation from W: "They stopped in front of me while suffering from not seeing me; I was taken aback."

106. Gab.[rieli], V.[ittorio]. "Stati Uniti: I Negri d'America," in Enciclopedia italiana di scienze, lettere ed arti 1938-1948. Ed. Mario Niccoli. Vol. 2. Rome: Instituto della enciclopedia italiana, pp. 902-903.
Mentions W briefly.

107. Glicksberg, Charles I. "The Furies in Negro Fiction." Western Review, 13 (Winter), 107-114.
Glicksberg considers black fiction of the forties to be obsessed with the subject of race. UTC examines pathological aggression caused by racism. NS provides the best portrait of racial hatred in a black character. BB stresses the same points and reveals how W came to write NS. Glicksberg also compares C. R. Offord's The White Face to NS.

108. Gomez, Ramuncho. "Richard Wright, el Dostoievsky negro." El Hogar (28 October), pp. 22-23, 75.
Essay-interview with W in Buenos Aires. Gomez sketches his literary career and describes his pleasing appearance and personality. W comments on life in Buenos Aires and Paris, the unimproved racial situation in the United States, French literary culture, and the filming of NS.

109. Green, Paul. "Symphonic Drama." College English, 10 (April), 359-365.
Comments briefly on the play NS, which "was symphonic in its use of music and musicalized sound effects especially."
Reprinted: 1953.141; 1965.73.

110. Hervin, Claude. "Un Grand Spectacle noir." Paris-Presse l'Intransigeant (19 July).
Notes that W is a sponsor of an exhibit of African art in Paris.

111. Hesse, Jean-Albert. "Misère, esclavage, et révolte." Paris Franc-Tireur (13 July).
Compares briefly the heroes of W and Alan Paton.

112. Hill, J. Newton. "The Achievement of the Negro in Drama." Negro History Bulletin, 12 (February), 100-102, 119.
    Mentions briefly the play NS.

113. Howlett, J.[acques]. "Le Musée vivant, (Numéro spécial, novembre 1948)." Présence Africaine, No. 6, pp. 178-180.
    Favorable review of the special issue on Africa edited by W and Michel Leiris.

114. _____. "Richard Wright, romancier de la liberté." Dakar L'A. O. F. (16 May).
    Favorable review of the French translation of NS. Howlett considers the novel in international perspective and focuses on its depiction of the effects of racism and repression on Bigger's personality. Praises W's powerful writing and racial commitment.

115. Hughes, Langston and Arna Bontemps. "Richard Wright," in their The Poetry of the Negro 1746-1949. Garden City, N. Y.: Doubleday, pp. 408-409.
    Biographical note. The anthology reprints "I Have Seen Black Hands" and "Between the World and Me."

116. Humboldt, Charles. "Communists in Novels." Masses & Mainstream, 2 (June), 13-31.
    Contains an analysis of NS (pp. 26-31) with special attention to the characterization of Bigger, Jan, and Max. Humboldt attacks W for arguing that Bigger's abnormal psychology is representative of black people. The characterization of Jan and Max is unnecessarily ambivalent. Max's defense of Bigger is incredible for a Communist lawyer. W errs in substituting the psychological for the ideological.

117. Jeanson, Francis. "Sartre et le monde noir." Présence Africaine, No. 7, pp. 189-214.
    Quotes from W's "Littérature noire américaine" (pp. 207, 210).

118. Jouvenel, Renaud de. "D'une bibliothèque américaine." Europe, 27 (March), 108-115.
    Accuses W of slanting in an effort to justify racial hatred.

119. L., P. "Contre l'immobilisme." Paris Aux Ecoutes (15 July).
    Quotes W's statement from "I Tried to Be a Communist" that Communists are more concerned with perfecting their propaganda than with the life of the masses.

120. Lash, John S. "The Race Consciousness of the American Negro Author: Toward a Reexamination of an Orthodox Critical Concept." Social Forces, 28 (October), 24-34.
    Mentions W's artistry in his short stories.

121. Lauras, A. "Richard Wright--Black Boy." Etudes, 260 (January), 157.
    Favorable review analyzing W's perspectives and literary art. Lauras finds the book to be "an authentic biography" and an "irrefutable piece of evidence" delivered "without passion but straightforwardly."

122. Le Breton, Maurice. "Une Jeune Génération de romanciers américains." France-Amerique [?], Nos. 25-30 (1947-1949 [?]), pp. 571-574.
    Mentions Caldwell, Farrell, and W as using realistic settings.

123. Levin, Harry. "Some European Views of Contemporary American Literature." American Quarterly, 1 (Fall), 264-279.
    Mentions Sartre's interest in W as an engaged writer (p. 275).
    Reprinted: 1950.173.

124. Lévy, Marguerite. "Aperçus sur le tragique américain." L'Age Nouveau (September), pp. 14-17.
    Mentions BB as an example of the genre of American tragedy.

125. Locke, Alain. "Dawn Patrol: A Review of the Literature of the Negro for 1948." Phylon, 10 (Second Quarter), 167-172.
    Mentions W in connection with Rebecca C. Barton's Witnesses for Freedom.

126. Lyons, Leonard. "The Lyons Den." New York Post (22 September), p. 28.
    Reports that W is leaving for Argentina to complete the filming of NS after secretly shooting exterior scenes in Chicago.

127. M., J. S. "Richard Wright blir parisare." Helsinki Hufvudstadsbladet (November).
    In this interview conducted in Paris, W discusses the failure of Franklin D. Roosevelt to effect real changes in American racial attitudes and recounts his relationship with Sartre. He names Himes, Petry, and Ellison as the best current black writers and praises Lillian Smith's Strange Fruit.

128. Maurois, André. "Para quem escrevemos?" Lisbon O Século Ilustrado (c. 9 July).
    Review of the second volume of

Sartre's Situations mentioning W.

129. Mistigri. "Entre cour et jardin." Paris Aux Écoutes (18 July). Mentions plans to produce the play NS at the Theatre Saint-Georges.

130. Mohrt, Michel. "Le Plus Grand Romancier américain William Faulkner a écrit un livre pour dire aux Yankees du Nord et aux Européens." Paris Carrefour (15 September), p. 8.
Review of Intruder in the Dust crediting BB with creating the European image of race relations in the United States.

131. Moon, Bucklin. "A Literature of Protest." The Reporter, 1 (6 December), 35-37.
Notes W's frustration and lack of productivity, caused in part by white expectations about black writing. Reprinted: 1950.185.

132. Morrison, Allan. "Twilight for Greenwich Village." Negro Digest, 7 (January), 27-37.
Mentions racial resentment directed at W and Robeson when they bought houses in the Village.

133. Nathan, Paul S. "Books Into Films." The Publishers' Weekly, 156 (1 October), 1586.
Discusses the filming of NS, noting the completed Chicago scenes, W's role as actor and scriptwriter, and his financial share of $6,000 and one-sixth of the profits.

134. Ozanne, Jean-Louis. "Aspects de la littérature américaine: Témoin du peuple noir écrivain de combat Richard Wright dénonce l'oppression raciale." Rouen Paris-Normandie (4 July).
Mainly a review of BB with extensive summary and quotations. Ozanne also sketches W's later career, emphasizing his theme of the psychological effect on blacks of white supremacy.

135. Padmore, George. "Afro American Writer Sends Greetings to African Nationalists--Richard Wright, Famous Novelist, Backs Self Government for the Colonies." The Gold Coast Observer (2 December).
Interweaves laudatory comment with W's message.

136. Parsons, Louella O. "Hollywood." Evening Journal (30 September).
Mentions that W was in Chicago filming background scenes for NS.

137. Paz, Magdeleine. "Littérature américaine: 'S'il Braille, Lache-le . . .'

par Chester Himes." Paru, No. 54 (October), pp. 31-32.
Favorable review of If He Hollers Let Him Go with a comparison to W.

138. Poore, Charles. "Books of the Times." The New York Times (8 January), p. 13.
Review of The Poetry of the Negro 1746-1949 mentioning W as a talented poet.

139. Radine, Serge. "Ecrivains américains non conformistes." Suisse Contemporaine, 9 (June), 287-295.
Contains a paragraph on NS (pp. 288-289) praising its objectivity, characterization, and sense of fatality.

140. Redding, Saunders. "American Negro Literature." The American Scholar, 18 (Spring), 137-148.
Argues that W is a new kind of Afro-American author because he writes for two audiences: black and white. Comments briefly on BB, NS, and UTC to support this thesis. Reprinted: 1949.141; 1969.201, 202; 1971.256.

141. _____. "The Fall and Rise of Negro Literature." Negro Digest, 7 (September), 41-49.
Reprint of 1949.140.

142. Rolo, Charles J. "Cultural Resistance." The Saturday Review of Literature, 32 (8 January), 25-26.
Review of Art and Action commenting on W's letters from Europe.

143. Romani, Bruno. "Il canto del 'gallo' è spento." La Turin gazetta del popolo (2 January).
Reprint of 1948.230.

144. _____. "Scritttori francesi a destra e a sinistra." Il mattino dell' Italia Centrale (8 January).
Reprint of 1948.230.

145. R.[osati], Sa.[lvatore]. "Stati Uniti: Letteratura," in Enciclopedia italiana di scienze, lettere ed arti 1938-1948. Ed. Mario Niccoli. Vol. 2. Rome: Instituto della enciclopedia italiana, p. 902.
Mentions W briefly.

146. _____. "Wright, Richard," in Enciclopedia italiana di scienze, lettere ed arti 1938-1948. Ed. Mario Niccoli. Vol. 2. Rome: Instituto della enciclopedia italiana, p. 1134.
Critical note.

147. Rosenfeld, Alvin. "Israel Diary." New York Post (22 May), p. 28.

Notes that W has a following in Israel.

148. Salomon, Michel. "An Interview in Paris with--Richard Wright: On U. S. Politics." Labor Action (30 May), pp. 1, 3.
Interview in a Trotskyist organ commenting on the RDR, the American left, the Communist Party and American blacks, and Truman's policies. See also 1949.11, 98, 100.

149. Sampiere, G. V. "Messaggi di Sartre e di Eleanora Roosevelt." Il giornale dell'Emilia-Bologna (1 May).
Quotes from the political statement signed by W, Sartre, and Merleau-Ponty.

150. Sartre, Jean-Paul. What Is Literature? Trans. Bernard Frechtman. New York: Philosophical Library, pp. 77-80, 107, 156, 241, 276.
Translation of 1947.273.

151. Sénard, Jean. "J. B. Moreau: 'l'objecteur.'" Unidentified clipping.
Sénard joins Camus, Bréton, and W in saluting Garry Davis.

152. Shachtman, Max. "RDR Muffed Its Chance to Take Clear Stand." Labor Action (23 May), pp. 1, 4.
Mentions the "excellent declaration" by W and Sartre.

153. Slocombe, George. "Reviews of New Books in Europe." New York Herald Tribune (Paris edition) (20 July), p. 6.
Reports that W is one of the sponsors of a projected literary review based in Paris.

154. Sullivan, Ed. "Little Old New York." New York Daily News (9 July).
Notes that "Wright, who quit the Commies in 1943, bawled out Paul Robeson in Paris interviews."

154a. Valori, Francesco. "Letteratura negra in America." Idea (7-14 August), p. 8.
Includes brief discussion of W's career, mentioning "Big Boy Leaves Home," Native Boy [sic], and BB.

155. Watson, Ted. "In Chicago." The Pittsburgh Courier (c. September).
Reports W's visit to Chicago to shoot outdoor scenes for NS. The main locale was "in and around Thirty-third and South Parkway."

156. Webb, Constance. "What Next for Richard Wright?" Phylon, 10 (Second Quarter), 161-166.
Repeats much of "Notes Preliminary to a Full Study of the Work of Richard Wright" (1946.280). Concentrates on BB and NS, drawing some parallels between W's characters and existentialist personalities. W needs a stimulus for his passion for equality to achieve even greater works.
Reprinted: 1971.147.

157. Weiler, A. H. "By Way of Report." The New York Times (9 October), Sec. 2, p. 5.
Reports the filming of NS.

158. Wilkerson, Doxey A. "Negro Culture: Heritage and Weapon." Masses & Mainstream, 2 (August), 3-24.
Criticizes W for his psychological emphasis instead of commitment to the class struggle. He "distorted the true character and aspirations and struggles of the Negro people" (p. 22).

1950

1. Abrahams, Peter. "Sans critique ni littérature." Paris Opera (29 November).
Article on Marcel Aymé praising W for his honesty.

2. Anon. "A la devanture du libraire: Le Dieu des ténèbres." Le Figaro Littéraire (24 June), p. 7.
Notice of the French translation of The God That Failed mentioning W.

3. Anon. "About This Book," in Native Son. Signet Book. New York: New American Library, p. [1].
Blurb emphasizing the novel's fascinating power and quoting from the novel itself and from favorable reviews.

4. Anon. "Argentine." Cinémonde (6 February).
Photograph with caption of a scene from the film NS.

5. Anon. "Arrivée du grand écrivain Richard Wright." Le Port-au-Prince Nouvelliste (25 July), p. 1.
Announces W's arrival in Haiti from Argentina.

6. Anon. "Auteur-acteur." Le Figaro Littéraire (9 September), p. 2.
Reports W's return to Paris after the filming of NS. He expresses satisfaction at working in the film medium.

7. Anon. "The Author." New York Post (13 July), p. 29.
Biographical sketch of W to accompany "From 'The God That Failed': Why I Quit Communism."

8. Anon. "The Best Sellers." The New York Times Book Review (5 March), p. 8.
Lists The God That Failed in sixteenth place in the general category.

9. Anon. "La Boîte à bouquins." Point de Vue Image du Monde (6 July).
Notice of the French translation of The God That Failed mentioning W.

10. Anon. "La Boîte aux lettres." Elisabethville L'Echo de Katanga (7 June).
Announcement of the French translation of The God That Failed mentioning W.

11. Anon. "Book Reviews." The Carlsbad Daily Current Argus (30 July), Sec. Two, p. 2.
Notice of The God That Failed mentioning W.

12. Anon. "Books We Should All Read: 'Uncle Tom's Children.'" The Cape Town Torch (30 January), p. 6.
Favorable review including a brief sketch of earlier developments in Afro-American literature. The reviewer emphasizes the theme of terror in "Big Boy Leaves Home" and the theme of human dignity in "Fire and Cloud."

13. Anon. "Le bottin de Marie-France." Paris Marie-France (5 June).
Quotes W's comment that one Orson Welles is enough.

14. Anon. "Calmann-Lévy." Cahiers du Monde Nouveau, 6, No. 44, back cover; No. 45, back cover.
Advertisement for the French translation of The God That Failed mentioning W.

15. Anon. "A Check List of 100 Worthy Books of 1950." The Milwaukee Journal (3 December), Christmas Book Sec., pp. 3, 6, 13, 15.
Contains a brief notice of The God That Failed (p. 13).

16. Anon. "Cinematografia." Unidentified clipping (26 July).
Photograph with caption of a scene from the film NS.

17. Anon. "Collection Liberté de l'Esprit." Les Temps Modernes, 6 (August), fourth unnumbered page after 384.
Advertisement for the French translation of The God That Failed mentioning W.

18. Anon. "Conversions anti-communistes." Casablanca Paris (10 November),
p. 7.
Review of the French translation of The God That Failed mentioning W.

19. Anon. "Crossman, R. H. S., ed. The God that failed." The Open Shelf (May), p. 9.
Notice mentioning W.

20. Anon. "Dans le livre 'Le Dieu qui Déçut' six écrivains expliquent pourquoi ils ne sont plus communistes." Paris L'Espoir (15 February).
Reprint of 1950.21.

21. _____. "Dans le livre: 'The God That Failed' six écrivains expliquent pourquoi ils ne sont plus communistes." U. S. A. (3 February), mimeographed flyer.
Review of the French translation of The God That Failed commenting on W's experience with Communism and citing a Washington Star review of the book.
Reprinted: 1950.20, 75.

22. Anon. "Le Dieu des ténèbres." Bibliographie de la France, No. 20 (19 May), pp. 1752-1753.
Advertisement for the French translation of The God That Failed.

23. Anon. "Le Dieu des ténèbres." Casablanca Maroc-Presse (14 July).
Review of the French translation of The God That Failed mentioning W.

24. Anon. "Le Dieu des ténèbres." Le Figaro Littéraire (24 June), p. 3.
Advertisement for the French translation of The God That Failed listing W as a contributor.

25. Anon. "Le Dieu des ténèbres." Rabat Maroc Matin (2 July).
Review of the French translation of The God That Failed mentioning W.

26. Anon. "Le Dieu des ténèbres." Revue de Paris (July), p. 177.
Advertisement for the French translation of The God That Failed mentioning W.

27. Anon. "Dieu (Le) des Ténèbres." Bibliographie de la France (22 September).
Brief notice of the French translation of The God That Failed mentioning W.

28. Anon. Dust Jacket of El negrito. By Richard Wright. Trans. Enrique Pascual. Madrid: Afrodisio Aguado.
Notes that despite his fame in America and the north of Europe, W

has heretofore been unknown in Spain.

29. Anon. "Entrevista com Richard Wright." Revista Branca.
Interview including comments on W's relationship with Sartre, the Cold War, the political responsibility of the writer, literary preferences and influences, works in progress, and the Franco-American fellowship.

30. Anon. "The God That Failed." The Monetary Times, 118 (September), 89-90.
Review mentioning W.

31. Anon. "The God That Failed." The New York Times Book Review (3 December), p. 66.
Brief notice mentioning W.

32. Anon. "The God That Failed." Time, 55 (27 February), 112.
Brief notice mentioning W.

33. Anon. "The God That Failed: A Confession." St. Petersburg Times (29 January), Magazine Sec., p. 13.
Review mentioning W.

34. Anon. "The God That Failed: A Confession." The Cresset, 13 (May), 54-55.
Review mentioning W, "the able Negro author."

35. Anon. "The God That Failed. Edited by Richard Crossman." Chicago American (18 February), p. 4.
Notice mentioning W.

36. Anon. "The God That Failed. Edited by Richard Crossman." Foreign Affairs, 28 (July), 679.
Notice mentioning W.

37. Anon. "The God That Failed, edited by Richard Crossman." The New Yorker, 25 (14 January), 89-90.
Review mentioning W.

38. Anon. Index Translationum 1. Paris: Unesco, pp. 127, 192, 296, 309, 316.
Lists translations of BB into Finnish, Italian, and Swedish, TMBV into French, and NS into Italian.

39. _____. Index Translationum 2. Paris: Unesco, pp. 153, 176.
Lists translations of BB into Hungarian and UTC into Italian.

40. Anon. "Livres reçus." Le Brussels Soir (9 December), p. 7.
Notice of the French translation of The God That Failed listing W as a contributor.

41. Anon. "Marche dans les ténèbres." Bibliographie de la France, No. 49 (8 December), 4346.
Advertisement for a novel by Hans Habe with a quotation mentioning W by Jean Rousselot from Les Nouvelles Littéraires.

42. Anon. "Le Matin se fait attendre." Bibliographie de la France, No. 49 (8 December), 4301.
Advertisement for the French translation of Nelson Algren's Never Come Morning mentioning W's preface.

43. Anon. "Movies: Native Son." Our World, 5 (19 December), 36-38.
Discusses the making of the film and includes seven captioned stills. Also comments on W's social success in Argentina, providing three captioned photographs in evidence.

44. Anon. "My First Lesson in How to Live as a Negro Came When I Was Quite Small," in Native Son. Signet Book. New York: New American Library, p. [416].
Consists of a quotation from "The Ethics of Living Jim Crow" and a blurb for UTC.

45. Anon. "Native Son," in Native Son. Signet Book. New York: New American Library, pp. [1], [414], and back cover.
Blurbs.

45a. Anon. "'Native Son' Pic Finished." Variety (14 June), p. 27.
Announces the completion of the film.

46. Anon. "Les Noirs, encore les noirs!" Le Cri de Paris (28 July).
Mentions the refusal of service to W by a Paris hotel.

47. Anon. "A Note on Signet Giants," in Native Son. Signet Book. New York: New American Library, p. [414].
Includes laudatory phrases by reviewers on NS.

48. Anon. "Noted US Author, Film Star Leaves for Haiti." Unidentified clipping.
Reports W's presence in Trinidad after the completion of the filming of NS.

49. Anon. "'A Novel of Tremendous Power and Beauty'--Newsweek," in Native Son. Signet Book. New York: New American Library, back cover.
Consists of a blurb, two quotations from reviews, and a biographical note.

50. Anon. "Una obra norteamericana en la pantalla argentina: 'Sangre negra.'" Unidentified clipping.
Amply illustrated article on the

filming of NS, the most expensively produced film yet by the Argentinian movie industry.

51. Anon. "Petites nouvelles." Paris Aux Ecoutes (22 December).
Comments on W's preface to the French translation of Nelson Algren's Never Come Morning. Notes W's belief that the book is honest and accurate in its depiction of Chicago.

52. Anon. "Première mondiale originale." La Cinématographie Française (25 November), p. 19.
Comments briefly on the filming of NS and its world premiere.

53. Anon. "Les Problèmes actuels." Bibliographie de la France, No. 51 (22 December), p. 4517.
Publisher's advertisement for the French translation of The God That Failed mentioning W.

54. Anon. "Prólogo," in El negrito. By Richard Wright. Trans. Enrique Pascual. Madrid: Afrodisio Aguado, S. A., pp. 9-10.
Notes W's fame elsewhere, emphasizes the racial theme of this translation of BB, and praises the work's prose style. If the Spanish example of racial tolerance had been followed, the racial problems revealed in the book would not exist. Notes that the translation is an expurgated version of the original.

55. Anon. "Que lirons-nous?" Le Parisien Libéré (6 September).
Notice of the French translation of The God That Failed mentioning W.

56. Anon. "Racisme yankee." Vivre d'Abord (January).
Partial reprint of 1945.590a.

57. Anon. "Reds." Life.
Photograph with caption of W and Gide.

58. Anon. "Reprints New Editions." New York Herald Tribune (19 November), p. 29.
Mentions the Signet Giant edition of NS.

59. Anon. "Richard Wright." Bibliographie de la France, No. 41 (13 October), p. 3285.
Advertisement for the French translations of NS and UTC.

60. Anon. "Richard Wright." Negro Digest, 8 (July), 52.
Note to accompany "Early Days in Chicago."

61. Anon. "Richard Wright." The Chicago Defender (2 September), p. 28.
Photograph with caption of W and friends on board the S. S. Argentina as he is leaving Buenos Aires for Trinidad.

62. Anon. "Richard Wright." Unidentified clipping.
Article in Spanish sketching W's life and analyzing NS. The year is conjectural.

63. Anon. "Richard Wright à Port-au-Prince." Haiti Journal (19 July).
Describes a meeting of W with two Haitian writers and comments favorably on W's personality.

64. Anon. "Richard Wright: I figli dello zio Tom." L'illustrazione italiana (26 February), p. 34.
Favorable review of the Italian translation of UTC mentioning each of the five stories.

64a. Anon. "Richard Wright: I figli dello zio Tom." Il Rome mondo (11 March), p. 8.
Favorable notice of the Italian translation of UTC praising W for his dramatic vigor and his lyricism.

65. Anon. "Richard Wright, interprète de Richard Wright, dans 'Un Enfant du pays' de Pierre Chenal." Paris Libération (30 November).
Interview with W on the circumstances behind the project to film NS.

66. Anon. "Richard Wright.--Mi vida de negro." El Mexico City Nacional (3 September), Suplemento Sec., p. 11.
After contrasting W's depiction of the serious social problems of black people with the exoticism of the Harlem Renaissance, this favorable review of the Spanish translation of BB notes its social protest and its artistry.

67. Anon. "Richard Wright Returns for Overnight Stay." Unidentified clipping (June).
Reports on W's visit to Trinidad after filming NS. He was greeted by his friend Dr. Eric Williams. He will proceed to Haiti "to look after some of the work the United Nations Organization is doing in that island and also to see the Great Exposition." Includes a photograph of W and Williams.

68. Anon. "Richard Wright se propose de revenir dans 3 mois." Le Port-au-Prince Nouvelliste (5 August), p. 1.
Reports that W will fly to the United

States on 6 August and sail for France on 16 August. Stresses W's interest in Haiti.

69. Anon. "Richard Wright: Un Enfant du pays." Bulletin du Club Français du Livre, No. 38 (July), p. 8.
Favorable review of the French translation of NS stressing that black suffering is symbolic of the human condition. In his plea for social justice, W achieves the power of a Biblical prophet.

70. Anon. "Rodada 'Sangre negra,' se ausentó Richard Wright." Antena (July).
Reports W's departure from Buenos Aires. He expresses satisfaction with the filming of his work.

71. Anon. "La Rue cases-nègres." Bibliographie de la France, 139 (22 September), 3044.
Advertisement for a novel by Joseph Zobel comparing it to W's work.

72. Anon. "La Rue cases nègres." La Gazette des Lettres (15 November), pp. 57-59.
Mentions W briefly as a writer who has dealt seriously with racial issues.

73. Anon. "'Sangre negra' puede mostrar al exterior la calidad lograda por el cine criollo." Unidentified clipping.
Amply illustrated article on NS with special praise for the technical skill of Argentinian moviemaking.

74. Anon. "Sangre negra . . . y almas blancas." Sintonia.
Laudatory illustrated article on the film NS, which could not have been filmed in W's native land. It is a triumph of the Argentinian movie industry.

75. Anon. "Six écrivains expliquent pourquoi ils ne sont plus communistes." Le Châlon-sur-Saône Courrier de Saône & Loire (15 February).
Reprint of the first part of 1950.21.

76. Anon. "Six écrivains avouent qu'ils ont cessé d'adorer Le dieu des ténèbres." La Paris Presse (11 June), p. 5.
Review of the French translation of The God That Failed containing a drawing and a biographical sketch of W and a quotation from the episode concerning Ross.

77. Anon. "Six témoignages sur les autocrates moscoutaires." Le Montagnard du Cantal (17 February).
Review of the French translation of The God That Failed commenting on W's

experience with Communism.

78. Anon. "'Son,' 1st English Film Made in Argent., Being Offered for U. S. Dates." Variety, 180 (15 November), p. 12.
Reports plans for distribution of NS.

79. Anon. "Sous la lune d'Argentine." L'Ecran Français (30 October), pp. 14-15.
Mentions briefly the filming of NS.

80. Anon. "Sur l'Amérique." Paris (April), p. 101.
Mentions W as an authority on American society.

81. Anon. 3ᶻᵒ Gran Premio Internationale Saint Vincent.
Lists W as a member of the jury for literature.

82. Anon. "Three in One." Air de Paris (11 January).
Lists W as a supporter of the "American Club Theatre."

83. Anon. "The Times Interviews Richard Wright." Port-au-Prince Times (28 July).
Mainly a sketch of W's life and literary career, not an interview. Alludes to a misunderstanding between W and the newspaper which both are eager to resolve.

84. Anon. "Tourisme et vacances: Le Dieu des ténèbres (Calmann-Lévy)." France-Illustration, 6 (8 July), [49].
Favorable review of the French translation of The God That Failed with special praise for W's contribution.

85. Anon. "Town Topics." The Buenos Aires Standard (5 May).
Describes the filming of the rooftop chase scene in the film NS. W himself, not a double, performed.

86. Anon. "3 livres bouleversants à propos de l'attribution du Prix Nobel de la paix à Ralph Bunche." Bibliographie de la France, 139 (13 October), 3285.
Advertisement for the French translations of NS, UTC, and Alan Paton's Cry, the Beloved Country.

87. Anon. "Two-Way Rebellion." The London Times Literary Supplement (3 February), p. 67.
Favorable review of The God That Failed focusing on Koestler, Silone, and W. W thought that the Communist Party would aid blacks, but he was made to feel unwelcome in its ranks.

88. Anon. "U. S. Author Praises Steel Band Music: 'Electric.'" Unidentified

clipping (June).
Reports W's visit to Trinidad after the filming of NS.

89. Anon. "The Ugly Leah." Time, 55 (9 January), 86, 89.
Favorable review of The God That Failed concentrating on the Koestler and Silone sections. W's contribution "is appealing for its passionate declaration of one Negro's reason for trying Communism, though a little boyish."

90. Anon. "Les Ultra-surréalistes peignent avec leurs doigts." Paris Samedi-Soir (21 January).
Reports that Christiane Alanare has spoken to W concerning a possible series of paintings of Harlem.

91. Anon. "Uncle Tom's Children," in Native Son. Signet Book. New York: New American Library, p. [416].
Blurb for the Signet edition.

92. Anon. Untitled article. Cinémonde (20 November), p. 4.
Brief illustrated account of the shooting of the film NS.

93. Anon. Untitled clipping.
Two photographs with captions from an Argentinian newspaper or magazine of scenes from the film NS.

94. Anon. Untitled clipping. Paris Franc-Tireur (11 December).
Notes that W attended a meeting of the Franco-American Fellowship at which Louis Fischer and Jean-Paul Sartre discussed liberty.

95. Anon. Untitled clipping. Tribune de Genève (12 August).
Notice of the French translation of The God That Failed mentioning W.

96. Anon. "When Richard Wright." The Chicago Defender (2 September), p. 28.
Photograph with caption of W and friends in Rio de Janiero.

97. Anon. "Wright," in Piccola enciclopedia Mondadori. Ed. Doro Rosetti. Verona: Mondadori, p. 1113.
Very brief biographical note with photograph.

98. Anon. "Wright," in Tidens Lexikon. Ed. Gunnar Dahlberg. Stockholm: Tidens Förlag, p. 3133.
Contains a brief biographical note.

99. Anon. "Wright, Riccardo," in Nuovissima enciclopedia illustrata. Ed. Giuseppe Maria Boccabianca. Vol. 5. Milan: Instituto Editoriale Italiano, p. 843.

Brief biographical note.

100. Anon. "Wright, Richard," in Chambers's Encyclopedia. New edition. Ed. M. D. Law. Vol. 14. New York: Oxford University Press, p. 758.
Biographical note.
Reprinted: 1959.47; 1968.33.

101. Anon. "Wright (Richard)," in Diccionario enciclopédico U. T. E. H. A. Vol. 10. Mexico, D. F.: Union Tipografica Editorial Hispano Americana, p. 1085.
Brief biographical note.

102. Anon. "Wright, Richard," in The Columbia Encyclopedia. Second edition. Ed. William Bridgwater and Elizabeth J. Sherwood. New York: Columbia University Press, p. 2176.
Biographical note.
Reprinted in revised form: 1975.14.

103. "Wright, Richard," in Who's Who in Colored America. Seventh edition. Ed. G. James Fleming and Christian E. Burckel. Yonkers-on-Hudson, N. Y.: Burckel & Associates, pp. 576-577.
Biographical sketch based on information received from W.

104. Armstrong, Alicia. "Writers Tell Why They Answered and Left Red Appeal." Davenport Times (c. 29 March).
Review of The God That Failed mentioning W.

105. Aron, Raymond. "Fidélité des apostats." La Table Ronde, No. 30 (June), pp. 52-65.
Notes that W, disillusioned with the Communist Party, continues to denounce the injustices of American society.
Reprinted: 1950.106.

106. _____. "Postface," in Le Dieu des ténèbres. Paris: Calmann-Lévy, pp. 289-307.
Reprint of 1950.105.

107. Bartlett, Vernon. "Dieu illusoire." Brussells Dernière Heure (14 June).
Review of the French translation of The God That Failed mentioning W.

108. Belcher, Fannin S., Jr. "The Negro Theater: A Glance Backward." Phylon, 11 (Second Quarter), 121-126.
Mentions Canada Lee in the play NS (p. 126).

109. Berger, Pierre. "Pierre Chenal a tourné." Paris-Presse l'Instransigeant (9 November).
Notes that Chenal praises W's writing and acting in the film version of NS.

110. Bitossi, Sergio. "Fermenti di ri-
volta del teatro negro: nei canti di
Harlem il grido di una razza." Rome
Avanti! (18 May), p. 3.
    Begins with a quotation from "I Have
    Seen Black Hands" and includes com-
    ments on the play NS.

111. Bondy, François. "The God That
Failed." Unidentified magazine clipping,
pp. 62-64.
    Review mentioning W and his "humane
    and true" voice.

112. Bontang, Pierre. "Six renégats du
communisme." Aspects de la France et du
Monde (15 June).
    Favorable review of the French trans-
    lation of The God That Failed.
    Although a "foolish Negro," W "has a
    real poetic sense." His story could
    have been better written by Faulkner,
    however.

113. Bontemps, Arna. "Famous WPA Authors." Negro Digest, 8 (June), 43-47.
    Emphasizes W's literary apprentice-
    ship and his subsequent success on
    the international level. NS, UTC, and
    BB are all important and influential
    books. His expatriation has somewhat
    dimmed W's power, Bontemps believes,
    but he remains the leading black
    writer.

114. _____. "Negro Poets, Then and Now."
Phylon, 11 (Fourth Quarter), 355-360.
    Mentions W's poetry and calls him
    "probably the most distinguished
    American now living on the Left Bank
    in Paris" (p. 360).
    Reprinted: 1969.40.

115. Bridier, Manuel. "Deuxième lettre à
mes anciens camarades." Liberté de l'Esprit (September).
    An ex-Communist, Bridier cites W as
    one of his predecessors in leaving
    the Party. Appeals to French Commu-
    nists to be more honest.

116. Brown, Jack E. "Crossman, Richard,
ed. The God That Failed." Library Journal, 75 (15 January), 106.
    Favorable notice with brief mention
    of W.

117. Burke, Kenneth. A Rhetoric of Motives. New York: Prentice-Hall, pp. 117,
194, 259.
    Comments on "social and sexual ten-
    sion" in NS, reversal of roles with
    the oppressor, and the doctrine of
    white supremacy in relation to econo-
    mic opportunity as exemplified in BB.

118. Butcher, Margaret Just. "What About
Negro Americans?" The Survey, 86 (Octo-

ber), 453-455.
    Mentions the acquaintance of Euro-
    peans with W's work.
    Reprinted: 1951.141.

119. C.[abrini], E.[milia]. "Cinque no-
velle che non piacciono al K. K. K."
Rome Avanti! (7 January), p. 3.
    Favorable review of the Italian
    translation of UTC. Focuses on "Fire
    and Cloud" and "Bright and Morning
    Star."

120. Cahen, Jacques-Fernand. La Littérature américaine. Paris: Presses Universitaires de France, p. 81.
    Refers to W and Farrell as "faithful
    imitators" of Dreiser who lack his
    "genius and power of sympathy."
    States that NS is an imitation of An
    American Tragedy.

121. Calta, Louis. "Random Items." The
New York Times (11 March), p. 8.
    Reports that Nicholas Joy will play
    Mr. Dalton in the film NS.

122. Chamberlin, William Henry. "Six Who
Found Communism a False, Treacherous
God." Chicago Sunday Tribune Magazine of
Books (22 January), p. 3.
    Favorable review of The God That
    Failed with a paragraph on W. W was
    made to feel like a pawn.

123. Chandler, G. Lewis. "A Major Prob-
lem of Negro Authors in Their March
Toward Belles-Lettres." Phylon, 11
(Fourth Quarter), 383-386.
    The major problem is segregation.
    Mentions W.

124. Clouard, Henri. "Le Mouvement in-
tellectuel." Revue Française de l'Elite
Européenne (April), pp. 46-48.
    Lists W as a writer whose work testi-
    fies to the continuing social revolt
    in America.

125. Coleman, William R. "Turning New
Leaves." The Canadian Forum, 30 (April),
18-19.
    Favorable review of The God That
    Failed with a brief mention of W.

126. Cook, Mercer. "The Negro in French
Literature: An Appraisal." The French
Review, 23 (March), 378-388.
    Mentions the interest of Césaire,
    Damas, and Senghor in W's verse.

127. Cothran, Tilman C. "White Stereotypes in Fiction by Negroes." Phylon, 11
(Third Quarter), 252-256.
    Sociological content analysis citing
    NS and BB to illustrate these stereo-
    types: low morals of rich white
    women, encouragement of black irres-

ponsibility by whites in order to feel superior, different physical characteristics and manners of Yankees and Southerners, better treatment of blacks by rich than by poor whites.

128. Cronenberg, Milton. "Seven Writers Analyse Communism's Failure." The Toronto Telegram (25 March), p. 39.
Favorable review of The God That Failed mentioning W.

129. Crowley, William. "Courant Books: The God That Failed Ed. Richard Crossman." The Hartford Courant (16 February), p. 12.
Favorable review noting that "Wright's personal appeal is the strongest in the book" and that "no understanding of the Communist evil cancels our own failures."

130. D., C. "The God that failed." La Fédération (July), p. 368.
Notice mentioning W.

131. D., L. "Roof-Top Hunt for Armed Killer!" Buenos Aires Herald (11 March), p. 8.
Detailed account of shooting the rooftop chase scene of the film NS. The reporter praises the acting of W in the live scene and Gloria Madison on film clips. He predicts "a spectacular success for the film."

132. Deacon, William Arthur. "Six Famous Writers Tell Why They Quit Communism." The Toronto Globe and Mail (4 March), p. 10.
Review of The God That Failed noting that when W discovered that Communism did not help minorities, "the dishonesty of the set-up was too much for him."

133. Delpech, Jeanine. "Avec l'enfant du pays." Les Nouvelles Littéraires (14 September), p. 1.
W comments on the film version of NS and future screen ventures. The interviewer comments on the film, especially W's acting ability and production plans. See 1950.134.

134. _____. "An Interview with Native Son." The Crisis, 57 (November), 625-626, 678.
Translation of 1950.133.
Reprinted: 1982.50.

135. Domenach, Jean-Marie. "Louis Fischer, Stephen Spender: Le Dieu des ténèbres." Esprit, 18 (November), 713-714.
Review of the French translation of The God That Failed comparing W's

unhappy experience with the Party following a miserable childhood with Silone's similar experience. Joining the Party to combat fear and injustice in society, they discovered their personal identity as well.

136. Dominique, Pierre. "Pèlerinage au dieu des ténèbres." Paris Samedi-Soir (18 July), p. 9.
Review of the French translation of The God That Failed mentioning W.

137. Drouin, Pierre. "Jazz et littérature." Le Paris Monde (c. 28 July).
Notes that W suggested a title for Milton Mezzrow's book.

138. Elliott, Mabel A. and Francis E. Merrill. Social Disorganization. Third edition. New York: Harper, pp. 412, 702.
Reprints 1941.712 and mentions W's withdrawal from Communism.

139. Elmquist, Carl Johan. "6 esk-kommunister fortoeller hoorfor." Copenhagen Politiken (20 January), p. 7.
Review of The God That Failed including a brief summary of W's chapter stressing the pressure directed against intellectuals in the Communist Party.

140. Elsen, Claude. "La Grande Illusion." La Table Ronde, No. 31 (July), pp. 119-122.
Review of the French translation of The God That Failed mentioning W.

141. _____. "Notes de lecture." Liberté de l'Esprit (September).
Contains a review of the French translation of The God That Failed mentioning W.

142. Emilio, Paolo. "Giro del mondo." L'Italia che scrive, 33 (March), 26.
Contains a favorable notice of the Italian translation of UTC comparing W to Goya and praising his "crudely and intensely lyric" stories.

143. Epin, Mathilde-Stéphane. "C'est dans la Bible que se trouve la première enquete criminelle." Paris Inter (20 January).
Notes that Lucien Prioly lists W among his predecessors as a writer of police stories.

144. Ezcurra. "Cine: 'Sangre negra.'" Unidentified clipping.
Brief illustrated notice of NS.

145. Farber, James. "Parade of Books." Baltimore News-Post (18 February), p. 34.
Contains a review of The God That

Failed mentioning W.
Reprinted: 1950.146.

146. ____. "Parade of Books." San Francisco Examiner (18 February), p. 16.
    Reprint of 1950.145.

147. Fontaine, André. "Un Dieu a
échoué': Six renégats parlent." Unidentified clipping (June).
    Favorable review of the French trans-
    lation of The God That Failed with
    two paragraphs summarizing W's ac-
    count, "undoubtedly the most moving"
    in the book.

148. Ford, Nick Aaron. "A Blueprint for
Negro Authors." Phylon, 11 (Fourth Quarter), 374-377.
    Claims that W was the first black
    author to deserve "a listing among
    first-rate American novelists" (p.
    374).
    Reprinted: 1969.86.

149. Fouchet, Max-Pol. "Les Livres
étrangers." Paris Carrefour (28 March),
p. 8.
    Contains a review of Gordon Merrick's
    Lancelot of Fifth Avenue mentioning
    W.

150. Gallois, A.[uguste]. "Le Dieu des
ténèbres." Force Ouvrière (22 June), p.
12.
    Review of the French translation of
    The God That Failed mentioning W.

151. Gardner, Martin. "The God That
Failed. Edited by Richard Crossman."
Ethics, 60 (July), 296-298.
    Favorable review mentioning W.

152. Gench, R. L. "New Books at the
Public Library." The Fort Scott Tribune
(3 April), p. 2.
    Review of The God That Failed claim-
    ing that W is the only one of the
    authors well known in the United
    States.

153. Glicksberg, Charles. "The Alienation of Negro Literature." Phylon, 11
(First Quarter), 49-58.
    Includes discussion of NS as a novel
    of suffering and protest. Fear,
    hatred, and alienation are character-
    istic of W's work.
    Reprinted: 1970.150.

154. Gloster, Hugh M. "Race and the
Negro Writer." Phylon, 11 (Fourth Quarter), 369-371.
    Argues that W helps to free the black
    writer to transcend strictly racial
    concerns by relating black suffering
    to that of all oppressed peoples,
    thereby combining the experiences of

class and race. Discusses NS in this
context.
    Reprinted: 1969.113.

155. Graham, Gladys P. "Author of 'Native Son' to Remain U. S. Citizen." The
Baltimore Afro-American (2 September),
p. 8.
    Partial reprint of 1950.157.

156. ____. "Author Richard Wright Back
from Buenos Aires." Unidentified clipping (c. 2 September).
    Reprint of 1950.157.

157. ____. "Native Son Richard Wright
Returns to America." Newton New Jersey
Herald (c. 26 August).
    Associated Negro Press report on W's
    visit to New York after the comple-
    tion of the film NS. W comments on
    the film and on blackface productions
    of the play NS in Europe and Israel.
    He states that he intends to remain a
    citizen of the United States. Graham
    comments on W's Haitian trip and on
    his interest in racial progress.
    Reprinted or partially reprinted:
    1950.155, 156, 158, 159, 160, 161.

158. ____. "'Native Son' Richard Wright
Returns to America for Visit." The New
Orleans Louisiana Weekly (2 September),
p. 2.
    Partial reprint of 1950.157.

159. ____. "Richard 'Black Boy' Wright
Returns to USA." Unidentified clipping
(c. 2 September).
    Partial reprint of 1950.157.

160. ____. "Richard Wright, 'Native
Son' Author, Returns to America." Atlanta Daily World (29 August), p. 2.
    Reprint of 1950.157.

161. ____. "Richard Wright Returns to
US." The Pittsburgh Courier (2 September), p. 13.
    Partial reprint of 1950.157.

162. H., Ed. "Le Dieu des ténèbres."
Arts (22 September), p. 2.
    Review of the French translation of
    The God That Failed noting that W's
    testimony is the most moving in the
    book.

163. H., R. F. "Six Agree That Communism
Can't Correct World's Ills." The Spring-
field (Mass.) Sunday Republican (29
January), p. 18A.
    Review of The God That Failed men-
    tioning and quoting from W.

164. Hart, James D. The Popular Book: A
History of America's Literary Taste. New
York: Oxford University Press, pp. 278,

317.
Notes that public concern about segregation and discrimination helped to
create a favorable climate for <u>BB</u>.

165. Hatch, Robert. "Studies in the
Permanent Crisis." <u>The</u> <u>New</u> <u>Republic</u>, 122
(13 March), 19-21.
Contains a review of <u>The</u> <u>God</u> <u>That</u>
<u>Failed</u> mentioning W.

166. Heuzé, Geneviève. "Conaissance des
Etats-Unis." <u>France-Etats-Unis</u> (November), p. 2.
Interview with W. The main topic is a
comparison of American and French
civilization.

167. Hill, Bob. "Looking at Books."
<u>Spokane</u> <u>Daily</u> <u>Chronicle</u> (9 March), p.
10.
Review of <u>The</u> <u>God</u> <u>That</u> <u>Failed</u> calling
W's experience with Communism "per-
haps the most disillusioning of all."

168. Hughes, Langston, Mozell C. Hill,
and M. Carl Holman. "Some Practical
Observations: A Colloquy." <u>Phylon</u>, 11
(Fourth Quarter), 307-311.
Hughes names W as one of the four
best black novelists of recent years.

169. Jarrett, Thomas D. "Toward Unfet-
tered Creativity: A Note on the Negro
Novelist's Coming of Age." <u>Phylon</u>, 11
(Fourth Quarter), 313-317.
Claims that W de-emphasizes the importance of Bigger's racial identity
in <u>NS</u>. "His experiences might well
have been those of a white youth in
the ghettoes of Chicago" (p. 315).

170. Lasky, Victor. "Knife Spree Alarm
Was Sounded Three Years Ago--And Forgot-
ten." New York <u>World</u> <u>Telegram</u> <u>and</u> <u>Sun</u>.
Compares a report on a mass murderer
with that on Bigger Thomas. The year
is conjectural.

171. Lee, Ulysses. "Criticism at Mid-
Century." <u>Phylon</u>, 11 (Fourth Quarter),
328-337.
Reviewing criticism of black writers,
Lee notes the controversy as to
whether or not W had the moral right
to risk reinforcing stereotyped views
of black people in <u>NS</u> and <u>BB</u>.

172. Leonardo, Sergio. "Los dos destinos
de Gloria Madison." Buenos Aires <u>Leoplan</u>
(15 February), pp. 32-33.
Article on the actress who played
Bessie in the film <u>NS</u>. She calls W "a
humanist who writes novels."

173. Levin, Harry. "Some European Views
of Contemporary American Literature," in
<u>The</u> <u>American</u> <u>Writer</u> <u>and</u> <u>the</u> <u>European</u>

Tradition. Ed. Margaret Denny and William H. Gilman. Minneapolis: University
of Minnesota Press, pp. 168-184.
Reprint of 1949.123.

174. Locke, Alain. "Self-Criticism: The
Third Dimension in Culture." <u>Phylon</u>, 11
(Fourth Quarter), 391-394.
Praises the first two parts of the
novel <u>NS</u> for reaching the level of
universal art. The last part, however, becomes "more and more involved
in propagandist formulae" (p. 392).

175. Loewel, Pierre. "De l'engagement."
Paris <u>L'Aurore</u> (27 June), p. 9.
Review of the French translation of
<u>The</u> <u>God</u> <u>That</u> <u>Failed</u> mentioning W.

176. Mallison, Dallas. "Red Threat and
How It Works." <u>The</u> <u>Raleigh</u> <u>News</u> <u>and</u>
<u>Observer</u> (17 September), Sec. IV, p. 5.
Review of <u>The</u> <u>God</u> <u>That</u> <u>Failed</u> claim-
ing that <u>W's</u> contribution is "of
especial value to us Southerners and
Americans."

177. Marietta. "Meeting Richard Wright."
<u>The</u> <u>Bulletin</u> <u>Board</u> (June).
Interview with W containing a brief
essay by him on writing for a film. W
comments also on important writers
and on his impressions of Argentina.

178. Marshall, Stanley. "'Native Son' as
Film Premieres in Italy; Author in Role
of 'Bigger.'" <u>The</u> <u>Chicago</u> <u>Defender</u> (2
September), p. 27.
Relates the story of the film version: the early Hollywood offer, the
stage version, the arrangement with
Sono films, W in the role of Bigger,
the other members of the cast, the
production on location in Chicago and
Argentina, and the premiere planned
for the Venice Film Festival.

179. Martens, Johannes Skancke. "Neger-
forfatter blir filmskuespiller." Oslo
<u>Aftenposten</u> (9 November), p. 3.
Reports briefly an interview with W
including his plans for the film
version of <u>NS</u> and his comments on
segregation and communism in the
United States. W refers briefly to
his interest in making a film concerning Toussaint L'Ouverture.

180. Maulnier, Thierry. "Les Ecrivains
devant le communisme." <u>Hommes</u> <u>et</u> <u>Mondes</u>,
12 (August), 592-596.
Review of the French translation of
<u>The</u> <u>God</u> <u>That</u> <u>Failed</u>. Comments at
length on W's personal motivations,
activities, and tragedy when he had
to leave the Party because they indicate, more clearly than those of
other contributors, the existential

dilemma people in his position had to face.

181. Mayer, Milton. "Six Former Communists Still Need Greater Faith." Chicago Sunday Sun-Times (4 June), Sec. Two, p. 7.

Review of The God That Failed mentioning W.

182. Miller, Merle. "Between Book Ends: The Disenchanted Ones." St. Louis Post Dispatch (14 January), p. 4A.

Reprint of 1950.183.

183. ____. "How They Became Communists, and How They Changed Their Minds." New York Herald Tribune Book Review (8 January), p. 7.

Favorable review of The God That Failed with a paragraph on W. Reprinted: 1950.182.

184. Montas, Lucien. "L'Histoire déchirante d'un Negre: R. Wright." Le Port-au-Prince Nouvelliste (2 August), pp. 1, 6; (8 August), pp. 1, 4; (12 August), pp. 1, 4.

Biographical-critical study with analyses of BB and NS. Essentially a realist, W also has a slight romantic streak. His main subject is race, but his approach is psychological and intensely individualistic. His literary power places him among the greatest of contemporary writers. Montas hopes that his influence on young Haitian writers will be as great as that of Langston Hughes.

185. Moon, Bucklin. "Is the Boom in Race Novels Over?" Negro Digest, 8 (March), 73-77.

Reprint of 1949.131.

186. Moussin, René. "Hugues Panassié." La Casserole (1 February).

Cites W as evidence of the affirmation of the human spirit.

187. Musard, François. "Le Dieu des ténèbres." Algiers Dernière Heure (19 July).

Review of the French translation of The God That Failed mentioning W.

188. N.[adeau], M.[aurice]. "A. Koestler, Silone, Wright, Gide, Fischer, Spender: Le Dieu des Ténèbres." Cahiers du Monde Nouveau, 6 (June), 123-125.

Review of the French translation of The God That Failed alluding to W's grandiose vision of human freedom and his subsequent moral suffering when he left the Communist Party.

189. ____. "Introduction," in Un Enfant du pays. By Richard Wright. Paris: Club Français du Livre, pp. i-v.

Based in part on Nadeau's other articles on W, this introduction to the French translation of NS stresses Bigger's social, economic, and psychological condition and the way in which murder could be affirmative for him. Nadeau also links his case with that of victims of racism elsewhere.

190. Nichols, Charles H., Jr. "The Forties: A Decade of Growth." Phylon, 11 (Fourth Quarter), 377-380.

Praises W's accomplishment: "Native Son has achieved a permanent place in American literature not only because its theme is universal, but because its prose is instinct with life, shorn of pretense and flabbiness, with all the freshness and tang of people talking."

191. Niebuhr, Reinhold. "To Moscow--And Back." The Nation, 170 (28 January), 88-90.

Review of The God That Failed noting that W was drawn to the universal fellowship offered by the Party.

192. Ott, Felix. "Götzendämmerung." Stimmen der Zeit, 146 (September), 443-452.

Review of the German translation of The God That Failed including a long quotation from W's contribution (pp. 449-450). Ott considers W and Silone more closely linked through their sympathy for the poor and oppressed to the Bolshevik Old Guard than are the four other writers in the collection. He finds the accounts of W, Silone, and Koestler more interesting than those of Gide, Fischer, and Spender.

193. Ottley, Roi. Black Odyssey: The Story of the Negro in America. New York: Scribner's, pp. 273-275.

Comments on W's background, achievement, and fame.

194. Pagosse, R. "Koestler (Arthur), Silone (Ignazio), Wright (Richard), Gide (André), Fischer (Louis), Spender (Stephen).--Le Dieu des ténèbres." La Revue Socialiste, N. S., No. 42 (December), pp. 587-588.

Review of the French translation of The God That Failed emphasizing W's contribution.

195. Panassié, H.[ugues]. "Really the Blues." Paris Opéra (26 July).

Favorable review of Milton Mezzrow's autobiography, which complements well W's books on American racism.

196. Parsons, Louella O. "Jean Wallace

Given Lead in 'Native Son.'" New York Journal-American (24 March), p. 25.
Notes also that W will play the lead in the film.

197. Pellizzi, Camillo. "Strada di ritorno dalla dittatura: Il dio che illuse." La fiera letteraria (9 April), p. 5.
Review of the Italian translation of The God That Failed mentioning W.

198. Petit, Henri. "Plaisir de lire." La Parisien Libéré (14 September).
Reports that W recommended a title for Hugues Panassié's Jazz Panorama.

199. Petitjean, A. "Jadis communistes ou communisants, Gide, Koestler, Silone, Richard Wright confessent leurs espérances et leurs déceptions." Paris Carrefour (27 June), p. 9.
Review of the French translation of The God That Failed mentioning W and including a photograph. W's testimony is poignant in its account of his confrontation with American racism and Stalinist imperialism.

200. Piquion, René. "Tonnerre dans la littérature." Haïti Journal (3 August).
Announces W's presence in Haiti, recalls meeting him at a party in Harlem in 1944, and sketches his life and literary career, ranking him with Langston Hughes as a leading black writer.

201. Pisko, Ernest. "The Loss of a False Faith." The Christian Science Monitor (14 January), p. 18.
Favorable review of The God That Failed including a paragraph on W.

202. Plamenatz, John. "To Be a Communist." The Spectator, 184 (10 February), 186.
Review of The God That Failed including a paragraph on W, whose contribution, along with Silone's, is the best in the collection. His account shows the attraction of Communism for the oppressed.

203. Prescott, Orville. "Books of the Times." The New York Times (13 January), p. 21.
Review of The God That Failed praising the contributions of W and Koestler.

204. Prisco, Michele. "I figli dello zio Tom hanno fatto la guerra." La fiera letteraria (15 January), p. 4.
Favorable review of the Italian translation of UTC in the context of the development of black art. W moves his material from the documentary to the artistic. Unlike Stowe, he writes of rebellious blacks in a driving, relentless prose. He may be one-sided, but his work has vitality.

205. Pritchett, V. S. "Books in General." The New Statesman and Nation, 39 (21 January), 68.
Review of The God That Failed with favorable discussion of W, "the most moving narrator in the book."

205a. [Quinn, Kerker]. "Accent."
Flyer listing W as a past contributor.

206. Reddick, L. D. "No Kafka in the South." Phylon, 11 (Fourth Quarter), 380-383.
Quotes W on the vivid, colorful quality of black speech.

207. Redding, Saunders. They Came in Chains: Americans from Africa. Philadelphia: Lippincott, pp. 279, 288.
Mentions W's Communist affiliation and points out that racial injustice prompted him to write.
Reprinted: 1969.205; 1973.249.

208. Riou, Gaston. "La Situation internationale." Hommes et Mondes, 13 (September), 129-134.
Includes a review of the French translation of The God That Failed mentioning W (p. 130).

209. [Rogers, W. G.]. (L. G.). "Commies Enticed Them But Briefly." Tulsa Daily World (12 March), Sec. 5, p. 9.
Reprint of 1950.212.

210. _____. "The God That Failed." Fremont (Neb.) Guide and Tribune (24 February), p. 7.
Reprint of 1950.212.

211. _____. "The God That Failed." The Tacoma Sunday Ledger-News Tribune (c. 19 March).
Reprint of 1950.212.

212. _____. "Literary Guidepost." Augusta (Maine) Daily Kennebec Journal (11 January), p. 6.
Review of The God That Failed mentioning W.
Reprinted: 1950.209, 210, 211, 213.

213. _____. "New Books." The Aberdeen (Wash.) Daily World (c. 19 March).
Reprint of 1950.212.

214. Rolo, Charles J. "Reader's Choice." The Atlantic Monthly, 185 (March), 74, 76, 78-82.
Contains a review of The God That Failed calling "the pieces by Silone

and Wright . . . deeply moving confessions" (p. 76).

215. Russell, Bertrand. "Came the Revo-
lution . . ." The Saturday Review of
Literature, 33 (25 March), 9-10, 36-37.
    Mentions W as a contributor to The
God That Failed.
    Translated: 1950.216.

216. _____. "Guddomen, der svigtede."
Copenhagen Politiken (9 April), pp. 14-
16.
    Translation of 1950.215 with a photo-
graph of W.

217. S., J.-P. "Sur les 'Book Clubs.'"
La Gazette des Lettres, No. 120 (5
August), p. 6.
    Lists W's works as Book-of-the-Month
Club selections.

218. Schlesinger, Arthur M., Jr. "Dim
Views of the Red Star." The Saturday
Review of Literature, 33 (7 January),
11.
    Review of The God That Failed with
specific comments on W's brutal experience with the Party.

219. Schmidt, Albert-Marie. "Littérature
engageante et littérature engagée."
Paris Réforme (24 June), p. 7.
    Includes a review of the French
translation of The God That Failed
mentioning W. Notes that W and Silone
can move the reader as well as interest him because their proletarian
origins made a tragedy of their break
with the Party.

220. Schuyler, George S. "What's Wrong
with Negro Authors." Negro Digest, 8
(May), 3-7.
    Contains disparaging remarks on the
exaggerated Communist propaganda in
W's work.

221. Schuyler, Josephine. "Looks at
Books: Big Writers Confess How Reds Won
Them." The Pittsburgh Courier (18
March), p. 19.
    Review of The God That Failed men-
tioning W.

222. Schweitzer, Leonard J. "America
Balances the Books." America, 83 (13
May), 175-178.
    Contains a favorable review of The
God That Failed mentioning W.

223. Simon, Jean. Le Roman américain au
XXe siècle. Paris: Boivin, p. 174.
    Mentions W and NS as exemplifying
social realism.

224. Slocombe, George. "Reviews of New
Books in Europe." New York Herald Tri-
bune, European Edition (27 April), p. 6.
    Favorable review of The God That
Failed mentioning and quoting from W.

225. Smith, William Gardner. "The Negro
Writer: Pitfalls and Compensations."
Phylon, 11 (Fourth Quarter), 297-303.
    Mentions W's bitter anger.
    Reprinted: 1969.223, 224; 1970.325;
1971.278.

226. Spaak, Paul-Henri. "Témoignages."
Le Brussels Peuple (20 September).
    Review of the French translation of
The God That Failed mentioning W.

227. Spaccarelli, M. "L'autrice de 'Bo-
cahe inutili' avrebbe fatto meglio a
tacere." La Rome libertà (9 March).
    Mentions W's friendship with Simone
de Beauvoir.

228. Squire, Sir John. "Novel Angles of
Approach to Contemporary Russia." The
Illustrated London News, 216 (4 March),
320.
    Contains an anti-Communist review of
The God That Failed with special
mention of W, "with whom one can
whole-heartedly sympathize," in contrast to the "stupidity and blindness" of the other contributors.

228a. Stammler, Heinrich. Amerikanische
Literaturgeschichte im Überblick. Bam-
berg: Verlag Bamberger Reiter G. M. B.
H., pp. 66-67.
    Contains brief comments on W as a
proletarian and black writer.

229. T., G. "Le Dieu des ténèbres, R.
Croosman [sic], Koestler, R. Wright, L.
Fischer, S. Spender, Silone, A. Gide."
Contacts Littéraires et Sociaux (Septem-
ber).
    Review of the French translation of
The God That Failed mentioning W.

230. Theis, E.[douard]. "Un Ecrivain:
Richard Wright." Présence Africaine,
Nos. 8-9 (March), pp. 141-148.
    Reprint of 1947.289.

231. Thérive, André. "Le Dieu des ténèbres." Paroles Françaises L'Alliance Nouvelle (3 July).
    Review of the French translation of
The God That Failed comparing W to
Rousseau.

232. Thomas, Norman. "Failing God." The
Call (24 February).
    Review of The God That Failed men-
tioning W.

233. Tillman, N. P. "The Threshold of
Maturity." Phylon, 11 (Fourth Quarter),
387-388.

Mentions W briefly.

234. Trédant, Paul. "Lettre de New York." Les Nouvelles Littéraires (26 January), p. 8.
Mentions plans for a New York revival of the play NS.

235. U., R. H. "The God That Failed. Edited by Richard Crossman." San Francisco Chronicle (26 March), This World Sec., p. 23.
Favorable review mentioning W.

236. Valentini, G.[iuseppe]. "Il grido di R. Wright è rivendicazione o vendetta?" Letture, 5 (February), 52-55.
Unfavorable review of the Italian translation of UTC. Valentini criticizes W for his vindictive bitterness and exaggeration. He compares W unfavorably to Ann Petry, who is more restrained in her racial protest.

237. Verdier, Robert. "Le Dieu des ténèbres." Montpellier Midi-Libre (14 June).
Review of the French translation of The God That Failed mentioning W.

238. W., E. "Marche dans les ténèbres de Hans Habe." Foi et Vie (c. December).
Briefly compares the Habe book to BB and Alan Paton's Cry, the Beloved Country.

239. Waldberg, Patrick. "Sur l'Amérique." Paru, No. 59 (April), pp. 101-103.
Names NS as a notable American book which appeared during the war.

240. Wallace, Jean. "Pierre Chenal nous a fait tourner 'Native Son' film sur Chicago, à Buenos Aires." Ciné Revue (18 August).
Illustrated article on the filming of NS by the actress who played Mary Dalton. She expresses admiration for W's idealism.

241. Warren, Virginia Lee. "Argentina Doubles as Chicago Locale for 'Native Son.'" The New York Times (21 May), Sec. 2, p. 5.
Detailed account of the filming of NS with information on the producer Jaime Prades, the director Pierre Chenal, and the cast, including W himself. Warren describes the extraordinary steps taken to ensure authenticity.

242. Weitz, Morris. Philosophy of the Arts. Cambridge, Mass.: Harvard University Press, pp. 137-141.
Uses NS as an example of a work of literature that embodies certain claims to truth through the presence

of depth-meaning. The last paragraphs are singled out for special analysis. Bigger is more than a symbol of exploitation. He represents all men who struggle for freedom.
Reprinted: 1971.147.

243. Werner, Alfred. "A Literary Letter About Israel." The New York Times Book Review (15 October), p. 33.
Lists W as an American writer popular in Israel.

244. West, Rebecca. "Roads to Communism and Back: Six Personal Histories." The New York Times Book Review (8 January), pp. 3, 29.
Favorable review of The God That Failed with special praise for W. He uses a bare style and several narrative voices. The result is a moving account.

245. Woolbert, Robert Gale. "Recent Books on International Relations." Foreign Affairs, 28 (July), 676-692.
Contains a notice of The God That Failed mentioning W.

246. Wright, Cobina. "Society as I See It." Unidentified clipping.
Reports Nicholas Joy's favorable appraisal of the Argentinian film industry using NS as a prime example.

247. Zobel, Joseph. "Richard Wright, témoin de la tragédie de 13 millions d'êtres." Liens (July), p. 4.
Tribute to W as a witness and advocate by a writer from Martinique.

248. _____. "Richard Wright: Un Enfant du pays." Liens (July), p. 4.
Favorable review of the French translation of NS. Zobel emphasizes W's achievement in creating a profound and representative character in Bigger.

1951

1. Algren, Nelson. Chicago: City on the Make. Garden City, N. Y.: Doubleday, pp. 63-64.
Praises W as the best Chicago writer since the middle twenties but criticizes his expatriation.

2. Altman, Georges. "Cette lèpre, le racisme." Paris Franc-Tireur (17 April).
Article on American racism quoting briefly W's comments on the relationships between white woman and black men.

3. Anon. "A. S. F. International Presents the Famous Novel by Richard Wright 'Native Son.'"

Promotional folder-poster for the film. Includes a plot summary, still photographs, and a list of the cast.

4. Anon. "A la biennale de Venise." Paris Aux Ecoutes (7 September).
Reports the consensus that NS is a successful and provocative film. Notes W's participation.

5. Anon. "A sens unique." Paris Franc-Tireur (7 February).
Mentions W's denunciation of American social evils.

6. Anon. "A Venise." Paris L'Aurore (23 August), p. 5.
Brief note on NS at the Venice Film Festival.

7. Anon. "A Venise Richard Wright a été consacré vedette de cinéma." Paris-Presse l'Intransigeant (1 September), p. 4.
Favorable review of the film NS. According to the Italian critics W is a good actor, but he does lack some credibility in the role of Bigger. Bigger becomes a black Raskolnikov.

8. Anon. ("Le Fanfarlo"). "Au festival de Venise." Le Paris Rassemblement (7 September), p. 11.
Contains a favorable notice of the film NS.

9. Anon. "Aurore actualités: Pas d'accord." Paris L'Aurore (8 June), p. 1.
Comments on W's unsuccessful intervention in a racial matter at the American Hospital in Neuilly.

10. Anon. "Author-Actor." Manchester Evening Chronicle (8 December).
Descriptive notice of the film NS.

11. Anon. "Bibliographie: Romans, récits, nouvelles." La Gazette des Lettres, 6 (15 January), 116.
Includes a notice of the French translation of Nelson Algren's Never Come Morning mentioning W's preface.

12. Anon. "Cinéma." Le Paris Monde (30 May), p. 9.
Notes that W was on the program of a meeting of the Franco-American Fellowship.

13. Anon. "Clima de intenso dramatismo tiene la nueva película 'Sangre negra.'" La Buenos Aires Razón (30 March).
Favorable review of the film NS. The theme of human solidarity is effectively realized. The reviewer expresses reservations about W's acting, however.

13a. Anon. "Club de 'l'Observateur.'" L'Observateur (26 April), p. 5.
Announces an appearance by W and Daniel Guérin to discuss racial and literary questions on 27 April.

14. Anon. "Club de 'l'Observateur.'" L'Observateur (3 May), p. 9.
Account of W's appearance at a dinner conference on 27 April, during which he responded to social and political questions from Daniel Guérin and the floor.

15. Anon. "Una conferenza dello scrittore negro: Richard Wright oggi a Torino." Unidentified clipping (January).
Announces W's lecture on "The Literature of the Negro in the United States" in Turin.

16. Anon. "Conferenziere." La libertà d'Italia (25 January).
Photograph with caption of W at the Eliseo Theater.

17. Anon. "Dal catalogo D. C. N. 1952-53." Cinemundus (March).
Comments with photographs of the film NS.

18. Anon. "Déception américaine." Paris France-Observateur (6 September), p. 33.
Unfavorable review of the film NS, "a bad film about a bad boy," with comparisons to the excellent novel.

19. Anon. "Depuis deux ans Daniel Guérin attend son visa pour les U. S. A." Le Paris Populaire (23 April), p. 3.
Notes that W signed a petition on behalf of Guérin.

20. Anon. "Le Dieu des ténèbres, par Arthur Koestler, Ignacio Silone, Richard Wright, André Gide, Louis Fischer, Stephen Spender." La Croix (21-22 January), p. 4.
Favorable review of the French translation of The God That Failed noting that W still believes in a socialist revolution.

21. Anon. "XII mostra internazionale d'arte cinematografica."
Playbill for the presentation of NS at the Venice Film Festival.

22. Anon. "XII mostra internazionale d'arte cinematografica." Carnet de Venezia, No. 17 (19-25 August), pp. 6-8.
Lists the film NS.

23. Anon. Dust jacket of Cinque uomini. By Richard Wright. Trans. Fernanda Pivano. Verona: Mondadori.
Publisher's blurb on the front inside flap of the Italian translation of

"Almos' a Man," "Early Days in Chicago," "The Man Who Lived Underground," "The Man Who Killed a Shadow," and "Silt."

24. Anon. "The Dynamite-Loaded Story of a Negro and a White Girl!" The Los Angeles Mirror (10 August), p. 38.
Advertisement for the film NS with a still photograph of W carrying Jean Wallace down the basement stairway.

25. Anon. "The Dynamite-Loaded Story of a Negro and White Girl!" The New York Times (15 June), p. 27.
Advertisement for the world premiere of the film NS at the Criterion Theater in New York on 16 June.

26. Anon. "L'Ecrivain Richard Wright se plaint de descriminations raciales à l'hôpital de Neuilly." Paris Combat (8 June), p. 8.
Account of a press conference held by W to protest racial discrimination by an American hospital in Paris which refused to hire a black nurse.

27. Anon. "Encore la respectueuse." Gazette de Lausanne (11 August).
Announces a new adaptation of La Putain respectueuse by W and Sartre.

28. Anon. "Excepcional realización ha dado Chenal a 'Sangre negra,' otra gran cinta." Unidentified clipping.
Comments on the production problems of the film NS and its generally favorable foreign reception. Praises the excellent directing of Pierre Chenal.

29. Anon. "Explodes on the Screen!" The Los Angeles Mirror (13 August), p. 7.
Advertisement for the film NS.

30. Anon. "Exploding Onto the Screen! Richard Wrights [sic] 'Native Son.'"
Large poster for the film.

31. Anon. "Le Festival de Venise." La Croix (25 August), p. 3.
Notes that W was mainly responsible for adapting NS from novel to film.

32. Anon. "Films de demain." L'Ecran Français (8-14 August).
Brief notice of the film NS. Pierre Chenal announces that it will show in Chile.

33. Anon. "France-Amérique." Gazette de Lausanne (3 March).
Announces the formation by W of the Franco-American Fellowship.

34. Anon. "I francesi ritirano i loro films dal Festival." Roma-Napoli (23 August).
Favorable review of the film NS noting its enthusiastic reception at the Venice Film Festival.

35. Anon. "Frente al crimen y la violencia." Unidentified clipping.
Advertisement for the film NS.

36. Anon. "Heat Slows Up B'way; Andrews Sis Tilt 'Angel' to Hep 80G, 'Sirocco' Plus Stage 42G, 'Native' Okay 17G." Variety (20 June), p. 9.
The film NS will gross $17,000 at the Criterion Theater in its first week.

37. Anon. "Heat Wilts B'way But 'He Ran' Plus Cavallaro-Juanita Hall Nice 60G, 'Angel'-Andrews Sis 58G, 'Samson' NG." Variety (27 June), p. 11.
Reports that in its second week the film NS grossed $6,000.

38. Anon. "Holiday Boosts Broadway Influx; 'Frogmen' Solid $102,000, 'Ace' Aces 29G, 'Dust'-Vaude 44G, 'Prowler' 17½G." Variety (4 July), p. 17.
The film NS grossed almost $8,000 in the second and last week of its New York run.

39. Anon. "Hommage à Louis Jouvet au Festival de Venise." La Casablanca Vigie Marocaine (28 [23?] August).
Notes that W's film NS was well received.

40. Anon. "Hommage à Louis Jouvet au Festival de Venise." Le Lyons Journal du Soir (23 August).
Reports that some critics consider the film NS amateurish.

41. Anon. Index Translationum 3. Paris: Unesco, pp. 95, 113, 128, 164, 227, 265.
Lists translations of BB into Spanish, NS into French, and The God That Failed into French, Italian, Dutch, and Swedish.

42. Anon. "International Bulletin."
Promotional flyer of International Film Distributors Ltd. for NS. Includes still photographs.

43. Anon. "Je choisis mes auteurs: Le Dieu des ténèbres." La Brussels Cité (13 February).
Review of the French translation of The God That Failed praising W's chapter as moving and informative.

44. Anon. "Les Journées de Carcassonne ou le cinéma dans la rue." La Croix (9 June), p. 3.
Reports that W attended a media party at the Ranelagh Theater in Paris on 5 June.

45. Anon. "'Kermesse héroïque' per com-
memorare Jouvet." Palermo L'Ora (24
August).
    Contains a favorable review of the
    film NS noting its good reception at
    the Venice Film Festival. The article
    also mentions W's press conference at
    the Hotel Excelsior.

46. Anon. "Le saviez-vous?" Le Populaire
de Paris (3 August), p. 2.
    Announces a new adaptation of La
    Putain respectueuse by W and Sartre.

47. Anon. "Logique du Pacte Atlantique:
A l'hôpital américain de Neuilly, on
cultive le virus raciste." Unidentified
clipping (15-21 June).
    Quotes W's statement of protest in
    L'Observateur.

48. Anon. "Le Matin se fait attendre,
par Nelson Algren." Arts (16 March), p.
2.
    Comments on W's excellent introduc-
    tion.

49. Anon. "Native Son." Kinematograph
Weekly, 416 (15 November), 23.
    Favorable review of the film noting
    its sordidness but praising its
    powerful delivery of its message.

50. Anon. "'Native Son.'" New York
Herald Tribune (10 June), Sec. 4, p. 3.
    Photograph with caption of W and
    Gloria Madison in a scene from the
    film. Announces its opening on Satur-
    day.

51. Anon. "Native Son." Newsweek, 38 (9
July), 94.
    Unfavorable review of the film com-
    plaining of stereotyped characteriza-
    tions, amateurish performances, and
    inadequate staging. Despite its sin-
    cerity, "the net effect of this pro-
    duction . . . is one of disappoint-
    ment and even embarrassment."

52. Anon. "Native Son." The Daily Film
Renter (14 November).
    Favorable review of the film noting
    its grimness but praising its drama-
    tic power and W's acting.

53. Anon. "'Native Son.'" The New York
Daily Compass (21 May), p. 18.
    Five still photographs with captions
    from the film.

54. Anon. "'Native Son' Among Week's New
Films." The New York Daily Compass (11
June), p. 20.
    Announces the first New York showing
    at the Criterion Theater.

55. Anon. "'Native Son' at the Gran

Rex." Buenos Aires Herald (30 March), p.
7.
    Favorable review of the film noting
    its outspoken theme and praising W's
    performance as Bigger.

56. Anon. "'Native Son' Filmed in Argentina." Ebony, 6 (January), 82-86.
    Amply illustrated account including
    details on the re-creation of Chicago
    slums in Buenos Aires and the shoot-
    ing of scenes in Chicago itself. W
    contributes "Wright Explains Ideas
    About Movie Making" (pp. 84-85). The
    article concludes with a report on
    W's life in Paris.

57. Anon. "'Native Son' Is International's New Offering." The Cinema News
and Property Gazette (14 November), p.
5.
    Announcement of the film.

58. Anon. "'Native Son' Now Reaches
Third Medium--Screen." New York Herald
Tribune (10 June), Sec. 4, p. 3.
    Notes the work's success as a novel
    and a play and announces its appear-
    ance as a film.

59. Anon. "'Native Son' Stars Richard
Wright Currently at the Criterion." New
York Inquirer (18 June), p. 7.
    Announcement of the film emphasizing
    the popularity of the novel in the
    original and in translation. It has
    become "something of a classic."
    Includes a still photograph from the
    film.

60. Anon. "Nelson Algren Le Matin se
fait attendre." Liens (1 April).
    Review quoting from W's introduction.

61. Anon. "Nouvelles brèves." Le Paris
Monde (c. 9 June).
    Mentions W's involvement with a
    racial problem at the American Hospi-
    tal in Neuilly.

62. Anon. "Of Local Origin." The New
York Times (18 April), p. 38.
    Announces that W will be present in
    May for the American premiere of the
    film NS.

63. Anon. "Of Local Origin." The New
York Times (7 June), p. 41.
    Announces the film NS.

64. Anon. "Okay 'Native Son.'" The
Hollywood Reporter (2 March).
    Reports that the film "has been
    passed by the state censors after
    deletion of several scenes."

65. Anon. "On en parlait hier: demandez
le programme (de Venise)." Paris L'Au-

rore (9 August), p. 5.
Notes the particular interest of NS because it stars its author.

66. Anon. "On projette." La Paris Presse (1 September).
Brief note on the production of the film NS.

67. Anon. "On the Screen Now: 'Native Son.'" The Buenos Aires Standard (2 April).
Favorable review of the film giving considerable attention to its production. Summarizes the plot and praises W's acting.

68. Anon. "Parla dei negri." Momento sera (25 January).
Notes W's lecture at the Eliseo Theater in Rome.

69. Anon. "Participation française à la biennale de Venise." Rabat L'Echo du Maroc (29 August).
Mentions the film NS. W attended its showing at the Venice Film Festival.

70. Anon. "Une Peau de couleur peut ne pas être un obstacle au succès." Femmes d'Aujourd'hui (2 August).
Reports W's comments on the expatriate and his rationale.

71. Anon. "Les Peintres noirs voient la vie en rose." Paris Samedi-Soir (7 July), p. 7.
Photograph with caption of the members of the Franco-American Fellowship. W is the president of the group.

72. Anon. "Pierre de Boisdeffre (Prix de la Critique 1950)." Unidentified clipping.
Mentions W as an example of the influence of the conditions of material life on literary creation. The year is conjectural.

73. Anon. "Portrait of an Existentialist." Paris News Post (January).
Photograph of Sartre with caption explaining that W helped to form the Franco-American Fellowship.

74. Anon. "Pour la famille de MacGee." Paris Franc-Tireur (10 May).
Lists W as a member of a committee soliciting contributions for the family of Willie MacGee, "executed by virtue of a racist sentence" in Jackson, Mississippi.

75. Anon. "Premiere mundial." Unidentified clipping.
Buenos Aires newspaper advertisement for the world premiere of the film NS.

76. Anon. "Les Producteurs français retirent leurs films de la Biennale de Venise." Le Lyons Progrès (23 August), p. 20.
Notes the appearance of NS at the Venice Film Festival.

77. Anon. "Ray Robinson jouera dans 'La P . . . respectueuse.'" Paris Ce Matin (3 August).
Notes that W adapted Sartre's material for the revival of the play La Putain respectueuse.

78. Anon. "Return of the Native Son." Ebony, 7 (December), 100.
Editorial refuting W's "The Shame of Chicago," which appears in the same issue. Admitting that slums exist, the editorialist argues that W neglects improving housing conditions for the black middle class and the promise of improvement for the black poor. W's account is one-sided and incomplete. See also 1952.20, 26, 47, 55, 60, 68.

79. Anon. "Richard Wright." Il tempo (1 September), p. 33.
Photograph of W with caption noting the film NS.

80. Anon. "Richard Wright," in I conferenziere dell'aci per l'anno 1950-1951. Turin-Geneva-Rome: Associazione culturale italiana, p. [20].
Biographical sketch emphasizing W's universal qualities.

81. Anon. "Richard Wright." Liens (1 March).
Announces the French translation of NS by Marcel Duhamel.

82. Anon. "Richard Wright Becomes Actor in His 'Native Son.'" Brooklyn Daily Eagle (10 June), p. 31.
Discusses W's varied experiences as good preparation for acting. Notes the original plan to cast Canada Lee as Bigger.

83. Anon. "Richard Wright è giunto a Torino." Gazzetta sera (18-19 January).
Brief account of W's life and literary career. Announces that he will speak in Turin on "The Literature of the Negro in the United States."

84. Anon. "Richard Wright 'La letteratura negro negli Stati Uniti.'" Turin-Geneva-Rome: Associazione culturale italiana, 3 pp.
Mimeographed pamphlet summary of W's lectures, delivered in English, on 19, 20, and 23 January 1951.

85. Anon. "Richard Wright: Un Enfant du pays." Rabat Le Journal du Maroc (10 February).
Favorable review of Marcel Duhamel's French translation of NS. The violent novel is not a pleasant book to read, but it is very moving.

86. Anon. "Richard Wright's verdensberømte Søn af de Sorte." Unidentified clipping.
Norwegian newspaper advertisement for the film NS. The year is conjectural.

87. Anon. "Richard Wrigth [sic]." Unidentified clipping.
Photograph with caption of W eating spaghetti.

88. Anon. Sangre negra.
Program for the film NS at the Venice Film festival, 22 August.

89. Anon. "Sangre negra." Unidentified clipping.
Still photograph from the film NS.

90. Anon. "'Sangre negra.'" Unidentified clipping.
Favorable review in a Buenos Aires newspaper or magazine of the film NS with reservations expressed about W's acting. Although it is a good film, it does not fully capture the novel's profoundly dramatic social significance.

91. Anon. "Sangre negra." Unidentified clipping.
Advertisement for the film NS at the Gran Rex Theater in Buenos Aires.

92. Anon. "'Sangre negra' ha sido objecto de una realización fluida y espectacular." El Montevideo Diario (April).
Favorable review of the film NS. It lacks the dramatic power and social significance of the novel, however.

93. Anon. "'Sangre negra' de Pierre Chenal." Milan Corriere della sera (23 August), p. 2.
Unfavorable review of the film NS, which attenuates the dramatic richness of the novel. W's acting is mediocre.

94. Anon. "La Semaine littéraire." Paris Combat (12 April), p. 4.
Reports a writers' congress which W attended held in Paris on 10 November 1950. Also mentions a book purge in Hungary including W.

95. Anon. "Le Sociologue Daniel Guérin n'obtient pas de visa pour les Etats-Unis." Paris Combat (25 April), p. 5.
Notes that W signed a petition to

have the case reconsidered.

96. Anon. "Some of the Explosive Showmanship of 'Native Son.'"
Printed folder of advertisements for the film published by the distributor.

97. Anon. "Søn af de Sorte." Unidentified clipping.
Advertisement for the film NS. The year is conjectural.

98. Anon. "Son av Sitt Land." Unidentified clipping.
Generally favorable Swedish review of the film NS calling it "uncompromising." W's acting is amateurish but intense.

99. Anon. "Stars in Own Story." New York Journal-American (10 June).
Photograph with caption of W and Gloria Madison in a scene from the film NS.

100. Anon. "Sur tous les rayons." La Croix (21 January), p. 4.
Review of the French translation of The God That Failed mentioning W.

101. Anon. "Un Télégramme du 'Franco-American Fellowship' à Joséphine Baker." La Dépêche Africaine (15 November).
Reports that a telegram of support was sent to Baker by W, Sartre, and others.

102. Anon. "10,000 Books Banned by Hungarian Regime." The New York Times (9 February), p. 23.
Notes that NS is among the bannned books.

103. Anon. "Tiene destreza y vigor el film 'Sangre negra.'" La Buenos Aires Nación (30 March), p. 6.
Highly favorable review of the film NS praising its cinematic effects, direction, and acting, especially that of W as Bigger.

104. Anon. "Trapped by an Impulsive Act of Fear." The New York Times (17 June), Sec. 2, p. 5.
Photograph with caption of W and Jean Wallace in a scene from the film NS.

105. Anon. "U. S. Negroes Chauvinists?" Unidentified clipping.
Reports an attack by René Maran on W, Himes, and others for never looking beyond "the narrow horizon of race."

106. Anon. "Ultimos estrenos: 'Sangre negra.'" Buenos Aires Clarín (30 March).
Favorable review of the film NS, which demonstrates the technical ex-

cellence of the Argentinian film industry as well as W's talent.

107. Anon. Unidentified clipping.
Caricature of W with caption from an Argentinian newspaper.

108. Anon. Untitled article. Le Canard Enchaîné (16 May), p. 3.
    Notice of the film NS showing in Buenos Aires.

109. Anon. Untitled article. The New York Times (11 June), p. 20.
    Announcement of the film NS.

110. Anon. Untitled article. The New York Times (16 June), p. 9.
    Announcement of the film NS.

111. Anon. Untitled clipping. Aux Ecoutes de la Finance (17 August).
    Notice of the French translation of "The Man Who Lived Underground."

112. Anon. Untitled clipping. Ciné-Revue (17 August).
    Notes that the film NS substantially addresses the black question in America.

113. Anon. Untitled clipping. Cleveland Plain Dealer (c. 29 April).
    Notes that "Communists have banned 10,000 bourgeois books in Hungary," including NS.

114. Anon. Untitled clipping. L'Ecran Français (16 [or 22?] May).
    Notes that Variety accused Pierre Chenal, director of the film NS, of being anti-American.

115. Anon. Untitled clipping. Liberté de l'Esprit (January).
    Summarizes the exchange between W and Joseph Zobel on racism.

116. Anon. Untitled clipping. Norristown Times Herald (10 September).
    Cites W's birthday.

117. Anon. Untitled clipping. Paris Franc-Tireur (5 March).
    Notes that W and others will speak at a meeting of the club of the "Lettres du Monde."

118. Anon. Untitled clipping. Paris Franc-Tireur (27 August).
    Comments on the film NS and its reception at the Venice Film Festival.

119. Anon. Untitled clipping. Le Paris Monde (c. 17 May).
    Reports that the family of Willie MacGee acknowledges the support of W and others.

120. Anon. Untitled clipping. Taunton (Mass.) Gazette (c. 10 February).
    Article on Paul Green mentioning W.

121. Anon. "Vie au ralenti." Paris-Press l'Intransigeant (24 August).
    Notes the excellence of the film NS.

122. Anon. "Wright e i negri." Daesesara (25 January).
    Photograph of W with caption.

123. Anon. "Wright (Richard)." Bibliographie de la France, 140 (5 January), 23.
    Notice of the French translation of NS.

124. Anon. "Wright, Richard," in Kunskapens Bok. Vol. 9. Stockholm: Bokförlaget Natur och Kultur, p. 4987.
    Biographical note.

125. Anon. "Wright, Richard," in Rassegna enciclopedica Labor 1935-1951. Ed. Arturo Barone. Milan: Edizioni Labor, p. 1171.
    Biographical note.

126. Anon. "Wright's 'Native Son.'" The New York Sunday Compass (15 April), p. 21.
    Announces the Hollywood premiere of the film in May.

127. Astre, Georges-Albert. "Le Roman aux Etats-Unis et la crise de l'homme américain." Age Nouveau, No. 60 (April), pp. 25-35.
    Mentions W (pp. 28, 30) as a writer who concentrates on "lost men."

128. B., A. "'Native Son,' di Richard Wright interpretato dallo scrittore stesso." Il gazzettino (23 August).
    Notes that the film NS, an artistic success, was well received at the Venice Film Festival.

129. Baldwin, James. "Many Thousands Gone." Partisan Review, 18 (November-December), 665-680.
    Detailed consideration of the structure, artistry, and impact of NS. Writing in a context of social struggle, W conveys with rage the monstrous stereotype of the black man existing in the white mind. To do so he must divorce Bigger from the complex reality of black group life. For this reason, the novel is unable to explore fully the issues it raises. Nevertheless, NS is "the most powerful and celebrated statement we have yet had of what it means to be a Negro in America" (p. 670).
    Reprinted: 1955.25; 1966.18; 1968.40; 1969.25; 1970.5, 51; 1971.34, 147;

1972.27; 1982.15.

129a. Balen, Šime. "O sjeveroameričkim crncima i njihovoj književnosti." Republika, 7 (June), 508-512.
    After a review of Afro-American history and literature, Balen sketches W's life and literary career. Surpassing other recent black writers, W clearly ranks with Douglass, Dunbar, and McKay. The occasion of this essay is the publication of Crnog djeĉaka, the Serbo-Croatian translation of BB.

130. Beck, Myer P. "Movie Talk: 'Native Son' Is International Job." The New York Sunday Compass (20 May), p. 31.
    Detailed account of the filming of NS, including the conditions W imposed: he would write the screenplay and dialogue; "there were to be no stars in the cast"; "the starkness of the story" would not be modified; some filming would be done in Chicago; and Canada Lee would play Bigger. Lee later withdrew because of production delays.

131. Bergagna, Laura. "Incontri Richard Wright." Stampa sera (19 January).
    Comments on W's personality and works, emphasizing racial protest.

132. Berry, Brewton. Race Relations. Boston: Houghton Mifflin, pp. 177, 178, 425-426.
    Notes W's use of art as a weapon and quotes from "The Ethics of Living Jim Crow."
    Reprinted: 1958.80; 1965.37.

133. Blanzat, Jean. "Les Romans de la semaine." Le Figaro Littéraire (13 January), p. 9.
    Review of the French translation of Nelson Algren's Never Come Morning mentioning W's preface.

134. Boisdeffre, Pierre de. "La Nouvelle Génération répudie J.-P. Sartre." Paris Ce Matin (10 August).
    Notes that W's treatment of the black problem anticipated Sartre's.

135. Bosc, Robert. "A. Koestler, I. Silone, R. Wright, A. Gide, L. Fischer, S. Spender.--Le Dieu des ténèbres." Etudes, 268 (January), 128-129.
    Review of the French translation of The God That Failed listing W as one of the authors.

136. Brewster, Dorothy and John Angus Burrell. "Symbol," in their Modern World Fiction. Paterson, N. J.: Littlefield, Adams, p. 187.
    Mentions Bigger Thomas as a social symbol.

137. Brin, Irene. "Corriere di Roma: Problema insolubile, per 'signore colte.'" Milan Corriere d'informazione (c. 26 January).
    Account of W's lecture on "The Literature of the Negro in the United States" at the Eliseo Theater in Rome.

138. Brown, Lloyd L. "Which Way for the Negro Writer?" Masses & Mainstream, 4 (March), 53-63; (April), 50-59.
    Characterizes the W-Himes school as having "a narrow range of frenzy, shock, brutality, frustration, in which the Negro character is reduced to an inhuman, helpless victim" (p. 52).

139. B.[rown], S.[terling] A. "Negro in the American Theatre," in The Oxford Companion to the Theatre. Ed. Phyllis Hartnoll. London: Oxford University Press, pp. 565-572.
    Contains a favorable brief evaluation of the play NS.
    Reprinted: 1957.152; 1967.19.

140. Buono, Oreste del. "La Francia si ritira dal Festival di Venezia?" Milano sera (23 August).
    Calls the film NS a powerful document of propaganda.

141. Butcher, Margaret Just. "What Europeans Are Asking About Negroes." Negro Digest, 9 (March), 65-69.
    Reprint of 1950.118.

142. Caillet, Gérard. "Connaissance du roman américain." La Vie Médicale (May), pp. 102-110.
    Lists W among postwar American writers read in France.

143. C.[aliver], A.[mbrose]. "Negro," in The World Book Encyclopedia. Ed. J. Morris Jones. Vol. 12. Chicago: Field Enterprises, pp. 5486-5492.
    Reprint of 1947.163.

144. _____. "Spingarn Medal," in The World Book Encyclopedia. Ed. J. Morris Jones. Vol. 15. Chicago: Field Enterprises, p. 7651.
    Reprint of 1947.164.

145. Cameron, Kate. "Wright's 'Native Son' on Criterion Screen." New York Daily News (18 June), p. 36.
    Unfavorable review asserting that the screen adaptation "has lost most of [the story's] dramatic power and its compassionate appeal to the heart." Cameron criticizes Chenal's direction as lacking in finesse, but praises W's "convincing performance" as Bigger. Provides a brief plot summary.

146. Canby, Henry Seidel. "Books That Are Milestones." The Atlantic Monthly, 187 (June), 75-78.
Refers to both NS and BB as autobiography in novel form.

147. Caorsi, Gigi. "'Sangue negro': Film argentino del romanzo di Wright." Gazetta del popolo (23 August).
Favorable review of the film NS praising W for his writing and acting.

148. Cayton, Horace R. "The Psychology of the Negro Under Discrimination," in Race Prejudice and Discrimination. Ed. Arnold M. Rose. New York: Knopf, pp. 276-290.
Partial reprint of 1946.171.

149. Chaunoise, M. "Richard Wright ou la foi en l'homme." La Paix du Monde (5 June).
Quotes W's opinions expressed at a political rally in Paris that neither the United States nor the Soviet Union could stand for freedom because of their commitment to nationalism and propaganda. The function of the writer is to get out of the "impersonal routine of big cities" in order to achieve self-expression and self-realization.

150. Contini, Ermanno. "La produzione argentina ha presentato il film 'Paura' dal romanzo di Wright." Unidentified clipping (23 August).
Rather favorable review of the film NS with extensive plot summary. Chenal's direction has a certain mechanical tone, but otherwise the film is effective.

151. Cook, Alton. "Author Plays Lead in 'Native Son' Film." New York World Telegram (18 June), p. 12.
Unfavorable review charging that the film fails either to convey a message of tolerance or to achieve suspense and polished melodrama. The acting and direction are amateurish. Cook states that he has been "told that the picture has been marred by some cuts made in deference to censors."

152. Corby, Jane. "'Native Son' at the Criterion with Richard Wright Starred." Brooklyn Eagle (18 June), p. 6.
Unfavorable review. Taking the theme to be "that children need decent home surroundings and a sense of security to grow up into good citizens," Corby thinks that the film's development is "on the lurid rather than the thoughtful side." As an actor W is not an adequate substitute for Canada Lee, though he "does an

honest and even impressive job."

153. Crowther, Bosley. "Good Intentions." The New York Times (24 June), Sec. 2, p. 1.
Contains an unfavorable review of the film NS: "the script is so clumsily constructed and it is so amateurishly played by Mr. Wright and a cast of virtual unknowns . . . that it loses all of the strange terror and authenticity of the original."

154. D., L. "Brève rencontre avec Pierre Chenal." La Casablanca Vigie Marocaine (16 January).
Brief interview with Chenal discussing the production of the film NS.

155. Derby, John B. "Novel, The Modern," in The Encyclopedia Americana. Ed. A. H. McDannald. Vol. 20. New York: Americana Corporation, pp. 474-476.
Reprint of 1945.876.

156. D'O., F. "Les Bons Spectacles et les autres." Paris France Journal (2 April), p. 3.
Favorable review of the film NS. The acting is generally remarkable.

157. Dufourcq, Norbert. "La Vie historique: Les Livres." Larousse Mensuel, 12 (January), [23].
Notice of the French translation of The God That Failed mentioning W.

158. Ei., T. "Richard Wright ai 'Sabati letterari.'" Il lavoro domenico (19 January).
Account of W's lecture in Genoa on "The Literature of the Negro in the United States."

159. Elsen, Claude. "Les Essais," in Almanach des Lettres 1951. Ed. André Billy. Paris: Les editions de Flore et La Gazette des Lettres, pp. 48-55.
Mentions W as a contributor to the French translation of The God That Failed.

160. Erval, François. "Intelligence du Monde." La Gazette des Lettres, 7 (15 March), 110-112.
Commenting on the award of the Nobel Prize to Faulkner, Erval notes that W expressed admiration for The Sound and the Fury.

161. Farrell, Frank. "New York--Day by Day: Time of His Life." New York World-Telegram (6 June), p. 23 [?].
Reports that NS was filmed in Argentina to avoid Hollywood racial taboos.

162. Fleg, Edmond. Untitled article.

Paris Droit et Liberté (9-15 February), p. 4.

Quotes BB on Jewish sympathy for blacks and urges protest of a racially unjust court sentence in the United States.

163. Fossati, Luigi. "Un povero film per un povero negro." Rome Avanti! (c. 23 August).

Unfavorable review of the film NS with extensive plot summary. Chenal has failed to realize the intimate dramatic aspects of the novel, and W's acting is not convincing.

164. Fouchet, Max-Pol. "Les Livres étrangers." Paris Carrefour (30 January), p. 8.

Reviewing a book by John Horne Burns, Fouchet quotes W on the "tragic vulgarity" of the life of the American masses.

165. Fréminville, Claude de. "De la part du feu à celle du lion à venir: Wright?" Le Paris Populaire (13 March), p. 4.

Review of Claude McKay's Banjo anticipating a future treatment of the same material by W.

166. Garlington, S. W. "Amusement Row." New York Amsterdam News (16 June), p. 23.

Explains some of the difficulties encountered in making the film NS, scheduled to open on 16 June in New York. Although Garlington considers the novel an American classic and has not seen the film, he fears that it will exacerbate race relations. Three still photographs from the film with captions appear adjacent to Garlington's column.

167. Gérard, Albert. "La Nuit de Jacob." Synthèses, 5 (May), 348-355.

Review of the French translation of The God That Failed discussing W's proletarian background and quoting at length from his contribution, especially to indicate his delight and exultation at the time he was writing his revolutionary poems in the thirties.

168. Giabar. "I 'Martedi letterari' all'Eliseo: Wright con i negri." La libertà d'Italia (25 January).

Reports W's speech at the Eliseo Theater.

169. Gibson, Richard. "Is the Negro Writer Free?" Negro Digest, 9 (September), 43-45.

Reprint of 1951.170.

170. _____. "A No to Nothing." The Kenyon Review, 13 (Spring), 252-255.

Contains a disparaging reference to W as a protest writer.
Reprinted: 1951.169.

171. Goodman, Ezra. "Ezra Goodman." New York Daily News (1 December).

Favorable review of NS, "a provocative and disturbing film."

172. Grey. "Vióse 'Sangre negra.'" La Buenos Aires Epoca.

Favorable notice of the film NS praising W's acting.

173. Gromo, Mario. "Romanzo negro." La schermo del lido (23 August).

Favorable review of the film NS. Powerful and realistic, it is an important work which deserves attention.
Reprinted: 1951.174.

174. _____. "Romanzo negro." La Turin stampa (23 August).

Reprint of 1951.173.

175. Guérin, Daniel. "La Révolte nègre," in his Où va le peuple américain? Vol. 2. Paris: Julliard, pp. 126, 127, 167, 168, 181, 246, 251, 311.

Mentions W, noting his relationship to the Communist Party, citing his opinions, and acknowledging his friendship and assistance.
Translated: 1956.176.

176. Guernsey, Otis L., Jr. "On the Screen." New York Herald Tribune (18 June), p. 10.

Unfavorable review of the film NS arguing that both the novel and the play are better. In the film, "the acting is spotty, the direction weak and the script a loosely organized collection of crises which fail to hold together on an emphatic line." Includes a plot summary.

177. H., M. "Men's Movie." Argosy, 333 (July), 79.

Favorable notice of the film NS with praise for W's acting. "Although technically weak in spots, the production is full of heart and almost painfully effective."

178. Hartung, Philip T. "The Screen." The Commonweal, 54 (29 June), 286.

Contains an unfavorable review of the film NS. Though W does a creditable job as Bigger, the acting is generally amateurish or worse. "In spite of the film's shortcomings, enough of the spirit of Wright's book comes through to make us ashamed of conditions which lead to such tragic ends."

179. Henniger, Paul. "'Native Son' Story Tops Its Actors." The Los Angeles Mirror (13 August), p. 22.
    Rather favorable review of the film. The value of the film's story, deriving from the novel, is high "even if the acting is secondary." Names four of the actors and summarizes the plot.

180. Hoffman, Frederick J. The Modern Novel in America 1900-1950. Chicago: Regnery, pp. 33, 136.
    Quotes disparaging comments on W by Blackmur and Kazin. See 1956.203 and 1963.110 for revised editions with additional remarks on W.

181. Hogan, Peter E., S. S. J. "Wright, Richard. Black Boy." Best Sellers, 11 (15 April), 27.
    Favorable review of the Signet reprint edition. Not for the weak, the work has great power.

182. Hurston, Zora Neale. "Negro, The, in the United States," in The Encyclopedia Americana. Ed. A. H. McDannald. Vol. 20. New York: Americana Corporation, pp. 47-52.
    Mentions W briefly (p. 51b). Reprinted: 1952.45; 1953.157.

183. Jackson, Blyden. "Faith Without Works in Negro Literature." Phylon, 12 (Fourth Quarter), 378-388.
    Contains a brief reference to NS.

184. Jolas, Eugene. "Latin Quarter Is Still Center of Cultural Life." New York Herald Tribune, European edition (Paris Bimillenary Special edition) (12 June), pp. 1, 14, 18.
    Mentions W's fame in France.

185. Jomaco. "Fué exhibida ayer en el cine gran Rex la versión de una novela de Richard Wright." Unidentified clipping.
    Favorable review of the film NS emphasizing the expose of American racism in this "cry of rebellion." Praises W for his portrayal of Bigger Thomas.

186. Jones, John Hudson. "Richard Wright's 'Native Son' a Distorted, Dreary Film." Daily Worker (21 June), p. 11.
    Unfavorable review criticizing the work artistically and politically. Anticlimaxes further weaken trite situations.

187. K., G. "Wright's 'Native Son' Acted by Own Author." Los Angeles Times (13 August), Part III, p. 7.
    Favorable review stating that "the

film's justification [for its brutal realism] is its pitifulness and a sort of rough, unembittered fairness." Praises the acting. Even W's is "spottily excellent."

188. Kann, Red, ed. 1951-52 International Motion Picture Almanac. New York: Quigley Publications, p. 554.
    Lists the film NS.

189. King. "Cinematografía: Fuerza dramatica en 'Sagre [sic] negra.'" El Buenos Aires Mundo (30 March), p. 7.
    Favorable review of the film NS praising its theme and its cinematic artistry. Chenal's direction receives special acclaim, but W's acting leaves something to be desired.

190. Knight, Arthur. "SRL Goes to the Movies: Sweet Are the Uses of Integrity." The Saturday Review of Literature, 34 (7 July), 24-25.
    Contains a rather favorable review of the film NS praising the acting of W and Gloria Madison but complaining of "technical defects." Bigger is more sympathetically presented and the social import is more implicit in the film than in either the novel or the play.

191. K.[nudsen], M.[ogens]. "Wright, Richard," in Vor Tids Leksikon. Ed. A. P. Hansen. Vol. 23. Copenhagen: Aschehoug Dansk Forlag, p. 302.
    Biographical sketch with photograph.

192. Lalou, René. "Le Cru de 1950," in Almanach des Lettres 1951. Ed. André Billy. Paris: Les Éditions de Flore et La Gazette des Lettres, pp. 9-16.
    Mentions W as a contributor to the French translation of The God That Failed (p. 11).

192a. Lamont, William H. F. and Lisle Rose. "Novels, 20th Century American," in Good Reading. Ed. Atwood H. Townsend. New York: The New American Library, pp. 127-131.
    Reprint of 1948.184a; revised reprint of 1941.786a.

193. M., A. "Buena técnica se aprecia en 'Sangre negra.'" El Buenos Aires Pueblo (30 March).
    Favorable review of the film NS praising its cinematic quality but noting that the racial theme has little urgency for an Argentinian audience.

194. Macé, Henri L. "Autour de 'L'Isle des hommes de fer': Il n'y a pas de romans-policiers, il y a seulement des romans." Montpellier Midi Libre (18

January).
    Contains a brief comment on W by Lucien Prioly.

195. Madrid, Francisco. "'Sangre negra' por Richard Wright." Unidentified clipping (May).
    Favorable Buenos Aires magazine review of the Spanish translation of the novel NS. Also praises the Buenos Aires production of the play and criticizes the film. W is not a deliberate prose stylist, but his novel is sincere, powerful, and disturbing.

196. Malavelle, Yvonne. "De Charlie à Orson Welles." La Toulouse Dépêche du Midi (2 January), pp. 1, 6.
    Quotes W's remark that a second Welles would be the end of civilization.

197. Mara, K. A. "Kintopp." Unidentified clipping.
    Brief German notice of the film NS.

198. Margot. "Native Son." Unidentified clipping.
    Favorable German review of NS calling it the first film to provide the black perspective on racial issues.

199. Martin, Mildred. "'Native Son' Is Drama on Earle Screen." Unidentified clipping.
    Unfavorable review complaining of bad acting and direction.

200. Matthiessen, F. O. Theodore Dreiser. The American Men of Letters Series. New York: William Sloane Associates, p. 230.
    Mentions Dreiser's interest in W.

201. Mauriac, Claude. "Le Cinéma: A Venise dans les lagunes du Festival." Le Figaro Littéraire (1 September), p. 10.
    Claims that the film NS bears a stronger impress from director Pierre Chenal than from W.

202. McDonald, Gerald D. "Native Son (Classic Pictures) Adapted from the Novel of Richard Wright." Library Journal, 76 (July), 1141.
    Unfavorable review of the film complaining of poor acting by the white members of the cast. "The film reflects" the good qualities of the novel "only dimly."

203. Michaut, Pierre. "La Biennale de Venise: Vue au jour le jour." La Cinématographie Française (1 September), pp. 3-4.
    Contains a brief note on the film NS.

204. Miller, Maud M. "The Week's New Films: 'Native Son' Does Not Spare Whites." Daily Dispatch (8 December).
    Favorable English review emphasizing W's conviction. "It makes a sincere film . . . even if it does not resolve any racial problems."

205. Mishkin, Leo. "'Native Son' an Amateurish Adaptation of Best Seller." New York Telegraph (18 June).
    Unfavorable review of the film. Though NS as a novel and a play pioneered in treating the racial issue, subsequent works on the same theme have been superior. Not only is the film version "almost embarrassingly awkward and amateurish," but "its themes today seem both hysterical and childish, its staging all in blacks and whites, and its examination of the Negro's place in society crude, one-sided and utterly illogical."

206. Mondadori, Alberto. "Terrore blanco." Epoca (1 September), pp. 56-57.
    Favorable illustrated Italian magazine review of the film NS. Mondadori, the publisher, begins with a personal anecdote of his meeting with W in Paris.

207. Musaraigne. "Martienne." Elle (11 June).
    Contains a brief mention of BB.

208. N., M. "A. Koestler, Silone, Wright, Gide, Fischer, Spender: Le Dieu des ténèbres." Cahiers Critques du Communisme, No. 1 (January), pp. 47-50.
    Review of the French translation of The God That Failed mentioning the grandiose perspective of the class struggle which W presents and his psychological depression when he is rejected by the Communist Party. "A real ex-Communist cannot find the integrity of his personality again," the reviewer remarks.

209. Nestor. "Lo que ví anoche: 'Sangre negra' es una asombrosa hazaña técnica del cine argentino." El Buenos Aires Laborista (30 March).
    Favorable review of the film NS praising the skillful realization in Argentina of an American theme and setting.

210. Nid. "Native Son." Variety (25 April), p. 14.
    Mixed review of the film praising W's performance as Bigger but deploring the work's anti-American perspective.

211. Nolan, William A. Communism Versus the Negro. Chicago: Regnery, p. 143.
    Notes W's opposition to war after the Nazi-Soviet pact.

211a. Nyland, Waino S. "Biography," in Good Reading. Ed. Atwood H. Townsend. New York: The New American Library, pp. 154-156.
   Reprint of 1946.282.

212. O'Hara, Frank Hurburt and Marguerite Harmon Bro. Invitation to the Theater. New York: Harper, p. 48.
   Cites NS as a propaganda play.

213. Oliver, W. E. "'Native Son' Spins Drama with Jolting Realism." Los Angeles Evening Herald & Express (13 August), p. A-14.
   Rather favorable review of the film stressing its documentary quality, which is enhanced by the awkward acting. The realism is grim and at times shocking in this "city tragedy born of fear and slum ignorance."

214. Ottley, Roi. No Green Pastures. New York: Scribner's, pp. 3, 11, 98, 119, 127, 205.
   W is mentioned several times in this account of racism abroad.

215. Panicucci, Alfredo. "La grande Venezia 1951: Capitale del cinema per ventidue giorni." Epoca (1 September?), pp. 51-54.
   Article on the Venice Film Festival mentioning NS and including a still photograph.

216. Pavese, Cesare. "Richard Wright," in his La letteratura americana e altri saggi. Turin: Einaudi, pp. 189-192.
   Originally delivered as a radio talk in May, 1947, this favorable review of BB places it in the context of the Italian response to modern American literature. Far from seeming exotic, W's autobiography will remind Italian readers of their own experience. W's style, praised for its energy and directness, is compared to that of Defoe and Cellini.
   Reprinted: 1971.147.
   Translated: 1970.286.

217. Peck, Seymour. "Today's Movie: Bigger Thomas Comes to Screen in Richard Wright's 'Native Son.'" The New York Daily Compass (18 June), p. 21.
   Extremely unfavorable review of the film. In contrast to the "deep insight" and "flashing illumination" of the novel, the film is "a crude and tawdry and unbalanced shocker" which fails to render dramatically "the vital matter of the forces and motivations in Bigger's life." Peck criticizes the use of an impersonal narrator, the elimination of Max's courtroom speeches, Chenal's direction, and the acting.

218. Peirce, Guglielmo. "Lanterna magica romana: Discorsetto a Wright sui negri." Il Rome tempo (24 January).
   Commentary on W's lecture in Rome.

219. Pelswick, Rose. "'Native Son': Wright Plays Top Role." New York Journal-American (18 June), p. 8.
   Notice of the film summarizing the plot without evaluation.

219a. [Quinn, Kerker]. "Accent."
   Flyer listing W as a contributor to Accent Anthology.

220. R., A. "A colloquio con Wright che scrisse 'Ragazzo negro.'" La Turin nuova stampa (19 January).
   Appraises W's personality. Although he seems cold at first, he is quite congenial on better acquaintance and an excellent conversationalist. Intellectually, he is very widely read, open-minded, and inquisitive.

221. _____. "R. Wright e la poesia negra." La Turin nuova stampa (20 January).
   Account of W's lecture on Afro-American literature.

222. Record, Wilson. The Negro and the Communist Party. Chapel Hill: The University of North Carolina Press, pp. 158, 305.
   Brief references to W.
   Reprinted: 1971.254.

223. Redding, Saunders. On Being Negro in America. Indianapolis: Bobbs-Merrill, pp. 90, 126-127.
   Mentions W's relation to the Communists and his absence from anthologies of American literature despite his worldwide fame.
   Second passage reprinted: 1970.295.

224. Rochefort, Christiane. "Calme à Venise où le Japon donne les leçons de cinéma à l'Occident." Paris Franc-Tireur (31 August).
   Mentions having a cocktail in honor of W and his film NS.

225. _____. "Calme sur le front du festival: Pas encore de gifles à Venise." Paris France-Soir (27 August), pp. 1, 3.
   Notes W's attendance at the Venice Film Festival.

226. Rondi, Gian Luigi. "Sangue negro, di Pierre Chenal." Il Rome tempo (23 August).
   Favorable review of the film NS with extensive plot summary.

227. Rutherford, William A. "Set Up Paris Groups to Battle U. S. Bias." New

York Amsterdam News (27 January).
    Reports that W is president of the
    Franco-American Fellowship and chair-
    man of its program committee.

228. S., D. J. "Expectante suspenso en
las escenas de 'Sangre negra.'" Democra-
cia.
    Favorable review of the film NS
    praising all aspects of the produc-
    tion, including W's acting. The re-
    viewer stresses the terror and sus-
    pense generated by the film.

229. Sala, Vittorio. "L'Argentino 'Sangre negra' presentato da Chenal." Unidentified clipping (23 August [?]).
    Favorable review of the film NS.
    Because of W's involvement, it is an
    excellent and faithful adaptation of
    the novel. Includes a plot summary
    and statements by W explaining the
    need for the film because of the lack
    of realistic treatments of racial
    tensions in the American cinema.
    Reprinted: 1951.230.

230. _____. "Un film argentino rializa
il tono della nostra." Il popolo (23
August).
    Reprint of 1951.229.

231. Sicor. "La letteratura negra
d'America nel pensiero di Richard
Wright." Il corriere di Trieste (1 February).
    Interview with W including discussion
    of his literary methods and comments
    on other writers.

232. Strassberg, Philip. "'Native Son'
at The Criterion." New York Daily Mirror
(18 June), p. 22.
    Unfavorable review of the film com-
    plaining of inadequate acting, espe-
    cially by W and Gloria Madison.

233. Straumann, Heinrich. American Literature in the Twentieth Century. London: Hutchinson's University Library,
pp. 49-50.
    Discusses W as a proletarian novel-
    ist. The best book on American race
    relations, NS is an impressive
    achievement characterized by a repor-
    torial method, consistent authorial
    attitude, and an important theme.
    Reprinted: 1965.119; 1968.198.

234. T., D. "Le Dieu des ténèbres." La
Antwerp Métropole (17 February).
    Review of the French translation of
    The God That Failed mentioning W.

235. Tallenay, Jean-Louis. "Le Douzième
Festival de Venise: un film 'argentin'
honorable." Unidentified clipping.
    Mentions the film NS. On seeing it,

one understands why it could not have
been made in the United States.

236. Tarvin, Harry. "'Native Son' Film
Held 'Terrifying.'" The Denver Post (6
August), p. 25.
    Favorable review summarizing the plot
    and commenting on the seriousness and
    honesty of the film. Though unpol-
    ished, W's acting is effective.

237. Temko, Allan. "An Interview with
'Expatriate' Richard Wright in Paris."
San Francisco Chronicle (30 December),
This World Sec., p. 19.
    W comments on his "feeling" for Eur-
    ope and its historical plight. Temko
    describes W's activities, especially
    with the Franco-American Fellowship.
    Discussing his work in progress, W
    states that he is completing a novel
    and a collection of short stories to
    be called Ten Men.

238. T.[hompson], C.[harles] H. "Wright,
Richard," in The World Book Encyclopedia. Ed. J. Morris Jones. Vol. 18.
Chicago: Field Enterprises, pp. 8932-
8933.
    Reprint of 1947.292.

239. Valentini, Giuseppe. "Cinque uomini
di R. Wright." Letture, 6 (May), 165.
    Review of Fernanda Pivano's transla-
    tion of five stories later collected
    in EM. W's earlier racial protest
    looked to a Marxist solution, but now
    he considers racism an insoluble
    problem.

240. Van Vechten, Carl. "A Note by the
Author," in his Nigger Heaven. New York:
Avon, pp. [187-190].
    Mentions W briefly.
    Reprinted: 1979.269.

241. Vicari, Giambattista. "Richard
Wright al Teatro Eliseo: an che per i
negri il dio rosso ha fallito." Il momento (24 March).
    Account of W's speech at the Eliseo
    Theater. Vicari notes W's disillu-
    sionment with Communism.

242. W., A. "The Screen in Review." The
New York Times (18 June), p. 19.
    Unfavorable review of the film NS, a
    sincere work but much less convincing
    than the novel or the play. In addi-
    tion to summarizing the plot, the
    reviewer complains of pedestrian
    direction and amateurish acting.

243. W., C. "Movies." Jamaica Public
Opinion.
    Favorable review of the film NS, "an
    exciting, disturbing experience for
    its audiences."

244. W., C. A. "Reviews: 'Native Son.'"
The Cinema News and Property Gazette (14
November), p. 6.
    Favorable review of the film praising
    the story, production, treatment,
    acting, and box-office appeal.

245. W., K. "Flucht aus dem Kommunismus." Le Strasbourg Nouvel Alsacien (6
January).
    Review of the French translation of
    The God That Failed mentioning W.

246. Walters, Raymond, Jr. "In Paper
Covers." The Saturday Review of Literature, 34 (17 February), 27.
    Lists the paperback edition of BB, an
    emotionally powerful autobiography.

247. Warfel, Harry R. American Novelists
of Today. New York: American Book Company, p. 468.
    Biographical-critical sketch of W
    with special attention to UTC and NS.
    W's dominant theme is racial protest.

248. Weiler, A. H. "By Way of Report."
The New York Times (13 May), Sec. 2, p.
5.
    Notes that the film NS has been
    booked for the Criterion Theater.

249. Whicher, George F. "The Resurgent
South," in The Literature of the American People. Ed. Arthur Hobson Quinn. New
York: Appleton-Century-Crofts, pp. 914-
926.
    Contains a favorable brief assessment
    of W (p. 920).

250. Winnington, Richard. "Close-Up."
London News Chronicle (30 November).
    Unfavorable review of the film NS
    charging it with an attempt to appeal
    to sentimentality. Bigger is "a bru-
    tal degenerate."

251. Winston, Archer. "Wright's 'Native
Son.'" New York Post (18 June), p.
32.
    Unfavorable review of the film prais-
    ing mildly W's performance and the
    Chicago scenes. Otherwise, the char-
    acterization of whites is superfi-
    cial, continuity is confusing, the
    acting is amateurish, and the pursuit
    of Bigger is melodramatic. All in
    all, the film is "a flat failure."

252. Zunser, Jessie. "Native Son." Cue
(16 June), p. 18.
    Extremely unfavorable review of the
    film calling it an "hysterical melo-
    drama" compared to the novel or the
    play. Complains about the weak acting
    and production. "Several [actors]
    were so bad their voices had to be
    redubbed in Hollywood."

1952

1. Anon. "American Literature. V. Twen-
tieth Century (1920-   ) Part II," in
The Book of Knowledge. Ed. E. V. Mc-
Loughlin. Vol. 14. New York: The Grolier
Society, pp. 5007-5025.
    Contains a paragraph on W (p. 5014)
    commenting on NS and BB.
    Reprinted: 1958.199; 1960.197.

2. Anon. "Black & Blue." Time, 59 (14
April), 112.
    Review of Invisible Man mentioning W
    briefly.

3. Anon. "Canada Lee, 45, Is Dead; Stage
and Film Star." New York Herald Tribune
(10 May), p. 10.
    Obituary of Lee mentioning his role
    in NS and contrasting his own career
    with that of Bigger Thomas.

4. Anon. "First Showing." Bristol (England) Evening Post (22 January).
    Review of the film NS commenting on
    the unusual situation of the author
    playing the lead.

5. Anon. Index Translationum 4. Paris:
Unesco, pp. 45, 223, 245, 291, 460.
    Lists translations of The God That
    Failed into German, BB into Hebrew
    and Serbo-Croatian, Five [sic] Men
    into Italian, and NS into Norwegian.

6. Anon. "'Native Son.'" Bristol (England) Evening World (2 February).
    Notice of the film praising W's act-
    ing. Includes a still photograph from
    the dream sequence.

7. Anon. "Native Son," in Masterpieces
of World Literature in Digest Form. Ed.
Frank N. Magill. New York: Harper, pp.
643-645.
    Reprint of 1949.41.

8. Anon. "'Native Son' Film Ban Upheld."
New York Herald Tribune (16 October), p.
27.
    Reports the banning of the film in
    Ohio because it allegedly would con-
    tribute to racial misunderstanding.

9. Anon. "'Native Son'--Richard Wright;
Tatler." Bristol (England) Evening World
(5 February).
    Brief notice of the film, "a grim
    drama."

10. Anon. "New Richard Wright Novel Out
in February." Jet (11 December), p. 41.
    Announcement of O with a comment from
    W: "People have been asking me why I
    didn't write a book about a Negro
    intellectual and in this book I've
    done it. His psychological problems

will make those of Bigger Thomas look like nothing."

11. Anon. "Novelist Stars." Bristol (England) Evening Post (2 February).
    Favorable notice of the film NS with a still photograph. W's acting is good, but NS is not as successful as Pinky or Intruder in the Dust.

12. Anon. "Ohio Film Ban Appealed." The New York Times (23 July), p. 19.
    Reports an appeal of the decision of the Ohio State Supreme Court banning the film NS because it would foment racial misunderstanding.

13. Anon. "Southern Writing Fills New Text." The Memphis Commercial Appeal (25 May), Sec. V, p. 12.
    Notes that W will be included in The Literature of the South.

14. Anon. Untitled clipping. Bristol (England) Observer (2 February).
    Announces the film NS and includes a photograph of Jean Wallace, who plays Mary Dalton.

15. Anon. "Wright (Ricardo)," in Diccionario enciclopédico U. T. E. H. A. Ed. Luis Doporto. Vol. 10. Mexico, D. F.: Unión Tipográfica Editorial Hispano Americana, p. 1085.
    Very brief biographical note.

16. Anon. "Wright, Richard," in Piccola enciclopedia Garzanti. Vol. 2. Milan: Garzanti, p. 991.
    Biographical note.
    Reprinted: 1956.86.

17. Arban, Dominique. "Romans américains, lecteurs français." Rapports France-Etats-Unis, No. 60 (March), pp. 25-34.
    Lists NS as an important American novel (p. 34). Includes a photograph of W with a caption noting his fame in France.

18. Aristarco, Guido. "Il negro è maggiorenne (ma non nel cinema americano)." Inventario, 4 (September-December), 158-164.
    Includes comparison of W to Chester Himes and Theodore Ward.

19. Armstrong, Alicia. "Writers Tell Why They Answered and Left Red Appeal." The Davenport Daily Times (29 March), p. 8-A.
    Notice of the paperback edition of The God That Failed mentioning W.

20. Barbee, Virginia. "The Shame of Chicago." Ebony, 7 (February), 8.
    Letter to the editor praising W's

essay on Chicago slums and applying his observations to Detroit.

21. Barrett, William. "Black and Blue: A Negro Celine." American Mercury, 74 (June), 100-104.
    Review of Invisible Man with a brief contrast between Ellison's protagonist and Bigger Thomas (p. 100).

22. Beatty, Richmond Croom, Floyd C. Watkins, and Thomas Daniel Young. "Richard Wright," in their The Literature of the South. Chicago: Scott, Foresman, p. 647.
    Headnote to an excerpt from BB.
    Reprinted: 1968.218.

23. Beauvoir, Simone de. America Day by Day. Trans. Patrick Dudley. London: Duckworth, pp. 20, 27, 33-34, 47, 49-50, 80, 85, 187, 191, 210-213, 214, 240, 243, 249, 250, 257, 262, 264, 265-266, 267-269.
    Translation of 1948.131.

24. Blackmur, R. P. Language as Gesture. New York: Harcourt, Brace, pp. 413-414.
    Unfavorable comments on NS, comparing it to The Grapes of Wrath and Crime and Punishment. It "is one of those books in which everything is undertaken with seriousness except the writing."

25. Bornet, Vaughn D. "Historical Scholarship, Communism, and the Negro." The Journal of Negro History, 38 (July), 304-324.
    Review of Wilson Record's The Negro and the Communist Party and William A. Nolan's Communism Versus the Negro including discussion of comments on W in The Journal of Negro History and reviews of NS in the white press (pp. 314-316).

26. Bowling, Mrs. G. E. "Shame of Chicago." Ebony, 7 (March), 10.
    Letter to the editor criticizing W's essay on Chicago slums for accentuating the negative. "I do believe he should spend more of his time writing good clean books about Negroes."

27. Brooks, Van Wyck. The Confident Years: 1885-1915. New York: Dutton, p. 550.
    Comments on W in relation to naturalism, calling NS a "masterly novel."
    Reprinted: 1955.31.

28. Brown, Lloyd L. "The Deep Pit." Masses & Mainstream, 5 (June), 62-64.
    Unfavorable review of Invisible Man. "Ellison is . . . a disciple of the Richard Wright-Chester Himes school and shares . . . their bitter aliena-

tion from the Negro people, their hatred and contempt of the Negro working masses, their renegades' malice--and their servility to the masters" (p. 64).
Partially reprinted: 1970.71.

29. C., B. R. "Richard Wright's 'Native Son.'" The Christian Science Monitor (8 May), p. 4.
Unfavorable review of the film complaining of poor acting by W and others, inadequate motivation, and static direction. With these defects the film is merely "a grisly and meaningless melodrama."

30. Cassidy, T. E. "A Brother Betrayed." The Commonweal, 56 (2 May), 99-100.
Review of Invisible Man ending with a brief contrast of Ellison and W.

31. Crossman, Richard. "Introduction," in his The God That Failed. New York: Bantam Books, pp. 1-10.
Reprint of 1949.92.

32. E., H. "Sort uheld." Oslo Tirsdag (5 February).
Unfavorable Norwegian review of the film NS. While noting its attempt to break down stereotyped screen images of blacks, the reviewer argues that it is disappointing because it fails to arouse indignation or sympathy.

33. Fanon, Frantz. Peau noire, masques blancs. Préface de Francis Jeanson. Paris: Editions du Seuil, pp. 140, 179.
Comments on fear as the motivation of Bigger's behavior and mentions a woman who rebuked W and Simone de Beauvoir for walking together on the streets of New York.
Translated: 1967.37.

34. Gibson, Rochelle. "Among Books and Authors." Wichita Daily Beacon (30 November), Sunday Magazine Sec., p. 1.
Includes an announcement of O and mention of W's residency in Paris.
Reprinted: 1952.35, 36.

35. _____. "Book Notes." Roanoke Times (30 November), p. 26.
Reprint of 1952.34.

36. _____. "Look Behind the Book--Notes Hopeful Facts About American Reds; 'Great Frontier' Due; Final Santayana Volume." Youngstown Vindicator (30 November), Sec. C., p. 17.
Reprint of 1952.34.

37. Glicksberg, Charles I. "Bias, Fiction, and the Negro." Phylon, 13 (Second Quarter), 127-135.
Contains three brief references to W.

38. _____. "Literature and Society." The Arizona Quarterly, 8 (Summer), 128-139.
Cites W among other writers who rejected Communism.
Reprinted: 1978.114.

39. H., H. "Ex-Communists." The Springfield (Mass.) Sunday Republican (27 January), p. 4D.
Favorable notice of the paperback edition of The God That Failed mentioning W.

40. Halper, Albert. "Foreword," in his This Is Chicago: An Anthology. New York: Holt, pp. v-x.
Mentions W as a member of the "Chicago School."

41. _____. "'South Side Boy' Richard Wright," in his This Is Chicago: An Anthology. New York: Holt, p. 130.
Headnote to an excerpt from NS sketching W's background. Before the novel, Halper asserts, W "had written hundreds of poems, dozens of short stories, and several novels."

42. Harkness, David J. "Greenville Holds High Spot in Mississippi's Literature." The Memphis Commercial Appeal (18 January), Sec. V, p. 12.
Survey of Mississippi writers includes a biographical paragraph on W.

43. Hazard, Eloise Perry. "The Author." The Saturday Review, 35 (12 April), 22.
Mentions W's influence on Ralph Ellison.

44. Hook, J. N., Ellen Burkhart, and Louise Lane. Illinois Authors and A Literary Map of Illinois. Urbana: The Illinois Association of Teachers of English, p. 26.
Contains a brief biographical note on W, who also appears on the map.

45. Hurston, Zora Neale. "Negro, The, in the United States," in The Encyclopedia Americana. Ed. Lavinia P. Dudley. Vol. 20. New York: Americana Corporation, pp. 47-52.
Reprint of 1951.182.

46. Kustermeier, Rudolf. "Ich besuchte Richard Wright." Die Welt, 11 (6 November).
Describes a visit to W's Paris apartment and summarizes W's career. Quotes W's praise of Paris as the world's greatest city.

47. Leavell, Rozell. "The Shame of Chicago." Ebony, 7 (February), 8.
Letter to the editor praising W's literary standing and his essay on Chicago slums, but expressing dismay

over his expatriation. "I would think that a man of Wright's ability and intelligence would remain right here in American and fight for the things he writes so well about."

48. Lennox, Roger. "Film on Color Bar." Bristol (England) Evening World (31 January).
    Favorable review of the film NS, "a triumph for Richard Wright."

49. Locke, Alain. "The High Price of Integration: A Review of the Literature of the Negro for 1951." Phylon, 13 (First Quarter), 7-18.
    Compares briefly Willard Motley to W.

50. _____. "The Negro in American Literature," in New World Writing. New York: The New American Library of World Literature, pp. 18-33.
    Includes brief comments on NS, "a masterpiece of realism." Locke regrets W's Communism.

51. _____. "Some Outstanding American Negroes," in The Book of Knowledge. Ed. E. V. McLoughlin. Vol. 12. New York: Grolier, pp. 4427-4433.
    Contains favorable comments on W as "the leading Negro writer of today." Reprinted: 1958.187; 1960.190.

51a. Logan, Rayford W. "The American Negro: Background and Contributions," in One America. Third edition. Ed. Francis J. Brown and Joseph S. Roucek. New York: Prentice-Hall, pp. 32-44.
    Mentions W briefly (p. 41).

52. M., W. "New York Times Book Critic Explores Contemporary Novel." The Dayton Daily News (4 May), Sec. 4, p. 23.
    Review of Orville Prescott's In My Opinion discussing his contention that W's own career contradicts the thesis of environmental determinism in NS.

53. Mandé, Philippe. Ecrivain U. S. A., écrivain U. R. S. S. Paris: Éditions Téqui, pp. 21, 28.
    Mentions W as a racial novelist.

54. Mayoux, Jean-Jacques. "Romans américains, lecteurs français." Rapports France-Etats-Unis, No. 60 (March), pp. 27-31.
    Quotes W on Faulkner as a Southern novelist.

55. Meriwether, Otis W. "Shame of Chicago." Ebony, 7 (March), 10, 13.
    Letter to the editor attacking W's "abortive and highly revolting attack upon the Negro citizens of the fair city of Chicago."

55a. Nyland, Waino S. "Biography," in Good Reading. Ed. Atwood H. Townsend. Mentor Books 76. New York: The New American Library, pp. 123-128.
    Revised reprint of 1946.282. Reprinted: 1954.151a; 1960.206a.

56. Ottley, Roi. "Blazing Novel Relates a Negro's Frustrations." Chicago Sunday Tribune Magazine of Books (11 May), p. 4.
    Review of Invisible Man noting that it "contains echoes of Richard Wright's shocking prose."

57. Parsons, Margaret. "Book Chat." The Worcester Evening Gazette (27 December), p. 5.
    Contains an announcement of O.

58. Prescott, Orville. "Books of the Times." The New York Times (16 April), p. 25.
    Review of Invisible Man comparing Ellison favorably to W.

59. _____. In My Opinion. Indianapolis: Bobbs-Merrill, pp. 40-49.
    Discusses W in a chapter entitled "The Power of Environment." Praises both NS and BB. W's talent enabled him to surpass the limits of literary naturalism.

60. Price, Gwendolyn. "The Shame of Chicago." Ebony, 7 (February), 7-8.
    Letter to the editor admitting W's literary skill, but arguing that his essay overemphasizes the ugly side of Chicago.

60a. [Quinn, Kerker]. "Start the New Year with a Subscription to Accent."
    Flyer listing W as a contributor to Accent Anthology.

61. Rahv, Philip. Image and Idea: Twenty Essays on Literary Themes. Norfolk, Conn.: New Directions, p. 146.
    Mentions NS as an example of "exposure-literature." Reprinted: 1969.198a.

61a. Rose, Lisle A. "20th Century American Novels," in Good Reading. Ed. Atwood H. Townsend. Mentor Books 76. New York: The New American Library, pp. 65-74.
    Reprint of 1948.184a; revised reprint of 1941.786a.

62. Scherman, David E. and Rosemarie Redlich. "Richard Wright," in their Literary America. New York: Dodd, Mead, p. 169.
    Consists of a note on Bigger, a passage from NS describing former mansions now slums on the South Side of Chicago, and a photograph of such

houses.

63. Sonderegger, Leo. "St. Cloud Board Keeps List Secret: Censors Brand Prize-winning Novels 'Unfit.'" The Minneapolis Star (24 December), pp. 1, 3.
Reports that NS is among books banned in St. Cloud, Minnesota.

64. Stevenson, David L. "Novel, The," in The Encyclopedia Americana. Ed. Lavinia P. Dudley. Vol. 20. New York: Americana Corporation, pp. 467-476.
Mentions W briefly (p. 472).
Reprinted: 1953.233; 1955.79; 1956. 312; 1957.329; 1958.256; 1960.244; 1963.174.

65. Temko, Allan. "Paris Letter: Many U. S. Literary Lights Are Summering on the Seine." San Francisco Chronicle (17 August), This World Sec., p. 23.
Mentions W and his work in progress.

66. Wagenknecht, Edward. Cavalcade of the American Novel. New York: Holt, p. 496.
Brief discussion of W in a section on authors not treated in the main text. Praises NS as social protest, mentions BB and UTC, and contrasts W with Langston Hughes.

66a. Ward, Matthew. Indignant Heart. New York: New Books, p. 182.
Mentions "Richard Wright's story of a trial in the Communist Party," comparing it to his own similar experience with Trotskyists.
Reprinted: 1978.75.

67. Webster, Harvey Curtis. "Inside a Dark Shell." The Saturday Review, 35 (12 April), 22-23.
Review of Invisible Man mentioning W briefly.

68. Winslow, Henry F. "The Shame of Chicago." Ebony, 7 (February), 8-9.
Letter to the editor praising W's essay and attacking the Ebony editorial ("Return of the Native Son") critical of it.

69. _____. "Unending Trial." The Crisis, 59 (June-July), 397-398.
Review of Invisible Man comparing Ellison unfavorably to W, who had an economic style and a "profound and sustained tragic sense."

70. Ynduráin, Francisco. "La novela norteamericana en los últimos treinta años. Ensayo de interpretación." Arbor, 22 (May), 67-88.
Mentions W as a protest novelist. BB and UTC indict both racist whites and passive blacks.

1. A., D. G. "Death and Violence." Winnipeg Evening Tribune (c. 30 May).
Review of O praising the narrative but complaining of theme and ideology.
Reprinted: 1953.2.

2. _____. "Death and Violence." Winnipeg Free Press (30 May), p. 13.
Reprint of 1953.1.

3. Adams, Phoebe. "Reader's Choice: The Wrong Road." The Atlantic Monthly, 191 (May), 77-78.
Unfavorable review of O viewing it mainly as a forum for W's conclusions on the nature of humanity and the future of society. His thesis is that "science and industrial society, by destroying the restraining power of traditional religion, give men of sufficient courage the opportunity to feel, and act, as gods." Cross is alienated and W is pessimistic, but the novel is disappointing because of "a hiatus between means and ends," between plot and theme.
Reprinted: 1978.209.

4. Ahorsey, Kofi. "Nkrumah Told: Go Ahead with Plan." Accra Daily Graphic (22 June), pp. 1, 8.
Reports that when W was introduced at a political rally, he said that he "was no stranger" and "felt at home" in the Gold Coast.

5. Algren, Nelson. "Jungle of Tenements." The Saturday Review, 36 (6 June), 16.
Review of Mark Kennedy's The Pecking Order comparing it to NS.

6. Allen, T. J. "Black God in Search of Himself." Saturday Night, 68 (25 July), 16.
Favorable review of O arguing that unlike many American novelists, W is both tragedian and artist. Damon's mind sets him apart from others. He looks for a rationale, not a credo. Of the two long discourses at the end, Damon's is successful, but Houston's fails. W is better with intense feeling than with profound thought.

7. Altshuler, Melvin. "An Important, But Exasperating, Book: Great Writer Wallows in Plot." The Washington Post (22 March), p. 6B.
Mixed review of O. After a brilliant beginning, the novel suffers from an excessively complicated and implausible plot and some sophomoric ideas. Nevertheless, it is an important work because W de-emphasizes the racial

angle, develops the important concept of the outsider, provides an excellent analysis of Communism, and writes and constructs the novel well "despite its wanderings and waste." Reprinted: 1978.209.

8. Anon. "Best Seller List." The New York Times Book Review (12 April), p. 18.
Lists O in sixteenth place in the fiction category.

9. Anon. "Black Boy Faces Reds." Toronto Daily Star (3 January), p. 7.
Announcement of O.

10. Anon. "Book of the Week: The Outsider by Richard Wright." Jet, 3 (26 March), 42.
Unfavorable review emphasizing the novel's similarity to NS. Despite some brilliant writing, the extremes of W's "almost psychopathic lust and violence" ruin O.
Reprinted: 1978.209.

11. Anon. "Book Review." The Philadelphia Tribune (3 March), pp. 12, 14.
Consists of an introductory paragraph and excerpts from W's letter to his publisher about O.

12. Anon. "Books-Authors." The New York Times (26 October), p. 19.
Notice of Carl Milton Hughes's The Negro Novelist mentioning W.

13. Anon. "Books: Seven Negro Books Set for Spring Publication." Jet, 3 (19 February), 47.
Contains an announcement of O and a photograph of W.

14. Anon. "The Bookseller's Almanac." The Retail Bookseller, 56 (March), 54-57.
Contains a notice of O emphasizing its power to shock and predicting good sales.

15. Anon. "Brief Notes on Recent Novels." Oakland Tribune (22 March), Knave Sec., p. 2-C.
Contains a favorable notice of O pointing out the theme of the novel as "the plight of man seeking freedom and individuality in an antagonistic society."

16. Anon. "Censorship Reported in Minnesota Cities." Publishers' Weekly, 163 (7 February), 757-758.
Reports that NS is among the books barred from sale in St. Cloud, Minnesota.

17. Anon. "Cross Section." The New York

Times Book Review (19 April), p. 8.
Notes the divided response to O and quotes from five reviews.

18. Anon. "A Decade of Negro Novelists." New York Herald Tribune (22 October), p. 23.
Notice of Carl Milton Hughes's The Negro Novelist mentioning NS.

19. Anon. Dust jacket of Negerjongen. By Richard Wright. Trans. J. N. C. Van Dietsch. Utrecht: Atlas Reeks.
Blurb on the back jacket of the Dutch translation of BB.

20. Anon. Dust jacket of The Outsider. New York: Harper.
Back cover is a large photograph of W. Front inside flap contains a publisher's blurb; back inside flap contains an unsigned autobiographical sketch by W.

21. Anon. "Grim Chicago, Harlem Scenes in Richard Wright's 'Outsider.'" Toronto Daily Star (28 March), p. 7.
Unfavorable review objecting to the novel's lack of morality and to the influence of Sartre. W stresses ideas more than characters. It is a brutal but sincere book.

22. Anon. "Horror, Violence Stalk 'Outsider.'" The Clarksdale Press Register (18 April), p. 2.
Mixed review of O criticizing its clumsy style and contrived plot but attesting to its shocking power and its concern with large themes. The review notes approvingly W's anti-Communism.

23. Anon. Index Translationum 5. Paris: Unesco, pp. 20, 226, 404, 410.
Lists translations of TMBV into German, BB into Japanese, an anthology containing W into Serbo-Croatian, and The God That Failed into Portuguese.

24. Anon. "Lamming, George. In the Castle of My Skin." Bulletin from Virginia Kirkus' Bookshop Service, 21 (15 August), 545.
Mentions W's introduction.

25. Anon. "Latest Novel." The Boston Guardian (14 February), p. 2.
Advance notice of O.

26. Anon. "Native Doesn't Live Here." Time, 61 (30 March), 90-92.
Unfavorable review of O noting W's past association with Communists, who will be displeased with this novel. W's universal protagonist sees the world "bereft of values and decency" and heading for world-wide totali-

tarianism. The novel's soapbox con-
glomerate of violence, coincidence,
and bombast leaves the reader bored.
Reprinted: 1978.209.

27. Anon. "New Books at Library." Hat-
boro (Pa.) Public Spirit (23 April), p.
C-5.
Mixed review of O praising the philosophical speculations but criticizing
the melodrama.

28. Anon. "New Richard Wright Novel to
be Reviewed in 'Worker.'" Daily Worker
(5 May), p. 4.
Announces Abner Berry's review of O,
forthcoming on 10 May. It will offer
"a convincing explanation of the
deterioration of a once promising
artist."

29. Anon. "Nkrumah, Supreme Head." The
Accra Spectator Daily (19 June).
Reports that W accompanied Nkrumah to
a public appearance and a private
celebration.

30. Anon. "'The Outsider,' by Richard
Wright." Montreal Daily Star (11 April),
p. 18.
Unfavorable review. "This sort of
story is unsatisfactory, melodramatic, and not calculated to enhance
the author's reputation in any way."

31. Anon. "The Outsider, by Richard
Wright." The Cleveland Press (2 December).
Brief notice of "a novel of the dark-
ness-and-blight school."

32. Anon. "The Outsider by Richard
Wright." The Monetary Times, 121 (May),
98.
Notice emphasizing the work's existentialism.

33. Anon. "The Outsider. By Richard
Wright." The Saturday Review, 36 (11
April), 9.
Advertisement.

34. Anon. "The Outsider. By Richard
Wright." The Saturday Review of Litera-
ture, 36 (11 April), 62.
Brief, nonevaluative notice.

35. Anon. "'The Outsider,' by Richard
Wright." Youngstown Vindicator (15
March), Sec. C, p. 21.
Brief notice mentioning the anti-
Communist theme.

36. Anon. "The Outsider, by Richard
Wright (Harper)." The New Yorker, 29 (28
March), 127-128.
Mixed review. Cross Damon's charac-
terization and the narrative of phy-

sical and mental flight are impressive, but W's "ideological debates"
impede the action, and the writing is
uneven.

37. Anon. "The Outsider. Richard
Wright." The Retail Bookseller, 56
(March), 76.
Favorable review finding the novel as
shocking as NS. It should become "a
bestseller and best renter."

38. Anon. "Publishers' Promotion Plans."
The Retail Bookseller, 56 (March), 44-
51.
Lists O and specifies plans (p. 47).

39. Anon. "Publishers' Row." The New
York Times Book Review (11 January), p.
8.
Contains an announcement of O.

40. Anon. "Ralph Ellison--Fiction Winner." The Crisis, 60 (March), 154-156.
Notes W's influence on Ellison's
early development.

41. Anon. "Reverie of Frustration." The
Nation, 176 (18 April), 331-332.
Unfavorable review of O finding it
disappointing. The story is similar
to that of Invisible Man, but more
pessimistic in theme. Cross Damon is
"an abstract monster" rather than a
credible character. In sum, "the book
is bad, but only as a work of genuine
talent can be bad, and nevertheless
full of interest."
Reprinted: 1978.209.

42. Anon. "Richard Wright." New Harper
Books (March-June), pp. 54-55.
Publisher's advertisement for O. The
following sales figures are cited:
NS--65,550 trade, 487,670 club and
reprint; BB--154,475 trade, 723,838
club and reprint.

43. Anon. "Richard Wright." The New York
Times Book Review (22 March), p. 7.
Large advertisement for O.

44. Anon. "Richard Wright." The New York
Times Book Review (12 April), p. 24.
Advertisement for O.

45. Anon. "Richard Wright." The Publishers' Weekly, 163 (28 February), [1027].
Full-page advertisement for O.

46. Anon. "Richard Wright." The Retail
Bookseller, 56 (March).
Advertisement for O.

47. Anon. "Richard Wright Has Two New
Novels." Jet, 3 (5 March), 49.
Announces O and a nearly completed
short novel. Also describes briefly

W's routine in Paris.

48. Anon. "Richard Wright to Publish New Novel." The Philadelphia Tribune (14 February), p. 9.
    Announcement of O.

49. Anon. "Scranton Public Library Notes." Scranton Sunday Scrantonian (26 April), p. 60.
    Contains a notice of O briefly summarizing the plot.

50. Anon. "Something Extra in 'Outsider.'" Little Rock Arkansas Gazette (21 June), p. 6F.
    Review of O commending the story's power but finding the ideological discussions and anti-Communist ideology superfluous, "something extra" that adds little. Cross Damon's situation is supraracial.

51. Anon. "Three Big Books of Next Week." The Roanoke Times (15 March), p. 28.
    Includes a brief announcement of O.

52. Anon. "Tips for the Bookseller." The Publishers' Weekly, 163 (3 January), 45-48.
    Announces publication date of 18 March for O, a novel about the struggles of a black man against both fascism and communism.

53. Anon. "U. S. Negro Novelist Arrives." Accra Daily Echo (19 June).
    Report on W's arrival in Accra noting that he is collecting material for a new book.

54. Anon. Untitled clipping. The New York Times.
    Announces the publication of O on 18 March.

55. Anon. Untitled clipping. The New Yorker, 29 (26 September), 139.
    Catalogs the several appearances of the phrase "woman as body of woman" in O.

56. Anon. Untitled clipping. Parsons Daily Sun (13 June), p. 9.
    Notice of O quoting from W's comments on it and emphasizing its violence.

57. Anon. Untitled clipping. Scranton Tribune (c. 25 April).
    Brief notice of O outlining the plot.

58. Anon. "What America Is Reading." New York Herald Tribune Book Review (19 April), p. 23.
    Lists O in eighteenth place in the fiction category.

59. Anon. "What America Is Reading." New York Herald Tribune Book Review (3 May), p. 15.
    Lists O in twenty-second place in the fiction category.

60. Anon. "What America Is Reading." New York Herald Tribune Book Review (10 May), p. 15.
    Lists O in twenty-first place in the fiction category.

61. Anon. "What America Is Reading." New York Herald Tribune Book Review (17 May), p. 35.
    Lists O in twenty-sixth place in the fiction category.

62. Anon. "Wright," in Bonniers Folklexikon. Ed. Axel Elvin. Vol. 5. Stockholm: Bonniers, pp. 1578-1579.
    Contains a biographical note on W.

63. Anon. "Wright, Richard," in The American Peoples Encyclopedia. Ed. Franklin J. Meine. Vol. 20. Chicago: Spencer Press, p. 403.
    Biographical sketch.
    Reprinted: 1967.7.

64. Anon. "Wright, Richard," in The Columbia-Viking Desk Encyclopedia. Ed. William Bridgwater. New York: Viking, p. 1078.
    Brief biographical note.
    Reprinted: 1960.107.

65. Anon. "Wright, Richard. The outsider." Book Review Digest (August).
    Excerpts or lists sixteen reviews.

66. Anon. "Wright, Richard. The outsider." The Booklist, 49 (1 March), 213-214.
    Review pointing out that for Cross Damon life is a succession of traps. The novel is too melodramatic, but it deals with important themes of man's freedom, isolation, and responsibility.

67. Anon. "Wright, Richard. The outsider." The Booklist, 49 (15 March), 238.
    Announces publication date of 18 March and refers to the review in the issue of 1 March.

68. Anon. "Wright, Richard. The Outsider." Bulletin from Virginia Kirkus Bookshop Service, 21 (15 January), 54.
    Review recognizing the "horrifying and disturbing" qualities of O but claiming that the novel's "muted" emotion leaves the reader "shocked--but unmoved."

69. Anon. "Wright, Richard. The outsider." The Publishers' Weekly, 163 (21

March), 1404.
   Brief, nonevaluative notice.

70. Anon. "Wright, Richard. The Outsider." The United States Quarterly Book
Review, 9 (June), 166-167.
   Mixed review. The use of violence and
   coincidence impedes the novel's credibility, but its ideas are important.
   It is a "nihilistic chronicle of
   modern man, not just the Negro man."
   W may not have advanced as a novelist, but O is too disquieting to be
   ignored.
   Reprinted: 1978.209.

71. Anon. "Wright Sees New Book 'Offensive' to Negroes." Jet, 3 (12 March),
43.
   Announces O and reports that although
   W considers the theme nonracial, he
   acknowledges that many black readers
   will find the work offensive.

72. Anon. "Wright's Second." Newsweek,
41 (23 March), 113.
   Mixed review of O comparing W to
   Victor Hugo and Dostoevsky, but most
   of all to himself. "Cross is a sharply drawn character, as valid as the
   Bigger of 'Native Son,' yet he is
   never so fearfully driven, impassioned, or motivated."

73. Arnavon, Cyrille. Histoire littéraire des Etats-Unis. Paris: Librarie
Hachette, p. 340.
   Refers unfavorably to W's "pamphlet-
   novels," which may be literally true
   but are too simplified to be artistic.

74. Asilijoe, E. K. "Negro Journalist on
Study Tour." Accra Daily Graphic (24
June), p. 2.
   Reports that W says that while he has
   no preconceptions about his six-month
   stay in the Gold Coast, his African
   descent makes it "inescapable" that
   he will view "things African" favorably.

75. B., M. H. "Clearing the Desk." The
El Paso Times (15 March), p. 6.
   Mentions W on the Harper spring list.

76. B., V. A. "Violent Story." Trenton
(N. J.) Evening Times (14 June), Part 4,
p. 12.
   Review of O emphasizing Sartre's
   existentialist influence. Communism
   controls Cross Damon, who learns too
   late to value freedom.

77. Baldwin, James. "Everybody's Protest
Novel." Perspectives USA, No. 2 (Win-
ter), pp. 93-100.
   Reprint of 1949.79.

78. Barkham, John. "Brief Reviews: The
Outsider, by Richard Wright." Buffalo
Evening News (21 March), Magazine Sec.,
p. 7.
   Unfavorable review objecting to the
   novel's extreme sensationalism but
   approving its anti-Communism.
   Reprinted: 1953.79, 80, 81, 82, 83,
   84, 85, 86.

79. _____. "Communism No Haven for U. S.
Negroes." Tucson Daily Citizen (21
March), p. 24.
   Reprint of 1953.78.

80. _____. "Kremlin Gods Shown Made of
Tin in Richard Wright's Violent Novel."
The Philadelphia Sunday Bulletin (12
April), Metropolitan Sec., p. 6.
   Reprint of 1953.78.

81. _____. "Negro Novelist Disillusioned
by Communism." The Charlotte Observer
(22 March), Sec. C, p. 21.
   Reprint of 1953.78.

82. _____. "Novel Bares Author's Rift
with Tin Gods." The Times-Picayune New
Orleans States (22 March), Sec. Two, p.
6.
   Reprint of 1953.78.

83. _____. "Red Line Rejected." The
Dallas Daily Times Herald (14 June),
Sec. 8, p. 5.
   Reprint of 1953.78.

84. _____. "The Tin Gods." The Roanoke
Times (22 March), p. 22.
   Reprint of 1953.78.

85. _____. "The World of Books: The
Outsider. By Richard Wright." Easton
(Pa.) Express (23 March), p. 23.
   Reprint of 1953.78.

86. _____. "Wright Turns on Tin Gods of
the Kremlin." Toledo Sunday Blade (22
March), Sec. 5, p. 2.
   Reprint of 1953.78.

87. Bedell, W. D. "Wright Grapples with
Machine Age Mankind." Houston Post (22
March), Sec. 7, p. 7.
   Favorable review of O as a philosophical novel concerning modern
   man's fearful confrontation of scientific and industrial reality without
   the sustaining myths of the past. The
   racial theme is unimportant in this
   novel.

88. Berry, Abner W. "The Freedom to
Murder." The Worker (10 May), pp. 8, 14.
   Unfavorable review of O attacking
   sharply its anti-Communism and its
   fictional implausibility. The message
   that freedom is achieved through

killing is abhorrent. From his early literary promise and commitment to his people, W has degenerated into a life-denying egoist. "He has squandered his talent, prostituted his art, and thereby deserted humanity."

89. _____. "Not So Simple." Masses & Mainstream, 6 (September), 55-58.
Review of Langston Hughes's Simple Takes a Wife containing references to "the 'arty' degeneracy" of W and to Cross Damon as a "fascistic killer."

90. Bixler, Paul. Untitled article. Newsletter on Intellectual Freedom, 1 (February), 5.
Mentions W among authors whose books were banned in St. Cloud, Minnesota.

91. Bontemps, Arna. "Three Portraits of the Negro." The Saturday Review, 36 (28 March), 15-16.
Review of O and two other novels. Exemplifying a new vogue of writing involving the "Negro problem," W in O has transcended the role of rebellious black boy from Mississippi and moved on to Parisian existentialism. Though treating a black protagonist from Chicago, the novel is not about the racial problem, but about universal corruption. Cross Damon "carries on his mind a problem which he cannot share"--woman. W uses melodrama as a device for the hero's conscious awakening. The conflict is that his consciousness seeks to drag him back to what he is attempting to flee. O is a gripping novel.
Reprinted: 1978.209.

92. Bowles, Patrick. "Everyman His Own Outsider." Points, No. 17 (Autumn), 51-55.
Unfavorable review of O comparing it to Camus's L'Etranger. W indulges excessively in verbose philosophizing, much of it intellectually confused. Nevertheless, he engages some of the basic issues of the middle of the twentieth century.

93. Boyle, Sarah Patton. "Some Racial Tensions." Richmond Times-Dispatch (22 March), p. A-9.
Mixed review of O praising W's literary skill but criticizing his lack of an ideological center. The novel movingly presents blacks as outsiders, but the philosophy implied is "negation for negation's sake."
Reprinted: 1978.209.

94. B.[radley], V.[an] A.[llen]. "The Book Browser: Violent Story." Trenton (N. J.) Sunday Times Advertiser (14 June), Part 4, p. 12.

Reprint of 1953.96.

95. _____. "Book Reflects Change in Richard Wright." The Indianapolis Times (29 March), p. 30.
Reprint of 1953.96.

96. _____. "'The Outsider': Story of Negro's Search for Meaning to Life." Chicago Daily News (25 March), p. 30.
Review summarizing W's transition from Communism to "Sartre's dark and brooding philosophy of existentialism." The novel itself is "absorbing but rarely convincing." The review ends with a plot summary.
Reprinted: 1953.94, 95.

97. Breit, Harvey. "In and Out of Books." The New York Times Book Review (19 April), p. 8.
Contains excerpts from reviews of O--ten favorable, ten unfavorable, ten noncommital.

98. _____. "Wright You Are." The New York Times Book Review (22 March), p. 8.
Recalls a chance meeting with W in Paris. The city has enabled W to think as an insider as well as an outsider. He has a particular affinity with existentialism.

99. Brooks, Van Wyck. The Writer in America. New York: Dutton, pp. 98-99.
Notes that France derives its impression of American race relations from the works of W.

100. Brown, Lloyd L. "Outside and Low." Masses & Mainstream, 6 (May), 62-64.
Unfavorable review of O denouncing W as a renegade from Communism. Brown reduces the ideas of the novel to the "simple and salable [sic]: homicide and anti-Communism." He also complains about critics who praise the work.
Reprinted: 1978.209.

101. Burley, Dan. "People Are Talking About." Jet, 3 (23 April), 51.
Notes that "Wright's new short novel [SH] . . . is already in the hands of his agents."

102. Butler, G. Paul. "Great Lakes Tycoon." New York Daily Mirror (22 March).
Contains a brief notice of O, "a hard story, disturbing, realistic."

103. Byam, Milton S. "Wright, Richard. The Outsider." Library Journal, 78 (15 April), 732.
Mixed review. According to W, man must seek his freedom through detachment. The method of the novel resembles that of Sartre or Celine, though

W is more of a pamphleteer than either of these authors. The writing is powerful, but it is marred by some fake dialogue and weak characterization.

104. Byrom, Elvin. "New Novel by Wright Is Study of Human Motives." Beckley Daily News Digest (18 August).
Favorable review of O with a full plot summary. The novel is superior to W's earlier work because it probes human motives more deeply. Byrom stresses the anti-Communist theme.

105. C., V. "Lack of Character." Pasadena Star-News (26 April), p. 43.
Review of O identifying Cross Damon's problems as personal or temperamental, not social or philosophical. What he really lacks is character. The novel is not a racial narrative.

106. C.[allaway], H. L. "Wright, Richard," in Cassell's Encyclopaedia of Literature. Ed. S. H. Steinberg. Vol. 2. London: Cassell, p. 2078.
Biographical note.

107. Cartwright, Marguerite. "Letter to the Editor: Descendants of Bigger Thomas." Phylon, 14 (First Quarter), 116-118.
Partial reprint of 1953.108 and 109.

108. _____. "The Neurotic Negro." New York Amsterdam News (14 March), p. 16.
Objects to Ellison and W for portraying the stereotype of "the neurotic Negro."
Partially reprinted: 1953.107.

109. _____. "S. P. D. N. M." New York Amsterdam News (7 March), p. 14.
Deplores W's influence in propagating unfavorable racial stereotypes. The protagonist of Invisible Man is an example.
Partially reprinted: 1953.107.

110. Cayton, Horace R. "The Psychology of the Negro Under Discrimination," in Race Prejudice and Discrimination. Ed. Arnold M. Rose. New York: Knopf, pp. 276-290.
Partial reprint of 1946.171.

111. Chaplin, Sid. "U. S. Negroes: A Great Novel." London Tribune (20 February), p. 6.
Favorable review of Invisible Man mentioning W briefly.

112. Church, Robert M. "Doomed to be an Outsider." Tulsa Sunday World (29 March), Magazine Sec., p. 23.
Favorable review of O finding it superior to NS and BB. W's "style is

fluent, clear, and correct," and his ideas have universal application. The "plot sounds like a blood and thunder mystery," but W portrays the protagonist well. Includes a plot summary.

113. Cowley, Malcolm. "American Books Abroad," in Literary History of the United States. Ed. Robert E. Spiller, Willard Thorp, Thomas H. Johnson, and Henry Seidel Canby. Revised edition. New York: Macmillan, pp. 1374-1391.
Reprint of 1948.151.

114. Davenport, Basil. "The Outsider by Richard Wright." Book-of-the-Month Club News (May), p. 7.
Mixed review finding the ideas intense and interesting, but the action too melodramatic. "Ranging from melodrama to philosophy, this is a powerful though uneven book."

115. De Toledano, Ralph. "New Work by Richard Wright: 'The Outsider' a Novel of Violence." Jamaica (N. Y.) Long Island Press (22 March).
Mixed but mainly favorable review. Failing "to weld together the novel of violence and the novel of ideas," W succeeds in portraying an extreme case of alienation. Cross Damon is a compelling, powerful character in his nihilism and revolt. W's style is clumsy like Dreiser's, but he is a more profound thinker.
Reprinted: 1978.209.

116. Dodson, Owen. "But Not Transformed." The New Republic, 128 (27 July), 21.
Review of Will Thomas's The Seeking quoting from the conclusion of BB and noting white reluctance to accept the veracity of W's account of his life in Mississippi.

117. D.[olbier], M.[aurice]. "Bookman's Galley: Young Writers, Young Readers." The Providence Sunday Journal (4 January), Sec. VI, p. 8.
Contains a brief announcement of O.

118. Duncan, Hugh Dalziel. Language and Literature in Society. Chicago: The University of Chicago Press, pp. 4-5.
Mentions W briefly.

119. Eastman, Max. "Man as a Promise." The Freeman, 3 (4 May), 567-568.
Mixed review of O. Cross Damon is incredible as a realistic character. On the other hand, the plot is "magnificently contrived and constructed." Ideologically, Eastman objects to W's existentialism but praises his anti-Communism. "What is man?" To this central question of the

novel, Cross Damon's final answer "is as great and memorable an aphorism as modern literature contains: 'Man is a promise that he must never break.'" Reprinted: 1978.209.

120. Eberle, Hans Ulrich. "Richard Wright: Ich Negerjunge. Die Geschichte einer Kindheit und Jugend." Bücherei und Bildung, 5 (March-April), 237-238.
    Favorable review of the German translation of BB comparing it to the autobiographies of Gorky and Nexö. Eberle thinks the sexual scenes too mature for young readers, but otherwise recommends the work. For those who find Faulkner too difficult, W's account of the racial problem, written in a realistic, powerful style, will be informative.

121. Ellison, Ralph. "Richard Wright's Blues," in The Antioch Review Anthology. Ed. Paul Bixler. Cleveland: World, pp. 263-275.
    Reprint of 1945.890.

122. _____. "Twentieth-Century Fiction and the Black Mask of Humanity." Confluence, 2 (December), 3-21.
    Contains a brief reference to W (p. 5.)
    Reprinted: 1964.49; 1966.47.

123. F., T. "America and Africa: Violence and Tenderness." Charlotte News (4 April), p. 6-A.
    Review of O and Blanket Boy, a book about South African life by Peter Lanham and A. S. Mopelis-Paulus. The reviewer contrasts W's violence with the tenderness of the other work. Cross Damon's problem is not mainly racial, but that of the protagonist of the other book is.

124. Flowers, Paul. "Those Gadabout Authors." The Memphis Commercial Appeal (14 June), Sec. V, p. 12.
    Lists W as an expatriate author.

125. Fontellio-Nanton, H. I. "Sad American?" Sepia USA, 1 (February), 35.
    Unfavorable review of O questioning its racial relevance and deploring Cross Damon's character.

126. Ford, Nick Aaron. "The Ordeal of Richard Wright." College English, 15 (November), 87-94.
    Analysis of W's literary career through O, which is more imaginative, challenging, and philosophical than NS. W has repudiated the ideological tenets of his early career; Ford argues that O is strongly anti-Communist and existentialist.
    Reprinted: 1970.131; 1971.120, 147.

127. Foree, James J. "About Books" (29 April).
    Mimeographed Associated Negro Press flyer containing a favorable review of O. Admitting its controversial nature, Foree thinks that the ideas outweigh the sensationalism. Includes a plot summary.
    Reprinted: 1953.128.

128. _____. "The Outsider by Richard Wright." The Philadelphia Tribune (9 May), p. 4.
    Reprint of 1953.127.

129. Fuller, Edmund. "The Outsider, by Richard Wright." Episcopal Churchnews, 119 (17 May), 20-21.
    Unfavorable review deploring W's existentialism. "This book epitomizes some of the most destructive thoughts and emotions current today."
    Reprinted: 1978.209.

130. Fuller, Hoyt W. "Native Son: A Group of Talented Young People Provide a Fine Evening of Theater." The Michigan Chronicle (21 March), p. 23.
    Favorable review of a Detroit production of the play NS, with special praise for Walter Mason's performance as Bigger. Includes a plot summary.

131. _____. "Reflections on 'Native Son,' Its Author and a Forthcoming Book: A Play and a Book." The Michigan Chronicle (14 March), p. 23.
    Announces O and a Detroit production of the play NS. Notes progress in race relations since the Depression.

132. Gallup, Donald. Untitled headnote, in his The Flowers of Friendship: Letters Written to Gertrude Stein. New York: Knopf, p. 379.
    Brief headnote to a letter from W to Stein dated 27 May 1945.

133. Gardner, Harold. "Some Thoughts on Recent Fiction." America, 89 (16 May), 191-193.
    Contains a notice of O complaining of W's dismissal of Christianity. The novel presents a quest which is not resolved.

134. Geismar, Maxwell. "A Cycle of Fiction," in Literary History of the United States. Ed. Robert E. Spiller, Willard Thorp, Thomas H. Johnson, and Henry Seidel Canby. Revised edition. New York: Macmillan, pp. 1296-1316.
    Reprint of 1948.168.

135. _____. Rebels and Ancestors: The American Novel, 1890-1915. Boston: Houghton Mifflin, pp. 19, 172.
    Compares NS to McTeague and BB to

Martin Eden.

136. Getze, George. "Harsh, Rough and Big." The Los Angeles Mirror (20 March), p. 35.
Favorable review of O comparing it to Crime and Punishment. It is "a great novel" even though it relies too much on concidence. Getze approves of W's rejection of Communism.

137. Gibson, Ellen. "Man Without a World." The Milwaukee Journal (22 March), Sec. V, p. 4.
Review of O consisting mostly of plot summary. The key to Cross Damon's character is apparently unmotivated violence. Gibson also calls attention to some autobiographical elements in the novel.

138. Gibson, Rochelle. "Among Books and Authors." The Roanoke Times (1 March), p. B-6.
Includes W's letter to his publisher about O, prefaced by a brief announcement of the impending publication of the novel.

139. Gillespie, Rey L. "Community Relations." Cleveland Plain Dealer (19 April), p. 13-C.
Favorable review of O consisting mostly of plot summary and quotation. Gillespie calls W "one of the most important writers of our times."

140. Grady, R. F., S. J. "Wright, Richard. The Outsider." Best Sellers, 13 (1 May), 24-25.
Favorable review praising W's honesty. W has made great artistic and intellectual progress since NS, and he will go farther.
Reprinted: 1978.209.

141. Green, Paul. "Symphonic Drama," in his Dramatic Heritage. New York: Samuel French, pp. 14-26.
Reprint of 1949.109.

142. Greenway, John. American Folksongs of Protest. Philadelphia: University of Pennsylvania Press, pp. 82-83.
Quotes W's definition of the blues.

143. Gregg, Charles. "The Book News of the Week." Oshkosh Daily Northwestern (4 April), p. 6.
Unfavorable review of O. The "dismal and depressing" plot is not redeemed by a social message, for Damon is largely responsible for his own troubles. The action is often illogical and the philosophical passages intrusive.

144. Hackett, Alice. "PW Buyer's Forecast: The Outsider. Richard Wright." The Publishers' Weekly, 163 (28 February), 1088.
Quotes from Harper's promotional release on the novel. It is bold, sexy, and violent.

145. Handley, H. T. "Wright Challenges Reader Anew with 'The Outsider.'" The Boston Herald (29 March), p. 46.
Favorable review. The novel is realistic and makes no attempt to propagandize. Damon is an individual, not a type.

146. Hansberry, Lorraine. Untitled clipping. Freedom, 14 (April), 7.
Extremely unfavorable review of O, "a story of sheer violence, death and disgusting spectacle, written by a man who has seemingly come to despise humanity." In contrast to his early career, W is now estranged from his people and their dignity. He is a futile nihilist.
Reprinted: 1978.209.

147. Harris, Arthur H., Jr. "The Jungle Under Veneer." Worcester Sunday Telegram (5 April), Sec. D, p. 11.
Mixed review concluding: "The Outsider is as profound as it is exciting, a very unusual book with an unsavory hero who somehow manages to carry the novel successfully for its four hundred odd pages." Earlier, however, Harris complains that unlike O'Neill and Conrad, who handled similar themes, W in this novel "seems more didactic than artistic, more melodramatic than dramatic."

148. Hicks, Granville. "Living with Books: James Baldwin's Promising First Novel, 'Go Tell It on the Mountain.'" The New Leader, 36 (1 June), 21-22.
Mentions W briefly.

149. _____. "Man's Search." The New York Times (22 March), International Edition.
Partial reprint of 1953.150.

150. _____. "The Portrait of a Man Searching." The New York Times Book Review (22 March), pp. 1, 35.
Review of O placing it in the context of W's career, summarizing the plot, and analyzing both the action and the ideas. The key ideological passages are Cross Damon's speech on Communism and Ely Houston's talk to Cross. W's position is subjective and existentialist, and the book has both intellectual and emotional power. The review ends with a brief comparison to Invisible Man.
Reprinted: 1953.149;1978.209; 1982.50.

151. Highet, Gilbert. "New Books: Lines of Communication." Harper's Magazine, 206 (May), 96, 98.

Review of O comparing it to a Dostoevskian novel: the hero rebels against traditional morality, against social distinctions, against friendship and love, against organized law and organized rebellion, and against religion. Highet also compares Cross Damon to Joe Christmas of Light in August. W is not successful in making Damon the vehicle of his anti-Communist position, however. The distance between Damon the postal clerk and Damon the philosopher quoting Nietzsche and Lenin is too great.
Reprinted: 1978.209.

152. House, Vernal. "A Welter of Senseless Living." The Toronto Globe and Mail (9 May), p. 27.

Unfavorable review of O complaining that Cross Damon is a sordid and repulsive character and that the ideological element of the novel is both intrusive and meaningless. After NS and BB, O is a disappointing book.

153. Hughes, Carl Milton. The Negro Novelist: A Discussion of the Writings of American Negro Novelists, 1940-1950. New York: The Citadel Press, pp. 41-68, 197-206.

In the section on NS, Hughes considers it a psychological novel under the general category of "Portrayals of Bitterness." Using biographical data, he treats Bigger as the embodiment of a particular type of neurotic black man. In the section on "Reputations," Hughes compares NS to The Grapes of Wrath and summarizes critical opinion on W's novel.
Reprinted: 1971.147.
Partially reprinted: 1973.256.

154. Hughes, Langston. "Negro Actors Have Enlivened the New York Stage Since 1821." New York Age Defender (18 April), p. 10.

Mentions briefly the play NS.

155. Hughes, Marjorie Crowe. "Anguish." The Commonweal, 58 (10 April), 29-31.

Generally favorable review of O comparing it as a novel of ideas to a morality play "with ideologies acting the vices--and the virtues left out." Though sometimes intellectually confusing, it is a work of great emotional power.
Reprinted: 1978.209.

156. Hughes, Riley. "The Outsider by Richard Wright, Far From the Customary Skies by Warren Eyster, The Boyds of Black River by Walter D. Edmonds." The

Catholic World, 177 (May), 154.

Mixed review of W's novel. The philosophy of O is romanticism; the method is a brutal and direct realism. These tend to cancel each other out. But Hughes admires W's treatment of the relation between Cross and the Communist Party.

157. Hurston, Zora Neale. "Negro, The, in the United States," in The Encyclopedia Americana. Ed. Lavinia P. Dudley. Vol. 20. New York: Americana Corporation, pp. 47-52.
Reprint of 1951.182.

158. Hyde, Frederic G. "Richard Wright Surveys Ills of Modern Man's World." The Philadelphia Inquirer (22 March), Society Sec., p. 18.

Review of O admiring the narrative drive and emotional power of the novel, but objecting to the negative theme, the melodramatic plot, and the reduction of most of the characters to ideological symbols. Cross Damon, however, is well drawn.

159. Jackson, Joseph Henry. "Bookman's Notebook: A Novel of Barbados." San Francisco Chronicle (17 December), p. 25.

Review of George Lamming's In the Castle of My Skin quoting from W's introduction.

160. Jackson, Luther P. "Wright's Outsider." Newark Sunday News (5 April), Sec. III, p. 42.

Review commenting on W's expatriation and exchange of Communism for existentialism, summarizing the plot of the novel, and concluding by praising W's narrative power but complaining about his didacticism. "The lickety split action of his novels bogs down in a slough of dialectics."

161. James, Mertice M. and Dorothy Brown. "Wright, Richard. The outsider." The Book Review Digest, 49 (May).
Lists or quotes from nine reviews.

162. _____. "Wright, Richard. The outsider." The Book Review Digest, 49 (August).
Lists or quotes from sixteen reviews.

163. Jessup, Lee Cheney. "Mature, Realistic." Nashville Banner (1 May), p. 30.

Favorable review of O, which Jessup considers W's best work. Violent like his earlier books, it shows more objectivity and realistic characterization. Cross Damon arouses compassion if not sympathy in his struggle against despair.

164. Jones, Carter Brooke. "New Richard Wright Novel Presents a Strange, Unforgettable Character." The Washington Sunday Star (22 March), p. E-7.
Favorable review of O stressing its mixture of melodrama and philosophy. "It's almost as if Henry James took over a plot devised by Mickey Spillane." Cross Damon is a strange character with complex motives. The story, with its melodrama and violence, is "an allegory of our times."

165. Kilgallen, Dorothy. "The Voice of Broadway: New Romance for Lew Ayres." New York Journal-American (23 October), p. 15.
Includes mention of W's work in progress that was to become SH.

166. Kogan, Herman. "Book Week: Chicagoans Prominent on Spring Book Lists." Chicago Sunday Sun-Times (8 February), Sec. Two, p. 6.
Contains an announcement of O and a photograph of W.

167. _____. "Wright's First Novel in 8 Years Is Like Cops-and-Robbers Tale." Chicago Sunday Sun-Times (22 March), Sec. Two, p. 6.
Unfavorable review of O interpreting Cross Damon as existential man, completely amoral and purposeless. W's discourses on dialectical issues detract considerably from the novel. Without its obvious symbols, O resembles "a surrealistic cops-and-robbers story." Cross is seldom a convincing character, and the reader feels little sympathy for him.

168. Kopke, Dick. "Novelist Does Another Book About Negroes." Buffalo Courier-Express (3 May), p. 30-C.
Favorable review of O viewing it as a blend of melodramatic violence and philosophical speculations, both "ingredients in [Wright's] questioning of whether man will learn to live decently in the world as it exists." Includes a plot summary.

169. Laski, Marghanita. "Look-How-Nasty!" The London Observer (11 January), p. 7.
Review of Invisible Man including the following statement: "As argument, as narrative, the book is less impressive than the true account of a very similar pilgrimage made by Richard Wright in 'The God That Failed.'"

170. Levin, Sid. "Shock, Power Prevail in Eyes of 'Outsider.'" The Davenport Daily Times (29 August), p. 6-A.
Highly favorable review of O comparing Cross Damon to Bigger Thomas, summarizing the plot, and praising W's style, ideas, and characterization. Despite his crimes, Damon is an attractive, even admirable, character.

171. Lewis, Sinclair. "Fiction Writing," in The American Peoples Encyclopedia. Ed. Franklin J. Meine. Vol. 8. Chicago: Spencer Press, p. 514.
Reprint of 1948.188a.

172. _____. "Gentlemen, This Is Revolution," in The Man From Main Street: A Sinclair Lewis Reader. Ed. Harry E. Maule and Melville H. Cane. New York: Random House, pp. 148-153.
Reprint of 1945.997.

173. _____. "No Flight to Olympus," in The Man From Main Street: A Sinclair Lewis Reader. Ed. Harry E. Maule and Melville H. Cane. New York: Random House, pp. 185-188.
Reprint of 1948.188a.

174. Locke, Alain. "From Native Son to Invisible Man: A Review of the Literature of the Negro for 1952." Phylon, 14 (First Quarter), 34-44.
The first paragraph praises Cane and NS as the first two "points of peak development in Negro fiction"; Invisible Man is the third. W's novel was marred only by his Communist ideology.
Reprinted: 1971.215.

174a. Lombardo, Agostino. "Invisible Man." Lo spettatore italiano, 6 (August), 364-366.
Contains several references to W as a proletarian naturalist.
Reprinted: 1957.256.

175. MacKell, Peter R. D. "Man's Inhumanity to Man." The Montreal Gazette (9 May), p. 21.
Unfavorable review of O finding W's message unclear and his style diffuse. "There is material here for at least three novels. The point of this theme, while obviously of the most pressing urgency, is lost in a sea of conflicting motivations and outside forces." In contrast to his previous work, W does not emphasize the racial theme in the novel.

176. Marcus, Steven. "The American Negro in Search of Identity." Commentary, 16 (November), 456-463.
Analysis of O, Invisible Man, and Go Tell It on the Mountain. Marcus considers O a continuation of NS and Cross Damon another Bigger Thomas. The story comes to life only when Damon is meditating or performing

some act of violence. In concentrating on violence, W fails to articulate black American life.
Partially reprinted: 1960.207; 1961.
219; 1963.150; 1971.218.

177. Marten, Johannes Skancke. "Richard
Wright tilbake efter åtte års taushet."
Oslo Aftenposten (31 March), Evening
Edition, p. 3.
    Reports a conversation with W in
    conjunction with the publication of
    O. W comments on his involvement with
    the film NS, denies that Sartre and
    Camus are Communists, and condemns
    Porgy and Bess as sentimental and
    unrealistic.

178. Martin, Gertrude Scott. "Book
Notes." The Michigan Chronicle (17 January), p. 20.
    Mentions W's long silence.

179. _____. "Book Notes." The Michigan
Chronicle (21 February), p. 22.
    Contains an announcement of O.

180. _____. "Book Notes." The Michigan
Chronicle (11 April), p. 20.
    Unfavorable review of O complaining
    of confused ideas and stereotyped
    characters. Martin insists that Cross
    Damon's blackness is important to the
    plot whether W wishes to acknowledge
    the fact or not.

181. Mason, Jack. "Disillusioned: Sense
of Outrage Dominates Outlook of Negro
Novelist." Oakland Tribune (14 June), p.
2-C.
    Unfavorable review of O, which Mason
    believes emphasizes a social and
    philosophical message at the expense
    of plausible characterization. W's
    literary existentialism is "less ef-
    fective . . . more brutal" than his
    literary Communism in NS.
    Reprinted: 1978.209.

182. McCain, Mary. "Violence Rules 'The
Outsider.'" The Memphis Commercial
Appeal (15 March), Sec. V, p. 12.
    Favorable review praising W's charac-
    terization and objectivity. Not a
    novel of race relations, O is "a
    serious probing of a man's soul," in
    which the main themes are hate and
    violence. In this novel W achieves
    "power, pathos and passion." Includes
    a plot summary.

183. McK., F. "The Bookshelf," The Vancouver Sunday Sun (28 March), p. 19.
    Contains a brief announcement of O.

184. Meyer, Frank. "New Novels." The
American Mercury, 76 (June), 143.
    Contains a favorable review of O

praising its power. "Every page reflects the agony of Mr. Wright's
effort to come to terms with the
meaning of life."

185. Moisimann, Denyse. "Some Notes on
Books." The Charleston News and Courier
(11 January), p. 6-B.
    Contains an announcement of O.

186. Monroe, Harold. "'The Outsider' Not
Up to Par." Fort Worth Star-Telegram (10
May), Sec. Three, p. 9.
    Unfavorable review complaining of
    inconsistency in the characterization
    of Cross Damon and uneven plot devel-
    opment. Furthermore, Damon rejects
    Communism for selfish reasons, not
    because of "its sham and its menace."
    Reprinted: 1978.209.

187. Montgomery, Althea P. "Man Can't
Live Alone--Though He Won His Way He
Lost World." The Birmingham News (5
April), Sec. E, p. 6.
    Favorable review of O consisting
    mostly of plot summary. Montgomery
    applauds W's "switch from the role of
    an alarmist [over racial problems] to
    the cool contemplation of a philo-
    sopher."

188. Moore, Marie. "The Story of a Grop-
ing Mind: Wright's 'The Outsider' Upholds His Reputation." The Houston
Chronicle (22 March), Feature Magazine
Sec., p. 16.
    Favorable review emphasizing the
    anti-Communist theme. W senses that
    something is profoundly wrong with
    the world, but he offers no solution.
    Moore notes an autobiographical ele-
    ment in the novel, for Damon's "view-
    point is that of a Negro in a white
    man's world."

188a. Moravia, Alberto. "La paura
negra." L'Europeo (21 May), p. 39.
    Somewhat unfavorable review of the
    film NS, which Moravia finds "more
    shocking than convincing." Comments
    also on W's career, including his
    break with Communism.

189. Morgan-Powell, S. "Among the New
Novels." Montreal Daily Star (11 April),
p. 18.
    Unfavorable review of O, which
    Morgan-Powell states is the first
    novel from W since The Naked Son
    [sic]. The unsatisfactory story is
    too "melodramatic, and not calculated
    to enhance the author's reputation in
    any way."

190. Munn, L. S. "'The Outsider':
Richard Wright's Novel of Cross Damon's
Melodramatic Journey to Destruction."

Springfield (Mass.) Sunday Republican (14 June), p. 9C.
Unfavorable review emphasizing W's existentialism. Though powerful, the work "is weakened and crippled by its dependence upon ideological concepts which twist the reality of the novel into a nightmarish fantasy." Cross Damon's problem mirrors W's.

191. Nelson, Boris E. "Books: Some Random Notes on Books." The Dayton Daily News (4 January), Sec. B, p. 7.
Contains an announcement of the forthcoming publication of O.

192. Nordhaus, Ruth. "Freedom Is Terrifying for Wright's New Hero." San Antonio Express (22 March), p. 2E.
Favorable review of O, which has "all the elements of greatness in its Dostoevskian attempt to define what man is in the most starkly realistic way." The central issue in the novel is individual as opposed to social moral responsibility. Includes a plot summary.

193. O'Connell, John Patrick. "Confusion and Despair of a 20th Century Man." Books on Trial, 11 (May), 294-295.
Unfavorable review of O complaining that W's ideas "are often too highly seasoned to be digestible." His despair and "futile godlessness" are unfortunate.
Reprinted: 1978.209.

194. O'Connor, Richard. "The Outsider." Los Angeles Evening Herald & Express (28 March), p. B-2.
Favorable review emphasizing the work's "power and vitality." O does not equal NS "as a work of art, but it is a thoroughly stimulating novel."

195. Olson, Lee. "A Gloomy View of Man's Future." The Denver Post (29 March), Roundup Sec., p. 18.
Review of O emphasizing the pessimism of W's world view compared to that of BB or that of his Marxist period. Damon kills "with the reasoned nihilism of a Raskolnikov and the gory efficiency of a Mike Hammer." The era of technology holds little hope for mankind.

196. O'Neill, Frank. "Inside of Books: Richard Wright in Savage Tale." Cleveland News (20 March), p. 15.
Review of O as "a savage commentary on the cynicism, confusion and despair abroad in the world." Cross Damon is unsympathetic but disturbing. Having rejected Communism, W is still searching for an ideology.

197. Ottley, Roi. "Wright Adds a New Monster to a Gallery of Dispossessed." Chicago Sunday Tribune Magazine of Books (22 March), p. 3.
Unfavorable review summarizing the plot of the "brutally explosive" work. Because Cross Damon acts without motives, Ottley suspects that "Wright is mocking us with a ghastly joke."
Reprinted: 1953.198; 1978.209.

198. _____. "Wright Adds New Monster." Washington Times-Herald (29 March), p. 2M.
Reprint of 1953.197.

199. Pearson, C. M. "A Disturbing Novel." The Hartford Courant (22 March), Magazine Sec., p. 19.
Review of O finding Cross Damon's negativism profoundly disturbing, for W's "skill makes it a tense, gripping horror." But some hope is offered by Ely Houston, who represents, Pearson believes, a way out of nihilism.

200. Pearson, R. M. "Conflict in Modern Society Pictured in 'The Outsider.'" The Windsor (Ont.) Daily Star (18 April), p. 14.
Favorable review calling the novel "frightening" but "interesting." Damon is overdrawn, but the contrast between him and Ely Houston is well executed. Pearson emphasizes Damon's alienation from "the herd."

201. Pickrel, Paul. "Outstanding Novels." The Yale Review, 42 (Summer), vi, viii, x, xii, xvi.
Contains an unfavorable notice of the "disappointing" O (p. x). The excessive use of coincidence and violence makes the characters appear less victims of fate and circumstances than "sinners in the hands of an angry author." In contrast, Jefferson Young's A Good Man is deemed a more credible story and James Baldwin's Go Tell It on the Mountain is lauded as a novel of "great force and vigor."

202. Poston, Ted. "Wright's Terrible 'Reality' Shocks in a Violent, Explosive New Novel." New York Post (22 March), p. 12M.
Favorable review of O finding it "even more violent and disturbing" than NS. Both a "philosophical treatise" and "a fast-moving murder story," O has well-drawn characters and is both engrossing and controversial.
Reprinted: 1978.209.

203. Power, Fremont. "When a Communist's Idols Fall, What Is There Left?" The

<u>Indianapolis</u> <u>News</u> (21 March), p. 2.
Unfavorable review of <u>O</u> acknowledging W's literary force but complaining of his nihilism. Cross Damon is compared to Bigger Thomas. Of W himself, Power opines that "Communism apparently has devoured him, leaving him a virtual man-without-a-country--and without a god."

204. Prescott, Orville. "Books of the Times." <u>The</u> <u>New</u> <u>York</u> <u>Times</u> (18 March), p. 29.
Review of <u>O</u> noting the new direction it represents in W's career--from naturalism to the novel of ideas. The characters of <u>O</u> are unreal and the plot implausible, but the ideas are fascinating. W's sympathy with Cross Damon's existentialist despair "is one of the symptoms of the intellectual and moral crisis of our times." Reprinted: 1978.209.

205. Pritchard, Alan. "Wright Uses Might for Right." <u>Dayton</u> <u>Daily</u> <u>News</u> (5 April), p. 17.
Unfavorable review of <u>O</u> complaining of excessive violence, poor plotting, and implausible use of coincidence. W has rejected Communism, but he is still looking for an ideology.

205a. [Quinn, Kerker]. "Accent Autumn 1953."
Flyer listing W as a contributor to <u>Accent</u> <u>Anthology</u>.

205b. _____. "Accent Spring 1953."
Flyer listing W as a contributor to <u>Accent</u> <u>Anthology</u>.

206. Raleigh, John Henry. "Escape and Sanctuary." <u>The</u> <u>New</u> <u>Republic</u>, 128 (4 May), 19.
Unfavorable review of <u>O</u>. It is interesting as a social novel, but W's symbolism is too simple and brutal. Cross Damon is Bigger Thomas intellectualized by French existentialism. In <u>O</u> W has become a nihilist.

207. Reagan, M. D. "Violent Search for Freedom." <u>America</u>, 89 (4 April), 20.
Favorable review of <u>O</u> praising its anti-Communism and its diagnosis of the spiritual malaise of modern man, but deploring its anti-Christianity. Impressive artistically as well as ideologically, it "is a raw, violent and lightning paced novel. A little too raw sexually, but otherwise a craftsmanlike job and tremendously exciting as a tale of modern adventure and suspense." Reprinted: 1978.209.

208. Reddick,, L. D. "A New Richard Wright?" <u>Phylon</u>, 13 [sic, but should be 14] (Second Quarter), 213-214.
Favorable review of <u>O</u> noting that the new W is philosopher as well as novelist. Reddick praises W's understanding of human motivation and narrative skill, almost as impressive here as in <u>NS</u>. The issues raised by <u>O</u> will be much debated. Includes a plot summary.
Reprinted: 1978.209.

209. Redding, J. Saunders. "Book Review." <u>The</u> <u>Baltimore</u> <u>Afro-American</u> (9 May), Magazine Sec., p. 2.
Unfavorable review of <u>O</u>, which Redding finds "often labored, frequently naive, and generally incredible," as well as structurally deficient. W fails to convey the illusion of reality except in Book One. Redding also disagrees with W's existentialism. Reprinted: 1978.209.

210. Rhea, James N. "Richard Wright's New Novel." <u>The</u> <u>Providence</u> <u>Sunday</u> <u>Journal</u> (22 March), Sec. VI, p. 10.
Unfavorable review of <u>O</u> finding it improbable in plot, uninformed about current American race relations, and pretentious in its "intellectual and symbolic trappings." Cross Damon is "pathetically insane, despite Wright's efforts to give him great intellectual powers."
Reprinted: 1978.209.

211. Riesman, David. "Marginality, Conformity, and Insight." <u>Phylon</u>, 14 (Third Quarter), 241-257.
Analyzes <u>BB</u> to show that a marginal position with respect to both the majority and the minority culture can lead to comprehension and self-development as well as alienation. Riesman also discusses W's attitudes toward puritanism and the Communist Party.

212. Rogers, W. G. "A Footloose Man, Empty, Hollow." <u>Bridgeport</u> <u>Sunday</u> <u>Post</u> (22 March), p. B-4.
Reprint of 1953.214.

213. _____. "Hollow Man." Omaha <u>Sunday</u> <u>World-Herald</u> (29 March), Magazine Sec., p. 29.
Reprint of 1953.214.

214. _____. "The Literary Guidepost." <u>Wausau</u> <u>Daily</u> <u>Record-Herald</u> (20 March), p. 9.
Review of <u>O</u> consisting mostly of plot summary. Expresses dissatisfaction with the characterization of Cross Damon: "Wright portrays a tragic figure, and so he succeeds; but he doesn't make you care, and so he fails."

Reprinted: 1953.212, 213, 215, 216, 217.

215. _____. "The Outsider, by Richard Wright." Chicago Herald-American (22 March), Pictorial Review, p. 12.
Reprint of 1953.214.

216. _____. "The Outsider, by Richard Wright." Manchester (N. H.) News (22 March).
Reprint of 1953.214.

217. _____. "'The Outsider' by Richard Wright." Walla Walla Union-Bulletin (22 March), p. 28.
Reprint of 1953.214.

217a. Rosati, Salvatore. "L'ultimo Wright." Il mondo (13 June), p. 6.
Review of O in the context of W's career. Rosati stresses W's spontaneous naturalism, his seriousness, and his naivete.
Reprinted: 1958.233.

217b. _____. "L'uomo invisibile di Ralph Ellison." Il mondo (27 October), p. 6.
Review of Invisible Man with a brief comparison to O.
Reprinted: 1958.232.

218. Rowan, Carl T. "How Do the Free Fight Would-Be Destroyers?" Minneapolis Sunday Tribune (22 March), Feature-News Sec., p. 6.
Review of O. It is a story filled with sex, tragedy, and violence, but it is devoid of the racial emphasis of NS. W's central concern is the fight of the free against both Communism and fascism.

219. Rugoff, Milton. "Richard Wright's New Novel of Negro Life in America." New York Herald Tribune Book Review (22 March), p. 4.
Unfavorable review of O emphasizing the lurid melodrama of the plot. Cross Damon is a psychopathic killer, and the interest he engenders is morbid. Much less impressive than his earlier books, this novel still has "moments of . . . naked intensity and unbearable frustration."
Reprinted: 1978.209.

220. Ruth, Kent. "An Outsider Queries Why?" The Oklahoma City Daily Oklahoman (29 March), Sunday Magazine, p. 20.
Somewhat favorable review of O considering Cross Damon a projection of W himself: "an outsider struggling blindly and tragically to find a purpose in life." The novel has power, but it presents a very negative view of reality.
Reprinted: 1978.209.

221. S., J. "Powerful Writing, Not Good Novel." Saskatoon Star-Phoenix (27 June), p. 15.
Mixed review of O complaining that it is more tract than novel, but admiring W's themes of "the inhumanity of communism, the cruelty of social injustice, the horror of the division in the world between the acceptable and the unacceptable."

222. Sablonière, Margrit de. "Afrekening van een buitenstaander." Litterair Paspoort, No. 68 (July-August), pp. 164-165.
Favorable review of O stressing its philosophical dimensions. Although W retains traces of the French influence of de Beauvoir and Sartre, he has "rejected all systems," creating a figure who typifies the fear-dominated man of contemporary industrial society.

223. Sawyer, Roland. "About a Monomaniac." The Christian Science Monitor (30 April), p. 11.
Extremely unfavorable review of O reacting sharply to the "sordid, sensual, sanguinary, story" of Cross Damon, who "became steeped in alcoholic and animal lusts." W handles language well, but the construction of the novel is weak. Above all, the theme of self-destruction through innate human weakness is repulsive.
Reprinted: 1978.209.

224. Schuyler, George S. "Views and Reviews: 'Liberal' French Face Full-fledged Race Problem." Unidentified clipping [The Pittsburgh Courier?].
Discusses the situation of the Algerians in France in disputing the claim of W and others that the French are racially tolerant. The year is conjectural.

225. Scott, Eleanor M. "This West Indian Novelist Writes as Van Gogh Painted." New York Herald Tribune Book Review (1 November), p. 3.
Review of In the Castle of My Skin claiming that W's introduction presents too limited and sociological a view of Lamming's work.

226. Sender, Ramón. "Wright y su última novela." El Bogota Tiempo (28 June), Suplemento Literario, p. 2.
Favorable review of O, a work of "diabolical beauty." Cross Damon is an amoral monster. Sender places W's work in the context of the American racial situation.

227. Silvera, John D. "Book of the Week." The Pittsburgh Courier (25

April), p. 6.
Unfavorable review of O, a novel "flavored with sex, race-hate, and communist ideology." W concocted the novel to sell, not to achieve literary stature.

228. Simpson, George Eaton and J. Milton Yinger. Racial and Cultural Minorities: An Analysis of Prejudice and Discrimination. New York: Harper, 773 pp.
Contains numerous references to W and extensive quotations, especially from BB, in chapters entitled "The Personality Functions of Prejudice," "The Consequences of Prejudice: The Responses of Minority-Group Members," and "Minorities and Art."
Reprinted: 1958.253; 1965.115; 1972.181.

229. Skelton, B. J. "Horror, Violence Stalk Outsider." The Clarksdale Press Register (18 April), p. 2.
Mixed review of O, which is exciting and ideologically interesting despite its contrived plot, manipulated characters, and clumsy style. Skelton dislikes W's nihilism but admires his anti-Communism.

230. Smith, William Gardner. "Black Boy in France." Ebony, 8 (July), 32-36, 39-42.
Account of W's expatriation, including comments on his activites, acquaintances, and attitudes toward France and America. Emphasizes Gertrude Stein's role in urging W to come to Paris. Smith concludes that W found freedom and a congenial life style only as an expatriate.
Reprinted: 1971.147.

231. Sprague, M. D. "Richard Wright: A Bibliography." Bulletin of Bibliography, 21 (September-December), 39.
First checklist of works by W includes sixty-two items, a few in collaboration with Frasconi, Green, and Hughes. The list is preceded by a headnote indicating W's importance.

232. Steele, Oliver. "Of Fury and Hate: 'The Outsider' Not Likely to Please Critics." The Richmond News Leader (13 April), p. 11.
Unfavorable review emphasizing the novel's existentialism. W overstates his case and borrows his ideas from Sartre.

233. Stevenson, David L. "Novel, The," in The Encyclopedia Americana. Ed. Lavinia P. Dudley. Vol. 20. New York: Americana Corporation, pp. 467-476.
Reprint of 1952.64.

234. Stokley, Wilma D. "Communist Appeal to Negro Race Is Disclosed in Vivid Description." Chattanooga Sunday Times (5 April), p. 20.
Unfavorable review of O arguing that W's merger of the novel of ideas and the novel of violence is not successful. The depiction of Communism is well done, but Cross Damon is not a plausible character.

235. Sylvester, Harry. "Changing Landscape in Barbados." The New York Times Book Review (1 November), pp. 4-5.
Review of George Lamming's In the Castle of My Skin concluding with a quotation from W's introduction.

236. Urban, Donald. Untitled clipping. Cincinnati Enquirer (c. May).
Mixed review of O. The plot is not credible, but "as a 'think piece'" the novel is impressive. The emphasis of the work is on the psychological problems of minority groups, not overt discrimination.
Reprinted: 1978.209.

237. Vaal, Hans de. "Interview met Richard Wright." Litterair Paspoort, 8 (July-August), 161-163.
Interview focusing on political conditions in the United States and their effect on black writing. W sees the "Negro problem" as a "social and economic problem" with psychological complications. "Negro literature" will exist as long as white attitudes remain unchanged. W also identifies a list of literary forebears and states that his favorite music includes jazz, Beethoven, and Schubert.

238. Van Vechten, Carl. Letter to Gertrude Stein, February [?] 1945, in The Flowers of Friendship: Letters Written to Gertrude Stein. Ed. Donald Gallup. New York: Knopf, p. 374.
Praises W's review of Stein's Wars I Have Seen.

239. _____. Letter to Gertrude Stein, 19 November 1945, in The Flowers of Friendship: Letters Written to Gertrude Stein. Ed. Donald Gallup. New York: Knopf, p. 393.
Mentions a package W is sending to Stein.

240. Vogler, Lewis. "Once Again Richard Wright Has Written a Controversial Novel." San Francisco Chronicle (5 April), This World Sec., p. 19.
Generally favorable review of O calling it violent, existentialist, troubled, and definitely not for squeamish readers or those who cannot admit

the psychological impact of the industrialization and mechanization of society. Cross Damon is weak-willed, sensitive, and intelligent, but he can no longer deal with the humiliating terms of his existence. Despite overplotting and unrealistic characterization, O is not dull. It is indeed a tribute to W's genius, especially the ideological portions of the book which are so stressed. Reprinted: 1978.209.

241. W., J. R. "The Outsider, by Richard Wright." The Calgary Herald (2 May), p. 4.
Mixed review finding the novel less impressive than NS and BB, but still "an exciting, violent, and, at times, compelling book." The reviewer objects strenuously to W's existential-ism, "a very murky, depressing and nihilistic philosophy at the best."

242. Walker, Danton. "Along Broadway." Buffalo Evening News (12 January), p. 15.
Reprint of 1953.243.

243. _____. "Broadway." New York Daily News (10 January), p. C12.
Contains an announcement of O, "an indictment against 'isms,' and an admission that the Negro gets better breaks in the U. S. than elsewhere." Reprinted: 1953.242.

244. Walters, Raymond, Jr. "The Critics Separate Wheat from Chaff." The Saturday Review, 36 (11 April), 62.
In a poll of the best books of the year, O received four votes in the fiction category.

245. Watts, Elizabeth W. "Wright Appraising; No Longer Angry." The Boston Sunday Globe (29 March), p. A-25.
Brief review of O finding it more mature but less compulsive than NS or BB. "Mr. Wright seems less to be making an impassioned plea for 'the outsider' . . . than he does to be making a measured judgment of the time we live in and the values we set."

246. Webster, Harvey Curtis. "Community of Pride." The Saturday Review, 36 (16 May), 14.
Review of Go Tell It on the Mountain mentioning W.

247. _____. "The Halls of Color." The Saturday Review, 36 (5 December), 36.
Review of George Lamming's In the Castle of My Skin quoting from W's introduction.

248. _____. "Richard Wright's Profound New Novel." The New Leader, 36 (6 April), 17-18.
Highly favorable review of O rating it higher than Invisible Man and ranking W "with Hemingway, Mann, Gide and Faulkner as one of the possibly great novelists of our time." After a general review of W's earlier work, Webster analyzes O, showing the thematic functions of implausibilities of plot and explaining Cross Damon's "thought-obsessed inability to feel" as characteristic of the modern intellectual. Reprinted: 1978.209.

249. White, Max. Letter to Gertrude Stein, 30 January 1938, in The Flowers of Friendship: Letters Written to Gertrude Stein. Ed. Donald Gallup. New York: Knopf, p. 326.
Praises W, mentions his interest in Stein, and discusses his politics.

250. White, Paul. "Paul White's Diary: Commotion Flows from an Eloquent Pen." Paris Daily Mail (1 April).
Announces O and quotes W's comments on it.

251. Wieck, David. "A Note on 'The Outsider.'" Resistance, 11 (August), 15.
Brief analysis of the novel from an anarchist point of view. W "has pictured very clearly and powerfully the basis for anarchism" by showing that both Communism and extreme individualism are equally futile. The only way is love and fraternity.

252. Williams, Ernest E. "Richard Wright Traces Man's Search for Meaning of Life." The Fort Wayne News-Sentinel (21 March), p. 4.
Favorable review of O comparing it to Crime and Punishment. It is controversial, violent, and provocative.

253. Winslow, Henry F. "Forces of Fear." The Crisis, 60 (June-July), 381-383.
Favorable review of O, a "tale of two cities," with an extensive plot analysis. When Cross Damon meets Eva, the novel becomes a classic work of art because the protagonist becomes multi-dimensional and a part of all he encounters as modern man. "What is here rendered is a true account of our times in humble and facile prose, an eloquently articulate reading of the handwriting on the iron walls of contemporary civilization." Reprinted: 1978.209.

254. Young, Margaret. "Marginalia." The Houston Post (4 January), Sec. 6, p. 5.
Contains an announcement of O, "the story of a young Negro's struggles

with Communism."

255. Zetlin, Florence Anshen. "All Mankind Indicted." Norfolk Virginian-Pilot (22 March), Sec. 2, p. 10.
    Review of O calling it "an appalling vision of the world as inferno," both in a naturalistic and philosophical sense. The Western world and its ideologies of right and left have failed, but W nevertheless retains a "confused belief that somehow better men in a better world are possible."

1954

1. Alexander, Charles. "Book Briefs and Best Sellers." Albany (Oregon) Democrat Herald (26 June), p. 7.
    Contains, s. v. "Poor Man's Library," an announcement of the paperback edition of O and reports that the paperback editions of UTC, NS, and BB have sold 1,300,000 copies.

2. Allen, Walter. "New Novels." The New Statesman and Nation, 48 (25 September), 370.
    Review of O and three other novels. Allen finds W's novel "powerful and impressive," though much below Dostoevsky and slightly below Sartre. The main problem is that "Mr. Wright's thesis overrides his characters; one isn't conscious of them as human beings as much as of exponents of ideas."

3. Allport, Gordon W. The Nature of Prejudice. Reading, Mass.: Addison-Wesley, pp. 147, 513.
    Cites BB to illustrate clowning by blacks.
    Reprinted: 1958.2.

4. Anderson, LaVere. "Under the Reading Lamp." Tulsa Daily World (7 November), Magazine Sec., p. 20.
    Contains a notice of BP along with an excerpt. W's views on Africa are strictly personal.

5. Anon. "An Act of Violence," in Savage Holiday. New York: Avon, back cover.
    Publisher's blurb with a photograph of W and quotations from The New York Times, Time, and The Yale Review.

6. Anon. "Africa and the West." The Edmonton Journal (16 October), p. 6.
    Review of BP praising W's description of African life and folkways, but finding his attitudes toward whites biased, his Marxism still present as a pattern of thought, and his prescription for the "militarization" of African life unacceptable.

7. Anon. "An American Negro--Author of Native Son--Views the African Gold Coast." Harper's Magazine, 209 (October), 21.
    Advertisement for BP.

8. Anon. "At the Library." Syracuse Herald-American (14 November), p. 31.
    Contains a notice of BP emphasizing the threat of Communism in Africa.

9. Anon. "'Black Boy' Visits Africa Gold Coast." Toronto Daily Star (9 October), p. 4.
    Review of BP noting that W has retained some Marxist elements in his thinking. The book is "ideologically debatable; reportorially vivid."

10. Anon. "'Black Power.'" Malden Evening News (10 November), p. 3.
    Favorable review noting the work's power and the advantages of W's perspective.

11. Anon. "Black Power." The Bookmark, 14 (October), 6.
    Very brief, nonevaluative notice.

12. Anon. "Black Power." The Dallas Morning News (26 September), Part VI, p. 7.
    Brief, nonevaluative notice.

13. Anon. "Black Power." Harper's Magazine, 209 (December), 106.
    Brief, nonevaluative notice.

14. Anon. "Black Power." The Saturday Review, 37 (25 September), 34.
    Notice emphasizing W's subjectivity.

15. Anon. "Black Power: An American Negro Views the African Gold Coast by Richard Wright." New Harper Books, pp. 26-27.
    Publisher's illustrated advertisement describing this "frank and brutal book" which "brings before the reader's eye every terrible and beautiful aspect of this country."

16. Anon. "Black Power. By Richard Wright." College English, 16 (December), 202-203.
    Favorable notice of an "important and well written" book.

17. Anon. "Black Power, by Richard Wright." Wichita Eagle (19 December), Magazine Sec., p. 8.
    Favorable notice of a "vivid, brutal, frank" report.

18. Anon. "Black Power, by Richard Wright (Harper)." The New Yorker, 30 (9 October), 167.
    Mixed review calling the book "af-

fecting and significant," despite W's "crude Marxism," "equally crude Freudianism," anxiety over the slave trade, and anthropological ignorance.

19. Anon. "'Black Power' Is New Richard Wright Book." The Indianapolis Times (13 June), p. 26.
Announcement of BP emphasizing its frankness.

20. Anon. "Black Power. Richard Wright." The Retail Bookseller, 57 (September), 132.
Notice predicting "probably good sales" and pointing out W's "predisposition against the British and Colonial rule."

21. Anon. "Books--Authors." The New York Times (25 May), p. 25.
Announcement of the publication of BP in the fall.

22. Anon. "The Bookseller's Almanac." The Retail Bookseller, 57 (September), 102-105.
Contains a notice of BP stressing W's anti-white prejudice.

23. Anon. "'De Buitenstaander' van Richard Wright." Rotterdamse Nieuwsblad (23 October).
Review of the Dutch translation of O. Although W's style makes Cross Damon a convincing character, the author is so concerned with creating a true outsider that the book will be condemned for its spiritual nihilism.

24. Anon. "Can't Find Answer: Africa's Puzzle Too Much for 2 American Authors." The Detroit News (31 October), p. 12-E.
Review of BP and Era Bell Thompson's Africa, Land of My Fathers emphasizing W's bewilderment over his reception by Africans and over the suitable means to achieve African independence.

25. Anon. "Capsule Review of Latest Arrivals on Literary Scene: Black Power." Oakland Tribune (26 September), p. 2-C.
Rather favorable notice emphasizing W's advantageous perspective with his African "racial inheritance" and his Western "cultural heritage."

26. Anon. Dust Jacket of Black Power. New York: Harper.
Back cover contains a photograph of W and a biographical note. Front and back inside flaps contain a publisher's blurb.

27. Anon. "Eastern Studies: 3 Negroes in

Search of Answer." Washington Times Herald (26 September), Sec. B, p. 7.
Review of BP, Era Bell Thompson's Africa, Land of My Fathers, and Saunders Redding's An American in India. W discovered little equality in Africa, but he believes in a bright future for those nations which seek independence.

28. Anon. "El Extraño." Novedades.
Notice of the Spanish translation of O. The protagonist and the author seem to have the same problem of identity.

29. Anon. "Fall Announcements." The Retail Bookseller, 57 (September), 171-193.
Lists BP (pp. 173, 193).

30. Anon. "Fiction Removal Is Rescinded by Board." The Galion Inquirer (15 March), p. 1.
Reports that "the superintendent requested and was granted the authority to eliminate from the school book shelves the three books, 'Anthony Adverse,' 'Toward the Morning,' and 'Native Son,' which precipitated the library book controversy." See 1954.134, 135.

31. Anon. "Frenchman Raps Black Americans: U. S. Negroes Chauvinists?" Unidentified clipping.
René Maran accuses W, Chester Himes, Alain Locke, and Mercer Cook of "racially centripetal tendencies." The year is conjectural.

32. Anon. "From Innocence to Nightmare," in Savage Holiday. New York: Avon, p. [1].
Brief description of the situation precipitating the crisis of the novel.

33. Anon. "Harper Books for Fall 1954." The Retail Bookseller, 57 (September), n. pag.
Lists BP for publication on 22 September.

34. Anon. Index Translationum 6. Paris: Unesco, pp. 18, 215.
Lists translations of The God That Failed into German and BB into Bengali.

35. Anon. "Let's Avoid Book Ban Reputation." The Galion Inquirer (10 March), p. 2.
Criticizes the action of the school board in removing all fiction from the junior and senior high school libraries. Makes no specific mention of NS. See 1954.134, 135.

36. Anon. "La Littérature noire: Richard Wright." Paris-Match (c. 29 May).
Photograph of W in a Paris cafe.

37. Anon. "Merchandising." The Publishers' Weekly, 166 (18 September), 1328-1333.
Contains an announcement of SH (p. 1332).

38. Anon. "'Native Son' in Africa." The Reporter, 11 (4 November), 48.
Mixed review of BP. The political analysis is superficial, but the reportage is superior. W is attentive to the nuances of hidden thoughts and emotions in the Africans he portrays. Reprinted: 1978.209.

39. Anon. "Native Son," in Masterplots. Ed. Frank N. Magill. First Series. Vol. 2. New York: Salem Press, pp. 643-645.
Reprint of 1949.41.

40. Anon. "The Negro in Society." The London Times Literary Supplement (24 September), p. 605.
Review of O and two other novels with black protagonists. O has continued the development of W's case against Communism begun in The God That Failed. Only partially a statement about the racial problem, the novel is mainly concerned with the isolationism that develops when society loses its morality. After rejecting God, family, and Communism, Cross Damon is left with nothing but the "anarchical will of solitary man." His tragedy is that he has to use the worst in himself to get rid of the worst in society. Somewhat deficient in characterization, O is fascinating "as an abstract discussion of the contemporary dilemma."

41. Anon. "Negro Writing: A Literature of Protest." The London Times Literary Supplement (17 September), pp. xxii, xxiv.
Contains a paragraph on NS complaining that Bigger is fictionally implausible and racially unrepresentative after he begins to cut up Mary's corpse. W "has written a deliberately sensational book, and yet he asks for our pity and our compassion." Reprinted: 1957.45.

42. Anon. "New Books at Public Library: Black Power. By Richard Wright." Santa Barbara News-Press (10 October), p. C-2.
Unfavorable review criticizing W's anti-white bias, his lack of recognition of the benefits brought to the Gold Coast by the British, and, especially, his attack on Christian missionaries.

43. Anon. "New Books at the City Library." Wichita Sunday Eagle (19 December), Magazine Sec., p. 8.
Contains a favorable notice of the "gripping . . . vivid, brutal, frank" BP.

44. Anon. "The New York Public Library Countee Cullen Branch Presents The Negro as Playwright, A Drama Reading Session Arranged by Raoul Abdul."
Mimeographed playbill including a reading of scene IV of NS, one of several presented on 27 May.

45. Anon. "One of the Most Important Books Written in Recent Years." The New York Times Book Review (3 October), p. 16.
Advertisement for BP containing laudatory comments by William Targ, Ralph Ellison, and Walter White.

46. Anon. "'Outsider' Republished." The Oklahoma City Daily Oklahoman (4 July), Sunday Magazine, p. 21.
Announces the Signet Giant edition of the novel.

47. Anon. "Poor Man's Library or Among the Paperbacks." Albany (Oregon) Democrat-Herald (26 June), p. 7.
Notice of the Signet Giant edition of O.

48. Anon. "Popular Books in New Format." Oakland Tribune (28 March), p. 2-C.
Contains a favorable notice of the paperback edition of UTC emphasizing its refutation of the romantic myth of Southern life.

49. Anon. "Richard Wright Black Power." Publishers' Weekly, 165 (29 May), [2216-2217].
Advertisement.

50. Anon. "Richard Wright Puissance Noire." France Observateur (24 November).
Advertisement.

51. Anon. "Richard Wright The Outsider." The London Observer (19 September), p. 13.
Advertisement for O with a quotation from Granville Hicks.

52. Anon. "Richard Wright Uses Lash in Writing of West in Africa." Dayton Journal Herald (20 November), p. 24.
Somewhat unfavorable review of BP objecting to the harsh bitterness of W's indictment of imperialism, which provokes resentment rather than concurrence.

53. Anon. "Richard Wright." Utanför

Unidentified clipping.
Advertisement for the Swedish translation of O.

54. Anon. "School Books Screened." The
New York Times (11 March), p. 25.
Reports that in Galion, Ohio, the
school board judged NS to be an obscene book.

55. Anon. "Search for Freedom." The
Hamilton (Ontario) Spectator (9 October), p. 12.
Mixed review of BP admiring W's reportorial skill but charging him with
bias toward the British. The latter
part of the book is superior to the
first part.

56. Anon. "Tips for the Bookseller."
Publishers' Weekly, 165 (5 June), 2480-
2486.
Contains an announcement of BP (p.
2480).

57. Anon. Untitled article. The New York
Times (25 May), p. 25.
Notice of BP emphasizing the importance of the issues with which W
deals in a personal way.

58. Anon. Untitled article. The Spokane
Spokesman-Review (6 June), Inland Empire
Magazine Sec., p. 15.
Announcement of BP.

59. Anon. Untitled article. Toledo Sunday Blade (30 May), Sec. 3, p. 6.
Announcement of BP.

60. Anon. Untitled article. The Wichita
Beacon (30 May), Home Magazine Sec., p.
1.
Announcement of BP.

61. Anon. Untitled clipping. Publishers'
Weekly.
Notes promotion plans for SH.

62. Anon. Untitled photograph. Vrij
Nederland (30 October), p. 1.
Photograph of W with caption mentioning Margrit de Sablonière's interview
with him.

63. Anon. "Utanför av Richard Wright."
Unidentified clipping.
Advertisement for the Swedish trans-
lation of O.

64. Anon. "Wright in Paris." Worcester
Sunday Telegram (11 July), p. B7.
Announcement of BP.

65. Anon. "Wright, Richard," in The New
Century Cyclopedia of Names. Ed. Clar-
ence L. Barnhart. Vol. 3. New York:
Appleton-Century-Crofts, p. 4182.

Brief biographical note.

66. Anon. "Wright, Richard," in unidentified book, pp. 736-737.
Summarizes W's work and life, stressing the progressive qualities and
freedom from hatred in his writing.
This is apparently from a German
biographical guide to American writers. The year is conjectural.

67. Anon. "Wright, Richard. Black
Power." Bulletin from Virginia Kirkus'
Bookshop Service, 22 (1 August), 511.
Favorable review summarizing the contents of the book, noting its subjective viewpoint and its differences
from other books on Africa, and stating that "it may frighten--but it
must be accepted as an important if
sometimes difficult contribution."

68. Anon. "Wright, Richard. Black power;
a record of reactions in a land of
pathos." The Booklist, 51 (1 September),
2.
Notice summarizing W's "militant report" and concluding that "the reader
of this subjective account learns as
much about the author's attitudes as
he does about race relations in the
Gold Coast."

69. Anon. "Wright, Richard. Black Power;
a record of reactions in a land of
pathos." The United States Quarterly
Book Review, 10 (December), 559-560.
Notice summarizing the contents of
the book and emphasizing W's account
of the Convention People's Party.

70. Anon. "Wright, Richard, 1908-." Wilson Library Bulletin, 29, Sec. 2 (November), 4-5.
Notice of BP pointing out W's observation of the range of ways of life
in the Gold Coast.

71. Anon. "Wright, Richard. Savage Holiday." Publishers' Weekly, 166 (4 December), 2244.
Notice stating that the protagonist
"comes agonizedly to grips with the
darkest forces of his being."

72. Anon. "Wright's Account Too Much
Wright." The Los Angeles Mirror (24
September), p. 14.
Unfavorable notice of BP complaining
of W's excessive subjectivity.

73. Apter, David E. "A Negro's Dim View
of Africa's Gold Coast." Chicago Sunday
Tribune Magazine of Books (10 October),
p. 6.
Unfavorable review of BP admitting
W's sincerity but criticizing his
alienation from Africans and his

misunderstanding of social changes in Africa. He does not give the people of the Gold Coast the credit due them.
Reprinted: 1978.209.

74. Arms, George and Louis Locke. "Reading, Interpretation, Topics for Writing," in their Symposium. New York: Rinehart, pp. 399-400.
Study aids to accompany an excerpt from BB.

75. Ashford, Gerald. "Pilgrims in Africa." San Antonio Evening News (26 September), p. 76.
Favorable review of BP and Era Bell Thompson's Africa, Land of My Fathers. W's book "is better written, more analytical, and strikes deeper."
Reprinted: 1978.209.

76. Aswell, James. "Famed Negro Novelist Takes Look at Africa." The Houston Chronicle (26 December), p. 21.
Review of BP stressing the contrast between W the cultivated writer and the "semi-savages" of Africa. Aswell prefers W's novelistic curiosity to his social and economic arguments.
Reprinted: 1978.209.

77. B., B. "Book of the Week: Black Power by Richard Wright." Jet, 6 (7 October), 48.
Mixed review criticizing W for being "still the impatient, impulsive radical," especially in advising Nkrumah to assume dictatorial power. But the reviewer praises W's splendid use of detail and observation in reporting African life.
Reprinted: 1978.209.

78. Bixler, Paul. "In Again, Out Again, Galion." Newsletter on Intellectual Freedom, 2 (June), 1-2.
Reports a censorship case in Galion, Ohio, in which NS was removed from school libraries.

79. B.[iyidi], A.[lexandre]. "L'Enfant noir." Présence Africaine, No. 16, pp. 419-420.
Review of Camara Laye's The Dark Child comparing it unfavorably to BB. Laye romanticizes African life, eschews protest, and supports art for art's sake. W has greater scope, depth, and significance.

80. Bl.[air], W.[alter]. "American Literature," in Encyclopaedia Britannica. Ed. Walter Yust. Vol. 1. Chicago: Encyclopaedia Britannica, pp. 784-794.
Mentions W briefly (p. 793).
Reprinted: 1956.117; 1957.143; 1958.84; 1959.59; 1960.119; 1962.40; 1963.53; 1965.39; 1968.46; 1970.59; 1973.63; 1976.37.

81. Bond, Harold L. "American Literature," in The International Year Book. Ed. Henry E. Vizetelly. New York: Funk & Wagnalls, pp. 20-22.
Mentions briefly O (p. 22).

81a. Bontemps, Arna. "Recent Writing by Negroes," in Literature in the Modern World. Ed. William J. Griffin. Nashville: George Peabody College for Teachers, pp. 113-123.
Includes consideration of O in the context of W's career. Notes the novel's existentialism, Cross Damon's problems with women, and W's use of melodramatic devices in exploring serious themes.

82. Bowman, Barc. "'Body' and 'Soul' Methods of Two Reports on Africa." Dayton Daily News (26 September), p. 19.
Review of BP and Era Bell Thompson's Africa, Land of My Fathers. The former urges self-help, the only way out for Africans. W finds the Gold Coast a disturbing setting.

83. B.[radley], V.[an] A.[llen]. "Literature," in The World Book Encyclopedia 1954 Annual Supplement. Ed. J. Morris Jones. Chicago: Field Enterprises, pp. 153-156.
Includes a favorable notice of O (p. 154).

84. _____. "A New Look at Some of the Recent Offerings: Autumn Days Bring New Books Whirling Off Presses Like the Leaves." The Binghamton Sunday Press (10 October), p. 10-B.
Contains a brief, favorable notice of BP.

85. Brown, Glenora W. and Deming B. Brown. A Guide to Soviet Russian Translations of American Literature. Columbia Slavic Studies, ed. Ernest J. Simmons. New York: King's Crown Press, Columbia University, p. 215.
Lists six items by W.

86. Brown, John. Panorama de la littérature contemporaine aux États-Unis. Paris: Gallimard, pp. 12, 65, 107, 145, 174-177, 231-232, 405.
Includes a biographical and interpretive account of W in a historical context. Discusses NS and O and emphasizes W's disillusionment with Communism. A photograph of W working on the film NS appears preceding p. 449.

87. C.[aliver], A.[mbrose]. "Negro," in

The World Book Encyclopedia. Ed. J.
Morris Jones. Vol. 12. Chicago: Field
Enterprises, pp. 5486-5492.
Reprint of 1947.163.

88. _____. "Spingarn Medal," in The
World Book Encyclopedia. Ed. J. Morris
Jones. Vol. 15. Chicago: Field Enter-
prises, p. 7651.
Reprint of 1947.164.

89. Cary, Joyce. "Catching Up with History." The Nation, 179 (16 October),
332-333.
Favorable review of BP emphasizing
W's reportorial skill. He poses the
right questions concerning African
survival, but Cary believes that he
errs in condoning violence and lies
to build a new civilization. The book
is vivid, factual, and honest in its
observations.
Reprinted: 1962.45; 1978.209; 1982.
50.

90. _____. "A Record of Reactions in a
Land of Pathos." The Book Find News, No.
162 (October), pp. 2-4.
Favorable review of BP praising W as
a reporter. So honest and direct is
he in his observations that he often
contradicts his own previous arguments.

91. Chapman, John. "Beware of the West,
Negro Writer Warns Africans." Minnea-
polis Star (1 October), p. 26.
Unfavorable review of BP deploring
W's insistent opposition to British
colonialism.
Reprinted: 1978.209.

92. Clark, Michael. "A Struggle for the
Black Man Alone?" The New York Times
Book Review (26 September), pp. 3, 26.
Unfavorable review of BP pointing out
that W's "passionate and subjective"
viewpoint results in unfairness to
British colonialism, especially missionary endeavors. His own racial
bias prevents him from seeing that
"the concept of assimilation" offers
the best "hope for true racial equality and peaceful 'co-existence.'"
Reprinted: 1978.209.

93. Coffman, Lillian. "Public Library
News." The Chico (Cal.) Enterprise-
Record (3 November), p. 3.
Contains a favorable notice of BP, "a
militant report" by an author of
stature.

94. Collins, L. M. "Power on Gold
Coast." The Nashville Tennessean (17
October), p. 19-D.
Favorable review of BP emphasizing
the danger of communism and the back-

wardness of Africans. In viewing the
African, "W is sometimes confused and
angry but more often fascinated and
entertained."
Reprinted: 1978.209.

95. Conkling, Fred. "Wright Sees West
Africa in Turmoil." Fort Wayne News
Sentinel (9 October), p. 4.
Unfavorable review of BP expressing
apprehension about the African unrest
the book reveals. Conkling calls BP
"a curious mixture."
Reprinted: 1978.209.

96. Cook, Mercer. "Race Relations as
Seen by Recent French Visitors." Phylon,
15 (Second Quarter), 121-138.
Refers to W in works by George Adam,
Simone de Beauvoir, Aline Caro-Dela-
vaille, and Daniel Guérin.

97. Cowley, Malcolm. The Literary Situation. New York: Viking, pp. 123-124.
Mentions W as a paperback author.

98. Cully, Kendig Brubaker. "U. S. Negro
in Africa: Wright's Impressions, Right
or Wrong?" Christian Advocate, 129 (28
October), 28.
Review of BP objecting to W's criticism of missionaries in Africa and
expressing the wish that "some real-
istically brilliant Christian apologist might make personal contact with
Mr. Wright to help him see that in
the Christian faith rather than in
secularistic democracy lies the
source of ultimate freedom for mankind."

99. D., M. "Yale Puts Rare Manuscripts
on Exhibition; Conferences and Other
Coming Events." The Providence Sunday
Journal (16 May), Sec. VI, p. 10.
Contains an announcement of BP.

100. Deicke, Hanna. "Richard Wright:
Schwarz unter Weiss--fern von Afrika."
Bücherei und Bildung, 6 (January-February), 96.
Review of the German translation of
TMBV stressing W's belief that black
people in America, deprived of their
African culture, have not been able
to replace it with new values. Deicke
warns against W's one-sided picture,
for whites have helped to diminish
racism.

101. Engberg, Harald. "Sin egen gud."
Unidentified clipping.
Favorable review of the Danish trans-
lation of O. Like Norman Mailer's
Barbary Shore, W's novel shows the
extent to which fear dominates the
United States. W, an American Dosto-
evsky, rejects all ideologies in

portraying the "barbaric twentieth century."

102. Faries, Belmont. "Exploring the Basic Problems of Foreign Diplomacy--." The Washington Sunday Star (5 December), Christmas Book Sec., p. 11.
Contains a brief notice of BP.

103. Ford, Nick Aaron. "Four Popular Negro Novelists." Phylon, 15 (First Quarter), 29-39.
Discusses the themes, philosophies, and techniques of W, Yerby, Motley, and Ellison. Ford treats NS, which he considers weak in design, and O, which he compares to Crime and Punishment.

104. _____. "Negro Novelists of the Forties." Phylon, 15 (First Quarter), 98-99.
Review of Carl Milton Hughes's The Negro Novelist mentioning W.

105. Gannett, Lewis. "Book Review." New York Herald Tribune (23 September), p. 19.
Review of BP and Era Bell Thompson's Africa, Land of My Fathers. W seems ambivalent toward the tactics of Nkrumah. Labeled a Western intellectual by Africans, W felt himself an outsider. His advice that Africa should be self-reliant is open to serious question.

106. Glicksberg, Charles I. "The Symbolism of Vision." Southwest Review, 39 (Summer), 259-265.
Essay on Invisible Man with a reference to NS as a novel "of unrelieved horror" (p. 260).
Reprinted: 1970.151.

107. Grassi, Franco. "The Outsider di Richard Wright." Il borghese (1 February), p. 94.
Brief notice.

108. H., H. J. "Africans' Problems." Winnipeg Evening Tribune (27 November), p. 16.
Somewhat favorable review of BP approving W's perspective and effort to find the truth, but noting that "it would be frightening to think he has found out or knows the answer to the African problem."

109. Hackett, Alice. "PW Buyers' Forecast." Publishers' Weekly, 166 (4 September), 846-851.
Contains a favorable notice of BP, "a timely and informative" (p. 846) book.

110. Hafner, Richard P., Jr. "American Negro on African Gold Coast." Oakland Tribune (3 October), p. 2-C.
Review of BP finding it subjective but vivid.

111. Hansen, Ann N. "Candid View of Africa's 'Gold Coast.'" Columbus (Ohio) Sunday Dispatch (24 October), Tab Sec., p. 15.
Somewhat favorable review of BP noting the confusion resulting from the mixture of Western and African cultures. Although W has rejected Communism, "he has not swung all the way to the right."

112. Hansen, Thorkild. "Den sorte Raskolnikof." Copenhagen Information (7 September), p. 2.
Favorable review of the Danish translation of O linking W's philosophical themes to those of Dostoevsky and Camus. With a "near demonic intensity," the novel demonstrates W's willingness to view critically the entire range of modern ideologies--religious, political, and economic. Hansen also praises W's artistry.

113. Harsham, Philip. "Richard Wright's Bitter Pen." The Louisville Courier-Journal (24 October), Sec. 3, p. 12.
Unfavorable review of BP complaining of the chip on W's shoulder and calling the book "one of the most subjective, most one-sided, and most emotional pieces of writing to be labeled nonfiction in many a moon." Personal racial resentment makes W unfair to whites. Harsham's own view is "that the Gold Coast is indeed an enchanting place, populated by charming and likeable natives."
Reprinted: 1954.114; 1978.209.

114. _____. "Richard Wright's Bitter Pen." St. Louis Post Dispatch (30 October), Sec. A, p. 4.
Reprint of 1954.113.

115. H.[ayford], H.[arrison] M. "American Literature," in 1954 Britannica Book of the Year. Ed. Walter Yust. Chicago: Encyclopaedia Britannica, pp. 41-45.
Mentions O, "a strange and sometimes unsatisfactory blend of violence and talkiness" (p. 43).

116. Henriques, Guy. "Paris Diary: Witch-hunting." London Tribune (14 May), p. 3.
Discusses efforts by the State Department to send home Americans in Paris who criticize the United States. Quotes W on the matter.

117. Hooper, Sarah S. "Views Its Problems--An American Negro Writes About

Africa." The Birmingham News (28 November), Sec. E, p. 7.
    Review of BP summarizing W's discussion of politics and religion in the Gold Coast. Hooper takes the title to refer to African religion and its taboos.

118. Horchler, R. T. "Wright, Richard. Black Power." Best Sellers, 14 (1 October), 97.
    Mixed review. W does present a personal narrative concerning his reaction to Africa, but much of his criticism is flawed by lack of knowledge and by prejudices of his own. His subjectivity is a source of both strength and weakness. Horchler criticizes W's treatment of Christian missionaries.
    Reprinted: 1978.209.

119. Hunter, Anna C. "Books: African Gold Coast Challenge to West." Savannah Morning News (26 September), p. 56.
    Favorable review of BP, "an important contribution to political science and literature." Hunter admires both W's passion and his reason in approaching his subject. Nevertheless, she thinks that he is too hard on British imperialism, especially the missionary endeavor.

120. Hutchens, John K. "Book Burning (Cont.)." New York Herald Tribune Book Review (28 March), p. 2.
    Notes that "the Board of Education of Galion, Ohio, has removed Richard Wright's 'Native Son' . . . from the local high school library."

121. Israel, Richard S. "The People of the High Rain Forest." San Francisco Chronicle (21 November), This World Sec., p. 26.
    Favorable review of BP finding it realistic, vivid, and impressionistic. W's emotions are strongly engaged. He helps to bring much needed knowledge about Africa to the West.
    Reprinted: 1978.209.

122. Italiaander, Rolf. "Dichter des schwarzen Erdteils." Die [Hamburg?] Welt (c. November).
    Reports on W's visit to the Gold Coast, stating that he has completed a manuscript on the journey. W comments that he now sees the great guilt of America and Europe toward Africa more clearly.

123. J.-Q., K. A. B. "Black Power: An Examination."
    Lengthy typescript in the Wright Archive at Yale criticizing BP for its "wholesale condemnnations" and

oppressive pessimism. Much of the book's distorted quality stems from "errors arising from both fact and fiction."

124. Jack, Homer A. "Three on Africa." The Progressive, 18 (December), 41-42.
    Favorable review of BP, Oden Meeker's Report on Africa, and Peter Abrahams's Mine Boy. BP "is easily half-Wright, only half-Africa," but nevertheless valuable, especially in its emphasis on the importance of Africa to the West, its advice to Nkrumah, and its analysis of the minor role of Communism in Africa.

125. Jackson, Blyden. "'Coloured' in South Africa." Phylon, 15 (Fourth Quarter), 410-411.
    Review of Peter Abrahams's Tell Freedom comparing it to BB.

126. Jackson, Luther P. "Wright in Africa." Newark Sunday News (14 November), Sec. III, p. E2.
    Unfavorable review of BP. W is too contemptuous of Ashanti culture, which he would wipe out without providing an alternative. W's racial kinship and a visit of a few months have not equipped him adequately to analyze African life.
    Reprinted: 1978.209.

127. Jackson, Margot. "Books: 'Black Power' Is Strong Work." Akron Beacon Journal (24 October), p. 40.
    Favorable review consisting mostly of summary. Jackson concludes that BP "is a powerful book . . . bitter and philosophical, funny and frank, rich in descriptions and interpretations."
    Reprinted: 1978.209.

128. James, Mertice M. and Dorothy Brown. "Wright, Richard. Black power; a record of reaction in a land of pathos." The Book Review Digest, 50 (November).
    Lists or quotes from eight early reviews.
    Reprinted: 1955.52.

129. _____. "Wright, Richard. The outsider," in their The Book Review Digest. New York: H. W. Wilson, pp. 1030-1031.
    Lists or quotes from nineteen reviews.

130. Jansen, William Hugh. "Pretentious Is the Term." Lexington (Ky.) Herald (7 November), p. 39.
    Mixed review of BP. W is honest but pretentious and somewhat confused. Nevertheless, the book is well written despite unevenness and occasional verbosity.
    Reprinted: 1978.209.

131. Jarrett, Thomas D. "Recent Fiction by Negroes." College English, 16 (November), 85-91.
Discusses NS and, especially, O. Less popular and well written than NS, O has a more complex theme, moving away from race toward a universal quest for identity. Jarrett approves this shift, apparent also in Himes and Ellison.

132. Jones, Mervyn. "Two Into One Won't Go." London Tribune (22 October), p. 5.
Contains a review of O expressing respect for W's talent and intention, but arguing that the novel does not unite "the philosophic drama" with "the sharply realistic crime story." But the characterization is good, the ideas are interesting if unclear, and the evocation of New York is brilliant.

133. Kilpatrick, Clayton E. "Your Library Calling--Exploring the 40's and 50's." Omaha Sunday World Herald (21 March), Magazine Sec., p. 37.
Mentions the power and critical success of NS.

134. Koehl, Edgar. "Board Orders All Fiction Removed." The Galion Inquirer (9 March), p. 1.
Reports the sweeping action after the previous removal of NS and two novels by Hervey Allen. Rev. Kenneth Hans of St. Joseph's Church condemned the moral level of W's book.

135. _____. "School Board Temporarily Pulls 3 'Obscene' Library Books; 'New Applicant' Screening Group Is Provided." The Galion Inquirer (9 February), pp. 1, 3.
Reports that NS was one of three books removed from the high school library by the school board on moral grounds and referred to a minister for evaluation.

136. Kroll, Harry Harrison. "Richard Wright Travels in Africa, Learns 'You Can't Go Home Again.'" The Memphis Commercial Appeal (10 October), Sec. V, p. 10.
Review of BP finding it fascinating mainly because it reveals what Kroll considers the savagery and depravity of the African way of life. He disagrees with W's indictment of British colonialism.

137. Lee, Charles. "Spotlight on Books." Wilmington (Del.) Journal-Every Evening (12 July), p. 15.
Notes the inclusion of NS, a "memorable tale of violence and social protest," in a Grosset reprint series.

138. L.[ocke], A.[lain] LeR.[oy]. "Negroes (American)," in 1954 Britannica Book of the Year. Ed. Walter Yust. Chicago: Encyclopaedia Britannica, pp. 498-499.
Lists O.

139. Mandel, Siegfried. "Off the Bookshelf: An Indictment of Western Colonialism." Garden City (N. Y.) Newsday (25 September), p. 34.
Favorable review of BP. W's prescription for the future of Africa is debatable, but he "writes with emotional persuasiveness and power, relentlessly probing men, motives, myths and history for a terrifying glimpse of a continent in turmoil." Reprinted: 1978.209.

140. Marshall, John. "Colored Writer Relates His Impressions of Africa." The Windsor (Ont.) Daily Star (23 October), p. 24.
Mixed review of BP placing it in the "return of the native" tradition. An ex-Communist, W is still opposed to colonialism and imperialism. He is a good writer and the book is "an excellent portrayal of life in the Gold Coast," but there is some intellectual confusion about the ability of Africans to rule themselves.

141. Martens, Johannes Skancke. "Samtale med Richard Wright." Oslo Aftenposten (12 August), p. 3.
Interview focusing on W's reactions to his trip to the Gold Coast. He expects no Mau-Mau type of activity there, but he states that whites in South Africa can expect it.

142. Martin, Fletcher. Our Great Americans: The Negro Contribution to American Progress. Chicago: Gamma Corporation, pp. 82-83.
Biographical sketch of W, viewed as one of the world's leading authors.

143. _____. "2 Tell Hostility in Africa, Land of Their Fathers." Chicago Sunday Sun-Times (26 September), Sec. Two, p. 4.
Review of BP and Era Bell Thompson's Africa, Land of My Fathers emphasizing the estrangement of American blacks in Africa. Summarizes the argument of W's book.

144. Maund, Alfred. "The Negro Novelist and the Contemporary Scene." The Chicago Jewish Forum, 13 (Fall), 28-34.
Contends that in O W moves away from the racial concerns of NS to a more dispassionate, intellectual position. He is trying to put aesthetic distance between himself and Bigger.

145. May, John Allan. "Return of the Native." The Christian Science Monitor (30 September), p. 11.
Review of BP and Era Bell Thompson's Africa, Land of My Fathers. W has written a powerful documentary which is somewhat weakened by his Marxist patterns of thought. Even if he generalizes too much, W must be taken seriously when he points out the challenge of Africa to the West.

146. McGrory, Mary. "Reading and Writing: High Altitude and Dark Continent Items Dominate Fall Book Lists." The Washington Sunday Star (29 August), p. E-9.
Includes brief mention of BP.

147. Meacham, William Shands. "Race and the Novel." The Virginia Quarterly Review, 30 (Winter), 134-139.
Review of O (pp. 137-139) and six other novels. W again demonstrates "his consummate skill as a novelist." Despite the dust jacket's disclaimer, O is a novel of race, and Cross Damon is another native son.

148. M.[onroe], H.[arold]. "Awakening of Africans on Gold Coast." Fort Worth Star-Telegram (28 November), Sec. Two, p. 9.
Review of BP calling W "a keen novelist and a disillusioned ex-Communist." Unable to understand the language or the mentality of the "natives," W nevertheless suggests some explosive answers to Africa's problems.

149. Moran, Charles E., Jr. "Richard Wright Reports on Gold Coast Colonies." The Richmond News Leader (26 November), p. 13.
Mixed review of BP praising W's sincerity but noting his "rather odd combination of anger and whimsical amusement, of doctrinaire Marxism and equally doctrinaire capitalism." Reprinted: 1978.209.

150. Mourey, Richard. "Gold Coast Turmoil." The Hartford Courant (10 October), Magazine Sec., p. 19.
Mixed review of BP calling it "a simultaneously fascinating and yet a disappointing work." Although it is "a moving, deep probing examination of the black man's mind and life," W "appears to have approached the African Negro with the same mental reservations the white man still entertains toward the American Negro." Reprinted: 1978.209.

151. Murray, Don. "Two Americans Recount Impressions of Africa." Boston Sunday Herald (26 September), Sec. II, p. 15.
Favorable review of BP and Era Bell Thompson's Africa, Land of My Fathers. Murray speaks of W's "ability to give ideas dramatic intensity, to illuminate in bold acts the meaning of subtle gestures and words. He is a writer of great skill."

151a. Nyland, Waino. "Biography," in Good Reading. Ed. Atwood H. Townsend. Mentor Books. New York: The New American Library, pp. 123-128.
Reprint of 1952.55a and revised reprint of 1946.282.

152. O'Mara, Roger. "Literary Lantern: Wright's 'Black Power' Studies Gold Coast." Tucson Arizona Daily Star (28 November), Sec. B, p. 5.
Mixed review noting W's subjectivity and questioning his political observations, but finding the work "in many respects . . . a highly interesting commentary on a strange land."

153. O'Neill, Frank. "Inside of Books: Honor Ohioans; Wright's Africa." Cleveland News (22 September), p. 11.
Contains a mixed review of BP. O'Neill has reservations about W's advice to militarize African life, but he admires W's seriousness and his anti-Communism.

154. Popkin, Henry. "The Outsider, by Richard Wright." The Chicago Jewish Forum, 12 (Spring), 192.
Unfavorable review conceding the excitement of W's narrative but finding the ideas oversimplified and the characterization inadequate. Cross Damon is "an intellectual type, a mere possibility who is not a real person."

155. Poston, Ted. "Travelers Report on India, Africa." New York Post (3 October).
Favorable review of BP and Saunders Redding's An American in India. Poston notes W's affirmation of revolution in achieving African independence. Reprinted: 1978.209.

156. Quigly, Isabel. "New Novels." Manchester Guardian (21 September), p. 4.
Contains a review of O pointing out its excessive length, repetitiousness, and confusion, but praising its sincere grappling with the ideological problems of an ex-Communist. "Man is worth the large scale of his suffering, it seems to be saying."

156a. [Quinn, Kerker]. "Accent Autumn 1954."

Flyer listing W as a contributor to Accent Anthology.

156b. _____. "Accent Spring 1954."
Flyer listing W as a contributor to Accent Anthology.

156c. _____. "Accent Winter 1954."
Flyer listing W as a contributor to Accent Anthology.

157. R., V. O. "Two Views of the Dark Continent." Charlotte News (20 November), Sec. A, p. 7.
Review of BP and Era Bell Thompson's Africa, Land of My Fathers. Quotes from BP, focusing on the role of Nkrumah, but offers no evaluation.

158. Ramsey, Joseph C. "The Problem of Freedom for Africa." The Charlotte Observer (17 October), Sec. C, p. 15.
Highly favorable review of BP by a sociologist. Ramsey points out the value of W's racial and political perspective on African problems. The book is "a work of art" showing "keen insight."

159. Randall, James R. "Wright on Africa." Greensboro Daily News (3 October), Feature Sec., p. 3.
Favorable review of BP admiring W's ability to penetrate an unfamiliar culture. W's literary ability enables the reader to have "knowledge by experience" rather than the sociologist's "knowledge by acquaintance." Blending "the travelogue and the socio-political analysis," BP is both good reading and a timely warning.
Reprinted: 1978.209.

160. Redding, Saunders. "Book Review." The Baltimore Afro-American (23 October), Magazine Sec., p. 2.
Unfavorable review of BP finding it both emotional and confused. It plunges the reader "into the dark complexity, not of the Gold Coast of Africa but of Wright's involvement with his own socio-political orientation and his own philosophical ambivalence." Having repudiated both Communism and existentialism, W "is adrift between the unfulfilled promises of Marxist politics and the unfulfilled principles of democratic dogma."
Reprinted: 1978.209.

161. _____. "Two Quests for Ancestors." The Saturday Review, 37 (23 October), 19-20.
Review of BP and Era Bell Thompson's Africa, Land of My Fathers. Redding finds W's book impenetrable because of poor writing, loose organization,

and confused thought.

162. Reed, Doris T. "Richard Wright Uses Lash in Writing of West in Africa." Dayton Journal Herald (20 November).
Review of BP stressing the bitterness of W's attack on British colonialism. Self-rule, W believes, is the only hope for Africa.
Reprinted: 1978.209.

163. Rhea, James N. "Two Views of a Continent in Conflict." Providence Journal (3 October), Sec VI, p. 8.
Review of BP and Era Bell Thompson's Africa, Land of My Fathers. W is too subjective and cynical. He psychologizes excessively, and his political advice to Nkrumah is gratuitous.
Reprinted: 1978.209.

164. Ricksecker, Robert S. "School Board Member States His Views on Library Book Question." The Galion Inquirer (11 March), p. 9.
Ricksecker, having agreed to the removal of NS but having voted against the banning of all fiction from the Galion schools, comments that "'Native Son,' while an excellent novel, is too far advanced for the average high school student. . . . The answer is not to burn 'Native Son,' but to acquire other books honestly telling of negro life with less raw bitterness." See 1954.134.

164a. _____. "Why I Voted Against the Removal of Fiction Books From Our School Libraries." The Galion Inquirer (c. March).
Mentions NS briefly.

164b. Rose, Lisle A. "20th Century American Novels," in Good Reading. Ed. Atwood H. Townsend. Mentor Books. New York: The New American Library, pp. 65-74.
Reprint of 1948.184a; revised reprint of 1941.786a.

165. Sablonière, Margrit de. "Wees vrij, werkelijk vrij!" Vrij Nederland (30 October), p. 3.
Interview with W about Paris, the experiences behind BP, American racism, and the filming of NS.

166. Scratch, Walter L. "The Scratch Pad: Warns Africa on Red Aims." Hollywood Citizen News (4 October).
Favorable review of BP emphasizing W's anti-Communism.

167. Senser, Bob. "Africa, As It Appears to a Negro Intellectual." Books on Trial, 13 (November), 66.
Mixed review of BP. The book is fas-

cinating reading, but Senser disparages W's political analysis and deplores his atheism.
Reprinted: 1978.209.

168. S.[ordo], E.[nrique]. "Richard Wright y la epopeya negra." Cuadernos Hispanoamericanos, No. 49 (January), pp. 110-114.
    Reviews W's early life, mistaking his birthplace as New Orleans and the year as 1907, and comments on UTC, NS, and BB. Compares W to the Afro-Caribbean writers Luis Palés Matos and Nicolás Guillén.

169. Taggart, Joseph. "A Man Who 'Died' Starts Life Again." The Star (17 September), p. 8.
    Favorable review of O. Written with power and conviction, the story is haunting.

170. Taylor, Robert S. "Wright, Richard. Black Power: An American Negro Views the Gold Coast." Library Journal, 79 (1 October), 1831.
    Favorable review of "the best recent study" of African nationalism. W shows insight and passion in analyzing Western ideals and black slavery, white materialism and black power.
    Reprinted: 1978.209.

171. Tetley, Gerard. "A History of Bitterness." Richmond Times-Dispatch (17 October), p. 6-F.
    Favorable review of BP, "the most brilliant" of recent books on Africa. An ex-Communist and a black man, W "pens history in bitterness and he paints a backdrop of racial martyrdom," as well as treating the contemporary situation.
    Reprinted: 1978.209.

172. T.[hompson], C.[harles] H. "Wright, Richard," in The World Book Encyclopedia. Ed. J. Morris Jones. Vol. 18. Chicago: Field Enterprises, p. 8733.
    Reprint of 1947.292.

173. Thorne, Nicholas. "Two Reports on Africa: Richard Wright Sees Gold Coast." Norfolk Virginian-Pilot (26 September), Part Three, p. 10.
    Review of BP consisting mostly of paraphrase of W's argument. The work is written in W's "usual compact, hard-hitting style."

174. Tove, Shirley Ruth. "Negro Views the Gold Coast." The Raleigh News and Observer (10 October), Sec. IV, p. 5.
    Favorable review of BP stressing W's fairness in depicting African primitivism as well as British exploitation. The work is vivid and informa-

tive on an important topic, and "it reads with the ease of a novel."

175. Turner, Lorenzo D. "The Outsider. By Richard Wright." The Journal of Negro History, 39 (January), 77-80.
    Favorable review comparing O to NS. A full plot summary emphasizes the causes of Cross Damon's frustration. Turner concludes by claiming that certain passages in W "in telling phrase, concentrated action, and dramatic suspense, achieve heights seldom equalled in English prose, early or modern" (p. 80).

176. V.[allette], J.[acques]. "Uncle Tom's Cabin, by R. Wright." Mercure de France, 321 (July), 532.
    Brief mention of the American paperback edition.

177. Walters, Raymond, Jr. "SR's Critics Poll for Fall." The Saturday Review, 37 (2 October), 56.
    Herman Kogan named the "intensely personal" BP one of the year's best books.

178. Warde, Josephine Maury. "Culture of Africa Subject of Studies." Chattanooga Daily Times (30 October), p. 10.
    Review of BP and Era Bell Thompson's Africa, Land of My Fathers. Warde admires W's "reflective, subjective, almost intimate style," but deplores his "political bias" which exaggerates the wrongs done to Africa by the white West and ignores the beneficial effects.

179. Watkins, Charlotte Crawford. "'A Stranger and Afraid.'" The Journal of Negro Education, 23 (Spring), 153-154.
    Favorable review of O stressing the theme of alienation and the use of a psychoanalytical method. The characters are types, Cross Damon being "a symbol of modern man and his problems." The novel is important for an understanding of modern literature and thought.

180. White, Theodore. "Black Power." The Book Find News, No. 162.
    Favorable blurb: "one of the most powerful studies in politics and people that has been written by an American since the war."

181. White, Walter. "A Major Report on Africa Today." New York Herald Tribune Book Review (26 September), pp. 1, 11.
    Favorable review of BP, "the most important, informative, and infuriating first-hand account of what is happening in today's Africa." Nevertheless, White criticizes W's Marxist

methodology and his propensity for generalizations about Africa.
Reprinted: 1978.209.

182. Wilson, Henry F. "'Black Power.'" The New York Times Book Review (31 October), p. 44.
Letter to the editor refuting Michael Clark's attack on W. Clark exhibits typical Western arrogance.

183. Woolridge, Nancy B. "English Critics and the Negro Writers." Phylon, 15 (Second Quarter), 139-146.
Discussion and quotation from reviews of UTC and NS in the Times Literary Supplement and New Statesman and Nation (pp. 145-146).

184. Yasuhara, Motosuke. "Hanko to Zetsubo no Kokujin Sakka--Richard Wright" ["The Negro Writer Richard Wright's Protest and Despair"]. Geibun Kenkyu [Studies in Arts and Literature], 4, pp. 105-120.
W is introduced as the first Negro writer recognized for his artistic talent and as one of the two most gifted American writers that emerged from the 40's, the other being Eudora Welty. His importance is in destroying the image of a humorous, gentle, uneducated black man. The article traces W's experience in Natchez, Miss., describes his relations with the Communist Party, and considers his short fiction a significant achievement. W succeeds in using a stream of consciousness technique in "Down by the Riverside"; the best short story is "Long Black Song" for his superb portrayal of Sarah, unlike that of any other woman character. Although a great stride in American race relations was made through W's work, his vision, unlike that of Dostoevski, became distorted because of his negritude and his life as a victim of racial segregation. [Y. H.]

1955

1. Algren, Nelson, Alston Anderson, and Terry Southern. "The Art of Fiction XI." The Paris Review, No. 11 (Winter), pp. 37-58.
Algren comments that W errs in trying to write intellectually rather than emotionally (pp. 51-52).
Reprinted: 1959.2.

2. Anon. Back cover of Bandoeng 1.500.000.000 d'hommes. By Richard Wright. Trans. Hélène Claireau. Paris: Calmann-Lévy.
Publisher's blurb for the French translation of CC emphasizing the importance of the Bandung conference

and stressing the personal quality of W's reporting.

3. Anon. Back cover of Great Tales of the Deep South. Introduction by Malcolm Cowley. New York: Lion Library Editions.
Mentions W's "tormented fugitives."

4. Anon. Back cover of Le Dieu de mascarade. By Richard Wright. Trans. Jane Fillion. Paris: Del Duca.
Plot summary of the French translation of SH and a biographical note on W.

5. Anon. Back cover of Le Transfuge. By Richard Wright. Trans. Guy de Montlaur. Paris: Gallimard.
Plot summary of the French translation of O pointing out the novel's pessimism.

6. Anon. "Bibliographie: Le Livre de Richard Wright: 'Black Power.'" Bulletin Interafrique Presse, No. 8 (9-16 January), pp. 17-19.
Contains a biographical note, extracts from W's introductory "Apropos Prepossessions" in BP, and excerpts from Joyce Cary's review of the work.

7. Anon. Dust jacket of Ho bruciato la notte. By Richard Wright. Trans. Cesare Salmaggi. Verona: Mondadori.
Front inside flap contains a blurb for the Italian translation of O. Back inside flap contains a biographical sketch of W.

8. Anon. "Editor's Note." The Saturday Review, 38 (2 July), 10.
Mention of W in an introductory note to an article on book censorship.

9. Anon. "Invitation."
Printed invitation to a talk by W on BP in Paris on 8 February.

10. Anon. "Je maudis le jour où pour la première fois j'ai entendu le mot 'politique.'" L'Express (18 October), p. 8.
Questionnaire with W's responses on motives, influences, favorite writers, relation of the writer to society and politics, and other topics.

11. Anon. "Native Son," in Masterplots. Ed. Frank N. Magill. First Series. Vol. 2. New York: Salem Press, pp. 643-645.
Reprint of 1949.41.

12. Anon. "Native Son," in The Reader's Encyclopedia. Ed. William Rose Benét. New York: Crowell, p. 760.
Reprint of 1948.62.

13. Anon. "Ein Neger zum ersten Male in Afrika." Die Woche (October), p. 7.

Headnote to an excerpt from the German translation of BP.

13a. Anon. "Nihon Eibun Gakkai dai 27-kai Taikai hōkoku." ["Report from the 27th Conference of the English Literary Society of Japan"]. Studies in English Literature, 32 (October), 154-161.
Includes brief abstracts of two papers on W: Sadami Hirose's "Illusion and Reality in Richard Wright" and Kiyoaki Nakao's "On Richard Wright as a Typical Negro Writer" (p. 159).

14. Anon. "Public Library." The Concord (N. H.) Daily Monitor (22 January), p. 4.
Contains a notice of BP, which "proves that a common color of skin is not a guarantee of easy understanding."

15. Anon. "Puissance noire." France Observateur (24 November).
Advertisement for the French translation of BP.

16. Anon. "Richard Wright Puissance noire." Le Figaro Littéraire (8 October), p. 2.
Advertisement for the French translation of BP.

17. Anon. "Richard Wright The Color Curtain." Publishers' Weekly, 168 (10 December), 2332-2333.
Advertisement.

18. Anon. "Trois écrivains font leurs rentrée." Le Figaro Littéraire (1 October), p. 10.
Includes a photograph of W autographing a copy of the French translation of BP.

19. Anon. Unidentified clipping.
Photograph of W with caption in Indonesian.

20. Anon. "What's New at the Library." The Regina Leader-Post (2 April), p. 26.
Contains a brief notice of BP emphasizing the importance of the African revolution.

21. Anon. "Wright, Riccardo," in Dizionare enciclopedico Sansoni. Ed. Mario Niccoli and Guido Martellotti. Vol. 4. Florence: Sansoni, p. 1284.
Biographical note.

22. Anon. "Wright, Richard," in The Reader's Encyclopedia. Ed. William Rose Benét. New York: Crowell, p. 1227.
Reprint of 1948.117.

23. Archer, Leonard B., Jr. "Books for

Vermonters." Rutland Daily Herald (4 January), p. 8.
Contains a favorable notice of BP praising W's literary skill.

24. Baldwin, James. "Life Straight in de Eye." Commentary, 19 (January), 74-77.
Mentions Bigger Thomas (p. 75). Reprinted: 1955.25.

25. _____. Notes of a Native Son. Boston: The Beacon Press, 175 pp.
Contains reprints of 1948.125; 1949.79; 1951.129; 1955.24.

26. Bontemps, Arna. Story of the Negro. Second edition. New York: Knopf, pp. 173, 202-203.
Reprint of 1948.137.

27. Bouma, Donald H. "Richard Wright, Black Power: An American Negro Views the African Gold Coast." The Calvin Forum, 20 (June-July), 235.
Unfavorable review. Although the book is "mediocre" and "ineffective," W's distinction between race and culture is valid. For this reason the book would be valuable to missionaries bound for Africa.

28. B.[radley], V.[an] A.[llen]. "Literature," in The World Book Encyclopedia 1955 Annual Supplement. Ed. J. Morris Jones. Chicago: Field Enterprises, pp. 148-151.
Mentions briefly BP (p. 150).

29. Breit, Harvey. "In and Out of Books." The New York Times Book Review (3 April), p. 8.
Notes that W is among the authors whose works have been considered objectionable in Brooklyn.

30. Brewer, W. M. "Black Power. By Richard Wright." The Journal of Negro History, 40 (January), 81-83.
Mixed review. Brewer finds the work a pioneering, honest study, but he has reservations about W's Marxist interpretations. The book does not reconcile observation and analysis.

31. Brooks, Van Wyck. The Confident Years: 1885-1915. Everyman's Library. New York: Dutton, p. 545.
Reprint of 1952.27.

32. Brown, Sterling A. "The New Negro in Literature (1925-1955)," in The New Negro Thirty Years Afterward. Ed. Rayford W. Logan, Eugene C. Holmes, and G. Franklin Edwards. Washington: Howard University Press, pp. 57-72.
Contains favorable discussion of UTC, NS, TMBV, and BB, as well as less favorable comments on O (pp. 64, 65-

66).
Reprinted: 1971.57.

33. Byrd, James W. "The Portrayal of White Character by Negro Novelists, 1900-1950." Ph.D. dissertation, George Peabody College for Teachers, pp. 244-248.
Includes consideration of NS.

34. Cady, Priscilla. "As Richard Wright Sees Africa." Labor Action (28 March), p. 7.
Mixed review of BP from an independent socialist perspective. W is perceptive as a reporter and observer, but his political advice is dubious and naive, especially when he suggests that Nkrumah "militarize" the life of the Gold Coast.

35. C.[ollins], D.[oug]. "Black Power, by Richard Wright." The Calgary Herald (19 February), p. 4.
Unfavorable review complaining bitterly of W's anti-British bias and his residual Marxism. The book is "a pot-pourri of emotion and blurred analysis." W overlooks British liberalism, which made possible abolition of slavery and gradual emancipation of the colonies.

36. Cowley, Malcolm. "Introduction," in his Great Tales of the Deep South. New York: Lion Library Editions, pp. vii-xii.
Contains brief mention of W (p. xii).

37. Davis, Kingsley. "Blankes Aleen: Race and Caste in Africa." The Yale Review, 44 (March), 469-476.
Review of BP and eight other books on Africa. W's work is informative, but if he had traveled elsewhere he would have realized how little white dominance is left in the Gold Coast. Davis emphasizes W's subjectivity.

38. Delpech, Jeanine. "Puissance noire par Richard Wright." Les Nouvelles Littéraires (3 November), p. 3.
Favorable review of the French translation of BP. Notable for his intellectual honesty, W is estranged from black Africans, but he depicts their problems compassionately.

39. D'Ucel, Jeanne. "Richard Wright. Black Power." Books Abroad, 29 (Summer), 309.
Notice praising the complexity of W's psychological probings. W should look at Liberia for a corrective to his tendency to place too much blame for African conditions on white colonialism.
Reprinted: 1978.209.

40. Ellison, Ralph, Alfred Chester, and Vilma Howard. "The Art of Fiction VIII." The Paris Review, No. 8 (Spring), pp. 54-71.
Ellison comments on his relation with W (pp. 56-57).
Reprinted: 1963.78; 1964.51; 1970. 117, 118; 1971.95.

41. E.[lovson], [Harald]. "Wright, Richard," in Svensk Uppslagsbok. Ed. Gunnar Carlquist and Josef Carlsson. Vol. 31. Malmö: Förlagshuset Norden Ab, pp. 789-790.
Biographical sketch with photograph.

42. Feliu, Jorge. "Richard Wright visita España." Imagenes (May), p. 20.
Interview with W, who discusses his impressions of Spain and his opinions of films on racial themes.

43. F.[ranklin], J.[ohn] H.[ope]. "Negro in America, History of the," in Collier's Encyclopedia. Ed. William T. Couch. Vol. 14. New York: P. F. Collier, pp. 461-462.
Mentions W briefly (p. 461J).
Reprinted: 1962.58; 1963.84; 1969.87; 1976.74; 1977.137.

44. Gard, Wayne. "Four Books on Uneasy Africa." The Dallas Morning News (30 January), Part 5, p. 11.
Contains a favorable notice of BP.

45. Girnon, Rochelle. "Books and Authors." Youngstown Vindicator (27 November), p. C-40.
Contains an announcement of CC.

46. Grana, Giani. "Oltre l'estetica della violenza: 'Quel fantastico giovedì' 'Ho bruciato la mia [sic] notte.'" Le fiera letteraria (30 October), p. 4.
Review of the Italian translations of O and John Steineck's Sweet Thursday. W's novel is bloodthirsty and not always coherent, but his prose has a tragic rhythm and his theme is important.

47. Grattan, C. Hartley. "Africa Masses and Elite." The New Leader, 38 (7 February), 22-24.
Unfavorable review of BP. Because of W's confused attitude regarding his own relationship to Marxism and Communism, the book is "exasperating." Its power stems from the author's ability to recreate his direct observations, particularly those relating to the disturbingly wide gap between the intelligentsia and the common people. But W's political analysis collapses because he fails, like most Marxists, to comprehend the realistic difficulties of autonomous economic

development.

48. Gunther, John. Inside Africa. New York: Harper, pp. 830, 894.
    Mentions meeting W in Paris and Accra. Comments on W's discussion of Afro-American genealogy with a Ghanaian journalist.

49. Haginome, Hiromichi. "Richard Wright nitsuite" ["On Richard Wright"]. Kobe Daigaku Bungaku Kai Kenkyu [Kobe University Literary Society Study], 7 (March), 202-214.
    An essay reflecting Haginome's enrollment in a college course in the United States in which three realistic novels were used for basic texts: The Grapes of Wrath, Arrowsmith, and NS. Provides a brief introduction to W's career, mentioning UTC, NS, TMBV, BB, The God That Failed, and O. Noting the usual comparison of NS to An American Tragedy, Haginome calls Bigger Thomas not so selfish a character as Clyde Griffiths. Defines W as a melodramatic novelist and classifies O as a thesis novel. [Y. H.]

50. Hesse, Jean-Albert. "Les Livres et les hommes: Richard Wright le grand écrivain noir d'Amèrique est allé en Afrique pour la première fois." Unidentified clipping.
    Favorable review of the French translation of BP, "a dramatic and powerful testimony."

51. Jackson, Blyden. "The Blythe Newcomers: Resumé of Negro Literature in 1954." Phylon, 16 (First Quarter), 5-12.
    Includes praise of BP as one of the best works of nonfiction by a black author of any year.

52. James, Mertice M. and Dorothy Brown. "Wright, Richard. Black power; a record of reactions in a land of pathos," in their The Book Review Digest. New York: H. W. Wilson, pp. 976-977.
    Lists or quotes from twelve reviews.

53. Johnson, Beulah Vivian. "The Treatment of the Negro Woman as a Major Character in American Novels 1900-1950." Ph.D. dissertation, New York University, pp. 345-346.
    Includes comments on W.

54. Johnson, Charles S. "Negro in America," in The Encyclopedia Americana. Ed. Lavinia P. Dudley. Vol. 20. New York: Americana Corporation, pp. 65-76.
    Mentions W briefly (p. 76).
    Reprinted: 1956.217; 1957.232; 1958.172; 1960.172; 1963.118; 1965.86; 1968.135.

55. _____. "The Negro Renaissance and Its Significance," in The New Negro Thirty Years Afterward. Ed. Rayford W. Logan, Eugene C. Holmes, and G. Franklin Edwards. Washington, D. C.: Howard University Press, p. 88.
    Refers briefly to BP.

56. Kunitz, Stanley J. "Wright, Richard," in his Twentieth Century Authors: First Supplement. New York: H. W. Wilson, pp. 1111-1112.
    Critical sketch of W's career from the mid-forties to the mid-fifties.

57. La Farge, John. "Afrika zwischen Steinzeit und Atomzeitalter." Die Kultur, 3 (January), 8.
    Includes several paragraphs on BP, including extended quotations. La Farge sharply questions W's criticism of the work of missionaries.

58. Lennartz, Frantz. "Wright, Richard," in his Ausländische Dichter und Schriftsteller unserer Zeit. Stuttgart: Alfred Kröner Verlag, pp. 736-737.
    Biographical-critical sketch.

59. Levi, Abramo. "R. Wright Ho bruciato la notte." Letture, 10 (November), 443-444.
    Favorable review of the Italian translation of O with excerpts from earlier reviews of the translations of UTC and Five Men (stories later included in EM). Rejecting Communism, O raises basic issues in an inspired way, even if it does not resolve them.

60. Lyons, Leonard. "The Lyons Den." New York Post (6 June), p. 24.
    Mentions W's visit to Bandung.

61. Mohrt, Michel. Le Nouveau Roman américain. Paris: Gallimard, p. 26.
    Mentions NS and BB as examples of committed literature.

62. O'Connell, Jeremiah Joseph, Frank S. Tavenner, Edwin E. Willis, and Gordon H. Scherer. "Testimony of Jeremiah Joseph O'Connell--Resumed," in Hearings Before the Committee on Un-American Activities, House of Representatives, Eighty-Fourth Congress, First Session. Washington: United States Government Printing Office, pp. 524-545.
    Tavenner, the committee counsel, claims (mistakenly) that the film Native Land was based on NS (p. 537).

63. Omari, Thompson Peter. "Wright, Richard. Black Power." Journal of Human Relations, 3 (Spring), 102-103.
    Mixed review conceding that the book is "very informative and provoca-

tive," especially to the African intellectual out of touch with the masses, but complaining of W's intellectual arrogance and his anti-white bias.

64. Ørel. "Jim Crows Leveregler." Copenhagen Kristeligt Dagbladet (22 August).
     UTC is a graphic demonstration of the Jim Crow rules facing American blacks. W, who experienced them himself, writes best when he focuses on characters such as Big Boy whose fate provides a clear picture of the brutal system.

65. Piel, Jean. "Richard Wright, Puissance noire." Critique, 11 (December), 1110-1112.
     Review from a sociohistorical point of view of the French translation of BP. After a summary and analysis of W's major discoveries in Africa and his reactions to them, Piel moves to a more general consideration of colonialism and racism, finding the book "a fine illustration of the absurdity of racism."

66. P.[orter], D.[orothy] B. "Negro," in The World Book Encyclopedia 1955 Annual Supplement. Ed. J. Morris Jones. Chicago: Field Enterprises, pp. 173-174.
     Mentions briefly BP.

66a. [Quinn, Kerker]. "Accent Autumn 1955."
     Flyer listing W as a contributor to Accent Anthology.

66b. _____. "Accent Winter 1955."
     Flyer listing W as a contributor to Accent Anthology.

67. Ricksecker, Robert S. "Censors and the Library: Galion, Ohio." The Saturday Review, 38 (2 July), 11.
     Analysis of the censorship problems of NS in Galion, where the novel is wrongly judged obscene. Ricksecker makes a plea for sensible censorship.

68. Riesman, David and Nathan Glazer. "The Intellectuals and the Discontented Classes," in The New American Right. Ed. Daniel Bell. New York: Criterion Books, pp. 56-90.
     Cites W's description in BB of the "sloganized cynicism" of the lower classes (p. 69).

69. Roditi, Edouard. "Book-Burying in East Berlin." The New Republic, 133 (17 October), 23.
     Reports that East German publishers regret their inability to obtain publishing rights to W.

70. Rousseaux, André. Littérature du vingtième siècle. Fifth series. Paris: Albin Michel, p. 32.
     Mentions W.

71. _____. "Tragédies raciales." Le Figaro Littéraire (22 October), p. 2.
     Review of the French translation of BP. Like all of W's books, it contributes to the liberation of blacks, but its most important theme is the confrontation of Westernized blacks with Africa. W himself is unable to communicate with or relate to the African people. Rousseaux agrees with most of W's conclusions, but finds his "attempt at explaining everything through psychology . . . perfectly monstrous."

72. Schmidt, Albert Marie. "Sombres Histoires." Réforme (29 October), p. 7.
     Contains a review of the French translation of BP. In relating the problems of emerging Africa, W retains his skill as a storyteller, but his basic attitude is ambivalent.

73. Schneider, Edgar. "L'Ecrivain William Faulkner: 'Je n'accepte pas ce verdict.'" Paris France-Soir (27 September), p. 5.
     Comments on the careers of Faulkner and W (especially BB and NS) and quotes the critical response of each to the acquittal of the murderers of Emmett Till. W notes that at least they were brought to trial. Winning this battle, Mississippi racists are nevertheless losing their war to maintain a racial caste system.

74. Sempronio. "Ha pasado un gran escritor: Wright, apóstol de los negros." Destino, No. 919 (19 March), p. 34.
     Having met W in Barcelona, the author discusses his Spanish vacation, his literary career, and his upcoming trip to Indonesia.

75. Shea, Vernon J. "Almos' a Man," in his Strange Barriers. New York: Lion Library, p. 116.
     Biographical headnote to the story.

76. Sh.[uck], E.[merson] C. "American Literature," in Collier's Encyclopedia. Ed. William T. Couch. Vol. 1. New York: P. F. Collier, pp. 480-485.
     Mentions W briefly (p. 485).

77. Sievers, W. David. Freud on Broadway: A History of Psychoanalysis and the American Drama. New York: Hermitage House, pp. 319-321.
     Contains an analysis of the play NS with a plot summary. The work is "based on the fusion of psychoanaly-

tic and sociological insights." Sievers compares NS to Dreiser's The Hand of the Potter.

78. Smith, Thelma M. and Ward L. Miner. Transatlantic Migration: The Contemporary American Novel in France. Durham, N. C.: Duke University Press, pp. 31, 55.
  Mentions W's popularity in France and Jean Kanapa's attack on him. See 1947.218; 1948.183.

79. Stevenson, David L. "Novel, The," in The Encyclopedia Americana. Ed. Lavinia P. Dudley. Vol. 20. New York: Americana Corporation, pp. 503-524.
  Reprint of 1952.64.

80. Tarry, Ellen. The Third Door: The Autobiography of an American Negro Woman. New York: David McKay, p. 149.
  Relates her acquaintance with W and the origin of her essay "Native Daughter."
  Reprinted: 1971.293.

81. Thompson, Roy. "Chip in Africa." Winston-Salem Journal and Sentinel (3 April), p. 5C.
  Unfavorable review of BP criticizing W's expatriation and biased perspective.
  Reprinted: 1978.209.

82. Udekwu, Fabian. "Africa." Catholic Interracialist, 14 (July-August), 7.
  Unfavorable review of BP by a Nigerian. W's Western perspective misunderstands Africa. Neither "rugged individualism" nor W's Marxist materialism is compatible with African needs.
  Reprinted: 1978.209.

83. V., M. J. "Black Power. By Richard Wright." Sociology and Social Research, 39 (January-February), 193-194.
  Favorable review summarizing W's prescription for Africa. The book is appealing as a tale of adventure.

84. Walker, Danton. "Broadway." New York Daily News (28 December), p. 14.
  Announces that W has completed CC.

85. Winslow, Henry F. "Beyond the Seas-- An Uneasy World." The Crisis, 62 (February), 77-80, 125.
  Review of BP and Saunders Redding's An American in India. Compares the careers of W and Redding. Winslow emphasizes W's emotional power deriving from his subjectivity. He also explains the circumstances of W's journey.
  Reprinted: 1978.209.

86. Wolfe, Bernard. "Ecstatic in Blackface: The Negro as a Song-and-Dance Man," in The Scene Before You: A New Approach to American Culture. Ed. Chandler Brossard. New York: Rinehart, pp. 51-70.
  Mentions W and Bigger Thomas (pp. 54, 59).

87. Wulkan, Ronnie. "Book Review." Boston Chronicle (19 March), p. 6.
  Favorable review of BP finding its style "frank, familiar, easy-going" and its content of great importance. The book "aids us in obtaining a deeper understanding and insight into the current African revolution."
  Reprinted: 1978.209.

1956

1. A., C. H. "Negro Point of View." New Commonwealth, 32 (29 October), 442.
  Review of BP noting the contrast between W's Western perspective and his political commitment to African nationalism. Other educated Western blacks must share his attitude.

2. Abella, Rafael. "Richard Wright, El Extrãno." Destino, No. 973 (31 March), p. 38.
  Biographical article on W with an accompanying photograph.

3. Ager. "Søn af de Sorte's Forfatter." Aftenbladet (24 November), p. 3.
  Interview with W upon his arrival in Denmark. He discusses BP, commenting that "the more Western you become, the more anti-Western you become." He calls himself a pessimist on American racial problems and discusses plans for a new novel on blacks in Europe.

4. Amadea. "Richard Wright vill finna vara hednatraditioner." Stockholms-Tidningen (25 November), pp. 1, 21.
  Report on W's visit to Stockholm noting the scope of his curiosity concerning Swedish culture.

5. Anon. "About the Author," in The Colour Curtain: A Report on the Bandung Conference. London: Dennis Dobson, p. [188].
  Biographical sketch of W, appearing also on the back inside flap of the dust jacket.

6. Anon. "Advice to Ghana." The Economist, 180 (22 September), 955.
  Unfavorable review of BP. Though W's reactions to modern Africans are interesting, the book as a whole is confusing and disappointing.

7. Anon. "American Literature," in The American Educator Encyclopedia. Ed.

Everette Edgar Sentman. Vol. 1. Lake Bluff, Ill.: The United Educators, pp. 120-130.
  Mentions W briefly.
  Reprinted: 1961.6; 1968.6.

8. Anon. "Asian Resentment is Revealed." The Wichita Beacon (25 March), Home Magazine Sec., p. 5.
  Rather favorable review of CC, a book that is "illuminating and disillusioning."

9. Anon. "Aspects of African Nationalism." The London Times Literary Supplement (21 September), p. 555.
  Review of BP and George Padmore's Pan-Africanism or Communism. W's aggressiveness and anti-British bias weaken his case. Nevertheless, the book is honest, however subjective.

10. Anon. "Book Review." Unidentified clipping.
  Advertisement for CC.

11. Anon. "Books and Authors." Pensacola News-Journal (4 March), p. 4-C.
  Includes an impressionistic review of CC expressing enjoyment in reading the book but noting its superficiality.

12. Anon. "Books of the Year: A Feast for West African Libraries." West African Review, 27 (December), 1147, 1149.
  Contains a mixed review of BP praising the description but criticizing the political and social analysis.

13. Anon. "Bookshelf of a Workingman: Assessing the Afro-Asian Conference at Bandung." Weekly People (7 April), p. 4.
  Favorable review of CC emphasizing W's perspective and literary skill. His appraisal of Bandung is good, except that he gives too much attention to race and not enough to class.

14. Anon. "Buch der Woche." Unidentified clipping (23 June).
  Advertisement for the German translation of BP.

15. Anon. "Claasen Verlag, Hamburg." SPÖ Vertrauensmann, 11 (December), 350.
  Contains a favorable notice of the German translation of BP stressing the disillusionment W experiences while researching the book.

16. Anon. "The Color Curtain." The Bookmark, 15 (July), 241.
  Brief notice calling the work a "thoughtful exploration" of its subject.

17. Anon. "The Color Curtain." Latin American Index (2 July).
  Brief notice mentioning the scope of the Bandung Conference.

18. Anon. "The Color Curtain. A Report on the Bandung Conference. By Richard Wright." Current History, 31 (July), 44-45.
  Review contrasting W's views to those of Carlos P. Romulo. Notes W's sensitivity to racial overtones of Bandung. The rise of the Third World will necessarily mean a lower standard of living for the white West.
  Reprinted: 1978.209.

19. Anon. "The Color Curtain: A Report on the Bandung Conference, by Richard Wright (World)." The New Yorker, 32 (31 March), 110-111.
  Favorable review emphasizing the importance of the event and calling W's interpretation "excited but by no means incoherent" (p. 110). His perspective is important and his warning to the white West timely, but his specific recommendations for action are questionable.

20. Anon. "The Color Curtain: A Report on the Bandung Conference. Richard Wright." The Retail Bookseller, 59 (March), 91.
  Notice stressing W's emphasis on the role of race and religion.

21. Anon. "The Color Curtain. By Richard Wright." Foreign Affairs, 34 (July), 685.
  Very brief, nonevaluative notice.

22. Anon. "The Color Curtain by Richard Wright." The Franklin Park (Ill.) Journal.
  Favorable review emphasizing the work's revelations to the white West.

23. Anon. "Color Curtain, by Richard Wright." Toronto Daily Star (5 May), p. 15.
  Notice stressing W's point that Bandung was the last call for the West to respond to Asian-African needs.

24. Anon. "The Color Curtain. Richard Wright." The Muslim Sunrise, 28 (Fourth Quarter), 27.
  Favorable review recapitulating W's argument.

25. Anon. "Conflict of Races." The London Times Literary Supplement (29 June), p. 390.
  Review of CC and J. F. Lipscomb's We Built a Country, a defense of white colonialism in Kenya. Both works are attacked, W's being called "almost hysterically over-written and indis-

criminately stressed." But the review considers credible W's claim that Asian Communists, free of racism, have an advantage over the West in appealing to Africans.

26. Anon. "Curtaining Material." The London Times Literary Supplement (11 May), p. 279.
Publisher's blurb for the British edition of CC.

27. Anon. "De la inocencia a la pesadilla." Editorial Sudamericana (July-August).
Publisher's blurb for the Spanish translation of SH. W is a "novelist of violence" in the spiritual rather than the physical sense.

28. Anon. Dust jacket of Black Power. London: Dennis Dobson.
Inside front flap contains a blurb noting W's "trained writer's eye" and quoting from favorable reviews by Joyce Cary and Walter White. Inside back flap contains a biographical sketch of W. Back calls CC "a very necessary book."

29. Anon. Dust jacket of The Color Curtain: A Report on the Bandung Conference. Cleveland: World.
Blurbs on front and on inside front and back flaps. Back contains a photograph and biographical sketch of W.

30. Anon. Dust jacket of The Colour Curtain: A Report on the Bandung Conference. By Richard Wright. London: Dennis Dobson.
Inside front flap contains a blurb calling the work "a necessary book of the political thinker, and for all those on both sides of the Colour Curtain who spare a thought for the human race." Back contains a blurb on BP with a comment by Walter White.

31. Anon. Dust jacket of De la inocencia a la pesadilla. By Richard Wright. Trans. Leon Mirlas. Buenos Aires: Editorial Sudamericana.
Inside front flap contains a blurb on the Spanish translation of SH and a biographical sketch of W.

32. Anon. Dust jacket of Ma nel settino giorno. By Richard Wright. Trans. Cesare Salmaggi. Verona: Mondadori.
Blurb for the Italian translation of SH on the inside front flap. Biographical sketch of W on the inside back flap.

33. Anon. Dust jacket of Schwarze Macht. By Richard Wright. Trans. Christian E. Lewalter and Werner von Grünau. Hamburg: Claasen Verlag.
Blurb for the German translation of BP on the inside front flap.

34. Anon. "Emergent Asia." Toledo Sunday Blade (1 April), Sec. 5, p. 7.
Unfavorable review of CC. Even after making allowances for W's atypicality as an expatriate and leftist, the reviewer finds the book disturbing in its revelation of the anti-Western attitudes and the low quality of American leadership of "Asia's emancipated millions."

35. Anon. "Europa ej längre hopp för undestry ekta folk." Göteborgs-Posten (1 December).
Report on W's Göteborg lecture stressing his pessimistic attitude toward establishing a bond between European workers and Third World revolutionaries.

36. Anon. "Die Farbige muss gleichberechtigt sein." Hamburger Echo (10 October).
Report on W's speech to the Congress for Cultural Freedom. Insists that solving the psychological problems brought about by colonialism is of as much interest to Europe as to Africa.

37. Anon. "A Feeling for Colour." The Economist, 179 (9 June), 989.
Favorable review of CC stressing W's qualifications and recapitulating his argument. He may overstate the danger to the West of the emotional attitudes of Asians and Africans, but his views provoke thought and deserve respect.

38. Anon. "Gerningsmanden var en hvid mand!" Copenhagen Politiken (c. 2 December).
Report on W's lecture on the psychology of oppressed peoples.

39. Anon. ("Polybios"). "Ein Hinweis auf Richard Wright." Der Freidenker, No. 39, pp. 56-60.
General survey of W's life and career with special attention to BB.

40. Anon. Index Translationum 7. Paris: Unesco, pp. 71, 144, 365, 442.
Lists translations of O into Spanish, Danish, Dutch, and Swedish.

41. Anon. "De Kleurbarrière. Richard Wright." De 3rd Weg (13 October).
Favorable notice of the Dutch translation of CC praising W for his insight into the tensions of the Third World.

42. Anon. "Die Kral--Verwandtschaften."

Der Spiegel, 10 (24 October), front cover.
Cover photograph of W with a brief identifying caption referring to the feature story. See 1956.47.

43. Anon. "Liebeserklarung an die Kultur." Morgenpost (10 October), p. 4.
Notice of W's speech to the Congress for Cultural Freedom. Includes a photograph of W.

44. Anon. "Ein Mann mit einer Toga stand auf." Hamburger Echo (7 December).
Headnote to an excerpt from BP. Refers to Nkrumah as a demagogue with a Hitleresque style.

45. Anon. "Medborgarhuset." Stockholms-Tidningen (25 November), p. 5.
Advertisement for W's lecture on the psychology of oppressed peoples.

45a. Anon. "Nihon Eigo Gakkai dai 28-kai Taikai hōkoku" ["Report from the 28th Conference of the English Literary Society of Japan"]. Studies in English Literature, 33 (July), 205-214.
Includes a brief abstract of Isao Sekiguchi's paper "Richard Wright and His Circumstances."

46. Anon. "Novedades 1956." Editorial Sudamericana (July-August).
Notice of the Spanish translation of SH praising W's insight into subconscious motives and his ability to create dramatic tension.

47. Anon. "Onkel Tom ist tot." Der Spiegel, 10 (24 October), 49-53.
Biographical sketch with accompanying photographs. Concentrates on W's recent journey to the Gold Coast. W had difficulty adjusting to the African reality because of his Western acculturation.

48. Anon. "One Last Call on the West." San Jose Mercury-News (8 April), Magazine Sec., p. 8.
Review of CC summarizing the contents. Stresses W's argument that if the West does not aid the Asian and African countries, China will do so.

49. Anon. Papa Bon Dieu. Paris.
Playbill with a statement by W.

50. Anon. "A Personal Report on the First International Conference of Colored Peoples." Unidentified clipping, p. 7.
Publisher's advertisement for CC.

51. Anon. "Prefaces: The Color Curtain, by Richard Wright." The Detroit News (6 May), Sec. E, p. 17.

Brief notice emphasizing the importance which W attaches to the Bandung Conference.

52. Anon. "The Problem of Color." Garden City (N. Y.) Newsday (17 March), p. 29.
Review of CC consisting mainly of recapitulation of W's argument.

53. Anon. "Publishers' Promotion Plans." The Retail Bookseller, 59 (March), 68-72.
Lists CC and specifies plans.

54. Anon. "Puissance Noire par Richard Wright." Unidentified clipping.
Favorable notice of the French translation of BP relating it to the East-West conflict. W's main concern is "the problem of liberty."

55. Anon. "Reception for Richard Wright." Paris Book News (Winter), p. 1.
Announces a reception and autograph party for W at The Mistral Bookshop in Paris.

56. Anon. "Richard Wright." Unidentified clipping.
Review of CC emphasizing the importance of W's description of events in the nonwhite world.

57. Anon. "Richard Wright.--Bandoeng. 1.500.000.000 d'hommes." Etudes, 290 (September), 306-307.
Review of the French translation of CC consisting mainly of summary.

58. Anon. "Richard Wright. Bandoeng, 1 milliard 500 millions d'hommes." Le Journal de Genève (25 May).
Favorable review of the French translation of CC. W's generous spirit sympathizes with the oppressed but is not blinded by his sympathy. W can be irritating and provocative, but he is always salutary.

59. Anon. "Richard Wright découvre 'Papa Bon Dieu.'" Temps de Paris (28 March).
Discusses plans for the Louis Sapin play and quotes W's enthusiastic reaction.

60. Anon. "Richard Wright på Oslo-besøk." Oslo Dagbladet (29 November).
Interview with W, who is called a well-known writer in Norway. He comments on Paris and his recent work, noting that while he begins many novels, he concludes few. W also gives his reactions to his Scandinavian lecture tour.

61. Anon. "Richard Wright Pagan Spain." Publishers' Weekly, 170 (15 October), 1850-1851.

Advertisement.

62. Anon. "Richard Wright road av heden-
dom i Sverige." Stockholm Dagens Nyheter
(25 November), p. 10.
     Interview with W upon his arrival in
     Sweden. He states that he is inter-
     ested in the pagan remnants of the
     Swedish countryside because of their
     similarities to those he saw in
     Spain. He also discusses political
     events in Hungary, Egypt, and Alge-
     ria, asserting that the role of the
     writer is to stand on the side of
     improvement.

63. Anon. "Richard Wright: Schwarze
Macht." Die Quelle, 7 (November), 542.
     Favorable notice of the German trans-
     lation of BP. Emphasizes W's support
     of African self-development without
     either Russian or American guidance.

64. Anon. Richard Wright The Psychological Reactions ot Oppressed Peoples.
     Printed program of lecture delivered
     by W in Stockholm on 26 November. The
     sponsor is Bonniers Folkbibliotek,
     W's Swedish publisher.

65. Anon. "Richard Wright to Stage All-
Negro Gallic Play." Jet, 10 (21 June),
62.
     Announces W's plans to adapt Louis
     Sapin's Papa Bon Dieu.

66. Anon. "Richard Wrights budskap:--Vi
moste forsta varam." Lungs Dagblad (4
December), pp. 1, 5.
     Report on a speech by W to students
     in Lund. He claims that the key to
     improved race relations is the accep-
     tance and understanding of non-West-
     ern traditions and standards. While
     stressing the need to "modernize"
     Africa, W recognizes that the obsta-
     cles are as much religious as poli-
     tical in nature.

67. Anon. "Schwarze Macht." Der Bonn
Flüchtling (December).
     Brief notice of the German transla-
     tion of BP mentioning W's motives for
     writing the book.

68. Anon. "Schwarze Macht." Steyrer Zeitung (1 November).
     Favorable review of the German trans-
     lation of BP stressing W's ability to
     cast light on Africa's primitive
     elements.

69. Anon. "Ein Schwarzer über Schwarze."
Die Zurich Weltwoche (23 November).
     Favorable review of the German trans-
     lation of BP. W's strangely mixed
     background, combining puritanism,
     Marxism, and Freudianism with speci-

fically racial feelings, makes BP a
peculiar but very interesting book.
Occasionally W makes an absurd mistake, but his love of truth compen-
sates.

70. Anon. "Son av sitt Land." Frihet,
No. 6.
     Headnote to a portion of the Swedish
     translation of NS. Stresses the power
     and political intent of the work.

71. Anon. "Traductions: Sous le signe de
la solitude." L'Express (9 March), pp.
18-19.
     Review of the French translation of
     SH praising W's theme of existential
     solitude but complaining that the
     translation is weak.

72. Anon. "Trumpet with Drummers." The
London Times Literary Supplement (31
August), p. 507.
     Dobson advertisement quoting a favor-
     able review of BP.

73. Anon. "U. S. Negro at Bandung Conference." The Miami Herald (11 March),
p. 4-G.
     Favorable review of CC, a "colorful
     and revealing" book. Emphasizes W's
     observations of the profound differ-
     ences between East and West.

74. Anon. Untitled clipping. Elseviers
Weekblad (16 June).
     Review of the Dutch translation of
     CC. Stresses W's condemnation of the
     Dutch role in the Third World and his
     observations about Red China. W's
     position is not strange considering
     his background.

75. Anon. Untitled clipping. Frankfürter
Rundschau (c. 3 November).
     Review of the German translation of
     BP. W is a clear-sighted man without
     prejudice for whom Africa is as exo-
     tic as for any European.

76. Anon. Untitled clipping. Herron
Journal (December).
     Notice of the German translation of
     BP calling it the most important book
     yet on the recent tensions in Africa.

77. Anon. Untitled clipping. Profils.
     Mentions briefly O, noting with
     approval that its scope is more than
     political.

78. Anon. Untitled typescript. Pullman:
State College of Washington, 23 April.
     Favorable review of CC, probably the
     transcript of a radio program.

79. Anon. ("Peeping Tom"). "Verdens-
berønt og verdensmann." Torsdag (29

November).
> Article based on a conversation with W. Briefly discusses his recent writings, including BP, CC, O, PS, and SH. Claims that W is now able to look at his past without bitterness.

80. Anon. "Voices in the Wind: Richard Wright." The Message Magazine, 22 (June), 8.
> Quotes several key sentences from CC.

81. Anon. "Vom Mississippi zur Seine." Hamburger Abendblatt (10 October), p. 1.
> Reports that in his speech on "The Psychology of Oppressed Peoples," delivered to the Congress for Cultural Freedom, W "feels with the blacks" but "thinks with the whites."

82. Anon. "Die Welt der gruñen Dämmerung." Kristall.
> Headnote to an excerpt from the German translation of BP.

83. Anon. "Wir lesen." Gleichheit (November), p. 438.
> Favorable review of the German translation of BP. The book is an interesting mixture of W's views as a socialist, a black, and an American. While honestly admitting the elements of backwardness in Africa, W maintains hope for its benign development into an industrial society.

84. Anon. "The World of Books: The Color Curtain. By Richard Wright." Easton (Pa.) Express (20 March), p. 27.
> Favorable review. Although as an expatriate leftist W is not a typical black American, his book is "illuminating and disillusioning in that it uncovers a resentment for the West on the part of Asian nations that seems beyond our powers to rectify." CC is a candid and disturbing book.

85. Anon. "The World-Famous Author of Native Son Richard Wright." The New York Times Book Review (25 March), p. 22.
> Advertisement for CC.

86. Anon. "Wright," in Piccola enciclopedia Garzanti. Vol. 2. Milan: Garzanti, p. 991.
> Reprint of 1952.16.

87. Anon. "Wright, Riccardo," in Enciclopedia Tumminelli. Sixth edition. Vol. 2. Rome: Tumminelli, p. 2381.
> Very brief biographical note.
> Reprinted: 1960.105.

88. Anon. "Wright, Richard," in Der grosse Herder. Vol. 9. Freiburg: Verlag Herder, p. 1301.
> Biographical note.

89. Anon. "Wright, Richard," in Skattkista. Ed. Hjalmar Helgesen and Nic. Stang. Vol. 4. Oslo: Forlagt av Johan Grundt Tanum, p. 467.
> Biographical note.

90. Anon. "Wright (Richard).--Bandoeng. 1.500.000.000 d'hommes." Bulletin du Livre Français (March).
> Favorable review of the French translation of CC. Praises W's clarity, precision, and magnanimity in presenting an excellent account of one of the world's major problems.

91. Anon. "Wright (Richard)--Bandoeng, 1.500.000.000 d'hommes." Revue Française de Science Politique, 6 (January-March), 249.
> Notice of the French translation of CC describing briefly the contents.

92. Anon. "Wright, Richard. Color Curtain: a report on the Bandung conference." Library Journal, 81 (1 February), 412.
> Brief, nonevaluative notice.

93. Anon. "Wright, Richard. Pagan Spain." Bulletin from Virginia Kirkus' Service, 24 (1 December), 890.
> Favorable review emphasizing that the work is "a sociological indictment," not a travel book.

94. Anon. "Wright, Richard. Pagan Spain." The Booklist and Subscription Books Bulletin, 53 (15 December), 190.
> Unfavorable notice claiming that "naïvete of tone and ineptness of style" weaken the book, despite W's sincerity.

95. Anon. "Wright, Richard/Schwarze Macht." Weiden Erlesenes (September).
> Brief notice of the German translation of BP mentioning W's African ancestry.

96. Anon. "Wright, Richard. The Color Curtain." Bulletin from Virginia Kirkus' Service, 24 (15 January), 64.
> Favorable review emphasizing the importance of the book because the Bandung Conference received inadequate attention in the Western press. After summarizing the contents, the review concludes: "A personal approach--this; but a book that needs to be pondered."
> Reprinted: 1978.209.

97. Anon. "Wright, Richard. The color curtain; a report on the Bandung Conference." The Booklist and Subscription Books Bulletin, 52 (15 April), 335.
> Notice summarizing the contents of the book and stating that it "comple-

ments the more formal report in [George McT.] Kahin's The Asian-African Conference."

98. Anon. "Wright, Richard. The Color Curtain: a report on the Bandung conference." Wisconsin Library Bulletin, 52 (March-April), 90.
Brief notice calling the book "a subjective but factual report."

99. Anon. "Wright, Richard. The Color Curtain; a report on the Bandung Conference; foreword by Gunnar Myrdal." Wilson Library Bulletin, 30 (May), Sec. 2, p. 6.
Quotes from the review in The Retail Bookseller.

100. Aptheker, Herbert. "Books: Wright's 'Color Curtain' a Spotty Work." Daily People's World (10 May), p. 7.
Reprint of 1956.101.

101. _____. "Richard Wright Gives Views on Bandung." Daily Worker (27 April), p. 7.
Unfavorable review of CC accusing W of subjectivism, mysticism, and cynicism. Nevertheless, W does recognize the unity of the Third World against imperialism and for peace.
Reprinted: 1956.100.

102. Araki, Hiroyuki. "Richard Wright Ron" ["A Study of Richard Wright with Special Reference to The Outsider"]. Kochi Joshi Daigaku Kiyo [Bulletin of Kochi Women's University], 5 (December), 26-37.
A discussion of Cross Damon as a modern man who transcends custom, morality, and God, but must assume responsibility for his actions. He is discarded by society and thus tragic; he speaks the same language, wears the same clothes, and acts the same as his countrymen, and yet lives in a different world. He is like an ancient man suddenly transported into the modern world. W seems determined to pursue such a life, and in so doing he attempts to deal with contemporary problems. [Y. H.]

103. Ashford, Gerald. "Books Off the Shelf." San Antonio Express Sunday San Antonio News (18 March), p. 14G.
Contains a favorable notice of CC. W is correct in his assessment of the importance of Bandung.

104. B., A. "Richard Wright.--Bandoeng." Paris Carrefour (c. 15 February).
Favorable notice of the French translation of CC. Praises W's success in recreating the atmosphere of the Bandung Conference. Whether or not

one agrees with W's opinions, one should read and study the book.

105. Barkham, John. "Bandung and Its Significance." The Roanoke Times (18 March), p. 18.
Reprint of 1956.108.

106. _____. "Bandung Parley Bares Asia's Dislike of West." The Hartford Times (24 March), p. 18.
Reprint of 1956.108.

107. _____. "'Color Curtain' Shows Asians' Hate of West." Santa Barbara News Press (8 April), p. D-6.
Reprint of 1956.108.

108. _____. "Emergent Asia." Mimeographed.
Favorable review of CC expressing concern at the hatred of the West revealed by W. The West is not giving adequate leadership to Asia's "emancipated millions."
Reprinted: 1956.105, 106, 107, 109.

109. _____. Untitled clipping. Record (12 March).
Reprint of 1956.108.

110. Beckedorf, Leo. "Tür zur Heimat wer Veniegelt." Samstag (15 December).
Review of the German translations of BP and Robert Ruark's Something of Value, both of which show that black Africans "remain barbarians" in the twentieth century. But W puts a larger share of the blame on whites, who have failed as "teachers of civilization."

111. Bekker, M. I. "Negritianskaia literatura," in Bol'shaia sovetskaia entsiklopediia. Ed. B. A. Vvedenskii. Vol. 39. Moscow: Bol'shaia sovetskaia entsiklopediia, pp. 641-642.
Mentions W, UTC, and NS. The novel shows signs of W's transition to reactionary politics and artistic decline.

112. Bengt. "Flygvardinnan dagens idealhustru." Stockholm Svenska Dagbladet (17 October), p. 14.
Brief interview. W praises Strindberg, recommends reading George Padmore, and refers to a new novel he is planning concerning blacks in Europe.

113. Berry, Abner. "Books: Much of Value, New Insights in Wright's 'The Color Curtain.'" Daily People's World (28 May), p. 7.
Reprint of 1956.115.

114. _____. "On the Way: Richard Wright and the Marxist 'Left.'" The Worker (1

July), p. 7.
Reviews W's relation to the Communist
Party, disputing the early Party
praise of NS, which Berry calls "the
powerfully written work of an extremely talented writer containing a
credo of cynicism and doubt." Berry
further criticizes W's elitism, especially in O. To BP and CC, however,
he gives qualified approval, rejecting Party criticism of these works.

115. _____. "On the Way: Richard
Wright's Report on Bandung." Daily Worker (15 May), p. 5.
Argues that despite Aptheker's opinion CC has value as accurate reporting, however wrong W's conclusions.
These conclusions derive from his
"subjectivism and his identification
with Western political aims." The
book provides good insights into the
thinking of the Third World.
Reprinted: 1956.113; 1978.209.

116. Bixler, Paul. Untitled article.
Newsletter on Intellectual Freedom, 5
(September), 2.
Reports that BB was one of the books
on reading lists of Tamalpais and
Drake High Schools in California
attacked as "obscene and subversive"
by Mrs. Anne Smart.

117. Bl.[air], W.[alter]. "American Lit-
erature," in Encyclopaedia Britannica.
Ed. Walter Yust. Vol. 1. Chicago:
Encyclopaedia Britannica, pp. 784-794.
Reprint of 1954.80.

118. Bradley, Sculley, Richmond Croom
Beatty, and E. Hudson Long. "An American
Chronology," in their The American Tra-
dition in Literature. Vol. 2. New York:
Norton, pp. 1254-1277.
Lists NS and BB among "significant
literary works."

119. Breit, Harvey. "In and Out of
Books." The New York Times Book Review
(1 January), p. 8.
Contains an announcement of CC.

120. Brenig. "Wright, Richard: Schwarze
Macht." Das Neue Buch, 2.
Unfavorable review of the German
translation of BP. Despite its wide
ranging concerns and often accurate
analysis, the book "is not suitable
for our libraries" because of its
anti-Christian and Marxist attitudes.

121. Brewer, Anita. "The Color Curtain
by Richard Wright." The Austin American
Statesman (8 April), Sec. C, p. 20.
Favorable review emphasizing W's reportorial objectivity and his stature
as a black writer.

122. Brièrre, Annie. "Sur quelques
romans américains." La Table Ronde, No.
106 (October), pp. 175-178.
Contains a discussion of the French
translations of CC, BP, SH, and O.
His reportage in the first two is
interesting, but his Marxist conclusions in BP are not convincing. The
novels are better, comparable to
works by Graham Greene and Dostoevsky. O, especially, is a great and
powerful existentialist novel.

123. Brogren, Peter. "Brunonia Book
Reviews: The Color Curtain. By Richard
Wright." Unidentified clipping, pp. 25-
26.
Favorable review of "a rewarding, if
upsetting" book. W's analysis is
superficial at times, however.

124. Burns, Ben. "'They're Not Uncle
Tom's Children.'" The Reporter, 14 (8
March), 21-23.
Blames W for creating a distorted
stereotype of black American life in
the minds of such Europeans as Henri
Cartier-Bresson. Burns also surveys
his previous commentary on W.
Partially reprinted: 1960.207;
1961.219; 1963.150.

125. Butcher, Margaret Just. The Negro
in American Culture. New York: Knopf,
pp. 178-179, 183, 196, 275-277.
Discusses briefly NS, BB, and O.
Reprinted: 1957.153; 1972.244.

126. Byam, Milton S. "Wright, Richard.
Color Curtain: a Report on the Bandung
Conference." Library Journal, 81 (15
January), 192.
Favorable notice. The reporting is
objective and timely. W provokes
thought on an important topic.

127. C., J. "Un 'Bandoeng' culturel noir
à la Sorbonne." Paris Demain (27 Septem-
ber), p. 15.
Article on the Congress of Black
Writers and Artists mentioning the
French translation of BP and quoting
W: "I am black but I am also a man of
the West."

128. _____. "Richard Wright, Bandoeng;
1.500.000.000 d'hommes." Christianisme
Social (March), pp. 279-280.
Favorable review recapitulating W's
argument and endorsing it. W's analysis of Bandung will help French readers to understand the Algerian situation. In the Third World, Communists
will win if Christians default.

129. Cannon, Poppy. A Gentle Knight: My
Husband, Walter White. New York: Rinehart, p. 298.

Notes that "although Walter admired the art and power of Richard Wright, it pained him that many people might gain from such books as Native Son their only glimpse of Negro life."

130. Carnall, Geoffrey. "African Politics." Peace News (28 September), p. 4.
Unfavorable review of BP stressing W's lack of understanding of Africans. Carnall objects sharply to W's prescription of regimentation for African countries.

131. Chapsal, Madeleine. "Le Livre de la semaine: Le Transfuge." L'Express (20 January), p. 11.
Rather unfavorable review of the French translation of O. W's narrative skill is apparent in this novel, but his philosophical ideas are imposed on the action rather than emergent from it. As a man divested of myth and devoid of fear, Cross Damon is not a credible character.

132. Christie, Walt. "Book Notes." The Honolulu Saturday Star-Bulletin (17 March), Hawaiian Life Week-End Magazine Sec., p. 2.
Contains a favorable review of CC recapitulating W's argument. "Summary: grim, challenging reading."

133. Clay, George. "Pan-African Emotion as Seed of Power." Cape Town Cape Times (3 October), p. 10.
Review of BP and George Padmore's Pan-Africanism or Communism finding them complementary. The former is an emotionally empathetic commentary on black African politics and the latter an intellectually astute analysis. Both agree that African nationalism is the only route to the redemption of the continent.

134. Colombo, Achille. "Ma nel settimo giorno . . . di R. Wright." Letture, 11 (July), 300-301.
Review of the Italian translation of SH with a plot summary. W's perspective is Freudian, but he is not as successful in developing psychological motivation here as he was in developing social motivation in his earlier work. He is still adept at describing confused, nightmarish fear, however.

135. Colquhoun, Iain. Untitled clipping. Daily Dispatch (20 August).
Contains an unfavorable notice of the English edition of BP.

136. Corda. "Myrdals litterär indespruta åt tystlåten Richard Wright." MT (25 November).

Report on W's visit to Stockholm mentioning his admiration for Myrdal. NS has sold 70,000 copies and BB 65,000 in Swedish translations.

137. Davis, Arthur P. "Integration and Race Literature." Phylon, 17 (Second Quarter), 141-146.
Traces the movement away from protest literature, citing O and SH among numerous other examples.
Reprinted: 1960.140; 1968.74.

138. _____. "'The Outsider' as a Novel of Race." The Midwest Journal, 7 (Winter), 320-326.
Argues that the novel is race fiction with an added dimension because W uses a black protagonist although he is not centrally concerned with the racial issue. The reader accepts Damon without emphasis on his race because W de-emphasizes stereotypes, employs irony, and maintains a detached authorial stance.

139. Delpech, Jeanine. "Un Noir chez les blancs." Les Nouvelles Littéraires (8 March), pp. 1, 6.
Interview with W, who comments on his work in progress (PS) as part of a trilogy including BP and CC, on African religions, on himself as an ordinary American who looks to the future, on male-female relations, and on the writer as exile. Delpech refers to W as "the black Dostoevsky."

140. DeMille, Amine. "2 U. S. Reports on Color Line." Little Rock Arkansas Gazette (6 May), p. 6F.
Favorable review of CC and Carl T. Rowan's The Pitiful and the Proud. Compared to Rowan, "Wright says less, organizes, savours, thinks through before he writes." W's mind is practical and Western even if his sympathies are with the East. He looks to a time of global unity when "there will be no East and West."

141. Derbyshire, S. Howe. "Reading Is Real." Junior Reviewers (January), pp. 3, 26-27.
Calls NS "rough reading" (p. 26) for teenagers.

142. Dh. "Es kommt auf Europäer." Hamburger Anzeiger (10 November)).
Reports W's lecture to the Congress for Cultural Freedom concentrating on his analysis of the psychological relationship between oppressors and oppressed.

143. Dolan, George. "American Negro Now Living in Paris Writes of Color Prob-

lem." Fort Worth Star-Telegram (1 April), Sec. Two, p. 7.

Unfavorable review of CC noting the West's choice to help Asian and African countries or "let them be swallowed into communism." Dolan objects to W's excessive preaching.

144. Dover, Cedric. "Bandung--Through a Curtain." United Asia, 8 (June), 214.

Extremely unfavorable review of CC, which Dover finds "neither scholarly analysis nor adequate reportage." The work reveals W to be a "tragic mulatto" who is condescending, confused, "clawing at 'curtains', projecting his own infirmities, and soaked in mystiques."

145. _____ . "Culture and Creativity." Presence Africaine, Nos. 8-10 (June-November), pp. 281-300.

Quotes approvingly from W's "Blueprint for Negro Writing."

146. Durdin, Tillman. "Peoples and Problems: Accent Asia: Richard Wright Examines the Meaning of Bandung." The New York Times Book Review (18 March), pp. 1, 33.

Moderately favorable review of CC stressing the vividness of W's reporting. W stresses color too much and is not always informed about Asian affairs, but he correctly poses the central question of Bandung. Will the Third World develop with the aid of Communism or the West?
Reprinted: 1978.209.

147. E. "Skeptisk met europeerna." Göteborgs Handels-Och Sjöfarts-Tidning (1 December).

Interview with W, who discusses the plight of American and European workers, insisting on psychological wounds inflicted by economic conditions. In the United States, the same forces which keep workers out of politics affect blacks even more strongly. No revolution of European workers is likely because there is no nationalistic underpinning and conditions are not desperate enough.

148. Ehnmark, Anders and Hemming Sten. "Richard Wright will lära de förgode leva i 'vita världen.'" Stockholm Expressen (28 November).

Reports a conversation with W, called a "man without a home" who "saw through communism." W comments on his exile, which was necessary for him to continue to respect himself.

149. Elgstrom, Anna Lenah. "Forgod Värld." Malmö Sydsvenska Dagbladet Snällposten (2 October), p. 4.

Lengthy review of CC concentrating on the tension between Communism and Christianity. W fails to present accurately the extent to which conflict between the two is inevitable.

150. F., A. "'Puissance noire' par Richard Wright." Presence Africaine, No. 5 (December-January), pp. 115-117.

Unfavorable review of the French translation of BP stressing W's incomprehension and self-contradictions. Discusses W's political perspective.

151. F., R. "Schwarzer über schwarze Brüder." Essen Westdeutsche Allgemeine (c. 15 November).

Favorable review of the German translation of BP. The work has a good deal of general interest, but it is most interesting as a record of the reaction of a Western black to his African brother. W finds Africans more alien to him than Englishmen.

152. F., S. "Richard Wright; Schwarze Macht." Das Leihbuch (October).

Favorable review of the German translation of BP. It is necessary reading because it powerfully pictures the internal struggles and misunderstandings of both blacks and whites regarding one another.

153. F., W. S., Jr. "Bandung's Historic Role." New Bedford Sunday Standard-Times (18 March), p. 36.

Favorable review of CC consisting mostly of summary and quotation. The book is "vividly authored by Richard Wright."

154. Falk, Roger. "More of Africa." Spectator, No. 6,690 (14 September), p. 358.

Unfavorable review of BP. As sustained journalism it has moments of sincerity, but the subject seems to elude the author. W is very American in his naïvete.

155. Falkner, Lamar. "A Mississippi-Born Negro Sees World-Wide Racism." The Clarion Ledger-Jackson (Miss.) Daily News (18 March), p. 6.

Review of CC. Falkner boasts that the fact that Mississippi's largest newspaper prints a review of this book proves that freedom of thought exists in the state. W has discovered that racism is a global problem, not one confined to his native state. He has not offered any solutions, however.

156. Fasel, Ida. "'Black Boy' in Bandung." Tulsa Sunday World (8 April), Magazine Sec., p. 26.

Favorable review of CC summarizing its contents, praising its vivid personal qualities, and placing it in the context of W's career.

157. Faulkner, William. Faulkner at Nagano. Ed. Robert A Jelliffe. Tokyo: Kenkyusha Ltd., pp. 171-172.
Responding to a question about black writers, Faulkner comments favorably on NS. Afterwards, Faulkner believes, W's artistic sense was submerged by his racial awareness.
Reprinted: 1958.118; 1968.74.

158. Franklin, John Hope. From Slavery to Freedom: A History of American Negroes. Second edition. New York: Knopf, pp. 506-507, 602.
Reprint of 1947.190 and mention of W's trip to the Gold Coast (p. 602).
Reprinted: 1967.42; 1974.73.

159. Freedley, George. "Of Books and Men." The New York Morning Telegraph (14 April).
Favorable review of CC, a "poignant, pointed and powerful book" which should be widely read by whites.

160. French, Warren. "Richard Wright Gives His Opinion of Afro-Asian Bandung Conference." The Lexington (Ky.) Sunday Herald-Leader (15 April), p. 43.
Unfavorable review of CC. French argues that W attached exaggerated importance to the Conference, was unduly disappointed by its results, and used it "as a center about which to organize [his] own ideas," those of a revolutionary impatient with the slowness of social and political change.

161. Freyss, Jean-Paul. "Chronique lit-téraire." Teletyped. Paris: Agence France-Presse (23 April).
Mixed review of the French transla-tion of CC. Despite W's effort to remain objective, the work is a high-ly subjective book which, because the author is blinded by his vision of its historical importance, fails to consider the dirty power politics which took place at Bandung. Never-theless, CC is valuable for its descriptions, and many of W's conclu-sions agree with those of better informed observers.

162. Fuller, Edmund. "The Color Curtain; A Report on the Bandung Conference. By Richard Wright." Episcopal Churchnews, 121 (29 April), 22.
Review asserting that the work is a mild and "softly understated account of his experiences, encounters and observations" while attending the Bandung Conference. White Christians should read it.

163. Fullerton, Garry. "Two Enlightening Books on a Momentous Development." Nash-ville Tennessean (1 April), p. 7-E.
Favorable review of CC and Guy Wint's Spotlight on Asia pointing out their complementary approaches to similar conclusions. Summarizes W's book.

164. Furnas, J. C. Goodbye to Uncle Tom. New York: William Sloane Associates, pp. 307, 418.
Refers to W's work as "earnest tra-vesty of Farrell or Dos Passos." Lists three books by W in the biblio-graphy.

165. Gallert, Myra P. "The Color Cur-tain: Richard Wright." The Ethical Out-look, 42 (September-October), 174.
Favorable review emphasizing W's sin-cerity and his attack on Communism.

166. George, John B. "A Few Holes in 'Color Curtain.'" Washington Post & Times-Herald (8 July), Sec. E, p. 6.
Unfavorable review emphasizing W's tendency to generalize.

167. Glissant, Edouard. "Notes sur le premier gongrès [sic] des écrivains et artistes noirs." Les Lettres Nouvelles, 4 (November), 667-681.
Includes a summary of the views ex-pressed by W at the congress and commentary on the dual identity of the Afro-American.

168. Goodland, Tim. "Africa in the Microscope." West African Review, 27 (October), 945, 947, 949.
Mixed review of BP with much quota-tion. W's political, social, and historical analysis is misguided, but "as author, whose job it is to exper-ience the feel and smell of places and people, he does well." Includes four photographs by W.

169. Gordon, Eugene. "Spirit of Bandung a Growing Force in the World." National Guardian (16 July), p. 4.
Review of CC and George McT. Kahin's The Asian-African Conference. Gordon criticizes the latter for following the United States State Department line and the former for invoking the "mysticism" of color instead of social, economic, and political fac-tors in explaining the Bandung Con-ference.

170. Granet, Marie. "Wright (Richard): Bandoeng. 1.500.000.000 d'hommes." La Revue Socialiste, No. 101 (November), pp. 438-440.

Unfavorable review of the French translation of CC. Although Granet concurs with W's assessment of the importance of the issues at the Bandung Conference and with a number of his observations, she questions his objectivity in denouncing Western colonialism while ignoring religious and colonial wars initiated by others, including China. She also disagrees with his characterization of the American Revolution as an anti-colonialist war. W seems to leave no choice to Third World countries except anarchy or dictatorship. The book closes on an expression of anguish which may not be justified by political realities.

171. Grant, Donald. "Bandung Seen as Last Call to West." St. Louis Post-Dispatch (1 April), p. 4C.
    Mixed review of CC. Although W "is a sensitive, good and intelligent human being," he exaggerates the importance of race and religion at Bandung. Nevertheless, the book is an important contribution to our understanding of the event.

172. Green, C. Sylvester. "Good Reporting." Durham Morning Herald (1 July), Sec. IV, p. 7.
    Favorable review of CC describing the aims of the Bandung Conference and praising W's objective reporting. Green emphasizes the disturbing revelations of the book for white readers.

173. Grimes, Alan and Janet Owens. "Civil Rights and the Race Novel." The Chicago Jewish Forum, 15 (Fall), 12-15.
    Comments on the didactic aspect of BB.

174. Grodzins, Morton. The Loyal and the Disloyal: Social Boundaries of Patriotism and Treason. Chicago: The University of Chicago Press, pp. 139-140, 146, 150.
    Discusses the appeal of Communism to W.

175. Guberina, Petar. "Message." Présence Africaine, No. 8-10 (June-November), pp. 392-393.
    Quotes from "I Have Seen Black Hands."

176. Guérin, Daniel. Negroes on the March: A Frenchman's Report on the American Negro Struggle. Trans. and ed. Duncan Ferguson. New York: George L. Weissman, pp. 15, 16, 55-56, 68, 125, 129, 186, 190.
    Translation of 1951.175.

177. _____. "Richard Wright à Bandoeng."

France Observateur, 7 (23 February), 13.
    Favorable review of the French translation of CC stressing W's analysis of colonialism and his skillful coverage of the Bandung Conference.

178. _____. "Richard Wright en Afrique." Les Lettres Nouvelles, 4 (January), 128-134.
    Favorable review of the French translation of BP by a Trotskyite friend of W. Guérin admires W's vigorous denunciation of colonialism in Africa. The major problem raised by the book is that of the Afro-American's relationship to the ancestral continent--the questions of African survivals and "negritude." W sincerely tries to analyze the causes of his misunderstandings with Africans, but there is some contradiction between his regret that the West has destroyed traditional African culture and his own rationalistic dislike of superstition. On the other hand, W proves to be a good anthropologist in observing the status of women in the struggle for national liberation, sexual customs, and old taboos. W's political analysis of the emergent Nkrumah regime partly fails because W's justified suspicion of Stalinists prevents him from integrating the liberation of the Gold Coast into a world revolutionary movement.

179. [H., E.]. "Die Fremde eigene Welt." Kiel Schleswig-Holsteinische Volkszeitung (17 November).
    Reprint of 1956.184.

180. _____. "Problem der Afrikanischen Revolution." Kasseler Post (15 December).
    Reprint of 1956.184.

181. _____. "Richard Wright: Schwarze Macht." Argentinisches Tageblatt (1 December), p. 4.
    Reprint of 1956.184.

182. _____. "Richard Wright: Schwarze Macht." Bielefeld Freie Presse (21 November).
    Reprint of 1956.184.

183. _____. "Richard Wright: Schwarze Macht." Bonn Politisch-Soziale Korrespondenz (1 November).
    Reprint of 1956.184.

184. _____. "Richard Wright: Schwarze Macht." Deutsche Presse Agentur (5 October).
    Favorable review of the German translation of BP, a valuable book because W reports on experiences inaccessible to white travelers. Himself alienated

from Africans, W nevertheless sympathizes with their desire for freedom while recognizing that their problems may be too great to be resolved.
Reprinted: 1956.179, 180, 181, 182, 183, 185, 186, 187, 188, 189, 190; 1957.197, 198, 199, 200.

185. _____. "Richard Wright: Schwarze Macht." Oberhausener Stadthefte (December).
Reprint of 1956.184.

186. _____. "Richard Wright: Schwarze Macht." Offenbach Post (10 November).
Reprint of 1956.184.

187. _____. "Richard Wright: Schwarze Macht." Wilhelmshavener Zeitung (24 November).
Reprint of 1956.184.

188. _____. "Schwarze Macht." Aargauer Tagblatt (8 November).
Reprint of 1956.184.

189. _____. "Schwarze Macht." Die Innsbruck Wochenpost (24 November).
Reprint of 1956.184.

190. _____. "Schwarze Macht." Der Wiesbaden Aussenhandels Kaufmann (December).
Reprint of 1956.184.

191. H., R. O. "'Color Curtain' by Richard Wright." Lewiston (Maine) Evening Journal (21 April), Magazine Sec., p. 2-A.
Favorable notice calling W "a talented and gifted writer" and emphasizing the importance of the Bandung Conference.

192. Haas, Willy. "'Beide Seiten tragen Wunden davon.'" Die Hamburg Welt (11 October), p. 8.
Summarizes W's lecture on "The Psychological Reactions of Oppressed People" delivered at the University of Hamburg.

193. Hackett, Alice Payne. 60 Years of Best Sellers, 1895-1955. New York: Bowker, p. 183.
Notes that BB, the leading autobiography of 1945, sold "195,000 copies, and, with book club, 546,000."

194. Hale, T. L. "Iron and Color." The Birmingham News.
Favorable review of CC noting the advantages of W's perspective. Hale derives consolation from the fact that the Third World will continue to rely on Western technology for some time.

195. Hall, Rufus G., Jr. "Afro-Asians Ask the Way." The Oklahoma City Daily Oklahoman (25 March), Magazine Sec., p. 30.
Favorable review of CC emphasizing W's excellent credentials as an interpreter of "the mind and emotions of the Asian and African." These, rather than the external activities of the Bandung Conference, are W's main concern.

196. Harrigan, Anthony. "Here's a Grim Story." The Charleston (S. C.) News and Courier (11 March), p. 11-C.
Extremely unfavorable review of CC disparaging the book's literary quality, disputing its ideas, and criticizing its emotionalism. Harrigan concedes, however, the point that W reflects the ideas and attitudes of Asian and African leaders.

197. Harris, Arthur S., Jr. "Reports Racial Tensions in Asia and Africa." Worcester Sunday Telegram (18 March), Sec. E, p. 11.
Review of CC stressing its personal quality and its strong warning to the West.

198. Harrison, Florence L. "Mission Reported." The Hartford Courant (25 March), Magazine Sec., p. 15.
Favorable review of CC stressing the vividness of W's reporting and the importance of his Third-World perspective. The book challenges the West "to pick our way in making our policies with understanding, sympathy, and skill."

199. Hart, James D. "Wright, Richard," in his The Oxford Companion to American Literature. Third edition. New York: Oxford University Press, p. 852.
Revised reprint of 1941.760.

200. Hashimoto, Fukuo. "Richard Wright Ron" ["An Essay on Richard Wright"]. Kindai Bungaku [Modern Literature], 11 (May), 20-28.
Although Cross Damon is W himself, O fails to portray W's life accurately. W's desire to be an outsider is first shown in BB, which indicates, more than any other work, why he had to alienate himself even from his black brothers. To be an outsider was an achievement for W, since his readers would feel relieved once he had reached Chicago. But he still wanted to return to the black world; this impression, Hashimoto says, is strictly his own and "may well be wrong." [Y. H.]

200a. Hellstrom-Kennedy, Marika. "Black Boy i Sverige." Folket i Bild, No. 49

(November), pp. 8-9, 47-49.
Building on a description of W's Scandinavian tour, this article reports W's comments on several issues, most notably the relationship between Afro-Americans and the African independence movement. Also compares W's achievement to Zola's.

201. Hilsbecher, Walter. "Erwachsenen-bildung/Natur und Wissen." Frankfort Hessischer Rundfunk (30 November).
Mimeographed radio review of the German translation of BP. Concentrates on the clash between tribal customs and "progressive" forces, arguing that W's American attitudes make it difficult for him to understand the indigenous African way of life.

202. Hinden, Rita. "We, The Accused." Socialist Commentary (June), pp. 30-31.
Review of the English edition of CC. W is too emotional. He does not offer specific suggestions to eliminate racism.

202a. Hirose, Sadami. "The Art of Richard Wright: The Literature of Fear." American Literary Review, 15 (July), 4-5.
Examines the relationship between reality and idealism in NS and BB. Considers the sense of fear underlying W's work as artistically viable and capable of expressing the humanity of black people. [Y. H. and T. K.]

203. Hoffman, Frederick J. The Modern Novel in America. Revised edition. Chicago: Regnery, pp. xiv, 36, 149.
Reprint of 1951.180 with a disparaging comment on O added.
Reprinted: 1963.110.

204. Huff, William Henry. "Between Book Covers." The Rockford Crusader (c. 23 June).
Favorable review of CC with quotations. W "is one of the most brilliant writers of the present age."

205. Hughes, Langston. "From Harlem to Paris." The New York Times Book Review (26 February), p. 26.
Review of Notes of a Native Son mentioning W.
Reprinted: 1974.95.

206. Huguenin, Jean-René. "Voici la legion étrangere de la littérature." Unidentified clipping (26 September-2 October).
Report on the Congress of Black Writers and Artists contrasting W and Camara Laye to underline the wide cultural range of the meeting.

207. Irvine, Keith. "The Challenge of Asia and Africa." The New Leader, 39 (23 April), 24-25.
Rather favorable review of CC. Whereas BP was analytical, the present volume "is a synthetic delineation of the problems afflicting newly independent nations which have emerged from colonial rule." W does not understand religion, but his discussion of racial problems is illuminating. Irving claims for CC "the virtue of dealing forthrightly with a delicate problem of great magnitude."

208. Irwin, Spencer D. "U Nu, U. S., U. S. S. R. & Rice." Cleveland Plain Dealer (8 April), Sec. B, p. 4.
Editorial containing brief reviews of CC and George Kahin's The Asian-African Conference. W is especially good at conveying the emotional tone at Bandung.

208a. Italiander, Rolf. Untitled clipping. Die Hamburg [?] Welt (November).
Notice of the German translation of BP.

209. Ivy, James W. "First Negro Congress of Writers and Artists." The Crisis, 63 (December), 593-600.
Mentions and quotes from W's speech.

210. Jack, Homer A. "Asia's Last Call to the West." The Saturday Review, 39 (17 March), 19-20.
Favorable review of CC commending W's sensitivity and insight.

211. Jackson, Blyden. "The Continuing Strain: Resume of Negro Literature in 1955." Phylon, 17 (First Quarter), 35-40.
Mentions BP.

212. Jackson, Luther P. "Wright on Race." Newark Sunday News (1 April), Sec. III, p. E2.
Unfavorable review of CC. Emphasizing East-West struggle, Jackson complains that W's own racial experience prevents his attaining journalistic objectivity. Instead, "he almost gleefully predicts that unity would result in the ascendancy of the colored majority over the erstwhile oppressors."

213. Jaeger, Hans. "Richard Wright, Schwarze Macht." Bulletin on German Questions (12 January).
Mimeographed review of the German translation of BP correcting misinterpretations about W's conceit and

condescension toward Africans. W is himself more anti-imperialist than the Africans.

214. James, Mertice M. and Dorothy Brown. "Wright, Richard. Color curtain; a report on the Bandung conference." The Book Review Digest, 52 (May).
Lists or quotes from ten early reviews.

215. _____. "Wright, Richard. Color curtain; a report on the Bandung conference." The Book Review Digest, 52 (August).
Lists or quotes from fourteen early reviews.

216. James, Weldon. "Observations from 'Behind the Color Curtain.'" The Louisville Courier-Journal (8 April), Sec. 4, p. 7.
Generally favorable review, but James considers W too naive and self-assured in his analysis, which tends to be too Marxist. But his skepticism about Russia and China, and his faith in the West's ability to help the Third World, are welcome. James is also favorably impressed by W's "muscular prose."

217. Johnson, Charles S. "Negro in America," in The Encyclopedia Americana. Ed. Lavinia P. Dudley. Vol. 20. New York: Americana Corporation, pp. 65-77.
Reprint of 1955.54.

218. Johnson, Paul. "Black Honour." The New Statesman and Nation, 52 (25 August), 221-222.
Favorable review of BP and George Padmore's Pan-Africanism or Communism written from the viewpoint of a European liberal. W stresses "the psychological background of the struggle for Negro freedom"; Padmore considers political and economic matters. Both emphasize that Africans must act for themselves in pursuing their own ends.

219. Jones, Jeanette T. "About Books." Mimeographed Associated Negro Press release (8 August).
Favorable review of CC accepting W's analysis, noting his objectivity, and praising the work as "a warm, vibrating human story."
Reprinted: 1956.220.

220. _____. "About Books." The Westchester County Press (11 August).
Reprint of 1956.219.

221. Jones, Mervyn. "Watch the Gold Coast!" London Tribune (24 August), p. 11.

Favorable review of BP finding that it combines a "compendium of useful facts," a political report, and "a penetrating investigation of the state of mind of Africa." W's special perspective makes him almost uniquely qualified to write such a book. Jones is hopeful for the future of black Africa.

222. Kaufmann, Herbert. "Ein Afro-Amerikaner in Afrika." Kölner Stadt-Anzeiger (10 November).
Favorable review of the German translation of BP emphasizing W's Marxist, Freudian, materialist, and Western perspective. He brilliantly exposes white cultural imperialism, which rests on the denial of African premises, especially those concerning cause and effect. W does overlook such honorable white exceptions as Albert Schweitzer, however.
Reprinted: 1956.223.

223. _____. "Gedanken zur Revolution in Ghana." Frankfurter Allgemeine Zeitung für Deutschland (10 November), Bilder und Zeiten Sec., p. 5.
Reprint of 1956.222.

224. Kazin, Alfred. On Native Grounds. Abridged edition. Anchor Books A69. Garden City, N. Y.: Doubleday, pp. 291, 295, 301-302.
Reprint of 1942.254.

225. Kitching, Jessie. "PW Buyers' Forecast." Publishers' Weekly, 169 (25 February), 1190.
Includes a favorable notice of CC, a "striking personal report."

226. Kozicki, Richard J. "Book Review." World Affairs Councilor, 7 (May).
Favorable review of CC. Although W does not have a profound knowledge of Asian affairs, he writes well and has historical insight.

227. L., J. "Afrikabücher--mit und ohne Vorurteile." Tages-Anzeiger für Stadt und Kanton Zurich (7 December).
Unfavorable review of the German translation of BP. Although the work is valuable as the report of a black American's reaction to his ancestral land, it is worthless as political analysis because of W's prejudices, which stem from an inadequate understanding of Africa.

228. L., R. D. "Story of Bandung Conference Highly Significant Reporting." San Rafael (Cal.) Independent-Journal (31 March), p. M2.
Favorable review of CC noting its subjectivity but stressing its inter-

pretive skill and its readability. Above all, it is provocative of thought.

229. Lalain, Odile de. "Richard Wright: Puissance Noire (Corréa)." La Nouvelle Nouvelle Revue Française, No. 38 (February), p. 352.
Brief favorable review of the French translation of BP. W is more American than black in his attitudes, however much he wishes to sympathize with Africans.

230. Lalou, René. "Le Livre de la semaine: Le Transfuge par Richard Wright." Les Nouvelles Littéraires (26 January), p. 3.
Review of the French translation of O summarizing the plot and analyzing some of the themes. Lalou finds the style a bit heavy with theoretical speeches at times impeding the flow of an otherwise exciting narrative.

231. Lamming, George. "The Negro Writer and His World." Présence Africaine, Nos. 8-10 (June-November), pp. 324-332.
Contains a brief reference to W (p. 324).

232. Lauras, A. "Richard Wright.--Le Transfuge." Etudes, 291 (November), 316.
Unfavorable review of the French translation of O finding fault with the writing but praising moments of "terrible lucidity." Includes a plot summary.

233. Lee, Charles. "The New Books-- Celebrities." Farm & Home News (20 March).
Contains a notice of CC, "an illuminating, sometimes explosive, and frequently belligerently pessimistic personal account."

234. Lessing, Doris. "Africa Illuminated." London Daily Worker (6 September), p. 2.
Favorable review of BP praising its "lively and vivid" portrayal of the Gold Coast. Lessing finds W's political position contradictory, however, because he condones black dictatorship in Africa after having repudiated Communism because of its curtailment of civil liberties.

235. Logue, Ellen. "The Color Curtain by Richard Wright." Books on Trial, 14 (April-May), 351-352.
Favorable review recapitulating W's emphasis on color as a crucial factor at Bandung. The issues W raises deserve attention.
Reprinted: 1978.209.

236. Lonnquist, Axel. "Racial Issues." New York Herald Tribune, European Edition (17 December), p. 4.
Letter to the editor protesting W's Swedish lectures on racism.

237. Lubis, Mochtar. "Through Coloured Glasses?" Encounter, 6 (March), 73.
Disagrees with the views expressed in W's "Indonesian Notebook" and accuses W of misquoting him. According to Lubis, race is not an important element of Asian life.

238. Lunger, Phil. "West Challenged to Moral Conscience: Sharp Focus Thrown on Racial Unrest." Buffalo Courier-Express (15 April), p. 24-D.
Mixed review of CC. Although Lunger praises W's "penetrating insight," he questions W's objectivity and believes that W underemphasizes the anti-Communism of many participants in the Bandung Conference.

239. Luskin, Michael M. "The Color Curtain by Richard Wright." The Greenville (N. C.) Daily Reflector (23 March), p. 7.
Favorable review sympathetic to W's assessment of Bandung. Luskin calls W's style "easy to read and clear."

240. Lyons, Leonard. "The Lyons Den." New York Post (25 September), p. 32.
Notes that W is completing a novel with a Paris setting and that he is changing publishers from Harper to Doubleday.

241. M., I. "The Magnitude of Bandung." Labour Monthly, 38 (November), 527.
Mixed review of CC. Although the book is shallow and superficial, it is useful because it is better than British reporting about Asian affairs.

242. Mandelin, Mary. "Mellan Svart Pojke och Mörk Kraft." Astra (c. December), pp. 286-287.
Profile of W's personality accompanied by vignettes of his domestic life and photographs of the W family.

243. Marguth, George. "Ein Arm voll Bücher." Koblenz Rhein-Zeitung (12 October).
Favorable review of the German translation of BP. W's black perspective is a necessary antidote to white views of Africa. W confronts the internal tensions facing Nkrumah and recommends militancy as a solution.

244. Marqués, Claudio. "Bandoeng, 1.500.000.000 de hombres." El Correo

Catalán (2 September).
Review of the Spanish translation of
CC. While welcoming the book because
of W's past accomplishments, the
reviewer claims that W contradicts
himself by calling the Third World
movement religious in nature while
maintaining that the West has destroyed all Eastern culture.

245. Martens, Johannes S. "Jeg er sort--
men en Mann fra Vesten." VG (18 November).
Lengthy interview with W, who calls
the Congress for Black Writers and
Artists "an extension of the Bandung
Conference." Insisting on the psychological impact of Western education,
W analyzes the relationship of intellectuals to African politics.

246. _____. Unidentified clipping.
Interview with W, who discusses the
links between paganism in Spain and
Africa, stressing the necessity to
colonialism of the religious domination of old ways, which never took
place in Spain or in Africa. The year
is conjectural.

247. Martin, Fletcher. "'Color Curtain'
Gives the West a Warning." Chicago Sunday Sun-Times (18 March), Sec. Two, p.
4.
Favorable review calling it an "un-
complicated volume" written with
"simple-minded honesty" from a perspective sympathetic to the Third
World. CC is an expansion of the
crusade against racism previously
fought in NS, BB, and BP.

248. McLaughlin, Richard. "'The Color
Curtain' by Richard Wright." Springfield
(Mass.) Sunday Republican (8 April), p.
10C.
Review summarizing the "very disturbing" argument of the book, emphasizing W's warning to the West.

249. Messiaen, Pierre. "Lettres américaines: Richard Wright, romancier noir."
La Croix (12-13 February), p. 3.
Review of the French translations of
O and BP. Less successful than NS or
BB, O is too sensationalistic in a
cinematic way and contains objectionable language. BP is unjustified in
its criticism of Christian missionaries in Africa.

250. Mohn, Bent. "Hvide kan ikke skildre
sorte." Information Mandag, 3 (December).
Interview with W, who discusses the
relationship between psychology and
realism in his writing and the treatment of black characters by white

writers such as Faulkner and Lillian
Smith.

251. Myrdal, Gunnar, "Foreword," in The
Color Curtain. Cleveland: World, pp.
7-8.
Notes that the book records W's im-
pressions of the Bandung Conference.
Not a documented scholarly analysis,
CC is valuable for its perspective,
honesty, and artistry.
Reprinted: 1956.252.

252. _____. "Foreword," in The Colour
Curtain. London: Dennis Dobson, pp. 7-8.
Reprint of 1956.251.

253. Ng. "Höchste Aktualität." Dortmund
Ruhr-Nachrichten (10 November).
Favorable review of the German translation of BP, a book which "rings
true" in its portrait of a new phase
in the history of colonialism.
Although now a "prominent anti-communist," W uses Marxist methods to
discover the gap between modern Africans and himself.

254. Nichols, Charles. "Personal Report
on Bandung." Dayton Daily News (11
March), Sec. 3, p. 21.
Favorable review of CC recapitulating
W's argument.

255. Nichols, Charles H. "The Ghost of
Caliban: Europe and the Negro." The
Antioch Review, 16 (December), 495-504.
Mentions W briefly (p. 503).

256. Nichols, Luther. "The Book Corner:
Bandung--Warning to West." San Francisco
Examiner (5 April), Sec. III, p. 3.
Rather favorable review of CC providing background on the Bandung Conference and on W's career as well as
sketching the main conclusions of the
book. W's criticism of both the West
and Communism gives him "a negative
kind of objectivity."

257. Nicol, Davidson. "The Soft Pink
Palms: On British West African Writers--
An Essay." Présence Africaine, Nos. 8-10
(June-November), pp. 107-121.
Contrasts the relatively gentle auto-
biographies of Camara Laye and Mbonu
Ojike to "the sombre, violent and
corrosive ones" of W, Baldwin, and
Peter Abrahams.

258. Nielsen, Johs. "Negerromanen i
amerikansk litteratur." Det Danske Maga-
sin, 4, pp. 408-414.
Contains a brief discussion of NS and
O.

259. Ochs, Martin. "Richard Wright Views
Bandung." Chattanooga Daily Times (22

March), p. 16.

    Favorable review of CC calling it "illuminating and periodically brilliant," but finding some inconsistencies and bitterness. Ochs praises W's "strongly anti-communist perspective."

260. Oka, Takashi. "What Happened at Bandung." The Christian Science Monitor (4 April), p. 9.

    Review of CC and George Kahin's The Asian-African Conference. Although "brilliantly written," W's book is marred by a subjectivity which leads him to overrate the importance of race to an understanding of the Third World. He overlooks difficulties caused by the subject-master relationship which are not specifically racial.

261. Öste, Sven. "Richard Wright, reporter." Stockholm Dagens Nyheter (29 June), p. 4.

    Review of BP and CC viewing them as companion works. Discusses the impact of W's Marxist attitudes and the presence of the Communist Chinese at Bandung.

262. P., F. W. "Forceful Report on Bandung Talks." The Boston Herald.

    Favorable review of CC emphasizing W's special qualifications and his literary skills.

263. P., L. "Licht im schwarzen Erdteil." Düsseldorf Handelsblatt (7 December).

    Review of the German translation of BP. W uses his powerful style to demand that Africa be allowed to develop on its own, but the book is one-sided in its condemnation of European colonialism.

264. Padmore, George. "Asian and African People Find Common Interests." Asia and Africa (July), pp. 2-4.

    Favorable review of CC summarizing extensively and quoting liberally. It "is a well-written, thought-provoking and challenging book" which "deserves the widest circulation, especially among policy makers," because "it poses in sharp focus the three greatest issues of our time--Nationalism, Colonialism, and Communism--in their Asian-African setting." Reprinted: 1956.265.

265. _____. "The Colour Curtain, by Richard Wright." Mankind, 1 (August), 91-94.

    Reprint of 1956.264.

266. Parker, John W. "Richard Wright

'The Color Curtain.'" The Charlotte Observer (5 August), p. 17-E.

    Favorable review stressing the historical importance of the Bandung Conference and W's "expanding perspective," which has moved from racism in Mississippi to problems of color on a global scale.

267. Parot, Jeanine. "Lumières et camouflage." Les Lettres Françaises (1 February), p. 3.

    Contains a review of the French translation of CC finding W's reportage brisk and full of revealing details. Although the book is accurate on the whole in its description of the general fight against colonialism, its angry anti-Communist mood is a defect. In spite of his "bad faith," W is forced to conclude that the lack of a Western solution to the problems of industrialization of the new nations will turn them to Communism for economic freedom.

268. Petree, Nellie. "The Bookshelf." The Clearwater Sun (22 March), p. 13.

    Favorable review of CC, a work of "very personal yet very objective reporting and analyzing." W articulates "hopes, dreams, yearnings heretofore unexpressed or misunderstood."

269. Pike, George M. "Richard Wright on Bandung." The Boston Sunday Globe (1 April), p. A-7.

    Unfavorable review of CC. Pike believes that "in his burning need to express his own thoughts on racial injustice and to discuss the broader implications of the Conference, Mr. Wright has given very brief and superficial coverage to this historic event."

270. Price, J. H. "The Gold Coast." Manchester Guardian (5 October), p. 9.

    Unfavorable review of BP criticizing W's distorting preconceptions. His Marxist thinking leads to unfair attacks on the British, and the combination of his consciousness of his African ancestry and his Western intellect leads him to confusion.

271. Puente, José V. Untitled clipping. Buenos Aires Clarín.

    Comments on the forthcoming PS, in which W sees a white country through his black eyes.

271a. [Quinn, Kerker]. "Accent Autumn 1956."

    Flyer listing W as a contributor to Accent Anthology.

271b. _____. "Accent Spring 1956."

Flyer listing W as a contributor to Accent Anthology.

271c. _____. "Accent Winter 1956."
Flyer listing W as a contributor to Accent Anthology.

272. R. "Richard Wright: Schwarze Macht." Täglicher Anzeiger Holzminden (25 December).
Notice of the German translation of BP mentioning the influence of Hollywood films on the self-image of the young in Ghana. W is "penetrating and candid" in this book.

273. Redding, Saunders. "The Color Curtain, by Richard Wright." Unidentified clipping (24 March).
Favorable review noting Western disparagement of the plan to meet at Bandung.

274. _____. "The Meaning of Bandung." The American Scholar, 25 (Autumn), 411-420.
Mentions approvingly W's views on the Bandung Conference.

275. Redfield, Malissa. "A Last Call to West: Wright's Report About Bandung." The Norfolk Virginian-Pilot and The Portsmouth Star (18 March), p. 6-C.
Favorable review of CC. Although "Wright's previous work has often been distinguished by a blind bitterness and hatred for America and the white West," the present volume "presents a valid and vital issue to the West, and many of its impressions and conclusions have been confirmed by observers of unquestioned objectivity and loyalty." Most of this review is a paraphrase of W's argument. Redfield emphasizes the danger of Communism if the West does not help both Asia and Africa.

276. Rétif, André. "Arthur Campbell.-- L'Ecole de la jungle; Richard Wright.-- Bandoeng. 1.500.000.000 d'hommes; Lion Chao-Tchi.--Pour être un bon communiste; Luce-Claude Maitre.--Introduction à la pensée d'Iqbal; Michel Leiris.--Contacts de civilisation en Martinique et en Guadeloupe." Etudes, No. 290 (September), pp. 306-307.
Contains a notice of the French translation of CC pointing out the important role of race and religion at Bandung and agreeing with W on the urgency of help to the Third World from the West. With "somewhat longish interviews," the book is not above the level of good reporting.

277. Rhea, James N. "Saigon and Bandung: Americans in S. E. Asia." The Providence Sunday Journal (18 March), Sec. VI, p. 10.
Somewhat favorable review of CC stressing W's warning to the West and considering the work "sensitively informative." But Rhea complains that the account of the author's preparations for the trip is too lengthy.

277a. Richards, Robert F. "Wright, Richard," in his Concise Dictionary of American Literature. Ames, Iowa: Littlefield, Adams, p. 250.
Biographical note.

278. Richardson, Ben. "Richard Wright," in his Great American Negroes. New York: Crowell, pp. 126-136.
Biographical sketch based mainly on BB, "Early Days in Chicago," and "I Tried to Be a Communist." Includes some comment on BP and CC.
Reprinted in revised form: 1976.158.

279. Richardson, Boyce. Untitled clipping. Winnipeg Free Press.
Unfavorable review of CC pointing out W's "indiscriminate lumping together of the peoples of Asia and Africa" and his "pompous sounding locutions." Nevertheless, the book may help to disturb the complacency of the West.

280. Rideout, Walter B. The Radical Novel in the United States, 1900-1954. Cambridge, Mass.: Harvard University Press, pp. 260-262, 268, 288, 290, 310.
Discusses W's career in relation to the Depression, Communism, and existentialism. Discusses or mentions UTC (especially "Fire and Cloud" and "Long Black Song"), NS, BB, and O. Notes that O reverses the environmental determinism of NS.

281. Robb, Helen. "Bandung Conference Report Interesting." The Montreal Star (19 May), p. 25.
Favorable review of CC consisting mostly of quotations on the significance of Bandung. The book is called "a well documented critical commentary" adding to the author's "impressive record."

282. Roberts, Henry L. "The Color Curtain. By Richard Wright." Foreign Affairs, 34 (July), 685.
Very brief, nonevaluative notice.

283. Rolf, Ch. Untitled clipping. Hamburger Anzeiger (1 December).
Review of the German translation of BP.

284. R.[orke], C.[ameron]. "The Color Curtain. By Richard Wright." Columbus (Ohio) Sunday Dispatch (3 June), Tab

Sec., p. 11.
Notice emphasizing the importance of the Bandung Conference and W's report of it. W's point of view is subjective and sympathetic.

285. Rousseaux, André. "Les Livres: L'Espagne impériale." Le Figaro Littéraire (7 January), p. 2.
Contains a short favorable review of the French translation of CC.

286. Roussel, Jean. "Bandoeng par Richard Wright." Les Nouvelles Littéraires (12 April), p. 3.
Review of the French translation of CC noting W's sociological and psychological approach. His optimism may be premature, but W is both a good reporter and a thoughtful analyst.

287. Roy, Tarachand. "Richard Wright: Schwarze Macht." Typescript.
Favorable review of the German translation of BP. Because of W's perspective, his book should open the eyes of many to East-West problems. His reaction to primitivism and irrationality leads to his condemnation of colonialism.

288. Ruin, Olaf. "Richard Wright och Afrika." Malmö Sydsvenska Dagbladet Snällposten (3 December), p. 4.
Review of the Swedish translation of BP beginning with a lengthy section on apparent continuities in black culture and character in Africa and the United States. Ruin then analyzes the reasons for alienation of various blacks from one another, including Ghana's elite from its masses. The review concludes with a full report on W's sympathetic view of Nkrumah.

289. Russell, Oland D. "Backstage at Bandung Parley: Wright Lifts the 'Color Curtain.'" Pittsburgh Press (18 March), Sec. V, p. 8.
Favorable review by a reviewer also at Bandung. Agrees with W's emphasis on the importance of racial consciousness at the Conference. A collective voice was raised by diverse peoples at Bandung, and W has analyzed it in a searching and absorbing way.
Reprinted: 1956.290, 291, 292, 293, 294.

290. _____. "Book About Bandung Challenges the West." The San Francisco News (24 March), p. 8T.
Reprint of 1956.289.

291. _____. "'The Color Curtain.'" The

Evansville Press (20 March), p. 20.
Reprint of 1956.289.

292. _____. "Food for U. S. Thought Found in Wright's Book." The Knoxville News-Sentinel (18 March), p. C-2.
Reprint of 1956.289.

293. _____. "A Searching Study of a Strange Gathering." The Washington News (20 March), p. 19.
Reprint of 1956.289.

294. _____. "Will This Call from Free Asia Be Answered?" The Cleveland Press (20 March), p. 18.
Reprint of 1956.289.

295. S., B. H. "Have You Read The Color Curtain by Richard Wright." The Meriden Record (3 July), p. 6.
Favorable review stressing the validity of W's perception of the historical importance of the Bandung Conference. The portraits of the participants are rendered with great literary skill as well as reportorial expertise.

296. Sablonière, Magrit de. "Boekenpaspoort en Boekennieuws: Negerliteratuur." Litterair Paspoort, 11 (August-September), 162-163.
Review of CC by its Dutch translator, who emphasizes its relationship to BP. In a sense both books are documentaries. But both suggest similar political programs, the main difference being that the program of CC is more ambitious and raises greater problems.

297. S.[aunders], D.[oris] E. "Book of the Week." Jet, 9 (19 April), 46.
Favorable review of CC. W believes that the West must provide to Asian and African countries an alternative to Communism. The book is required reading for thoughtful people.

298. Schonfeld, Herbert. "Eine grosse Unbekannte: Die schwarze Macht." Esslinger Zeitung (22 November).
Favorable review of the German translation of BP. It is a valuable work even though W remained an outsider in Ghana and never made real contact outside the elite. Includes a lengthy discussion of the role of Christianity and the opposition of segments of African society to "progressive" forces.

299. Schubert, Ludwig. Untitled typescript. N. D. R. Rundfunkhaus (9 October).
Transcript of a radio review of the German translation of BP.

300. Schumann, Werner. "Richard Wright: Schwarze Macht." SPD Pressedienst (5 December), pp. 4-5.
Notice of the German translation of BP referring to W's Marxist modes of analysis and his alienation from his African past.

301. Schuyler, George S. "Richard Wright on Bandung." The Pittsburgh Courier (7 July), Magazine Sec., p. 7.
Unfavorable review of CC accusing W of poor organization, "unsupported generalizations, and dubious interpretations." Schuyler disputes W's emphasis on the importance of race in Asia.

302. Schuyler, Joseph B. "America Balances the Books." America, 95 (19 May), 200-204.
In a semi-annual survey, Schuyler comments on CC. Not a scholarly work, it nevertheless provides insight into the importance of color in the Third World.

303. Scott, Nathan A. "Search for Beliefs: Fiction of Richard Wright." The University of Kansas City Review, 23 (Autumn), 19-24; (Winter), 131-138.
Traces W's journey from the sociological to the metaphysical, discussing NS and O as the primary texts. He is still searching for a way to rebel that is not self-destructive. Scott dismisses SH as "a curiously incoherent little potboiler."
Reprinted: 1971.147.

304. Sekiguchi, Isao. "Richard Wright no Shosetsu--Haigo to Naru Kankyo o Cushin toshite" ["Richard Wright's Fiction: A Study of Its Environment"]. Meiji Daigaku Eibei Bungaku [Meiji University English and American Literature], 2 (July), 77-91.
Points out that abolishing slavery resulted in more social restriction for blacks and stimulated more protest from them. As argued by W, NS is a sharper attack on racial prejudice than UTC. NS, however, is not merely a protest novel but a demonstration of a black man's self-determination, suggesting W's interest in existentialism as further seen in O. [Y. H.]

305. Shaw, Van B. "Color Curtain." The Colorado Springs Free Press (8 April), Sunday Review Sec., p. 11.
Mixed review agreeing on the importance of Bandung and praising the objective reporting of racialism and religion at the Conference, but complaining of padding in the first part of the book.

306. Simmons, Walter. "Arrested Case of Communism Looks at Asia." Chicago Sunday Tribune Magazine of Books (25 March), p. 2.
Unfavorable review of CC noting that W's observations differed from those of other reporters at the Bandung Conference. W utilizes his old Marxist vocabulary in this book.
Reprinted: 1978.209; 1982.50.

307. Snelling, Paula. "Import of Bandung." The Progressive, 20 (June), 39-40.
Favorable review of CC calling it "a good journalistic account of an extraordinary and significant event . . . written in a simple, straightforward manner." Snelling emphasizes the urgency of W's warning to the West.
Reprinted: 1978.209; 1982.5.

308. Sohier, A. "A la rencontre des hommes." Eglise Vivante, 8 (28 November), 75-76.
Review of the French translation of CC objecting to W's antireligious rationalism. He particularly fails to understand Catholics. His analysis of Chinese Communist tactics at Bandung is perceptive, however.

309. Spearman, Walter. "The Literary Lantern: Richard Wright's 'The Color Curtain' Seen as 'Must' Reading on Bandung Conference." Rocky Mount Telegram (25 March), Sec. B, p. 2.
Mixed review. Some of W's views lack clarity, but his warning to the West is timely and should be considered by whites.

310. Spiro, Robert H., Jr. "By Ex-Mississippian: A Search for Dignity Is Noted at Bandung." Jackson (Miss.) State Times (29 April), p. 3C.
Review of CC consisting mostly of summary. It is "a strange book, affording an intimate glimpse into not only the Bandung Conference of 1955 but into the emotional and sensitive mind of a Mississippi-born Negro expatriate." Includes two brief biographical paragraphs.

311. Steele, A. T. "Color of Asia." New York Herald Tribune Books (22 April), p. 9.
Somewhat unfavorable review of CC. W's views on the racial issue are interesting, but his overall conclusions are vague and undocumented.
Reprinted: 1978.209.

312. Stevenson, David L. "Novel, The," in The Encyclopedia Americana. Ed. Lavinia P. Dudley. Vol. 20. New York:

Americana Corporation, pp. 503-524.
Reprint of 1952.64.

313. Stråhle, Bo. "Sweden ett vitt land, sa Wright." Stockholm Dagstidningen (26 November), p. 1.
Interview with W including a quick survey of his literary career and intellectual background. He has always been a religious skeptic. W comments on O as his literary break with Communism, mentions his diffi-culties in completing works in prog-ress, and attributes racial problems to the outlook of whites.

314. Strandberg, Olle. "Vit Man under svart hud." Unidentified clipping (c. December), pp. 14-15.
Lengthy report on a conversation with W comparing the nature of his exper-ience with Africa with Hemingway's. W is far more conscious of the nature and extent of his alienation.

315. Swalm, Neal Chapline. "Book Re-views." Sarasota News (8 April), p. 6.
Contains a favorable review of CC consisting mostly of quotation. It "is a significant book on our turbu-lent times."

316. T., B. J. "Schwarze macht." Hagen Hessische Nachrichten (19 December).
Notice of the German translation of BP. Notes the clash of two worlds in W's individual experience.

317. Tate, Merze. "The Color Curtain: A Report on the Bandung Conference. By Richard Wright." The Journal of Negro History, 41 (July), 263-265.
Unfavorable review. W's knowledge of international affairs is deficient, and his racial consciousness impairs his objectivity.

318. Thom. "Göteborg och Buenos Aires modiga städer tycker Wright." Göteborg Ny Tid (1 December).
Article on W's visit to Göteborg reporting his condemnation of England and France for intervention in Egypt. W also explains why industrialization is beneficial to American blacks.

319. Thomas, Norman. "Kalmuck." The New York Times Book Review (20 May), p. 32.
Reminded of the Kalmucks by Tillman Durdin's review of CC, Thomas in a letter to the editor reports that two representatives of this lost nation were unofficial delegates to the Bandung Conference.

320. Tügel, Peter W. Untitled clipping. Hamburg B. P. Kurier (December).
Review of the German translation of BP.

321. T.[urner], D.[echerd]. "Tragic Divisions of Our Times." The Dallas Times Herald (18 March), Sec. E, p. 10.
Favorable review of CC and another book calling the Bandung Conference "the greatest event of our century." W recognizes the complexity of Third World problems and stimulates the reader's thoughts about them.

322. V., S. "Negro Cultural Congress Is Proposed." Intro Bulletin, 1 (March-April), 12.
Notes the call for a black cultural congress by W, Senghor, and Cesaire.

323. V.[allette], J.[acques]. "Puissance noire, par R. Wright, trad. Giroux." Mercure de France, 326 (January), 199.
Very favorable notice of the French translation of BP.

324. _____. "Le Transfuge, par R. Wright, trad. de Montlaur." Mercure de France, 326 (March), 593.
Favorable review of the French trans-lation of O. A man of his time, W has written a novel of isolation.

325. Vecchi, Massimo. "Esce in italiano l'ultimo Wright: Ho bruciato la notte." La fiera letteraria (22 April), p. 2.
Review of the Italian translation of O preceded by a survey of W's pre-vious literary career. Unlike the militant but optimistic earlier work, this novel is a statement of extreme disillusionment, even nausea.

326. Vegetti, Mario. "Richard Wright, Bandoeng: 1.500.000.000 d'hommes." Aut Aut, No. 36 (November), 504-510.
Review in Italian of the French translation of CC. Vegetti admires W's sense of engagement, his recogni-tion of the importance of Bandung, and his stimulation of the reader to consider the larger implications of the event. On the other hand, W is not sympathetic enough toward the movement of the Third World and he misunderstands the role of China in Asia and on the world scene.

327. W., H. A. "Bandung." Trenton Sunday Times-Advertiser (15 April), Part Four, p. 14.
Favorable review of CC consisting mostly of summary.

328. W., R. G. "An American Negro in Africa." The London Financial Times (27 August), p. 8.
Favorable review of BP. The work's two central issues are identity and politics. As to the first, W dis-

covers that he is a Western intellectual, not an African. As to the second, he supports Nkrumah's policies. Despite some bias and hasty generalizations, W has produced "a brilliant perception of the Gold Coaster's psychological problems, a realistic analysis of his needs and potentialities--and, above all, a style of writing that is compelling, and leavens a sustained piece of matchless reportage with moments of sheer poetry."

329. Wicker, Tom. "The Loyal and the Disloyal . . . A Sensible Lesson for Our Times." Winston-Salem Journal and Sentinel (12 August), p. 4C.
Review of Morton Grodzins's The Loyal and the Disloyal mentioning W's relation to Communism.

330. W.[illiams], D.[avid]. "Afro-Asia and the West." West Africa (20 October), p. 822.
Mixed review of CC praising W's lively writing but objecting to some of his ideas. "His talent for descriptive writing and his insight into individual psychology are not matched by powers of political or economic analysis, or by knowledge of history or the world."

331. ____. "One Man's Gold Coast." West Africa (29 September), p. 755.
Unfavorable review of BP, "an important book: absorbing and vivid; revealing and infuriating; contradictory and passionate." W's extreme subjectivity causes him to misinterpret much of what he saw in Africa, but his impressions are nevertheless interesting.

332. W.[int], G.[uy]. "The Asian Prospect." Manchester Guardian (15 May), p. 4.
Unfavorable review of CC complaining of W's "impressionist manner of writing and his apparent distaste for fact." Nevertheless, the book casts light on Third World attitudes.

333. ____. "Impatience of the East." The Nation, 182 (14 April), 324.
Review of CC noting that the subtitle is misleading because W does not report in detail the actual proceedings of the Bandung Conference. Instead, he concentrates on background and on the psychology of the delegates, especially their bitter feelings toward the West. The work is highly subjective.
Reprinted: 1978.209.

334. Wisley, Charles. "Bandung Report."

Masses & Mainstream, 9 (June), 50-53.
Unfavorable review of CC conceding W's special qualifications but arguing that reductive emotionalism leads him to overestimate the role of race and religion at Bandung and underestimate the issues of colonialism and peace. W's treatment of Chou En-Lai is biased.
Reprinted: 1978.209.

335. ____. "Richard Wright's Bandung Report." The Worker (9 July), p. 4.
Letter to the editor rejecting Abner W. Berry's criticism of Wisley's review of CC. See 1956.114.

336. Woodman, Dorothy. "Report on Bandung." The New Statesman and Nation, 52 (15 September), 321.
Review of CC and George Kahin's The Asian-African Conference criticizing W's excessive color-consciousness. The issue of race, Woodman believes, is relevant to African nationalism but not to Asian nationalism.

337. Wright, Eric. "American Eyes on Africa." Reynolds News and Sunday Citizen (14 October), p. 8.
Unfavorable British review of BP. W is too American and too critical of the British role in Africa.

338. Young, James D. "Wright's Report on Bandung." The Houston Post (25 March), Now Sec., p. 21.
Favorable review of CC noting that W's intellectual perspective is Western but his emotional sympathies are with the Asian-African nations. This combination leads to a "perceptive and informed" discussion of the Bandung Conference.

339. Zardoya, Concha. Historia de la literatura norteamericana. Barcelona: Editorial Labor, pp. 308-309.
Surveys W's literary career through BB. NS is notable for its psychological insight into Bigger's character. W's purpose in his writing is propagandistic, but his work is artistically satisfying.

340. Zerbo, J.[oseph] Ki. "'Bandoeng': 1,500,000,000 d'hommes par R. Wright." Présence Africaine, No. 6 (February-March), pp. 168-169.
Mixed review of the French translation of CC. Zerbo praises the perception, accuracy, and finesse of W's reportage as well as his sympathy for the Third World. But W oversimplifies by excessive emphasis on religious and racial feelings in the East. His use of psychoanalysis is vague. He offers no real solution to the prob-

lems of the Third World, for his advocacy of Western help outside the framework of capitalism is unrealistic.

341. Ziprin, Nathan. "Of the Record." The Jersey City Jewish Standard (18 May).
Comments favorably on CC, but deplores W's failure to criticize the exclusion of Israel from the Bandung Conference and the appearance there of the former Mufti of Jerusalem.

1957

1. A., C. L. Untitled clipping. Labor Daily (20 February).
Favorable notice of PS, a "quietly passionate story of an emotionally retarded nation."

2. Abdoulaye, Sadji. "Puissance noire." Unidentified clipping.
Review of the French translation of BP emphasizing W's racial consciousness. The year is conjectural.

3. Ahemm, Hildegard. "Zur afrikanischen Revolution." Stuttgart Deutsche Rundschau, 83 (June), 648-649.
Favorable review of the German translation of BP stressing W's analysis of the conflict between tribal culture and Western thought. Poetic as well as incisive, the book helps the reader to understand the African revolution.

4. Akanji. "Black Power by Richard Wright." Black Orpheus: A Journal of African and Afro-American Literature, No. 1 (September), pp. 48-51.
Unfavorable review stressing W's estrangement from Africans and his condescension toward them. Critical of white colonial attitudes toward "natives," he adopts some of these attitudes himself. His efforts to identify with the people of the Gold Coast fail: "I was black and they were black but it did not help me."

5. Anon. "Afrika im Aufbruch." Würzburg Frankisches Volksblatt (3 July).
Mixed review of the German translation of BP. Although the book presents the uncomfortable facts of African hostility toward European institutions--including church missions--it is an important perspective on Africa. W attacks Christianity too harshly since he fails to consider any positive impact it has made.

6. Anon. "Afrikaner zwischen den Kulturen." Evangelische Missiones Zeit-schrift (January), pp. 8-14.
Headnote to an excerpt from the German translation of BP giving the background of the book and stressing its importance to the European understanding of Africa.

7. Anon. "American Literature Reflects American Life," in Compton's Pictured Encyclopedia and Fact-Index. Ed. Guy Stanton Ford. Vol. 1. Chicago: F. E. Compton, pp. 240-263.
Mentions W briefly (p. 262).
Reprinted: 1958.6; 1970.16; 1973.12.

8. Anon. "Analysen der farbigen Kontinente." Stuttgart Junge Stimme (5 January).
Review of the German translation of BP and several other books on the Third World. W's work shows Europeans that the roots of their fear of the new Africa lie in their lack of understanding of the old Africa.

9. Anon. "Begegnungen mit Büchern." Schweizer Radio Zeitung, No. 16 (21-27 April), p. 29.
Contains a brief notice of the German translation of BP stressing its topical interest.

10. Anon. "A Bitter Book by Wright." Chicago Daily News (27 February), p. 20.
Notice of PS stressing the controversy it will stimulate.

11. Anon. "Boeiend boekje van Wright over de kleurbarrière." Nieuwe Rotterdamse Courant (6 August), p. 4.
Favorable review of the Dutch translation of CC. More influenced by his Western identity than by his race, W nevertheless emphasizes color consciousness as the key to understanding the Third World. A book of great narrative skill, CC is the best work on the Bandung Conference.

12. Anon. "Books--Authors." The New York Times (2 January), p. 25.
Announces that W's book on Spain is scheduled for publication in February.

13. Anon. "Books--Authors." The New York Times (10 October), p. 30.
Announces the publication of WML "next Thursday."

14. Anon. "Books: Richard Wright Authors New Book on Spain." Jet, 11 (14 March), 26.
Announces PS as a sociological and political work.

15. Anon. "The Bookseller's Almanac." The Retail Bookseller, 60 (February),

105-107.
  Predicts a good sale for PS, but expresses the hope that "it will be toned down a little before it's put into book form" (p. 107).

16. Anon. "Brief Looks at Newest of the Autumn Books." The Times-Picayune New Orleans States (3 November), Sec. Three, p. 5.
  Contains a notice of WML. The work has sound observations but lacks continuity.

17. Anon. "Buch des Monats." Das Leih-buch (May).
  Reports that the Darmstadt jury has named the German translation of BP the Book-of-the-Month for April.

18. Anon. "Crucial Stage in Ghana." Peace News (6 September), p. 4.
  Using BP as a focal point, the editorialist argues for quick self-rule in Ghana.

19. Anon. Dust jacket of Pagan Spain. New York: Harper.
  Front and back inside flaps contain a blurb stressing W's insight into aspects of Spanish life neglected by other writers on Spain. Photograph and biographical sketch are on back.

20. Anon. Dust jacket of Potenza nera. By Richard Wright. Trans. Quirino Maffi. Milan: Mondadori.
  Blurbs on front inside flap and back jacket of this Italian translation of BP.

21. Anon. Dust jacket of White Man, Listen! Garden City, N. Y.: Doubleday.
  Blurb on front and back inside flaps. Biographical sketch on back inside flap. Photograph of W with his comment on his book on the back.

22. Anon. "Erwachendes Afrika." Der Gewerkschaften Monatsschrift für die Funktionare der IG Metall (5 January).
  Favorable review of the German translation of BP. Praises W for his consideration of the spiritual, as well as the economic, exploitation of Africa. W stresses the difficulty of attaining true freedom and recommends militancy and self-reliance.

23. Anon. "Erwachendes Afrika." Heidenheimer Zeitung (6 March).
  Favorable review of the German translation of BP with laudatory comments on W's insight, writing style, and balanced consideration and conclusions.

24. Anon. "Les Etats-Unis sont-ils une nation, une loi, un peuple?" La Nef, 14 (November), 57-60.
  Biographical headnote to an interview with W. Notes the author's attachment to Paris. The interview concerns the racial situation in the United States, especially Little Rock. Reprinted: 1971.147.

25. Anon. Fiche de lecture: Richard Wright Black Boy. Paris: Peuple et Culture, 24 pp.
  Reader's guide with summary of the narrative, comments on theme and form, biographical sketch of W, bibliography, and study suggestions.

26. Anon. "Ghana's Silent Hero." The Crisis, 64 (April), 214, 252-253.
  Biographical sketch of George Padmore including W's remarks on him.

27. Anon. "Harper Books for Spring 1957." The Retail Bookseller, 60 (February), n. pag.
  Lists PS for publication on 20 February.

28. Anon. "Historical News." The Journal of Negro History, 42 (October), 301-303.
  Includes a favorable notice of WML. "Its pungent message reflects the feeling and thinking of darker people who constitute the majority of the world's population" (p. 303).

29. Anon. "In einem afrikanischen Kino." Der Pfälzer (1 March).
  Excerpt from the German translation of BP followed by a short postscript describing the book's genesis.

30. Anon. Index Translationum 8. Paris: Unesco, pp. 68, 170, 285, 591.
  Lists translations of O into Spanish, Finnish, and Japanese, UTC into Japanese, and NS into Serbo-Croatian.

31. Anon. "Journey Into Spain." Newsweek, 49 (25 February), 120, 122.
  Review of PS placing it in the context of books on Spain by Emmet J. Hughes, Gerald Brenan, and V. S. Pritchett, all of whom agree with W that Spain is out of touch with the modern world. PS consists of "passionate reporting and debatable theorizing about Franco's land."

32. Anon. "De Kleurbarrière." Friese Koerier (30 March).
  Review of the Dutch translation of CC. Despite the lack of balance in W's treatment of the Dutch, the book is an interesting topical work. W's subject and attitude both seem inevitable given his past experiences.

33. Anon. "De Kleurbarrière--Richard Wright." De Evenras, No. 2, p. 27.
Review of the Dutch translation of CC. The work expresses the deep hatred of the Third World for the West and poses important questions, particularly in the chapter devoted to the role of Communism.

34. Anon. "'Kraal-Relationships.'" The Crisis, 64 (January), 29.
Quotes from reviews of the German translation of BP in Der Spiegel and the Frankfurter Allgemeine Zeitung.

35. Anon. "The Library Shelf." The Centralia-Chelalis (Wash.) Daily Chronicle (16 November), p. 6.
Contains a notice of WML pointing out that "no one is better qualified to interpret" the colored races than W.

36. Anon. "A List of 250 Outstanding Books of the Year . . . A Christmas Guide." The New York Times Book Review (1 December), p. 71.
Describes WML as a "blunt warning on the dangers inherent in prejudice and imperialism."

37. Anon. "Mais l'homme blanc reste sourd." Paris France Observateur (7 November), p. 24.
Favorable review of the French translation of WML stressing W's expatriation and the importance of his message.

38. Anon. "Meet Famous Author Richard Wright." Mimeographed.
Flyer announcing an appearance by W at "Base Library" on 17 July.

39. Anon. "Meet Mr. Richard Wright." Mimeographed.
Flyer announcing an appearance by W at "Base Library" on 17 July.

40. Anon. "Movie Cowpoke Long Lariat Throw From Real Article." The Portland Sunday Oregonian (20 October), p. 37.
Contains a brief notice of WML calling W "eloquent."

41. Anon. "Native Son," in Masterplots. Ed. Frank N. Magill. First Series. Vol. 2. New York: Salem Press, pp. 643-645.
Reprint of 1949.41.

42. Anon. "Naviglio: il colore non fa differenza." Il giorno (2 June), p. 12.
Summarizes an interview with W in Italy. He contends that color has no importance for the civilized individual.

43. Anon. "Negro Progress 1956." Ebony, 12 (January), 58-59, 61-62.

Mentions W (p. 62).

44. Anon. "Negro States Case for Non-Whites." Fayetteville Northwest Arkansas Times (25 October), p. 10.
Unfavorable review of WML finding fault with the origin of the book as speeches and criticizing W's habit of reading psychological significance into minor events.

45. Anon. "Negro Writing: A Literature of Protest," in American Writing Today: Its Independence and Vigor. Ed. Allan Angoff. New York: New York University Press, pp. 96-110.
Reprint of 1954.41.

46. Anon. "Negroes in American Life," in Compton's Pictured Encyclopedia and Fact-Index. Ed. Guy Stanton Ford. Vol. 10. Chicago: F. E. Compton, pp. 124-127.
Mentions W briefly (p. 125).
Reprinted: 1958.36; 1970.28.

47. Anon. "New Light on an Important Area." The Charleston (W. Va.) Gazette (10 November), State Magazine Sec., p. 23m.
Review of WML conceding the importance of W's message but claiming that he is too inclusive in condemning whites.

48. Anon. "No Castles in Spain." Charlotte News (23 February), Sec. A, p. 5.
Implicitly favorable review of PS recapitulating W's argument. The Spain he reveals is a Spain oppressed by church and state, not the colorful Spain of the tourist.
Reprinted: 1978.209.

49. Anon. "One Hundred of the Year's Outstanding Books: A Selected Guide to Summer Reading." The New York Times Book Review (9 June), pp. 42-43.
Contains a brief notice of PS.

50. Anon. "Pagan Spain." Denver Rocky Mountain Telegraph (24 March).
Favorable notice stressing W's rejection of the past. "He describes the people and the places vividly, sometimes with lyricism, sometimes with indignation."

51. Anon. "'Pagan Spain.'" Springfield (Mass.) Sunday Republican (17 September), p. 15C.
Brief, nonevaluative notice.

52. Anon. "Pagan Spain. By Richard Wright." Current History, 32 (April), 240.
Unfavorable review. Admitting W's literary talent, the reviewer finds the work "too superficial to be

classed as a political or social study, too subjective to be a travel book." Its chief value is autobiographical.
Reprinted: 1978.209.

53. Anon. "Pagan Spain, by Richard Wright (Harper)." The New Yorker, 33 (23 March), 150-151.
Favorable notice finding W's facts about Spanish life brutal and his theories explaining them provocative and forceful.

54. Anon. "Pagan Spain. Richard Wright." The Retail Bookseller, 60 (February), 111.
Notice mentioning the good sales expected. Points out that W's research included conversations with all social classes in Spain.

55. Anon. "A Personal Report on Spain Today." The New York Times Book Review (24 February), p. 15.
Advertisement for PS.

56. Anon. "Programme." Unidentified clipping (29 June).
Reports that W was one of the sponsors for a charity concert at the Moulin d'Andé.

57. Anon. "Publishers' Promotion Plans." The Retail Bookseller, 60 (February), 98-101.
Lists PS.

58. Anon. "Réception américaine." L'Observatoire (6 September).
Claims that NS was not well received in America.

59. Anon. "Richard Wright." Het Missionwerk, No. 36 (July), p. 190.
Review of the Dutch translation of CC. Written in a concrete and expressive style, the book argues that white vs. nonwhite, not Communist vs. non-Communist, is the world's central conflict. This review concentrates on the unforeseen consequences of this development for Christian missionaries.

60. Anon. "Richard Wright." Jet, 11 (21 March), 30.
Quotes from W on his philosophy of life.

61. Anon. "Richard Wright."
Poster announcing W's lecture on "The Psychological Reactions of Oppressed People" at Medborgarhuset.

62. Anon. "Richard Wright." Münchner Merkur (7 April).
Review of the German translation of

BP. Filled with anger at his alienation, but motivated by love for the African people, W condemns colonialism, singling out Christianity for special attack.

63. Anon. "Richard Wright." Publishers' Weekly, 172 (26 August), [4].
Publisher's advertisement for WML. It is "not a comfortable book but a startling and important one."

64. Anon. "Richard Wright." Unidentified clipping.
Advertisement for WML.

65. Anon. "Richard Wright Biased on Spain." Houston Chronicle (17 February), p. 31.
Unfavorable review of PS pointing out W's Communist background and questioning his bias.

66. Anon. "Richard Wright Completes Study of Pagan Spain." Winston-Salem Journal and Sentinel (10 March), p. 5C.
Favorable review emphasizing W's penetrating observation of Spain's inner reality.

67. Anon. "Richard Wright Pens Novel [sic] About Spain." The Memphis Commercial Appeal (3 February), Sec. V, p. 10.
Nonevaluative notice of PS pointing out the diversity of W's experiences and acquaintances in Spain.

68. Anon. "Richard Wright: Potenza nera." Il Rome mondo (17 September), p. 9.
Notice of the Italian translation of BP stressing the competition between East and West for the allegiance of postcolonial Africa.

69. Anon. "Richard Wright Schwarze Macht." Die Friedens Rundschau, 2 (April), 24.
Favorable review of the German translation of BP. One of the best books on Africa, it is notable for W's keen understanding of the difficulty of moving the African people into the modern world.

70. Anon. "Richard Wright: Schwarze Macht." Essen Deutsches Pfarrerblatt (15 June).
Unfavorable review of the German translation of BP. Despite his feelings of alienation from Africans, W sympathizes with their movement and hates whites. W's agnosticism, acceptable in itself, leads him to caricature deplorably the church's efforts in Africa.

71. Anon. "Richard Wright/Schwarze

Macht." Erlesenes (June).
   Notice of the German translation of
   BP stressing the fact that W is able
   to observe events not accessible to
   whites.

72. Anon. "Richard Wright: Schwarze
Macht--zur afrikanischen Revolution."
Die Kultur, 5 (15 February), 13.
   Notice of the German translation of
   BP emphasizing W's inability to iden-
   tify with the African personality.
   Nevertheless, his politically rele-
   vant book includes many observations
   which could not be made by whites.
   The afterword is of special interest.

73. Anon. "Richard Wright--Von anderen
Erdteilen." Basler Nachrichten (25
January).
   Review of the German translation of
   BP. Though no longer a Communist, W
   remains militant in his approach to
   black emancipation. BP demonstrates
   his inability to think in other than
   Marxist political terms. Still, the
   solution to problems is, for W, a
   psychological concern.

74. Anon. "Richard Wright White Man,
Listen!" Publishers' Weekly, 172 (26
August), 4.
   Advertisement.

75. Anon. "Richard Wright's Pagan
Spain." Unidentified clipping.
   Advertisement.

76. Anon. "Schwarze Macht." Die Industrie, No. 21 (27 November).
   Favorable review of the German translation of BP. Despite the simplifications stemming from W's Marxist
   attitudes, the book is a significant
   work which portrays the alienated
   position of the black American in
   Africa.

77. Anon. "Schwarze Macht." Mitteilungen
der Industrie und Handelskammer zu Neuss
(April).
   Review of the German translation of
   BP. W, identified as the spiritual
   leader of the African Congress of
   Paris, tempers his enthusiasm in the
   work with an honest recognition of
   the difficulties of racial awareness.

78. Anon. "Schwarze Macht." Nordwest-
deutsche Allgemeine Stadten Tagesblatt
(31 March).
   Notice of the German translation of
   BP stressing W's deep understanding
   of African affairs despite his feeling of alienation.

79. Anon. "Schwarze Macht." Schweizer
Radio Zeitung (16 November).

Notice of the German translation of
BP praising the work's topicality.

80. Anon. "Ein Schwarzer versteht seine
schwarzer Brüder nicht." Basel National-
Zeitung (9 November).
   Review of the German translation of
   BP summarizing W's reasons for leaving the Communist Party and noting
   his alienation from Africa. The book
   culminates in lectures to both Africa
   and the West, though W has little
   hope that they will be heeded.

81. Anon. "Spain Still Pagan Place Says
'Black Boy' Wright." Toronto Daily Star
(2 March), p. 30.
   Review of PS stressing its vigorous
   style and its potential for controversy.

82. Anon. "Spaniards Underfed, Says
Writer." The Miami Herald (2 June), p.
4-G.
   Favorable review of PS quoting comments by W on Protestants, malnutri-
   tion, and women in Spain. Though
   hardly objective, W has "a deep compassion, a quixotic turn of mind and
   a vivid style."

83. Anon. "Spring Announcements." The
Retail Bookseller, 60 (February), 152-
180.
   Lists PS (pp. 171, 180).

84. Anon. "Their Books Told Story of
Negro in America." Ghana Salute (9
March).
   Lists W among praiseworthy Afro-
   American writers.

85. Anon. "This Is Richard Wright's
Spain." The New York Times (13 March),
p. 29.
   Advertisement for PS.

86. Anon. Unidentified clipping.
   Favorable review of PS emphasizing
   W's effort to avoid tourist spots and
   his observation of the ubiquity of
   sex in Spain.

87. Anon. Unidentified clipping (15 September).
   Favorable notice of PS commenting on
   its poetic qualities. W tries to
   understand the inner life of Spaniards.

88. Anon. Unidentified clipping (August-
December), p. 27.
   Advertisement for WML, perhaps from
   the Doubleday catalog.

89. Anon. Unidentified clipping. Ashtabula Star Beacon (17 November).
   Notice of WML.

90. Anon. Untitled clipping. Haagsch Dagblad (1 February).
Favorable review of the Dutch translation of CC. It is a well-written book which gives Europeans and Americans a fresh look at a highly topical problem.

91. Anon. Untitled clipping. Kerkblad (July), p. 5.
Excerpt from a review in Afrikaans of the Dutch translation of CC. Stresses W's identification with the Third World.

92. Anon. Untitled clipping. Manchester (N. H.) Union and Leader (c. 30 November).
Brief, nonevaluative notice of WML.

93. Anon. Untitled clipping. Washington-ville (N. Y.) Orange County Post (21 November).
Notice of WML praising "The Literature of the Negro in the United States" as the best section of the book.

94. Anon. Untitled clipping. Wirtschaft und Wissen (February).
Favorable review of the German translation of BP. The book makes the reader feel W's own emotions of dislocation and recognize the great guilt of colonialism. It is one of the best works on the racial question.

95. Anon. "Volume Destined for Controversy." The Dallas Times Herald (24 February), Roundup Sec., p. 19.
Favorable review of PS stressing the controversial nature of the subject but calling the book "a capable, sensitive, at times heart-rending picture of a people caught in the tentacles of poverty and fear." W's descriptions of Spanish landscapes are excellent.
Reprinted: 1978.209.

96. Anon. "Von negern geschreiben." Der Standpunkt (March).
Brief review of the German translation of BP summarizing the background of the book and quoting W's warning to the West.

97. Anon. "Weekly Record." Publishers' Weekly, 172 (21 October), 82-98.
Contains a brief notice of WML (p. 96).

98. Anon. "Weltproblem." Akademie Coccum [?] (February).
Notice of the German translation of BP mentioning its highly topical nature.

99. Anon. "White Man, Listen!" The New York Times (28 October), p. 25.
Advertisement.

100. Anon. "'White Man, Listen' by Richard Wright." Cedar Rapids Gazette (15 December), Sec. III, p. 9.
Unfavorable notice calling W "indignant and argumentative."

101. Anon. "White Man, Listen by Richard Wright." The Dallas Times Herald (3 November), Roundup Sec., p. 18.
Brief, favorable notice.

102. Anon. "'White Man, Listen!' by Richard Wright." Garden City (N. Y.) Newsday (19 October), p. 25.
Brief, nonevaluative notice.

103. Anon. "White Man, Listen!, by Richard Wright (Doubleday)." The New Yorker, 33 (26 October), 187.
Unfavorable notice. While agreeing that white supremacy is deplorable, the reviewer states that "the ungainly blend of intellectual jargon and strident emotionalism . . . reduces [the message] to the level of a street-corner harangue."

104. Anon. "Wright," in Das kluge Alphabet. Vol. 3. Berlin: Ullslein, p. 888.
Brief biographical notice.

105. Anon. "Wright," in Der grosse Brockhaus. Vol. 12. Wiesbaden: F. A. Brockhaus, pp. 601-602.
Contains a biographical note.
Reprinted in revised form: 1974.17.

106. Anon. "Wright a Milano." Epoca (23 June).
Profusely illustrated account of W's visit to Arnoldo Mondadori, his Italian publisher.

107. Anon. "Wright or Wrong? World's Colored Peoples Stirring." The Miami Herald (29 December), p. 4-G.
Unfavorable review of WML. Conceding W's brilliance, the reviewer criticizes his tendency to overlook cultural differences in the Third World and his truculent antiwhite position. Despite his "passionate fanaticism," his book is "provocative reading."

108. Anon. "Wright, Riccardo," in Enciclopedia universale Curcio. Ed. Francesco Acerbo. Vol. 8. Rome: Armando Curcio Editore, p. 5920.
Biographical note.

109. Anon. "Wright, Richard." Beiblatt zum Amtsblatt der Bayerischen Staats-

ministeriums für Unterricht und Kultur
(29 June).
   Brief notice of the German translation of BP.

110. Anon. "Wright, Richard," in Alge-
mene Nederlandse Systematisch Ingerichte
Encyclopedie. Ed. J. Buys. Vol. 3. Am-
sterdam: N. V. Amsterdamsche Boek -en
Courantmaatschappij, p. 1772.
   Biographical note.

111. Anon. "Wright, Richard," in Ras-
segna enciclopedica Labor 1935-1957. Ed.
Arturo Barone. Seventh edition. Milan:
Edizioni Labor, pp. 1171-1172.
   Biographical note.

112. Anon. "Wright, Richard." Unidentified clipping.
   Brief notice of the Dutch translation
   of CC pointing out its interpretive
   nature.

113. Anon. "Wright, Richard Nathaniel,"
in Compton's Pictured Encyclopedia and
Fact-Index. Ed. Guy Stanton Ford. Vol.
15. Chicago: F. E. Compton, p. 461.
   Brief biographical note.
   Reprinted: 1958.68.

114. Anon. "Wright, Richard. Pagan
Spain." Book Review Digest (April).
   Excerpts or lists eight reviews.

115. Anon. "Wright, Richard. Pagan
Spain." Book Review Digest (August).
   Excerpts or lists twelve reviews.

116. Anon. "Wright, Richard. Pagan
Spain." Bulletin from Virginia Kirkus
Service, 25 (15 August), 890.
   Favorable review of "a sociological
   indictment, impassioned, emotionally
   keyed, high-lighted with some of
   the--to him--symbolic events characteristic of the Spain he saw."

117. Anon. "Wright, Richard. Pagan
Spain." Library Journal, 82 (1 Febru-
ary), 353.
   Brief, nonevaluative notice.

118. Anon. "Wright, Richard. Pagan
Spain." The Booklist and Subscription
Books Bulletin, 53 (1 March), 353.
   Announcement.

119. Anon. "Wright, Richard. Pagan
Spain." Wilson Library Bulletin, 31
(April), Sec. Two, 6.
   Brief, nonevaluative notice.

120. Anon. "Wright, Richard. Pagan
Spain." Wisconsin Library Bulletin, 53
(July), 450.
   Favorable notice. The book is "writ-
   ten with sincerity and sympathy."

121. Anon. "Wright, Richard: Schwarze
Macht." Literarischer Ratgeber.
   Notice of the German translation of
   BP mentioning W's quasi-Communist and
   anti-Christian leanings.

122. Anon. "Wright, Richard: Schwarze
Macht." Literaturanzeiger (January).
   Review of the German translation of
   BP. Employing Marxist methods, the
   book is a discomforting but clear
   report on an important world confrontation.

123. Anon. "Wright, Richard. White Man,
Listen!" Book Review Digest (December).
   Excerpts or lists six reviews.

124. Anon. "Wright, Richard. White Man,
Listen!" Bulletin from Virginia Kirkus
Service, 25 (15 August), 614.
   Favorable review summarizing briefly
   each of the four lectures. "A valu-
   able book to inform our thinking on a
   most controversial subject."
   Reprinted: 1978.209.

125. Anon. "Wright, Richard. White Man,
Listen!" Library Journal, 82 (1 October), 2431.
   Favorable notice emphasizing the
   timeliness of the book.

126. Anon. "Wright, Richard. White man,
listen!" The Booklist and Subscription
Books Bulletin, 54 (1 November), 128-
129.
   Notice calling W's plea to the West
   "articulate, outspoken, and vehement"
   and his analysis of white racism
   "unflinching."

127. Anon. "Wright 'Schwarze Macht.'"
Schwäbische Landeszeitung (10 April).
   Announcement of the German transla-
   tion of BP.

128. Anon. "Writers' Colony." Ebony, 13
(November), 114, 116, 118.
   Reports that Lowney Handy, sponsor of
   the colony at Marshall, Illinois,
   accuses W of excessive bitterness.

129. Anon. "Zum Buch des Monats April."
Kiel Schleswig-Holsteinische Volkszeitung (10 April).
   Reports that the Darmstadt jury has
   selected the German translation of BP
   as the book of the month for April.

130. Ashford, Gerald. "Books Off the
Shelf: Book Labels Racism as Modern
Error." San Antonio Sunday Express and
News (24 February), p. 16-G.
   Contains a favorable notice of PS.
   Although W opposes Franco's regime,
   he shows that racism is absent from
   the country, free speech is possible

"in ordinary conversation," and freedom of travel by an admitted ex-
Communist is possible.

131. Ault, Phil. "Books From These
Pages." Los Angeles Mirror-News (4
March), Part II, p. 3.
    Contains a notice of PS emphasizing
    the subjectivity of this "angry book,
    mellowed at times with shafts of
    humor and tightly drawn narrative."

132. B., D. "Richard Wright." Freiburg-
Breisgau Atlantis Verlag (April).
    Review of the German translation of
    BP noting that W was motivated to
    research the book by parallel urges
    to observe the independence movement
    in the Gold Coast and to return to
    his ancestral home. But gradually
    the two quests merge into a synthesis
    culminating in his awareness of the
    importance of Africa to the West as a
    whole.

133. B., H. "Afrikanische Revolution."
Köln Vorwärts (16 August).
    Favorable review of the German trans-
    lation of BP. Despite W's sympathy
    with the African freedom movement,
    the work avoids sentimentality and
    remains objective. Aware of the
    internal tensions in the Gold Coast,
    W undertakes to study the nature and
    possibilities of Nkrumah's political
    and social programs.

134. B., L. "Book of the Week." Jet (5
December), p. 44.
    Unfavorable review of WML charging W
    with supporting black totalitarian-
    ism. His expatriation has caused W to
    lose touch with reality.

135. B., R. "Geheimnisvolle Kräfte."
Berliner Morgenpost (9 May).
    Notice of the German translation of
    BP pointing out that it was chosen
    the April book of the month by the
    Darmstadt jury.

136. Baldwin, James. "Letter from Paris:
Princes and Powers." Encounter, 8 (January), 52-60.
    Report on the Congress of Black
    Writers and Artists in Paris in Sep-
    tember 1956. Corrects Senghor's em-
    phasis on the African quality of BB,
    which Baldwin considers "one of the
    major American autobiographies." In
    reporting W's speech, Baldwin notes
    his ambiguous position in providing
    liaison between the American and
    African delegations. Expresses skep-
    ticism about W's reliance on the good
    faith of Africans to relinquish power
    after using it to achieve necessary
    goals.

Reprinted: 1961.110a; 1962.35; 1975.
21.

137. Ballard, Loretta. "Shaking Finger."
Chattanooga Sunday Times (24 November),
p. 16.
    Unfavorable review of WML complaining
    that W is too shrill in his denuncia-
    tion of white exploiters of the Third
    World. The discussion of the "tragic
    elite" of Western-educated African
    and Asian leaders is the most valu-
    able part of the book.

138. Banks, Richard. "'Mystique.'" New
York Herald Tribune.
    Letter to the editor commenting on
    W's description of bullfighting and
    the Black Virgin in PS.

139. Bekker, M.[eri Iosifovna]. Progres-
sivnaia negritianskaia literatura SShA.
Leningrad: Sovetskii pisatel', pp. 199-
203.
    Interprets W's literary career as the
    movement of a black petit bourgeois
    intellectual from progressivism in
    the thirties to decadence in the
    forties and fifties. Bekker praises
    the early poetry and UTC, but criti-
    cizes W's work thereafter, especially
    "The Man Who Lived Underground," for
    replacing social with psychological
    themes. BP and CC, however, provide
    hopeful signs that W is moving back
    toward humanity.

140. Bendiner, Elmer. "'Pagan Spain':
Wright on Wright." National Guardian (1
April), p. 10.
    Unfavorable review of PS complaining
    of W's extreme subjectivity, his
    unfamiliarity with Spain and its
    language, his obsession with sex, and
    his factual inaccuracies. "The book
    produces a somber, desperate mood.
    But how much of it is Spain's and how
    much Richard Wright's is hard to
    say."

141. Bergin, Thomas G. "Misery and Sex."
The Saturday Review, 40 (16 March), 60-
62.
    Review of PS considering it naive and
    narrow in scope, but honest and pro-
    vocative nevertheless. W condemns
    both state and church for reducing
    the Spanish people to misery and
    sexual obsession.

142. Binderup, Hortense. "Richard Wright
Describes Spain as Pagan Country." The
Portland Sunday Oregonian (17 March),
Sec. Three, p. 11.
    Favorable review of PS praising W's
    literary skill and his social con-
    science. The work is "startlingly
    frank and vigorously alive." In sum-

marizing W's observations, Binderup emphasizes the role of women and paganism.

143. Bl.[air], W.[alter], "American Literature," in Encyclopaedia Britannica. Ed. Walter Yust. Vol. 1. Chicago: Encyclopaedia Britannica, pp. 784-794.
Reprint of 1954.80.

144. Bo. "Schwarzer Aufstand." Geist und Tat (December), p. 416.
Favorable review of the German translation of BP. It is a book of lasting value because it could have been written by no one else. W's sympathy and exact reporting make it the best book on white injustices and black reactions in Africa.
Reprinted: 1957.145.

145. _____. "Schwarzer Aufstand." Der Selbständig Schaffende (December).
Reprint of 1957.144.

146. Bowman, Barc. "'Pagan Spain' Seen as Living Paradox." Dayton Daily News (24 February), Sec. 3, p. 4.
Contains a favorable review dwelling on the relation of prostitution to Spanish Catholicism. Bowman praises W's descriptive power.

147. _____. "Richard Wright's New Book Too Deep." Ft. Lauderdale News (3 November), p. 14-F.
Unfavorable review of WML. Conceding W's talent and intelligence, Bowman complains that the book is too difficult to understand.

148. Breit, Harvey. "In and Out of Books." The New York Times Book Review (9 June), p. 8.
Announces the forthcoming WML. "The book will tell us a little of what we don't know, a great deal of what we do know but don't want to know, all mixed with a normal share of wrongheadedness about our bad mistakes everywhere in the world."

149. Bridges, Kenneth. "White Man, Listen! By Richard Wright." El Paso Herald-Post (7 December), p. 4.
Unfavorable review stressing W's hatred of the white world. "This is a highly controversial book, in which most of the material is obscured by emotionalism."

150. Brie, Peter. "Die Enttauschung des Richard Wright." Frankfürter Neue Presse (2 February).
Review of the German translation of BP. The complex background of both Ghana and W himself makes the work sometimes confusing. But W's powers

of observation lead him to the clear and unequivocal conclusion that the first barrier to African freedom is psychological.

151. Brièrre, Annie. "Rencontres a Paris." Les Nouvelles Littéraires (25 July), p. 4.
Mentions W briefly.

152. B.[rown], S.[terling] A. "Negro in the American Theatre," in The Oxford Companion to the Theatre. Ed. Phyllis Hartnoll. Second edition. London: Oxford University Press, pp. 565-572.
Reprint of 1951.139.

153. Butcher, Margaret Just. The Negro in American Culture. Mentor Book. New York: The New American Library, pp. 142-143, 155, 215, 216.
Reprint of 1956.125.

154. Byam, Milton S. "Wright, Richard. Pagan Spain." Library Journal, 82 (15 February), 553.
Mixed review. W presents an interesting, if "somewhat awry," picture of Spain. His characterization of the country as pagan is not convincing, but his view of Spanish politics is, especially his revelation of methods of indoctrination.
Reprinted: 1978.209.

155. _____. "Wright, Richard. White Man, Listen!" Library Journal, 82 (15 September), 2138.
Favorable review praising W's insight into Third World psychology.
Reprinted: 1978.209.

156. Byrne, Harry J. "Spain." The New York Times Book Review (14 April), p. 31.
Letter to the editor critical of PS and Herbert L. Matthews's review of it.

157. C.[aliver], A.[mbrose]. "Negro," in The World Book Encyclopedia. Ed. J. Morris Jones. Vol. 12. Chicago: Field Enterprises, pp. 5486-5492.
Reprint of 1947.163.

158. _____. "Spingarn Medal," in The World Book Encyclopedia. Ed. J. Morris Jones. Vol. 15. Chicago: Field Enterprises, p. 7651.
Reprint of 1947.164.

159. Carman, Harry J. "Richard Wright in Spain." New York Herald Tribune Book Review (10 March), p. 8.
Review of PS. Subjective and often inaccurate, the work is nevertheless "a highly illuminating and provocative report by one of America's live-

liest writers." According to W's analysis, poverty resulting from a primitive economy has been perpetuated by oppressive political and religious institutions, preventing the development of secular culture. Reprinted: 1978.209.

160. Carter, Luther. "Africa and Asia: Whites' Racist Example May Well be Followed." The Norfolk Virginian-Pilot and the Portsmouth Star (20 October), p. 4-C.
Favorable review of WML with extensive quotations. Finds "The Miracle of Nationalism in the African Gold Coast" to be "the most interesting and important" of the four selections. The overall theme is the indivisibility of freedom.

161. Chambers, Lucille Arcola. "The Arts," in her America's Tenth Man. New York: Twayne, pp. 178, 186.
Brief mention of the novel and the play NS.

162. C.[imatti], P.[ietro]. "Libri Nuovi: Richard Wright: Potenza Nera." Il popolo Rome (3 August), p. 4.
Generally favorable review of the Italian translation of BP. As a rebellious black man, W understands emerging Africa. W's style is incisive and colorful, but his recurrent polemics against religion are displeasing.

163. Cockey, Sarah F. "New Adult Books for Young People: Fall 1957." Library Journal, 82 (15 October), Junior Libraries Sec., 113-114.
Contains a favorable notice of WML (p. 122).

164. Colombo, Achille. "Africa: continente da conoscere." Letture, 12 (August), 611-617.
Review of the Italian translation of BP and four other books on Africa. Colombo criticizes W for his attack on the historical role of the Catholic Church in slavery.

165. Comans, Grace P. "An Unhappy People." The Hartford Courant (24 February), Magazine Sec., p. 16.
Favorable review of PS consisting mainly of summary. It is "vigorous and controversial, beautifully and dramatically written." A photograph of W appears with the review.

166. Cori, Carl F. and Gerty T. Cori. Untitled note, in Doctors' Choice. Ed. Phyllis and Albert Blaustein. New York: Wilfred Funk, p. 253.
Statement by two research physicians

explaining their choice of W's "What You Don't Know Won't Hurt You" for an anthology of medical stories.

167. Cronberg, Gilbert. "Two Writers Look at Complex Spain." Des Moines Register (21 April), p. 11-G.
Favorable review of Herbert L. Matthews's The Yoke and the Arrows and W's PS. In contrast to Matthews's journalistic perspective, W is personal and pessimistic about Spain's future. Cronberg notes W's emphasis on sex in Spanish life.

168. D.[atisman], D.[on] F. "Richard Wright Presents Case for African Negro." The Gary Post-Tribune (20 October), Panorama Sec., p. 7.
Unfavorable review of WML calling it "excitably written, often confused and confusing." The chapter on black literature is better and clearer, however.

168a. Davis, Robert Gorham. "Art and Anxiety," in Art and Psychoanalysis. Ed. William Phillips. New York: Criterion Books, pp. 440-453.
Reprint of 1945.873.

169. Davis, Saville R. "Voice for the Colored World." The Christian Science Monitor (17 October), p. 11.
Favorable review of WML praising W's imaginative insight and the quality of his writing. Rather than reciting facts, he asks suggestive questions. The book is frank and fresh. Reprinted: 1978.209.

170. Deedy, John. "White Man, Listen! By Richard Wright." The Ave Maria, 86 (28 December), 27-28.
Unfavorable review praising W's message of freedom, but accusing the book of emotionalism and incoherence. W is biased in one way; the West is biased in another. "The result is a book as confused in exposition as the situation it discusses is in reality" (p. 28).

171. Dolbier, Maurice. "Books and Authors: 'Alwayes a Note-Booke in His Pocket.'" New York Herald Tribune Book Review (6 January), p. 2.
Contains an announcement of the scheduled publication of PS in February.

172. Donahue, John. "Spain's Case Is Traced to 'Pagan Past.'" The Washington Post and Times Herald (24 February), p. E7.
Favorable review of PS noting the remarkable restraint of W's criticism of Franco. W goes deeper to discover

the causes of Spain's plight in Spanish character and tradition.

173. Dulck, Jean. "Richard Wright.--Black Power." Les Langues Modernes, 51 (May-June), 107-108.
Review of the English edition focusing on W's gradual discovery of Africa and the final difficulty he encounters in trying to penetrate non-Western types of knowing. The book mirrors the problems of Afro-Americans when they come to Africa with the illusion that they will establish immediate kinship with Africans. W depicts this situation with much deftness and poignancy.

174. Ebert, Wolfgang. "Von schwarzer Haut und Macht." Die Hamburg Zeit (21 February), p. 6.
Review of the German translation of BP emphasizing W's anticolonialism, especially its psychological dimension. If the West does not accept its guilt and aid the African revolution, Africa will become Communist.

175. Eckman, Frederick. "Neither Tame nor Fleecy." Poetry, 90 (September), 386-397.
Reviewing Allen Ginsberg's Howl and Other Poems, Eckman relates him to W and other Depression poets.

176. Elliott, John K. "Warning Words to White Men." London (Ontario) Free Press (1 November), p. 6.
Favorable review of WML stressing W's focus on the psychological aspects of race relations. With his perspective as both Western and black man, W's message is important to whites.

177. Ellis, Frederick E. "Pagan Spain. By Richard Wright." The Churchman, 171 (15 May), 13.
Favorable review stressing the lesson that church and state should be separated.
Reprinted: 1978.209.

178. Exum, Kinchen. "'Polite Nod for 'Thesis' 'Withdrawn.'" Chattanooga News-Free Press (30 October), p. 6.
Unfavorable review of WML urging W to return to Natchez, where racial harmony prevails.

179. _____. "Wright Shows True Picture of Spaniards." Chattanooga News-Free Press (12 March), p. 6.
Favorable review of PS, "the most thought-provoking book on Spain to appear in decades." Exum particularly admires W's account of a bullfight.

180. F., R. "Labor Looks at Africa and Asia." Labor's Daily (5 November), p. 9.
Favorable review of WML praising W's analysis of the racial situation and stressing the need for better understanding among the races.

181. Fabian, Walter. "Geheimnis des Afrikaners." Frankfürter Rundschau (16 March), Zeit und Bild Sec., p. 3.
Favorable review of the German translation of BP emphasizing the advantages of W's perspective as a black American and his skill as a writer. He was able to penetrate the African personality and comprehend African problems.

182. Ferree, H. Clay. "Awakening Is Urged by Wright." Winston-Salem Journal and Sentinel (27 October), p. 7C.
Favorable review of WML calling it "frank, hard-hitting, revealing." Ferree emphasizes W's point of the difficulty of communication between the West and the colored races. Self-protective dissimulation on the part of the darker peoples is a main cause.

183. Flowers, Paul. "Restrained Richard Wright." The Memphis Commercial Appeal (13 October), Sec. IV, p. 10.
Favorable notice of WML finding it more temperate than his other books. "Instead of being inflammatory, the argument is reasoned and restrained, free of the bitterness and venom that characterized the author's novels."

184. F.[ranklin], J.[ohn] H.[ope] and R.[ayford] W.[hittingham] L.[ogan]. "Negro, American," in Encyclopaedia Britannica. Ed. Walter Yust. Vol. 16. Chicago: Encyclopaedia Britannica, pp. 194-201.
Mentions W briefly (p. 200).
Reprinted: 1958.125; 1959.83; 1960. 148; 1962.59; 1963.85; 1965.65; 1968. 100; 1970.134.

185. G., P. "Dissection of Racial Complex." Columbia Missourian (4 December), p. 4.
Mixed review of WML. W oversimplifies history, but he succeeds in conveying black emotions.

186. G., R. J. "An Alarm and a Human Victory." San Francisco Chronicle (24 November), Christmas Book Sec., p. 6.
Favorable review of WML emphasizing the unconventional and urgent nature of W's warning to the West.
Reprinted: 1978.209.

187. Galen Last, H. van. "Richard Wright: Appel van Bandung wacht op antwoord." Unidentified clipping.

Mixed review of the Dutch translation of CC, a book that is "half journalistic reportage, half polemical pamphlet."

188. Gensecke, Hanns. "Schwarz und Weiss." Berlin Telegraf (24 November), p. 19.
Favorable notice of the German translation of BP concentrating on W's fascination with Nkrumah and his methods of emotional appeal.

189. Gibson, Ellen. "Mr. Wright's Spain." The Milwaukee Journal (17 March), Part 5, p. 4.
Mixed review of PS emphasizing the work's controversial opinions, especially antifascism and anti-Catholicism. "Wright does appear to have written what for him is an honest report on Spain. Surely it is intense and dramatic."
Reprinted: 1978.209; 1982.50.

190. Gibson, Rochelle. "Among Books and Authors: Writer's Position: No Decision." St. Petersburg Times (19 May), Sunday Magazine Sec., p. 15.
Quotes Langston Hughes at the National Assembly of Authors and Dramatists on black expatriates, including W.

191. Graham, Robert A. "America Balances the Books." America, 97 (11 May), 202, 204-209, 211-212.
Contains an unfavorable notice of PS (p. 206) objecting to W's treatment of Catholicism.

192. _____. "World Scene." America, 98 (7 December), 319-322.
Contains a notice of WML, a shocking book in which W "expounds his ideas on the future of the relationship of Western culture with the non-white world" (p. 322).

193. Grebstein, Sheldon. "Some Recent Nonfiction, In Brief." Lexington (Ky.) Sunday Herald-Leader (1 December), p. 55.
Contains an unfavorable review of WML complaining of structural defects resulting from the work's origin as separate speeches. Grebstein also accuses W of excessive emotionalism and ranting demagoguery.

194. Greiff, John B. "Food for Thought Provided in Race Relations Inquiry." Newport News Daily Press (20 October), p. 4D.
Favorable review of WML finding W's special perspective valuable in interpreting the East to the West. Greiff is disturbed by W's recommendation that Afro-Asian leaders assume extraordinary powers in modernizing their nations.

195. Griffith, Albert J. "White Man, Listen! by Richard Wright." Austin (Tex.) American Statesman (3 November), p. A-7.
Somewhat favorable review stressing the importance of W's message of the global interrelatedness of racial issues. Although WML "is not as powerful or consistent a plea as it might have been," W's voice will be heard.

196. Grove, Harold Edward. "Wright." The New York Times Book Review (24 November), p. 41.
Letter to the editor agreeing with Oscar Handlin's review of WML and reproving W for categorizing whites. Instead of hatred, W should use Martin Luther King's "weapon of love."

197. H., E. "Ein Kontinent erwacht." Allgemeine Wochenzeitung der Juden in Deutschland (18 January), p. 7.
Reprint of 1956.184.

198. _____. "Richard Wright." Aachener Prisma (January).
Reprint of 1956.184.

199. _____. "Schwarze Macht." Johannesburg Afrika Post (May).
Reprint of 1956.184.

200. _____. "Schwarze Macht." Westfälisch-Lippische Beamtenworte (April).
Reprint of 1956.184.

201. H., R. F. "'White Man, Listen!' on Racial Tensions." Springfield (Mass.) Republican (17 November).
Mixed review calling the work "not one of Mr. Wright's better efforts, being uneven in tempo and disconnected in thought, but nevertheless . . . a quite eloquent and intelligent summary of a tragic situation."

202. Hackett, Walter. "Spain: Land of Contrasts." Worcester (Mass.) Sunday Telegram (17 February), p. D9.
Mixed review of PS praising W's powers of observation and expression, but disputing his slanted ideological and political analysis. If Franco did not rule, Hackett believes, the Communists would.

203. Hahn, K. J. "Richard Wright---voor of tegen rassendiscriminatie." De Cunie [?] (9 February).
Unfavorable review of the Dutch translation of CC objecting at length to W's condemnation of the Dutch impact in Asia and Africa. Praises

W's past work and his detailed reporting of his experiences in the book under review, however.

204. Handlin, Oscar. "Patterns of Prejudice." The New York Times Book Review (20 October), p. 3.
Review of WML emphasizing the importance of W's theme and perspective, but calling the book "argumentative, belligerent and often wrong-headed." W oversimplifies complex issues, especially the attitudes of whites toward dark races, and underestimates the threat of Communism.
Reprinted: 1978.209; 1982.50.

205. Hanscom, Leslie. "Spain--Religious But Pagan." New York World-Telegram and The Sun (25 February), p. 19.
Favorable review of PS, "Richard Wright's intellectual travelogue," quoting freely from the book while emphasizing the religiosity W found. Hanscom also comments on W's use of the Falangist political catechism. "Vivid for its sightseeing as well as its thinking, the book makes the Spanish--with all their strange faults--sound like the most alive of people and their country sound like one of the earth's most fascinating."
Reprinted: 1978.209.

206. Harris, Arthur S., Jr. "A Coherent Comment; Emphatic Not Angry." Worcester (Mass.) Sunday Telegram (20 October), Sec. E, p. 9.
Favorable notice of WML stressing W's calmness and rationality in presenting the case against racism.

207. Harrison, Joseph G. "Richard Wright on Spain." The Christian Science Monitor (21 February), p. 13.
Favorable review of PS. Although at times biased and prone to exaggeration, W confronts aspects of Spanish life with frankness and courage.
Reprinted: 1978.209; 1982.50.

208. H.[ayford], H.[arrison] M. "American Literature," in 1957 Britannica Book of the Year. Ed. Walter Yust. Chicago: Encyclopaedia Britannica, pp. 102-105.
Mentions briefly CC.

209. Hetherly, [Van]. "Explosive!: Wright Assails Racism." The Houston Chronicle (15 December), Feature Magazine Sec., p. 38.
Favorable review of WML, urging that W's message be heard.

210. Hicks, Granville. "Richard Wright: Spain the Fossil." New York Post (24 February), p. M11.
Somewhat favorable review of PS

emphasizing W's analytical rather than touristic interest in the country with which, as an "emancipated cosmopolitan," he so sharply differed. Hicks agrees that Spain is fossilized, but thinks that W "has misdated the fossil" by calling it pagan.
Reprinted: 1978.209.

211. Hicks, John. "Between Book Ends: Not Free for Treason." St. Louis Post-Dispatch (13 November), p. 2E.
Favorable review of WML, a "terse and poignant" explanation of the emotional reactions of the world's darker peoples to racism. Hicks explains the origin of the book in W's European lectures.

212. Hilsenbeck. "Wright, Richard: Schwarze Macht." Stadtliche Beratungsstelle für Volksbüchereien (15 February).
Favorable review of the German translation of BP. W's description of the tension between old and new ways is applicable to all of black Africa.

213. Ho. "Schwarze Macht." Kultur und Unterricht (August).
Favorable notice of the German translation of BP pointing out its condemnation of colonial brutality and its call for a new order in Africa.

214. Hoffmann, Siegfried. "Afrikanische Freiheitsbewegung." Die Hamburg andere Zeitung (19 September).
Lengthy review of the German translation of BP summarizing W's observations on colonialism and his recommendations for new attitudes toward Africa. The book is particularly timely because it should help German readers to come to terms with their fears stemming from African independence.

215. Hogan, William. "A Bookman's Notebook: A Gloomy Report on Present-Day Spain." San Francisco Chronicle (20 February), p. 23.
Favorable review of PS. Controversial but honest, the book is an artfully written, unconventional work emphasizing the country's preoccupation with sex, its "pagan" Catholicism, and its oppressive government. Hogan compares W's use of juxtaposition to that of Dos Passos.
Reprinted: 1978.209.

216. Holland, E. L., Jr. "Agree or Not--Wright on Racial Issues Enigmatic." The Birmingham News (20 October), Sec. E, p. 7.
Mixed review of WML, a book that is

thoughtful but difficult to understand. "It is so elevated in linguistic trickery that even thoughtful
Southerners would undoubtedly have
trouble with it." Holland considers
the first part of the book the most
penetrating.

217. _____. "Non-Political Report on
Spain Is Timely." Little Rock Arkansas
Gazette.
    Favorable review of PS praising W's
    reportorial skill. The book is good
    writing on a difficult subject.

218. _____. "'Platero y Yo' Is Rated
'57's Best by Reviewer." The Birmingham
News (15 December), Sec. E, p. 6.
    Includes comments on PS, a tough and
    incisive book, and WML, an ambitious
    and at times brilliant work.

219. Holmberg, Ted. "Spain and Richard
Wright." The Providence Sunday Journal
(24 February), Sec. VI, p. 8.
    Rather unfavorable review of PS find-
    ing it lively as a travel book but
    not profound or original as a social,
    political, and cultural interpreta-
    tion. Holmberg dislikes W's comments
    on Spanish religion and his Freudian
    analysis of the bullfight.
    Reprinted: 1978.209.

220. [Howe, Irving]. Untitled note. Dissent, 4 (Autumn), 358.
    Prefatory remarks to an excerpt from
    W's "Tradition and Industrializa-
    tion." Includes an explanation of the
    origins of WML.

221. _____ and Lewis Coser. The American
Communist Party: A Critical History
(1919-1957). Boston: Beacon Press, p.
394.
    Lists W as one of the leaders of the
    American Peace Mobilization in 1940.

222. Howe, Lee A. "Book Report."
    Radio script of a review of WML
    presented on the Religion in Life
    series of station WVET in Rochester,
    New York, on 27 October 1957. Howe
    agrees with W's emphasis on race
    relations as the paramount world
    problem and values W's empathetic
    treatment.

223. Hughes, Langston. "The Spectator:
The Black List." National Guardian (3
June), p. 12.
    Discusses the problem of censorship
    encountered by the black writer.
    Expatriation is sometimes the result,
    as in W's case.

224. Ito, Kenji. "Teiko to Dasshutsu--
Richard Wright nitsuite" ["Richard

Wright's Protest and Freedom"]. Kaichoon
[Tidal Sound], 13 (September), 46-54.
    A description of W's life and work as
    a black man who views American
    society from the inside. First
    attracted to Communism, W launched on
    a writing career through its philo-
    sophy, but soon departed from it to
    create his own vision. Says that
    BP constitutes his final vision.
    [Y. H.]

225. Ivy, James W. "Promise and Failure." The Crisis, 64 (December), 640.
    Favorable review of WML with special
    praise for "The Psychological Reac-
    tions of Oppressed People." Empha-
    sizes W's point that understanding on
    the part of whites is necessary for a
    rapprochement between Western and
    Asian-African nations.
    Reprinted: 1978.209.

226. _____. "Spanish Journey." The
Crisis, 64 (May), 313-314.
    Review of PS. After summarizing the
    contents, Ivy concludes that although
    some of W's interpretations are
    questionable, he has written "a
    lively and provocative book" that
    shows "intuitive understanding of a
    people who have a psychological
    affinity in many ways with American
    Negroes."

227. Jacobs, Rudolf. Untitled article.
Westdeutscher Rundfunk (19 July).
    Radio review of the German transla-
    tion of BP.

228. Jahn, Janheinz. Schwarze Ballade:
Moderne afrikanische Erzähler beider
Hemisphären. Düsseldorf-Köln: Eugen
Diederichs Verlag, pp. 242-243.
    Biographical sketch of W and a list
    of German translations of his work.

229. _____. "World Congress of Black
Writers." Black Orpheus, No. 1 (September), pp. 39-46.
    Discusses the disagreement between W
    and Césaire on the issue of African
    culture versus Westernization.
    Includes a photograph of W.

230. James, Mertice M. and Dorothy
Brown. "Wright, Richard. Color Curtain;
a report on the Bandung conference," in
their The Book Review Digest. New York:
The H. W. Wilson Company, p. 1029.
    Lists or quotes from eighteen
    reviews.

231. _____. "Wright, Richard. Pagan
Spain," in their The Book Review Digest,
53 (April).
    Lists or quotes from eight early
    reviews.

232. Johnson, Charles S. "Negro in America," in The Encyclopedia Americana. Ed. Lavinia P. Dudley. Vol. 20. New York: Americana Corporation, pp. 65-77.
Reprint of 1955.54.

232a. Joly, Pierre. "James Baldwin évoque Harlem, sa patrie." Rouen Paris-Normandie (5 April), p. 11.
Mentions W briefly.

233. Jones, Carter Brooke. "Spain Today." The Washington Sunday Star (24 February), p. D-21.
Unfavorable review of PS. W writes well, but his "patent bias and prejudice weaken all his findings."
Reprinted: 1978.209.

234. Jones, Marjorie B. "Life in Franco's Spain." The Baltimore Sun (24 February), Sec. A, p. 16.
Review of The Face of Spain and PS favoring Gerald Brenan's book over W's, which overemphasizes sex and is too prolix. Jones praises the chapter on persecution of Protestants, however.
Reprinted: 1978.209.

235. K., R. "Books and Authors." Lewiston-Auburn Maine Independent (26 November).
Reprint of 1957.236.

236. _____. "Books and Authors." Lewiston (Maine) Sun (21 November).
Review of WML emphasizing the work's power and frankness.
Reprinted: 1957.235.

237. Kim, Jean-Jacques. "La Culpabilité multiple des noirs américains." Critique, 13 (January), 80-88.
Review of the French·translation of O summarizing the major stages in the development of Cross Damon's awareness of the entanglements of life and his own desires. Kim does not stress existentialism in the work, but he does comment on W's interest in a variety of human relationships.

238. Kincheloe, Henderson. "The World of Books." The Raleigh News and Observer (3 November), Sec. III, p. 5.
Contains a mildly favorable notice of WML pointing out W's "emotional involvement in his subject."

239. Kitching, Jessie. "PW Forecast for Booksellers." Publishers' Weekly, 172 (16 September), 281-284.
Includes a favorable notice of WML, "a very angry book."

240. Kl. "Zur kolonial Frage." Die neue Verdenig (January).

Review of the German translation of BP. Although W makes many incisive political observations, his socialist perspective often leads him to overlook approaches which could increase the book's value.

241. Kleffel, Helmut. Untitled article. Baden-Baden Sudwestfunk (23 June).
Radio review of the German translation of BP.

242. Knox, George. "The Negro Novelist's Sensibility and the Outsider Theme." Western Humanities Review, 11 (Spring), 137-148.
Compares O and Invisible Man as novels of estrangement and alienation. W and Ellison treat a black protagonist who suffers the problems of modern cosmopolitan man. Both writers develop the symbolic properties of blackness, and both maintain tension between individual self-reliance and societal determinism.

243. Krebs, Patricia. "Between Book Ends: Misery Is the Spaniard." St. Louis Post-Dispatch (16 April), p. 2C.
Favorable review of PS praising the vivid writing but noting also W's subjectivism and emotionalism. Spain's plight is due mainly to religious influence and to the irrationality of the Spanish personality.

244. Küster, Ingeborg. "Buchbesprechungen." Das andere Deutschland (June).
Notice of the German translation of BP.

245. L., F. M. "Pagan Spain. By Richard Wright." The Spokane Spokesman-Review (c. 24 March).
Reprint of 1957.246.

246. _____. "Pagan Spain. By Richard Wright." The Tacoma Sunday News Tribune and Sunday Ledger (24 March), Pacific Parade Magazine Sec., p. 2.
Favorable review of a controversial and exciting book praising the quality of the writing and emphasizing W's political perspective.
Reprinted: 1957.245.

247. L., M. "An Uncomfortable, Probing Look at Modern Spain." New Bedford Sunday Standard-Times (21 April), p. 36.
Favorable review of PS, a thought-provoking book recalling "the intensity, the restless searching and painful candor" of W's earlier works.

248. L., R. E. "Pagan Spain, by Richard Wright." Albuquerque Tribune (16 March), p. 4.

Favorable review of "a beautifully written, lucid book" that is also disturbing and controversial.

249. Langhammer-Köllmer, Ella. "Richard Wright: Schwarze Macht." Neue Volksbildung, 8 (February), 59.
Favorable notice of the German translation of BP mentioning W's activities since his break with Communism and his expatriation. The reviewer is especially interested in W's accounts of his meetings with Nkrumah.

250. Lash, John. "A Long, Hard Look at the Ghetto." Phylon, 18 (First Quarter), 21-22.
Survey of Afro-American literature in 1956 including a brief summary of CC emphasizing the potential power of the Afro-Asian alliance.

251. Le. "Politische Bücher: Indien und Afrika." Stuttgarter Zeitung (29 August), p. 12.
Contains a favorable review of the German translation of BP. Although W's insights are by no means original, the book is interesting for its descriptions of the tensions between primitive and progressive tendencies in Ghana's everyday life.

252. Lee, Charles. "Books: Mayflower Bears New Manuscript." Cincinnati Times-Star (21 May), p. 22.
Notes that W is included in Doctor's Choice, edited by Phyllis and Albert Blaustein, "an unusual anthology consisting of 16 favorite medical stories by 16 prominent men of medicine."

253. Lerner, Max. "The Lost Country." New York Post (21 July), p. M8.
Mentions W as an interpreter of Spanish life.

254. Lindau, Betsy. "'White Man, Listen.'" Asheville Citizen-Times (17 November), Sec. D, p. 3.
Favorable review calling W "probably the world's most articulate Negro." White readers will disagree with many of his points, but they should not neglect the "rare opportunity" this book provides to understand a black perspective.

255. Locke, W. R. "Personal Report on Conditions in Spain." Oakland Tribune (14 April), p. 14-C.
Review of PS detecting subjectivity and predicting controversy. Locke emphasizes W's linking of church and state and his discussion of Spain's agricultural problems.

256. Lombardo, Agostino. "Il romanzo e la polemica: Ralph Ellison e Herbert Gold," in his Realismo e simbolismo. Saggi di letteratura americana contemporanea. Biblioteca di studi americani 3, ed. Agostino Lombardo. Rome: Edizioni di storia e letteratura, pp. 231-243.
Contains a reprint of 1953.174a.

257. Lunger, Phil. "Angry Author Clouds Issue of Nationalism." Buffalo Courier-Express (22 December), p. 8-D.
Mildly favorable review of WML finding W's arguments "well-informed and effectively presented," but believing that the book's angry tone may alienate some readers. Lunger also thinks that W tends to underestimate the danger of Communism to the Third World.

258. M., B. "Richard Wright. Schwarze Macht." Schweizerische Arbeiterbildungszentrale (12 March).
Favorable review of the German translation of BP. Despite many questionable political conclusions, the book is recommended reading. It is particularly interesting because it records W's reaction to the land of his ancestors.

259. Malecek, F. T., S. J. "Negro Writer's Record of an Emotional State." The Denver Post (20 October), Roundup Sec., p. 12.
Somewhat unfavorable review of WML complaining of oversimplification and subjectivity. The book is "rather a broad human document."

260. Maloney, Joseph F. "Wright, Richard. White Man, Listen." Best Sellers, 17 (15 November), 280.
Review including a detailed summary with quotations. W's lectures are more emotional than intellectual, leaving the reader somewhat disappointed. But Maloney singles out the chapters on Afro-American literature and Ghana for special praise. He does not believe that W is a representative black American.
Reprinted: 1978.209.

261. Manchester, Paul. "Books on Spain Sharp in Contrasts." The Nashville Tennessean (3 March), p. 5-E.
Unfavorable review of PS and favorable review of Gerald Brenan's The Face of Spain. Criticizes W for his ignorance of the language and the culture, his glib generalizations, and his own personal background.

262. Mannhardt, Joh. W. "Richard Wright: Schwarze Macht. Zur Afrikanischen Revolution." Das Historisch-Politische Buch,

5, No. 10, 320.
Somewhat unfavorable review of the German translation of BP stressing the difficulty of understanding Africa from an outsider's position. As an American W frequently fails to recognize the intricacies of the European-African relationship.

263. Marsh, Robert C. "Two Writers Look at Spain--Before and After Its Civil War." Chicago Sun-Times (17 March), Sec. Three, p. 12.
Unfavorable review of PS complaining of W's lack of knowledge of the country, his subjectivity, his undue selectivity in his materials, and his neglect of the Spanish middle class. Reprinted: 1978.209.

264. Maslin, Marsh. "The Browser: Beauty and Bitterness in Spain." San Francisco Call-Bulletin (24 February).
Favorable review of PS stressing the variety of people W met. "A writer of great sensitivity and force," the author has produced "a deeply moving book."

265. _____. "Difference Between Black and White." San Francisco Call-Bulletin (18 October), p. 9.
Favorable review of WML, a powerful plea for understanding between the races. Considers the section on Afro-American literature especially good.

266. Matthews, Herbert L. "How It Seemed to Him." The New York Times Book Review (24 February), p. 7.
Favorable review of PS calling it "fascinating, intense, subjective, emotional . . . somewhat naive, bitterly anti-Franco and very anti-Spanish Catholic." Not always factually accurate, W is a vivid and immensely talented writer. Reprinted: 1978.209.

267. McCarthy, Helen. "Between the Book-ends." The Ayer (Mass.) Public Spirit (17 October), p. 7.
Favorable review of WML, which "isn't a pretty book," but is one which merits close study. Its analysis of black mentality is penetrating.

268. McCormick, John. Catastrophe and Imagination: An Interpretation of the Recent English and American Novel. London: Longmans, p. 201.
Mentions briefly W's "savage naturalism."

269. McGrory, Mary. "Reading and Writing: TV Not Real Culprit in Decline of Reading." The Washington Sunday Star (10 February), p. E-5.

Contains an announcement of PS.

270. McMahon, Francis E. "Spain Through Secularist Spectacles." America, 96 (9 March), 648, 653.
Unfavorable review of PS. Because of his limited experience in Spain and his lack of knowledge about the country, W fails in his analysis of Spanish culture. McMahon sharply criticizes W's anti-Catholicism. PS reveals more about its author than its subject.
Reprinted: 1978.209.

271. Miller, Albert H. "White Man, Listen! by Richard Wright." The Critic, 16 (November), 13-14.
Favorable review. "Wright is a self-conscious, brutally honest, and awfully lonely cosmopolitan intellectual." Miller agrees with most of W's analyses.

272. Minchero Vilasaró, Angel. "Wright, Richard," in his Diccionario universal de escritores. San Sebastian: Edidhe, pp. 335-336.
Biographical-critical sketch.

273. Molden, Virginia. "All Spain Maladjusted to Wright." The Fort Wayne News-Sentinel (23 February), p. 4.
Unfavorable review of PS accusing W of bias, exaggeration, and ignorance. With unreliable informants and without knowledge of the language, he "finds Spain peopled with neurotics, under the domination of Church and State or a combination thereof, and solely preoccupied with sex and paganism."

274. Mondadori, Alberto. "Tre americhe." Epoca (1 September), pp. 55-56.
Mentions the film NS and includes photographs.

275. Morrison, Joseph L. "Spain's Plight." Greensboro Daily News (24 March), Feature Sec., p. 3.
Favorable review of PS calling it a "raw and grim" but accurate account of class hatred between the masses and the aristocracy. This hatred "forebodes the classic explosion" of renewed civil war.

276. Moskowitz, Gene. "American Negroes' Impact on Parisian Show Biz." Variety (9 January), p. 204.
Includes two paragraphs on W's expatriation, which Moskowitz believes has been beneficial in expanding and universalizing W's art.

277. Motley, Mary Penick. "White Man, Listen!" Detroit Metro Shopper's Guide

(9 November).
Favorable review commenting on the excellence of the writing and the absorbing interest of the material.

278. Nichols, Luther. "Wright Warns White Race." San Francisco Examiner (17 October), Sec. III, p. 3.
Review of WML noting W's subjective approach. The message of the book should be heeded.

279. Norris, Hoke. "Wright Sounds Dire Warning for Whites." Chicago Sun-Times (20 October), Sec. 3, p. 6.
Review of WML stressing the global nature of the problems W treats.

280. O., R. P. "Titillating Spain." National Review, 4 (3 August), 141-142.
Unfavorable review of PS objecting to W's obscenities and irreligion.
Reprinted: 1978.209.

281. Ottley, Roi. "He Should Stick to Fiction." Chicago Sunday Tribune Magazine of Books (3 March), p. 10.
Unfavorable review of PS complaining of W's subjectivity. Despite his literary abilities, he does not have the skills of a reporter or the depth of understanding necessary in treating an alien culture. He should turn his attention to the struggle for civil rights at home.
Reprinted: 1978.209.

282. _____. "Reasoned Passion Against Racism." Chicago Sunday Tribune Magazine of Books (10 November), p. 11.
Favorable review of WML summarizing W's argument, which is couched in "his most trenchant prose" and advanced with "reasoned passion."
Reprinted: 1978.209.

283. Owens, William A. "Introduction," in Native Son. Harper's Modern Classics. New York: Harper, pp. vii-xii.
Considers NS a naturalistic novel, emphasizing its determinism and comparing it to An American Tragedy, The Grapes of Wrath, Martin Eden, and The Jungle.

284. Parker, Jane A. B. "Richard Wright Explores a Nation in Candid Report." Jackson (Miss.) Daily News (24 February), p. 40.
Favorable review of PS, a "vigorous, compassionate and engrossing" book that is bound to be controversial. Notes W's emphasis on sex and religion in Spain.
Reprinted: 1978.209.

285. Petree, Nellie. "The Bookshelf." The Clearwater Sun (17 October), p. 30.

Includes a favorable review of WML consisting mainly of summary and quotation. Petree considers W's viewpoint well suited to achieve his "literate, rational discussion of a problem which now is foremost in the minds and hearts of many," but she admits that "some will discuss it as Negro propaganda without reading all of it or any of it."

286. Pickrel, Paul. "Over the Pyrenees." Harper's Magazine, 214 (May), 84, 86, 88.
Review of PS and Herbert L. Matthews's The Yoke and the Arrows noting that W's vivid and personal sketches of Spanish people complement Matthews's more abstract presentation of Spain's problems.

287. Pillsbury, F. W. "Equal Rights Move Traced." The Boston Herald (18 November).
Favorable review of WML noting that the work is impassioned but factual.

288. Pivano, Fernanda. "L'autore di 'Paura' e enthusiasta della piaggia." Letteratura e arta nel mondo (14 June).
Reports on W's visit to Italy for consultation on translations of BP and O.

289. _____. "Richard Wright." Il giorno (19 January).
Describes W's life style in Paris. Surrounded by creature comforts, he recalls the hardships of his youth. His literary career, however, has moved from social protest to psychological exploration.
Reprinted: 1964.104.

290. Plum, Werner. "Ein amerikanischer Negerschriftsteller fährt nach Afrika." Die europäische Zeitung (20 November).
Favorable review of the German translation of BP agreeing with W that Europe is to blame for Africa's problems. The unique quality of the book stems from W's open recognition of his Western attitudes.

291. Polsby, Allen J. Untitled clipping. Brown Daily Herald (c. November).
Review of WML.

292. Price, Emerson. "Russian's Novel Hailed as Literature." The Cleveland Press (22 October), p. 7.
Contains a favorable notice of WML. Price accepts W's argument, stating that "the nature and proportions of one of the larger problems facing western civilization are clearly revealed here."

293. Przywara, Erich. "Mythos und Mys-
terum." Besinnung, pp. 236-237.
Contains a paragraph on the German
translation of BP, which exemplifies
a "contradictory" variety of social-
ism. Although W seems to have an
iconoclastic temperament, his recommendations for Ghana amount to support for a "new colonialism."

293a. [Quinn, Kerker]. "Accent Spring
1957."
Flyer listing W as a contributor to
the Spring 1942 issue of Accent.

293b. ____. "Accent Winter 1957."
Flyer listing W as a contributor to
the Spring 1942 issue of Accent.

294. R. "Richard Wright, De kleurbarrière." Tijdschrift von Economische en
sociale Geographie, 48 (March), 88.
Brief notice of the Dutch translation
of CC.

295. Rausch, Jurgen. "Brücke über die
Jahrhunderte." Bremer Nachrichten (20
November).
Review of the German translation of
BP stressing the importance of the
temporal, rather than spatial,
journey--the clash between modern and
traditional ways in Africa. W's main
interests are psychological, but he
places his studies against a penetrating analysis of Ghana's social
conflicts and corruptions.

296. Redding, Saunders. "Book Review."
The Baltimore Afro-American (9 March),
Magazine Sec., p. 2.
Favorable review of PS considering it
in the context of W's literary
career, especially in comparison to
O, BP, and CC. In his rejection of
both politics and religion, W
approaches nihilism, and PS seems to
support his position. "But it is an
interesting--indeed, a fascinating
book; for Wright's skill in handling
sharp dramatic incident and in portraying people is coupled with a
descriptive skill he rarely uses, and
both operate to produce the emotional
intensity of fiction."
Reprinted: 1978.209.

297. ____. "Book Review." The Baltimore
Afro-American (26 October), Magazine
Sec., p. 2.
Favorable review of WML identifying
"the unity of man" as the
intellectual concept which governs
W's examination of relations
between the West and the Third
World. The social failure to
implement this intellectually valid
concept has been psychologically

disastrous for both the rejectors and
the rejected. "Wright has never written more poignantly or more brilliantly, but he has not written to
catch only the ear of the white man:
he wants the colored man to listen
too."

298. Reinhold, Kurt von. "Ghana." Darm-
stadter Echo (6 March).
Lengthy analysis of the newly independent Ghana followed by a brief
comment on the German translation of
BP pointing out W's condemnation of
white colonial influence.

299. Roberts, Henry L. "Recent Books on
International Relations." Foreign Affairs, 35 (July), 704-720.
Contains a very brief notice of PS
(p. 714).

300. Rogers, J. A. "Your History." The
Pittsburgh Courier (30 March), Magazine
Sec., p. 8.
Includes a drawing of W and a brief
biographical sketch describing him as
a famous expatriate and world
traveller.

301. Rose, Ruth G. "Literary Guide-
posts." Scranton Scrantonian (3 November).
Favorable review of WML, a book that
should receive serious thought. W has
not changed his feelings about the
race issue.

302. Ross, Eva J. "Pagan Spain, by
Richard Wright." Books on Trial, 15
(March), 307-308.
Unfavorable review complaining of W's
anti-Catholicism, sexual obsession,
and ignorance of the Spanish lan-
guage.
Reprinted: 1978.209

303. Rowe, Leonard. "White Man, Listen!
By Richard Wright." The Cincinnati
Enquirer (24 November), p. 21.
Rather favorable notice stressing the
vehemence of this "flaming Jeremiad,"
but noting that W supports his case
well and responds to the exigencies
of the time.

304. Rudolf, Ernst. "Richard Wright:
Schwarze Macht. Zur afrikanischen Revolution." Wirtschaftsdienst, 37 (January), 54.
Favorable review of the German translation of BP. The book serves as a
reminder that no solution to Africa's
problems can afford to ignore the
human factor. Although at times W
stands too prominently in the foreground and his experiences and
beliefs sometimes dominate his inter-

pretations, he raises important issues concerning social and political relationships.

305. S., C. "Die Emanzipation Afrikas." Das Bücherblatt, 21 (5 April), 7.
Favorable review of the German translation of BP emphasizing W's concern for human treatment of all black people. He does not thoroughly understand African religion and he ignores the flora and fauna, but he reports alertly and intelligently on the freedom movement in the Gold Coast.

306. S., H. M. "Pagan Spain by Richard Wright." Wilmington (Del.) Morning News (25 February), p. 11.
Favorable review stating that W finds the Spanish people "sensitive and sensual." His comments on Spanish politics and religion may be controversial, but his "descriptions, especially that of the bullfight, are extremely beautiful."

307. S., R. "Hinweise auf Bücher." Neues Winterthürer Tagblatt (3 January).
Favorable review of the German translation of BP. Despite W's alienation, it is a highly interesting political book, notable for its analysis of the relation between Communism and the developing political awareness of the African masses.

308. S., S. "Ein Negerstaat wird selbständig." Welt der Abeit, No. 9 (c. February).
Review of the German translation of BP consisting largely of a general summary of social and political conditions in Ghana. The historical insight of BP makes it an important book on Africa.

309. Sabbath, Lawrence. "The Protest Technique." The Montreal Gazette (9 March), p. 31.
Unfavorable review of PS finding its protest technique anachronistic, its viewpoint narrow, and its subjectivity apparent. Sabbath does praise W's description of a bullfight, however.

310. Sadoya, Shigenobu. "Richard Wright no Sakuhin to Style" ["Richard Wright's Work and Style"]. Jiji Eigo Kenkyu [The Study of Current English], 12 (August), 50-52.
The value of W's work can be appreciated once W is recognized as a black individual as well as a representative of the race. Both UTC and NS succeeded in attracting public attention, for they described the problem of race more directly than before.

Claims the influences of Dreiser and Farrell on W to be superficial and suggests that naturalism was merely fashionable in the 40s. [Y. H.]

310a. Saito, Tadatoshi. "An Essay on Richard Wright." Essays, 4 (April), 46-56.
Suggests that black literature should be evaluated not for its success as protest literature but as work of artistic merit. W, through UTC, NS, and O, provides a new direction in dealing with black humanism. [Y. H. and T. K.]

311. _____. "Richard Wright Ron--Native Son nitsuite" ["Richard Wright's Native Son"]. Gaikoku Bungaku [Foreign Literature], 6, pp. 1-15.
Bigger's accidental killing of Mary is interpreted as his first meaningful action as a man, but it also means a tragedy for the entire race. The novel is successful not only as protest literature but in W's organization of fictional material. His basic philosophy in the book is Communism but its structure indicates his desire to explore existentialism. [Y. H.]

312. Salisbury, Harrison E. "Writers in the Shadow of Communism." The New York Times Magazine (9 June), pp. 10, 28, 30, 33-34.
Mentions W (p. 10) and includes a photograph (p. 34).

313. Schlyter, Herman. "Att tänka svart." Den Evangeliska Missionen (November-December), pp. 176-180.
Pamphlet on missionary work in Africa discussing the relevance of BP to the problems facing Christian missionaries.

314. Schürenberg, Sven. Untitled clipping. Frankfurt Hessischer Rundfunk (7 June).
Radio review of the German translation of BP, an important work, though often perplexing and sometimes irritating. Quotes extensively to demonstrate W's distrust of whites and alienation from Africans.

315. Schuyler, George S. "Richard Wright Sees Spain." The Pittsburgh Courier (23 March), Magazine Sec., p. 2.
Unfavorable review of PS complaining of subjectivity and superficiality. The book is readable, however.

316. Seeberger, Kurt. "Gute Bücher gute Freunde." Bayerischer Rundfunk (10 March).
Radio review of the German trans-

lation of BP. Although there is some truth in the work's attack on European colonialism, W overlooks the sincere efforts of missionaries such as Schweitzer to teach Africans European ideals.

317. Seidkin, Phyllis. "Spanish Quartet: Four Views of That Enigmatic Land." San Francisco Examiner (28 April), p. 11.
Includes a brief, unfavorable notice of PS complaining of its subjectivity and lack of factual material.

318. Sellenthin, H. G. "Wright, Richard: Schwarze Macht." Arbeitskreis Berliner Volksbibliothekäre.
Favorable review of the German translation of BP. The book represents an extension of the Harriet Beecher Stowe school of humanitarian literature into African affairs. Its value lies in the fact that it considers the Gold Coast with the sensibility of a Walt Whitman.

319. Silverman, Joseph H. "Three Windows on Spain." The Nation, 185 (7 September), 113-116.
Review of PS, Gerald Brenan's The Face of Spain, and Herbert L. Matthews's The Yoke and the Arrows. Silverman praises W's literary ability and his treatment of the bullfight and Spanish Protestantism. W also has "brilliant intuitive observations" (p. 114) on politics and Catholicism. On the other hand, he overemphasizes sex, dismisses important scholarship on Spain, and perpetuates the black legend of Spanish imperialism.

320. Smith, Guy E. American Literature: A Complete Survey. Ames, Iowa: Littlefield, Adams, pp. 149, 227.
Contains a general paragraph on W and a paragraph summarizing the plot of NS.

321. Smith, Woodrow. "Life in Spain Found Oppressive." Chattanooga Sunday Times (10 March), p. 26.
Mixed review of PS, "a remarkably sensitive, preceptive [sic] and informative book," but one whose sexual and religious perspectives are idiosyncratically subjective.

322. Smythe, Hugh H. "Pervasive Racialism." The Crisis, 64 (January), 58-59.
Review of CC and Carl T. Rowan's The Pitiful and the Proud. Smythe is more favorable to W than to Rowan. W, "with his longer years of experience, deeper feeling, and own personal complexes," stresses race as the dominant factor in the Bandung Conference.

323. Snelling, Paula. "Warning Voice." The Progressive, 21 (December), 42-43.
Favorable review of WML discussing the need of cooperation between the white West and the dark East so as to avoid massive violence. The best hope resides in the "tragic elite" of Western-educated African and Asian leaders. Snelling also comments on W's lecture on Afro-American literature.
Reprinted: 1978.209.

324. Spingarn, Arthur B. "Books by Negro Authors in 1956." The Crisis, 64 (February), 76-82.
Lists CC.

325. Spletz, Oskar. "Der Schwarze Kontinent im Spiegel." Munich Süddeutsche Zeitung (30-31 March), p. 43.
Unfavorable review of the German translation of BP. W's disappointment at not being able to establish a bond with his African past leads him to two extremes. On the one hand he rails in hatred against the British while on the other he demands that Nkrumah make Ghana a totally modern, "civilized" nation.

326. Sprigge, Elizabeth. Gertrude Stein: Her Life and Work. London: Hamish Hamilton, p. 260.
Notes that Stein "was a member of the reception committee for the visit of the Negro author, Richard Wright, who had early praised Melanctha."

327. Starkey, Marion L. "White Man, Listen! by Richard Wright." The Boston Sunday Globe (24 November), p. A-19.
Brief notice expressing fear that the book will be unread by those who need to read it most.

328. Stephenson, Mary Ellen. "Spain Gets Bitter Barbs from Visitor." Richmond News Leader (28 August), p. 13.
Mixed review of PS noting the author's bitterness and violence, but conceding his sympathy for the Spanish people. The book is both fascinating and repulsive.
Reprinted: 1978.209.

329. Stevenson, David L. "Novel, The," in The Encyclopedia Americana. Ed. Lavinia P. Dudley. Vol. 20. New York: Americana Corporation, pp. 503-524.
Reprint of 1952.64.

330. Stewart, Ollie. "Report from Europe: Richard Wright Pens New Tome." The Baltimore Afro-American (6 July), p. 8.
Reports a visit with W including discussion of his book sales and his Italian tour. Stewart emphasizes W's

interest in Africa and black nationalism.

331. Stover, Carl F. "White Man Is Intrusive." The Washington Post and Times
Herald (29 December), Sec. E, p. 6.
     Somewhat favorable review of WML
     calling it "a bitter and vituperative
     book." Stover claims that the work
     reflects W's "own plight as a tal-
     ented and sensitive American Negro"
     more than the plight of Africans and
     Asians.

332. Strandberg, Olle. "Vit man under
svart hud." Unidentified article (c.
January), pp. 14-15.
     Swedish article on W reporting his
     visits to several Paris tourist at-
     tractions, where he reflects on Afri-
     can and European cultures. W says
     that he understands "nothing" of
     African culture. Strandberg compares
     W with Hemingway in the distance from
     which they encountered Africa.

333. Strout, Richard. "Richard Wright's
Spanish Excursion." The New Republic,
136 (18 February), 18.
     Favorable review of PS noting W's
     observations on prostitution, reli-
     gion, bullfights, and fascism. With a
     "terse, lucid dramatic style" similar
     to Hemingway's, "Wright is a citizen
     of the world writing compassionately
     about Spain's poverty and self-hatred
     and fanaticism."

334. Sulzer, Peter. "Kairos in Afrika."
Schweizer Monatshefte, 37 (September),
538-541.
     Contains a review of the German
     translation of BP pointing out that
     it contains contradictory impulses.
     While defending the old African ways
     against missionaries and colonialism,
     W also wants to force Africa to adopt
     modern ways. Although he is no longer
     a Communist, the implications of his
     attitude leave an unchristian Africa
     with no defense against world Commu-
     nism.

335. Thomas, Sidney S. "Ramstein Air
Base Library Notes." The Ramjet, 5 (12
July).
     Announces that W will visit Ramstein
     Air Base, where he will serve as a
     judge in the annual United States Air
     Force short story contest.

336. T.[hompson], C.[harles] H. "Wright,
Richard," in The World Book Encyclo-
pedia. Ed. J. Morris Jones. Vol. 18.
Chicago: Field Enterprises, p. 8933.
     Reprint of 1947.292.

337. V., P. "Richard Wright: De kleur-

barrière." Het Vrije Volk (12 January).
     Favorable review of the Dutch trans-
     lation of CC. Its strength, compar-
     able to that of BP, lies in the hon-
     esty with which W approaches racial
     matters.

338. Vries, Henk de. "De Kleurbarrière--
een verslag van de Conferentie van Bandung." Unidentified clipping.
     Unfavorable review of the Dutch
     translation of CC, which sometimes
     suffers from contradictory implica-
     tions because of W's insufficient
     understanding of colonialism.

339. Walker, Danton. "Broadway." New
York Daily News (8 July), p. 39.
     Notes that W's next book will be
     entitled WML.

340. Wanek, Alwin. "Richard Wright."
Wiener Bücherbriefe (June).
     Favorable review of the German trans-
     lation of BP. It is recommended for
     all libraries because of its treat-
     ment of the impact of modern civili-
     zation on African culture. Although
     written with understandable resent-
     ment against all whites, it explains
     much concerning African affairs.

341. Watts, Richard, Jr. "Two on the
Aisle." New York Post (26 March), p. 49.
     Contains a favorable review of PS. W
     "has a sharp eye, an observant intel-
     ligence, an independent judgment, and
     writes beautifully."

342. _____. "Two on the Aisle: Random
Notes on This and That." New York Post
(20 November), p. 67.
     Contains brief comments on WML. The
     section on black poets is good, but
     in general W is unfair to the West.

343. Webb, Robert. "Wright Speaks on
Race." Jackson (Miss.) State Times (3
November), p. 8-B.
     Review of WML stressing W's effort to
     reveal the black mind to the white
     mind. Webb is noncommital on W's case
     against white racism and imperialism.

344. Weber, H. R. "Schwarzer Amerikaner
schwarzer Afrika." Der Trier Sonntag (8
December).
     Review of the German translation of
     BP discussing W's ambivalence toward
     Europe, which accurately reflects the
     tensions of the Third World attitude.
     Inasmuch as he is a black "victim," W
     hates Europe. Inasmuch as he is ali-
     enated and repelled by African
     "primitivism," he wishes to "Europe-
     anize" the continent.

345. White, Fredus A. "Wright in Spain."

Newark Sunday News (24 February), Sec.
III, p. E2.
Review of PS noting that W's judgment
of the country was preconditioned by
his racial and political experience.
Attracted to the landscape, he disliked the Spanish people and their
religious, sexual, and political attitudes.

346. Wright, W. Archer, Jr. "Emotional
Undertones of Today's Spanish Life."
Richmond Times-Dispatch (9 June), p.
L-9.
Favorable review of PS, "a book of
moving power and magnetism." The
reviewer emphasizes the work's subjectivity and vividness. It concentrates on people and their emotional
lives. The indictment of Spanish
religion and government will provoke
controversy.
Reprinted: 1978.209.

347. Wyllie, John. "Mr. Wright's Harangue on Race Topics." The Montreal
Star and Herald (30 November), p.
28.
Unfavorable review of WML. Professing
to agree with some of W's ideas,
Wyllie nevertheless complains about
"the book's hysteria, turbulence and
passages of hyperbole." These ex-
cesses will alienate potential allies
of W's cause.

348. York, Rosemary. "The Bookworm--
Schlesinger Starts Series on Roosevelt."
The Indianapolis Times (3 March), p. 33.
Contains a brief notice of PS.

349. Zorn, Fritz. "Mystik und Wirklichkeit der Tropen." Süddeutschen Rundfunk
(25 June).
Radio review of the German translation of BP, the best book to appear
on the new Africa. Although W's life
adds a personal meaning to his journey, there is not a single sentimental sentence in the book. W sees
clearly immaturity in the Gold Coast.

1958

1. Allen, Madge. "White Man, Listen!"
Greenville (S. C.) Daily Reflector (1
March).
Review stressing W's bitterness. The
book reveals the author.

2. Allport, Gordon W. The Nature of
Prejudice. Anchor Books. Garden City,
N. Y.: Doubleday, pp. 144, 475.
Reprint of 1954.3.

3. Amundson, Robert H. "White Man, Listen by Richard Wright." The Catholic
World, 187 (April), 79.

Unfavorable review objecting to W's
positivism and emotionalism. Some
good antiracist points are made, but
"a pale brand of humanism with a
hysterical tic is not enough."

4. Anderson, Albert. "About Books."
Mimeographed Associated Negro Press
release (5 November).
Unfavorable review of LD. It "is one
long nightmare for the Negroes involved in this explosive, power-
packed story." Flight is not the
answer to improved race relations.

5. Ankenbruck, John. "Author Projects
Note of Powerful Protest." The Fort
Wayne News-Sentinel (25 October), p. 8.
Favorable review of LD emphasizing
the theme of racial injustice. The
book is readable and powerful, "sometimes coarse, sometimes brutal, often
really humorous in dialogue."

6. Anon. "American Literature Reflects
American Life," in Compton's Pictured
Encyclopedia and Fact-Index. Ed. Guy
Stanton Ford. Vol. 1. Chicago: F. E.
Compton, pp. 240-263.
Reprint of 1957.7.

7. Anon. "L'Amérique est une terre pro-
pice aux écrivains mais Paris est le
rendez-vous de nombreux écrivains américains." Informations et Documents
(March).
United States Information Service
release including photographs of W
with a caption.

8. Anon. "Amid the Alien Corn." Time, 72
(17 November), 28.
Article on black expatriates, mainly
in Paris, with a photograph of W and
a paragraph about him. W is "quoted,"
but he had given no interview to Time
reporters.

9. Anon. "Among the Outstanding Books of
1958: Some Holiday Suggestions." New
York Herald Tribune Book Review (30 November), pp. 10, 12, 14, 16, 18, 24, 26.
Contains a notice of LD (p. 16).

10. Anon. "Banner Book Shelf." Bennington Evening Banner (29 October), p. 11.
Contains a notice of LD, a story of a
young black man "growing up without
human rights."

11. Anon. "Bishop Prevented from Going
to Lambeth." The Christian Century, 75
(6 August), 894.
Mentions W's comments on the plight
of Spanish Protestants in PS.

12. Anon. "Book Marks." The Dallas Times
Herald (26 October), Roundup Sec., p.

20.
Contains a favorable notice of LD stressing its painful truthfulness.

13. Anon. "Book Shelf: White Man, Listen! by Richard Wright." The International Blue Printer, 31 (March), 52.
Notice emphasizing W's treatment of the impact of the white man on black culture.

14. Anon. "Books--Authors." The New York Times (10 October), p. 29.
Announces the publication of LD on 21 October.

15. Anon. "The Brutal Awakening of 'Fish.'" Charleston (W. Va.) Sunday Gazette-Mail (26 October), Show Time Sec., p. 18m.
Review of LD with a plot summary. It is "an angry book" which "brings home the plight of the Negro in the South today."

16. Anon. Dust jacket of Os Filhos do Pai Tomás. By Richard Wright. Trans. Manuel de Seabra. Lisbon: Editore Arcádia.
Biographical sketch of W on the front and back inside flaps of this Portuguese translation of UTC.

17. Anon. Dust jacket of The Long Dream. Garden City, N. Y.: Doubleday.
Blurb on the front inside flap calling the work "a powerful story of terrible truths." Back inside flap contains a biographical note. A large photograph of W appears on the back.

18. Anon. "Edward C. Aswell Dies; Was Doubleday Editor." New York Herald Tribune (6 November), p. 18.
Mentions W as one of the writers edited by Aswell.

19. Anon. "L'Espagne vue par Richard Wright." Le Figaro Littéraire (5 April), p. 14.
Favorable review of the French translation of PS, "a beautiful book, quivering with anger, color, and life."

20. Anon. "Even More Explosive Than His Native Son!" The New York Times (30 October), p. 29.
Advertisement for LD.

21. Anon. "Even More Explosive Than His Native Son." Unidentified clipping.
Magazine advertisement for LD.

22. Anon. "Fall Titles to Be Especially Noted." Publishers' Weekly, 174 (22 September), 50-51.
Contains a publisher's advertisement

for LD.

23. Anon. "Gemingsmanden van en hird mand--!" Copenhagen Politiken (2 December).
Report on W's lecture on "The Psychological Reactions of Oppressed People."

24. Anon. "Das grüne Buch des rebellischen Fraulein Carmen: Im Reiche des Caudillo--Ein farbiger Amerikaner sieht Spanien / Von Richard Wright." Die Hamburg Zeit (3 October), p. 21.
Headnote to an excerpt from the German translation of PS.

25. Anon. "Heidnisches Spanien." Atlantis (c. 28 November).
Reprint of 1958.150.

26. Anon. Index Translationum 9. Paris: Unesco, pp. 25, 67, 70, 191, 194, 220, 270, 322, 343, 438, 630.
Lists translations of BP into German, French, and Dutch, SH into Spanish and French, The God That Failed into German and Hebrew, O into French, Italian and Swedish, NS into French, CC into French and Dutch, and UTC into Slovenian.

27. Anon. "Internationaler Hörspielkunst." Norddeutscher Rundfunk (February-March), p. 3.
Radio schedule announcing the broadcast of "Man, God Ain't Like That" on 6 March.

28. Anon. "Library News." The Hamilton (Ont.) Spectator (10 May), p. 45.
Contains a favorable notice of WML, a "stimulating" and "impassioned" plea for racial justice.

29. Anon. "The Long Dream. By Richard Wright." Cleveland Plain Dealer (26 October), p. 40-E.
Favorable brief notice.

30. Anon. "The Long Dream. By Richard Wright." The Sunday Denver Post (26 October), Roundup Sec., p. 29.
Brief, nonevaluative notice.

31. Anon. "The Long Dream, by Richard Wright (Doubleday)." The New Yorker, 34 (8 November), 210.
Brief, unfavorable notice calling the novel "a facile, mechanically written story."

32. Anon. "The Long Dream: Powerful Story of Negro Life in the Deep South." The St. Catherines Standard (15 November), p. 6.
Favorable review praising W's literary skill and social message. The

novel "is easy to read, gripping, and at times so powerful it is frightening." Governor Orval Faubus of Arkansas should read it.

33. Anon. "Major Fall Books October-December: 185 Highspot Promotions." Publishers' Weekly, 174 (22 September), 186-225.
Contains a favorable notice of LD pointing out that it is "more hopeful" than NS (p. 190). Also contains a photograph of the front dust jacket of the novel (p. 197).

34. Anon. "Miscellaneous." Chelsea (Mass.) Evening Record (4 April), p. 3.
Favorable notice of WML.

35. Anon. "Negro Progress." Ebony, 13 (January), 82-84, 86.
Notes that W published WML and PS during the year 1957. Includes a photograph of W.

36. Anon. "Negroes in American Life," in Compton's Pictured Encyclopedia and Fact-Index. Ed. Guy Stanton Ford. Vol. 10. Chicago: F. E. Compton, pp. 124-127.
Reprint of 1957.46.

37. Anon. "Negroes of the Year--1957." New York Teacher News (25 January), p. 6.
W is one of twenty-five listed.

38. Anon. "New Books at Library Are Listed." Niagara Falls (N. Y.) Gazette (14 December), p. 10-B.
Contains a brief notice of LD.

39. Anon. "Pagan Spain, by Richard Wright." The Virginia Quarterly Review, 34 (Winter), xxxvi.
Favorable notice calling the writing "journalism of a high order." W is honest in his observations of Spanish life.

40. Anon. "Papa Bon Dieu et la critique." L'Avant-Scène, No. 168 (15 February), p. 33.
Notes that W is adapting the play as Daddy Goodness.

41. Anon. "A propos d'Espagne païenne par Richard Wright." Journal de Genève (12-13 July), p. 6.
Contains excerpts from a letter by Victor de la Serna, a Spaniard, responding to P.-O. Walzer's review of the French translation of PS. De la Serna attacks W bitterly for bias and mendacity. Walzer replies to this and another letter from a Spaniard. See 1958.261.

42. Anon. "Punk and Incense." Trenton (N. J.) Sunday Times-Advertiser (2 November), Part Four, p. 16.
Contains a notice of LD, "the story of a Negro boy growing up without human rights."

43. Anon. "Résumé." Paris L'Aurore (3 June), p. 11.
Brief notice of the French translation of PS.

44. Anon. "Richard Wright," in Cyclopedia of World Authors. Ed. Frank N. Magill. New York: Harper, pp. 1176-1177.
Biographical-critical sketch with brief bibliographical references.

45. Anon. "Richard Wright." Paris Arts (12-18 February), p. 3.
Photograph with caption of W and Senghor.

46. Anon. "Richard Wright." Übersee-Rundschau (January).
Favorable review of the German translation of BP. A kind of imaginary journey into a primitive world, the book is an artistically powerful view of a situation with tragic overtones.

47. Anon. "Richard Wright Destroyed Self, Says Faulkner." Jet, 15 (18 December), 52.
Quotes from Faulkner's comments on W in Japan as reported in Esquire.

48. Anon. "Richard Wright: Heidnisches Spanien." Osnabrück Neue Tagespost (14 November).
Favorable review of the German translation of PS praising W's sympathy for the Spanish plight while noting the problems arising from his extreme subjectivity.

49. Anon. "Richard Wright: Heidnisches Spanien." Grünberg Heimat-Zeitung (28 October).
Brief notice of the German translation of PS. It is an aggressive, polemical corrective to romantic views of Spain.

50. Anon. "Richard Wright: Heidnisches Spanien." Politische Jahrkorrespondenz [?] (December).
Review of the German translation of PS stressing the controversial nature of W's analytical methods, which represent those of a leading American intellectual group. Notes the work's consideration of obscure aspects of Spanish social reality.

51. Anon. "Richard Wright: Ich Negerjunge." Die Quelle, 9 (August), 392.
Notice of the German translation of BB stating that it shows that blacks

retain their humanity despite their degradation by whites.

52. Anon. "Der Schwarze Erdteil." Mannheimer Morgen (19 April).
Favorable review of the German translation of BP, in which W's subjectivity results in a perfect melting together of form and content. He has an unusual attitude, in part resulting from his "tragic" alienation from his African brothers.

53. Anon. "Der schwarze Mann hat ausgeschlafen." Bücherschiff, 8 (January), 5.
Review of the German translation of BP and other books on Africa. Praises W for his honesty, accuracy, and perception. For European readers the book is "noble . . . extraordinarily stimulating."

54. Anon. "Das 'Schwarze Spanien' eines Amerikaners." Badisches Neuste Nachrichten (28 November).
Unfavorable review of the German translation of PS stressing W's distortions and oversimplifications. He has provided a sometime grotesque caricature, especially of Spain's religious life.

55. Anon. "10 Negro Best Sellers." Unidentified clipping (Jet?).
Advertisement stating that LD can be ordered from the Ebony bookstore.

56. Anon. "They Dared to Fight." The Rebel (Fall).
Review of LD in the literary magazine of East Carolina College. Mainly favorable, the review considers some of the dialogue implausible.

57. Anon. "Tous les soirs ressuscitera 'Papa Bon Dieu.'" Radar (19 January).
Mentions W and includes a photograph of him.

58. Anon. "Tract in Black & White." Time, 72 (27 October), 94, 96.
Review of LD with a plot summary. Lacking art and subtlety, the novel has crude power in expressing its anger.
Reprinted: 1978.209.

59. Anon. Unidentified clipping (c. October).
Review of Martha Foley and David Burnett's The Best American Short Stories 1958 noting that "Big Black Good Man" stands out like a straight tap dance in an off-beat revue, for it is the only story in the lot that is standard short in the stout old-fashioned form, complete with twist-eroo."

60. Anon. Untitled clipping. Arts et Spectacles (5 November).
Notice of LD.

61. Anon. Untitled clipping. Das Cologne deutsche Wort (2 November).
Notice of the German translation of PS. It is a "polemical and aggressive" work.

62. Anon. Untitled clipping. Frankfürter Rundschau (11 October), p. 35.
Photograph of W with a caption on the publication of the German translation of PS.

62a. Anon. "Voici les écrivains étrangers qui ont choisi de vivre en France." France-Soir (6 September), p. 8.
Lists W among twenty writers from various countries living in France. UTC and WML are listed as his principal works.

63. Anon. "Vous devriez avoir lu." Réalités, No. 150 (July), p. 86.
Lists the French translation of PS.

64. Anon. "Weekly Record." Publishers' Weekly, 174 (27 October), 64-80.
Contains a favorable notice of LD, "a poignant story" (p. 79).

65. Anon. "Wright," in Der neue Brockhaus. Vol. 5. Wiesbaden: F. A. Brockhaus, p. 561.
Biographical note.

66. Anon. "Wright," in Diccionario enciclopédico compendiado. Vol. 3. Barcelona: Spes, p. 1214.
Brief biographical note.

67. Anon. "Wright, Richard," in Kiepen-Lexikon des Wissens und der Bildung. Koln: Kiepenheuer & Witsch, p. 1348.
Biographical note.

68. Anon. "Wright, Richard Nathaniel," in Compton's Pictured Encyclopedia and Fact-Index. Ed. Guy Stanton Ford. Vol. 15. Chicago: F. E. Compton, p. 461.
Reprint of 1957.113.

69. Anon. "Wright, Richard / Schwarze Macht." Benediktinische Monatschrift, 34 (September-October), 420.
While warning against W's negative portrayal of the church, this review of the German translation of BP praises it as an important source of insight into Africa. The most important element of the book is its examination of the mixture of modern politics and tribal customs.

70. Anon. "Wright, Richard / Schwarze Macht." Bücherschau.

Review of the German translation of BP. Despite W's biased treatment of Christianity and his dislike of pagan African religion, it is a very important book on emerging Africa.

71. Anon. "Wright, Richard. The Long Dream." Bulletin from Virginia Kirkus Service, 26 (15 August), 624.
Unfavorable review. "It is a powerful indictment," but hopeless in attitude. The novel is candid, but "crude and violent and bitter."

72. Anon. "Wright, Richard. The Long Dream." Patients' Library Bureau Book Cart (October-November).
Notice arguing that the novel is too grim, especially in the autopsy scene, for reading by hospital patients.

73. Archer, Leonard B., Jr. "Books for Vermonters." Rutland Herald (14 January), p. 8.
Includes a favorable notice of WML, "a powerful indictment of the white man's domination of the world."

74. Armstrong, Jerry. "Explosive Adventures Told of Mississippi Negro Boy." Columbus (Ga.) Enquirer (17 November), p. 5.
Favorable review of LD consisting mostly of plot summary. It is "an explosive novel in attitude but wholly the thoughts and understandings of his race." It is "deeply moving" and a "tragic saga."

75. Ballentine, Ruth. "Richard Wright Pens a Shocker." The Memphis Commercial Appeal (23 November), Sec. IV, p. 10.
Favorable review of LD, a "shocking and compassionate story." Includes a brief plot summary.

76. Barnett, A. N. "Wright, Richard. The Long Dream." Library Journal, 83 (15 October), 2843-2844.
Favorable review noting the ambiguity of W's attitude toward his people. The novel starts slowly and contains worn phrases and awkward prose, but the characterization is true and deep. The conclusion implies that a choice must be made between flight and staying in the United States to fight for equality. Recommends the book for all libraries.
Reprinted: 1978.209.

77. Barth, Heinz F. "Spanien auf der Anklagebank." Der Berlin Tagesspiegel (26 October), p. 30.
Unfavorable review of the German translation of PS. Admitting the vivid impressions W provides of com-

mon life in Spain, Barth complains of distortion, zealous onesiddedness, factual errors, and excessive subjectivity.

78. Baumier, Jean. "Richard Wright: Espagne païenne." Europe, No. 353 (September), 137.
Unfavorable review of the French translation of PS. W's Spain is a tourist's Spain, and his political conclusions are weak.

79. Bernkopf, Elizabeth. "Touches Dignity Once." The Boston Sunday Globe (19 October), p. A-31.
Review of LD, an "explosive, bitter novel." Bernkopf asserts that W's "anger sometimes gets in the way of his message," but she is impressed by Tyree's revelation of racial truths to the white liberal, a scene in which "the novel achieves greatness."

80. Berry, Brewton. Race and Ethnic Relations. Second edition. Boston: Houghton Mifflin, pp. 140, 281, 487-488.
Reprint of 1951.132.

81. Berry, Thomas, C. P. "White Man, Listen! By Richard Wright." The Sign, 37 (February), 73-74.
Unfavorable review pointing out W's emotionalism and redundancy. His own secularism is an example of the damage done to black people by the West.
Reprinted: 1978.209.

82. Bittner, Markus. "Wright, Richard." Die Zeit im Buch (7 February).
Unfavorable review of the German translation of BP complaining of W's sympathy with the leftist demagogue Nkrumah and his slanderous misrepresentation of Christianity.

83. Blackford, Frank. "Mississippi: Negro Boy in the South." The Norfolk Virginian-Pilot and The Portsmouth Star (19 October), p. 6-F.
Unfavorable review of LD complaining of outmoded leftist clichés about black life in the South. W's expatriation has resulted in "a false, cheap thriller, compounded out of literary sweat and a written-out talent."

84. Bl.[air], W.[alter]. "American Literature," in Encyclopaedia Britannica. Ed. Walter Yust. Vol. 1. Chicago: Encyclopaedia Britannica, pp. 784-794.
Reprint of 1954.80.

85. Bone, Robert A. The Negro Novel in America. Yale Publications in American Studies, 3. New Haven, Conn.: Yale University Press, pp. 4, 81, 101, 110, 113,

115, 117, 128, 140-152, 156-160, 164, 165-166, 168, 169, 170, 173, 176, 179, 180, 184, 185, 188, 197-198, 218, 245.
The main entry on W (pp. 140-152) provides a biographical account and a full analysis of NS. O and LD are dismissed in a footnote. The three major influences on NS are literary naturalism, the author's life in Chicago, and Marxism. The chief weakness of the novel is Book III, in which "Wright has failed to digest Communism artistically" (p. 150). Elsewhere Bone discusses the "Wright School" of black protest fiction: Himes, Smith, Savoy, Offord, Bland, Petry, Lucas, Kaye, and Brown. Finally, Bone ranks NS with Cane and Invisible Man as one of the major achievements of the Afro-American novel.
Partially reprinted: 1969.64; 1970.5; 1972.27; 1973.256.

86. Bonnefoi, Geneviève. "Espagne païenne, par Richard Wright, traduit par Roger Giroux." Les Lettres Nouvelles, 6 (June), 929-932.
Review of the French translation of PS. Bonnefoi analyzes at length W's attempt to connect subconscious motivation and cultural trends, especially concerning his perception of the link between Church and State, between the sacred and sexuality. The reviewer praises W's angry warning against Franco's political system.

87. Bontemps, Arna. "Introduction," in The Book of Negro Folklore. Ed. Langston Hughes and Arna Bontemps. New York: Dodd, Mead, pp. vii-xv.
Notes that W was "born into a folk culture" (p. xiv).
Reprinted: 1969.39.

88. _____. Story of the Negro. Third edition. New York: Knopf, pp. 202-203.
Reprint of 1948.137.

89. Bradley, Van Allen. "Negro Author Shuns Reality in Third Novel." Syracuse Post-Standard (9 November), p. 4.
Reprint of 1958.90.

90. _____. "Richard Wright Wastes Talent in His 'Dream.'" Chicago Daily News (29 October), p. 16.
Unfavorable review of LD arguing that W's expatriation has isolated him from the reality of American racial relations, leading to exaggeration, sensationalism, and excessive violence in the novel.
Reprinted: 1958.89; 1959.63.

90a. Browning, D. C. "Wright, Richard," in his Everyman's Dictionary of Literary

Biography: English and American. London: J. M. Dent & Sons, p. 740.
Biographical sketch.

91. Bucaille, Victor. "Espagne païenne par Richard Wright." Les Nouvelles Littéraires (15 May), p. 3.
Mixed review of the French translation of PS. Although biased, the work is lively and colorful.

92. Byrd, James W. "Ineffective Sequel to Brilliance." The Phylon Quarterly, 19 (Fourth Quarter), 433-435.
Review of Willard Motley's Let No Man Write My Epitaph mentioning W.

93. Collier, Tarleton. "Excess of Racial Antipathy." The Louisville Courier-Journal (23 November), Sec. 4, p. 7.
Unfavorable review of LD complaining of "an impression of unrelieved evil, not only in white hatred and harassment but also in Negro collaboration." W's treatment of black life strips it of both dignity and hope, making the author seem racist.

94. Cook, Mercer. "The Last Laugh," in Africa Seen by American Negroes. Ed. John A. Davis. Paris: Présence Africaine, pp. 199-214.
Mentions W briefly (p. 207).

95. _____. "Lend Me Your Ears." The Journal of Negro Education, 27 (Winter), 44-45.
Favorable review of WML. More than a native son, W is now "a spokesman for a billion and a half colored people." His message deserves to be heard.

96. Coolhaas, W. "Richard Wright, De Kleurbarrière." De Jicks [?], pp. 144-145.
Review of the Dutch translation of CC noting that in W's view Dutch colonists are comparable to white American Southerners in their racism.

97. Coyle, John. "Mainly About Books." The East Northport (N. Y.) News (30 October).
Favorable notice of LD admiring W's power.

98. D'Agostino, Nemi. "Pavese e l'America." Studi americani, 4, pp. 399-413.
Mentions Cesare Pavese's essay on W (p. 403).

99. Datisman, Don F. "Venemous Approach to Case." The Gary Post-Tribune (26 October), p. D-6.
Unfavorable review of LD, a book "more revolting than convincing."

100. Davis, John A. "Introduction," in

his Africa Seen by American Negroes.
Paris: Présence Africaine, pp. 1-8.
   Mentions W (p. 8).

101. Dickenberger, Georg. "Paul Vesey."
Black Orpheus, No. 4 (October), pp. 5-8.
   Contrasts Vesey's favorable view of
   Africa with W's unfavorable feelings.

102. Dieterich, Anton. "Ein Amerikaner
sieht Spanien." Düsseldorf Rheinische
Post (6 December), p. [38].
   Reprint of 1958.105.

103. _____. "Das 'Schwarze Spanien'
eines Amerikaners." Kölnische Rundschau
(28 December), Am Sonntag Sec., p. [4].
   Reprint of 1958.105.

104. _____. "Das 'Schwarze Spanien'
eines Amerikaners." Trierer Landeszeitung (30 November).
   Reprint of 1958.105.

105. _____. "Das Schwarze Spanien
Richard Wrights." Aachener Volkszeitung
(15 October).
   Very unfavorable review of the German
   translation of PS by a Catholic
   critic.
   Reprinted: 1958.102, 103, 104; 1959.
   75.

106. _____. "Spanisches--das uns 'spanisch' verkommt." Süddeutscher Rundfunk
(21 October).
   Unfavorable radio review of the German translation of PS. W correctly
   identifies the religious roots of
   Spanish life, but his American mentality has difficulty adjusting to
   Spain and his viewpoint causes difficulties for European readers.

107. Diop, Thomas. "White man, listen,
de Richard Wright." Présence Africaine,
No. 20 (June-July), pp. 128-129.
   Favorable review describing the book.
   W elucidates several aspects of the
   psychological situation in Africa
   contributing to a dialogue between
   blacks and whites.

108. Dixon, Edwina Streeter. "Richard
Wright's Latest." The Pittsburgh Courier
(20 December), Magazine Sec., p. 6.
   Notice of LD finding it interesting,
   controversial, and, in parts, obscure. The father-son relationship is
   the core of the book.

109. Dunlea, William. "Wright's Continuing Protest." The Commonweal, 69 (31
October), 131.
   Unfavorable review of LD emphasizing
   W's attack on blacks for submitting
   to white racist oppression. The style
   is heavy and thesis-ridden. Angrier

even than W's work of the forties, LD
offers little valid insight into the
present racial situation in the
United States.
   Reprinted: 1978.209.

110. Dvorak, Margaret. "Wright as Before: Novel Packed with Violence." Lincoln (Neb.) Sunday Journal and Star (26
October), p. 11 B.
   Unfavorable review of LD considering
   it "another agonizing psychological
   study of one of his race." W's racial
   protest would be more effective if
   violence, outrage, and shock were
   used less frequently.

111. E., B. S. "De Kleurbarrière." Vox
Veritas, No. 9 (1 February), pp. 6-7.
   Unfavorable review of the Dutch
   translation of CC. Racism and colonialism alone, according to this
   reviewer, do not seem sufficient to
   explain the East-West cleavage that W
   describes. Furthermore, W often lacks
   clarity in his own analysis.

112. Easton, Elizabeth. "The Long Dream
by Richard Wright." Book-of-the-Month
Club News (November), pp. 10-11.
   Review noting that in this "crudely
   violent" novel, W traces the black-
   white relationships in a small
   Southern town. It succeeds in shocking the reader, who realizes, however, that the conditions it
   describes are not typical.

113. Edes, Mary Elizabeth. "Fiction
Forecast: The Long Dream." Publishers'
Weekly, 174 (15 September), 60.
   Favorable notice of "a strong, tense
   drama of urban Negro life" scheduled
   for publication on 16 October.

114. _____. "Fiction Forecast: The Long
Dream." Publishers' Weekly, 174 (22
September), 276-277.
   Favorable notice pointing out that
   the publication date has been changed
   to 21 October.

115. Elgström, Anna Lenah. "Spansk
stinx." Perspektiv, 9 (March), 128-130.
   Unfavorable review of the Swedish
   translation of PS. Admiring W's previous books, Elgström notes that in
   the present work his lack of perspective renders his analysis of Spain
   unconvincing. Specifically, W regards
   the link of church and state as too
   recent a development.

116. Ellison, Ralph. "Change the Joke
and Slip the Yoke." Partisan Review, 25
(Spring), 212-222.
   Comments on the role of Shorty as
   scapegoat in BB (p. 215). See

1958.163.
Reprinted: 1964.44; 1970.113.

117. Erpel, Philipp. "Spanische Paradox-
ien." Darmstädter Echo (4 December), p.
5.

Favorable review of the German translation of PS. In spite of the occasional lack of necessary context, it
is an extremely well-written book
which points directly to the importance of the state-army-church association in Spanish life. The clash of
Spain's irrational reality and W's
highly rational mind exemplifies the
meeting of "extremes" which characterizes the book.

118. Faulkner, William. "Faulkner in
Japan." Esquire, 50 (December), 139,
141-142.
Reprint of 1956.157.

119. Ferbert, A. "Espagne païenne par
Richard Wright." Unidentified clipping.
Favorable review of the French translation of PS. It is a "powerful
study" of the country.

120. Figueroa, Agustín de. "En defensa
de España." ABC (17 December), pp. 69-
70.
Extremely unfavorable review of the
French translation of PS. The reviewer, who is the Marqués de Santo
Floro, complains bitterly of W's
bias, hostility, and insensitivity.
His obsession with prostitutes in
Spain must derive from "indelible
maternal memories," and his "soul is
as black as his face."

121. Ford, Nick Aaron. "Blunders and
Failures of the White Man." Phylon, 19
(First Quarter), 125-126.
Favorable review of WML noting that W
has always addressed a white
audience. The present work is "a
merciless analysis of the white man's
blunders" (p. 125), timely but also
profound. "The Miracle of Nationalism
in the African Gold Coast" is the
best chapter; "The Literature of the
Negro in the United States" is the
least satisfactory because of factual
errors.
Reprinted: 1978.209.

122. _____. "The Long Dream. By Richard
Wright." CLA Journal, 2 (December), 143-
144.
Unfavorable review arguing that the
novel subordinates artistic considerations to its social message. That
message posits white fear of black
people as the cause of white racism.
The secondary message is that money
to favored blacks does not compensate

for their systematic degradation.

123. _____. "'A Long Way from Home.'"
Phylon, 19 (Fourth Quarter), 435-436.
Unfavorable review of LD noting the
decline of W's artistic power and the
limited scope of the novel, which
confines itself to Southern sex and
Jim Crow.
Reprinted: 1978.209.

124. _____. "White Man, Listen! By
Richard Wright." CLA Journal, 1 (March),
110-111.
Favorable review describing the book
as an analysis of the results of
white exploitation of colored peoples
and a justification of the forceful
methods of such leaders as Nasser,
Nkrumah, and Nehru to counteract the
feeling of dependency and inferiority
in Africa and Asia.

125. F.[ranklin], J.[ohn] H.[ope] and
R.[ayford] W.[hittingham] L.[ogan]. "Ne-
gro, American," in Encyclopaedia Britan-
nica. Ed. Walter Yust. Vol. 16. Chicago:
Encyclopaedia Britannica, pp. 194-201.
Reprint of 1957.184.

126. Frisé, Adolf. "Äussert spanisch."
Frankfürter Hefte, 13 (December), 885-
888.
Review of the German translations of
PS and a book on Spain by Americo
Castro. Frisé finds them complemen-
tary, for W emphasizes the minor-
ities, the exceptions, the darker
Spanish reality. His view is reso-
lutely anti-Romantic.

127. Fuller, Edmund. Man in Modern Fiction. New York: Random House, pp. 55-56.
Contains a paragraph on NS as a protest novel.

128. G., H. Untitled clipping. Bremer
Tageblatt (20 December).
Favorable notice of the German trans-
lation of PS.

129. G., N. "Wright's Saga Hard to
Believe." The Chicago American (2 November), p. 31.
Unfavorable review of LD emphasizing
the autobiographical element but expressing skepticism about the degree
of white racist oppression portrayed.

130. Gardiner, Harold C. "Fiction."
America, 100 (29 November), 291-293,
295.
Contains a notice of LD (p. 293)
commenting on its stridency and confused values. Nevertheless, W's moral
indignation is genuine.

131. Gasseling, Helmut. "Richard Wright:

Schwarze Macht." Bücherei und Bildung, 10 (April), 257-258.
Favorable review of the German translation of BP. Gasseling admires W's blend of art and sociology in depicting the vivid contrasts of the Gold Coast. The work is important as a document and analysis of the African revolution.

132. _____. Untitled clipping. Buchanzeiger (February).
Favorable notice of the German translation of BP.

133. Geerts, F. "Richard Wright, De Kleurbarrière." Kerk en Missie (January).
Notice of the Dutch translation of CC stressing its function in making readers more aware of racial injustice.

134. Geismar, Maxwell. American Moderns: From Rebellion to Conformity. New York: Hill and Wang, pp. 97, 117.
Contains brief references to W in discussions of Faulkner and Sinclair Lewis.

135. _____. "Growing Up in Fear's Grip." New York Herald Tribune Book Review (16 November), p. 10.
Mixed review of LD. Inferior to W's other fiction, it is nevertheless powerful in its tragic reality. It shows the American dream for blacks to be a "long nightmare of thwarted power, of obsessive fear and cruelty."
Reprinted: 1978.209.

136. Glicksberg, Charles I. "Existentialism in The Outsider." Four Quarters, 7 (January), 17-26.
Argues that W's novel was strongly influenced by Sartre and Camus, especially by the latter's The Rebel. Glicksberg analyzes the steps by which Cross Damon becomes a god controlling his own destiny.

137. _____. "The God of Fiction." The Colorado Quarterly, 7 (Autumn), 207-220.
Considers O (pp. 217-219) in terms of W's debt to Sartre and Camus. W uses the premise set forth in The Rebel: What happens to the will to power if a man tries to become a god? W creates a criminal hero who becomes the source of his own value, therefore literally an outsider.
Reprinted: 1960.159.

138. Goodheart, Eugene. "In a Paris Cafe." Midstream, 4 (Spring), 104-108.
Account of conversations with black intellectuals in the Café Tournon. W,

called "J. R.," comments on his expatriation and on African affairs.

139. Grade, Ed. "Wright's New Plot Misses." Los Angeles Evening Mirror-News (8 December), p. 12.
Unfavorable review of LD praising the plot construction and characterization, but finding the depiction of white racism too extreme to be credible. Grade also criticizes W's expatriation.

140. Green, C. Sylvester. "Race Problem Interpreted." Durham Morning Herald (23 February), Sec. D, p. 5.
Favorable review of WML. Green considers W's approach to be comprehensive and objective, resulting in surprising and revealing analyses.

141. Greiff, John B. "A Sadly Out-Dated Picture of Negroes in Deep South." Newport News Daily Press (28 December), p. 4D.
Unfavorable review of LD considering W's portrayal of Southern racism anachronistic, for conditions have improved, even in Mississippi. Young black readers of the novel will have their resentments unduly intensified; white Northern and foreign readers will be misled; white Southern readers will learn something about black "defense mechanisms" in dealing with whites.

142. Guérin, Daniel. "Controverse autour de l'héritage africain aux U. S. A." Présence Africaine, Nos. 17-18 (February-May), pp. 166-172.
Mentions W's change of opinion about African survivals in America after visiting the Gold Coast (pp. 171-172).

143. Harris, Arthur S., Jr. "New Novel by Wright." Worcester (Mass.) Sunday Telegram (26 October), Sec. D, p. 11.
Mixed review of LD. After a glance at W's career, Harris applauds his return to fiction from sociology. Reminiscent of NS, LD is, however, less exciting and moving.

144. Harrison. "Way of Life Is Told in Long Dream." Lake Charles American Press (23 November), p. 42.
Highly favorable review of LD comparing it to Uncle Tom's Cabin and NS. W tells "terrible truths" about the denial of dignity, respect, and opportunity to black people in the South, and he tells them with eloquence and power.

145. Hartlaub, Geno. "Hinter den Kulissen des Fremdenverkehrs." Hamburg Lau-

tersblatt (7 December).
Favorable review of the German translation of PS summarizing W's thesis
and stressing his sympathy for all of
the Spanish people. The chapter on
Protestantism is particularly rich.

146. Hatch, Robert. "Either Weep or
Laugh." The Nation, 187 (25 October),
297-298.
Favorable review of LD. W emphasizes
ideas more than art, but the structure of the novel is sound and the
characterization is impressive even
if the plot is somewhat contrived.
W's understanding of the racial issue
has grown over the years. "It is in
the poignant vision of the two races
locked in terrible, degrading embrace
that Wright, a truly proud Negro, has
isolated the essence of the tragedy."
Reprinted: 1978.209.
Partially reprinted: 1960.207.

147. Hayes, E. Nelson. "Of Blackest
Pessimism." The Boston Sunday Herald (2
November), Sec. III, p. 9.
Favorable review of LD with a plot
summary. Hayes concludes: "With its
characters vibrant with life, with
its almost miraculous ability to
arouse emotion in the reader, and
with its highly communicative style,
this is a novel of profound depths,
of great power and of blackest pessimism, pointing as it does to no answer for the Negro except exile."

148. Heipen, J. J. Van. Algemeine Ver-
eeniging Radio OMROED (24 August).
Dutch radio review of SH.

149. Held, Robert. "Richard Wright be-
gegnet Spanien." Frankfurter Allgemeine
Zeitung für Deutschland (25 October),
Bilder und Zeiten Sec., p. 5.
Mixed review of the German translation of PS. Not suitable as an introductory volume on Spain because of
its historical and analytical oversimplifications, it is nevertheless a
well-written book which utilizes
skillfully a reportorial technique.
Held has some reservations about W's
anti-Western point of view.

150. Helwig, Werner. "Unterbelichtetes
Spanien." Munich Süddeutsche Zeitung (31
October, 1-2 November), p. [52].
Unfavorable review of the German
translation of PS. Like Marco Polo,
W, despite his intelligence, does not
understand the complexities of the
country he visits. The result is an
unintended ironic effect. But the
writing is brilliant and the interviewing careful.
Reprinted: 1958.25; 1959.92.

151. Hermann, Rudolf. "Frappierendes
Bild Spaniens." Die Hamburg Zeit (28
November), p. 12.
Favorable review of the German translation of PS. W's persistent, probing
curiosity overcame the obstacles to
understanding, resulting in an illuminating, provocative book. Spain's
essential paganism is at the root of
its problems.

152. Hetherly, Van. "Wright Raps Bigotry; Probes Faults of Race." The Houston
Chronicle (30 November), Feature Magazine Sec., p. 30.
Favorable review of LD admitting the
shocking, controversial nature of the
novel. "Wright is a master at depicting the evils of bigotry and ignorance. But he doesn't stop with that.
He also brutally probes the faults of
his own race, and therein lies part
of his greatness.

153. Hicks, Granville. "The Art of the
Short Story." Saturday Review, 41 (20
December), 16.
Comments that although W evokes fear
successfully in "Big Black Good Man,"
the story is spoiled by an incredible
resolution.

154. _____. "The Power of Richard
Wright." Saturday Review, 41 (18 October), 13, 65.
Favorable review of LD with comparisons to NS, BB, and O. Flawed by
melodrama and purple prose, LD nevertheless has great power because
"Wright is telling the truth about
the situation of the American Negro,
and the truth cannot fail to shock
us." He touches both the emotions and
the consciousness of the reader.
Reprinted: 1978.209.

155. Hirose, Sadami. "Richard Wright
Ron" ["On Richard Wright"]. Kokujin
Kenkyu [Negro Study], 5 (October), 2-4.
A brief essay stating that W's work
is not only protest literature but an
unusual emotional appeal to the public conscience; W's outlook is humanistic. Finds that fear, underlying
his work, is transformed into art.
[Y. H.]

156. Hoehl, Egbert. "Das Leben nach dem
Tode." Die Kultur, 7 (1 December), 6.
Favorable review of the German translation of PS praising the publisher
for issuing such a controversial
work. Hoehl finds W's analysis of
Spain both brilliantly written and
essentially convincing.

157. _____. Untitled clipping. Die Hamburg andere Zeitung (11 December).

Favorable review of the German translation of PS.

157a. Hoover, J. Edgar. Masters of De-
ceit: The Story of Communism in America
and How to Fight It. New York: Holt,
Rinehart and Winston, pp. 247-248.
    Quotes from W's contribution to The
    God That Failed.

158. Howe, Lee A. "Book Report." Mimeographed.
    Radio review of LD on the Religion in
    Life series of station WVET in
    Rochester, New York, on 7 December
    1958. Howe includes a biographical
    sketch of W and recommends the novel
    to honest readers who wish to under-
    stand racism.

159. Hoyt, Elizabeth N. "New Books."
Cedar Rapids Gazette (23 November), Sec.
III, p. 2.
    Contains a favorable notice of LD, a
    novel by "one of the most articulate
    spokesmen of his race."

160. Hughes, Langston. "Langston Hughes'
Speech at National Assembly of Authors
and Dramatists Symposium: 'The Writer's
Position in America,' Alvin Theatre, New
York City, May 7, 1957," in his The
Langston Hughes Reader. New York: George
Braziller, pp. 483-485.
    Mentions W's expatriation.

161. _____ and Milton Meltzer. A Pictorial History of the Negro in America.
New York: Crown, pp. 281, 286.
    Quotes W on housing conditions and
    mentions him as an employee of the
    Writers Project.

162. Hurst, Louise F. "Timely Story of
'Man's Inhumanity to Man.'" Charleston
(West Va.) Sunday Gazette-Mail (c. 16
November).
    Review of LD finding it unpleasant to
    read but powerful and stirring.

163. Hyman, Stanley Edgar. "The Negro
Writer in America: An Exchange: The Folk
Tradition." Partisan Review, 25
(Spring), 197-211.
    Relates BB, O, and "The Man Who Lived
    Underground" to the complicated,
    ironic folk tradition of blacks.
    Compares W to Hughes and Baldwin. See
    1958.116.
    Reprinted: 1963.115; 1970.186.

164. _____. "Some Trends in the Novel."
College English, 20 (October), 1-9.
    Discusses "The Man Who Lived
    Underground" as an example of a
    favorable trend. It reveals black
    experience to be "pre-existentialist"
    (pp. 5-6).

165. Inglesby, Edith. "Tragic Refutation
of Legend." Savannah Morning News (21
December), Magazine Sec., p. 13.
    Review of LD calling it a "tragic
    refutation of the notion that black
    people are lucky by birth." By exag-
    geration and sensationalism, W has
    weakened the novel. "It lacks the
    conviction of Native Son."

166. Ivy, James. "Seules les anciennes
cultures africaines méritaient ce nom."
Preuves, No. 86 (April), pp. 34-35.
    Mentions W briefly.

167. Jack, Homer A. "'Who Hath Ears
. . .'" The Christian Century, 75 (16
July), 830.
    Favorable review of WML calling it
    "Wright at his best--impressionistic,
    hardly systematic. . . . Wright is
    the rootless prophet and his role is
    to deal in feelings, not formulas; in
    meaning, not happiness." Jack stres-
    ses W's message to the pundits, mis-
    sionaries, club women, and racists of
    the white West.

168. Jacob, Gerhard. "Wright, Richard:
Schwarze Macht." Welt und Wort, 13
(April), 121.
    Somewhat unfavorable notice of the
    German translation of BP. Jacob
    questions W's basic attitudes as an
    Afro-American, his materialistic
    philosophy, and his tendency to
    generalize about Africa.

169. Jahn, Janheinz. Muntu. Düsseldorf-
Koln: Eugen Diederichs Verlag, pp. 189,
197, 208, 235-238.
    Quotes from TMBV, BB, and BP.
    Translated: 1961.184.

170. James, Mertice M. and Dorothy
Brown. "Wright, Richard. Pagan Spain,"
in their The Book Review Digest. New
York: H. W. Wilson, p. 1014.
    Lists or quotes from fourteen re-
    views.

171. _____. "Wright, Richard. White man,
listen!" in their The Book Review
Digest. New York: H. W. Wilson, p. 1014.
    Lists or quotes from nine reviews.

172. Johnson, Charles S. "Negro in Amer-
ica," in The Encyclopedia Americana. Ed.
Lavinia P. Dudley. Vol. 20. New York:
Americana Corporation, pp. 65-77.
    Reprint of 1955.54.

173. J.[ones], C.[arter] B.[rooke].
"Richard Wright Returns to the Deep
South." The Washington Sunday Star (26
October), p. C-14.
    Unfavorable review of LD conceding
    the plausibility of the racism

depicted in the episodes of the novel, but finding their combined effect overdrawn. Furthermore, the novel overemphasizes sex and contains some improbabilities of plot. The story moves fast and Tyree Tucker is well portrayed, but on the whole "the author seems to have let his indignation run away with his artistic judgment."

174. Jones, Edgar L. "Author Out of Touch." The Baltimore Sunday Sun (14 December), Sec. A, p. 32.
Unfavorable review of LD admitting W's literary skill and emotional power, but complaining that his vision of Southern black life is too degrading and sordid, ignoring progress since World War II.

175. Kelly, James. "Stories That Cope with Universals." The New York Times Book Review (28 September), p. 47.
In a review of Martha Foley's Best American Short Stories 1958 Kelly mentions unfavorably W's contribution ("Big Black Good Man").

176. Kentera, George. "Passionate Outcry." Newark Sunday News (23 November), Sec. 4, p. S14.
Unfavorable review of LD admitting the significance of its social protest, but complaining of its preoccupation with sex and of its structural problems, including the anticlimactic quality of Part III.

177. Kiniery, Paul. "Wright, Richard. The Long Dream." Best Sellers, 18 (1 November), 296-297.
Unfavorable review complaining of excessive sex and slangy dialogue. W's solution of flight from racist America may not solve anything. "This is strong fare."
Reprinted: 1978.209.

178. L., C. E. "Eleventh Book: Novelist Writes Again of Interracial Strife." Durham Morning Herald (23 November), p. 5-D.
Favorable review of LD comparing it to NS and BB as a narrative of interracial conflict. After summarizing the plot, the reviewer offers this evaluation: "It is a brutal, violent, dramatic story, yet compassionate and tender in its wistful hope."

179. L., E. H. "Antithese des Christentums." Die Hamburg andere Zeitung (11 December).
Favorable review of the German translation of PS. Although it is shocking at first because of its attacks on all established institutions, it

serves as another expression of W's humanistic outlook. Brilliantly written, the book indicts the "absolute triumvirate" of Spain's church, state, and army, which forces her people into a "living death," a phrase which is "not metaphysical but an exact diagnosis of Spain's physical and spiritual condition."
Reprinted in a condensed version: 1959.108.

180. Lash, John. "The Conditioning of Servitude: A Critical Summary of Literature by and About Negroes in 1957: Part II." Phylon, 19 (Third Quarter), 247-257.
Contains a brief review of WML and mentions W elsewhere. Criticizes W's radicalism.

181. Las Vergnas, Raymond. "Richard Wright." La Revue de Paris, 65 (August), 124-131.
After a biographical sketch, Las Vergnas discusses all of W's major works. He considers O a flawed but important book. W needs to develop new territory in his writing.
Reprinted: 1971.147.

182. Lembourn, Hans Jørgen. "Menneske--Lyt!" Copenhagen Berlingske Tidende (7 January), p. 10.
Mixed review of the Danish translation of WML. W merits praise for his psychological insight, but he occasionally reveals his ignorance of the larger political implications of his recommendations concerning Africa and Asia.

183. Lenz, Siegfried. "Bücher für den Weinachtstisch. Hannover Funkhaus (22 December).
Radio review of the German translation of PS. Lenz believes that W's background conditions his belief that it is a misfortune to be Spanish. Like Americo Castro, Salvador de Madariaga, and Hemingway, W discovers his own Spain. His book reveals more of himself than it does of his subject. The book is unjust, but it does give us a "new Spain."

184. _____. "Spanien, gemalt in schwarzen Farben." Die Hamburg Welt (4 October), Die Geistige Welt Sec., p. 2.
Review of the German translation of PS stressing the subjectivity of W's account. If it leads to distortion, it also leads to a penetrating boldness in developing W's thesis that it is a misfortune to be Spanish.

185. Lincoln, Phil. "Wright Grinds Racial Ax to Dull Ineffective Edge."

Columbia Missourian (2 November), p. 7b.
Unfavorable review of LD with a plot
summary. W brings nothing new to
racial protest. Repetition of such
protest results in the loss of its
original force.

186. Lindau, Bill. "Books." The Asheville Citizen (4 December), p. 23.
Contains a favorable notice of LD.
The novel is shocking and powerful in
its racial protest. "Few, if any,
white people can possibly judge how
much basis he has for the picture he
draws with such strength and
ability."

187. Locke, Alain. "Some Outstanding
American Negroes," in The Book of Know-
ledge. Ed. E. V. McLoughlin. Vol. 12.
New York: The Grolier Society, pp. 4427-
4433.
Reprint of 1952.51.

188. Lytle, Andrew. "Man or Symbol?"
National Review, 6 (6 December), 375.
Review of LD and Brainard Cheyney's
This Is Adam. W's novel is contrived
and unconvincing. In it "fear and
hatred become the only conventions of
intercourse between the races."

189. M., T. B. "The Long Dream by
Richard Wright." Wilmington (Del.) Morning News (27 October), p. 15.
Favorable review of "another block-
buster by Wright." It is truthful and
bitter.

190. Magill, Frank N. "Richard Wright,"
in his Cyclopedia of World Authors. New
York: Harper & Brothers, pp. 1176-1177.
Brief biographical and literary survey with three bibliographical references.
Reprinted: 1958.191.

191. _____. "Richard Wright," in his
Masterplots Cyclopedia of World Authors.
New York: Salem Press, pp. 1176-1177.
Reprint of 1958.190.

192. Marchand, Jean-José. "La Culture
noire." Prevues, No. 86 (April), pp. 32-
33.
Mentions W as one of the respondents
to Marchand's questionnaire.

193. _____. "Richard Gibson: La culture
noire, c'est notre lutte pour la libération." Prevues, No. 87 (May), p. 41.
Headnote contrasting Gibson and W.

194. _____. "Richard Wright: Le 'Noir'
est une création du Blanc." Prevues, No.
87 (May), p. 40.
Headnote to W's response to Marchand's questionnaire.

195. Maslin, Marsh. "The Browser." The
San Francisco Call-Bulletin (12 November), p. 15.
Unfavorable review of LD and favorable review of Langston Hughes's
Tambourines to Glory. W needs more
restraint in expressing his bitterness against racial injustice. Maslin
quotes the final sentence of the
novel and calls it "bad writing." W
has lost touch with American reality.

196. McCartney, Charlotte. "Banner Book
Shelf: New Book on Jewish State Problems
Is Powerful." Bennington Evening Banner
(29 October).
Contains a brief notice of LD.

197. McCarty, Helen. "The Long Dream."
Ayer (Mass.) Public Spirit (30 October).
Favorable review relating the novel
to the civil rights struggle. The
book is bitter and brutal, "but
Wright can certainly express himself
and the emotions of his people!"
Reprinted: 1958.198.

198. _____. "The Long Dream." Groton
Landmard (31 October), p. 3.
Reprint of 1958.197.

199. McDowell, Louise and Helen Merrick.
"American Literature: Twentieth Cen-
tury," in The Book of Knowledge. Ed. E.
V. McLoughlin. Vol. 14. New York: The
Grolier Society, pp. 4997-5025.
Reprint of 1952.1

200. McIntyre, Bruce. "Wright's Fish-
belly--He's Native Son All Over Again."
Akron Beacon Journal (7 December), p.
8D.
Unfavorable review of LD complaining
that in it W, cut off by his expatriation from recent developments on
the American racial scene, is rewriting both NS and BB. "Generally, the
story does not ring true, although it
contains a number of effectively
written vignettes." W relies too much
on melodrama and violence.

201. McManis, John. "By Author of
'Native Son': A 'Long Dream' Ends in
Flight." The Detroit News (26 October),
The Passing Show Sec., p. 22.
Mixed review of LD comparing it to
NS, to which it is technically superior but thematically inferior because
it presents escape as the only solution to racial problems. McManis
compares Bigger and Fishbelly and
provides some biographical information on W.

202. McPherson, Flora. "Books and
Things." The Galt Evening Reporter (31
January).

Review of PS stressing W's subjectivity.

203. Me. "Richard Wright: Schwarze Macht." Frankfort Allegemeine Deutsche Lehrerzeitung (9 April).
Brief review of the German translation of BP noting that W had access to experiences in Ghana unavailable to whites. Stresses his conclusion that Africa must follow a course separate from either Communism or the West.

204. ____. "Richard Wright: Schwarze Macht." Frankfort Allgemeine Deutsche Lehrerzeitung (15 September).
Review of the German translation of BP. Although it is too extreme in its criticism of Christianity, the work does not support Communism. Despite his alienation from Africa, W recommends that Ghana follow its "individual path."

205. Nadeau, Maurice. "'Espagne païenne' par Richard Wright." France Observateur, 9 (24 April), 19-20.
Mixed review of the French translation of PS. Nadeau concentrates on the paradox of calling so Catholic a country as Spain pagan. W's point of view, emphatically not French, is "curious, inventive, and profoundly human," but it leads him to some distortions, such as the notion that Spain is incapable of change.

206. Naguère, Jean. "Espagne païenne." Le Petit Matin (5 March), p. 5.
Favorable review of the French translation of PS. Naguere, agreeing with W's method and approach, considers the work a "perfect achievement" uniting warm understanding with a lucid and fascinating vision.

207. Neumann, Günter. "Richard Wright: Schwarze Macht." Unidentified clipping (February).
Review of the German translation of BP. The book chronicles W's developing feeling of alienation from the Gold Coast. He has access to experiences closed to whites and does not spare Western civilization in his conclusions.

208. Norris, Hoke. "Wright--A Master Who Has Failed to Go On." Chicago Sunday Sun-Times (26 October), Sec. Three, p. 4.
Unfavorable review of LD finding it similar in several respects to NS but less powerful. W tends to melodrama and propaganda, presenting almost all his characters as "stupid, venal or brutal." Perhaps he should have looked for some solution to the racial situation other than flight.

209. Oboler, Eli M. "Foley, Martha & Burnett, David, eds. The Best American Short Stories 1958; and the Yearbook of the American Short Story." Library Journal, 83 (15 October), 2841.
Mentions W briefly.

210. Ottley, Roi. "Wright's New Novel Isn't for Squeamish." Chicago Sunday Tribune Magazine of Books (26 October), p. 3.
Favorable review of LD praising W's characterization of both Fishbelly and Tyree Tucker. The work's social protest is powerful and provocative, but valid. Disturbing, even nightmarish, the book "reveals some awful truths."
Reprinted: 1978.209.

211. P., B. "Book Review." Africa Weekly, 9 (3 September).
Review of Freda Wolfson's Pageant of Ghana mentioning the inclusion of W.

212. Perry, Al. "Wright Has Powerful New Novel." Winston-Salem Journal and Sentinel (7 December), p. 7C.
Favorable review of LD, "a first-rate novel" though too repetitive in its attack on Jim Crow and not as effective as NS. Perry admires W for "the crackling realism of his narrative and the power of his dialogue."

213. Pickrel, Paul. "Dark City." Harper's Magazine, 217 (November), 114.
Unfavorable review of LD complaining of structural defects, inept use of dream passages, unsatisfactory conclusion, and stylistic excess in the final paragraph. Nevertheless, "the central episodes of the story are strong and firmly written," and Tyree Tucker is a convincing character.

214. Pittman, John. "Books: 4 Lectures by Richard Wright." Daily Worker (1 July), p. 4.
Mixed review of WML praising "The Literature of the Negro in the United States," "Tradition and Industrialization," and "The Miracle of Nationalism in the African Gold Coast," but criticizing "The Psychological Reactions of Oppressed People" for its reliance on psychological speculation and its rejection of Marxism.

215. Plastrik, Stanley. "Lonely Outsiders." Dissent, 5 (Spring), 191-192.
Generally favorable review of WML emphasizing the role of the "tragic elite" in Africa and Asia. Plastrik is skeptical that these leaders can

realize adequate economic gains and is disturbed by W's notion that their power will not become self-serving, but he urges that communication be kept open between them and the West. "Wright himself is a precious example of what this means."
Reprinted: 1978.209.

216. Porter, Dorothy B. "A Bibliographical Checklist of American Negro Writers About Africa," in Africa Seen by American Negroes. Ed. John A. Davis. Paris: Présence Africaine, pp. 379-399.
Lists BP, Puissance Noire, and WML (p. 398).

217. Poston, Ted. "Wright: He's Out of Touch." New York Post (26 October), p. M10.
Somewhat unfavorable review of LD admitting the graphic power of the novel but arguing that W's expatriation has caused him to lose contact with the current realities of racial relations in Mississippi. The evaluation is made in the context of W's entire career.
Reprinted: 1978.209.

218. Powell, Dawn. "They Got the Blue Ribbon, But Why?" New York Post (14 September), p. M11.
Review of The Best American Short Stories 1958 singling out "Big Black Good Man" as one of the three good stories in an otherwise disappointing collection. Includes a photograph of W.

219. Price, Emerson. "War Child's Story Filled with Horror, Beauty." The Cleveland Press (21 October), p. 13.
Contains a favorable notice of LD, an "unlovely but compelling tale." It is realistic, not didactic.

219a. [Quinn, Kerker]. "Accent Winter 1958."
Flyer listing W as a contributor to Accent Anthology.

220. Railsback, Jo Helen. "Novels of Negro Life in U. S." The Houston Post (9 November), Houston Now Magazine Sec., p. 12.
Review of LD and Julian Mayfield's The Long Night. W's novel is a convincing presentation of racial problems from a black perspective, but its message has a diminished impact because of its repetition.

221. Randolph, Peggy. "Racial Round-Up." Tulsa Sunday World (16 February), Magazine Sec., p. 29.
Unfavorable review of WML objecting to the stridency of W's tone. The

"frog perspective" may be personal as well as racial, the reviewer argues. Many whites are on W's side, but they may be alienated by his "rudeness." He should instead "shout in a whisper."

222. Rauch, Karl. "Heidnisches Spanien?" Die Bücherkommentare, 7 (15 September), 21.
Favorable review of the German translation of PS finding it far superior to all other travel books, both for its literary artistry and its incisive social and political commentary. Rauch predicts that it will be attacked as subjective and unjust, but he defends W's view of the contradictions of Spanish character and history.
Reprinted: 1958.223.

223. _____. "Das solten Sie lesen." Berlin Telegraf (12 October), p. 26.
Reprint of 1958.222.

224. Record, Jane Cassels. "Warning to the White West." New York Herald Tribune Book Review (23 February), p. 10.
Review of WML analyzing each of its four sections. Record considers W most provocative in discussing the Western response to Third World leaders.

225. Redding, Saunders. The Lonesome Road: The Story of the Negro's Part in America. Garden City, N. Y.: Doubleday, p. 281.
Mentions and quotes W in a section on Paul Robeson to illustrate the appeal of Marxism to black intellectuals.

226. _____. "The Way It Was." The New York Times Book Review (26 October), pp. 4, 38.
Unfavorable review of LD. After analyzing the opening episode, Redding identifies the theme of the novel as the fragmentation of personality. In developing this theme, W is guilty of sensationalism and loose writing. His expatriation has weakened his understanding of American reality.
Reprinted: 1978.209.

227. Renaud, P.-A. "Les Revues: Wright s'adresse à l'homme blanc." France Observateur (23 October), pp. 20-21.
Favorable notice of an extract published in Les Lettres Nouvelles of the forthcoming French translation of WML.

228. Rennert, Leo. "Wright Is Obsessed Writer But a Fine One." The Sacramento Bee (25 October), pp. L-26-L-27.
Favorable review of LD consisting

mostly of plot summary. Rennert places the novel in the context of W's life and career, calling it "a clearly reasoned and powerfully documented apologia" by a "mesmeric storyteller."

229. Richards, Robert. "Let's Talk About Books." Duarte (Cal.) Dispatch (6 November), p. 5.
Review of LD admitting the veracity of W's picture of the South in the twenties, but claiming that is is "overblown" for the fifties because it ignores the progress that has been made in decreasing violence. Still, the potential for violence does abide in racist attitudes.

230. Richardson, Boyce. "Behind the Color Curtain." Winnipeg Free Press (12 July), p. 43.
Mixed review of WML. Valuable in its challenge to white righteousness, the book is oversimplified because W leaves China out of his black-white equation. Richardson also objects to W's psychological jargon.

231. Rogge, Heinz. "Die amerikanische Negerfrage im Lichte der Literatur von Richard Wright und Ralph Ellison." Die neueren Sprachen, No. 2, pp. 56-69; No. 3, pp. 103-117.
Discussing W's presentation of the American racial question, Rogge emphasizes the theme of fear, with comparisons to Swift, Kafka, Nietzsche, Kierkegaard, and Dostoevsky. Rogge also comments on other matters, including W's relationship to Simone de Beauvoir and Daniel Guérin and his participation in the First Congress of Black Artists and Writers in Paris.

232. Rosati, Salvatore. "L'uomo invisibile di Ralph Ellison," in his L'ombra dei padri. Studi sulla letteratura americana. Biblioteca di studi americani 4, ed. Agostino Lombardo. Rome: Edizioni di storia e letteratura, pp. 135-141.
Reprint of 1953.217b.

233. _____. "Richard Wright," in his L'ombra dei padri. Studi sulla letteratura americana. Biblioteca di studi americani 4, ed. Agostino Lombardo. Rome: Edizioni di storia e letteratura, pp. 149-153.
Reprint of 1953.217a.

234. _____. "Tendenze della prosa narrativa," in his L'ombra dei padri. Studi sulla letteratura americana. Biblioteca di studi americani 4, ed. Agostino Lombardo. Rome: Edizioni di storia e letteratura, pp. 69-78.

Reprint of 1947.261a.

235. Rowland, Jeanette. "Book Reviews." Santa Cruz Citizen News (9 November).
Contains an unfavorable notice of LD complaining of improbability.

236. Rumley, Larry. "Richard Wright's Latest Book Renews Old Theme." Baton Rouge Morning Advocate (9 November), p. 5-E.
Review of LD comparing it somewhat unfavorably to the play NS and to BB. "Mr. Wright writes well although he is guilty of contrivance at times. He is also a man with an obsession and, I think, has worked the same vein almost to bare ground."

237. S., Dr. "Schwarze Macht." Volkswerke (19 December).
Favorable review of the German translation of BP, which is worth reading even when one cannot accept W's conclusions. Of high political and psychological interest, it reflects both its author's Western patterns of thought and his deep commitment to understanding Africa.

238. Sablonière, Margrit de. "Richard Wrights nieuwste boek." Vrij Nederland (25 January), p. 8.
Favorable review of the Dutch translation of WML. The result of W's long concern with various racial problems, the book deserves notice for its analysis of the development of a black elite, its vignettes concerning the effect of Dutch exploitation of Indonesians, and the chapter on Afro-American literature. WML provides a key to understanding W's personality, which is both humane and uncompromising.

239. Saito, Tadatoshi. "America Kokujin Bungaku Kanken--Richard Wright, Ralph Ellison o Chushin ni" ["A View of Black American Literature: Richard Wright and Ralph Ellison"]. Utsunomiya Daigaku Kenkyu Ronshu [Utsunomiya University Studies], 7 (January), 97-110.
Although literature should not be propaganda, contemporary black American literature, best represented by W and Ellison, cannot help being protest literature. The distinction of the two novelists is (1) W's fiction must entail action, (2) action in W's work is used to alleviate one's fear and doubt, (3) W's fiction is based on fact. While these characteristics make W's earlier works successful as protest literature, the failure of O is attributed to his failure to adhere to the principles. [Y. H.]

240. Sanders, David. "Native Son Unloads More Dice." The Washington Post and Times Herald (19 October), p. E7.
    Favorable review of LD, an angry and despairing but impressive book. Set in the present, it views flight as the only recourse for a Southern black man. W has earned the right to this conclusion, for he "has worked as heroically as any other writer toward the amelioration of his people."

241. Schulze, Andrew. "White Man, Listen! By Richard Wright." Cresset, 21 (June), 25-26.
    Favorable review emphasizing the importance of the work to white Christian readers. The ambiguous relationship of the African and Asian elite (and of W himself) to Western civilization yields profound insights.

242. Schürenberg, Dr. "Am Büchertisch." Mimeographed (2 September).
    Radio review of the German translation of PS, a book which provides a realistic counterbalance to romantic images of Spain. W insists on his thesis, applying it to all incidents.

243. Schuyler, George S. "A Negro Who Preaches Racism." American Mercury, 86 (April), 148-149.
    Extremely hostile review of WML accusing W of ignoring Soviet imperialism while castigating the white West. Far from exploiting Africa and Asia, the colonial powers brought improved living conditions. W to the contrary notwithstanding, African and Asian leaders know that cooperation with the West is necessary for survival.

244. Scott, Nathan A., Jr. Modern Literature and the Religious Frontier. New York: Harper & Brothers, pp. 59, 60, 98-99.
    Mentions O as an existentialist novel. Contrasts NS and O to show W's altered view of social reality.

245. [Seigler, Milledge Broadus]. "American Literature," in Britannica Junior. Ed. Don A. Walter. Vol. 2. Chicago: Encyclopaedia Britannica, pp. 216-227.
    Mentions NS and BB as "novels that portray the sordid side of Negro life" (p. 225).
    Reprinted: 1960.240;1961.262; 1962. 99; 1963.168; 1964.114.

246. Sekiguchi, Isao. "Richard Wright to Kokujin Kihyo--Shitsurakuseru Kami to Kuroi Chikara" ["Richard Wright and Negro Criticism: The God That Failed and Black Power"]. Meiji Daigaku Eibei Bungaku [Meiji University English and American Literature], 3 (January), 2-17.
    Suggests that The God That Failed is not W's attack on Communism as often claimed, but rather an autobiography of his formative years. During this period W joined the Communist Party to seek out humanity in cooperation with workers. A similar quest is made in BP. [Y. H.]

247. Seton, Marie. Paul Robeson. London: Dennis Dobson, pp. 124, 134.
    Mentions W as a WPA writer and notes the mistaken allegation of Martin Dies that the film Native Land was based on NS.

248. Shands, Bill. "An Intimate Look at Negro's Troubled World." San Mateo Times (25 October), Weekend Sec., p. 3A.
    Favorable review of LD emphasizing its power and candor but objecting to the ending as escapist and hopeless.

249. Shapiro, Charles. "A Slow Burn in the South." The New Republic, 139 (24 November), 17-18.
    Favorable review of LD comparing it to NS, An American Tragedy, and The Grapes of Wrath. Its power compensates for some stylistic excesses. Fishbelly learns that a black man cannot combine success and sensitivity in the South.
    Reprinted: 1978.209.

250. Shaw, Fred. "Fine Reading, Fine Comments." The Miami News (9 November), p. 6B.
    Contains a review of LD. The novel is powerful, but its author is out of touch with recent racial progress.

251. Shaw, Mildred Hart. "Between Book Ends." Grand Junction Daily Sentinel (9 November), p. 4.
    Contains a review of LD. The novel is vivid and honest, but less important than some of W's other work.

252. Shroyer, Frederick. "Powerful Richard Wright Novel Rages at Inequality." Los Angeles Times (26 October), Part V, p. 6.
    Review of LD. Compared to this novel, "Dante's Inferno is nothing but a description of a pleasure jaunt through Disneyland." Shroyer is impressed by W's power, but he suspects some exaggeration in the account of the racial situation.

253. Simpson, George Eaton and J. Milton Yinger. Racial and Cultural Minorities: An Analysis of Prejudice and Discrimination. Revised edition. New York: Harper, 881 pp.

Revised reprint of 1953.228.

254. Skard, Sigmund. American Studies in Europe. Vol. 2. Philadelphia: University of Pennsylvania Press, p. 578.
Refers to essays issued by the Gorky Institute in 1950 classifying W as a bourgeois reactionary.

255. Stauffer, William H. "A Sordid Picture of Life in the South." Richmond Times-Dispatch (19 October), p. L-11.
Unfavorable review of LD, a "sordidly and sloppily sensual" book. Such unwholesome sensationalism, distortion, and racial bias will "fan the flames of racial differences that unhappily confront the South today."

256. Stevenson, David L. "Novel, The," in The Encyclopedia Americana. Ed. Lavinia P. Dudley. Vol. 20. New York: Americana Corporation, pp. 503-524.
Reprint of 1952.64.

256a. Strachey, John. "Expiring Laws Continuance Bill," in Parliamentary Debates: House of Commons. Vol. 595. London: Her Majesty's Stationery Office, pp. 1351-1355.
In a November debate on immigration policy, Strachey urges reconsideration of a decision to exclude W.

257. Tidwell, Lyda P. "The Long Dream, by Richard Wright." The Albuquerque Tribune (8 November), p. 4.
Unfavorable review. The social protest is valid, but the novel "abounds in violence and filth."

258. Tilliette, X.[avier]. "Richard Wright.--Espagne païenne. Jean Créac'h.--Chroniques espagnoles. Luis Romero.--Les Autres. Jesús Fernandez Santos.--Les Fiers. Carmen de Icaza.--Avant qu'il soit trop tard." Etudes, 299 (December), 429.
Contains an unfavorable review of the French translation of PS complaining of distortion.

259. Underwood, Carol K. "Modern Fiction by Negro Authors." The Houston Post (21 December), Houston Now Sec., p. 37.
Favorable review of Robert Bone's The Negro Novel in America praising its evaluation of NS.

260. W., B. "Fishbelly Tackles a Strange World." The Fayetteville (N. C.) Observer (7 December), p. 5C.
Rather favorable review of LD praising W's power, but finding it somewhat excessive. Because of the amelioration of the racial situation in Mississippi, a more oblique protest could have been more effective.

261. Walzer, P.-O. "Gens du sud." Journal de Genève (14-15 June), p. 3.
Contains a favorable review of the French translation of PS. Not satisfied with a tourist's impressions, W explores social and moral conditions. Not content with a political indictment, W probes the irrational core of Spanish reality.

262. Washburn, Beatrice. "Books in Review: Seething Racial Story Blends Anger, Truth." The Miami Herald (9 November), p. 6-G.
Review of LD with quotations. W's depiction of race relations in the South is true, but his racial anger may impede interracial understanding and sympathy.

263. Wellejus, Ed. "The Bookshelf." Erie Times-News (23 November), p. 15-E.
Contains a notice of LD, not "a good book, but . . . a powerful one."

264. Wells, Robert W. "In a Racial Jungle." The Milwaukee Journal (26 October), Part 5, p. 4.
Somewhat unfavorable review of LD. It is a gripping story, but more polemical than artistic. Segregationists will have their racism confirmed by "Fishbelly's yen for blonds."

265. Wickert, Ulrich. "Richard Wright." Murmures 5. Mimeographed, pp. 3-4.
Interview with W concentrating on his travels but touching also on his life, works, and the availability of translations. Murmures is a periodical of the École de la Source, Meudon-Bellvue, S.-O.

266. W.[illis], C.[arol]. "Richard Wright at Best in Novel About Injustice." Buffalo Evening News (25 October), p. 10.
Favorable review of LD emphasizing its universality, especially as compared to NS. W's characters "are first of all men, good or evil." Though not pretty, the novel presents "a true picture of an important part of America."

267. Wolfson, Freda. "Introduction," in her Pageant of Ghana. London: Oxford University Press, pp. 1-36.
Mentions W's "unusual slant to the Gold Coast in Black Power" (p. 35).

268. Wyrick, Green D. "Book Review." The Emporia Daily Gazette (29 November), p. 4.
Unfavorable review of LD complaining of lack of originality. Often W's style is no better than Dreiser's.

269. Z., I. "Richard Wright: 'Heidnisches Spanien.'" _Der_ Landau _Pfälzer_
(19 December).
Review of the German translation of
PS. W inverts the usually pleasant
approach to Spain and stresses the
psychological and political darkness
in which its people live.

270. Zöller, J. O. "Gerne Grossinquisi-
tor." _Echo_ _der_ _Zeit_ (21 September).
Unfavorable review of the German
translation of PS. W's thesis is
almost entirely unconvincing, and sex
is overemphasized. Although some of
the descriptive passages surpass even
Hemingway's, W's prejudices render
him incapable of dealing effectively
with Spain's religion.

1959

1. Abrahams, Peter. "The Blacks." _Holi-_
day, 25 (April), 74-75, 112-114, 118-
122, 124-126.
Discusses African life, particularly
political developments in Ghana and
Kenya and the role of tribal man.
Relates meeting with W in Accra. W
was shocked by the casualness of sex
in Africa and bewildered by his lack
of acceptance on the basis of color.
He did not understand tribalism.
Reprinted: 1960.2; 1963.1; 1973.3.

2. Algren, Nelson, Alston Anderson, and
Terry Southern. "Nelson Algren," in
Writers at Work. Ed. Malcolm Cowley. New
York: The Viking Press, pp. 233-249.
Reprint of 1955.1.

3. Allen, Samuel W. "La Negritude et ses
rapports avec le Noir américain." _Pré-_
sence Africaine, No. 2 (August-November), pp. 16-26.
Mentions W briefly (p. 21).

4. Ames, Alfred C. "Books of the Year,"
in _The American Peoples Encyclopedia_
Yearbook. Ed. Carroll Chouinard. Chicago: Spencer Press, pp. 289-292.
Mentions briefly LD (p. 289).

5. Anon. "Ace Books." _Publishers' Week-_
_ly_, 176 (16 November), 46.
Announces a paperback edition of LD.

6. Anon. "The American Theatre Associa-
tion of Paris Monthly Meetings."
Flyer announcing a meeting on 19
February 1959 featuring a talk by W
and a reading of scenes from _Daddy_
Goodness.

7. Anon. "AMSAC Notes." _AMSAC News-_
letter, 1 (28 February), 2.
Contains an announcement of the
French translation of WML.

7a. Anon. "Away from the Ghetto." _The_
London _Times_ _Literary_ _Supplement_, No.
2,976 (13 March), p. 146.
Favorable review of Robert A. Bone's
The Negro Novel in America mentioning
briefly NS, W's relation to the Communist Party, and his expatriation.

8. Anon. "Bauern, Bürger und Beduinen."
Aachener _Volkszeitung_ (4 May).
Notice of the German translation of
BP, "an intelligent and surprisingly
objective book."

9. Anon. "Books for Businessmen." _The_
Financial _Post_ (5 September), p. 33.
Contains a notice of LD relating it
to W's previous work on the racial
situation in the brutal Southern
environment.

10. Anon. "Das Bücherfenster." Cologne
Rheinischer _Merkur_ (20 March), p. 24.
Contains a very unfavorable notice of
the German translation of PS wondering why the work was published by a
"serious German press." Complains of
W's preconceptions and his excessive
interest in prostitution.

11. Anon. "Christus lebt im Untergrund:
Die Leidengeschichte der Protestanten in
Franco-Spanien / Von Richard Wright."
Bonn _Vorwärts_ (6 March), p. 4.
Headnote to an excerpt from the Ger-
man translation of PS.

12. Anon. "Daddy Goodness." _Newsletter_
_of_ _the_ _American_ _Theatre_ _Association_, No.
3 (April).
Notice of the adaptation by W of
Louis Sapin's play.

13. Anon. "Ghana und Israel." Göttingen
Deutsche _Universitätszeitung_ (14 February).
Contains a review of the German
translation of BP, a book in which
there are a number of unresolved
contradictions. W seems unaware of
the effect of Marxist analysis on his
"independent" conclusions. His desire
that Ghana modernize does not seem
consistent with his wish that it
overthrow European influence.

14. Anon. "Ein heidnisches Land." _Zeit-_
schrift _für_ _Gemeinschaft_ _und_ _Politik_
(July-August), pp. 19-23.
Favorable review of the German translation of PS. Discusses in detail W's
treatment of Protestantism, prostitution, and economic deprivation under
Franco. Notes the irony of an American presenting such a devastating
picture of a country whose government
survives with the help of American
power. See also the condensed version

in 1959.34.

15. Anon. "Heidnisches Spanien." Magnum, 23 (April), 42.
    Commentary on the German translation of PS with illustrations. Notes W's hostility to Christianity and summarizes his conclusions on the pagan nature of Spanish Catholicism.

16. Anon. "Heidnisches Spanien. Von Richard Wright." Die Barbe (February).
    Review of the German translation of PS consisting mostly of summary.

17. Anon. "Hinweise." Deutsche Rundschau, 85 (August), 761-764.
    Contains a notice of the German translation of PS describing it as a serious work, not a tourist's book.

18. Anon. "'An Important and Valuable Book,'" in The God That Failed. Ed. Richard Crossman. Bantam Fifty F2011. New York: Bantam Books, back cover.
    Mentions W briefly and includes a photograph.

19. Anon. Index Translationum 10. Paris: Unesco, pp. 134, 287, 289, 462, 464, 632.
    Lists translations of UTC into Danish and Swedish, SH into Italian, BP into Italian and Serbo-Croatian, The God That Failed into Italian, NS into Swedish, and BB into Swedish.

20. Anon. "The Long Dream--Richard Wright." Berkeley Daily Gazette (c. 1 March).
    Notice of "a bitter book" portraying black men enmeshed in corruption.

21. Anon. "Negro Boy's Unhappy Life in South Revealed in Book." Wichita Eagle (23 January), p. 12C.
    Favorable review of LD identifying W as "one of the leading spokesmen for the Negro in America," summarizing the plot, and concluding with emphasis on the autobiographical authenticity of this "powerful and dramatic novel."

22. Anon. "Negro Playwrights." Ebony, 14 (April), 95-96, 98-100.
    Includes a photograph of W with caption.

23. Anon. "Neu in Deutschland." Der Spiegel, 13 (18 February), 57-58.
    Contains a notice of the German translation of PS stressing the role of force--guns--in maintaining the power of state, army, and church. The book is "as subjective as it is humanistic."

24. Anon. "Nota," in Razza umana. By Richard Wright. Trans. Attilio Landi. Milan: Il Saggiatore, pp. 7-8.
    Introductory note to the Italian translation of "Tradition and Industrialization."

25. Anon. "Partner for Play." The New York Times (c. November).
    Announces that Cheryl Crawford will be joined by Joel W. Schenker as a partner for the production of a dramatic version of LD.

26. Anon. "Rajt, Richard," in Mala entsiklopedija prosveta. Ed. Oto Bikhalji-Merin, Borislav Blagojević, Radivoj Davidović, Ilija Ćurichić, and Dragi Milenković. Vol. 2. Belgrade: Prosveta, p. 396.
    Biographical note.

27. Anon. "Red and Black: Paradoxical Freedom Born of the Outsider." The London Times Literary Supplement, No. 3,010 (6 November), pp. xxviii-xxix.
    Mentions W briefly.

28. Anon. "Richard Wright: El largo sueño." Sudamericana (November).
    Advertisement for the Spanish translation of LD.

29. Anon. "Richard Wright: 'Heidnisches Spanien.'" Das Menschenrecht (April).
    Favorable review of the German translation of PS. The book is quite subjective and unconventional, but interesting.

30. Anon. "Richard Wright: Heidnisches Spanien." Leutkirch-Allgäu Schwäbischen Zeitung (19 December).
    Review of the German translation of PS, an "aggressive," subjective work, perhaps based on too short a stay in Spain.

31. Anon. "Richard Wright signera son livre Ecoute, homme blanc."
    Printed invitation to an autograph party at L'Escalier bookstore in Paris on 26 June.

32. Anon. "Société africaine de culture." Présence Africaine, Nos. 24-25 (February-May), p. [431].
    List of officers of the organization with W included on the executive council and the executive committee.

33. Anon. "Spanien und Portugal." Bücherschiff, 9 (June), 14.
    Review of the German translation of PS and three other books on the Iberian peninsula. Praises W's intellect, but notes his ignorance of the Spanish language and European history

and tradition. The picture that W paints of Spain is gloomy.

34. Anon. "Spaniens Uhren gehen falsch." Der Ruf, No. 12 (June), p. 5.
    Slightly condensed version of 1959.14.

35. Anon. "Spanische Wirklichkeit." Munich Deutsche Woche (1 July).
    Review of the German translation of PS concentrating on W's analysis of the connections between political repression and sexuality. Points out that the author's extensive interviewing is an effective means of getting to the truth behind the stereotyped image of picturesque Spain.

36. Anon. Untitled article. Editorial Sudamericana (1 November), p. 26.
    Publisher's review of the Spanish translation of LD. In relating terrible truths of cruelty and frustration, W champions a noble cause.

37. Anon. Untitled article, in Ecoute, homme blanc. By Richard Wright. Trans. Dominique Guillet. Paris: Calmann-Lévy, back cover.
    Publisher's blurb.

38. Anon. Untitled article, in ¡Escucha, hombre blanco! By Richard Wright. Trans. Floreal Mazía. Buenos Aires: Editorial Sudamericana, front inside flap of cover.
    Publisher's blurb.

39. Anon. Untitled article, in Sangre negra. By Richard Wright. Trans. Pedro Lecuona. Colección Horizonte. Buenos Aires: Editorial Sudamericana, front inside flap of cover.
    Publisher's blurb emphasizing the theme of racial resentment in NS. Includes a brief biographical sketch of W.

40. Anon. Untitled clipping. Basel National-Zeitung.
    Review of the German translation of PS consisting mostly of summary.

41. Anon. Untitled clipping. Jet (c. August), pp. 28-29.
    Notes that the dramatic version of LD is being cast and directed by Lloyd Richards.

42. Anon. Untitled clipping. Niagara Falls Gazette (c. 14 December).
    Mentions briefly LD.

43. Anon. Untitled clipping. Wiener Bücherbriefe (May).
    Favorable review of the German trans-

lation of BP noting W's anti-Communist stand.

44. Anon. Untitled clipping. Würzberg Deutsche Tagespost (7-8 August).
    Review of the German translation of PS stressing W's subjectivity.

45. Anon. "Weltreisender Wright." Wir, Schulerzeitung Sterde (1 July), pp. 1-3.
    Considers W as a travel writer on the basis of BP and PS. Emphasizing the corruption of Spain and the tensions between W and Africa, the article concludes that W is far more than a reporter: he is a discoverer.

46. Anon. "Wright," in Kleines Lexikon A-Z. Leipzig: Verlag Enzyklopaedie, p. 1084.
    Very brief biographical note.

47. Anon. "Wright, Richard," in Chambers's Encyclopedia. New Edition. Ed. M. D. Law. Vol. 14. London: George Newnes Limited, p. 758.
    Reprint of 1950.100.

48. Anon. "Wright, Richard," in Enciclopedia Garzanti. Vol. 5. Milan: Garzanti Editore, p. 4335.
    Biographical note.

49. Anon. "Wright, Richard," in Focus. Ed. Sven Lidman. Vol. 4. Stockholm: Almquist & Wiksell, p. 2377.
    Biographical note.

50. Anon. "Wright, Richard," in The Macmillan Everyman's Encyclopedia. Fourth edition. Ed. E. F. Bozeman. Vol. 12. New York: Macmillan, p. 137.
    Biographical note.

51. Anon. "Wright (Richard): Ecoute, homme blanc!" 2 pp.
    A "fiche bibliographique," apparently from the publisher, reviewing enthusiastically the French translation of WML and sketching W's life.

52. Anon. "Wright, Richard: Heidnisches Spanien." Literarische Ratgeber, 40.
    Review of the German translation of PS emphasizing W's subjectivity and his analysis of the debased quality of sexual love in Spain. His attitudes derive largely from his racial and political experiences.

53. Antignac, Golda G. "'Daddy Goodness.'" The American Theatre Association of Paris News Letter, No. 3 (April), p. 1.
    Explains production plans for W's adaptation of Louis Sapin's play and appeals for funds.

54. Baldus, Alexander. "Richard Wright: Heidnisches Spanien." Begegnung (July), p. 191.
    Favorable review of the German translation of PS emphasizing W's subjectivity.

55. Bardolph, Richard. The Negro Vanguard. New York: Rinehart, pp. 276-284.
    Considers W the most famous black expatriate. Comments on BB and NS and notes W's relation to Communism.
    Reprinted: 1961.120.

56. Barry, Joseph. "An American in Paris--I." New York Post (23 March), Magazine Sec., p. 4.
    Discussing American literary expatriation in Paris beginning in the twenties, Barry comments on W and his relation to Gertrude Stein. Quotes W on his residence in Paris: "I may not work better, but I sure live better." Stein has advised him: "You will find prejudice in Paris, Dick, but you won't find a problem."

57. Bauer, Arnold. "Wie lebt und denkt man in Spanien?" Berliner Stimme (28 February).
    Favorable review of the German translation of PS. W uses the methods of empirical sociology to provide a clear, penetrating analysis of the country. He allows things to speak for themselves in a way which condemns the Franco regime without direct commentary.

58. Becher, H., S. J. "Wright, Richard: Heidnisches Spanien." Stimmen der Zeit, 163 (February), 397.
    Unfavorable review of the German translation of PS. Becher concedes W's stylistic skill, but considers his view of Spain worthless--distorted, negative, Godless. The book reveals more about the author than the subject.

59. Bl.[air], W.[alter]. "American Literature," in Encyclopaedia Britannica. Ed. Walter Yust. Vol. 1. Chicago: Encyclopaedia Britannica, pp. 784-794.
    Reprint of 1954.80.

60. Bock, Hans-Joachim. "Richard Wright: Heidnisches Spanien." Bücherei und Bildung, 11 (January), B22.
    Review of the German translation of PS. Bock admits W's bias and distortions, but finds some value in his sensitivity to threats to humanity in Spain. The summary stresses W's preparation for his travels, his observations, and his interviews.

61. Bonosky, Phillip. "Man Without a People." Mainstream, 12 (February), 49-51.
    Unfavorable review of LD complaining of subjectivity and immaturity. W's art has suffered greatly from his estrangement from his people. LD, in which the black characters seem inferior to their white oppressors, is neither credible nor realistic.
    Reprinted: 1978.209.

62. Booker, Simeon. "Ticker Tape U. S. A." Jet.
    Notes that W is working on a sequel to LD.

63. Bradley, Van Allen. "'The Long Dream': A Situation Magnified Beyond All Reason." Binghamton Press (18 January), p. 12-B.
    Reprint of 1958.90.

64. Brenner, Hans-Georg. "Begegnung mit einem Buch." Mimeographed (23 August).
    Radio review of the German translation of PS. The strengths of the book stem from W's unique background and his insistence on observation as a basis of analysis. Even when his observations closely resemble those which have been made before, W's role of stranger charges his book with an unusual intensity, especially in the highly subjective political sections.

65. Brewer, Anita. "The Long Dream by Richard Wright." The Austin American-Statesman (22 March), p. B-14.
    Unfavorable review arguing that W's depiction of the South is anachronistic because of recent racial progress. Nevertheless, the novel has power.

66. Brinnin, John Malcolm. The Third Rose: Gertrude Stein and Her World. Boston: Little, Brown, pp. 120-121, 394.
    Points out W's friendship with Stein and his admiration for "Melanctha," quoting from W's account of reading the story to black stockyard workers in Chicago.

67. Browne, Jack A. "Letter to the Editor." The New York Times Book Review (15 February), p. 42.
    Criticizes W's expatriation while praising Baldwin's "The Discovery of What It Means to Be an American."

68. Burnham, Louis E. "The Negro Writer in U. S. Is Finding His Way." National Guardian (4 May), p. 12.
    After sketching the development of Afro-American literature and pointing out some of its problems, Burnham reviews five recent books by black

writers, including LD. W's novel is so unrelievedly nightmarish as to be more allegorical than realistic.

69. C.[aliver], A.[mbrose]. "Spingarn Medal," in The World Book Encyclopedia. Ed. J. Morris Jones. Vol. 15. Chicago: Field Enterprises, p. 7651.
    Reprint of 1947.164.

70. Clark, John Abbot. "American Literature," in Collier's Encyclopedia 1959 Year Book. Ed. William T. Couch. New York: P. F. Collier & Son, pp. 54-56.
    Contains an unfavorable reference to LD.

71. Clayton, Ed. "West Coast Round Up." Jet, 16 (8 October), 28-29.
    Mentions LD.

72. Collins, Marion. "One for the Books: Latest Wright Novel Powerful." Albany (N. Y.) Times-Union (4 January), p. E4.
    Favorable review of LD and Robert Bone's The Negro Novel in America deeming W's novel "a well-conceived, well-executed story that satisfies the demands both of artistic and racial loyalty." Collins believes that W's view of Southern race relations is still valid.

73. Crossman, Richard. "Introduction," in his The God That Failed. Bantam Fifty F2011. New York: Bantam Books, pp. 1-10.
    Reprint of 1949.92.

74. Decraene, Philippe. Le Panafricanisme. Paris: Presses Universitaires de France, p. 29.
    Mentions W's presence at the First Congress of Black Writers and Artists in Paris.

75. Dieterich, Anton. "Ein Amerikaner sieht Spanien." Düsseldorf Rheinische Post (c. 6 January).
    Reprint of 1958.105.

76. Doerig, J. A. "Bemerkungen zu einem Spanienbuch." Neue Zürcher Nachrichten (22 May), pp. 5-6.
    Reprint of 1959.77.

77. _____. "Bemerkungen zu einem Spanienbuch." Die St. Gallen Ostschweiz (28 April).
    Unfavorable review of the German translation of PS placing it in the context of Spanish history and historiography. Doerig stresses W's ignorance of Spain's history and language, his strange attraction to prostitutes, and his unfair attack on Franco's regime. The book should not have been published, for it damages

W's own literary reputation as well as the reputation of the Spanish people.
    Reprinted: 1959.76.

78. D.[ouglass], J.[oseph] H. "Negro," in The World Book Encyclopedia. Ed. J. Morris Jones. Vol. 12. Chicago: Field Enterprises, pp. 5486-5492.
    Mentions W briefly.
    Reprinted: 1960.141; 1961.138.
    Reprinted in revised form: 1962.49; 1963.73; 1964.42; 1965.56.

79. Dreyfus, Remy. "'Ecoute, Homme Blanc.'" France Observateur (2 July), p. 19.
    Favorable review of the French translation of WML analyzing each of the four lectures. W's background as a Western black man leads to a duality of perspective which both partakes of and evaluates the thoughts and aspirations of the Third World.

80. E., M. "Spanien." Das Bücherblatt, 23 (13 March), 3.
    Favorable review of the German translation of PS emphasizing its difference from the usual travel book. The reviewer praises W's description of the bullfight and his effort to penetrate to the core of Spanish opinions on important topics.

81. Elkins, Stanley M. Slavery: A Problem in American Institutional and Intellectual Life. Chicago: The University of Chicago Press, pp. 132-133.
    Uses Shorty from BB as an example of manipulation of the strong by the weak.
    Reprinted: 1963.76; 1968.81; 1976.65.
    Partially reprinted: 1969.69.

82. Fontaine, William T. "Toward a Philosophy of the American Negro Literature." Présence Africaine, Nos. 24-25 (February-May), pp. 165-176.
    Contains an analysis of the symbolism and characterization of NS. According to Fontaine, W uses materialism, Marxism, and "the psychoanalytic mechanisms of fear-shame-guilt-hate" to explore the behavior of both races.

83. F.[ranklin], J.[ohn] H.[ope] and R.[ayford] W.[hittingham] L.[ogan]. "Negro, American," in Encyclopaedia Britannica. Ed. Walter Yust. Vol. 16. Chicago: Encyclopaedia Britannica, pp. 194-201.
    Reprint of 1957.184.

84. Frisé, Adolf. "Richard Wright: Heidnisches Spanien." Hessischer Rundfunk (15 February).

Radio review of the German translation of PS, best understood as an attack on Américo Castro's interpretation of Spain's religious nature. Although W's oppressed background prevents him from romanticizing Spain, some of his interpretations are questionable because the travel book format keeps him from including pertinent background material on the folk psychology of the country. Such material would explain Spanish attitudes in terms of the conventional ideals of courage and heroism which W rejects.

85. G., B. H. "New Wright Novel Held Powerful." New Bedford Sunday Standard-Times (4 January), p. 37.
     Mixed review of O. Admitting W's "consummate mastery as a novelist and his force and vitality," the reviewer complains of the repetitious theme of racism in his novels, his propagandizing, his bias, and his implausible characterization.

86. Gardiner, John. "Aspects of Racial Curbs." The Windsor (Ont.) Daily Star (31 January), p. 41.
     Favorable review of LD emphasizing its frankness, power, and applicability to current racial problems in the United States. W's chief theme in the novel is "man's inhumanity to man."

87. Geismar, Maxwell. "Novelists Up From Slavery." The New York Times Book Review (29 March), p. 6.
     Review of Robert Bone's The Negro Novel in America mentioning W as "perhaps our only true novelist of the Dostoevskian depths."

88. Gibson, Richard. "The Color of Experience." The Nation, 188 (7 February), 123.
     Review of Robert Bone's The Negro Novel in America mentioning its assessment of NS as a "major" novel.

89. Haislip, Bryan. "Poignance, Frustrations, Withering Hopes." The Raleigh News and Observer (4 January), Sec. III, p. 5.
     Somewhat unfavorable review of LD complaining of oversimplified characterization and excessive propaganda. Nevertheless, W presents in the first half of the novel "a revealing picture of a Negro youth coming of age," and the book, though it lacks compassion, is at least "a signal across the gulf" that separates the races.

90. Harrington, Michael. "The Literary Tradition of the Negro." The Commonweal, 70 (1 May), 132.

Favorable review of Robert A. Bone's The Negro Novel in America mentioning briefly NS.

91. Haselden, Kyle. The Racial Problem in Christian Perspective. New York: Harper, pp. 40, 146.
     Uses "Fire and Cloud" and NS to illustrate points.

91a. Hashimoto, Fukuo. "The Novel of Sex and Feud: The Long Dream." Jiji Eigo Kenkyu [The Study of Current English], 14 (1 August), 62-64.
     Though provocative, the novel is marred by an exaggeration of the fear of black people and the violence of white rule. [Y. H. and T. K.]

92. Helwig, Werner. "Heidnisches Spanien?" St. Gallen Tagblatt (12 April). Reprint of 1958.150.

93. Hesse, Franz. "Katholisch-heidnisches Spanien." Die Hannover Freigeistige Aktion (7 August), p. 56.
     Favorable review of the German translation of PS with summary and quotation. Emphasizes W's view of the connections between religion, sex, and politics in Spain.

93a. Hicks, Granville. "Literary Horizons: From the Academy." Saturday Review, 42 (20 June), 18.
     Contains a notice of Robert A. Bone's The Negro Novel in America mentioning briefly NS.

94. Hicks, John H. "Between Book-Ends: No Holds Barred." St. Louis Post-Dispatch (24 January), p. 4.
     Favorable review of LD praising the uninhibited power and the dramatic quality of W's attack on Mississippi racism. Hicks provides a plot summary and notes the possibility of a sequel.

95. Hirose, Sadami. "Richard Wright no Sakuhin" ["Richard Wright's Work"]. Kokujin Kenkyu [Negro Study], 10 (December), 16-18.
     A brief statement that W's finest achievement is BB, a work which might remind one of Rousseau. [Y. H.]

96. Hofstadter, Richard, William Miller, and Daniel Aaron. The American Republic. Vol. 2. Englewood Cliffs, N. J.: Prentice-Hall, p. 485.
     Mentions W briefly.
     Reprinted: 1967.58.

97. Holt, Simma. "Negro's 'Long Dream' More of a Nightmare." The Vancouver Sunday Sun (21 February), p. 5.
     Favorable review stressing W's emo-

tional power in developing his racial protest. The tale develops slowly, but has a "dramatic and horrifying climax" and "a sad conclusion."

98. Hopper, Hedda. "Hollywood." New York Daily News (20 February), p. 45.
Announces that Anthony Quinn and Karl Malden will play in the dramatization of LD.

99. Howe, Irving. "Realities and Fictions." Partisan Review, 26 (Winter), 130-136.
Contains a mixed review of LD. W may have lost touch with America, but he remembers how it was. "The reality pressing upon the novel is a nightmare of remembrance."

100. Howlett, Jacques. "Le Livre de la semaine: Ecoute, homme blanc de Richard Wright." Les Lettres Nouvelles, 7 (27 May), 9-10.
Favorable review of the French translation of WML. Analyzes some of W's central arguments, which it defines as liberal humanism as opposed both to racial irrationality and dialectical Marxism.

100a. Ichikawa, Shigejiro. "America's First Black Writer Richard Wright." Nihon Daigaku Gakuho [Nihon University Study Report], 2 (31 December), 1-13.
An introduction to W's personality and work. BB is an accurate mirror of W's upbringing. NS powerfully portrays black struggle. UTC successfully depicts American society from a black point of view. O demonstrates that W after all is an American, while BP reminds him that he is an outsider in Africa. [Y. H. and T. K.]

101. Ivy, James W. "Ecrits nègres aux Etats-Unis." Présence Africaine, No. 26 (June-July), pp. 67-77.
Refers only briefly to W because he is already well known in France.

102. Jackson, Blyden. "A Golden Mean for the Negro Novel." CLA Journal, 3 (December), 81-87.
Refers briefly to W and NS.

103. Kennedy, Gerald. "The Long Dream, by Richard Wright." Together, 3 (May), 58.
Favorable review agreeing with W's tactic of presenting unattractive black protagonists instead of paragons. Kennedy warns the reader, however, that "this book is tough and deals with the seamy side of life."

104. Kimura, Michio. "Richard Wright Zakkan" ["Impressions of Richard Wright"]. Kokujin Kenkyu [Negro Study], 7 (February), 17-18.
Brief mention of W's later works. Focusing on SH, Kimura can hardly believe that such a work was written by the author who had produced NS. [Y. H.]

105. Ks., J. "Diese Woche gelesen." Neue Zürcher Nachrichten (6 February).
Unfavorable review of the German translation of PS by a Catholic reviewer complaining that W's rationalism and Freudianism prevent him from understanding Spanish Catholicism on its own terms.
Reprinted: 1959.106.

106. _____. Untitled clipping. Zurich Christliche Kultur (6 February), p. 2.
Reprint of 1959.105.

107. L., A. F. "'The Lone [sic] Dream' Wright's Latest." Lewiston (Maine) Evening Journal (2 May), Magazine Sec., p. 8.
Favorable review emphasizing the candor of W's depiction of "naked brutality and lust" in revealing the sordid consequences of racism. The novel is "an appeal to conscience" without being didactic.

108. L., E. H. "Heidnisches Spanien." Deutsche Volkszeitung (7 March).
Condensed reprint of 1958.179.

109. Lash, John S. "Dimension in Racial Experience: A Critical Summary of Literature by and About Negroes in 1958." Phylon, 20 (Second Quarter), 115-131.
Includes a paragraph on LD with a brief plot summary (pp. 119-120). Lash concedes the plausibility of the doomed quality of black life in the South, but concludes that "somehow, though, strong as is its presentation of racial effects unquestionably is, W's work does not get far beyond the South of sex and segregation."

110. Learned, Barry. "U. S. Lets Negro Explain Racial Ills, Wright Declares." The American Weekend (24 January).
Interview containing W's reaction to such recent developments as the desegregation struggle in Little Rock. W discusses his plans for a trip to French Africa.

110a. Lee, Ulysses. "The Negro Novel in America. By Robert A. Bone." The Journal of Negro History, 44 (April), 183-185.
Review mentioning W briefly.

111. Lehan, Richard. "Camus' American Affinities." Symposium, 13 (Fall), 255-270.

Includes a brief comparison of Camus and W (p. 268). The world of BB is "absurd, irrational, and malevolent." Cross Damon may be influenced by Camus's Meursault.

112. _____. "Existentialism in Recent American Fiction: The Demonic Quest." Texas Studies in Literature and Language, 1 (Summer), 181-202.
Discusses O as the most explicitly existential novel in American fiction, comparable to Camus's The Stranger. W's novel is flawed by sentimentalism and editorializing.

112a. Lipton, Lawrence. The Holy Barbarians. New York: Julian Messner, p. 232.
"John Steinbeck and Richard Wright lead a kind of twilight existence in the literary experience of the beat generation writers, but Nelson Algren is very vivid, very much in the foreground."

113. Loetscher, Hugo. "Diagnose eines Negers." Die Zurich Weltwoche (23 January).
Review of the German translation of PS. W insists that no understanding of Spain's politics and economics is possible without comprehending its religion. By inverting the usual stereotype held by whites that sees African tribes as pagan, W reminds his readers of the heathen roots of modern European "tribes."

114. Ludwig, Richard M. "Richard Wright," in his Literary History of the United States: Bibliography Supplement. New York: Macmillan, p. 216.
Lists seven primary and seven secondary sources.
Reprinted: 1963.172; 1974.165.

115. Meier, August. "Some Reflections on the Negro Novel." CLA Journal, 2 (March), 168-177.
Favorable essay-review of Robert Bone's The Negro Novel in America containing several references to W.

116. O., E. C. "Richard Wright: Heidnisches Spanien." Der Lehrbuchhandler (7 August).
Unfavorable review of the German translation of PS. Although W covers a wide range of material and performs a service in examining the extent and causes of Spanish poverty, he does not provide a good introduction to Spain in this book because his Freudianism and Marxism lead him into distortions of the significance of Catholicism in Spanish civic life.

117. Olivan, Federico. "A propósito de 'La España Pagana.': el negro que tenía el alma negra inspira una versión grotesca de la opera 'Carmen.'" Unidentified clipping.
Extremely hostile review of PS calling W "the Negro with black soul" and the book "stupid and base . . . a fabric of dull slanders and diatribes against our country." Olivan cites favorably Agustín de Figueroa's similar review, adding that Spain was exporting civilization while W's ancestors were naked in African jungles, that Spain freed slaves before the United States did, that W did not suffer discrimination in Spain as he would have at home, and that Spain has never lynched a black man.

118. Ouchi, Yoshikazu. "Kokujin Sakka Richard Wright nitsuite" ["Concerning Black Writer Richard Wright"]. Waseda Daigaku Kyoyo Shogaku Kenkyu [Waseda University General Studies], No. 9, pp. 21-36.
Notes that by a critic like David Daiches, W is ranked among such minor figures as Meyer Levin and Kay Boyle. Traces W's career from the John Reed Club through his Communist Party involvement to the exile in Paris. Unfortunately W alienated himself from the black world, the South, and finally the world itself. LD, however, indicates his latent wish to return to the real world. [Y. H.]

119. Parker, Dorothy. "Dorothy Parker on Books." Esquire, 51 (February), 16, 18.
Includes a notice of LD, "a grim and stunning report" which should jar the consciences of white racists.
Reprinted: 1978.209.

120. Pierre-Louis, Ulysse. "Le Roman français contemporain dans une impasse: Perspectives communes du roman d'Haïti des peuples noirs et de l'Amérique latine." Présence Africaine, Nos. 27-28 (August-November), pp. 51-68.
Mentions W and NS (p. 59).

121. Poster, William S. "Black Man's Burden." The New Leader, 42 (31 August), 23-24.
Unfavorable review of LD. Poster admits W's raw narrative talent, but complains of his lack of "a unified stylistic surface" and convincing characters, his cliché-ridden racial attitudes, and the absence of both "a perception of the weakness of the white world and an appreciation of the inner strength of Negro life."
Reprinted: 1978.209.

122. Priestly, Lee. "Violent, Bitter Is

the Dream." The Oklahoma City Daily Oklahoman (29 March), Sunday Oklahoman Magazine Sec., p. 23.

Unfavorable review of LD admitting W's power but complaining that his depiction of Southern race relations is shocking and atypical. W's basic motive is misguided because racist attitudes are beyond the reach of rational or fictional persuasion.

123. R., H. "Die Kehrseite von Spanien." Freiburg Badische Zeitung (17 February).

Unfavorable review of the German translation of PS. Although it does serve as a corrective of romantic views of Spain, the book should not be taken as a true picture of the country. W's sympathy with nonconformists leads him to find evidence to support a preconceived thesis.

124. Rabemananjara, Jacques. "The Foundations of Our Unity Arising from the Colonial Epoch." Présence Africaine, Nos. 24-25 (February-May), pp. 73-88.

Notes that W, Césaire, Lamming, and Senghor would be more at home in Europe than in Africa (p. 81).

125. Raymond, Sally. "Evil Footsteps Lead to Flight." Chattanooga Sunday Times (4 January), p. 14.

Mixed review of LD wishing that it had been better edited, for it "is a raw novel, written of a world of almost total depravity. Yet it has moments of real power and insight." Fishbelly's story is more like a nightmare than a dream.

126. Redding, Saunders. "Contradictions de la littérature negro-américaine." Présence Africaine, Nos. 27-28 (August-November), pp. 11-15.

Argues that W's expatriation has severed him from his roots.

127. Reifenrath, J. W. "Ein ganz anderes Bild von Spanien." Kölner Stadtanzeiger (10 January).

Favorable review of the German translation of PS praising W's realism, intellectual honesty, and objectivity. Reifenrath denies that W is anti-Catholic or even antireligious.

128. Reitz, Helmuth. "Kritik an Spanien." Welt und Wort, 14 (July), 212.

Review of the German translation of PS admiring W's social conscience but criticizing the book for lack of historical perspective and excessive rationality. W finds the key to the Spanish situation in the bond between state and church.

129. Rev. "Heidnisches Spanien." Der Vienna Rundblick (7 May).

Review of the German translation of PS noting W's effort to clarify the enigma of the country.

130. Sablonière, Margrit de. "Boekenpaspoort en Boekenniews." Litterair Paspoort, 64 (February), 44.

Favorable review of the Dutch translation of LD by the translator. Well written and penetrating, particularly in its description of black-white psychological relations, the novel shows that W has attained the necessary distance to treat his youthful experiences artistically.

131. Sabourin, Clemence. "Fiction: The Long Dream by Richard Wright." The Cresset (January), p. 27.

Favorable review confirming the veracity of W's portrait of white racism in the South.

132. Schickel, Richard. "Search for Value." The Progressive, 23 (March), 48-50.

Contains an unfavorable review of LD. Because W lacks the fictional techniques to communicate the existential meaning of LD, he remains "a Negro novelist." His early works overcame his lack of style with raw power, but now his obsession with childhood experiences is surface mannerism.

133. Sellenthin, H. G. "Onkel Toms Hütte steht leer." Bonn Vorwärts (16 January), p. 12.

Contains a favorable review of the German translation of PS. Mixing common sense and controversy, the book is both a political polemic and something more.

134. Senghor, Léopold Sédar. "Eléments constructifs d'une civilisation d'inspiration négro-africaine." Présence Africaine, Nos. 24-25 (February-May), pp. 249-279.

Quotes Sartre on W (p. 250).

135. Siebenmann, Gustav. "Spanien im Verhör." Neue Zürcher Zeitung (19 April), Sec. 3, p. 1.

Unfavorable review of the German translation of PS complaining about W's method of interviewing, his ignorance of Spanish, his lack of a sense of history, and his emphasis on sex. But Siebenmann is pleased by W's avowal of his own confusion and by the dramatic quality of his encounter with an alien culture.

135a. Söderberg, Lasse. "Möte med Richard Wright." Folket i Bild (18 September), pp. 4-5.

Report of a meeting with W in his Paris apartment including a sampling of W's comments on the difference between the American North and South, the nature of the color problem as seen in Algeria, and the relationship between politics and self-realization.

136. T.[hompson], C.[harles] H. "Wright, Richard," in The World Book Encyclopedia. Ed. J. Morris Jones. Vol. 18. Chicago: Field Enterprises, p. 8933.
Reprint of 1947.292.

136a. Ueda, Kazuko. "An Essay on R. Wright's The Outsider." Jissen Bungaku [Jissen Literature], 8 (30 October), 61-70.
Although W strives for objectivity in O, Cross Damon turns out to be neither a genuine outsider nor a man with an objective vision of himself. Unlike Meursault in Camus' Stranger, Damon is not free of fear. [Y. H. and T. K.]

137. W., E. "The Long Dream--Richard Wright." The Auburn (N. Y.) Citizen-Advertiser (24 January), p. 4.
Favorable review consisting mostly of plot summary. As good as NS, LD shows that W is "a superb writer with a remarkable descriptive power and enviable command of English." Also comments favorably on W's expatriation.

138. W., G. "Richard Wright: Heidnisches Spanien." Kirchenblatt für die reformierte Schweiz, 115 (19 February), 62.
Mixed review of the German translation of PS. The thesis of the book is not convincing, and W must be approached cautiously because of his cultural and religious bias. But he is a close observer and should be read. His insights concerning Spanish Protestants are particularly revealing.

139. Winchell, Walter. "Walter Winchell of New York." New York Mirror (20 March), p. 10.
Announces that Anthony Quinn and Lena Horne may be cast in the dramatic version of LD.

140. Winslow, Henry F. "Nightmare Experiences." The Crisis, 66 (February), 120-122.
Review of LD placing it in the context of W's career and central ideas. The latter are the white racist taboo on sexual contact between black men and white women and the fundamental materialism of American society. Winslow notes W's fire imagery and com-

pares the fire in the novel to the actual conflagration in the Rhythm Nite Club in Natchez in 1940.
Reprinted: 1978.209; 1982.50.

141. Wyrick, Green D. "The Long Dream, by Richard Wright." A William Allen White Library Book Review, Kansas State Teachers College, No. 110. Mimeographed.
Review praising W's emphasis on the ineluctable racial problem. Compares W to Dreiser and Dickens, but notes that he is a romantic melodramatist, not a realist like Dreiser, and a tragic Dickensian, not a comic Dickens.

142. Young, Stark. "Book Basis," in his Immortal Shadows: A Book of Dramatic Criticism. New York: Hill and Wang, pp. 204-207.
Reprint of 1941.1058.

143. Zanelli, Giannino. "Un Boccaccio danese e il 'negro' Wright." L'Osservatore politico letterario, 5 (November), 109-111.
Contains a favorable review of Bruno Fonzi's Italian translation of BB.

144. Zöller, J. O. "Bücher der Zeit." Wort und Wahrheit, 14 (February), 148.
Extremely unfavorable review of the German translation of PS complaining of W's subjectivity and impertinence. Zoller dismisses W's charge of religious persecution and objects to his obsession with sex. Although brilliantly written, the book is essentially a worthless exercise in yellow journalism.

145. Zolotow, Sam. "Broadway Debut for Lucille Ball." The New York Times (27 October), p. 41.
Notes (s. v. "Partner for Play") that Joel W. Schenker will join Cheryl Crawford in producing LD.

1960

1. A., Z. "Richard Wright: Der schwarze Traum." Basler Volksblatt (20 December).
Review of the German translation of LD. The novel continues W's battle against injustice which he has carried out not as a fiery revolutionary or a wide-eyed idealist, but as a black man who overcame his environment as shown in this final, largely autobiographical work.

2. Abrahams, Peter. "The Blacks," in An African Treasury. Ed. Langston Hughes. New York: Crown, pp. 42-55.
Reprint of 1959.1.

3. Albert, O. K. "Das andere Amerika."

Heidelberg Rhein-Neckar-Zeitung [?] (7 September).
Favorable review of the German translation of LD. W avoids distracting his readers from the attack on racism which is the novel's primary focus. Only after registering its moral point does the reader notice its artistic strength.

4. Allen, Samuel W. "Négritude and Its Relevance to the American Negro Writer," in The American Negro Writer and His Roots. New York: The American Society of African Culture, pp. 8-20.
Contains a brief mention of W (p. 14).
Reprinted: 1971.6, 7.

5. Anon. "Aber wir haben doch nichts getan." Die Hamburg Welt (13 September), p. 9.
Introductory note to an excerpt from the German translation of LD. Stresses the theme of racial hatred in the novel.

6. Anon. "Amis abonnés, lisez ceci attentivement: pour paraître le 1er mai, Les lettres nouvelles 3, Richard Wright, Fishbelly (The Long Dream), roman traduit de l'américain par Hélène Bokanowski." Les Lettres Nouvelles, 8 (March-April), 158-160.
Announces the French translation of the novel and provides a detailed plot summary.

7. Anon. "Asking for It." New York Sunday News (14 February), Sec. 2, p. 1.
Photograph of a scene from the play LD.

8. Anon. "Avec Richard Wright qui parle de 'Fishbelly.'" Paris France Observateur (9 June), p. 19.
Interview with W by his French publisher. W stresses the social meaning of LD.

9. Anon. "Brute Force." New York Journal-American (14 February), p. 24-L.
Photograph with caption of a scene from the play LD.

10. Anon. "C'était le plus grand écrivain noir U. S." Paris Libération (1 December), p. 8.
Obituary notice summing up the highlights of W's literary career. Points out that he was an expatriate because he refused to be a propagandist for American "democracy."

11. Anon. "Cheryl Crawford and Joel Schenker Present The Long Dream." The New York Times (24 January), Sec. 2, p. 2.

Large advertisement for the play.

12. Anon. "Closing." New York Post (21 February).
Lists LD as one of the plays closing.

13. Anon. "Deaths at Large: Death's Figure a Familiar Sight." The Baltimore Afro-American (31 December), p. 19.
Contains a photograph and a brief obituary of W.

14. Anon. "Le Dernier Roman de Richard Wright écrivain noir U. S. qui vient de mourir à Paris a été traduit par Mme Bokanowski femme du ministre français des P. et T." Paris France-Soir (1 December), p. 5.
Obituary stressing the hardships of W's childhood and his continuing struggle against racism.

15. Anon. "'Dream' Ends." New York Daily News (20 February), p. 21.
Announces the closing of the play LD after five performances.

16. Anon. "'Dream' Tonight." New York Daily News (17 February), p. 55.
Announces the opening of the play LD at the Ambassador Theater.

17. Anon. Dust jacket of Der schwarze Traum. By Richard Wright. Trans. Werner von Grünau. Hamburg: Classen Verlag.
Blurb on front inside flap and biographical sketch on back inside flap.

18. Anon. Dust jacket of Fishbelly. By Richard Wright. Trans. Hélène Bokanowski. Les Lettres nouvelles 3. Paris: Julliard.
Blurbs on front and back inside flaps and on the back cover.

19. Anon. Dust jacket of Pagan Spain. London: The Bodley Head.
Back cover quotes W on PS. Front inside flap contains a publisher's blurb and a quotation from V. S. Pritchett; back inside flap has favorable quotations from The Nation, New York Herald Tribune, and Figaro Littéraire.

20. Anon. Dust jacket of The Long Dream. London: Angus and Robertson.
Blurb for a "powerful story of terrible truths" on front inside flap.

21. Anon. "È morto Richard Wright." Il Rome popolo (30 November), p. 5.
Obituary-eulogy of W stressing his intellectual and moral honesty.

22. Anon. "Entretien avec Richard Wright." L'Express, No. 479 (18 August), pp. 22-23.

Interview with W on a number of topics. He discusses the growing awareness of the world of color and his own fight for a world free of racism. American racism prompted his European exile. Little progress has been made to implement school desegregation. Other signs of continuing racism are the poor reception in the United States of BP, the paternalistic attachment of whites to blacks, Dutch rule in Indonesia. W also comments on American expatriates black and white, the liking of the French for Afro-Americans, and sexual freedom in France.
Translated abridgement: 1960.23.

23. _____. "Die Farbe ist nicht mein Vaterland." Die Kultur, 9 (November), 6.
Abridged translation of 1960.22.

24. Anon. "Fiction The Long Dream Richard Wright," in Angus and Robertson Spring Books. London: Angus and Robertson, p. 14.
Publisher's advertisement commenting on the novel and on W.

25. Anon. "Harlem par Richard Wright." Les Parisiens, No. 3 (December), p. 24.
Headnote to W's article stating that it was the last thing he wrote. Sent to the magazine only twelve hours before his death, it shows his nostalgia for Harlem.

26. Anon. "Heidnisches Spanien." Berliner Rundfunk (February).
Favorable radio review of the German translation of PS. Praises W's method of interviewing people from all walks of Spanish life and the illuminating results obtained. "Richard Wright's critically enlightening mind, his brilliance, his belief in reason, his suspicion of the dark, medieval tirade of state propaganda, and his distinguished understanding of the history of the country have led him to many valuable insights into the 'secrets.'" Not a typical travel book, PS links psychological and political irrationality in Spain.

27. Anon. "Il est mort à 52 ans: 'Pour moi il est trop tard . . .'" disait Richard Wright." Paris-Presse-Intransigeant (1 December), p. 22.
Obituary quoting a remark by W a few days after the election of President Kennedy. "I won't return to the United States. For me, it's too late."

28. Anon. "In Memoriam." Présence Africaine, Nos. 34-35 (October-January), p. 247.
Obituary of W praising his aid to the magazine, to French-speaking Africans, and to liberty.

29. Anon. Index Translationum 11. Paris: Unesco, pp. 109, 235, 271, 354, 381, 417, 492.
Lists translations of PS into Flemish, Dutch, and Swedish, UTC into French and Portuguese, The God That Failed into Indonesian, NS into Norwegian, BB into Norwegian, and SH into Dutch.

30. Anon. "Lawrence Winters Paces 'Long Dream' Reading." New York Herald Tribune (4 January), p. 14.
Comments on the opening rehearsals for the play LD.

31. Anon. "Livres et auteurs pour vos vacances." L'Express (21 July), p. 26.
Contains an advertisement for Fishbelly, the French translation of LD.

32. Anon. "'The Long Dream.'" Chicago Daily News (c. 22 February).
Reports the critical response to the New York opening of the play.

33. Anon. "The Long Dream." Cue (29 February).
Mixed review of the play praising its acting, staging, and intentions, but criticizing its structure and focus, which "lend an air of unreality to the proceedings."

34. Anon. "The Long Dream." The New York Times (24 January), Sec. 2, p. 2.
Large advertisement for the opening of the play.

35. Anon. "The Long Dream by Richard Wright," in Ace Star Books (January).
Publisher's advertisement with blurb for the paperback edition.

36. Anon. "Milestones." Time, 76 (12 December), 84.
Contains an obituary stating that "Wright took the position: 'In America there is no Negro problem but a white problem. Any time the white wants to change it, it will be solved. The Negro is powerless.'"

37. Anon. "La Mort de Richard Wright." L'Express (1 December), p. 36.
Obituary stressing that the theme of W's work was always the position of blacks in American society.

38. Anon. "La Mort de Richard Wright." Le Figaro Littéraire (3 December), p. 2.
Obituary stressing W's racial themes. Living in France, he maintained a spiritual identification with his

black brothers in Mississippi.

39. Anon. "Mort de Richard Wright." Le Parisien Libéré (30 November), p. 6.
Notice of W's death explaining his medical condition.

40. Anon. "Mort de Richard Wright." L'Humanité (30 November), p. 2.
Brief notice of W's death.

41. Anon. "Mr. Richard Wright." The London Times (30 November), p. 16.
Obituary pointing out that W is best known in England for BB. Emphasizes W's early life and career through his break with the Communist Party, but mentions also PS.

42. Anon. "N. Y. Critics Report." The Philadelphia Inquirer (21 February), Sec. D, p. 4.
Quotes from seven reviews of the play LD.

43. Anon. "NAACP Mourns Death of Richard Wright." 2 December.
Typescript of NAACP press release including a message of condolence sent by Roy Wilkins to Ellen Wright.

44. Anon. "A Native Son Dies Abroad." Chicago Daily Defender (5 December), p. 14.
Editorial eulogy of W emphasizing his social criticism, sketching his life, and praising his literary achievement.

45. Anon. "New on Broadway." Newark Sunday News (14 February), p. E5.
Photograph of a scene from the play LD.

46. Anon. "New York Stage Openings." Newark Sunday News (14 February), Sec. 3, p. E1.
Announces the opening of LD.

47. Anon. "Obituary Notes." Publisher's Weekly, 178 (12 December), 31-32.
Sketches W's literary career emphasizing NS and BB (p. 32). Notes the decline in W's critical and commercial success and provides a partial list of editions of W's work currently available.

48. Anon. "The Openings." The New York Times (14 February), Sec. 2, p. 1.
Announces the opening of the play LD at the Ambassador Theater.

49. Anon. "Openings This Week." New York Journal-American (14 February), p. 26-L.
Announces the opening of the play LD.

50. Anon. "The Outsider," in The Out-sider. London: Panther Books, back cover.
Publisher's blurb for the English paperback edition with a quotation from a review in The Star.

51. Anon. "Pagan Spain. Richard Wright." New Statesman, 59 (2 April), 492.
Advertisement with a quotation from V. S. Pritchett's review.

52. Anon. "Racial Problem Plays in Rehearsal." The New York Times (24 January), Sec. 2, p. 3.
Includes a photograph with caption from LD.

53. Anon. "Red Rag to Spain." The London Times Literary Supplement (15 April), p. 243.
Favorable review of PS reviewing briefly W's career, explaining his motives for visiting Spain, and evaluating the result as "in a class by itself" among books on the country. "Mr. Wright sees modern Spain clearly, and sees it whole."

54. Anon. "Richard Wright." Bonn Vorwärts (9 December).
Obituary stressing W's polemical writing but noting that he considered himself a "man" before either an American or a black.

55. Anon. "Richard Wright." Classen Verlag (9 December).
"Eulogy-advertisement" from W's German publisher containing a biographical sketch praising W's contribution to the "self-understanding of humanity."

56. Anon. "Richard Wright." Die Hamburg Welt (1 December), p. 11.
Obituary stressing the inevitability of W's major theme of racial protest. In addition to protesting, W sought better understanding between blacks and whites.

57. Anon. "Richard Wright." New York Daily News (30 November), p. 52.
Two-paragraph Associated Press obituary.

58. Anon. "Richard Wright." The Baltimore Afro-American (10 December), p. 2.
Photograph and obituary note.

59. Anon. "Richard Wright." The Baltimore Afro-American (17 December), p. 4.
Editorial praising W, especially his role in organizing the Franco-American Fellowship.

60. Anon. "Richard Wright." Mimeographed press release (2 December).

Obituary from the NAACP.

61. Anon. "Richard Wright." Westdeutsche Bücherkritisch betrachtet (25 December).
Combined review of the German translations of BB and LD pointing out that both works attack the inconsistencies and hypocrisies of bourgeois democracy. Although LD uses many autobiographical elements from BB, it is also an "epic of the American Negro."

62. Anon. "Richard Wright, Author of Native Son, Dies." Chicago Daily Defender (30 November), p. 3.
United Press International obituary with a photograph. Discusses W's childhood and literary career. Mentions the scheduled publication of EM on 23 January 1961.

63. Anon. "Richard Wright. Der schwarze Traum." Classen Verlag.
Enthusiastic review of the German translation of LD in the publisher's catalog. W is one of the most fascinating of contemporary authors. Here he writes on a major contemporary social problem.

64. Anon. "Richard Wright: Der schwarze Traum." Der O. T. V. Vertrauensmann (December).
Review of the German translation of LD. Although some will find it too one-sided, many will find it exciting and will admit its topical impact.

65. Anon. "Richard Wright: 'Der schwarze Traum.'" Der Spiegel, 14 (28 September), 82.
Notice of the German translation of LD summarizing the plot and emphasizing the theme of racial conflict.

66. Anon. "Richard Wright: Der schwarze Traum." Die Kultur, 9 (November), 12.
Favorable notice of the German translation of LD consisting mainly of plot summary. W does not solve the racial problem, but he exposes its roots. The novel is brilliant and tense.

67. Anon. "Richard Wright: Der schwarze Traum." Die Quelle, 11 (December), 553.
Favorable review of the German translation of LD. Emphasizes the work's racial protest, expressing the hope that W's outcry will be heard in America. Praises W's literary skill, especially his avoidance of stereotypes.

68. Anon. "Richard Wright: Der schwarze Traum." Mainz Freiheit (15 December), p.

13.
Review of the German translation of LD. A well-conceived, well-written fable, the novel is mainly a work of social criticism.

69. Anon. "Richard Wright: Der schwarze Traum." Offenbach-Post (3 December).
Favorable notice of the German translation of LD emphasizing the book's narrative power.

70. Anon. "Richard Wright: Der schwarze Traum." Wiener Börsen-Kurier (29 October).
Favorable notice of the German translation of LD stressing W's dynamic style and narrative.

71. Anon. "Richard Wright Dies in Paris; American Negro Author, 52." New York Herald Tribune, European Edition (30 November), p. 3.
Obituary reviewing W's life and career. NS "established him as one of the foremost American contemporary authors."

72. Anon. "Richard Wright écrivain solitaire." Paris Combat (4 December), p. 9.
Obituary with a favorable assessment of W's literary career, especially in its concern with the suffering of American blacks. Includes a photograph of W.

73. Anon. "Richard Wright El Sueño Largo." Editorial Sudamericana, p. 3.
Publisher's advertisement for the Spanish translation of LD.

74. Anon. "Richard Wright ¡Escucha, Hombre Blanco!" Editorial Sudamericana S. A. Boletin (February), p. 1.
Publisher's announcement of the Spanish translation of WML.

75. Anon. "Richard Wright est mort." La Paris Croix (1 December), p. 6.
Obituary emphasizing W's struggle for the independence of colonized peoples everywhere and his resolve never to return to the United States to live.

76. Anon. "Richard Wright est mort." Paris Jour (1 December).
Brief obituary mentioning the influence of Sartre and Simone de Beauvoir.

77. Anon. "Richard Wright Fishbelly."
Flyer advertising the French translation of LD and containing a note on W. Points out that the black bourgeoisie is a new subject for the author.

78. Anon. "Richard Wright Fishbelly."

Bulletin Julliard (July), p. 2.
Advertisement for the French translation of LD.

79. Anon. "Richard Wright Fishbelly."
L'Edition chez Julliard, No. 111 (May),
p. 3.
Advertisement for the French translation of LD claiming that W is a
"philosopher and a humorist" as well
as a novelist.

80. Anon. "Richard Wright gestorben."
Frankfürter Rundschau (1 December), p.
1.
Brief notice of W's death.

81. Anon. "Richard Wright Is Dead,
Author of 'Native Son.'" New York Herald
Tribune (30 November), p. 23.
Obituary stating that "Mr. Wright had
joined the Communist Party in 1934."
Mentions several of W's works.

82. Anon. "Richard Wright n'est plus."
Le Paris Figaro (30 November), p. 17.
Obituary emphasizing his exile in
France. He appealed to the conscien-
ces of both blacks and whites.

83. Anon. "Richard Wright. Pagan Spain."
New Statesman, 59 (7 May), 684.
Advertisement with a quotation from
the Times Literary Supplement. "The
quality of the writing" is "in a
class by itself."

84. Anon. "Richard Wright Will Be Buried
in France." New York Amsterdam News (3
December), p. 9.
Obituary recounting W's life and
praising him as literary genius and
racial spokesman.

85. Anon. "Richard Wright, Writer, 52,
Dies." The New York Times (30 November),
p. 37.
Obituary noting that while all W's
works were reviewed with "respect,"
he was unable to match the critical
or commercial success of NS and BB.
Reprinted: 1982.50.

86. Anon. "Says Whites' Guilt Complex
Folds 2 Plays." Jet, 17 (10 March), 59.
Producer Joel Schenker makes the
point about LD and The Cool World.

87. Anon. "Schwarz und Weiss." Basel
National-Zeitung (13 November), pp. 5-6.
Headnote to an excerpt from the German translation of LD. Praises the
book as one of a very few which are
equally powerful on social and aesthetic grounds.

88. Anon. "Die schwarze Haut." Das grüne
Blatt (23 December).
Notice of the German translation of
LD praising W for avoiding self-pity
and for contributing to our under-
standing of racial problems.

89. Anon. "Der schwarze Traum." Twen,
No. 9 (September).
Notice of the German translation of
LD claiming that "world opinion is
demanding a Nobel Prize" for W.

90. Anon. "This Week's Openings." Newark
Sunday News (14 February).
Announcement of the play LD.

91. Anon. "Tonight's Premiere on Broadway." New York Herald Tribune (17 February), p. 18.
Announces the opening of the play LD
at the Ambassador Theater.

92. Anon. "Transition." Newsweek, 56 (12
December), 86.
Obituary stating that W wrote "real-
istically harsh novels" because he
was "embittered by his own life."

93. Anon. Untitled article. Paris Combat
(30 November), p. 3.
Brief note on W's death.

94. Anon. Untitled clipping. Bulletin on
German Questions (1 March).
Favorable review in English of the
German translation of PS stressing
W's nonconformist point of view. The
book "contains thousands of beau-
ties."

95. Anon. Untitled clipping. Chicago
Daily News [?].
Unfavorable review of the play LD.
Although engrossing for some members
of the audience, it caused critic
John Chapman to walk out. The adapta-
tion from the novel is poorly done.

96. Anon. Untitled clipping. L'Express,
No. 456 (10 March), p. 28.
Contains an announcement of the
French translation of LD.

97. Anon. Untitled clipping. Der Leih-
buchhandler (October).
Favorable review of the German translation of LD. W's personal experience, easily discernible in this
novel, makes him an unparalleled
interpreter of black-white tensions.

98. Anon. Untitled radio broadcast
script. Berliner Welle (25 December).
Review of the German translation of
LD containing also discussion of BB.

99. Anon. "Warten auf hohe Auflagen."
Saarbrucker Zeitung (24 September), p.
[35].

Mentions the success of Werner von Grünau's translation of LD.

100. Anon. "Warum musste er im Dunkel leben?" Der Berlin Kurier (1 December). Review of the German translation of LD with extracts.

101. Anon. "West Africa." Die neue Bund (January), p. 13.
Notice of the German translation of BP summarizing its contents.

102. Anon. "What's New." New York Journal-American (17 February), p. 18.
Announces the opening of LD at the Ambassador Theater.

103. Anon. "World Mourns Death of Richard Wright." Jet, 19 (15 December), 18-19.
Obituary with a biographical sketch. W is most memorable as a racial spokesman. His expatriation was both necessary and detrimental to his literary development. Nothing in his later career matched the value of NS and BB.

104. Anon. "Wright," in Piccola enciclopedia Mondadori. Ed. Doro Rosetti. Vol. 2. Verona: Arnoldo Mondadori Editore, p. 1378.
Very brief biographical note.

105. Anon. "Wright, Riccardo," in Enciclopedia Tumminelli. Sixth edition. Vol. 2. Rome: Tumminelli, p. 2381.
Reprint of 1956.87.

106. Anon. "Wright, Richard," in Gyldendals Opslagsbog. Ed. A. P. Hansen and Anders Svarre. Vol. 4. Copenhagen: Gyldendal, p. 538.
Biographical note.

107. Anon. "Wright, Richard," in The Columbia-Viking Desk Encyclopedia. Ed. William Bridgwater. Second edition. New York: Viking, p. 1120.
Reprint of 1953.64.

108. Anon. "Wright, Richard. Eight Men." Bulletin from Virginia Kirkus' Service, 28 (1 November), 973.
Favorable review calling the work "haunting . . . powerful and disturbing." Notes the basic situation in each of the eight pieces.

109. Aschauer, Josef. "Wright, Richard: Der schwarze Traum." Die Zeit in Buch (Spring).
Favorable notice of the German translation of LD emphasizing its autobiographical content.

110. Aston, Frank. "'Long Dream' Opens at the Ambassador." New York World-Telegram and The Sun (18 February), p. 18.
Mixed review with a plot summary of the Ketti Frings adaptation. "The subject is overwhelming. The dramatics are uneven. The writing is lucid. The acting and directing couldn't be better." All in all, the work "is engrossing, but not as theatrical as it might be."

111. Atkinson, Brooks. "Theatre: Ketti Frings' 'Long Dream.'" The New York Times (18 February), p. 36.
Unfavorable review of the play. Although W "has a hard mind and a taut style," the adaptation of the novel "is heavy . . . seldom comes alive." The play has good acting and sets, but the script and the direction are unsatisfactory.

112. Baldwin, James and Marisa Bulgheroni. "Incontro con James Baldwin," in Il nuovo romanzo americano 1945-1959. By Marisa Bulgheroni. Milan: Schwarz editore, pp. 243-250.
Baldwin acknowledges his debt to W (p. 245).

113. Banks, Richard. "Mystique." New York Herald Tribune (c. 6 September).
Letter to the editor praising W's description of bull fighting and mentioning W's visit to the statue of the black Virgin.

114. Baumier, Jean. "Richard Wright: Fishbelly." Europe, No. 377 (September), 150-151.
Generally favorable review of the French translation of LD. W exaggerates the bleakness of his subject, however.

115. Beaufort, John. "On and Off Broadway: Drama Desk Debates Negro's Story." The Christian Science Monitor (29 February), p. 9.
Discussion of the prospects for plays about blacks. Beaufort thinks that LD failed for dramatic reasons, not because of its unpopular theme.

116. B.[eer], J.[ohannes]. "Wright, Richard Nathaniel," in his Der Romanführer. Vol. 11. Stuttgart: Anton Hiersemann, pp. 367-368.
Summarizes the five stories of UTC.

117. Bell, Daniel. The End of Ideology. Glencoe, Ill.: The Free Press, p. 287.
Mentions W briefly.

118. Benét, Stephen Vincent. Selected Letters of Stephen Vincent Benét. Ed. Charles A. Fenton. New Haven: Yale Uni-

versity Press, pp. 340-341.
    In a letter to Edward Weeks dated 10
    January 1940, Benét praises W: "He
    has lots of stuff."

119. Bl.[air], W.[alter]. "American
Literature," in Encyclopaedia Britan-
nica. Ed. Walter Yust. Vol. 1. Chicago:
Encyclopaedia Britannica, pp. 784-794.
    Reprint of 1954.80.

120. Borel, Jacques. "Un Noir face à
l'Europe." Les Beaux-Arts, No. 888 (11
March).
    Favorable review of the French trans-
    lation of WML. Borel stresses his
    agreement with W's point that Western
    aid to Africa and Asia should be
    given fraternally, not paternalis-
    tically. W is a better novelist than
    polemicist, but WML is an important
    book.

121. Bosschère, Guy de. "Fishbelly, de
Richard Wright." Synthèses, No. 174
(November), pp. 63-66.
    Reprint of 1960.122 with a preamble
    on the racial question.

122. _____. "Fishbelly, par Richard
Wright." Présence Africaine, No. 31
(April-May), pp. 125-127.
    Favorable review of the French trans-
    lation of LD with a plot summary and
    an analysis of the themes of fear and
    dreaming. Explains the compromise
    achieved by Tyree Tucker and its
    psychic cost. W's style and power are
    admirable.
    Reprinted: 1960.121.

123. Braem, Helmut M. "Fern von Onkel
Toms Hütte." Stuttgarter Zeitung (7
December), Literaturblatt Sec., p. [2].
    Unfavorable review of the German
    translation of LD. The book is an
    effort to justify the author's expat-
    riation, but it seems also an attack
    on human dignity itself. W reveals
    the tragically divided consciousness
    of the Afro-American, but the novel
    subordinates artistry to agitation.
    Broadcast by radio: 1961.128.

124. _____. "Zwischen Schwarz und
Weiss." Cologne Deutsche Zeitung (1
December).
    Obituary praising W as an author who
    expressed the truth without resent-
    ment and hate in a body of work cen-
    tered on the "tragedy of his race."

125. Brièrre, Annie. "L'Amérique n'est
pas conformiste, elle se renouvelle sans
cesse." France-U.S.A., Nos. 141-142
(September-October), p. 2.
    Discusses LD and O. The latter is
    Dostoevskian. Quotes W as saying that

he did not intend O to be specifically existentialist, but to reflect his wider philosophy. W believes that human creativity will
triumph over technology, prefers
Dreiser to most other American novelists, and considers Freud and Marx as
poets.

126. Bryer, Jackson R. "Richard Wright
(1908-1960): A Selected Checklist of
Criticism." Wisconsin Studies in Contemporary Literature, 1 (Fall), 22-33.
    Lists 192 reviews without annotation
    and 82 annotated items.

127. Bulgheroni, Marisa. Il nuovo romanzo americano 1945-1959. Milan: Schwarze
editore, pp. 26, 47, 111-114, 117, 119,
122, 126, 131, 145, 234, 245, 256.
    Discusses W as a protest novelist
    (especially in NS) and indicates his
    influence on the "scuola di Wright"
    (pp. 111-114). Notes W's relation to
    Baldwin (pp. 114, 126, 245) and Elli-
    son (pp. 119, 134). Mentions W brief-
    ly elsewhere.

128. Byam, Milton S. "Wright, Richard.
Eight Men." Library Journal, 85 (1
December), 4394.
    Favorable review, but Byam finds the
    collection old-fashioned. The best
    pieces are "The Man Who Lived Under-
    ground" and "Man, God Ain't Like That
    . . . ." The range in time and tone
    is remarkable in this collection.
    Although it shows W at his best, it
    presents a slightly distorted version
    of American blacks at present.

129. Carr, Raymond. "See Those Bull-
fights." The London Observer (20 March),
p. 20.
    Mixed review of PS praising it for
    "the power of fresh observation, the
    brightness of immediacy," and for its
    treatment of Spanish urban life. But
    W's combination of "outraged liberal-
    ism and sex-blood-bulls-and-death
    school" leads to distortion, espec-
    ially compared to books on Spain by
    British writers.

130. Cayton, Horace. "World at Large."
The Pittsburgh Courier (17 December), p.
8.
    Cayton recalls his friendship with W,
    mentioning W's concern over the im-
    pact of NS, his break with the Commu-
    nists, his plans for literary pro-
    jects with Cayton. "To me he was a
    great American writer and a Negro who
    refused to accept subordination with-
    out fighting back."

131. Chapman, John. "1st Act of 'Long
Dream' Shoddy and Lascivious." New York

Daily News (18 February), p. 66.
Extremely unfavorable review of the first act of the play, after which the reviewer left the theater. Chapman complains of bad taste, sexual explicitness, and harsh depiction of race relations.

132. Cimatti, Pietro. "In morte dello scrittore americano Richard Wright." La fiera letteraria (11 December), pp. 1-2.
Evaluation of W's career emphasizing his radicalism and racial protest. With Erskine Caldwell, he was one of the chief spokesmen of American naturalism of the Depression. Discusses briefly NS, BB, and BP.

133. Clark, Edward. "Images of the Negro in the American Novel." Jahrbuch für Amerikastudien, 5, pp. 175-184.
Treats NS briefly.

134. Clarke, John Henrik. "Transition in the American Negro Short Story." Phylon, 21 (Fourth Quarter), 360-366.
Contains a brief discussion of W as a craftsman in the short story, the best since Chesnutt.
Partially reprinted: 1966.36.

135. Coleman, Robert. "'Long Dream' Sketchy, Rough." New York Mirror (18 February), p. 24.
Mixed review of the play praising the production and acting, but complaining that the Ketti Frings script is weak, with obvious effects and stereotyped characters. The theme is important, but its dramatic expression is not.

136. ____. "Theatre News and Views: Kit Cornell to Star in Play on Shaw." New York Mirror (15 February), pp. 24-25.
Mentions the opening of the play LD.

137. Cooke, Richard P. "The Theater: Mississippi Tragedy." The Wall Street Journal (19 February), p. 12.
Unfavorable review of the play LD. Ketti Frings presents a strong theme with sincerity, but with too much melodrama and sentimentality. LD is a less effective play than Raisin in the Sun.

138. Cotton, Lettie Jo. "The Negro in the American Theatre." The Negro History Bulletin, 23 (May), 172-178.
Contains a brief discussion of the play NS as a work of social protest (p. 174).

139. Crist, Judith. "Ketti Frings Crosses Fingers on New Play." New York Herald Tribune (14 February), Sec. 4,
pp. 1, 3.
Article-interview including comments by Frings on the adaptation of LD from novel to play. The center of dramatic interest is Tyree Tucker. Quotes from a letter by W to the play's producers expressing his great satisfaction with the script.

140. Davis, Arthur P. "Integration and Race Literature," in The American Negro Writer and His Roots. New York: The American Society of African Culture, pp. 34-40.
Reprint of 1956.137.

141. Douglass, Joseph H. "Negro," in The World Book Encyclopedia. Ed. J. Morris Jones. Vol. 13. Chicago: Field Enterprises, pp. 106-112.
Reprint of 1959.78.

142. Dusenbury, Winifred L. The Theme of Loneliness in Modern American Drama. Gainesville: University of Florida Press, p. 113.
Mentions NS as a protest play.

143. Edes, Mary Elizabeth. "Fiction Forecast." Publisher's Weekly, 178 (5 December), 40.
Contains a favorable prepublication notice of EM stressing the theme of racial conflict. Some of the plots are too fantastic, however.

144. Ellison, Ralph and Marisa Bulgheroni. "Incontro con Ralph Ellison," in Il nuovo romanzo americano 1945-1959. By Marisa Bulgheroni. Milan: Schwarz editore, pp. 231-241.
Ellison mentions W's encouragement early in his literary career.

145. Farnsworth, T. A. "The Negro in American Literature." Contrast, 1 (Summer), 61-63.
Prefers Faulkner's treatment of the racial theme to that of W, Ellison, or Baldwin because "at present the Negro writer is too personally involved in the issues to think of himself as a writer rather than as a Negro" (p. 63).

146. Fenton, Charles. "The Last Years of Twentieth-Century American Literature." South Atlantic Quarterly, 59 (Summer), 332-338.
Not well suited to study by modern critical methods, W nevertheless needs to be studied.

147. Fiedler, Leslie A. Love and Death in the American Novel. New York: Criterion Books, p. 470.
Compares Invisible Man favorably to "the passionate, incoherent books of

Richard Wright," who relied on realism and on "formulas of protest and self-pity."
Reprinted: 1966.54; 1967.39.

148. F.[ranklin], J.[ohn] H.[ope] and R.[ayford] W.[hittingham] L.[ogan]. "Negro, American," in Encyclopaedia Britannica. Ed. Walter Yust. Vol. 16. Chicago: Encyclopaedia Britannica, pp. 194-201.
Reprint of 1957.184.

149. Frayn, Michael. "Ends of the Earth." The Spectator, 204 (22 April), 587-588.
Review of PS and four other travel books. Frayn thinks that "Wright has remained so much an outsider . . . that his indictment has the flat unreality of a bad Left-wing novel," but his use of the Falangist catechism and the description of the bullfight receive praise.

150. Frisé, Adolf. "Abschied von Amerikas schwarzen Sänger." Der Berlin Tagesspiegel (11 December), p. 37.
Favorable review of the German translation of LD. Surveying W's entire career, Frisé finds the central theme to be racial relations. W's view of racial reality is more relevant to present issues than Ellison's or Faulkner's, and it is expressed with great and probing power.
Reprinted: 1960.151; 1961.150.

151. _____. "Ein schwarzer Traum." St. Galler Tagblatt (28 December), pp. 2-3, 5.
Reprint of 1960.150.

152. Funke, Lewis. "News and Gossip of the Rialto." The New York Times (14 February), Sec. 2, p. 1.
Includes comment on the musical talent in the stage version of LD. A photograph of a scene from the play also appears on this page.

153. _____. "News and Gossip Gathered at the Rialto." The New York Times (21 February), Sec. 2, p. 1.
Note, s. v. "Scoreboard," on the unfavorable critical reception of the play LD. Only Richard Watts praised it highly.

154. Misdated duplicate item deleted here. See 1961.154.

155. Galen Last, H. van. "Bij de Dood

van Richard Wright." Het Parool (3 December), p. 6.
Eulogy emphasizing W's interest in the Third World. Mentions his friendship with Gunnar Myrdal and his lukewarm feelings toward Baldwin and Ellison.

156. Garland, Phyl. "Skill and Maturity Mark Negro Writer of Today." The Pittsburgh Courier (17 September), Sec. 3, p. 4.
Contains a paragraph on W and NS. "If one were to name the three or four greatest Negro writers up to the present, Richard would have to be one of them by virtue of this book." A photograph of W accompanies the article.

157. Gaver, Jack. "Two New Plays are Disappointing." Wichita Daily Beacon (6 March), p. 2D.
Contains an unfavorable review of LD, "a racial melodrama that has nothing new to say in this line and says what it does in a rather routine way." The direction is weak, but some of the acting is good.

158. Gérard, Albert. "Négritude et humanité chez Richard Wright." La Revue Nouvelle, 32 (15 October), 337-343.
Deals with W's important novels, especially O. Gerard argues that W's concerns transcended race. They focused on the larger dilemma of modern man facing his existential condition in a void without traditional values.

159. Glicksberg, Charles I. Literature and Religion: A Study in Conflict. Dallas: Southern Methodist University Press, pp. 190-191.
Reprint of 1958.137.

160. H., H. "Flucht aus dem Getto." Düsseldorf Deutsche Volkszeitung (16 December).
Review of the German translation of LD. Discusses W's expatriation in relation to the theme of the novel. Praises W's continuing commitment to racial justice.

161. H., W. "Richard Wright: Der schwarze Traum." Neues Winterthürer Tagblatt (21 November).
Favorable review of the German translation of LD. Beginning with an outline of W's biography which is recapitulated in the novel, the reviewer comments on the careful dramatic and dialectical structuring of the book and attempts to define the symbolic meanings W attaches to "black" and "white."

161a. Hamamoto, Takeo. "Asia and the Two Writers: Richard Wright and Yoshie Hotta." Sekai Bungaku [World Literature], 22, pp. 48-56.
Although both Asians and black Americans are colored peoples, Asians are separated from white culture by Eastern religions whereas black Americans must adhere to European civilization. [Y. H. and T. K.]

162. Hampaté-Ba, A.[madou]. "Richard Wright, mon frère." Democratie 60, No. 59 (8 December), p. 26.
Obituary emphasizing W's universal appeal and his commitment to the struggle for African independence. "Your death makes human culture poorer. Black Africa recognizes you and claims you back." Reprinted: 1961.167.

163. Hampton, Chester. "He Fought a Bitter Battle with Words." Washington Afro-American (10 December), p. 5.
Obituary article tracing W's career from Mississippi to Paris and praising his early books. Includes four photographs.

164. Häusermann, H. W. "'Der schwarze Traum': Der letze Roman von Richard Wright." Neue Zürcher Zeitung (7 December), pp. 19-20.
Favorable review of the German translation of LD. After a brief survey of W's career, Häusermann identifies the central theme of the novel as racism, particularly as it inculcates fear and distorts the sexual impulse. W's treatment of the theme is not propagandistic but artistic, especially in its psychological insights and its use of symbols.

165. Hetwig, Werner. "Afrikanische Unerschöpflichkeit." Merkur, 14, pp. 91-94.
Survey of books on Africa mentioning briefly W's pervasive skepticism in BP.

166. Hutchens, John K. "The Great Old Day of the Little Magazines Is Back." San Francisco Chronicle (24 July), This World Sec., p. 22.
Lists W as a writer who got his start in little magazines.

167. Isaacs, Harold R. "Five Writers and Their African Ancestors." Phylon, 21 (Third Quarter), 243-265; (Fourth Quarter), 317-336.
Discusses W's treatment of Africa in BP, CC, and WML (pp. 254-265). Reprinted: 1963.116; 1970.189.

167a. Ishida, Yuriko. "Richard Wright's White Man, Listen!" Kokujin Kenkyu

[Negro Studies], 12 (May), 14-15.
WML is a psychological analysis of the Asian and African elite, who are attempting to blend European culture into their lives under white rule. [Y. H. and T. K.]

168. J., G. "Richard Wright: Heidnisches Spanien." Buch und Volk (December).
Notice of the German translation of PS stressing that it is more than a travel book.

169. Jackson, Blyden. "The Negro's Image of the Universe as Reflected in His Fiction." CLA Journal, 4 (September), 22-31.
Compares NS and Invisible Man to illustrate Jackson's view that black fiction divides the world between the ghetto and the outside. At the end of NS, Bigger's world has not really expanded. Reprinted: 1965.82; 1968.130; 1972.102.

170. Jahn, Janheinz. "Richard Wright: Tragiker zwischen Schwarz und Weiss." Christ und Welt (8 December), p. 4.
Obituary emphasizing W's lifelong struggle against injustice in several of its forms. Despite his global perspective, he was quintessentially American, however much rejected by white racism. His fiction develops the theme of suffering from the viewpoint of the sufferer.

171. James, Stuart. "Race Relations in Literature and Sociology." Dissertation Abstracts, 21 (December), 1565.
Abstracts a 1960 University of Washington dissertation treating in Chapter I black characters in works by W, Welty, and Faulkner.

172. Johnson, Charles S. "Negro in America," in The Encyclopedia Americana. Ed. Lavinia P. Dudley. Vol. 20. New York: Americana Corporation, pp. 65-77.
Reprint of 1955.54.

173. Juin, Hubert. "'Fishbelly' un grand roman." Les Lettres Françaises (2-8 June), p. 3.
Favorable descriptive review of the French translation of LD. Juin emphasizes the book's treatment of racism.

174. J.[ulien], C.[laude]. "Richard Wright." Paris France Observateur (1 December), p. 18.
Obituary-editorial noting the irony of W's exile. In contrast to the rising hope of the civil rights movement in the United States, W was more violently bitter in LD than in his earlier works.

175. _____. "Richard Wright est mort."
Le Paris Monde (1 December), p. 6.
Obituary-eulogy commenting on the
irony of W's death at a time when
blacks are just beginning to liberate
themselves. Although he attained personal fame, W was never satisfied
with the political effect of his
writings.

176. Kerr, Walter. "Authors Hurt in
Debris of Fast-Folding Flops." New York
Herald Tribune (27 March), Sec. 4, pp.
1, 4.
Laments the practice of closing plays
prematurely, citing LD as an
example.

177. _____. "First Night Report: 'The
Long Dream.'" New York Herald Tribune
(18 February), p. 14.
Mixed review of the play praising the
honest presentation of the Tucker
family. The acting is good, especially that of Lawrence Winters as
Tyree. But the white characters are
too brutal and venal to be credible.
In sum: "A valid theme, and much
accuracy; but without the intimacy of
deep personal involvement."

178. Kessel, Patrick. "Romans: 'Fishbelly' de Richard Wright." Paris France
Observateur (9 June), p. 18.
Generally favorable review of the
French translation of LD consisting
mostly of summary. W's view of race
relations is somewhat anachronistic,
but the narrative is exciting and
fascinating.

179. Killens, John O. "Opportunities for
Development of Negro Talent," in The
American Negro Writer and His Roots. New
York: The American Society of African
Culture, pp. 64-70.
Claims that W overemphasized tragic
dehumanization in his portraiture of
black people.

180. Kl., St. "Richard Wright: Der
schwarze Traum." Vienna Informationer
für Alle (13 December).
Favorable review of the German translation of LD. Despite the novel's
portrayal of harsh racial oppression,
W in no way incites racial hatred.
Rather he appeals for better actions
from both sides.

181. Las Vergas, Raymond. "Images en
noir et blanc." Les Nouvelles Littéraires (26 May), p. 2.
Favorable review of the French translation of LD with a lengthy plot
summary and an analysis of Fishbelly's moral and psychological
drama. Includes an account of W's

literary evolution.

182. Lennig, Walter. "Irgendwo im Staate
Mississippi." Westermanns Monatshefte,
101 (December), 96, 98.
Favorable review of the German translation of LD endorsing W's credentials as a commentator on the American racial situation and as a novelist. Both the defender and the critic of black Americans, W reveals
their almost incomprehensible problems in the South.

183. Lennon, Peter. "One of Uncle Tom's
Children." The Guardian (8 December), p.
8.
Interview with W conducted in Paris
commenting on his self-education (including the reading of Joseph Conrad), his role as a writer, and his
views on political and racial matters. Includes a photograph.

184. Lenz, Siegfried. "Der schwarze
Traum." Baden Südwestfunk (10 October).
Radio review of the German translation of LD. After emphasizing the
subjectivity of PS, Lenz reviews the
novel as a desperate plea for the
oppressed. Black dreams are doomed to
frustration. But Fishbelly and Tyree
are corrupt, not noble.
Reprinted: 1960.185.

185. _____. Untitled transcript. Kultur
wort Red. Asche (10 October).
Reprint of 1960.184.

186. Lewis, Emory. "The Theatre: Lawrence Winters Offers Memorable Portrayal." Cue (29 February).
Mixed review of the play LD. The
adaptation from the novel is weak and
unrealistic, but the play represents
new trends in American theatre and is
revealing in its presentation of
segregation.

187. Lissner, Erich. "Dem Kämpfer für de
Black Boys." Frankfurter Rundschau (1
December), p. 9.
Obituary outlining W's career and
emphasizing his struggle for equality
for blacks and his notion that race
was an "accident." Lissner, an
acquaintance, also stresses W's personal warmth.

188. Little, Stuart W. "Producer Holds
Dim View for Future of Negro Play." New
York Herald Tribune (25 February), p.
12.
Argues that the early closing of LD
and The Cool World will discourage
producers from presenting plays on
racial themes.

189. _____. "Theater News: Drama Desk to Discuss Negro's Role." New York Herald Tribune (15 February), p. 10.
Mentions LD.

190. Locke, Alain. "Some Outstanding American Negroes," in The Book of Knowledge. Ed. Lowell A. Martin. Vol. 12. New York: The Grolier Society, pp. 4427-4433.
Reprint of 1952.51.

191. Lomax, Louis E. The Reluctant African. New York: Harper, pp. 15-16.
Recounts a conversation about Africa with W, who resented the snobbishness of Africans toward Afro-Americans. W tells of being asked to serve as an intermediary between an African leader and a businessman, but refusing. He also speaks of the "dependency mentality" of Africans.

192. Lyons, Leonard. "The Lyons Den." New York Post (1 December), p. 33.
Mentions W's death and recounts discrimination against him in a Washington restaurant.

193. Mannes, Marya. "The Dark Side of the Street." The Reporter, 22 (17 March), 38-39.
Includes an analysis of the play LD. It fails because the protagonists are so unattractive that the audience cannot pity them. Lawrence Winters gives a good performance in the role of Tyree, a corrupt, shoddy man.

194. Marja, A. "Lezend en Luisterend Links en Recht." De Nieuwe Stem, 15 (May), 326-335.
Reprint of 1960.195.

195. _____. "Richard Wright slaapt niet." Friese Koerier (5 March).
Highly favorable review of the Dutch translation of LD, considered the best of W's novels. Though not "political," it is committed to the struggle against racial injustice, the most serious problem of the twentieth century. W is uncompromising and objective in revealing the degradation of black life.
Reprinted: 1960.194.

196. McClain, John. "'The Long Dream': Shades of Corruption Fail to Become Clear." New York Journal-American (18 February), p. 20.
Unfavorable review of the play, which reveals man's moral nature regardless of race or society. Despite good acting, the play fails.

197. McDowell, Louise and Helen Merrick. "American Literature: Twentieth Century," in The Book of Knowledge. Ed. Lowell A. Martin. Vol. 14. The Grolier Society, pp. 4997-5025.
Reprint of 1952.1.

198. McKechnie, Logan. "Real People Emerge from Short Stories." Amarillo Sunday News-Globe (18 December), p. 15.
Favorable review of EM emphasizing the variety of setting, mood, characterization, and treatment in the stories. Without being "'racial problem' stories, they provide considerable food for thought on one of the most important problems in the world today."

199. Menck, Clara. "Verirrt in einem Ghetto." Frankfurter Allgemeine Zeitung für Deutschland (22 November), Literaturblatt Sec., p. 4.
Favorable review of the German translation of LD comparing it to Uncle Tom's Cabin and Invisible Man. The novel depicts with cold objectivity the degradation ghetto life imposes on both blacks and whites.

200. Moget, M.[arie] Th.[erese]. "Richard Wright: 'Fishbelly.'" La Nouvelle Critique, No. 119 (October), pp. 143-145.
Favorable review of the French translation of LD noting the lack of social opportunities for American blacks.

201. Moon, Henry Lee. "Spingarn Medal," in The World Book Encyclopedia. Ed. J. Morris Jones. Vol. 16. Chicago: Field Enterprises, p. 617.
Lists W as a winner.
Reprinted: 1961.212; 1962.88; 1963.143; 1964.97; 1965.102; 1975.135; 1977.235; 1978.174.

202. Moore, Geoffrey. "Amerikanische Literatur," in Lexikon der Weltliteratur. Vol. 1. Freiburg: Herder, pp. 30-54.
Mentions W briefly (p. 39).

203. Murdock, Henry T. "'The Long Dream' at Walnut: Race Violence Study Explodes Into Fierce and Bitter Melodrama." The Philadelphia Inquirer (2 February), p. 14.
Favorable review of the premiere of Ketti Frings's stage version of LD praising the tenseness of the scenes and the performances of the actors. Murdock notes the shift in emphasis in the play from Fishbelly to his father.

204. Nadeau, Maurice. "Portrait: La Vérité de Richard Wright." L'Express (8 December), pp. 47-48.

Eulogy emphasizing W's service in substituting truthful for transitional images of race relations. His interest in Africa and Asia was inspired by the same impulses behind his earlier works and shared their sense of urgency. Nadeau recalls his first meeting with W, explains the importance of Marxism to the writer, and comments on UTC and NS.

205. _____. "Richard Wright s'explique sur son oeuvre et sur 'The Long Dream.'" Les Lettres Nouvelles, 8 (April), 9-15.
Interview with W, who discusses American political pressures on Afro-American literature and his intentions in LD. Nadeau provides a prefatory note on W's career.

206. Niemeyer, Carl. "Wright, Richard," in The World Book Encyclopedia. Ed. J. Morris Jones. Vol. 19. Chicago: Field Enterprises, p. 420.
Biographical sketch.
Reprinted: 1961.218; 1962.91; 1963. 149; 1964.99; 1965.106.

206a. Nyland, Waino S. "Biography," in Good Reading. Ed. J. Sherwood Weber. New York: R. R. Bowker, pp. 157-162.
Reprint of 1952.55a and revised reprint of 1946.282.

207. Nyren, Dorothy, ed. A Library of Literary Criticism: Modern American Literature. New York: Frederick Ungar, pp. 550-552.
Contains excerpts on W from 1938.164, 181; 1940.583, 784; 1948.170; 1951. 233; 1953.176; 1956.124; 1958.146.

208. O., H. "Richard Wright." Bremer Nachrichten (19 November).
Favorable review of the German translation of LD. A powerful expression of the hatred of the black world for the white, it adds a new dimension to discussions of racial problems. It portrays the necessity of repressing one's racial awareness in order to succeed, as does Tyree Tucker, and it demonstrates the tragic result.

209. Ohff, Heinz. "Die Sorge der Schwarzen." Die Bücher-Kommentare, 9 (15 September), 9.
Favorable review of the German translation of LD. Though complaining that too many black writers deal with racial themes, Ohff praises W's treatment of racial problems. Dispensing with pity, W shows the effects of racial oppression on both blacks and whites.

210. Okano, Hisaji. "America no Higeki-- Theodore Dreiser to Richard Wright no Aida" ["American Tragedies: Theodore Dreiser and Richard Wright"]. Doshisha Joshi Daigaku Kenkyu Nenpo [Annual Study Report of Doshisha Women's College], 11 (December), 182-206.
Despite the obvious similarities between An American Tragedy and NS, there are some fundamental differences. Chicago for Bigger is a haven from fear and hate, while for Clyde it is the place where he could realize his dreams of success. The difference also exists in the two characters: Clyde is a gentle soul but Bigger is a hard, cruel individual. The two books also differ in social criticism: W wants to disclose only social evils, but Dreiser's interest is in probing the mystery of life itself. In general, NS directly deals with the tragedy of a black American, while An American Tragedy is primarily concerned with a tragedy that results from the failure of materialistic dreams. [Y. H.]

211. Omori, Norikazu. "Richard Wright Shoron" ["A Commentary on Richard Wright"]. Kokujin Kenkyu [Negro Study], 13 (September), 14-16.
A brief discussion of W as the only black American writer who is able to reveal the racial injustice in American society. [Y. H.]

212. Ortlepp, Gunar. "Onkel Sams Farbige Stiefkinder." Cologne Deutsche Zeitung (12 November).
Favorable review of the German translation of LD. The novel returns to W's central concern with blacks in the South. Its literary and social importance is enhanced by its avoidance of a simplified picture of "bad whites" oppressing "good blacks."

213. Ouchi, Giichi. "Richard Wright nio-keru Kyofu nitsuite" ["Fear in Richard Wright"]. Waseda Daigaku Eibungaku [Waseda University English Literature], 19, pp. 313-325.
A discussion of fear in W's canon. BB is an illustration of the young W's efforts to transcend his innate fear. As he grew older W was attracted to existentialism and ultimately came to the belief that life is beyond human conception. O is a clear example of his attempt to escape life entirely; LD indicates his desire to seek freedom by making a distinction between him and those blacks who share the same destiny. These actions lead to various results. In BB his transcendence of fear is made into creation. In both NS and O protest is a private matter and crime is a defense mechanism to alleviate fear. But NS results

in a triumph while O becomes a defeat. In LD Fishbelly, being in an ambiguous status of a black as well as an occidental, becomes a "negative American"; consequently the novel produces a tragic disaster. [Y. H.]

214. P., B. "Rencontre avec Richard Wright." Le Figaro Littéraire (14 May), p. 3.
   Interview with W, who states that his writings have aided interracial understanding and explains the failure of LD in the United States. Also discusses W's correspondence with a Danish girl who committed suicide.

215. Patterson, Ray. "From Our Past: Roi Ottley--Black Odysseus; Richard Wright--Native Son." New York Citizen-Call (10 December), p. 14.
   Compares and contrasts W and Ottley, both of whom died in 1960.

216. Petersen, Hans. "Literatur-Journal." Berliner Welle (21 November).
   Unfavorable review of the German translation of LD. Although there are legitimately tragic elements in the stories of Tyree and Fishbelly, the novel is a "neurotic" book. W has lost contact with his black brothers and abandoned his commitment for a form of escapism.

217. Poston, Ted. "Richard Wright Dies." New York Post.
   Obituary.

218. Pritchett, V. S. "Books to Amplify a Foreigner's Image of America." Life International, 28 (1 February), 137.
   Includes NS in a list of thirty books.

219. ____. "Pagan Spain," in Bodley Head Books for Spring and Summer 1960. London: Bodley Head, p. 8.
   Favorable review stressing the book's controversial quality. The central paradox of Spain, W believes, is its religion.

220. R., M. "Der schwarze Westler." Frankfurter Allgemeine Zeitung für Deutschland (1 December), p. 14.
   Obituary emphasizing W's struggle for personal and racial freedom.

221. R., M. D. "Warten auf hohe Auflagen." Saarbrücker Zeitung (24 September), p. 33.
   Mentions the German translation of LD.

222. Redding, Saunders. "The Negro Writer and His Relationship to his Roots," in The American Negro Writer and His Roots. New York: American Society of African Culture, pp. 1-8.
   Includes comments on W's alienation and on NS.
   Reprinted: 1968.183; 1969.203; 1971.256a.

223. ____. "Negro Writing in America." The New Leader, 43 (16 May), 8-10.
   Mentions W, stressing his American identity even in exile.

224. ____. "Richard Wright: An Evaluation." AMSAC Newsletter, 3 (30 December), 3-6.
   General assessment of W emphasizing the power and value of his early works and their biographical and social matrix. In France W achieved personal fulfillment, but his deracination hurt his writing.

225. ____. "What's New in Books: Genius of Dick Wright." The Baltimore Afro-American (24 December), Afro Magazine Sec., p. 2.
   Obituary-eulogy emphasizing W's power in writing against racial injustice. Redding believes that by cutting him off from his roots, W's expatriation damaged his art.

226. Reeves, Edward. "Richard Wright Hits U. S. Racial Hypocrisy." Chicago Daily Defender (28 November), p. 13.
   Account of a lecture W gave to the American church in Paris, in which he commented on racial relations in the United States and in Africa.

227. Rétif, André. "Richard Wright.--Ecoute, homme blanc." Etudes, 304 (February), 279.
   Unfavorable review of the French translation of WML complaining of W's lay point of view.

228. Rhea, James N. "A Native Son's Mistaken Exile." The Providence Sunday Journal (11 December), Sec. H, p. 12.
   Because of W's exile, Rhea argues, he never fulfilled the promise of NS and BB, which were "magnificent" from both literary and social perspectives. Preoccupied with large philosophical issues but unable to handle them adequately, W lost contact with the American black movement which he had helped to propel.

229. Rideout, Walter B. "An American Dilemma," in his Instructor's Manual for The Experience of Prose. New York: Crowell, pp. 29-36.
   Mentions NS and analyzes briefly "The Ethics of Living Jim Crow."

230. ____. "Questions," in his The

Experience of Prose. New York: Crowell, pp. 495-496.
    Study questions to accompany "The Ethics of Living Jim Crow."

231. _____. "Richard Wright The Ethics of Living Jim Crow: An Autobiographical Sketch," in his The Experience of Prose. New York: Crowell, pp. 485-486.
    Biographical headnote.

232. Ross, Don. "Lorraine Hansberry Interviewed: 'Whites Dreadfully Ignorant of Negro Life.'" New York Herald Tribune (13 March), Sec. 4, p. 3.
    Mentions briefly LD, which Hansberry had neither read nor seen.

233. Rousseaux, André. "'Fishbelly' de Richard Wright." Le Figaro Littéraire (4 June), p. 2.
    Favorable review of the French translation of LD analyzing the social and psychological elements of the novel.

234. Rovit, Earl H. "Ralph Ellison and the American Comic Tradition." Wisconsin Studies in Contemporary Literature, 1 (Fall), 34-42.
    Mentions the theme of the underground man in W (p. 40).
    Reprinted: 1970.309, 310.

235. Sablonière,, Margrit de. "In Memoriam Richard Wright." Vrij Nederland (10 December), p. 6.
    Obituary-eulogy with a summary of W's career. Whether arguing against totalitarianism or racial discrimination, he always defended the oppressed. Includes several personal reminiscences, among them W's reaction to the Netherlands as "dull."

236. Saito, Kazue. "Richard Wright to Sono Sakuhin." ["Richard Wright and His Works"]. Waseda Hogakkaishi [Waseda Journal of Philosophy, Literature and Natural Science], 11, pp. 1-26.
    An essay stating her personal reactions to W's career. W is introduced as one of the two most celebrated black American writers, the other being Ralph Ellison. Traces his life from Natchez to Memphis, where he learned of Lewis, Dreiser, and Mencken. Concludes that W was convinced of the necessity to liberate the South; agreeing with Faulkner, she asserts that it could be liberated only by people of the South. It is ironic that W was first recognized by French critics rather than by Southern critics. [Y. H.]

237. Schier, Ernie. "At the Walnut: 'The Long Dream' Glosses Over Moral Issue." The Philadephia Evening Bulletin (2 February), p. 22.
    Unfavorable review of the play complaining of melodrama, oversimplification, and special pleading.

238. Schneider, Douglas H. "Le Souvenir de Richard Wright." France-U.S.A., No. 144 (December), p. 2.
    Obituary-eulogy recalling Schneider's meeting with W when the author arrived in Paris. Driving around the city with Gertrude Stein, he responded to its beauty.

239. Schreckenbach, Walter. "Sind alle Spanier Heiden?" Ja und Nein (July), p. 4.
    Unfavorable review of the German translation of PS. Despite its brilliant style, the book is flawed by half-truths and by W's rage and hate. It has much the same type of interest and philosophy as Sartre's No Exit.

240. [Seigler, Milledge Broadus]. "American Literature," in Britannica Junior. Ed. Don A. Walter. Vol. 2. Chicago: Encyclopaedia Britannica, pp. 216-227.
    Reprint of 1958.245.

241. Sekiguchi, Isao. "Cross Damon wa Naze Kokujin de Nakereba Naranaika" ["Why Cross Damon Has to Be a Negro"] Kokujin Kenkyu [Negro Study], 12 (May), 1-3.
    As BP indicates, W realizes that he is not only an American but a Negro. Focusing on O, Sekigucchi argues that since a man like Cross Damon is a black American, he is destined to be a second class citizen. He cannot deny this fact no matter how much intellect he may acquire, or how hard he may try to live among white Americans. [Y. H.]

242. Snyder, Mary Rennels. "Behind the Backs of Books & Authors." The Gary Post-Tribune (11 December), Sec. D, p. 4.
    Obituary recalling a conversation with W in 1945. He denied that his works had brought about significant progress for blacks, but he reiterated his identification with and commitment to "the little fellow."

243. Spanehl, Werner. "Christentum und Abendland." Frankfort Deutsche Post (5 January), pp. 17-18.
    Favorable review of the German translation of PS accompanied by an excerpt. Spanehl claims that despite W's rationalist method, his conclusions resemble those of Catholic writer Georges Bernanos.

244. Stevenson, David L. "Novel, The,"

in The Encyclopedia Americana. Ed.
Lavinia P. Dudley. Vol. 20. New York:
Americana Corporation, pp. 503-524.
Reprint of 1952.64.

245. Stewart, Ollie. "Report from Europe: Happiest Years of His Life." The
Baltimore Afro-American (17 December),
p. 4.
  Tribute to W as a "soft-spoken family
  man who jealously guarded, and provided for, Ellen and their two daughters, the humorous cafe-sitter, the
  hater of sham and prejudice, and the
  uncompromising intellectual."

246. _____. "Report from Europe: 1961
Inheriting Troubles of '60." The Balti-
more Afro-American (31 December), p. 4.
Mentions W's death.

247. Stil, André. "Les Livres et la vie:
Noir sur noir." L'Humanité (28 July), p.
2.
  Unfavorable review of the French
  translation of LD. Although it starts
  very well, the novel becomes ambiguous and presents a black life so
  corrupted as to seem almost to justify white racist repression. It is
  true that W shows where the ultimate
  responsibility for racism lies, but
  the latter part of the book is too
  melodramatic. Stil compares W to
  Eugène Sue.

248. T., H. "Un Grand Romancier noir est
mort." Le Paris Populaire Dimanche (11
December), p. 2.
  Obituary referring to W as "a man
  liberated from all racial and ideological prejudices."

249. Tanaka, Yoshiko. "Black Literature:
Richard Wright." Kokujin Kenkyu [Negro
Study], 12 (May), 8-13.
  "Richard Wright has deserted his
  fellow Southern Negroes, the Communist Party and, at least, his mother-
  land, America, in order to pursue the
  path of a complete outsider." This
  experience, she claims, inevitably
  led to the failure of his later
  works. [Y. H.]

250. Thorp, Willard. American Writing in
the Twentieth Century. Cambridge, Mass.:
Harvard University Press, p. 261.
  A paragraph sketching W's life and
  career appears in a chapter on the
  "Southern Renaissance."

251. Tynan, Kenneth. "Deaths and Entran-
ces." The New Yorker, 36 (5 March), 120.
  Favorable review of the play LD
  lamenting its early closing. Although
  the third act is too melodramatic,
  most of the play is tense and power-

ful. It is also a valid indictment of
Mississippi racism.

252. Umemura, Shigehiro. "Richard Wright
no Bungaku Shiso (1)" ["Richard Wright's
Literary Thought I"]. Kokujin Kenkyu
[Negro Study], 12 (May), 4-7.
  A discussion of W's thoughts that
  inform his works ranging from UTC to
  LD. The early works through BB are
  considered protest literature whereas
  the later ones can be called "revi-
  sional literature." The earlier period coincided with W's involvement
  with Communism; the later period,
  with his interest in existentialism.
  Notes that NS is his most successful
  attempt to deal with the racial
  issue. Continued in 1960.253 and
  1961.276. [Y. H.]

253. _____. "Richard Wright no Bungaku
Shiso (2)" ["Richard Wright's Literary
Thought II"]. Kokujin Kenkyu [Negro
Study], 13 (September), 11-14.
  Continuation of 1960.252.

254. Vernon, Françoise. "Traduit de
l'américain." Informations & Documents
(1 September), pp. 34-39.
  Contains a highly favorable notice of
  the French translation of LD (p. 37)
  calling it W's masterpiece and emphasizing its universal meaning.

255. Vilaine, Anne-Marie. "Richard
Wright: La Rééducation des blancs est
plus urgente que celle des noirs." L'Express, No. 463 (28 April), p. 34.
  Interview with W commenting on LD, a
  novel about the corruption bred by
  racism. Crippling the psychological
  processes of whites as well as
  blacks, the affliction is present in
  Asia and Africa as well as America.
  France is comparatively free of racism, however.

256. Vuyk, Beb. "Mensen en Plaatsen:
Weekinde met Richard Wright." Vrij
Nederland (19 November), p. 19.
  Report of a visit with W including
  discussions of CC and colonialism in
  general. W reasserts his view of the
  importance of Nkrumah to the Third
  World as a whole.

257. _____. "Mensen en Plaatsen: Weekinde met Richard Wright (2)." Vrij
Nederland (26 November), p. 8.
  Report of Mochtar Lubis's impressions
  of W emphasizing that even though no
  longer a "black boy," he continues to
  emphasize color consciousness in his
  world view. Although there are differences in American, Indonesian, and
  Japanese approaches to color questions, W overlooks them, thus provid-

ing evidence that the world is in fact "color crazy."

258. W., H. "Protest, Traum und Resignation." Deutsche Woche (December).

Obituary claiming that LD provides the clue to the nature of W's career. Even while protesting the destruction of the dreams of his race, he is resigned to the inevitability of the process.

259. War. "Rassenkampf--Alkoholismus--Wehrlosigkeit." Der Dusseldorf Mittag (8 October).

Review of the German translation of LD. Although W's portrayal of white mentality is somewhat limited by the tight thematic focus of the novel, it is a powerful autobiographical statement on the destruction of black hope. Fishbelly is shaped more by his harsh environment than by his father's influence.

259a. Ward, John William. "20th Century American Novels," in Good Reading. Ed. J. Sherwood Weber. New York: R. R. Bowker, pp. 123-132.

Reprint of 1941.786a.

260. Wartenweiler, Fritz. Schwarze in USA. Zurich: Rotapfel Verlag, pp. 89-121.

W is one of seven prominent black Americans to whom chapters in this book are devoted. The account of W's life and career is popularized and contains much quotation from his works.

261. Waters. "The Long Dream." Unidentified clipping.

Favorable review of the Philadelphia production of the play. Waters praises the dramatic excitement, acting, and staging.

262. Watts, Richard, Jr. "Gang War, Dope and Sex in the Harlem Jungles." New York Post (23 February), p. 46.

Review of the play The Cool World comparing it unfavorably to LD even though it is more successful.

263. _____. "Two on the Aisle." New York Post (23 February), p. 44.

Commenting on the reaction to the play LD, Watts found the hostility to it shocking. He was not shocked by the play itself.

264. _____. "Two on the Aisle." New York Post (1 March), p. 48.

Contrasts the sensationalism of The Cool World to the honesty of LD.

265. _____. "Two on the Aisle: A Father and Son in Mississippi." New York Post (18 February), p. 56.

Favorable review of the play LD. The Frings adaptation of the novel sprawls somewhat, but it is engrossing as theater--well acted and staged. Watts emphasizes the conflict of generations under the pressure of a racist society.

266. _____. "Two on the Aisle: Two New Plays, One Already Gone." New York Post (28 February), p. 15.

Laments the early closing of LD and its hostile critical reception. Watts reaffirms his view that it "was one of the season's few striking plays" and stresses the generational conflict between the subservient father and the proud son.

267. Webb, Constance. "A Few Words About Richard Wright." Correspondence, 4 (24 December), 41.

Eulogy stressing the spiritual and intellectual independence that made W "forever incompatible with any radical group."

268. Widmer, Kingsley. "The Existential Darkness: Richard Wright's The Outsider." Wisconsin Studies in Contemporary Literature, 1 (Fall), 13-21.

Analysis of "one of the very few consciously existentialist works in American literature" (p. 13). Indebted to Kierkegaard, Nietzsche, and Sartre, O inverts such emotions as love and hate in an existentalist dialectic. Other existentialist characteristics in the novel are dread, ambiguity, disbelief, and hopelessness.

Reprinted: 1970.362; 1971.147, 315.
Partially reprinted: 1980.259.

269. Wimmer, Paul. "Der Abgrund der Schande." Vienna Heute (24 December).

Favorable review of the German translation of LD together with a sketch of W's career. Praises the realism with which W portrays both the physical and the psychological violence of Fishbelly's environment.

270. Wolter, Beverly. "Twin City Reviewer Appraises Broadway." Winston-Salem Journal and Sentinel (28 February), p. D4.

Review of LD, Raisin in the Sun, and seven other plays. LD is sociologically valid but dramatically weak despite good acting. Raisin in the Sun is a better play on a similar theme.

1961

1. A. "Acht Negerschicksale." Hamburger Abendblatt (29 September), p. 9.
  Favorable review of the German translation of EM praising its portrayal of racial tragedy and its handling of diction and dialogue.

2. Aaron, Daniel. Writers on the Left: Episodes in American Literary Communism. New York: Harcourt, Brace & World, pp. 281-282, 385.
  Treats briefly W's experience with the John Reed Club and the fourth congress of the League of American Writers.

3. Algren, Nelson. "Remembering Richard Wright." The Nation, 192 (28 January), 85.
  Discusses W and Chicago, quoting from letters by W. His message, still valid, was the responsibility of society for those like Bigger who must resort to violence to achieve manhood.
  Reprinted: 1971.147; 1972.27.

4. Anderson, Robert E., Jr. "Short Stories to Haunt America's Conscience." The Atlanta Journal and The Atlanta Constitution (19 February), p. 2-B.
  Review of EM. The central theme of the volume as a whole is the feeling of inferiority in blacks inculcated by racism.

5. Angoff, Allan. "Protest in American Literature Since the End of World War II." CLA Journal, 5 (September), 31-40.
  Cites the scant attention paid to W's death as an example of the decline of the protest tradition (p. 32).

6. Anon. "American Literature," in The American Educator Encyclopedia. Ed. Everette Edgar Sentman. Vol. 1. Lake Bluff, Ill.: The United Educators, pp. 120-130.
  Reprint of 1956.7.

7. Anon. "At War with Reality." Newsweek, 57 (9 January), 82-83.
  Mixed review of EM placing it in the context of W's career. Even though W lacks verbal wit, the collection shows his "increasingly subtle insight" into the emotional and psychological complexities of black lives. "The Man Who Lived Underground" is the most impressive story in EM.

8. Anon. "Aus dem Weihnachtsbücherberg." Der Berlin Tagesspiegel (16 December), p. 14.
  Contains a notice of the German translation of EM emphasizing the theme of racial conflict and its tone of despair.

9. Anon. "Black and White." The London Times Literary Supplement, No. 3,113 (27 October), p. 765.
  Unfavorable review of LD. Some of the dialogue has a sense of immediacy, but the book is badly written in the main. The reviewer emphasizes W's violence, comparing it to Faulkner's.

10. Anon. "'Black Boy' One of Forty on Blacklist." Newsletter on Intellectual Freedom, 10 (March), 7.
  Reports that Rev. Riley F. Marquis, Jr., a Church of Christ minister in Garden Grove, California, objected to the presence of BB in the Bolsa Grande High School library and had its card removed from the catalog.

11. Anon. "Book Briefs." Greensburg (Pa.) Tribune-Review (27 January), p. 12.
  Reprint of 1961.27.

12. Anon. "Books of Interest at Fargo Library." Fargo Forum (23 April).
  Mentions EM.

13. Anon. "Christmas Books for Varied Tastes." The Saturday Review, 44 (2 December), 32.
  Contains a notice of EM stressing the theme of black struggle to survive in a racist world.

14. Anon. "Collected Tales Are Author's Last." The Indianapolis Star (19 February), Sec. 9, p. 4.
  Reprint of 1961.27.

15. Anon. "Collection by Wright." The Detroit News (26 February), p. 3-E.
  Reprint of 1961.27.

16. Anon. "Deaths of Notable Persons," in The World Book Encyclopedia 1961 Annual Supplement. Ed. Roy M. Fisher. Chicago: Field Enterprises, pp. 68-73.
  Contains an obituary notice of W (p. 73).

17. Anon. Dust jacket of Der Mann, der nach Chikago ging. By Richard Wright. Trans. Enzio von Cramon and Erich Freed. Hamburg: Classen Verlag.
  Blurb on front and back inside flaps.

18. Anon. Dust jacket of Eight Men. Cleveland: World.
  Unsigned blurb and autobiographical sketch by W on front and back inside flaps. Photograph of W with note on back.

19. Anon. Dust jacket of Zoon van Amer-ika. By Richard Wright. Trans. A. W. Ebbinge-Van Nes. The Hague: Zuid-Hollandsche Nitgeners Mij.
Blurb on front and back inside flaps of this Dutch translation of NS emphasizing its social import and relating it to the new Kennedy administration.

20. Anon. "Eight Men." Ashtabula Star Beacon (22 January).
Reprint of 1961.27.

21. Anon. "Eight Men." Bad Axe (Mich.) Huron Daily Tribune (27 January).
Reprint of 1961.27.

22. Anon. "Eight Men." DeLand Sun News (22 January).
Reprint of 1961.27.

23. Anon. "Eight Men." Dowagiac Daily News (25 January).
Reprint of 1961.27.

24. Anon. "Eight Men." Eureka Standard (8 March).
Reprint of 1961.27.

25. Anon. "Eight Men." Irwin (Pa.) Standard (6 April).
Reprint of 1961.27.

26. Anon. "Eight Men." Morganton News-Herald (20 January).
Reprint of 1961.27.

27. Anon. "Eight Men." Ocean City (N. J.) Citizen (19 January).
Favorable United Press International review ranking the collection with NS. Mentions "The Man Who Lived Underground" and "The Man Who Was Almost a Man." Notes variations in style and mood in the eight pieces. Reprinted: 1961.11, 14, 15, 20, 21, 22, 23, 24, 25, 26, 28, 30, 31, 32, 34, 37, 51, 81, 53, 237.

28. Anon. "Eight Men." Orange (Cal.) News (20 January).
Reprint of 1961.27.

29. Anon. "Eight Men." Westwood Hills Citizen (26 January).
Favorable notice emphasizing the originality and variety of the collection.

30. Anon. "Eight Men." Wilkes-Barre Independent (22 January).
Reprint of 1961.27.

31. Anon. "Eight Men, by Richard Wright." Coos Bay World (20 January), p. 4.
Reprint of 1961.27.

32. Anon. "Eight Men, by Richard Wright." Humboldt Standard (8 March), p. 8.
Reprint of 1961.27.

33. Anon. "Eight Men, by Richard Wright." The Bookmark, 20 (April-May), 169.
Notice praising W's "forceful simplicity" in treating his "universal themes."

34. Anon. "Eight Men, by Richard Wright." The Honolulu Sunday Advertiser (22 January), Weekly Sec., p. 10.
Reprint of 1961.27.

35. Anon. "Eight Men, by Richard Wright." Wichita Eagle and Beacon (19 February), Magazine Sec., p. 11.
Favorable notice stressing the reality of W's characters. The pieces lodge in the reader's imagination.

36. Anon. "Eight Men Richard Wright." The Book Buyer's Guide, 64 (January), 56.
Favorable notice praising W's realism.

37. Anon. "Eight Stories on Negro Life." The Hayward Daily Review (22 January), The Sunday Previewer Sec., p. 4.
Reprint of 1961.27.

38. Anon. "Fiction Shelf." Wilmington (Del.) Journal (23 January).
Contains a favorable notice of EM.

38a. Anon. "5 of the Greatest," in Quintet. New York: Pyramid Books, back cover.
Contains a brief blurb on "The Man Who Lived Underground."

38b. Anon. "Fugitive--Genius--Judge--Girl--Man," in Quintet. New York: Pyramid Books, p. [1].
Contains a brief note on "The Man Who Lived Underground."

39. Anon. "Garden Grove School News: Books in Bolsa Grande Library Criticized; Quality of Teaching Discussed." The Santa Ana (Cal.) Register (15 February), p. C17.
Reports the compilation of a list of "lewd and subversive works" in a high school library by Frank McDonald, "chairman of the committee for fundamental education." The only work specifically mentioned is BB, "so offensive that certain passages could not be recited aloud in public."

40. Anon. "Historical News." The Journal of Negro History, 46 (January), 56-58.
Contains a brief obituary of W (p.

56).

41. Anon. "Il y a un an, Richard Wright." La Vie Africaine, No. 20 (December), p. 42.
    Homage emphasizing W's interest in Africa.

42. Anon. Index Translationum 12. Paris: Unesco, pp. 56, 69, 148, 244, 315, 382, 473.
    Lists translations of BB into German and Italian, WML into Spanish and French, LD into Danish, Dutch and Swedish, NS into Danish and Italian, and PS into French.

43. Anon. "Last Book." The Cedar Rapids Gazette (22 January), Sec. 3, p. 11.
    Review of EM. Less assertive than some of W's works, the stories in this collection nevertheless demonstrate W's racial commitment. "The Man Who Went to Chicago" is autobiographical.

44. Anon. "Letteratura," in Nuovissima enciclopedia pratica Bompiani. Twentieth edition. Vol. 1. Milan: Bompiani, tavola 44.
    Mentions W briefly.

45. Anon. "Der Mann, der das Hochwasser sah. Von Richard Wright." Deutsche Zeitung (September), p. 22.
    Headnote to the German translation of "The Man Who Saw the Flood." W was both socially engaged and poetically inclined.

46. Anon. "Der Mann, der nach Chikago ging." Wiener Borsenkurier (4 November).
    Notice of the German translation of EM stressing the psychological elements.

47. Anon. "Melancholie und Humor." Stuttgarter Nachrichten (14 October), p. 39.
    Favorable review of the German translation of EM. Melancholy and conscious monotony are the prevailing moods of the stories in the collection, but "The Man Who Was Almost a Man" is the best because it adds some humor. W's careful technique clarifies what is complex but at the same time leaves a resonance of something deeper.

48. Anon. "Native Son by Richard Wright," in Native Son. Afterword by Richard Sullivan. Signet Classic CT81. New York: The New American Library, back cover.
    Publisher's blurb placing the novel "among the first American works of fiction to portray an existential

hero in the process of self-transcendence." Quotes from The New Yorker and The New York Times.

49. Anon. "Necrologio," in Almanaco italiano 1961. Vol. 61. Florence: Bemporad-Marzocco, pp. 501-511.
    Includes a brief obituary of W (p. 511).

50. Anon. "Necrology . . . 1960," in The Americana Annual 1961. Ed. Lavinia P. Dudley and John J. Smith. New York: Americana Corporation, pp. 839-852.
    Contains a biographical sketch of W (p. 852).

51. Anon. "New Books." Philadelphia Daily News (16 March), p. 41.
    Reprint of 1961.27.

52. Anon. "New York Beat." Jet, 19 (19 January), 63.
    Reports at the time of his death W was planning a series of broadcasts on blues and jazz for African radio.

53. Anon. "Nota," in La letteratura negra negli Stati Uniti. By Richard Wright. Trans. Attilio Landi. Milan: Il Saggiatore, pp. 7-10.
    Sketches W's life and comments on his translated essay.

54. Anon. "Obituaries," in Britannica Book of the Year. Ed. Harry S. Ashmore and Robert W. Murphey. Chicago: Encyclopaedia Britannica, pp. 509-522.
    Includes a brief obituary of W, "one of the most important Negro writers and spokesmen" (p. 522).

55. Anon. "Obituaries," in The New International Year Book. Ed. Drenka Willen. New York: Funk & Wagnalls, pp. 525-539.
    Contains a brief obituary of W (p. 539).

56. Anon. "Paperbacks." Publisher's Weekly, 180 (13 November), 38-39.
    Announces the Avon paperback edition of EM, scheduled for publication early in 1962.

57. Anon. "People." Time, 77 (10 February), 31.
    Quotes from Ollie Harrington's "The Last Days of Richard Wright."

58. Anon. "Pick of the Paperbacks." Saturday Review, 44 (18 November), 28-29.
    Contains a favorable notice of the Signet edition of NS. "In many ways it's a crude book, but the author's raw energy and youthful anger has [sic] lost none of its brilliance in

the succeeding years."

59. Anon. "Release Richard Wright's Last Short Story Anthology." Jet, 19 (2 March), 22.
    Favorable notice of EM. Quotes W. G. Rogers calling W one of the most distinguished sons of Mississippi.

60. Anon. "Richard Wright," in Native Son. Afterword by Richard Sullivan. Signet Classic CT81. New York: The New American Library, p. [1].
    Biographical sketch.

61. Anon. "Richard Wright." The Crisis, 68 (January), 35.
    Editorial-obituary stressing W's racial protest "in a lyrically savage prose." As an expatriate, he lost touch with improvements in American race relations. Still, he was true to his own experience--"the great incorruptible among American writers."

62. Anon. "Richard Wright." Wilson Library Bulletin, 35 (January), 344.
    Obituary notice.

63. Anon. "Richard Wright: Der Mann, der nach Chikago ging." Berliner Welle (18 October), 2 pp.
    Favorable radio review of the German translation of EM. W appeals for human sympathy for his characters, whose fates in between the black and white worlds are predetermined. He directs his attack on whites who contribute to the psychological oppression of blacks.

64. Anon. "Richard Wright: Der Mann, der nach Chikago ging." Heidenheimer Zeitung (21 November).
    Reprint of 1961.89.

65. Anon. "Richard Wright: Der Mann, der nach Chikago ging." Israel Freiheit (7 December).
    Favorable review of the German translation of EM, which demonstrates once again that W is among the foremost contemporary writers. The book emphasizes the unresolved racial tensions of the United States.

66. Anon. "Richard Wright: 'Der Mann, der nach Chikago ging.'" Der Spiegel, 15 (18 October), 84.
    Favorable notice of the German translation of EM. The racial theme is paramount, but W asserts an appeal based on humor as a defensive weapon. W's spare prose style derives from Hemingway and Faulkner [sic].

67. Anon. "Richard Wright: Der schwarze Traum." Berner Tagblatt (20 January).

Review of the German translation of LD. Its extreme subjectivity is both its strength and its weakness. It interests readers but will not necessarily convince them.

68. Anon. "Richard Wright: Der schwarze Traum." Du und die Welt (March).
    Favorable notice of the German translation of LD stressing the white brutality depicted.

69. Anon. "Richard Wright: Der schwarze Traum." Die Hamburg andere Zeitung (7 February).
    Favorable review of the German translation of LD stressing the links between W's studies of American racism and his commitment to the black freedom movement on a worldwide scale.

70. Anon. "Richard Wright: Der schwarze Traum." Mitarbeiterhilfe, No. 4.
    Review of the German translation of LD from a religious perspective. The novel calls to mind similar oppression of the German Jews. The dark tone of the book derives in part from the fact that its characters know no God, but W increases our awareness in a way which should increase our dedication to the message of Christ.

71. Anon. "Richard Wright: Der schwarze Traum." Die Vienna Wochen-Presse (18 February).
    Favorable notice of the German translation of LD emphasizing its stark consideration of the possibility of freedom.

72. Anon. "Richard Wright: Der schwarze Traum." Wiener Wochenhausgabe, No. 9 (25 February-3 March).
    Advertisement for the German translation of LD.

73. Anon. "Richard Wright, le plus grand romancier noir américain, est mort." Horizons, 10 (January), 121-123.
    Obituary article emphasizing W's role as racial spokesman and commenting on UTC, NS, BB, and LD.

74. Anon. "Der schwarze Traum." Der Regensburger (April).
    Favorable notice of the German translation of LD calling it the best of W's novels.

75. Anon. "Der schwarze Traum." Das Sozialsblatt (February).
    Brief favorable notice of the German translation of LD.

76. Anon. "Der schwarze Traum." Wirtschaft und Wissen (2 February).

Favorable review of the German translation of LD noting that Fishbelly's real conflict is not with society but with himself.

77. Anon. "Selected Bibliography," in Native Son. Afterword by Richard Sullivan. Signet Classic CT81. New York: The New American Library, p. [400].
Lists twelve primary and five secondary items.

78. Anon. "A Selected List of 250 Books of the Year." The New York Times Book Review (3 December), p. 71.
Lists and describes briefly EM.

79. Anon. "Spotlight on Books: 'Gone with Wind' Not; Reissues Due." Wilmington (Del.) Evening Journal (23 January), p. 15.
Contains a favorable notice of EM pointing out the theme of racial conflict and praising some of the stories for ingenious technique.

80. Anon. "Stories by Wright." Sioux Falls Argus-Leader (1 January), p. 7C.
Brief announcement of EM.

81. Anon. "Stories of Negro Life." The St. Catherines Standard (21 January), p. 14.
Reprint of 1961.27.

82. Anon. "This Week's Books." Denver Rocky Mountain News (22 January), p. 14A.
Contains a notice of EM stressing the geographical range of the stories.

83. Anon. "Today's Book." The Grand Rapids Press (7 February), p. 18.
Reprint of 1961.27.

84. Anon. "Die Tragödie des schwarzen Mannes." Jugendrotkreuz und Eizicher (May-June).
Review of the German translation of BP. Although W's harsh attitude toward Christianity is not entirely justifiable, particularly in the light of his picture of African paganism, the book does help to explain the problems faced by contemporary missionaries in the Congo.

85. Anon. Untitled article. Erlesenes-Verlag (c. April).
Review of the German translation of LD. A "document of reality" rather than a novel, it continues W's preoccupation with the black-white conflict.

86. Anon. Untitled clipping. Congrès Information Form [?] la Liberté de la Culture (February), p. 4.

Short obituary mentioning W's commitment to justice and dignity and his interest in Africa and Asia.

87. Anon. Untitled clipping. Constance Südkurier (11 July).
Favorable notice of the German translation of PS stressing W's subjectivity.

88. Anon. Untitled clipping. Neue Bücherdienst (April).
Notice of the German translation of EM. Its psychological insights help to explain the struggle of black people against their hostile environment.

89. Anon. Untitled clipping. Neue Bücherdienst (4 September).
Notice of the German translation of EM stressing the difference between black and white psychological reactions.
Reprinted: 1961.64.

90. Anon. Untitled clipping. Neue Bücherdienst (October).
Favorable notice of the German translation of LD stressing its strong support of humanistic principles.

91. Anon. Untitled clipping. Neue Zürcher Nachrichten (28 November).
Notice of the German translation of EM.

92. Anon. Untitled clipping. Wiener Wochenausgabe, No. 9 (25 February).
Mentions briefly the German translation of LD.

93. Anon. Untitled clipping. Wiesbaden Illuspress (28 March).
Review of the German translation of LD. It must be seen in the historical context of race relations in the United States, but ultimately it focuses on Fishbelly's inner conflict.

94. Anon. Untitled clipping. Zurich Christliche Kultur (28 October), p. 2.
Review of the German translation of LD.

95. Anon. "View from Paris." High Point (N. C.) Enterprise (15 January), p. 10C.
Photograph of W accompanied by an announcement of EM.

96. Anon. "Wright," in Dictionnaire universel des lettres. Ed. Pierre Claroc. Paris: Société d'édition de dictionnaires et encyclopédies, p. 930.
Biographical note.

97. Anon. "Wright, Richard." Current Biography, 22 (January), 47.
  Obituary note.
  Reprinted: 1962.26.

98. Anon. "Wright, Richard," in Dizionario enciclopedico italiano. Ed. Umberto Bosco. Vol. 12. Rome: Instituto della Enciclopedia Italiana, p. 940.
  Biographical note.

99. Anon. "Wright, Richard," in Enciclopedia italiana di scienze, lettere ed arti 1949-1960. Ed. Umberto Bosco. Appendix 3. Vol. 2. Rome: Instituto della Enciclopedia Italiana, p. 1141.
  Very brief notice of W's death.

100. Anon. "Wright, Richard," in Lilla Focus. Ed. Sven Lidman. Stockholm: Almqvist & Wiksell, p. 933.
  Brief biographical note.

101. Anon. "Wright, Richard," in The American Educator Encyclopedia. Ed. Everette Edgar Sentman. Vol. 10. Lake Bluff, Ill.: The United Educators, p. 3917.
  Biographical sketch.
  Reprinted: 1968.32.

102. Anon. "Wright, Richard. Eight Men." The Booklist and Subscription Books Bulletin, 57 (15 January), 294.
  Brief notice pointing to troubled racial relations as the theme of the collection.

103. Anson, Cherrill. "Eight Wright Short Stories." The Baltimore Sunday Sun (22 January), Sec. A, p. 7.
  Favorable review of EM praising W's narrative skill and characterization. The book "is bold and bitter at times, but it is laced with a bubbling humor as well. At all times it is simply and powerfully written."

104. B., H. "Die Sonne der untern Welt." Cologne Rheinischer Merkur (17 November), pp. 25-26.
  Favorable review of the German translation of EM. Praises "The Man Who Lived Underground" for its treatment of the modern theme of universal guilt. Unaware that "Man, God Ain't Like That" is a radio play, the reviewer complains that it has too much dialogue.

105. B., H. R. "Richard Wright: Der Mann der nach Chikago ging." Neues Winterthürer Tagblatt (30 December).
  Favorable review of the German translation of EM. The beauty of the stories does not overshadow their political value. Although not all of the stories are tragic, W sees no

possibility for happy endings.

106. Baldus, Alexander. "Richard Wright: Der schwarze Traum." Begegnung (November).
  Mixed review of the German translation of LD. While arguing that the novel overemphasizes hatred and is not adequately resolved in Fishbelly's flight, Baldus nevertheless praises W's verbal power which makes the work an "artistic accomplishment."

107. Baldwin, James. "Alas, Poor Richard," in his Nobody Knows My Name: More Notes of a Native Son. New York: Dial Press, pp. 200-215.
  Account of Baldwin's friendship with W in Paris and their estrangement, with special attention to the Franco-American Fellowship. Baldwin argues that W became generally alienated from black people during his Paris years.
  Reprinted: 1971.147.

108. _____. "Eight Men," in his Nobody Knows My Name: More Notes of a Native Son. New York: Dial Press, pp. 181-189.
  Reprint of 1961.116.

109. _____. "The Exile," in his Nobody Knows My Name: More Notes of a Native Son. New York: Dial Press, pp. 190-199.
  Reprint of 1961.113.

110. _____. "Notes for a Hypothetical Novel: An Address," in his Nobody Knows My Name: More Notes of a Native Son. New York: Dial Press, pp. 141-154.
  Mentions W briefly as an urban novelist comparable to James T. Farrell. Delivered as a speech at the third annual Esquire symposium on "The Role of the Writer in America."

110a. _____. "Princes and Powers," in his Nobody Knows My Name: More Notes of a Native Son. New York: Dial Press, pp. 13-55.
  Reprint of 1957.136.

111. _____. "Richard Wright." Encounter, 16 (April), 58-60.
  Reprint of 1961.113.

112. _____. "Richard Wright," in The Nonconformers: Articles of Dissent. Ed. David Evanier and Stanley Silverzweig. New York: Ballantine Books, pp. 143-149.
  Reprint of 1961.113.

113. _____. "Richard Wright: A Personal Memoir." New America (1 January), pp. 3, 5.
  Discusses the most important elements of the Baldwin-W relationship from

their first encounter until W's death. Baldwin acknowledges his debt to W, but emphasizes their profound ideological and artistic differences.
Reprinted: 1961.109, 111, 112.
Translated: 1961.114, 115.

114. _____. "El Richard Wright que conocí." Cuadernos, No. 48 (May), pp. 47-50.
Translation of 1961.113. Includes a sketch of W by Zamorano.

115. _____. "Richard Wright tel que je l'ai connu." Preuves, No. 120 (February), pp. 42-45.
Translation of 1961.113.

116. _____. "The Survival of Richard Wright." The Reporter, 24 (16 March), 52-55.
Generally favorable review of EM with reservations expressed about W's notions of society, politics, and history. The Depression stories do not seem dated, and "Man of All Work" and "The Man Who Lived Underground" are excellent. "The Man Who Killed a Shadow" fails, however, because W's violence is obsessive. Whatever his faults, his loss to literature will be deeply felt. "Wright's unrelentingly bleak landscape was not merely that of the Deep South, or of Chicago, but that of the world, of the human heart."
Reprinted: 1961.108.
Partially reprinted: 1969.64.
Translated: 1963.48.

117. _____. "Theatre: On the Negro Actor." The Urbanite, 1 (April), 6, 29.
Mentions the adaptation of LD by Ketti Frings.
Reprinted: 1962.36; 1969.24; 1976.30.

118. _____, Nat Hentoff, Alfred Kazin, Lorraine Hansberry, Emile Capouya, and Langston Hughes. "The Negro in American Culture." Cross Currents, 11 (Summer), 205-224.
Panel discussion focusing on black literature. Baldwin contends that W lacks true literary artistry.
Reprinted: 1969.25a; 1971.34a.

119. Bannon, Barbara. "Forecast of Paperbacks." Publishers' Weekly, 180 (11 September), 63-64.
Contains a favorable notice of the Signet edition of NS.

120. Bardolph, Richard. The Negro Vanguard. Vintage Books V-198. New York: Random House, pp. 291, 373, 374, 379, 380, 381, 383, 384.
Reprint of 1959.55.

121. Barley, Rex. "Symphony Orchestra in a Mythical War." Los Angeles Mirror (23 January), Part 3, p. 3.
Contains an unfavorable notice of EM complaining that the unreality of most of the stories makes them seem "almost parodies of his previous work."

122. Benét, Rosemary. "Eight Men by Richard Wright." Book-of-the-Month Club News (March), p. 10.
Favorable review stressing the theme of racial hostility or misunderstanding. Praises W's effective development of his plots.

123. Bolinder, Barbo. "Onkel Toms barn." Femina, No. 1 (8 January), 36, 73-76.
Report of a visit with W in Paris stressing his "humanistic" approach to life. W discusses the failure of the United States to provide true equality for blacks and comments on the parallels between his own life and Fishbelly's in LD.

124. Bond, Alice Dixon. "Eight Men." Boston Traveller (14 February), p. 42.
Quotes favorable comments on EM by Ruth Wolfe Fuller praising most highly "The Man Who Was Almost a Man."

125. Bontemps, Arna. "The New Black Renaissance." Negro Digest, 11 (November), 52-58.
Compares Lorraine Hansberry to W and notes that W's power overcame his stylistic awkwardness.

126. Braem, Helmut M. "Blues in Prosa." St. Galler Tagblatt (12 November).
Reprint of 1961.127.

127. _____. "Blues in Prosa." Stuttgarter Zeitung (4 November), Sunday Supplement Sec., p. 4.
Review of the German translation of EM and of novels by Alston Anderson and Frank London Brown. Braem is generally favorable to W, but believes that his social commitment is greater that his literary commitment. He is more interested in ideas than in literary form.
Reprinted: 1961.126.

128. _____. "Bücherecke." Österreichischer Rundfunk (8 May), 3 pp.
Radio transcript of 1960.123.

129. Bramwell, Gloria. "Articulated Nightmare." Midstream, 7 (Spring), 110-112.
Unfavorable review of EM with discussion of W's early hardships and his relation to the Communist Party. His

typical motifs are guilt and fear. "The Man Who Lived Underground" fails in comparison to Invisible Man. Reprinted: 1978.209.

130. Brenner, Hans-Georg. "Begegnung mit einem Buch: Wright: Der schwarze Traum." Radio Bremen (9 March), 5 pp.
Typescript of a radio review of the German translation of LD together with recollection of a personal meeting with W in Hamburg. Both personally and artistically W "lived between the races," at home with Western culture but yearning toward an African culture.

130a. Burtis, Mary Elizabeth and Paul Spencer Wood. "Richard Wright, 1908--," in their Recent American Literature. Paterson, N. J.: Littlefield, Adams, pp. 343-344.
Biographical-critical sketch calling W "the leader of many young Negro writers" and claiming that he was "unconcerned with technique."

131. Buskes, J. J. "In memoriam: Richard Wright." Hervormd Nederland (4 February), p. 13.
Eulogy stressing that despite W's pessimistic outlook on human nature and his harsh attitude toward himself, he continued to struggle against injustice.

132. Butler, Shepperd. "Oddment of Venom and Hate." Bridgeport (Conn.) Sunday Herald (22 February).
Review of EM emphasizing the heterogeneity of the collection.

133. Cimatti, Pietro. "Un poeta negro: Langston Hughes e il risveglio dei popoli di colore." La fiera letteraria (17 September), p. 3.
Mentions briefly W's trip to Africa.

134. Clarke, Dick. "A Memory of Haiti and Richard Wright." New York Citizen-Call (4 February), p. 12.
Personal recollection of a meeting with W in Haiti.

135. Dai, Bingham. "Minority Group Membership and Personality Development," in Race Relations: Problems and Theory. Ed. Jitsuichi Masuoka. Chapel Hill: The University of North Carolina Press, pp. 181-199.
Quotes W and cites him as an example of the difficulty of intraracial friendship and intimacy (pp. 189-190).

136. Dawkins, Cecil. "Richard Wright Men." The Milwaukee Journal (22 January), Part 5, p. 4.

Unfavorable review of EM. Except for "The Man Who Went to Chicago" and "The Man Who Lived Underground," the stories are melodramatic or sentimental, and "the writing is strangely amateurish." W treats the racial problem well in his novels, "but he seems crowded and ill at ease in the short story form."

137. D'Dée "'Native Son' ou le film interdit." La Vie Africaine, No. 20 (December), pp. 43-46.
Photo essay on the film with extensive plot summary. Notes that the uncut, uncensored version was shown only in Argentina.

138. Douglass, Joseph H., Ina Corinne Brown, and John Hope Franklin. "Negro," in The World Book Encyclopedia. Ed. J. Morris Jones. Vol. 13. Chicago: Field Enterprises, pp. 106-112.
Revision of 1959.78.

139. Doyle, Paul A. "Wright, Richard. Eight Men." Best Sellers, 20 (1 February), 416-417.
Favorable review sketching W's life and commenting on the bitter sincerity, the simple and impassioned prose, and the psychological subtlety to be found in this book's treatment of the major theme of white racism.

140. E., M. "Von Neger-Schriftstellern: Richard Wright: Der Mann, der nach Chikago ging." Das Bücherblatt, 25 (1 December), 4.
Favorable review of the German translation of EM emphasizing W's skill in interpreting black mentality to whites. The reviewer mentions "The Man Who Went to Chicago," "Man, God Ain't Like That . . .," "Man of All Work," and "The Man Who Lived Underground" (the best story in the volume).

141. E., R. "Der schwarze Traum." Goslarche Zeitung (4 February).
Notice of the German translation of LD calling W the spokesman of the oppressed.

142. Egger, Eugen. "Wright, Richard: Der schwarze Traum." Der neue Büch (October).
Favorable review of the German translation of LD recommending it for libraries. The novel demonstrates that blacks have taken on the corrupt values of white society.

143. Ellison, Ralph and Richard G. Stern. "That Same Pain, That Same Pleasure." December, 3 (Winter), 30-46.
Ellison discusses his relation with W

and comments on the composition of NS (pp. 41-42).
Reprinted: 1964.53; 1968.84.

144. Emmerling, Hans. "Richard Wright: Der schwarze Traum." Süddeutscher Rundfunk (9 May).
Radio review of the German translation of LD. Although W writes well, this novel is important less for its literary value than for its documentary elements. Emmerling points out the brutality of many scenes but praises them for increasing the power of W's message.

145. F., K. P. "Fesselnd." Welt der Arbeit (21 April).
Favorable notice of the German translation of LD stressing its bitterness.

146. Faber, Gustav. "Wir sprechen über neue Bücher." Süddeutscher Rundfunk (16 June).
Radio review of the German translation of LD. It resembles many American novels in its harshness, but it uses the macabre elements as part of its powerful appeal.

147. Fanon, Frantz. Les Damnés de la terre. Preface by Jean-Paul Sartre. Paris: F. Maspéro, p. 162.
Mentions W briefly.
Reprinted: 1966.51.
Translated: 1968.96; 1975.72.

148. Fehse, Willi. "Heimisch im fremden Land." Wiesbadener Kurier (1 November).
Review of the German translation of EM. Mixing tragic and comic elements, W uses apparently simple methods to attain a complex "melancholy" effect. "The Man Who Was Almost a Man" is one of the best pieces in the book because of its humor.
Reprinted: 1962.56.

149. Ford, Nick Aaron. "Battle of the Books: A Critical Survey of Significant Books by and About Negroes Published in 1960." Phylon, 22 (Second Quarter), 119-134.
Notes W's death and reviews EM. Like UTC, EM is a collection of stories about the victimization of blacks by whites. The new collection is not as strong as the earlier one, however.
Reprinted: 1978.209.

150. Frisé, Adolf. "Richard Wright und die Charta der Menschenrechte." Munich Süddeutsche Zeitung (21-22 January), SZ am Wochenende Sec., p. 66.
Reprint of 1960.150.

151. Fuller, Hoyt. "On the Death of

Richard Wright." Southwest Review, 46 (Autumn), vi-vii, 334-337.
Reminisces about a meeting with W in November 1959, and discusses a mutual acquaintance, William Harper, who knew W much earlier. Discusses also Baldwin's comments on W. Fuller believes that W remained essentially an American despite his forced expatriation.
Reprinted: 1971.147.

152. _____ and Doris E. Saunders. "Perspectives." Negro Digest, 10 (July), 50.
Notes that W was responsible for publication of the French translation of Kyle Onstott's novel Mandingo.

153. Fürst, Ludwig. "Flucht aus Mississippi." Die Hamburg Zeit (27 January), U. S. edition, p. 9.
Favorable review of the German translation of LD stressing both its artistic power and its racial theme. Blinded by racism, whites commit outrages which otherwise they would shrink from, and blacks such as Tyree Tucker survive as best they can. Fürst compares Tyree Tucker's self-justification to that of the king in Grillparzer's Jews of Toledo. For Fishbelly, flight seems the only response to Mississippi racial oppression.

154. G., D. "Richard Wright." Théâtre, No. 15 (January), p. 3.
Obituary stressing that despite W's residence in France, he remained committed to his homeland and race both in his work and his emotions.

155. G., U. "Der Negerjunge Fishbelly." Stuttgarter Nachrichten (21 January).
Favorable review of the German translation of LD. Although the novel at times falls into cynicism and mannerism, these faults are overshadowed by scenes such as Fishbelly's encounter with the police chief. W clearly depicts the unacceptable price of success in his treatment of Tyree Tucker.

156. Gannett, Lewis. "A Ten Dollar Shelf." New York Herald Tribune Book Review (15 January), Paperback Sec., pp. 32, 33.
BB is one of ten titles in the biography category.

157. Gasseling, Helmut. "Richard Wright: Der schwarze Traum." Bücherei und Bildung, 13 (October), 610-611.
Favorable review of the German translation of LD. Gasseling expresses reservations about the formlessness of some of the novel's parts and the

macabre quality of some episodes and details, but he argues that these recede before the fascinating view it gives of American racial conflict.

158. _____. "Wright, Richard: Der schwarze Traum." Buchanzeiger, No. 163 (September), p. 5.
Notice of the German translation of LD. Although not suitable for children, LD is recommended for all libraries.

158a. Gérard, Albert. "Ralph Ellison et le dilemme noir." Revue générale belge, 97 (October), 89-104.
Notes plot resemblances between O and Invisible Man (pp. 89-90).

159. _____. "Vie et vocation de Richard Wright." Revue générale belge, 97 (January), 65-78.
Obituary-article summarizing and defining the major trends and characteristics of W's career as an embattled writer, stressing his humanistic and existential interests, his political commitment, and the problems raised in his fiction.

160. Gilman, Richard. "The Immediate Misfortunes of Widespread Literacy." The Commonweal, 74 (28 April), 130-131.
Review of EM and three other collections of short fiction. Gilman finds W's book much the worst--embarrassing, inept, self-conscious, unsubtle. Reprinted: 1978.209.

161. Giordano, Ralph. "Freiheit und Gleichberechtigung." Allgemeine Wochenzeitung der Juden in Deutschland (23 January).
Favorable review of the German translation of LD discussing the intricacies of the relationship of Fishbelly to W. Not merely an autobiography, the book uses details to force the reader to accept its authenticity. W and Fishbelly finally come together at the point where Fishbelly realizes that he must either give in or flee the United States.

162. Gorlier, Claudio. "I figli dello zio Crow: appunti sulla narrativa negra negli Stati Uniti." Paragone, 12 (August), 20-32.
Includes discussion of W as a protest writer with special attention to LD. Comments also on W's expatriation and death.

163. Gould, Helen. "Bookmarks." Springfield (Vermont) Reporter (1 March), p. B2.
Contains a notice of EM. Gould favors the earlier stories and disparages

the expatriate stories.

164. Gysling, Erich W. "Der schwarze Traum." Zurich Tages-Anzeiger für Stadt und Kanton (8 October).
Review of the German translation of LD. Like Joyce, W in this novel considers history a nightmare from which he is trying to awake. For Fishbelly there is no awakening in the United States, only a flight to Europe motivated by fear and hatred.

165. H. "Richard Wrights vorletztes Werk." Die Vienna Presse (c. January).
Favorable review of the German translation of LD noting parallels with W's life. Praises W's description of the physical and emotional environment of Clintonville.

166. H., E. "Richard Wright: Der schwarze Traum." Munich Deutsche Woche (1 November).
Favorable notice of the German translation of LD commenting on the representative nature of Fishbelly's fate.

167. Hampaté-Ba, Amadou. "Richard Wright, mon frère." La Vie Africaine, No. 10 (10 January), p. 5.
Reprint of 1960.162.

168. Hanrahan, Virginia. "American Negro's Tragedy Told in Eight Short Stories." The Napa Register (25 February), p. 3-A.
Favorable notice of EM. The stories are powerful and shocking, "but they carry the tremendous impact of realism" in presenting the condition of blacks in a hostile white world.

169. Harrington, Ollie. "The Last Days of Richard Wright." Ebony, 16 (February), 83-86, 88, 90, 92-94.
Illustrated personal account of W's death and funeral by a close friend. Includes comments on W's home, style of life, and leisure activities.

170. Hassan, Ihab. Radical Innocence: Studies in the Contemporary American Novel. Princeton, N. J.: Princeton University Press, pp. 168-169.
Mentions W in a discussion of Ellison.

171. Hayman, Allen. "The Reader's Corner: Eight Men by Richard Wright." Purdue University, WBAA (9 February), 3 pp.
Favorable radio review placing the collection in the context of "the career of one of our most compelling authors."

172. Helbig, Karl. "Wright, Richard: Der

schwarze Traum." <u>Der Übersee-Rundschau</u> (February).

Review of the German translation of <u>LD</u> arguing that W's arduous but successful battle for inner freedom caused his death. This largely autobiographical novel is part of his contribution to the struggle of other blacks.

173. Hindels, Josef. "Der Fluch des Rassenhasses: Die Geschichte eines schwarzen Jugendlichen." Vienna <u>Arbeiter-Zeitung</u> (20 May), p. 3.

Favorable review of the German translation of <u>LD</u> comparing it to white protest literature by Zola, Hauptmann, Gorky, and Toller. The depth of white racism which W's novel reveals will require more than superficial civil rights legislation to remedy. Hindels emphasizes sexual terror and awareness of Africa in choosing specific episodes for comment.

174. Hö. "Richard Wright: Der Mann, der nach Chikago ging." Deutsche Presse-Agentur (20 November).

Favorable review of the German translation of <u>EM</u>. Each story in the collection is a masterful psychological study demonstrating W's pessimism concerning the possibility of overcoming racial problems.

175. Hoehl, Egbert. "Richard Wright: Der Mann, der nach Chikago ging." Die Hamburg <u>andere Zeitung</u> (29 September).

Favorable review of the German translation of <u>EM</u> praising W's psychological insights into blacks trapped in a hostile world. Sartre's statement that "words are loaded pistols" applies well to W's writing.

175a. Holmes, Eugene C. "In Memoriam-- Richard Wright." <u>Dasein</u>, 1 (March), 2.

Eulogy comparing W to Byron as a "poet-seeker." As an old friend, Holmes considers W "one of the most humorous and wittiest of individuals despite his lurking cynicism."

176. Howe, Glynova. "<u>Eight Men</u>. By Richard Wright." <u>Interracial Review</u>, 34 (November), 296.

Favorable review emphasizing W's readable style and noting his "elusive humor." Nevertheless, he has thought deeply about racism.

177. H.[owe], I.[rving]. "Richard Wright." <u>Dissent</u>, 8 (Winter), inside front cover.

Obituary tribute stressing W's association with <u>Dissent</u> and his permanence as the author of <u>NS</u> and <u>BB</u>.

178. ____. "Richard Wright: A Word of Farewell." <u>The New Republic</u>, 144 (13 February), 17-18.

Literary obituary reviewing <u>EM</u> and analyzing W's career. "The Man Who Lived Underground" is the best piece in the collection. "Big Black Good Man" reveals W's humorous side. "The best stories are marked by a strong feeling for the compactness of the form, so that even when the language is scraggly or leaden there is a sharply articulated pattern of event." Emphasizes W's "nightmare of remembrance" as the key to his work. Reprinted: 1978.209;1979.134; 1982.50.

179. Hoyer, Franz A. "Der Minderwertigkeitskomplex zu Richard Wrights letztem Roman." <u>Saarbrücker Zeitung</u> (8 April), p. [28].

Favorable review of the German translation of <u>LD</u> stressing its autobiographical character. W accuses both whites and blacks, the latter for their propensity for living in a dream world. The novel is sensational and reportorial, but well written.

180. Hughes, Langston. <u>Ask Your Mama</u>. New York: Knopf, p. 44.

Mentions W's exile and death in Paris.

181. ____. "Richard Wright's Last Guest at Home." <u>Ebony</u>, 16 (February), 94.

Account of Hughes's visit three days before W's death. W gave him a manuscript of <u>Daddy Goodness</u>.

182. ____, Nat Hentoff, James Baldwin, Alfred Kazin, Lorraine Hansberry, and Emile Capouya. "The Negro in American Culture." <u>Cross Currents</u>, 11 (Summer), 205-224.

Includes comments by Hughes on W's expatriation (p. 222).
Reprinted: 1969.139; 1976.192.

183. Isaacs, Harold R. "A Reporter at Large: Back to Africa." <u>The New Yorker</u>, 37 (13 May), 105-106, 108, 110, 112, 114, 116, 119-122, 124, 126, 129-130, 132, 134-136, 138, 140-143.

Includes comments on W's sense of estrangement in Africa.
Reprinted: 1963.116.

184. Jahn, Janheinz. <u>Muntu: An Outline of the New African Culture</u>. Trans. Marjorie Grene. New York: Grove Press, pp. 185, 192, 230, 232, 233.

Translation of 1958.169.

185. ____. "Neoafrikanische Literatur," in <u>Lexikon der Weltliteratur im 20. Jahrhundert</u>. Vol. 2. Freiburg: Herder,

pp. 494-507.
Mentions W briefly (p. 502).

186. _____. "Wright, Richard," in Lexikon der Weltliteratur im 20. Jahrhundert. Vol. 2. Freiburg: Herder, pp. 1288-1289.
Biographical sketch. W's photograph appears following p. 512.

187. K. "Die Tragik des schwarzen Mannes." Kiel Morgenzeitung (11 October).
Review of the German translation of EM and a summary of W's career. His death took a leading spokesman not only from blacks, but from America and humanity at large.

188. Kala-Lobé, Iwiyé. "Un des vieux amis de 'Présence Africaine.'" La Vie Africaine, No. 20 (December), pp. 42-43.
Reminscence of W's association with Présence Africaine.

189. Kazin, Alfred, Nat Hentoff, James Baldwin, Lorraine Hansberry, Emile Capouya, and Langston Hughes. "The Negro in American Culture." Cross Currents, 11 (Summer), 205-224.
Kazin compares O unfavorably to NS. Reprinted: 1969.139; 1971.192.

190. Kenny, Howard N. "Hatred Blunts His Point." Peoria Journal Star (11 March), p. B-6.
Unfavorable review of EM. Kenny admits W's artistry, but complains that the short story allows less scope for the theme of anger than the novel does. Therefore, his ubiquitous anger in the stories "at times imposes a severe stricture upon his skill."

191. Knox, George. "Eight Men." Riverside (Cal.) Press-Enterprise (12 February), p. C-8.
Review placing the work in the context of W's career and emphasizing the grotesque, emotional, and shocking elements. "At his best he achieves haunting pathos and irony, at his worst tedious didacticism and lack of objectivity." "The Man Who Lived Underground," like Invisible Man indebted to Dostoevsky, is the best story in EM.

192. Ks. J. "Diese Woche gelesen." Neue Zürcher Nachrichten (28 October).
Review of the German translation of LD together with a sketch of W's life. W's was an art committed to the struggle for black rights, but he chastised the submissiveness of blacks as well as the arrogance of whites.

193. L., H. B. "Richard Wright: Der schwarze Traum." Israel-Forum (July-August).
Favorable notice of the German translation of LD. Notes the similarity between the social situation of blacks in the novel and that of Jewish minorities.

194. LaFarge, John. "Eight Men by Richard Wright." America, 104 (28 January), 573-574.
Favorable review emphasizing the pointed, astringent humor with which W treats the theme of the "psychology of habitual uncertainty" brought about by racism.

195. Lamm, Hans. "Zur Einführung," in Die psychologische Lage unterdrückter Völker. By Richard Wright. Vom Gestern zum Morgan--Band 7. Munich: Ner-Tamid Verlag, p. [3].
Brief introductory note explaining that the lecture here reprinted was delivered on 9 October 1956 in Hamburg under the auspices of the Congress for Cultural Freedom.

196. Leavell, Rozell. "Last Days of Richard Wright." Ebony, 16 (April), 15-16.
Letter to the editor on the impact of W's death. Praises W's work, which made readers more aware than bitter.

197. Lee, Lawrence. "Evident Art Diluted by Uncontrolled Anger." Chicago Sunday Tribune Magazine of Books (22 January), p. 4.
Review of EM admitting W's artistry but arguing that it is diminished by his anger at "the white man who was the evil figure of Wright's first works [and] the unelaborated and unmotivated villain of the last stories." Compares "Big Black Good Man" to Stephen Crane's "The Blue Hotel" and praises "Man, God Ain't Like That . . . ."
Reprinted: 1978.209.

198. Lemaire, Marcel. "Fiction in U. S. A.: From the South . . . ." Revue des Langues Vivantes, 27, No. 3, 244-253.
Includes a review of LD (pp. 246-248). The novel is melodramatic and sordid, but it points up the moral problems in Southern racism.

199. Logan, Floyd. "Negro Author Pens Vehement Stories About His Own Race." The Fort Wayne News-Sentinel (11 March), p. 4.
Rather favorable review of EM predicting that the stories will endure even though "the seeming indictment

and raw exposure of the unfortunate protagonists" might have been written by a white racist.

200. Loney, Myra. "Last Days of Richard Wright." Ebony, 16 (May), 13-14.
Letter to the editor disagreeing with Ollie Harrington's comments about the house in which W lived in Jackson. The editor comments supporting Harrington and rebutting Loney. Includes a photograph of the back of the house in question.

201. Lovell, John, Jr. Digests of Great American Plays. New York: Crowell, pp. 344-348.
Detailed summary of the plot of NS, an "expressionistic sociological drama," together with a statement of the theme, a list of characters, a historical note, and other information.

202. L.[yman], H.[elen] H. "Wright, Richard. Eight Men." Wisconsin Library Bulletin, 57 (September-October), 309.
Favorable notice.

202a. Lytle, Charlotte, ed. Index to Selected Periodicals: Decennial Cumulation 1950-1959. Boston: G. K. Hall, p. 496.
Lists ten items by or about W.

203. M., F. "Helle und Dämonie." Die Allgemeine Sonntagzeitung (30 July).
Favorable review of the German translation of LD. Emphasizes the overwhelming forces which W shows working against emerging human dignity.

204. M., S. "Ein länger Traum." Der Berlin Tag (27 February).
Review of the German translation of LD. Fishbelly represents W himself and symbolizes humanity as a whole. The novel expresses the dream of blacks everywhere which is beginning to be realized.

205. M., T. "Richard Wright: Der schwarzer Traum." Die Freidensrundschau, No. 10.
Review of the German translation of LD. Arguing that W's "attack on American democracy" fails to consider the more severe conditions faced by the peoples of Hitler's Germany and Stalin's Russia, the reviewer nevertheless recognizes the power behind W's "cheerless picture."

206. Maly, Karl Anton. "Richard Wright: Der schwarze Traum." Neue Volksbildung, 12 (March), 141.
Favorable review of the German translation of LD. It is a novel of devel-

opment (Entwicklungsroman) of great objectivity despite W's struggle against racism. W's break with Communism is mentioned.
Reprinted: 1961.207.

207. _____. "Richard Wright: Der schwarze Traum." Wiener Bücher Briefe (May).
Reprint of 1961.206.

208. Mauro, Walter. "Dolore e rivolta nella letteratura dei negri d'America." Il calendario del popolo (April), p. 4536.
Contains a paragraph criticizing W for abandoning the racial identification and protest of his early work for the estrangement and defeatism of O and SH. Contrasts W unfavorably to Langston Hughes.

209. McCloy, Shelby T. The Negro in France. Lexington: University of Kentucky Press, p. 185.
Contains a paragraph on W, whose residence in Paris "entitles him to be called a French writer as well as American."

210. Michels, Josef. "Wenn der Wind darüber geht." Düsseldorf Rheinische Post (28 October), RP am Samstag Sec., p. [10].
Contains a favorable review of the German translation of EM. Emphasizes W's moral power in showing the conflict between the sense of exclusion blacks feel and the superficiality of white values. Mentions specifically "The Man Who Went to Chicago," "The Man Who Lived Underground," The Man Who Saw the Flood," and "The Man Who Killed a Shadow."

211. Miller, Bill. "Bias Is Cast Aside." Denver Rocky Mountain News (29 January), p. 16A.
Favorable review of EM praising W for putting literary professionalism above racial propaganda. Both color and justice are his themes, but he "does not infer that injustice and color are synonymous." Miller comments on "The Man Who Lived Underground," "Man, God Ain't Like That . . .," and "The Man Who Was Almost a Man."

212. Moon, Henry Lee. "Spingarn Medal," in The World Book Encyclopedia. Ed. J. Morris Jones. Vol. 16. Chicago: Field Enterprises, p. 617.
Reprint of 1960.201.

213. Mphahlele, Ezekiel. "The Cult of Négritude." Encounter, 16 (March), 50-

52.
    Contains a disparaging reference to
W's opinions in BP.

214. N. "Der schwarze Traum." Badische
Zeitung (28 April).
    Favorable review of the German trans-
    lation of LD. The book demonstrates
    both W's artistic power and his wide
    human sympathies. He does not believe
    that the American dream is dead, but
    he sees it as still a distant hope.

215. N., J. K. "Von der Not des schwarzen Mannes." Zürische Zeitung (16 October).
    Review of the German translation of
    EM. All the stories deal with the
    quest of blacks in the white world.
    "The Man Who Went to Chicago" most
    clearly articulates the problem,
    which can quite often be reduced to a
    sexual difficulty. Comments also on
    "The Man Who Killed a Shadow" and
    "The Man Who Lived Underground."

216. Neumann, Michael. "Die Klage eines
schwarzen Mannes." Westermanns Monatshefte, 102 (December), 90, 92.
    Favorable review of the German trans-
    lation of EM concentrating on the
    social relevance of the stories to
    the unhappy American racial situa-
    tion. "The Man Who Went to Chicago"
    and "The Man Who Lived Underground"
    receive special mention.

217. Nichols, Charles H. "Color, Conscience and Crucifixion: A Study of
Racial Attitudes in American Literature
and Criticism." Jahrbuch für Amerikastudien, 6, pp. 37-47.
    Contains a brief comment on W (p.
    45), emphasizing his rage and pro-
    test, in the context of longer treat-
    ments of Melville, Twain, Faulkner,
    Redding, Ellison, and Baldwin.

218. Niemeyer, Carl. "Wright, Richard,"
in The World Book Encyclopedia. Ed.
J. Morris Jones. Vol. 19. Chicago: Field
Enterprises, p. 420.
    Reprint of 1960.206.

219. Nyren, Dorothy, ed. A Library of
Literary Criticism: Modern American
Literature. Second edition. New York:
Frederick Ungar, pp. 550-552.
    Reprint of 1960.207.

220. O'Connor, Willian Van. "Wright
Stories Tell of Torment." Minneapolis
Sunday Tribune (12 February) Upper Mid-
west Sec., p. 6.
    Unfavorable review of EM. O'Connor
    argues that W's obsession with racial
    questions, his hatred of whites, and
    his "Communist 'esthetic'" prevented

his artistic growth. He lacks "the
detachment that art, serious art,
requires." O'Connor exemplifies his
points with "Man, God Ain't Like
That . . ." and "The Man Who Went to
Chicago."

221. Ohff, Heinz. "Ein neuer Neger-
autor." Die Bücher-Kommentare, 10
(Fourth Quarter), 8.
    Review of the German translation of
    Frank London Brown's Trumbull Park
    mentioning W.

222. _____. "Die Psyche der Neger." Die
Bücher-Kommentare, 10 (15 September), 7.
    Favorable review of the German trans-
    lation of EM stressing W's effort to
    interpret black life to the white
    world with both literary artistry and
    social commitment. "The Man Who Lived
    Underground," "Man of All Work," "The
    Man Who Went to Chicago," and "Big
    Black Good Man" receive individual
    comment.

223. Ouchi, Yoshikazu. "Richard Wright
no Black Power nitsuite" ["On Richard
Wright's Black Power"]. Waseda Daigaku
Kyoyo Shogaku Kenkyu [Waseda University
General Studies], No. 13, pp. 1-16.
    The article was occasioned by W's
    death in the previous year. Notes
    that W's purpose in BP was to dis-
    cover negritude in his heritage. In
    his own country blacks suffered from
    the lack of freedom, as well as their
    fear and inferiority complex. He
    tried to escape this fear and complex
    by joining the Communist Party, going
    into exile, and finally travelling to
    Africa. But in Africa, just as in
    the Communist Party and in the United
    States, he discovered the same fear
    and inferiority complex. His journey
    into Africa thus ended in great dis-
    appointment. [Y. H.]

224. Ozawa, Fumio. "Negro Bungaku no
Honshitsuo Sasaeru Mono Sono 3--Richard
Wright no Sakuhin The Long Dream nit-
suite" ["That Which Sustains the Essence
of Negro Literature, III: Richard
Wright's The Long Dream"]. Showa Joshi
Daigaku Gakuen [Showa Women's College
Instruction], No. 256 (April), 94-104.
    Much like W's own life after leaving
    the United States for France, Fish-
    belly's journey into an exile signals
    W's abandonment of the native strug-
    gle. LD repeats a black man's self-
    defense, protest, celebration, and
    finally despair, suggesting what hap-
    pens to a majority of black Ameri-
    cans. The novel also points to a
    narrow view of the racial question
    widely held by the blacks: the blacks
    are perpetually pitted against the

whites. Unless this vicious cycle is broken, there would not be a new development in Negro literature. [Y. H.]

225. P. "Richard Wright: Der Mann, der nach Chikago ging." Der Leihbuchhändler (11 November).

Highly favorable notice of the German translation of EM with special praise for "The Man Who Lived Underground."

226. P. "Richard Wright: Der Mann, der nach Chikago ging." Salzburger Volksblatt (25-26 November).

Favorable notice of the German translation of EM. It amounts to a symbolic statement of the life of blacks in the United States and stands in the mainstream of the American short story tradition because of the dominance of dialogue.

227. P., M. "Richard Wright: Heidnisches Spanien." Familie und Heim (August).

Notice of the German translation of PS stressing its polemical nature.

228. P., M. "Die Welt der Neger." Saarbrücker Zeitung (4 November), p. [39].

Favorable review of the German translation of EM praising W's literary technique, especially his use of dialogue. He opens up the seemingly "exotic" inner world of blacks to white readers, focusing on situations of confrontation.

229. Paepke, Lotte. "Das Buch der Woche." Baden Südwestfunk (19 March), 7 pp.

Radio review of the German translation of LD. The novel demonstrates that the root of the racial problem lies not in the social-racial hierarchy as such, but in the fact that black values have been obliterated by the values of a corrupt white society. A weakness of the book is its failure to portray any humane whites, but this is not accompanied by sentimentalizing of blacks.

230. _____. "Mississippi ist überall." Frankfürter Hefte, 16 (August), 570-572.

Favorable review of the German translation of LD contrasting Fishbelly's escape from racial problems to W's lifelong engagement with them. Paepke emphasizes the hostility of the white world to the blacks in the novel and their consequent alienation.

231. Peeples, William. "He Aspired to Break Out." Louisville Times (23 January), p. 7.

Review of EM pointing out that it demonstrates both W's strengths and

his weaknesses. He is at his best when he writes from personal experience; his attempts at symbolism and allegory are unsuccessful. The best piece in the collection is "The Man Who Went to Chicago."

232. Poston, Ted. "Wright's Last Book." New York Post (22 January), Magazine Sec., p. 11.

Review of EM comparing it to UTC. Believing that W's expatriation damaged his talent and estranged him from American realities, Poston points out that most of his stories in EM were written before he went to Paris.

Reprinted: 1978.209.

233. Powers, Bob. "Powers of Books." The Huntington (W. Va) Herald-Advertiser (5 February), p. 35.

Contains a tribute to W and a favorable review of EM. Powers especially likes "The Man Who Lived Underground," "The Man Who Was Almost a Man," and "Man of All Work." W struggled against racism, but he was a storyteller, not a sermonizer.

234. _____. "Powers of Books." The Huntington (W. Va.) Herald-Advertiser (17 December), p. 23.

Favorable review of the Signet paperback edition of NS glancing at W's career and quoting from James Baldwin and from Richard Sullivan's afterword. Though rejecting the Communist message in the novel, Powers praises highly W's power and literary artistry, especially "the beauty of its composition, the brilliance of its dialogue."

235. Price, Eileen. "Eloquence to Remember." The Sunday Denver Post (19 March), Roundup Sec., p. 13.

Review of EM praising both the collection and the literary career of its author. Dealing with racial themes, W raises universal questions. Price also admires his literary craftsmanship. "His stories are easy to read, but hard to forget."

236. Price, Emerson. "'Future of Mankind' Offers Two Choices: Life, or Death for All." The Cleveland Press (24 January), p. 4-B.

Contains a notice of EM calling it "a collection of powerful and compelling stories describing the travail of Negro characters in a predominantly white world."

237. R., L. "Eight Men. By Richard Wright." Durham Morning Herald (5 March), p. 5D.

Reprint of 1961.27.

238. Rauch, Karl. "Romane--deutsch und amerikanisch." Berlin Telegraf (27 May), p. 23.
Contains a notice of the German translation of LD, which Rauch considers a high point of W's art and racial protest.

239. Raymond, Sally. "Raw Experience with Feeling." Chattanooga Sunday Times (19 February), p. 14.
Favorable review of EM noting the variety and power of the collection. "The Man Who Went to Chicago," "The Man Who Lived Underground," and "Man of All Work" receive special praise.

240. Redding, Saunders. "Home Is Where the Heart Is." The New Leader, 44 (11 December), 24-25.
Criticizes W's expatriation, which Redding believes has damaged his art. Always an American, he should have returned home.
Revised version: 1963.160; 1970.293; 1978.209.

241. _____. "Last Work of Richard Wright." The Baltimore Afro-American (18 February), Magazine Sec., p. 2.
Review of EM praising the early pieces--"The Man Who Saw the Flood," "The Man Who Killed a Shadow," and "The Man Who Lived Underground"--but finding the others weak, ambiguous, or bizarre. W's expatriation brought him personal comfort, but damaged him as an artist by estranging him from his most vital material.

242. _____. "Richard Wright's Posthumous Stories." New York Herald-Tribune Book Review (22 January), p. 33.
Unfavorable review of EM. The theme of the stories is rootlessness, but the best of them were written before W's expatriation. "Man, God Ain't Like That . . ." and "Man of All Work" are unsuccessful experiments. "The Man Who Lived Underground" is an impressive failure.
Reprinted: 1978.209.

243. Reding, Josef. "Männer gehen nach Irgendwo." Rechlinghausen Echo der Zeit (26 November).
Mixed review of the German translation of EM. "Big Black Good Man" merits high praise for its subtle control of tone, but other stories, especially "Man of All Work," fall so far short that one is forced to think that W was overrated at the end of his life. He is successful, however, in keeping the didactic elements from dominating his work.

244. Rexroth, Kenneth. "Who Am I? Where Am I Going???" The Urbanite, 1 (March), 6-7.
Reminiscence of the author's friendship with W and comments, mostly negative, about his exile. W's main virtue was telling the truth about American racism.
Reprinted: 1961.245.

245. _____. "Who Am I? Where Am I Going???" in Assays. Norfolk, Conn.: New Directions, pp. 14-18.
Reprint of 1961.244.

246. Rivers, Conrad Kent. "To Richard Wright." The Antioch Review, 20 (Winter), 464-465.
Poem on W's expatriation and the current racial situation in the United States.
Reprinted: 1962.95c; 1972.173.

247. Rogers, W. G. "From a Social Nether World." Saturday Review, 44 (21 January), 65-66.
Favorable review of EM. The final words of the best story in the collection, "The Man Who Went to Chicago," summarize the work. W tends to emphasize artistry more than race. Includes a sympathetic summary of W's life and career.

248. Rousseaux, André. Littérature du vingtième siècle. Seventh series. Paris: Editions Albin Michel, pp. 220-228.
Discusses LD with emphasis on the theme of black fear of whites. Whatever W's literary limitations, he speaks irresistibly to the white conscience.

249. Rubin, Louis D., Jr. and Robert D. Jacobs. "Introduction: Southern Writing and the Changing South," in their South: Modern Southern Literature in Its Cultural Setting. Garden City: N. Y.: Doubleday, pp. 11-25.
Contains an unfavorable comparison of W to Faulkner and Ellison (pp. 19-20). Unlike them, W subordinates his literary artistry to his message.

250. Ryan, Stephen P. "Eight Men, by Richard Wright." The Critic, 19 (February-March), 37.
Favorable review praising W's "feeling for language and . . . narrative sense." W's characters achieve universality.

251. S. "Richard Wright: Der schwarze Traum." Moderne Literatur (November).
Favorable notice of the German translation of LD stressing its topi-

cality.

252. S., C. "Neue 'Farbige' Bücher." St. Galler Tagblatt (22 January).
Review of the German translation of LD. Although its record of the sexual pressures faced by American blacks makes it worth reading, the novel shows that W stayed away from the United States too long and ultimately lost his natural writing style.

253. S., E. "Wrights letztes Werk." Basel Vörwarts (19 May).
Highly favorable review of the German translation of LD singling out the first third of the novel for special praise. The entirely convincing description of the milieu prepares us for W's final statement that racial problems cannot be solved within a capitalist system.

254. S., W. L. "Eight Men." Los Angeles Citizen News (14 January).
Favorable review praising W's characterization. The reviewer objects to W's expatriation, however.

255. Sablonière, Margrit de. "Laatste verhalen von Richard Wright." Litterair Paspoort, 142 (January), 7.
Eulogy of W and a review of EM. Stresses the autobiographical tensions, emphasizing "The Man Who Went to Chicago." EM comes closer to reality than LD, and W's sparse style makes several of the stories at once subtle and grotesquely humorous.

256. Sanders, David. "Wright: A Last Word." The Washington Post (29 January), p. E7.
Favorable review of EM finding W's universality and individualism more important than his protest. "Bigger Thomas, Fishbelly and Wright himself . . . are figures who represent . . . an existential individual given little chance in a hostile world." W had a narrative gift and a concern for language. Sanders mentions "Man, God Ain't Like That . . ." and "Man of All Work" as exemplifying W the literary professional.

257. Sch., H. "Richard Wright: Der Mann, der nach Chikago ging." Schweiz Arbeitsbildungszentrale (July).
Notice of the German translation of EM identifying "The Man Who Went to Chicago" as autobiographical and noting the similar patterns in each story.

258. Schürenberg, Dr. "Ein Leser gibt Auskunft." Sender Freies Berlin (14 May).

Radio review of the German translation of LD arguing that it is W's "most powerful novel." Schürenberg also summarizes W's life and works. He was a symbol of the fight for human dignity.

259. Schwab-Felisch, Hans. "Richard Wright: Der schwarze Traum." Neue Deutsche Hefte, No. 81 (May-June), 150-153.
Favorable review of the German translation of LD. After an introductory discussion of the complex American racial problem, the reviewer praises W for not succumbing to reverse racism. LD, however, is his most pessimistic novel of race relations. With great emotional power he presents a story of the need to attain black rights and the difficulty of doing so.

260. Scott, Nathan A., Jr. "No Point of Purchase." The Kenyon Review, 23 (Spring), 337-343.
Review of EM and a general assessment of W's career explicating the psychological and philosophical ramifications of the writing. Scott's judgment is largely unfavorable. In EM, "The Man Who Lived Underground" is brilliant and self-contained, but the other stories suffer because of W's radical perspective.
Partially reprinted: 1969.64.

261. Seelmann-Eggebert, Ulrich. "Richard Wrights letzter Traum." Därmstadter Echo (22 April).
Review of the German translation of LD. Too intelligent to believe in Europe as an actual Utopia which can solve all of Fishbelly's problems, W focuses his novel on the dark psychological forces which drive blacks away from identifying with themselves and their fates. He concludes that however much man flees he is condemned to playing out new versions of the ancient story of Cain and Abel.

262. [Seigler, Milledge Broadus]. "American Literature," in Britannica Junior. Ed. Don A. Walter. Vol. 2. Chicago: Encyclopaedia Britannica, pp. 216-227.
Reprint of 1958.245.

263. Sekiguchi, I. and T. Hamamoto. Introduction and notes, in their Man of All Work. Muse Library 79. Kyoto: Apollon-Sha.
Introduction and notes in Japanese to the English texts of "The Man Who Was Almost a Man" and "Man of All Work."

264. S.[mith], B.[lanche] H.[ixson]. "Have You Read Collections of Short

Stories by Noted Writers." The Meriden Record (16 September), p. 7.

Contains a favorable notice of EM. Smith praises "Man of All Work" as "a tale of loving devotion that knew no limits to its exercise." Smith admires W's dialogue, characterization, and atmosphere.

265. Smith, William Gardner. "Richard Wright, 1908-1960: The Compensation for the Wound." Two Cities, No. 6 (Summer), pp. 67-69.

Considers W's color to be his wound. He became a great writer to compensate for the suffering his color caused in a racist society. Poverty also played a major role in developing W's literary material and perspective.
Reprinted: 1971.147.

266. Steinberg, Steve. "Deaths," in The American Peoples Encyclopedia Yearbook. Ed. Ruth C. Hunt. Chicago: Spencer Press, pp. 322-334.

Includes a brief obituary of W (p. 334).

267. Stern, Richard G. "That Same Pain, That Same Pleasure . . .: An Interview with Ralph Ellison." December, 3 (Winter), 30-32, 37-46.

Ellison discusses his early relation with W (pp. 41-42).
Reprinted: 1964.53.

268. Stewart, Ollie. "The Richard Wright I Knew." Ave Maria, 93 (6 May), 9-11.

Memoir of W in Paris stressing the happiness of the last decade of his life in contrast to the bitterness of his early years. Stewart mentions the Franco-American Fellowship, W's Normandy farm, and his pleasant family and intellectual life.

269. Sullivan, Richard. "Afterword," in Native Son. Signet Classic CT81. New York: The New American Library, pp. 394-399.

Emphasizes the truthfulness and power of the novel while admitting the crudity of the style. Didacticism mars the third section. Nevertheless, Bigger is comparable to Raskolnikov of Crime and Punishment. Lacking wisdom, the novel is still revelation.

270. _____. "Lives of More Than Quiet Desperation." The New York Times Book Review (22 January), p. 5.

Favorable review of EM with special praise for "The Man Who Lived Underground" and "The Man Who Went to Chicago." All the pieces are remarkable for their truth and insight into racial discrimination.
Reprinted: 1978.209.

270a. Taylor, Clyde R. "His Gift Was Fire." Dasein, 1 (March), 3.

Poetic eulogy to W. The central metaphor is the fire of his suffering and his protest.

271. Thorpe, Earl E. The Mind of the Negro: An Intellectual History of Afro-Americans. Baton Rouge: Ortlieb Press, pp. 44, 113, 135, 228, 480.

Discusses W and his career and mentions BP, NS, BB, and O.

272. Tim. "Rich. Wright: Der schwarze Traum." Buch und Volk (December).

Notice of the German translation of LD calling it an "epic" with the pace but not the tone of a melodrama.

273. Tinkle, Lon. "Reading and Writing: Mossiker Book Leads Unusual Spring List." The Dallas Morning News (8 January), Sec. 7, p. 7.

Contains an announcement of EM.

274. Turner, Darwin T. "The Negro Dramatist's Image of the Universe, 1920-1960." CLA Journal, 5 (December), 106-120.

Comments briefly on the play NS (p. 109).
Partially reprinted: 1965.120.
Reprinted: 1968.204; 1969.238; 1971.300; 1976.194.

275. Turner, Jim. "Best of the Week." The Cleveland Press (24 January), p. 4-B.

Contains a brief, favorable notice of EM.

276. Umemura, Shigehiro. "Richard Wright no Bungaku Shiso (3)" ["Richard Wright's Literary Thought III"]. Kokujin Kenkyu [Negro Study], 15 (April), 5-8.

Continuation of 1960.252.

276a. Uchida, Shoichiro. "An Essay on Richard Wright." Rikkyo Daigaku Kenkyu Hokoku [Rikkyo University Study Report], 10 (30 June), 37-49.

The anger of the oppressed finds a congenial form of expression in UTC as it does in Tobacco Road and Of Mice and Men, two books by white writers published in the 1920s and '30s. W portrays black people's search for salvation in religion, drink, and wandering as epitomized, respectively, by Bigger Thomas's mother, Bessie Mears, and W himself. Though essentially romantic, W was disenchanted by Communism, and as LD indicates, he failed to fulfill his dreams. [Y. H. and T. K.]

277. Vaal, Hans de. "In memoriam Richard Wright." Litterair Paspoort, 16 (January), 10-12.

Assessment of W's career arguing that O is his most important book even though NS is his greatest novel. Reflecting the pressures on W from his increasing European popularity and his decreasing impact on America, O speaks to the condition of all Western men of the twentieth century.

278. Vogel, Wolfgang. "Träume enttäuschen." Diskus (June).

Review of the German translation of LD. The work of a "moralist," the novel registers almost scientifically the workings of the "inferiority complex" which gives birth to fear in black Americans. Vogel discusses the ways in which W's metaphors and plot structure contribute to the strength of his call to action.

279. W., H. H. "Der schwarze Traum." Salzburger Volksblatt (8 April).

Favorable review of the German translation of LD noting parallels with W's biography. Fishbelly's basic conclusion is that he must not be like his father.

280. W., J. "Eight Men--By Richard Wright." Auburn (N. Y.) Citizen-Advertiser (c. 21 June).

Favorable review praising especially "Big Black Good Man" but criticizing "The Man Who Lived Underground" as "wordy and pretentious."

281. W., T. "Richard Wright: Der schwarze Traum." Schweiz Arbeitsbildungszentrale (July).

Favorable review of the German translation of LD. It is a fascinating novel of development because of the treatment of Fishbelly's conflict with his father and the accurate description of the psychology of the oppressed.

282. Walker, Warren S. Twentieth-Century Short Story Explication. Hamden, Conn.: The Shoe String Press, p. 366.

Lists two items on W.
Reprinted: 1967.102.

283. Weissensteiner, Fritz. "Die Männer mit der anderen Haut." Vienna Heute (9 December).

Favorable review of the German translation of EM. Even though the stories in the collection sometimes resemble essays, W makes "every experience convincing" in a way whites writing on black life cannot. The reader's confrontation with W's open attack on the perverse white culture is both

overwhelming and distressing.

284. Wendland, Heinz. "Der schwarze Traum." Berliner Stimme (29 January).

Favorable review of the German translation of LD. While making the hatred and fear of blacks toward whites comprehensible, the work avoids all traces of self-pity. It is an effective protest against racial discrimination.

285. Wickert, Erwin. "Ein Neger in Paris." Frankfürter Allgemeine (8 February), p. 24.

Personal reminiscence with many anecdotes concerning W's contradictory attitudes toward his racial identity. Although he did not hate whites, he resented their preoccupation with his racial rather than human characteristics and significance.

286. Wolff, Maria. "Klagen des schwarzen Mannes." Müncher Merkur (23-24 September).

Review of the German translation of EM comparing W to Frank London Brown, who is less stylistically ambitious than W but has a more hopeful outlook on racial relations.

287. Wyatt, Bob. "Nine [sic] Vivid Short Tales." Tulsa Sunday World (29 January), Your World Magazine Section, p. 17.

Review of EM commenting on the plots of six of the eight stories. Wyatt finds most interesting "Man of All Work" and "Man, God Ain't Like That . . . ."

288. Y. "Richard Wright: Der Mann, der nach Chikago ging." ÖGB-Bildungsfunktionär (October-December).

Favorable notice of the German translation of EM emphasizing W's role as a racial spokesman.

289. Y. Untitled article. Konkret (April).

Notice of the German translation of LD, pointing out that it does nothing to alter the status of NS as the best novel of W, who is called America's Sartre.

1962

1. Anon. "Bücherbrief." Bücherweisen in Holstein (September).

Review of the German translation of EM. All of the pieces in the collection consider the inner needs of blacks in a society based on racial mistrust. "The Man Who Lived Underground" mingles reality and dream in its treatment of this theme.

2. Anon. Dictionary Catalog of the Schomburg Collection of Negro Literature & History. Vol. 9. Boston: G. K. Hall, pp. 8396-8400.
Reproduces ninety-four catalog cards on W.

3. Anon. Dust jacket of Huit Hommes. By Richard Wright. Trans. Jacqueline Bernard and Claude-Edmonde Magny. Les Lettres Nouvelles 30. Paris: Julliard.
Front inside flap sketches W's literary career and calls LD "perhaps his best book." Back inside flap compares some of the stories in EM to LD and notes their diversity of form.

4. Anon. Dust jacket of Spagna pagana. By Richard Wright. Trans. Giuliana De Carlo. Verona: Arnoldo Mondadori.
Blurb on front inside flap. Biographical sketch on back inside flap.

5. Anon. "Farbiges Amerika." Bücherschiff, 12 (February), 16.
Review of the German translation of LD and EM and two other books. Laments W's early death. He lectures too much in some of the stories, but the novel, somewhat autobiographical, conveys its message with implicit accusation.

6. Anon. "Four Books Banned in Savannah." Newsletter on Intellectual Freedom, 10 (January), 7.
Reports that BB was among four books removed from school libraries upon recommendation of the Chatham County Grand Jury.

7. Anon. Index Translationum 13. Paris: Unesco, pp. 81, 86, 145, 223, 250, 319, 345.
Lists translations of WML into Spanish, LD into Spanish, Finnish, and French, BB into Korean, UTC into Italian, "Tradition and Industrialization" into Italian, and "Bright and Morning Star" and "Down by the Riverside" into Japanese.

8. Anon. "Der Kampf mit dem schwarzer Schatter." Freiburg Badische Zeitung (20 August).
Favorable review of the German translation of EM stressing the recurring shadow figures. Points out parallels between "The Man Who Lived Underground" and Invisible Man. The mixture of emotional textures in the story is highly effective.

9. Anon. "Il lungo sogno," in Il Lungo sogno. By Richard Wright. Trans. Maria Luisa Cipriani Fagioli. Verona: Arnoldo Mondadori, front inside cover.
Blurb for the Italian translation of LD.

10. Anon. "Der Mann, der nach Chikago ging." Bonn Dienstag [?] (18 December), Sec. B/18, p. 16.
Notice of the German translation of EM pointing out similarities to LD and praising W's style.

11. Anon. "Der Mann, der nach Chikago ging." De Brussels Linie (30 March).
Review of the German translation of EM commenting on the dark comedy which underlies the theme of the complexity of guilt and innocence.

12. Anon. "Der Mann, der nach Chikago ging." Klarer Kurs (6 September).
Favorable notice of the German translation of EM mentioning "Man of All Work" and "Man, God Ain't Like That . . ." as keys to W's central themes. Praises W's psychological insight.

13. Anon. "Negerschicksale." Kristall, No. 9 (September).
Brief notice of the German translation of EM.

14. Anon. "Richard Wright," in Il lungo sogno. By Richard Wright. Trans. Maria Luisa Cipriani Fagioli. Verona: Arnoldo Mondadori, back cover.
Biographical sketch.

15. Anon. "Richard Wright." Zurich Tages-Anzeiger für Stadt und Kanton (1 December).
Obituary emphasizing that W's books increased white understanding of black people.

16. Anon. "Richard Wright: Der Mann, der nach Chikago ging." Bielefeld Freie Press (6 January).
Notice of the German translation of EM. W takes the position of neutral observer to reveal the deep tensions of race relations.

17. Anon. "Richard Wright: Der Mann, der nach Chikago ging." Bücherschiff (2 November).
Review of the German translation of EM. The book is impressive for its "forceful urgency," but W "lectures too much" and fails to recognize improvements in race relations resulting from recent legislative advances.

18. Anon. "Richard Wright: Der Mann, der nach Chikago ging." Die Quelle, 13 (February), 96.
Favorable notice of the German translation of EM praising W's talent and commitment.

19. Anon. "Richard Wright: Der schwarze Traum." Bücherschiff, No. 2.
Favorable review of the German translation of LD. Notes that W treats experiences overlooked by white American writers.

20. Anon. "Richard Wright: Der schwarze Traum." Heimat und Welt (March).
Favorable notice of the German translation of LD.

21. Anon. Untitled clipping. Basel Vorwärts (21 December).
Very favorable brief review of the German translation of EM.

22. Anon. Untitled clipping. Lady (February).
Contains a notice of the German translation of EM commenting on its clear and sober style.

23. Anon. Untitled note, in Ocho hombres. By Richard Wright. Trans. Leon Mirlas. Buenos Aires: Editorial Sudamericana, front inside flap of cover.
Blurb for the Spanish translation of EM.

24. Anon. Untitled radio script. Berlin Deutschlandsender (9 April).
Favorable radio review of the German translation of EM. Notes that all the pieces in the collection focus on the existential feelings of fear and anxiety. W analyzes the responsibility of whites for black fears, but ultimately sees only death or tragic renunciation as solutions.

25. Anon. Untitled radio script. Süddeutscher Rundfunk (4 September), p. 11.
Unfavorable radio review of the German translation of EM. While praising W's style, the reviewer dismisses the work as a polemical pamphlet with predictable themes.

26. Anon. "Wright, Richard," in Current Biography Yearbook 1961. Ed. Charles Moritz. New York: The H. W. Wilson Company, p. 483.
Reprint of 1961.97.

27. Anon. "Wright, Richard," in Der kleine Brockhaus. Vol. 2. Wiesbaden: F. A. Brockhaus, p. 671.
Brief bio-bibliographical note.

28. Anon. "Wright Richard," in Dizionario universale della letteratura contemporanea. Ed. Orlando Bernardi. Vol. 4. Milan: Arnoldo Mondadori, pp. 1197-1199.
Full biographical sketch with photograph and a bibliography of primary and secondary sources.

29. Anon. "Wright, Richard,," in Új Magyar Lexikon. Vol. 6. Budapest: Akademiai Kiadó, p. 744.
Biographical note.

30. Anon. "Wright, Richard: Der schwarze Traum." Büchereiwesen in Holstein (September).
Notice of the German translation of LD, a book not suitable for children.

31. Anon. "Wright, Richard: Der schwarze Traum." Walhaller und Traeberia [?] Klug [?].
Notice of the German translation of LD.

32. Arnold, Paula. "Der Mann, der nach Chikago ging. Von Richard Wright." Israel-Forum, 4 (July), 30.
Favorable review of the German translation of EM stressing the "grotesque humor" and bitterness of the stories. Notes W's parallel between blacks and Jews as outsiders.

33. Aschauer, Josef, S. J. "Wright: Richard: Der Mann, der nach Chikago ging." Die Zeit im Buch (October), p. 9.
Favorable review of the German translation of EM. The work leads to a better understanding of racial conflict because it demonstrates the psychological impact of racism on blacks.

34. Baldwin, James. Another Country. New York: The Dial Press, p. 195.
NS is one of three books belonging to the character Eric in France. Reprinted: 1963.47.

35. _____. Nobody Knows My Name: More Notes of a Native Son. Delta Book. New York: Dell, pp. 141-154, 181-215.
Reprints of 1957.136; 1961.107, 110, 113, 116.

36. _____. "Theatre: The Negro In and Out," in The Angry Black. Ed. John A. Williams. New York: Lancer Books, pp. 13-22.
Reprint of 1961.117.

37. Bartsch, Wolfgang. "Der Buchertisch." Hessischer Rundfunk (20 January).
Favorable radio comments on W, whose career helped to improve race relations. He focused clearly on the nature of the problem without illusions.

38. Benot, Yves. "Richard Wright et la condition du romancier noir américain." Europe, No. 398 (June), pp. 134-143.
Introductory note to William Alphaeus Hunton's "Richard Wright et la condi-

tion noire américaine" explaining that it is a translation of a lecture Hunton delivered at Conakry on 18 January 1961.

39. Birbaumer, Alfred. Untitled clipping. Neue Wege, 175 (May).
    Review of the German translation of EM.

40. Bl.[air], W.[alter]. "American Literature," in Encyclopaedia Britannica. Ed. Harry S. Ashmore. Vol. 1. Chicago: Encyclopaedia Britannica, pp. 784-794.
    Reprint of 1954.80.

40a. Breman, Paul. "Preface," in his Sixes and Sevens: An Anthology of New Poetry. Heritage Series, No. 2. London: Paul Breman Limited, pp. 6-8.
    Mentions briefly W and his haiku.

41. Brooks, A. Russell. "The Comic Spirit and the Negro's New Look." CLA Journal, 6 (September), 35-43.
    Mentions W as a protest writer. Humor appears even in his most tragic novels, however.

42. Brown, Deming. Soviet Attitudes Toward American Writing. Princeton, N. J.: Princeton University Press, pp. 34, 109, 128-130, 133, 144, 275.
    Discusses the Soviet critical reception of UTC and NS. The main issue in discussion of the novel was W's use of an unsympathetic protagonist. Ideological problems were not emphasized.
    Partially reprinted: 1971.147.

43. Browning, D. C. "Wright, Richard," in his Everyman's Dictionary of Literary Biography: English & American. Revised edition. London: J. M. Dent, p. 756.
    Biographical sketch.

44. Burke, W. J., Will D. Howe, and Irving K. Weiss. "Black Boy," in their American Authors and Books 1640 to the Present Day. Second edition. New York: Crown, p. 68.
    Note identifying author and theme.
    Reprinted: 1972.42.

44a. _____. "Native Son," in their American Authors and Books 1640 to the Present Day. Second edition. New York: Crown, p. 521.
    Reprint of 1943.24.

44b. _____. "Wright, Richard," in their American Authors and Books 1640 to the Present Day. Second edition. New York: Crown, p. 826.
    Revised reprint of 1943.24a.

45. Cary, Joyce. "Catching Up with His-

tory," in his The Case for African Freedom and Other Writings on Africa. Austin: University of Texas Press, pp. 221-224.
    Reprint of 1954.89.

46. Dempf, Anneliese. "Vision des Südens." Steyrer Zeitung (22 February).
    Favorable review of the German translation of EM. Like all of W's books, it expresses the plight of the outcast. Concentrating on blacks in hopeless situations, these brilliantly written stories avoid hatred even while viewing the doomed attempts of blacks to find a new world free from humiliation.

47. Do., Dr. "R. Wright erzählt." Essen Neue Ruhr Zeitung (15 March), p. [13].
    Favorable notice of the German translation of EM mentioning the two radio plays and emphasizing W's social message.

48. Dortmunder, Wilhelm. "Richard Wright: Der Mann, der nach Chikago ging." Das Schönste, 8 (March), 72.
    Rather favorable review of the German translation of EM identifying W's basic theme as the role of black people in white society. Less artistically accomplished than Hemingway or Faulkner, W nevertheless has some striking qualities, especially humor.

49. [Douglass, Joseph], Ina Corinne Brown, and John Hope Franklin. "Negro," in The World Book Encyclopedia. Ed. David C. Whitney. Vol. 13. Chicago: Field Enterprises, pp. 106-112.
    Revised reprint of 1959.78.

50. Drake, St. Clair and Horace R. Cayton. "Authors' Preface to the Torchbook Edition," in their Black Metropolis: A Study of Negro Life in a Northern City. Revised and enlarged edition. Vol. 2. New York: Harper & Row, pp. ix-xiv.
    Comments on W's introduction and reviews his career. He rejected both American racism and the urban black ghettoes which were its result. He "would hardly have felt that the changes occurring in Bronzeville since he wrote his essay constitute 'Progress'" (p. xiii).

51. _____. "Suggestions for Collateral Reading," in their Black Metropolis: A Study of Negro Life in a Northern City. Revised and enlarged edition. Vol. 2. New York: Harper & Row, pp. 797-798.
    Mentions favorably TMBV.

52. Dvorak, Jarmila. "Richard Wright. Eight Men." Books Abroad, 36 (Spring), 208.

Favorable review. "The Man Who Killed a Shadow" is a characteristic expression of W's "preoccupation with crime." "Man of All Work" is uncharacteristically humorous. W was stimulated by his contact with French culture.

53. Eichler, Willi. "Das unheimliche Missverständis." Geist und Tat (February), p. 64.
Favorable review of the German translation of EM. According to W, the main difficulty of race relations lies in the fact that blacks no longer exist as an actual "folk." They have been oppressed to the point that, as the excellent story "Big Black Good Man" shows, misunderstanding is inevitable.

54. F., B. E. "Ein Amerikaner erlebt Spanien." Volkestimme (20 December).
Favorable review of the German translation of PS summarizing W's analysis of the stultifying influences on the Spanish personality. W's "rational realism" makes him a typical American spokesman while his political and psychological interests broaden his perspective.

55. Faris, Kenneth. "A Small Portrait of Richard Wright." The Negro History Bulletin, 25 (April), 155-156.
Essay-interview with W. Meeting W in April of 1959, Faris found him to have an unusually vigorous personality. Quotes W on expatriation, politics (including Communism), and works in progress.
Reprinted: 1971.147.

56. Fehse, Willi. "Mann der Gegensätze." Der Berlin Tag (4 March).
Reprint of 1961.148.

57. Ford, Nick Aaron. "Richard Wright, A Profile." The Chicago Jewish Forum, 21 (Fall), 26-30.
Discusses W as a tortured writer whose work reflected his pain. He was primarily a social critic and secondarily a writer of fiction.

58. Franklin, John Hope. "Negro," in Collier's Encyclopedia. Ed. Louis Shores. Vol. 17. New York: The Crowell-Collier Publishing Company, pp. 276-292.
Reprint of 1955.43.

59. _____ and R.[ayford] W.[hittingham] L.[ogan]. "Negro, American," in Encyclopaedia Brittanica. Ed. Harry S. Ashmore. Vol. 16. Chicago: Encyclopaedia Britannica, pp. 192-200.
Reprint of 1957.184.

60. Fyfe, Christopher. "Introduction," in The Case for African Freedom and Other Writings on Africa. By Joyce Cary. Austin: University of Texas Press, pp. ix-xiv.
Mentions Cary's review of BP (p. xiii).

61. Gasseling, Helmut. "Der Mann, der nach Chikago ging." Buchanzeiger, 169 (May).
Notice of the German translation of EM pointing out the continuity of the collection with W's previous works.

62. _____. "Richard Wright: Der Mann, der nach Chikago ging." Bücherei und Bildung, 14 (April), 261.
Favorable review of the German translation of EM with special praise for "The Man Who Lived Underground." The central theme of the collection is racial conflict.

63. Geismar, Maxwell. "Society and the Novel," in A Time of Harvest: American Literature 1910-1960. Ed. Robert E. Spiller. American Century Series AC50. New York: Hill and Wang, pp. 33-41.
Mentions W and Henry Miller as "underground writers" who were "the two new major literary voices in the United States of the 1940's" (p. 40).

64. Gérard, Albert. "Humanism and Negritude: Notes on the Contemporary Afro-American Novel." Diogenes, No. 37 (Spring), pp. 115-133.
Concerns mainly Ellison and Baldwin, but discusses W and his relation to Communism, finding here an "emotional personalism" that is of the essence of blackness.

65. Gonfiantini, Loriano. "Richard Wright, Spagna pagana." Il ponte, 18 (October), 1407-1408.
Review of the Italian translation of PS pointing out that in its sociological, political, and Freudian dimensions it transcends the genre of the travel book. It reveals more about its author than about Spain, however.

66. H., H. W. "Richard Wrights Erzählungen." Neue Zürcher Zeitung (20 January), Sec. 2, p. 1.
Unfavorable review of the German translation of EM. The stories in the collection deserve notice as social protest, but their didactic tone spoils them as art.

67. Hakel, Hermann. "Buchkritik." Neue Welt (May), p. 14.
Contains a favorable review of the German translation of EM praising

both W's literary skill and his social and international importance as a racial spokesman. Hakel compares W to Hemingway in style, but stresses the former's spiritual quality.

68. Heil, Piet. "Randsel Heidendom." Het Vrije Volk (21 July).
Stressing the similarity W sees between African and Spanish religions, this review of the Dutch translation of PS praises its economic and political insights. W suggests more than he states in condemning Spanish political mysticism.

69. Heise, H.-J. "Der Mann, der nach Chikago ging." Konkret, 2 (January), 22.
Notice of the German translation of EM calling Hughes a greater black writer than W but praising W's use of literature as a weapon.

69a. Herzberg, Max J. "Wright, Richard [Nathaniel]," in his The Reader's Encyclopedia of American Literature. New York: Thomas Y. Crowell Company, p. 1257.
Biographical sketch with photograph.

70. Huet, G. H. M. van. "De verwesterste kleurling." Algemeen Indisch Dagblat (17 March).
Favorable review of the Dutch translation of WML. It reinforces the perception that W's most important contribution was his insight into the dilemma of the "emancipated" black. It is clear, especially in the sections dealing with the Third World, that W is not comfortable with non-Western traditions.

71. Hughes, Everett C. "Introduction to the Torchbook Edition," in Black Metropolis: A Study of Negro Life in a Northern City. By St. Clair Drake and Horace R. Cayton. Revised and enlarged edition. Vol. 1. New York: Harper & Row, pp. xxxv-xl.
Mentions W (p. xxxv).

72. Hunton, William Alphaeus. "Richard Wright et la condition du romancier noir américain." Trans. Eric Lévy and Yves Benot. Europe, No. 398 (June), 134-143.
Discusses W in relation to American racism, with some attention to his interest in the Third World. Emphasizes W's radicalism and social protest.

73. Jackson, Esther Merle. "The American Negro and the Image of the Absurd." Phylon, 23 (Fourth Quarter), 359-371.
Compares NS extensively to Light in August and briefly to Crime and Punishment. W's novel now seems less

a deterministic study of racial and social injustice than an existential exploration of human responsibility in a world where all things are possible.
Reprinted: 1970.192.
Partially reprinted: 1971.147.

73a. [James, C. L. R. ("J. Meyer")]. "The Revolutionary Answer to the Negro Problem in the U. S.," in Documents on the Negro Struggle. Bulletin of Marxist Studies, No. 4. New York: Pioneer Publishers, pp. 26-35.
Reprint of 1948.179a.

74. J.[eanpierre], W. A. "Young Blood [sic], par John O. Killens." Présence Africaine, No. 41 (Second Quarter), pp. 186-187.
Notes that the style of the novel recalls the W of the early forties.

75. Jürgen, Ingeborg. "Neues junges Afrika." Berlin Telegraf (4 March), p. 23.
Contains a favorable review of the German translation of EM emphasizing W's mediation between blacks and whites. Mentions "The Man Who Lived Underground," "Man of All Work," and "The Man Who Went to Chicago."

76. Kaiser, Ernest. "On Heightening the Social Muse." Freedomways, 2 (Spring), 119-132.
Quotes W quoting Shakespeare in his introduction to Black Metropolis.

77. Katzenschlager, Hans. "Richard Wright: Der Mann, der nach Chikago ging." Neue Volksbildung, 13 (February), 95.
Favorable notice of the German translation of EM stressing the realism, pessimism, and objectivity of W's presentation of racial conflict. The review quotes from "The Man Who Went to Chicago."

78. Kleffel, Helmut. "Neues vom "Büchermarkt." Hamburg N. V. B. (18 September), pp. 6-7.
Radio review of the German translation of EM identifying hatred as the central theme. W analyses the origins of the emotion both in white pressure and in internalized black self-images.

79. Krim, Seymour. "Ask for a White Cadillac," in The Angry Black. Ed. John A. Williams. New York: Lancer Books, pp. 99-115.
Mentions W briefly (p. 111).

80. L., F. R. "Richard Wright: Der Mann, der nach Chikago ging." Neues Afrika,

No. 4 (April).
Review of the German translation of EM noting that, as in all his work, W explores the extent of the effect of European influence on blacks. The reviewer briefly summarizes each story to demonstrate his contention that W is arguing that blacks must shape their own lives.

81. Lacouture, Jean and Jean Baumier. Le Poids du tiers monde. Paris: Arthaud, pp. 32-34.
Discusses CC noting W's experiential qualifications to analyze the political and psychological processes of the oppressed.

82. Luce, Phillip Abbott. "Communications on James Baldwin: 'Abruptly Banal.'" Mainstream, 15 (May), 45-48.
Discusses briefly Baldwin's attitude toward W.

83. M., E. "Der schwarze Traum." Vienna Volkstimme (6 January), p. [13].
Favorable review of the German translation of LD analyzing the word nigger as a clue to the book's meaning. Unlike Harriet Beecher Stowe, W is devoid of sentimentality. Blacks must struggle to achieve self-knowledge and become free.

84. M., F. "Der Autor und sein Werk." Dortmund Westfälische Rundschau (12-13 May), Rundschau Wochenend Sec., p. 3.
Note on W accompanying a reprint of the German translation of "The Man Who Saw the Flood." W lacks the humor of Langston Hughes in depicting race relations, but he achieves a tragic quality.

85. M., H. "Wright, Der Mann, der nach Chikago ging." Junge Europäer diskutieren (12 October).
Review of the German translation of EM noting the strength of W's picture of unjust conditions. Underlying W's works is the hope that these conditions can be improved.

86. McDonnell, Thomas. "The Emergence of the Negro in Literature." The Critic, 20 (December-January), 31-34.
Comments on W's attitude toward Africa and his relation to Baldwin.

87. Metkin, Gunter. "Abt. Literatur." Saarländisches Rundfunk (1 February).
Radio review of the German translation of EM, which reveals the seamy side of American optimism by spotlighting the situation of blacks. Unlike Faulkner, who views the South from a historical perspective, W takes a militant political view.

88. Moon, Henry Lee. "Spingarn Medal," in The World Book Encyclopedia. Ed. David C. Whitney. Vol. 16. Chicago: Field Enterprises, p. 617.
Reprint of 1960.201.

89. Mphahlele, Ezekiel. The African Image. New York: Praeger, pp. 46-47, 49-50, 133, 177.
Discusses W's response to Africa, especially in BP; mentions W's poetry; and points out his influence on Alan Paton and Peter Abrahams. Revised: 1974.136.

90. Myrdal, Gunnar. An American Dilemma: The Negro Problem and Modern Democracy. Twentieth anniversary edition. New York: Harper & Row, pp. 656, 734, 735, 936, 989, 992.
Reprint of 1944.127.

91. Neimeyer, Carl. "Wright, Richard," in The World Book Encyclopedia. Ed. David C. Whitney. Vol. 19. Chicago: Field Enterprises, p. 420.
Reprint of 1960.206.

92. P., R. "Richard Wright: Der schwarze Traum." Atlantis (July), p. 13.
Review of the German translation of LD stressing its topicality. Discusses the extreme tension surrounding the relations of white women and black men.

93. P., U. "Amerika wird immer wieder neu entdeckt." Salzburger Nachrichten (28 July), p. 21.
Contains a favorable notice of the German translation of EM praising W's dramatic quality. Mentions "Man of All Work."

94. R., H. "Der Mann, der nach Chikago ging." Die Tat (17 November).
Review of the German translation of EM emphasizing the recurring patterns of racial ambivalence. Notes the influence of Mencken, Dreiser, and Sinclair Lewis on W.

95. Riecke, Charlotte. "Richard Wright: Schwarze Macht." Literarische Arbeitsgemeinschaft (9 January), pp. 1-8.
Discussion of the German translation of BP relating the book's thesis to events after W's death and pointing out that unrest in Africa does not necessarily reflect Russian agitation. Summarizes the contents of BP.

95a. Rivers, Conrad Kent. "Postscript," in Sixes and Sevens: An Anthology of New Poetry. Ed. Paul Breman. Heritage Series, No. 2. London: Paul Breman Limited, pp. 32-33.
Poem commenting on "To Richard

Wright" (1961.246) and praising W's vision and literary form.
Reprinted: 1972.173.

95b. _____. "To Richard Wright," in his These Black Bodies and This Sunburnt Face. Wilberforce, Ohio: The Free Lance, p. 6.
Poem on W stressing racist oppression.
Reprinted: 1963.162b; 1970.5; 1972.173.

95c. _____. "To Richard Wright," in Sixes and Sevens: An Anthology of New Poetry. Ed. Paul Breman. Heritage Series, No. 2. London: Paul Breman Limited, pp. 31-32.
Reprint of 1961.246.

96. Rosenfeld, Isaac. "The Young Richard Wright," in his An Age of Enormity: Life and Writing in the Forties and Fifties. Ed. Theodore Solotaroff. Cleveland: World, pp. 100-103.
Reprint of 1945.1115.

97. S., M. H. "Wright, Schwarze Macht." Junge Europäer diskutieren (12 October).
Review of the German translation of BP. Although it is unfortunate that W retained the Communist hatred for religion, BP is interesting because of its subjective view of blacks.

98. Schiffman, Joseph, S. V. Baum, Sylvia E. Bowman, Marvin Klotz, and J. Albert Robbins. "American Literature." PMLA, 77 (May), 213-240.
Bibliography listing six items on W (p. 240).

99. [Seigler, Milledge Broadus]. "American Literature," in Britannica Junior. Ed. Harry S. Ashmore. Vol. 2. Chicago: Encyclopaedia Britannica, pp. 216-227.
Reprint of 1958.245.

100. Serpieri, Alessandro. "Richard Wright, La letteratura negra negli Stati Uniti." Il ponte, 18 (June), 752.
Favorable review of the Italian translation of "The Literature of the Negro in the United States." W identifies the source of the uniqueness of Afro-American literature as social oppression.

101. Strong, Augusta. "Notes on James Baldwin." Freedomways, 2 (Spring), 167-171.
Mentions Baldwin's quarrel with W.

102. Sykes, Gerald. The Hidden Remnant. New York: Harper, p. 176.
Relates that a publisher noted that W's work in exile would deteriorate "because he won't suffer so much."

103. Thompson, James W. "Black Boy: In Memory of Richard Wright." The Negro History Bulletin, 26 (October), 70-71.
Poem on the pain and love of W's childhood, together with his resolve to avenge racial wrongs.

104. Wagner, Jean. Les Poètes nègres des Etats-Unis. Paris: Librairie Istra, pp. XIV, 36, 184, 200-201, 254-255, 404, 490, 520, 542, 606, 608.
Contains several references to and quotations from W, who knew the author and discussed the subject with him.
Translated: 1973.288.

105. Werth, Wolfgang. "Wrights Erzählungen." Cologne Deutsche Zeitung (17-18 May).
Favorable review of the German translation of EM. Praises W's literary artistry in the short story form, reminiscent of Hemingway's, and his effort to interpret blacks to whites. As "Big Black Good Man" shows, whites need more understanding.

106. Wien, Werner. "Schwarz-Weiss." Bremer Nachrichten (9 January).
Review of the German translation of EM. Written from the perspective of the victim, the collection mirrors a society mired in distrust. It should remind the German reader that racial questions transfer from race to race and that black and Jewish persecution are similar. "The Man Who Lived Underground" typifies W's position in both its power and hopelessness.

107. Williams, John A. "Introduction," in his The Angry Black. New York: Lancer Books, pp. 7-9.
Mentions W as "the first Angry Man."

108. _____. "Richard Wright," in his The Angry Black. New York: Lancer Books, p. 142.
Headnote to an excerpt from NS.

109. Winslow, Henry F. "Richard Nathaniel Wright: Destroyer and Preserver (1908-1960)." The Crisis, 69 (March), 149-163, 187.
Critical-biographical essay with special concern for the themes and sources of W's fiction. Discusses LD, O, and WML. Winslow makes a strong case for W's integrity in exposing racism in America. No Afro-American writer matches his achievement.
Reprinted: 1971.147.

1963

1. Abrahams, Peter. "Nkrumah, Kenyatta, and the Old Order," in African Heritage.

Ed. Jacob Drachler. New York: The Crowell-Collier Press, pp. 131-144.
Partial reprint of 1959.1.

2. Adams, Frank T., Jr. "Miscellany Shows Sense of Creativity." The Norfolk Virginian-Pilot (7 July), p. B-6.
Favorable review of Herbert Hill's Soon, One Morning with special praise for W's "Five Episodes."

3. Algren, Nelson. Who Lost an American? New York: Macmillan, p. 305.
Mentions W briefly.

4. Anon. "American Ambassador Books Chosen by the Books-Across-the-Sea Selection Panel, N. Y." The English Speaking Union.
Recommends LT as a book interpreting American life to readers abroad because of its "wit and insight" in treating black experience.

5. Anon. "Athenaeum Notes: Lawd Today." The St. Johnsbury Caledonian Record (28 June), p. 2.
Favorable notice. Written with "compassion and humor," the novel reveals Jake Jackson's "brutality, immorality and gusto."

6. Anon. "Book Notes: Characters to the Right of Us." Chicago Sunday Sun-Times (26 May), Sec. Three, p. 2.
Notice of Herbert Hill's Soon, One Morning listing W as a contributor.

7. Anon. "Books." Playboy, 10 (June), 48, 50.
Contains an unfavorable review of LT. Considered as a new novel it is uninteresting, but its place in W's career lends it "a certain fascination." It evinces the anger but not the skill of the later works.

8. Anon. "Books Ahead: New Books This Week." The National Observer (25 March), p. 17.
Contains a nonevaluative notice of LT.

9. Anon. "Current Racial Tensions." Publishers' Weekly, 184 (9 September), 58.
New American Library advertisement listing BB and NS.

10. Anon. "Dream is Reality." Duluth News-Tribune (17 March), Cosmopolitan Sec., p. 2.
Notice of LT speaking of its "brutal realism" and its nightmarish quality.

11. Anon. Dust jacket of Der schwarze Traum. By Richard Wright. Trans. Werner von Grünau. Zurich: Buchclub ex Libris.

Blurb on back.

12. Anon. Dust jacket of Lawd Today. New York: Walker.
Blurb on front and back inside flaps.

13. Anon. "Ebony Book Shelf: Lawd Today, by Richard Wright." Ebony, 18 (June), 22.
Favorable review noting that the novel is valuable for its humor as well as the "brutal style which made the author famous." It is based in part on W's employment in the Chicago post office during the thirties.

14. Anon. "800 Literature." The Booklist and Subscription Books Bulletin, 59 (15 June), 845.
Lists W as a contributor to Herbert Hill's Soon, One Morning.

15. Anon. "Estados Unidos," in Enciclopedia Cultural. Vol. 6. Mexico, D. F.: Union Editorial Hispano Americana, pp. 466-495.
Mentions W as a novelist born in the twentieth century (p. 495). Adapted from Compton's Pictured Encyclopedia.

16. Anon. "An Exile No Longer." The New York Times (3 June), p. 19.
Article on James Baldwin referring to his rupture with W. Baldwin returned to the United States in 1957 because he did not want to "live in limbo" like W.

17. Anon. "Illustrated Topical Chronology of World Events 1958-1962," in The Encyclopedia Americana. Ed. Lavinia P. Dudley. Vol. 30. New York: Americana Corporation, pp. 1-56.
Contains a brief obituary of W (p. 28).

18. Anon. Index Translationum 14. Paris: Unesco, pp. 79, 167, 317, 443, 506, 685.
Lists translations of LD into German and Swedish, EM into Danish, BB into Danish and Hebrew, NS into Portuguese, and BP into Slovenian.

19. Anon. "Julliard." Le Paris Monde (16 January), p. 13.
Contains an advertisement for the French translation of EM.

20. Anon. "Lawd Today." St. Paul Pioneer-Press (24 February), TV, Theater, Entertainment Magazine Sec., p. 6.
Notice pointing out the novel's realism.

21. Anon. "Lawd Today, by Richard Wright." The Fresno Bee (14 April), p. 30-F.
Brief notice calling the novel a

"grim story."

22. Anon. "Lawd Today. Richard Wright."
The Book Buyer's Guide, 66 (March), 112.
    Brief notice emphasizing the novel's
    determinism.

23. Anon. "National Literatures: Anglo-
American Literature," in The Concise
Encyclopedia of Modern World Literature.
Ed. Geoffrey Grigson. New York: Hawthorn
Books, pp. 13-15.
    Mentions W briefly.

24. Anon. "Native Sons." Time, 81 (5
April), 106.
    Review of LT, memorable because of
    its truthful depiction of Chicago in
    the thirties. Of the protagonist of
    the novel, the reviewer writes: "Jake
    is no left-wing stereotype of a good
    man. He and society match each other
    in crude nastiness." Discusses also
    Baldwin and W.
    Reprinted: 1978.209.

25. Anon. "New Writings by American
Negroes." Omaha Star (31 May), p. 4.
    Review of Herbert Hill's Soon, One
    Morning containing a brief reference
    to W.

26. Anon. "Notes Without Comment."
Albany (N. Y.) Times Union (26 May), p.
I-7.
    Contains a notice of LT pointing out
    that it was an apprentice work.

27. Anon. "Ocho Hombres." Editorial Sudamericana (26 March).
    Favorable publisher's notice of the
    Spanish translation of EM. Although
    W uses racial materials, his idea
    of "essential humanity" is beyond
    color.

28. Anon. "On the Shelves of the Owosso
Public Library." The Owosso Argus-Press
(18 July), p. 13.
    Contains a notice of LT pointing out
    that "Jake is no hero."

29. Anon. "The Open Door Book Club."
Saturday Review, 46 (20 April), 17.
    Advertisement for a black book club
    offering LT as the initial selection.

30. Anon. "Pick of the Paperbacks: The
American Negro." Saturday Review, 46 (26
October), 46-47.
    Survey of black autobiography calling
    BB a "burning and indignant" book
    which "is triumphant proof that man
    indeed can prevail."

31. Anon. "Public Library Notes." The
Sioux City Sunday Journal (12 May), p.
C4.

Contains a brief notice of LT calling
it "bitter."

32. Anon. "Richard Wright." Trenton
(N. J.) Sunday Times Advertiser (28
July), Part Three, p. 8.
    Brief notice of LT.

33. Anon. "Show Selects." Show, 3 (September), 59.
    Mentions Herbert Hill's Soon, One
    Morning and lists W as a contri-
    butor.

34. Anon. "Some New Writing by American
Negroes." Bridgeport (Conn.) Sunday
Herald (16 June), Feature Magazine and
TV Sec., p. 20.
    Contains a brief reference to W call-
    ing NS "one of the important and
    perhaps grossly underrated novels of
    our time."

35. Anon. "Soon, One Morning." Manhattan
(Kansas) Mercury (18 August), p. 4.
    Notice of Herbert Hill's anthology
    listing W as a contributor.

36. Anon. "Soon, One Morning." Syracuse
Sunday Herald-American (7 July), Stars
Magazine Sec., p. 4.
    Notice of Herbert Hill's anthology
    listing W as a contributor.

37. Anon. "Spring Book Index, 1963."
Publishers' Weekly, 183 (28 January),
[366].
    Announces 29 March as the publication
    date for LT.

38. Anon. "3 Big New Bestsellers from
Avon." Chicago Tribune Magazine of Books
(6 October), p. 9A.
    Advertisement for LT stressing W's
    Chicago connections.

39. Anon. "Two Novels on the Negro Highlight a Spring List." The Detroit Free
Press (21 April), Sec. B, p. 5.
    Contains a favorable review of LT, a
    book comparable in quality to W's
    other unquestionably important works.
    Even at this early stage W was most
    concerned with the "economic priva-
    tion" of blacks.

40. Anon. "2,600 Books Get White House
O. K." U. S. News and World Report, 55
(26 August), 8.
    Reports that the Kennedy administra-
    tion has approved a list of books on
    American culture and history includ-
    ing NS and BB.

41. Anon. "Weekly Record." Publishers'
Weekly, 183 (1 April), 87.
    Contains a brief nonevaluative notice
    of LT with bibliographical details.

41a. Anon. "Wright," in Enciclopedia Universal Sopena. Vol. 9. Barcelona: Editorial Ramón Sopena, pp. 9191-9192.
Contains a brief bibliographical note.

42. Anon. "Wright, Richard," in The Columbia Encyclopedia. Third edition. Ed. William Bridgwater and Seymour Kurtz. New York: Columbia University Press, p. 2358.
Biographical note.

43. Anon. "Wright, Richard. Lawd Today." The Booklist and Subscription Books Bulletin, 59 (15 April), 680-681.
Notice pointing out that "Wright's understanding of the pressures on Jackson and his inimitable style compounded of humor, compassion, rhythmic dialog, and irony make Jackson's brutality, immorality, fecklessness, and gusto all of a piece and understandable."

44. Anon. "Wright, Richard. Lawd Today." Bulletin from Virginia Kirkus' Service, 31 (15 February), 202.
Favorable review praising the work as one of W's best, notable especially for its high-spirited wit. "Mr. Wright whips his bile so smoothly into the cream of his humor that most readers, Northern or Southern, will take the bitter with the butter and like it." LT is "a work of more consistent artistry" than Invisible Man.

45. Antonini, Giacomo. "Un romanziere negro americano: Baldwin dopo Wright." La fiera letteraria, Nos. 33-34 (11 August), pp. 1-2.
Review of the Italian translation of Another Country mentioning W briefly.

46. Baisier, Leon. "Hill, Herbert (Editor). Soon, One Morning." Best Sellers, 23 (1 July), 127.
Contains a brief reference to W.

47. Baldwin, James. Another Country. New York: Dell, p. 167.
Reprint of 1962.34.

48. _____. "Ce qui survivra de Richard Wright." Prevues, No. 146 (April), pp. 76-79.
Translation by Jean Bloch-Michel of 1961.116.

49. Bannon, Barbara A. "Forecast of Paperbacks: Lawd Today. Richard Wright." Publishers' Weekly, 184 (5 August), 71.
Notice of "a grim and gripping story."

50. Barnes, L. "The Proletarian Novel." Mainstream, 16 (July), 51-57.
Praises UTC but criticizes the treatment of Communists in NS. "L. Barnes is the pseudonym of an American author and critic" (p. 2).

50a. Baumbach, Jonathan. "Nightmare of a Native Son: Ralph Ellison's Invisible Man." Critique, 6 (Spring), 48-65.
Mentions W briefly.
Reprinted: 1965.34; 1970.52; 1971.38.

51. Beauvoir, Simone de. La Force des choses. Paris: Gallimard, 686 pp.
Mentions W numerous times, especially in connection with the political activity of the Rassemblement Démocratique Revolutionnaire. Her friendship with the Wrights began in 1946 and continued, though she disagreed with W's open anti-Communism of the late fifties. His death grieved her.
Translated: 1965.35.

52. Bitker, Marjorie M. "Day in an Anguished Life." The Milwaukee Journal (26 May), Part 5, p. 4.
Favorable review of LT. Though not up to the standard of his later works, it is a powerful novel and compelling social commentary, Bitker gives special praise to the dialogue.

53. Bl.[air], W.[alter]. "American Literature," in Encyclopaedia Britannica. Ed. Harry S. Ashmore. Vol. 1. Chicago: Encyclopaedia Britannica, pp. 764-776.
Reprint of 1954.80.

54. Boardman, Kathryn. "Producer Tells of Agonizing Struggle to Save Play." St. Paul Pioneer Press (24 February), TV Tab Sec., p. 6.
Contains a brief announcement of the publication of LT in March with a note on W's life and career.

55. Boatner, Maxine Tull. "A Window Opens." Hartford Courant (23 June), The Courant Magazine Sec., p. 14.
Favorable review of Herbert Hill's Soon, One Morning with a brief mention of W.

56. Bojarski, H. T. "Lawd Tomorrow." Time, 81 (19 April), 22.
Letter to the editor praising James T. Farrell and W while disparaging Baldwin.

57. Bontemps, Arna. "Biographical Notes," in his American Negro Poetry. New York: Hill and Wang, pp. 187-194.
Contains a note on W (p. 194) and mentions W in a note on Samuel Allen (p. 187).
Reprinted: 1964.30; 1974.31.

58. _____. "Introduction," in his Ameri-

can Negro Poetry. New York: Hill and Wang, pp. xiii-xviii.
 Mentions W's method of securing books from the Memphis Public Library (p. xviii).
 Reprinted: 1964.31; 1974.32.

59. _____. "Preface," in his Personals. Heritage Series 4. London: Paul Breman, pp. 6-11.
 Mentions W briefly.
 Reprinted: 1971.47.

60. Bosschère, Guy de. "Huit Hommes by Richard Wright (Julliard-Collection 'Les Lettres Nouvelles.')." Présence Africaine, 18 (Second Quarter), 231-232.
 Favorable review of the French translation of EM. Emphasizes the work's statement against racism, comparing it to BB and LD.

61. Bradbury, John M. Renaissance in the South: A Critical History of the Literature, 1920-1960. Chapel Hill: The University of North Carolina Press, p. 148.
 Contains a brief evaluation of W praising his power and thematic seriousness, but complaining of his lack of objectivity and artistry. W is also mentioned briefly elsewhere.

62. Brooks, Gwendolyn. "One of God's Rawest Creatures." Chicago Sunday Sun-Times (28 April), Sec. 3, p. 2.
 Favorable review of LT insisting that it is an accurate depiction of some, not all or most, black life.
 Reprinted: 1972.35.

63. Buckmaster, Henrietta. "Double Service from an Anthology." Chicago Tribune Magazine of Books (26 May), p. 7.
 Favorable review of Herbert Hill's Soon, One Morning containing laudatory comments on W and his contribution.

64. Burgum, Edwin Berry. "The Art of Richard Wright's Short Stories," in his The Novel and the World's Dilemma. New York: Russell and Russell, pp. 241-259.
 Reprint of 1944.64.

65. _____. "The Promise of Democracy in Richard Wright's Native Son," in his The Novel and the World's Dilemma. New York: Russell and Russell, pp. 223-240.
 Reprint of 1943.23.

66. Cargas, Harry J. "Lawd Today." The Sign, 42 (July), 61-62.
 Mixed review of the novel. Although it contains "too much technique," the author's "sincerity and passion" demand the reader's attention. Like many of W's works, LT is "more pamphlet than novel."

67. Charney, Maurice. "James Baldwin's Quarrel with Richard Wright." American Quarterly, 15 (Spring), 65-75.
 Analyzes the personal and artistic sources of the quarrel. Baldwin thought that W overemphasized the writer's social responsibilities at the expense of his artistic responsibilities. Charney defends W against Baldwin's charges, but concludes with analysis and praise of Baldwin, especially Another Country.
 Reprinted: 1970.86; 1971.147.

68. Colombo, Furio. "James Baldwin, la voce nuova dei negri d'America." La stampa (24 July), p. 7.
 Mentions briefly W's Parisian exile.

69. Conant, Mike. "Good Try." The Sunday Olympian (23 June), p. 6.
 Review of Herbert Hill's Soon, One Morning dismissing W's contribution as "lacking in style and imagination."

70. Conroy, Jack. "A Vivid Dramatization." Focus/Midwest, 2 (August), 22-23.
 Favorable review of LT calling it "an impressive performance" in spite of "its frequent gaucheries." Though unpolished, the novel has good dialogue, descriptions, and characterizations. Conroy provides a detailed plot summary.

71. Cowley, Malcolm. "American Books Abroad," in Literary History of the United States: History. Ed. Robert E. Spiller, Willard Thorp, Thomas H. Johnson, Henry Seidel Canby, and Richard M. Ludwig. Third edition. New York: Macmillan, pp. 1374-1391.
 Reprint of 1948.151.

72. Dadoun, Roger. "Retour à Richard Wright." Jeune Afrique, No. 119 (28 January-3 February), pp. 25, 28.
 Favorable review of the French translation of EM tracing W's success to his intimate knowledge of both black and white spheres of life. W achieves unity through subject matter and imagery. Discusses "The Man Who Lived Underground," "Big Black Good Man," and "The Man Who Killed a Shadow."

72a. Davis, Robert Gorham. "Art and Anxiety," in Art and Psychoanalysis. Ed. William Phillips. Meridian Books M161. Cleveland: The World Publishing Company, pp. 440-453.
 Reprint of 1945.873.

73. [Douglass, Joseph H.], Ina Corinne Brown, and John Hope Franklin. "Negro," in The World Book Encyclopedia. Ed. David C. Whitney. Vol. 13. Chicago:

Field Enterprises, pp. 106-112.
Revision of 1959.78.

74. Downey, Mary. "Younger Set Likes Action." The Portland Sunday Oregonian (19 May), Sec. Two, p. 6.
Lists LT.

75. Eisinger, Chester E. Fiction of the Forties. Chicago: The University of Chicago Press, pp. 68-70.
Discusses NS in relation to naturalism, Communism, and the sociology and psychology of race. Affronted by his denial of human dignity, Bigger turns to violence as a desperate means of self-realization. W, a "literary survivor from the thirties," does not control his outrage.

76. Elkins, Stanley M. Slavery: A Problem in American Institutional and Intellectual Life. Intro. Nathan Glazer. New York: Universal Library, pp. 132-133.
Reprint of 1959.81.

77. Ellison, Ralph. "The World and the Jug." The New Leader, 46 (9 December), 22-26.
Response to Irving Howe's "Black Boys and Native Sons." Ellison discusses W's relation to Mississippi and his use of art as a weapon. He rejects Howe's view that W influenced him. Reprinted: 1964.50; 1970.5, 115, 116; 1971.147.

78. _____, Alfred Chester, and Vilma Howard. "The Art of Fiction: An Interview," in Writers at Work: The Paris Review Interviews. Second Series. Introduction by Van Wyck Brooks. New York: Viking, pp. 320-334.
Reprint of 1955.40.

79. Emanuel, James A. "The Invisible Men of American Literature." Books Abroad, 37 (Autumn), 391-394.
Essay-review of Herbert Hill's Soon, One Morning containing a paragraph on "Five Episodes." Emanuel points out the new directions of ironic humor that W's death ended.

79a. English, Charles. "Another Viewpoint." Jubilee, 11 (September), 43-46.
Essay on Baldwin commenting on his "preoccupation with Richard Wright."

80. Fabre, Michel. "Richard Wright's First." The Boston Sunday Globe (7 July), p. A-55.
Favorable review of LT analyzing W's technique and placing the novel in the context of relevant literary traditions--Afro-American, Joycean, and picaresque. Fabre praises W's "genuine ability to recreate real-

istically the varied texture of life in universal terms."

81. Filler, Louis. "Introduction," in his The Anxious Years: America in the Nineteen Thirties: A Collection of Contemporary Writings. New York: Putnam's, pp. 1-29.
Contains a reference to UTC (p. 24).

82. _____. "Wright, Richard," in his A Dictionary of American Social Reform. New York: Philosophical Library, pp. 844-845.
Calls W a "writer of rebellious temperament" whose NS "argues the bitter thesis that a Negro treated like a rat could act only like a rat." Reprinted: 1969.83.

83. Fogarty, Robert S. "A Protesting Voice of Life." The Sunday Denver Post (14 April), Roundup Sec., p. 11.
Favorable review of LT asserting that the novel will enhance the reputation of W, who was a trailblazer for Baldwin and Ellison. "Lawd Today is at once funny and pathetic; cruel and vibrant since the voice of protest is the voice of life."

84. Franklin, John Hope. "Negro," in Collier's Encyclopedia. Ed. Louis Shores. Vol. 17. New York: Crowell-Collier, pp. 276-292.
Reprint of 1955.43.

85. _____ and R.[ayford] W.[hittingham] L.[ogan]. "Negro, American," in Encyclopaedia Britannica. Ed. Harry S. Ashmore. Vol. 16. Chicago: Encyclopaedia Britannica, pp. 192-200.
Reprint of 1957.184.

86. Frémy, Dominique. Quid? Encyclopedie annuelle. Paris: Librairie Plon, p. 21.
Lists W and three of his works. Reprinted: 1964.58; 1965.66; 1966.58; 1967.44; 1968.101; 1969.88; 1970.138; 1971.126; 1972.76; 1973.151; 1974.74; 1975.81; 1976.77; 1977.142; 1978.103; 1979.108.

87. Fuller, Edmund. "Slice of Life Cut by an Apprentice's Hand." Chicago Tribune Magazine of Books (14 April), p. 8.
Favorable review of LT. Despite structural defects, W shows detachment, objectivity, and candor in this novel, a "vivid, harrowing document that rings absolutely true within its strict limits of a small segment of observed behavior."

88. Gannett, Lewis. "Lawd Today. By Richard Wright." New York Herald Tribune Books (5 May), p. 10.

Unfavorable review emphasizing that the novel is an apprentice work. Reprinted: 1978.209.

89. Geismar, Maxwell. "A Cycle of Fiction," in Literary History of the United States: History. Ed. Robert E. Spiller, Willard Thorp, Thomas H. Johnson, Henry Seidel Canby, and Richard M. Ludwig. Third edition. New York: Macmillan, pp. 1296-1316.
    Reprint of 1948.168.

90. Giles, Louise. "Hill, Herbert, ed. & intro. by. Soon, One Morning: New Writing by American Negroes, 1940-1962." Library Journal, 88 (1 May), 1884.
    Mentions W.

91. _____. "Wright, Richard. Lawd Today." Library Journal, 88 (1 April), 1549.
    Mixed review comparing the novel unfavorably to NS. Equally sordid, it is less powerful. W's environmental determinism is now anachronistic. Reprinted: 1978.209.

92. Gorlier, Claudio. "Della repetizione: ossia Salinger, Baldwin, Roth, Hawkes, Updike." L'approdo letterario, 9 (January-March), 150-155.
    Contains a review of Another Country mentioning W briefly (p. 152).

93. _____. Storia dei negri degli Stati Uniti. Universale Cappelli 84/85. Bologna: Cappelli, pp. 36, 282-291, 295, 300, 302.
    Includes an account of W's career with emphasis on the themes of racial protest and revolt. Emphasizes NS and LD. Mentions W elsewhere, especially in connection with Baldwin.

94. Grant, William A. "Early Wright Book Is Raw." The Louisville Courier-Journal (12 May), Sec. 4, p. 5.
    Unfavorable review of LT calling it "a raw little volume, with a static quality punctuated here and there by flashes of overdone violence." The dated effect of the novel attests to the progress made by black people since the thirties. The basic point of LT is that "the Jake Jacksons of the world are a trial to themselves, as well as to society."

95. G.[ray], M.[argaret]. "Richard Wright's 'The Man Who Was Almost a Man.'" The Horn Book Magazine, 39 (December), 656.
    Recounts a successful teaching experience with the story noting that the boys in the class were interested in the subject matter and discussed the question of who was to blame for Dave's troubles.

96. Grumbach, Doris. "Fiction Shelf: Lawd Today, by Richard Wright." The Critic, 21 (June-July), 82.
    Mixed review. Like W's other books, LT is "raw, violent, blasphemous, painfully direct and honest," but it seems dated. It is an honest portrait of a victim of society, but W's realism is excessive and tedious. Reprinted: 1978.209.

97. Guérin, Daniel. Décolonisation du noir américain. Paris: Les Editions de Minuit, 219 pp.
    Dedicated to W, Padmore, Fanon, and Du Bois, this study cites W several times in support of particular points about race relations in the United States. Guérin notes that W paid tribute to Communist support of the black cause in the thirties.

98. H., E. N. "Essays, Poems, Short Fiction." The New Haven Register (9 June), Sec. 4, p. 6.
    Review of Herbert Hill's Soon, One Morning mentioning W.

99. Hagopian, J. V. "Die amerikanische Literatur," in Herders Zeitbericht. Freiburg: Verlag Herder, pp. 1371-1374.
    Mentions W briefly (p. 1371).

100. Hairston, Loyle. "Fine Collection of New Writing." Freedomways, 3 (Summer), 451-452.
    Favorable review of Herbert Hill's Soon, One Morning commenting on the centrality of protest in W.

101. Harris, Arthur S. "Interesting Negro Book." Worcester Sunday Telegram (21 July), p. 10E.
    Mixed review of Herbert Hill's Soon, One Morning commenting on Saunders Redding's appraisal of W's "Five Episodes" as worthwhile new work.

102. Hayes, Mary Anne. "New Negro Writing: A Mismatched Collection." The Houston Post (23 June), Sec. 7, p. 7.
    Unfavorable review of Herbert Hill's Soon, One Morning calling the W selection "a bad piece of writing."

103. Helyar, Thelma. "New City Library Books." Lawrence (Kansas) Daily Journal-World (11 May), p. 4.
    Contains a brief notice of LT.

104. Hentoff, Nat. "Negro Writing: More Literary Than Polemical." New York Herald Tribune Books (9 June), p. 7.
    Review of Herbert Hill's Soon, One Morning mentioning W.

105. Hicks, Granville. "Dreiser to Farrell to Wright." The Saturday Review, 46 (30 March), 37-38.
Review of LT with a plot summary. Notes the influence of Dreiser and Farrell. Despite Baldwin's quarrel with W's political emphasis, this novel is not Communist propaganda. LT conveys knowledge of Jake's society and creates a feeling for Jake himself.
Reprinted: 1978.209; 1982.50.

106. Hill, Herbert. "Acknowledgements," in his Soon, One Morning: New Writing by American Negroes, 1940-1962. New York: Knopf, pp. ix-x.
Mentions Hill's discussion with W about this book in the summer of 1960. Soon, One Morning is dedicated "to the memory of Richard Wright."

107. ____. "Introduction," in his Soon, One Morning: New Writing by American Negroes, 1940-1962. New York: Knopf, pp. 3-18.
Reprint of 1963.108.

108. ____. "The New Directions of the Negro Writer." The Crisis, 70 (April), 205-210.
Discusses and quotes from NS (pp. 206, 207-208). Compares "The Man Who Lived Underground" and Invisible Man (p. 209).
Reprinted: 1963.107.

109. Himelstein, Morgan Y. Drama Was a Weapon: The Left-Wing Theatre in New York 1929-1941. New Brunswick, N. J.: Rutgers University Press, pp. 120-122, 224.
Discusses the play NS in a chapter on the Mercury Theatre. It is a stirring melodrama with social significance. Himelstein discusses the play's reception on the mistaken assumption that W had already left the Communist Party.

110. Hoffman, Frederick J. The Modern Novel in America. Third edition. Chicago: Regnery, pp. xiv, 36, 149, 246-247, 248-249.
Reprint of 1956.203 with additional comments deploring the hatred W expressed in his fiction. EM and LT mitigate that hatred, however.

111. Hogan, William. "A Bookman's Notebook: New Writing by American Negroes." San Francisco Chronicle (29 May), p. 43.
Favorable review of Herbert Hill's Soon, One Morning calling NS "one of the most important and perhaps grossly underrated novels of our time" and containing a photograph of W.

112. Holmesly, Sterlin. "Depression Novel Bitter, Brilliant." San Antonio Express and News (5 May), p. 4-G.
Favorable review of LT giving special praise to W's use of dialogue. W is unsparing both to the black characters and to the society which produced them. Provides a brief plot summary.

113. Howe, Irving. "Black Boys and Native Sons." Dissent, 10 (Autumn), 353-368.
Examines favorably W's contribution to literature, especially NS and BB, comparing it to the less socially committed work of Baldwin and Ellison. Notes the criticism of W's work by Kazin and Rosenfeld. "The day Native Son appeared, American culture was changed forever. No matter how much qualifying the book might later need, it made impossible a repetition of the old lies. In all its crudeness, melodrama and claustrophobia of vision, Richard Wright's novel brought out into the open, as no one ever had before, the hatred, fear and violence that have crippled and may yet destroy our culture" (pp. 354-355).
Reprinted: 1963.114; 1970.5, 182, 183, 184, 185; 1971.147, 174; 1972.27; 1982.72.
Partially reprinted: 1974.92; 1975.104.

114. ____. "Black Boys and Native Sons," in his A World More Attractive: A View of Modern Literature and Politics. New York: Horizon Press, pp. 98-122.
Reprint of 1963.113.

115. Hyman, Stanley Edgar. "American Negro Literature and the Folk Tradition," in his The Promised End. Cleveland: World, pp. 295-315.
Expanded version of 1958.163.

116. Isaacs, Harold R. The New World of Negro Americans. New York: John Day, pp. 58, 113, 237, 247-260, 261, 262, 263, 266, 267, 268, 269, 304, 306, 321, 338.
Reprints 1960.167 and 1961.183 and comments on W elsewhere.
Reprinted: 1964.76.

117. Jahn, J.[anheinz]. "Die neoafrikanische Literatur," in Herders Zeitbericht. Freiburg: Verlag Herder, pp. 1407-1410.
Mentions W briefly (p. 1407).

118. Johnson, Charles S. "Negro in America," in The Encyclopedia Americana. Ed. Lavinia P. Dudley. Vol. 20. New York: Americana Corporation, pp. 65-74.
Reprint of 1955.54.

119. Jones, Anita. "Tortured Soul Bared in 'A Buried Land.'" Palm Beach Post-Times (c. July).
   Favorable review of LT calling W Baldwin's predecessor as black spokesman. Jake's story is emblematic of the fate of many other Afro-Americans.

120. Jones, LeRoi. Blues People: Negro Music in White America. New York: William Morrow, pp. 112-113.
   Quotes and comments on the list of topics in BB proscribed in interracial conversation in the South.

121. _____. "Problems of the Negro Writer: 2. The Myth of a 'Negro Literature.'" Saturday Review, 46 (20 April), 20-21.
   Contains a disparaging comparison of W, Toomer, Ellison, and Baldwin to Somerset Maugham. Such black writers have not yet reached the level of Melville or Joyce.
   Reprinted:1966.88; 1969.133; 1970. 207, 208, 209, 210; 1971.187.

122. Kaiser, Ernest. "The Literature of Harlem." Freedomways, 3 (Summer), 276-291.
   Mentions W and places Lorraine Hansberry and John O. Killens in the W tradition.
   Reprinted: 1969.135a.

123. _____. and John H. Clarke. "Recent Books." Freedomways, 3 (Fall), 580-591.
   Contains a brief notice of LT, a book in which "the author's formative literary prowess is clearly shown" (p. 586).

124. Keown, Don. "A Novel Indicts 'Ghetto System.'" San Rafael Independent-Journal (18 May), p. M14.
   Review of LT finding it a bitterly honest social indictment, but less impressive as a story. W presents his black characters unfavorably, but he shows the responsibility of society for them.

125. Kesteloot, Lilyan. Les Ecrivains noirs de langue française: naissance d'une littérature. Brussels: L'Institut de Sociologie de l'Université Libre de Bruxelles, pp. 65, 66, 72, 73, 81, 254, 258, 266, 267, 275, 276, 282, 287.
   Quotes WML and mentions W's relation to Présence Africaine and his influence on Francophone black writers.
   Reprinted: 1965.88.
   Translated: 1974.104.

126. Killens, John Oliver. And Then We Heard the Thunder. New York: Knopf, pp. 362, 407.

Mentions TMBV.
Reprinted: 1964.83.

127. Kinzer, H. M. "Yesterday's Classics: 12 Million Black Voices." Popular Photography, 52 (May), 59.
   Favorable review concentrating on the photography but mentioning W's "searing" text.

128. Kitching, Jessie. "Fiction Forecast." Publishers' Weekly, 183 (11 February), 131.
   Contains a prepublication notice of LT, a novel remarkable for its compassion for its unattractive characters. "While not as powerful as 'Native Son,' this is an acute, intense documentary story about unhappy, submerged and smoldering people."

129. Konishi, Tomoshichi. "Hashigaki," in Eight Men. Tokyo: Charles E. Tuttle, pp. i-vi.
   Introduction in Japanese to an English language edition of "The Man Who Went to Chicago" and "Big Black Good Man" with Japanese and English annotation. Konishi reviews W's life and literary career, quoting Sartre at length to explain W's viewpoint as a writer. He also comments briefly on the essay and the short story included.

129a. _____. "A Note on Negro Dialect: Richard Wright's 'The Man Who Went to Chicago.'" Kokujin Kenkyu [Negro Studies], 20 (December), 7-9.
   Discusses and illustrates three prevalent forces in Negro dialect: (1) courtesy ("I thought maybe you needed a porter"), (2) mixing ("Those who condemn them seek the basest goals of any people on the surface of the earth"), and (3) analogy ("slammed the windows shut"). [Y. H. and T. K.]

130. Kuniczak, W. S. "Negro Writers Join the Main Stream." The Cleveland Plain Dealer (26 May), p. 11-H.
   Favorable review of Herbert Hill's Soon, One Morning mentioning its dedication to W and W's contributions.

131. LaHoud, John. "Anthologies Reflect a New Negro Maturity." The National Observer (22 July), p. 17.
   Contains a review of Herbert Hill's Soon, One Morning calling W's contribution "a bad piece" which "still stands above much of the rest of the book, indicative of the late writer's talent." Includes a photograph of W.

132. Langnas, I. A. and J. A. List.

"Wright, Richard," in their Major Writers of the World. Paterson, N. J.: Littlefield, Adams, p. 516.
  Biographical sketch.

133. Leaks, Sylvester. "From Prison--A Cry." Freedomways, 3 (Spring), 230-232.
  Review of Paul Crump's Burn, Killer, Burn calling it "unquestionably a distinguished, worthy successor to Native Son. In many cases it is its superior" (p. 232).

134. _____. "James Baldwin--I Know His Name." Freedomways, 3 (Winter), 102-105.
  Asserts that Baldwin shares W's lack of love for black people. Quotes from BB to show W's attitude.

134a. LePape, Pierre. "La prochaine fois le feu de James Baldwin." Rouen Paris-Normandie (20 December), p. 9.
  Mentions W briefly.

135. Lynd, Stoughton. "The New Negro Radicalism." Commentary, 36 (September), 252-256.
  Contains a review of LT stressing the parallels between W's thought and that of Martin Luther King. In this early novel, W had not yet explicitly rejected Christianity, choosing to emphasize the collective suffering of his people. Like the young militants of the sixties, W in essence uses a "Christian vocabulary" to express "post-Christian" thoughts.
  Partially reprinted: 1969.64.

136. MacInnes, Colin. "Dark Angel: The Writings of James Baldwin." Encounter, 21 (August), 22-33.
  Mentions Baldwin's essays on W.
  Reprinted: 1970.252.

137. Magill, Frank N. "Native Son," in his Cyclopedia of Literary Characters. New York: Harper & Row, pp. 760-761.
  Lists and identifies nine of the characters of the novel.

138. Maloff, Saul. "The Negro Writer: A Long, Painful Search for Identity." The Commonweal, 78 (6 September), 540-541.
  Mentions W as a contributor to Herbert Hill's Soon, One Morning.

139. Martin, Ron. "Two Novels on the Negro Highlight a Spring List." The Detroit Free Press (21 April), Sec. B, p. 5.
  Contains a favorable review of LT considering it equal to his other books. It lacks eloquence, but it tells the truth.

140. Mayfield, Julian. "And Then Came Baldwin." Freedomways, 3 (Spring), 143-155.
  Contains three brief references to W.

141. Mélèze, Josette. "Huit Hommes par Richard Wright." Les Nouvelles Littéraires (24 January), p. 5.
  Favorable review of the French translation of EM commenting specifically on five of the pieces. Mélèze notes a lyrical vein as well as the protest mode and praises "The Man Who Saw the Flood" and "The Man Who Lived Underground."

142. Mitchell, Loften. "The Negro Theatre and the Harlem Community." Freedomways, 3 (Summer), 384-394.
  Mentions the play NS as a significant achievement (p. 390).
  Reprinted: 1969.174, 175; 1976.130.

143. Moon, Henry Lee. "Spingarn Medal," in The World Book Encyclopedia. Ed. David C. Whitney. Vol. 16. Chicago: Field Enterprises, p. 617.
  Reprint of 1960.201.

144. Morris, Willie. "Despair in Mississippi; Hope in Texas." Dissent, 10 (Summer), 220-226.
  Recalls a meeting with W in Paris (p. 221). See also 1967.77.

145. Morse, Carl. "All Have Something to Say." The New York Times Book Review (6 October), pp. 4, 28.
  Review of Arna Bontemps's American Negro Poetry and Gwendolyn Brooks's Selected Poems. In the former, "Wright appears as a good writer but not an especially good poet."

146. Mphahlele, Ezekiel. "African Culture Trends," in African Independence. Ed. Peter Judd. New York: Dell, pp. 109-139.
  Mentions the influence of W on Peter Abrahams, Richard Rive, and Bloke Modisane.

147. Murphy, William S. "Two Negroes Throw Light on Race Issue." Los Angeles Times (8 September), Calendar Sec., p. 15.
  Contains a review of paperback editions of BB and NS stressing the obstacles in the development of W's literary career.

148. Negri, Alfred. "A Negro's Turbulent Day in Depression-Era Chicago." Redwood City Tribune (11 May), Peninsula Living Sec., p. 29.
  Favorable review of LT summarizing the story of Jake's day, an episode in the continual battle of his life. Although not comparable to NS or BB,

LT "is representative of the genius of a man who wrote about the people he understood because he was one of them."

149. Niemeyer, Carl. "Wright, Richard," in The World Book Encyclopedia. Ed. David C. Whitney. Vol. 19. Chicago: Field Enterprises, p. 420.
    Reprint of 1960.206.

150. Nyren, Dorothy, ed. A Library of Literary Criticism: Modern American Literature. Third edition. New York: Frederick Ungar, pp. 550-552.
    Reprint of 1960.207.

151. O'Daniel, Therman B. "James Baldwin: An Interpretive Study." CLA Journal, 7 (September), 37-47.
    Comments on the Baldwin-W relationship.

152. P., G. J. "Lawd Today." Boston Traveller (c. 9 May).
    Favorable review of a novel that shares some of the themes of NS without attaining its quality. Still, it is a "good and often vital story."

153. Parks, Gordon. "Books They Value Most." Popular Photography, 52 (May), 59.
    The two books Parks lists are TMBV and You Have Seen Their Faces.

154. Parot, Jeanine. "Nouvelles en noir et blanc." Les Lettres Françaises (14-20 February), p. 3.
    Favorable descriptive review of the French translation of EM mentioning each of the eight pieces.

155. Pollak, Felix. "Landing in Little Magazines--Capturing (?) a Trend." The Arizona Quarterly, 19 (Summer), 101-115.
    Mentions W briefly (p. 109).

156. Ray, David. "Negro Authors Breaking Bonds with New Books." The Miami Herald (23 June), p. 7-F.
    Reprint of 1963.159.

157. _____. "Negro Changes Self-Pity and Rage Into Great Art." The Vancouver Sun (7 June), Leisure Sec., p. 8.
    Reprint of 1963.159.

158. _____. "Negro Writer Assumes New Dimensions." Toledo Blade (16 June), p. 7.
    Reprint of 1963.159.

159. _____. "Top Writing Displayed in Anthology." Buffalo Evening News (1 June), Sec. B, p. 8.
    Favorable review of Herbert Hill's

Soon, One Morning comparing NS to Nelson Algren's Never Come Morning. W was "a giant whose last book of stories took on dimensions even 'Native Son' had not promised, created a new pride and a new universe of possibilities in the work of other Negroes."
    Reprinted: 1963.156, 157, 158.

160. Redding, Saunders. "The Alien Land of Richard Wright," in Soon, One Morning: New Writing by American Negroes, 1940-1962. Ed. Herbert Hill. New York: Knopf, pp. 50-59.
    Revised version of 1961.240.
    Reprinted: 1970.293; 1971.147.
    Partially reprinted: 1969.64; 1973.256.

161. Reed, W. A., Jr. "Oft Brutal Offering of Life in the Raw." The Nashville Tennessean (24 March), p. 8-F.
    Favorable review of LT locating it in W's career, summarizing the plot, and praising its tragic realism and social protest.

162. Rhodes, Richard. "Integration Need Not Be So Solemn." The Kansas City Star (14 April), p. 3E.
    Contains a favorable review of LT comparing W to Steinbeck and Upton Sinclair in the tradition of protest fiction and contrasting him to Baldwin. Rhodes praises W's dialogue and his stylistic experimentation.

162a. Rivers, Conrad Kent. "For Richard Wright." Umbra, No. 2 (December), p. 37.
    Poem expressing the poet's resolve to leave the Paris of his and W's expatriation and return to America.
    Reprinted: 1972.173.

162b. _____. "To Richard Wright," in American Negro Poetry. Ed. Arna Bontemps. New York: Hill and Wang, pp. 177-178.
    Reprint of 1962.95b.

163. Sablonière, Margrit de. "Blanke man, luister!" Nieuwe Rotterdamse Courant (1 June), Amerikaanse boeken Sec., p. 7.
    Survey of W's career in the context of the history of Afro-American literature. Emphasizes W's understanding of both political and psychological problems. Includes a photograph.

164. _____. "Boekenpaspoort en Boekennieuws: Negerlitteratuur." Litterair Paspoort, 18 (August-September), 141-142.
    Review of Charles Wright's The Messenger mentioning W.

165. _____. "Negerlitteratuur." Litterair Paspoort, 18 (June-July), 139-
140.
Review of LT, which is interesting
primarily because it fills a historical gap in our knowledge of W's
development. Reading like an early
version of LD, the novel presents the
black man's dilemma in a manner less
crystallized than NS.

165a. Sainville, Léonard and M. Haron.
"Richard Wright," in Anthologie de la
littérature négro-africaine: romanciers
et conteurs. Ed. Léonard Sainville. Vol.
1. Paris: Présence Africaine, pp. 381-
406.
Excerpts with commentary from French
translations of UTC, NS, and BB. The
commentary emphasizes the social and
racial dimensions of W's work.

165b. Saito, Tadatoshi. "Freedom as Escape: Richard Wright and His Work."
Hitosubashi Ronshu [Hitosubashi Trea-
tises], 50 (1 July), 53-70.
A survey of W's career up to Paris.
Discusses his style in UTC, NS, BB,
and O, and concludes that to W freedom means escape and that escape,
accomplished for the sake of understanding the world to which one escapes, eventually leads to defeatism.
[Y. H. and T. K.]

166. Schlueter, Paul. "Collection of
Negro Writing Is Best Yet." The Sunday
Denver Post (6 October), Roundup Sec.,
p. 16.
Review of Herbert Hill's Soon, One
Morning listing W as a contributor.

167. Scott, Julius S., Jr. "Essays,
Fiction, Poetry by 27 Negro Authors."
Houston Chronicle (2 June), Zest Maga-
zine Sec., p. 11.
Favorable review of Herbert Hill's
Soon, One Morning mentioning W.

168. [Seigler, Milledge Broadus]. "Amer-
ican Literature," in Britannica Junior.
Ed. Harry S. Ashmore. Vol. 2. Chicago:
Encyclopaedia Britannica, pp. 216-227.
Reprint of 1958.245.

169. Shaw, Fred. "The Negro Writers."
Miami Daily News (26 May), p. 6B.
Favorable review of Herbert Hill's
Soon, One Morning citing W's life
work as "a landmark in Negro writing," but praising the contributors
to the anthology for moving from
protest to universal themes.

170. Shay, Arthur. "The Novel Wright
Suppressed." Chicago Daily News (30
March), Panorama Sec., p. 10.
Favorable review of LT praising its

resonant power. Shay attacks W for
his expatriation, but compares Baldwin unfavorably to W. "The impotence
of Wright's Negro, one sighs, is
organic, the impotence of Baldwin,
the new impotence, one might scoff,
is neurotic."

171. Smith, Welton. "'Gnawing' View of
the Negro." San Francisco Examiner (21
April), Highlight Sec., p. 18.
Review of LT considering it better
than NS and almost as good as UTC. W
communicates effectively "his sprawl-
ing hurt and his screeching anger,
made in America." The social message
is one of black unity.

171a. Smith, William Gardner. The Stone
Face. New York: Farrar, Straus & Giroux,
p. 135.
Novel mentioning W briefly as an
expatriate novelist.
Reprinted: 1964.116a; 1975.183a.

172. Spiller, Robert E., Willard Thorp,
Thomas H. Johnson, Henry Seidel Canby,
and Richard M. Ludwig. "Richard Wright,"
in their Literary History of the
United States: Bibliography. Third edition. New York: Macmillan, pp. 789, 216.
Reprint of 1948.251, 1959.114.

173. Stafford, Philip. "The Book Mark."
Oakland Tribune (7 July), El Dorado
Sec., p. 3-EL.
Mentions W as a contributor to Arna
Bontemps's American Negro Poetry.

174. Stevenson, David L. "Novel, The,"
in The Encyclopedia Americana. Ed.
Lavinia P. Dudley. Vol. 20. New York:
Americana Corporation, pp. 503-524.
Reprint of 1952.64.

175. Strout, Cushing. The American Image
of the Old World. New York: Harper &
Row, p. 260.
Mentions W as Baldwin's "literary
father."

176. Thompson, Francis J. "The Quality
of Negro Literati." The Tampa Tribune
(28 July), p. 6-E.
Review of Herbert Hill's Soon, One
Morning referring to Redding's
article on W as "highly informative."

177. Thorp, Willard and Robert E.
Spiller. "End of an Era," in Literary
History of the United States: History.
Ed. Robert E. Spiller, Willard Thorp,
Thomas H. Johnson, Henry Seidel Canby,
and Richard M. Ludwig. Third edition.
New York: Macmillan, pp. 1395-1411.
Mentions W as an "unreconstructed"
literary naturalist of power and
honesty (p. 1401).

Reprinted: 1974.169.

178. Toklas, Alice B. What Is Remembered. New York: Holt, Rinehart and Winston, pp. 170-171.
Discusses W's friendship with Gertrude Stein and their admiration for each other's writing.

179. W., H. A. "Negro Writing in America." Trenton (N. J.) Sunday Times Advertiser (22 September), Part Four, p. 8.
Favorable review of Herbert Hill's Soon, One Morning mentioning W's contribution and pointing to the publication of NS as a watershed in black literature.

180. Walker, Gerald. "20 Years of Good Writing." New York Post (9 June), Magazine Sec., p. 13.
Favorable review of Herbert Hill's Soon, One Morning commenting on W's contribution in comparison to Ellison's.

181. Watson, Madeline. "Can a Man Not Rise Above His Own Faults?" The Raleigh News and Observer (5 May), Sec. III, p. 5.
Somewhat unfavorable review of LT calling it a "sociological novel." After a plot summary, however, Watson asserts that the protagonist himself, "not society, is responsible for his many troubles." Thus Jake is an unsympathetic character.

182. Weisner, Peter. "Early Novel by Wright Is Published." The Sacramento Bee (10 March), p. L14.
Review of LT emphasizing the repulsiveness of Jake's character and the sordidness of his life. "His world, reproduced without sociological asides, is dull, ugly, and terrifying." Jake and "the forces crushing him" still exist, but the situation has improved since W wrote LT.

183. Wershba, Joseph. "Closeup: NAACP Labor Aide." New York Post (14 June), p. 39.
Reports that Herbert Hill credits W, whose work is the "turning point in Negro literature," with inspiring Soon, One Morning. W had promised to write an introduction to the volume but died before he had done so.

184. West, Paul. The Modern Novel. London: Hutchinson, pp. 297, 298, 303.
Comments briefly on W.

185. Williams, John A. "Negro in Literature Today." Ebony, 18 (September), 73-76.
Mentions W briefly and includes a photograph of W in Paris.

186. _____. "Problems of the Negro Writer 3: The Literary Ghetto." Saturday Review, 46 (20 April), 21, 40.
Notes that in the esteem of white critics and publishers James Baldwin "replaced Richard Wright, who, in turn, may have replaced Langston Hughes."
Reprinted: 1969.253; 1970.364; 1971.316.

187. Winslow, Henry F. "The Life of the Poor." St. Louis Post-Dispatch (24 March), p. 4C.
Favorable review of LT calling it a "mock-epic-folk drama." W indicts the society responsible for the suffering of the poor and the black. "The tragedy and the comedy here are human misery relieved by irony and mordant, scornful laughter." Winslow compares the novel to Mark Twain's Letters from the Earth.

188. _____. "Stating the Case: Negro Writing Since 1940." St. Louis Post-Dispatch (30 June), p. 4B.
Favorable review of Herbert Hill's Soon, One Morning containing a defense of W against Saunders Redding's attack.

1964

1. Adams, Russell L. "Richard Wright (1908-1960): A Sound of Thunder," in his Great Negroes Past and Present. Ed. David P. Ross, Jr. Chicago: Afro-Am Publishing Company, p. 126.
Biographical sketch emphasizing W's racial protest.
Reprinted: 1969.3.

2. Allen, Walter. The Modern Novel in Britain and the United States. New York: Dutton, pp. 155-158, 317.
American edition of 1964.3.

3. _____. Tradition and Dream: The English and American Novel from the Twenties to Our Time. London: Phoenix House, pp. 155-158.
Treats W in the context of the "bottom-dog novel" of Dahlberg, Farrell, and Algren. Allen concentrates on NS, "a most powerful novel both of Negro assertion and of radical protest" (p. 156). Quite unlike W himself, Bigger is nevertheless so fully realized that the reader becomes immersed in his experience. The third part of the novel is weaker, however, because it is too explicit. Allen also treats O briefly, judging it a failure. See 1964.2.

3a. André, Robert. "James Baldwin: La Prochaine Fois, le Feu--Personne ne saît mon Nom." La Nouvelle Revue Française, 12 (April), 722-723.
Mentions W briefly.

4. Anon. "Bontemps to Take Part in California Conference." Unidentified clipping, probably from a Nashville newspaper.
Reports that Bontemps will participate in a panel discussion on W.

5. Anon. "Books and Authors: Negro Resistance Tradition." The New York Times (15 December), p. 39.
Lists W as a contributor to Harvey Wish's The Negro Since Emancipation.

6. Anon. Dust jacket of Der schwarze Traum. By Richard Wright. Trans. Werner von Grünau. Frankfort am Main: Buchergilde Gutenberg.
Blurb on front inside flap with quotations from reviews in the Wiener Börsenkurier and Die Welt.

7. Anon. Dust jacket of Der schwarze Traum. By Richard Wright. Trans. Werner von Grünau. Zurich: Buchclub ex Libris.
Blurb on back.

8. Anon. Index Translationum 15. Paris: Unesco, pp. 75, 82, 230, 306, 328, 384, 487, 645.
Lists translations of EM into German and Dutch, BB into Spanish, French, Japanese, and Russian, "The Literature of the Negro in the United States" into Italian, and SH into Swedish.

9. Anon. "Literature," in Reading & Study Guide to Be Used with The World Book Encyclopedia. Chicago: Field Enterprises, pp. 250-259.
Lists W as a regionalist.

10. Anon. "Paperbacks." Best Sellers, 24 (1 September), 208-212.
Contains an announcement of WML (p. 210).

11. Anon. "Parade of Interesting Paperback Publications." Pasadena Star News (18 October).
Contains a notice of WML. W insists that the problem is not "racial" but "human."

12. Anon. "'Tell It Like It Is.'" Newsweek, 64 (24 August), 84-85.
Report on the University of California conference on black literature. W was the only significant figure to emerge from the Harlem Renaissance, and his "ghost still hovers over Negro literature like a presiding deity."

13. Anon. Untitled note in Que día Señor. By Richard Wright. Trans. León Mirlas. Buenos Aires: Editorial Sudamericana, front inside flap of cover.
Blurb for the Spanish translation of LT.

14. Anon. "Wright," in De kleine Oosthoek. Vol. 2. Utrecht: Nv. A. Oosthoek's Uitgeversmaatschappij, p. 691.
Very brief biographical note.

15. Anon. "Wright Biography." Buffalo Evening News (21 March), p. B-12.
Reports that Putnam's has contracted with Louis Lomax for an authorized biography of W.

16. Anon. "Wright, Riccardo," in Enciclopédia brasiliera mérito. Vol. 20. São Paulo: Editôra Mérito, p. 603.
Biographical sketch.

17. Anon. "Wright, Richard," in Enciklopedija Leksikografskog Zavoda. Ed. Marko Kostrenčić and Miroslav Krleža. Vol. 7. Zagreb: Izdanje i Naklada Jugoslavenskog Leksikografskog Zavoda, p. 725.
Biographical note.

18. Anon. "Wright, Richard," in Encyclopedia International. Ed. George A. Cornish. Vol. 19. New York: Grolier, p. 500.
Biographical note.
Reprinted: 1968.36.

19. Anon. "Wright (Richard)," in Grand Larousse encyclopédique. Ed. Claude Dubois. Vol. 10. Paris: Librarie Larousse, p. 965.
Biographical note.

20. Anon. "Wright, Richard," in Das grosse Nymphenburger Volkslexikon. Vol. 2. Munich: Nymphenburger Verlagshandlung, p. 1355.
Biographical note.

21. Anon. "Wright, Richard," in Meyers neues Lexikon. Vol. 8. Leipzig: Veb Bibliographisches Institut, p. 802.
Biographical note.

22. Anon. "Wright, Richard," in Nordisk Konversations Leksikon. Ed. Harald W. Møller. Copenhagen: Nordisk Konversations Leksikon, p. 475.
Biographical note.

23. Anon. "Wright (Richard)," in Pequeño Larousse ilustrado. Ed. Miguel de Toro y Gisbert and Ramón García-Pelayo y Gross. Buenos Aires: Editorial Larousse, p. 1654.
Very brief biographical note.

24. Antonicelli, Franco. "'Il nero è un colore terribile.'" La Turin stampa (23 September), p. 11.
Article on James Baldwin mentioning briefly NS.

25. Baker, William D. "Suggestions for Writing," in his Prose for Effective Composition. Englewood Cliffs, N. J.: Prentice-Hall, p. 341.
Follows a reprinting of the Mencken episode from BB.

26. Bannon, Barbara A. "Forecast of Paperbacks: White Man, Listen! Richard Wright." Publishers' Weekly, 186 (27 July), 74.
Notice pointing out that although much has changed since the time of the first publication of the book, its indignation is still important for providing insight into the psychology of oppressed people.

27. Beja, Morris. "It Must Be Important: Negroes in Contemporary American Fiction." The Antioch Review, 24 (Fall), 323-336.
Analyzes categories of black characterization in relation to the theme of identity. Discusses NS and O.

28. Bennett, Lerone, Jr. "Blues and Bitterness," in New Negro Poets U. S. A. Ed. Langston Hughes. Bloomington: Indiana University Press, p. 53.
Poem to Billie Holiday containing these lines: "She was Bigger / Before Wright wrote."

29. ____. "Tea and Sympathy: Liberals and Other White Hopes," in his The Negro Mood and Other Essays. Chicago: Johnson Publishing Company, p. 75-104.
Discusses the Bigger Thomas-Mary Dalton relationship as exemplifying the difficulty of achieving private solutions to problems involving "the mutually exclusive worlds of the oppressed and the oppressor" (p. 93).

29a. Bhely-Quenum, Olympe. "'Personne ne sait mon nom,' 'La prochaine fois, le feu' par James Baldwin." La Vie Africaine (February), p. 43.
Mentions W briefly.

30. Bontemps, Arna. "Biographical Notes," in his American Negro Poetry. American Century Series. New York: Hill and Wang, pp. 187-194.
Reprint of 1963.57.

31. ____. "Introduction," in his American Negro Poetry. American Century Series. New York: Hill and Wang, pp. xiii-xviii.

Reprint of 1963.58.

32. ____. Story of the Negro. Fourth edition. New York: Knopf, pp. 202-203.
Reprint of 1948.137.

32a. Bourniquel, Camille. "Librairie du Mois: James Baldwin." Esprit, 32 (April), 681-685.
Mentions W briefly.

33. Brent, Stuart. "Issue of Concern to Everyone." Chicago Tribune Books Today (11 October), p. 7A.
Lists UTC, NS, and BB as books helpful to understanding the Civil Rights movement.

34. Bronz, Stephen H. Roots of Negro Racial Consciousness: The 1920's: Three Harlem Renaissance Authors. New York: Libra, pp. 15, 93.
Contrasts W briefly to the genteel writers of the Harlem Renaissance.

35. Caute, David. Communism and the French Intellectuals, 1914-1960. New York: Macmillan, p. 361.
Mentions W as a contributor to The God That Failed.

35a. Cazemajou, J. "Baldwin (James).--La Prochaine fois, le feu." Livres (December), pp. 28-29.
Notes that W is better known in France than Baldwin.

36. Cecchi, Emilio. "Richard Wright," in his Scrittori inglese e americani. Vol. 2. Saggi di arte e di letteratura 21, ed. C. Garboli and M. T. Giannelli. Milan: Mondadori, pp. 346-349.
Reprint of 1948.144.

37. Clarke, John Henrik. "The Alienation of James Baldwin." Journal of Human Relations, 12 (First Quarter), 30-33.
Mentions W briefly.
Reprinted: 1969.56.

38. Collier, Eugenia W. "The Phrase Unbearably Repeated." Phylon, 25 (Third Quarter), 288-296.
Mentions a published comment by James Baldwin on a story by W (p. 292).
Reprinted: 1977.94.

39. Couch, William, Jr. "Sinclair Lewis: Crisis in the American Dream." CLA Journal, 7 (March), 224-234.
Mentions W briefly.

40. D'Avack, Massimo. "Solitudine negra." La fiera letteraria, No. 15 (12 April), p. 3.
Compares Baldwin to W and Ellison.

41. Donohue, H. E. F. Conversations with

Nelson Algren. New York: Hill and Wang, pp. 65, 95, 237-238, 250, 251, 257.
   Algren comments on W as a member of the Illinois Writers Project, as a spokesman for the inarticulate, and as a radical. He also relates a conversation with James Baldwin and others about W.
   Reprinted: 1965.55.

42. [Douglass, Joseph H.], Ina Corinne Brown, and John Hope Franklin. "Negro," in The World Book Encyclopedia. Ed. David C. Whitney. Vol. 14. Chicago: Field Enterprises, pp. 106-112.
   Revised reprint of 1959.78.

43. Ellison, Ralph. "Beating That Boy," in his Shadow and Act. New York: Random House, pp. 95-101.
   Reprint of 1945.889.

44. _____. "Change the Joke and Slip the Yoke," in his Shadow and Act. New York: Random House, pp. 45-59.
   Reprint of 1958.116.

45. _____. "Hidden Name and Complex Fate: A Writer's Experience in the U. S.," in The Writer's Experience. By Ralph Ellison and Karl Shapiro. Washington: Library of Congress, pp. 1-15.
   Discusses Ellison's friendship with W, who directed his reading to Henry James, Conrad, Joseph Warren Beach, and Dostoevsky.
   Reprinted: 1964.46; 1968.83; 1971.91, 92.

46. _____. "Hidden Name and Complex Fate: A Writer's Experience in the United States," in his Shadow and Act. New York: Random House, pp. 144-166.
   Reprint of 1964.45.

47. _____. "A Rejoinder." The New Leader, 47 (3 February), 15-22.
   Replying to Irving Howe, Ellison comments on his relationship to W and takes issue with Howe's defense of LD.
   Reprinted: 1964.50.

48. _____. "Richard Wright's Blues," in his Shadow and Act. New York: Random House, pp. 77-94.
   Reprint of 1945.890.
   Partially reprinted: 1969.64.

49. _____. "Twentieth-Century Fiction and the Black Mask of Humanity," in his Shadow and Act. New York: Random House, pp. 24-44.
   Reprint of 1953.122.

50. _____. "The World and the Jug," in his Shadow and Act. New York: Random House, pp. 107-143.

Reprint of 1963.77; 1964.47.

51. _____, Alfred Chester, and Vilma Howard. "The Art of Fiction: An Interview," in Ellison's Shadow and Act. New York: Random House, pp. 167-183.
   Partial reprint of 1955.40.

52. _____ and Allen Geller. "An Interview with Ralph Ellison." The Tamarack Review, No. 32 (Summer), pp. 3-24.
   Ellison claims that UTC is better existentialist fiction than O. W presents ideas in his fiction discursively rather than dramatically.
   Reprinted: 1969.71.

53. _____ and Richard G. Stern. "That Same Pain, That Same Pleasure," in Ellison's Shadow and Act. New York: Random House, pp. 3-23.
   Reprint of 1961.143.

53a. Elsen, Claude. "D'un monde à l'autre." Ecrits de Paris (January), pp. 117-121.
   Contains a review of Nobody Knows My Name and The Fire Next Time comparing Baldwin unfavorably to W.

54. Evans, Oliver. "The Pad in Brooklyn Heights." The Nation, 199 (13 July), 15-16.
   Reminiscence mentioning W's residence in Brooklyn Heights.

55. Fiedler, Leslie A. Waiting for the End. New York: Stein and Day, pp. 106-107.
   Contains disparaging remarks about W. Bigger, "identified by his very name as a reaction to Uncle Tom, [is] the imaginary Negro who has seemed to most Negroes the most offensive travesty of their long history and current plight." As a protest writer, W is "incapable of outliving the causes that occasioned his wrath."

56. Ford, Nick Aaron. "The Fire Next Time? A Critical Survey of Belles Lettres by and About Negroes Published in 1963." Phylon, 25 (Second Quarter), 123-134.
   Contains an extremely unfavorable review of LT (pp. 129-130), "a dull, unimaginative novel" that is "melodramatic, disjointed, padded with a multitude of hackneyed episodes . . . devoid of any unified relevance." The style is W's, but the vision is not. Ford finds it difficult to believe that W is the author.
   Reprinted: 1978.209.

57. _____. "Lawd Today. By Richard Wright." CLA Journal, 7 (March), 269-270.

Unfavorable review complaining of dullness and melodrama. Unless the work is read as an apprentice novel, it will damage W's reputation.

58. Frémy, Dominique. Quid? Tout pour tous. Paris: Librairie Plon, p. 22.
Reprint of 1963.86.

59. Fuller, Hoyt W. "The Negro Writer in the United States." Ebony, 20 (November), 126-128, 130-132, 134.
Report on the Asilomar conference mentioning the session on W.

60. Gibson, Rochelle. "Mutations in the Body Politic." Saturday Review , 47 (29 August), 74, 76, 78, 80, 82, 84, 86, 127-128.
J. Ben Lieberman credits W with providing "A fair symbol" of "erupting racial consciousness" (p. 76) in this survey of the "most important books" of the last four decades.

61. Gorlier, Claudio. "La linea Mason-Dixon (e quel che ne è rimasto)." Paragone, 15 (June), 84-91.
Mentions W as a protest writer (p. 88).

62. Grau, Shirley Ann. "The Southern Mind--Black/White." Cosmopolitan, 157 (August), 34-48.
Mentions W briefly.

63. Gross, Theodore. "The World of James Baldwin." Critique, 7 (Winter), 139-149.
Mentions W briefly.

64. Grossman, Walter. "Der Negerroman in den USA." Norddeutscher Rundfunk (23 March).
Discusses the Afro-American novel beginning with NS, which first poses the central question: "Who am I?" Through his contact with a hostile environment, Bigger is led to assert himself in existential violence. At the end it is apparent that he is "invisible," suggesting Ellison's basic theme.

65. Haas, Robert Bartlett. "Gertrude Stein Talking--A Trans-Atlantic Interview." UCLAN Review, 9 (Winter), 44-48.
Stein gives high praise to W as a stylist: "I think in the first place he has a great mastery of the English language, and I think, to my mind, he has succeeded in doing the most creative work that has been done in many a year" (p. 45).
Reprinted: 1973.161.

66. Hackett, Alice. "Popular Books 1924-1964: Do You Remember . . ." Saturday Review, 47 (29 August), 109-125.

Identifies BB as the leading autobiography of 1945 (p. 115).

67. Hansberry, Lorraine. "Village Intellect Revealed." The New York Times (11 October), Sec. 2, pp. 1, 3.
Notes that her generation "came to maturity drinking in the forebodings of the Silones, Koestlers, and Richard Wrights. It had left us ill-prepared for decisions that had to be made in our time about Algeria, Birmingham or the Bay of Pigs" (p. 3).

68. Hansen, Harry. "Depression-Born Durability." Chicago Tribune Books Today (12 April), p. 6.
Review of the reissues of WPA Guides noting that W worked on the staff of the New York City Guide.

69. _____. "Tenacity of Ideals." Chicago Tribune Books Today (28 June), p. 2.
Notes the increasing sales of W's books.

70. Heermance, J. Noel. "The Modern Negro Novel." Negro Digest, 13 (May), 66-76.
Uses W and NS as points of departure for a discussion of Ellison and Baldwin. Includes a photograph of W in his Paris apartment.

71. Hicks, Granville. "Signatures to the Significance of the Self." Saturday Review, 47 (29 August), 67, 70, 72.
Mentions Baldwin's criticism of NS.

72. Howe, Irving. "A Reply to Ralph Ellison." The New Leader, 47 (3 February), 12-14.
Argues that W's shocking brutality is a more effective vehicle of protest than literary niceties.

73. Hughes, Langston. "Biographical Notes," in his New Negro Poets: U. S. A. Bloomington: Indiana University Press, pp. 117-126.
The entry on Samuel Allen (p. 117) mentions W.

74. _____. "Negroes Abroad." New York Post (13 November), p. 4.
Mentions W briefly.

75. Hyman, Stanley Edgar. "Ralph Ellison in Our Time." The New Leader, 47 (26 October), 20-21.
Mentions Ellison's contention that W freed himself from his environment through will and imagination.
Reprinted: 1974.96.

76. Isaacs, Harold R. The New World of Negro Americans. Compass Books edition. New York: Viking, pp. 231-287.

Reprint of 1963.116.

77. Itazu, Yukio. "Richard Wright Shoron" ["An Essay on Richard Wright"]. Hosei Daigaku Kyoyobu Kenkyu [Hosei University School of General Studies Report], 8 (March), 73-80.
    W's finest achievement is NS. His intention was to illustrate the struggle of man through the example of Bigger Thomas, though ironically the book was taken as a protest novel. The essay also discusses W's relations with the Communist Party as shown in BB and NS. Notes that although LD is interesting as an entertainment, it fails as a serious novel. [Y. H.]

78. Jones, LeRoi. "A Dark Bag." Poetry, 103 (March), 394-401.
    Review of Arna Bontemps' American Negro Poetry praising W's "Between the World and Me" and the haiku poems.
    Reprinted: 1966.85.

79. _____. Dutchman and The Slave. New York: William Morrow, p. 57.
    In the play The Slave Grace calls the protagonist Walker "a second-rate Bigger Thomas."

80. _____. "In the Ring (2)." The Nation, 198 (29 June), 661-662.
    Mentions W as a "bad nigger" driven from his country.
    Reprinted: 1966.86.

81. Kaiser, Ernest. "Literature on the South." Freedomways, 4 (Winter), 149-167.
    Mentions UTC, BB, and LD, noting their power.

82. Kempton, Murray. "Black and White: But Whose Great Society?" The New Republic, 151 (7 November), 75-79.
    Cites the fact that BB did not alter white indifference toward racial problems as evidence of the basic difficulty facing Afro-Americans.

83. Killens, John Oliver. And Then We Heard the Thunder. New York: Pocket Books, pp. 372, 419.
    Reprint of 1963.126.

84. _____. "Explanation of the 'Black Psyche.'" The New York Times Magazine (7 June), pp. 37-38, 42, 47-48.
    Quotes TMBV.
    Reprinted: 1965.90; 1970.230.

85. Klein, Marcus. "Ralph Ellison," in his After Alienation: American Novels in Mid-Century. Cleveland: World, pp. 71-146.

Contains several references to W and Bigger Thomas. "Even Native Son, although it ends in creating a new stereotype, the Negro-as-a-proletarian-grotesque, contributed to the revolt against protest by trying the Negro problem both in terms invented by American naturalism and in terms of a Marxist analysis, terms which were nonracial" (p. 76).
Partially reprinted: 1970.236; 1971.205.

85a. Las Vergnas, Raymond. "Vision insolites." Les Nouvelles Littéraires (29 October), p. 5.
    Mentions W in a review of the French translation of Baldwin's Another Country.

86. Lee, Carleton L. "Religious Roots of the Negro Protest," in Assuring Freedom to the Free. Ed. Arnold M. Rose. Detroit: Wayne State University Press, pp. 45-71.
    Discusses the prophetic strain in W with particular reference to "Bright and Morning Star" and "Big Boy Leaves Home."

87. Leibson, Paula. "Just Browsing." The El Paso Times (15 March), Sunday Magazine Sec., p. 19.
    Notes that Louis Lomax is working on a biography of W.

88. Levin, David. "Baldwin's Autobiographical Essays: The Problem of Negro Identity." The Massachusetts Review, 5 (Winter), 239-247.
    Mentions Baldwin's references to W.

89. Lindegren, Erik. "Son av sitt land," in Son av sitt land. By Richard Wright. Trans. Gösta Olson. Delfinböckerna. Stockholm: Bonniers, back of dust jacket.
    Blurb.

90. Lissovoy, Peter de. "The Visible Ellison." The Nation, 199 (9 November), 334-336.
    Review of Shadow and Act referring to "Wright's limited, propagandistic depiction of Negro life" (p. 335).

91. MacGregor, Martha. "The Week in Books." New York Post (20 September), p. 47.
    Reports that Herbert Hill called the W symposium at the University of California conference on Afro-American literature "very moving."

92. Materassi, Mario. "La difficile lezione di Baldwin." Il ponte, 20 (March), 384-386.
    Review of the Italian translation of

The Fire Next Time mentioning W briefly.
Reprinted: 1977.220.

93. Mauro, Walter. "L'America negra di Baldwin." Il pensiero nazionale (31 May), pp. 22-23.
Includes discussion of W's literary career and his influence on other black intellectuals.

94. Mendel'son, Moris Osipovich. Sovremennyi amerikanskii roman. Moscow: Izdatel'stvo "nauka," pp. 5, 13, 18, 25, 26, 31, 96, 195, 196, 197, 201, 353, 445, 447-455, 458, 481, 486, 493, 494.
In addition to numerous brief references to W, Mendel'son reviews W's career (pp. 447-455) with specific commentary on UTC, NS, "The Man Who Lived Underground," and LD. Mendel'son deplores W's shift from radicalism in the first two to decadent modernism in the novella. LD is better but still deeply flawed.

94a. Merton, Thomas. "The Legend of Tucker Caliban," in his Seeds of Destruction. New York: Farrar, Straus and Giroux, pp. 72-90.
Essay on William Melvin Kelley's A Different Drummer mentioning W briefly.

95. Minakawa, Soichi. "Richard Wright no Hito to Sakuhin" ["Richard Wright's Personality and Work"]. Eigo Seinen [The Rising Generation], 110 (February), 90-91.
O vividly shows how W himself led the life of an outsider. Not only is the novel similar to Ralph Ellison's Invisible Man, but both novels closely reflect the lives of both authors respectively. The chief difference is in style: Ellison describes a man living in the present while W turns the same man into a symbol. [Y. H.]

96. Monicelli, Mino. "La legge della paura." L'Europeo, 20 (4 October), 62-69.
Article on James Baldwin mentioning W's expatriation in Paris.

97. Moon, Henry Lee. "Spingarn Medal," in The World Book Encyclopedia. Ed. David C. Whitney. Vol. 17. Chicago: Field Enterprises, p. 617.
Reprint of 1960.201.

98. Myrdal, Gunnar. An American Dilemma. Paperback edition. 2 vols. New York: McGraw-Hill, pp. 656, 734, 735, 936, 989, 992.
Reprint of 1944.127.

99. Niemeyer, Carl. "Wright, Richard," in The World Book Encyclopedia. Ed. David C. Whitney. Vol. 20. Chicago: Field Enterprises, p. 420.
Reprint of 1960.206.

99a. Ozawa, Fumio. "That Which Sustains the Essence of Negro Literature, V: Native Son as Naturalist Literature." Showa Joshi Daigaku Gakuen [Showa Women's College Instruction], 292 (April), 67-78.
W's adoption of realism and naturalism in writing his protest literature was influenced by Dreiser, Mencken, and Lewis, and his method of expression suited NS. [Y. H. and T. K.]

100. Peden, William. The American Short Story: Front Line in the National Defense of Literature. Boston: Houghton Mifflin, pp. 158, 159.
Contains a paragraph on EM deeming it artistically unsatisfactory because of stereotyped characters but "memorable and disturbing . . . as a sad and often moving testimonial to the result of racial intolerance on a gifted and bitterly disillusioned human being." Peden prefers such Langston Hughes stories as "Who's Passing for Who?" to W's "savage denunciations."

101. Pettigrew, Thomas F. A Profile of the Negro American. The University Series in Psychology, ed. Davis C. McClelland. Princeton, N. J.: Van Nostrand, pp. 4, 9, 44, 46, 234.
Cites BB to illustrate sociological points.

101a. Piccioni, Leone. "Letteratura negra," in Antologia dei poeti negri d'America. Ed. Leone Piccioni and Perla Cacciaguerra. Verona: Arnoldo Mondadori Editore, pp. 635-676.
Contains a critical sketch of W with specific comments on "The Man Who Lived Underground," BB, and NS (pp. 672-674).

101b. _____. "Taccuino d'un viaggio 1962," in Antologia dei poeti negri d'America. Ed. Leone Piccioni and Perla Cacciaguerra. Verona: Arnoldo Mondadori Editore, pp. 7-36.
Mentions briefly W's communism (p. 31).

102. Piovene, Guido. "Baldwin voce nuova dei negri d'America." La Turin stampa (11 October), p. 3.
Discusses Baldwin as W's successor in racial protest.

103. Pivano, Fernanda. "Letteratura negra U. S. A.," in her America rossa e nera. Florence: Vallecchi Editore, pp.

155-167.
    Contains a section on W (pp. 162-164)
    showing how his work exemplifies
    three black characteristics: expres-
    sion of concepts through image or
    action (as in BB), repetition (as in
    UTC), and a non-Western comic sense.
    Pivano also comments on W's idea of
    "life structure."

104. _____. "Richard Wright," in her
America rossa e nera. Florence: Vallecchi Editore, pp. 183-186.
    Reprint of 1957.289.

105. Quarles, Benjamin. The Negro in the
Making of America. New York: Collier
Books, pp. 248-249.
    Mentions W as a protest writer.
    Reprinted: 1969.198.

106. Redding, Saunders. "Modern African
Literature." CLA Journal, 7 (March),
191-201.
    Refers briefly to BB.

107. _____. "The Problems of the Negro
Writer." The Massachusetts Review, 6
(Autumn-Winter), 57-70.
    Contains several references to W,
    including comments on his loss of
    power as a consequence of his expat-
    riation.
    Reprinted: 1969.204; 1972.167.

108. Riva, Franco. "Letteratura negra:
la svolta di Baldwin." Humanitas, 19
(May), 586-591.
    Mentions briefly W and BP.

109. Rose, Peter I. They and We: Racial
and Ethnic Relations in the United
States. New York: Random House, pp. 102,
119, 132-134, 145, 147.
    Contains several quotations from W to
    illustrate sociological points.
    Reprinted: 1968.189.

110. Sandle, Floyd L. The Negro in the
American Educational Theatre. Ann Arbor:
Edwards Brothers, pp. 21-23.
    Treats NS as novel and play with
    quotations from "How 'Bigger' Was
    Born" and Hugh M. Gloster's Negro
    Voices in American Fiction.

111. Schiffman, Joseph, Sylvia E. Bowman, Marvin Klotz, Joseph V. Ridgely,
and J. Albert Robbins, with the help of
Philip R. Headings. "American Literature." PMLA, 79 (May), 187-212.
    Bibliography listing two items on W.

112. Schneider, Betty. "An Old Wright."
Community, 23 (January), 14.
    Mixed review of LT pointing out that
    W's apprentice naturalism is out-
    moded. "The story is undeviatingly

honest and forceful," but it is awkward at times.

113. Scott, Nathan A., Jr. "The Dark and
Haunted Tower of Richard Wright." Graduate Comment, 7 (July), 93-99.
    General discussion of W's fiction,
    especially UTC, NS, O, and EM. In NS
    W's rage causes him to project Bigger
    as an archetype of the black man in
    America, but actually he is a stereo-
    type of the bestial black. W lacks a
    humane vision, as O demonstrates, and
    he lacks artistry, but his testimony
    is moving.
    Reprinted: 1969.218; 1970.314, 315;
    1971.147.
    Partially reprinted: 1973.256.

114. [Seigler, Milledge Broadus]. "American Literature," in Britannica Junior
Encyclopaedia. Ed. John V. Dodge. Vol.
2. Chicago: Encyclopaedia Britannica,
pp. 216-227.
    Reprint of 1958.245.

115. Senghor, Léopold Sédar. "La Poésie
négro américaine," in his Liberté I:
Négritude et humanisme. Paris: Éditions
du Seuil, pp. 104-121.
    At the end of this 1950 lecture,
    Senghor quotes from "I Have Seen
    Black Hands" and comments briefly on
    the proletarian poetry of W and
    others.

116. Silberman, Charles E. Crisis in
Black and White. New York: Random House,
pp. 4, 48, 53, 58, 101-102, 115-118,
182-183, 186, 225, 229.
    Mentions and quotes W to illustrate
    sociological points. Uses NS to
    illustrate the point that blacks
    believe that whites control every-
    thing. Bigger Thomas is a by-product
    of this belief.

116a. Smith, William Gardner. The Stone
Face. New York: Pocket Books, p. 117.
    Reprint of 1963.171a.

117. Solotaroff, Theodore. "Afterword,"
in Native Son. New York: New American
Library, pp. 393-400.
    Uses "How 'Bigger' Was Born" to gain
    access to the novel's meaning. W
    attempted to find a general social
    meaning for black violence. Solo-
    taroff is also concerned with the
    theme of freedom within the context
    of Bigger's fear, flight, and fate. W
    raised issues that American society
    still confronts.
    Reprinted: 1970.327; 1979.238.
    Partially reprinted: 1973.256.

118. _____. "Irving Howe--The Socialist
Imagination." Commentary, 37 (June), 61-

64.
Criticizes severely Howe's "Black Boys and Native Sons." Reprinted: 1979.239.

119. Spingarn, Arthur B. "Books by Negro Authors in 1963." The Crisis, 71 (February), 82-91.
Contains a notice of LT (p. 91).

120. Steinem, Gloria. "James Baldwin, An Original." Vogue, 144 (July), 78-79, 129, 138.
Mentions W briefly in connection with Nobody Knows My Name.

121. Talbot, William. "Every Negro in His Place: The Scene on and off Broadway." Drama Critique, 7 (Spring), 92-96.
Mentions LD (p. 93).
Reprinted: 1969.227; 1976.185.

122. Talese, Gay. "W. P. A. City Guide Will Be Updated." The New York Times (1 April), p. 41.
Notes that W contributed to the original New York City Guide of 1939.

123. Tucker, Martin. "American Literature," in The New International Year Book. Ed. Virginia Carew. New York: Funk and Wagnalls, pp. 27-28.
Comments briefly on LT.

124. Tv.[eterås], E.[gil]. "Wright, Richard," in Norsk Allkunnebok. Ed. Arnulv Sudmann. Vol. 10. Oslo: Fonna Forlag, p. 1233.
Biographical sketch.

125. Warren, Robert Penn. "Race." The New York Review of Books, 3 (8 October), 7-9.
Quotes approvingly comments by W on resistance to serious and candid discussion of racial issues.

126. Wasserstrom, William. "Introduction," in his Civil Liberties and the Arts: Selections from Twice a Year 1938-48. Syracuse: Syracuse University Press, pp. xi-xli.
Mentions W briefly (p. xxvi, xl).

127. _____. "Notes on Contributors," in his Civil Liberties and the Arts: Selections from Twice a Year 1938-48. Syracuse: Syracuse University Press, pp. 307-322.
Contains a biographical sketch of W (p. 322).

128. Weeks, Edward. "The Peripatetic Reviewer: The Spirit Takes Wings." The Atlantic Monthly, 214 (September), 116.
Review of the writings of Margaret Laurence using NS as an example of a

work on racial issues marred by an "overload of dark hatred" which "threw everything out of proportion."

129. Wertham, Frederic. "An Unconscious Determinant in Native Son," in Psychoanalysis and Literature. Ed. Hendrick M. Ruitenbeck. New York: Dutton, pp. 321-325.
Reprint of 1944.156.

130. Williams, John A. "Introduction," in White Man, Listen! Anchor Books. New York: Doubleday, pp. ix-xii.
Favorable evaluation of W's prophetic powers in showing the universality of the problems of race. He deserves more recognition than he has received.

131. _____. "Learning to See Invisible Men." New York Herald Tribune Book Week (20 December), p. 2.
Reports on a class on "The Negro in American Literature" taught by Dave Owen at Syracuse University. Notes that the "greatest emphasis" in the section on black writers is on W.

132. Wish, Harvey. "Richard Wright," in his The Negro Since Emancipation. Englewood Cliffs, N. J.: Prentice-Hall, pp. 114-115.
Headnote to an excerpt from W's contribution to The God That Failed. Sketches W's life to 1940 and comments on Communist-black relations.

133. Witham, W. Tasker. The Adolescent in the American Novel, 1920-1960. New York: Frederick Ungar, pp. 16, 81, 92, 97, 98, 201, 211, 212-213, 270, 276.
Discusses NS in a chapter on the influence of community environment on the protagonist of the novel of adolescence. Emphasizes the Northern urban dimension of W's treatment of racial problems.

134. Woodley, Richard. "A Recollection of Michael Schwerner." The Reporter, 31 (16 July), 23-24.
Reports that CORE worker Schwerner made W's books available to blacks in Meridian, Mississippi, before he was murdered.

1965

1. Anon. "Baptist Church Seeks Own School After Losing Censorship Plea." Library Journal, 90 (15 December), 5487.
Reports that the Lake Ponds Baptist Church of Waterford, Connecticut, petitioned the school board to remove twelve books, including BB and NS, from the recommended reading list for high school.

2. Anon. "Bon sang de bonsoir." Echo de Lanion (23 October).
Favorable review of the French translation of LT. Revealing W's forceful technique, it deals with twenty-four hours of the life of a black man in racist America. Of intense topical interest, it shows that W was many years ahead of his time.

3. Anon. "Bon sang de bonsoir." Reflets du Luxembourg (1 July).
Review of the French translation of LT. Although it shows traces of crudity, it affirms our basic conception of W's message and his art. Jake is involved in the confrontation with being, but he is the victim of himself as well as of society.

4. Anon. "Bon sang de bonsoir de R. Wright." Panorama Chrétien (October).
Favorable review of the French translation of LT noting especially W's success in creating sympathy for a brutal protagonist.

5. Anon. "Bon sang de bonsoir de R. Wright." Sélection des Librairies de France (July).
Notice of the French translation of LT pointing out its lack of didacticism in depicting Jake's terrible condition.

6. Anon. "Bon sang de bonsoir de R. Wright." Syndicalisme (July-August).
Notice of the French translation of LT. As a black man, the protagonist has not found his place in society.

7. Anon. "Books to Come." The London Times Literary Supplement (1 April), p. 260.
Announces the publication of the English edition of LT on 19 April.

8. Anon. "Broadway: A Man for All Scenes." Time, 85 (19 March), 86, 88.
Article on the stage designer Oliver Smith noting that he had been a member of the Brooklyn Heights group to which W belonged.

9. Anon. "Charles Wright, Ulysses in Manhattan." Bücherschiff, 15 (March-April), 53.
Review comparing Charles Wright unfavorably to W.

10. Anon. "La Chronique littéraire de 'République.'" La République de Toulon (16 July).
Notice of the French translation of LT. The protagonist is so unattractive in his violence and insolence that he seems to constitute a reason for racism.

11. Anon. "Une Colère noire." Le Nouveau Candide (23 May), p. 26.
Favorable review of the French translation of LT suggesting that W's pessimism on racial issues is the "incurable pessimism of all true novelists."

12. Anon. "Crime: Hayneville Justice." Newsweek, 66 (11 October), pp. 36, 41.
Reports that the possession of a copy of NS was admitted as evidence against the character of a white seminarian murdered in Hayneville, Alabama.

13. Anon. Dust jacket of Lawd Today. London: Anthony Blond.
Quotation from Baldwin on front and back. Blurb on front inside flap.

14. Anon. Index Translationum 16. Paris: Unesco, pp. 186, 422, 470, 703, 735.
Lists translations of NS into Danish, Dutch, and Serbo-Croatian, BB into Norwegian, EM into Russian, and LD into Serbo-Croatian.

15. Anon. "Lawd Today," in Lawd Today. London: Anthony Blond, p. [1].
Publisher's blurb which also appears on the front inside flap of the dust jacket.

16. Anon. "Martyr or Traitor?" The London Times Literary Supplement (29 April), p. 324.
Unfavorable review of the English edition of LT. Points out artistic defects in the novel and rejects W's theme of societal responsibility for such people as Jake Jackson. Nevertheless, the reviewer praises certain scenes: the bout of the dozens, the tedium of working at the post office, the revelry at the brothel.

17. Anon. "Mercure de France," in Bon sang de bonsoir. By Richard Wright. Trans. Hélène Bokanowski. Paris: Mercure de France, back cover.
Blurb for the French translation of LT.

18. Anon. "Mrs. Blake's Apartment," in Savage Holiday. Award Books A131X. New York: Universal Publishing and Distributing Corporation, p. [3].
Blurb explaining the basic situation of the novel.

19. Anon. "Native Son," in The Reader's Encyclopedia. Ed. William Rose Benét. Second edition. New York: Crowell, p. 703.
Brief plot summary.

20. Anon. "New Books: Fifty Best Ameri-

can Short Stories 1915-1965, edited by Martha Foley." Des Moines Sunday Register (4 July), p. 7-F.
  Review noting the inclusion of "Bright and Morning Star."

21. Anon. "Un Noir à New York" [sic]. Paris Aux Ecoutes.
  Inaccurate review of the French translation of LT placing the time in the twenties and the setting in Harlem. Notes that W was the black spokesman before Baldwin.

22. Anon. "The Outsider Richard Wright," in The Outsider. Perennial Library P22. New York: Harper & Row, back cover.
  Publisher's blurb.

23. Anon. "Pick of the Paperbacks: The American Negro." Saturday Review, 48 (17 April), 52-53.
  Mentions the inclusion of W, a "master" of "imperious protest," in Harvey Wish's The Negro Since Emancipation.

24. Anon. "Restrictions in Richmond Schools." Newsletter on Intellectual Freedom, 14 (September), 56.
  Reports that BB is among the books attacked by the group Parents for Educational Decency in Richmond, California.

25. Anon. "Storm Over Book Selection Proposal." Berkeley Daily Gazette (30 July), p. 16.
  Reports that BB is among books questioned by Parents for Educational Decency at a meeting of the Richmond Unified School District.

26. Anon. "Wright (Ricardo)," in Diccionario enciclopédico abreviado. Appendix. Madrid: Espasa-Calpe, pp. 1520-1521.
  Brief biographical note.

27. Anon. "Wright, Richard. Lawd Today." L'Epicerie Française (26 November).
  Favorable review of the French translation of a moving, realistic study of an ordinary black man. Ironically, dreams make Jake find escape in violent actions.

28. Anon. "Wright, Richard [Nathaniel]," in The Reader's Encyclopedia. Ed. William Rose Benét. Second edition. New York: Crowell, p. 1104.
  Biographical note.

29. Anon. "'You've had many men, haven't you?'" in Savage Holiday. Award Books A131X. New York: Universal Publishing and Distributing Corporation, back cover.
  Publisher's blurb.

30. Aptheker, Herbert. "The Watts Ghetto Uprising." Political Affairs, 44 (November), 28-44.
  Includes a passage (p. 39) arguing that Bigger Thomas is not representative of black people and that the novel NS and its reception were "fuzzy" on the issue of the responsibility of the dominant social class.
  Reprinted: 1971.26.

30a. Arscott, John R. "From Black Boy Richard Wright," in his Introduction to Nonfiction. Cincinnati: McCormick-Mathers Publishing Company, p. 10.
  Brief headnote.

30b. _____. "Questions and Comments, Word Study, Composition," in his Introduction to Nonfiction. Cincinnati: McCormick-Mathers Publishing Company, pp. 15-16.
  To accompany an excerpt from BB.

31. B., B. Untitled clipping. Garden City (N. Y.) Newsday (c. 26 June).
  Lists W as a contributor to Martha Foley's Fifty Best American Short Stories 1915-1965.

32. Baldwin, James. "Previous Condition," in his Going to Meet the Man. New York: Dial, pp. 83-100.
  Reprint of 1948.126.

33. Bannon, Barbara. "Forecast of Paperbacks: Uncle Tom's Children. Richard Wright." Publishers' Weekly, 188 (26 July), 51.
  Favorable notice of a paperback reprint calling the collection "powerful and memorable."

34. Baumbach, Jonathan. "Nightmare of a Native Son: Invisible Man by Ralph Ellison," in his The Landscape of Nightmare: Studies in the Contemporary American Novel. New York: New York University Press, pp. 68-86.
  Reprint of 1963.50a.

35. Beauvoir, Simone de. Force of Circumstance. Trans. Richard Howard. New York: Putnam's, 658 pp.
  Translation of 1963.51.
  Reprinted: 1977.55.

36. Bennett, Lerone J. Confrontation: Black and White. Chicago: Johnson Publishing Company, pp. 65, 150, 171-172, 191, 209-210, 216.
  Refers to W and discusses "Bigger the symbol and Wright the apostle of a new racial sensibility" (p. 170). Also treats the W-Baldwin relationship.
  Partially reprinted: 1970.5.

37. Berry, Brewton. Race and Ethnic Relations. Third edition. Boston: Houghton Mifflin, pp. 118-119, 387-388.
Reprint of 1951.132.

38. Bisol, Gaetano. "Richard Wright: Drama raziale e narrativa negra di protesta." Letture, 20, pp. 259-276.
Argues that by employing the contrast of the visible "white reality" and the unseen "black reality," W both protests social attitudes and states an "essential symbolism." Violence is the most compelling aspect of W's vision. Ultimately W's "parables" admit no solution because he sees the black-white contrast only in terms of war, never admitting spiritual values.

39. Bl.[air], W.[alter]. "American Literature," in Encyclopaedia Britannica. Ed. Warren E. Preece. Vol. 1. Chicago: Encyclopaedia Britannica, pp. 764-776.
Reprint of 1954.80.

40. Blake, Pamella. "A Dream Deferred." Harvard Journal of Negro Affairs, 1, No. 1, pp. 6-16.
Quotes from NS to illustrate a point about the relation of parents and children in a black family (pp. 9-10).

41. Bokanowski, Hélène. "Introduction," in Bon sang de bonsoir. By Richard Wright. Trans. Hélène Bokanowski. Paris: Mercure de France, pp. 7-11.
Analyzes LT as a characteristic Wrightian work in theme and technique.

42. Bone, Robert A. The Negro Novel in America. Revised edition. New Haven, Conn.: Yale University Press, pp. 4, 101, 110, 113, 115, 117, 140-152, 164, 165-166, 168, 170, 173, 176, 179, 180, 184, 185, 188, 197-198, 218, 231, 245.
Reprint of 1958.85.

43. _____. "The Novels of James Baldwin." Tri-Quarterly (Winter), pp. 3-20.
Attributes the shift in Baldwin's career from shame to wrathful prophecy to his acceptance of W as a father-surrogate. Also compares Rufus of Another Country to Bigger.
Reprinted: 1965.42; 1966.21; 1970.60; 1974.29.

44. Bowen, John. "Lawd Today." London Sunday Times (18 [?] April).
Review pointing out that the novel includes powerful passages but is often tedious. Although W suggests that capitalist society is to blame for Jake's degradation, he himself presents Jake as "a stereotype of

what a racist would want us to believe."

45. Bracy, William. "Wright, Richard," in Encyclopedia Americana. Ed. David C. Whitney. Vol. 29. New York: Americana Corporation, p. 555.
Biographical sketch. "His writing may be said to contain more anger than art, but despite some unevenness of style, he sustained in his works a narrative power and a disturbing emotional impact that brought lasting recognition."
Reprinted: 1968.49; 1970.65; 1977.69; 1978.45.

46. Brulé, Claude. "Elle a tout vu-entendu-lu." Elle, No. 1025 (12 August), p. 13.
Contains an unfavorable notice of the French translation of LT.

47. Cabau, Jacques. "Etranger." L'Express (6 September), p. 50.
Contains a favorable review of the French translation of LT emphasizing its hard realism and comparing W to Dos Passos.

48. Cayton, Horace R. Long Old Road. New York: Trident Press, pp. 247-250, 253.
Recounts Cayton's meeting and friendship with W, the Communist reception of NS, the trip of Cayton and W to Fisk University, and their plans for intellectual collaboration.
Reprinted: 1970.80.

49. Chisholm, Lawrence Washington. "Signifying Everything." The Yale Review, 54 (Spring), 450-454.
Review of Shadow and Act noting Ellison's distinction between literary ancestors (such as Hemingway) and literary relatives (such as W).
Reprinted: 1974.44.

50. Clark, Kenneth B. Dark Ghetto: Dilemmas of Social Power. New York: Harper & Row, pp. 191, 195.
Mentions W briefly.

51. Copans, Sim. "Le Problème noir aux Etats-Unis." Les Langues Modernes, 59 (July-August), 66-72.
Contains a review of Herbert Hill's Soon, One Morning mentioning W.

52. Darnall, Albert. "René Maran cet homme pareil aux autres," in Hommage à René Maran. Paris: Présence Africaine, pp. 77-89.
Contains a comparison of Maran and W emphasizing the differences in their backgrounds.

53. De Franciscis, Umberto. "La protesta

di Baldwin." L'Europa letteraria, 6 (May-June), 167, 169-171.
Comments on the Baldwin-W relationship.

54. Dennison, George. "Voices of the Dispossessed." Show, 5 (May), 28-33.
Includes a discussion of NS emphasizing the work's universal dimension, which transcends the category of racial protest. Fear is the main theme of this work "in the front ranks of the Existential Novel" (p. 29).

54a. Dommergues, Pierre. Les Ecrivains américains d'aujourd'hui. Paris: Presses Universitaires de France, p. 110.
Comments briefly on W's racial consciousness in contrast to such later black novelists as Motley and Baldwin.

55. Donohue, H. E. F. Conversations with Nelson Algren. Berkley Medallion S1134. New York: Berkley, pp. 62, 87, 204, 212, 214, 218.
Reprint of 1964.41.

56. [Douglass, Joseph], John Hope Franklin, and Thurgood Marshall. "Negro," in The World Book Encyclopedia. Ed. Robert O. Zeleny. Vol. 14. Chicago: Field Enterprises, pp. 106-112b.
Reprint of 1959.78.

57. Esnor, Henri. "Bon sang de bonsoir." Le Brussels Drapeau Rouge (25 September).
Reprint of 1965.113.

58. Fabre, Michel. "Ou en est l'écrivain noir aux Etats-Unis?" Lettres (28 April-4 May), pp. 5-7.
Examination of the main trends in the public reception of black writing. Notes that throughout his career W was subjected to criticism from many sides and that his "humane" attitude is no longer prevalent among black writers.

59. _____ and Edward Margolies. "Richard Wright (1908-1960): A Bibliography." Bulletin of Bibliography and Magazine Notes, 24 (January-April), 131-133, 137.
Lists 173 primary items divided into the following categories: fiction, poetry, nonfiction, newspaper contributions, and miscellaneous--introductions to books, letters, sketches, etc.
Reprinted: 1968.94; 1969.76; 1971. 112; 1973.137, 138, 139.

60. Fair, Ronald L. "The Task of the Negro Writer as Artist." Negro Digest, 14 (April), 69, 72.

Attests to the influence of W's example on a younger writer.

61. Farrell, James T. "Richard Wright." The Smith, 2 (November), 62-65.
Farrell summarizes his relationship with W and evaluates some of W's works. He mentions a manuscript called "The Outcast" which he thought was weak and which W abandoned. Praises UTC and BB but criticizes some portions of NS. Predicts that W will be increasingly recognized as a great writer.

61a. Finestone, Harry. "Miscellaneous," in American Literary Scholarship: An Annual/1963. Ed. James Woodress. Durham, N. C.: Duke University Press, pp. 209-224.
Mentions W briefly (p. 216).

62. Finkelstein, Sidney. Existentialism and Alienation in American Literature. New York: International Publishers, p. 212.
Mentions W briefly.

63. Flowers, Paul. "Map and Booklet List 200 Tennessee Authors." The Memphis Commercial Appeal (25 April), Sec. 5, p. 6.
Includes W in a list of Tennessee authors.

64. Foley, Martha. "Richard Wright," in her Fifty Best American Short Stories 1915-1965. Boston: Houghton Mifflin, p. 214.
Headnote to "Bright and Morning Star" mistakenly calling it W's first published story.

65. F.[ranklin], J.[ohn] H.[ope], R.[ayford] W.[hittingham] L.[ogan], and S.[terling] A. Br.[own]. "Negro, American," in Encyclopaedia Britannica. Ed. Warren E. Preece. Vol. 16. Chicago: Encyclopaedia Britannica, pp. 188-201.
Reprint of 1957.184.

66. Frémy, Dominique. Quid? Tout pour tous. Paris: Librairie Plon, p. 71.
Reprint of 1963.86.

67. Freustié, Jean. "Chicago Story." Le Nouvel Observateur (10 June), pp. 21-22.
Favorable review of the French translation of LT including a detailed plot summary. Expressing indebtedness to Hélène Bokanowski's excellent introduction to the novel, Freustie points out that the unflattering portrait of blacks caused the Communist Party to advise W not to publish it. But the work conveys forcefully, with the aid of authorial objectivity and techniques derived from Dos Passos, the idea that American

society is responsible for the degradation of blacks.

68. Fuller, Hoyt W. "Contemporary Negro Fiction." Southwest Review, 50 (Autumn), 321-335.
Contends that W was the literary ancestor of contemporary Afro-American writing. NS is the work to which recent novelists are most indebted. Also mentions O and LD.
Reprinted: 1969.93; 1971.128.

69. Fuller, John G. "Trade Winds." Saturday Review, 48 (15 May), 12-13.
Includes W in a list of authors "fostered" by Paris publisher Maurice Girodias.

70. Gayle, Addison, Jr. "The Literature of Protest." Negro History Bulletin, 29 (December), 61-62.
Refers to Bigger Thomas and to BB.

71. Gilenson, Boris. "A Book About the Modern American Novel." Soviet Literature, No. 8 (August), pp. 174-178.
Mentions W briefly in a review of Moris Mendelson's The Modern American Novel.

72. Gleason, Judith. "A Proletarian Novelist." African Forum, 1 (Fall), 106-108.
Review of Sembene Ousmane's L'Harmattan, Referendum comparing his first novel, Le Docker noire, to NS.

73. Green, Paul. "Symphonic Drama," in American Playwrights on Drama. Ed. Horst Frenz. New York: Hill and Wang, pp. 68-78.
Reprint of 1949.109.

74. Hart, James D. "Native Son," in his The Oxford Companion to American Literature. Fourth edition. New York: Oxford University Press, pp. 584-585.
Partial reprint of 1941.760.

75. _____. "Wright, Richard," in his The Oxford Companion to American Literature. Fourth edition. New York: Oxford University Press, pp. 949-950.
Revised and expanded reprint of 1941.760.

76. Hernton, Calvin C. Sex and Racism in America. Garden City, N. Y.: Doubleday, pp. 81-82, 85, 93.
Discusses O and "Man of All Work." Reprinted: 1966.72.

77. Hicklin, Fannie Ella Frazier. "The American Negro Playwright, 1920-1964." Ph.D. dissertation, University of Wisconsin, pp. 334-339.
Discusses the novel and the play NS

emphasizing their brutal power. Considers both naturalism and symbolism in the works. Includes comments on the threat of censorship in 1942.

78. Hicks, Granville. Part of the Truth. New York: Harcourt, Brace & World, p. 164.
In this autobiography Hicks mentions introducing W "at a left-wing tea" in Boston while Hicks was at Harvard in 1937-1938.

78a. Holman, C. Hugh. "Fiction: 1900-1930," in American Literary Scholarship: An Annual/1963. Ed. James Woodress. Durham, N. C.: Duke University Press, pp. 132-142.
Mentions W briefly as a radical writer.

79. Hoppes, Stephanie. "Short Story Anthology Fitting Commemoration." The Indianapolis Star (4 July), Sec. 7, p. 5.
Review of Martha Foley's Fifty Best American Short Stories 1915-1965 claiming that "Bright and Morning Star" marked the "emergence of Negro authors as major contributors to American literature."

80. Hubbell, Jay B. "The Southern Literary Renaissance," in his South and Southwest: Literary Essays and Reminiscences. Durham, N. C.: Duke University Press, pp. 73-89.
Mentions W briefly as a Communist who became disillusioned and as "perhaps the most gifted of the Negro writers" (p. 82).

81. Huie, William Bradford. "The Trial of Hayneville." New York Herald Tribune (30 September), pp. 1, 16.
Reports that at the trial of a man for the murder of a seminarian working for civil rights in Alabama, the defense used the possession of a copy of NS by a priest who was also shot as evidence of the victim's fanaticism.

82. Jackson, Blyden. "The Negro's Image of the Universe as Reflected in His Fiction," in Images of the Negro in America. Ed. Darwin T. Turner and Jean M. Bright. Boston: Heath, pp. 85-90.
Reprint of 1960.169.

83. _____. "The Negro's Negro in Negro Literature." The Michigan Quarterly Review, 4 (Fall), 290-295.
Discusses "Big Boy Leaves Home." The protagonist of this story, a "sentimental ironist," is a prototype of most black protagonists in Afro-American literature. Jackson discusses Bigger Thomas briefly.

Reprinted: 1970.191.

84. Jahn, Janheinz. A Bibliography of Neo-African Literature from Africa, America, and the Caribbean. New York: Praeger, pp. 320-327.
   Lists chronologically ninety-five W items, including dissertations.

85. _____. "Black Boy," in Kindlers Literatur Lexikon. Ed. Gert Woerner. Vol. 1. Zurich: Kindler Verlag, p. 1663.
   Summary with critical comments and a brief bibliography.

85a. Johnson, Albert. "The Negro in American Films: Some Recent Works." Film Quarterly, 18 (Summer), 14-30.
   Mentions W briefly (p. 28).
   Reprinted: 1975.110a.

86. Johnson, Charles S. "Negro in America," in Encyclopedia Americana. Ed. David C. Whitney. Vol. 20. New York: Americana Corporation, pp. 65-74.
   Reprint of 1955.54.

87. Kaufman, Bob. "Blues Note," in his Solitudes Crowded with Loneliness. New Directions Paperbooks NDP199. New York: New Directions, p. 20.
   Poem mentioning "Bessie's crushed black skull."
   Reprinted: 1972.107.

88. Kesteloot, Lilyan. Les Ecrivains noirs de langue française: Naissance d'une littérature. Second edition. Brussels: L'Institut de Sociologie de l'Université Libre de Bruxelles, pp. 65, 66, 72, 73, 81, 254, 258, 266, 267, 275, 276, 282, 287.
   Reprint of 1963.125.

89. Killens, John Oliver. Black Man's Burden. New York: Trident Press, pp. 17-18, 73-74.
   Uses TMBV to support points about white ignorance of black reality and the strength of black familial love. Partially reprinted: 1970.229; 1972.119.

90. _____. "We Refuse to Look at Ourselves Through the Eyes of White America," in Negro Protest Thought in the Twentieth Century. Ed. Francis L. Broderick and August Meier. The American Heritage Series, ed. Leonard W. Levy and Alfred Young. Indianapolis: Bobbs-Merrill, pp. 348-357.
   Reprint of 1964.84.

91. Kinnamon, Keneth. "Richard Wright Items in the Fales Collection." Bulletin of the Society for the Libraries of New York University, No. 66 (Winter).
   Describes the page proofs of NS,

noting differences from the novel as published. Lists other W items in the Fales Library.

92. Kyria, [Pierre]. "Derniers parus, derniers lus." Paris Aux Ecoutes (15 April).
   Notice of the French translation of LT. A social document as well as an individual confession, the novel evokes the difficulties of American cities, particularly Harlem.

93. Landor, Mikhail. "Faulkner in the Soviet Union." Soviet Literature, No. 12 (December), pp. 178-185.
   Mentions W briefly (p. 178).
   Reprinted: 1972.134.

94. Las Vergnas, Raymond. "Bon sang de bonsoir par Richard Wright." Les Nouvelles Littéraires (26 August), p. 5.
   Favorable review of the French translation of LT with a plot summary. It shows the emerging talent of a great Afro-American novelist.

95. L.[e] C.[lec'h], G.[uy]. "Romans." Le Figaro Littéraire (15-21 July), p. 4.
   Favorable brief review of the French translation of LT. Although blacks today have more political awareness than in 1938, the novel is otherwise timely.

96. _____. "Wright, Richard (1909 [sic]-1960," in Ecrivains contemporaines. Ed. Georges-Emmanuel Clancier. Paris: Editions d'art Lucien Mazenod, p. 608.
   Brief biographical sketch.

97. Lehan, Richard D. "The Strange Silence of Ralph Ellison." California English Journal, 1, pp. 63-68.
   Mentions NS briefly.

97a. Levidova, I. M. Khudozhestvennaïa Literatura SSHA. Moscow, pp. 22, 113.
   Mentions W as a writer of the thirties (p. 22). Includes an annotated listing of LT (p. 113).

98. Magid, Marion. "The Death of Hip." Esquire, 63 (June), 89-103, 138.
   Quotes Ollie Harrington on W and the Cafe Tournon crowd.

99. Marks, Robert. "News About Books: Cry of Anguish." High Point Enterprise (29 August).
   Discussing the riot in Watts, Marks points out that black writers had warned of tensions before the outbreak and notes that W had written of problems in both the North and the South.

100. Martin, Kenneth K. "Richard Wright

and the Negro Revolt." Negro Digest, 14 (April), 39-48.

Emphasizes the depth of W's literary anger and its influence on the subsequent development of black literature. Discusses UTC, NS, WML, O, and LD. Only by changing the conditions of American life can the accusing voice of Bigger Thomas be silenced.

101. Maunick, E. J. "Bon Sang de bonsoir." Les Bonnes Feuilles, No. 46.

Notice of the French translation of LT. W's premature death removed a writer who achieved universality through his desire to rectify injustice wherever found.

102. Moon, Henry Lee. "Spingarn Medal," in The World Book Encyclopedia. Ed. Robert O. Zeleny. Vol. 17. Chicago: Field Enterprises, p. 617.

Reprint of 1960.201.

103. Neal, Lawrence P. "The Black Writer's Role: Richard Wright." Liberator, 5 (December), 20-22.

Discusses W as a precursor of black literary nationalism.

104. Neuvéglise, Paule. "Roman posthume de Richard Wright." Paris France-Soir (17 June), p. 2.

Review of the French translation of LT placing it in the context of W's development and quoting from Hélène Bokanowski's introduction on the way the novel reveals W's technique. Bokanowski also states that the novel's publication was discouraged by the Communist Party when it was written.

105. Nichols, Charles H. "The Emancipation of the American Negro Author." Neusprachliche Mitteilungen aus Wissenschaft und Praxis, 18 (August), 121-129.

Mentions W as a literary pioneer (p. 123) and as an observer of Africa (p. 125). Discusses W's achievement, focusing on NS. "Richard Wright is for the Negro writer what Martin Luther King is for the Negro's political struggle" (p. 126).

106. Niemeyer, Carl. "Wright, Richard," in his The World Book Encyclopedia. Ed. Robert O. Zeleny. Vol. 20. Chicago: Field Enterprises, p. 420.

Reprint of 1960.206.

107. Oliver, Clinton Forrest, Jr. "The Name and Nature of American Negro Literature: An Interpretive Study in Genre and Ideas." Ph.D. dissertation, Harvard University.

Comments on W's "Introduction" to Black Metropolis as a donnée for O

and Invisible Man (p. 253), on NS as a naturalistic novel (p. 313), on BB as a "spiritual autobiography" in the tradition of A Portrait of the Artist as a Young Man and George Moore's Confessions of a Young Man (p. 314), and on the influence of W on subsequent black writers (p. 318).

107a. Otomo, Yoshiro. "On Uncle Tom's Children and Eight Men." Tohoku Daigaku Kyoyobu Kiyo [Bulletin of Tohoku University School of General Studies], 1 (March), 144-160.

The five short stories contained in UTC are well linked and well reflect both W's experience and the spirit of the 1930s. EM is more modern than UTC in terms of its style and technique. "The Man Who Lived Underground," included in EM, is by far the best story in the collection; it deals with the theme of alienation as well as the theme of salvation through crime. The changes between the two collections reflect those of W and black literature [Y. H. and T. K.]

108. P., M. "White Man, Listen!" Calgary Herald (20 February).

Notice pointing out that the book contains little ideology but shows racial problems on the personal level.

109. Paolini, Alcide. "James Baldwin: 'Mio padre doveva essere bellissimo.'" La fiera letteraria (19 September), p. 4.

Mentions NS briefly.

110. Plessner, Monika. "Richard Wright, Vorkämpfer der Zweiten Amerikanischen Revolution." Frankfürter Hefte, 20 (December), 840-852.

After an introductory section establishing a social and historical context, Plessner reviews comprehensively W's career with special attention to the issue of identity. She examines W's existentialism and his relations to Sartre. She analyzes UTC, NS, and O, touching on other works as well. Concludes with an account of W's childhood and youth, which shaped the identity of this prophet of the second American revolution.

Reprinted: 1971.147.

111. Randall, Dudley. "The Task of the Negro Writer as Artist." Negro Digest, 14 (April), 59, 77.

Mentions W briefly.

112. Redding, Saunders. "The Task of the Negro Writer as Artist." Negro Digest, 14 (April), 66, 74.

Cites W as a favorable example of a black writer's "dual commitment: to his people and to his art."

113. Ronse, Henri. "La Négritude americaine." Courrier du Littoral (24 September).
Favorable review of the French translation of LT noting W's cinematic technique. Jake Jackson suffers from alienation and self-hatred.
Reprinted: 1965.57.

113a. Rubin, Louis D., Jr. "Fiction: 1930 to the Present," in American Literary Scholarship: An Annual/1963. Ed. James Woodress. Durham, N. C.: Duke University Press, pp. 143-164.
Comments on Maurice Charney's article on Baldwin and W (pp. 150-151).

114. Sablonière, Margrit de. "Ook Dorothy Padmore." De Nieuwe Stem, 20 (January), 29-32.
Review of Dorothy Padmore's book on Ghana noting the Padmore friendship with W and the influence of BP.

115. Simpson, George E. and J. Milton Yinger. Racial and Cultural Minorities: An Analysis of Prejudice and Discrimination. Third edition. New York: Harper & Row, 582 pp.
Revised reprint of 1953.228.

116. Sloan, Irving J. The American Negro: A Chronology and Fact Book. Dobbs Ferry, N. Y.: Oceana Publications, pp. 40-41, 53.
Lists the publication of NS, the award of the Spingarn Medal, and W's death.
Reprinted: 1968.196; 1971.277; 1977.289.

116a. Smith, Lewis. "Existentialism in the Work of Richard Wright." Hiroshima Amerika Bungaku Kenkyu [Hiroshima Studies in American Literature], 3 (April), 1-10.
Despite society's denial of the existence of Bigger and Damon as men, they are able to assert their dignity and freedom. Fishbelly, on the other hand, "has never really lived because he has surrendered the one quality which makes him a man--freedom." Unlike most existentialist work, W's work exhibits "a passionate cry for freedom for a whole people." In English. [Y. H. and T. K.]

117. Smith, Sherwin. "Boondoggle That Helped 38 Million People." The New York Times Magazine (2 May), pp. 37, 68, 72, 74, 76.
Includes W in a list of artists and writers aided by WPA.

118. Smith, William Gardner. "Black Man in Europe." Holiday, 37 (January), 22, 24-26, 28-29.
Quotes a remark by W on the solidarity of the Third World with African and Asian expatriates in Europe.

119. Straumann, Heinrich. American Literature in the Twentieth Century. Third revised edition. Harper Torchbooks. New York: Harper & Row, pp. 31, 37.
Reprint of 1951.233.

120. Turner, Darwin T. "The Negro Dramatist's Image of the Universe, 1920-1960," in Images of the Negro in America. Ed. Darwin T. Turner and Jean M. Bright. Boston: Heath, pp. 91-99.
Partial reprint of 1961.274.

121. _____ and Jean M. Bright. "Introduction," in their Images of the Negro in America. Boston: Heath, pp. vii-xi.
Mentions W briefly (p. x).

122. _____. "Suggestions for Library Work," in their Images of the Negro in America. Boston: Heath, pp. 112-113.
Mentions NS and BB.

122a. Turpin, Waters E. "The Contemporary American Negro Playwright." CLA Journal, 9 (September), 12-24.
Includes a paragraph on the play NS, which was important in presenting its protagonist "as a product of socio-economic determinism" rather than as an exotic primitive.

123. Wardle, Irving. "Victims of the White Trap." The London Observer (18 April), p. 27.
Favorable review of LT. W uses the degradation of blacks, expressed in a style reminiscent of Dos Passos, to indict the society responsible for it. W is superior to Baldwin because his "social indignation is free from private rancour."

124. Warren, Robert Penn. "The Unity of Experience." Commentary, 39 (May), 91-96.
Mentions the role of W in the literary debate between Irving Howe and Ralph Ellison.
Reprinted: 1974.175.

125. _____. Who Speaks for the Negro? New York: Random House, pp. 83, 285, 287, 349.
W is mentioned in interviews with Aaron Henry, James Baldwin, and Ralph Ellison. Warren himself refers to W's mention of black anti-Semitism in BB.
Reprinted: 1966.146.

126. Welsch, Erwin K. The Negro in the

United States: A Research Guide. Bloomington: Indiana University Press, pp. 6,
76, 77, 80, 83-84.
  Contains a brief evaluation of WML
  (p. 6) and other references to W.

127. Wüstenhagen, Heinz. "James Baldwins
Essays und Romans Versuch einer ersten
Einschätzung." Zeitschrift für Anglistik
und Amerikanistik, 12, pp. 117-157.
  Discusses Baldwin's relationship with
  W emphasizing the latter's positive
  accomplishments. Baldwin's approach
  to NS reveals his own paradoxical
  tendency to reject social approaches
  and mythologize the past more than it
  reveals shortcomings in W.

128. X, Malcolm, with the assistance of
Alex Haley. The Autobiography of Malcolm
X. New York: Grove Press, p. 360.
  Recounts meeting W's widow and
  daughters.
  Reprinted: 1966.150.

1966

1. Aaron, Daniel. "The Thirties--Now and
Then." The American Scholar, 35 (Summer), 490-494.
  Quotes W on the Scottsboro case (p.
  493).

2. Alexander, Charlotte A. James Bald-
win's Go Tell It on the Mountain and
Aother Country, The Fire Next Time,
Giovanni's Room, and Notes of a Native
Son. Monarch Notes and Study Guides
Series. New York: Monarch Press, p. 15.
  Mentions W in a comment on "Many
  Thousands Gone."

3. Anon. "Books-Authors: Wide-Ranging
Negro Humor." The New York Times (21
January), p. 44.
  Lists W as a contributor to Langston
  Hughes's The Book of Negro Humor.

4. Anon. Dust jacket of Der Mann, der
nach Chikago ging. By Richard Wright.
Trans. Enzio von Cramon and Erich Fried.
Frankfurt am Main: Fischer Bücherei.
  Blurb on back cover.

5. Anon. Index Translationum 17. Paris:
Unesco, pp. 82, 99, 398, 600, 618.
  Lists translations of BB into German,
  LD into German (2) and Italian, LT
  into Spanish, PS into Italian, and NS
  into Swedish.

6. Anon. "Der Mann, der nach Chikago
ging," in Der Mann, der nach Chikago
ging. By Richard Wright. Trans. Enzio
von Cramon and Erich Fried. Frankfurt am
Main: Fischer Bücherei, p. [2].
  Blurb and biographical sketch. A list
  of W's other works in German trans-

lation appears on p. [237].

7. Anon. "Native Son Revival." Danbury
News-Times (30 April), p. 6.
  Announces that John Berry will direct
  Sidney Bernstein's revival of the
  play NS in the fall.

8. Anon. "Necrology," in The Biographi-
cal Encyclopaedia & Who's Who of the
American Theatre. Ed. Walter Rigdon. New
York: James H. Heineman, pp. 995-1101.
  Contains a brief entry on W (p.
  1100).

9. Anon. "Negro Humor Book Covers Many
Years." The Memphis Commercial Appeal
(30 January), Sec. 5, p. 4.
  Lists W as as contributor to Langston
  Hughes's The Book of Negro Humor.

10. Anon. "Richard Wright: Der Mörder
und die Schuldigen." Unidentified clipping (c. October).
  Notice of the German translation of O
  referring to it as a novel about the
  black-white conflict in America.

11. Anon. "Das Stichwort." Berliner
Welle (27 August).
  Review of the German translation of
  O. W sees Communism as "political
  gangsterism." The fate of Cross Damon
  demonstrates that "justice through
  violence" is a contradiction in
  itself.

12. Anon. Untitled essay in Spagna
pagana. By Richard Wright. Trans.
Giuliana De Carlo. I Record. Verona:
Mondadori, pp. 5-7.
  Sketch of W's life and career.

13. Anon. Untitled note in Spagna
pagana. By Richard Wright. Trans.
Giuliana De Carlo. I Record. Verona:
Mondadori, back cover.
  Blurb.

14. Anon. "Wright, Richard," in Uusi
Tietosanakirja. Ed. Veli Valpola. Vol.
23. Helsinki: Tietosanakirja Oy, p. 723.
  Biographical note.

15. Anon. "Zwei schwarze Erzähler."
Bücherschiff, 16 (July-August), 20.
  Review of Cyprian Ekwensi's Jagua
  Nana and the German translation of O.
  Summarizes the plot of W's novel and
  makes the following judgment:
  "Naturalistic in its approach, this
  novel, in its wonderful compactness,
  projects into the realm of the
  irrational."

16. B., O. "Richard Wright: Der Mörder
und die Schuldigen." Die Zurich Tat (10
December).

Favorable review of the German translation of O, a powerful document and great novel on American social problems. There is much of W's own hope, fear, and desire in the character of Cross Damon, but the story indicates that the difficult struggle will be lost.

17. Baldwin, James. "James Baldwin . . . in Conversation." Ed. Dan Georgakas. Arts in Society, 3 (Summer), 550-557.
"I check in USIS Libraries to see if they have my books and books by Wright, Ellison, Hughes, and Du Bois."
Reprinted: 1968.39.

18. ____. "Many Thousands Gone: Richard Wright's 'Native Son,'" in Images of the Negro in American Literature. Ed. Seymour L. Gross and John Edward Hardy. Patterns of Literary Criticism, No. 5, ed. Marshall McLuhan, R. L. Schoeck, and Ernest Sirluck. Chicago: The University of Chicago Press, pp. 233-248.
Reprint of 1951.129.

19. Boegner, Karl. "Wright: Der Mörder und die Schuldigen." Die Bücherkommentare, 15 (15 March), 5.
Highly favorable review of the German translation of O calling it one of the great books of the century. Emphasizing the novel's treatment of Communism, Boegner compares W to Arthur Koestler and Manes Sperber. Chris [sic] Damon is an autobiographical character.

20. Boles, Robert. "Negro Writer: His Restrictions, Triumphs." The Boston Sunday Globe (13 February), p. 28-A.
Review of Herbert Hill's Anger, and Beyond noting that W is discussed at length.

21. Bone, Robert A. "The Novels of James Baldwin," in Images of the Negro in American Literature. Ed. Seymour L. Gross and John Edward Hardy. Patterns of Literary Criticism, No. 5, ed. Marshall McLuhan, R. L. Schoeck, and Ernest Sirluck. Chicago: The University of Chicago Press, pp. 265-288.
Reprint of 1965.43.

22. ____. "Ralph Ellison and the Uses of Imagination," in Anger, and Beyond: The Negro Writer in the United States. Ed. Herbert Hill. New York: Harper & Row, pp. 86-111.
Mentions Irving Howe's discussion of W and Ellison.
Reprinted: 1970.61; 1971.45, 46; 1974.30.

23. Bontemps, Arna. "The Negro Contribu-

tion to American Letters," in The American Negro Reference Book. Ed. John P. Davis. Englewood Cliffs, N. J.: Prentice-Hall, pp. 850-878.
Reviews W's career (pp. 875-877) emphasizing the importance of its American phase.
Reprinted: 1976.40.

24. ____. "The Negro Renaissance: Jean Toomer and the Harlem Writers of the 1920's," in Anger, and Beyond: The Negro Writer in the United States. Ed. Herbert Hill. New York: Harper & Row, pp. 20-36.
Mentions briefly UTC and SH.
Partially reprinted: 1969.38.
Reprinted: 1970.63; 1971.48.

25. ____, Herbert Hill, Horace Cayton, and Saunders Redding. "Reflections on Richard Wright: A Symposium on an Exiled Native Son," in Anger, and Beyond: The Negro Writer in the United States. Ed. Herbert Hill. New York: Harper & Row, 196-212.
Bontemps review W's career and influence and compares his early works with the expatriate books. The Paris years added little to W's stature.
Partially reprinted: 1969.64.
Reprinted: 1970.64; 1976.147.

26. Boskin, Joesph [sic]. "The Duality of Consciousness." Phylon, 27 (Second Quarter), 203-204.
Review of Herbert Hill's Anger, and Beyond: The Negro Writer in the United States mentioning the symposium on W.

27. Braem, Helmut M. "Nicht einmal Blumen des Bösen." St. Galler Tagblatt (21 August).
Unfavorable review of the German translation of O, a book which marked a decline of W's talent. Unable to resolve the questions he raises, W blatantly contrives several incidents to illustrate his theme that rage is without cause beyond the inevitable fact of man's confrontation with a senseless world.

28. Brignano, Russell Carl. "Richard Wright: The Major Themes, Ideas, and Attitudes in His Works." Ph.D. dissertation, The University of Wisconsin.
"This study of Wright's works is literary-critical, historical, and biographical. It isolates for close examination four of the author's major concerns in his publications: race relations in America, Marxism, international affairs, and personal and social philosophy" (Brignano in Dissertations Abstracts). Brignano's conclusions focus on the vitality of W's idealism. See 1967.16.

29. Brown, Adger. "Book World: Negro Humor." The State and the Columbia (S. C.) Record (30 January), p. 12-D.
  Lists W as a contributor to Langston Hughes's The Book of Negro Humor.

30. Brown, Sterling A. "A Century of Negro Portraiture in American Literature." The Massachusetts Review, 7 (Winter), 73-96.
  Includes discussion of W. Influenced by Marxism, he excelled in portraying the victims of racism and indicting racial injustice. During his expatriation he lost touch with the American realities even as he was interpreting them to Europeans. Mentions UTC, NS, and BB.
  Reprinted: 1968.53; 1969.43a; 1971.56, 56a.

31. Buttlar-Moscon, Alfred. "Sprengstoff im amerikanischen Alltag." Die Vienna Presse (15-16 October).
  Favorable review of the German translation of O. Like Macbeth and the works of Nietzsche, Hobbes, Kierkegaard, and the apostle Paul, W's novel provides a profound glimpse into the hell of the spirit. In the tragic story of Cross Damon, W combines the numerous explosive tensions of everyday life in the United States and analyzes their consequences.

32. Cayton, Horace R. "Ideological Forces in the Work of Negro Writers," in Anger, and Beyond: The Negro Writer in the United States. Ed. Herbert Hill. New York: Harper & Row, pp. 37-50.
  Discusses Herbert Hill's remarks on W and Ellison, W as prophet in TMBV, and the influence of Communism on his development. Quotes from "Blueprint for Negro Writing." W's works are exemplary for black writing.

33. _____, Herbert Hill, Arna Bontemps, and Saunders Redding. "Reflections on Richard Wright: A Symposium on an Exiled Native Son," in Anger, and Beyond: The Negro Writer in the United States. Ed. Herbert Hill. New York: Harper & Row, pp. 196-212.
  Cayton recalls his meeting with W at the University of Chicago and recounts their personal relationship. He discusses TMBV and mentions briefly UTC and NS.
  Reprinted: 1970.82; 1971.147.

34. Chapman, Abraham. The Negro in American Literature and A Bibliography of Literature by and About Negro Americans. Oshkosh: Wisconsin Council of Teachers of English, pp. 8, 23, 57-58, 77, 83, 85, 90, 118.
  Mentions W twice in the introductory essay. The bibliography has entries, some of them annotated, for W's books.

35. Clarke, John Henrik. "Biographical Notes," in his American Negro Short Stories. American Century Series. New York: Hill and Wang, pp. 349-355.
  Contains a note on W (p.355). Reprints "Bright and Morning Star" on pp. 75-108.

36. _____. "Introduction," in his American Negro Short Stories. American Century Series. New York: Hill and Wang, pp. xv-xix.
  Partial reprint of 1960.134.

37. Cleaver, Eldridge. "Notes on a Native Son." Ramparts, 5 (June), 51-52, 54-56.
  Personal response to Baldwin's attacks on W. Because Baldwin was himself too personally and emotionally involved with W to be objective, he distorted and tarnished his literary reputation. "Of all black American novelists, and indeed of all American novelists of any hue, Richard Wright reigns supreme for his profound political, economic, and social reference."
  Reprinted: 1968.65; 1969.57; 1970.88, 89; 1971.70; 1974.46.

38. _____. "On Becoming." Ramparts, 5 (August), 16, 18-20.
  Cleaver mentions the help NS provided in understanding his attitudes toward black women and white women.
  Reprinted: 1968.66; 1971.71.

39. Corry, John. "An American Novelist Who Sometimes Teaches." The New York Times Magazine (20 November), pp. 54-55, 179-180, 182-187, 196.
  Article on Ralph Ellison noting his friendship with W (p. 180).
  Reprinted: 1970.94.

40. Cramon, Enzio von and Erich Fried. Untitled article in their translation of Der Mann, der nach Chikago ging. By Richard Wright. Frankfurt am Main: Fischer Bücherei, p. [6].
  Note on the translation of EM.

41. D., R. "Kein alltägliches Thema." Wiesbadener Kurier (29 September).
  Review of the German translation of O. Although W gives the reader an interesting glimpse of the inner workings of the Communist Party, his attempt to justify philosophically Cross Damon's violence is unconvincing. The novel reflects the harsh conflicts of everyday American

life.

42. Davis, David Brion. "Violence in American Literature." The Annals of the American Academy of Political and Social Science, 364 (March), 28-36.
   Contains a brief discussion of NS in comparison to The Clansman and Light in August. Max's reference to Bigger's killing of Mary as "an act of creation" is cited as an example of the relation between violence and antirationalism.

43. Dommergues, Pierre. "Les Intellectuels dans la société américaine: II.--La négritude." Le Paris Monde (13 April), p. 3.
   Mentions W briefly.
   Reprinted: 1966.44.

44. _____. "Le Problème noir aux Etats-Unis." Les Langues Modernes, 60 (May-June), 94-98.
   Reprint of 1966.43.

45. _____, Michel Fabre, Langston Hughes, Paule Marshall, and William Melvin Kelley. "Table ronde: Le problème noir aux Etats-Unis." Trans. and condensed by Michel Fabre. Les Langues Modernes, 60 (May-June), 108-116.
   Hughes and Marshall argue that W's expatriation did not harm his writing. Together with Kelley, they comment on SH, LD, and O in relation to the American racial situation.
   Reprinted: 1967.27b.

46. Eckman, Fern Marja. The Furious Passage of James Baldwin. New York: M. Evans, pp. 103-105, 121-122.
   Discusses Baldwin's first meeting with W and the appearance of "Everybody's Protest Novel."
   Reprinted: 1968.79.

47. Ellison, Ralph. "Twentieth-Century Fiction and the Black Mask of Humanity," in Images of the Negro in American Literature. Ed. Seymour L. Gross and John Edward Hardy. Patterns of Literary Criticism, No. 5, ed. Marshall McLuhan, R. J. Schoeck, and Ernest Sirluck. Chicago: The University of Chicago Press, pp. 115-131.
   Reprint of 1953.122.

48. Evans, Oliver. The Ballad of Carson McCullers. New York: Coward McCann, pp. 10, 56, 57, 82, 148.
   Discusses W's review of The Heart Is a Lonely Hunter and his acquaintance with McCullers.

49. F., L. "Lawd Today." Publishers' Weekly, 190 (5 September), 71.
   Notice of the paperback edition of

LT. It lacks the genius of W's later novels.

50. Fabre, Michel. "Panorama critique: Le problème noir aux Etats-Unis." Les Langues Modernes, 60 (May-June), 119-129.
   Contains a favorable review of the French translation of LT (pp. 125-126) placing it in the context of W's career, noting its Joycean parallels, and emphasizing its tough humor.

51. Fanon, Frantz. Les Damnés de la terre. Preface by Jean-Paul Sartre. Paris: F. Maspero, p. 162.
   Reprint of 1961.147.

52. Fassbinder, Fritz. "Bücherecke." Osterreicher Rundfunk (8 August).
   Favorable radio review of the German translation of O stressing the extent to which Cross Damon, without religious or philosophical restraints on his emotions, plays the role of "God without God's greatness."

53. Ferguson, Blanche E. Countee Cullen and the Negro Renaissance. New York: Dodd, Mead, pp. 168-169, 182, 194.
   Discusses W's impact on the literary scene and his rejection of the earlier emphasis on the black middle class.

54. Fiedler, Leslie. Love and Death in the American Novel. Revised edition. New York: Stein and Day, p. 493.
   Reprint of 1960.147.

55. Förster, I. "Richard Wright: Schwarze Macht." Der Deutsche Lehrer im Ausland (October).
   Favorable review of the German translation of BP. It has justly become a standard work on Africa and still has much to teach concerning African psychology.

56. Franke, Konrad. "Neue Bücher." Süddeutscher Rundfunk (3 October).
   Radio review of the German translation of O. Cross Damon embodies many of the basic literary myths of our time; the novel is W's attack on these myths. Cross is able to penetrate the delusions of the ideologies of other people but lacks the courage to look critically at himself.

57. Fremont-Smith, Eliot. "Books of the Times: Native Sons." The New York Times (16 February), p. 41.
   Review of Herbert Hill's Anger, and Beyond using W's death in exile to question whether it is possible to be true to one's self as an American, a black man, and an artist.

58. Frémy, Dominique and Michèle Frémy. Quid? Tout pour tous. Paris: Librairie Plon, p. 73.
    Reprint of 1963.86.

59. French, Warren. The Social Novel at the End of an Era. Crosscurrents Modern Critiques, ed. Harry T. Moore. Carbondale and Edwardsville: Southern Illinois University Press, pp. 17, 171-180.
    Discusses LT and NS. French believes that W was victimized by his own talent and ability with language. Partially reprinted: 1971.147.

60. Friedman, Saul. "Books Limited Under Pressure." Detroit Free Press (6 March), Sec. B, pp. 1, 11.
    Reports that NS is among the books placed in restricted use at the Grosse Pointe public libraries because of pressure from ultra-conservative groups. Reprinted in abridged form: 1966.61.

61. _____. "Books Limited Under Pressure." Newsletter on Intellectual Freedom, 15 (May), 28.
    Abridged reprint of 1966.60.

62. G., S. "Richard Wright: Der Mörder und die Schuldigen." Bildungsarbeit (September).
    Review of the German translation of O, a book recommended for readers interested in the racial problem in the United States. Cross Damon is doomed because he carries his fear into his new life.

63. Green, Gerald. "Back to Bigger." The Kenyon Review, 28 (September), 521-539.
    Revaluation of the social novel of the thirties and forties. NS is the supreme example of this genre, and Bigger Thomas is the most memorable protagonist. Social novels of the present fade in comparison to W's book. Reprinted: 1968.118.

64. Gross, Seymour L. "Introduction: Stereotype to Archetype: The Negro in American Literary Criticism," in Images of the Negro in American Literature. Ed. Seymour L. Gross and John Edward Hardy. Patterns of Literary Criticism, No. 5, ed. Marshall McLuhan, R. J. Schoeck, and Ernest Sirluck. Chicago: The University of Chicago Press, pp. 1-26.
    Discusses briefly the impact of NS (pp. 18-19). Mentions "Blueprint for Negro Writing" (p. 16) and WML (p. 25). Reprinted: 1966.65.

65. _____. "Stereotype to Archetype: The Negro in American Literary Criticism." Midway, No. 28 (Autumn), 99-128.
    Reprint of 1966.64.

66. _____ and John Edward Hardy, eds. Images of the Negro in American Literature. Patterns of Literary Criticism, No. 5, ed. Marshall McLuhan, R. J. Schoeck, and Ernest Sirluck. Chicago: The University of Chicago Press, p. [vii].
    One of the two epigraphs is W's statement that "the Negro is America's metaphor."

67. H., J. "Bon sang de bonsoir par Richard Wright." Perspectives (19 March).
    Unfavorable review of the French translation of LT complaining of excessive brutality.

68. Hausdorff, Don. "Negroes as Authors." The Detroit News (1 May), p. 3-G.
    Review of Herbert Hill's Anger, and Beyond referring to the symposium on W as "largely historical" and "gently nostalgic."

69. Hentoff, Nat. "The Other Side of the Blues," in Anger, and Beyond: The Negro Writer in the United States. Ed. Herbert Hill. New York: Harper & Row, pp. 76-85.
    Mentions W briefly (p. 79).

70. Hernton, Calvin C. "Blood of the Lamb: The Ordeal of James Baldwin," in his White Papers for White Americans. Garden City, N. Y.: Doubleday, pp. 105-128.
    Compares Baldwin and W, finding similarities in their early lives and in their expatriation. Discusses the estrangement of the two authors. Reprinted: 1970.178.

71. _____. "Postscript: A Fiery Baptism," in his White Papers for White Americans. Garden City, N. Y.: Doubleday, pp. 129-147.
    Notes that Blues for Mister Charlie is "brute [sic], crude, violent, and bold, more in the fashion of Richard Wright" (p. 130) than Baldwin's earlier works had been. Reprinted: 1970.179; 1974.90.

72. _____. Sex and Racism in America. Evergreen Black Cat Edition BC-113. New York: Grove Press, pp. 81-82, 85, 93.
    Reprint of 1965.76.

73. _____. White Papers for White Americans. Garden City, N. Y.: Doubleday, p. [ix].
    The epigraph is W's haiku "I Am Nobody."

74. Hicks, Granville. "Racial Reality and the American Dream." Saturday Review, 49 (12 February), 27-28.
Review of Herbert Hill's Anger, and Beyond noting that W is seen as an "important pioneer" although there are "large doubts" about his late work.

75. Hill, Herbert. "Introduction," in his Anger, and Beyond: The Negro Writer in the United States. New York: Harper & Row, pp. xiii-xxii.
In a discussion of the relation between the artist and society, Hill cites W as an example of the close ties between freedom and the creative imagination. As his personal life was degraded, his artistic talent developed its potential.

76. ____, Horace Cayton, Arna Bontemps, and Saunders Redding. "Reflections on Richard Wright; A Symposium on an Exiled Native Son," in Anger, and Beyond: The Negro Writer in the United States. Ed. Herbert Hill. New York: Harper & Row, pp. 196-212.
Hill moderates the discussion and comments on W and Communism (pp. 204-205) and W's response to Redding's criticism of his expatriation (p. 206).
Reprinted: 1970.180; 1971.147.

77. Hilliard, Robert L. "The Drama and American Negro Life." Southern Theatre, 10 (Winter), 9-14.
Includes a long statement by John Randolph of the cast of the road show version of NS describing problems encountered because of racism and discrimination together with efforts to overcome them (pp. 11-13).

78. Hoyer, Franz A. "Für sie gelesen--aus neue Büchern." Bayerischer Rundfunk (19 September).
Radio review of the German translation of O stressing Sartre's influence. W achieves only mixed success in blending his mystery story with his philosophical treatise. The novel now seems dated.

79. Hughes, Langston. "The Negro and American Entertainment," in The American Negro Reference Book. Ed. John P. Davis. Englewood Cliffs, N. J.: Prentice-Hall, pp. 835, 847.
Refers briefly to the dramatic versions of NS and LD.
Reprinted: 1976.103.

80. Hughes, Langston. "The Twenties: Harlem and Its Negritude." African Forum, 1 (Spring), 11-20.
W is mentioned frequently in this discursive essay on the Harlem Renaissance. Hughes introduced Ellison to W, who influenced the younger man as he had been influenced by Hughes. Hughes also discusses W's connection with the Writers Project, his residence in Harlem and Brooklyn, and his literary career, especially NS.

81. Huguet, Jean and Georges Belle. La Bibliothèque idéale de poche. Paris: Editions Universitaires, p. 325.
Lists French pocket editions of W and provides a brief critique of the writer.

82. Jacobs. "Die Mörder und die Schuldigen." Bonn General-Anzeiger (2 September).
Review of the German translation of O stressing the novel's link with the central themes of W's prior work--alienation, fear, and the fatal accident of skin color. The work is not one of W's great ones because, although social chaos is behind Cross Damon's actions, W de-emphasizes the social criticism which is his forte.

83. J.[ahn], J.[anheinz] H. "Eight Men," in Kindlers Literatur Lexikon. Ed. Gert Woerner. Vol. 2. Zurich: Kindler Verlag, pp. 1894-1895.
Summary with critical comments and a brief bibliography.

84. Jones, LeRoi. "Black Writing," in his Home: Social Essays. New York: William Morrow, pp. 161-165.
Mentions favorably BB and NS.

85. ____. "A Dark Bag," in his Home: Social Essays. New York: William Morrow, pp. 121-132.
Reprint of 1964.78.

86. ____. "The Dempsey-Liston Fight," in his Home: Social Essays. New York: William Morrow, pp. 155-160.
Reprint of 1964.80.

87. ____. "LeRoi Jones Talking," in his Home: Social Essays. New York: William Morrow, pp. 179-188.
Mentions W's exile (p. 179).
Reprinted: 1971.186.

88. ____. "The Myth of a 'Negro Literature,'" in his Home: Social Essays. New York: William Morrow, pp. 105-115.
Reprint of 1963.121.

89. ____. "Philistinism and the Negro Writer," in Anger, and Beyond: The Negro Writer in the United States. Ed. Herbert Hill. New York: Harper & Row, pp. 51-61.
States that "the most completely

valid social novels and social criti-
cisms of South and North, non-urban
and urban Negro life, are Wright's
Black Boy and Native Son" (p. 59).

90. Jürgen, Ingeborg. "Abenteuer und
Utopie in Roman." Berlin Telegraf (28
August), p. 18.
    Review of the German translation of
    O, a novel which proves that W was
    concerned with internal tensions and
    the struggle between good and evil in
    addition to social questions.
    Although Cross Damon sees murder as
    a way of correcting the world order
    and feels innocent, the novel leaves
    the reader with many unanswered
    questions.

91. Kallen, Horace M. "'Color-Blind.'"
The Emory University Quarterly, 22 (Summer), 110-122.
    Refers briefly to W's idea that the
    "negro is both inside and outside the
    white man's culture" (p. 119).

92. Kattan, Naim. "Rencontre avec Ralph
Ellison." Les Langues Modernes, 60 (May-
June), 99-101.
    Introductory note to an interview
    with Ellison mentions W briefly.

93. Kinnamon, Keneth. "The Emergence of
Richard Wright: A Literary, Biographi-
cal, and Social Study." Ph.D. thesis,
Harvard University.
    Early version of 1972.123.

94. Kramer, Dale. Chicago Renaissance:
The Literary Life in the Midwest 1900-
1930. New York: Appleton-Century, pp.
347-348.
    Contains a paragraph on W in Chicago.

95. Langhammer-Köllmer, Ella. "Richard
Wright: Die Mörder und die Schuldigen."
Neue Volksbildung, 17 (October), 465-
466.
    Favorable review of the German trans-
    lation of O stressing the Dostoev-
    skyan parallels. W criticizes both
    American society and the Communist
    Party in the larger context of an
    embittered search for value in a
    hostile world.

96. Liptzin, Sol. The Jew in American
Literature. New York: Block, pp. 153,
170-171.
    Comments on NS, especially the char-
    acterization of Boris Max.

97. Littlejohn, David. Black on White: A
Critical Survey of Writing by American
Negroes. New York: Grossman, p. 4, 8, 9,
10, 15, 17, 18, 21, 33, 37, 54, 62, 65,
67, 80n, 83-84, 86-89, 101, 102-110,
120-121, 127, 138, 141, 142, 144, 161,
166, 170.
    The main section on W (pp. 102-110)
    emphasizes his "primeval simplicity"
    (p. 102). He relies more on sensa-
    tionalism and protest than on artis-
    tic technique and psychological or
    moral insight. His theme is race war.
    With these presuppositions Littlejohn
    discusses BB, UTC, and NS and men-
    tions other works by W.
    Reprinted: 1969.160.
    Partially reprinted: 1970.249; 1978.
    148.

98. Margolies, Edward L. "A Critical
Analysis of the Works of Richard
Wright." Dissertation Abstracts, 27
(December), 1829A-1830A.
    Based on the aesthetic premise that
    art should lead to social action, W's
    work derives from his experience as a
    black man and from his reading in the
    social sciences. Moving from Marxism
    to existentialism to color national-
    ism, W exemplifies historical pat-
    terns affecting millions of people.
    As a writer of fiction he excels in
    narrative skill, especially in situa-
    tions of suspense and fear. His
    greatest imaginative theme is racism
    and its consequences. He is at once
    universal and quintessentially Ameri-
    can.

98a. Masuda, Aogu. "Understanding of a
Segment of the Racial Problem by Refer-
ring to Richard Wright's Black Boy."
Orio Joshi Keizai Tanki Daigaku Ronshu
[Orio Women's Junior College of Econo-
mics Treatises], 1 (June), 139-145.
    The problems of race W copes with in
    BB are so complicated that, given the
    Rev. M. L. King's efforts, they are
    beyond solution. In English. [Y. H.
    and T. K.]

99. Materassi, Mario. "James Baldwin, un
profeta del nostro tempo." Il ponte, 22
(March), 359-369.
    Notes Baldwin's rejection of the W
    tradition (p. 363).
    Reprinted: 1977.220.

100. _____. "Mito e realtà del negro
americano." Il ponte, 22 (July), 951-
961.
    Mentions W briefly (p. 951).
    Reprinted: 1977.220.

101. Mauro, Walter. "'Gridalo forte' di
James Baldwin." Il Naples mattino (15
September), p. 3.
    Mentions W briefly.

102. McElrath, Edith Anne. "Speaking of
Books." The Seattle Rainier District
Times (25 May), p. 5.
    Cites W's haiku in Arna Bontemps's

American Negro Poetry as proof that
"good poetry is universal."

103. Meier, August and Elliott M. Rudwick. From Plantation to Ghetto: An
Interpretive History of American
Negroes. New York: Hill and Wang, p.
210.
    Mentions W as "the dominant literary
    figure" of his time. His social and
    racial themes are presented with
    "bitter sociological and psychologi-
    cal realism."

104. Meltzer, Milton and August Meier.
Time of Trial, Time of Hope: The Negro
in America, 1919-1941. Garden City,
N. Y.: Doubleday, p. 102.
    Discusses briefly W's early protest
    writing through NS.

105. Miller, Elizabeth W. The Negro in
America: A Bibliography. Cambridge,
Mass.: Harvard University Press, pp. 8,
10, 44, 50.
    Lists eight of W's books with brief
    annotations.
    Reprinted: 1970.265.

105a. Montague, Gene and Marjorie Hen-
shaw. "For Analysis," in their The
Experience of Literature: Anthology and
Analysis. Englewood Cliffs, N. J.: Prentice-Hall, p. 109.
    Three brief study questions on
    "Almos' a Man."

105b. ____. "The Short Story," in their
The Experience of Literature: Anthology
and Analysis. Englewood Cliffs, N. J.:
Prentice-Hall, pp. 5-16.
    Includes brief comments on setting
    and symbol in "Almos' a Man" (pp. 15,
    16).

106. Murray, Albert. "Something Differ-
ent, Something More," in Anger, and
Beyond: The Negro Writer in the United
States. Ed. Herbert Hill. New York:
Harper & Row, pp. 112-137.
    Discusses Baldwin's quarrel with W.
    Baldwin overstates his case against
    W. Murray also comments on W's expat-
    riation and Ellison's relation to W.
    Reprinted: 1968.170; 1970.269.

107. N. "Richard Wright: Der Mörder und
die Schuldigen." Die Kirrke [?] (c.
August).
    Favorable notice of the German trans-
    lation of O viewing it as an unveil-
    ing of the inhumanity of Communism.
    It contains elements of W's spiritual
    autobiography.

108. Neal, Lawrence P. "The Black
Writer's Role: James Baldwin." Liberator, 6 (April), 10-11, 18.
    Mentions W briefly.

109. ____. "The Black Writer's Role:
Ralph Ellison." Liberator, 6 (January),
9-11.
    Includes comments on W.

110. ____. "The Black Writer's Role:
Richard Wright," in Afro-American Festi-
val of the Arts Magazine. Newark: Jihad
Productions, pp. [7-13].
    Discusses NS and, more extensively,
    "Blueprint for Negro Writing." W
    tried to reconcile black nationalism
    and Communism.
    Reprinted: 1967.78; 1969.183.

111. Newman, Charles. "The Lesson of the
Master: Henry James and James Baldwin."
The Yale Review, 56 (October), 45-59.
    Mentions W briefly (p. 45).
    Reprinted: 1974.138.

112. Obiechina, Emmanuel. "Three New
Novels by Negro Americans." African
Forum, 1 (Winter), 107-111.
    Mentions briefly NS.

113. O'Neal, Robert. Teachers' Guide to
World Literature for the High School.
Champaign, Ill.: National Council of
Teachers of English, pp. 14, 311, 406.
    Mentions NS briefly in comparison to
    Corrado Alvaro's Revolt in Aspro-
    monte, Jean-Paul Sartre's The Res-
    pectful Prostitute, and Oscar Wilde's
    The Ballad of Reading Gaol.

114. Parks, Gordon. A Choice of Weapons.
New York: Harper & Row, pp. 232, 241,
243-244.
    Parks states that "12 Million Black
    Voices became my bible" at a crucial
    period of his development as a writer
    and photographer. He also describes a
    1942 meeting with W, "neat, soft-
    spoken, well-groomed and scholarly
    looking, seemingly free of the scars
    of his terrible Southern boyhood. Yet
    a sort of terror lurked in his soft
    eyes."
    Reprinted: 1967.81.

115. Pendexter, Faunce. "Between the
Bookends." Lewiston (Maine) Evening
Journal (12 February), p. 2-A.
    Lists W as a contributor to Langston
    Hughes's The Book of Negro Humor.

116. Pinot, Germaine. "Bon sang de bonsoir." Postale des Posteset Telecommuni-
cations (15 January).
    Favorable review of the French trans-
    lation of LT. W is one of the great
    American novelists, and this book is
    an important addition to his canon.

117. Plessner, Monika. "James Baldwin

and das Land der Verheissung." Merkur, 20, pp. 515-533.

Baldwin's feud with W reveals tensions similar to those inherent in his relationship with his father. Baldwin grows out of the Puritan tradition of the "promised land"; W is a "native son" of the American revolution (pp. 520-521).

118. Poore, Charles. "Books of the Times: The Proletarian Writers and Scarlett O'Hara." The New York Times (26 May), p. 45.

Review of The American Writer and the Great Depression noting that it contains a selection from TMBV.

119. Pouzot, Henri. "Bon Sang de Bonsoir (R. Wright)." Présence des Lettres et des Arts.

Review of the French translation of LT noting that W condemns both white racism in the North and black submission to it. All must accept responsibility for the racial situation.

120. R., W. G. "Die Tragik des Aussenseiters." Badisches Tagblatt (September).

Review of the German translation of O, one of W's most significant works. It continues his consideration of the question of individual versus social responsibility. The key to the book lies in the interaction of Cross Damon and Ely Houston, which leads to the perception that only affirmation of the individual can help break down the walls between self and world.

121. Ra. "Schicksal eines Aussenseiters." Allgemeine Wochenzeitung der Juden in Deutschland (2 September).

Favorable review of the German translation of O. W's analysis of society and the soul makes the novel a nearly overpowering experience. Filled with brutality like all of W's books, O deals with the American racial problem by attacking society as a whole and individual citizens.

122. Ravitz, Abe C. "Negro Writers Blaze Trail." The Cleveland Plain Dealer (27 February), p. 7-F.

Review of Herbert Hill's Anger, and Beyond mentioning briefly its consideration of W.

123. Redding, Saunders. "The Negro Writer and American Literature," in Anger, and Beyond: The Negro Writer in the United States. Ed. Herbert Hill. New York: Harper & Row, pp. 1-19.

Includes a discussion of UTC, NS, and BB emphasizing W's universalism. W treats "only incidentally, for drama-

tic purposes, and because of the authenticity of empiricism, the subject of Negro and white. What he deals with is prejudice" (p. 17). Reprinted: 1970.294.

124. _____. "Since Richard Wright." African Forum, 1 (Spring), 21-31.

Surveys the Afro-American literary scene since W's death with some attention to deviations from the W "Negro norm."

125. _____, Herbert Hill, Arna Bontemps, and Horace Cayton. "Reflections on Richard Wright: A Symposium on an Exiled Native Son," in Anger, and Beyond: The Negro Writer in the United States. Ed. Herbert Hill. New York: Harper & Row, pp. 196-212.

Redding recalls meeting W at a performance of Othello in 1943. Although W suffered from discrimination in the United States, including New York, in Paris he grew homesick. Redding discusses critically W's expatriation and its literary consequences. W was committed and humorless, but his best books have the compensating qualities of "their moral integrity, their social force, their truth" (p. 212). Reprinted: 1970.296; 1971.147.

126. Reilly, John M. "Afterword," in Black Boy: A Record of Childhood and Youth. New York: Harper & Row, pp. 286-288.

W's autobiography is agonizingly painful to read. In the genre of spiritual autobiography, it is nevertheless a socially factual document.

127. _____. "Afterword," in Native Son. New York: Harper & Row, pp. 393-398.

NS is a powerful, realistic novel deserving of the praise it has received. It is an exposé of social injustice, not an objective report. Reilly approves of W's literary method.

128. Robbins, J. Albert, Jackson R. Bryer, Philip R. Headings, Joseph V. Ridgely, and Donald B. Stauffer, with the help of Haskell S. Springer. "American Literature." PMLA, 81 (May), 172-197.

Bibliography listing four items on W (p. 197).

129. Salk, Erwin A. A Layman's Guide to Negro History. Chicago: Quadrangle Books, pp. 12, 44, 92, 118, 123, 154.

Lists W and some of his books under various categories. Reprinted: 1967.90.

130. Samuels, Gertrude. "Huck, Jim and Mary Jane." The New York Times Book Review (8 May), pp. 3, 44.
Notes that W is being read by a junior honors class at an all-black boys' high school.

131. Schwabeneder, Franz. "Machtrausch mit Mord vergolten." Oberösterreichsche Nachrichten (31 December).
Review of the German translation of O. W makes the astoundingly violent materials of his novel cohere by placing Cross Damon at the midpoint of the conflict of larger forces. Murder provides the path for entering into the inescapable human guilt.

132. Seibert, Claus. "Der Mörder und die Schuldigen." Unidentified clipping.
Review of the German translation of O. Developing from a realistic into a visionary novel, it shows the influence of Dostoevsky, Zola, and Dreiser.

133. Séjourné, Philippe. "La Carrière littéraire de Richard Wright et l'évolution du problème noir aux Etats-Unis." Annales de la Faculté des Lettres et Sciences Humaines d'Aix, 41 (December), 133-154.
Retrospective essay on W's literary career with discussion of his major novels. Calls for a revaluation of his major importance.

133a. Shafer, Boyd C., Richard A. McLemore, and Everett Augspurger. United States History for High Schools. River Forest, Ill.: Laidlaw Brothers, p. 675.
Mentions briefly W and WML.
Reprinted: 1967.95a.

134. Silber, Hans. "Neue Buecher." La Montevideo Voz del Día (10 October).
Unfavorable review of the German translation of O. W's typical stance as a plaintiff rather than as an accuser is inappropriate to this novel because he does not treat Cross Damon as an oppressed black man but as a self-assertive individual.

135. Spearman, Walter. "Books." The Chapel Hill Weekly (28 December), p. 8.
Contains a review of David Littlejohn's Black on White mentioning its consideration of W.

135a. Stafford, William. "Fiction: 1930 to the Present," in American Literary Scholarship: An Annual/1964. Ed. James Woodress. Durham, N. C.: Duke University Press, pp. 154-178.
Mentions W briefly (pp. 155, 157, 158).

135b. Stone, Edward. Voices of Despair: Four Motifs in American Literature. Athens: Ohio University Press, pp. 74-75, 81.
Comments on the symbolic use of whiteness in NS and quotes Malcolm Cowley on the same novel.

136. Swados, Harvey. "Introduction," in his The American Writer and the Great Depression. The American Heritage Series, No. 63, ed. Leonard W. Levy and Alfred Young. Indianapolis: Bobbs-Merrill, pp. xi-xxxvi.
Mentions W briefly (pp. xv-xvi).

137. _____. "Speech from a Forthcoming Play E. E. Cummings," in his The American Writer and the Great Depression. The American Heritage Series, No. 63, ed. Leonard W. Levy and Alfred Young. Indianapolis: Bobbs-Merrill, pp. 379-380.
Compares briefly W, Faulkner, and Cummings as protest writers.

138. _____. "These Are Our Lives," in his The American Writer and the Great Depression. The American Heritage Series, No. 63, ed. Leonard W. Levy and Alfred Young. Indianapolis: Bobbs-Merrill, pp. 47-48.
Mentions W's connection with the Writers Project.

139. _____. "12 Million Black Voices Richard Wright," in his The American Writer and the Great Depression. The American Heritage Series, No. 63, ed. Leonard W. Levy and Alfred Young. Indianapolis: Bobbs-Merrill, pp. 368-369.
Biographical sketch asserting that W is still relevant.

140. Taiyosha Editorial Department. Notes in Black Boy. Tokyo: The Taiyosha Press, 106 pp.
The text is in English; the notes are in Japanese.

141. Thorp, Willard. "Whit Burnett and Story Magazine." The Princeton University Library Chronicle, 27 (Winter), 107-112.
Mentions W material in the Whit Burnett papers at Princeton.

142. Tolson, M.[elvin] B. "Miles to Go with Black Ulysses." The New York Sunday Herald Tribune (20 February), Book Week Sec., pp. 2, 12.
Mentions W briefly.

143. Turner, Darwin T. "The Negro Novel in America: In Rebuttal." CLA Journal, 10 (December), 122-134.
Mentions W briefly (pp. 124, 133).

Reprinted: 1971.301.

144. Vo. "Rassenproblem in den USA."
Westdeutsche Allgemeine (c. 16 August).
Review of the German translation of
O. The novel pleads not for political
and legal rights, but for human and
civil ones. Though the protagonist
commits murder, the guilt belongs to
white society.

145. Vogel, Albert W. "The Education of
the Negro in Richard Wright's Black
Boy." The Journal of Negro Education, 35
(Spring), 195-198.
Uses BB to support the thesis that
education for blacks in America is
designed to suppress the aspirations
and capabilities of the group. In W's
autobiography the process of education is carried out by suffering
poverty and racial discrimination as
well as by going to school.

146. Warren, Robert Penn. Who Speaks for
the Negro? Vintage Books V-323. New
York: Random House, pp. 83, 285, 289,
349.
Reprint of 1965.125.

147. Weisenburger, Hansjörg. "Die Last
der Versprechen." Allgemeine Zeitung (10
August).
Review of the German translation of
O. The novel focuses on W's disillusionment with the Communist Party by
demonstrating that brutal absurdity
results when Cross Damon transfers
totalitarian principles into the
sphere of his personal life.

148. Wertham, Frederic, M. D. A Sign for
Cain: An Exploration of Human Violence.
New York: Macmillan, pp. 332-333.
Discusses NS as the greatest modern
novel about violence. W correctly
depicts Bigger's violence as a psychological necessity.

149. Wolff, Geoffrey A. "After Their
Fire, the Half-Baked." Book Week (27
March), pp. 3, 17.
Review of Herbert Hill's Anger, and
Beyond arguing that W is inextricably
bound to other black writers by race.
When he ignores this fact, as in SH,
he fails.

150. X, Malcolm, with the assistance of
Alex Haley. The Autobiography of Malcolm
X. Evergreen Black Cat Book B-146. New
York: Grove Press, pp. 354-355.
Reprint of 1965.128.

151. Young, Margaret B. The First Book
of American Negroes. New York: Franklin
Watts, p. 57.
Mentions W and NS.

1967

1. Anon. "Afrika," in Das kleine Lexikon
der Weltliteratur. Ed. Hermann Pongs.
Stuttgart: Union Verlag, pp. 25-29.
Mentions briefly W and some of his
works.

2. Anon. Dictionary Catalog of the
Schomburg Collection of Negro Literature
and History: First Supplement. Vol. 2.
Boston: G. K. Hall, p. 869.
Reproduces nine catalog cards on W.

3. Anon. Index Translationum 18. Paris:
Unesco, pp. 290, 387, 443, 487, 597.
Lists translations of LT into French,
Dutch, and Swedish, BB into Italian
and Norwegian, and PS into Italian.

4. Anon. "Richard Wright: A Biography."
Publishers' Weekly, 192 (28 August),
242.
Notice of the biography by Constance
Webb.

5. Anon. "Wright," in Bonniers Lexikon.
Ed. Axel Elvin. Vol. 15. Stockholm:
Albert Bonniers förlag, pp. 563-565.
Contains a biographical sketch with
photograph.

6. Anon. "Wright, Richard," in Alverdens
viden. Odense: Skandinavisk Bogforlag,
p. 831.
Biographical note.

7. Anon. "Wright, Richard," in The American Peoples Encyclopedia. Ed. Edward
Humphrey. Vol. 19. New York: Grolier, p.
415.
Revised reprint of 1953.63.

8. Anon. "Wright, Richard," in Novissima
enciclopedia Ceschina. Milan: Casa Edi-
trice Ceschina, p. 1476.
Biographical note.

9. Anon. "Wright, Richard," in Priručni
Leksikon. Ed. Milan Salakovic, Ivo Vran-
cic, and Sime Balen. Zagreb: Nakladni
Zavod Znanje, p. 978.
Biographical note.

9a. Baldwin, James, Julia Hervé, and
Jean Duflot. "James Baldwin: 'Il y a
plusieurs manières de tuer un Noir.'"
Jeune Afrique, No. 340 (16 July), pp.
30-34.
In this interview with W's daughter
and another journalist, Baldwin mentions W briefly.

10. Banton, Michael. Race Relations. New
York: Basic Books, pp. 148, 415.
Mentions the elevator operator in BB.

11. Baur, Esther. "The Fader Plan:

Detroit Style." Library Journal, 92 (15 September), 3119-3121.

Lists BB on a list of most popular paperbacks and mentions NS favorably in an accompanying quotation from Hooked on Books by Daniel Fader and Morton Shavitz.

12. Bayliss, John F. "Native Son: Protest or Psychological Study?" Negro American Literature Forum, 1 (Fall), 5-6.

Argues that Bigger is disoriented and disturbed, but not mainly for racial reasons. Rather he is neurotic to begin with. The novel is more a psychological study than a work of protest.
Reprinted: 1970.53.

13. Bensky, Lawrence M. "What's New on Campus." The New York Times Book Review (26 February), Part II, pp. 2-3, 14.
Notes that W is the most popular writer among black college students.

14. Bigsby, C. W. E. "The Committed Writer: James Baldwin as Dramatist." Twentieth Century Literature, 13 (April), 39-48.
Mentions Baldwin's attack on W as a protest novelist (p. 39).
Reprinted: 1968.45.

15. Borges, Jorge Luis. Introducción a la literatura norteamericana. Colección Esquemas 77. Buenos Aires: Editorial Columba, p. 51.
Contains a long paragraph on W providing a sketch of his life and literary career through O. W's "theme [is] man harassed by a hostile society."
Translated: 1971.49.

16. Brignano, Russell Carl. "Richard Wright: The Major Themes, Ideas, and Attitudes in His Works." Dissertation Abstracts, 28 (August), 666A-667A.
See 1966.28.

17. Britt, David. "Native Son: Watershed of Negro Protest Literature." Negro American Literature Forum, 1 (Fall), 4-5.
Analysis of the novel as a work of protest which reveals the realities of racial life in America. The controlling metaphor is nightmare. Each problem that Bigger faces is compounded because of his color. To discuss Bigger in "human" or "universal" terms and not as a social phenomenon is to misinterpret the novel.

18. Brooks, Charlotte. "Introduction," in her The Outnumbered. New York: Dell,

pp. 7-10.
Includes a brief comment on a passage from NS reprinted on pp. 144-156.

19. Brown, Sterling A. "Negro in the American Theatre," in The Oxford Companion to the Theatre. Ed. Phyllis Hartnoll. Third edition. London: Oxford University Press, pp. 672-679.
Reprint of 1951.139.

20. Bussey, Virginia. "Best Short Stories of Negro Writers Collected." The Bakersfield Californian (18 February), The Golden Empire Sec., p. 19A.
Review of Langston Hughes's The Best Short Stories by Negro Writers calling "Almos' a Man" a bitter treatment of the struggle of youth to attain manhood.

21. Chapman, Abraham. "The Harlem Renaissance in Literary History." CLA Journal, 11 (September), 38-58.
Mentions W several times.

22. Clarke, John Henrik. "The Origin and Growth of Afro-American Literature." Negro Digest, 17 (December), 54-67.
Points out that W's critical success forced subsequent black writers to be evaluated by the same standards applied to white writers.
Reprinted: 1968.64; 1971.69a.

23. Cleaver, Eldridge. "My Father and Stokely Carmichael." Ramparts, 5 (April), 10-14.
Contains a brief comment on W.
Reprinted: 1969.56a.

24. Cowley, Malcolm. "Richard Wright: The Case of Bigger Thomas," in his Think Back on Us . . . A Contemporary Chronicle of the 1930's. Ed. Henry Dan Piper. Carbondale and Edwardsville: Southern Illinois University Press, pp. 355-357.
Reprint of 1940.614.

25. Cruse, Harold. The Crisis of the Negro Intellectual. New York: William Morrow, pp. 3, 51, 69, 115, 181-189, 237, 267, 269, 271, 273, 275-277, 500, 510.
The chapter on W analyzes his relationship to Communism, especially his position in "Blueprint for Negro Writing" and his affiliation with New Challenge. Because W did not understand his white comrades' desire to keep blacks in a subordinate status in the revolutionary movement, he never realized the revolutionary potential of black nationalism. Mentions W frequently, notably in a discussion of Lorraine Hansberry's review of O.
Reprinted: 1968.69.

Partially reprinted: 1971.147.

26. Davis, Arthur P. "Trends in Negro American Literature (1940-65)." The Promethean (May), pp. 30-34.
Mentions NS, O, SH, and LD.

27. Dickinson, Donald C. A Bio-Bibliography of Langston Hughes 1902-1967. Archon Books. Hamden, Ct.: Shoe String Press, pp. 54, 67-68, 79, 100-101, 113.
Mentions and quotes W.
Reprinted: 1972.59.

27a. Dommergues, Pierre. "Fiches d'identité," in his Les U. S. A. à la recherche de leur identité. Paris: Editions Bernard Gresset, pp. 399-476.
Contains a bio-bibliographical note on W (pp. 475-476).

27b. ____, William Melvin Kelley, Paule Marshall, and Langston Hughes. "Statut et responsibilité de l'ecrivain noir," in Les U. S. A. à la recherche de leur identité. Ed. Pierre Dommergues. Paris: Editions Bernard Gresset, pp. 142-156.
Reprint of 1966.45.

28. Ellison, Martha. "Velvet Voices Feed on Bitter Fruit: A Study of American Negro Poetry." Poet and Critic, 4 (Winter), 39-49.
Mentions and quotes from "I Have Seen Black Hands" (p. 39) and "In the Falling Snow" (p. 42).

28a. Ellison, Ralph. "L'Integration de l'esprit," in Les U. S. A. à la recherche de leur identité. Ed. Pierre Dommergues. Paris: Editions Bernard Gresset, pp. 177-193.
Emphasizes Ellison's personal friendship but ideological and artistic disagreement with W. Ellison prefers W to Bigger. Notes that W introduced Ellison to Dostoevsky.

29. ____, James Thompson, Lennox Raphael, and Steve Cannon. "A 'Very Stern Discipline': An Interview with Ralph Ellison." Harper's Magazine, 234 (March), 76-80, 83-86, 88, 90, 93-95.
Ellison notes that W competed on the international literary scene, not merely among black writers. Ellison also points out that his literary intention differs from W's.

30. Emerson, Donald. "American Literature," in Encyclopedia of World Literature in the 20th Century. Ed. Wolfgang Bernard Fleischmann. Vol. 1. New York: Ungar, pp. 32-44.
Mentions briefly UTC (p. 38).

31. Fabre, Michel "Des taudis et des rats," in his Les Noirs américains.

Paris: Colin, p. 187.
Headnote to a selection from NS.

32. ____. "Du haut de la chaire," in his Les Noirs américains. Paris: Colin, p. 237.
Headnote to a selection from LD.

33. ____. "L'Inoubliable Obsession," in his Les Noirs américains. Paris: Colin, p. 208.
Headnote to "Between the World and Me."

34. ____. Les Noirs américains. Paris: Colin, p. 81, 98, 105, 107, 109, 120-21.
Mentions W frequently in chapters entitled "Racism and the Personality of the American Black" and "The Forces of the Black Revolution." Provides headnotes to passages from TMBV, NS, and LD and to "Between the World and Me."

35. ____. "Passer sa rage," in his Les Noirs américains. Paris: Colin, p. 221.
Headnote to a selection from NS.

36. ____. "Sous le sceptre du roi coton," in his Les Noirs américains. Paris: Colin, p. 156.
Headnote to a selection from TMBV.

37. Fanon, Frantz. Black Skin, White Masks. Trans. Charles Lam Markmann. New York: Grove Press, pp. 139, 183.
Translation of 1952.33
Reprinted: 1968.95.

38. Farmer, James. "The 'Movement' Now." Lincoln University Bulletin (Winter), pp. 6-9.
Quotes W on the black sense of exclusion from society.
Reprinted: 1972.70.

39. Fiedler, Leslie A. Love and Death in the American Novel. Revised edition. New York: Dell, p. 493.
Reprint of 1960.147.

39a. Flanagan, John T. "Some Middle-western Literary Magazines." Papers on Language and Literature, 3 (Summer), 237-257.
Mentions W briefly as a contributor to Accent (p. 251).

40. Fleming, Robert Edward. "The Chicago Naturalistic Novel: 1930-1966." Ph.D. dissertation, University of Illinois, pp. 67-109.
In a chapter entitled "The Negro in the Promised Land," Fleming treats NS and subsequent novels of black life in Chicago.

41. Fontaine, William T. Reflections on

Segregation, Desegregation, Power and Morals. Springfield, Ill.: Charles C. Thomas, pp. 22-30.

In a section entitled "Richard Wright's 'Native Son': The Promise of Communism," Fontaine emphasizes Bigger's development as a human being under Max's tutelage.

42. Franklin, John Hope. From Slavery to Freedom: A History of Negro Americans. Third edition. New York: Knopf, pp. 515-516, 647.

Reprint of 1956.158.

43. _____. "Negro," in Merit Students Encyclopedia. Ed. Bernard S. Cayne. Vol. 13. New York: Crowell-Collier Educational Corporation, pp. 156-164.

Mentions W briefly (p. 164).

44. Frémy, Dominique et Michèle Frémy. Quid? Tout pour tous. Paris: Librairie Plon, p. 75.

Reprint of 1963.86.

45. French, Warren. "The Thirties--Fiction," in his The Thirties: Fiction, Poetry, Drama. Deland, Fla.: Everett/Edwards, pp. 5-10.

Comments on W, especially as a precursor of literary existentialism. Praises LT highly.

46. Fuller, Hoyt W. "Books Noted." Negro Digest, 17 (November), 86-87.

Contains a brief reference to W.

47. Gayle, Addison, Jr. "A Defense of James Baldwin." CLA Journal, 10 (March), 201-208.

In defending Baldwin against Robert Bone and Eldridge Cleaver, Gayle analyzes the attitudes toward W held by Baldwin and Cleaver. W should be honored as a cultural hero--"every Negro Boy who ever set pen to paper since Native Son has harbored a desire to grow up to be another Richard Wright" (p. 207)--but Baldwin's criticism of NS is valid.

48. _____. "Langston Hughes: A Simple Commentary." Negro Digest, 16 (September), 53-57.

Contains a brief comparison of Hughes and W.

49. _____. "White Experts and Black Subjects." Rights and Reviews, 3 (Fall-Winter), 27-30.

Compares briefly Norman Mailer's "The White Negro" to NS.

49a. Goldstein, Malcolm. "Drama," in American Literary Scholarship: An Annual/1965. Ed. James Woodress. Durham, N. C.: Duke University Press, pp. 231-246.

Mentions briefly the play NS (p. 246).

50. Green, Constance McLaughlin. The Secret City: A History of Race Relations in the Nation's Capital. Princeton, N. J.: Princeton University Press, pp. 202, 256.

Refers to W's "hatred of all white America" and to discriminatory treatment of him by a Washington restaurant.

51. Gussow, Mel. "And Now, Diana at the Stake." The New York Times (31 December), Sec. 2, pp. 1, 4.

The actress Diana Sands recalls being moved as a child by Canada Lee's performance in NS.

52. Haas, Victor P. "From a Bookman's Notebook." Omaha Sunday World-Herald (21 May), Sec. I, p. 46.

Includes W in a list of novelists who have made important contributions to the genre since 1910.

53. Hagelberg, Günter. "Von Büchern und Schriftstellern." Berlin RIAS (2 and 14 January).

Favorable review of the German translation of O. One of the most important literary examinations of Communism since Koestler, the novel shows that W no longer places the racial issue in the foreground but reduces all questions to that of man's place in the world.

54. Hand, Clifford. "The Struggle to Create Life in the Fiction of Richard Wright," in The Thirties: Fiction, Poetry, Drama. Ed. Warren French. Deland, Fla.: Everett/Edwards, pp. 81-87.

Analyzes W's technique of developing characters. The general pattern is one of a struggle to be born, to break out of a world of fear and hate. Hand treats this pattern in UTC, NS, and O, commenting also on W's essay "The Literature of the Negro in the United States." W's purpose is to make the reader aware of possibilities once a character is reborn.

Partially reprinted: 1969.64.

54a. Hashimoto, Fukuo. "Richard Wright's Escape" and "The Outsider," in his Kokujin Bungaku no Sekai [The World of Black Literature]. Tokyo: Miraisha, pp. 61-77, 77-85.

Notes that W, through his works, defines the essential nature of twentieth-century man; from a black man's point of view the twentieth century is an age of violence. Suggests that the difference between Camus's Meursault and W's Cross stems from their racial backgrounds and the two authors' views of existentialism [Y. H. and T. K.]

55. Hayden, Robert. "El-Hajj Malik El-Shabazz," in For Malcolm: Poems on the Life and death of Malcolm X. Ed. Dudley Randall and Margaret G. Burroughs. Preface and Eulogy by Ossie Davis. Detroit: Broadside Press, pp. 14-16.
    Mentions "Native Son" in the subtitle of this poem.
    Reprinted: 1970.170.

56. Hicks, Granville. "Expression of the Negro Experience." Saturday Review, 50 (14 January), 79-80.
    Review of David Littlejohn's Black on White, Seymour Gross and John Edward Hardy's Images of the Negro in American Literature, and John Henrik Clarke's American Negro Short Stories, noting W's presence in all three. "Bright and Morning Star" is the best story in Clarke's volume.

57. Hoffman, Frederick J. The Art of Southern Fiction: A Study of Some Modern Novelists. Preface by Harry T. Moore. Crosscurrents Modern Critiques, ed. Harry T. Moore. Carbondale and Edwardsville: Southern Illinois University Press, pp. 112, 165.
    Mentions briefly BB.

58. Hofstadter, Richard, William Miller, and Daniel Aaron. The United States. Second edition. Englewood Cliffs, N. J.: Prentice-Hall, p. 762.
    Reprint of 1959.96.

59. Hooker, James R. Black Revolutionary: George Padmore's Path from Communism to Pan-Africanism. New York: Praeger, pp. 104, 123-124, 127.
    Though denied access to W's papers, Hooker comments on the W-Padmore friendship, notes Padmore's reactions to BP, and discusses the circumstances of W's frank foreword to Padmore's Pan-Africanism or Communism?, which was deleted from a Nigerian edition.

60. Hughes, Langston. "Biographical Notes," in his The Best Short Stories by Negro Writers: An Anthology from 1899 to the Present. Boston: Little, Brown, pp. 497-508.
    Contains a brief sketch of W (p. 507).

61. _____. "Editor's Note," in his The Best Short Stories by Negro Writers: An Anthology from 1899 to the Present.

Boston: Little, Brown, pp. viii. Mentions W.

62. _____. "Introduction," in his The Best Short Stories by Negro Writers: An Anthology from 1899 to the Present. Boston: Little, Brown, pp. ix-xiii.
    Comments briefly on W. The anthology includes "Almos' a Man" (pp. 91-103).

63. Hungerford, Edward B. "All Sides of the Negro Suppression Revealed." Chicago Tribune (12 March), Books Today Sec., p. 8.
    Review of Langston Hughes's The Best Short Stories by Negro Writers naming W as one of the best-known contributors.

64. Jackson, Esther Merle. "A 'Tragic Sense' of the Negro Experience." Freedomways, 7 (First Quarter), 16-25.
    Comments on NS as "perhaps the most nearly tragic exposition of the theme of racial discrimination." Bigger may not achieve the awareness of the true tragic hero, however.

64a. Jones, Howard Mumford. Violence and the Humanist. Middlebury, Vermont: Middlebury College, 24 pp.
    Contains an unfavorable paragraph on NS (p. 17), which is important as a case study of "self-destructive rage" but not as art.

65. Jones, LeRoi. "The Screamers," in his Tales. New York: Grove, pp. 71-80.
    Contains a brief reference to Bigger Thomas on the last page.
    Reprinted: 1968.136.

66. Josephson, Matthew. Infidel in the Temple: A Memoir of the Nineteen-Thirties. New York: Knopf, pp. 363, 377-378.
    Comments briefly on W's connection with the John Reed Club and the Writer's Project.

67. Kaiser, Ernest. "Negro Images in American Writing." Freedomways, 7 (Second Quarter), 152-163.
    Review of Seymour Gross and John Edward Hardy's Images of the Negro in American Literature mentioning W.

68. Kauffmann, Stanley. "Torn Loose." The New Republic, 156 (24 June), 18, 36.
    Review of Carlene Hatcher Polite's The Flagellants mentioning W briefly.

69. Kent, George E. "Ethnic Impact in American Literature: Reflections on a Course." CLA Journal, 11 (September), 24-37.
    Mentions W's grim view of racial life in BB, UTC, and NS.
    Reprinted: 1968.140.

69a. Kesteloot, Lilyan, ed. Anthologie Negro-Africaine. Verviers: Marabout Université, pp. 28, 124, 128, 175, 176-179, 225, 376, 379.
Contains a critical headnote and an excerpt from "Long Black Song." Mentions W briefly elsewhere and includes a photograph following p. 225.

69b. Kinnamon, Keneth. "Anger, and Beyond: The Negro Writer in the United States. Edited by Herbert Hill." Journal of English and Germanic Philology, 66 (January), 165-168.
Comments on the symposium on W included in the work.

70. Lewis, Sinclair. "Fiction Writing," in The American Peoples Encyclopedia. Ed. Edward Humphrey. Vol. 7. New York: Grolier, pp. 521-522.
Reprint of 1948.188a.

71. MacGregor, Martha. "The Week in Books." New York Post (1 April), Magazine Sec., p. 15.
Notice of Constance Webb's Richard Wright pointing out that Ellen Wright "doesn't believe in authorized biographies."

71a. McGrady, Mike. "Found: A Nonprotester." Newsday (28 October), pp. 3W, 36W.
Article on Ellison mentioning his exchange with Irving Howe. "Unlike many of today's most successful Negro writers, Ellison's artistic lineage does not begin with Richard Wright."

72. Meltzer, Milton. Untitled headnote, in his In Their Own Words: A History of the American Negro, 1916-1966. Vol. 3. Apollo Editions A-148c. New York: Crowell, pp. 6-7.
Headnote to an excerpt from "The Ethics of Living Jim Crow." Contains a photograph of W.

73. _____. Untitled headnote, in his In Their Own Words: A History of the American Negro, 1916-1966. Vol. 3. Apollo Editions A-148c. New York: Crowell, p. 15.
Headnote to an excerpt from TMBV.

73a. Miller, James E., Jr. Quests Surd and Absurd: Essays in American Literature. Chicago: The University of Chicago Press, p. 20.
Compares Invisible Man favorably to W's work.

74. Milner, Ronald. "Black Magic: Black Art." Negro· Digest, 16 (April), 8-12, 93-94.
Mentions W briefly (p. 9).
Reprinted: 1970.266; 1973.223.

75. Mims, A. Grace. "Nervous Nellies on Race Relations?" Library Journal, 92 (15 March), 1291-1293, 1299.
Includes BB in a list of books on blacks recommended for school libraries.

76. Mitchell, Loften. Black Drama: The Story of the American Negro in the Theatre. New York: Hawthorn Books, pp. 109, 114-117.
Discusses W's career and the play NS, especially in terms of the careers of W, Green, Welles, and Lee.

77. Morris, Willie. North Toward Home. Boston: Houghton Mifflin, p. 8.
Somewhat different version of 1963.144.

78. Neal, Lawrence P. "The Black Writer's Role: Richard Wright," in Afro-Arts Anthology. Newark: Jihad Productions, pp. [7-13].
Reprint of 1966.110.

79. Niles, Olive Stafford, Edythe Daniel, Edmund J. Farrell, Alfred H. Grommon, and Robert C. Pooley. "The Kitten," in their Teacher's Resource Book to Accompany Counterpoint in Literature. Glenview, Ill.: Scott, Foresman, pp. 75-76.
Study and teaching aids for an excerpt from BB.
Reprinted: 1976.53, 139.

80. O'Daniel, Therman B. "The Image of Man as Portrayed by Ralph Ellison." CLA Journal, 10 (June), 277-284.
Discusses Ellison's relation to W (pp. 280, 282-283).
Reprinted: 1970.278, 279.

80a. Palmer, Helen H. and Jane Anne Dyson. American Drama Criticism: Interpretations, 1890-1965 Inclusive, of American Drama Since the First Play Produced in America. Hamden, Conn.: The Shoe String Press, pp. 227-228.
Lists eleven items on the play NS.

81. Parks, Gordon. A Choice of Weapons. Berkley Medallion S1399. New York: Berkley Publishing, pp. 190, 197, 199.
Reprint of 1966.114.

82. Ploski, Harry A. and Roscoe C. Brown, Jr. The Negro Almanac. New York: Bellwether Publishing Company, pp. 169, 683, 698, 719.
Contains a biographical entry on W (p. 698) and brief mention elsewhere.
Reprinted: 1971.249; 1976.146.

83. Pooley, Robert C., Edythe Daniel, Edmund J. Farrell, Alfred H. Grommon,

and Olive Stafford Niles. "Discussion, The Author," in their Projection in Literature. Glenview, Ill: Scott, Foresman, p. 279.
    Study questions for an excerpt from BB ("Hunger") and a biographical sketch emphasizing W's youth.
    Reprinted: 1976.147.

84. ____. "Discussion, Word Study, The Author," in their Counterpoint in Literature. Glenview, Ill.: Scott, Foresman, p. 145.
    Study aids for an excerpt from BB ("The Kitten") and a sketch of W's youth.

85. Porter, James A. "One Hundred and Fifty Years of Afro-American Art," in The Negro in American Art. Los Angeles: UCLA Art Galleries, pp. 5-12.
    Mentions W's influence on black painters of his generation.

86. Quinn, Arthur Hobson and Anon. "United States Literature," in The American Peoples Encyclopedia. Ed. Edward Humphrey. Vol. 18. New York: Grolier, pp. 418-426.
    Mentions briefly NS (p. 420).

87. Redding, Saunders. The Negro. The U. S. A. Survey Series. Washington: Potomac Books, p. 78.
    Contains a brief reference to W.

88. Revueltas, José. Obra literaria. Vol. 1. Mexico, D. F.: Empresas Editoriales, p. 12.
    Contains a brief reference to W.

89. Rideout, Walter B. "Wright, Richard," in Merit Students Encyclopedia. Ed. Bernard S. Cayne. Vol. 20. New York: Crowell-Collier Educational Corporation, p. 34.
    Biographical note.
    Reprinted: 1973.255.

90. Salk, Erwin A. A Layman's Guide to Negro History. Revised edition. A Ramparts book. New York: McGraw-Hill, pp. 22, 26, 59, 92, 140, 161.
    Reprint of 1966.129.

91. Schöne, Annemarie. Abriss der amerikanischen Literaturgeschichte in Tabellen. Frankfurt am Main: Athenäum Verlag, pp. 194, 195, 260, 282-283.
    Biographical-bibliographical note on W (p. 194) and brief mention elsewhere.

92. Schulberg, Budd. "Introduction," in his From the Ashes: Voices of Watts. New York: The New American Library, pp. 1-24.
    Reprint of 1967.93.

93. ____. "The Watts Workshop." Playboy, 14 (September), 111, 162, 164, 166-167, 170-172, 175-179.
    Mentions W briefly (p. 162).
    Reprinted: 1967.92; 1969.217.

94. Scott, Nathan A., Jr. "Judgment Marked by a Cellar: The American Negro Writer and the Dialectic of Despair." The Denver Quarterly, 2 (Summer), 5-35.
    Following the thesis of Richard Chase, Scott contends that W's fiction, especially "Long Black Song" and NS, constitutes "the most drastic instances of the wounded Adam in American literature." This myth leads W to indulge a gratuitous violence beyond which he could not reach because of the racial split between black and white in his experience and imagination. This impasse hindered W's further development, as O shows.
    Reprinted: 1968.195a; 1969.219; 1971.270.

95. Segal, Ronald. The Race War. New York: Viking, p. 216.
    Notes that NS "reflected the hatred and violence swelling within black America."

95a. Shafer, Boyd C., Richard A. McLemore, and Everett Augspurger. 1865 to the Present: A United States History of High Schools. River Forest, Ill.: Laidlaw Brothers, p. 423.
    Reprint of 1966.133a.

96. Sostre, Martin. "Letter from a Buffalo Prison--A Black Frame-Up Victim's Reply." Workers World (17 August), p. 4.
    Claims that Sostre's bookstore is the only place in the black community where the works of W and other black writers could be purchased.

97. Spear, Allan H. Black Chicago: The Making of a Negro Ghetto, 1890-1920. Chicago: The University of Chicago Press, p. viii.
    Mentions W briefly.

97a. Stafford, William T. "Fiction: 1930 to the Present," in American Literary Scholarship: An Annual/1965. Ed. James Woodress. Durham, N. C.: Duke University Press, pp. 180-203.
    Mentions W briefly (p. 184).

98. Tindall, George Brown. The Emergence of the New South 1913-1945. A History of the South, vol. 10, ed. Wendell Holmes Stephenson and E. Merton Coulter. Baton Rouge: Louisiana State University Press, pp. 664-665.
    Sketches W's career through BB.

99. Treworgy, Mildred L. and Paul B.

Foreman. Negroes in the United States: A Bibliography of Materials for Schools-- Approvable for Purchase in Pennsylvania Under NDEA Provisions. The Pennsylvania State University Libraries School Series No. 1. University Park: The Pennsylvania State University Libraries, pp. 10, 12, 16.
> Lists and briefly annotates six books by W.

99a. Tucker, Martin. Africa in Modern Literature: A Survey of Contemporary Writing in English. New York: Ungar, pp. 15, 19, 243, 249.
> Quotes from BP.

100. Turner, Darwin T. "The Negro Novelist and the South." Southern Humanities Review, 1 (Spring), 21-29.
> Cites W along with Chesnutt, Hurston, and Yerby as favorable examples of black novelists treating the South. Nevertheless, they all have defects.

101. Vecchi, Massimo. "Baldwin e il problema negro." Il Rome popolo (27 May), p. 3.
> Mentions briefly W, NS, and BB.

102. Walker, Warren S. Twentieth-Century Short Story Explication. Hamden, Conn.: The Shoe String Press, p. 689.
> Reprint of 1961.282.

103. Ward, Francis. "Books Noted." Negro Digest, 16 (September), 94-95.
> Review of John Henrik Clarke's American Negro Short Stories mentioning W.

104. Wilber, Rhona Ryan. "Negro Stories." The Houston Post (2 April), Spotlight Sec., p. 17.
> Review of Langston Hughes's The Best Short Stories by Negro Writers citing W as a "familiar name."

105. Williams, John A. The Man Who Cried I Am. Boston: Litle, Brown, 403 pp.
> The character Harry Ames in this novel is a thinly disguised portrait of W. Ames is a black American expatriate writer in Paris critical of both America and Communism. He is portrayed as a rebel, an outsider, and a much misunderstood individual.

106. Wirzberger, Karl-Heinz. Probleme der Bürgerrechtsbewegung in der amerikanischen Prosaliteratur der Gegenwart. Sitzungsberichte der Deutscher Akademie der Wissenschaften zu Berlin, 2. Berlin: Akademie Verlag, pp. 11-12.
> Discusses W as a forerunner of the civil rights movement with special attention to the issue of frank portrayal of brutalized black characters.

107. Zietlow, Edward Robert. "Wright to Hansberry: The Evolution of Outlook in Four Negro Writers." Dissertation Abstracts, 28 (August), 701-A.
> Discusses W and Ellison as absurdist writers--in contrast to Baldwin. Each has absurd protagonists cut off from tradition and God. Their social criticism is presented in terms of pathological irrationality.

1968

1. Adoff, Arnold. "Biographical Notes," in his Black on Black: Commentaries by Negro Americans. New York: Macmillan, pp. 235-236.
> Emphasizes W's life and career in the United States. The anthology reprints excerpts from BB and "The Psychological Reactions of Oppressed People."
> Reprinted: 1970.11.

2. _____. "Richard Wright," in his I Am the Darker Brother: An Anthology of Modern Poems by Negro Americans. New York: Macmillan, p. 124.
> Biographical sketch.
> Reprinted: 1970.13.

3. Algren, Nelson. "Native Son." The Critic, 26 (June-July), 66-67.
> Ostensibly a review of Constance Webb's biography of W, which Algren dislikes, this essay is mainly Algren's own interpretation of the meaning of W's life, career, and role in racial protest.

4. Anderson, Jervis. "Black Writing: The Other Side." Dissent, 15 (May-June), 233-242.
> Includes comments on W by William Melvin Kelley and Lawrence Neal. Kelley praises O for rejecting both Left and Right. Neal points out that in speaking to whites in NS W does not achieve his own goals enunciated in "Blueprint for Negro Writing."

5. _____. "Race, Rage & Eldridge Cleaver." Commentary, 46 (December), 63-69.
> Discusses Cleaver's essay attacking Baldwin and defending W (pp. 67-68). Mentions and quotes from W elsewhere.

6. Anon. "American Literature," in The American Educator Encyclopedia. Ed. Everette Edgar Sentman. Vol. 1. Lake Bluff, Ill.: The United Educators, pp. A 185-A 195.
> Reprint of 1956.7.

7. Anon. "Black Boy," in Dictionnaire des oeuvres contemporaines de tous les pays. Paris: Société d'édition de dic-

tionnaires et encyclopédies, p. 70.
  Summary of the autobiography. A
  photograph of W appears on p. 71.

8. Anon. "'Daddy' Opens." New York Daily
News (4 June), p. 59.
  Announces the opening of the play
  Daddy Goodness at the St. Mark's
  Playhouse.

9. Anon. Dust jacket of Richard Wright:
A Biography. By Constance Webb. New
York: Putnam's.
  Blurb on inside flaps. Photographs of
  W on front and back cover.

10. Anon. "Un Enfant du pays," in Dictionnaire des oeuvres contemporaines de
tous les pays. Paris Société d'édition
de dictionnaires et encyclopédies, p.
221.
  Plot summary of the novel NS with a
  photograph from the film.

11. Anon. "Les Enfants de l'oncle Tom,"
in Dictionnaire des oeuvres contemporaines de tous les pays. Paris: Société
d'édition de dictionnaires et encyclopédies, p. 222.
  Plot summary of the five stories of
  the enlarged edition of UTC.

12. Anon. "Finale." New York Sunday News
(2 June), Sec. Two, p. S3.
  Photograph with caption of a scene
  from Daddy Goodness.

13. Anon. "Fishbelly," in Dictionnaire
des oeuvres contemporaines de tous les
pays. Paris: Société d'édition de dictionnaires et encyclopédies, p. 280.
  Plot summary of LD.

14. Anon. Index Translationum 19. Paris:
Unesco, pp. 176, 278.
  Lists translations of NS into Danish,
  BB into Danish and Finnish, and O
  into Danish.

15. Anon. "Negro Ensemble Company to
Alternate Plays." New York Post (18
June), p. 28.
  Announces a summer repertory produc-
  tion of Daddy Goodness.

16. Anon. "Um negro que quis viver," in
Um negro que quis viver. By Richard
Wright. Trans. Luísa Sampaio. Lisbon:
Editora Ulisseia, front inside flap of
cover.
  Blurb for the Portuguese translation
  of BB with John Reilly's "After-
  word."

17. Anon. "1966 Bibliography of Missis-
sippi Writers." Notes on Mississippi
Writers, 1 (Spring), 32-39.
  Lists one item on W.

18. Anon. "Opening Tonight." New York
Post (4 June), p. 67.
  Announces the opening of the play
  Daddy Goodness at the St. Mark's
  Playhouse.

19. Anon. "Pictorial Highlights." Negro
Digest, 18 (December), 38-44.
  Thirteen photographs with a brief
  narrative of W's life.

20. Anon. "Problème noir aux Etats-
Unis." Afrique Contemporaine, No. 37
(May-June), pp. 37-38.
  Contains a favorable notice of the
  French translation of LT.

21. Anon. "Puissance noire," in Dictionnaire des oeuvres contemporaines de tous
les pays. Paris: Société d'edition de
dictionnaires et encyclopédies, pp. 600-
601.
  Summary of BP with a photograph of W.

22. Anon. "Rait, Richard," in Ukrain-
s'kyi radians'kyi entsiklopedichayi
slovnyk. Ed. M. P. Bazhan. Vol. 3. Kiev:
Holovna Redaktsiia Ukrains'koi Radian-
s'koi Entsiklopedii, p. 101.
  Brief biographical note.

23. Anon. "Revues de livres et des
revues." Afrique Contemporaine, No. 37
(May-June), pp. 31-36.
  Contains a notice of the French
  translation of LT. Its style is that
  of an apprentice work.

24. Anon. "Richard Wright, by Constance
Webb." The New Yorker, 44 (20 April),
196.
  Unfavorable notice complaining of
  Webb's fictionalizing.

25. Anon. "Webb, Constance. Richard
Wright." AB Bookman's Weekly, 41 (3-10
June), 2200.
  Notice pointing out the author's
  friendship with W, who was "a literary intellectual as well as a political adventurer."

26. Anon. "Webb, Constance. Richard
Wright; a biography." The Booklist and
Subscription Books Bulletin, 64 (1
June), 1124.
  Unfavorable notice pointing out that
  the work "is marred by a personal and
  sometimes sentimental approach."

27. Anon. "Whiff of 'The Problem.'"
Time, 91 (22 March), 82.
  Review of Constance Webb's Richard
  Wright concluding that she is an
  "overprotective" biographer, espe-
  cially in her treatment of W's pri-
  vate life. The reviewer states that
  W's existentialist tendencies re-

deemed him from the protest tradition and placed him "in the mainstream of contemporary literature."

28. Anon. "Will the Real Nat Turner Please Stand Up?" Time, 92 (12 July), 80.
Quotes W on Gertrude Stein's Melanctha.

29. Anon. "Wright," in Das grosse Duden-Lexikon. Vol. 8. Mannheim: Bibliographisches Institut, p. 686.
Biographical note.

30. Anon. "Wright," in Der grosse Knaur. Ed. Hans Joachim Störig. Munich: Droemer Knaur, p. 645.
Biographical note.

31. Anon. "Wright," in Diccionario enciclopédico Salvat. Thirteenth edition. Vol. 12. Barcelona: Salvat Editores, pp. 700-701.
Biographical note.

32. Anon. "Wright, Richard," in The American Educator Encyclopedia. Ed. Everette Edgar Sentman. Vol. 14. Lake Bluff, Ill.: The United Educators, p. W·179.
Reprint of 1961.101.

33. Anon. "Wright, Richard," in Chambers's Encyclopaedia. Ed. M. D. Law and M. Vibart Dixon. New revised edition. Vol. 14. London: International Learning Systems, p. 733.
Reprint of 1950.100.

34. Anon. "Wright (Richard)," in Dictionnaire des littératures. Ed. Philippe Van Tieghem. Vol. 3. Paris: Presses universitaires de France, pp. 4201-4202.
Biographical note.

35. Anon. "Wright, Richard," in Enciclopedia Hoepli. Ed. Aldo L. Cerchiari and Carlo Zommattio. Vol. 7. Milan: Editore Ulrico Hoepli, p. 1007.
Biographical headnote.

36. Anon. "Wright, Richard," in Encyclopedia International. Ed. George A. Cornish. Vol. 19. New York: Grolier, p. 500.
Reprint of 1964.18.

37. Bailey, Peter. "Daddy Goodness." Black Theatre, 1, p. 30.
Unfavorable review complaining of stereotyped characters and trite situations.

38. _____. "Is the Negro Ensemble Company Really Black Theater?" Negro Digest, 17 (April), 16-19.
Contains a brief reference to Daddy Goodness.

39. Baldwin, James. "James Baldwin . . . in Conversation," ed. Dan. Georgakas, in Black Voices: An Anthology of Afro-American Literature. Ed. Abraham Chapman. Mentor Books MW866. New York: The New American Library, pp. 660-668.
Reprint of 1966.17.

40. _____. "Many Thousands Gone," in Black Voices: An Anthology of Afro-American Literature. Ed. Abraham Chapman. Mentor Books MW866. New York: The New American Library, pp. 590-604.
Reprint of 1951.129.

41. _____. Tell Me How Long the Train's Been Gone. New York: The Dial Press, p. 147.
Leo Proudhammer, the protagonist of this novel, is called "native son."

42. Barnes, Clive. "Theater: 'Daddy Goodness' Has St. Marks Premiere." The New York Times (5 June), p. 37.
Mixed review of the play. It "is full of very bright ideas, and is often sharply funny, but in the final accounting is neither polished, nor meaningful, nor pertinent enough to make the effect it might have." W and Sapin were unable to decide whether to be satirical of money-making religion or serious about God inhabiting a common man. Barnes praises the production and the acting, especially that of Moses Gunn in the title role.

43. [Bayliss, John F.]. "Editorial." Negro American Literature Forum, 2 (Spring), 3.
Mentions the theme of endurance in UTC in response to the Red Summer of 1919. The context is the assassinations of King and Robert Kennedy.

44. Berry, Faith. "On Richard Wright in Exile: Portrait of a Man as Outsider." Negro Digest, 18 (December), 26-37.
Analyzes W's expatriation. Escaping American racism, W was a cultural interloper in France. He lived between two worlds. He became more social critic than social protester. The nonfiction of his years in exile is interesting, but his fiction is weak. Berry compares the Pan-Africanism of W and Fanon and contrasts W to Baldwin.

45. Bigsby, C. W. E. "James Baldwin," in his Confrontation and Commitment: A Study of Contemporary American Drama 1959-66. Columbia: University of Missouri Press, pp. 126-137.
Reprint of 1967.14.

46. Bl.[air], W.[alter]. "American Literature," in Encyclopaedia Britannica.

Ed. Warren E. Preece. Vol. 1. Chicago: Encyclopaedia Britannica, pp. 764-774.
Reprint of 1954.80.

47. Blanch, Antonio, S. J. "El problema negro en la novela norteamericana." Razón y Fe, 178 (September-October), 203-222.
Contains a sketch of W's career with some factual errors (pp. 213-215).

48. Bone, Robert. "Magnificent Failure." The New York Times Book Review (7 April), pp. 10, 12.
Mixed review of Constance Webb's Richard Wright with a summary of W's life. Although "a portrait of considerable warmth and intimacy," it fails to reveal W's inner life. Webb identifies too closely with her subject's point of view, even when it is self-deceptive.

49. Bracy, William. "Wright, Richard," in The Encyclopedia Americana. Ed. George A. Cornish. Vol. 29. New York: Americana Corporation, p. 555.
Reprint of 1965.45.

50. Britt, David Dobbs. "The Image of the White Man in the Fiction of Langston Hughes, Richard Wright, James Baldwin and Ralph Ellison." Dissertation Abstracts, 29 (November), 1532-A.
Considers W as a protest novelist, noting that two-thirds of his work consists of essays and lectures.

51. Brown, Cecil M. "Books Noted." Negro Digest, 17 (February), 51-52, 89-91.
Review of William Styron's The Confessions of Nat Turner mentioning W.

52. _____. "The Lesson and the Legacy: Richard Wright's Complexes and Black Writing Today." Negro Digest, 18 (December), 45-50, 78-82.
Unfavorable assessment of W's art. His protest is "negative" and his characters are subhuman. Discusses much of W's fiction, but ignores O. Praises Ellison, Baldwin, Jones, and Cleaver at the expense of W.
Reprinted: 1970.5; 1971.147.
Partially reprinted: 1970.70.

53. Brown, Sterling A. "A Century of Negro Portraiture in American Literature," in Black Voices: An Anthology of Afro-American Literature. Ed. Abraham Chapman. Mentor Books MW866. New York: The New American Library, pp. 564-589.
Reprint of 1966.30.

54. Bryer, Jackson, Philip R. Headings, Lewis A. Lawson, Joseph V. Ridgely, Donald B. Stauffer, and John E. Todd, with the help of Ronald Leatherbarrow.

"American Literature." PMLA, 83 (June), 718-744.
Bibliography listing four items on W (p. 744).

55. Burnier, Michel-Antoine. Choice of Action: The French Existentialists on the Political Front Line. Trans. Bernard Murchland. New York: Random House, pp. 61, 63.
Mentions W in connection with the Rassemblement Democratique Revolutionnaire.

56. Byam, Milton S. "Webb, Constance. Richard Wright: a Biography." Library Journal, 93 (15 February), 747.
Favorable review. Nevertheless, Webb glosses over W's Communist connections and attempts to elevate him to heroic stature.

57. Campbell, Dick. "Is There a Conspiracy Against Black Playwrights?" Negro Digest, 17 (April), 11-15.
Contains a brief reference to Daddy Goodness.

58. Campbell, Mary. "'Daddy Goodness' in Off-Broadway Run." Unidentified clipping (c. June).
Favorable Associated Press review noting the play's "surprisingly moderate" tone toward cult religion. Daddy Goodness' message is that people should forgive themselves their sins; the author's message is that people are confused by so simple an idea.

59. Cayton, Horace. "The Curtain: A Memoir." Negro Digest, 18 (December), 11-15.
Memoir of a Jim Crow incident W and Cayton experienced on a trip by train from Chicago to Nashville in 1943. They were segregated from white passengers in the dining car by a curtain drawn around their table.
Reprinted: 1971.147.

60. Chapman, Abraham. "Bibliography," in his Black Voices: An Anthology of Afro-American Literature. Mentor Books MW866. New York: The New American Library, pp. 700-718.
Lists W's books (pp. 717-718).

61. _____. "Black Poetry Today." Arts in Society, 5, pp. 401-408.
Quotes a poem by Don L. Lee mentioning W.

62. _____. "Introduction," in his Black Voices: An Anthology of Afro-American Literature. Mentor Books MW866. New York: The New American Library, pp. 21-49.

Contains several references to W and lengthy quotations from "The Literature of the Negro in the United States."
Condensation: 1970.85.

63. ____. "Richard Wright (1908-1960)," in his Black Voices: An Anthology of Afro-American Literature. Mentor Books MW866. New York: The New American Library, pp. 113-114, 288, 436, 538.
Headnotes to "The Man Who Lived Underground," "The Ethics of Living Jim Crow: An Autobiographical Sketch," "Between the World and Me," and "How 'Bigger' Was Born."

64. Clarke, John Henrik. "The Origin and Growth of Afro-American Literature," in Black Voices: An Anthology of Afro-American Literature. Ed. Abraham Chapman. Mentor Books MW866. New York: The New American Library, pp. 632-645.
Reprint of 1967.22.

64a. ____. "The Origin and Growth of Afro-American Literature." Journal of Human Relations, 16 (Third Quarter), 368-384.
Reprint of 1967.22.

65. Cleaver, Eldridge. "Notes on a Native Son," in his Soul on Ice. New York: McGraw-Hill, pp. 97-111.
Reprint of 1966.37.
Reprinted: 1970.5; 1971.147.

66. ____. "On Becoming," in his Soul on Ice. New York: McGraw-Hill, pp. 3-17.
Reprint of 1966.38.

67. ____. "To All Black Women, From All Black Men," in his Soul on Ice. New York: McGraw-Hill, pp. 205-210.
Mentions W as a black hero (p. 209).
Reprinted: 1970.90; 1972.52.

68. Corrington, John William. "Why Richard Wright Fell Short of Greatness." The National Observer (1 April), p. 19.
Unfavorable review of Constance Webb's Richard Wright complaining of poor writing, excessive generalization, and a lack of scholarly development. Includes Faulkner's letter to W about BB in an abbreviated version.

69. Cruse, Harold. The Crisis of the Negro Intellectual. Apollo Editions. New York: William Morrow, pp. 3, 51, 69, 115, 181, 183-184, 187, 237, 267, 269, 271, 273, 275-277, 500, 510.
Reprint of 1967.25.

70. ____. "Introduction," in his Rebellion or Revolution? New York: William Morrow, p. 11.
Cruse acknowledges his youthful

intellectual indebtedness to W.

71. Dale, Joanne. "Integrating Literature by Minority Writers in the Literature Program." Curriculum Exchange, 10 (April), 1-3.
Comments briefly on NS.
Reprinted: 1968.72.

72. ____. "Integrating Literature by Minority Writers in the Literature Program." Negro American Literature Forum, 2 (Spring), 8-9.
Reprint of 1968.71.

73. David, Jay. "From Black Boy by Richard Wright (1909 [sic]-1960)," in his Growing Up Black. New York: William Morrow, p. 231.
Biographical-critical headnote.

74. Davis, Arthur P. "Integration and Race Literature," in Black Voices: An Anthology of Afro-American Literature. Ed. Abraham Chapman. Mentor Books MW866. New York: The New American Library, pp. 606-611.
Reprint of 1956.137.

75. Davis, James. "Along the Backstage Beat." New York Daily News (10 June), p. 60.
Mentions Daddy Goodness.

76. ____. "Far-Out Faith Is Key to 'Daddy Goodness.'" New York Daily News (5 June), p. 103.
Unfavorable review. Moses Gunn gives a good performance in the title role, but the play is incoherent in its mixture of dramatic styles.

77. Dodds, Barbara. Negro Literature for High School Students. Champaign, Ill.: National Council of Teachers of English, pp. 23, 33, 121, 126, 127.
Brief references to W.

78. Dodson, Owen. "Dissenting Viewpoint: Playwrights in Dark Glasses." Negro Digest, 17 (April), 31-36.
Praises W's early work about "the terror, the hurt, the crushed spirits and the laughter through tears of the Negro's state," points out his artistic decline during his expatriation, and criticizes the play NS as "now dated because of the blatant propagandistic theme and projection."

79. Eckman, Fern Marja. The Furious Passage of James Baldwin. London: Michael Joseph, pp. 105-107, 123.
Reprint of 1966.46.

80. Eisinger, Chester E. "Character and Self in Fiction on the Left," in Proletarian Writers of the Thirties. Ed.

David Madden. Crosscurrents Modern Critiques, ed. Harry T. Moore. Carbondale and Edwardsville: Southern Illinois University Press, pp. 158-183.
Mentions briefly W's introduction to Nelson Algren's Never Come Morning.

81. Elkins, Stanley M. Slavery: A Problem in American Institutional and Intellectual Life. Second edition. Chicago: The University of Chicago Press, pp. 132-133.
Reprint of 1959.81.

82. Ellison, Ralph. "A Dialogue with His Audience." The Barat Review, 3 (January), 51-53.
Ellison criticizes the characterization of Bigger Thomas because he is "brutalized by Wright," stripped of his culture by the author.

83. _____. "Hidden Name and Complex Fate," in Dark Symphony: Negro Literature in America. Ed. James A. Emanuel and Theodore L. Gross. New York: The Free Press, pp. 279-295.
Reprint of 1964.45.

84. _____ and Richard G. Stern. "That Same Pain, That Same Pleasure," in Black Voices: An Anthology of Afro-American Literature. Ed. Abraham Chapman. Mentor Books MW866. New York: The New American Library, pp. 645-659.
Reprint of 1961.143.

85. Emanuel, James. "Fever and Feeling: Notes on the Imagery in Native Son." Negro Digest, 18 (December), 16-24.
Analyzes W's imagery in the novel to show its function in characterizing Bigger as a black "man of feeling." Includes discussion of such recurrent images as the furnace, Bigger standing in the middle of the floor, the cross, blindness, blotting out, the white blur, the wall, and the curtain.
Reprinted: 1970.5; 1971.147.

86. _____ and Theodore L. Gross. "Bibliography," in their Dark Symphony: Negro Literature in America. New York: The Free Press, pp. 564-600.
Contains a bibliography of W listing twenty primary and twenty-one secondary sources (pp. 584-586).

87. _____. "Contemporary Literature: Introduction," in their Dark Symphony: Negro Literature in America. New York: The Free Press, pp. 350-373.
Discusses the place of UTC and EM in the development of the Afro-American short story (pp. 351-353). Mentions NS (p. 354) and O (p. 359).

88. _____. "Ernest Gaines 1933-," in their Dark Symphony: Negro Literature in America. New York: The Free Press, pp. 427-428.
Reports that "Gaines believes that Richard Wright 'had to get his material out of the American soil, not out of a European library.'"

89. _____. "James Baldwin 1924-," in their Dark Symphony: Negro Literature in America. New York: The Free Press, pp. 296-300.
Mentions Baldwin's friendship with W.

90. _____. "Preface," in their Dark Symphony: Negro Literature in America. New York: The Free Press, pp. ix-x.
Quotes W's statement that "the Negro is America's metaphor."

91. _____. "Ralph Ellison 1914-," in their Dark Symphony: Negro Literature in America. New York: The Free Press, pp. 249-253.
Mentions Ellison's friendship with W.

92. _____. "Richard Wright 1908-1960," in their Dark Symphony: Negro Literature in America. New York: The Free Press, pp. 222-226.
Biographical-critical headnote emphasizing W's early career and commenting specifically on "The Man Who Killed a Shadow" and "The Ethics of Living Jim Crow," reprinted on pp. 227-248. W is mentioned in passing elsewhere in this anthology.
Reprinted: 1971.147.

93. Fabio, Sarah Webster. "Who Speaks Negro? What Is Black?" Negro Digest, 17 (September-October), 33-37.
Mentions W briefly.

94. Fabre, Michel and Edward Margolies. "Bibliography," in Richard Wright: A Biography. By Constance Webb. New York: Putnam, pp. 423-429.
Reprint of 1965.59.

95. Fanon, Frantz. Black Skin, White Masks. Trans. Charles Lam Markmann. Black Cat Edition. New York: Grove Press, pp. 139, 183.
Paperback reprint of 1967.37.

96. _____. The Wretched of the Earth. Trans. Constance Farrington. Black Cat Edition. New York: Grove Press, p. 216.
Translation of 1961.147.

97. Faulkner, William. Lion in the Garden: Interviews with William Faulkner, 1926-1962. Ed. James Meriwether and Michael Millgate. New York: Random House, pp. 185-186.
Reprint of 1956.157.

98. Fiedler, Leslie. "The Two Memories: Reflections on Writers and Writing in the Thirties," in Proletarian Writers of the Thirties. Ed. David Madden. Crosscurrents Modern Critiques, ed. Harry T. Moore. Carbondale and Edwardsville: Southern Illinois University Press, pp. 3-25.
    Reprint of 1968.99.

99. _____. "The Two Memories: Reflections on Writers and Writing in the Thirties," in The Thirties: A Reconsideration in the Light of the American Political Tradition. Ed. Morton J. Frisch and Martin Diamond. De Kalb: Northern Illinois University Press, pp. 44-67.
    Mentions W briefly (p. 56).
    Reprinted: 1968.98.

99a. Finestone, Harry. "Themes, Topics, and Criticism," in American Literary Scholarship: An Annual/1966. Ed. James Woodress. Durham, N. C.: Duke University Press, pp. 250-266.
    Mentions briefly the symposium on W in Anger, and Beyond.

100. F.[ranklin], J.[ohn] H.[ope], R.[aymond] W.[hittingham] L.[ogan], and S.[terling] A. B.[rown]. "Negro, American," in Encyclopaedia Britannica. Ed. Warren E. Preece. Vol. 16. Chicago: Encyclopaedia Britannica, pp. 188-201.
    Reprint of 1957.184 with a photograph of W.

101. Frémy, Dominique and Michèle Frémy. Quid? Tout pour tous. Paris: Librairie Plon, p. 86.
    Reprint of 1963.86.

101a. French, Warren. "Fiction: 1900 to the 1930's," in American Literary Scholarship: An Annual/1966. Ed. James Woodress. Durham, N. C.: Duke University Press, pp. 147-166.
    Mentions W briefly (p. 150).

102. Fuller, Hoyt W. "An Informal Survey: Black Theater in America." Negro Digest, 17 (April), 83-93.
    Mentions Daddy Goodness.

103. _____. "Perspectives." Negro Digest, 17 (June), 49-50.
    Mentions W briefly.

104. _____. "Richard Wright: The Most Important Black American Writer of All Time?" Chicago Sunday Sun-Times Book Week (31 March), pp. 1, 9.
    Review of Constance Webb's Richard Wright consisting mainly of a summary of W's life. Fuller notes a lack of "the immediacy and the excitement" the subject should develop and com-

plains of Webb's neglect of W's relationships with other black writers.

105. _____. "A Survey: Black Writers Views on Literary Lions and Values." Negro Digest, 17 (January), 10-48, 81-89.
    Announces that "of 38 black writers polled, more than half named the dead novelist [W] as the most important black American writer of all time" (pp. 12-13).

106. Gaffney, Floyd. "Is Your Door Really Open?" Drama & Theatre, 7 (Fall), 4-7.
    Mentions the play NS.

107. Galloway, David and John Whitley. "Bright and Morning Star," in their Ten Modern American Short Stories. London: Methuen Educational Ltd., pp. 109-112.
    Biographical-critical introductory essay to a reprinting of the story. Aunt Sue is an heroic character, asserting personal will in an admirable way. Notes Biblical parallels to the story.

108. Gayle, Addison, Jr. "The Children of Bigger Thomas." Liberator, 8 (August), 4-8.
    Discussing the problems facing black professors of literature delegated as racial spokesmen, Gayle asserts that the life and trial of Bigger Thomas may be an appropriate image of the modern black man. Summarizes Baldwin's discussion, agreeing with his notion that Bigger exists in the private selves of blacks.

109. _____. "Perhaps Not So Soon One Morning." Phylon, 29 (Fourth Quarter), 396-402.
    Contains an unfavorable comparison of Baldwin to W.
    Reprinted: 1969.102.

110. _____. "Richard Wright: Beyond Nihilism." Negro Digest, 18 (December), 4-10.
    Relates W's work to the current mood of blacks. W began as a naturalist, but he always recognized the possibility of transcendence through violence, as in NS. But if hope is too long denied, nihilistic man (e.g., Cross Damon) will rise. W conveyed this message to white men who would not listen. Now blacks no longer try to make whites listen.
    Reprinted: 1970.5; 1971.147.

111. Geismar, Maxwell. "Introduction," in Soul on Ice. By Eldridge Cleaver. New York: McGraw-Hill, pp. xi-xv.

Notes Cleaver's reaction to W.

112. Giachetti, Romano. "Jimmy hai per-
so il treno." La fiera letteraria, No.
32 (8 August), pp. 16-17.
     Review of the Italian translation of
     Tell Me How Long the Train's Been
     Gone mentioning briefly W and NS.

113. Gibson, Donald B. "Richard Wright:
A Biography, by Constance Webb." Negro
American Literature Forum, 2 (Summer),
32.
     Generally favorable review discount-
     ing the claims of other reviewers
     that Webb was too close to her sub-
     ject and weak as a critic. The book
     has flaws, but it is badly needed.

114. Gilbert, James Burkhart. Writers
and Partisans: A History of Literary
Radicalism in America. New York: John
Wiley, p. 128.
     Mentions W briefly.

115. Gilman, Richard. "White Standards
and Negro Writing." The New Republic,
158 (9 March), 25-28, 30; (13 April),
25-28.
     Contains brief references to W.
     Reprinted: 1969.111, 112; 1971.150.

116. Graham, James D. "Negro Protest in
America, 1900-1955: A Bibliographical
Guide." The South Atlantic Quarterly, 67
(Winter), 94-107.
     Contains a paragraph on NS stressing
     its Dostoevskian elements.

117. Gray, Yohma. "An American Metaphor: The Novels of Richard Wright."
Dissertation Abstracts, 28 (April),
4175-A.
     Denying that W is either a naturalist
     or an innovator, Gray relates him to
     the American literary tradition
     "which focuses upon the exact rela-
     tionship between the drive toward
     personal identity, or the need to
     feel separated from all the rest of
     the knowable world, and the drive
     toward human community, or the need
     to feel united to all the rest of the
     knowable world." The frustrations of
     attempting to reconcile the two im-
     pulses appear in all of W's protag-
     onists.

118. Green, Gerald. "Back to Bigger," in
Proletarian Writers of the Thirties. Ed.
David Madden. Crosscurrents Modern Critiques, ed. Harry T. Moore. Carbondale
and Edwardsville: Southern Illinois University Press, pp. 26-45.
     Reprint of 1966.63.

119. Gross, Theodore L. "His Art Shack-
led to Suffering." Saturday Review, 51

(13 April), 43-44.
     Mixed review of Constance Webb's
     Richard Wright. Her account of W's
     expatriation is quite valuable. She
     lacks objectivity and does not go
     beyond W's own self-understanding,
     but her book is helpful as a source.

120. _____. "Our Mutual Estate: The
Literature of the American Negro." The
Antioch Review, 28 (Fall), 293-303.
     Complains of neglect of W and criti-
     cizes some of W's critics--Webb,
     Ellison, Bone, and others. W changed
     the comic image of the black man
     created by white writers. Along with
     Hughes, he pioneered in the serious
     treatment of blacks.
     Reprinted: 1969.117; 1971.157.

121. Handlin, Oscar. "Reader's Choice:
Native Son." The Atlantic Monthly, 221
(March), 130-131.
     Ostensibly a review of Constance
     Webb's Richard Wright, this is a
     survey of W's life and analysis
     of the reasons for his expatria-
     tion.

122. Harding, Vincent. "Blueprint for
National Renewal: The Uses of the Afro-
American Past." Negro Digest, 17 (Feb-
ruary), 4-9, 81-84.
     Mentions and quotes from W.

123. _____. "Preface to the Atheneum
Edition," in The Negro's God as Reflect-
ed in His Literature. By Benjamin Mays.
New York: Atheneum, pp. [i-v].
     Mentions W briefly.

124. Hernton, Calvin C. "Dynamite Grow-
ing Out of Their Skulls," in Black Fire:
An Anthology of Afro-American Writing.
Ed. LeRoi Jones and Larry Neal. New
York: William Morrow, pp. 78-104.
     Mentions W briefly (p. 82).
     Reprinted: 1969.125.

125. Hill, Herbert. "The Negro Writer
and the Creative Imagination." Arts in
Society, 5, pp. 245-255.
     Mentions W several times and dis-
     cusses NS as a protest novel (pp.
     245-246). Concludes with a quotation
     from TMBV.

126. Holmes, Eugene C. "Alain Locke and
the New Negro Movement." Negro American
Literature Forum, 2 (Fall), 60-68.
     Mentions W briefly (p. 68).

127. Howe, Irving. "James Baldwin: At
Ease in Apocalypse." Harper's Magazine,
237 (September), 92, 95-100.
     Praises NS as "a crude but overwhelm-
     ing book" (p. 92).
     Reprinted: 1974.93.

128. Humm. "Off-Broadway Reviews." Variety (26 June), p. 57.
Unfavorable review of Daddy Goodness. Apparently suggested by the career of Father Divine and by Eugene O'Neill's The Emperor Jones, the play almost works as a satire on bogus religion but fails because of poor characterization and an inconsistent approach.

129. Ihde, Horst. "Black Writer's Burden: Bemerkungen zu John Oliver Killens." Zeitschrift für Anglistik und Amerikanistik, 16, pp. 117-137.
Contrasts W and Killens, generally to the advantage of the latter. Killens gives more prominence to the role of the family in black life and has a better sense of humor. Bigger's revolt in NS is individual and instinctive; the action of Youngblood is collective.

130. Jackson, Blyden. "The Negro's Image of the Universe as Reflected in His Fiction," in Black Voices: An Anthology of Afro-American Literature. Ed. Abraham Chapman. Mentor Books MW866. New York: The New American Library, pp. 623-631.
Reprint of 1960.169.

131. _____. "A Word About Simple." CLA Journal, 11 (June), 310-318.
Mentions Bigger Thomas (p. 316). Reprinted: 1971.179.

132. Jackson, Miles M., Jr. A Bibliography of Negro History and Culture for Young Readers. Pittsburgh: University of Pittsburgh Press for Atlanta University, p. 33.
Contains annotated entries for BB and Constance Webb's Richard Wright.

133. Jahn, Janheinz. A History of Neo-African Literature. Trans. Oliver Coburn and Ursula Lehrburger. London: Faber, pp. 131, 151, 185, 201-203, 205, 209, 213, 278.
Among several brief mentions of W, he is treated in a section on Depression writers, where he is classified as the most militant of the group. Jahn discusses briefly UTC and NS.

134. _____. "The Long Dream," in Kindlers Literatur Lexikon. Ed. Rolf Geisler. Vol. 4. Zurich: Kindler Verlag, p. 1610.
Summary with critical comments and a brief bibliography.

135. Johnson, Charles S. "Negro in America," in The Encyclopedia Americana. Ed. George A. Cornish. Vol. 20. New York: Americana Corporation, pp. 65-74.
Reprint of 1955.54.

136. Jones, LeRoi. "The Screamers," in his Tales. Evergreen E-469. New York: Grove Press, pp. 71-80.
Reprint of 1967.65.

137. Joye, Barbara. "Satire and Alienation in Soulsville." Phylon, 29 (Fourth Quarter), 410-412.
Contains a review of John Williams's The Man Who Cried I Am noting that "Max [sic] Ames . . . in many ways represents Richard Wright."

138. Kamarck, Edward L. "Art or Social Protest?" Arts in Society, 5, pp. 388-389.
Mentions NS.

139. Kellner, Bruce. Carl Van Vechten and the Irreverent Decades. Norman: University of Oklahoma Press, p. 314.
Lists W under the year 1945 in a catalog of Van Vechten photographs.

140. Kent, George E. "Ethnic Impact in American Literature (Reflections on a Course)," in Black Voices: An Anthology of Afro-American Literature. Ed. Abraham Chapman. Mentor Books MW866. New York: The New American Library, pp. 691-697.
Reprint of 1967.69.

141. Kirsch, Robert. "Paperback Edition of the 50 Best Short Stories." Los Angeles Times (3 January), Part V, p. 5.
Notes that W is included in Martha Foley's Fifty Best American Short Stories 1915-1965.

142. _____. "Prophet of Black Man's Experience in U. S." Los Angeles Times (2 June), Calendar Sec., p. 34.
Mixed review of Constance Webb's Richard Wright claiming that it veils the central fact of W's confrontation with race in America. Although Webb does depict W's human qualities, she does not reveal the real significance of his exile, which harmed his work by "drying the taproots."

143. Kitching, Jessie B. "Richard Wright. Constance Webb." Publishers' Weekly, 193 (8 January), 61.
Mixed review stating that the work "vividly delineates the affronts and indignities and suffering the man endured." Unfortunately, however, it reads like an apologia.

144. Kloman, William. "Moses Gunn: A Brilliant Black Star." The New York Times (16 June), Sec. 2, pp. 1, 3.
Discusses Gunn's performance in the title role of Daddy Goodness.

145. Knipp, Thomas. "Introduction," in

his Letters to Joe C. Brown. By Richard Wright. Occasional Papers No. 1, Kent, Ohio: Kent State University Libraries, pp. 3-5.
Emphasizes W's alienation from the Communist Party and from the South during the period of the letters (1938-1945). Knipp fully annotates the ten letters.

146. Kritzer, Hyman W. "Preface," in Letters to Joe C. Brown. By Richard Wright. Ed. Thomas Knipp. Occasional Papers No. 1. Kent, Ohio: Kent State University Libraries, p. 2.
Emphasizes the timeliness of W's black pride.

147. Lawrence, Paul, Florence Randall, Takako Endo, and Esther McStay. Negro American Heritage. Ed. Arna Bontemps. San Francisco: Century Communications, p. 112.
Comments briefly on W and NS.

148. Lee, Don L. "Black Poetry: Which Direction?" Negro Digest, 17 (September-October), 27-32.
Mentions W briefly (p. 31).

149. _____. "Books Noted: The Man Who Cried I Am." Negro Digest, 17 (March), 51-52, 77-79.
Notes that the character Harry Ames corresponds to W.

150. _____. "Needed: A Native Son to Write About a Native Son." Negro Digest, 17 (July), 85-88.
Unfavorable review of Constance Webb's Richard Wright. The personal element is interesting, but Webb fails to provide interpretation of W's works and his place in world literature.

151. _____. "The Self-Hatred of Don L. Lee," in his Black Pride. Detroit: Broadside Press, p. 19.
Poem naming W as a writer who helped Lee to realize his blackness.
Reprinted: 1971.210.

152. Leinwald, Gerald. "Black Boy," in his The Negro in the City. New York: Pocket Books, p. 77.
Headnote to an excerpt from BB mentioning NS and stressing W's revelation of "the deep hatred many black men feel toward whites."

152a. Lester, Julius. "Not in Memory of Robert Kennedy." Guardian (15 June), p. 11.
Poem mentioning W.
Reprinted: 1969.157b; 1970.243a.

153. Lewis, Theophilus. "Theatre: Daddy

Goodness." America, 118 (22 June), 800.
Mixed review of the play praising the acting but calling the script diffuse and the authors' purpose unclear.

154. Lipton, Lawrence. "Richard Wright: The Agony of Integration." Los Angeles Free Press (26 April), Living Arts Sec., pp. 18-19.
Mixed review of Constance Webb's Richard Wright criticizing the book for failing to record adequately the paradox of W's ambivalent attitude toward his race. The reviewer includes several anecdotes concerning his contact with W in the early thirties in Chicago.

155. Llorens, David. "Books Noted." Negro Digest, 17 (June), 37-39.
Review of Eldridge Cleaver's Soul on Ice mentioning W.

156. Lottman, Herbert. "The Action Is Everywhere the Black Man Goes." The New York Times Book Review (21 April), pp. 6-7, 48-49.
Mentions W in a discussion of such black expatriates in Paris as Margaret Butcher, Carlene Polite, William M. Kelley, and William Gardner Smith.

157. Madden, David. "Introduction," in his Proletarian Writers of the Thirties. Crosscurrents Modern Critiques, ed. Harry T. Moore. Carbondale and Edwardsville: Southern Illinois University Press, pp. xv-xlii.
Mentions NS briefly (p. xxxiv).

158. Maloff, Saul. "Native Son." Newsweek, 71 (April), 92.
Unfavorable review of Constance Webb's Richard Wright. Despite Webb's labor of love, the book is poorly organized and inconclusive. It pays little attention to W's works.

159. Marden, Charles F. and Gladys Meyer. Minorities in American Society. Third edition. New York: American Book Company, p. 223.
Mentions briefly NS.

160. Margolies, Edward. Native Sons: A Critical Study of Twentieth Century Negro American Authors. Philadelphia: Lippincott, pp. 19-20, 22, 33-34, 44, 48, 50, 65-86, 87, 91, 192, 197, 198.
In Chapter IV, "Richard Wright: Native Son and Three Kinds of Revolution," Margolies reviews W's life and career and analyzes NS. Though sharing many of the characteristics of proletarian fiction, the novel is more psychological than sociological. The basic question W raises concerns

what human responsibility is "in a world devoid of meaning and purpose." The three kinds of revolution the novel expresses are Communist, black nationalist, and metaphysical. Elsewhere Margolies quotes W and comments on his relation to Himes and LeRoi Jones.
Reprinted: 1969.168.

161. Mason, Philip. "The Revolt Against Western Values," in Color and Race. Ed. John Hope Franklin. Boston: Houghton Mifflin, pp. 50-74.
Cites and quotes from W to explain the alienation of Black Muslims from white American society.
Reprinted: 1969.171.

162. Mata, G.[onzalo], H.[umberto]. And Now What My Dr. King? ¿Y ahora que, mi Dr. King? Memoria a Richard Wright. Cuenca, Ecuador: Biblioteca "Cenit," 34 pp.
The last six pages of this pamphlet are a highly subjective meditation on W emphasizing the American racism which he suffered and depicted. W lacked faith in black people, Mata asserts, but events after his death have been more hopeful for the redemption of the race.

163. Materassi, Mario. "Al di qua del 'Black Power': il grido di John A. Williams." Il ponte, 24 (November-December), 1545-1559.
Article on The Man Who Cried I Am mentioning W (p. 1549) and noting his depiction in the novel as Harry Ames (p. 1550).
Reprinted: 1977.220.

164. _____. "Building Up Somebody Else's Civilization: sul concetto di cultura negra americana." Quartiere, 10 (31 March), 16-24.
Quotes W on George Moses Horton and mentions him as a protest writer.
Reprinted: 1977.220.

165. _____. "La faccia nascosta della letteratura nordamericana." Il ponte, 24 (January), 62-78.
Mentions W briefly (p. 62).
Reprinted: 1977.220.

166. _____. "Poesia del Black Power." La nazione (12 December), p. 3.
Quotes from W's "The Literature of the Negro in the United States."
Reprinted: 1977.220.

167. McAleer, John J. "Richard Wright. By Constance Webb." America, 118 (27 April), 585.
Favorable review noting W's initial cooperation with the author. "It is

more than the biography of one man, however; it emblemizes the plight of the Negro race in modern America."

168. Meltzer, Milton. Langston Hughes: A Biography. New York: Crowell, p. 225.
Comments on W's review of The Big Sea and his friendship with Hughes.

169. Mitchell, Loften. "An Informal Memoir: For Langston Hughes and Stella Holt." Negro Digest, 17 (April), 41-43, 74-77.
Mentions W briefly.

170. Murray, Albert. "Something Different, Something More," in Anger, and Beyond: The Negro Writer in the United States. Ed. Herbert Hill. Perennial Library. New York: Harper and Row, pp. 112-137.
Reprint of 1966.106.

171. Neal, Larry. "And Shine Swam On," in Black Fire: An Anthology of Afro-American Writing. Ed. LeRoi Jones and Larry Neal. New York: William Morrow, pp. 638-656.
Discusses "Blue Print for Negro Writing" and WML in relation to black nationalism (pp. 649-652).
Reprinted: 1969.181.

172. _____. "Sinner Man Where You Gonna Run To?" in Black Fire: An Anthology of Afro-American Writing. Ed. LeRoi Jones and Larry Neal. New York: William Morrow, pp. 510-518.
Short story with an epigraph from O.
Reprinted: 1969.184.

173. The New York Public Library. Books, Films, Recordings by and About the American Negro. New York: The New York Public Library, 24 pp.
Lists BB and Constance Webb's Richard Wright. Mentions W elsewhere.

174. Nkrumah, Kwame. Dark Days in Ghana. New York: International Publishers, p. 6.
Uses a quotation from W's letter to Nkrumah in BP as a preface.

175. Novick, Julius. "Theatre: Daddy Goodness." The New York Village Voice (13 June), pp. 41, 43.
Unfavorable review. Though Moses Gunn's performance in the title role helps to emphasize Daddy Goodness's humor, the play fails because the authors have no idea about how to handle their theme and fall back on empty sentimentality and nonfunctional plot conventions.

176. Oliver, Edith. "The Theatre: Off Broadway." The New Yorker, 44 (15 June),

65.
   Unfavorable review of Daddy Goodness, "a feeble affair, lacking satiric, comic, and dramatic force." The acting is good, however.

177. Osborne, John. The Old South. Time-Life Library of America. New York: Time-Life Books, pp. 149, 151, 159.
   Comments on W and includes a photograph.

177a. Patterson, Lindsay. "'It's Gonna Blow Whitey's Mind.'" The New York Times (25 August), Sec. II, p. 13.
   Mentions NS briefly.
   Reprinted: 1975.142b.

178. Pearson, Norman Holmes. "American Literature," in The Encyclopedia Americana. Ed. George A. Cornish. Vol. 1. New York: Americana Corporation, pp. 691-709.
   Mentions W briefly (p. 706).
   Reprinted: 1970.288; 1977.255; 1978.188.

179. [Perosa, Sergio]. "Richard Wright," in Dizionario di centouno capolavori della letteratura americana. Ed. Claudio Gorlier. Guide culturali Bompiani. Milan: Bompiani, pp. 149-151.
   Biographical note and a plot summary of NS.

180. Pitcole, Marcia. "Black Boy and Role Playing: A Scenario for Reading Success." English Journal, 57 (November), 1140-1142.
   Describes an experiment to induce students to read W's book.

181. Redding, Saunders. "Black, Male and American." The New Leader, 51 (26 August), 22.
   Unfavorable review of Constance Webb's Richard Wright. In her concern for detail, the author loses sight of the truth.

182. _____. "Literature and the Negro." Contemporary Literature, 9 (Winter), 130-135.
   Review of Loften Mitchell's Black Drama, David Littlejohn's Black on White, and Seymour Gross and John Edward Hardy's Images of the Negro in American Literature. Redding criticizes the treatment of W in the first two.

183. _____. "The Negro Writer and His Relationship to his Roots," in Black Voices: An Anthology of Afro-American Literature. Ed. Abraham Chapman. Mentor Books MW866. New York: The New American Library, pp. 612-618.
   Reprint of 1960.222.

184. Reilly, John Marsden. "Insight and Protest in the Works of Richard Wright." Dissertation Abstracts, 28 (April), 4185A-4186A.
   Contends that W's basic philosphical outlook was existential. His works reflect that outlook. W's identification with the outcast developed his sympathy for the suffering of all humanity. The dissertation examines first BB and then W's other major works, concluding with a chapter on critical opinion about W.

185. Relyea, Harold C. "'Black Power': The Genesis and Future of a Revolution." Journal of Human Relations, 16 (Fourth Quarter), 502-513.
   Considers BP an important source of the movement of the sixties, for it "anticipated certain of the ideas which would be embodied in the ideology of Pan-Africanism and the extension of that ideology to the United States as 'black power'" (p. 505).

186. Riley, Clayton. "Theatre Review." Liberator, 8 (July), 21.
   Mixed review of Daddy Goodness praising the production and acting but finding fault with the writing, especially the characterization of the protagonist.

186a. Rivers, Conrad Kent. "A Mourning Letter from Paris," in his The Still Voice of Harlem. Heritage Series, No. 5. London: Paul Breman Limited, p. 9.
   A poem for W about his expatriation.
   Reprinted: 1971.261a; 1972.173.

187. Robinson, Vivian. "'Daddy Goodness' Message to Spread Joy; It Does." New York Amsterdam News (8 June), p. 20.
   Favorable review emphasizing the play's comic qualities. Praises the production and the cast. Includes a photograph of a scene.

188. Romerstein, Herbert, John M. Ashbrook, and Chester D. Smith. "Testimony of Herbert Romerstein," in Hearings Before the Committee on Un-American Activites, Ninetieth Congress, Second Session. Washington: U. S. Government Printing Office, pp. 2036-2048.
   Quoting Martin Sostre, imprisoned bookstore owner, that his store was the only place where W and other black writers could be purchased, Romerstein points out that W is available elsewhere in Buffalo (pp. 2038-2039).

189. Rose, Peter I. They and We: Racial and Ethnic Relations in the United States. Second edition. New York: Random

House, pp. 102, 119n, 132-134, 145, 147n.
Reprint of 1964.109.

190. Rubenstein, Annette T. "Amerikanische Negerschriftsteller Heute." Sinn und Form, 20, pp. 1264-1274.
Mentions W in relation to Communism and existentialism. Also alludes to his exile and feud with Baldwin.

190a. Sainville, Léonard. "Auteurs des Ameriques et des Antilles," in his Anthologie de la littérature negro-africaine: romanciers et conteurs. Vol. 2. Paris: Présence Africaine, pp. 611-627.
Contains a biographical sketch of W and excerpts from BB.

190b. Saito, Tadatoshi. "Wright's First Biography: Constance Webb's Richard Wright: A Biography." Bungaku Kai [Literary Circle], 22 (September), 199-202.
Webb's work elucidates, through new evidence, the background of W's escape to the North and the motive behind his withdrawal from the Communist Party. His exile in France was prompted by a concern for his daughter. [Y. H. and T. K.]

191. Sanders, Ronald. "Relevance for the Sixties: Richard Wright Then and Now." Negro Digest, 18 (December), 83-98.
Reprint of 1968.192.

192. ____. "Richard Wright and the Sixties." Midstream, 14 (August-September), 28-40.
Examines W's connection with the Jewish community and with the Communist Party in relation to his search for his own literary identity. Analyzes "Joe Louis Uncovers Dynamite," UTC, BB, NS, O and EM. Reprinted: 1968.191.

193. Sayre, Nora. "New York's Black Theatre." New Statesmen, 76 (25 October), 556.
Summarizes the plot of Daddy Goodness.

194. Schafer, William J. "Ralph Ellison and the Birth of the Anti-Hero." Critique: Studies in Modern Fiction, 10, No. 2, pp. 81-93.
Mentions W briefly (pp. 81, 82). Reprinted: 1971.266; 1974.154.

195. Schoener, Allon, ed. Harlem on My Mind: Cultural Capital of Black America 1900-1968. New York: Random House, p. 163.
Contains a photograph of W. Reprinted: 1979.228a.

195a. Scott, Nathan A., Jr. "Judgment

Marked by a Cellar: The American Negro Writer and the Dialectic of Despair," in The Shapeless God: Essays on Modern Fiction. Ed. Harry J. Mooney, Jr., and Thomas F. Staley. Pittsburgh: University of Pittsburgh Press, pp. 139-169.
Reprint of 1967.94.

196. Sloan, Irving J. The American Negro: A Chronology and Fact Book. Second edition. Dobbs Ferry, N. Y.: Oceana Publications, pp. 40-41, 53.
Reprint of 1965.116.

196a. Stafford, William T. "Fiction: The 1930's to the Present," in American Literary Scholarship: An Annual/1966. Ed. James Woodress. Durham, N. C.: Duke University Press, pp. 167-186.
Mentions the chapter on W in Warren French's The Social Novel at the End of an Era and two articles on W.

197. Sterling, Dorothy. "The Soul of Learning." English Journal, 57 (February), 166-180.
Mentions W briefly.

198. Straumann, Heinrich. American Literature in the Twentieth Century. Third revised edition. Perennial Library. New York: Harper and Row, pp. 31, 39.
Reprint of 1951.233.

199. ____. "Zum Wandel des Menschenbildes in der zeitgenössischen amerikanischen Literatur," in Amerika: Vision und Wirklichkeit. Ed. Franz H. Link. Frankfurt am Main: Athenäum Verlag, pp. 471-480.
Discussing Baldwin, Straumann mentions W and Ellison.

199a. Sutherland, Bill. "Bill Sutherland: Tanzania," in The Black Expatriates: A Study of American Negroes in Exile. Ed. Ernest Dunbar. New York: E. P. Dutton, pp. 88-109.
States that Africa was not at fault because W failed to find a "psychological home" there.

200. Takahashi, Masao. Higeki no Henrekisha--Richard Wright no Shogai [The Tragic Wanderer: The Life of Richard Wright]. Tokyo: Chuo University Press.
A monograph with a translation of part of The God That Failed, ed. Richard Crossman. Traces W's life with some references to the John Reed Club and his tragic death in Paris. Notes on the basis of BB that by 1944 W had cut off his relations with the Communist Party. Sees his literary life after leaving the United States as a failure, but argues that W, being a black, must have felt he had to leave his own country. Concludes

that he failed because he was a black writer. [Y. H.]

201. Tanaka, Hiroshi. "Osore to Nikushimi-- Native Son o Megutte" ["Fear and Hatred in Native Son"]. Kyoto Daigaku Shikai [Kyoto University View], 10 (Spring), 14-25.
    Mentions UTC, in which tragic theme is well demonstrated by action, and states that Max's word in NS is devoid of meaning for Bigger. Bigger's protest, dramatized by his fear and hatred, becomes more significant than Max's [Y. H.]

202. [Temple, Herbert]. "Richard Wright: His Life and Works." Negro Digest, 18 (December), front cover.
    Front cover of the special W issue listing some of the contributors and presenting a collage of seven photographs of W.

203. Tischler, Nancy M. "The Negro in Modern Southern Fiction: Stereotype to Archetype." Negro American Literature Forum, 2 (Spring), 3-6.
    Compares Ellison and W.

204. Turner, Darwin T. "The Negro Dramatist's Image of the Universe, 1920-1960," in Black Voices: An Anthology of Afro-American Literature. Ed. Abraham Chapman. Mentor Books MW866. New York: The New American Library, pp. 677-690.
    Reprint of 1961.274.

205. ____. "Past and Present in Negro American Drama." Negro American Literature Forum, 2 (Summer), 26-27.
    Mentions briefly the play NS.

206. Watkins, Mel. "In the Ghettos." The New York Times Book Review (25 February), Part 2, p. 24.
    Survey of ghetto reading habits noting that W is popular among younger readers and occasionally read by older residents.

207. Watts, Daniel H. "The Hustlers." Liberator, 8 (June), 3.
    Points out that in covering Stokely Carmichael's use of the term "Black Power" the white press ignored the W antecedent.

208. Watts, Richard, Jr. "Random Notes on This and That." New York Post (11 June), p. 75.
    Contains laudatory comments on W's gift for comedy in Daddy Goodness.

209. ____. "Two on the Aisle: The Miracle That Got Out of Hand." New York Post (5 June), p. 63.
    Highly favorable review of Daddy

Goodness praising W's comic sense directed at human gullibility. The theme of "the sadness and wistful hopes of man's stubborn dreaming" is universal. Watts admires Moses Gunn's performance in the title role.

210. ____. "Two on the Aisle: The Religion of Daddy Goodness." New York Post (15 June), p. 22.
    Praises the play, comparing it to The Playboy of the Western World. Like Synge, W will be criticized for traducing his people, but in both cases the satire is directed toward universal human traits. The title character has great vitality and human appeal.

211. Webb, Constance. Richard Wright: A Biography. New York: Putnam's, 443 pp.
    The first full-length biography of W, Webb's sympathetic memoir brings to light much new information, especially on his childhood and exile. The biography does not always follow the chronological order of events in W's life; dates are infrequently cited. More of an interpretation of W's personality than an assessment of his work, Richard Wright: A Biography draws from the author's personal friendship with the subject as well as from documentary records and from interviews. Webb presents W in an extremely favorable way. The book contains thirty-four illustrations, notes, and the Fabre-Margolies bibliography of primary sources.

212. Webb, Howard W., Jr. "The Modern Range," in his Illinois Prose Writers: A Selection. Carbondale and Edwardsville: Southern Illinois University Press, pp. 113-116.
    Reviews W's connection with Chicago and his early career. Webb calls Bigger Thomas "the definitive portrait" of the urban black rebel.

213. Weiss, M. Jerry. "Literature for Teenagers." The New York Times Book Review (25 February), Part 2, p. 26.
    Contains a notice of Charlotte Brooks's anthology The Outnumbered mentioning W.

214. Wertham, Frederic, M. D. "The Virus of Violence." San Francisco Sunday Examiner and Chronicle (28 April), This World Sec., pp. 20-21.
    Wertham's point of departure is a meeting between W and Martin Luther King, Jr., in March of 1959.

215. Williams, John A. "On Wright, Wrong and Black Reality." Negro Digest, 18 (December), 25.
    Appreciation of W as the most im-

portant Afro-American writer. His
focus moved from the oppression of
blacks to a concern for all oppressed
people in his last works. Williams
urges that black writers, in honor
of W, cease quarreling among themselves.

216. Willis, John. Theatre World. Vol.
24. New York: Crown, p. 149.
    Lists members of the cast and pro-
    vides other information about Daddy
    Goodness. Includes three photographs
    from the play.

217. Woodress, James. Dissertations in
American Literature 1891-1966. Durham,
N. C.: Duke University Press, items
2835-2838.
    Lists dissertations on W by Bakish,
    Brignano, Kinnamon, and Margolies.

218. Young, Thomas Daniel, Floyd C.
Watkins, and Richmond Croom Beatty.
"Richard Wright 1908-1960," in their The
Literature of the South. Revised edi-
tion. Glenview, Ill.: Scott, Foresman,
p. 663.
    Reprint of 1952.22.

1969

1. Abdul, Raoul. "The Negro Playwright
on Broadway," in Anthology of the American Negro in the Theatre: A Critical
Approach. Ed. Lindsay Patterson. New
York: Publishers Company, pp. 59-63.
    Mentions NS and refers to two favor-
    able reviews (p. 61).
    Reprinted: 1976.1.

2. Abramson, Doris E. Negro Playwrights
in the American Theatre 1925-1959. New
York: Columbia University Press, pp. 3,
4, 44-45, 93, 95, 136-156, 157, 160,
242, 243, 266, 270, 279, 301.
    The section on the play NS (pp. 136-
    156) sketches W's career, explains
    the circumstances of W's collabora-
    tion with Paul Green, analyzes the
    play scene by scene, and comments
    briefly on its critical reception.
    Elsewhere Abramson quotes W on the
    plight of blacks in the Depression
    (from LT), on Theodore Ward, and on
    Bigger Thomas. She also compares the
    play NS and A Raisin in the Sun.
    Partially reprinted: 1971.147.

3. Adams, Russell L. "Richard Wright
(1908-1960): A Sound of Thunder," in his
Great Negroes Past and Present. Ed.
David P. Ross, Jr. Third edition. Chicago: Afro-Am Publishing Company, p.
156.
    Revised reprint of 1964.1.

4. Allen, Michael. "Some Examples of

Faulknerian Rhetoric in Ellison's 'Invisible Man,'" in The Black American
Writer. Ed. C. W. E. Bigsby. Vol. 1.
DeLand, Fla.: Everett/Edwards, pp. 143-
151.
    Refers to W's naturalism and its
    influence on Ellison.
    Reprinted: 1971.5.

5. Anderson, S. E. "For Black Students
1969." Negro Digest, 18 (September), 38.
    Poem mentioning W.

6. Anon. "Back in Print." Wichita Falls
Times, (7 December), Features Magazine
Sec., p. 4.
    Notice of Harper reprints of UTC, BB,
    NS, and O.

7. Anon. "The Blacks and the Churches."
New York Post (c. 12 May).
    Photograph of W's daughter Julia
    Hervé at a SNCC rally in Paris.

8. Anon. "Children's Books." Publishers'
Weekly, 196 (14 July), 148-154.
    Contains a favorable review of John
    A. Williams's The Most Native of Sons
    stressing that W maintained touch
    with the United States during his
    expatriation.

9. Anon. Demands of San Francisco State
College Black Students Union. San Francisco: Privately printed.
    Leaflet mentioning W briefly.
    Reprinted: 1971.13.

10. Anon. Dust jacket of The Art of
Richard Wright. By Edward Margolies.
Carbondale and Edwardsville: Southern
Illinois University Press.
    Blurb, summary, and note on Margolies
    on the inside flaps. Biographical
    note and a drawing of W on the back
    cover.

11. Anon. Dust jacket of The Example of
Richard Wright. By Dan McCall. New York:
Harcourt, Brace & World.
    Blurb on the front inside flap; bio-
    graphical note on McCall on back
    inside flap. The back cover contains
    a quotation from page 6 of the book
    that is taken without permission or
    acknowledgement from Keneth Kinna-
    mon's 1966 dissertation on W. See
    1971.203, 219, 202.

12. Anon. "The Example of Richard
Wright." Book Buyer's Guide, 72 (March),
124.
    Brief notice of McCall's critical
    study.

13. Anon. "The Example of Richard Wright
by Dan McCall." Unidentified clipping.
    Favorable notice of a "provocative

critical study."

14. Anon. "Four Wright Books Being Republished." Buffalo Evening News (8 November), p. B-12.
Notice of Harper reprints of UTC, NS, BB, and O.

15. Anon. "Freedom by Festival." El Manjabit [?] (13 August).
Notes that W's daughter Julia Hervé participated in the opening of the French "Afro-American Center."

16. Anon. Index Translationum 20. Paris: Unesco, pp. 85, 134, 461, 534, 559.
Lists translations of O into German, NS into Portuguese, UTC into Arabic and Dutch, LT into Dutch, and LD into Polish.

17. Anon. "Library Notes." The Redmond (Ore.) Spokesman (13 August), p. [4].
Mentions a selection from W in Arnold Adoff's Black on Black.

18. Anon. "Margolies, Edward. The Art of Richard Wright." The Booklist and Subscription Books Bulletin, 65 (1 May), 991.
Notice pointing out that Margolies assesses W's strengths and weaknesses, "explores his fiction and nonfiction, and delves into his themes with full treatment." The book is careful and scholarly.

19. Anon. "Margolies, Edward. The Art of Richard Wright." Choice, 6 (May), 368.
Complementing Webb's biography, Margolies attempts to evaluate W's art. "His effort to discriminate between W's craft and esthetics is conscientious and evocative." The book clarifies W's literary status.

20. Anon. "A Uniform Edition of Four Major Books by Richard Wright." The New York Times Book Review (2 November), p. 49.
Advertisement for Harper reprints of BB, NS, O, and UTC.

21. Anon. "Wright (Richard)," in Nouveau Larousse universel. Ed. Claude DuBois. Vol. 2. Paris: Librairie Larousse, p. 857.
Brief biographical note.

22. Anudsen, Kristin. "The Art of Richard Wright." The New York University Alumni News.
Favorable notice of Margolies's book.

23. Arnez, Nancy L. "Racial Understanding Through Literature." English Journal, 58 (January), 56-61.
Contains a brief reference to a pas-

sage in BB exemplifying the importance of education in black values.

24. Baldwin, James. "James Baldwin on the Negro Actor," in Anthology of the American Negro in the Theatre: A Critical Approach. Ed. Lindsay Patterson. New York: Publishers Company, pp. 127-130.
Reprint of 1961.117.

25. _____. "Many Thousands Gone," in Black Expression: Essays by and About Black Americans in the Creative Arts. Ed. Addison Gayle, Jr. New York: Weybright and Talley, pp. 325-339.
Reprint of 1951.129.

25a. _____ et al. "The Negro in American Culture," in The Black American Writer. Ed. C. W. E. Bigsby. Vol. 1. DeLand, Fla.: Everett/Edwards, pp. 79-108.
Reprint of 1961.118.

26. Bazelon, David T. "Burgum's Play," in his Nothing But a Fine Tooth Comb: Essays in Social Criticism, 1944-1969. New York: Simon and Schuster, pp. 202-203.
Reprint of 1947.144.

27. Bergman, B. A. "Books and Authors: Huzzahs to Harper's." The Sunday Philadelphia Bulletin (16 November), Sec. 2, p. 3.
Notice of Harper reprints of UTC, NS, BB, and O, books which are "bitter indictments" of American conditions.

28. Bergman, Peter M. The Chronological History of the Negro in America. New York: Harper & Row, pp. 355-356, 480, 482, 492, 509.
Contains a biographical sketch (pp. 355-356), mainly of W's early life and career, with critical comments on UTC and NS.

29. Bigsby, C. W. E. "The Black American Writer," in his The Black American Writer. Vol. 1. DeLand, Fla.: Everett/Edwards, pp. 5-33.
General discussion of modern Afro-American literature containing several references to W.
Reprinted: 1971.42.

30. Blake, Nelson Manfred. "The Volcano of Anger: Richard Wright," in his Novelists' America: Fiction as History, 1910-1940. Syracuse, N. Y.: Syracuse University Press, pp. 226-253.
Analyzes the characters of NS against the social background. Includes much paraphrase. Blake defends W's Communist rhetoric as a function of his idealism rather than his ideology.

31. Blum, Daniel. A Pictorial History of

the American Theatre 1860-1970. Third edition enlarged and revised by John Willis. New York: Crown Publishers, pp. 291, 293.
    Mentions Canada Lee in NS and includes a photograph.
    Reprinted: 1977.65.

32. Bogart, Max. "Fiction," in his The Bitter Years: The Thirties in Literature. The American Character Series, ed. John C. Schweitzer. New York: Scribner's, pp. 137-139.
    Contains two study questions on W.

33. _____. "Introduction," in his The Bitter Years: The Thirties in Literature. The American Character Series, ed. John C. Schweitzer. New York: Scribner's, pp. 3-15.
    Mentions W briefly (pp. 3, 13, 14).

34. _____. "Richard Wright (1908-1960)," in his The Bitter Years: The Thirties in Literature. The American Character Series, ed. John C. Schweitzer. New York: Scribner's, p. 53.
    Biographical headnote to an excerpt from NS.

35. Bogle, Donald. "Black and Proud Behind Bars." Ebony, 24 (August), 64-66, 68, 70, 72.
    Concerns the activities of the Black Cultural Development Society at the Colorado State Penitentiary. NS is one of three books mentioned that the group acquired for its library.

36. Bone, Robert A. Richard Wright. University of Minnesota Pamphlets on American Writers No. 74, ed. Leonard Unger and Ted Wright. Minneapolis: University of Minnesota Press, 48 pp.
    After a biographical sketch, Bone provides a critique of W's American period and French period. Extended treatment is given only to BB, NS, "The Man Who Lived Underground," "Tradition and Industrialization," and O. Bone points out a pattern of the picaresque in W's work, discusses his theory of history, pays respect to him as a thinker, and tries to see W's life and art as a whole. He deemphasizes W's protest and dislikes his Marxism.
    Reprinted: 1974.30a.

37. Boning, Richard A. Profiles of Black Americans. Rockville Centre, N. Y.: Dexter & Westbrook, p. 107.
    Biographical sketch with a drawing by Joseph Forte.

38. Bontemps, Arna. "Introduction," in Cane. By Jean Toomer. New York: Harper & Row, pp. vii-xvi.

Partial reprint of 1966.24.

39. _____. "Introduction to The Book of Negro Folklore," in Black Expression: Essays by and About Black Americans in the Creative Arts. Ed. Addison Gayle, Jr. New York: Weybright and Talley, pp. 29-36.
    Reprint of 1958.87.

40. _____. "Negro Poets, Then and Now," in Black Expressions: Essays by and About Black Americans in the Creative Arts. Ed. Addison Gayle, Jr. New York: Weybright and Talley, pp. 82-89.
    Reprint of 1950.114.

41. _____. "The Slave Narrative: An American Genre," in his Great Slave Narratives. Boston: Beacon Press, pp. vii-xix.
    Notes W's indebtedness to the tradition of the slave narrative (pp. x, xix).

42. _____. Story of the Negro. Fifth edition. New York: Knopf, pp. 203, 221.
    Reprint of 1948.137 with an additional reference to BP.

43. Bourniquel, Camille. "Ralph Ellison: Homme invisible, pour qui chantes-tu?" Esprit, 37 (September), 368-370.
    Review of the French translation of Invisible Man mentioning W briefly.

43a. Brown, Sterling A. "A Century of Negro Portraiture in American Literature," in Black & White in American Culture: An Anthology from The Massachusetts Review. Ed. Jules Chametsky and Sidney Kaplan. Amherst: The University of Massachusetts Press, pp. 333-359.
    Reprint of 1966.30.

44. _____. "Contemporary Negro Poetry: 1914-1936," in An Introduction to Black Literature in America from 1746 to the Present. Ed. Lindsay Patterson. International Library of Negro Life and History. New York: Publishers Company, pp. 146-154.
    Reprint of 1937.17, 18.

45. _____. Negro Poetry and Drama and The Negro in American Fiction. Preface by Robert Bone. Studies in American Negro Life, ed. August Meier. New York: Atheneum, pp. 78, 187.
    Reprint of 1937.17, 18.

46. Bryer, Jackson R. "Richard Wright (1908-1960)," in A Bibliographical Guide to the Study of Southern Literature. Ed. Louis D. Rubin, Jr. Baton Rouge: Louisiana State University Press, pp. 333-334.
    Comments on W's career and on the critical and scholarly response to

his work. Lists twenty-one secondary items.

47. _____, Philip R. Headings, Joseph V. Ridgely, Donald B. Stauffer, John E. Todd, and Peter G. Van Egmond, with the help of Ronald Leatherbarrow. "American Literature." PMLA, 84 (June), 878-908.
    Bibliography listing five items on W.

48. Carbine, Francis A. "Richard Wright: What His Stories Say About Dixie." Inscape (Greater Philadelphia Council of Teachers of English), 8 (December), 6-7, 12-14.
    Argues that protest against Southern racism was the abiding theme of W's short fiction. Like Joyce in exile from Ireland, W as artist could not forget his homeland--the South.

49. Cargill, Oscar. "American Literature," in Collier's Encyclopedia. Ed. Louis Shores. Vol. 2. New York: Crowell-Collier Educational Corporation, pp. 42-74.
    Includes comments on W (pp. 71-72). Reprinted: 1976.47; 1977.84; 1979.58.

50. Carlsen, G. Robert, Anthony Tovatt, Ruth Christoffer Carlsen, and Patricia O. Tovatt. "Plain Sense, Implications, Reading Literature, Words," in their Focus: Themes in Literature. St. Louis: McGraw-Hill, p. 547.
    Study questions for "The Right to the Streets of Memphis," reprinted from Chapter 2 of BB.

51. _____. "Richard Wright," in their Focus: Themes in Literature. St. Louis: McGraw-Hill, p. 620.
    Brief biographical sketch.

52. Cartey, Wilfrid G. O. "Images of the Negro in American Literature. Seymour Gross and John E. Hardy." Pan-African Journal, 2 (Winter), 129-135.
    Includes comments on Baldwin's treatment of W in "Many Thousands Gone."

53. Cartosio, Bruno. "Due scrittori afroamericani: Richard Wright e Ralph Ellison." Studi americani, 15, pp. 395-431.
    Considers NS the culmination of the protest novel of the thirties. Characterized by W's desire to incite political action, it is at times overly didactic. Nevertheless it attains a greater degree of universality than BB, which is too much limited to W's personal experience.

54. Childs, James. "Wright and Bellow." New Haven Register.
    Dual review of Edward Margolies's The Art of Richard Wright and a book on

Saul Bellow in the same series. Praises the Margolies book.

55. Christian, Barbara. "Ralph Ellison: A Critical Study," in Black Expression: Essays by and About Black Americans in the Creative Arts. Ed. Addison Gayle, Jr. New York: Weybright and Talley, pp. 353-365.
    Refers to W's relation to Ellison. Reprinted: 1972.51.

56. Clarke, John Henrik. "The Alienation of James Baldwin," in Black Expression: Essays by and About Black Americans in the Creative Arts. Ed. Addison Gayle, Jr. New York: Weybright and Talley, pp. 350-353.
    Reprint of 1964.37.

56a. Cleaver, Eldridge. "My Father and Stokely Carmichael," in his Post-Prison Writings and Speeches. Ed. Robert Scheer. Vintage Books V-567. New York: Random House, pp. 43-56.
    Reprint of 1967.23.

57. _____. "Notes of a Native Son," in Black Expression: Essays by and About Black Americans in the Creative Arts. Ed. Addison Gayle, Jr. New York: Weybright and Talley, pp. 339-349.
    Reprint of 1966.37.

58. Comans, Grace P. "Critical Viewpoints." The Hartford Courant (29 June), Parade Sec., p. 21.
    Contains a review of Edward Margolies's The Art of Richard Wright. Treating both W's fiction and nonfiction, Margolies shows how his major themes--"freedom, existential horror, and black nationalism"-- emerge from childhood experience.--The book is "a long-needed, thought-provoking study."

58a. Conroy, Jack. "An Anthology of WPA Creative Writing," in New Masses: An Anthology of the Rebel Thirties. Ed. Joseph North. New York: International Publishers, pp. 217-220.
    Reprint of 1937.20.

59. Cook, Mercer. "African Voices of Protest," in The Militant Black Writer in Africa and the United States. By Mercer Cook and Stephen E. Henderson. Madison: University of Wisconsin Press, pp. 3-62.
    Compares BB and Camara Laye's The African Child (p. 22).

60. Corona, Mario. "La saggistica di James Baldwin." Studi americani, 15, pp. 433-463.
    Discusses Baldwin's unfavorable attitudes toward W and NS, especially as

revealed in "Many Thousands Gone" (pp. 440-448). Notes also Baldwin's tribute to W in "Alas, Poor Richard" (p. 457).

61. Coudert, Marie-Louise. "Martha Foley: Cinquante ans de nouvelles américains." Europe, Nos. 478-479 (February-March), 340.
   Very favorable account of "Bright and Morning Star" in an otherwise unfavorable review.

62. Coulthard, G. R. "La literatura de las Antillas Británicas." Inter-American Review of Bibliography, 19 (January-March), 38-55.
   Mentions W briefly.

63. Cunningham, James. "The Case of the Severed Lifeline." Negro Digest, 18 (October), 23-28.
   Deplores the infighting among black writers, citing Cleaver's attitude toward Baldwin and W.

64. Curley, Dorothy Nyren and Maurice Kramer, eds. A Library of Literary Criticism: Modern American Literature. Fourth edition. Vol. 3. New York: Frederick Ungar, pp. 416-417, 463.
   Reprint of 1960.207 and excerpts from 1958.85; 1961.116, 260; 1963.135, 160; 1964.48; 1966.25; 1967.54.

65. DaSilva, Benjamin, Milton Finkelstein, and Arlene Loshin. The Afro-American in United States History. New York: Globe Book Company, pp. 365-366, 367.
   Comments on NS and BB. Includes a photograph of W.
   Reprinted: 1972.57a.

66. Davis, Bertha, Dorothy S. Arnof, and Charlotte Croon Davis. Background for Tomorrow: An American History. New York: Macmillan, p. 630.
   Mentions briefly W and NS. Includes a photograph.

67. Drimmer, Melvin. "Gilbert Osofsky," in his Black History: A Reappraisal. Anchor Books AO-8. Garden City, N. Y.: Doubleday, pp. 372-374.
   Mentions NS.

68. Dunning, Stephen, Elsie Katterjohn, and Olive Stafford Niles. "His Life in His Books," in their Focus. Glenview, Ill.: Scott, Foresman, p. 71.
   Biographical sketch focusing on W's early years.

69. Elkins, Stanley M. "Slavery and Personality," in Black History: A Reappraisal. Ed. Melvin Drimmer. Anchor Books AO-8. Garden City, N. Y.: Double-

day, pp. 182-204.
   Partial reprint of 1959.81.

70. Ellison, Ralph. "Richard Wright's Blues," in Black Expression: Essays by and About Black Americans in the Creative Arts. Ed. Addison Gayle, Jr. New York: Weybright and Talley, pp. 311-325.
   Reprint of 1945.890.

71. _____ and Allen Geller. "An Interview with Ralph Ellison," in The Black American Writer. Ed. C. W. E. Bigsby. Vol. 1. DeLand, Fla.: Everett/Edwards, pp. 153-168.
   Reprint of 1964.52.

72. Emanuel, James A. "America Before 1950: Black Writers' Views." Negro Digest, 18 (August), 26-34, 67-69.
   Comments on W and his followers. NS is unique in its influence on subsequent black writers, who have responded to its emotional quality, its indictment of racism, and its naturalism.

73. _____. "Item: Black Men Thinking." Negro Digest, 18 (September), 57.
   Poem on reading that W was poisoned by the CIA.

74. E.[vans], P.[amela]. "Wright, Richard (1908-1960)," in Twentieth Century Writing: A Reader's Guide to Contemporary Literature. Ed. Kenneth Richardson. London: Newnes Books, p. 666.
   Brief biographical note.
   Reprinted: 1971.99.

75. Fabio, Sarah Webster. "A Black Paper." Negro Digest, 18 (July), 26-31, 76-89.
   Mentions W in an attack on David Littlejohn.

76. Fabre, Michel and Edward Margolies. "Richard Wright (1908-1960): A Bibliography." Negro Digest, 18 (January), 86-92.
   Reprint of 1965.59.

77. Faderman, Lillian and Barbara Bradshaw. "Introduction," in their Speaking for Ourselves: American Ethnic Writing. Glenview, Ill.: Scott, Foresman, pp. 3-9.
   Contains a paragraph on W (p. 7).

78. _____. "Richard Wright," in their Speaking for Ourselves. Glenview, Ill.: Scott, Foresman, p. 11.
   Biographical headnote to accompany "The Man Who Saw the Flood" and "Hokku Poems."

79. _____. "Suggestions for Discussion,"

in their Speaking for Ourselves. Glenview, Ill.: Scott, Foresman, pp. 15-16,
92.
    To accompany "The Man Who Saw the
    Flood" and "Hokku Poems."

80. ____. "Suggestions for Writing and
Comparison," in their Speaking for Ourselves. Glenview, Ill.: Scott, Foresman,
pp. 16, 92.
    To accompany "The Man Who Saw the
    Flood" and "Hokku Poems."

81. Farnsworth, Robert. "Testing the
Color Line--Dunbar and Chesnutt," in The
Black American Writer. Ed. C. W. E.
Bigsby. Vol. 1. DeLand, Fla.: Everett/
Edwards, pp. 111-124.
    Contains brief references to W.

82. Farrison, W. Edward. "Richard
Wright: A Biography. By Constance Webb."
CLA Journal, 12 (June), 371-373.
    Unfavorable review. Though important
    as the first life of W, the book
    omits much. Its style is undistin-
    guished.

83. Filler, Louis. "Wright, Richard," in
his A Dictionary of American Social
Reform. New York: Greenwood Press, pp.
844-845.
    Reprint of 1963.82.

84. F.[leischmann], U.[lrich]. "Native
Son," in Kindlers Literatur Lexikon. Ed.
Rolf Geisler. Vol. 5. Zurich: Kindler
Verlag, pp. 290-291.
    Summary with critical comments and a
    brief bibliography.

85. ____. "The Outsider," in Kindlers
Literatur Lexikon. Ed. Rolf Geisler.
Vol. 5. Zurich: Kindler Verlag, pp.
1204-1205.
    Summary with critical comments and a
    brief bibliography.

86. Ford, Nick Aaron. "A Blueprint for
Negro Authors," in Black Expression:
Essays by and About Black Americans in
the Creative Arts. Ed. Addison Gayle,
Jr. New York: Weybright and Talley, pp.
276-280.
    Reprint of 1950.148.

87. Franklin, John Hope. "Negro," in
Collier's Encyclopedia. Ed. Louis
Shores. Vol 17. New York: Crowell-
Collier Educational Corporation, pp.
276-293.
    Reprint of 1955.43 without the photo-
    graph.

88. Frémy, Dominique and Michèle Frémy.
Quid? Tout pour tous. Paris: Librairie
Plon, p. 74.
    Reprint of 1963.86.

89. F.[rench], W.[arren]. "June 16,
1940," in his The Forties: Fiction,
Poetry, Drama. DeLand, Fla.: Everett/
Edwards, p. 85.
    Mentions W's enthusiasm for Carson
    McCullers's The Heart Is a Lonely
    Hunter.

90. ____. "The Lost Potential of
Richard Wright," in The Black American
Writer. Ed. C. W. E. Bigsby. Vol. 1.
DeLand, Fla.: Everett/Edwards, pp. 125-
142.
    After reviewing W's career and W
    criticism, French speculates that the
    author wrote best in his early
    career, when he could exercise his
    "kinesthetic" sensibility in depict-
    ing the people and environment with
    which he was in daily contact. In the
    final section of the essay French
    applies this theory to W's work,
    mainly in the light of Margolies's
    practical criticism in The Art of
    Richard Wright. W's protest was much
    more personal than racial, French
    believes. The essay also compares W
    and Steinbeck.
    Reprinted: 1971.127.

91. ____. "A Montage of Minorities:
Some Waspish Remarks." Kansas English,
55 (December), 6-13.
    Mentions W briefly (p. 12).

91a. Fujita, Takemasa. "Ralph Ellison's
Relationships to Richard Wright." Numazu
Kogyo Kotogakko Kenkyu Hokoku [Numazu
Technical College Study Report], 4 (10
March), 141-151.
    The differences in style and content
    between the writings of W and Ellison
    derive from their experiences: while
    W witnessed only ugliness in Southern
    life, Ellison also sought beauty.
    Although Ellison learned his fiction-
    al technique from W, Ellison attempt-
    ed to internalize black men's pro-
    test, as shown in Invisible Man. As a
    result, W's style is "hard-boiled,"
    whereas Ellison's is surrealistic and
    symbolic. [Y. H. and T. K.]

92. Fulks, Bryan. Black Struggle: A
History of the Negro in America. Laurel-
Leaf Library. New York: Dell, pp. 228-
312.
    Mentions W briefly.

93. Fuller, Hoyt W. "Contemporary Negro
Fiction," in The Black American Writer.
Ed. C. W. E. Bigsby. Vol. 1. DeLand,
Fla.: Everett/Edwards, pp. 229-243.
    Reprint of 1965.68.

94. ____. "He told the black man's
story." The New York Times Book Review
(18 May), pp. 8, 10.

Favorable review of Dan McCall's The Example of Richard Wright crediting NS with lifting "the smothering shadow" of Western literature" from black writing. W helped win the freedom which has allowed some "universal-oriented" black writers to rebel against his example.

95. _____. "Perspectives." Negro Digest, 18 (February), 49-50, 86-89.
Mentions a work in progress on W by John A. Williams.

96. Fullinwider, S. P. The Mind and Mood of Black America: 20th Century Thought. Homewood, Ill.: Dorsey Press, pp. 187-193, 194, 195, 205, 209, 218.
Examines W's sense of isolation and his evaluation of American society in a discussion of "Early Days in Chicago," "How 'Bigger' Was Born," and NS. Also notes Ellison's debt to W.

96a. Furukawa, Hiromi. "Eight Men: A Chronicle of Richard Wright's Writings." Kokujin Kenkyu [Negro Studies], 38 (October), 36-41.
"The Man Who Was Almost a Man" is based on escape psychology. "The Man Who Lived Underground," thriving on a tense atmosphere, is experimental and poetical; it deals with the problems of modern civilization and alienation. "Big Black Good Man," though analyzing white men's depth psychology, fails to portray man. "The Man Who Saw the Flood," despite its shortness, is an excellent story. "Man of All Work" is an excellent comedy while "Man, God Ain't Like That . . ." is not. "The Man Who Killed a Shadow" is a successful tragedy with a psychological vision. "The Man Who Went to Chicago," tne collection's final story, is significant; it suggests W's return to the launching of his career. [Y. H. and T. K.]

97. Furukawa, Hiromi. Introduction, notes, and bibliography in his The Man Who Lived Underground. By Richard Wright. Osaku: Aoyoma, 90 pp.
The text is in English; the introduction, notes, and bibliography are in Japanese.

98. Galway, Trevor. "Paperback Panorama." The Oakland Skyline Beacon (17 September).
Contains a notice of the paperback edition of EM. W "not only survived--but seemed to prevail."

99. Garland, Phyl. The Sound of Soul. Chicago: Henry Regnery, pp. 75-76.
Quotes from W's introduction to Paul

Oliver's Blues Fell This Morning.

100. Gayle, Addison, Jr. "Cultural Nationalism: The Black Novel and the City." Liberator, 9 (July), 14-17.
Places W and NS in the context of American and European racism--a "concentration camp environment" (p. 16). Unlike Baldwin and Ellison, W is in the militant black tradition of Martin Delany.
Reprinted and expanded: 1970.144.

101. _____. "Cultural Strangulation: Black Literature and the White Aesthetic." Negro Digest, 18 (July), 32-39.
Mentions W briefly.
Reprinted: 1971.133; 1972.80.

102. _____. "Perhaps Not So Soon One Morning," in his Black Expression: Essays by and About Black Americans in the Creative Arts. New York: Weybright and Talley, pp. 280-288.
Reprint of 1968.109.

103. _____. "Preface," in his Black Expression: Essays by and About Black Americans in the Creative Arts. New York: Weybright and Talley, pp. vii-xv.
Discusses W's belief that racial oppression results in racial consciousness and protest on the part of black writers.

104. Geismar, Maxwell. "Introduction," in New Masses: An Anthology of the Rebel Thirties. Ed. Joseph North. New York: International Publishers, pp. 5-13.
Mentions W briefly as poet and essayist (pp. 7, 8).

105. Gerald, Carolyn. "Black Expression." Negro Digest, 18 (July), 51-52, 71-72.
Review of Addison Gayle's anthology mentioning W.

106. Gérard, Albert. Les Tambours de néant: Le problème existentiel dans le roman américaine. Brussels: La Renaissance du Livre, pp. 12, 147, 149-163, 164, 165, 168, 169, 171, 183, 186.
In a chapter entitled "Fils de Cham," Gérard analyzes the structure of "Big Boy Leaves Home" as similar to classical tragedy. He compares W's style to Hemingway's. He also comments on Cross Damon as a frustrated idealist. Partially translated: 1971.142.

107. Gibson, Donald B. "Richard Wright: A Bibliographical Essay." CLA Journal, 12 (June), 360-365.
Expressing his "intention of suggesting in broad outline what has so far been accomplished in regard to the life and work of Wright" (p. 260),

Gibson includes sections on bibliography, editions, biography, criticism, and influence.

108. _____. "Richard Wright and the Tyranny of Convention." CLA Journal, 12 (June), 344-357.
Taking W's major theme to be "the individual in conflict with social convention" (p. 344), Gibson discerns in the novels and stories a consistent pattern: violation of convention; a consequent sense of freedom, fear, or indifference; and confession, capture, or flight. Usually W opposes the restraints of convention, but O is an exception. See also 1970.149.
Reprinted: 1971.147.

109. _____. "Wright's Invisible Native Son." American Quarterly, 21 (Winter), 728-738.
Gibson argues that most critics have seen Bigger as a social symbol, but not as an individual person. Yet W is careful to delineate Bigger's individuality, especially at the end when Bigger comes to terms with his impending death. For all his good will, Max and his view are limited, and W is aware of the limitations of Communism. Although NS grew out of naturalism, it is also a "prototype of the modern existentialist novel" and other more recent fiction.
Reprinted: 1972.27.

110. Gilbert, Zack. "For Richard Wright." Negro Digest, 18 (January), 85.
Poem paying tribute to the emotional and intellectual power of NS.
Reprinted: 1970.5.

111. Gilman, Richard. "White Standards and Negro Writing," in The Black American Writer. Ed. C. W. E. Bigsby. Vol. I. DeLand, Fla.: Everett/Edwards, pp. 35-49.
Reprint of 1968.115.

112. _____. "White Standards and Negro Writing." Negro American Literature Forum, 3 (Winter), 111-116.
Reprint of 1968.115.

113. Gloster, Hugh M. "Race and the Negro Writer," in Black Expression: Essays by and About Black Americans in the Creative Arts. Ed. Addison Gayle, Jr. New York: Weybright and Talley, pp. 255-258.
Reprint of 1950.154.

114. Greenlee, Sam. "Report on Black Theater: Chicago." Negro Digest, 18 (April), 23-24.
Mentions W in connection with Theo-dore Ward and the Negro Playwrights Company.

115. Gross, Robert A. "The Black Novelists: 'Our Turn.'" Newsweek, 73 (16 June), 94, 96B, 98, 100.
Mentions W as one of the older black novelists who have "long been recognized as important figures."

116. Gross, Theodore L. "The Idealism of Negro Literature in America." Phylon, 30 (Spring), 5-10.
Argues that since black writers are intensely aware of history and politics, they tend to be more complex in their treatment of these areas than white writers. W is a case in point. His treatment of historical, political, and racial themes in EM, UTC, O, and LD is almost Gothic in its complexity.

117. _____. "Our Mutual Estate: The Literature of the American Negro," in The Black American Writer. Ed. C. W. E. Bigsby. Vol. 1. DeLand, Fla.: Everett/Edwards, pp. 51-61.
Reprint of 1968.120.

118. H. "The Art of Richard Wright." Long Beach Independent-Press-Telegram.
Notice of the Margolies book emphasizing W's importance in the development of Afro-American literature.

119. Haas, Joseph. "Best of the Paperbacks." Chicago Daily News (15 February), Panorama Sec., p. 11.
Mentions an excerpt from BB in Gerald Leinwald's The Negro in the City.

120. Hagopian, John V. "Negro American Authors." Contemporary Literature, 10 (Summer), 416-420.
Review of Edward Margolies's Native Sons with comments on NS.

121. Harris, Janet and Julius Hobson. Black Pride: A People's Struggle. New York: McGraw-Hill, pp. 105, 156.
Mentions W and lists BB.

122. Haslam, Gerald W. "Two Traditions in Afro-American Literature." Research Studies (Washington State University), 37 (September), 183-193.
W was the product of the oral and written traditions, becoming "the most influential single figure in all American Negro literature." He transcended naturalism through his use of symbols "rooted in the most clandestine corners of the Afro-American psyche."

123. Henderson, David. "The Man Who Cried I Am: A Critique," in Black Ex-

pression: Essays by and About Black Americans in the Creative Arts. Ed. Addison Gayle, Jr. New York: Weybright and Talley, pp. 365-371.
Identifies the character Harry Ames as W.

124. Henderson, Stephen E. "'Survival Motion': A Study of the Black Writer and the Black Revolution in America," in The Militant Black Writer in Africa and the United States. By Mercer Cook and Stephen E. Henderson. Madison: University of Wisconsin Press, pp. 63-129.
Includes brief discussion of "How 'Bigger' Was Born" (p. 99).

125. Hernton, Calvin C. "Dynamite Growing Out of Their Skulls," in Black Fire: An Anthology of Afro-American Writing. Ed. LeRoi Jones and Larry Neal. Apollo Editions A-220. New York: William Morrow, pp. 78-104.
Reprint of 1968.124.

126. Hicks, Granville. "Literary Horizons." Saturday Review, 52 (5 April), 34.
Review of Nelson Manfred Blake's Novelists' America mentioning W.

127. Huberman, Edward. "Minireviews." The CEA Critic, 32 (November), 10.
Contains a notice of Robert Bone's Richard Wright.

128. _____. "Minireviews: Something for Almost Everybody." The CEA Critic, 31 (May), 6.
Contains a favorable notice of Edward Margolies's The Art of Richard Wright.

129. Jackson, Blyden. "Richard Wright: Black Boy from America's Black Belt and Urban Ghettos." CLA Journal, 12 (June), 287-309.
The first chapter of a proposed biography of W, this essay discusses the significant facts his life. Jackson emphasizes the lasting effects of W's identification with the Black cultures of Mississippi and Chicago.
Reprinted: 1976.104b.

130. Jarab, Josef. "The Drop of Patience of the American Negro." Philologica Pragensia, 12, No. 3, 159-170.
Mentions W briefly.

131. Jones, Harry L. "The Art of Richard Wright. By Edward Margolies." CLA Journal, 12 (June), 373-375.
Favorable review in the main. Expresses reservations about Margolies's style and his lack of attention to existentialism and to folklore.

132. Jones, Howard Mumford. "Violence and the Humanist," in his Violence and Reason. New York: Atheneum, pp. 17-39.
Reprint of 1967.64a.

133. Jones, LeRoi. "The Myth of a 'Negro Literature,'" in Black Expression: Essays by and About Black Americans in the Creative Arts. Ed. Addison Gayle, Jr. New York: Weybright and Talley, pp. 190-197.
Reprint of 1963.121.

134. _____. "That Mighty Flight," in his Black Magic. Indianapolis: Bobbs-Merrill, p. 161.
A poem attributing prophetic powers to Bigger Thomas in NS.

135. Jordan, June. "Black Studies: Bringing Back the Person." Evergreen Review, 13 (October), 39-41, 71-72.
Cites Bigger Thomas as an example of violence as a possible means of black liberation.
Reprinted: 1971.188.

135a. Kaiser, Ernest. "The Literature of Harlem," in Black Expression: Essays by and About Black Americans in the Creative Arts. Ed. Addison Gayle, Jr. New York: Weybright and Talley, pp. 239-255.
Reprint of 1963.122.

136. _____. "Margolies, Edward. The Art of Richard Wright." Freedomways, 9 (Spring), 187.
Brief notice.

137. _____. "Recent Literature on Black Liberation Struggles and the Ghetto Crisis (A Bibliographical Survey)." Science & Society, 33 (Spring), 168-196.
Mentions BP (p. 173) and "The Literature of the Negro in the United States" (p. 193).

138. Kakonis, Thomas E. and Barbara G. T. Desmarais, eds. The Literary Artist as Social Critic. Beverly Hills, Cal.: Glencoe Press, pp. [i], 350, 379, 381.
The editors briefly compare BB to William Blake's "The Little Black Boy," provide a headnote to an excerpt from BB, include a study question on the excerpt, and list NS and UTC among "Suggestions for Further Reading."

139. Kazin, Alfred et al. "The Negro in American Culture," in his The Black American Writer. Ed. C. W. E. Bigsby. Vol. 1. DeLand, Fla.: Everett/Edwards, pp. 79-108.
Reprint of 1961.189.

140. Kent, George E. "On the Future Study of Richard Wright." CLA Journal,

12 (June), 366-370.
Suggests directions for scholarly and critical inquiry under the following categories: biography and bibliography, collected works and other collections, full-length studies, and the briefer essay or monograph. Reprinted: 1972.114.

141. _____. "Richard Wright: Blackness and the Adventure of Western Culture." CLA Journal, 12 (June), 322-343.
Explores "three sources of Wright's power: his double-consciousness, his personal tension, and his dramatic articulation of black and white culture" in the major works of the author's American phase: BB, UTC, LT, and NS.
Reprinted: 1971.147, 196; 1972.117.
Partially reprinted: 1972.27.

142. Kilgore, James C. "The Case for Black Literature." Negro Digest, 18 (July), 22-25, 66-69.
Mentions W briefly.

142a. Killens, John Oliver. "The Writer and Black Liberation," in In Black America: 1968: The Year of Awakening. Ed. Patricia W. Romero. A Pioneer Paperback. Washington, D. C.: United Publishing Corporation, pp. 265-271.
Mentions briefly W and NS.

143. King, Woodie, Jr. "A Poet of the Black Theater." Negro Digest, 18 (April), 27-32, 95-96.
Mentions W briefly.

144. Kinnamon, Keneth. "Native Son: The Personal, Social, and Political Background." Phylon, 30 (Spring), 66-72.
Analyzes the genesis of the novel in episodes of W's life in Mississippi and Chicago, his knowledge of the urban ecology of the South Side, the Nixon trial, and Communist doctrine. "The nice balance of subjective and objective elements in Native Son prevents the work from becoming either a purely personal scream of pain on the one hand, or a mere ideological tract on the other" (p. 72).
Reprinted: 1970.5; 1971.147; 1982.83.
Reprinted in revised form: 1972.123.

145. _____. "The Pastoral Impulse in Richard Wright." Midcontinent American Studies Journal, 10 (Spring), 41-47.
Examines W's use of "a retrospective rural nostalgia from the vantage point of the author's urban present" in LT and UTC. W uses the tranquility of Southern rural scenes to contrast with the racial violence occurring in them, but his pastoral nostalgia is a genuine and deeply felt emotion.

Reprinted: 1971.147.
Partially reprinted in revised form: 1972.123.

146. _____. "Richard Wright: A Biography. By Constance Webb." American Literature, 40 (January), 575-576.
Unfavorable review complaining of subjectivity, poor organization, factual errors, and simplistic criticism.

147. _____. "Richard Wright: Proletarian Poet." Concerning Poetry, 2 (Spring), 39-50.
Analyzes W's early poetry for its intrinsic interest and "as an instructive example of some of the problems and opportunities faced by a young writer deeply committed to the ideological left" (p. 39). Kinnamon considers "Between the World and Me" to be W's best early poem.
Reprinted: 1971.147; 1982.84.
Partially reprinted in revised form: 1972.123.

148. _____. "Richard Wright's Use of Othello in Native Son." CLA Journal, 12 (June), 358-359.
Argues that W established parallels with Othello, especially concerning race and sex, in designing his novel. "Stated bluntly, Bigger Thomas is Othello to Mary Dalton's Desdemona," and Buckley "is a treacherous Iago."

149. Knowles, A. S., Jr. "Six Bronze Petals and Two Red: Carson McCullers in the Forties," in The Forties: Fiction, Poetry, Drama. Ed. Warren French. DeLand, Fla.: Everett/Edwards, pp. 87-98.
Mentions favorably W's review of The Heart Is a Lonely Hunter.

150. Kostelanetz, Richard. "The Politics of Unresolved Quests in the Novels of Richard Wright." Xavier University Studies, 8 (Spring), 31-64.
Examines W's fictional themes and the relation of his works of fiction to each other, finding that he "consistently, but unsystematically, undercuts the political alternatives espoused in earlier works. If both UTC and BB favored emigration from the South to the North, both LT and NS showed how dreadful life in Chicago could be for a Southern-born Negro. If NS and, to a lesser extent, UTC dramatized that the Communists could be a Negro's truest friend among the whites, I Tried to Be a Communist and O described the Communists as exploiters of Negro hopes. If LD implicitly advised the Southern

Negro to go to Europe, then the unfinished novel portrayed him as lost
in an alien culture" (p. 63). Nevertheless, an overriding theme does
emerge--"the utter horror of living
with no purpose at all" (p. 63).
Reprinted: 1971.147.

151. Krim, Seymour. "The American Novel
Made Us." Playboy, 16 (June), 121, 124,
202, 204, 206, 208, 211.
    Mentions W briefly (p. 121).
    Reprinted: 1970.238.

152. Kubbel', F. L. and L. M.
Eidel'kind. "Predislovie," in their Deti
diadi Toma. By Richard Wright. Leningrad: Izdatel'stvo "Prosveshchenie," pp.
3-4.
    Introduction to the English language
    Russian edition of UTC. States that a
    dramatic adaptation of "Bright and
    Morning Star" (entitled "Faraway
    Brothers") was staged in the Soviet
    Union in 1940. Sketches W's life as a
    worker and his early literary career.
    Growing out of a radical vision and
    repudiating the somewhat subservient
    posture of Uncle Tom, the stories in
    UTC depict blacks demanding their
    rights. Comments on all the stories
    except "Long Black Song," praising
    their literary qualities and their
    identification with the people.

153. Laker, J. H. C. [?] "The Art of
Richard Wright." Unidentified clipping
(11 July).
    Notice of Edward Margolies's book.
    Reprinted: 1969.154.

154. _____. "The Art of Richard Wright."
Unidentified clipping (19 September).
    Reprint of 1969.153.

155. Larson, Charles R. "African-Afro-
American Literary Relations: Basic
Parallels." Negro Digest, 19 (December),
35-42.
    Mentions W briefly (p. 41).

156. Lee, Don L. "The Measure and Meaning of the Sixties." Negro Digest, 19
(November), 11-14.
    Contains a brief reference to Bigger
    Thomas.

157. _____. "Understanding But Not For-
getting (for the Non-Colored of the
World)," in his Think Black. Detroit:
Broadside Press, pp. 12-14.
    Poem mentioning that the poet's
    mother read W and Himes.
    Reprinted: 1971.211.

157a. Lehan, Richard D. "Fiction: The
1930's to the Present," in American
Literary Scholarship: An Annual/1967.

Ed. James Woodress. Durham, N. C.: Duke
University Press, pp. 190-209.
    Mentions W briefly in connection with
    Baldwin.

157b. Leibson, Paula. "Just Browsing."
The El Paso Times (9 November), Sundial
Sunday Magazine Sec., p. 17.
    Contains a notice of the Harper re-
    prints of UTC, BB, NS, and O.

158. Lester, Julius. "Not in Memory of
Robert Kennedy," in his Revolutionary
Notes. New York: Richard W. Baron, pp.
112-115.
    Reprint of 1968.152a.

159. Libman, Valentina. Russian Studies
of American Literature. Trans. Robert V.
Allen. Ed. Clarence Gohdes. Chapel Hill:
University of North Carolina Press, pp.
33, 213-214.
    Lists twenty-one secondary items on
    W, mostly on UTC and NS.

159a. Lipton, Lawrence. "The Barbarian
Is at the Gates," in The American Novel
Since World War II. Ed. Marcus Klein.
Greenwich, Conn.: Fawcett, pp. 177-185.
    Reprint of 1959.112a.

160. Littlejohn, David. Black on White:
A Critical Survey of Writing by American
Negroes. Compass Edition. New York:
Viking, pp. 4, 8, 9, 10, 15, 17, 18, 21,
33, 37, 54, 62, 65, 67, 80n, 83-84, 86-
89, 101, 102-110, 120-121, 127, 138,
141, 142, 144, 161, 166, 170.
    Reprint of 1966.97.

161. Llorens, David. "Ameer (LeRoi
Jones) Baraka." Ebony, 24 (August), 75-
78, 80-83.
    Mentions W briefly.

162. Lynn, Kenneth S. "Violence in Amer-
ican Literature and Folk Lore," in The
History of Violence in America: Histori-
cal and Comparative Perspectives. Ed.
Hugh Davis and Ted Robert Gurr. A Report
Submitted to the National Commission on
the Causes and Prevention of Violence.
New York: Praeger, pp. 226-242.
    Reprint of 1969.164.

163. _____. "Violence in American Liter-
ature and Folk Lore," in Violence in
America: Historical and Comparative Per-
spectives. Ed. Hugh Davis Graham and Ted
Robert Gurr. A Report Submitted to the
National Commission on the Causes and
Prevention of Violence. New York: Bantam
Books, pp. 226-242.
    Reprint of 1969.164.

164. _____. "Violence in American Literature and Folk Lore," in Violence in
America: Historical and Comparative Per-

spectives. Ed. Hugh Davis Graham and Ted Robert Gurr. A Report Submitted to the National Commission on the Causes and Prevention of Violence. Vol. 1. Washington: United States Government Printing Office, pp. 181-191.
> The penultimate paragraph treats NS, an "implacable novel" of interracial violence and hostility.
> Reprinted: 1969.162, 163; 1973.214.

165. Major, Clarence. All-Night Visitors. New York: The Olympia Press, p. 169.
> Near the end of this novel the protagonist reads a book by W, "the black master writer who saw the human condition as a poet."

166. Mangione, Jerre. "Speaking of Books: Federal Writers' Project." The New York Times Book Review (18 May), pp. 2, 32.
> Mentions W briefly.

167. Margolies, Edward. The Art of Richard Wright. Crosscurrents Modern Critiques, ed. Harry T. Moore. Carbondale and Edwardsville: Southern Illinois University Press, 180 pp.
> After an introductory chapter on W's life and works, Margolies devotes three chapters to the nonfiction and five to the fiction. The point of view inclines more to W's existentialism and universalism than to his protest and radicalism. Margolies frequently disparages W's Marxism. He examines W's use of the concept of the outsider as an analytical tool that led to incisive, even prophetic insights, despite or perhaps because of its extreme subjectivity. Margolies includes notes and a brief selected bibliography of fifteen primary and two secondary sources. Harry T. Moore contributes a preface.
> Partially reprinted: 1971.147; 1982. 96.

168. _____. Native Sons: A Critical Study of Twentieth-Century Negro American Authors. Paperback edition. Philadelphia: Lippincott, pp. 19-20, 22, 33-34, 44, 48, 50, 65-86, 87, 91, 192, 197, 198.
> Reprint of 1968.160.

169. _____. "Soul on Ice. By Eldridge Cleaver." The Michigan Quarterly Review, 8 (January), 68-69.
> Comments on Cleaver's admiration of W.

170. Marshall, Carol and John A. Myers, Jr. "Pictures in the Mind's Eye," in their Designs for Reading: Poems. Boston: Houghton Mifflin, pp. 73-94.
> Includes brief comments on haiku, with three of W's as examples.

171. Mason, Philip. "The Revolt Against Western Values," in Color and Race. Ed. John Hope Franklin. Boston: Beacon Press, pp. 50-74.
> Reprint of 1968.161.

172. McCall, Dan. The Example of Richard Wright. New York: Harcourt, Brace & World, 202 pp.
> Sketches W's career, analyzes his major work, and assesses favorably his importance as writer and social critic. McCall finds the confrontation with racism to be W's main subject. He deplores W's association with Communism, which he believes intensified the violence of W's prose. In violation of his signed pledge, McCall made extensive unauthorized and unacknowledged use of Keneth Kinnamon's 1966 dissertation on W. See 1971.202, 203, 219.
> Partially reprinted: 1970.5; 1971. 147.

173. Meyer, Howard N. "Preface," in Let Me Live. By Angelo Herndon. New York: Arno Press, pp. iii-x.
> Concedes that Herndon's autobiography "may lack, as literature, the poetry and passion" (p. v) of BB.

174. Mitchell, Loften. "The Negro Theatre and the Harlem Community," in Anthology of the American Negro in the Theatre: A Critical Approach. Ed. Lindsay Patterson. New York: Publishers Company, pp. 177-184.
> Reprint of 1963.142.

175. _____. "The Negro Theatre and the Harlem Community," in Black Expression: Essays by and About Black Americans in the Creative Arts. Ed. Addison Gayle, Jr. New York: Weybright and Talley, pp. 82-89.
> Reprint of 1963.142.

176. Mitra, B. K. "The Wright-Baldwin Controversy." Indian Journal of American Studies, 1 (July), 101-105.
> Emphasizes W as a novelist of unrestrained rage and Baldwin as a novelist of artistically controlled anger. Reviews the W-Baldwin relationship and traces Baldwin's references to W in his essays.

177. Moore, Harry T. "Preface," in The Art of Richard Wright. By Edward Margolies. Crosscurrents Modern Critiques, ed. Harry T. Moore. Carbondale and Edwardsville: Southern Illinois University Press, pp. v-vi.
> Describes Margolies's book with em-

phasis on its timeliness and judi-
ciousness.

178. Moore, Robert H. "Constance Webb,
Richard Wright: A Biography." American
Quarterly, 21 (Summer), 406.
    Mixed review. Despite flaws in
    scholarship and perspective, the work
    is valuable in correcting neglect of
    W and in providing much new infor-
    mation.

179. Myrdal, Gunnar. An American
Dilemma: The Negro Problem and Modern
Democracy. 2 vols. Harper Torchbooks TB
1443. New York: Harper & Row, pp. 656,
734, 735, 936, 989, 992.
    Reprint of 1944.127.

180. Nagel, James. "Images of 'Vision'
in Native Son." University Review, 36
(December), 109-115.
    Examines the work as a novel of per-
    ception relying heavily on the image-
    ry of vision. Both plot and point of
    view depend on the extensive develop-
    ment of this pattern of images.
    Reprinted: 1971.147; 1982.107.

181. Neal, Larry. "And Shine Swam On,"
in Black Fire: An Anthology of Afro-
American Writing. Ed. LeRoi Jones and
Larry Neal. Apollo Editions A-220. New
York: William Morrow, pp. 638-656.
    Reprint of 1968.171.

182. _____. "Any Day Now: Black Art and
Black Liberation." Ebony, 24 (August),
54-58, 62.
    Mentions W briefly (p. 56).

183. _____. "The Black Writer's Role:
Richard Wright," in Afro-Arts Anthology.
Newark: Jihad Productions, pp. [7-13].
    Reprint of 1966.110.

184. _____. "Sinner Man Where You Gonna
Run To?" in Black Fire: An Anthology of
Afro-American Writing. Ed. LeRoi Jones
and Larry Neal. Apollo Editions A-220.
New York: William Morrow, pp. 510-518.
    Reprint of 1968.172.

185. Nin, Anaïs. The Diary of Anaïs Nin
1939-1944. Ed. Gunther Stuhlmann. New
York: Harcourt, Brace & World, pp. 279,
281.
    Nin mentions her friendship with
    Richard and Ellen Wright during their
    residence in the "February House" in
    Brooklyn and gives accounts of par-
    ties which the Wrights attended.
    "Richard Wright is handsome, quiet,
    simple, direct. His speech is beauti-
    ful, modulated and smooth. His ideas
    clear." She includes comments by
    W on the situation of the American
    writer.

186. Norman, Dorothy. The Hero: Myth/
Image/Symbol. New York and Cleveland:
World Publishing Company, pp. 172-174.
    Quotes from the end of BB with a
    brief comment.

187. North, Joseph. "Prologue," in his
New Masses: An Anthology of the Rebel
Thirties. New York: International Pub-
lishers, pp. 19-33.
    Mentions publication of W's first
    poem in order to encourage a young
    black writer (p. 31).

188. Nower, Joyce. "The Traditions of
Negro Literature in the United States."
Negro American Literature Forum, 3
(Spring), 5-12.
    Comments on the themes of violence
    and loss of identity in NS.

188a. Ohashi, Kenzaburo. "Humor and an
Overwhelming Sense of Dissociation."
Gungo, 24 (June), 318-320.
    "The Man Who Went to Chicago" is
    autobiographical, and the tension
    created in the story is greater than
    that of fiction. Although the collec-
    tion exhibits W's talent and range of
    social criticism, it falls short of
    an artistic achievement and suffers,
    as does Baldwin's writing, from "an
    overwhelming sense of dissociation."
    [Y. H. and T. K.]

189. Olson, Ivan. "A Critic Examines
Works of Richard Wright." The Fresno Bee
(16 March), p. 6-C.
    Review of Edward Margolies's The Art
    of Richard Wright focusing on its
    treatment of the fluctuations of W's
    reputation, which declined before his
    death. Disfavor with the protest mode
    and reaction against W's radicalism
    led to the decline, but his fame will
    now increase.

190. Oster, Harry. "The Afro-American
Folktale in Memphis: Theme and Function." Negro American Literature Forum,
3 (Fall), 83-87.
    Mentions W briefly (p. 84).

191. Ozawa, Fumio. "Richard Wright--
Sayoku tono Seshoku to Ridatsu"
["Richard Wright and the Left Wing:
Contact and Detachment"]. Showa Joshi
Daigaku Gakuen [Showa Women's College
Instruction], No. 352 (April), 126-
133.
    States that W joined the Communist
    Party because he had found an affi-
    nity between workers and blacks. He
    left the Party when he became con-
    vinced that it was not concerned with
    the liberation of the blacks. Con-
    siders W's attitude toward Communism
    too idealistic; as war grew intense

he became disillusioned with Communist politics. Argues that his leaving the Party does not mean his departure from Communist doctrine.
[Y. H.]

192. Patterson, Lindsay. "Introduction,"
in his An Introduction to Black Literature in America from 1746 to the Present. International Library of Negro
Life and History. New York: Publishers
Company, p. [101].
    In this introduction to the twen-
    tieth-century section of his antho-
    logy, Patterson emphasizes W's impact
    and influence.

193. _____. "Introduction," in his An
Introduction to Black Literature in
America from 1746 to the Present. International Library of Negro Life and History. New York: Publishers Company, p.
xvii.
    Mentions W's political activity as a
    means of coping with his alienation
    as a black man.

194. Piccioni, Leone. "1962: Popolo nel
popolo," in his Troppa morte, troppa
vita: viaggi e pensieri intorno agli
USA. Firenze: Vallecchi Editore, pp.
167-199.
    Mentions briefly W's communism (p.
    193).

195. Pinkney, Alphonso. Black Americans.
Englewood Cliffs, N. J.: Prentice-Hall,
pp. 149-150.
    Comments briefly on W in a chapter
    entitled "Contributions to American
    Life."

195a. Pirie, James W. Books for Junior
College Libraries. Chicago: American
Library Association, pp. 67, 213.
    Lists WML, BB, and NS.

196. Price, E. Curmie. "The Ballad of
Bigger Thomas." Negro Digest, 18
(April), 48.
    A poem on violence in NS and its
    relation to existentialism.
    Reprinted: 1970.5.

197. Quantic, Diane Dufva. "Black
Authors in Kansas." Kansas English, 55
(December), 14-17.
    Mentions W briefly (p. 16).

198. Quarles, Benjamin. The Negro in the
Making of America. Revised edition. New
York: Collier Books, pp. 248-249.
    Reprint of 1964.105.

198a. Rahv, Philip. "Notes on the De-
cline of Naturalism," in The American
Novel Since World War II. Ed. Marcus
Klein. Greenwich, Conn.: Fawcett, pp.

27-38.
    Reprint of 1952.61.

199. Record, Wilson. "The Negro Writer
and the Communist Party," in The Black
American Writer. Ed. C. W. E. Bigsby.
Vol. 1. DeLand, Fla.: Everett/Edwards,
pp. 217-228.
    Contains several brief references to
    W.

200. Redding, Saunders. "Absorption with
Blackness Recalls Movement of '20s." The
Washington Sunday Star (25 May), p. E-3.
    Mentions briefly Dan McCall's The
    Example of Richard Wright and in-
    cludes a photograph of W.

201. _____. "American Negro Literature,"
in Black American Literature: Essays.
Ed. Darwin T. Turner. Charles E. Merrill
Literary Texts, ed. Matthew J. Bruccoli
and Joseph Katz. Columbus, Ohio: Charles
E. Merrill, pp. 91-102.
    Reprint of 1949.140.

202. _____. "American Negro Literature,"
in Black Expression: Essays by and About
Black Americans in the Creative Arts.
Ed. Addison Gayle, Jr. New York: Weybright and Talley, pp. 229-239.
    Reprint of 1949.140.

203. _____. "The Negro Writer and His
Relationship to His Roots," in An Introduction to Black Literature in America
from 1746 to the Present. Ed. Lindsay
Patterson. International Library of
Negro Life and History. New York: Publishers Company, pp. 287-290.
    Reprint of 1960.222.

204. _____. "The Problems of the Negro
Writer," in Black & White in American
Culture: An Anthology from The Massa-
chusetts Review. Ed. Jules Chametzky and
Sidney Kaplan. Amherst: The University
of Massachusetts Press, pp. 360-371.
    Reprint of 1964.107.

205. _____. They Came in Chains: Americans from Africa. Philadelphia: Lippincott, pp. 279, 288.
    Reprint of 1950.207.

206. Rees, Robert A. and Barry Menikoff.
"Richard Wright," in their The Short
Story: An Introductory Anthology. Bos-
ton: Little Brown, p. 165.
    Biographical headnote to "The Man Who
    Lived Underground."
    Reprinted: 1975.157.

207. _____. "Study Questions," in their
The Short Story: An Introductory Anthology. Boston: Little, Brown, p. 214.
    To accompany "The Man Who Lived
    Underground."

Reprinted: 1975.157.

208. Reeves, Paschal et al. "A Checklist of Scholarship on Southern Literature for 1968." Mississippi Quarterly, 22 (Spring), 155-180.
Lists two items on W (p. 176).

209. Rehder, Jessie and Wallace Kaufman. "Questions," in their The Act of Writing. New York: Odyssey, p. 177.
To accompany an excerpt from TMBV. Emphasizes W's use of repetition.

210. Robinson, Wilhelmena S. "Wright, Richard," in her Historical Negro Biographies. International Library of Negro Life and History. New York: Publishers Company, pp. 265-266.
Biographical sketch emphasizing W's early life. Includes a photograph. Reprinted: 1976.161.

211. Rodgers, Carolyn M. "Black Poetry-- Where It's At." Negro Digest, 18 (September), 7-16.
Includes comments on W's signifying (pp. 14, 15).
Reprinted: 1972.176.

212. Rodnon, Stewart. "Ralph Ellison's Invisible Man: Six Tentative Approaches." CLA Journal, 12 (March), 244-256.
Discourages comparison of Ellison's novel to the inferior works of W and Baldwin (p. 255).
Reprinted: 1971.262.

213. Rowell, Charles H. "A Bibliography of Bibliographies for the Study of Black American Literature and Folklore." Black Experience: A Southern University Journal (Bulletin Southern University and A. & M. College), 60 (June), 95-111.
Lists four items on W (p. 106).

214. Rubin, Steven Joel. "Richard Wright and Ralph Ellison: Black Existential Attitudes." Dissertation Abstracts International, 30, p. 2041A.
Argues that W's concern with existential themes and problems reflects his own experience more than the direct influence of Sartre, Malraux, or Camus. Although O, written during the time of W's friendship with Sartre, attempts to incorporate directly the French writer's philosophy, similar themes had been present throughout W's work.

215. Saal, Rollene W. "Pick of the Paperbacks." Saturday Review, 52 (25 October), 42-43.
Contains a brief notice of paperback reprints of LT and LD.

215a. Saito, Tadatoshi. "The Birth of Bigger Thomas: Notes on Native Son." Hitotsubashi Ronshu [Hitotsubashi Treatises], 62 (1 November), 598-603.
Argues on the basis of "How 'Bigger' Was Born" that his problems are not only his own but those of the entire nation. Though alienated and deprived of his birthright, Bigger is a genuine native son. [Y. H. and T. K.]

215b. Sakamoto, Masayuki. "The Mechanics of Fear: Richard Wright's Native Son." Kikan Eibungaku [English Literature Quarterly], 6 (Spring), 166-181.
Bigger's murder of Mary is caused by his sensibility, in which fear dominates. The fear creates tension between the outside world and his inner world, where he even excludes black people; consequently he has no alternative but to murder Mary [Y. H. and T. K.]

216. Salsini, Barbara. "A Double Winner Leads Off a Fertile Paperback Month." The Milwaukee Journal (4 May), Part 5, p. 4.
Mentions W as a contributor to Langston Hughes's anthology The Best Short Stories by Negro Writers.

217. Schulberg, Budd. "Introduction," in his From the Ashes: Voices of Watts. Meridian M272. Cleveland: The World Publishing Company, pp. 1-24.
Reprint of 1967.93.

218. Scott, Nathan A., Jr. "The Dark and Haunted Tower of Richard Wright," in Black Expression: Essays by and About Black Americans in the Creative Arts. Ed. Addison Gayle, Jr. New York: Weybright and Talley, pp. 296-311.
Reprint of 1964.113.

219. _____. "Judgment Marked by a Cellar: The American Negro Writer and the Dialectic of Despair," in The Shapeless God: Essays on Modern Fiction. Ed. Harry J. Mooney, Jr., and Thomas F. Staley. Pittsburgh: University of Pittsburgh Press, pp. 139-169.
Reprint of 1967.94.

220. Scruggs, Otey M. "Why Study Afro-American History?" in Seven on Black: Reflections on the Negro Experience in America. Ed. William G. Shade and Roy C. Herrenkohl. Philadelphia: Lippincott, pp. 9-23.
Quotes approvingly a passage from WML on the value of the black American's quest for freedom (p. 22).

221. Singh, Raman K. "Some Basic Ideas and Ideals in Richard Wright's Fiction." CLA Journal, 13 (September), 78-

84.
     Argues that W's Marxism continued to
     influence his thought even after he
     withdrew from the Communist Party.
     Christianity is also an important
     element. Singh analyzes NS and O to
     emphasize these two elements. He
     argues that ideology enabled W to
     transcend racial issues.

222. Smith, Gloria. A Slice of Black
Americana: A Regional Survey of History,
A Chronology of Publications from 1746
to 1940, A Survey of Literary Genres for
Teachers or Students of Literature and
History. Champaign, Ill.: Privately
printed, pp. 23, 28, 29, 31, 32.
     Comments briefly on W.

223. Smith, William Gardner. "The Negro
Writer: Pitfalls and Compensations," in
Black Expression: Essays by and About
Black Americans in the Creative Arts.
Ed. Addison Gayle, Jr. New York: Wey-
bright and Talley, pp. 288-295.
     Reprint of 1950.225.

224. _____. "The Negro Writer: Pitfalls
and Compensations," in The Black American Writer. Ed. C. W. E. Bigsby. Vol. I.
DeLand, Fla.: Everett/Edwards, pp. 71-
78.
     Reprint of 1950.225.

225. Sofian, Naid. "SR's Check List of
the Week's New Books." Saturday Review,
52 (8 March), 10.
     Lists The Art of Richard Wright by
     Edward Margolies.

226. Stanton, Robert. "Outrageous Fiction: Crime and Punishment, The Assistant, and Native Son." Pacific Coast
Philology, 4, pp. 52-58.
     Argues that close similarities of
     plot and theme relate NS to Crime and
     Punishment. W's work explores and
     extends some of Dostoevsky's most
     "outrageous" ideas, especially the
     notion that society can deprive a
     person of selfhood, which can then be
     recovered only through revolt.

227. Talbot, William. "Every Negro in
His Place: The Scene on and off Broad-
way," in Anthology of the American Negro
in the Theatre: A Critical Approach. Ed.
Lindsay Patterson. New York: Publishers
Company, pp. 207-211.
     Reprint of 1964.121.

228. Tischler, Nancy M. Black Masks:
Negro Characters in Modern Southern
Fiction. University Park: The Pennsylvania State University Press, pp. 20,
25, 26, 54, 59, 60, 61, 106, 111, 115,
116, 127, 129, 133, 134, 144, 161, 163-
164, 169, 172, 180, 183, 189.

     Brief comments on W's characters and
     other matters.

229. _____. "Negro Literature and Classic Form." Contemporary Literature, 10
(Summer), 352-365.
     Mentions W.

230. Toppin, Edgar Allan. "Negro," in
The World Book Encyclopedia. Ed. William
H. Nault. Vol. 14. Chicago: Field Enter-
prises, pp. 106-112e.
     Mentions W briefly (p. 112).
     Reprinted: 1975.194; 1977.323; 1979.
     265

231. Turner, Darwin T. "The Black Playwright in the Professional Theatre of
the United States of America 1858-1959,"
in The Black American Writer. Ed.
C. W. E. Bigsby. Vol. 2. DeLand, Fla.:
Everett/Edwards, pp. 113-128.
     Includes a discussion of NS relating
     the plot and analyzing the differen-
     ces between the play and the novel.
     In the play "Bigger was humanized,"
     thus changing the theme of social
     determinism.
     Reprinted: 1970.338; 1971.299.
     Partially reprinted: 1970.343.

232. _____. "Collections of Stories by
Individual Authors," in his Black Ameri-
can Literature: Fiction. Charles E.
Merrill Literary Texts, ed. Matthew J.
Bruccoli and Joseph Katz. Columbus,
Ohio: Charles E. Merrill, p. 142.
     Lists EM and UTC.
     Reprinted: 1970.339.

233. _____. "Dark Symphony: Negro Liter-
ature in America. Edited by James A.
Emanuel and Theodore L. Gross." CLA
Journal, 12 (June), 375-377.
     Mentions W briefly.

234. _____. "Introduction," in his Black
American Literature: Essays. Charles E.
Merrill Literary Texts, ed. Matthew J.
Bruccoli and Joseph Katz. Columbus,
Ohio: Charles E. Merrill, pp. 1-8.
     Mentions "The Ethics of Living Jim
     Crow" (p. 6) and WML (p. 7).
     Reprinted: 1970.340.

235. _____. "Introduction," in his Black
American Literature: Fiction. Charles E.
Merrill Literary Texts, ed. Matthew J.
Bruccoli and Joseph Katz. Columbus,
Ohio: Charles E. Merrill, p. 1-6.
     Contains a paragraph on W (p. 5) and
     mentions him elsewhere.
     Reprinted: 1970.342.

236. _____. "Introduction," in his Black
American Literature: Poetry. Charles E.
Merrill Literary Texts, ed. Matthew J.
Bruccoli and Joseph Katz. Columbus,

Ohio: Charles E. Merrill, pp. 1-8.
Discusses briefly W's importance in
demonstrating that literary craft
must be applied to protest themes.
Reprinted: 1970.341.

237. _____. "Native Sons." Negro Digest,
18 (February), 51-52, 68.
Review of the book by Edward Margolies mentioning W.

238. _____. "The Negro Dramatist's Image
of the Universe, 1920-1960," in Anthology of the American Negro in the Theatre: A Critical Approach. Ed. Lindsay
Patterson. New York: Publishers Company,
pp. 65-74.
Reprint of 1961.274.

239. _____. "The Outsider: Revision of
an Idea." CLA Journal, 12 (June), 310-
321.
Compares NS and O noting similarities
in plot, structure, characterization,
and theme. In both novels the individual is destroyed by organized institutions. O is more intellectually
persuasive, but NS is more successful
emotionally and artistically.
Reprinted: 1970.345; 1971.147.

240. _____. "Richard Wright (1908-
1960)," in his Black American Litera-
ture: Fiction. Charles E. Merrill Liter-
ary Texts, ed. Matthew J. Bruccoli and
Joseph Katz. Columbus, Ohio: Charles E.
Merrill, pp. 71-72.
Biographical headnote to accompany
"The Man Who Was Almost a Man."
Reprinted: 1970.346.

241. _____. "Significant Collections of
Essays by Individual Black Writers," in
his Black American Literature: Essays.
Charles E. Merrill Literary Texts, ed.
Matthew J. Bruccoli and Joseph Katz.
Columbus, Ohio: Charles E. Merrill, p.
153.
Lists WML.

242. Tuttleton, James W. "The Negro
Writer as Spokesman," in The Black American Writer. Ed. C. W. E. Bigsby. Vol.
I. DeLand, Fla.: Everett/Edwards, pp.
245-259.
Argues that since as a spokesman the
black writer represents the dilemma
of black people in a racist society,
he must reconcile the conflicting
claims of propaganda and art. W exemplifies the problem. In this context,
Tuttleton discusses NS and the W-
Baldwin controversy.
Reprinted: 1971.304.

243. Vince, Thomas L. "McCall, Dan. The
Example of Richard Wright. Margolies,
Edward. The Art of Richard Wright."

Library Journal, 94 (1 April), 1500.
Favorable review of the two books.
McCall emphasizes NS and BB; Margolies discusses also the minor
works. McCall stresses protest; Margolies focuses on W's art.

244. Webb, Constance. "Wright, Richard
Nathaniel," in Collier's Encyclopedia.
Ed. Louis Shores. Vol. 23. New York:
Crowell-Collier Educational Corporation,
p. 638.
Biographical sketch.
Reprinted: 1976.201a; 1977.341; 1979.
277.

245. Weimer, David. "'Big Boy Leaves
Home' Richard Wright," in his Modern
American Classics: An Anthology of Short
Fiction. New York: Random House, p. 216.
Headnote commenting on setting, mood,
and social meaning. The story is
"reportorial and prophetic rather
than contemplative and tragic."

246. _____. "Black Realities and White:
The City and the Imagination Gap."
Southwest Review, 54 (Spring), 105-119.
Discusses W while arguing that black
and white literary concepts of the
city differ.

247. _____. "Introduction," in his
Modern American Classics: An Anthology
of Short Fiction. New York: Random
House, pp. xi-xv.
Mentions briefly "Big Boy Leaves
Home" and its naturalism.

248. W.[eitzel], K.[arl]. "Der Mann, der
nach Chikago ging," in Der Romanführer.
Ed. Johannes Beer. Vol. 14. Stuttgart:
Anton Hiersemann, pp. 336-337.
Summarizes the stories of EM.

249. _____. "Der schwarze Traum," in Der
Romanführer. Ed. Johannes Beer. Vol. 14.
Stuttgart: Anton Hiersemann, p. 336.
Plot summary of LD.

250. Welburn, Ronald. "Native Sons: A
Critical Study of Twentieth-Century
Negro American Authors. By Edward Margolies." Arizona Quarterly, 25 (Summer),
182-184.
Unfavorable review charging that Margolies does not understand design and
characterization in NS.

251. Wesley, Charles H. The Quest for
Equality: From Civil War to Civil
Rights. International Library of Negro
Life and History. New York: Publishers
Company under the auspices of The Asso-
ciation for the Study of Negro Life and
History, pp. 200, 201.
Mentions W briefly and includes a
photograph.

Reprinted: 1976.202.

252. West, Earle H. A Bibliography of
Doctoral Research on the Negro 1933-
1966. Ann Arbor, Mich: Xerox University
Microfilms, p. 95.
    Includes an annotated listing of
    Edward L. Margolies's dissertation.

253. Williams, John A. "The Literary
Ghetto," in The Black American Writer.
Ed. C. W. E. Bigsby. Vol. 1. DeLand,
Fla.: Everett/Edwards, pp. 67-69.
    Reprint of 1963.186.

254. Wright, Charles. "Dear Dead
Richard!" Chicago Tribune Book World (4
May), Part I, p. 13.
    Favorable review of Dan McCall's The
    Example of Richard Wright. Accuses W
    of weakness, carelessness, and com-
    mercialism in his later work.

255. Yamagata, Toshio. "A Revolt Against
Protest Literature." Komazawa Daigaku
Bungaku Kenkyu Kiyo [Bulletin of Kama-
zawa University School of Literature],
27 (15 March), 1-16.
    Argues that W was the father of pro-
    test literature in America, that
    Baldwin revolted against W, and that
    Ellison eliminated social and racial
    problems from black literature.
    [Y. H. and T. K.]

1970

1. Aaron, Daniel and Robert Bendiner.
Headnote to "Joe Louis Uncovers Dynamite," in their The Strenuous Decade: A
Social and Intellectual Record of the
1930s. Documents in American Civilization Series. Garden City, N. Y.: Anchor
Books, p. 392.
    Provides information on W and Joe
    Louis, stressing political overtones.

2. Abcarian, Richard. "Bibliography," in
his Richard Wright's Native Son: A Critical Handbook. Belmont, Cal.: Wadsworth,
pp. 255-261.
    Lists 134 items.

3. _____. "Chronology: Richard Wright
(1908-1960)," in his Richard Wright's
Native Son: A Critical Handbook. Belmont, Cal.: Wadsworth, pp. 247-254.
    Detailed chronology.

4. _____. "Preface," in his Richard
Wright's Native Son: A Critical Handbook. Belmont, Cal.: Wadsworth, pp. v-
vii.
    Sketches the changing reputation of W
    and explains the organization of the
    book.

5. _____, ed. Richard Wright's Native

Son: A Critical Handbook. Belmont, Cal.:
Wadsworth, 261 pp.
    Contains a preface, chronology, and
    bibliography by Abcarian. Reprints
    W's "A World View of the American
    Negro," "The Ethics of Living Jim
    Crow," "How 'Bigger' Was Born," "I
    Bite the Hand That Feeds Me," "Ras-
    coe-Baiting," and the following items
    on W: 1940.396, 572, 592, 608, 614,
    620, 625, 644, 651, 727, 735, 736,
    769, 784, 794, 842, 858, 873, 919,
    921; 1946.202; 1947.159; 1951.129;
    1958.85; 1962.95b; 1963.77, 113;
    1965.36; 1968.52, 65, 85, 110;
    1969.110, 144, 172, 196.

6. Abe, Daisei. "Jinshushugi to Kokujin
Bungaku--Bigger Thomas to Rufus Scott"
["Black Literature and White Racism:
Bigger Thomas and Rufus Scott"]. Gifu
Daigaku Ron [The Journal of Gifu
College of Economics], 3 (March), 189-
207.
    A discussion of racism in two of the
    "most controversial" novels: NS and
    Another Country. Bigger is seen as a
    victim of white racism; Rufus as a
    black man who fails to establish a
    permanent relationship with a white
    girl. Comments on white racism, which
    results in murder in NS, and which
    brings about a suicide in Another
    Country. [Y.H.]

7. Adams, William, Peter Conn, and Barry
Slepian. "For Discussion," in their
Afro-American Literature: Nonfiction.
Boston: Houghton Mifflin, p. 76.
    Study questions following "The Man
    Who Went to Chicago."

8. _____. "For Discussion," in their
Afro-American Literature: Poetry. Boston: Houghton Mifflin, p. 64.
    Study question following "Between the
    World and Me."

9. _____. "Richard Wright (1908-1960),"
in their Afro-American Literature: Non-
Fiction. Boston: Houghton Mifflin, p.
64.
    Biographical headnote to "The Man Who
    Went to Chicago."

10. _____. "Richard Wright (1908-1960),"
in their Afro-American Literature:
Poetry. Boston: Houghton Mifflin, p.
128.
    Biographical sketch.

11. Adoff, Arnold. "Biographical Notes,"
in his Black on Black: Commentaries by
Black Americans. Collier Books. New
York: Macmillan, p. 265.
    Reprint of 1968.1.

12. _____. "Richard Wright," in his

Brothers and Sisters: Modern Stories by Black Americans. New York: Macmillan, p. 237.
　　Biographical note. "The Man Who Was Almost a Man" is reprinted on pp. 214-228.
　　Reprinted: 1975.2.

13. ____. "Richard Wright," in his I Am the Darker Brother: An Anthology of Modern Poems by Black Americans. Collier Books. New York: Macmillan, pp. 128-129.
　　Reprint of 1968.2.

14. Amedekey, E. Y. The Culture of Ghana: A Bibliography. Accra: Ghana Universities Press, p. 31.
　　Contains an annotated entry for BP.

15. Anderson, S. E. "Revolutionary Black Nationalism and the Pan-African Idea," in The Black Seventies. Ed. Floyd B. Barbour. Boston: Porter Sargent, pp. 99-126.
　　Mentions W's assessment of the Communist Party (pp. 102-103).

16. Anon. "American Literature Reflects American Life," in Compton's Encyclopedia and Fact-Index. Ed. Donald E. Lawson. Vol. 1. Chicago: F. E. Compton, pp. 342-367.
　　Reprint of 1957.7.

16a. Anon. "Baldwin (James)," in La Littérature. Ed. Bernard Gross. Paris: Centre d'Etude et de Promotion de la Lecture, p. 27.
　　Biographical sketch mentioning W.

17. Anon. "Biography." Durham Morning Herald (15 November), p. 5D.
　　Contains a notice of John A. Williams's The Most Native of Sons.

18. Anon. "Black Boy, (35 s.), Native Son (42 s.) by Richard Wright." Nottingham Guardian Journal (12 August).
　　Favorable review of these "classics of negro literature." Compares W favorably to "some of his latter-day followers."

19. Anon. "Black Metropolis." The San Diego Voice and Viewpoint (15 September).
　　Quotes W's statement that Black Metropolis is "a document of agony."

20. Anon. "Books for Brotherhood." National Conference for Christians and Jews (July-August).
　　Favorable notice of John A. Williams's The Most Native of Sons stressing W's posthumous importance.

21. Anon. "The Case of Bigger Thomas." Wolverhampton Chronicle.

Favorable review of the reprint of NS praising the novel's prophetic quality, vividness, and sincerity.

22. Anon. "Children's Books for Spring." Publishers' Weekly, 197 (23 February), 92-124.
　　Contains a favorable notice of John A. Williams's The Most Native of Sons. W's "novels and non-fiction books paved the way for present-day black writers" (p. 100).

23. Anon. Dictionary Catalog of the Jesse E. Moorland Collection of Negro Life and History. Vol. 9. Boston: G. K. Hall, pp. 423-425, 848.
　　Reproduces sixty-one catalog cards on W.

24. Anon. Index Translationum 21. Paris: Unesco, pp. 77, 542, 548, 733.
　　Lists translations of EM into German, UTC into German, BB into Portuguese, Arabic, and Georgian.

25. Anon. "Mississippi--Heart of the Deep South," in Compton's Encyclopedia and Fact-Index. Ed. Donald E. Lawson. Vol. 15. Chicago: F. E. Compton, pp. 372-388.
　　Includes a photograph of W (p. 384).
　　Reprinted: 1973.28.

26. Anon. "The Most Native of Sons: A Biography of Richard Wright by John A. Williams." Pensacola News-Journal (6 September), p. 11E.
　　Unfavorable review complaining of superficiality and unwarranted influences. Praises W, "a major American writer," while disparaging this biography.

27. Anon. "The Most Native of Sons: A Biography of Richard Wright by John A. Williams." Publishers' Weekly, 197 (1 June), 67.
　　Favorable notice recommending the book because it is accurate without falling into sentimentality.

28. Anon. "Negroes in American Life," in Compton's Encyclopedia and Fact-Index. Ed. Donald E. Lawson. Vol. 16. Chicago: F. E. Compton, pp. 124-126d.
　　Reprint of 1957.46.

29. Anon. "New Books." The New York Times (20 January), p. 40.
　　Lists Russell C. Brignano's Richard Wright: An Introduction to the Man and His Works.

30. Anon. "New Books for the Juniors." San Rafael Daily Independent-Journal (13 June), p. M16.
　　Contains a favorable notice of John

A. Williams's biography of W, which should lead to increased awareness of the latter's gifts.

31. Anon. "New Books: Updike in 'Bech' Satirizes Author." The Burlington (Vt.) Free Press (22 July), p. 6.
Contains a favorable brief notice of John A. Williams's biography of W.

32. Anon. "Pick of Pack of Paperbacks." St. Louis Globe-Democrat (10-11 January), p. 5C.
Contains a short notice of SH, a "novel of violence."

33. Anon. "A Return to Schomburg: Richard Wright's Papers Acquired." Bulletin of the New York Public Library, 79 (May), 284.
Announces the acquisition of the original typescript of NS, an unpublished novel entitled "Monument to Memory," the second draft of LD, the typescript of Webb's biography, a copy of the screenplay of NS, and other papers. Includes also a biographical sketch of W.

34. Anon. "Richard Wright." New World Review, 38 (Winter), 173.
Headnote to the poem "Transcontinental."
Reprinted: 1970.260.

35. Anon. "Richard Wright; an introduction to the man and his works." The Booklist, 66 (1 April), 949.
Descriptive notice of the book by Russell C. Brignano.

36. Anon. "Shorter Notices." Church Times (31 July), p. 7.
Contains a favorable notice of reprints of NS and BB.

37. Anon. "Situation Report." Time, 95 (6 April), 100.
Survey of blacks in the publishing industry pointing out that it took NS twenty years to sell a million copies. Forty percent of these sales occurred in the last three years.

38. Anon. "Uncle Tom's Children." The San Diego Voice and Viewpoint News (15 December).
Favorable review praising W as a skilled writer who "knows intimately what he is writing about."

39. Anon. Untitled article. The Glasgow Herald (26 September), Saturday-Extra Sec., p. 4.
Favorable notice of the reprints of NS and BB, including special mention of "How 'Bigger' Was Born." W's "stature and importance" have increased.

since his death.

40. Anon. Untitled clipping. Book Gleanings [?] (Fall).
Favorable review of John A. Williams's The Most Native of Sons. W's work is now receiving recognition as great American literature.

41. Anon. "Williams, John A. The Most Native of Sons." Kirkus Reviews, 38 (1 June), 614.
Unfavorable review. Williams's biography lacks W's "brutal honesty" and fails to explore adequately his involvement with Communism, existentialism, or Pan-Africanism.

42. Anon. "Williams, John Alfred. The most native of sons; a biography of Richard Wright." The Booklist, 67 (15 September), 98.
Notice emphasizing that the book is directed to a juvenile audience.

43. Anon. "Williams, John Alfred. The most native of sons; a biography of Richard Wright." The Booklist, 67 (1 October), 149.
Very brief notice.

43a. "Wright (Richard)," in La Littérature. Ed. Bernard Gross. Paris: Centre d'Etude et de Promotion de la Lecture, pp. 539-540.
Biographical sketch.

44. Anon. "Wright, Richard Nathaniel," in Compton's Encyclopedia and Fact-Index. Ed. Donald E. Lawson. Vol. 24. Chicago: F. E. Compton, pp. 304-305.
Biographical sketch with photograph.

45. Aptheker, Herbert. "Afro-American Superiority: A Neglected Theme in the Literature." Phylon, 31 (Winter), 336-343.
Mentions W as a conveyer of the notion of black superiority.

46. Arndt, Clinton. "Life Related of Black Child." Pittsburg (Cal.) Post Dispatch (18 March).
Review of Maya Angelou's I Know Why the Caged Bird Sings placing it alongside BB.

47. Austin, Lettie J., Lewis H. Fenderson, and Sophia P. Nelson. "Richard Wright (1908-1960)," in their The Black Man and the Promise of America. Glenview, Ill.: Scott, Foresman, p. 321.
Biographical headnote to "The Ethics of Living Jim Crow." W is quoted elsewhere (p. 231), and an excerpt from NS appears on pp. 432-436.

48. Bailey, Peter. "The Last Poets: A

Sharp Insight Into Blackness." The New York Times (31 May), Sec. 2, p. 20.
Contains a favorable review of Brock Peters' recording of BB emphasizing its relevant insights into the problems of black parent-child relationships.

49. Bakewell, Dennis C. The Black Experience in the United States: A Bibliography Based on Collections of the San Fernando Valley State College Library. Northridge, Cal.: San Fernando Valley State College Foundation, pp. 8, 21, 85, 122, 123.
Lists twelve books by W and six books on W.

50. Baldwin, James. "Everybody's Protest Novel," in The Black Novelist. Ed. Robert Hemenway. Charles E. Merrill Literary Texts, ed. Matthew J. Bruccoli and Joseph Katz. Columbus, Ohio: Merrill, pp. 220-226.
Reprint of 1949.79.

51. _____. "Many Thousands Gone," in Five Black Writers. Ed. Donald B. Gibson. New York: New York University Press, pp. 230-242.
Reprint of 1951.129.

51a. _____ and Nabile Farès. "James Baldwin." Jeune Afrique, No. 504 (1 September), pp. 20-24.
In this interview Baldwin pays high tribute to W and accepts blame for the quarrel between the two. Baldwin prefers BB to NS.

52. Baumbach, Jonathan. "Nightmare of a Native Son: Invisible Man, by Ralph Ellison," in Five Black Writers. Ed. Donald B. Gibson. New York: New York University Press, pp. 73-87.
Reprint of 1963.50a.

53. Bayliss, John. "Native Son: Protest or Psychological Study," in Instructor's Guide for Forgotten Pages of American Literature. By Gerald W. Haslam. Boston: Houghton Mifflin, pp. 73-77.
Reprint of 1967.12.

54. Beauvoir, Simone de and Michel Fabre. "Impressions of Richard Wright: An Interview with Simone de Beauvoir." Studies in Black Literature, 1 (Autumn), 3-5.
Beauvoir discusses W's contributions to Les Temps Modernes and his intellectual relationship with Sartre. She admires W's mind.
Reprinted: 1971.147.

55. Bell, Bernard William. "The Afro-american Novel and Its Tradition." Dissertation Abstracts International, 31

(November), 2373-A.
Examines W and six other black novelists as racial spokesmen and as literary craftsmen.

56. Bell, James K. and Adrian A. Cohn. "The Black Experience," in their Toward the New America. Lexington, Mass.: D. C. Heath, p. 112.
Headnote to "The Ethics of Living Jim Crow."

57. _____. "Richard Wright," in their Toward the New America. Lexington, Mass.: D. C. Heath, p. 353.
Biographical note.

58. Bigsby, C. W. E. "From Protest to Paradox: The Black Writer at Mid-Century," in The Fifties: Fiction, Poetry, Drama. Ed. Warren French. DeLand, Fla.: Everett/Edwards, pp. 217-240.
Discusses NS (pp. 226-227) as an ambiguous ideological statement. Unable to make his characters bear the weight of his thought, W finds this predicament even more severe in O (pp. 228-229). His chief importance is as a precursor of Ellison and Baldwin.

59. Bl.[air], W.[alter]. "American Literature," in Encyclopaedia Britannica. Ed. Warren E. Preece. Vol 1. Chicago: Encyclopaedia Britannica, pp. 764-774.
Reprint of 1954.80.

60. Bone, Robert. "The Novels of James Baldwin," in The Black Novelist. Ed. Robert Hemenway. Charles E. Merrill Literary Texts, ed. Matthew J. Bruccoli and Joseph Katz. Columbus, Ohio: Merrill, pp. 113-133.
Reprint of 1965.43.

61. _____. "Ralph Ellison and the Uses of Imagination," in Twentieth Century Interpretations of Invisible Man. Ed. John M. Reilly. Spectrum Book S-872. Englewood Cliffs, N. J.: Prentice-Hall, pp. 22-31.
Partial reprint of 1966.22.

62. Bontemps, Arna. "Negro in America: Contributions to American Culture," in The Encyclopedia Americana. Ed. George A. Cornish. Vol. 20. New York: Americana Corporation, pp. 74-77.
Mentions W briefly.
Reprinted: 1977.66; 1978.44.

63. _____. "The Negro Renaissance: Jean Toomer and the Harlem Writers of the 1920's," in The Black Novelist. Ed. Robert Hemenway. Charles E. Merrill Literary Texts, ed. Matthew J. Bruccoli and Joseph Katz. Columbus, Ohio: Mer-

rill, pp. 153-165.
Reprint of 1966.24.

64. ____, Herbert Hill, Horace Cayton, and Saunders Redding. "Reflections on Richard Wright: A Symposium on an Exiled Native Son," in Five Black Writers. Ed. Donald B. Gibson. New York: New York University Press, pp. 58-69.
Reprint of 1966.25.

65. Bracy, William. "Wright, Richard," in The Encyclopedia Americana. Ed. George A. Cornish. Vol. 29. New York: Americana Corporation, p. 555.
Reprint of 1965.45.

65a. Bragdon, Henry W., Charles W. Cole, and Samuel P. McCutchen. A Free People: The United States in the Twentieth Century. New York: Macmillan, pp. 328-329, 582.
Mentions W and NS, quoting Bigger to exemplify black alienation.

66. Brasmer, William and Dominick Consolo. "Paul Green," in their Black Drama: An Anthology. Columbus, Ohio: Merrill, pp. 71-72.
Headnote to Paul Green's "revised dramatization" of the play Native Son. Quotes from a letter from Green to Brasmer explaining the method of collaboration between Green and W in the original version.

67. Brignano, Russell Carl. Richard Wright: An Introduction to the Man and His Works. Critical Essays in Modern Literature. Pitt Paperback-59. Pittsburgh: University of Pittsburgh Press, 201 pp.
Reprint of 1970.68.

68. ____. Richard Wright: An Introduction to the Man and His Works. Critical Essays in Modern Literature. Pittsburgh: University of Pittsburgh Press, 201 pp.
Study combining "literary criticism, biography, and historical matter" (p. x). The first four chapters discuss the four concerns Brignano considers most central in W's career: racial relations in America, Marxism, the role of the Third World, and the philosophical conflict between rationalism and the absurd. A brief final chapter glances at the transitional character of his work of the late fifties. The main thesis is that W was essentially a latter-day eighteenth-century rationalist in spite of the recurrent demonic aspects of his thought. Treats all of W's major works, often in more than one chapter, and includes a bibliography of fifty-three primary and sixty-seven secondary sources.

Reprinted: 1970.67.
Partially reprinted: 1975.29.

69. Brown, Cecil M. "Black Literature and LeRoi Jones." Black World, 19 (June), 24-31.
Contains brief references to W.
Reprinted: 1978.50.

70. ____. "Richard Wright's Complexes and Black Writing Today," in Black Dialogues: Topics in Afro-American History. Ed. George Ducas. Chicago: Encyclopaedia Britannica Educational Corporation, pp. 445-447.
Partial reprint of 1968.52.

71. Brown, Lloyd L. "The Deep Pit," in Twentieth Century Interpretations of Invisible Man. Ed. John M. Reilly. Spectrum Book S-872. Englewood Cliffs, N. J.: Prentice-Hall, pp. 97-99.
Partial reprint of 1952.28.

72. Brown, Lloyd W. "Black Entitles: Names as Symbols in Afro-American Literature." Studies in Black Literature, 1 (Spring), 16-44.
Discusses the onomastic significance of Cross Damon (p. 23) and Bigger Thomas (pp. 33-37). "In essence, 'Bigger' denotes the gradual expansion of young Thomas' perceptual faculties, from inherited, one-dimensional stereotypes of himself and whites, to human perspectives."

73. ____. "Stereotypes in Black and White: The Nature of Perception in Wright's Native Son." Black Academy Review, 1 (Fall), 35-44.
Argues that Bigger's sense of his own identity is initially defined by the stereotypes imposed by white racism, but these are challenged by his encounters with the white "outsiders" Mary, Jan, and Max. Finally, Bigger achieves an intensely introspective discovery of his real human self. While presenting his view of Bigger's individual development, Brown does not minimize the importance of the novel's social themes.

74. Brown, Sterling A., Arthur P. Davis, and Ulysses Lee. "Richard Wright (1909 [sic]-   )," in their The Negro Caravan. New York: Arno Press and The New York Times, pp. 105-106, 401, 1050.
Reprint of 1941.668.

75. ____. "The Short Story," in their The Negro Caravan. New York: Arno Press and The New York Times, pp. 10-17.
Reprint of 1941.669.

76. Burgum, Edwin Berry. "The Art of Richard Wright's Short Stories," in Five

Black Writers. Ed. Donald B. Gibson. New York: New York University Press, pp. 36-49.
Reprint of 1944.64.

77. Burns, Landon C. "A Cross-Referenced Index of Short Fiction and Author-Title Listing." Studies in Short Fiction, 7 (Winter), 1-218.
Lists three stories by W.

78. Bush, Joseph Bevans. "The Alienated Richard Wright: A Native Son Remembered," in A Galaxy of Black Writing. Ed. R. Baird Shuman. Durham, N.C.: Moore Publishing Company, pp. 63-66.
Praises NS as the definitive statement of racial protest. Nothing that W wrote subsequently is comparable. His expatriation damaged his talent.

79. Cain, Eugene. The Black Hero Teaching Guide. New York: Scholastic Book Services, pp. 34-38, 60-67, 128.
Contains a sketch of W's literary career emphasizing the damaging effect of his exile, a detailed guide for teaching an excerpt from NS, and a checklist of W's books.
Reprinted: 1970.353.

79a. Carruth, Gordon and Associates, ed. The Encyclopedia of American Facts and Dates. Fifth edition. New York: Crowell, pp. 516, 524, 550.
Chronicles the publication of W's first three books.

80. Cayton, Horace R. Long Old Road. Seattle: University of Washington Press, pp. 247-250, 253.
Reprint of 1965.48.

81. _____. "The Psychology of the Negro Under Discrimination," in Being Black: Psychological-Sociological Dilemmas. Ed. Robert V. Guthrie. San Francisco: Canfield Press, pp. 50-65.
Partial reprint of 1946.171.

82. _____, Herbert Hill, Arna Bontemps, and Saunders Redding. "Reflections on Richard Wright: A Symposium on an Exiled Native Son," in Five Black Writers. Ed. Donald B. Gibson. New York: New York University Press, pp. 58-69.
Reprint of 1966.33.

83. Chace, William M. and Peter Collier. "Preface," in their Justice Denied: The Black Man in White America. New York: Harcourt, Brace & World, pp. v-vii.
Quotes W.

84. _____. "Richard Wright 'The Ethics of Living Jim Crow,'" in their Justice Denied: The Black Man in White America. New York: Harcourt, Brace & World, pp. 270-271.
Headnote praising W's social observations in this essay and in NS.

85. Chapman, Abraham. "The Black American Contribution to Literature," in The Negro Impact on Western Civilization. Ed. Joseph S. Roucek and Thomas Kiernan. New York: Philosophical Library, pp. 361-397.
Condensed reprint of 1968.62

86. Charney, Maurice. "James Baldwin's Quarrel with Richard Wright." in Five Black Writers. Ed. Donald B. Gibson. New York: New York University Press, pp. 243-253.
Reprint of 1963.67.

87. Clarke, John Henrik. "The Visible Dimensions of Invisible Man." Black World, 2 (December), 27-30.
Mentions W's strong influence on Ellison.

88. Cleaver, Eldridge. "Notes on a Native Son," in On Being Black: Writings by Afro-Americans from Fredrick Douglass to the Present. Ed. Charles T. Davis and Daniel Walden. Greenwich, Conn.: Fawcett, pp. 313-317.
Reprint of 1966.37.

89. _____. "Notes on a Native Son," in The Black Novelist. Ed. Robert Hemenway. Charles E. Merrill Literary Texts, ed. Matthew J. Bruccoli and Joseph Katz. Columbus, Ohio: Merrill, pp. 233-242.
Reprint of 1966.37

90. _____. "To All Black Women, From All Black Men," in Black Literature in America: A Casebook. Ed. Raman K. Singh and Peter Fellowes. New York: Crowell, pp. 170-174.
Reprint of 1968.67.

91. Clements, Clyde C., Jr. "Black Studies for White Students." Negro American Literature Forum, 4 (March), 9-11.
Mentions W briefly.

92. Corrigan, Robert A. "Afro-American Fiction: A Checklist, 1853-1970." Midcontinent American Studies Journal, 11 (Fall), 114-135.
Revised reprint of 1970.93.

93. _____. "Bibliography of Afro-American Fiction: 1853-1970." Studies in Black Literature, 1 (Summer), 51-86.
Lists eight items by W (pp. 84-85).
Reprinted in revised form: 1970.92; 1971.79.

94. Corry, John. "Profile of an American Novelist." Black World, 20 (December), 116-125.

Reprint of 1966.39.

95. Curry, Gladys J. "Questions for Discussion and Writing," in her Viewpoints from Black America. Englewood Cliffs, N. J.: Prentice-Hall, p. 63.
    To accompany W's "Psychological Reactions of Oppressed People."

96. ____. "Richard Wright," in her Viewpoints from Black America. Englewood Cliffs, N. J.: Prentice-Hall, pp. 56-57.
    Biographical headnote to "Psychological Reactions of Oppressed People."

97. ____. "Suggestions for Further Reading," in her Viewpoints from Black America. Englewood Cliff, N. J.: Prentice-Hall, pp. 234-236.
    Lists WML.

97a. Davenport, F. Garvin, Jr. The Myth of Southern History: Historical Consciousness in Twentieth-Century Southern Literature. Nashville: Vanderbilt University Press, p. 187.
    Mentions and quotes from BB.

98. Davis, Charles T. and Daniel Walden. "Early Moderns," in their On Being Black: Writings by Afro-Americans from Frederick Douglass to the Present. Greenwich, Conn.: Fawcett, pp. 185-186.
    Mentions NS.

99. ____. "Introduction," in their On Being Black: Writings by Afro-Americans from Frederick Douglass to the Present. Greenwich, Conn.: Fawcett, pp. 13-39.
    Discusses NS (pp. 28-31), especially its effect on white and black readers, its relation to naturalistic traditions, its use of language (influenced by Gertrude Stein), and its political ideology.
    Reprinted: 1982.33.

100. ____. "James Baldwin," in their On Being Black: Writings by Afro-Americans from Frederick Douglass to the Present. Greenwich, Conn.: Fawcett, p. 225.
    Mentions W's influence on Baldwin.

101. ____. "Ralph Ellison," in their On Being Black: Writings by Afro-Americans from Frederick Douglass to the Present. Greenwich, Conn.: Fawcett, p. 213.
    Mentions W's influence on Ellison.

102. ____. "Richard Wright," in their On Being Black: Writings by Afro-Americans from Frederick Douglass to the Present. Greenwich, Conn.: Fawcett, p. 187.
    Biographical headnote to a selection from NS.

103. Demarest, David P. and Lois S.

Lamdin. "Parents and Children," in their The Ghetto Reader. New York: Random House, pp. 105-106.
    Mentions W.

104. ____. "Richard Wright," in their The Ghetto Reader. New York: Random House, p. 138.
    Headnote to a selection from BB.

105. Dennis, R. Ethel. The Black People of America: Illustrated History. Ed. Victor B. Lieberman, Elliott H. Kone, and Grace Ann Kone. New York: McGraw-Hill, pp. 271, 275, 284, 315.
    Contains several references to W, including a brief biographical sketch and a photograph (p. 315).

106. Depestre René. "Les metamorphoses de la négritude en Amérique." Présence Africaine, No. 75 (Third Quarter), pp. 19-33.
    Lists W as a proponent of Black Power.

106a. Diagne, Pathé. "Homme invisible, pour qui chantes-tu? par Ralph Ellison." Présence Africaine, No. 74 (Second Quarter), pp. 223-225.
    Review of the French translation of Invisible Man mentioning W briefly.

107. Donlan, Dan M. "The White Trap: A Motif." English Journal, 59 (October), 943-944.
    Catalogs white color symbolism in NS, used to express Bigger's predetermined destruction by white racism.

108. Drake, St. Clair. "Introduction," in A Long Way from Home. By Claude McKay. Harvest Book HB 172. New York: Harcourt Brace & World, pp. ix-xxi.
    Mentions W briefly (p. ix).

109. Ducas, George. "Native Son," in his Black Dialogues: Topics in Afro-American History. Chicago: Encyclopaedia Britannica Educational Corporation, pp. 443-445.
    Note on Bigger to accompany partial reprinting of W's "I Bite the Hand That Feeds Me."

110. ____ with Charles Van Doren. "How 'Bigger' Was Born," in their Great Documents in Black American History. New York: Praeger, pp. 230-232.
    Headnote reviewing W's career with special attention to NS and "How 'Bigger' was Born." A photograph of W with caption appears in a section of photographs following p. 240.

111. Ellis, Edward Robb. A Nation in Torment: The Great American Depression

1929-1939. New York: Coward-McCann, p. 512.
  Contains a paragraph on W in a discussion of the WPA.

112. Ellison, Ralph. "Beating That Boy," in Viewpoints from Black America. Ed. Gladys J. Curry. Englewood Cliffs, N. J.: Prentice-Hall, pp. 103-107.
  Reprint of 1945.889.

113. _____. "Change the Joke and Slip the Yoke," in Black Literature in America: A Casebook. Ed. Raman K. Singh and Peter Fellowes. New York: Crowell, pp. 228-238.
  Reprint of 1958.116.

114. _____. "Richard Wright's Blues," in Forgotten Pages of American Literature. Ed. Gerald W. Haslam. Boston: Houghton Mifflin, pp. 313-327.
  Reprint of 1945.890.

115. _____. "The World and the Jug," in Five Black Writers. Ed. Donald B. Gibson. New York: New York University Press, pp. 271-295.
  Reprint of 1963.77.

116. _____. "The World and the Jug," in On Being Black: Writings by Afro-American from Fredrick Douglass to the Present. Ed. Charles T. Davis and Daniel Walden. Greenwich, Conn.: Fawcett, pp. 241-253.
  Reprint of 1963.77.

117. _____, Alfred Chester, and Vilma Howard. "The Art of Fiction: An Interview," in The Black Experience: An Anthology of American Literature for the 1970s. Ed. Francis E. Kearns. New York: Viking, pp. 552-565.
  Reprint of 1955.40.

118. _____, Alfred Chester, and Vilma Howard. "The Art of Fiction: An Interview," in The Black Novelist. Ed. Robert Hemenway. Charles E. Merrill Literary Texts, ed. Matthew J. Bruccoli and Joseph Katz. Columbus, Ohio: Merrill, pp. 207-217.
  Reprint of 1955.40.

119. _____ and James Alan McPherson. "Indivisible Man." The Atlantic, 226 (December), 45-60.
  Mentions the W-Baldwin conflict (p. 52) and W's difficult relationship with the Communist Party (p. 53). Discusses NS and O (p. 56). Reprinted: 1974.64.

120. Emanuel, James A. "Lines for Richard Wright." Studies in Black Literature, 1 (Autumn), 2.
  Poem on W's racial pain, his expat-

riation, and his sense of his home.

121. Epstein, Seymour. "Politics and the Novelist." Denver Quarterly, 4 (Winter), 1-18.
  Contains a discussion of NS, which is both a political tract and great literature. W's politics are valid, but he departed from realism in restricting Bigger's character.

122. Fabre, Michel. "The Black Expatriates: A Study of American Negroes in Exile. By Ernest Dunbar." Negro American Literature Forum, 4 (March), 35-36.
  Mentions W briefly.

123. _____. "Pères et fils dans Go Tell It on the Mountain de James Baldwin." Études Anglaises, 23, pp. 47-61.
  Includes discussion of Baldwin's relationship to W.
  Translated: 1971.105; 1974.66.

124. _____. "The Poetry of Richard Wright." Studies in Black Literature, 1 (Fall), 10-22.
  Examines not only the agitprop verse but the poetic qualities of prose works such as TMBV and BB and the haiku poems to which W turned at the end of his life. Fabre stresses W's "intimate sense of the universal harmony, his wonder before life, his thirst for a natural existence" (p. 21).
  Reprinted: 1971.147; 1982.49.

125. _____. "Richard Wright (1908-1960): Essai de biographie critique." Doctoral thesis, Université de Paris.
  Full-scale biography of W. See 1973. 133.

126. [Falk, Robert]. "Richard Wright," in American Poetry and Prose. Ed. Norman Foerster, Norman S. Grabo, Russel B. Nye, E. Fred Carlisle, and Robert Falk. Fifth edition. Vol. 2. Boston: Houghton Mifflin, pp. 1358-1359.
  Biographical-critical headnote to "Fire and Cloud" stressing W's relation to the South and his influence on subsequent black writers.

126a. Farrison, W. Edward. "The Black Novelist. Edited by Robert Hemenway." CLA Journal, 14 (December), 214-216.
  Mentions W briefly.

126b. Finestone, Harry. "Themes, Topics, and Criticism," in American Literary Scholarship: An Annual/1968. Ed. J. Albert Robbins. Durham, N. C.: Duke University Press, pp. 300-312.
  Comments briefly on W in a section on black literature (pp. 308, 310, 311).

127. Fleming, Robert E. "Black American Literature: Essays. Edited by Darwin T. Turner. Black American Literature: Fiction. Edited by Darwin T. Turner." Negro American Literature Forum, 4 (March), 38, 40.
Mentions W briefly.

128. ____. "Contemporary Themes in Johnson's Autobiography of an Ex-Coloured Man." Negro American Literature Forum, 4 (Winter), 120-124, 141.
Contrasts Johnson's depiction of the black mother and W's.

129. ____. "Dark Symphony: Negro Literature in America, edited by James A. Emanuel and Theodore L. Gross." Negro American Literature Forum, 4 (March), 37-38.
Mentions W briefly.

130. Foote, Bird. "Native Son Took Place in Literature." Atlanta Journal (16 February).
Favorable review of John A. Williams' The Most Native of Sons. The book avoids condescending to its young readers. It is useful to mature readers as well.

131. Ford, Nick Aaron. "The Ordeal of Richard Wright," in Five Black Writers. Ed. Donald B. Gibson. New York: New York University Press, pp. 26-35.
Reprint of 1953.126.

132. Foster, Frances. "The Black and White Masks of Frantz Fanon and Ralph Ellison." Black Academy Review, 1 (Winter), 46-58.
Contains a paragraph on Bigger Thomas as perceived by whites projecting their fantasies (p. 48).

133. Franklin, John Hope. An Illustrated History of Black Americans. New York: Time-Life Books, pp. 114, 116.
Praises and quotes from TMBV.

134. ____, R.[ayford] W.[hittingham] L.[ogan], and S.[terling] A. Br.[own] "Negro, American," in Encyclopaedia Britannica. Ed. Warren E. Preece. Vol. 16. Chicago: Encyclopaedia Britannica, pp. 189-201.
Reprint of 1957.184 with a photograph of W.

135. Frazier, Thomas R. "Suggestions for Further Reading," in his Afro-American History: Primary Sources. New York: Harcourt, Brace & World, p. 329.
Recommends BB and NS.
Reprinted: 1971.125.

136. Freedman, Frances S. "From Native Son by Richard Wright," in his The Black American Experience: A New Anthology of Black Literature. Bantam Pathfinder Edition NP 4426. New York: Bantam, p. 155.
Biographical headnote. The inside front cover contains a photograph of W.

137. ____. "Suggestions for Further Reading," in his The Black American Experience: A New Anthology of Black Literature. Bantam Pathfinder Edition NP4426. New York: Bantam, pp. 275-278.
Lists and comments briefly on BB.

137a. Freidel, Frank and Henry N. Drewry. America: A Modern History of the United States. Lexington, Mass.: D. C. Heath, p. 643.
Mentions W and NS. Includes a photograph.

138. Frémy, Dominique and Michèle Frémy. Quid? Tout pour tous. Paris: Librairie Plon, p. 105.
Reprint of 1963.86.

139. French, Warren. "The Age of Salinger," in The Fifties: Fiction, Poetry, Drama. DeLand, Fla.: Everett/Edwards, pp. 1-39.
Mentions O and LD, which "lack the concentrated power of his early stories" (p. 14).

139a. ____. "Fiction: 1900 to the 1930's," in American Literary Scholarship: An Annual/1968. Ed. J. Albert Robbins. Durham, N. C.: Duke University Press, pp. 177-200.
Comments on a book, a chapter in a book, and a dissertation on W (pp. 198-199).

139b. Furukawa, Hiromi. "Richard Wright's Native Son." Kokujin Kenkyu [Negro Studies], 40 (June), 15-20.
Dalton is also to blame for Mary's death; he is a symbol of what Hashimoto calls "contradictory American crime." [Y. H. and T. K.]

140. Fussell, Edwin. "Foreword," in American Literature: Essays and Opinions. By Cesare Pavese. Trans. Edwin Fussell. Berkeley and Los Angeles: University of California Press, pp. v-xxii.
Mentions Pavese's essay on W.

141. Gaffney, Kathleen. "Bigger Thomas in Richard Wright's Native Son." Roots, 1, pp. 81-85.
Emphasizes fear and hatred as constant elements in Bigger's oppressive ghetto environment. Not a hero at the beginning of the novel, Bigger develops cleverness and achieves a sense of power and pride. The system of white supremacy requires his death at

the end.

142. Gasseling, Helmut. "Wright, Rich-ard: _Sohn Dieses Landes_." Bücherei und Bildung, 22 (June), 417.
 Favorable review of the German trans-lation of _NS_ commending the novel as social criticism despite its sensa-tionalism and psychologizing. It is still revelant to racial unrest in the United States thirty years after its original publication.

143. Gayle, Addison, Jr. "Cultural Hege-mony: The Southern White Writer and American Letters," in _Amistad 1._ Ed. John A. Williams and Charles F. Harris. Vintage Books V-605. New York. New York: Random House, pp. 3-24.
 Mentions W briefly (p. 22).

144. _____. "Cultural Nationalism: The Black Novelist in America," in his _The Black Situation_. New York: Horizon Press, pp. 189-209.
 Revision and expansion of 1969.100.

145. _____. "The Expatriate." _Black World_, 19 (May), 54-65.
 Mentions W briefly.

146. _____. "The Son of My Father," in his _The Black Situation_. New York: Hori-zon Press, pp. 11-25.
 Refers to W's creation of Bigger Thomas as a catharsis for his emo-tions engendered by white racism. Reprinted: 1972.85.

147. _____. "White Experts--Black Sub-jects," in his _The Black Situation_. New York: Horizon Press, pp. 36-42.
 Compares Mailer's ideas in "The White Negro" to W's in _NS_ (pp. 39-40).

148. Gibson, Donald B. "Bibliography," in his _Five Black Writers_. New York: New York University Press, pp. 303-310.
 Contains a section on W (pp. 303-305) listing fifty-six secondary sources.

149. _____. "Introduction," in his _Five Black Writers: Essays on Wright, Elli-son, Baldwin, Hughes, and LeRoi Jones_. New York: New York University Press, pp. xi-xxviii.
 Contains a discussion of W (pp. xii-xv) drawing from Gibson's "Richard Wright and the Tyranny of Convention" (1969.108).

150. Glicksberg, Charles I. "The Alien-ation of Negro Literature," in _Black Literature in America: A Casebook_. Ed. Raman K. Singh and Peter Fellowes. New York: Crowell, pp. 238-249.
 Reprint of 1950.153.

151. _____. "The Symbolism of Vision," in _Twentieth Century Interpretations of Invisible Man_. Ed. John M. Reilly. Spec-trum Book S-872. Englewood Cliffs, N. J.: Prentice-Hall, pp. 48-55.
 Reprint of 1954.106.

152. Goede, William. "On Lower Frequen-cies: The Buried Men in Wright and Elli-son." _Modern Fiction Studies_, 15 (Win-ter), 483-501.
 Examines W's influence on Ellison, which Goede considers more a matter of conception than style or tech-nique. Analyzes "The Man Who Lived Underground" and compares it to _Invi-sible Man_.

153. Guiney, Elizabeth M. "Brignano, Russell Carl. _Richard Wright: An Intro-duction to the Man and His Works_." _Library Journal_, 95 (15 May), 1842.
 Favorable notice praising Brignano's analyses, documentation, and biblio-graphy. As a critical study the work complements Webb's biography.

154. Haas, Joseph. "African-American Library Provides Black Insights." _The Salt Lake Tribune_ (30 August), p. 2E.
 Mentions W as one of the few well-known black writers of the past.

155. Hach, Clarence W. "Introduction to Syllabus on Afro-American Literature." _Illinois English Bulletin_, 58 (November), 2-4.
 Mentions the teaching of _BB_, _The Outsiders_ [sic], _UTC_, and _NS_ in Evanston Township High School.

156. Halcrow, J. M. "Black Power's Ar-moury." _The London Daily Telegraph_ (16 July), p. 6.
 Review of new editions of _NS_ and _BB_ comparing them favorably to books by Rap Brown and Julius Lester.

157. Halper, Albert. _Good-bye, Union Square_. Chicago: Quadrangle Books, pp. 231-239.
 Narrates Halper's acquaintance with W. In addition to a detailed account of their first meeting soon after the publication of _NS_, Halper mentions several subsequent meetings and dis-cusses W's exile, which damaged him as a writer. But _NS_ and _BB_ are major contributions.

158. Hamalian, Leo and Edmond L. Volpe. "Now That You've Read Wright's _The Man Who Lived Underground_," in their _Eleven Modern Short Novels_. Second edition. New York: Putnam's, pp. 672-679.
 Biographical sketch of W and an analysis of the novella followed by a brief bibliography. Hamalian and

Volpe emphasize existential elements, especially alienation, identity, and oppression.

159. Harris, Charles F. and John A. Williams. "Introduction," in their Amistad 1. Vintage Books V-605. New York: Random House, pp. vii-ix.
Mentions W briefly.

160. Hashimoto, Fukuo. "Wright to Baldwin" ["Wright and Baldwin"]. Kozo [Structure], No. 87 (March), pp. 78-91.
Argues that in view of the current racial tension in the United States, W's position in racial matters is more appropriate than Baldwin's. Though W dealt with a generation earlier than Baldwin's, W's work more closely reflects the racial violence at present than Baldwin's. Remarks that W's racial protest seems to differ with what a critic such as Irving Howe has expected of contemporary black writers. Concludes that W was neither a Marxist nor a socialist, as expected and advocated by leftist critics. [Y. H.]

161. Haslam, Gerald W. "American Literature: The Forgotten Pages'" in his Forgotten Pages of American Literature. Boston: Houghton Mifflin, pp. 1-11.
Comments on W's haiku (p. 9).

162. _____. Instructor's Guide for Forgotten Pages of American Literature. Boston: Houghton Mifflin, pp. 7, 35, 41-44, 46, 73-77.
Mentions W, discusses the teaching of "Long Black Song" and Ellison's "Richard Wright's Blues," and reprints 1967.12.

163. _____. "James Baldwin," in his Forgotten Pages of American Literature. Boston: Houghton Miffin, p. 332.
Mentions W's encouragement of Baldwin.

164. _____. "Preface," in his Forgotten Pages of American Literature. Boston: Houghton Mifflin, p. vii.
Calls NS a "masterwork."

165. _____. "Ralph Ellison," in his Forgotten Pages of American Literature. Boston: Houghton Mifflin, p. 313.
Mentions W's influence on Ellison.

166. _____. "Richard Wright," in his Forgotten Pages of American Literature. Boston: Houghton Mifflin, p. 288.
Biographical headnote to "Long Black Song."

167. _____. "The Subtle Thread: Asian-American Literature," in his Forgotten Pages of American Literature. Boston: Houghton Mifflin, pp. 79-90.
Comments on W's haiku (p. 85) and thematic parallels between W and Richard Kim (p. 86).

168. _____. "Two Traditions: Afro-American Literature," in his Forgotten Pages of American Literature. Boston: Houghton Mifflin, pp. 239-252.
Discusses NS, especially its use of symbols (pp. 247-248).

169. Hatch, James V. Black Image on the American Stage: A Bibliography of Plays and Musicals 1770-1970. New York: DBS Publications, p. 73.
Lists the play NS.

170. Hayden, Robert. "El-Hajj Malik El-Shabazz," in his Words in the Mourning Time. New York: October House, pp. 37-40.
Reprint of 1967.55.

171. Hemenway, Robert. "Introduction," in his The Black Novelist. Charles E. Merrill Literary Texts, ed. Matthew J. Bruccoli and Joseph Katz. Columbus, Ohio: Merrill, pp. 1-6.
Comments on W and his "school" and on NS.

172. _____. "James Baldwin 'Everybody's Protest Novel,'" in his The Black Novelist. Charles E. Merrill Literary Texts, ed. Matthew J. Bruccoli and Joseph Katz. Columbus, Ohio: Merrill, pp. 218-219.
Headnote explaining the Baldwin-W relationship.

173. _____. "Nathan A. Scott, Jr. 'The Dark and Haunted Tower of Richard Wright,'" in his The Black Novelist. Charles E. Merrill Literary Texts, ed. Matthew J. Bruccoli and Joseph Katz. Columbus, Ohio: Merrill, pp. 72-73.
Headnote emphasizing the theme of violence in W.

174. _____. "Richard Kostelanetz 'The Politics of Ellison's Booker: Invisible Man as Symbolic History,'" in his The Black Novelist. Charles E. Merrill Literary Texts, ed. Matthew J. Bruccoli and Joseph Katz. Columbus, Ohio: Merrill, pp. 88-89.
Headnote mentioning W.

175. _____. "Richard Wright 'How 'Bigger' Was Born,'" in his The Black Novelist. Charles E. Merrill Literary Texts, ed. Matthew J. Bruccoli and Joseph Katz. Columbus, Ohio: Merrill, p. 166.
Headnote pointing out both the political and aesthetic elements of W's essay.

176. _____. "Robert Bone 'The Novels of James Baldwin,'" in his The Black Novelist. Charles E. Merrill Literary Texts, ed. Matthew J. Bruccoli and Joseph Katz. Columbus, Ohio: Merrill, pp. 111-112.
Headnote mentioning W.

177. _____. "Selected Bibliography," in his The Black Novelist. Charles E. Merrill Literary Texts, ed. Matthew J. Bruccoli and Joseph Katz. Columbus, Ohio: Merrill, pp. 243-245.
Lists fifteen primary and fifteen secondary works on W.

178. Hernton, Calvin C. "Blood of the Lamb: The Ordeal of James Baldwin," in Amistad 1. Ed. John A. Williams and Charles F. Harris. Vintage Books V-605. New York: Random House, pp. 183-199.
Reprint of 1966.70.

179. _____. "Postscript: A Fiery Baptism," in Amistad 1. Ed. John A. Williams and Charles F. Harris. Vintage Books V-605. New York: Random House, pp. 200-225.
Mentions W briefly (p. 224).
Reprint of 1966.71.

180. Hill, Herbert, Horace Cayton, Arna Bontemps, and Saunders Redding. "Reflections on Richard Wright: A Symposium on an Exiled Native Son," in Five Black Writers. Ed. Donald B. Gibson. New York: New York University Press, pp. 58-69.
Reprint of 1966.76.

181. Hofstadter, Richard, William Miller, and Daniel Aaron. The American Republic. Second edition. Vol. 2. Englewood Cliffs, N. J.: Prentice-Hall, p. 433.
Contains two paragraphs on W and his influence.
Reprinted: 1972.99a; 1976.99.

182. Howe, Irving. "Black Boys and Native Sons," in Five Black Writers. Ed. Donald B. Gibson. New York: New York University Press, pp. 254-270.
Reprint of 1963.113.

183. _____. "Black Boys and Native Sons," in his A World More Attractive: A View of Modern Literature and Politics. Freeport, N. Y.: Books for Libraries Press, pp. 98-122.
Reprint of 1963.113.

184. _____. "Black Boys and Native Sons," in his Decline of the New. New York: Harcourt, Brace & World, pp. 167-189.
Reprint of 1963.113 with additional comments.

185. _____. "Black Boys and Native

Sons," in Twentieth Century Interpretations of Invisible Man. Ed. John M. Reilly. Spectrum Book S-872. Englewood Cliffs, N. J.: Prentice-Hall, pp. 100-102.
Reprint of 1963.113.

186. Hyman, Stanley Edgar. "American Negro Literature and the Folk Tradition," in Black Literature in America: A Casebook. Ed Raman K. Singh and Peter Fellowes. New York: Crowell, pp. 210-228.
Reprint of 1963.115.

187. _____. "Richard Wright Reappraised." The Atlantic, 225 (March), 127-132.
Beginning with the premise that the major problem of the black writer is to control his hate within his art rather than to express it through his art, Hyman concludes that W's greatest work is "The Man Who Lived Underground," which he calls "a radically symbolist and fantasist work, finding the perfect metaphor for Negro identity in life under the streets in a sewer." Discounting racial and social protest, Hyman considers "the constraints of Negro life in the South" depicted in BB to be "metaphoric for Stalinist restraints," and he avers that "The Long Dream represents a melodramatic South which never existed." Considers also W's Freudianism and his obsession with violence and includes a mixed review of Brignano's book.

188. Ihde, Horst. "Richard Wright: Sohn dieses Landes. Übersetzt von Klaus Lambrecht. Mit einem nachwort von Karl-Heinz Schönfelder." Zeitschrift fur Anglistik und Amerikanistik, 18 (April), 211-213.
Review of the German translation of NS complaining of the expurgated translation and a misleading dust jacket. After placing the novel in the context of W's career, Ihde discusses the characterization of Bigger as an oppressed black man who expresses openly his hatred of the oppressor. Ihde also stresses the influence of An American Tragedy and points out the relevance of NS to recent black literature and protest.

189. Isaacs, Harold R. "Five Writers and Their African Ancestors," in Black Literature in America: A Casebook. Ed. Raman K. Singh and Peter Fellowes. New York: Crowell, pp. 249-298.
Reprint of 1960.167.

190. Jackson, Blyden. "The Art of Richard Wright. By Edward Margolies, with a Preface by Harry T. Moore." Amer-

ican Literature, 41 (January), 616.
    Favorable review pointing out that
    Margolies does demonstrate W's artis-
    try. Jackson praises the work's read-
    able style and its comprehensiveness,
    but points out some errors of fact.

191. _____. "The Negro's Negro in Negro
Literature," in Black Literature in
America: A Casebook. Ed. Raman K. Singh
and Peter Fellowes. New York: Crowell,
pp. 299-308.
    Reprint of 1965.83.

192. Jackson, Esther Merle. "The American Negro and the Image of the Absurd,"
in Twentieth Century Interpretations of
Invisible Man. Ed. John M. Reilly. Spectrum Book S-872. Englewood Cliffs,
N. J.: Prentice-Hall, pp. 64-72.
    Reprint of 1962.73.

193. James, Charles L. "Additional Reading," in his From the Roots: Short Stories by Black Americans. New York: Dodd,
Mead, pp. 178-179.
    Lists UTC.

194. _____. "Additional Reading," in his
From the Roots: Short Stories by Black
Americans. New York: Dodd, Mead, p. 242.
    Lists NS and BB.

195. _____. "Additional Reading," in his
From the Roots: Short Stories by Black
Americans. New York: Dodd, Mead, pp.
363-366.
    Lists five works by W.

196. _____. "Historical Information,
1950-1969," in his From the Roots: Short
Stories by Black Americans. New York:
Dodd, Mead, pp. 366-370.
    Notes W's death.

197. _____. "Introductory Comments," in
his From the Roots: Short Stories by
Black Americans. New York: Dodd, Mead,
pp. 117-118.
    Mentions W briefly.

198. _____. "Introductory Comments," in
his From the Roots: Short Stories by
Black Americans. New York: Dodd, Mead,
pp. 183-184.
    Emphasizes the social and historical
    context of "Almos' a Man" and other
    stories.

199. _____. Notes for Teaching From the
Roots: Short Stories by Black Americans.
New York: Dodd, Mead, pp. 13-14, 16-17.
    Analyzes "Big Boy Leaves Home" and
    "Almos' a Man" emphasizing themes of
    fear, flight, and violence.

200. _____. "Questions," in his From the
Roots: Short Stories by Black Americans.

New York: Dodd, Mead, pp. 171-172.
    Ten study questions on "Big Boy
    Leaves Home."

201. _____. "Questions," in his From the
Roots: Short Stories by Black Americans.
New York: Dodd, Mead, p. 200.
    Seven study questions on "Almos' a
    Man."

202. _____. "Tales of the Black Six-
ties," in his From the Roots: Short
Stores by Black Americans. New York:
Dodd, Mead, pp. 284-286.
    Mentions W briefly.

203. _____. "Two Young Protestors," in
his From the Roots: Short Stories by
Black Americans. New York: Dodd, Mead,
pp. 137-139.
    Biographical headnote on W and John
    Henrik Clarke to accompany "Big Boy
    Leaves Home" and "Santa Claus Is a
    White Man."

204. _____. "The War Years," in his From
the Roots: Short Stories by Black Americans. New York: Dodd, Mead, pp. 200-201.
    Mentions W briefly.

205. Jeffers, Lance. "The Death of the
Defensive Posture: Toward Grandeur in
Afro-American Letters," in The Black
Seventies. Ed. Floyd B. Barbour. Boston:
Porter Sargent, pp. 253-263.
    Praises W for his candor and honesty,
    rather than defensiveness, in depict-
    ing black life. Confronting the hell
    within and without, W achieves in
    such works as "Big Boy Leaves Home,"
    "Down by the Riverside," "Long Black
    Song," NS, and BB an intensity and
    grandeur reminiscent of the spiri-
    tuals.

206. Jones, Junemary. "Teaching Afro-
American Literature." Illinois English
Bulletin, 57 (February), 1-10.
    Comments on the teaching of NS and
    BB.

207. Jones, LeRoi. "The Myth of a 'Negro
Literature,'" in Black Literature in
America: A Casebook. Ed. Raman K. Singh
and Peter Fellowes. New York: Crowell,
pp. 308-315.
    Reprint of 1963.121.

208. _____. "The Myth of a 'Negro Literature,'" in On Being Black: Writings
by Afro-Americans from Frederick Douglass to the Present. Ed. Charles T.
Davis and Daniel Walden. Greenwich,
Conn.: Fawcett, pp. 293-301.
    Reprint of 1963.121.

209. _____. "The Myth of a 'Negro Literature,'" in The Ghetto Reader. Ed.

David P. Demarest and Lois S. Lamdin. New York: Random House, pp. 294-301.
Reprint of 1963.121.

210. _____. "The Myth of a 'Negro Literature,'" in Viewpoints of Black America. Ed. Gladys J. Curry. Englewood Cliffs, N. J.: Prentice-Hall, pp. 109-115.
Reprint of 1963.121.

211. Jordan, June. "Richard Wright," in her Soulscript: Afro-American Poetry. Garden City, N. Y.: Doubleday, p. 144.
Biographical note.

211a. Justus, James H. "Fiction: The 1930's to the Present," in American Literary Scholarship: An Annual/1968. Ed. J. Albert Robbins. Durham, N. C.: Duke University Press, pp. 201-227.
Mentions W briefly in connection with an article on Killens (p. 224).

212. Kahle, Roger. "The Case for Black Literature." This Day, 22 (November), 16-19, 32-33.
Contains a brief sketch of W.

213. Kaiser, Ernest. "A Critical Look at Ellison's Fiction and at Social and Literary Criticism by and About the Author." Black World, 20 (December), 53-59, 81-97.
Examines Ellison's views of W.

214. _____. "Recent Books." Freedomways, 10 (Second Quarter), 183-192.
Includes an unfavorable notice of Robert Bone's Richard Wright mentioning other recent books on W.

214a. Kawabe, Koichi. "A Study of Black Literature, II: Protest and Fear in Richard Wright." Nagasaki Gaikokugo Tanki Daigaku Ronshu [Nagasaki Junior College for Foreign Studies Treatises], 12 (5 February), 45-60.
W's motive for writing was fear rather than protest. W struggled with the internal problems of self. [Y. H. and T. K.]

215. Kearns, Francis E. "Bibliography," in his The Black Experience: An Anthology of American Literature for the 1970s. New York: Viking, pp. 639-650.
Includes six items on W.

216. _____. "Chester Himes (1909-)," in his The Black Experience: An Anthology of American Literature for the 1970s. New York: Viking, pp. 593-594.
Places If He Hollers Let Him Go in the W tradition.

217. _____. Instructor's Manual for

Black Identity: A Thematic Reader. New York: Holt, Rinehart and Winston, pp. 3-4, 21.
Contains answers to the "Questions" for "Our Strange Birth" and a comment on "The Ethics of Living Jim Crow."

218. _____. "Introduction," in his The Black Experience: An Anthology of American Literature for the 1970s. New York: Viking, pp. xii-xx.
Mentions W briefly (pp. xv, xvii, xix).

219. _____. "James Baldwin (1924-)," in his The Black Experience: An Anthology of American Literature for the 1970s. New York: Viking, pp. 566-568.
Comments on Baldwin's relation to W.

220. _____. "Margaret Walker (1915-)," in his The Black Experience: An Anthology of American Literature for the 1970s. New York: Viking, p. 497.
Compares the theme of "For My People" to W's work.

221. _____. "Questions," in his Black Identity: A Thematic Reader. New York: Holt, Rinehart and Winston, pp. 13-14.
To accompany "Our Strange Birth," an excerpt from TMBV.

222. _____. "Ralph Ellison (1914-)," in his The Black Experience: An Anthology of American Literature for the 1970s. New York: Viking, pp. 550-552.
Mentions W's influence on Ellison, but contrasts their political and social attitudes.

223. _____. "Richard Wright (1908-1960)," in his The Black Experience: An Anthology of American Literature for the 1970s. New York: Viking, pp. 451-452.
Biographical headnote to "The Man Who Went to Chicago."

224. Kelly, Mary. "In Black and White." London Catholic Herald (4 September).
Favorable review of the new edition of NS praising its use of point of view and its prophetic quality.

225. Kendricks, Ralph and Claudette Levitt. "Modern Times," in their Afro-American Voices 1770's-1970's. New York: Oxford Book Company, pp. 240-242.
Includes brief mention of W and "Fire and Cloud."

226. _____. Untitled footnote, in their Afro-American Voices 1770's-1970's. New York: Oxford Book Company, p. 243.
Biographical note on W.

227. Kent, George. "Ralph Ellison and Afro-American Folk and Cultural Tradi-

tion." CLA Journal, 13 (March), 265-276. Quotes from Ellison's "Richard Wright's Blues" (p. 266). Reprinted: 1972.116

228. Kgositsile, Keorapetse. "The Relevance of Bigger Thomas to Our Time." Roots, 1, pp. 79-80.
Summarizes and comments on the plot of NS emphasizing W's understanding of the necessity of violence as a means of achieving black liberation and the futility of individual as opposed to collective effort in realizing that goal. The theme of black-white brotherhood and the portrayal of Jan and Max may represent W's "wishful thinking" or "personal hangups in the guise of ideological convictions." In either case, they are irrelevant to the present. But the book as a whole is still a true picture of American racial conditions.

229. Killens, John Oliver. "The Black Psyche," in Being Black: Psychological-Sociological Dilemmas. Ed. Robert V. Guthrie. San Francisco: Canfield Press, pp. 26-35.
Partial reprint of 1965.89.

230. _____. "Explanation of the 'Black Psyche,'" in From a Black Perspective: Contemporary Black Essays. Ed. Douglas A. Hughes. New York: Holt, Rinehart and Winston, pp. 67-74.
Reprint of 1964.84.

231. King, Woodie, Jr. "The Dilemma of Black Theater." Negro Digest, 19 (April), 10-15, 86-87.
Mentions briefly the play NS (p. 10).

232. Kinnamon, Keneth. "Afro-American Literature, the Black Revolution, and Ghetto High Schools." English Journal, 59 (February), 189-194.
Contains brief comments on W.
Reprinted: 1971.201.

232a. _____. "Nancy M. Tischler, Black Masks: Negro Characters in Modern Southern Fiction." American Quarterly, 22 (Summer), 321.
Notes that the work contains six factual errors about W.

233. Kitzhaber, Albert R., Stoddard Malarkey, Barbara Drake, Donald MacRae, and Jacqueline Snyder. "'Hokku Poems' Richard Wright," in their Literature V: Teacher's Guide. New York: Holt, Rinehart and Winston, pp. 238-240.
Analysis of the poems keyed to 1970.234.

234. _____. "Questions for Discussion,"

in their Literature V. New York: Holt, Rinehart and Winston, p. 640.
To accompany W's "Hokku Poems."

235. _____. "Richard Wright," in their Literature V. New York: Holt, Rinehart and Winston, p. 727.
Biographical sketch.

236. Klein, Marcus. "Ralph Ellison's Invisible Man," in Five Black Writers. Ed. Donald B.Gibson. New York: New York University Press, pp. 88-101.
Reprint of 1964.85.

237. Klotman, Phyllis Rauch. "The Running Man as Metaphor in Contemporary Negro Literature." Dissertation Abstracts International, 30 (March), 3946-A.
Includes treatment of BB, NS, O, LD.

238. Krim, Seymour. "The American Novel Made Me," in his Shake It for the World, Smartass. New York: The Dial Press, pp. 3-25.
Reprint of 1969.151.

238a. Kyria, Pierre. "L'Homme qui muert de James Baldwin." Paris Combat (15 October), p. 7.
Review of the French translation of Tell Me How Long the Train's Been Gone noting that Baldwin is less intellectual than W.

239. Lacy, Leslie Alexander. The Rise and Fall of a Proper Negro: An Autobiography. New York: Macmillan, pp. 13, 173-174.
Mentions W and his daughter Julia.

240. Lara, José Gerardo Manrique de. El mundo negro. Madrid: Ediciones y Publicaciones Españolas, pp. 12-13.
Contains comments on W emphasizing his social message in UTC, NS, and BB.

241. LeClair, Thomas. "The Blind Leading the Blind: Wright's Native Son and a Brief Reference to Ellison's Invisible Man." CLA Journal, 13 (March), 315-320.
Traces the imagery of blindness and sight, which is metaphorically crucial to the novel's thematic development. In conclusion, LeClair relates W's pattern to Invisible Man.

242. Lee, Don L. "Dedication or To Those Who Helped Create a New Consciousness," in his We Walk the Way of the New World. Detroit: Broadside Press, pp. 5-6.
Calls W, Robeson, and E. Franklin Frazier "the dynamiters, makers of new words/ideas that did more than just walk the page, they jumped at us

with unrelenting force that wdn't
wait."
Reprinted: 1971.209.

243. Lehan, Richard D. "The Strange
Silence of Ralph Ellison," in Twentieth Century Interpretations of Invisible Man. Ed. John M. Reilly. Spectrum Book S-872. Englewood Cliffs,
N. J.: Prentice-Hall, pp. 106-110.
    Partial reprint of 1965.97.

243a. Lester, Julius. "Not in Memory of
Robert Kennedy," in his Revolutionary
Notes. Evergreen Black Cat Book B-241.
New York: Grove Press, pp. 112-115.
    Reprint of 1968.152a.

244. _____. "Richard Wright," in Young
and Black in America. Ed. Rae Pace Alexander and Julius Lester. New York: Random House, pp. 19-21.
    Biographical headnote to an excerpt
from BB.

245. Lewis, David L. King: A Critical
Biography. New York: Praeger, p. 266.
    Mentions W briefly.
    Reprinted: 1978.147.

246. Liebman, Arthur. "Patterns and
Themes in Afro-American Literature."
English Record, 20, No. 3, pp. 2-12.
    Mentions W's emphasis on an oppres-
sive environment for blacks.

247. L. [imbacher], J. [ames] L. "Richard Wright. Black Boy." Library Journal,
95 (15 June), 2242-2243.
    Favorable review of Brock Peters's
recording of BB calling it the "story
of triumph against great odds."

248. Lincoln, C. Eric. "Introduction,"
in Great Documents in Black American
History. Ed. George Ducas with Charles
Van Doren. New York: Praeger, pp. ix-xv.
    Concludes with a tribute to the pro-
phetic quality of Bigger Thomas as a
"social construct."

249. Littlejohn, David. "From Black on
White," in Black Literature in America:
A Casebook. Ed. Raman K. Singh and Peter
Fellowes. New York: Crowell, pp. 316-
325.
    Reprint of pp. 157-170 of 1966.97.

250. Lockwood, Lee. Conversation with
Eldridge Cleaver--Algiers. New York:
Dell, p. 88.
    Cleaver reports that he never joined
the Communist Party because he was
influenced by W's resignation from
it.

251. Ludington, Charles T.[ownsend], Jr.
"Protest and Anti-Protest: Ralph Elli-

son." Southern Humanities Review, 4
(Winter), 31-39.
    Discusses Ellison's attitudes toward
W (pp. 33-34).

252. MacInnes, Colin. "Dark Angel: The
Writings of James Baldwin," in Five
Black Writers. Ed. Donald B. Gibson. New
York: New York University Press, p. 119-
142.
    Reprint of 1963.136.

253. Margolies, Edward. "Anger," in his
A Native Sons Reader. Philadelphia: Lippincott, p. 303.
    Cites Bigger Thomas as an example of
black anger.

254. _____. "The City," in his A Native
Sons Reader. Philadelphia: Lippincott,
p. 141.
    Mentions "The Man Who Went to Chi-
cago."

255. _____. "The Image of the Primitive
in Black Letters." Midcontinent American
Studies Journal, 11 (Fall), 67-77.
    Notes that W was the first black
writer to use the image of the primitive in a pejorative sense.

256. _____. "Migration," in his A Native
Sons Reader. Philadelphia: Lippincott,
p. 88.
    Mentions "Big Boy Leaves Home."

257. _____. "Richard Wright (1908-
1960)," in his A Native Sons Reader.
Philadelphia: Lippincott, p. 361.
    Biographical note to accompany "Big
Boy Leaves Home" and "The Man Who
Went to Chicago."

258. Mason, Clifford. "Native Son
Strikes Home." Life, 68 (8 May), 18.
    Celebrates the thirtieth anniversary
of the publication of NS, a novel
which has proved to be prophetic. W
is the most important of black writers. Compares him briefly to Ellison
and Baldwin.

259. _____. "Ralph Ellison and the
Underground Man." Black World, 20 (December), 20-26.
    Comments on the relation of "The Man
Who Lived Underground" to Invisible
Man. Moreover, Bigger Thomas and the
protagonist of Ellison's novel are
also comparable.

260. Mason, Daniel and Jessica Smith.
"Richard Wright," in their Lenin's Im-
pact on the United States. New York: NWR
Press, p. 173.
    Reprint of 1970.34.

261. May, John R., S. J. "Images of

Apocalypse in the Black Novel." Renascence, 23 (Autumn), 31-45.
    Considers NS, Invisible Man, Go Tell
    it on the Mountain, and The System of
    Dante's Hell. NS is probably the most
    apocalyptic of these works.

262. McElderry, Bruce R., Jr. "American." Modern Fiction Studies, 15 (Winter), 550-556.
    Includes a favorable notice of Ed-
    ward Margolies's The Art of Richard
    Wright.

263. Meltzer, Milton. "In the American
Grain: The Most Native of Sons: A Bio-
graphy of Richard Wright. By John A.
Williams." Chicago Tribune (17 May),
Children's Book World Sec. (9A), p.
10.
    Favorable review praising Williams's
    warmth and penetration. The book
    explains how and why W became a
    writer.

264. Meyer, Shirley. "The Identity of
'The Man Who Lived Underground.'" Negro
American Literature Forum, 4 (July), 52-
55.
    Uses quotation and plot summary to
    show that the story "carries the
    universal message that only the ac-
    ceptance of one's responsibility in
    an absurd world can result in self-
    realization."

265. Miller, Elizabeth W. and Mary L.
Fisher. The Negro in America: A Biblio-
graphy. Revised and enlarged edition.
Cambridge, Mass.: Harvard University
Press, pp. 10, 80, 81, 105.
    Reprint of 1966.105.

266. Milner, Ronald. "Black Magic, Black
Art," in Five Black Writers. Ed. Donald
B. Gibson. New York: New York University
Press, pp. 296-301.
    Reprint of 1967.74.

267. Mitarai, Hiroshi. "Umarenagara no
Outsider Higeki" ["The Tragedy of a Born
Outsider"]. Kita-Kyushu Daigaku Gaiko-
kugo Gakubu Kiyo [Bulletin: Faculty of
Foreign Languages, Kita-kyushu Univer-
sity], 20 (October), 185-210.
    States that Cross Damon's disadvan-
    tage is being an outsider as deter-
    mined by his race. As Prosecutor
    Houston argues, hovever, Cross as a
    black man stands inside and outside
    of society. At the end of the story
    Cross remains merely a protesting
    individual, not a revolutionary hero.
    O is not an existential novel that
    transcends race and color of skin,
    but the tragedy of a Negro who, deny-
    ing his negritude, struggles and
    ultimately fails. [Y. H.]

268. Morsberger, Robert E. "Segregated
Surveys: American Literature." Negro
American Literature Forum, 4 (March), 3-
8.
    Laments inadequate representation of
    black writers in anthologies of Amer-
    ican literature and urges their in-
    clusion. Calls BB "possibly the most
    eloquent and moving autobiography in
    American literature, certainly more
    so than Benjamin Franklin's."

269. Murray, Albert. The Omni-Americans:
New Perspective on Black Experience and
American Culture. New York: Outerbridge
& Dienstfrey, 227 pp.
    Contains numerous references to W,
    especially in the chapter entitled
    "James Baldwin, Protest Fiction, and
    the Blues Tradition" (pp. 142-168), a
    revised version of 1966.106. Murray
    objects to W's Marxism, his existen-
    tialism, and his tendency to deper-
    sonalize black people by politicizing
    their problems.

270. Murray, Alma and Robert Thomas.
"Richard Wright," in their The Black
Hero. New York: Scholastic Book Ser-
vices, p. 208.
    Biographical note to accompany an
    excerpt from NS.
    Reprinted: 1970.271.

271. _____. "Richard Wright," in their
The Journey. New York: Scholastic Book
Services, p. 192.
    Reprint of 1970.270.

272. Neal, Larry. "Ellison's Zoot Suit."
Black World, 20 (December), 31-52.
    Comments on W's Marxism and compares
    it to Ellison's own political devel-
    opment.
    Reprinted: 1974.137.

273. Nevius, Blake. The American Novel:
Sinclair Lewis to the Present. Golden-
tree Bibliographies in Language and
Literature, ed. O. B. Hardison, Jr. New
York: Appleton-Century-Crofts, pp. 107-
108.
    Lists thirty-four secondary sources
    on W, some of them briefly annotated.

274. Nilon, Charles. "Introduction," in
The Sport of The Gods. By Paul Laurence
Dunbar. African/American Library, ed.
Charles R. Larson. Collier Books. New
York: Macmillan, pp. 6-16.
    Mentions the W-Baldwin controversy
    over protest fiction.

275. Noble, Peter. The Negro in Films.
The Literature of Cinema series, ed.
Martin S. Dworkin. New York: Arno Press
& The New York Times, pp. 22, 45, 154.
    Reprint of 1948.213.

276. O'Brien, Eileen. "Books of the Day: Blackest Shadow." The Dublin Irish Times (10 July), p. 11.
Review of new editions of NS and BB. The former is too didactic, but the "diamond lucidity" and "crushing power" of the latter make it an important book.

277. O'Connor, Francine M. "To Be Black and Write." St. Louis Post-Dispatch (12 July), p. 4D.
Favorable review of John A. Williams's The Most Native of Sons maintaining that W "never lost his faith in his native country."

278. O'Daniel, Therman B. "The Image of Man as Portrayed by Ralph Ellison," in Five Black Writers. Ed. Donald B. Gibson. New York: New York University Press, pp. 102-107.
Reprint of 1967.80.

279. _____. "The Image of Man as Portrayed by Ralph Ellison," in Twentieth Century Interpretations of Invisible Man. Ed. John M. Reilly. Spectrum Book S-872. Englewood Cliffs, N. J.: Prentice-Hall, pp. 89-95.
Reprint of 1967.80.

280. Ohashi, Kenzaburo. "Wright to Baldwin--Sono Danzetsu ga Imishita Mono" ["Wright and Baldwin: The Meaning of Their Separation"]. Bungaku [Literature], 38 (March), 8-15.
W's vision was based on one's fear and hatred toward society; W always sought to leave society in quest of a dream and its realization in the future. Baldwin, on the other hand, dealt with the present and his own community in Harlem. What W searched for in the North, Europe, and Africa, Baldwin tried to find in the deep South. Baldwin, rather than alienating himself from the South as did W, regarded himself as a descendant of the South. In Ohashi's view Baldwin, declaring that W's world had vanished, nevertheless realized that it would return in the 70's. [Y. H.]

281. Ozawa, Fumio. "Richard Wright no Tanpen Shosetsu--1" ["Richard Wright's Short Fiction, I"]. Showa Joshi Daigaku Gakuen [Showa Women's College Instruction], No. 364 (April), 94-103.
UTC was written while W was closely connected with the Communist Party; thus it is best appreciated in terms of that relationship. The success of the short fiction can be attributed to the technique of a thriller on the one hand and the mood of black language and action on the other. [Y. H.]

282. Padmore, Dorothy. "A Letter from Dorothy Padmore." Studies in Black Literature, 1 (Fall), 5-9.
Letter to Michel Fabre concerning the relationship between W and George Padmore. Most of her remarks concern W's non-fiction and his political development in the last decade of his life.
Reprinted: 1971.147.

283. Panwitt, Barbara, Mary Jane Richeimer, Malcolm E. Stern, Elizabeth White, and Clarence W. Hach. "Appendix." Illinois English Bulletin, 58 (November), 24-26.
Lists four works by W.

284. _____. "Teachers' Bibliography." Illinois English Bulletin, 58 (November), 19-24.
Annotated list including EM and Constance Webb's Richard Wright.

285. Patrick, John J. The Progress of the Afro-American. Westchester, Ill.: Benefic Press, p. 158.
Comments briefly on W's career. "Few writers have surpassed Wright in calling the attention of the world to the social problems in the U. S."

286. Pavese, Cesare. "Richard Wright," in his American Literature: Essays and Opinions. Trans. Edwin Fussell. Berkeley: University of California Press, pp. 192-195.
Translation of 1951.216.

287. Payne, Lois. "He Saw Strife." Austin (Tex.) American-Statesman.
Unfavorable review of John A. Williams's The Most Native of Sons. Although W's life is compelling, Williams tries to crowd too much into too small a space.

288. Pearson, Norman Holmes. "American Literature," in The Encyclopedia Americana. Ed. George A. Cornish. Vol. 1. New York: Americana Corporation, pp. 691-709.
Reprint of 1968.178.

289. Peek, Charles A. A Bibliography of Afro-American Literature. Freshman English Experimental Materials. Lincoln: University of Nebraska, pp. 10, 29-30.
Mentions W and lists fourteen primary sources. The entry for NS is annotated.

290. Perkins, Eugene. "The Changing Status of Black Writers." Black World, 19 (June), 18-23, 95-98.
Mentions and quotes W (pp. 19, 95).

291. Price, E. Curmie. "The Ballad of

Bigger Thomas," in his The State of the Union. Surrey, B. C.: Sono Nis Press, p. 27.
Poem attesting to the impact of NS on Price's imagination.

292. Pugh, Griffith T. "Three Negro Novelists: Protest and Anti-Protest--A Symposium: Introduction." Southern Humanities Review, 4 (Winter), 17-18.
Comments briefly on the relation of Ellison and Baldwin to W.

293. Redding, Saunders. "The Alien Land of Richard Wright," in Five Black Writers. Ed. Donald B. Gibson. New York: New York University Press, pp. 3-11.
Reprint of 1963.160.

294. ____. "The Negro Writer and American Literature," in Viewpoints from Black America. Ed. Gladys J. Curry. Englewood Cliffs, N. J.: Prentice-Hall, pp. 91-99.
Reprint of 1966.123.

295. ____. "On Being Negro in America," in Viewpoints from Black America. Ed. Gladys J. Curry. Englewood Cliffs, N. J.: Prentice-Hall, pp. 65-70.
Reprint of second passage of 1951.223.

296. ____, Herbert Hill, Horace Cayton, and Arna Bontemps. "Reflections on Richard Wright: A Symposium on an Exiled Native Son," in Five Black Writers. Ed. Donald B. Gibson. New York: New York University Press, pp. 58-69.
Reprint of 1966.125.

297. Reed, Ishmael. "Introduction," in his 19 Necromancers from Now. Anchor Books A 743. Garden City, N. Y.: Doubleday, pp. xi-xxvi.
Mentions W briefly.
Reprinted: 1972.169.

298. Reed, Kenneth T. "Native Son: An American Crime and Punishment." Studies in Black Literature, 1 (Summer), 33-34.
Points out similarities in plot of the two novels and compares the characterization of Bigger and Raskolnikov. The protagonists are similar in motivation and psychology.
Reprinted: 1971.147.

299. Reeves, Paschal et al. "A Checklist of Scholarship on Southern Literature for 1969." Mississippi Quarterly, 23 (Spring), 181-217.
Lists twelve items on W (pp. 211-212).

300. Reilly, John M. "Chronology of Important Dates," in his Twentieth Century Interpretations of Invisible Man.

Spectrum Book S-872. Englewood Cliffs, N. J.: Prentice-Hall, pp. 113-116.
Mentions NS and Ellison's meeting with W.

301. ____. "Introduction," in his Twentieth Century Interpretations of Invisible Man. Spectrum Book S-872. Englewood Cliffs, N. J.: Prentice-Hall, pp. 1-9.
Contains brief references to W.

302. Rickels, Milton and Patricia Rickels. Richard Wright. Southern Writers Series No. 11, ed. Sam H. Henderson and James W. Lee. Austin: Steck-Vaughn, 44 pp.
Surveys all of W's books, interweaving biography with criticism. The main emphasis is on W's Southernness: "The great themes of Wright's art--alienation, suffering, fear and anger, the psychology of oppressor and oppressed, the passion for freedom, the compulsion to rebel--grow from Southern soil" (p. 1). Includes a "Selected Bibliography" of fifteen primary and ten secondary items.

303. Ridenour, Ronald. "The Man Who Lived Underground: A Critique." Phylon, 31 (Spring), 54-57.
Analyzes the story emphasizing universality and existentialism while disparaging protest. W's brand of existentialism is more hopeful than most.

304. Root, Shelton L., Jr. "The Most Native of Sons. By John A. Williams." Elementary English, 47 (November), 1025.
Favorable review summarizing the contents and calling the work "informative and absorbing."

305. Rose, Karel. "The Role of Black Literature in Teacher-Education." Afro-American Studies: An Interdisciplinary Journal, 1 (May), 61-67.
Comments on NS as a slum novel (p. 63) and on "The Ethics of Living Jim Crow" (p. 65).

306. Rosenblatt, George. "Richard Wright's Biography--Too Succinct?" Houston Chronicle (5 July), Zest Sec., p. 27.
Mixed review of John A. Williams's The Most Native of Sons praising its treatment of W's hostile environment but asking for greater depth in the treatment of his involvement with communism.

307. Rosenblatt, Roger. "Black as the Color of Chaos," in The Interpretation of Narrative: Theory and Practice. Ed. Morton W. Bloomfield. Harvard English

Studies. Vol. 1. Cambridge, Mass.: Harvard University Press, pp. 249-261.
Uses "Big Boy Leaves Home," "Fire and Cloud," "Long Black Song," and NS as examples of the special significance attached to the colors black and white in black fiction.

308. Ross, Ishbel. The Expatriates. New York: Crowell, p. 292.
Mentions W's expatriation, especially his frequenting the Café de Tournon in Paris.

309. Rovit, Earl H. "Ralph Ellison and the American Comic Tradition," in Five Black Writers. Ed. Donald B. Gibson. New York: New York University Press, pp. 108-115.
Reprint of 1960.234.

310. _____. "Ralph Ellison and the American Comic Tradition," in Twentieth Century Interpretations of Invisible Man. Ed. John M. Reilly. Spectrum Book S-872. Englewood Cliffs, N. J.: Prentice-Hall, pp. 56-63.
Reprint of 1960.234.

311. Salzman, Jack. Untitled footnote, in his Years of Protest: A Collection of American Writings of the 1930's. Indianapolis: Bobbs-Merrill, p. 354.
Biographical sketch emphasizing W's experience with Communism to accompany "I Have Seen Black Hands."

312. Samples, Ron. "Bigger Thomas and His Descendants." Roots, 1, pp. 86-93.
Examines themes of fear and failure in NS in relation to imagery of light, brightness, fire, and darkness. The usual racist symbolism of white and black is inverted.

313. Saporta, Marc. Histoire du roman américain. Paris: Seghers, pp. 167, 171, 173, 174, 175, 246-248, 251, 252, 254, 298, 313, 317, 318, 319, 346.
In addition to numerous brief mentions of W, Saporta provides a brief sketch of his literary career (pp. 246-247)
Reprinted: 1976.170.

313a. Schatz, Walter, ed. Directory of Afro-American Resources. New York: R. R. Bowker Company, pp. 27, 103, 112, 186, 220, 266, 304.
Lists W items in depositories in Connecticut, Illinois, Nevada, New York, Ohio, and Tennessee.

314. Scott, Nathan A., Jr. "The Dark and Haunted Tower of Richard Wright," in Five Black Writers. Ed. Donald B. Gibson. New York: New York University Press, pp. 12-25.

Reprint of 1964.113.

315. _____. "The Dark and Haunted Tower of Richard Wright," in The Black Novelist. Ed. Robert Hemenway. Charles E. Merrill Literary Texts, ed. Matthew J. Bruccoli and Joseph Katz. Columbus, Ohio: Merrill, pp. 74-87.
Reprint of 1964.113.

316. Seymour-Smith, Martin. "An American Masterpiece." The Edinburgh Scotsman (15 August), The Week-end Scotsman Sec., p. 3.
Contains a laudatory review of the reprint of NS comparing the novel favorably to An American Tragedy and Invisible Man. Seymour-Smith praises W's power and poignancy.

317. Shaw, Arnold. The World of Soul: Black America's Contribution to the Pop Music Scene. New York: Cowles Book Company, pp. 45, 47.
Quotes W on the blues.

318. Shaw, Fred. "Black America Reveals Itself in Its Literature." The Miami Herald (31 May), p. 7-H.
Points out that NS first showed white America the depths of black life which engender anger and violence.

319. Shaw, Mildred Hart. "Variety of Books Satisfy Interest." Grand Junction (Col.) Daily Sentinel (11 July), p. 10.
Contains a favorable notice of John A. Williams's The Most Native of Sons. As one of America's best black writers, W deserves attention.

320.S.[ingh], R.[aman] K. "Editor's Note." Studies in Black Literature, 1 (Fall), inside front cover.
Acknowledges help received from Michel Fabre and Ellen Wright in putting together this special issue on W.

321. _____. "Notes on Contributors." Studies in Black Literature, 1 (Fall), 27.
Notes on the contributors to the special W issue.

322. _____. "Wright's Tragic Vision in 'The Outsider.'" Studies in Black Literature, 1 (Autumn), 23-27.
Shows relations between W's modern existentialist tragedy and ancient Greek tragedy.
Reprinted: 1971.147.

323. _____ and Peter Fellowes. "Richard Wright (1908-1960)," in their Black Literature in America: A Casebook. New York: Crowell, p. 348.
Biographical note.

324. Smith, Gery E. _American Literature: A Complete Survey_. Totowa, N. J.: Littlefield, Adams, pp. 149, 227.
Comments on NS and BB.

325. Smith, William Gardner. "The Negro Writer--Pitfalls and Compensation," in _The Black Novelist_. Ed. Robert Hemenway. Charles E. Merrill Literary Texts, ed. Matthew J. Bruccoli and Joseph Katz. Columbus, Ohio: Merrill, pp. 198-204.
Reprint of 1950.225.

326. _____. _Return to Black America_. Englewood Cliffs, N. J.: Prentice-Hall, pp. 59-62, 106-107.
Provides an account of a conversation in 1954 between W and other black expatriates in Paris. Comments on W's advice to Nkrumah.

327. Solotaroff, Theodore. "The Integration of Bigger Thomas," in his _The Red Hot Vacuum and Other Pieces on the Writing of the Sixties_. New York: Atheneum, pp. 122-132.
Reprint of 1964.117.

328. Spearman, Marie. _Richard Nathaniel Wright_. CAAS Bibliography No. 4. Atlanta: Center for African and African-American Studies, 19 pp.
Selected enumerative bibliography of primary and secondary sources without annotations.

329. Standley, Fred L. "James Baldwin: The Artist as Incorrigible Disturber of the Peace." _Southern Humanities Review_, 4 (Winter), 18-30.
Discusses Baldwin's attitudes toward W (pp. 22-24).

330. Stimpson, Catherine R. "Black Culture/White Teacher." _Change_, 2 (May-June), 35-40.
Uses NS and BB to illustrate differences in the responses of black and white students.
Reprinted: 1971.291.

331. Summerfield, Geoffrey. "Introduction," in _Black Boy_. London: Longman, pp. v-viii.
Introduction to an illustrated edition. Summerfield claims that BB can be read as a tragic story concerning the plight of a young black or simply as a story of growing up. The similarities between white and black are more important than the differences. The book takes on greater importance as Britain develops into a multiracial society.

332. Tatham, Campbell. "Double Order: The Spectrum of Black Aesthetics." _Midcontinent American Studies Journal_, 11 (Fall), 88-100.
Is black literature to be judged by the same criteria as white literature? In examining this question, Tatham uses NS as an example of the controversy.

333. Terkel, Studs. _Hard Times: An Oral History of the Great Depression_. New York: Pantheon Books, p. 438.
Notes that Horace Cayton is at work on a book about W.

334. Thorpe, Earl E. _The Mind of the Negro: An Intellectual History of Afro-Americans_. Westport, Conn.: Negro Universities Press, pp. 44, 113, 135, 215, 228, 337, 421, 439, 478.
Reprint of 1961.271.

335. Tischler, Nancy M. "Brignano, Russell Carl. _Richard Wright: An Introduction to the Man and His Works_. Margolies, Edward. _The Art of Richard Wright_." _Studies in the Novel_, 2 (Fall), 365-368.
Review rating Brignano's book higher than Margolies's. Concentrating on patterns of thought in the major works, Brignano is sensitive and penetrating. Spending too much time on minor works, Margolies writes a useful introduction but does not generate much enthusiam for W. Brignano is the critic; Margolies is the scholar.

336. Turner, Darwin T. "Afro-American Literary Critics." _Black World_, 19 (July), 54-67.
Comments on W as a literary essayist (p. 62) and mentions him elsewhere.

337. _____. _Afro-American Writers_. Goldentree Bibliographies in Language and Literature, ed. O. B. Hardison, Jr. New York: Appleton-Century-Crofts, pp. 77-80.
Lists twelve primary and fifty-nine secondary items on W.

338. _____. "The Black Playwright in the Professional Theatre of the United States of America, 1858-1959," in _Black Drama: An Anthology_. Ed. William Brasmer and Dominick Consolo. Columbus, Ohio: Merrill, pp. 1-18.
Reprint of 1969.231.

339. _____. "Collections of Stories by Individual Authors," in his _Black American Literature: Essays, Poetry, Fiction, Drama_. Charles E. Merrill Literary Texts, ed. Matthew J. Bruccoli and Joseph Katz. Columbus, Ohio: Charles E. Merrill, p. 432.
Reprint of 1969.232.

340. ____. "Introduction," in his Black American Literature: Essays, Poetry, Fiction, Drama. Charles E. Merrill Literary Texts, ed. Matthew J. Bruccoli and Joseph Katz. Columbus, Ohio: Charles E. Merrill, pp. 1-8.
Reprint of 1969.234.

341. ____. "Introduction," in his Black American Literature: Essays, Poetry, Fiction, Drama. Charles E. Merrill Literary Texts, ed. Matthew J. Bruccoli and Joseph Katz. Columbus, Ohio: Charles E. Merrill, pp. 157-164.
Reprint of 1969.236.

342. ____. "Introduction," in his Black American Literature: Essays, Poetry, Fiction, Drama. Charles E. Merrill Literary Texts, ed. Matthew J. Bruccoli and Joseph Katz. Columbus, Ohio: Charles E. Merrill, pp. 291-296.
Reprint of 1969.235.

343. ____. "Introduction: The Afro-American Playwright in the New York Professional Theatre, 1923-1959," in his Black American Literature: Essays, Poetry, Fiction, Drama. Charles E. Merrill Literary Texts, ed. Matthew J. Bruccoli and Joseph Katz. Columbus, Ohio: Charles E. Merrill, pp. 435-451.
Partial reprint of 1969.231.

344. ____. "Introduction to the Perennial Edition," in Mules and Men. By Zora Neale Hurston. New York: Harper & Row, pp. 6-20.
Calls Hurston "one of the most talented black novelists before Richard Wright" (p. 11).

345. ____. "The Outsider: Revision of an Idea." Southern Humanities Review, 4 (Winter), 40-50.
Reprint of 1969.239.

346. ____. "Richard Wright (1908-1960)," in his Black American Literature: Essays, Poetry, Fiction, Drama. Charles E. Merrill Literary Texts, ed. Matthew J. Bruccoli and Joseph Katz. Columbus, Ohio: Charles E. Merrill, pp. 361-362.
Reprint of 1969.240.

347. ____. "Significant Collections of Essays by Individual Black Writers," in his Black American Literature: Essays, Poetry, Fiction, Drama. Charles E. Merrill Literary Texts, ed. Matthew J. Bruccoli and Joseph Katz. Columbus, Ohio: Merrill, p. 153.
Reprint of 1969.232.

348. ____. "The Teaching of Afro-American Literature." College English, 31 (April), 666-670.

Mentions W briefly.
Reprinted: 1971.302; 1972.193.

349. Vogler, Thomas A. "Invisible Man: Somebody's Protest Novel." The Iowa Review, 1 (Spring), 64-82.
Relates Ellison to the protest tradition, especially to W.
Reprinted: 1971.308; 1974.172.

350. Waldmeir, Joseph J. "Only an Occasional Rutabaga: American Fiction Since 1945." Modern Fiction Studies, 15 (Winter), 467-481.
Mentions W briefly (p. 469).

350a. Walker, Margaret. "The Humanistic Tradition of Afro-American Literature." American Libraries, 1 (October), 849-854.
Mentions W and quotes from WML.

351. Walker, Warren S. Twentieth-Century Short Story Explication: Supplement I to Second Edition, 1967-1969. Hamden, Conn.: The Shoe String Press, p. 258.
Lists two items on W.

352. Ward, A. C. "Wright, Richard," in Longman Companion to Twentieth Century Literature. London: Longman, p. 583.
Biographical note.
Reprinted: 1975.200.

353. Washington, William. The Journey Teaching Guide. New York: Scholastic Book Services, pp. 126-127.
Contains a reprint of 1970.79, a guide for teaching an excerpt from LD, and a checklist of W's books.

354. Waterman, A.[rthur] E. A Chronology of American Literary History. Columbus, Ohio: Charles E. Merrill, pp. 46, 64, 65, 75.
Lists W's birth, publication of UTC, NS, and BB, and W's death.

355. Watkins, Mel and Jay David. "Biographies of Contributors," in their To Be a Black Woman: Portraits in Fact and Fiction. New York: William Morrow, pp. 281-285.
Contains a sketch of W's life (p. 285).

356. ____. "'The Ethics of Living Jim Crow,'" in their To Be a Black Woman: Portraits in Fact and Fiction. New York: William Morrow, p. 28.
Headnote to a passage from W's essay depicting the brutalization of a black woman.

357. W.[ebb], C.[onstance] W. "Wright, Richard," in Encyclopaedia Britannica. Ed. Warren E. Preece. Vol. 23. Chicago: Encyclopaedia Britannica, p. 817.

Biographical sketch.
Reprinted: 1973.298.

358. Weinberg, Helen. The New Novel in
America: The Kafkan Mode in Contemporary
Fiction. Ithaca, N. Y.: Cornell Univer-
sity Press, pp. xii-xiii, 190.
   Mentions W briefly.

359. Welburn, Ron. "The Trailblazing Art
of Richard Wright." Southwest Review, 55
(Spring), 208-209.
   Review of Russell C. Brignano's Richard Wright: An Introduction to the
   Man and His Works comparing it to
   treatments of W by Bone, Margolies,
   and McCall. Brignano treats W ideologically and speculates on his unpublished work.

360. Weser, Deborah. "Volumes on Blacks
Designed for Insight." San Antonio Sun-
day Express and News (20 December),
Sunday One Sec., p. 35.
   Mentions selections by W in Rae Pace
   Alexander's Young and Black in Amer-
   ica and Mel Watkins and Jay David's
   To Be a Black Woman.

361. White, Walter. A Man Called White:
The Autobiography of Walter White. Mid-
land Book 135. Bloomington: Indiana
University Press, p. 174.
   Reprint of 1948.259.

362. Widmer, Kingsley. "The Existential
Darkness: Richard Wright's The Outsider," in Five Black Writers. Ed. Donald B. Gibson. New York: New York University Press, pp. 50-57.
   Reprint of 1960.268.

363. Williams, Jim. "Survey of Afro-
American Playwrights." Freedomways, 10
(First Quarter), 26-45.
   Quotes Doris Abramson on the play NS
   (p. 42).
   Reprinted: 1977.348.

364. Williams, John A. "The Literary
Ghetto," in The Black Novelist. Ed.
Robert Hemenway. Charles E. Merrill
Literary Texts, ed. Matthew J. Bruccoli
and Joseph Katz. Columbus, Ohio: Mer-
rill, pp. 229-230.
   Reprint of 1963.186.

365. _____. The Most Native of Sons: A
Biography of Richard Wright. A Perspective Book. Garden City, N. Y.: Doubleday, 141 pp.
   Biography for juvenile readers. The
   emphasis throughout is biographical
   rather than critical, but the warm
   appreciation of PS is noteworthy.
   Williams provides some fresh details
   on the W-Himes friendship. The tone
   throughout is highly laudatory. The

narrative is divided into three sections: "The Mississippi Mud," "Free
at Last . . . Free at Last," and
"European Sojourn."

366. _____. "My Man Himes: An Interview
with Chester Himes." Amistad 1. Ed. John
A. Williams and Charles F. Harris. Vintage Books V-605. New York: Random
House, pp. 25-93.
   Himes recounts his friendship with W,
   assesses W's literary stature and
   influence, regrets W's abandonment of
   American themes, evaluates the quarrels between Time magazine and W and
   between Baldwin and W, and reminisces
   in some detail (pp. 85-91) on W in
   Paris.

367. Williams, Kenny J. They Also Spoke:
An Essay on Negro Literature in America,
1787-1930. Nashville: Townsend Press, p.
246.
   Contains brief discussion of "The
   Literature of the Negro in the United
   States." Mentions W briefly else-
   where.

1971

1. Aaron, Daniel. "Richard Wright and
the Communist Party." New Letters, 38
(Winter), 170-181.
   Account of the circumstances, commit-
   ments, and consequences of W's experience with the party. Examines NS in
   the light of the author's political
   affiliation and his discomfort with
   it.
   Reprinted: 1973.2, 3.

2. Abcarian, Richard. "Brignano, Russell
C. Richard Wright: An Introduction to
the Man and His Works." Journal of
Modern Literature, 1 (Summer), 958-
961.
   Unfavorable review complaining that
   Brignano ignores W's central theme of
   the effect of white racism on black
   psychology. His thematic organization
   fragments his treatment of W's fiction.

3. Abrahams, Peter. "The Blacks," in
Race Awareness: The Nightmare and the
Vision. Ed. Ruth Miller and Paul J.
Dolan. New York: Oxford University
Press, pp. 84-95.
   Reprint of 1959.1.

4. Alexander, Margaret Walker. "Richard
Wright." New Letters, 38 (Winter), 182-
202.
   Personal account of the author's
   relationship with W, whom she first
   met in February 1936. The friendship
   continued until his expatriation. She
   discussed NS with W, and he commented

on Jubilee. Alexander also considers
the literary and philosophical influences on W's writing.
Reprinted: 1973.10, 11.

5. Allen, Michael. "Some Examples of
Faulknerian Rhetoric in Ellison's Invisible Man," in The Black American Writer. Ed. C. W. E. Bigsby. Vol. 1. Baltimore: Penguin Books, pp. 143-151.
Reprint of 1969.4.

6. Allen, Samuel W. "Negritude and Its
Relevance for the American Negro Writ-
er," in Backgrounds to Blackamerican
Literature. Ed. Ruth Miller. Chandler
Publications in Backgrounds to Litera-
ture, ed. Richard A. Levine. Scranton,
Pa.: Chandler Publishing Company, pp.
136-144.
Reprint of 1960.4.

7. ____. "Negritude and Its Relevance
to the American Negro Writer," in Cavalcade: Negro American Writing from 1760
to the Present. Ed. Arthur P. Davis and
Saunders Redding. Boston: Houghton Mifflin, pp. 617-626.
Reprint of 1960.4.

8. Amis, Lola Jones. Native Son Notes.
Lincoln, Neb.: Cliff's Notes, 54 pp.
Student guide to the novel with a
full summary of the plot and analysis
of the characters.

9. Anon. "The Afro-American in Films
1902-1967," in Richard Wright and His
Influence. Ed. Robert A. Corrigan. Third
Annual Institute for Afro-American Culture. Iowa City: The University of Iowa,
pp. [474-494].
Lists the film NS (p. 486).

10. Anon. "Books." Dallas Morning News
(25 April), Sec. D., p. 2.
Includes The Most Native of Sons
among books for younger readers.

11. Anon. "Books for Brotherhood." Commonweal, 93 (26 February), 520-523.
Contains a notice of John A. Williams's The Most Native of Sons.

11a. Anon. Index to Periodical Articles
by and About Negroes: Cumulated 1960-
1970. Boston: G. K. Hall, pp. 241, 371,
605.
Lists two items on NS and fifteen
items on W.

12. Anon. Index Translationum 22. Paris:
Unesco, pp. 201, 450, 499, 574, 663,
804.
Lists translations of NS into Danish
and Polish, BB into Danish and Italian, EM into Japanese, WML into
Japanese, O into German, and LD into

Serbo-Croatian.

13. Anon. "'It Is Detrimental to Us as
Black Human Beings to Be Controlled by
Racists,'" in Black Protest Thought in
the Twentieth Century. Ed. August Meier,
Elliott Rudwick, and Francis L. Brod-
erick. Second edition. The American
Heritage Series, ed. Leonard W. Levy and
Alfred F. Young. Indianapolis: Bobbs-
Merrill, pp. 528-535.
Reprint of 1969.9.

14. Anon. "Letter Comes to the Defense
of Wright After July 9, 1971, Article
Attacking Him." Muhammed Speaks (30
July), p. 20.
Defends W against Leon Forrest's
criticism. See 1971.123.

15. Anon. "'Native Son.'" New Letters,
38 (Winter), 46.
Advertisement for the film.
Reprinted: 1973.29, 30.

15a. Anon. "1971: A Selection of Noteworthy Titles." The New York Times Book
Review (5 December), pp. 78-88.
Contains a notice of The Autobiography of Miss Jane Pittman pointing
out that Ernest Gaines is "a writer
whose style is closer to Charles
Dickens and Langston Hughes than to
Richard Wright or Ralph Ellison" (p.
82). See 1971.308a.

16. Anon. "Richard Wright at Wading
River, L. I., 1947." New Letters, 38
(Winter), 97.
Photograph of W and his cat.
Reprinted: 1973.32, 33.

17. Anon. "Richard Wright in Chicago,
1928." New Letters, 38 (Winter), 41.
Photograph.
Reprinted: 1973.34, 35.

18. Anon. "Richard Wright's Native Son."
New Letters, 38 (Winter), 47.
Photograph of Bigger and Bessie in
a scene from the film.
Reprinted: 1973.37, 38.

19. Anon. "Richard Wright's Native Son."
New Letters, 38 (Winter), 48.
Photograph of W as Bigger in a scene
from the film.
Reprinted: 1973.39, 40.

20. Anon. "Richard Wright's Native Son."
New Letters, 38 (Winter), 98.
Photograph of Gloria Madison as Bes-
sie in a scene from the film.
Reprinted: 1973.41, 42.

21. Anon. "Richard Wright's Native Son:
A Critical Handbook." Mississippi Quarterly, 24 (Spring), 212.

Brief notice of Abcarian's book.

22. Anon. "Rocky Mount, N. C." News-letter on Intellectual Freedom, 20 (March), 33-34.
Reports that fundamentalist ministers caused New Worlds in Literature and Voices in Literature to be removed from junior high schools because they include works by W and other Commu-nists.

23. Anon. "Wright, Richard. Black Boy. Read by Brock Peters." The Booklist, 67 (15 March), 599.
Favorable review of the Caedmon recording with special praise for the skill of the abridgement.

24. Anon. "Wright, Richard (1908-1960)," in The New Book of Knowledge. Ed. Martha Glauber Shapp. Vol. 20. New York: Grolier, p. 316.
Biographical sketch.

25. Appel, Benjamin. "Personal Impres-sions." New Letters, 38 (Winter), 20-23.
Recalls friendship with W in Brooklyn in the forties, explaining W's atti-tude toward the war and military service. Comments on whiteness as a theme in W's imagination.
Reprinted: 1973.48, 49.

26. Aptheker, Herbert. Afro-American History: The Modern Era. New York: The Citadel Press, pp. 259-260.
Reprint of 1965.30.

27. Atkinson, Brooks. "'Native Son,'" in The New York Times Theater Reviews 1920-1970. Vol. 4. New York: The New York Times & Arno Press, p. [644].
Reprint of 1941.636.

28. ____. "'Native Son,' by Paul Green and Richard Wright, Put On by Orson Welles and John Houseman," in The New York Times Theater Reviews 1920-1970. Vol. 4. New York: The New York Times & Arno Press, pp. [640-641].
Reprint of 1941.638.

29. Baker, Houston A., Jr. "Black Ameri-can Literature: An Overview," in his Black Literature in America. New York: McGraw-Hill, pp. 2-18.
Discusses W's place in black literary tradition.

30. ____. "Completely Well: One View of Black American Culture," in Key Issues in the Afro-American Experience. Ed. Nathan I. Huggins, Martin Kilson, and Daniel M. Fox. Vol. 1. New York: Har-court Brace Jovanovich, pp. 20-33.
Refers to Bigger Thomas as a trick-ster.

Reprinted: 1972.24.

31. ____. "Richard Wright (1908-1960)," in his Black Literature in America. New York: McGraw-Hill, p. 436.
Biographical sketch to accompany "Bright and Morning Star" and "The Ethics of Living Jim Crow."
Partially reprinted: 1973.256.

32. ____. "The Thirties and Forties," in his Black Literature in America. New York: McGraw-Hill, pp. 204-208.
Discusses W's place in the depression and war years.

33. Bakish, David. "Underground in an Ambiguous Dreamworld." Studies in Black Literature, 2 (Autumn), 18-23.
Summarizes the plot and analyzes the symbols of "The Man Who Lived Under-ground." Most of the symbols in the story are ambiguous: light, darkness, fire, childhood, diamonds, movies, church, sewer. The theme is the nightmare world of blacks and the difficulty of distinguishing between dream and reality.

34. Baldwin, James. "Many Thousands Gone," in Backgrounds to Blackamerican Literature. Ed. Ruth Miller. Chandler Publications in Backgrounds to Litera-ture, ed. Richard A. Levine. Scranton, Pa.: Chandler, pp. 218-229.
Reprint of 1951.129.

34a. ____ et al. "The Negro in American Culture," in The Black American Writer. Ed. C. W. E. Bigsby. Vol. 1. DeLand, Fla.: Everett/Edwards, pp. 79-108.
Reprint of 1961.118.

35. Baldwin, Richard E. "The Art of The Conjure Woman." American Literature, 43 (November), 385-398.
Compares Chesnutt's choice of Uncle Julius as a negative stereotype to W's choice of Bigger Thomas.
Partially reprinted: 1979.33.

36. Baritz, Loren. "The Black Begin-ning," in his The American Left: Radical Political Thought in the Twentieth Cen-tury. New York: Basic Books, pp. 271-273.
Comments on "Bright and Morning Star" as a work of "literary power and black rage."

37. ____. "The Literary Class Strug-gle," in his The American Left: Radical Political Thought in the Twentieth Cen-tury. New York: Basic Books, pp. 189-191.
Mentions W briefly.

38. Baumbach, Jonathan. "Nightmare of a

Native Son: Invisible Man, by Ralph
Ellison," in Modern Black Novelists: A
Collection of Critical Essays. Ed. M. G.
Cooke. Englewood Cliffs, N. J.: Pren-
tice-Hall, pp. 64-78.
    Reprint of 1963.50a.

38a. Beja, Morris. "Bibliography," in
his Psychological Fiction. Glenview,
Ill.: Scott, Foresman, pp. 489-499.
    Includes three items on W.

38b. _____. "Eros," in his Psychological
Fiction. Glenview, Ill.: Scott, Foresman, pp. 84-86.
    Comments on "The Man Who Killed a
    Shadow," relating it to Jungian psy-
    chology.

39. Bennett, Stephen B. and William W.
Nichols. "Violence in Afro-American Fic-
tion: An Hypothesis." Modern Fiction
Studies, 17 (Summer), 221-228.
    Uses "Bright and Morning Star," NS,
    and O as examples of the character-
    istic violence of black fiction. In
    W's case the violence is creative.
    Reprinted: 1974.25.

40. Benoit, Bernard and Michel Fabre. "A
Bibliography of Ralph Ellison's Published Writings." Studies in Black Literature, 2 (Autumn), 25-28.
    Lists three items on W.

41. Bergen, Daniel Patrick. "In Fear of
Abstraction: The Southern Response to
the North in Twentieth-Century Fiction
and Non-Fiction." Dissertation Abstracts
International, 31 (April), 5389-A.
    Uses W and others to show a Southern
    predilection toward concrete detail
    and a fear of an abstract world view.

42. Bigsby, C. W. E. "The Black American
Writer," in his The Black American Writer. Vol. 1. Baltimore: Penguin Books,
pp. 5-33.
    Reprint of 1969.29.

43. Bilbo, Theodore G. Untitled speech.
New Letters, 38 (Winter), 16.
    Reprint of 1945.773.

44. Birdoff, Harry. "Personal Impressions." New Letters, 38 (Winter), 24-27.
    Recalls meeting W in the spring of
    1941 and comments on W's experience
    with the theater. Also relates anec-
    dotes about W's work habits
    Reprinted: 1973.61, 62.

45. Bone, Robert. "Ralph Ellison and the
Uses of Imagination," in Modern Black
Novelists: A Collection of Critical
Essays. Ed. M. G. Cooke. Twentieth Cen-
tury Views Series. Englewood Cliffs,
N. J.: Prentice-Hall, pp. 45-63.

Reprint of 1966.22.

46. _____. "Ralph Ellison and the Uses
of Imagination," in The Merrill Studies
in Invisible Man. Ed. Ronald Gottesman.
Charles E. Merrill Studies, ed. Matthew
J. Bruccoli and Joseph Katz. Columbus,
Ohio: Merrill, pp. 16-36.
    Reprint of 1966.22.

47. Bontemps, Arna. "Harlem, the Beau-
tiful Years," in Bondage, Freedom, and
Beyond: The Prose of Black Americans.
Ed. Addison Gayle, Jr. Zenith Books
Z19, ed. Milton Meltzer. Garden City,
N. Y.: Doubleday, pp. 76-82.
    Reprint of 1963.59.

48. _____. "The Negro Renaissance:
Jean Toomer and the Harlem Writers
of the 1920's," in Backgrounds to
Blackamerican Literature. Ed. Ruth
Miller. Chandler Publications in Back-
grounds to Literature, ed. Richard A.
Levine. Scranton, Pa.: Chandler, pp.
165-176.
    Reprint of 1966.24.

49. Borges, Jorge Luis. An Introduction
to American Literature. Trans. and ed.
L. Clark Keating and Robert O. Evans.
Lexington: The University Press of Kentucky, pp. 71-72.
    Translation of 1967.15.

50. Bracey, John H., Jr. "Black Nation-
alism since Garvey," in Key Issues in
the Afro-American Experience. Ed. Nathan
I. Huggins, Martin Kilson, and David M.
Fox. Vol. 2. New York: Harcourt Brace
Jovanovich, pp. 259-279.
    Mentions BP (p. 273).

51. Bradbury, Malcolm, Eric Mottram, and
Jean Franco. "Negro Literature," in
their The Penguin Companion to American
Literature. New York: McGraw-Hill, pp.
186-189.
    Mentions W briefly.

52. _____. "Wright, Richard (1908-
1960)," in their The Penguin Companion
to American Literature. New York:
McGraw-Hill, p. 276.
    Biographical sketch.

53. Bridges, Lloyd. "Flight in the American Novel." Dissertation Abstracts
International, 32 (December), 3243-A.
    Mentions W's fiction as a black quest
    for identity.

54. Brignano, Russell C. "Richard
Wright: A Bibliography of Secondary
Sources." Studies in Black Literature, 2
(Summer), 19-25.
    Lists 178 items under the following
    categories: books about W, pamphlets

about W, books containing individual chapters or major sections on W, other books offering significant discussions of W, journal special numbers devoted to W, essays about W, and other essays containing discussions of W.

55. Briscoe, Alden F. The WPA: What Is to Be Learned. Issues Paper No. 2. Washington, D. C.: Center for Governmental Studies, p. 19.
    Mentions W's employment by the WPA.

56. Brown, Sterling A. "A Century of Negro Portraiture in American Literature," in Afro-American Literature: An Introduction. Ed. by Robert Hayden, David J. Burrows, and Fredrick R. Lapides. New York: Harcourt Brace Jovanovich, pp. 249-271.
    Reprint of 1966.30.

56a. ____. "A Century of Negro Portraiture in American Literature," in Black Insights: Significant Literature by Black Americans--1760 to the Present. Ed. Nick Aaron Ford. Waltham, Mass.: Ginn, pp. 66-78.
    Reprint of 1966.30.

57. ____. "The New Negro in Literature (1925-1955)," in Cavalcade: Negro American Writing from 1760 to the Present. Ed. Arthur P. Davis and Saunders Redding. Boston: Houghton Mifflin, pp. 410-427.
    Reprint of 1955.32.

58. Bruchac, Joseph. "Black Autobiography in Africa and America." Black Academy Review, 2 (Spring-Summer), 61-70.
    Compares BB and Camara Laye's The Dark Child.
    Reprinted: 1971.59.

59. ____. "Black Autobiography in Africa and America," in Modern Black Literature. Ed. S. Okechukwu Mezu. Buffalo: Black Academy Press, pp. 61-70.
    Reprint of 1971.58.

60. Bryant, Jerry H. "Politics and the Black Novel." The Nation, 213 (20 December), 660-662.
    Stresses the primacy of NS as a novel of black protest.

61. Budd, Louis J. "Richard Wright: An Introduction to the Man and His Works. By Russell Carl Brignano." The South Atlantic Quarterly, 70 (Winter), 131-132.
    Favorable review praising Brignano's balanced assessment and pointing out his emphasis on W's belief that rational human society is possible.

62. [Bullins, Ed]. Untitled footnote. Black Theatre, No. 5, p. 47.
    Claims that W was driven from the United States by whites.

63. Burnett, Whit. "Preface: The Long Shadow," in his Black Hands on a White Face: A Timepiece of Experiences in a Black and White America. New York: Dodd, Mead, pp. vii-x.
    Refers to W's central position in the development of Afro-American literature.

64. ____. "Richard Wright 'How 'Bigger' Was Born,'" in his Black Hands on a White Face: A Timepiece of Experience in a Black and White America. New York: Dodd, Mead, p. 215.
    Biographical headnote.

64a. Burns, Ben. "Gertrude Stein on Race, Racists and Racism." Sepia, 2 (July), 56-62.
    Includes an account of the Stein-W relationship, noting their high opinion of each other and their personal quarrels in Paris. Burns quotes from interviews with Stein and W and from a letter from W to Joe C. Brown.

64b. Burns, Landon C. , Jr. "The 1970 Supplement to a Cross-Referenced Index of Short Fiction Anthologies and Author-Title Listing." Studies in Short Fiction, 8 (Spring), 351-409.
    Lists three W stories in five anthologies.

64c. Cahill, Tom and Susan Cahill. "Introduction," in their Big City Stories by Modern American Writers. New York: Bantam, pp. viii-x.
    Mentions W briefly.

64d. ____. "Selected Bibliography," in their Big City Stories by Modern American Writers. New York: Bantam, pp. 403-405.
    Lists seven of W's books.

65. Camus, Albert. "Letter to Richard Wright." New Letters, 38 (Winter), 132.
    Concerns a project for Twice a Year, to which W, Camus, and others were asked to contribute. The date of the letter is 16 October [1946 or 1947]. Reprinted: 1973.79, 80.

66. Carmichael, Stokely. "At Morgan State," in his Stokely Speaks: Black Power Back to Pan-Africanism. New York: Random House, p. 74.
    In a speech on 28 January 1967, Carmichael urges Morgan State students to read W and other militant black writers.

67. Cayton, Horace and Sidney Williams. "Personal Impressions." New Letters, 38 (Winter), 37-40.
Transcript of a tape recording made in August of 1967. Concerns mainly W's African experience and his status as an expatriate writer in Paris. Reprinted: 1973.91, 92.

68. Chapman, Frank E., Jr. "Pages from the Life of a Black Prisoner." Freedomways, 11 (Third Quarter), 332-345.
Contains a favorable mention of W. Reprinted: 1977.88.

68a. Cherry, Richard L., Robert J. Conley, and Bernard A. Hirsch. "Suggestions for Further Reading," in their A Return to Vision. Boston: Houghton Mifflin, pp. 397-400.
Lists NS.
Reprinted: 1974.43.

69. Childress, Alice. "Biographies," in her Black Scenes. Zenith Books Z21, ed. Milton Meltzer. Garden City, N. Y.: Doubleday, pp. 147-152.
Contains a sketch of Theodore Ward mentioning W.

69a. Clarke, John Henrik. "The Origin and Growth of Afro-American Literature," in Afro-American Literature: An Introduction. Ed. Robert Hayden, David J. Burrows, and Frederick R. Lapides. New York: Harcourt Brace Jovanovich, pp. 283-294.
Reprint of 1967.22.

70. Cleaver, Eldridge. "Notes on a Native Son," in Backgrounds to Blackamerican Literature. Ed. Ruth Miller. Chandler Publications in Backgrounds to Literature, ed. Richard A. Levine. Scranton, Pa.: Chandler, pp. 230-238.
Reprint of 1966.37.

71. _____. "On Becoming," in Black Insights: Significant Literature by Black Americans--1760 to the Present. Ed. Nick Aaron Ford. Waltham, Mass.: Ginn, pp. 347-352.
Reprint of 1966.38.

72. Cocteau, Jean. "Letter to Richard Wright." New Letters, 38 (Winter), 133.
In a letter of 1950 Cocteau declines an invitation and asks W for documents on Harlem for an article Cocteau is writing. Reprinted: 1973.95, 96.

72a. Cohn, David L. "The Negro Novel," in Makers of America. Ed. Wayne Moquin. Vol. 9: Refugees and Victims 1939-1954. Chicago: Encyclopaedia Britannica Educational Corporation, pp. 188-190.
Partial reprint of 1940.608.

73. Coles, Robert, M. D. Migrants, Sharecroppers, Mountaineers. Vol. 2 of Children of Crisis. Boston: Little, Brown, p. 626.
Mentions briefly NS.

73a. _____. The South Goes North. Vol. 3 of Children of Crisis. Boston: Little, Brown, pp. 660, 667.
Mentions W briefly.

74. Conroy, Jack. "Personal Impressions." New Letters, 38 (Winter), 33-36.
Recalls W in Chicago, especially his associations with The Anvil and The New Anvil.
Reprinted: 1973.97, 98.

75. Cooke, M. G. "Biographical Notes," in his Modern Black Novelists: A Collection of Critical Essays. Twentieth Century Views Series. Englewood Cliffs, N. J.: Prentice-Hall, pp. 210-212.
Includes a biographical sketch of W.

76. _____. "Introduction," in his Modern Black Novelists: A Collection of Critical Essays. Twentieth Century Views Series. Englewood Cliffs, N. J.: Prentice-Hall, pp. 1-12.
Comments on W's symbolic fiction and use of violence.

77. Cornish, Sam. "Bigger Thomas Says Some Bad Niggers Is Over Thirty," in his Generations. Boston: Beacon Press, pp. 76-77.
Poem comparing W's protagonist to rebellious blacks thirty years later.

78. _____. "My Brother Is Homemade," in his Generations. Boston: Beacon Press, p. 29.
Poem mentioning W.
Reprinted: 1974.49.

79. Corrigan, Robert A. "Afro-American Fiction: A Checklist 1853-1970," in his Richard Wright and His Influence. Third Annual Institute for Afro-American Culture. Iowa City: The University of Iowa, pp. [70-198].
Revised reprint of 1970.93.

80. _____. "Richard Wright Criticism: A Checklist," in his Richard Wright and His Influence. Third Annual Institute for Afro-American Culture. Iowa City: The University of Iowa, pp. [5-68].
Lists 472 items under the following categories: bibliographies, books, pamphlets, journal issues, portions of books, essays, and reviews.

81. Cripps, Thomas. "Native Son in the Movies." New Letters, 38 (Winter), 49-63).
Traces the film history of NS from

W's initial encounter with Hollywood to its reception on the international scene. Cripps explains such matters as contracts, casting, production, and financial considerations.
Reprinted: 1973.107, 108.

82. Davis, Arthur P. and Saunders Redding. "The New Negro Renaissance and Beyond 1910-1954," in their Cavalcade: Negro American Writing from 1760 to the Present. Boston: Houghton Mifflin, pp. 228-235.
Discusses W briefly, focusing on NS (pp. 234-235).

83. _____. "Ralph Ellison," in their Cavalcade: Negro American Writing from 1760 to the Present. Boston: Houghton Mifflin, p. 532.
Headnote mentioning Ellison's acquaintance with W.

84. _____. "Richard Wright," in their Cavalcade: Negro American Writing from 1760 to the Present. Boston: Houghton Mifflin, pp. 459-460.
Biographical-critical headnote.

85. _____. "Selective Bibliography," in their Cavalcade: Negro American Writing from 1760 to the Present. Boston: Houghton Mifflin, pp. 873-897.
Lists twelve titles by W.

85a. Denisoff, R. Serge. Great Day Coming: Folk Music and the American Left. Urbana: University of Illinois Press, p. 56.
Quotes W on the Communist Party.

86. Deodene, Frank and William P. French. Black American Poetry Since 1944: A Preliminary Checklist. Chatham, N. J.: The Chatham Bookseller, pp. 39, 44.
Lists W's The F. B. Eye Blues and advertises a reprint edition of LD.

87. Dickstein, Morris. "Wright, Baldwin, Cleaver." New Letters, 38 (Winter), 117-124.
Discusses NS and BB in terms of their influence on later black writers. The basic pattern is that of a Bildungsroman. For W theme and material continually clashed.
Reprinted: 1973.113, 114.

88. Dodson, Owen. "Personal Impressions." New Letters, 38 (Winter), 30-32.
Comments on W's self-education, especially in horticulture; notes his magnanimous attitude toward other writers; defines Bigger's tragedy; mentions W's affinity for existentialism; and praises his sense of

"the mystery and wonder of childhood." Dodson calls him "one of the warmest, and most generous and gentle writers I have ever met."
Reprinted: 1973.115, 116.

89. Elam, Julia Corene. "The Afro-American Short Story: From Accommodation to Protest." Dissertation Abstracts International, 32 (November), 2683-A.
Anthology with "General Introduction" and "Course Evaluation." Through no authors are mentioned, W is presumably included.

90. Ellison, Curtis William. "Black Adam: The Adamic Assertion and the Afro-American Novelist." Dissertation Abstracts International, 32 (September), 1508-A.
Studies the response of six black writers to the American dream. "Of this group, only Richard Wright evolves a firm rejection of adamic innocence as an influence destructive to human community."

91. Ellison, Ralph. "Hidden Name and Complex Fate," in Backgrounds to Black-american Literature. Ed. Ruth Miller. Chandler Publications in Backgrounds to Literature, ed. Richard A. Levine. Scranton, Pa.: Chandler, pp. 183-196.
Reprint of 1964.45.

92. _____. "Hidden Name and Complex Fate: A Writer's Experience in the United States," in Cavalcade: Negro American Writing from 1760 to the Present. Ed. Arthur P. Davis and Saunders Redding. Boston: Houghton Mifflin, pp. 550-565.
Reprint of 1964.45.

93. _____. "Richard Wright's Blues," in Black Insights: Significant Literature by Black Americans--1760 to the Present. Ed. Nick Aaron Ford. Waltham, Mass.: Ginn, pp. 186-192.
Reprint of 1945.890.

94. _____. "Richard Wright's Blues," in Criticism: Some Major American Writers. Ed. Lewis Leary. New York: Holt, Rinehart and Winston, pp. 392-403.
Reprint of 1945.890.

95. _____, Alfred Chester, and Vilma Howard. "The Art of Fiction: An Interview," in The Merrill Studies in Invisible Man. Ed. Ronald Gottesman. Charles E. Merrill Studies, ed. Matthew J. Bruccoli and Joseph Katz. Columbus, Ohio: Merrill, pp. 38-49.
Reprint of 1955.40.

96. Emanuel, James A. "Blackness Can: A Quest for Aesthetics," in The Black

Aesthetic. Ed. Addison Gayle, Jr. Garden City, N. Y.: Doubleday, pp. 192-223.
Contains a rebuttal of Cecil Brown's attack in "The Lesson and the Legacy: Richard Wright's Complexes and Black Writing Today."
Reprinted: 1972.62.

97. Essien-Udom, E. U. "Black Identity in the International Context," in Key Issues in the Afro-American Experience. Ed. Nathan I. Huggins, Martin Kilson, and Daniel M. Fox. Vol. 2. New York: Harcourt Brace Jovanovich, pp. 233-258.
Quotes Baldwin on W (p. 237).

98. Esslinger, Pat M. and Thomas A. Green. "Content Analysis in Black and White: A Research Note." Negro American Literature Forum, 5 (Winter), 123-125, 139.
Arguing that Afro-American culture is oriented toward "patterns of dramatic performance" rather than goals, the authors cite "The Man Who Saw the Flood" in support of their thesis.

98a. Evans, Oliver and Harry Finestone. "Richard Wright: The Man Who Was Almost a Man," in their Instructor's Manual for The World of the Short Story: Archetypes in Action. New York: Knopf, pp. 78-79.
Comments on the story and on W's career in general. Includes study questions.

99. E.[vans]. P.[amela]. "Wright, Richard (1908-1960)," in Twentieth Century Writing: A Reader's Guide to Contemporary Literature. Ed. Kenneth Richardson. Levittown, N. Y.: Transatlantic Arts, p. 666.
Reprint of 1969.74.

100. Fabio, Sarah Webster. "Tripping with Black Writing," in The Black Aesthetic. Ed. Addison Gayle, Jr. Garden City, N. Y.: Doubleday, pp. 173-181.
Contains brief references to Bigger and W (p. 181).
Reprinted: 1972.64.

101. Fabre, Michel. "'The American Problem--Its Negro Phase' Richard Wright." New Letters, 38 (Winter), 9.
Brief headnote to a previously unpublished essay by W.
Reprinted: 1973.123, 124.

102. _____. "Bibliographie choisie," in his bilingual edition of L'Homme qui vivait sous terre. By Richard Wright. Paris: Aubier-Flammarion, pp. 53-57.
Lists twenty-six primary and secondary items, including some in progress.

103. _____. "Black Cat and White Cat: Richard Wright's Debt to Edgar Allan Poe." Poe Studies, 4 (June), 17-19.
Notes similarities between the methods of Poe and W, especially in atmosphere, tone, and the technique of doubling. Discusses "Superstition" and NS.

104. _____. "Chronologie," in his bilingual edition of L'Homme qui vivait sous terre. By Richard Wright. Paris: Aubier-Flammarion, pp. 9-12.
Contains thirty-two entries, most of them for the period beginning in 1932.

105. _____. "Fathers and Sons in James Baldwin's Go Tell It on the Mountain," in Modern Black Novelists: A Collection of Critical Essays. Ed. M. G. Cooke. Twentieth Century Views Series. Englewood Cliffs, N. J.: Prentice-Hall, pp. 88-104.
Translation by Katherine P. Mack of 1970.123.

106. _____. "Note." New Letters, 38 (Winter), 131.
Note to a letter from Andre Gide to W.
Reprinted: 1973.127, 128.

107. _____. "Notes." New Letters, 38 (Winter), 132.
Notes to a letter from Albert Camus to W.
Reprinted: 1973.129, 130.

108. _____. "Préface," in his bilingual edition of L'Homme qui vivait sous terre. By Richard Wright. Paris: Aubier-Flammarion, pp. 15-51.
After discovering and discussing the source of "The Man Who Lived Underground" in a story appearing in True Detective magazine, Fabre reviews its reception and explores its artistry and its philosophical profundities. "The Man Who Lived Underground" in a fable of human destiny carefully crafted and copiously imagined.
Translated in abridged form: 1971.110.

109. _____. "Présentation," in Violence II. Paris: Editions du seuil, pp. 21-24.
Mentions W briefly as a militant poet. Fabre's translation of "Between the World and Me" appears on pp. 27-28.

110. _____. "Richard Wright: The Man Who Lived Underground." Studies in the Novel, 3 (Summer), 165-179.
Abridged translation of 1971.108.

111. _____. "Wright's Exile." New Let-

ters, 38 (Winter), 136-154.
Discusses W's attitudes toward America before and after his self-imposed exile in France. Fabre contends that his expatriation resulted more from white America's attitude toward him than from his discovery of a freer and richer culture in France. Reprinted: 1973.135, 136.

112. _____ and Edward Margolies. "A Bibliography of Richard Wright's Works." New Letters, 38 (Winter), 155-169.
Reprint of 1965.59 with additions. Reprinted: 1973.137, 138.

113. Fanon, Frantz. "Letter to Richard Wright." New Letters, 38 (Winter), 135.
Letter dated 6 January 1953 introducing himself and asking W for titles of his works unknown to Fanon. Reprinted: 1973.140, 141.

114. Farnsworth, Robert M. "Introduction." New Letters, 38 (Winter), 5-7.
Introducing the special issue on "The Life and Work of Richard Wright," Farnsworth explains how it developed from the University of Iowa conference on W. He hopes that the issue will stimulate further study of W.

114a. Farrison, W. Edward. "Black Literature in America. By Houston A. Baker." CLA Journal, 15 (September), 90-93.
Review taking issue with Baker's judgement of BB and his dating of the editions of UTC.

115. Faulkner, William. "Letter to Richard Wright." New Letters, 38 (Winter), 128.
Comments favorably on BB and more favorably on NS. Advises W to be less personal, more universal. Reprinted: 1973.146, 147.

115a. Fenderson, Lewis H. "The New Breed of Black Writers and Their Jaundiced View of Tradition." CLA Journal, 15 (September), 18-24.
Mentions W briefly.

116. Fischer, William C. "The Aggregate Man in Jean Toomer's Cane." Studies in the Novel, 3 (Summer), 190-215.
Quotes BB in a note to corroborate Toomer's representation of Kabnis' state of mind.

116a. F.[ohlen], C. "Noirs (États-Unis)," in Encyclopaedia Universalis. Ed. Claude Gregory. Vol. 11. Paris: Encyclopaedia Universalis France, pp. 837-840
Mentions briefly W and three other writers.

117. Ford, Nick Aaron. "Claude Brown (1937-   )," in his Black Insights: Significant Literature by Black Americans--1760 to the Present. Waltham, Mass.: Ginn, pp. 310-311.
Compares Manchild in the Promised Land to BB.

118. _____. "Comments and Questions," in his Black Insights: Significant Literature by Black Americans--1760 to the Present. Waltham, Mass.: Ginn, pp. 299-302.
Contains seven items on W (p. 300).

119. _____. "Introduction," in his Black Insights: Significant Literature by Black Americans-- 1760 to the Present. Waltham, Mass.: Ginn, pp. xiii-xix.
Mentions the novel NS as the pinnacle of black fiction (p. xv). Mentions also the play NS (p. xviii).

120. _____. "The Ordeal of Richard Wright," in his Black Insights: Significant Literature by Black Americans--1760 to the Present. Waltham, Mass.: Ginn, pp. 123-128.
Reprint of 1953.126.

121. _____. "Ralph Ellison (1914-   )," in his Black Insights: Significant Literature by Black Americans-- 1760 to the Present. Waltham, Mass.: Ginn, p. 177.
Mentions Ellison's friendship with W.

122. _____. "Richard Wright (1908-1960)," in his Black Insights: Significant Literature by Black Americans--1760 to the Present. Waltham, Mass.: Ginn, pp. 164-166.
Biographical-critical essay mentioning most of W's works. His expatriation put him in touch with the Third World but out of touch with his own country.

123. Forrest, Leon. "Scholars, Authors Study Contradictions of Richard Wright." Muhammed Speaks (9 July), pp. 23-24.
Announces the W conference at the University of Iowa. Forrest criticizes W for not realizing Bigger's humanity in NS. Includes a photograph of W.

124. Forsythe, Dennis. "Roll-Call of the Negro Intellectual." Présence Africaine, No. 77 (First Quarter), pp. 240-249.
Critique of The Crisis of the Negro Intellectual contrasting Cruse's elitist view to W's underdog perspective, especially in their explanations of black attitudes toward Jews.

125. Frazier, Thomas R. "Suggestions for Further Reading," in his Afro-American

History: Primary Sources. Shorter edition. New York: Harcourt Brace Jovanovich, p. 169.
Reprint of 1970.135.

125a. Freese, Peter. Die Initiationsreise: Studien zum jugendlichen Helden im modernen amerikanischen Roman. Neumünster: Karl Wachholtz Verlag, pp. 64-65, 67, 86, 88, 172, 174.
Contains a paragraph on the theme of Bigger's rebirth through violence (pp. 64-65). Elsewhere Freese mentions briefly W, Bigger, and BB.

126. Frémy, Dominique and Michèle Frémy. Quid? Tout pour tous. Paris: Librairie Plon, p. 50.
Reprint of 1963.86.

126a. French, Warren. "Fiction: 1900 to the 1930's," in American Literary Scholarship: An Annual/1969. Ed. J. Albert Robbins. Durham, N. C.: Duke University Press, pp. 200-223.
Discusses two books, a monograph, and eleven articles on W (pp. 220-223) and mentions W briefly elsewhere (p. 201).

127. _____. "The Lost Potential of Richard Wright," in The Black American Writer. Ed. C. W. E. Bigsby. Vol. 1. Baltimore: Penguin, pp. 125-142.
Reprint of 1969.90.

128. Fuller, Hoyt W. "Contemporary Negro Fiction," in The Black American Writer. Ed. C. W. E. Bigsby. Vol 1. Baltimore: Penguin Books, pp. 229-243.
Reprint of 1965.68.

129. _____. "The New Black Literature: Protest or Affirmation," in The Black Aesthetic. Ed. Addison Gayle, Jr. Garden City, N. Y.: Doubleday, pp. 346-369.
Notes that W wrote a book (SH) with no black characters.
Reprinted: 1972.77.

130. _____. "The Turning of the Wheel." The Black Position, No. 1, pp. 4-5.
Mentions briefly "those vulgar Bigger Thomases whose rising fury takes sporadic shape in murder and flames."

131. Galloway, David D. "Helen Weinberg. The New Novel in America: The Kafkan Mode in Contemporary Fiction; Barry H. Leeds. The Structured Vision of Norman Mailer; Russell Carl Brignano. Richard Wright: An Introduction to the Man and His Works." Modern Fiction Studies, 16 (Winter), 566-571.
Brignano "richly evokes the drama continuously enacted within the artist, but he is less successful in appraising the art that springs from that drama." Brignano does succeed in showing W's prophetic quality.

132. Gayle, Addison. "Cultural Nationalism: The Black Novelist in America." Black Books Bulletin, 1 (Fall), 4-9.
Praises W as the first black novelist to "affirm his commitment to reality." Examining this reality by means of the "concentration camp metaphor" appropriate to his time, W in NS demolishes the "American myth" and presents a "nationalistic formula" for avoiding racial war.

133. _____. "Cultural Strangulation: Black Literature and the White Aesthetic," in his The Black Aesthetic. Garden City, N. Y.: Doubleday, pp. 38-45.
Reprint of 1969.101.

134. _____. "The Function of Black Literature at the Present Time," in his The Black Aesthetic. Garden City, N. Y.: Doubleday, pp. 407-419.
Quotes approvingly "Blueprint for Negro Writing."
Reprinted: 1972.81.

135. _____. "I Was in the South Where Neither Law nor Tradition Was on My Side," in his Bondage, Freedom, and Beyond: The Prose of Black Americans. Garden City, N. Y.: Doubleday, p. 82.
Headnote to an excerpt from "How Jim Crow Feels."

136. _____. "Introduction," in his The Black Aesthetic. Garden City, N. Y.: Doubleday, pp. xv-xxiv.
Comments on Henry Dalton as a hypocritical Northern white liberal.
Reprinted: 1972.82.

137. _____. "Richard Wright," in his Bondage, Freedom, and Beyond: The Prose of Black Americans. Garden City, N. Y.: Doubleday, p. 151.
Biographical note.

138. _____. "Richard Wright," in his The Black Aesthetic. Garden City, N. Y.: Doubleday, p. 400.
Biographical note.
Reprinted: 1972.84.

139. Geisinger, Marion. Plays, Players, & Playwrights. New York: Hart, p. 556.
Mentions the play NS.

140. Geismar, Peter. Fanon. New York: The Dial Press, pp. 147, 152.
Mentions W briefly in connection with the Congress of Black Writers and Artists.

141. George, Felicia. "Black Woman,

Black Man." Harvard Journal of Afro-American Affairs, 2, No. 2, pp. 1-17.
    Discusses "Long Black Song," "Man of All Work," and NS. W "treats the Black man's problem as a result of a historical castration, arising primarily from the impact of the world the white man has imposed upon the Black."

142. Gérard, Albert. "The Sons of Ham." Studies in the Novel, 3 (Summer), 148-164.
    Partial translation by Judith H. McDowell of 1969.106.

142a. Gibb, Carson. Exposition and Literature. New York: Macmillan, pp. 34, 216, 222.
    Quotes Therman O'Daniel mentioning W, states that the message of NS "is that the white man has made a monster of the black man," and lists W among seven famous naturalists.

143. Gibson, Donald B. "Ralph Ellison and James Baldwin," in The Politics of Twentieth-Century Novelists. Ed. George A. Panichas. New York: Hawthorn Books, pp. 307-320.
    Comments briefly on W as a "political" writer.

144. _____ and Carol Anselment. "Introduction," in their Black and White: Stories of American Life. New York: Washington Square Press, pp. ix, xii.
    Mentions W briefly. "The Man Who Saw the Flood" is reprinted on pp. 60-65.

145. _____. "Richard Wright," in their Black and White: Stories of American Life. New York: Washington Square Press, pp. 256-257.
    Biographical note.

146. _____. "The Victim," in their Black and White: Stories of American Life. New York: Washington Square Press, p. 41.
    Mentions W briefly.

147. _____ and Robert A. Corrigan with the assistance of Lynn Munro, eds. Richard Wright's Fiction: The Critical Response 1940-1971. Third Annual Institute for Afro-American Culture. Iowa City: The University of Iowa.
    Photographic reprints of 1940.916, 917, 918; 1943.23; 1944.64; 1945.845, 890; 1946.198,202; 1949.156; 1950. 242; 1951.129, 216; 1953.126, 153, 230; 1956.303; 1957.24; 1958.181; 1960.268; 1961.3, 107, 151, 265; 1962.42, 55, 73, 109; 1963.67, 77, 113,160;1964.113; 1965.110; 1966. 59, 76; 1967.25; 1968.52, 59, 65, 85, 92, 110; 1969.2, 108, 141, 144, 145,

147, 150, 167, 172, 239; 1970.54, 124, 282, 298, 322; 1971.178, 203.

148. Gide, André. "Letter to Richard Wright," New Letters, 38 (Winter), 131.
    Expresses his sympathy with black people and praises W as their spokesman.
    Reprinted: 1973.153, 154.

149. Gilbert, Zack. "For Angela." Black World, 20 (June), 69.
    Poem mentioning W and The God That Failed.
    Reprinted: 1973.155.

150. Gilman, Richard. "White Standards and Negro Writing," in The Black American Writer. Ed. C. W. E. Bigsby. Vol. 1. Baltimore: Penguin, pp. 35-49.
    Reprint of 1968.115.

151. Giovanni, Nikki. Gemini. Indianapolis: Bobbs-Merrill, pp. 80, 110, 141.
    Autobiography mentioning the author's reading of "Bright and Morning Star" and BB. Giovanni also alleges a conspiracy to murder W.

152. Gordon, Allan Moran. "Cultural Dualism and the Themes of Certain Afro-American Artists." Dissertation Abstracts International, 31 (February), 4059-A.
    Includes analysis of NS.

153. Gottesman, Ronald. "Preface," in his The Merrill Studies in Invisible Man. Charles E. Merrill Studies, ed. Matthew J. Bruccoli and Joseph Katz. Columbus, Ohio: Merrill, pp. iii-v.
    Mentions Steven Marcus' essay on W, Ellison, and Baldwin.

154. Green, Rita. "Your Library Calling: These Fine Autobiographies Tell How It Is to Grow Up as a Black in America." Omaha Sunday World Herald (7 November), Entertainment Sec., p. 47.
    Mentions BB.

154a. Greenspan, Charlotte and Lester M. Hirsch. "Richard Wright Big Black Good Man," in their Instructor's Manual for All Those Voices: The Minority Experience. New York: Macmillan, pp. 24-25.
    Brief commentary and study questions on the story emphasizing its irony and its allegory of race relations.

155. _____. "Wright, Richard," in their All Those Voices: The Minority Experience. New York: Macmillan, p. xxiii.
    Brief bibliographical note to accompany "Big Black Good Man."

156. Gross, Theodore L. The Heroic Ideal in American Literature. New York: The

Free Press, pp. 132, 148-157, 167, 169, 180, 183, 186.
>Discusses the hero of W's works from UTC through LT. W's protagonists are arrested heroes because they die before reaching truly heroic proportions.

157. _____. "Our Mutual Estate: The Literature of the American Negro," in The Black American Writer. Ed. C. W. E. Bigsby. Vol. 1. Baltimore: Penguin, pp. 51-61.
>Reprint of 1968.120.

158. _____. "Religion: Belief and Disbelief," in his A Nation of Nations: Ethnic Literature in America. New York: The Free Press, pp. 241-242.
>Mentions W's rejection of his family's religion.

159. Grumbach, Doris. "Christianity and Black Writers." Renascence, 23 (Summer), 198-212.
>Includes a discussion of W's dismissal of Christianity.

159a. Guttmann, Allen. The Jewish Writer in America: Assimilation and the Crisis of Identity. New York: Oxford University Press, p. 162.
>Mentions NS in a discussion of Norman Mailer.

160. Hagopian, John V. "Mau-Mauing the Literary Establishment." Studies in the Novel, 3 (Summer), 135-147.
>Comments unfavorably on W, especially in comparison to Ellison.

161. Harper, Michael S. "Poems for Richard Wright: A Sequence." New Letters, 38 (Winter), 83-87.
>Sequence of eight poems on various aspects of W's work and career: "The Meaning of Protest," "Near the Whitehouse," "Bigger's Blues," "Tree Fever," "Parable," "Heartblow: Messages," "History as Diabolical Materialism," and "Rat Fever: History as Hallucination."
>Reprinted: 1973.169.
>Partially reprinted ("The Meaning of Protest" and "Heartblow Messages"): 1977.160, 161.

162. Hart, Henry. "Discussion and Proceedings of the American Writers' Congress," in The American Left: Radical Political Thought in the Twentieth Century. New York: Basic Books, pp. 196-213.
>Partial reprint of 1935.8.

163. Hayden, Robert, David J. Burrows, and Frederick R. Lapides. "Autobiography," in their Afro-American Literature:

An Introduction. New York: Harcourt Brace Jovanovich, p. 187.
>Mentions W briefly.

164. _____. "Fiction," in their Afro-American Literature: An Introduction. New York: Harcourt Brace Jovanovich, pp. 3-4.
>Comments on "The Man Who Lived Underground," which "raises questions about psychic freedom, the illusory values of materialism, and the dehumanization of the individual."

165. _____. "Introduction," in their Afro-American Literature: An Introduction. New York: Harcourt Brace Jovanovich, pp. 1-2.
>Calls NS "a novel in the naturalistic mode pioneered by Frank Norris and Theodore Dreiser."

166. _____. "Notes on the Authors," in their Afro-American Literature: An Introduction. New York: Harcourt Brace Jovanovich, pp. 299-304.
>Contains a biographical sketch of W (p. 304).

167. _____. "Questions," in their Afro-American Literature: An Introduction. New York: Harcourt Brace Jovanovich, pp. 59-60.
>Study questions to accompany "The Man Who Lived Underground."

168. _____. "Questions," in their Afro-American Literature: An Introduction. New York: Harcourt Brace Jovanovich, p. 196.
>Study questions to accompany Chapter XIII of BB.

169. _____. "Richard Wright (1908-1960)," in their Afro-American Literature: An Introduction. New York: Harcourt Brace Jovanovich, p. 304.
>Biographical sketch.

170. Higgins, Judith. "Biographies They Can Read." Library Journal, 96 (15 April), 1431-1432.
>Contains a favorable notice of John A. Williams's The Most Native of Sons. "Crisply sketched," the book shows why W had to become a writer.
>Reprinted: 1971.171.

171. _____. "Biographies They Can Read." School Library Journal, 17 (April), 33-34.
>Reprint of 1971.170.

172. Hillocks, George, Bernard J. McCabe, and James F. McCampbell. The Dynamics of English Instruction Grades 7-12. New York: Random House, pp. 368-385.

Mentions W several times in a section on "The Literature of Black Protest." Quotes a passage from the first part of NS and provides study questions for it and for "The Ethics of Living Jim Crow."

173. Houseman, John. "Native Son on Stage." New Letters, 38 (Winter), 71-82.
Slightly edited excerpt from Houseman's autobiography Run-Through (1972) concerning the writing and production of the stage version of the novel. Houseman emphasizes the different outlooks of W and his collaborator Paul Green, which led to differences between the published version of the play and the version actually performed. Houseman also describes his personal relationship with W, including an account of a Jim Crow incident in Washington, D. C., and a letter from W to Houseman. Reprinted: 1972.100; 1973.183, 184.

174. Howe, Irving. "Black Boys and Native Sons," in Criticism: Some Major American Writers. Ed. Lewis Leary. New York: Holt, Rinehart and Winston, pp. 445-462.
Reprint of 1963.113.

175. Huggins, Nathan I. "Afro-American History: Myths, Heroes, Reality," in Key Issues in the Afro-American Experience. Ed. Nathan I. Huggins, Martin Kilson, and Daniel M. Fox. Vol. 1. New York: Harcourt Brace Jovanovich, pp. 5-19.
Notes W's relation to Dreiserian naturalism (p. 18).

176. _____. Harlem Renaissance. New York: Oxford University Press, p. 239.
Comments on NS in relation to its audience.

177. Jackson, Blyden. "The Ghetto of the Negro Novel: A Theme with Variations," in The Discovery of English: NCTE 1971 Distinguished Lectures. Urbana, Ill.: National Council of Teachers of English, pp. 1-12.
Includes a brief discussion of NS as an archetypal novel of "the ghetto as a city of dreadful night."
Reprinted: 1976.104.

178. _____. "Richard Wright in a Moment of Truth." The Southern Literary Journal, 3 (Spring), 3-17.
Detailed analysis of "Big Boy Leaves Home" with emphasis on the sources, symbols, plot pattern, and recurrent themes. Because the story conveys an essential truth about black life in the South, Jackson considers it one of W's finest contributions and a major American short story.

Reprinted: 1971.147; 1972.103; 1975. 109; 1976.105.

179. _____. "A Word About Simple," in Langston Hughes: Black Genius: A Critical Evaluation. Ed. Therman O'Daniel. New York: William Morrow, pp. 110-119.
Reprint of 1968.131.

180. Jacobs, Paul and Saul Landau with Eve Pell. "Joe Louis Uncovers Dynamite," in their To Serve the Devil. Vol. 1: Natives and Slaves. New York: Random House, p. 178.
Headnote to a reprinting of W's essay.

181. James, C. L. R. "Black Studies." Radical America, 5 (September-October), 79-96.
Includes comments on the author's friendship with W and the latter's interest in Kierkegaard.

182. James, Charles. "Bigger Thomas in the Seventies: A Twentieth-Century Search for Significance." The English Record, 22 (Fall), 6-14.
Analyzes NS as a novel about the black search for maturity in an absurd world. Like other blacks, Bigger is confounded by American hypocrisy. Includes a plot summary.

183. Jeffers, Lance. "Afro-American Literature, The Conscience of Man." The Black Scholar, 2 (January), 47-53.
Discusses NS as a prophecy of man's self-transcendence, "Big Boy Leaves Home" as a positive analysis of reaction to oppression, and "Bright and Morning Star" as a story of the struggle for social justice.
Reprinted: 1972.105.

184. Johnson, Siddie Joe. "Black is Booming in Younger Books." The Dallas Morning News (25 April), Sec. D, p. 2.
Contains a brief notice of John A. Williams's The Most Native of Sons comparing its theme of the search for identity with the same theme in juvenile biographies of Langston Hughes and Frederick Douglass.

185. Jones, Iva G. "Research in Afro-American Literature." CLA Journal, 15 (December), 240-244.
Lists three items on W (p. 241).

186. Jones, LeRoi. "LeRoi Jones Talking," in Black Insights: Significant Literature by Black Americans--1760 to the Present. Ed. Nick Aaron Ford. Waltham, Mass.: Ginn, pp. 323-326.
Reprint of 1966.87.

187. _____. "The Myth of a Negro Litera-

ture," in Cavalcade: Negro American Writing from 1760 to the Present. Ed. Arthur P. Davis and Saunders Redding. Boston: Houghton Mifflin, pp. 651-657.
Reprint of 1963.121.

188. Jordan, June. "Black Studies: Bringing Back the Person," in New Perspectives on Black Studies. Ed. John W. Blassingame. Urbana: University of Illinois Press, pp. 28-39.
Reprint of 1969.135.

188a. Justus, James H. "Fiction: The 1930's to the Present," in American Literary Scholarship: An Annual/1969. Ed. J. Albert Robbins. Durham, N. C.: Duke University Press, pp. 224-251.
Comments on William Goede's article on Ellison and W (p. 248).

189. Kaiser, Ernest. "Recent Books." Freedomways, 11 (Second Quarter), 211-226.
Contains an unfavorable review of John A. Williams's The Most Native of Sons criticizing his treatment of the Communist Party. "His writing is very confusing . . . for young people" (p. 226).

190. Kaminsky, Marc. "Wright, Richard," in Encyclopedia of World Literature in the Twentieth Century. Ed. Wolfgang Bernard Fleischmann. Vol. 3. New York: Frederick Ungar, pp. 545-547.
Biographical-critical essay with a brief bibliography of primary and secondary sources. Focusing on UTC, NS, and BB, Kaminsky stresses W's themes of identity and race, his narrative skill, and his Gothicism.

191. Karl, Frederick R. and Leo Hamalian. Untitled headnote, in their The Naked I: Fictions for the Seventies. Greenwich, Conn.: Fawcett, p. 90.
Brief biographical headnote to "The Man Who Went to Chicago."

191a. Katz, William Loren. Teachers' Guide to American Negro History. Revised edition. Chicago: Quadrangle Books, pp. 12, 162, 170.
Mentions W briefly.

192. Kazin, Alfred et al. "The Negro in American Culture," in The Black American Writer. Ed. C. W. E. Bigsby. Vol. 1. Baltimore: Penguin, pp. 79-108.
Reprint of 1961.189.

193. Kearns, Edward. "The 'Fate' Section of Native Son." Contemporary Literature, 12 (Spring), 146-155.
Defends the last section of the novel against previous critics. It has a closer relation to the first two

sections than previously assumed, pursuing the theme of the conflict between abstraction and concreteness and carrying out the motif of blindness. W's use of irony is pervasive. Partially reprinted: 1973.256.

194. Kenny, Vincent S. Paul Green. Twayne United States Authors Series 186, ed. Sylvia E. Bowman. New York: Twayne, pp. 40, 66, 69-73, 108.
Analyzes the play NS as an artistic failure, noting defects in characterization and theme. Disagreeing with W and Orson Welles over the issues of communism and determinism, Green withdrew from the project at a late stage.

195. Kent, George E. "The Poetry of Gwendolyn Brooks: Part II." Black World, 20 (October), 36-48, 68-71.
Mentions NS briefly (p. 71).
Reprinted: 1972.115.

196. _____. "Richard Wright: Blackness and the Adventure of Western Culture." Black Review, No. 1, pp. 11-34.
Reprint of 1969.141.

197. Kgositsile, William Keorapetse. "Paths to the Future," in The Black Aesthetic. Ed. Addison Gayle, Jr. Garden City, N. Y.: Doubleday, pp. 234-245.
Contains a brief reference to W (p. 242).
Reprinted: 1972.118.

198. Killens, John Oliver. The Cotillion or One Good Bull Is Half the Herd. New York: Trident Press, p. 93.
Mentions W briefly.
Reprinted: 1972.120.

199. _____. "Rappin' with Myself." Amistad 2. Ed. John A. Williams and Charles F. Harris. Vintage Books V-660. New York: Random House, pp. 97-136.
Refers to W several times, including an extended tribute to "the awesome, unadulterated power of his writing, his word power, his righteous anger, his indignation, his great success, his impact on the western world" (p. 100).

200. _____. "'We Refuse to Look at Ourselves Through the Eyes of White America,'" in Black Protest Thought in the Twentieth Century. Ed. August Meier, Elliott Rudwick, and Francis L. Broderick. Second edition. The American Heritage Series, ed. Leonard W. Levy and Alfred F. Young. Indianapolis: Bobbs-Merrill, pp. 420-429.
Reprint of 1964.84.

201. Kinnamon, Keneth. "Afro-American

Literature, the Black Revoluton and Ghetto High Schools," in Challenge and Change in the Teaching of English. Ed. Arthur Daigon and Ronald T. LaConte. Boston: Allyn and Bacon, pp. 187-195.
    Reprint of 1970.232.

201a. _____. "Albert Murray, The Omni-Americans: New Perspectives on Black Experience and American Culture." American Quarterly, 23 (August), 322-323.
    Mentions W briefly.

202. _____. "Correspondence." Journal of English and Germanic Philology, 70 (October), 753-754.
    Replies to Dan McCall's response to Kinnamon's review of McCall's The Example of Richard Wright.

203. _____. "The Example of Richard Wright, by Dan McCall." Journal of English and Germanic Philology, 70 (January), 180-186.
    Unfavorable review. Praises McCall's analysis of "Big Boy Leaves Home" and his understanding of the significance of W's career, but complains of the book's flippant tone, digressions, treatment of W's communism, and factual errors. Kinnamon reveals that McCall made extensive unauthorized and unacknowledged use of Kinnamon's 1966 dissertation.
    Reprinted: 1971.147.

204. _____. "Lawd Today: Richard Wright's Apprentice Novel." Studies in Black Literature, 2 (Summer), 16-18.
    Analyzes structure and personal and social themes in the novel, relating them to W's theory of fiction expressed in "Blueprint for Negro Writing." Though flawed in its execution, Lawd Today "stakes out some of the major concerns and attitudes that its author was to develop further in his later fiction" (p. 18).
    Reprinted in revised form: 1972.123.

205. Klein, Marcus. "Ralph Ellison's 'Invisible Man,'" in The Merrill Studies in Invisible Man. Ed. Ronald Gottesman. Columbus, Ohio: Merrill, pp. 74-88.
    Reprint of 1964.85.

206. Lamar, Wilmer A. "Black Literature in High Schools in Illinois (English Teachers Speak for Themselves)." Illinois English Bulletin, 58 (May), 1-41.
    Mentions W (p. 22) and cites BB and NS among the twenty "books most often taught" (p. 41).

207. Lawson, Lewis A. "Cross Damon: Kierkegaardian Man of Dread." CLA Journal, 14 (March), 298-316.
    Analyzes the use of Kierkegaardian

concepts, especially dread, in O to show that the novel's existentialism is more Christian than atheistic. The Concept of Dread and The Sickness Unto Death constitute the primary philosophical sources of O, but Sartre's Being and Nothingness is also cited.

208. Leary, Lewis. "Richard Wright," in his Criticism: Some Major American Writers. New York: Holt, Rinehart and Winston, pp. 389-390.
    Bibliographical headnote to Ralph Ellison's "Richard Wright's Blues."

209. Lee, Don L. "Dedication or to those who helped create a New Consciousness," in his Directionscore: Selected and New Poems. Detroit: Broadside Press, pp. 132-133.
    Reprint of 1970.242.

210. _____. "The Self-Hatred of Don L. Lee," in his Directionscore: Selected and New Poems. Detroit: Broadside Press, pp. 55-56.
    Reprint of 1968.151.

211. _____. "Understanding but Not Forgetting (for the Non-Colored of the World," in his Directionscore: Selected and New Poems. Detroit: Broadside Press, pp. 36-39.
    Reprint of 1969.157.

212. Levidova, J. M. "Wright, Richard," in Kratkaia literaturnaia entsiklopediia. Ed. A. A. Surkov. Vol. 6. Moscow: Sovetskaia entsiklopediia, p. 166.
    Biographical sketch with brief bibliography.

213. Levi-Strauss, Claude. "Letter to Richard Wright." New Letters, 38 (Winter), 130.
    Invites W to visit France as an official guest with expenses paid. The letter is dated 25 April 1946.
    Reprinted: 1973.208, 209.

214. Lieber, Todd M. and Maurice J. O'Sullivan. "'Native Sons?' Black Students on Black Literature." Negro American Literature Forum, 5 (Spring), 3-7.
    Mentions W briefly.

215. Locke, Alain. "From Native Son to Invisible Man: A Review of the Literature of the Negro for 1952," in The Merrill Studies in Cane. Ed. Frank Durham. Columbus Ohio: Merrill, pp. 56-57.
    Reprint of 1953.174.

216. Lynn, Kenneth S. "American Literature," in The New Book of Knowledge. Ed. Martha Glauber Shapp. Vol. 1. New York: Grolier, pp. 195-216.

Mentions W briefly (p. 216).

217. Lyons, Thomas T. Black Leadership in American History. Menlo Park, Cal.: Addison-Wesley, p. 121.
Mentions W as a "descendent" of the Harlem Renaissance.

217a. Madgic, Robert F., Stanley S. Seaberg, Fred H. Stopsky, and Robin W. Winks. The American Experience: A Study of Themes and Issues in American History. Menlo Park, Cal.: Addison Wesley, p. 165.
High-school history text mentioning W briefly.

218. Marcus, Steven. "The American Negro in Search of Identity," in The Merrill Studies in Invisible Man. Ed. Ronald Gottesman. Columbus, Ohio: Merrill, pp. 1-14.
Reprint of 1953.176.

219. McCall, Dan. "Correspondence." Journal of English and Germanic Philology, 70 (October), 750-753.
Responds to charges of improper and unacknowledged use of a doctoral dissertation brought by Keneth Kinnamon in his review of McCall's The Example of Richard Wright. See 1971. 202, 203.

220. McDowell, Robert E. and George Fortenberry. "A Checklist of Books and Essays About American Negro Novelists." Studies in the Novel, 3 (Summer), 219-236.
Includes fifty-one entries on W (pp. 234-236).

221. McPherson, James M., Laurence B. Holland, and James M. Banner, Jr., Nancy J. Weiss, and Michael D. Bell. Blacks in America: Bibliographical Essays. Garden City, N. Y.: Doubleday, pp. xii, 225, 233, 253, 254-255, 256-258, 262.
In addition to mentioning W and his work several times, the authors include three paragraphs (pp. 254-255) listing and commenting on primary and secondary sources.
Reprinted: 1972.150.

222. Mellard, James M. "Racism, Formula, and Popular Fiction." Journal of Popular Culture, 5 (Summer), 10-37.
Comments on Bigger as scapegoat and on W's conscious manipulation of popular myths about black sex and violence (p. 31).

223. Merkle, Donald R. "The Furnace and the Tower: A New Look at the Symbols of Native Son." English Journal, 60 (September), 735-739.

Argues that the major symbols of the novel are the furnace and water tower. Both contain elements which are totally opposite to each other.

224. Miller, Henry. "Letter to Richard Wright." New Letters, 38 (Winter), 129.
In a letter dated 3 November 1946 Miller expresses his admiration for BB and urges Wright to have the work translated into French and Italian. Reprinted: 1973.221, 222.

225. Miller, Ruth. "Bibliography," in her Blackamerican Literature 1760-Present. Beverly Hills, Cal.: Glencoe Press, pp. 761-771.
Contains a section on W (p. 768) listing nine primary and six secondary sources.

226. ____. "Introduction," in her Backgrounds to Blackamerican Literature. Chandler Publications in Backgrounds to Literature, ed. Richard A. Levine. Scranton, Pa.: Chandler, pp. 1-2.
Mentions W briefly.

227. ____. "James Baldwin 1924-," in her Blackamerican Literature 1760-Present. Beverly Hills, Cal.: Glencoe Press, pp. 510-511.
Mentions W briefly.

228. ____. "1915-1939," in her Blackamerican Literature 1760-Present. Beverly Hills, Cal.: Glencoe Press, pp. 423-425.
Chronological table listing NS.

229. ____. "Ralph Ellison 1914-," in her Blackamerican Literature 1760-Present. Beverly Hills, Cal.: Glencoe Press, pp. 481-483.
Mentions Ellison's friendship with W.

230. ____. "Richard Wright 1908-1960," in her Blackamerican Literature 1760-Present. Beverly Hills, Cal.: Glencoe Press, pp. 425-426.
Biographical-critical headnote to "Down by the Riverside" emphasizing W's recurrent theme of social protest and analyzing the story briefly. A photograph of W appears following p. 304.

231. ____. "Significant Events, 1501-1968," in her Backgrounds to Blackamerican Literature. Chandler Publications in Backgrounds to Literature, ed. Richard A. Levine. Scranton, Pa.: Chandler, pp. 272-285.
Lists the publication of NS.

232. Minor, Delores. "Public Schools and Black Materials." Negro American Litera-

ture Forum, 5 (Fall), 85-87, 107.
    Discussing the role of black litera-
    ture in the schools at a time of
    black activism, Minor notes that
    although NS is very popular among
    black students, it is addressed main-
    ly to white readers.

233. Mirer, Martin. "About the Author,"
in his Modern Black Stories. Woodbury,
N. Y.: Barron's Educational Series, p.
101.
    Biographical note on Ellison mention-
    ing W's influence on him.

234. _____. "From Native Son," in his
Modern Black Stories. Woodbury, N. Y.:
Barron's Educational Series, pp. 133,
141-144.
    Headnote about the novel, "Questions
    for Discussion," "Vocabulary," re-
    marks on the characters, topics for
    themes, and a biographical sketch of
    W.

235. _____. "Introduction," in his Modern Black Stories. Woodbury, N. Y.:
Barron's Educational Series, pp. vii-ix.
    Mentions NS briefly.

236. _____. "Selected Bibliography," in
his Modern Black Stories. Woodbury,
N. Y.: Barron's Educational Series, p.
196.
    Lists EM.

237. Mizener, Arthur. "Richard Wright,
'Big Boy Leaves Home,'" in his A Hand-
book of Analyses, Questions, and a Dis-
cussion of Technique for Use with Modern
Short Stories: The Uses of Imagination.
New York: Norton, pp. 134-137.
    Analysis of the story with study
    questions. Mizener emphasizes W's
    simplification of characterization
    and action to achieve a generalized
    narrative with social implications.
    He discusses also Big Boy's matura-
    tion.

237a. Moquin, Wayne. "A Premonition of
Black Militancy," in his Makers of America. Vol. 9: Refugees and Victims 1939-
1954. Chicago: Encyclopaedia Britannica
Educational Corporation, p. 188.
    Headnote to partial reprints of David
    L. Cohn's "The Negro Novel" and W's
    "I Bite the Hand That Feeds Me."

238. Mphahlele, Ezekiel, Ian Munro,
Richard Priebe, and Reinhard Sander. "An
Interview with Ezekiel Mphahlele."
Studies in Black Literature, 2 (Autumn),
6-8.
    Mphahlele acknowledges W's influence.

239. Munro, Lynn. "Periodicalized and
Anthologized Afro-American Short Fic-

tion," in Richard Wright and His Influence. Ed. Robert A. Corrigan. Third
Annual Institute for Afro-American Culture. Iowa City: The University of Iowa,
pp. [200-322].
    Lists sixteen items by W with re-
    prints (pp. 316-320).

240. Murray, Alma and Robert Thomas.
"Richard Wright (1908-1960)," in their
Major Black Writers. New York: Scholas-
tic Books, p. 210.
    Biographical sketch to accompany "The
    Man Who Saw the Flood." W is the most
    important of black writers.

241. Musgrave, Marian E. "Triangles in
Black and White: Interracial Sex and
Hostility in Black Literature." CLA
Journal, 14 (June), 444-451.
    Discusses O and "The Man Who Killed a
    Shadow," calling the latter "a kind
    of Exhibit A in the pathology of
    interracial sex relations" (p. 449).

242. Nichols, Charles H. Instructor's
Guide to Accompany Cavalcade: Negro
American Writing from 1760 to the Present. Boston: Houghton Mifflin, pp. 48,
86, 96.
    Includes study questions on W and
    course outlines listing W.

243. Nin, Anaïs. The Diary of Anaïs Nin
1944-1947. Ed. Gunther Stuhlmann. New
York: Harcourt Brace Jovanovich, pp.
102, 145, 186, 189-191.
    Nin records a visit by W, mentions
    having him in mind in her story "The
    Child Born Out of the Fog," records a
    visit with Bill Howell to W, and
    describes a party she gave for W at
    which he spoke of going to Europe. Of
    W, Nin says: "I have tried to be his
    friend, but I find him reserved and
    full of mistrust" (p. 191).

244. O'Brien, John. "'Becoming' Heroes
in Black Fiction: Sex, Iconoclasm, and
the Immanence of Salvation." Studies in
Black Literature, 2 (Autumn), 1-5.
    Includes comments on NS, especially
    Bigger's quest for self-understand-
    ing.

245. Oliver, Clinton F. "An Introductory
Essay: The Negro and the American Thea-
ter," in Contemporary Black Drama from A
Raisin in the Sun to No Place to Be
Somebody. Ed. Clinton F. Oliver and
Stephanie Sills. New York: Scribner's,
pp. 3-25.
    Mentions the play NS (pp. 16, 21) and
    quotes W's statement that "the Negro
    is America's metaphor" (p. 23).

246. _____. "James Baldwin (1924-)," in
Contemporary Black Drama from A Raisin

in the Sun to No Place to Be Somebody.
Ed. Clinton Oliver and Stephanie Sills.
New York: Scribner's, pp. 235-236.
Mentions Baldwin's friendship with W.

247. Ozawa, Fumio. "Richard Wright no
Tenpen Shosetsu--2" ["Richard Wright's
Short Fiction, II"]. Showa Joshi Daigaku
Gakuen [Showa Women's College Instruc-
tion], No. 376 (April), pp. 87-96.
    Focuses on EM and observes that these
    short stories, unlike those in UTC,
    reflect the changing attitude of
    blacks toward the protest movement.
    The most significant piece is "The
    Man Who Lived Underground," where
    race is treated not as a black prob-
    lem but as a white problem. [Y. H.]

248. Pavese, Cesare. "Letter to Richard
Wright." New Letters, 38 (Winter), 129-
130.
    In a letter dated 29 August 1947
    Pavese comments on the Italian recep-
    tion of BB and places W "among the
    greatest and most serious writers of
    to-day."
    Reprinted: 1973.236, 237.

249. Ploski, Harry A., Otto J. Linden-
meyer, and Ernest Kaiser. Reference
Library of Black America. Vol. 3. New
York: Bellwether Publishing Company, pp.
13, 37.
    Reprint of 1967.82.

250. Randall, Dudley. "The Black Aesthetic in the Thirties, Forties, and Fifties," in The Black Aesthetic. Ed. Addison Gayle, Jr. Garden City, N. Y.:
Doubleday, pp. 212-221.
    Mentions W's politics (p. 214).

251. _____. "Black Bards and White
Reviewers." The Black Position, No. 1,
pp. 3, 15.
    Mentions W briefly.

251a. Ray, David and Robert M. Farnsworth, eds. The Life and Work of Richard
Wright. New Letters, 38 (Winter), 1-204.
    Special issue of New Letters. For
    contents see 1971.1, 4, 15, 16, 17,
    18, 19, 20, 25, 43, 44, 65, 67, 72,
    74, 81, 87, 88, 101, 106, 107, 111,
    112, 113, 114, 115, 148, 161, 173,
    213, 224, 248, 252, 253, 264, 265,
    271, 281, 295, 310, 312, 314, 320.
    Reprinted: 1973.245.

252. _____. "A Note on the Photography,
Calligraphy, and Music." New Letters, 38
(Winter), 204.
    Note on the special W issue of New
    Letters.

253. _____. "Notes on Contributors." New
Letters, 38 (Winter), 203.

Notes on contributors to the special
W issue of the magazine.
Reprinted: 1973.242, 243.

254. Record, Wilson. The Negro and the
Communist Party. New York: Atheneum, pp.
158, 305.
    Reprint of 1951.222.

255. _____. "The Negro Writer and the
Communist Party," in The Black American
Writer. Ed. C. W. E. Bigsby. Vol. 1.
Baltimore: Penguin, pp. 217-228.
    Reprint of 1969.199.

256. Redding, Saunders. "American Negro
Literature," in Afro-American Literature: An Introduction. Ed. Robert Hayden, David J. Burrows, and Frederick R.
Lapides. New York: Harcourt Brace Jovanovich, pp. 273-282.
    Reprint of 1949.140.

256a. _____. "The American Negro Writer and His Roots," in Cavalcade: Negro
American Writing from 1760 to the Present. Ed. Arthur P. Davis and Saunders
Redding. Boston: Houghton Mifflin, pp.
438-444.
    Reprint of 1960.222.

257. _____. "Negro History," in The New
Book of Knowledge. Ed. Martha Glauber
Shapp. Vol. 13. New York: Grolier, pp.
89-105.
    Mentions W briefly (p. 101).

258. Reeves, Paschal et al. "A Checklist
of Scholarship on Southern Literature
for 1970." Mississippi Quarterly, 24
(Spring), 175-222.
    Lists eight items on W (pp. 212-213).

259. Reilly, John M. "Lawd Today: Richard Wright's Experiment in Naturalism."
Studies in Black Literature, 2 (Autumn),
14-17.
    Steeped in the naturalist tradition,
    W emphasizes environmental determin-
    ism and authorial detachment in LT.
    This experiment showed to W, however,
    that naturalism was not wholly ade-
    quate to his literary needs.

260. _____. "Richard Wright: An Essay in
Bibliography." Resources for American
Literary Study, 1 (Autumn), 131-180.
    Analytical and evaluative discussion
    of W scholarship and criticism divid-
    ed into the following categories:
    bibliography, editions, manuscripts
    and letters, biography, and criti-
    cism. The last category is subdivided
    as follows: first responses--W's
    career in the United States, exile
    and the post-war mood, and the major
    writer: recent criticism. The last
    category is further subdivided as

follows: books, pamphlets, and parts of books; general estimates: articles; and studies of the works.

261. _____. "Self-Portraits by Richard Wright." The Colorado Quarterly, 20 (Summer), 31-45.
Argues that self-portraiture is at the center of W's art. All of his works are to some degree self-portraits, but BB and "The Man Who Lived Underground," merging personal and social details, are the most prominent examples.

261a. Rivers, Conrad Kent. "A Mourning Letter from Paris," in The Black Poets. Ed. Dudley Randall. New York: Bantam, p. 199.
Reprint of 1968.186a.

262. Rodnon, Stewart. "Ralph Ellison's Invisible Man: Six Tentative Approaches," in The Merrill Studies in Invisible Man. Ed. Ronald Gottesman. Columbus, Ohio: Merrill, pp. 109-120.
Reprint of 1969.212.

263. Rose, Karel. A Gift of the Spirit: Readings in Black Literature for Teachers. New York: Holt, Rinehart and Winston, pp. 3-4, 17, 18, 19, 105, 107, 108, 185, 187, 188, 262.
Contains many comments and discussion questions on W to accompany "The Man Who Lived Underground" and portions of NS and BB.

264. Safford, Frank, M. D. (as told to Elizabeth Hill Downey). "Personal Impressions." New Letters, 38 (Winter), 32-33.
Recalls renting a cottage in Wading River, Long Island, to W, who was the only black resident. W left for Paris soon after being rebuffed in his attempts to buy property there.
Reprinted: 1973.258, 259.

265. Sartre, Jean Paul. "Letter to Richard Wright." New Letters, 38 (Winter), 132-133.
Offers a loan to W.
Reprinted: 1973.260, 261.

266. Schafer, William J. "Ralph Ellison and the Birth of the Anti-Hero," in The Merrill Studies in Invisible Man. Ed. Ronald Gottesman. Columbus, Ohio: Merrill, pp. 89-100.
Reprint of 1968.194.

267. Schorer, Mark. "Richard Wright (1908-1960)," in The Literature of America. Ed. Irving Howe, Mark Schorer, and Larzer Ziff. Vol. 2. New York: McGraw-Hill, pp. 1103-1104.
Biographical-critical headnote with suggestions for further reading to accompany "Big Boy Leaves Home." Schorer stresses W's naturalism.

268. Schraufnagel, Noel Clark. "The Negro Novel: 1940-1970." Dissertation Abstracts International, 32 (December), 3330A-3331A.
Treats NS as the dominant novel in the protest tradition which it initiated. After Ellison, Baldwin, and other accommodationists repudiated W, the militant novelists of the sixties revived protest.

269. _____. "A Visible Native Son." Prairie Schooner, 44 (Winter), 361-363.
Mixed review of Russell Carl Brignano's Richard Wright: An Introduction to the Man and His Works preceded by a general discussion of W's career. The strength of the book is its analysis of W's intellectual development, but Brignano slights aesthetic issues.

270. Scott, Nathan A., Jr. "Judgment Marked by a Cellar: The American Negro Writer and the Dialectic of Despair," in Cavalcade: Negro American Writing from 1760 to the Present. Ed. Arthur P. Davis and Saunders Redding. Boston: Houghton Mifflin, pp. 821-842.
Reprint of 1967.94.

271. Senghor, Léopold Sédar. "Letter to Richard Wright." New Letters, 38 (Winter), 134.
Letter dated 21 July 1959 expressing admiration for WML but defending Christianity, especially Roman Catholicism, against W.
Reprinted: 1973.269, 270.

272. Senna, Carl. Black Boy Notes. Lincoln, Neb.: Cliff's Notes, 53 pp.
Study guide followed by a selective bibliography.

273. Sherr, Paul C. "Richard Wright: The Expatriate Pattern." Black Academy Review, 2 (Spring-Summer), 81-90.
Discusses O, SH, and LD in relation to the theme of flight.
Reprinted: 1971.274.

274. _____. "Richard Wright: The Expatriate Pattern," in Modern Black Literature. Ed. S. Okechukwu Mezu. Buffalo, N. Y.: Black Academy Press, pp. 81-90.
Reprint of 1971.273.

275. Singh, Raman K. "The Black Novel and Its Tradition." Colorado Quarterly, 20 (Summer), 23-29.
Includes comments on Bigger's quest for identity.

276. ____. "Richard Wright: Novelist of Ideas." Dissertation Abstracts International, 32, p. 3332A.

Argues that W's work focuses on three major ideas--Christianity, Marxism, and Existentialism. His concern with racial problems is always expressed in connection with the persective and insight of one or more of these ideas.

277. Sloan, Irving J. Blacks in America 1492-1970: A Chronology & Fact Book. Third edition. Dobbs Ferry, N. Y.: Oceana Publications, pp. 33, 43.

Reprint of 1965.116.

278. Smith, William Gardner. "The Negro Writer: Pitfalls and Compensations," in The Black American Writer. Ed. C. W. E. Bigsby. Vol. 1. Baltimore: Penguin, pp. 71-78.

Reprint of 1950.225.

279. [Snow, Royall]. "American Literature," in The Lincoln Library of Essential Information. Ed. William J. Redding. Vol. 1. Columbus, Ohio: The Frontier Press, pp. 207-213.

Mentions and lists W (pp. 210-213). Reprinted: 1972.186.

280. Spradling, Mary Mace, ed. In Black and White: Afro-Americans in Print. Kalamazoo: Kalamazoo Library System, p. 102.

Lists thirteen secondary sources on W.

281. Sprandel, Katherine. "The Long Dream." New Letters, 38 (Winter), 88-96.

Analysis of LD focusing on the characters of Tyree and Fishbelly. Identifies the main themes of the novel as "Fish's love-hatred of the white world and its misuse of him; his isolation from his own people; and, the transfer of a legacy from Tyree to Fish." Sprandel also makes a number of comments on W's earlier works. Reprinted: 1973.277, 278.

282. Stanford, Barbara Dodds. "Biographies," in her I, Too, Sing America: Black Voices in American Literature. New York: Hayden Book Company, pp. 299-305.

Includes a brief sketch of W.

283. ____. "The Depression and World War II," in her I, Too, Sing America: Black Voices in American Literature. New York: Hayden Book Company, pp. 118-119.

Comments on W as "the leader in the new style of writing," on his deprived background and on NS.

284. ____. "For Further Reading," in her I, Too, Sing America: Black Voices

in American Literature. New York: Hayden Book Company, p. 180.

Lists four books by W.

285. ____. "The Modern Age: Integration," in her I, Too, Sing America: Black Voices in American Literature. New York: Hayden Book Company, pp. 213-215.

Mentions W briefly.

286. ____. "Questions," in her I, Too, Sing America: Black Voices in American Literature. New York: Hayden Book Company, p. 138.

Study questions to accompany an excerpt from BB.

287. Starke, Catherine Juanita. Black Portraiture in American Fiction. New York: Basic Books, pp. 8-9, 117, 118-119, 197, 200-204, 225.

Comments on W in Africa and analyzes characterization in NS and O. Bigger suffers "the problem of environmental constriction and internalized aggression" (p. 118). Cross Damon is comparable to the protagonist of Invisible Man.

288. Stein, Allen F. and Thomas N. Walters. "Afterword," in their The Southern Experience in Short Fiction. Glenview, Ill.: Scott, Foresman, pp. 57-59.

Brief comment on "Long Black Song" and a biographical sketch of W, followed by "Questions for General Discussion" and "Suggestions for Writing."

289. ____. "Afterword," in their The Southern Experience in Short Fiction. Glenview, Ill.: Scott, Foresman, pp. 68-69.

Brief comment on "The Man Who Was Almost a Man" followed by "Questions for General Discussion" and "Suggestions for Writing."

290. Stephens, Martha. "Richard Wright's Fiction: A Reassessment." The Georgia Review, 25 (Winter), 450-470.

Reviews W's reputation, disputing the Ellison-Baldwin disparagement of W. Argues for the artistic superiority of LT and UTC to W's later fiction. Partially reprinted: 1973.256.

291. Stimpson, Catherine R. "Black Culture/White Teacher," in New Perspectives on Black Studies. Ed. John W. Blassingame. Urbana: University of Illinois Press, 169-184.

Reprint of 1970.330.

291a. Tanaka, Hiroshi. "Constance Webb's Richard Wright: A Biography." Albion, 17 (November), 118-120.

States that Webb's biography is a

detailed account of the processes that led W to a lonely exile in Paris, but regrets that it contains no account of Baldwin. [Y. H. and T. K.]

292. Tanaka, Hiroshi. "Kokujin Sakka niokeru Rentai to Kodoku-Hughes to Wright no Baai" ["Kinship and Estrangement Among the Black Writers: The Case of Hughes and Wright"] Kyoto Daigaku Shikai [Kyoto University View], 14 (Autumn), 58-70.

The works of black writers can be interpreted in terms of their responses to the black masses. Hughes portrays blacks who have friendly relations with whites; he favors those blacks who are poor and have little education, and considers them the backbone of their survival. W, on the other hand, seeks estrangement not only from whites but from blacks; as a result his later works lack strength and durability. [Y. H.]

293. Tarry, Ellen. The Third Door: The Autobiography of an American Negro Woman. Westport, Conn.: Negro Universities Press, p. 149.

Reprint of 1955.80.

294. Thomas, Peter. "African, American-- Or Human?" Présence Africaine, No. 79 (Third Quarter), pp. 144-147.

Mentions W briefly.

295. Thomas, Winburn T. "Personal Impressions." New Letters, 38 (Winter), 27-29.

Thomas, a clergyman and missionary, recalls meeting W at Bandung and comments on W's attitudes toward missionaries, his behavior in Africa, his sympathy with Spanish protestants and Algerian revolutionaries. Reprinted: 1973.282, 283.

296. Timmerman, John. "Symbolism as a Syndetic Device in Richard Wright's 'Long Black Song.'" CLA Journal, 14 (March), 291-297.

Interprets Sarah's character in the story in terms of her inability to cope with reality. Both escapist and materialistic, she cannot understand her husband's proud commitment to the land, which represents his freedom. The symbol of the clock is analyzed in relation to this argument.

297. Toppin, Edgar A. "Wright, Richard (1908-1960), Novelist," in his A Biographical History of Blacks in America Since 1528. New York: David McKay, pp. 475-479.

Biographical sketch, mainly on W's American years.

298. Turner, Darwin T. "Afro-American Literary Critics: An Introduction," in The Black Aesthetic. Ed. Addison Gayle, Jr. Garden City, N Y.: Doubleday, pp. 57-74.

Mentions work on W by Nathan A. Scott and James Baldwin (pp. 63, 66) and comments briefly on "The Literature of the Negro in the United States." Reprinted: 1972.193.

299. _____. "The Black Playwright in the Professional Theatre of the United States of America 1858-1959," in The Black American Writer. Ed. C. W. E. Bigsby. Vol. 2. Baltimore: Penguin, pp. 113-128.

Reprint of 1969.231.

300. _____. "The Negro Dramatist's Image of the Universe, 1920-1960," in Backgrounds to Blackamerican Literature. Ed. Ruth Miller. Chandler Publications in Backgrounds to Literature, ed. Richard A. Levine. Scranton, Pa.: Chandler, pp. 145-156.

Reprint of 1961.274.

301. _____. "The Negro Novel in America: In Rebuttal," in Backgrounds to Blackamerican Literature. Ed. Ruth Miller. Chandler Publications in Backgrounds to Literature, ed. Richard A. Levine. Scranton, Pa.: Chandler, pp. 249-258.

Reprint of 1966.143.

302. _____. "The Teaching of Afro-American Literature," in New Perspectives on Black Studies. Ed. John W. Blassingame. Urbana: University of Illinois Press, pp. 185-193.

Reprint of 1970.348.

303. _____ and Barbara Dodds Stanford. Theory and Practice in the Teaching of Literature by Afro-Americans. NCTE/ERIC Studies in the Teaching of English. Urbana, Ill.: National Council of Teachers of English, pp. 9, 27, 30, 37, 40, 44-45, 89.

Turner mentions W several times and provides a critical sketch emphasizing UTC and NS (p. 27). Stanford mentions BB briefly (p. 89).

304. Tuttleton, James W. "The Negro Writer as Spokesman," in The Black American Writer. Ed. C. W. E. Bigsby. Vol. 1. Baltimore: Penguin, pp. 245-259.

Reprint of 1969.242.

305. U.[hlmann], W.[ilfried]. "Wright, Richard," in Literaturlexikon 20. Jahrhundert. Ed. Helmut Olles. Hamburg: Rowohlt, p. 839.

Biographical sketch.

306. Van Vechten, Carl. "A Portfolio of

Photographs." Amistad 2. Ed. John A. Williams and Charles F. Harris. Vintage Books V-660. New York: Random House, pp. [323-336].
Includes a photograph of W on p. [328].

307. Velling, Rauno. "Richard Wrightin romaani Native Son," in Kirjallisuuden-tutkijain Seuran Vuosikirja 25. Ed. Vaino Kaukosen. Helsinki: Suomalaisen Kirjallisuuden Seura, pp. 217-227.
Published in Finnish translation more than twenty years after its first publication, NS is America's finest example of socialist realism. Placing the novel in the contexts of its critical reception in America and of the critical ideas of Michael Gold, Velling explains that its Communist point of view prevented its earlier appearance in Finland. NS is also related to Sartrean existentialism and the black militancy of Eldridge Cleaver and Angela Davis.

308. Vogler, Thomas A. "Invisible Man: Somebody's Protest Novel," in The Merrill Studies in Invisible Man. Ed. Ronald Gottesman. Columbus, Ohio: Merrill, pp. 51-74.
Reprint of 1970.349.

308a. Wagner, Jean. "Noirs des U. S. A." La Quinzaine Littéraire, No. 110 (16-31 January), pp. 7-8.
Review of books by Chester Himes, James Baldwin, and LeRoi Jones mentioning W in connection with each of them.

308b. Walker, Alice. "The Autobiography of Miss Jane Pittman." The New York Times Book Review (23 May), pp. 6, 12.
Review noting that "Gaines is much closer to Charles Dickens . . . and Langston Hughes than he is to Richard Wright or Ralph Ellison."
See 1971.15a.

309. _____. "A Sudden Trip Home in the Spring." Essence, 2 (September), 59, 78-79.
Short story about a young woman's reaction to her father's death. Uses W's relation to his father as a means of understanding for the protagonist.
Reprinted: 1975.198.

310. Watson, Edward A. "Bessie's Blues." New Letters, 38 (Winter), 64-70.
Analyzes the characterization of Bessie Mears in NS as an embodiment of the blues. Watson discusses Bessie's speech and compares it to the songs of Bessie Smith.
Reprinted: 1973.295, 296.

311. Weber, Diane Judith Downs. "The Autobiography of Childhood in America." Dissertation Abstracts International, 32 (August), 936-A.
Mentions W.

312. Weigel, Henrietta. "Personal Impressions." New Letters, 38 (Winter), 17-20.
Comments on Weigel's friendship with W in the thirties and forties. Notes W's literary projects, racial attitudes, and personal characteristics.
Reprinted: 1973.299, 300.

313. Welburn, Ronald. "Richard Wright. By Robert Bone; The Art of Richard Wright. By Edward Margolies; The Example of Richard Wright. By Dan McCall." Arizona Quarterly, 27 (Spring), 81-83.
Favorable review of three pioneering critical studies of W which will bring him into the literary mainstream. "What we have in Richard Wright, despite the fears that plagued him, is an Afro-American writer whose life was a continuous search for personal identity and a corresponding search for the meaning of freedom for all men and for himself" (p. 83).

314. White, Grace McSpadden. "Wright's Memphis." New Letters, 38 (Winter), 105-116.
Discusses the influence of the city on W and his literary use of it. Much of White's material comes from interviews with people who knew Wright during his Memphis years.
Reprinted: 1973.304, 305.

315. Widmer, Kingsley. "Black Existentialism: Richard Wright," in Modern Black Novelists: A Collection of Critical Essays. Ed. M. G. Cooke. Englewood Cliffs, N. J.: Prentice-Hall, pp. 79-87.
Revision of 1960.268 with added paragraphs on "The Man Who Lived Underground."
Partially reprinted in revised form: 1980.259.

316. Williams, John A. "The Literary Ghetto," in The Black American Writer. Ed. C. W. E. Bigsby. Vol. 1. Baltimore: Penguin, pp. 67-69.
Reprint of 1969.253.

317. _____ and Charles F. Harris. Footnote, in their Amistad 2. Vintage Books V-660. New York: Random House, p. 3.
Note to "Blueprint for Negro Literature" explaining that it is a longer version of "Blueprint for Negro Writing."

318. _____. "To Richard Wright," in

their Amistad 2. Vintage Books V-660.
New York: Random House, front matter.
   Dedication of the book.

319. Williams, Shirley. "Bookends." The
Louisville Courier-Journal & Times (31
January), p. E5.
   Notice of John A. Williams's The Most
   Native of Sons accompanied by a brief
   summary of W's career.

320. Williams, Sidney and Horace Cayton.
"Personal Impressions." New Letters, 38
(Winter), 37-40.
   Transcribed from a tape recording
   made in August 1967. Williams and
   Cayton discuss W's African experience
   and his life in Paris.

321. Winks, Robin W. The Blacks in Canada: A History. New Haven, Conn.: Yale
University Press, pp. 462-463.
   Discusses W's visit to Quebec in 1945
   and its impact on his thought.

322. Wood, Forrest. "Afro-American History: Selected Books," in Richard Wright
and His Influence. Ed. Robert A. Corrigan. Third Annual Institute for Afro-
American Culture. Iowa City: The University of Iowa, pp. [388-422].
   Lists WML (p. 406), BB (p. 410), and
   W's fiction (p. 418).

323. The Yound Lords Party and Michael
Abramson. Palante: Young Lords Party.
New York: McGraw-Hill, p. 23.
   An epigraph is W's "You're either a
   victim or a rebel."

1972

1. Adams, William. "For Discussion," in
his Afro-American Authors. Boston:
Houghton Mifflin, p. 59.
   Three study questions to accompany
   "The Man Who Went to Chicago."

2. _____. "Introduction," in his Afro-
American Authors. Boston: Houghton Mif-
flin, pp. 1-6.
   Comments briefly on the boldness of
   W's racial protest.

3. _____. "Richard Wright," in his Afro-
American Authors. Boston: Houghton Mif-
flin, p. 46.
   Biographical headnote to "The Man Who
   Went to Chicago."

4. Adelman, Irving and Rita Dworkin.
"Wright, Richard, 1908-1960," in their
The Contemporary Novel: A Checklist of
Critical Literature on the British and
American Novel Since 1945. Metuchen,
N. J.: The Scarecrow Press, pp. 579-
584.
   Contains 101 items.

5. Anon. "American Literature," in The
Lincoln Library of Language Arts. Second
edition. Vol. 1. Columbus, Ohio: The
Frontier Press, pp. 193-199.
   Mentions W briefly.

6. Anon. "Critics' Prize Goes to 'Watch
on Rhine,'" in The New York Times Theater Reviews 1920-1970. Vol. 9. New York:
The New York Times and Arno Press, pp.
[40-41].
   Reprint of 1941.160.

7. Anon. Dictionary Catalog of the
Schomburg Collection of Negro Literature
and History: Second Supplement. Vol. 4.
Boston: G. K. Hall, pp. 521-522.
   Reproduces twenty-two catalog cards
   on W.

8. Anon. Dust jacket of The Emergence of
Richard Wright: A Study in Literature
and Society. By Keneth Kinnamon. Urbana:
University of Illinois Press.
   Front cover contains a close-up
   photograph of W's face; back cover
   describes the book and contains a
   favorable comment by Warren French.

9. Anon. "The Emergence of Richard
Wright: A Study in Literature and Soci-
ety. Keneth Kinnamon," in Fall-Winter
Books 1972/73. Urbana: University of
Illinois Press, p. 7.
   Publisher's notice with a favorable
   comment by Warren French.

10. Anon. "The Example of Richard
Wright. Dan McCall." Indian Journal of
American Studies Reviews (March), p. 26.
   Favorable notice of McCall's "unpre-
   tentious book." W's early career is
   more important than his expatriate
   years.

11. Anon. Index Translationum 23. Paris:
Unesco, pp. 342, 513, 716.
   Lists translations of BB into Fin-
   nish, UTC into Japanese, and NS into
   German.

12. Anon. "New Book on Life of Wright."
The Champaign-Urbana News-Gazette (31
December), p. 44.
   Notice of Keneth Kinnamon's The Emer-
   gence of Richard Wright: A Study in
   Literature and Society.

13. Anon. "1941," in The New York Times
Theater Reviews 1920-1970. Vol. 9. New
York: The New York Times and Arno Press,
pp. [117-118].
   Reprint of 1941.481.

14. Anon. "1943," in The New York Times
Theater Reviews 1920-1970. Vol. 9. New
York: The New York Times and Arno Press,
pp. [118-119].

Reprint of 1943.9.

15. Anon. "Richard Wright," in The Emerging Minorities in America: A Resource Guide for Teachers. Ed Sophie E. Schnitter. Santa Barbara, Cal.: American Bibliographical Center--Clio Press, p. 81.
 Biographical note.

16. Anon. Untitled clipping. University Press Books for Secondary Schools.
 Favorable notice of Russell Carl Brignano's Richard Wright: An Introduction to the Man and His Works.

17. Anon. "Wright, Richard," in Gran diccionario enciclopédico ilustrado. Vol. 3. Mexico, D. F.: Selecciones del Reader's Digest, p. 316.
 Biographical sketch.

18. Anon. "Wright Richard," in Leksykon PWN. Ed. Adam Karowski. Warsaw: Panstwowe Wydawnictwo Naukowe, p. 1298.
 Brief biographical note.

19. Anon. Wright, Richard," in Új Magyar Lexikon. Ed. Ákos Károly. Vol. 7. Budapest: Akadémiai Kiadó, p. 465.
 Very brief notice of W's death.

20. Anon. "Wright, Richard (1908-60)," in The Lincoln Library of Language Arts. Second edition. Vol. 2. Columbus, Ohio: The Frontier Press, p. 763.
 Biographical sketch.

21. Arnez, Nancy L. "Enhancing the Black Self-Concept Through Literature," in Black Self-Concept: Implications for Education and Social Science. Ed. James A. Banks and Jean Dresden Grambs. New York: McGraw-Hill, pp. 93-116.
 Mentions Wright (p. 108).

22. Baker, Houston A., Jr. "Black Folklore and the Black American Literary Tradition," in his Long Black Song: Essays in Black American Literature and Culture. Charlottesville: The University Press of Virginia, pp. 18-41.
 Quotes W on the meaning of the word Negro (p. 20) and comments on the relation of NS and BB to black folklore (p. 39).

23. ____. "The Black Man of Culture: W. E. B. Du Bois and The Souls of Black Folk," in his Long Black Song: Essays in Black American Literature and Culture. Charlottesville: The University Press of Virginia, pp. 96-108.
 States that W, together with Ellison and Baldwin, exemplifies "the norm of the black man of culture established for this century by W. E. B. Du Bois" (pp. 107-108).

24. ____. "Completely Well: One View of Black American Culture," in his Long Black Song: Essays in Black American Literature and Culture. Charlottesville: The University Press of Virginia, pp. 1-17.
 Reprint of 1971.30.

25. ____. "Conclusion," in his Long Black Song: Essays in Black American Literature and Culture. Charlottesville: The University Press of Virginia, pp. 142-144.
 Views W as the culmination of black folkloric and literary tradition.

26. ____. "Racial Wisdom and Richard Wright's Native Son," in his Long Black Song: Essays in Black American Literature and Culture. Charlottesville: The University Press of Virginia, pp. 122-141.
 Sketch of W's life and literary career followed by an analysis of NS. Baker stresses W's immersion in black folk culture and his reflection of it in the novel. Bigger "is intelligible as a conscious literary projection of the folk hero who embodies the survival values of a culture"--he is both trickster and rebel. Baker discounts W's own statements of alienation from black culture in "How 'Bigger' was Born" and BB.
 Reprinted: 1972.27; 1982.14.

27. ____, ed. Twentieth Century Interpretations of Native Son: A Collection of Critical Essays. Englewood Cliffs, N. J.: Prentice-Hall, 124 pp.
 Includes a chronology, notes on contributors, and a bibliography of twelve annotated secondary items. Reprints "How 'Bigger' was Born" and the following: 1940.614, 651; 1951.129; 1958.85 (partial reprint); 1961.3; 1963.113; 1969.109, 141 (partial reprint), 172 (partial reprint); 1972.26.

28. ____. "Utile, Dulce and the Literature of the Black American." Black World, 21 (September), 30-35.
 Cites Irving Howe as an example of white critical unfairness. As Wright states in NS, whites seem unable to recognize the humanity of black people.

29. Bakish, David J. "Richard Wright: Dreams and the Ambiguity of Existence." Dissertation Abstracts International, 32 (May), 6412A.
 Abstracts a 1971 University of Delaware dissertation arguing that W's central theme is "the concept of a thoroughly ambiguous existence in a world between fantasy and reality, a

world apart, a world buried underground." Bakish summarizes briefly the nine chapters of the dissertation.

29a. Baldwin, James. "Everybody's Protest Novel," in Black Writers of America: A Comprehensive Anthology. Ed. Richard Barksdale and Keneth Kinnamon. New York: Macmillan, pp. 725-729.
Reprint of 1949.79.

30. _____. No Name in the Street. New York: The Dial Press, p. 50.
Mentions seeing W in Paris in the fall of 1956.

31. [Barksdale, Richard K.]. "The Present Generation: Since 1945," in Black Writers of America: A Comprehensive Anthology. Ed. Richard Barksdale and Keneth Kinnamon. New York: Macmillan, pp. 653-667.
Comments on Bigger Thomas as "an Everyman prototype for Black Youth" (p. 653) and on NS as an exemplary literary expression of the black mood of the forties.

32. Bell, Bernard. "The Quest for a Black Aesthetic." The Massachusetts Review, 13 (Autumn), 715-717.
Review of Addison Gayle's The Black Aesthetic mentioning W.

33. Bluefarb, Sam. "Bigger Thomas: Escape Into the Labyrinth," in his The Escape Motif in the American Novel: Mark Twain to Richard Wright. Columbus: Ohio State University Press, pp. 135-153.
Unlike previous escape in American fiction, Bigger's is not spatial and geographical, for he remains within the labyrinth of the Chicago ghetto. His most significant escape is into a larger self-understanding.
Partially reprinted: 1975.25.

34. Bontemps, Arna. "Letters to Jack Conroy." New Letters, 39 (Fall), 23-25.
Two letters, one dated 17 July 1947 and the other undated but probably from 1963, mention W. The first comments on his attraction to the existentialists; the second concerns the W-Baldwin relationship.

35. Brooks, Gwendolyn. Report from Part One. Detroit: Broadside Press, pp. 31-32, 74-75.
Mentions WML and BB. Reprints 1963.62.

36. Brooks, Mary Ellen. "Behind Richard Wright's 'Artistic Conscience.'" Literature & Ideology, No. 13, pp. 21-30.
Very strong denunciation of W as a bourgeois opportunist. The point of

view is rigidly Marxist.

37. Brown, Lloyd W. "The Expatriate Consciousness in Black American Literature." Studies in Black Literature, 3 (Summer), 9-12.
Mentions W briefly.

37a. Brown, Roscoe C., Mae Gwendolyn Henderson, and Mathias B. Freese. The Black Experience. New York: Thomas A. Hearn, p. 92.
Mentions W.

38. Bryant, Jerry H. "Individuality and Fraternity: The Novels of William Gardner Smith." Studies in Black Literature, 3 (Summer), 1-8.
Mentions W briefly.

39. Bryer, Jackson R. "Richard Wright: An Introduction to the Man and His Works. By Russell Carl Brignano." American Literature, 43 (January), 672-673.
Mixed review pointing out that Brignano's thematic approach precludes aesthetic judgments. Nevertheless, the book is essential for future W scholars.

40. _____, Jean Downey, Philip R. Headings, Joseph V. Ridgely, Donald B. Stauffer, and Peter G. Van Egmond, with the help of Matthew O'Brien and Donald P. Wharton. "American Literature," in 1970 MLA International Bibliography. Compiled by Harrison T. Meserole. Vol. 1. New York: Modern Language Association, pp. 99-139.
Lists seventeen items on W.

41. Burgess, Françoise. "James Baldwin," in Littérature de notre temps: Ecrivains américains. Ed. Pierre Dommergues. Paris: Casterman, pp. 33-35.
Mentions W as Baldwin's spiritual father.

42. Burke, W. J., Will D. Howe, Irving Weiss, and Anne Weiss. "Black Boy," in their American Authors and Books 1640 to the Present Day. Third edition. New York: Crown, p. 58.
Reprint of 1962.44.

42a. _____. "Native Son," in their American Authors and Books 1640 to the Present Day. Third edition. New York: Crown, p. 453.
Reprint of 1943.24.

42b. _____. "Wright, Richard," in their American Authors and Books 1640 to the Present Day. Third edition. New York: Crown, p. 712.
Revised reprint of 1943.24a.

43. Burke, William Martin. "Modern Black

Fiction and the Literature of Oppression." Dissertation Abstracts International, 32 (May), 6415-A
Abstracts a University of Oregon doctoral dissertation examining Ellison, W, Baldwin, and Williams. W stresses the psychological effect of racism, including the propensity for violence.

44. Butcher, Margaret Just. The Negro in American Culture. Second edition. New York: Knopf, pp. 178-179, 183, 196, 275, 276-277.
Reprint of 1956.125.

45. Cargas, Harry J. Daniel Berrigan and Contemporary Protest Poetry. New Haven, Conn.: College and University Press, pp. 12, 84.
Mentions briefly W and NS.

46. Carr, John C. "My Brother's Keeper: A View of Blacks in Secondary-School Literature Anthologies," in Black Image: Education Copes with Color. Ed. Jean Dresden Grambs and John C. Carr. Dubuque, Iowa: William C. Brown, pp. 122-137.
Notes the inclusion or exclusion of W in textbooks.

46a. Casmier, Adam A. and Sally Souder. "About the Authors," in their Coming Together: Modern Stories by Black and White Americans. Encino and Belmont, Cal.: Dickenson Publishing Company, pp. 411-420.
Includes a biographical sketch of W (p. 420).

46b. _____. "To Our Readers," in their Coming Together: Modern Stories by Black and White Americans. Encino and Belmont, Cal.: Dickenson Publishing Company, pp. xiii-xv.
Mentions briefly "Big Boy Leaves Home."

47. Chapman, Abraham. "Introduction," in his New Black Voices: An Anthology of Contemporary Afro-American Literature. Mentor Books MW1116. New York: The New American Library, pp. 25-53.
Quotes W on the blues (p. 42) and on the exclusion of black people from Western culture (p. 48).

48. Chavis, Helen De Lois. "The New Decorum: Moral Pespectives of Black Literature." Dissertation Abstracts International, 32 (January), 3993-A.
Discovers moral awareness to be the common denominator of world black literature. No black writer is explicitly mentioned, but W is presumably included.

49. Childers, Emily, Joan Heaton, Jean Holder, Lynda Lancaster, and Zeb Shook. Black American Culture Bibliography: A List of Books and Periodicals on Black American Culture Located in the Belk Library, Appalachian State University. Boone, N. C.: Appalachian State University, pp. 31, 138, 164.
Lists six works by W.

50. Chisholm, Shirley. "Foreword," in White Racism and Black Americans. Ed. David G. Bromley and Charles F. Longino, Jr. Cambridge, Mass.: Schenkman, pp. xv-xxiii.
Quotes approvingly from BB on the effects of racism.
Reprinted: 1979.64.

50a. Christadler, Martin. "Ralph Ellison Invisible Man," in Der Amerikanische Roman: Von den Anfängen bis zur Gegenwart. Ed. Hans-Joachim Lang. Düsseldorf: August Bagel Verlag, pp. 333-369, 417-421.
Comments on the role of NS and Bigger Thomas in the establishment of black protest fiction, against which Ellison and Baldwin reacted (pp. 335-336).

51. Christian, Barbara. "Ralph Ellison: A Critical Study," in The American Novel: Criticism and Background Readings. Ed. Cristof Wegelin. New York: The Free Press, pp. 512-525.
Reprint of 1969.55.

52. Cleaver, Eldridge. "To All Black Women, From All Black Men," in Black Writers of America: A Comprehensive Anthology. Ed. Richard Barksdale and Keneth Kinnamon. New York: Macmillan, pp. 884-886.
Reprint of 1968.67.

53. Conn, Annette. "Comment." College English, 34 (November), 284-286.
Replying to an article by James G. Kennedy (1972.110), Conn, also a Marxist, distinguishes between class, national, and racial oppression. Kennedy's view of Bigger as proletarian hero, she feels, is oversimplified.

54. Coombs, Norman. The Black Experience in America. New York: Twayne, p. 166.
Mentions briefly NS and W's connection with the Writers Project.

55. Cowan, Kathryn Osburn. "Black/White Stereotypes in the Fiction of Richard Wright, James Baldwin and Ralph Ellison." Dissertation Abstracts International, 33 (December), p. 2926-A.
Abstracts a St. Louis University doctoral dissertation examining two of W's black characters as reflec-

tions of white stereotypical attitudes using Gordon Allport's The
Nature of Prejudice. Like those of
other black writers, Wright's characters tend to be "flat" to serve the
needs of social protest.

56. Crunden, Robert M. From Self to
Society, 1919-1941. Englewood Cliffs,
N. J.: Prentice-Hall, pp. 103-105.
Comments on W's politics and his
perspective as a marginal man. NS
achieves greatest success as a psychological study of "a conflict of
stereotypes."

56a. Curling, R. Maud. "Presentación de
Richard Wright y Bigger Thomas." Anales
del Departamento de Lenguas Modernas,
Universidad de Costa Rica, No. 1
(August), pp. 19-24.
Sketches W's life and analyzes NS
with emphasis on the social signifi-
cance of its characterization of
Bigger.

56b. Curry, Richard O., John G. Sproat,
and Kenyon C. Cramer. The Shaping of
America. New York: Holt, Rinehart and
Winston, pp. 585, 754.
High-school history text commenting
briefly on NS and on W's influence on
Baldwin.

57. Dance, Daryl Cumber. "Wit and Humor
in Black American Literature." Dissertation Abstracts International, 32 (February), 4458A-4459A.
Covers W and many others in a survey
of black literary humor.

57a. DaSilva, Benjamin, Milton Finkel-
stein, and Arlene Loshin. The Afro-
American in United States History.
Second edition. New York: Globe Book
Company, pp. 365, 366, 367.
Reprint of 1969.65.

57b. Davis, George. "We Can't Breathe.
By Ronald Fair." The New York Times Book
Review (6 February), p. 6.
Briefly compares Fair's novel to NS.

58. Demby, William and John O'Brien.
"Interview with William Demby." Studies
in Black Literature, 3 (Autumn), 1-7.
Demby disavows influence by W (p. 1).
Reprinted: 1973.112.

59. Dickinson, Donald C. A Bio-Biblio-
graphy of Langston Hughes 1902-1967.
Second edition. Archon Books. Hamden,
Conn.: The Shoe String Press, pp. 54,
67-68, 79, 100-101, 113.
Reprint of 1967.27.

60. Dickstein, Morris. "The Black Aesthetic in White America." Partisan

Review, 38 (Winter), 376-395.
Argues that W is not really a naturalistic writer and that BB and NS are
structurally unsound.

61. Dommergues, Pierre. "Points de vue,"
in his Littérature de notre temps: Ecrivains américains. Paris: Casterman, pp.
17-24.
Includes a passage from "Blueprint
for Negro Writing" translated into
French (p. 22).

62. Emanuel, James A. "Blackness Can: A
Quest for Aesthetics," in The Black
Aesthetic. Ed. Addison Gayle, Jr. Anchor
Books A822. Garden City, N. Y.: Double-
day, pp. 182-211.
Reprint of 1971.96.

63. Emerson, O. B. "Cultural Nationalism
in Afro-American Literature," in The Cry
of Home: Cultural Nationalism and the
Modern Writer. Ed. H. Ernest Lewald.
Knoxville: University of Tennessee
Press, pp. 211-244.
Comments on W (pp. 219-222), especially NS and its social and literary
effect.

64. Fabio, Sarah Webster. "Tripping with
Black Literature," in The Black Aesthe-
tic. Ed. Addison Gayle, Jr. Anchor Books
A822. Garden City, N Y.: Doubleday, pp.
173-181.
Reprint of 1971.100.

65. Fabre, Michel. "A Case of Rape."
Black World, 21 (March), 39-48.
Article on Chester Himes's novel
mentioning W's situation as the leading black expatriate in Paris.

66. _____. "Jack Conroy as Editor." New
Letters, 39 (Winter), 115-137.
Mentions W as a contributor to The
Anvil and as a fund raiser for The
New Anvil (pp. 134, 136).

67. _____. Note to "Ethnographical Aspects of Chicago's Black Belt." New
Letters, 39 (September), 61-62.
Note to a previously unpublished
essay by W derived from research in
the George Cleveland Hall Branch of
the Chicago Public Library. A novice
sociologist, W nevertheless demonstrates intellectual inquisitiveness
and clarity.

68. _____. "Richard Wright," in Littérature de notre temps: Ecrivains
américains. Ed. Pierre Dommergues.
Paris: Casterman, pp. 245-248.
Consists of a critical sketch relating W's work to Afro-American social
history and to an existentialist
perspective, brief critical comments

on six essential works by W, bibliographies of primary and secondary works, and a biographical chronology.

69. Fair, Ronald. "Introduction," in The Wright Poems. By Conrad Kent Rivers. Heritage Series, No. 18. London: Paul Breman, pp. 3-5.
    Concerns the difficulty of the role of black writer in America, Rivers's admiration of W ("He was a god, man. He really was a god."), and the favorable environment that W found in Paris.

70. Farmer, James. "The 'Movement' Now," in The Voice of Black America: Major Speeches by Negroes in the United States, 1797-1971. Ed. Philip S. Foner. New York: Simon and Schuster, pp. 1041-1048.
    Reprint of 1967.38.

71. Farrison, W. Edward. "Black Writers of America: A Comprehensive Anthology. Edited by Richard Barksdale and Keneth Kinnamon." CLA Journal, 16 (December), 264-267.
    Demurs at the editors' excessive claims for W's influence.

72. Fax, Elton C. Garvey: The Story of a Pioneer Black Nationalist. New York: Dodd, Mead, pp. 283-284.
    Compares W's views on African redemption to Garvey's.

73. Fleming, Robert E. "'Playing the Dozens' in the Black Novel." Studies in Black Literature, 3 (Autumn), 23-24.
    Discusses W's use of the dozens in "Big Boy Leaves Home" and LT.

74. Frazier, Levi, Jr. "The Black Students Association and the Department of Communication Arts of Southwestern Present a Tribute to Richard Wright." Mimeographed flyer, 17-18 March.
    Announces a presentation of dramatic readings from W by students and a lecture by Michel Fabre at Southwestern University in Memphis.

75. Freeman, Melissa McRee. "A Critical Study of the Short Stories of Richard Wright." Masters Abstracts, 10 (March), 76.
    Claims that any revaluation of W's success as an artist demands careful consideration of his short stories. These demonstrate a sureness not always present in his work, effectively employing imagery and symbolism to support action and dialogue.

76. Frémy, Dominique and Michèle Frémy.

Quid? Tout pour tous. Paris: Librairie Plon, p. 54.
    Reprint of 1963.86.

76a. French, Warren. "Fiction: 1900 to the 1930s," in American Literary Scholarship: An Annual/1970. Ed. J. Albert Robbins. Durham, N. C.: Duke University Press, pp. 223-252.
    Discusses two books and nine articles on W (pp. 250-252).

76b. Fujii, Motoharu. "A Technique of Repetition: The Rhetoric of R. Wright's Early Work." Meiji Daigaku Eibei Bungaku [Meiji University English and American Literature], 67 (1 February), 60-78.
    The chief characteristic of W's style is syntactic repetition in the use of parts of speech (nouns, adjectives, adverbs), phrases, and sentences. Also cites examples of phonological repetition. [Y. H. and T. K.]

77. Fuller, Hoyt W. "The New Black Literature: Protest or Affirmation," in The Black Aesthetic. Ed. Addison Gayle, Jr. Anchor Books A822. Garden City, N. Y.: Doubleday, pp. 327-348.
    Reprint of 1971.129.

78. _____. "Perspectives." Black World, 21 (March), 49-50.
    Contains an unfavorable review of the special W issue of New Letters. Fuller praises the black contributions and criticizes the white contributions.

79. _____. The Turning of the Wheel/or Are Black Men Serious. Chicago: Institute of Positive Education, p. 5.
    Refers to "those vulgar Bigger Thomases" as violent rebels.

79a. Gasarch, Pearl and Ralph Gasarch. "Richard Wright (1908-1960)," in their Fiction: The Universal Elements. New York: Van Nostrand Reinhold, pp. 45-46.
    Biographical headnote to "Big Boy Leaves Home."

79b. _____. "Some Notes on Form in Fiction," in their Fiction: The Universal Elements. New York: Van Nostrand Reinhold, pp. 443-455.
    Comments briefly on the function of setting in NS (p. 448).

80. Gayle, Addison, Jr. "Cultural Strangulation: Black Literature and the White Aesthetic," in his The Black Aesthetic. Anchor Books A822. Garden City, N. Y.: Doubleday, pp. 38-45.
    Reprint of 1969.101.

81. _____. "The Function of Black Literature at the Present Time," in his The

Black Aesthetic. Anchor Books A822. Garden City, N. Y.: Doubleday, pp. 383-394.
Reprint of 1971.134.

82. _____. "Introduction," in his The Black Aesthetic. Anchor Books A822. Garden City, N. Y.: Doubleday, pp. xv-xxiv.
Reprint of 1971.136.

83. _____. "The Politics of Revolution: Afro-American Literature." Black World, 21 (June), 4-12.
Contains brief comments on W and Bigger Thomas as the image of the "bad nigger."

84. _____. "Richard Wright," in his The Black Aesthetic. Anchor Books A822. Garden City, N. Y.: Doubleday, p. 400.
Reprint of 1971.138.

85. _____. "The Son of My Father," in New Black Voices: An Anthology of Contemporary Afro-American Literature. Ed. Abraham Chapman. Mentor Books MW1116. New York: The New American Library, pp. 525-538.
Reprint of 1970.146.

86. _____ and Saundra Towns. "Addison Gayle Interviewed." The Black Position, No. 2, pp. 4-36.
Gayle comments on NS (p. 10-11), W's knowledge of white literature (pp. 18-19), Himes and W (p. 23), and Baldwin's evolution to a position close to W's (p. 24).

87. Gecau, Kimani. "An Idea on Wright's Native Son." Busara, 4, No. 1, 57-58.
Discusses briefly Bigger's killing of Mary Dalton as emotional release and as self-definition through challenge of the social order of white racism.

88. Gibson, Donald B. "Wright, R." in 1970 MLA Abstracts of Articles in Scholarly Journals. Compiled by John H. Fisher and Walter S. Achtert. Vol. 1. New York: Modern Language Association, p. 157.
Abstract of 1969.109.

89. Gilzinger, Donald, Jr. "Kinnamon, Keneth. The Emergence of Richard Wright: A Study in Literature and Society." Library Journal, 97 (1 November), 3591.
Favorable notice.

90. Gotoh, Tomokuni. "Wright no Jidenteki Shosetsu Black Boy nitsuite' ["On Wright's Autobiographical Novel, Black Boy"]. Kobe Gakuin Daigaku Kiyo [Annals of Kobe Gakuin University], 3 (October), 93-106.
Considers BB predominantly autobio-

graphic and explains that it is an objective psychological analysis of himself rather than a protest novel. The ultimate image W wants to create in the book is that of an outsider: he escaped his own family, the South, and finally the United States. [Y. H.]

91. Graham, Louis. "The White Self-Image Conflict in Native Son." Studies in Black Literature, 3 (Summer), 19-21.
Discusses the question of identity throughout the novel. Not only does Bigger undergo a conflict between the appearance and reality of what he is, but the white characters do as well.

91a. Groh, George W. The Black Migration: The Journey to Urban America. New York: Weybright and Talley, pp. 5, 44-45, 255.
Mentions W and quotes from TMBV.

92. Hajek, Friederike. "American Tragedy--zwei Aspekte. Dargestellt in Richard Wrights Native Son und in Theodore Dreisers An American Tragedy." Zeitschrift für Anglistik und Amerikanistik, 20 (July), 262-279.
Detailed comparison of the two novels focusing on the protagonists. Because Clyde Griffiths, a petty bourgeois, is too closely identified with capitalism and its individualism to develop a revolutionary perspective on his own exploitation, he dies a depressing and ignorant sacrifice to his oppressor. As a despised and deprived black man, the proletarian Bigger Thomas can reject and rebel against his society and its values. With the help of communist spokesmen such as Max, Bigger achieves a truly revolutionary class consciousness.

93. Harrison, Paul Carter. The Drama of Nommo. Evergreen E-603. New York: Grove Press, pp. 164, 181-182.
Quotes from "Blueprint for Negro Writing" and discusses the relation of Bigger Thomas to black nationalism. Compares NS to Imamu Amiri Baraka's The Slave.

94. Hayashi, Susanna Campbell. "Dark Odyssey: Descent Into the Underworld in Black American Fiction." Dissertation Abstracts International, 32 (April), 5790-A.
W is one of five writers treated.

95. Heller, Arno. "Ralph Ellison's 'Invisible Man': Das Rassenproblem als Analyse moderner Existenz." Die neuren Sprachen, 21, pp. 2-9.
Mentions NS as the "high point" of the protest novel of the thirties.

96. Henderson, Stephen. "Biographical Notes," in his Understanding the New Black Poetry. New York: William Morrow, pp. 377-394.
    The entry on Samuel Allen (p. 379) mentions W.

97. Himes, Chester. The Quality of Hurt: The Autobiography of Chester Himes. Vol. 1. Garden City, N. Y.: Doubleday, pp. 100, 101, 114-117, 140-144, 169, 177-183, 187-188, 194-203, 207, 211, 216-217, 220.
    Covering Himes's life through 1954, this work describes his relationship with W during the Paris years.

98. _____ and Hoyt W. Fuller. "Traveler on the Long, Rough, Lonely Old Road: An Interview with Chester Himes." Black World, 21 (March), 4-22, 87-98.
    Himes discusses the W-Baldwin quarrel, W's relationship with the Communist Party, and Himes's friendship with W.

99. Hoffman, Nancy Y. "The Annunciation of William Demby." Studies in Black Literature, 3 (Spring), 8-13.
    Contrasts Demby's treatment of the black man with W's and comments on Bigger Thomas.

99a. Hofstadter, Richard, William Miller, and Daniel Aaron. The United States. Third edition. Englewood Cliffs, N. J.: Prentice-Hall, p. 700.
    Reprint of 1970.181.

100. Houseman, John. Run-Through: A Memoir. New York: Simon and Schuster, pp. 461-475.
    Reprint of 1971.173.

100a. Howard, Daniel F. "Richard Wright 1908-1960," in his The Modern Tradition: An Anthology of Short Stories. Second edition. Boston: Little, Brown, pp. 307-308.
    Biographical headnote to "Big Boy Leaves Home" and "The Man Who Lived Underground." A full-page photograph of W appears on p. 306.
    Reprinted: 1976.99.

101. Howe, Florence. "Feminism and Literature," in Images of Women in Fiction: Feminist Perspectives. Ed. Susan Koppelman Cornillon. Bowling Green, Ohio: Bowling Green University Popular Press, pp. 253-277.
    Includes discussion of Howe's experiences teaching NS. She speculates that W may be aware "that sexual identification [is] sharper even than racial" (p. 272).

102. Jackson, Blyden. "The Negro's Image

of the Universe as Reflected in His Fiction," in White Racism and Black Americans. Ed. David G. Bromley and Charles F. Longino. Cambridge, Mass.: Schenkman, pp. 628-636.
    Reprint of 1960.169.

103. _____. "Richard Wright in a Moment of Truth," in The Poetry of Community: Essays on the Southern Sensibility of History and Literature. Ed. Lewis P. Simpson. Spectrum Monograph Series, Vol. 2. Atlanta: Georgia State University School of Arts and Sciences, pp. 55-66.
    Reprint of 1971.178.

104. Jahn, Janheinz. "Die neoafrikanische Literatur," in Kindlers Literatur Lexikon. Ed. Rudolf Radler and Johanna Zeitler. Vol. 7. Zurich: Kindler Verlag, pp. 694-700.
    Mentions W briefly (p. 698).

105. Jeffers, Lance. "Afroamerican Literature: The Conscience of Man," in New Black Voices: An Anthology of Contemporary Afro-American Literature. Ed. Abraham Chapman. Mentor Books MW1116. New York: The New American Library, pp. 506-513.
    Reprint of 1971.183.

105a. Justus, James H. "Fiction: The 1930s to the Present," in American Literary Scholarship: An Annual/1970. Ed. J. Albert Robbins. Durham, N. C.: Duke University Press, pp. 253-279.
    Mentions W briefly (p. 263).

106. Kaiser, Ernest. "Recent Books." Freedomways, 12 (Fourth Quarter), 347-359.
    Includes notices of Houston A. Baker's Long Black Song (commenting on the essay on W) and Keneth Kinnamon's The Emergence of Richard Wright (pp. 347, 354).

107. Kaufman, Bob. "Blues Note," in Understanding the New Black Poetry. Ed. Stephen Henderson. New York: William Morrow, pp. 209-210.
    Reprint of 1965.87.

108. Kelly, Ernece B. "Point of View: Whose American Literature?" The Chronicle of Higher Education, 6 (30 May), 12.
    Cites W as a literary giant largely neglected by the white literary establishment.

109. _____ et al. Searching for America. Urbana, Ill.: National Council of Teachers of English, pp. 11, 34, 41-42, 52, 67.
    Mentions W in a review of anthologies and critical works in American liter-

ature under the auspices of the NCTE Task Force on Racism and Bias in the Teaching of English.

110. Kennedy, James G. "The Content and Form of Native Son." College English, 34 (November), 269-283.
    Marxist analysis arguing that the novel's content is working class in character, therefore antagonistic to middle-class values. As expressed in Bigger's story, W's world view, or class philosophy, reacts to the social reality in America of imperialism, which Lenin called the highest stage of capitalism. The form of the novel consists of a main plot of action showing "the virtual impossibility of any personal relationship across class or race lines" (p. 278) and a sub-plot of character showing the development in Bigger of a revolutionary consciousness.

111. Kent, George. "Before Ideology: Reflections on Ralph Ellison and the Sensibility of Younger Black Writers," in his Blackness and the Adventure of Western Culture. Chicago: Third World Press, pp. 184-202.
    Comments on the W-Baldwin relationship (pp. 184-185) and discusses briefly Ellison's essays on W (pp. 189, 190).

112. ____. "Books Noted: Shaping Up the Field of Black Literature: Reviews of a Guide and a Bibliography: Theory and Practice in the Teaching of Literature by Afro-Americans; Black American Poetry Since 1944." Black World, 21 (September), 51-52, 87-89.
    Review mentioning W.

113. ____. "Introduction," in his Blackness and the Adventure of Western Culture. Chicago: Third World Press, pp. 9-14.
    Comments briefly on W.

114. ____. "On the Future Study of Richard Wright," in his Blackness and the Adventure of Western Culture. Chicago: Third World Press, pp. 98-103.
    Reprint of 1969.140.

115. ____. "The Poetry of Gwendolyn Brooks," in his Blackness and the Adventure of Western Culture. Chicago: Third World Press, pp. 104-138.
    Reprint of 1971.195.

116. ____. "Ralph Ellison and Afro-American Folk and Cultural Traditon," in his Blackness and the Adventure of Western Culture. Chicago: Third World Press, pp. 152-163.
    Reprint of 1970.227.

117. ____. "Richard Wright: Blackness and the Adventure of Western Culture," in his Blackness and the Adventure of Western Culture. Chicago: Third World Press, pp. 76-97.
    Reprint of 1969.141.

118. Kgositsile, William Keorapetse. "Paths to the Future," in The Black Aesthetic. Ed. Addison Gayle, Jr. Anchor Books A822. Garden City, N. Y.: Doubleday, pp. 234-245.
    Reprint of 1971.197.

119. Killens, John Oliver. "The Black Psyche," in Voices from the Black Experience: African and Afro-American Literature. Ed. Darwin T. Turner, Jean M. Bright, and Richard Wright. Lexington, Mass.: Ginn, pp. 5-10.
    Partial reprint of 1965.89.

120. ____. The Cotillion or One Good Bull Is Half the Herd. New York: Pocket Books, p. 108.
    Reprint of 1971.198.

121. ____. "Introduction: The Smoking Sixties," in Black Short Story Anthology. Ed. Woodie King. New York: Columbia University Press, pp. xi-xviii.
    Notes the transition in black literature "from the posture of Richard Wright's White Man Listen! [sic] to one of Black Man Speaks to Black people in particular but for humanity to listen" (pp. xiv-xv).

122. [Kinnamon, Keneth]. "Ann Petry (1911-   )," in Black Writers of America: A Comprehensive Anthology. Ed. Richard Barksdale and Keneth Kinnamon. New York: Macmillan, pp. 762-763.
    Notes that critics placed Petry in the "School of Wright" after the publication of The Street.

123. ____. The Emergence of Richard Wright: A Study in Literature and Society. Urbana: University of Illinois Press, 200 pp.
    "A study of the life, literary career, and social milieu of Richard Wright from his birth in 1908 through the publication of Native Son in 1940, with a glance in the final chapter at his withdrawal from the Communist movement and the beginning of his expatriation. The effort throughout has been to reconcile the varying claims of literary and social criticism, to examine Wright's early poetry and fiction both as works of the aesthetic and moral imagination and as events in the history of American racial protest" (p. vii). The five chapters are entitled "The Burdens of Caste and Class," "A Literary

Apprenticeship," "Lawd Today and Uncle Tom's Children" "Native Son," and "Epilogue." A selected bibliography lists 153 primary and 468 secondary items.
Partially reprinted: 1979.150.

124. _____. "James Baldwin (1924-   )," in Black Writers of America: A Comprehensive Anthology. Ed. Richard Barksdale and Keneth Kinnamon. New York: Macmillan, pp. 722-725.
Discusses the Baldwin-W relationship.

125. _____. "Preface," in Black Writers of America: A Comprehensive Anthology. Ed. Richard Barksdale and Keneth Kinnamon. New York: Macmillan, pp. xi-xii.
Mentions W.

126. _____. "Ralph Ellison (1914-   )," in Black Writers of America: A Comprehensive Anthology. Ed. Richard Barksdale and Keneth Kinnamon. New York: Macmillan, pp. 683-686.
Discusses the Ellison-W relationship.

127. _____. "Renaissance and Radicalism: 1915-1945," in Black Writers of America: A Comprehensive Anthology. Ed. Richard Barksdale and Keneth Kinnamon. New York: Macmillan, pp. 467-479.
Sketches the early literary career of W, "the central figure in Black literature during the 1930's and early 1940's" (p. 478).

128. _____. "Richard Wright (1908-1960)," in Black Writers of America: A Comprehensive Anthology. Ed. Richard Barksdale and Keneth Kinnamon. New York: Macmillan, pp. 538-542.
Biographical, critical, and bibliographical headnote to selections by W. Emphasizes W's deprived childhood and youth and his Chicago and New York periods.

129. Kishino, Junko. "'Fear' of Richard Wright--Laying Stress on His Early Works" ["Richard Wright niokeru Kyofu (Fear) nitsuite--Tokuni Shoki no Sakuhin o Chushin ni"]. Chuo-Gakuin Daigaku Rongyo [The Chuo-Gakuin Review], 7 (November), 163-188.
An examination of how W's concept of fear functions as a springboard in his philosophy. Comments on his unsuccessful attempt in escaping his own fear. This fear has two phases: fear of whites in the South and fear of himself who did not hesitate to revolt against the whites, and of the violence that accompanied his action. [Y. H.]

130. Klotman, Phyllis R. "The Passive Resistant in A Different Drummer, Day of

Absence, and Many Thousands Gone." Studies in Black Literature, 3 (Autumn), 7-12.
Quotes W's statement that "the Negro is America's metaphor" (p. 7). Reprinted in revised form: 1977.206.

131. _____ and Melville Yancey. "Gifts of Double Vision: Possible Political Implications of Richard Wright's 'Self-Consciousness' Thesis." CLA Journal, 16 (September), 106-116.
Examines W's concept of "double vision" in O for its application to politics.

132. Lacy, Dan. The White Use of Blacks in America. New York: Atheneum, p. 169.
Mentions W briefly.
Reprinted: 1973.203.

133. Lamming, George. Natives of My Person. New York: Holt, Rinehart and Winston, page following the copyright page.
Dedicatory note "for Margaret Gardiner and in memory of Richard Wright."

134. Landor, M.[ikhail]. "Faulkner in the Soviet Union," in Soviet Criticism of American Literature in the Sixties: An Anthology. Ed. Carl R. Proffer. Ann Arbor, Mich.: Ardis, pp. 173-180.
Reprint of 1965.93.

135. Larsen, R. B. V. "The Four Voices of Richard Wright's Native Son." Negro American Literature Forum, 6 (Winter), 105-109.
Identifies the four narrative voices of the novel as "first, the dominant and more or less continuous voice of the third-person limited narrator; second, the inarticulate voice (speech and closely-rendered thought) of Bigger himself; third, the biased voice of the supposedly 'objective' Establishment, principally news accounts and the utterance of state prosecutor Buckley; and fourth, the highly articulate and humane voice of the lawyer Boris Max, supremely analytical" (p. 105). Larsen analyzes each of these voices.

135a. Laye, Camara and J. Steven Rubin. "The Writer and His World: Laye: Commitment to Timeless Values." Africa Report, 17 (May), 20, 22, 24.
Laye comments on BB and BP. W's understanding of Africa was imperfect.

136. Leary, Lewis. "Lawd Today: Notes on Richard Wright's First/Last Novel." CLA Journal, 15 (June), 411-420.
Appreciation of LT preferring it to NS. The story of Jake Jackson reveals

both "the essential bleakness of black life" and the barrenness of white American culture. Repulsive yet amiable, Jake "emerges from his day neither pathetic nor tragic, only insistently, tediously alive," an everyman as well as a black man. Reprinted: 1982.90.

137. Lee, Brian and David Murray. "American Literature: The Twentieth Century." The Year's Work in English Studies 1970. Ed. Geoffrey Harlow. Vol. 51, pp. 407-448.
 Contains notices of books on W by Brignano and Abcarian and an article by Kenneth Reed. Abcarian's Richard Wright's Native Son: A Critical Handbook is "in every way an excellent compilation" (p. 441).

137a. Levin, Harry. "A Literary Enormity: Sartre on Flaubert." Journal of the History of Ideas, 33 (October-December), 643-649.
 Mentions W briefly.
 Reprinted 1980.149.

137b. LeVot, André. "James T. Farrell," in Littérature de notre temps: Ecrivains américains. Ed. Pierre Dommergues. Paris: Casterman, pp. 93-96.
 Mentions briefly W and NS.

138. _____. "Richard Wright: L'Homme qui vivait sous terre." Esprit, 40 (January), 142-143.
 Favorable review of Michel Fabre's edition of the French translation of "The Man Who Lived Underground." Le Vot praises the mixture of "the sordid and the marvelous, the lyric and the realistic" with which W, anticipating Ellison and Himes, presents his subject.

139. Lieber, Todd M. "Ralph Ellison and the Metaphor of Invisibility in Black Literary Tradition." American Quarterly, 24 (March), 86-100.
 Discusses metaphors of blindness and invisibility in NS (pp. 89-91). "The power and freedom that lie within invisibility have been major themes of Richard Wright" (p. 89).

140. Lohner, Edgar. "Die amerikanische Literatur," in Kindlers Literatur Lexikon. Ed. Rudolf Radler and Johanna Zeitler. Vol. 7. Zurich: Kindler Verlag, pp. 315-331.
 Mentions W briefly (p. 323).

141. Lomax, Michael L. "Fantasies of Affirmation: The 1920's Novel of Negro Life." CLA Journal, 16 (December), 232-246.
 Comments on W's social protest (p.

234)

142. Longstreet, Stephen. "Richard Wright--Black Exile," in his We All Went to Paris: Americans in the City of Light: 1776-1971. New York: Macmillan, pp. 430-440.
 Account of W's Paris years emphasizing the problems and difficulties of living and working there.

142a. Louit, Robert. "Ralph Ellison," in his Littérature de notre temps: Ecrivains américains. Ed. Pierre Dommergues. Paris: Casterman, pp. 89-92.
 Mentions briefly W and "The Man Who Lived Underground."

143. Mangione, Jerre. The Dream and the Deal: The Federal Writers' Project, 1935-1943. Boston: Little, Brown, pp. 121, 123-126, 255-256.
 Among many references to W, Mangione provides accounts of his friendships with Nelson Algren, Margaret Walker, and Ralph Ellison.

144. Mapp, Edward. Blacks in American Films: Today and Yesterday. Metuchen, N. J.: Scarecrow Press, p. 48.
 Contains a paragraph on the film NS emphasizing the social theme. Bigger is called "a young Negro man of limited intelligence."

144a. Margolies, Edward. "Experiences of the Black Expatriate Writer: Chester Himes." CLA Journal, 15 (June), 421-427.
 Mentions W briefly.

145. Martin, Katherine Anne. "Naturalism and Existentialism in the Novels of Richard Wright." Masters Abstracts, 10 (March), 77-78.
 W identifies two stages in the black man's quest for freedom: one of determinism and one of self-determination. LT and LD portray the first stage; NS and O the second.

146. Mauro, Walter. Jazz e universo negro. Milan: Rizzoli Editore, pp. 59-60, 83, 99, 110-115, 160, 236, 259.
 In addition to quoting and mentioning W, Mauro compares his Kafkaesque sensibility to developments in black music (pp. 110-113) and to his proteges Ellison (pp. 113-114) and Baldwin (p. 115). Includes W in the bibliography (p. 259).

147. May, John Richard. "Apocalypse in the American Novel." Dissertation Abstracts International, 32 (January), 4009A-4010A.
 Includes treatment of NS. See 1972.148.

148. _____. Toward a New Earth: Apocalypse in the American Novel. Notre Dame, Indiana: University of Notre Dame Press, pp. 161-171.
    Treats W in a chapter entitled "Ellison, Baldwin, and Wright: Vestiges of Christian Apocalypse."

149. McCarthy, Harold T. "Richard Wright: The Expatriate as Native Son." American Literature, 44 (March), 97-117.
    Describes and analyzes W's attitudes toward other expatriates, his encounters with the Communist Party, and the effect of transcendentalist and existentialist theories on his writing. W's childhood alienation anticipated his mature expatriation and his sympathy for the oppressed.
    Reprinted in revised form: 1974.122.
    Partially reprinted: 1975.130.

150. McPherson, James M., Laurence B. Holland, James M. Banner, Jr., Nancy J. Weiss, and Michael D. Bell. Blacks in America: Bibliographical Essays. Anchor Books AO-54. Garden City, N. Y.: Doubleday, pp. xii, 225, 233, 253, 254-255, 256-258, 262.
    Reprint of 1971.221.

150a. Meserve, Walter. "Drama," in American Literary Scholarship: An Annual/ 1970. Ed. J. Albert Robbins. Durham, N. C.: Duke University Press, pp. 330-346.
    Mentions W briefly (p. 343).

151. Miller, Eugene E. "Voodoo Parallels in Native Son." CLA Journal, 16 (September), 81-95.
    Traces extensive parallels between Haitian voodoo rituals and Bigger's killing of Mary in NS. These parallels represent an intuitive, emotional element derived from black folk tradition that complements W's rational, Western approach to social reality.

152. Miller, Wayne Charles. "Introduction," in his A Gathering of Ghetto Writers: Irish, Italian, Jewish, Black and Puerto Rican. New York: New York University Press, pp. 1-71.
    Mentions W briefly (p. 51).

153. Munro, John M. "The Arab Response to the Black Writers of America," in Asian Response to American Literature. Ed. C. D. Narasimhaiah. Delhi: Vikas Publications, pp. 281-288.
    Munro admits W's power in UTC and NS, but complains of sentimentality in the former and propaganda in the latter. The Arab student "response to Wright tends to be reasoned, cool and fairly objective" (p. 286).

154. Nagase, Hiroshi and Tsutomu Kanashiki. Introduction and notes to "The Ethics of Living Jim Crow," in their What the Negro Wants and Other Essays. By W, Langston Hughes, George S. Schuyler, James Baldwin, and Chester Himes. Tokyo: Kaitakusha, pp. 1-27.
    The introduction and notes are in Japanese; the text is in English.

155. Neal, Larry. "Into Nationalism, Out of Parochialism." Performance, 1 (April), 32-40.
    Mentions "Blueprint for Negro Writing."
    Reprinted: 1980.182.

156. Oleson, Carole W. "The Symbolic Richness of Richard Wright's 'Bright and Morning Star.'" Negro American Literature Forum, 6 (Winter), 110-112.
    Arguing that "Bright and Morning Star" is more than a mere protest story, Oleson analyzes the symbols of rain, the airplane beacon, the rich earth, and the star of the title.

156a. Ozawa, Fumio. "'Essays on Richard Wright' in Five Black Writers (New York: New York University Press, 1970)." Showa Joshi Daigaku Gakuen [Showa Women's College Instruction], 388 (1 April), 109-118.
    An introduction to the collected essays. Notes a change in W criticism and points out that there has been a great deal of "negative criticism" in recent years. The essays, Ozawa maintains, suggest a transition in W criticism. [Y. H. and T. K.]

157. Ozick, Cynthia. "Literary Blacks and Jews." Midstream, 18 (June-July), 10-24.
    Mentions W in connection with the Ellison-Howe controversy.

158. Phillips, Elizabeth C. Richard Wright's Native Son. New York: Monarch Press, 99 pp.
    Study guide with biographical sketch; thematic, structural, and stylistic analysis; plot summary; character analysis; survey of criticism; study questions; and bibliography.

159. Plante, P. R. "American Courage." Novel: A Forum on Fiction, 5 (Winter), 180-181.
    Review of Albert Gérard's Les Tambours du néant mentioning O.

160. Plumpp, Sterling. Black Rituals. Chicago: Third World Press, p. 21.
    Plump acknowledges W's influence in college and afterwards.

161. Priebe, Richard. "The Search for

Community in the Novels of Claude McKay." Studies in Black Literature, 3 (Summer), 22-30.
> Compares briefly Jake in Home to Harlem to Bigger Thomas.

162. Primeau, Ronald. "Imagination as Moral Bulwark and Creative Energy in Richard Wright's Black Boy and LeRoi Jones' Home." Studies in Black Literature, 3 (Summer), 12-18.
> Places both W and Jones in the tradition of romantic literature. Although BB essentially concerns racism, it is also about the power of the imagination to create and sustain personal identity. Primeau traces this theme through the autobiography and then compares W's work to Jones's.

163. Prior, Linda T. "A Further Word on Richard Wright's Use of Poe in Native Son." Poe Studies, 5 (December), 52-53.
> After noting similarities pointed out by Fabre and McCall, Prior focuses on W's use of "The Murders in the Rue Morgue." W employs irony in drawing from Poe's story in the furnace scene, newspaper coverage of the crime, and the emphasis on apelike savagery.

164. Proffer, Carl R. "Introduction: American Literature in the Soviet Union," in his Soviet Criticism of American Literature in the Sixties: An Anthology. Ann Arbor, Mich.: Ardis, pp. xiii-xxxii.
> Lists the translation of Selected Stories by W in 1962.

165. Raghavacharyulu, D. V. K. "A Perspective on the Fiction of the Minorities," in Asian Response to American Literature. Ed. C. D. Narasimhaiah. Delhi: Vikas Publications, pp. 289-292.
> Includes comparison of W, Baldwin, and Ellison. "Whereas, to use Kenneth Burke's structural formula . . . Richard Wright emphasizes 'purpose', and Baldwin 'passion', Ellison concentrates on 'perception' . . ." (p. 292).

166. Rather, Ernest R. "Richard Wright," in his Chicago Negro Almanac and Reference Book. Chicago: Chicago Negro Almanac Publishing Company, p. 8.
> Biographical sketch.

167. Redding, Saunders. "The Problems of the Negro Writer," in White Racism and Black Americans. Ed. David G. Bromley and Charles F. Longino, Jr. Cambridge, Mass.: Schenkman, pp. 617-627.
> Reprint of 1964.107.

168. Reed, Ishmael. "Chester Himes:

Writer." Black World, 21 (March), 23-38, 83-86.
> Contains several references to W. Reprinted: 1978.201.

168a. ____. Mumbo Jumbo. Garden City, N. Y.: Doubleday, p. 209.
> Mentions W briefly. Reprinted: 1978.202.

169. ____. "19 Necromancers from Now Introduction," in New Black Voices: An Anthology of Contemporary Afro-American Literature. Ed. Abraham Chapman. Mentor Books MW1116. New York: The New American Library, pp. 513-524.
> Reprint of 1970.297.

170. Reeves, Paschal et al. "A Checklist of Scholarship on Southern Literature for 1971." Mississippi Quarterly, 25 (Spring), 199-246.
> Lists fourteen items on W (pp. 237-238).

171. Reilly, John M. "Richard Wright's Apprenticeship." Journal of Black Studies, 2 (June), 439-460.
> Focuses on W's early poetry and journalism, noting the important influence of radical politics. The relationship between ideology and art was central in W's work throughout his life.

171a. Ricard, Alain. Théâtre et Nationalisme: Wole Soyinka et LeRoi Jones. Paris: Présence Africaine, pp. 23-24, 46, 128.
> Mentions W's attitude toward Africa, the play NS, and Bigger Thomas.

172. Rivers, Conrad Kent. "A Mourning Letter from Paris (for Richard Wright)," in Understanding the New Black Poetry. Ed. Stephen Henderson. New York: William Morrow, p. 256.
> Partial reprint of 1972.173.

173. ____. The Wright Poems. Introduction by Ronald Fair. Heritage Series, No. 18. London: Paul Breman, 20 pp.
> Collects poems by Rivers paying tribute to W and acknowledging his importance and influence.
> Partially reprinted: 1972.172.

174. Robinson, William H. "Biographical Sketches," in his Nommo: An Anthology of Modern Black African and Black American Literature. New York: Macmillan, pp. 475-485.
> Includes a brief entry for W (p. 485).

175. ____. "Introduction," in his Nommo: An Anthology of Modern Black African and Black American Literature. New York:

Macmillan, pp. 1-35.
    Mentions W's attitude toward black
    consciousness (p. 23) and comments on
    W's universality in NS, O, "Big Black
    Good Man," and "The Man Who Lived
    Underground."

176. Rodgers, Carolyn M. "Black Poetry--
Where It's At," in Rappin' and Stylin'
Out: Communication in Urban Black America. Ed. Thomas Kochman. Urbana: University of Illinois Press, pp. 336-345.
    Reprint of 1969.211.

176a. Royer, Michel and Paulette Schubert. "Chronologie des événements poli-
tiques, scientifiques, littéraires et
artistiques de 1900 à 1971," in Littérature de notre temps: Ecrivains américaines. Ed. Pierre Dommergues. Paris:
Casterman, pp. 1-16.
    Lists UTC, NS, BB, O, WML, LD, and
    LT.

177. Sadoul, Georges. "Chenal, Pierre
(P. Cohen)," in his Dictionary of Film
Makers. Trans., ed., and updated by
Peter Morris. Berkeley: University of
California Press, p. 44.
    Lists NS among Chenal's films.

178. Scheub, Harold. "Study Topics and
Notes," in his African Images. New York:
McGraw-Hill, pp. 368-372.
    One pertains to "I Have Seen Black
    Hands" (reprinted on pp. 342-343).

178a. Schulberg, Budd. The Four Seasons
of Success. Garden City, N. Y.: Doubleday, p. 14.
    Notes that W, like certain other
    American writers, did not match his
    early literary success in his later
    works.

179. Shima, Hideo. "Seishin no Horosha
toshiteno Richard Wright" ["Richard
Wright as a Spiritual Pilgrim"]. Kana-
gawa Kenritsu Gaigo Tanki Daigaku Kiyo
[Bulletin of the Kanagawa College of
Foreign Studies], 4 (October), 39-58.
    WML is W's final word on his spiri-
    tual pilgrimage. He discovered that
    alienation and loneliness are man's
    ultimate lot; his own life journey
    from the South to France demonstrates
    a poignant understanding of human
    life [Y. H.]

180. Shulman, Irving. "A Study of the
Juvenile Delinquent as Depicted in the
Twentieth-Century American Novel." Dis-
sertation Abstracts International, 33
(July), 329A-330A.
    Includes consideration of NS.

181. Simpson, George Eaton and J. Milton
Yinger. Racial and Cultural Minorities:

An Analysis of Prejudice and Discrimination. Fourth edition. New York: Harper &
Row, 775 pp.
    Revised reprint of 1953.228.

182. Singh, Raman K. "Christian Heroes
and Anti-Heroes in Richard Wright's
Fiction." Negro American Literature
Forum, 6 (Winter), 99-104, 131.
    Analyzes the protagonists of "Fire
    and Cloud," NS, O, and "Man, God
    Ain't Like That . . ." to study "the
    rejection-selection-definition pro-
    cess that marks W's fictional por-
    trayal of Christianity (and gener-
    alized religion)" (p. 99).

182a. Skeeter, Sharyn J. "The Quality of
Hurt: The Autobiography of Chester
Himes." Essence, 3 (August), 81.
    Mentions W briefly.

182b. _____. "Reprints." Essence, 3
(May), 24.
    Lists TMBV.

183. Smith, Sidonie Ann. "Patterns of
Slavery and Freedom in Black American
Autobiography." Dissertation Abstracts
International, 32 (March), 5245-A.
    Includes treatment of BB. See 1972.
    184.

184. _____. "Richard Wright's Black Boy:
The Creative Impulse as Rebellion." The
Southern Literary Journal, 5 (Fall),
123-136.
    In the tradition of the slave nar-
    rative, W's autobiography relates
    his self-realization through rebel-
    lion against an oppressive environ-
    ment. He first strikes out against
    his family, then against Southern
    white society, utilizing words as
    weapons.
    Reprinted in revised form: 1974.164.

185. Snelling, Paula. "Three Native
Sons," in From the Mountain. Ed. Helen
White and Redding S. Sugg, Jr. Memphis:
Memphis State University Press, pp. 203-
210.
    Reprint of 1940.930.

186. [Snow, Royall]. "American Literature," in The Lincoln Library of Essential Information. Ed. William J. Redding. Vol. 1. Columbus, Ohio: The Frontier Press Company, pp. 207-213.
    Reprint of 1971.279.

187. Spiller, Robert E., Willard Thorp,
Thomas H. Johnson, Henry Seidel Canby,
and Richard M. Ludwig. "Richard Wright,"
in their Literary History of the United
States: Bibliography Supplement II. New
York: Macmillan, pp. 285-286.
    Lists three primary and twenty-five

secondary sources.

188. Takaki, Ronald T. Violence and the Black Imagination: Essays and Documents. New Perspectives on Black America, ed. Herbert Hill. New York: Capricorn Books, pp. 17, 348.

Quotes from NS as an epigraph to Part I and mentions in the bibliographical essay the novel's perceptive analysis of violence.

188a. Tanaka, Hiroshi. "Richard Wright's The Outsider, trans. Fukuo Hashimoto." Kokujin Kenkyu [Negro Studies], 44 (25 December), 27.

Points out that W's idea of "escape" is consciously reflected in the plot of O; after the subway accident, the novel lacks reality, and Cross's tragedy is unconvincing [Y. H. and T. K.]

189. Tatham, Campbell. "Vision and Value in Uncle Tom's Children." Studies in Black Literature, 3 (Spring), 14-23.

After reviewing recent critical commentary on UTC, Tatham analyzes all of the five stories of the enlarged edition for content and authorial intention. The central metaphor of the collection is racial war.

190. Taylor, Clyde. "Black Folk Spirit and the Shape of Black Literature." Black World, 21 (August), 31-40.

Mentions W briefly.

191. Tener, Robert L. "Role Playing as a Dutchman." Studies in Black Literature, 3 (Autumn), 17-21.

Very briefly compares Clay in Dutchman to Bigger Thomas (p. 19).

191a. Thompson, G. R. "Themes, Topics, and Criticism," in American Literary Scholarship: An Annual/1970. Ed. J. Albert Robbins. Durham, N. C.: Duke University Press, pp. 376-401.

Mentions W several times in connection with essays on general topics on Afro-American literature.

192. Timmerman, John. "Trust and Mistrust: The Role of the Black Woman in Three Works by Richard Wright." Studies in the Twentieth Century, No. 10 (Fall), pp. 33-45.

Contrasts Sarah of "Long Black Song," who escapes from reality, and Aunt Sue of "Bright and Morning Star," who confronts it. In LT, Jake Jackson fails to realize his own humanity by failing to love his wife Lil.

193. Turner, Darwin T. "Afro-American Literary Critics: An Introduction," in The Black Aesthetic. Ed. Addison Gayle,

Jr. Anchor Books A822. Garden City, N. Y.: Doubleday, pp. 57-74.

Reprint of 1971.298.

194. _____. "The Teaching of Afro-American Literature," in New Black Voices: An Anthology of Contemporary Afro-American Literature. Ed. Abraham Chapman. Mentor Books MW1116. New York: The New American Library, pp. 499-505.

Reprint of 1970.348.

195. _____, Jean M. Bright, and Richard Wright (of Detroit). "Richard Wright (1908-1960)," in their Voices from the Black Experience: African and Afro-American Literature. Lexington, Mass.: Ginn, p. 275.

Biographical note emphasizing the "migratory pattern" of W's life and work.

196. _____. Untitled headnote and study questions, in their Voices from the Black Experience: African and Afro-American Literature. Lexington, Mass.: Ginn, pp. 171, 177.

To accompany "The Ethics of Living Jim Crow."

197. Uchiyama, Tetsujiro. "Uncle Tom no Kodomotachi ni Mirareru Tatakai to Sono Hoko" ["Uncle Tom's Children: How Negroes Were Fighting"]. Niigata Daigaku Jinbun Kagaku Kenkyu [Niigata University Studies in Cultural Sciences], No. 43 (December), 193-227.

A discussion and explanation of W's treatment of various racial struggles depicted in the collection. "Big Boy Leaves Home" is concerned with the protagonist's successful escape; "Down by the Riverside" is faced with a dilemma between escaping the white world alone and with family; "Long Black Song" creates a hero out of Silas, who resorts to rebellion and violence; "Fire and Cloud" dramatizes a coalition of blacks and white workers in their common struggle; "Bright and Morning Star" becomes the struggle of an individual and not of the Party. W's protagonist suffers estrangement from the black community as he gains experience and maturity; this pattern of development also applies to W's career. [Y. H.]

198. Vickery, John B. and J'nan M. Sellery. "Literary Works for Further Study," in their The Scapegoat: Ritual and Literature. Boston: Houghton Mifflin, pp. 385-386.

Lists NS.

199. Wade, Melvin and Margaret Wade. "The Black Aesthetic in the Black Novel." Journal of Black Studies, 2

(June), 391-408.
    Mentions NS as the greatest American
    naturalistic novel.

200. Wager, Willis. "American Negro
Writing,"in Asian Response to American
Literature. Ed. C. D. Narasimhaiah.
Delhi: Vikas Publications, pp. 399-405.
    Contains a paragraph on W comparing
    NS to An American Tragedy (p. 404).

201. Walcott, Ronald. "The Early Fiction
of John A. Williams." CLA Journal, 16
(December), 198-213.
    Mentions Williams's biography of W
    (p. 198).

202. _____. "The Man Who Cried I Am:
Crying in the Dark." Studies in Black
Literature, 3 (Spring), 24-32.
    Notes that the character Harry Ames
    is based on W.

203. _____. "Some Notes on the Blues
Style and Space: Ellison, Gordone, and
Tolson." Black World, 22 (December), 4-
29.
    Mentions "The Man Who Lived Under-
    ground" and NS in relation to con-
    cepts of space and time in black
    culture.

203a. Walker, Alice. "A Talk: Convoca-
tion 1972." Sarah Lawrence Alumni Magazine (Summer), pp. 6-8.
    Contrasts briefly NS and Their Eyes
    Were Watching God.

204. Washington, William D. and Samuel
Beckoff. "Do You Dig It?" in their Black
Literature: An Anthology of Outstanding
Black Writers. New York: Simon and
Schuster, pp. 245-246.
    Study questions for "The Man Who Was
    Almost a Man."

205. _____. "Richard Wright," in their
Black Literature: An Anthology of Outstanding Black Writers. New York: Simon
and Schuster, p. 232.
    Headnote to "The Man Who Was Almost a
    Man."

206. Whitlow, Roger. "The Two Hundred
Most Important Works of Black American
Literature: A Bibliography." Illinois
English Bulletin, 60 (October), 11-20.
    Lists BB, NS (the novel), EM, and NS
    (the play).

207. Williams, Sherley Anne. Give Birth
to Brightness: A Thematic Study in Neo-
Black Literature. New York: The Dial
Press, pp. 84, 215.
    Comments briefly on NS.

208. Young, James Owen. "The Talented
Tenth and the Great Depression." Disser-

tation Abstracts International, 32 (February), 4546A-4547A.
    Not explicitly mentioned in the ab-
    stract, W is treated in the disserta-
    tion. See 1973.312.

1973

1. Aaron, Daniel. "The Emergence of
Richard Wright: A Study in Literature
and Society. By Keneth Kinnamon." American Literature, 45 (November), 474-475.
    Favorable review pointing out the
    combination of sociological and aes-
    thetic approaches to W's life and
    work.

2. _____. "Richard Wright and the Communist Party," in Richard Wright: Impressions and Perspectives. Ed. David Ray
and Robert M. Farnsworth. Ann Arbor
Paperbacks AA189. Ann Arbor: The University of Michigan Press, pp. 34-46.
    Reprint of 1971.1.

3. _____. "Richard Wright and the Communist Party," in Richard Wright: Impressions and Perspectives. Ed. David Ray
and Robert M. Farnsworth. Ann Arbor: The
University of Michigan Press, pp. 34-
46.
    Reprint of 1971.1.

4. Abcarian, Richard and Marvin Klotz.
"Questions," in their Literature: The
Human Experience. New York: St. Martin's
Press, p. 305.
    Study questions to accompany "The Man
    Who Lived Underground."
    Reprinted: 1975.118; 1978.1; 1980.1.

5. _____. "Richard Wright, The Man Who
Lived Underground," in their Instruc-
tor's Manual to Accompany Literature:
The Human Experience. New York: St.
Martin's Press, pp. 27-29.
    Analysis emphasizing the theme of
    universal existential guilt. Comments
    on the upper vs. the lower world and
    on W's use of dreams in the story.
    Reprinted: 1975.119; 1978.2; 1980.2.

6. Achtert, Walter S., comp. 1971 MLA
Abstracts of Articles in Scholarly Jour-
nals. Vol. I. New York: Modern Language
Association, p. 228.
    Abstracts of articles on W by Blyden
    Jackson, Edward A. Kearns, Lewis A.
    Lawson, John M. Reilly, Martha T.
    Stephens, and John H. Timmerman.

7. Adoff, Arnold. "Biographical Notes,"
in his The Poetry of Black America:
Anthology of the 20th Century. Introduction by Gwendolyn Brooks. New York:
Harper & Row, pp. 517-538.
    Contains a note on W (p. 538).

8. Ahern, Camille. "The Emergence of Richard Wright: A Study in Literature and Society by Kenneth [sic] Kinnamon." What's New in Scholarly Books, Fall, p. [3].
Notice summarizing the contents.

9. Alexander, Margaret Walker. "J. Baldwin," in Encyclopedia of World Biography. Ed. David Eggenberger. Vol. 1. New York: McGraw-Hill, pp. 359-360.
Mentions W briefly.

10. ____. "Richard Wright," in Richard Wright: Impressions and Perspectives. Ed. David Ray and Robert M. Farnsworth. Ann Arbor Paperbacks AA189. Ann Arbor: The University of Michigan Press, pp. 47-67.
Reprint of 1971.4.

11. ____. "Richard Wright," in Richard Wright: Impressions and Perspectives. Ed. David Ray and Robert M. Farnsworth. Ann Arbor: The University of Michigan Press, pp. 47-67.
Reprint of 1971.4.

12. Anon. "American Literature Reflects American Life," in Compton's Encyclopedia and Fact-Index. Ed. Donald E. Lawson. Vol. 1. Chicago: F. E. Compton, pp. 342-367.
Reprint of 1957.7.

13. Anon. "Baker, Houston A., comp. Twentieth century interpretations of Native son; a collection of critical essays." Choice, 10 (July-August), 772.
Favorable notice describing briefly the contents of the collection.

14. Anon. "Baker, Houston A., comp., Twentieth century interpretations of Native son; a collection of critical essays." The Booklist, 69 (15 May), 884.
Notice describing the contents of the collection.

15. Anon. "Bakish, David. Richard Wright." The Booklist, 69 (15 June), 967.
Favorable notice describing the contents and praising their balance.

16. Anon. "Bakish, David. Richard Wright." The Booklist, 69 (15 June), 1016.
Favorable notice pointing out that the book is more informative than Houston Baker's collection of essays.

17. Anon. "Book by Kinnamon on Richard Wright." The Champaign-Urbana Courier (3 January), p. 3.
Notice of The Emergence of Richard Wright.

18. Anon. Dust jacket of Der schwarze Traum. By Richard Wright. Trans. Karl-Heinz Schönfelder. Berlin: Verlag Volk und Welt.
Front inside flap summarizes the plot, especially the father-son relationship.

19. Anon. Dust jacket of Richard Wright. By David Bakish. New York: Ungar.
Front cover contains a photograph of W. Inside flaps contain a blurb and a biographical note on Bakish.

20. Anon. Dust jacket of The Unfinished Quest of Richard Wright. By Michel Fabre. New York: William Morrow.
Front cover has a color photograph of W; back cover has a black and white photograph of Fabre. Inside flaps contain a summary of the book, a blurb by Anaïs Nin, and a biographical note on Fabre.

21. Anon. "The Emergence of Richard Wright, by Keneth Kinnamon." The Virginia Quarterly Review, 49 (Spring), cxv.
Generally favorable review expressing reservations about Kinnamon's reluctance to analyze W's complex mind.

22. Anon. "Expressions: Reviews: Books." The Black Collegian, 3 (March-April), 17.
Highly favorable review of Keneth Kinnamon's The Emergence of Richard Wright.

23. Anon. "Fabre, Michel. The unfinished quest of Richard Wright." Choice, 10 (December), 1548.
Favorable review expressing reservations about Fabre's critical analysis of W's work.

24. Anon. Index to Periodical Articles by and About Negroes: 1971. Boston: G. K. Hall, p. 538.
Lists four items on W.

25. Anon. Index Translationum 24. Paris: Unesco, pp. 107, 184, 243, 727, 766.
Lists translation of LD into German, BB into Bulgarian and Turkish (2), and UTC into Danish and Arabic.

26. Anon. "Kinnamon, Keneth. The Emergence of Richard Wright: A Study in Literature and Society." American Ambassador Books Chosen by the Books-Across-the-Sea Selection Panel (4 May), p. 2.
Favorable notice of "a sensitive and important appraisal" in a mimeographed newsletter of The English-Speaking Union.

27. Anon. "Kinnamon, Keneth. The emergence of Richard Wright; a study in

literature and society." Choice, 10 (September), 979.
    Favorable notice praising the work's treatment of W's early years and his agitprop writings.

28. Anon. "Mississippi--Heart of the Deep South," in Compton's Encyclopedia and Fact-Index. Ed. Donald E. Lawson. Vol. 14. Chicago: F. E. Compton, pp. 372-388.
    Reprint of 1970.25.

29. Anon. "'Native Son,'" in Richard Wright: Impressions and Perspectives. Ed. David Ray and Robert M. Farnsworth. Ann Arbor Paperbacks AA189. Ann Arbor: The University of Michigan Press, following p. 115.
    Reprint of 1971.15.

30. _____. "'Native Son,'" in Richard Wright: Impressions and Perspectives. Ed. David Ray and Robert M. Farnsworth. Ann Arbor: The University of Michigan Press, following p. 115.
    Reprint of 1971.15.

31. Anon. "Negro, American: Cultural Status," in Encyclopaedia Britannica. Ed. Warren E. Preece. Vol. 16. Chicago: Encyclopaedia Britannica, pp. 198-200C.
    Mentions W.

32. Anon. "Richard Wright at Wading River, L. I., 1947," in Richard Wright: Impressions and Perspectives. Ed. David Ray and Robert M. Farnsworth. Ann Arbor Paperbacks AA189. Ann Arbor: The University of Michigan Press, following p. 115.
    Reprint of 1971.16.

33. _____. "Richard Wright at Wading River, L. I., 1947," in Richard Wright: Impressions and Perspectives. Ed. David Ray and Robert M. Farnsworth. Ann Arbor: The University of Michigan Press, following p. 115.
    Reprint of 1971.16.

34. Anon. "Richard Wright in Chicago, 1928," in Richard Wright: Impressions and Perspectives. Ed. David Ray and Robert M. Farnsworth. Ann Arbor Paperbacks AA189. Ann Arbor: The University of Michigan Press, following p. 115.
    Reprint of 1971.17.

35. _____. "Richard Wright in Chicago, 1928," in Richard Wright: Impressions and Perspectives. Ed. David Ray and Robert M. Farnsworth. Ann Arbor: The University of Michigan Press, following p. 115.
    Reprint of 1971.17.

36. Anon. "Richard Wright Under Study."

The Kansas City Star (30 September), Sec. E, p. 3.
    Notice of the scheduled publication of Michel Fabre's The Unfinished Quest of Richard Wright.

37. Anon. "Richard Wright's Native Son," in Richard Wright: Impressions and Perspectives. Ed. David Ray and Robert M. Farnsworth. Ann Arbor Paperbacks AA189. Ann Arbor: The University of Michigan Press, following p. 115.
    Reprint of 1971.18.

38. _____. "Richard Wright's Native Son," in Richard Wright: Impressions and Perspectives. Ed. David Ray and Robert M. Farnsworth. Ann Arbor: The University of Michigan Press, following p. 115.
    Reprint of 1971.18.

39. Anon. "Richard Wright's Native Son," in Richard Wright: Impressions and Perspectives. Ed. David Ray and Robert M. Farnsworth. Ann Arbor Paperbacks AA189. Ann Arbor: The University of Michigan Press, following p. 115.
    Reprint of 1971.19.

40. _____. "Richard Wright's Native Son," in Richard Wright: Impressions and Perspectives. Ed. David Ray and Robert M. Farnsworth. Ann Arbor: The University of Michigan Press, following p. 115.
    Reprint of 1971.19.

41. Anon. "Richard Wright's Native Son," in Richard Wright: Impressions and Perspectives. Ed. David Ray and Robert M. Farnsworth. Ann Arbor Paperbacks AA189. Ann Arbor: The University of Michigan Press, following p. 115.
    Reprint of 1971.20.

42. _____. "Richard Wright's Native Son," in Richard Wright: Impressions and Perspectives. Ed. David Ray and Robert M. Farnsworth. Ann Arbor: The University of Michigan Press, following p. 115.
    Reprint of 1971.20.

43. Anon. Right On: A List of Books by and About the American Negro. North Las Vegas, Nev.: North Las Vegas Library, pp. 3, 18, 21, 39.
    Lists books by W.

44. Anon. "This Week." The Christian Century, 90 (26 September), 953.
    Contains a brief, favorable notice of Michel Fabre's The Unfinished Quest of Richard Wright.

45. Anon. "The Unfinished Quest of Richard Wright. Michel Fabre." Publishers Weekly, 204 (16 July), 107.
    Favorable notice of "a stunning portrait of a life" and "a chronicle of

the triumphs and agonies of a writer."

46. Anon. "The University of Michigan
Press." CLA Journal, 17 (September),
following p. 100.
    Contains an advertisement for Richard
    Wright: Impressions and Perspectives,
    ed. David Ray and Robert M. Farns-
    worth.

47. Anon. "Wright, Richard Nathaniel,"
in Compton's Encyclopedia and Fact-
Index. Ed. Donald E. Lawson. Vol. 22.
Chicago: F. E. Compton, pp. 304-305.
    Biographical sketch with photograph.

48. Appel, Benjamin. "Personal Impressions," in Richard Wright: Impressions
and Perspectives. Ed. David Ray and
Robert M. Farnsworth. Ann Arbor Paperbacks AA189. Ann Arbor: The University
of Michigan Press, pp. 74-77.
    Reprint of 1971.25.

49. ____. "Personal Impressions," in
Richard Wright: Impressions and Perspec-
tives. Ed. David Ray and Robert M.
Farnsworth. Ann Arbor: The University of
Michigan Press, pp. 74-77.
    Reprint of 1971.25.

50. Bakish, David. Richard Wright.
Modern Literature Monographs. New York:
Ungar, 114 pp.
    Chronological survey of W's life and
    works. Chapter 1 sketches W's youth-
    ful years in the South and his liter-
    ary apprenticeship in Chicago, devot-
    ing special attention to "Big Boy
    Leaves Home" and LT. Chapter 2 treats
    the New York period, analyzing the
    short stories, NS, and "The Man Who
    Lived Underground." Examines TMBV as
    a statement of black nationalism. BB
    and some of the essays receive brief-
    er treatment. A brief third chapter
    concerns the initial phase of W's
    expatriation and comments on four
    pieces later included in EM. Chapter
    4 (1953-1957) analyzes O and SH,
    which Bakish considers failures, and
    examines W's interest in Africa and
    Asia. PS receives detailed analysis
    as the author's best travel book. The
    final chapter interprets LD as a
    skillful synthesis of "the style and
    themes of his earlier fiction" (p.
    90), describes the unpublished
    "Island of Hallucination" in the
    context of black intrigue in Paris,
    points out the unhappiness of W's
    last years, and assesses briefly his
    continuing importance. A chronology
    and brief bibliography are included.

51. Baldwin, James and Nikki Giovanni. A
Dialogue. Philadelphia: Lippincott, pp.
16, 64, 76, 78, 81.
    Includes discussion of Baldwin's
    relation to W and comments on LT (p.
    64).

52. Baldwin, Richard E. "The Creative
Vision of Native Son." The Massachusetts
Review, 14 (Spring), 378-390.
    Analyzes W's development of Bigger's
    perspective and personality. The
    novel presents the dark side of the
    American dream. Despite the social
    obstacles, however, Bigger does
    create a vision of self that is full
    of meaning.

52a. Barksdale, Richard K. "Black America and the Mask of Comedy," in The
Comic Imagination in American Literature. Ed. Louis D. Rubin, Jr. New Brunswick, N. J.: Rutgers University Press,
pp. 349-360.
    Mentions W briefly (p. 352).

53. Baskin, Wade and Richard N. Runes.
Dictionary of Black Culture. New York:
Philosophical Library, pp. 322-323, 484.
    Contains entries for NS and W.

54. Bell, Bernard W. "Contemporary Afro-
American Poetry as Folk Art." Black
World, 22 (March), 16-26, 74-87.
    Cites "Blueprint for Negro Writing"
    for W's comments on the black oral
    tradition.

54a. Bennett, James R. "American Literature and the Acquisitive Society; Background and Criticism: A Bibliography."
Bulletin of Bibliography, 30 (October-
December), 175-184.
    Contains two annotated items on W.

55. Benson, Joseph. "At Last, a Defini-
tive Biography of Richard Wright."
Greensboro Daily News (28 October), p.
B3.
    Highly favorable review of Michel
    Fabre's The Unfinished Quest of
    Richard Wright. It is an exemplary
    literary biography, carefully
    researched and documented. It is of
    major importance in W studies.

56. ____. "The Short Fiction of Richard
Wright." Dissertation Abstracts International, 33, p. 5713A.
    Argues that W's short fiction matches
    NS in quality and is among the best
    in the American tradition. UTC con-
    centrates on the movement from sub-
    mission to rebellion; EM deals with
    the quest for personal identity. W's
    strengths as a writer are his ability
    to create realistic dialogue and to
    deal with scenes of violent action.

57. Berkley, Saundra Gould. "Problems

for Discussion," in her The Short Story Reader. Third edition. Indianapolis: Bobbs-Merrill, p. 361.
  Includes seven study questions on "The Man Who Was Almost a Man."

58. Bianchi, Ruggero and Claudio Gorlier. "Wright, Richard," in Grande dizionario enciclopedico utet. Vol. 19. Turin: Unione tipografico-Editrice Torinese, p. 747.
  Biographical sketch.

59. Bilbo, Theodore G. Untitled speech, in Richard Wright: Impressions and Perspectives. Ed. David Ray and Robert M. Farnsworth. Ann Arbor Paperbacks AA189. Ann Arbor: The University of Michigan Press, p. 16.
  Reprint of 1945.773.

60. _____. Untitled speech, in Richard Wright: Impressions and Perspectives. Ed. David Ray and Robert M. Farnsworth. Ann Arbor: The University of Michigan Press, p. 16.
  Reprint of 1945.773.

61. Birdoff, Harry. "Personal Impressions," in Richard Wright: Impressions and Perspectives. Ed. David Ray and Robert M. Farnsworth. Ann Arbor Paperbacks AA189. Ann Arbor: The University of Michigan Press, pp. 81-84.
  Reprint of 1971.44.

62. _____. "Personal Impressions," in Richard Wright: Impressions and Perspectives. Ed. David Ray and Robert M. Farnsworth. Ann Arbor: The University of Michigan Press, pp. 81-84.
  Reprint of 1971.44.

63. Bl.[air], W.[alter]. "American Literature," in Encyclopaedia Britannica. Ed. Warren E. Preece. Vol. 1. Chicago: Encyclopaedia Britannica, pp. 764-774.
  Reprint of 1954.80.

64. Bode, Carl. "The Unsteady Journey of a Native Son." Washington Star-News (30 September), p. H-3.
  Favorable review of Michel Fabre's The Unfinished Quest of Richard Wright with special praise for its thorough research.

65. Bogle, Donald. Toms, Coons, Mulattoes, Mammies, and Bucks: An Interpretive History of Blacks in American Films. New York: The Viking Press, pp. 183-184.
  Unfavorable discussion of the film NS calling it "ill conceived and technically poor." Bogle complains especially about W's performance.

66. Boitani, Piero. "Richard Wright: i

damnati della terra," in his Prosatori negri americani del novecento. Rome: Edizioni di Storia e Letteratura, pp. 123-164.
  Analyzes in detail NS as a naturalistic novel. Considers "The Man Who Lived Underground" and BB at length, but does not treat the later fiction. Partially translated: 1979.42.

67. Bontemps, Arna. "3 Pennies for Luck," in his The Old South. New York: Dood, Mead, pp. 221-238.
  Relates an anecdote of lending W two cents for carfare in Chicago.

68. _____. "Arna Bontemps," in Interviews with Black Writers. Ed. John O'Brien. New York: Liveright, pp. 4-15.
  Includes brief comments on W's involvement with Communism (p. 11).

69. Boyd, G. N. and L. A. Boyd. Religion in Contemporary Fiction: Criticism from 1945 to the Present. San Antonio: Trinity University Press, p. 53.
  Lists three items on W.

70. Breman, Paul. "Richard Wright," in his You Better Believe It: Black Verse in English from Africa, the West Indies and the United States. Baltimore: Penguin, pp. 107-109.
  Biographical-critical sketch emphasizing W's search for freedom throughout his career. Breman includes "Between the World and Me" and "In the Falling Snow" in this anthology.

71. Brignano, Russell C. "Autobiographical Books by Black Americans: A Bibliography of Works Written Since the Civil War." Negro American Literature Forum, 7 (Winter), 148-156.
  Lists five works by W.

72. Brooks, A. Russell. "A Dialogue. By James Baldwin and Nikki Giovanni." CLA Journal, 17 (December), 291-294.
  Review mentioning the author's conversation on "black literature from Richard Wright to the present" (p. 293).

73. Brooks, Cleanth, R. W. B. Lewis, and Robert Penn Warren. "Richard Wright (1908-1960)," in their American Literature: The Makers and the Making. Vol. 2. New York: St. Martin's Press, pp. 2726-2731.
  Critical and biographical headnote to accompany "The Man Who Was Almost a Man" and a selection from BB. Focuses on UTC, NS, and BB, deeming the autobiography W's finest work. Includes biographical chronology and sugges-

tions for further reading.

74. Brown, Linda Weaver. "The Design and Development of an Introductory Course in Afro-American Literature." Dissertation Abstracts International, 33 (January), 3633-A.
    NS is included as a text in the course.

75. Bryant, Jerry H. "The Return of Richard Wright." The Nation, 217 (5 November), 470-472.
    Favorable review of Michel Fabre's The Unfinished Quest of Richard Wright. The biography is a "vast accumulation of Wright's everday activity." W was obsessed with the idea of bringing all races together, of improving the national life as well as the black condition. The "narrative has a curious surface quality" and Fabre maintains scholarly objectivity. Nevertheless, the book is a penetrating and brilliant account of W's life and career.

76. Bryer, Jackson R., Eddy Dow, Philip R. Headings, Joseph V. Ridgley, and Peter G. Van Egmond, with the help of Matthew O'Brien and Donald P. Wharton. "American Literature," in 1971 MLA International Bibliography. Compiled by Harrison T. Meserole. Vol. 1. New York: Modern Language Association, pp. 116-164.
    Lists twenty-two items on W.

77. Bullins, Ed. "Introduction: Black Theater: The '70's--Evolutionary Changes," in his The Theme Is Blackness: 'The Corner' and Other Plays. New York: William Morrow, pp. 3-15.
    Mentions W as an intellectual ancestor of black revolutionary nationalism (p. 4).

78. Busacca, Basil. "Checklist of Black Playwrights: 1823-1970." The Black Scholar, 5 (September), 48-54.
    Lists NS.

79. Camus, Albert. "Letter to Richard Wright," in Richard Wright: Impressions and Perspectives. Ed. David Ray and Robert M. Farnsworth. Ann Arbor Paperbacks AA189. Ann Arbor: The University of Michigan Press, p. 147.
    Reprint of 1971.65.

80. _____. "Letter to Richard Wright," in Richard Wright: Impressions and Perspectives. Ed. David Ray and Robert M. Farnsworth. Ann Arbor: The University of Michigan Press, p. 147.
    Reprint of 1971.65.

81. Carlsen, G. Robert and Anthony Tovatt. "Biographical Notes," in their Insights: Themes in Literature. Second edition. Themes and Writers Series. New York: McGraw-Hill, pp. 490-493.
    Includes an entry on W (pp. 490-491). Reprinted: 1979.59.

82. _____. "The Fight," in their Teacher's Resource Guide for Second Edition Insights: Themes in Literature. New York: McGraw-Hill, p. 199.
    Teaching aids for an excerpt from BB. Reprinted: 1979.60.

83. _____. "He Passed the Test, Implications, Techniques," in their Insights: Themes in Literature. Second edition. Themes and Writers Series. New York: McGraw-Hill, p. 510.
    Study aids for an excerpt from BB. Reprinted: 1979.61.

84. _____. "Hokku Poems," in Teacher's Resource Guide for Second Edition Insights: Themes in Literature. New York: McGraw-Hill, p. 174.
    Brief comments on teaching the poems. Reprinted: 1979.62.

85. Carlsen, G. Robert, Edgar H. Schuster, and Anthony Tovatt. "'. . . The Poor Get Poorer,' Implications, Techniques, Words," in their American Literature: Themes and Writers. Second edition. New York: McGraw-Hill, pp. 406-407.
    Study notes and questions on "The Man Who Saw the Flood."

86. _____. "Richard Wright 1908-1960," in their American Literature: Themes and Writers. Second edition. New York: McGraw-Hill, pp. 400-403.
    Biographical-critical sketch preceding "The Man Who Saw the Flood," "The Man Who Was Almost a Man," and an excerpt from BB. Includes a photograph.

87. _____. "To Become a Man, Implications, Techniques, Words," in their American Literature: Themes and Writers. Second edition. New York: McGraw-Hill, pp. 414-415.
    Study notes and questions on "The Man Who Was Almost a Man."

88. _____. "Who Is to Blame, Implications, Techniques, Words," in their American Literature: Themes and Writers. Second edition. New York: McGraw-Hill, pp. 432-433.
    Study notes and questions on BB.

89. Carson, David L. "Ralph Ellison: Twenty Years After." Studies in American Fiction, 1 (Spring), 1-23.

Interview with Ralph Ellison, who denies that "The Man Who Lived Underground" influenced Invisible Man. "Wright's approach was Dreiserian, from the Chicago school."

90. Cash, Earl A. "The Narrators in Invisible Man and Notes from Underground: Brothers in the Spirit." CLA Journal, 16 (June), 505-507.
    Compares briefly "The Man Who Lived Underground" to Notes from Underground and NS to Crime and Punishment.

91. Cayton, Horace and Sidney Williams. "Reminiscences," in Richard Wright: Impressions and Perspectives. Ed. David Ray and Robert M. Farnsworth. Ann Arbor Paperbacks AA189. Ann Arbor: The University of Michigan Press, pp. 154-157.
    Partial reprint of 1971.67.

92. _____. "Reminiscences," in Richard Wright: Impressions and Perspectives. Ed. David Ray and Robert M. Farnsworth. Ann Arbor: The University of Michigan Press, pp. 154-157.
    Partial reprint of 1971.67.

93. Chapman, Abraham. "Concepts of the Black Aesthetic in Contemporary Black Literature," in The Black Writer in Africa and the Americas. Ed. Lloyd W. Brown. University of Southern California Studies in Comparative Literature, Vol. 6. Los Angeles: Hennessey & Ingalls, pp. 11-43.
    Quotes from and comments briefly on W's "Tradition and Industrialization" (pp. 27-28).

94. Cherry, Richard L., Robert J. Conley, and Bernard A. Hirsch. "'Psychological Reactions of Oppressed People' Richard Wright," in their Instructor's Manual The Shadow Within. Boston: Houghton Mifflin, pp. 19-20.
    Compares W's essay to Baldwin's "Stranger in the Village." Includes study aids.

95. Cocteau, Jean. "Letter to Richard Wright," in Richard Wright: Impressions and Perspectives. Ed. David Ray and Robert M. Farnsworth. Ann Arbor Paperbacks AA189. Ann Arbor: The University of Michigan Press, p. 148.
    Reprint of 1971.72.

96. _____. "Letter to Richard Wright," in Richard Wright: Impressions and Perspectives. Ed. David Ray and Robert M. Farnsworth. Ann Arbor: The University of Michigan Press, p. 148.
    Reprint of 1971.72.

96a. Colter, Cyrus. The Hippodrome. Chi-

cago: The Swallow Press, p. [vii].
    One of the four epigraphs is from "The Man Who Lived Underground."

97. Conroy, Jack. "A Reminiscence," in Richard Wright: Impressions and Perspectives. Ed. David Ray and Robert M. Farnsworth. Ann Arbor Paperbacks AA189. Ann Arbor: The University of Michigan Press, pp. 31-34.
    Reprint of 1971.74.

98. _____. "A Reminiscence," in Richard Wright: Impressions and Perspectives. Ed. David Ray and Robert M. Farnsworth. Ann Arbor: The University of Michigan Press, pp. 31-34.
    Reprint of 1971.74.

99. _____. "Richard Wright: As Writer, a Truly Representative Man." Chicago Tribune (28 October), Sec. 7, p. 3.
    Favorable review of Michel Fabre's The Unfinished Quest of Richard Wright. Based on extensive research, it seems definitive.

100. Cook, Mercer A. "Some Literary Contacts: African, West Indian, Afro-American," in The Black Writer in Africa and the Americas. Ed. Lloyd W. Brown. University of Southern California Studies in Comparative Literature, Vol. 6. Los Angeles: Hennessey & Ingals, pp. 119-140.
    Includes discussion of W's role in the Presence Africaine group.

100a. Cooke, Michael G. "Modern Black Autobiography in the Tradition," in Romanticism: Vistas, Instances, Continuities. Ed. David Thorburn and Geoffrey Hartman. Ithaca, N. Y.: Cornell University Press, pp. 255-280.
    Includes a discussion of BB, in which W "surpasses all writers . . . in the naturalistic, non-Kafkaesque evocation of the physical dimensions of incertitude, its simple separation from the operations of interpretive reason and purposive will" (p. 271).

101. Cooper, Wayne. "Introduction," in his The Passion of Claude McKay: Selected Poetry and Prose, 1912-1948. New York: Schocken Books, pp. 1-41.
    Argues that W's dominance after 1940 has discouraged adequate investigation of earlier black writers (p. 2).

102. _____. "Selected Poems, 1912-1925," in his The Passion of Claude McKay: Selected Poetry and Prose, 1912-1948. New York: Schocken, pp. 107-109.
    Mentions W briefly.

103. Cortese, Giuseppina. Letteratura e conscienza nera. Milan: U. Mursia & C.,

pp. 13, 15, 19-20, 24-25, 29, 39-79, 84,
85, 86, 87-88, 91, 93, 96, 97, 99, 100,
105, 106, 109, 110, 111, 112, 124, 124-
125, 126, 128-129, 136, 138, 140-141,
142, 143, 146, 147, 149, 155, 163, 166,
170, 170-171, 183, 185, 188-189, 191,
192.
> The chapter on W emphasizes social
> oppression and dehumanization as
> major themes and treats W's intel-
> lectual evolution, which retained
> elements of Marxism even after he
> left the Party. W added race to the
> concept of class struggle. Cortese
> discusses NS and O, mentioning other
> works. Elsewhere she cites or quotes
> W and comments on his relation to
> Ellison, Baldwin, Jones, and Cleaver.

104. Cosgrove, William. "Modern Black
Writers: The Divided Self." Negro American Literature Forum, 7 (Winter), 120-
122.
> Uses NS and Invisible Man in a dis-
> cussion of recent black writers. The
> W tradition stresses the "American-
> ness of native blacks" (p. 120).

105. Cowley, Malcolm. A Second Flower-
ing: Works and Days of the Lost Generation. New York: The Viking Press, p.
240.
> Mentions W briefly.

106. _____. "What Books Survive from the
1930's?" Journal of American Studies, 7
(December), 293-300.
> Cites NS, The Male Animal, and The
> Heart Is a Lonely Hunter as the three
> outstanding works published in 1940.

107. Cripps, Thomas. "Native Son in the
Movies," in Richard Wright: Impressions
and Perspectives. Ed. David Ray and
Robert M. Farnsworth. Ann Arbor Paperbacks AA189. Ann Arbor: The University
of Michigan Press, pp. 101-115.
> Reprint of 1971.81.

108. _____. "Native Son in the Movies,"
in Richard Wright: Impressions and Perspectives. Ed. David Ray and Robert M.
Farnsworth. Ann Arbor: The University of
Michigan Press, pp. 101-115.
> Reprint of 1971.81.

109. Davidson, Marshall B. and the Editors of American Heritage. The American
Heritage History of the Writers' America. New York: American Heritage Publishing Company, pp. 377, 379.
> Contains a photgraph of W and a para-
> graph about him mainly concerning NS.

110. Davis, Charles T. "Introduction,"
in Richard Wright: Impressions and Perspectives. Ed. David Ray and Robert M.
Farnsworth. Ann Arbor Paperbacks AA189.

Ann Arbor: The University of Michigan
Press, pp. 1-6.
> Reprint of 1973.111.

111. _____. "Introduction," in Richard
Wright: Impressions and Perspectives.
Ed. David Ray and Robert M. Farnsworth.
Ann Arbor: The University of Michigan
Press, pp. 1-6.
> Notes the revival of interest in W
> and disputes the reductive interpre-
> tation of his career, especially the
> notion that his expatriation ended
> his importance as a writer and poli-
> tical thinker. Instead, W's imagina-
> tion and life have unity as well as
> relevance to the present.
> Reprinted: 1973.110.

112. Demby, William and John O'Brien.
"William Demby," in Interviews with
Black Writers. Ed. John O'Brien. New
York: Liveright, pp. 37-53.
> Reprint of 1972.58.

113. Dickstein, Morris. "Wright, Baldwin, Cleaver," in Richard Wright: Impressions and Perspectives. Ed. David
Ray and Robert M. Farnsworth. Ann
Arbor Paperbacks AA189. Ann Arbor: The
University of Michigan Press, pp. 183-
190.
> Reprint of 1971.87.

114. _____. "Wright, Baldwin, Cleaver,"
in Richard Wright: Impressions and Perspectives. Ed. David Ray and Robert M.
Farnsworth. Ann Arbor: The University of
Michigan Press, pp. 183-190.
> Reprint of 1971.87.

115. Dodson, Owen. "Personal Impressions," in Richard Wright: Impressions
and Perspectives. Ed. David Ray and
Robert M. Farnsworth. Ann Arbor Paperbacks AA189. Ann Arbor: The University
of Michigan Press, pp. 78-79.
> Reprint of 1971.88.

116. _____. "Personal Impressions," in
Richard Wright: Impressions and Perspec-
tives. Ed. David Ray and Robert M.
Farnsworth. Ann Arbor: The University of
Michigan Press, pp. 78-79.
> Reprint of 1971.88.

117. _____ and John O'Brien. "Owen Dodson," in Interviews with Black Writers.
Ed. John O'Brien. New York: Liveright,
pp. 56-61.
> Dodson contrasts Coin, the protagon-
> ist of his novel Boy at the Window,
> with Bigger Thomas (p. 61).

118. Dorsinville, Max. "Caliban Without
Prospero: The Novels of Black America
and French Canada." Dissertation Abstracts International, 33 (January),

3641-A.
Does not mention specific authors, but W is treated in this study of "corresponding attitudes of aliena-tion, revolt and lucidity" in the fiction of the two groups. See 1974.60.

119. Edwards, Margaret A. "Reading for Young Adults," in Compton's Encyclopedia and Fact-Index. Ed. Donald E. Lawson. Chicago: F. E. Compton, pp. 111f-112f.
Lists and describes briefly BB, "one of the finest autobiographies in American literature" (p. 111h).

120. Ellison, Ralph and John O'Brien. "Ralph Ellison," in Interviews with Black Writers. Ed. John O'Brien. New York: Liveright, pp. 63-77.
O'Brien quotes from Ellison's "Richard Wright's Blues."

121. Ellmann, Richard and Robert O'Clair. "Richard Wright (1908-1960)," in their The Norton Anthology of Modern Poetry. New York: Norton, pp. 784-785.
Critical-biographical headnote to "I Have Seen Black Hands," "Between the World and Me," and "Four Haiku." The authors criticize W for seldom ex-ploiting in his poetry "the energies of the anonymous folk art of which he was heir."

122. Emanuel, James A. "The Challenge of Black Literature: Notes on Interpreta-tion," in The Black Writer in Africa and the Americas. Ed. Lloyd W. Brown. Uni-versity of Southern California Studies in Comparative Literature, Vol. 6. Los Angeles: Hennessey & Ingalls, pp. 85-100.
Suggests the need for revaluation of NS with more emphasis on its artistry (p. 96).

123. Fabre, Michel. "'The American Prob-lem--Its Negro Phase' Richard Wright," in Richard Wright: Impressions and Per-spectives. Ed. David Ray and Robert M. Farnsworth. Ann Arbor Paperbacks AA189. Ann Arbor: The University of Michigan Press, p. 9.
Reprint of 1971.101.

124. _____. "'The American Problem--Its Negro Phase' Richard Wright," in Richard Wright: Impressions and Perspectives. Ed. David Ray and Robert M. Farnsworth. Ann Arbor: The University of Michigan Press, p. 9.
Reprint of 1971.101.

125. _____. "Black Literature in France." Studies in Black Literature, 4 (Autumn), 9-14.

Shows that W is the best-known Afro-American writer among French authors. Lists French translations of Wright's works.

126. _____. "Keneth Kinnamon.--The Emer-gence of Richard Wright; Houston A. Baker, Jr.--Twentieth Century Interpre-tations of 'Native Son'; David Bakish.--Richard Wright." Etudes Anglaises, 26 (October-December), 491-492.
Favorable review of the three works. Kinnamon's book notes W's debt to Joyce and Poe, documents the Nixon case, and contains an excellent bib-liography. Baker's collection, com-parable to Abcarian's, and Bakish's monograph, comparable to Bone's, are useful to students beginning a study of W.

127. _____. "Note," in Richard Wright: Impressions and Perspectives. Ed. David Ray and Robert M. Farnsworth. Ann Arbor Paperbacks AA189. Ann Arbor: The Uni-versity of Michigan Press, p. 146.
Reprint of 1971.106.

128. _____. "Note," in Richard Wright: Impressions and Perspectives. Ed. David Ray and Robert M. Farnsworth. Ann Arbor: The University of Michigan Press, p. 146.
Reprint of 1971.106.

129. _____. "Notes," in Richard Wright: Impressions and Perspectives. Ed. David Ray and Robert M. Farnsworth. Ann Arbor Paperbacks AA189. Ann Arbor: The Univer-sity of Michigan Press, p. 147.
Reprint of 1971.107.

130. _____. "Notes," in Richard Wright: Impressions and Perspectives. Ed. David Ray and Robert M. Farnsworth. Ann Arbor: The University of Michigan Press, p. 147.
Reprint of 1971.107.

131. _____. "René Maran, trait-d'union entre deux négritudes," in Les Littéra-tures d'expression française: Négritude africaine, négritude caraïbe. Ed. Jeanne-Lydie Gore. Université Paris-Nord, Centre d'Etudes Francophones. Nivelles: Havaux, pp. 55-61.
Discusses Albert Darnal's contrast of Maran and W (p. 60).

132. _____. "Richard Wright's First Hun-dred Books." CLA Journal, 16 (June), 458-474.
Discusses W's readings to 1940. Mencken, Poe, Henry James, Dreiser, Stephen Crane, Sinclair Lewis, Sher-wood Anderson, James T. Farrell, Dos Passos, Algren, Hemingway, Stein, Shakespeare, Conrad, Hardy, George

Moore, H. G. Wells, Joyce, Lawrence, Dostoevsky, Gorky, Proust, and Malraux were among his favorite authors. W's early development as a writer was influenced especially by Conrad, James, Stein, and Dostoevsky.

133. _____. The Unfinished Quest of Richard Wright. Trans. Isabel Barzun. New York: William Morrow, 652 pp.
Full-scale biography based on Fabre's doctoral thesis (1970). The text includes a preface, introduction, twenty-one chapters, a conclusion, notes, a selected bibliography excluding criticism but including an enlarged version of the Fabre-Margolies checklist of primary works and secondary sources of biographical importance, and a thorough index. In each chapter he uses much unpublished material--manuscripts, letters, journals, interviews. The resulting portrait of W shows both a spokesman for blacks castigating white racism and a seeker of humanistic perspectives universally applicable. "Richard Wright was attempting more than entertainment or even political enlightenment . . . . he was grappling with a definition of man. Although his solitary quest ended prematurely and did not allow him to find one, his achievement as a writer and a humanist makes him, in the Emersonian sense, a truly 'representative man' of our time" (p. 531).
Passage reprinted: 1976.68.

134. _____. "Wright (Richard) 1908-1960," in Encyclopedia Universalis. Vol. 16. Paris: Encyclopedia Universalis France, pp. 1010-1011.
Traces W's life and career from racist Mississippi to Depression Chicago to success in New York to exile in Paris with existentialist and Third World interests. W's narrative power distinguishes his style, and his thought has sincerity and a prophetic quality. His themes include both the horrors of racism and the humanistic and revolutionary potentialities of the world's people of color.

135. _____. "Wright's Exile," in Richard Wright: Impressions and Perspectives. Ed. David Ray and Robert M. Farnsworth. Ann Arbor Paperbacks AA189. Ann Arbor: The University of Michigan Press, pp. 121-139.
Reprint of 1971.111.

136. _____. "Wright's Exile," in Richard Wright: Impressions and Perspectives. Ed. David Ray and Robert M. Farnsworth. Ann Arbor: The University of Michigan

Press, pp. 121-139.
Reprint of 1971.111.

137. _____ and Edward Margolies. "A Bibliography of Richard Wright's Works," in Richard Wright: Impressions and Perspectives. Ed. David Ray and Robert M. Farnsworth. Ann Arbor Paperbacks AA189. Ann Arbor: The University of Michigan Press, pp. 191-205.
Reprint of 1965.59 with additions and revisions.

138. _____. "A Bibliography of Richard Wright's Works," in Richard Wright: Impressions and Perspectives. Ed. David Ray and Robert M. Farnsworth. Ann Arbor: The University of Michigan Press, pp. 191-205.
Reprint of 1965.59 with additions and revisions.

139. _____. "Selected Bibliography," in The Unfinished Quest of Richard Wright. By Michel Fabre. New York: William Morrow, pp. 625-638.
Contains a reprint of 1965.59 with additions and revisions.

140. Fanon, Frantz. "Letter to Richard Wright," in Richard Wright: Impressions and Perspectives. Ed. David Ray and Robert M. Farnsworth. Ann Arbor Paperbacks AA189. Ann Arbor: The University of Michigan Press, p. 150.
Reprint of 1971.113.

141. _____. "Letter to Richard Wright," in Richard Wright: Impressions and Perspectives. Ed. David Ray and Robert M. Farnsworth. Ann Arbor: The University of Michigan Press, p. 150.
Reprint of 1971.113.

142. Farnsworth, Robert M. "Preface," in Richard Wright: Impressions and Perspectives. Ed. David Ray and Robert M. Farnsworth. Ann Arbor Paperbacks AA189. Ann Arbor: The University of Michigan Press, pp. vii-viii.
Reprint of 1973.143.

143. _____. "Preface," in Richard Wright: Impressions and Perspectives. Ed. David Ray and Robert M. Farnsworth. Ann Arbor: The University of Michigan Press, pp. vii-viii.
Acknowledges aid of Charles T. Davis, Michel Fabre, and Ellen Wright. Contains an appreciation of W.
Reprinted: 1973.142.

144. Farrison, W. Edward. "Blackness and the Adventure of Western Culture. By George E. Kent." CLA Journal, 16 (March), 383-386.
Contains two paragraphs on Kent's "informed and judicious" (p. 384)

treatment of W.

145. _____. "The Emergence of Richard Wright: A Study in Literature and Society. By Keneth Kinnamon." CLA Journal, 17 (September), 120-122.
Favorable review, but Farrison expresses reservations about Kinnamon's comments on W's use of dialect and symbolism.

146. Faulkner, William. "Letter to Richard Wright," in Richard Wright: Impressions and Perspectives. Ed. David Ray and Robert M. Farnsworth. Ann Arbor Paperbacks AA189. Ann Arbor: The University of Michigan Press, p. 143.
Reprint of 1971.115.

147. _____. "Letter to Richard Wright," in Richard Wright: Impressions and Perspectives. Ed. David Ray and Robert M. Farnsworth. Ann Arbor: The University of Michigan Press, p. 143.
Reprint of 1971.115.

148. Fleming, Robert E. "Overshadowed by Richard Wright: Three Black Chicago Novelists." Negro American Literature Forum, 7 (Fall), 75-79.
Discusses Waters E. Turpin, Alden Bland, and Frank London Brown with frequent comparisons to W.

149. Ford, Nick Aaron. "Attitudes and Actions of English Departments Toward the Promotion of Black Studies." CLA Journal, 16 (March), 334-344.
Mentions W (p. 336).

150. _____. Black Studies: Threat-or-Challenge? Port Washington, N. Y.: Kennikat Press, pp. 16, 85, 129, 207.
Mentions W's encounter with a racist conductor on a segregated train. Notes briefly the study of W at various universities.

151. Frémy, Dominique and Michèle Frémy. Quid? Tout pour tous. Paris: Librairie Plon, p. 89.
Reprint of 1963.86.

151a. French, Warren. "Fiction: 1900 to the 1930s," in American Literary Scholarship: An Annual/1971. Ed. J. Albert Robbins. Durham, N. C.: Duke University Press, pp. 209-244.
Comments on ten articles on W (pp. 239-240).

151b. Furukawa, Hiromi. "Richard Wright's Personality and Work," in his Kokujin Bungaku Nyumon [Introduction to Black Literature]. Osaka: Sogensha, pp. 183-209.
Discusses W's involvement in and withdrawal from the Communist Party,

and interprets NS and EM. Sees that his final years, devoted to haiku, were lonely. [Y. H. and T. K.]

151c. Garrett, George. "The South," in Regional Perspectives: An Examination of America's Literary Heritage. Ed. John Gordon Burke. Chicago: American Library Association, pp. 49-75.
Mentions BB (p. 66).

152. Gaskill, Gayle. "The Effect of Black/White Imagery in Richard Wright's Black Boy." Negro American Literature Forum, 7 (Summer), 46-48.
W inverts the usual association of evil with black and good with white.

152a. Gendzier, Irene L. Frantz Fanon: A Critical Study. New York: Pantheon Books, pp. 34, 42, 263.
Mentions W briefly.

153. Gide, André. "Letter to Richard Wright," in Richard Wright: Impressions and Perspectives. Ed. David Ray and Robert M. Farnsworth. Ann Arbor Paperbacks AA189. Ann Arbor: The University of Michigan Press, p. 146.
Reprint of 1971.148.

154. _____. "Letter to Richard Wright," in Richard Wright: Impressions and Perspectives. Ed. David Ray and Robert M. Farnsworth. Ann Arbor: The University of Michigan Press, p. 146.
Reprint of 1971.148.

155. Gilbert, Zack. "For Angela," in The Poetry of Black America: Anthology of the 20th Century. Introduction by Gwendolyn Brooks. New York: Harper & Row, pp. 196-197.
Reprint of 1971.149.

156. Gilenson, Boris. "Afro-American Literature in the Soviet Union." Soviet Life, No. 203 (August), pp. 60-61.
Notes the Soviet response to NS, a 1962 edition of W's stories, and a dissertation on W.
Reprinted: 1975.88.

157. Giles, James R. "Richard Wright's Successful Failure: A New Look at Uncle Tom's Children." Phylon, 34 (September), 256-266.
Artistically superior to NS, the enlarged edition of UTC develops the theme of increasing militancy as a response to white racist oppression. Giles examines such recurrent motifs as the hostility of nature and sexual taboos to show the work's unity.

158. Gilmore, Al-Tony. "Essence and Soul." The American Scholar, 42 (Summer), 531-533.

Favorable review of Keneth Kinnamon's The Emergence of Richard Wright: A Study in Literature and Society, "by far the best book written on and about the life and writings of Wright."

159. Gotoh, Tomokuni. "American Kokujin Sakka Wright to Africa--Wright no Africa Sobyo Black Power of Chushin toshite" ["The American Negro Wright and Africa-- With Priority Given to Wright's African Sketches, Black Power"]. Africa Kenkyu [Journal of African Studies], 13 (March), 10-21.
    When W "came across the faces whose reactions were riddles to him . . . he found that Africans were more alien to him than white Americans. Such being the case, the result of Wright's fact-finding travel in Africa seemed to fall short of expectations." [Y. H.]

159a. Gotoh, Tomokuni. "Symbolism in Wright's Native Son." Kokujin Kenkyu [Negro Studies], 45 (20 June), 8-13.
    The killing of a rat in the opening scene of NS symbolizes Bigger's fate; the plan to rob a white store, a challenge to white society; the fireplace at the Dalton's, the bloody incident; Mrs. Dalton's blindness, the blindness of white people. [Y. H. and T. K.]

160. Guérin, Daniel. De l'oncle Tom aux Panthères: Le drame des Noirs américains. Paris: Les Editions de Minuit, pp. 72, 168.
    Dedicated to W, this book refers to him several times. Guerin quotes from W's letter to Roger Hagnauer of 12 March 1951 and recounts W's tribute to the work of the Communist Party in the thirties.

161. Haas, Robert Bartlett. "A Transatlantic Interview 1946," in his A Primer for the Gradual Understanding of Gertrude Stein. Los Angeles: Black Sparrow Press, pp. 15-35.
    Reprint of 1964.65.

162. Haas, Rudolf. "Über die Rezeption amerikanischer Romane in der Bundesrepublik 1945-1965," in Nordamerikanische Literatur im deutschen Sprachraum seit 1945. Ed. Horst Frenz and Hans-Joachim Lang. Munich: Winkler, pp. 20-46.
    Identifies W, Baldwin, and Ellison as the foremost black writers for Germans and mentions translations of NS and BB.

163. Hamalian, Leo and Frederick R. Karl. "Richard Wright Big Black Good Man," in their Short Fiction of the

Masters. Second edition. New York: G. P. Putnam's Sons, p. 423.
    Biographical headnote.

164. ____. "Wright Big Black Good Man," in their Short Fiction of the Masters. Second edition. New York: G. P. Putnam's Sons, p. 435.
    Study questions on the story.

165. Harper, Michael. "Afterword: A Film," in his Debridement. Garden City, N. Y.: Doubleday, pp. 61-63.
    Partial reprint of 1973.167.

166. ____. "Afterword: A Film," in Richard Wright: Impressions and Perspectives. Ed. David Ray and Robert M. Farnsworth. Ann Arbor Paperbacks AA189. Ann Arbor: The University of Michigan Press, pp. 162-163.
    Reprint of 1973.167.

167. ____. "Afterword: A Film," in Richard Wright: Impressions and Perspectives. Ed. David Ray and Robert M. Farnsworth. Ann Arbor: The University of Michigan Press, pp. 162-163.
    Poem on Bigger Thomas.
    Reprinted: 1973.166; 1977.159.
    Partially reprinted: 1973.165.

168. ____. "Heartblow," in his Debridement. Garden City, N. Y.: Doubleday, pp. 45-63.
    Reprint of 1973.169.

169. ____. "Heartblow: A Sequence for Richard Wright," in Richard Wright: Impressions and Perspectives. Ed. David Ray and Robert M. Farnsworth. Ann Arbor Paperbacks AA189. Ann Arbor: The University of Michigan Press, pp. 158-163.
    Reprint of 1971.161 and two additional poems: "Spiritual" and "Afterword: A Film."
    Reprinted: 1973.168, 170.

170. ____. "Heartblow: A Sequence for Richard Wright," in Richard Wright: Impressions and Perspectives. Ed. David Ray and Robert M. Farnsworth. Ann Arbor: The University of Michigan Press, pp. 158-163.
    Reprint of 1971.161 and two additional poems: "Spiritual" and "Afterword: A Film."
    Reprinted: 1973.168, 169.

171. ____. "Spiritual," in his Debridement. Garden City, N. Y.: Doubleday, p. 60.
    Reprint of 1973.173.

172. ____. "Spiritual," in Richard Wright: Impressions and Perspectives. Ed. David Ray and Robert M. Farnsworth. Ann Arbor Paperbacks AA189. Ann Arbor:

The University of Michigan Press, p. 162.
   Reprint of 1973.173.

173. _____. "Spiritual," in Richard Wright: Impressions and Perspectives. Ed. David Ray and Robert M. Farnsworth. Ann Arbor: The University of Michigan Press, p. 162.
   Brief poem on W's childhood.
   Reprinted: 1973.171, 172.

174. Harrington, Ollie. "Look Homeward Baby." Freedomways, 13 (Third Quarter), 200-215.
   Mentions and quotes W in the Cafe Monaco in Paris (p. 204).
   Reprinted: 1977.165.

175. Harvey, Emily Dennis. Teachers Guide to Black Boy by Richard Wright. New York: Harper & Row, 17 pp.
   Consists of a synopsis of the work, an introductory comment, and the following discussion topics, all accompanied by suggested questions, activities, and assignments: "Black in America: Prejudice," "Black Culture," "Poverty and Society," "Revolt of Youth," "The Formation of a Writer," and "Black Boy as a Work of Literature." A biographical sketch and a "Selected Bibliography" conclude this pamphlet, designed mainly for high school teachers.

176. _____. Teachers Guide to Native Son by Richard Wright. New York: Harper & Row, 17 pp.
   Consists of a synopsis of the entire novel, followed by analyses of each of the three books, with "Questions for Discussion" and "Activities and Assignments" appended to each analysis. A biographical sketch and a "Selected Bibliography" conclude this pamphlet, designed mainly for high school teachers.

177. Hassan, Ihab. "American Literature," in World Literature Since 1945. Ed. Ivar Ivask and Gero von Wilpert. New York: Ungar, pp. 1-64.
   Reprint of 1973.178.

178. _____. Contemporary American Literature 1945-1972: An Introduction. New York: Ungar, pp. 73-74, 76, 133.
   Notes W's formative role in developing these themes for black fiction: "memories of slavery, protest and fury, the contradictory search for dignity in a world dominated by white values, the conflict between the artistic and political natures of the writer, his sexual complexities, the existential quality of his life, his need for an ethnic definition of himself" (pp. 73-74). Mentions W briefly elsewhere.
   Reprinted: 1973.177.

179. Henderson, Stephen. "Introduction: The Forms of Things Unknown," in his Understanding the New Black Poetry: Black Speech and Black Music as Poetic References. New York: William Morrow, pp. 3-69.
   Contains several brief references to W, including praise of "The Literature of the Negro in the United States" as "the clearest and most intriguing statement" (p. 5) on black oral poetry.

180. Hoard, Walter B. Anthology: Quotations and Sayings of People of Color. San Francisco: R and E Research Associates, pp. 7, 9, 25, 80, 87, 93.
   Includes quotations from W under the following headings: Betrayal, Black Power, Desperation, Prison, Rootless, Snow.

181. Hogan, William. "Life and Death of Richard Wright." San Francisco Chronicle (10 September), p. 43.
   Favorable review of Michel Fabre's The Unfinished Quest of Richard Wright. Emphasizes W's intellectual problems as an ex-Marxist.

182. Holden, Matthew, Jr. The White Man's Burden. New York: Chandler Publishing Company, pp. 32, 41.
   Mentions W briefly.

183. Houseman, John. "Native Son on Stage," in Richard Wright: Impressions and Perspectives. Ed. David Ray and Robert M. Farnsworth. Ann Arbor Paperbacks AA189. Ann Arbor: The University of Michigan Press, pp. 89-100.
   Reprint of 1971.173.

184. _____. "Native Son on Stage," in Richard Wright: Impressions and Perspectives. Ed. David Ray and Robert M. Farnsworth. Ann Arbor: The University of Michigan Press, pp. 89-100.
   Reprint of 1971.173.

185. Howard, Patsy C. Theses in American Literature 1896-1971. Ann Arbor: The Pierian Press, pp. 45, 53, 59, 255-256.
   Lists thirteen unpublished master's theses wholly on W and ten partially on W. The earliest is dated 1939.

186. Hudson, Theodore R. From LeRoi Jones to Amiri Baraka: The Literary Works. Durham, N. C.: Duke University Press, pp. 19, 155.
   Quotes David Llorens mentioning W and comments briefly on the use of NS in The Slave.

187. Hughes, Langston. "Democracy and Me," in his Good Morning Revolution: Uncollected Social Protest Writings. Ed. Faith Berry. New York: Lawrence Hill, pp. 127-130.
Reprint of 1939.86.

188. Janaro, Richard Paul and Paul E. Gearhart. "'Between the World and Me' Richard Wright," in their Human Worth. New York: Holt, Rinehart and Winston, p. 153.
Critical headnote relating the poem's theme of social protest to W's fiction.

189. Jewkes, W. T. Untitled questions, in his The Perilous Journey. New York: Harcourt Brace Jovanovich, p. 27.
To accompany "The Street," an excerpt from BB.

190. Jones, Harry L. "Long Black Song: Essays in Black American Literature. By Houston A. Baker." CLA Journal, 16 (March), 395-397.
Praises Baker's interpretation of W.

191. Justus, James H. "Fiction: The 1930s to the Present," in American Literary Scholarship: An Annual/1971. Ed. J. Albert Robbins. Durham, N. C.: Duke University Press, pp. 245-276.
Mentions W briefly (p. 273).

191a. Kaname, Hiroshi. "Richard Wright's The Outsider: The Problems of Freedom." Eibei Bungaku Kenkyu to Kansho [Studies in British and American Literature], 20 (1 April), 95-111.
A study of Cross Damon's purpose in life in accord with his version of existentialism. For Cross, freedom from God becomes a burden; in the end he realizes that freedom lies in solidarity. He has not given up hope. [Y. H. and T. K.]

192. Karrer, Wolfgang and Eberhard Kreutzer. Daten der englischen und amerikanischen Literatur von 1890 bis zur Gegenwart. Munich: Deutscher Taschenbuch Verlag, pp. 54, 207.
Includes a brief summary of NS, mentions W as a Southern writer, and points out his influence on Ellison.

192a. Kazin, Alfred. Bright Book of Life: American Novelists and Storytellers from Hemingway to Mailer. Boston: Little, Brown, p. 243.
Use a quotation from "The Man Who Went to Chicago" as an epigraph to a chapter on "The Absurd as a Contemporary Style: Ellison to Pynchon."

193. Kesteloot, Lilyan. "La Négritude et son expression littéraire," in Les Littératures d'expression française: Négritude africaine, négritude caraïbe. Ed. Jeanne-Lydie Gore. Université Paris-Nord, Centre d'Etudes Francophones. Nivelles: Havaux, pp. 94-102.
Mentions W (p. 97).

194. Killinger, John. The Fragile Presence: Transcendence in Modern Literature. Philadelphia: Fortress Press, pp. 129-134, 135, 139, 146, 153.
Discussing religious themes in modern literature, Killinger considers NS, which he deems one of the most important novels of the century, in terms of protest and denial of conventional Christianity. Quotes and analyzes Bigger's comments on the church.

195. Kirsch, Robert. "The High Cost of Heightened Sensibility." Los Angeles Times (28 October), pp. 52, 62.
Includes a favorable review of Michel Fabre's The Unfinished Quest of Richard Wright.

195a. Kitamura, Takao, Hiroka Sato, Isao Sekiguchi, Takeo Hamamoto, and Koichiro Fujikura. "Wright's Attitude," in Kokujin Bungaku no Shuhen: Symposium [Around Black Literature: A Symposium]. Tokyo: Kenkyusha, pp. 218-223.
A discussion of W's major works in terms of the historical significance of NS, W's involvement in the Communist Party, his exile in France, and his harrassment by the F. B. I. [Y. H. and T. K.]

196. Klise, Thomas S. "The Odyssey of Richard Wright." Peoria: Thomas S. Klise.
Filmstrip with sound track on W's career.

197. Klotman, Phyllis R. "An Examination of the Black Confidence Man in Two Black Novels: The Man Who Cried I Am and dem." American Literature, 44 (January), 596-611.
Quotes from O and comments on W's relation to the novel by Williams. Reprinted in revised form: 1977.206.

198. _____. "The Slave and the Western: Popular Literature of the Nineteenth Century." North Dakota Quarterly, 41 (Autumn), 40-54.
Mentions W briefly (p. 41). Reprinted in revised form: 1977.206.

199. Koehmstedt, Carol L. Plot Summary Index. Metuchen, N. J.: The Scarecrow Press, pp. 106, 310.
Lists three items for the novel NS and one item for the play.

200. Kriegel, Leonard and Abraham H.

Lass. "Author Profiles," in their
Stories of the American Experience.
Mentor Books ME1605. New York: New Amer-
ican Library, pp. 495-500.
    Includes a biographical sketch of W
    (p. 500).

201. _____. "Introduction," in their
Stories of the American Experience.
Mentor Books ME1605. New York: New Amer-
ican Library, pp. ix-x.
    Calls W "still the most important
    writer to have been produced by black
    America."

202. _____. "Race and Reality," in their
Stories of the American Experience.
Mentor Books ME1605. New York: New Amer-
ican Library, pp. 367-372.
    Comments on W and "Bright and Morning
    Star." The story is didactic but
    believable.

203. Lacy, Dan. The White Use of Blacks
in America. McGraw-Hill Paperbacks. New
York: McGraw-Hill, p. 169.
    Reprint of 1972.132.

204. L.[eary], L.[ewis] and J.[oseph]
H.[arris] S.[chiffman]. "American Liter-
ature," in Cassell's Encyclopaedia of
World Literature. Ed. S. H. Steinberg
and J. Buchanan-Brown. Second edition.
Vol. 1. London: Cassell, pp. 24-30.
    Comments briefly on W and NS (pp. 29,
    30).
    Reprinted: 1973.205.

205. _____. "American Literature," in
Cassell's Encyclopaedia of World Litera-
ture. Ed. S. H. Steinberg and J.
Buchanan-Brown. Second edition. Vol. 1.
New York: William Morrow, pp. 24-30.
    Reprint of 1973.204.

206. Lehan, Richard. A Dangerous Cross-
ing: French Literary Existentialism and
the Modern American Novel. Carbondale
and Edwardsville: Southern Illinois University Press, pp. 95-106.
    In Chapter Four, "The Outer Limits:
    Norman Mailer and Richard Wright,"
    Lehan provides a biographical sketch
    of W and discusses NS, O, and "The
    Man Who Lived Underground" in rela-
    tion to existentialism. Mentions more
    briefly LD.

207. Lenz, Günter H. "James Baldwin," in
Amerikanische Literatur der Gegenwart.
Ed. Martin Christadler. Stuttgart:
Alfred Kröner Verlag, pp. 174-176.
    Survey of Baldwin's career noting the
    "paradox" of his attitude toward W.
    Although Baldwin's essays reject W's
    "mixing of literature and sociology,"
    Another Country can be seen as an
    attempt to rewrite NS in the context

of changed social circumstances.

208. Levi-Strauss, Claude. "Letter to
Richard Wright," in Richard Wright:
Impressions and Perspectives. Ed. David
Ray and Robert M. Farnsworth. Ann Arbor
Paperbacks AA189. Ann Arbor: The Univer-
sity of Michigan Press, p. 145.
    Reprint of 1971.213.

209. _____. "Letter to Richard Wright,"
in Richard Wright: Impressions and Perspectives. Ed. David Ray and Robert M.
Farnsworth. Ann Arbor: The University of
Michigan Press, p. 145.
    Reprint of 1971.213.

210. Lieberman, Laurence. "New Poetry:
The Muse of History." The Yale Review,
63 (Autumn), 113-136.
    Includes discussion of Michael Har-
    per's poetry on W (pp. 123-124).
    Reprinted: 1977.212.

211. Loftis, N. J. Black Anima. New
York: Liveright, pp. 54, 69, 100, 116.
    Sequence of poems mentioning or al-
    luding to W.

212. Ludwig, Richard M. "Ellison," in
Encyclopedia of World Biography. Ed.
David I. Eggenberger. Vol. 3. New York:
McGraw-Hill, pp. 570-571.
    Mentions W briefly.

213. Lynch, Hollis R. "Black People in
the United States," in Compton's Encyclopedia and Fact-Index. Ed. Donald E.
Lawson. Vol. 15. Chicago: F. E. Compton,
pp. 124-126j.
    Mentions W briefly (p. 126f).

214. Lynn, Kenneth S. "Violence in Amer-
ican Literature and Folklore," in his
Visions of America: Eleven Literary
Historical Essays. Contributions in
American Studies, No. 6, ed. Robert H.
Walker. Westport, Conn.: Greenwood
Press, pp. 189-205.
    Reprint of 1969.164.

215. Macebuh, Stanley. James Baldwin: A
Critical Study. New York: Third Press,
pp. 34-36, 49-50.
    Includes comments on Baldwin's
    friendship with and dissent from W.

216. Margolies, Edward. "The Letters of
Richard Wright," in The Black Writer in
Africa and the Americas. Ed. Lloyd W.
Brown. University of Southern California
Studies in Comparative Literature, Vol.
6. Los Angeles: Hennessey & Ingalls, pp.
101-116.
    Analyzes the whole range of W's let-
    ters in historical perspective, em-
    phasizing their intellectual content.
    Valuable to the biographer, the cri-

tic, and the historian for their revelation of W's social, political, and racial ideas, the letters tell us less about his emotional life and personal relationships. Margolies also comments on the style of the letters and on W's correspondents.

217. Martin, Herbert W. The Shit-Storm Poems. Grand Rapids, Mich.: Pilot Press, p. [6].
Uses the following epigraph from W: "'Lawd, Man! Ef it wuzn't fer them policies [sic] 'n them ol' lynch-mobs, there wouldn't be nothing but uproar down here!'"

218. Mayfield, Julian and John O'Brien. "Julian Mayfield," in Interviews with Black Writers. Ed. John O'Brien. New York: Liveright, pp. 143-151.
Mayfield mentions reading W, a "literary giant," at an early age (p. 143).

219. McCollum, Kenneth G. Nelson Algren: A Checklist. Introduction by Studs Terkel. A Bruccoli-Clark Book. Detroit: Gale, pp. 16, 47, 64, 72.
Mentions W's introduction to Never Come Morning, states that W borrowed the title NS from Algren, and lists two pieces on W by Algren.

220. McWilliams, Wilson Carey. The Idea of Fraternity in America. Berkeley and Los Angeles: University of California Press, pp. 576, 578, 601, 602, 610, 614.
Cites and quotes from W to illustrate various historical points. Discusses the W-Ellison-Baldwin disagreements.

221. Miller, Henry. "Letter to Richard Wright," in Richard Wright: Impressions and Perspectives. Ed. David Ray and Robert M. Farnsworth. Ann Arbor Paperbacks AA189. Ann Arbor: The University of Michigan Press, p. 144.
Reprint of 1971.224.

222. _____. "Letter to Richard Wright," in Richard Wright: Impressions and Perspectives. Ed. David Ray and Robert M. Farnsworth. Ann Arbor: The University of Michigan Press, p. 144.
Reprint of 1971.224.

223. Milner, Ron. "Black Magic, Black Art," in The Rhetoric of Yes. Ed. Ray Fabrizio, Edith Karas, and Ruth Menmur. New York: Holt, Rinehart and Winston, pp. 289-294.
Reprint of 1967.74.

224. Mitchell, Louis D. "The Picaresque Element in Richard Wright's Two Major Novels." The Journal of Afro-American Issues, 1 (Summer-Fall), 384-394.

Examines the picaresque format of both BB and NS. In both works the picaresque element tends toward an existentialist perspective.

225. Mizuta, Hisakazu. "Richard Wright Saiko--America no Musoko Ron" ["Richard Wright: A Reconsideration of Native Son"]. Rikkyo Daigaku Eibei Bungaku [The Rikkyo Review], 33 (March), 73-85.
A critical survey of W's life and work. Mentions the attitude of James Baldwin, who now regards W as a pioneer who accurately portrayed the racial struggle in the United States rather than as a protest writer. Speculates that Bigger's bitter smile at the end of the novel suggests his struggle in finding identity and his failure to achieve it. [Y. H.]

226. Munro, C. Lynn. "LeRoi Jones: A Man in Transition." CLA Journal, 17 (September), 57-78.
Mentions Jones's opinion of W (p. 60).

227. Murray, Albert. The Hero and the Blues. Columbia: University of Missouri Press, pp. 45, 93-97.
Mostly unfavorable treatment of NS, which is not a tragedy but merely "a social science-oriented melodrama with an unhappy ending" (p. 95). Despite W's intentions, Bigger is not symbolically representative of black people.

228. Myers, Miles and Bernard R. Tanner. "Explorations," in their The Meanings of Literature. Menlo Park, Cal.: Addison-Wesley, p. 180.
Study questions on "The Kitten," an excerpt from BB.

229. _____. "The Role of the Psychological Critic," in their The Meanings of Literature. Menlo Park, Cal.: Addison-Wesley, p. 175.
Comments briefly on "The Kitten," an excerpt from BB.

230. Nichols, Charles N. [sic]. "'To Help Humanity Prevail,'" in A Commemorative Celebration in Honor of James Weldon Johnson. Hampton, Va.: Hampton Institute Press, pp. 29-36.
Mentions W briefly (p. 34).

231. Norris, Hoke. "Richard Wright, Buried in Trivia." Chicago Daily News (22-23 September), Panorama Sec., p. 7.
Unfavorable review of Michel Fabre's The Unfinished Quest of Richard Wright complaining of excessive detail which diffuses the effect of the biography. Fabre should have relied more on condensation and synthesis.

232. Nyang'aya, Elijah M. "Richard Wright's Commitment," in Standpoints on African Literature: A Critical Anthology. Ed. Chris L Wanjala. Nairobi, Kampala, and Dar es Salaam: East African Literature Bureau, pp. 374-389.
Overview of W's career identifying his early experience as a member of a "depressed" group as the primary shaping force of his work. NS resembles the works of Alex la Guma and Ezekiel Mphahlele in its portrayal of maladjusted youths turning to violence.

233. O'Brien, John. "Introduction," in his Interviews with Black Writers. New York: Liveright, pp. vii-xii.
Includes a paragraph arguing that NS is existential, not naturalistic (pp. viii-xi).

234. Page, James A. "Black Literature." English Journal, 62 (May), 709-717.
Contains a brief sketch of W's literary career (p. 714) emphasizing the early period. W was the first black writer to achieve "major rank among American writers, without respect to race."
Partially reprinted: 1975.142.

235. Parker, J. A. Angela Davis: The Making of a Revolutionary. New Rochelle, N. Y.: Arlington House, pp. 24-27.
Discusses W's relation to Communism, quoting extensively.

236. Pavese, Cesare. "Letter to Richard Wright," in Richard Wright: Impressions and Perspectives. Ed. David Ray and Robert M. Farnsworth. Ann Arbor Paperbacks AA189. Ann Arbor: The University of Michigan Press, pp. 129-130.
Reprint of 1971.248.

237. ____. "Letter to Richard Wright," in Richard Wright: Impressions and Perspectives. Ed. David Ray and Robert M. Farnsworth. Ann Arbor: The University of Michigan Press, pp. 129-130.
Reprint of 1971.248.

238. Pells, Richard H. Radical Visions and American Dreams: Culture and Social Thought in the Depression Years. New York: Harper & Row, pp. 194, 221, 229-232, 238.
Points out that NS is less a sociological novel than a treatment of the quest for personal freedom. W is more concerned with the individual than the masses.

239. Plessner, Monika. Onkel Tom verbrennt seine Hütte: Die literarische Revolution der schwarzen Amerikaner. Frankfurt am Main: Insel Verlag, pp.

151-175.
Argues that W became the leading voice for black liberation because of his statement of the problem of racial identity for all Americans. Reaching a solution parallel to those of Lincoln, Thoreau, Douglass, and Du Bois, W supports a progression from revolution through definition to identity. Plessner considers NS a "Marxist, but not a socialist novel," but also one which introduces the existential themes later developed in O. Both works embody W's vision of revolt.

240. Pütz, Manfred. "'Black Literature' in der neueren Kritik." Die neueren Sprachen, 22 (March), 159-168.
Mentions W as a black writer encouraging the social function of literature (p. 162) and seeking self-understanding (p. 164).

241. Ray, David. "Books of the Day." The Kansas City Star (14 January), Sec. I, p. 3.
Favorable review of Keneth Kinnamon's The Emergence of Richard Wright: A Study in Literature and Society. The work demonstrates W's relevance to the present. Ray compares NS to An American Tragedy.

242. ____ and Robert M. Farnsworth. "Notes on Contributors," in their Richard Wright: Impressions and Perspectives. Ann Arbor Paperbacks AA189. Ann Arbor: The University of Michigan Press, p. 207.
Reprint of 1971.253.

243. ____. "Notes on Contributors," in their Richard Wright: Impressions and Perspectives. Ann Arbor: The University of Michigan Press, p. 207.
Reprint of 1971.253.

244. ____, eds. Richard Wright: Impressions and Perspectives. Ann Arbor Paperbacks AA189. Ann Arbor: The University of Michigan Press, 207 pp.
Reprint of 1973.245.

245. ____, eds. Richard Wright: Impressions and Perspectives. Ann Arbor: The University of Michigan Press, 207 pp.
Reprint of 1971.251a, with the contents rearranged and with a new introduction by Charles T. Davis.
Reprinted: 1973.244.

246. Rayson, Ann Louise. "Black American Autobiography." Dissertation Abstracts International, 34 (September), 1292-A.
Considers BB the greatest achievement of black biography, the dominant mode of which is confessional.

247. Redding, Saunders. "L. Hughes," in Encyclopedia of World Biography. Ed. David I. Eggenberger. Vol. 5. New York: McGraw-Hill, pp. 399-400.
Mentions W briefly.

248. ____. "R. Wright," in Encyclopedia of World Biography. Ed. David I. Eggenberger. Vol. 11. New York: McGraw-Hill, pp. 454-455.
Biographical-critical article praising the early work. Includes suggestions for secondary reading.

249. ____. They Came in Chains: Americans from Africa. Revised edition. Philadelphia: Lippincott, pp. 279, 288.
Reprint of 1950.207.

250. Reed, Ishmael. "Bird Lives!" The New York Times Book Review (25 March), p. 4.
Mentions W briefly.
Reprinted: 1978.200.

251. ____. "Haitians," in his Chattanooga. New York: Random House, pp. 17-18.
Poem mentioning Fishbelly and The [sic] Island of Hallucinations.

252. ____ and John O'Brien. "Ishmael Reed," in Interviews with Black Writers. Ed. John O'Brien. New York: Liveright, pp. 167-183.
Includes comments on the relation of W and his politics to white "radical liberal" critics.
Reprinted: 1974.150.

253. Reeves, Paschal et al. "A Checklist of Scholarship on Southern Literature for 1972." Mississippi Quarterly, 26 (Spring), 185-242.
Lists six items on W (p. 229).

254. Reilly, John M. "The Emergence of Richard Wright: A Study in Literature and Society. By Keneth Kinnamon." Journal of English and Germanic Philology, 72 (October), 581-584.
Favorable review praising Kinnamon's placement of W in his social context. Kinnamon's personal and social treatment of W does not fully merge with his critical analyses, however.

255. Rideout, Walter. "Wright, Richard," in Merit Students Encyclopedia. Ed. Emanuel Friedman. Vol. 20. New York: Macmillan Educational Corporation, p. 34.
Reprint of 1967.89.

256. Riley, Carolyn, ed. "Wright, Richard 1908-1960," in her Contemporary Literary Criticism. Detroit: Gale, pp. 377-380.
Contains partial reprints of writings by Baker (1971.31), Bone (1958.85), Hughes (1953.153), Kearns (1971.193), Redding (1963.160), Scott (1964.113), Solotaroff (1964.117), and Stephens (1971.290).

256a. Robertson, Wilmot. The Dispossessed Majority. Cape Canaveral, Fla.: Howard Allen, p. 239.
Mentions W briefly.

257. Rollin, Roger B. "The Quest for Social Order," in his Hero/Anti-Hero. New York: McGraw-Hill, pp. 181-184.
Includes a paragraph on "Fire and Cloud" (p. 183).

258. Safford, Frank K., M. D. (as told to Elizabeth Hill Downey). "Personal Impressions," in Richard Wright: Impressions and Perspectives. Ed. David Ray and Robert M. Farnsworth. Ann Arbor Paperbacks AA189. Ann Arbor: The University of Michigan Press, pp. 80-81.
Reprint of 1971.264.

259. ____. "Personal Impressions," in Richard Wright: Impressions and Perspectives. Ed. David Ray and Robert M. Farnsworth. Ann Arbor: The University of Michigan Press, pp. 80-81.
Reprint of 1971.264.

260. Sartre, Jean Paul. "Letter to Richard Wright," in Richard Wright: Impressions and Perspectives. Ed. David Ray and Robert M. Farnsworth. Ann Arbor Paperbacks AA189. Ann Arbor: The University of Michigan Press, p. 147.
Reprint of 1971.265.

261. ____. "Letter to Richard Wright," in Richard Wright: Impressions and Perspectives. Ed. David Ray and Robert M. Farnsworth. Ann Arbor: The University of Michigan Press, p. 147.
Reprint of 1971.265.

262. Savory, Jerold J. "Descent and Baptism in Native Son, Invisible Man, and Dutchman." Christian Scholar's Review, 3 (Winter), 33-37.
Examines the influence of the Book of Job on NS. Bigger derives self-knowledge from crime.

263. Schatt, Stanley. "You Must Go Home Again: Today's Afro-American Expatriate Writers." Negro American Literature Forum, 7 (Fall), 80-82.
Schatt's point of departure is a brief discussion of W's expatriation.

264. Scheer-Schäzler, Brigette. "Ralph Ellison," in Amerikanische Literatur der Gegenwart. Ed. Martin Christadler. Stuttgart: Alfred Kröner Verlag, pp.

190-209.
Notes that Ellison's temperament is essentially unlike W's (pp. 192, 194). Also remarks that BB anticipates the invisibility motif of Invisible Man (pp. 200-201).

265. Schönfelder, Karl-Heinz. "Nachwort," in Der schwarze Traum. By Richard Wright. Trans. Werner von Grünau. Berlin: Verlag Volk und Welt, pp. 479-486.
After an historical sketch of the development of class structure in Afro-American society, especially the rise of the black bourgeoisie, Schönfelder analyzes LD from a Marxist point of view. Fishbelly rejects his father's role of modern Uncle Tom, but decides that he must escape the South to live in dignity. Now, however, young blacks are pursuing the same goal through collective struggle rather than individual flight.

266. Schraufnagel, Noel. From Apology to Protest: The Black American Novel. DeLand, Fla.: Everett/Edwards, pp. 19-32, 91-93, 102, 110-112.
Treats W extensively, especially in the chapter "Wright and the Protest Novel." With its social protest, violence, and psychological insight, NS is the pivotal work in the history of the genre. Schraufnagel also analyzes "Big Boy Leaves Home," O as an "accommodationist novel," SH as an "assimilationist novel," and LD as a return to protest fiction.

267. Schroth, Raymond A. "Footnotes." Commonweal, 99 (26 October), 90.
Review of Michel Fabre's The Unfinished Quest of Richard Wright noting that NS and Invisible Man have a strong influence on college students.

268. Scruggs, Charles W. "The Emergence of Richard Wright: A Study in Literature and Society. By Keneth Kinnamon." The Arizona Quarterly, 29 (Autumn), 286-288.
Unfavorable review complaining about the work's "pedestrian New Criticism." Scruggs denies that W's communist ideology plays an important role in NS. Praises the treatment of W's early poetry and the Nixon case.

269. Senghor, Léopold Sédar. "Letter to Richard Wright," in Richard Wright: Impressions and Perspectives. Ed. David Ray and Robert M. Farnsworth. Ann Arbor Paperbacks AA189. Ann Arbor: The University of Michigan Press, p. 149.
Reprint of 1971.271.

270. _____. "Letter to Richard Wright," in Richard Wright: Impressions and Perspectives. Ed. David Ray and Robert M.
Farnsworth. Ann Arbor: The University of Michigan Press, p. 149.
Reprint of 1971.271.

271. Shafer, Boyd C., Richard A. McLemore, and Everett Augspurger. United States History for High Schools. River Forest, Ill.: Laidlaw Brothers, p. 675.
Mentions briefly W and NS.

271a. Shimizu, Takeo. "A Commentary on Richard Wright: What Is 'Crime' to Black Americans?" Kyushu Shika Daigaku Shingaku Katei Kenkyu Kiyo [Bulletin of Kyushu Dental College], 4 (31 March), 34-36.
For black men in the South, not to commit a crime is a crime; murder is necessary for them to achieve identity and vision. [Y. H. and T. K.]

271b. Shiratani, Nobuhiko. "The Repetition of Synonymous Words in the Works of Richard Wright." Kyushu Kogyo Daigaku Kenkyu Hokoku [Kyushu Institute of Technology Study Report], 21 (31 March), 71-89.
A linguistic study of W's use of pleonasm. Cites, for example, 124 examples of pleonasm in NS. Also cites synonymous words joined by and and or. [Y. H. and T. K.]

272. Shucard, Alan R. "Richard Wright's Life and Works Elucidated." Library Journal, 98 (15 April), 1286.
Favorable review of Michel Fabre's The Unfinished Quest of Richard Wright praising the use of source material.

273. Simonson, Harold P. "Richard Wright," in his Instructor's Manual to Accompany Quartet: A Book of Stories, Plays, Poems, and Critical Essays, Second Edition. New York: Harper & Row, pp. 6-7.
Comments, study questions, and suggestions for further reading to accompany "The Man Who Was Almost a Man."

274. _____. "Richard Wright," in his Quartet: A Book of Stories, Plays, Poems, and Critical Essays. Second edition. New York: Harper & Row, p. 1084.
Headnote to "The Man Who Was Almost a Man."

274a. Skeeter, Sharyn J. "Black Women Writers: Levels of Identity." Essence, 4 (May), 58-59, 76, 89.
Mentions W briefly.

275. Smith, James Frederick. "From Symbol to Character: The Negro in American Fiction of the Twenties." Dissertation Abstracts International, 33 (January),

3672A-3673A.
Mentions W briefly.

276. Spady, James G. "Memorial Services for Arna Bontemps." CLA Journal, 17 (September), 117-119.
Discusses a eulogy by Lawrence D. Reddick which commented on Bontemps' relation to W.

277. Sprandel, Katherine. "The Long Dream," in Richard Wright: Impressions and Perspectives. Ed. David Ray and Robert M. Farnsworth. Ann Arbor Paperbacks AA189. Ann Arbor: The University of Michigan Press, pp. 174-182.
Reprint of 1971.281.

278. _____. "The Long Dream," in Richard Wright: Impressions and Perspectives. Ed. David Ray and Robert M. Farnsworth. Ann Arbor: The University of Michigan Press, pp. 174-182.
Reprint of 1971.281.

279. Swindell, Larry. "The Year's 100 Best Books." The Philadelphia Inquirer (2 December), Sec. H, p. 18.
States that Michel Fabre's The Unfinished Quest of Richard Wright is "likely to stand as the definitive study of perhaps the foremost Black American writer of the century."

280. Tanaka, Hiroshi. "Wright's The Outsider--Jinshusei to Fuhensei"["Wright's The Outsider: Racial Quality and Universality"]. Kyoto Daigaku Eibungaku Hyoron [Kyoto University Review of English Literature], 30 (March), 83-105.
W's purpose in O is to create a Bigger Thomas of universality, but Cross Damon's development is arrested by W's existentialism. In content and form, the novel mirrors W's own struggle. [Y. H.]

281. Terrier, Michel. Individu et société dans le roman américain de 1900 à 1940: essai de poetique sociale. (EA 52). Paris: Didier, pp. 23-24, 46, 51-53, 74-75, 86, 94, 101, 104, 105, 111-112, 136, 164, 213, 245-246, 252, 255, 264, 268, 279, 286, 293, 346, 360, 414, 422.
Numerous brief mentions of W, especially in the sections on literary naturalism.

282. Thomas, Winburn T. "Reminiscences," in Richard Wright: Impressions and Perspectives. Ed. David Ray and Robert M. Farnsworth. Ann Arbor Paperbacks AA189. Ann Arbor: The University of Michigan Press, pp. 151-153.
Reprint of 1971.295.

283. _____. "Reminiscences," in Richard Wright: Impressions and Perspectives. Ed. David Ray and Robert M. Farnsworth. Ann Arbor: The University of Michigan Press, pp. 151-153.
Reprint of 1971.295.

284. Thompson, G. R. "Themes, Topics, and Criticism," in American Literary Scholarship: An Annual/1971. Ed. J. Albert Robbins. Durham, N. C.: Duke University Press, pp. 369-390.
Mentions W briefly (p. 389).

285. Thune, Ensaf and Ruth Prigozy. "'Bright and Morning Star' Richard Wright," in their Instructor's Manual Short Stories: A Critical Anthology. New York: Macmillan, pp. 30-32.
Analyzes the story emphasizing its power, its psychological interest, and "its writing and construction." Includes study questions.

286. _____. "Richard Wright," in their Short Stories: A Critical Anthology. New York: Macmillan, pp. 67, 368.
Includes a paragraph of analysis of "Bright and Morning Star" and a biographical headnote to the story.

287. Towns, Saundra. "The Black Woman as Whore: Genesis of the Myth." The Black Position, No. 3, pp. 39-59.
Discusses Bessie in NS and Sarah in "Long Black Song" as "simple, sexual animals, incapable of any kind of transcendence" (p. 40). Also comments on W's relation to his mother as depicted in BB (p. 51).

288. Wagner, Jean. Black Poets of the United States from Paul Laurence Dunbar to Langston Hughes. Trans. Kenneth Douglas. Bibliographical supplement by Kenneth Kinnamon. Urbana: University of Illinois Press, pp. xv, 172, 187, 235, 368, 482.
Translation of 1962.104.

289. Walker, Alice and John O'Brien. "Alice Walker," in Interviews with Black Writers. Ed. John O'Brien. New York: Liveright, pp. 185-211.
Walker mentions W briefly (p. 209).

290. W.[alker], I. M. "Wright, Richard," in Cassell's Encyclopaedia of World Literature. Ed. S. H. Steinberg and J. Buchanan-Brown. Second edition. Vol. 3. London: Cassell, p. 761.
Biographical-bibliographical note. Reprinted: 1973.291.

291. _____. "Wright, Richard," in Cassell's Encyclopaedia of World Literature. Ed. S. H. Steinberg and J. Buchanan-Brown. Second edition. Vol. 3. New York: William Morrow, p. 761.

Reprint of 1973.290.

292. _____. "Wright, Richard," in Webster's New World Companion to English and American Literature. Ed. Arthur Pollard and Ralph Willett. New York: World Publishing Company, pp. 748-749, 849.
Biographical sketch and lists of primary and secondary works.

293. Walker, Warren S. Twentieth-Century Short Story Explication: Supplement II to Second Edition, 1970-1972. Hamden, Conn.: The Shoe String Press, pp. 159-161.
Lists thirty-three items on W.

293a. Walling, William. "'Art' and 'Protest': Ralph Ellison's Invisible Man Twenty Years After." Phylon, 34 (Second Quarter), 120-134.
Comments on the relation of Invisible Man to "The Man Who Lived Underground."

294. Walton, Martha R. Ballard. "Major Concerns of the Black Novel in America in Relation to the American Mainstream." Dissertation Abstracts International, 34 (November), 2660A-2661A.
Gives "intensive treatment" to the novels of W.

295. Watson, Edward A. "Bessie's Blues," in Richard Wright: Impressions and Perspectives. Ed. David Ray and Robert M. Farnsworth. Ann Arbor Paperbacks AA189. Ann Arbor: The University of Michigan Press, pp. 167-173.
Reprint of 1971.310.

296. _____. "Bessie's Blues," in Richard Wright: Impressions and Perspectives. Ed. David Ray and Robert M. Farnsworth. Ann Arbor: The University of Michigan Press, pp. 167-173.
Reprint of 1971.310.

297. Weatherhead, A. Kingsley. "Poetry: The 1930s to the Present," in American Literary Scholarship: An Annual/1971. Ed. J. Albert Robbins. Durham, N. C.: Duke University Press, pp. 299-321.
Mentions the bibliography of Wright by Fabre and Margolies (p. 321).

298. We.[bb], C.[onstance]. "Wright, Richard," in Encyclopaedia Britannica. Ed. Warren E. Preece. Vol. 23. Chicago: Encyclopaedia Britannica, p. 817.
Reprint of 1970.357.

298a. Weber, Brom. "The Mode of 'Black Humor,'" in The Comic Imagination in American Literature. Ed. Louis D. Rubin, Jr. New Brunswick, N. J.: Rutgers University Press, pp. 361-371.

Mentions W briefly (p. 364).

299. Weigel, Henrietta. "Personal Impressions," in Richard Wright: Impressions and Perspectives. Ed. David Ray and Robert M. Farnsworth. Ann Arbor Paperbacks AA189. Ann Arbor: The University of Michigan Press, pp. 71-74.
Reprint of 1971.312.

300. _____. "Personal Impressions," in Richard Wright: Impressions and Perspectives. Ed. David Ray and Robert M. Farnsworth. Ann Arbor: The University of Michigan Press, pp. 71-74.
Reprint of 1971.312.

301. Weisbord, Robert G. Ebony Kinship: Africa, Africans, and the Afro-American. Westport, Conn.: Greenwood Press, p. 135.
Mentions W's visit to Africa in a chapter entitled "Back-to-Africanism Since Garvey."

302. West, Earle H. A Bibliography of Doctoral Research on the Negro. Supplement 1967-1969. Ann Arbor, Mich.: Xerox University Microfilms, p. 23.
Lists Edward R. Zeitlow's "Wright to Hansberry: The Evolution of Outlook in Four Negro Writers." The year of publication is uncertain.

303. West, Hollie I. and Ralph Ellison. "Through a Writer's Eyes." The Washington Post (21 August), pp. B1, B3.
Ellison comments on his early literary relation to W.

304. White, Grace McSpadden. "Wright's Memphis," in Richard Wright: Impressions and Perspectives. Ed. David Ray and Robert M. Farnsworth. Ann Arbor Paperbacks AA189. Ann Arbor: The University of Michigan Press, pp. 19-30.
Reprint of 1971.314.

305. _____. "Wright's Memphis," in Richard Wright: Impressions and Perspectives. Ed. David Ray and Robert M. Farnsworth. Ann Arbor: The University of Michigan Press, pp. 19-30.
Reprint of 1971.314.

306. Whitlow, Roger. Black American Literature: A Critical History. Chicago: Nelson Hall, pp. 107-117, 141, 185.
Sketches Wright's youth, discusses NS, and comments on BB, TMBV, WML, and "Between the World and Me."

307. _____. "The Harlem Renaissance and After: A Checklist of Black Literature of the Twenties and Thirties." Negro American Literature Forum, 7 (Winter), 143-146.
Lists UTC.

308. Wideman, John. "The Most Important Book on One of Our Most Important Writers." The New York Times Book Review (7 October), pp. 31-32.
Highly favorable review of Michel Fabre's The Unfinished Quest of Richard Wright. Fabre establishes W's stature and shows the integrity of his quest.

309. _____ and John O'Brien. "John Wideman," in Interviews with Black Writers. Ed. John O'Brien. New York: Liveright, pp. 213-223.
Wideman acknowledges W as an influence on his writing (p. 216).

310. Williams, John A. and John O'Brien. "John Williams," in Interviews with Black Writers. Ed. John O'Brien. New York: Liveright, pp. 225-243.
Williams and O'Brien both mention W in relation to white literature (p. 227) and as a model for Harry Ames in The Man Who Cried I Am (p. 235).

311. Wiltz, John Edward. The Search for Identity: Modern American History. Philadelphia: Lippincott, p. 506.
Mentions briefly W and NS.

312. Young, James O. Black Writers of the Thirties. Baton Rouge: Louisiana State University Press, pp. xii, 127-131, 134, 148-149, 155, 158, 159-164, 165, 179-180, 203, 219, 223, 225, 229-235, 240, 241-242.
Discusses and mentions W as historian, literary critic, novelist, poet, and, especially, his relation to the Communist Party. Discusses UTC and NS in some detail.

313. Zara, Louis. "Show Case: Marvelous Study of Richard Wright." Chicago Sun-Times (14 October), Sec. 3, p. 17.
Highly favorable review of Michel Fabre's The Unfinished Quest of Richard Wright.

1974

1. Achtert, Walter S. and Eileen M. Mackesy, comps. 1972 MLA Abstracts of Articles in Scholarly Journals. Vol. 1. New York: Modern Language Association, p. 201.
Abstracts of articles on W by James G. Kennedy, Phyllis R. Klotman and Melville Yancey, Lewis Leary, Harold T. McCarthy, Eugene E. Miller, and Sidonie A. Smith.

2. Alford, Sterling G. Famous First Blacks. New York: Vantage Press, p. 104.
Lists NS as one of "the first black plays by black authors to reach Broadway."

3. Algren, Nelson. "Traveling a No Man's Land in the War Between the Races." Los Angeles Times (24 February), Book Review Sec., pp. 1-2, 9.
Ostensibly a somewhat unfavorable review of Michel Fabre's The Unfinished Quest of Richard Wright, this consists mainly of Algren's recollections of W. Fabre did not take sufficient note of W's stubbornness, abrasiveness, and other unpleasant traits.

4. Amis, Lola Jones. "Richard Wright's Native Son: Notes." Negro American Literature Forum, 8 (Fall), 240-243.
Comments on the first two books of the novel, emphasizing the contrast between white illusion and black reality, and exploring Bigger's negative "self-concept."

5. Anderson, David D. "Chicago as Metaphor." The Great Lakes Review, 1 (Summer), 3-15.
Mentions BB and NS.

6. Anderson, Dorothy W., Marieta L. Harper, J. Flagg Kris, James P. Johnson, and Dolores C. Leffall. Recent Notable Books: A Selected Bibliography in Honor of Dorothy Burnett Porter. Washington, D. C.: Howard University, 16 pp.
Lists Keneth Kinnamon's The Emergence of Richard Wright.

6a. Angelou, Maya. Gather Together in My name. New York: Random House, p. 207.
Mentions W among the author's books when she was a teenager.

7. Anon. "Allen, Samuel," in Afro-American Encyclopedia. Ed. Martin Rywell. Vol. 1. North Miami: Educational Book Publishers, p. 120.
Mentions W briefly.

8. Anon. "Conroy Himself." American Libraries, 5 (December), 606.
Mentions Jack Conroy's early publication of W.

9. Anon. "Ellison, Ralph W.," in Afro-American Encyclopedia. Ed. Martin Rywell. Vol. 3. North Miami: Educational Book Publishers, pp. 884-885.
Mentions W briefly.

10. Anon. "General Chronology 1492-1973," in Afro-American Encyclopedia. Ed. Martin Rywell. Vol. 10. North Miami: Educational Book Publishers, pp. 2909-2967.
Lists the publication of BB (p. 2952).

11. Anon. "Harlem," in Afro-American Encyclopedia. Ed. Martin Rywell. Vol. 4.

North Miami: Educational Book Publishers, pp. 1136-1139.
Mentions W briefly.

12. Anon. Index to Periodical Articles by and About Negroes: 1972. Boston: G. K. Hall, p. 822.
Lists four items on W.

13. Anon. "Lee, Canada," in Afro-American Encyclopedia. Ed. Martin Rywell. Vol. 5. North Miami: Educational Book Publishers, pp. 1456-1457.
Mentions W briefly.

14. Anon. "Ray, David and Robert M. Farnsworth, eds. Richard Wright; impressions and perspectives." Choice, 11 (July-August), 762.
Favorable notice praising the collection's effort to appreciate W's human qualities and to dispel some myths of W criticism. The documentation and bibliography are sound.

15. Anon. "Richard Wright." Journal of Modern Literature, 3 (February), 832-833.
Review of W issue of New Letters.

16. Anon. Untitled essay, in Black Boy. Trans. Marcel Duhamel. Paris: Gallimard, pp. 7-8.
Biographical sketch.

17. Anon. "Wright," in Brockhaus Enzyklopädie. Vol. 20. Wiesbaden: F. A. Brockhaus, pp. 494-495.
Revised reprint of 1957.105 with a photograph.

18. Anon. "Wright," in Petit Larousse illustré. Paris: Librairie Larousse, p. 1786.
Brief biographical note.

19. Anon. "Wright, Richard," in Afro-American Encyclopedia. Ed. Martin Rywell. Vol. 10. North Miami: Educational Book Publishers, pp. 2865-2866.
Biographical sketch with photograph.

20. Anon. "Wright, Richard," in Leksikon JLZ. Ed. Miroslav Krleža. Zagreb: Jugoslavenski Leksikografski Zavod, p. 1072.
Biographical note with a photograph.

21. Aptheker, Herbert. Untitled headnote to "I Have Seen Black Hands," in his A Documentary History of the Negro People in the United States 1933-1945. Secaucus, N. J.: The Citadel Press, p. 60.
Brief note stating that the poem "captures so much of the anguish and hope of the 1930's."

22. ____. Untitled headnote to "Joe Louis Uncovers Dynamite," in his A Docu-mentary History of the Negro People in the United States 1933-1945. Secaucus, N. J.: The Citadel Press, p. 194.
Brief note on the social context of the essay.

23. Baker, Houston A., Jr. "The Emergence of Richard Wright. By Keneth Kinnamon." Journal of Popular Culture, 8 (Summer), 202-203.
Mixed review praising Kinnamon's research but questioning some of his interpretations and conclusions.

24. Bell, Bernard W. The Folk Roots of Contemporary Afro-American Poetry. Detroit: Broadside Press, pp. 132-135.
Praises W's effort to work with his folk roots. His sensibility is unexcelled by Afro-American writers of fiction.

25. Bennett, Stephen B. and William W. Nichols. "Violence in Afro-American Fiction: An Hypothesis," in Ralph Ellison: A Collection of Critical Essays. Ed. John Hersey. Englewood Cliffs, N. J.: Prentice-Hall, pp. 171-175.
Reprint of 1971.39.

26. Bianchi, Ruggero. La dimensione narrativa (Ipotesi sul romanzo americano). Il Portico biblioteca di lettere e arti 50, ed. Antonio Piromalli. Ravenna: Longo editore, pp. 37, 40, 52, 143-146, 148.
Includes comments on NS focusing on the characterization of Bigger Thomas. Mentions W briefly elsewhere.

27. Bigsby, C. W. E. "Houston Baker, Jr., Twentieth Century Interpretations of Native Son; Keneth Kinnamon, The Emergence of Richard Wright: A Study in Literature and Society." Journal of American Studies, 8 (December), 406-408.
Mixed review of Baker's collection. It is uneven, but the Gibson, Howe, and Baldwin essays are rewarding. Mixed review of Kinnamon's work. Although it is well researched and documented, it does not succeed in reconciling social and literary criticism.

28. Blassingame, John W. "Black Autobiographies as History and Literature." The Black Scholar, 5 (December 1973-January 1974), 2-9.
Mentions W (pp. 7, 8, 9).

29. Bone, Robert A. "James Baldwin," in James Baldwin: A Collection of Critical Essays. Ed. Keneth Kinnamon. Englewood Cliffs, N. J.: Prentice-Hall, pp. 28-51.
Reprint of 1965.43.

30. ____. "Ralph Ellison and the Uses

of the Imagination," in Ralph Ellison: A
Collection of Critical Essays. Ed. John
Hersey. Englewood Cliffs, N. J.: Pren-
tice-Hall, pp. 95-114.
   Reprint of 1966.22.

30a. _____. "Richard Wright," in Ameri-
can Writers: A Collection of Literary
Biographies. Ed. Leonard Unger. Vol. 4.
New York: Scribner's, pp. 474-497.
   Reprint of 1969.36 with an updated
   bibliography.

31. Bontemps, Arna. "Biographical
Notes," in his American Negro Poetry.
Revised edition. American Century
Series. New York: Hill and Wang, pp.
215-227.
   Revised reprint of 1963.57.

32. _____. "Introduction," in his American Negro Poetry. Revised edition. American Century Series. New York: Hill and
Wang, pp. xv-xx.
   Revised reprint of 1963.58.

33. Brignano, Russell C. Black Americans
in Autobiography: An Annotated Bibliography of Autobiographies and Autobiographical Books Written Since the Civil
War. Durham, N. C.: Duke University
Press, pp. 84-85.
   Lists six works by W.

34. Brisbane, Robert H. Black Activism:
Racial Revolution in the United States
1954-1970. Valley Forge, Pa.: Judson
Press, pp. 269-272, 276.
   Notes the impact of NS. In that work
   and BB W "had singlehandedly closed
   out an era. He had wrung [sic] down
   the curtain on the plantation themes
   and moods of the Harlem Renaissance."

35. Brivic, Sheldon. "Conflict of
Values: Richard Wright's Native Son."
Novel: A Forum on Fiction, 7 (Spring),
231-245.
   Contends that Bigger Thomas has a
   split personality deriving from the
   conflict of values which W himself
   experienced. The most revealing episode is the killing of Mary Dalton,
   an act both accidental and inten-
   tional, representing the two sides of
   Bigger's mind. The essay concludes
   with a political postscript analyzing
   W's prophecy of black liberation.
   Partially reprinted: 1978.49.

36. Brooks, Thomas R. Walls Come Tum-
bling Down: A History of the Civil
Rights Movement 1940-1970. Englewood
Cliffs, N. J.: Prentice-Hall, p. 43.
   Refers to and quotes from the con-
   cluding passage of BB.

37. Brown, Lloyd W. "The Cultural Revo-

lution in Black Theatre." Negro American
Literature Forum, 8 (Spring), 159-164.
   Comments briefly on NS as exemplifying "the Afro-American writer's
   interest in mythic stereotypes as
   social reality."

38. _____. "The Portrait of the Artist
as a Black American in the Poetry of
Langston Hughes." Studies in Black Literature, 5 (Spring), 24-27.
   Mentions W briefly.

39. Broyard, Anatole. "Books of the
Times: No Color Line in Cliches." The
New York Times (17 May), p. 37.
   Unfavorable review of James Baldwin's
   If Beale Street Could Talk claiming
   that Baldwin is even more dated than
   W.

39a. Bryer, Jackson R., Eddy Dow, Philip
R. Headings, Matthew O'Brien, Joseph V.
Ridgely, Peter G. Van Egmond, and Leo
Weigant, with the help of Joanne Giza
and Donald Wharton. "American Literature," in 1972 MLA International Bibliography. Vol. 1. New York: Modern Language Association, pp. 128-173.
   Lists fifteen items on W.

40. Burger, Mary M. Williams. "Black
Autobiography--A Literature of Celebration." Dissertation Abstracts International, 34 (June), 7740-A.
   Considers NS as well as BB.

41. Butterfield, Stephen. Black Autobiography in America. Amherst: University
of Massachusetts Press, pp. 7, 19, 37,
86, 87, 93, 95, 108, 109, 110-111, 122,
127, 130-131, 155-179, 184, 198, 203,
206, 208, 225, 231, 233, 273.
   Chapter 8 (pp. 155-179) treats BB as
   the finest autobiography in American
   literature. Its themes are characteristic of black autobiography: identity, alienation, rebellion, desire
   for knowledge, and restlessness. In
   structure and style, too, BB is
   related to traditional black autobiography, especially the slave narrative. The structure alternates between factual detail and interpretation as it develops W's need to free
   his spirit from the imprisonment of
   his surroundings. The style is characterized by "terse clarity, serious
   tone, loaded rhetorical questions,
   plain verbs and syntax, short sentences, rapid accumulation of clauses"
   (p. 177). Butterfield frequently refers to W elsewhere in the volume.

41a. Cavanaugh, William C. "Purpose and
Form," in his Introduction to Poetry.
Dubuque, Iowa: Wm. C. Brown Company, pp.
15-38.

Quotes "In the Falling Snow" as "one of our best haiku" (p. 24).

42. Chapman,, Dorothy H. Index to Black Poetry. Boston: G. K. Hall, pp. 21, 92, 102, 373.
   Lists "Between the World and Me," "Hokku Poems," and "I Have Seen Black Hands."

43. Cherry, Richard L., Robert J. Conley, and Bernard A. Hirsch. "Suggestions for Further Reading," in their A Return to Vision. Second edition. Boston: Houghton Mifflin, pp. 433-437.
   Reprint of 1971.68a.

44. Chisholm, Lawrence Washington. "Signifying Everything," in Ralph Ellison: A Collection of Critical Essays. Ed. John Hersey. Englewood Cliffs, N. J.: Prentice-Hall, pp. 31-35.
   Reprint of 1965.49.

45. [Clampit, Maryellen Hains]. "Folklore and Literature in Mississippi," in Mississippi: Conflict and Change. Ed. James W. Loewen and Charles Sallis. New York: Pantheon, pp. 219-235.
   Contains a sketch of W's early career (pp. 232-233) and mentions W elsewhere. Quotes a passage from "Down by the Riverside" in a discussion of the Great Flood of 1927.

46. Cleaver, Eldridge. "Notes on a Native Son," in James Baldwin: A Collection of Critical Essays. Ed. Keneth Kinnamon. Englewood Cliffs, N. J.: Prentice-Hall, pp. 66-76.
   Reprint of 1966.37.

47. Conroy, Jack. "Memories of Arna Bontemps, Friend and Collaborator." American Libraries, 5 (December), 602-606.
   Mentions the play NS (p. 604).
   Reprinted: 1979.71.

48. Cooke, Michael G. "The Descent Into the Underworld and Modern Black Fiction." Iowa Review, 5 (Fall), 72-90.
   Includes brief discussion of NS and "The Man Who Lived Underground."

49. Cornish, Sam. "My Brother Is Homemade," in My Black Me. Ed. Arnold Adoff. New York: Dutton, p. 39.
   Reprint of 1971.78.

50. Cortada, Rafael L. Black Studies: An Urban and Comparative Curriculum. Lexington, Mass.: Xerox College Publishing, pp. 95-122.
   In a chapter entitled "The New Humanities" Cortada mentions W several times (see especially p. 112) while proposing greater attention to black

topics in humanities curricula.

51. Covo, Jacqueline. The Blinking Eye: Ralph Waldo Ellison and His American, French, German and Italian Critics, 1952-1971. Metuchen, N. J.: The Scarecrow Press, pp. 16, 22, 26, 27, 28, 47, 48, 49, 58, 59, 67, 69, 71, 72, 80, 101, 103, 106, 115, 118, 122.
   Cites references to W in Ellison criticism.

52. Cowley, Malcolm. "American Books Abroad," in Literary History of the United States: History. Fourth edition. Ed. Robert E. Spiller, Willard Thorp, Thomas H. Johnson, Henry Seidel Canby, Richard M. Ludwig, and William M. Gibson. New York: Macmillan, pp. 1374-1391.
   Reprint of 1948.151.

53. Crewdson, Arlene J. "Invisibility: A Study of the Works of Toomer, Wright and Ellison." Dissertation Abstracts International, 35, pp. 1092A-1093A.
   Like Cane and Invisible Man, NS is an important work of American literature which considers serious moral questions. W writes of an underground man who undergoes an initiation rite in order to discover his existential self and survive in a dehumanized industrial society.

54. Dance, Daryl C. "You Can't Go Home Again: James Baldwin and the South." CLA Journal, 18 (September), 81-90.
   Cites a comment by Saunders Redding on W's response to Africa (p. 82) and notes W's appreciation of "the physical beauty of the South" (p. 86).

55. Davis, Arthur P. From the Dark Tower: Afro-American Writers 1900 to 1960. Washington, D. C.: Howard University Press, pp. 10, 13, 55, 133, 139-140, 142, 147-157, 193, 207, 215-217, 221-223, 267-270.
   Reviews W's life and career with evaluative comments on the fiction (except SH) and BB. W's basic purpose is "to express the great social crime that America perpetrated upon the black masses and the effects of that crime on the life and personality of the Negro" (p. 149). Davis mentions W frequently throughout. The bibliographical entry (pp. 267-270) lists nineteen primary and fifty-nine secondary sources. Includes Van Vechten's photograph of W.

56. Demarest, David P., Jr. "Richard Wright: The Meaning of Violence." Negro American Literature Forum, 8 (Fall), 236-239.
   Analyzes "Between the World and Me" and selected episodes in BB to show

that the violence imposed by white America on black life creates both black racial solidarity and an intensified awareness of self.

57. Dixon, Melvin. "Richard Wright: Native Father and His Long Dream." Black World, 23 (March), 91-95.
Favorable review of Michel Fabre's The Unfinished Quest of Richard Wright noting that it is more social, historical, and biographical than literary and critical.

58. Dolan, Paul J. and Joseph T. Bennett. "Race: Arrangements in Black and White," in their Introduction to Fiction. New York: John Wiley, pp. 207-208.
Comments briefly on "The Man Who Went to Chicago."

59. _____. "Richard Wright 1908-1960," in their Introduction to Fiction. New York: John Wiley, p. 521.
Biographical note.

60. Dorsinville, Max. Caliban Without Prospero: Essay on Quebec and Black Literature. Erin, Ontario: Press Porcepic, 227 pp.
Analysis of the parallel between French-Canadian and Afro-American literature and culture in terms of the Caliban-Prospero metaphor. W's visit to Quebec is the point of departure for Dorsinville's introduction, and W is mentioned and discussed throughout. Bigger is the central figure in a chapter entitled "The Revolted Black," which shows the influence of NS on The Street, Blood on the Forge, If He Hollers Let Him Go, Last of the Conquerors, Beetlecreek, and Invisible Man. Dorsinville also discusses the role of Christianity in NS (pp. 137-139) and O as "Wright's vision of a post-revolt attitude on the part of the American Negro" (p. 162).

61. Dybek, Caren. "Black Literature for Adolescents." English Journal, 63 (January), 64-67.
Mentions W briefly.

62. Edmonds, Randolph. "The Black in the American Theatre, 1700-1969." Pan-African Journal, 7 (Winter), 297-322.
Comments briefly on Bigger in the play NS as a "Bad Nigger."

63. Ellison, Mary. The Black Experience: American Blacks Since 1865. New York: Barnes & Noble, pp. 127-128, 138.
Mentions W in connection with the WPA and Communist efforts to recruit blacks.

64. Ellison, Ralph and James Alan McPherson. "Invisible Man," in Ralph Ellison: A Collection of Critical Essays. Ed. John Hersey. Englewood Cliffs, N. J.: Prentice-Hall, pp. 43-57.
Reprint of 1970.119.

65. Everette, Mildred W. "The Death of Richard Wright's American Dream: 'The Man Who Lived Underground.'" CLA Journal, 17 (March), 318-326.
Argues that this pessimistic story of universal guilt and meaninglessness refutes the hope of human dignity and meaning expressed at the end of BB. W develops his theme carefully through imagery of rats, corpses, and death.

66. Fabre, Michel. "Fathers and Sons in James Baldwin's Go Tell It on the Mountain," in James Baldwin: A Collection of Critical Essays. Ed. Keneth Kinnamon. Englewood Cliffs, N. J.: Prentice-Hall, pp. 120-138.
Translation by Keneth Kinnamon of 1970.123.

67. Felgar, Robert. "Black Content, White Form." Studies in Black Literature, 5 (Spring), 28-31.
Mentions briefly W and NS.

68. _____. "'The Kingdom of the Beast': The Landscape of Native Son." CLA Journal, 17 (March), 333-337.
Points out that W uses animal and jungle imagery in the novel to show how destructive white stereotypes promote violence, cunning, and ferocity in the ghetto among such blacks as Bigger.

69. _____. "Soul on Ice and Native Son." Negro American Literature Forum, 8 (Fall), 235.
Applies Cleaver's myth of racial-sexual roles to NS: "Buckley corresponds to the Omnipotent Administrator, Mary Dalton to the Ultra-feminine, Bessie Mears to the Amazon, and of course Bigger Thomas to the Supermasculine Menial."

70. Fischer, Russell G. "Invisible Man as History." CLA Journal, 17 (March), 338-367.
Mentions W's involvement with the Communist Party (p. 360).

71. Flanagan, John T. "Folklore," in American Literary Scholarship: An Annual/1972. Ed. J. Albert Robbins. Durham, N. C.: Duke University Press, pp. 372-400.
Mentions W briefly (p. 390).

72. Fleming, Robert E. "The Emergence of Richard Wright: A Study in Lit-

erature and Society. By Keneth Kinnamon." Negro History Bulletin, 37 (January), 207.
    Favorable review praising Kinnamon's
    scholarship. The chapter on NS is the
    strongest.

73. Franklin, John Hope. From Slavery to
Freedom: A History of Negro Americans.
Fourth edition. New York: Knopf, pp.
386-387, 506.
    Reprint of 1956.158.

74. Frémy, Dominique and Michèle Frémy.
Quid? Tout pour tous. Paris: Editions
Robert Laffont, p. 91.
    Reprint of 1963.86.

75. French, Warren. "Fiction: 1900 to
the 1930s," in American Literary Scholarship: An Annual/1972. Ed. J. Albert
Robbins. Durham, N. C.: Duke University
Press, pp. 237-263.
    Comments on one book and sixteen
    articles on W (pp. 257-260).

76. Fullinwider, S. P. "Black Writers of
the Thirties. By James O. Young." The
Journal of Southern History, 40 (August), 507-508.
    Mentions W briefly.

77. Geismar, Maxwell. "A Cycle of Fic-
tion," in Literary History of the United
States: History. Fourth edition. Ed.
Robert E. Spiller, Willard Thorp, Thomas
H. Johnson, Henry Seidel Canby, Richard
M. Ludwig, and William M. Gibson. New
York: Macmillan, pp. 1296-1316.
    Reprint of 1948.168.

78. Gibson, Donald B. "More About
Wright." Novel: A Forum on Fiction, 7
(Spring), 283-284.
    Favorable review of Keneth Kinnamon's
    The Emergence of Richard Wright call-
    ing it "a detailed, well-documented,
    sensitive and sensible study." Never-
    theless, Kinnamon relies too much on
    BB for biographical details and em-
    phasizes literary over social con-
    siderations in his analyses of W's
    work.

79. _____. "Wright, Richard," in Encyclopedia of American Biography. Ed. John
A. Garraty. New York: Harper & Row, pp.
1231-1232.
    Biographical sketch followed by a
    critical evaluation stressing the
    conflict in W's mind between the
    autonomy of the individual and social
    determinism.

80. Giovanni, Nikki and Margaret Walker.
A Poetic Equation: Conversations Between
Nikki Giovanni and Margaret Walker.
Washington, D. C.: Howard University

Press, pp. 80-101.
    Walker discusses her early relation-
    ship with W, comments extensively on
    Michel Fabre's The Unfinished Quest
    of Richard Wright, and mentions the
    questions surrounding W's death.

81. Goldstein, Malcolm. The Political
Stage: American Drama and Theater of the
Great Depression. New York: Oxford Uni-
versity Press, pp. 298, 447.
    Discusses the play NS in the context
    of the Mercury Theater.

82. Gounard, J.-F. "La Carrière singu-
lière de James Baldwin: 1924-1970."
Revue de l'Université d'Ottawa, 44
(October-December), 507-518.
    Comments on the W-Baldwin relation-
    ship (pp. 510-511).

83. _____. "Richard Wright as a Black
American Writer in Exile." CLA Journal,
17 (March), 307-317.
    Reviews W's life and career during
    his expatriation. Losing some of the
    power that characterized his earlier
    work on racial themes, his writing in
    France demonstrated initially a weak-
    ness in handling the novel of ideas,
    then a deep concern for the Third
    World, and finally a new maturity,
    humor, and sensitivity to physical
    nature.

84. Graham, Don B. "Lawd Today and the
Example of The Waste Land." CLA Journal,
17 (March), 327-332.
    Claims that W derived his sense of
    form from Eliot's poem, from which
    imagery, symbolism, and motifs are
    noted in LT. "Spiritual death and the
    possibility of rebirth" (p. 329) are
    major themes in both the poem and the
    novel.

85. Gross, Seymour L. "'Dalton' and
Color-Blindness in Native Son." The
Mississippi Quarterly, 27 (Winter 1973-
1974), 75-77.
    Argues that the use of the name Dal-
    ton, derived from Daltonism, to sug-
    gest distortion of racial perception
    was probably deliberate on W's part.

86. Guilford, Virginia N. Brown. "The
Black Contemporary Novel: Social Index."
Dissertation Abstracts International, 35
(December), 3680-A.
    A chapter on "The Forerunners" pre-
    sumably includes treatment of W.

87. H., J. "Richard Wright," in Dictionnaire des litteratures étrangères contemporaines. Ed. Dominique de Roux.
Paris: Editions Universitaires, pp. 321-
322.
    Biographical-critical sketch.

87a. Haas, Rudolf. Amerikanische Literaturgeschichte 2. Uni-Taschenbücher 199.
Heidelberg: Quelle & Meyer, pp. 333-334.
Mentions UTC, NS, and BB, and quotes
from "The Ethics of Living Jim Crow."

88. Hassan, Ihab. "Fiction," in Literary
History of the United States: History.
Fourth edition. Ed. Robert E. Spiller,
Willard Thorp, Thomas H. Johnson, Henry
Seidel Canby, Richard M. Ludwig, and
William M. Gibson. New York: Macmillan,
pp. 1460-1475.
Mentions the existential element in
NS and calls W "father of the modern
Black novel" (p. 1467).

89. Hatch, James V. and Ted Shine. "Na-
tive Son 1941," in their Black Theater,
U. S. A.: Forty-Five Plays by Black
Americans 1847-1974. New York: The Free
Press, p. 393.
Headnote to the play discussing it as
characteristic of its time and rele-
vant to the present.

90. Hernton, Calvin C. "A Fiery Bap-
tism," in James Baldwin: A Collection of
Critical Essays. Ed. Keneth Kinnamon.
Englewood Cliffs, N. J.: Prentice-Hall,
pp. 109-119.
Reprint of 1970.179.

91. Hicks, Granville. "Richard Wright's
Prize Novellas," in Granville Hicks in
the New Masses. Ed. Jack Alan Robbins.
Port Washington, N. Y.: Kennikat Press,
pp. 130-132.
Reprint of 1938.222.

92. Howe, Irving. "Black Boys and Native
Sons," in Ralph Ellison: A Collection of
Critical Essays. Ed. John Hersey. Engle-
wood Cliffs, N. J.: Prentice-Hall, pp.
36-38.
Partial reprint of 1963.113.

93. _____. "James Baldwin: At Ease in
Apocalypse," in James Baldwin: A Collec-
tion of Critical Essays. Ed. Keneth
Kinnamon. Englewood Cliffs, N. J.: Pren-
tice-Hall, pp. 96-108.
Reprint of 1968.127.

94. Hughes, Douglas A. "Richard Wright
(1908-1960)," in his Studies in Short
Fiction. Second edition. New York: Holt,
Rinehart and Winston, p. 324.
Biographical-critical headnote to
"Bright and Morning Star" stressing
W's white audience.

95. Hughes, Langston. "From Harlem to
Paris," in James Baldwin: A Collection
of Critical Essays. Ed. Keneth Kinnamon.
Englewood Cliffs, N. J.: Prentice-Hall,
pp. 9-10.
Reprint of 1956.205.

96. Hyman, Stanley Edgar. "Ralph Ellison
in Our Time," in Ralph Ellison: A Collection of Critical Essays. Ed. John
Hersey. Englewood Cliffs, N. J.: Prentice-Hall, pp. 39-42.
Reprint of 1964.75.

97. Jackson, Blyden. "The Emergence of
Richard Wright: A Study in Literature
and Society. By Keneth Kinnamon." The
South Atlantic Quarterly, 73 (Summer),
409.
Favorable review noting Kinnamon's
sympathy with his subject and praising his research and analyses.

98. _____. "A Survey Course in Negro
Literature." College English, 35
(March), 631-636.
Jackson divides his course into six
chronological periods, one of which
is the "Age of Wright," for W is its
greatest writer.
Reprinted: 1976.106a.

99. _____. "The Unfinished Quest of
Richard Wright. By Michel Fabre." American Literature, 46 (November), 412-414.
Favorable review praising Fabre's
research but noting some factual
errors. The work is indispensable to
the serious student, but Fabre does
not manage to enter into the black
world.

100. Jackson, Bruce. "Get Your Ass in
the Water and Swim Like Me": Narrative
Poetry from Black Oral Tradition. Cambridge, Mass.: Harvard University Press,
p. 123.
Mentions LT.

101. John-Kanem, A. U. "How Can We De-
velop the Feeling of Solidarity Between
the Different Communities of the Black
World?" Présence Africaine, No. 92
(Fourth Quarter), pp. 113-121.
Mentions W's attendance at the First
Congress of Negro Artists and Writers
in Paris in 1956.

102. Jordan, June. "On Richard Wright
and Zora Neale Hurston: Notes Toward a
Balancing of Love and Hatred." Black
World, 23 (August), 4-8.
Contrasts W and Hurston. Their Eyes
Were Watching God expresses black
affirmation; NS expresses black pro-
test.
Reprinted: 1981.70.
Partially reprinted: 1980.132.

103. Justus, James H. "Fiction: The
1930s to the Present," in American Lit-
erary Scholarship: An Annual/1972. Ed.
J. Albert Robbins. Durham, N. C.: Duke
University Press, pp. 264-311.
Mentions W briefly (p. 304).

103a. Kasunose, Yoshiko. "Keneth Kinnamon's The Emergence of Richard Wright: A
Study in Literature and Society." Kokujin Kenkyu [Negro Studies], 46 (20
June), 10-11, 19.
Considers the study well annotated
and supported by evidence. Provides a
summary of each chapter as well as a
brief biography of Kinnamon. [Y. H.
and T. K.]

104. Kesteloot, Lilyan. Black Writers in
French: A Literary History of Negritude.
Trans. Ellen Conroy Kennedy. Philadelphia: Temple Univeristy Press, pp. 58,
59, 73, 281, 292, 293, 298, 299, 307,
350.
Translation of 1963.125.

105. Kim, Kichung. "Wright, The Protest
Novel, and Baldwin's Faith." CLA Journal, 17 (March), 387-396.
Maintains that the literary quarrel
between Baldwin and W grew out of
different conceptions of man's nature. W believed that racial oppression had dehumanizing effects on
black personality; Baldwin held to a
human ideal which survived and triumphed over injustice. In his recent
development Baldwin has lost faith in
love, racial reconciliation, and the
American Dream, thus moving closer to
W's position.

106. Kinnamon, Keneth. "Introduction,"
in his James Baldwin: A Collection of
Critical Essays. Englewood Cliffs,
N. J.: Prentice-Hall, pp. 1-8.
Notes W's aid to the young Baldwin
(p. 4).

107. Kirby, John B. "Black Writers of
the Thirties. By James O. Young." The
Journal of American History, 61 (December), 828-829.
Mentions briefly W and NS.

108. Kishimoto, Hisao. "Black Boy ni
Mirareru Richard Wright" ["Richard
Wright as Seen in Black Boy"]. Soka Daigaku Bungakubu Ronshu [Soka University
Treatises of the Literary Faculty], 3
(March), 21-32.
Mentions the timing of BB, which
comes between the two periods in W's
creative work, before and after his
departure from the United States. The
experiences described in BB are typical of human experiences where innate
character is inevitably strangled by
social forces: W's struggle is that
of all men. [Y. H.]

109. _____. "From Black Boy to The Outsider." Soka Daigaku Bungakubu Ronshu
[Soka University Treatises of the Literary Faculty], 4 (December), 95-106.

An examination of diction in O in
comparison with BB. Indicates that
protesting against whites is considerably less in O than in BB. In BB
fear leads to self-assertion, while
in O self-denial predominates, and
social injustice and battle are replaced by inner struggle and alienation. [Y. H.]

110. Kitano, Harry H. L. Race Relations.
Englewood Cliffs, N. J.: Prentice-Hall,
pp. 125-126.
To illustrate a step in the development of ethnic identity, Kitano
quotes from "The Ethics of Living Jim
Crow" the episode in which W was
beaten by his mother for fighting
with white boys.

111. Klinkowitz, Jerome. "The Dark and
the Feeling, essays by Clarence
Major." Chicago Review, 26, No. 3,
194-195.
Mentions W briefly.

112. Klotman, Phyllis R. "Moral Distanc-
ing as a Rhetorical Technique in Native
Son: A Note on 'Fate.'" CLA Journal, 18
(December), 284-291.
Applying a critical concept of Wayne
Booth, Klotman argues that W arranges
"the events in the novel in order to
set up a moral distance between those
events and the reader at the specific
times when he wants the reader to
make moral judgments. On the other
hand, he reduces the distance . . .
when he wants the judgment suspended"
(p. 285). This technique subserves
W's purpose of forcing white readers
to recognize their social guilt. In
support of her thesis, Klotman analyzes parallels between the rat scene
early in the novel and Bigger's
flight and capture, and comments on
the cell scene involving Bigger and
Max at the end of the work.

113. Knickerbocker, Kenneth L. and H.
Willard Reninger. "Preface," in their
Interpreting Literature. Fifth edition.
New York: Holt, Rinehart and Winston,
pp. vi-viii.
Mentions briefly W, whose "Bright and
Morning Star" is included (pp. 121-
137).

114. Lederer, Norman. Unidentified clipping.
Favorable review of Richard Wright:
Impressions and Perspectives, ed.
David Ray and Robert Farnsworth. The
biographical contributions to the
collection are the most valuable.
Lederer comments on most of the
essays included and praises the bibliography.

115. Lowry, Lois. "Richard Wright," in her Black American Literature. Portland, Maine: J. Weston Walch Publisher, pp. 74-77.
    Biographical-critical sketch including commentary on "Big Boy Leaves Home" and NS.

116. Major, Clarence. The Dark and Feeling: Black American Writers and Their Work. New York: The Third Press, pp. 61-71, et passim.
    In a chapter entitled "Richard Wright: The Long Hallucination," Major states: "I will examine here the activities of Wright's writing career, some aspects of his personal life, the actual works he produced, and touch on correlations among these aspects in the hope of achieving not only a better understanding of his life as a writer but also with the suggestion of what such a life means for a black writer in a culture that is largely white" (p. 61).

117. Mannucci, Loretta Valtz. I negri americani dalla depressione al dopoguerra. Milan: Feltrinelli, pp. 21-27, 71, 98-107, 111, 124, 126, 158, 159, 160, 162, 163-164, 175.
    Includes a detailed analysis of the Time review of BB showing how it reinforced white prejudice (pp. 21-27) and a discussion of NS in its social context with a plot summary (pp. 98-107). Bigger is a character of such power that he breaks out of W's own ideological framework. Manucci mentions W elsewhere in relation to Himes, Ellison, and Cleaver.

118. Margolies, Edward. "Kinnamon, Kenneth [sic]. The Emergence of Richard Wright: A Study in Literature and Society." Journal of Modern Literature, 3 (February), 831-832.
    Mixed review praising Kinnamon's treatment of the racism of W's youth and his evaluation of W's works. He is less successful in achieving the promise of his title or in dealing with W's Chicago and New York years.

119. Martin, S. Rudolph, Jr. "A New Mind: Changing Black Consciousness, 1950-1970." Dissertation Abstracts International, 35 (December), 3752-A.
    Considers W as a pivotal figure whose view is "that black Americans will be free only when they can relate with others directly and humanely, with full recognition of the differences their histories have produced in their world outlooks."

120. Matheus, John F. "The Unfinished Quest of Richard Wright. By Michel Fabre." CLA Journal, 18 (September), 130-133.
    Favorable review comparing the work to Marie Bonaparte's life of Poe. Matheus praises Fabre's psychological insight and his scholarship.

121. McAleer, John J. "The Unfinished Quest of Richard Wright." America, 130 (26 January), 56-57.
    Favorable review of the biography by Fabre emphasizing its scholarly character.

122. McCarthy, Harold T. "Richard Wright: The Expatriate as Native Son," in his The Expatriate Perspective: American Novelists and the Idea of America. Rutherford, Madison, Teaneck, N. J.: Fairleigh Dickinson University Press, pp. 175-196.
    Revised reprint of 1972.149.

123. McClane, Kenneth A. "For Saunders Redding and Myself." The Crisis, 81 (February), 58-59.
    Poem inspired by a Redding lecture on W.

124. McConnell, Frank D. "Black Words and Black Becoming." The Yale Review, 63 (Winter), 193-210.
    Includes a discussion of NS. Ultimately an absurdist "comic movement," the novel focuses on working out the positive (expansionist) and negative (racist) implications of Bigger's name. By exploiting the connection between language and identity, Bigger gains control of his own fate. While a failure in the terms of the realistic and protest novel, NS succeeds in transforming realism into a larger imaginative context.

125. McMichael, George. "James Baldwin 1924-," in his Anthology of American Literature. Vol. 2. New York: Macmillan, pp. 1773-1774.
    Headnote mentioning W's relation to Baldwin.
    Reprinted: 1980.162.

126. _____. "Ralph Ellison 1914-," in his Anthology of American Literature. Vol. 2. New York: Macmillan, pp. 1580-1581.
    Headnote mentioning W's friendship with Ellison.
    Reprinted: 1980.163.

127. _____. "Richard Wright," in his Instructor's Manual for Anthology of American Literature. New York: Macmillan, pp. 150-151.
    Study questions to accompany "The Man Who Was Almost a Man."

128. _____. "Richard Wright 1908-1960," in his Anthology of American Literature. Vol. 2. New York: Macmillan, pp. 1569-1570.
Biographical-critical headnote to "The Man Who Was Almost a Man" emphasizing W's early career. Includes suggestions for reading. Reprinted: 1980.164.

129. McQuade, Donald and Robert Atwan. "Richard Wright/Black Boy," in their Popular Writing in America: The Interaction of Style and Audience. New York: Oxford University Press, p. 632.
Reprinted: 1980.166.

130. Mebane, Mary E. "The Family in the Works of Charles W. Chesnutt and Selected Works of Richard Wright." Dissertation Abstracts International, 34, pp. 5982A-5983A.
W describes the black family under attack by environmental forces in both the North and the South. Only when family members respond collectively rather than individually can they hope to be effective. W's last novel marks a departure from previous patterns because it focuses on a Southern family in contact with whites.

131. Mills, Moylan Chew. "The Literary Reputation of Richard Wright." Dissertation Abstracts International, 35 (October), 2286A.
Examines the original reception of all of Wright's works of fiction and BB. Analyzes later commentary on NS, O, and "The Man Who Lived Underground." The final chapter is entitled "Wright's Literary Reputation: Pertinent Factors and Current Status."

132. Minakawa, Soichi. "Richard Wright to Haiku" ["Richard Wright and Haiku"]. Shin Nihon Bungaku [New Japanese Literature], 29 (June), 101-105.
An account of the circumstances in which W, gaining access to R. H. Blyth's four volume introduction to Japanese haiku, tried his hand in composing haiku in English toward the very end of his life. Translates and comments on the four of W's 4,000 haiku quoted in Michel Fabre's The Unfinished Quest of Richard Wright. Finds one of these, "I am nobody / A red sinking autumn sun / Took my name away," comparable, in form, structure, theme, and imagery, to any one of the three haiku by Taniguchi Buson, a celebrated eighteenth-century Japanese poet, which Minakawa quotes. Though Minakawa considers another of W's haiku, "It is Septem-

ber / The month in which I was born / And I have no thought," a relative failure as a haiku, he maintains that it delineates "the tired, disillusioned Wright" shortly before his death in Paris. [Y. H.]

133. Mitchell, Louis D. "Invisibility--Permanent or Resurrective." CLA Journal, 17 (March), 379-386.
Compares briefly the protagonist of Invisible Man to the protagonist of NS (p. 381).

134. Moorer, Frank E. "Fabre, Michel. The Unfinished Quest of Richard Wright, translated from the French by Isabel Barzun." MLN, 89 (December), 1072-1075.
Favorable review praising Fabre's research and his placement of W in the relevant contexts. Moorer himself stresses the nuturing influence on W of the Communist Party and of white women.

135. Mootry, Maria Katella. "Studies in Black Pastoral: Five Afro-American Writers." Dissertation Abstracts International, 35 (December), 3757-A.
Treats W "to demonstrate the psychological implications of pastoral."

136. Mphahlele, Ezekiel. The African Image. Revised edition. London: Faber and Faber, pp. 12, 101-102, 159.
Revised reprint of 1962.89.

137. Neal, Larry. "Ellison's Zoot Suit," in Ralph Ellison: A Collection of Critical Essays. Ed. John Hersey. Englewood Cliffs, N. J.: Prentice-Hall, pp. 58-79.
Reprint of 1970.272.

138. Newman, Charles. "The Lesson of the Master: Henry James and James Baldwin," in James Baldwin: A Collection of Critical Essays. Ed. Keneth Kinnamon. Englewood Cliffs, N. J.: Prentice-Hall, pp. 52-65.
Reprint of 1966.111.

139. Nin, Anaïs. The Diary of Anaïs Nin 1947-1955. Ed. Gunther Stuhlmann. New York: Harcourt Brace Jovanovich, pp. 206-207.
Records a visit to W in Paris in the fall of 1954. W discussed his life in Brooklyn and France, the response of critics to NS, and the role of the black American writer.

140. Nyabongo, Virginia Simmons. "Keneth Kinnamon. The Emergence of Richard Wright: A Study in Literature and Society." Books Abroad, 48 (Spring), 375.
Favorable notice.

141. Ouchi, Yoshikazu. "Richard Wright,"

in his Afro-America Bungaku [Afro-American Literature]. Tokyo: Hyoronsha, pp. 82-119.

A historical and critical discussion of W's life and work. Does not see W as a pioneer bent on attacking hypocrisy in a democratic society. His anger and protest were not necessarily motivated by the race issue, but by a universal awareness of man's plight. The depression that gave rise to protest literature made the public regard the problem of race as that of man as a whole. W's characters--Bigger, Cross, and Fishbelly--all want to be Americans, but they are not accepted as Americans for their color of skin. As long as racial prejudice and injustice continue to exist in American society, Ouchi observes, they remain what W calls "negative Americans." [Y. H.]

142. [Perkins, George]. "Richard Wright (1908-1960)," in The American Tradition in Literature. Fourth edition. Ed. Sculley Bradley, Richmond Croom Beatty, E. Hudson Long, and George Perkins. New York: Grosset & Dunlap (distributed by Norton), pp. 1496-1497.

Biographical-critical headnote to "Big Black Good Man." Perkins considers BB W's best book.

142a. Pickering, James H. Instructor's Manual Fiction 100. New York: Macmillan, p. 115.

Lists three items on W.

143. _____. "Questions for Study," in his Fiction 100: An Anthology of Short Stories. New York: Macmillan, p. 1027.

To accompany "The Man Who Was Almost a Man."

144. _____. "Wright," in his Fiction 100: An Anthology of Short Stories. New York: Macmillan, p. 1048.

Biographical note.

145. Prakken, Sarah L., ed. The Reader's Adviser: A Layman's Guide to Literature. Twelfth edition. Vol. 1. New York: Bowker, pp. 600-601.

Contains a biographical sketch of W and brief primary and secondary bibliographies.

146. Primeau, Ronald. "Slave Narrative Turning Midwestern: Deadwood Dick Rides Into Difficulties." Midamerica I, pp. 16-35.

Includes a discussion of W (pp. 22-25) in his transition from South to Midwest, from BB to NS. Chicago both aroused and frustrated the expectations of the black migrant from the South.

147. Prosen, Rose Mary. "'Ethnic Literature'--of Whom and for Whom; Digressions of a Neo-American Teacher." College English, 35 (March), 659-669.

Contains a brief discussion of Bigger Thomas (p. 666).

147a. Pryse, Marjorie. "Ralph Ellison's Heroic Fugitive." American Literature, 46 (March), 1-15.

Mentions briefly UTC (p. 4) and quotes Ellison on NS (p. 7).

148. Puckett, John R. "The Book of Dispossession: A Study of the Photo-Textual Documentary." Dissertation Abstracts International, 35 (October), 2292-A.

Abstracts a University of Iowa dissertation containing a chapter on TMBV.

149. Rampersad, Arnold. "The Unfinished Quest of Richard Wright by Michel Fabre." Harvard Advocate, 107, No. 4, 56-57.

Review of Fabre's biography in relation to previous W scholarship. Though indispensable, the work leaves many serious questions unanswered, especially those concerning W's psychology after his emergence as a public figure.

149a. Reed, Ishmael. The Last Days of Louisiana Red. New York: Random House, p. 18.

A character in this novel named Maxwell Kasavubu is "writing a critical book on Richard Wright's masterpiece, Native Son."

Reprinted: 1976.153a.

150. _____ and John O'Brien. "Ishmael Reed," in The New Fiction: Interviews with Innovative American Writers. Ed. Joe David Bellamy. Urbana: University of Illinois Press, pp. 130-141.

Reprint of 1973.252.

151. Reeves, Paschal et al. "A Checklist of Scholarship on Southern Literature for 1973." Mississippi Quarterly, 27 (Spring), 225-272.

Lists eight items on W (pp. 264-265).

152. Rich, Andrea L. Interracial Communication. New York: Harper & Row, pp. 91, 139.

Uses BB to illustrate conflicts of belief and racist language in interracial communication.

153. Rosenblatt, Roger. Black Fiction. Cambridge, Mass.: Harvard University Press, pp. 2, 4, 5, 6, 8, 17-19, 19-36, 43, 64, 68, 69, 70-76, 87-88, 90, 130, 138, 157, 161-167, 172, 173, 178, 198-199.

Rosenblatt's thesis is that the heroes of black fiction are trapped in a cyclical, nightmarish history and society from which all efforts to break free are doomed. Within this conceptual framework he analyzes NS and "Big Boy Leaves Home," with briefer comments on "Long Black Song," O, and other works by W.

154. Schafer, William J. "Ralph Ellison and the Birth of the Anti-Hero," in Ralph Ellison: A Collection of Critical Essays. Ed. John Hersey. Englewood Cliffs, N. J.: Prentice-Hall, pp. 115-126.
Reprint of 1968.194.

155. Scott, Nathan A., Jr. "The Emergence of Richard Wright: A Study in Literature and Society. By Keneth Kinnamon." The Journal of Ethnic Studies, 1 (Winter), 109-110.
Favorable review praising Kinnamon's scholarship and focus.

156. Seyersted, Per. "A Survey of Trends and Figures in Afro-American Fiction." American Studies in Scandinavia, 6, pp. 67-86.
Includes discussion of W as the central figure of the protest tradition. Traces briefly W's influence on subsequent writers.

157. Shrodes, Caroline, Harry Finestone, and Michael Shugrue. "Richard Wright," in their The Conscious Reader: Readings Past and Present. New York: Macmillan, p. 1037.
Brief biographical note.

158. Siegel, Paul N. "The Conclusion of Richard Wright's Native Son." PMLA, 89 (May), 517-523.
Argues against conventional interpretations, maintaining that Boris Max is more reformer than radical. He seeks to avert the disaster toward which American racism is taking the country. Bigger, on the other hand, finds meaning in his existence by accepting his feelings of hatred.
Reprinted in revised form: 1979.235.

159. Singh, Amritjit. "Misdirected Responses to Bigger Thomas." Studies in Black Literature, 5 (Summer), 5-8.
Refutes charges that Bigger is too melodramatically violent, that his characterization is more sociological than artistic, and that he is an example of "negative" rather than "positive" protest. Singh finds Bigger's intensified awareness at the end of the novel implausible, but otherwise considers him "one of the most powerful creations in twentieth-century American fiction" (p. 8).

160. Singh, Raman K. "Marxism in Richard Wright's Fiction." Indian Journal of American Studies, 4 (June and December), 21-35.
Argues that as the chief ideological influence on W, Marxism influences each stage of his career. His early works criticize capitalist society in a manner which prepares for the explicit search for Marx in NS. Paradoxically, O at once rejects communism and upholds Marxist ideals.

161. Skerrett, Joseph. "Fabre, Michel: The Unfinished Quest of Richard Wright. Kinnamon, Keneth: The Emergence of Richard Wright: A Study in Literature and Society." Kritikon Litterarum, 3, pp. 202-204.
Review pointing out that Fabre's biography is excellent in its analysis of W's intellectual development. Psychological areas are not fully explored by either Fabre or Kinnamon. The latter's book is well researched also and useful for its relation of W's early works to their political context. What is most needed in W criticism, however, is a psychological approach.

162. Smith, Charles Kay. Styles and Structures: Alternative Approaches to College Writing. New York: Norton, pp. 62-86.
After reprinting from NS (pp. 13-19) an early scene between Bigger and Gus, Smith analyzes its style in a chapter entitled "How Form and Content Work Together in a Psychological Style." Smith points out W's use of symbolism, especially in its Freudian and Marxist dimensions.

163. Smith, Dwight L., ed. Afro-American History: A Bibliography. Santa Barbara, Cal.: ABC-CLIO, Inc., pp. 58, 72-73, 461, 655-656, 755, 756, 766.
Contains abstracts of seven articles touching on W from historical journals.

164. Smith, Sidonie. Where I'm Bound: Patterns of Slavery and Freedom in Black American Autobiography. Westport, Conn.: Greenwood Press, pp. 49-71.
Revised reprint of 1972.184. References to W elsewhere in this book compare him to other black autobiographers.

165. Spiller, Robert E., Willard Thorp, Thomas H. Johnson, Henry Seidel Canby, Richard M. Ludwig, and William M. Gibson. Literary History of the United States: Bibliography. Fourth edition.

New York: Macmillan, pp. 150, 789, 1010, 1323-1324.
> Reprint of 1948.251 and 1959.114 together with an updated entry listing three primary and twenty-three secondary items.

166. Sprandel, Katherine R. "Richard Wright's Hero: From Initiate and Victim to Rebel and Isolate (An Achronological Study)." Dissertation Abstracts International, 34 (June), 7786A-7787A.
> Argues that the critical climate has changed to the point where we can now see W not as a black novelist but as a writer who supplies a central metaphor for modern man in the figure of the "rebel-victim." BB and LD present basic patterns of metaphysical rebellion which are explored in depth in W's other works. See 1977.131.

167. Tatham, Campbell. "Reflections: Sutton Griggs' Imperium in Imperio." Studies in Black Literature, 5 (Spring), 7-15.
> Uses a quotation from TMBV as an epigraph.

168. Terry, Esther A. "The Long and Unaccomplished Dream of Richard Wright." Dissertation Abstracts International, 35 (July), 420-A.
> Although W knew and wrote of the culture of black America, he considered it a burden rather than a source of strength. His career consisted of a succession of experiments with substitute involvements ranging from politics to philosophy to travel. But his failure to embrace black culture "cheats" his characters "of the possibility of becoming universally great."

169. Thorp, Willard and Robert E. Spiller. "End of an Era," in Literary History of the United States: History. Ed. Robert E. Spiller, Willard Thorp, Thomas H. Johnson, Henry Seidel Canby, Richard M. Ludwig, and William M. Gibson. Fourth edition. New York: Macmillan, pp. 1392-1411.
> Reprint of 1963.177.

170. Towns, Saundra. "Black Autobiography and the Dilemma of Western Artistic Tradition." Black Books Bulletin, 2 (Spring), 17-23.
> Includes an analysis of BB as an example of the "disengaged" form of black autobiography.

171. Uchiyama, Tetsujiro. "America no Musuko no Mondaiten--Deguchi o Fusaida Kikujin no Drama" ["A Study of Native Son: The Tragedy of a Negro Without Any Place to Live In"]. Niigata Daigaku Jinbun Kagaku Kenkyu [Niigata University Studies in Cultural Sciences], No. 46 (December), pp. 51-73.
> The more vigorously Bigger Thomas seeks freedom the more harshly it is denied him. His murder of Mary Dalton inevitably leads to his tragedy; the flight section demonstrates the denial of freedom by virtue of his returning to the South Side and intentionally killing Bessie. The final section of the book also denies him an outlet since Max dominates his story. As Bigger becomes an individual his freedom is ironically taken away from him. Notes this development is similar to what happens to Aunt Sue in "Bright and Morning Star." [Y. H.]

171a. Uchiyama, Tetsujiro. "The Structure of Uncle Tom's Children: Fiction and History," Kokujin Kenkyu [Negro Studies], 46 (20 June), 1-6.
> The collection is based on the structure of a novel. Relating the growth of individuals to that of a group, W demonstrates their historical development from slaves through tenant farmers and city workers to bourgeoisie. [Y. H. and T. K.]

172. Vogler, Thomas A. "Invisible Man: Somebody's Protest Novel," in Ralph Ellison: A Collection of Critical Essays. Ed. John Hersey. Englewood Cliffs, N. J.: Prentice-Hall, pp. 127-150.
> Reprint of 1970.349.

173. Walker, S. Jay. "John O'Brien, ed. Interviews with Black Writers; David Bakish. Richard Wright; Keneth Kinnamon. The Emergence of Richard Wright: A Study in Literature and Society; Stanley Macebuh. James Baldwin: A Critical Study." Modern Fiction Studies, 20 (Summer), 284-287.
> Unfavorable review of Bakish complaining of excessive condensation. Favorable review of Kinnamon praising his studies of W's sources and his emphasis on W's artistry.

174. W.[aring], N.[ancy] W. "Ray, David & Farnsworth, Robert, eds. Richard Wright; impressions and perspectives." Kliatt Paperback Book Guide, 8 (April), 68.
> Favorable review of a collection presenting "a composite portrait of a compelling personality and a literary figure." Praises especially the contributions of Michel Fabre and Margaret Walker Alexander.

175. Warren, Robert Penn. "The Unity of Experience," in Ralph Ellison: A Collec-

tion of Critical Essays. Ed. John Hersey. Englewood Cliffs, N. J.: Prentice-Hall, pp. 21-26.
Reprint of 1965.124.

176. Weiss, Adrian. "A Portrait of the Artist as a Black Boy." Rocky Mountain MLA Bulletin, 28 (December), 93-101.
Emphasizes W's use of imagination and experience to develop his self-awareness in his creative efforts.

177. Whitlow, Roger. Black American Literature: A Critical History. Totowa, N. J.: Littlefield, Adams, pp. 107-117, 141, 185.
Devotes more space to W than to any other author, with emphasis on NS, BB, and the poetry. Whitlow also discusses Chester Himes, Ann Petry, Curtis Lucas, Willard Savoy, Philip B. Kaye, Lloyd Brown, William Attaway, Willard Motley, and Nathan Heard as members of "The Wright School."

178. Willingham, John R. "Minireviews." The CEA Critic, 37 (November), 48.
Contains a favorable notice of Richard Wright: Impressions and Perspectives, ed. David Ray and Robert M. Farnsworth.

179. Winchell, Carol. "A-W Library Pathfinder: Literature--Richard Wright." Reading, Mass.: Addison-Wesley Publishing Co., 2 pp.
Bibliographical guide.

180. Woodress, James. "Richard Wright (1908-1960)," in his American Fiction, 1900-1950. Detroit: Gale, pp. 229-233.
After a biographical paragraph, Woodress provides a selective bibliographical essay with the following rubrics: Bibliography and Manuscripts, Works of Fiction, Editions and Reprints, Biography, and Criticism.

1975

1. Achtert, Walter S. and Eileen M. Mackesy, comps. 1973 MLA Abstracts of Articles in Scholarly Journals. Vol. 1. New York: Modern Language Association, pp. 209-210.
Abstracts of articles on W by Thomas Cripps, Michel Fabre, and Gayle Gaskill.

2. Adoff, Arnold. "Richard Wright," in his Brothers and Sisters: Modern Stories by Black Americans. New York: Dell, pp. 252-253.
Reprint of 1970.12.

3. Allen, Shirley S. "Religious Symbolism and Psychic Reality in Baldwin's Go

Tell It on the Mountain." CLA Journal, 19 (December), 173-199.
Contrasts briefly Baldwin's novel to NS.

4. Anon. "Butterfield, Stephen. Black autobiography in America." Choice, 12 (April), 203.
Mentions BB briefly.

5. Anon. "Davis, Arthur P. From the dark tower; Afro-American writers, 1900-1960." Choice, 11 (January), 1628.
Mentions W briefly.

6. Anon. Index Translationum 25. Paris: Unesco, pp. 169, 302, 345, 493, 800.
Lists translations of NS into Danish, Finnish, Japanese, and Georgian, BB into Finnish, "The Man Who Lived Underground" into French, and O into Japanese.

7. Anon. "Literatura norteamericana," in Nueva enciclopedia autodidactica Quillet. Vol. 1. Buenos Aires: Aristides Quillet, pp. 477-482.
Mentions W briefly.

8. Anon. "Major, Clarence. The dark and feeling; black American writers and their work." Choice, 11 (January), 1633.
Praises the chapter on W.

9. Anon. "Rait (Wright) Richard," in Bol'shaia Sovetskaia Entsiklopediia. Ed. A. M. Prokhorov. Vol. 21. Moscow: Sovetskaia Entsiklopediia, p. 439.
Biographical note emphasizing NS. Translated: 1978.32.

10. Anon. "Rosenblatt, Roger. Black Fiction." Choice, 12 (July-August), 684.
Mentions W briefly.

11. Anon. "Smith, Sidonie. Where I'm bound; patterns of slavery and freedom in black American autobiography." Choice, 11 (February), 1762.
Mentions W briefly.

12. Anon. "The Way of the New World: The Black Novel in America. Addison Gayle, Jr." Publishers Weekly, 207 (13 January), 56.
Mentions W briefly.

13. Anon. "Wright, Richard," in Lexikon der Weltliteratur. Ed. Gero von Wilpert. Vol. 1. Stuttgart: Alfred Kröner Verlag, p. 1762.
Biographical-bibliographical note.

14. Anon. "Wright, Richard," in The New Columbia Encyclopedia. Fourth edition. Ed. William H. Harris and Judith S. Levey. New York: Columbia University Press, p. 3012.

Revised reprint of 1950.102.

15. Anon. "Wright (Richard)," in Pluri dictionnaire Larousse. Ed. Claude Du Bois. Paris: Librairie Larousse, p. 1456.
Biographical note.

16. Anon. "Wright, Richard," in Who Was Who in American History--Arts and Letters. Chicago: Marquis Who's Who, p. 599.
Brief biographical sketch.

17. Anon. "Wright, Richard Nathaniel," in Grote Winkler Prins. Ed. J. F. Staal, R. F. Lissens, A. Devreker, J. Presser, and A. J. Wiggers. Vol. 20. Amsterdam: Elsevier, p. 273.
Biographical note.

18. Aubert, Alvin. "Useful Collection of Critical and Biographical Essays." Freedomways, 15 (First Quarter), 55-57.
Review of Arthur P. Davis's From the Dark Tower mentioning W.

19. Baker, Houston A., Jr. "Where I'm Bound: Patterns of Slavery and Freedom in Black American Autobiography. By Sidonie Smith." American Literature, 47 (May), 296-298.
Comments on Smith's treatment of W.

20. Bakish, David. "Himes, Chester Bomar," in Encyclopedia of World Literature in the 20th Century. Ed. Wolfgang Bernard Fleischmann. Vol. 4. New York: Ungar, pp. 159-161.
Mentions briefly W's influence on Himes.

21. Baldwin, James. "Black Colloquium in Paris," in Black Homeland/Black Diaspora: Cross-Currents of the African Relationship. Ed. Jacob Drachler. Port Washington, N. Y.: Kennikat Press, pp. 99-111.
Reprint of 1957.136.

22. Bennett, Lerone, Jr. The Shaping of Black America. Chicago: Johnson Publishing Company, p. 220.
Quotes from W's introduction to Black Metropolis.

22a. Benston, Kimberly W. "Architectural Imagery and Unity in Paule Marshall's Brown Girl, Brownstones." Negro American Literature Forum, 9 (Fall), 67-70.
Mentions briefly W's anticipation of Marshall's imagery of blindness.

22b. ____. "Sought by the Whale." The Alternative, 8 (May), 27-28.
Favorable review of Roger Rosenblatt's Black Fiction mentioning NS and Bigger Thomas.

23. Billingsley, Ronald G. "The Burden of the Hero in Modern Afro-American Fiction." Black World, 25 (December), 38-45, 66-73.
Includes discussion of Bigger Thomas as a black hero trapped by racism and ashamed of his degraded role. Nevertheless, he manages to reject the definitions of white society through a self-liberating violence.
Reprinted in revised form: 1975.24.

24. ____. "Forging New Definitions: The Burden of the Hero in Modern Afro-American Literature." Obsidian, 1 (Winter), 5-21.
Revised reprint of 1975.23.

25. Bluefarb, Sam. "Wright, Richard 1908-1960," in Contemporary Literary Criticism. Ed. Carolyn Riley. Vol. 3. Detroit: Gale, p. 546.
Partial reprint of 1972.33.

26. Bolton, H. Philip. "The Role of Paranoia in Richard Wright's Native Son." Kansas Quarterly, 7 (Summer), 111-124.
Analyzes Bigger as a paranoid with special attention to his dream in Book Two. His mental condition is imposed by a racist society.

27. Bone, Robert. Down Home: A History of Afro-American Short Fiction from Its Beginnings to the End of the Harlem Renaissance. New Perspectives on Black America, ed. Herbert Hill. New York: Putnam's, pp. xiii, xxi, xxii, 246, 264, 280, 285, 287.
Contains several references to W as the leader of the "antipastoral" group that changed the direction of the black short story. Notes also W's relation to Langston Hughes and Arna Bontemps.

28. Bonin, Jane F. Major Themes in Prize-Winning American Drama. Metuchen, N. J.: The Scarecrow Press, p. 171.
Lists the play NS.

29. Brignano, Russell Carl. "Wright, Richard 1908-1960," in Contemporary Literary Criticism. Ed. Carolyn Riley. Vol. 4. Detroit: Gale, pp. 594-597.
Partial reprint of 1970.68.

30. Brooks, Cleanth, John Thibaut Purser, and Robert Penn Warren. "Exercises," in their An Approach to Literature. Fifth edition. Englewood Cliffs, N. J.: Prentice-Hall, p. 164.
To accompany "The Man Who Was Almost a Man."

31. ____. Untitled note, in their An Approach to Literature. Fifth edition.

Englewood Cliffs, N. J.: Prentice-Hall, p. 164.
> Explanatory note on "The Man Who Was Almost a Man" stressing the gun as a symbol of manhood and the racial implications of the story.

32. Brooks, Gwendolyn, Keorapetse Kgositsile, Haki R. Madhubuti, and Dudley Randall. A Capsule Course in Black Poetry Writing. Detroit: Broadside Press, p. 6.
> Brooks comments on W's effort "to attract, stun, charm and enlist white sympathy, to stimulate white empathy."

33. Brown, Richard Maxwell. Strain of Violence: Historical Studies of American Violence and Vigilantism. New York: Oxford University Press, pp. 185, 224-225.
> Quotes from W's introduction to Black Metropolis and discusses NS as a depiction of the violent ghetto experience.

34. Bruck, Peter. Von der 'Store Front Church' zum 'American Dream': James Baldwin und der amerikanische Rassenkonflikt. Amsterdam: Verlag B. R. Grüner, pp. 2, 8, 10-13, 83, 118, 142.
> Includes a discussion of Baldwin's relationship with W (pp. 10-13). Whereas W emphasizes the power of rage, Baldwin seeks to analyze it and to transcend it through love.

35. Brüning, Eberhard. "Progressive American Writer's Organizations and Their Impact on Literature During the Nineteen Thirties." Zeitschrift für Anglistik und Amerikanistik, 23, pp. 208-216.
> Survey citing W as one example of the strength of American proletarian writing in the thirties. Brüning considers W's activity as a member of the Chicago John Reed Club crucial to his development as a writer.

35a. Bryer, Jackson R., Eddy Dow, Philip R. Headings, James Nagel, Matthew O'Brien, Joseph V. Ridgely, Peter G. Van Egmond, and Leo Weigant, with the help of Joanne Giza and Donald Wharton. "American Literature," in 1973 MLA International Bibliography. Vol. I. New York: Modern Language Association, pp. 128-181.
> Lists twenty-eight items on W.

36. Budd, Louis J. "Objectivity and Low Seriousness in American Naturalism." Prospects. Ed. Jack Salzman. Vol. 1. New York: Burt Franklin, pp. 41-61.
> Quotes W on Dreiser and comments briefly on NS (p. 59).

37. Bullock, Charles, III and Harrell R. Rodgers, Jr. Racial Equality in America: In Search of an Unfulfilled Goal. Pacific Palisades, Cal.: Goodyear Publishing Company, p. 11.
> Cites BB.

37a. Burger, Mary W. "I, Too, Sing America: The Black Autobiographer's Response to Life in the Midwest and Mid-Plains." Kansas Quarterly, 7 (Summer), 43-57.
> Mentions W briefly.

38. Burns, Glen. "How the Devil Helped Leroi Jones Turn Into Imamu Amiri Baraka," in Amerikanisches Drama und Theater im 20. Jahrhundert. Ed. Alfred Weber and Siegfried Neuweiler. Göttingen: Vandenboeck & Ruprecht, pp. 261-288.
> Mentions Philip Roth's knowledge of W.

39. Carey, Glenn O. "Richard Wright," in his Quest for Meaning: Modern Short Stories. New York: David McKay, p. 75.
> Biographical-critical headnote to "Big Boy Leaves Home."

40. Carr, Virginia Spencer. The Lonely Hunter. New York: Doubleday, pp. 127-128, 129, 220, 224, 282-283, 290, 291, 394.
> Biography of Carson McCullers discussing her friendship with W in Brooklyn and Paris.

40a. Carter, Tom. "Ernest Gaines." Essence, 6 (July), 52-53, 71-72.
> Mentions NS briefly.

41. Caselli, Ron. The Minority Experience: A Basic Bibliography of American Ethnic Studies. Revised and enlarged edition. Santa Rosa, Cal.: Sonoma County Office of Education, p. 23.
> Lists three works by W.

42. Cheatwood, Kiarri. "Die Nigger Die!" Black World, 24 (October), 51-52, 82-87.
> Mentions briefly Baldwin's attack on W.

43. Clark, James I. and Robert V. Remini. Freedom's Frontiers: The Story of the American People. Beverly Hills, Cal.: Benziger, p. 346.
> Cites TMBV on black urban life. Reprinted: 1975.44.

44. _____. We the People: A History of the United States. Combined edition. Beverly Hills, Cal.: Glencoe Press, p. 346.
> Reprint of 1975.43.

45. Clark, Marden J., Soren F. Cox, and Marshall R. Craig. "Questions," in their

About Language: Contexts for College Writing. Second edition. New York: Scribner's, p. 55.
    To accompany an excerpt from the penultimate chapter of BB.

46. _____. "Questions," in their About Language: Contexts for College Writing. Second edition. New York: Scribner's, pp. 431-432.
    To accompany "The Man Who Was Almost a Man."

47. _____. "Richard Wright," in their About Language: Contexts for College Writing. Second edition. New York: Scribner's, p. 47.
    Headnote to an excerpt from the penultimate chapter of BB.

48. _____. "Richard Wright," in their About Language: Contexts for College Writing. Second edition. New York: Scribner's, p. 421.
    Headnote to "The Man Who Was Almost a Man."

49. _____. "Suggestions for Writing," in their About Language: Contexts for College Writing. Second edition. New York: Scribner's, p. 55.
    To accompany an excerpt from the penultimate chapter of BB.

50. Cobb, Nina Kressner. "Alienation and Expatriation: Afro-American Writers in Paris After World War II." Dissertation Abstracts International, 36 (September), 1736-A.
    Abstracts a City University of New York dissertation focusing on W, Himes, and Baldwin. Cobb emphasizes their alienation from traditional black culture.

51. Cone, James H. God of the Oppressed. New York: The Seabury Press, pp. 3, 186.
    Mentions W briefly and quotes from WML.

52. Cosgrove, William. "Strategies of Survival: The Gimmick Motif in Black Literature." Studies in the Twentieth Century, No. 15 (Spring), pp. 109-127.
    Discusses methods of survival in a hostile white world used by fictional protagonists of W, Baldwin, and Baraka.

53. Cox, Martha Heasley and Wayne Chatterton. Nelson Algren. Boston: Twayne Publishers, pp. 27, 32-33, 93-94, 135.
    Relates W's indebtedness to Algren for the title NS, comments on their friendship and literary affinity, and quotes W's inscription of a copy of NS to Algren: "Who I believe is still the best writer of good prose in the

U. S. A."

54. Crocker, Edith. "Biographical Notes," in her How It Is: Growing Up Black in America. New York: Grosset & Dunlap, pp. 171-175.
    Contains a sketch of W emphasizing his early life (p. 175).

55. _____. "Introduction," in her How It Is: Growing Up Black in America. New York: Grosset & Dunlap, pp. v-viii.
    Mentions W briefly.

56. _____. "'Street Rights' Richard Wright," in her How It Is: Growing Up Black in America. New York: Grosset & Dunlap, p. 17.
    Brief headnote to a selection from BB.

57. Daniels, Lee A. "Notes Toward a Definition of a Black Aesthetic." The Washington Post Book World (30 March), p. 2.
    Review of Roger Rosenblatt's Black Fiction and Addison Gayle's The Way of the New World contrasting the bleakness of W's vision in NS to the celebration of the black music of Ellington and others.

58. Davis, Vivian I. "The Genius of Fantastic Feebleness (With Apologies to Richard Wright)." Proceedings of the Comparative Literature Symposium, 8, pp. 99-116.
    Compares "Down by the Riverside" and NS with The Plague and The Stranger. Both W and Camus "write of man's despair, estrangement, separateness, fear, suffering and hopelessness in a world where there is neither God, nor the promise that he will come."

59. Day, Martin S. A Handbook of American Literature. New York: Crane, Russak, & Company, pp. 247, 401, 433, 442-443, 474, 556.
    In addition to brief mentions of W, Day provides a short analysis of NS (pp. 442-443) stressing Bigger's brutalization and W's attack on liberal whites as represented by the Daltons. Books I and II "dose out perhaps the most visceral writing in the American novel," but Book III is too propagandistic.

60. Doner, Dean. "Wright, Richard," in The World Book Encyclopedia. Ed. William H. Nault. Vol. 21. Chicago: Field Enterprises, p. 420.
    Biographical sketch.
    Reprinted: 1978.80; 1979.82.

61. Drachler, Jacob. "Introduction," in his Black Homeland/Black Diaspora:

Cross-Currents of the African Relationship. Port Washington, N. Y.: Kennikat
Press, pp. 3-14.
    Notes W's expatriation and his skep-
    ticism about African cultural sur-
    vivals in Afro-American life.

62. _____. "James Baldwin," in his Black
Homeland/Black Diaspora: Cross-Currents
of the African Relationship. Port Washington, N. Y.: Kennikat Press, pp. 97-
99.
    Comments on Baldwin's response to W
    at the Congress of Black Writers and
    Artists in Paris in 1956.

63. _____. "Richard Wright," in his
Black Homeland/Black Diaspora: Cross-
Currents of the African Relationship.
Port Washington, N. Y.: Kennikat Press,
pp. 87-89.
    Headnote to a selection from BP.
    Drachler emphasizes W's "relentlessly
    inquiring and agonizingly ambivalent"
    response to Africa. He was finally
    too Western to understand African
    society.

64. Dunn, Lynn P. Black Americans: A
Study Guide and Sourcebook. San Francisco: R and E Research Associates, pp.
3, 6, 7, 44, 46, 84, 112.
    Mentions W and his works to illus-
    trate historical or sociological
    points. The bibliography lists five
    items by W.

65. Dunning, Stephen and Alan B. Howes.
Literature for Adolescents: Teaching
Poems, Stories, Novels, and Plays. Glenview, Ill.: Scott, Foresman, pp. 269,
271-272, 281, 283-284, 285, 291-292.
    Comments on and quotes from BB. Men-
    tions NS and TMBV.

66. Eden, Walter Anthony. "A Critical
Approach to Autobiography: Techniques
and Themes in Sherwood Anderson, Bene-
detto Croce, Jean-Paul Sartre, and
Richard Wright." Dissertation Abstracts
International, 36 (December), 3649-A.
    Abstracts a New York University dis-
    sertation containing a segment show-
    ing how W sees his personal struggle
    to aid the cause of the oppressed as
    an "arduous" one.

67. Edward, Sister Ann. "Three Views on
Blacks: The Black Woman in American
Literature." CEA Critic, 37 (May), 14-
16.
    Mentions briefly W's portrait of his
    mother in BB.

68. Emanuel, James A. "Racial Fire in
the Poetry of Paul Laurence Dunbar," in
A Singer in the Dawn: Reinterpretations
of Paul Lawrence Dunbar. Ed. Jay Martin.

New York: Dodd, Mead, pp. 75-93.
    Quotes W on Dunbar (p. 76) and men-
    tions W in connection with grinning
    as a racial defense mechanism (p.
    91).

69. Everett, Chestyn. "Tradition in
Afro-American Literature." Black World,
25 (December), 20-35.
    Refers to NS as a protest novel and
    cites Baldwin on W.

70. Fabre, Michel. "James O. Young.--
Black Writers of the Thirties." Etudes
Anglaises, 28 (October-December), 496.
    Mentions W briefly.

71. _____. "Richard Wright: Beyond
Naturalism?" in American Literary Natur-
alism: A Reassessment. Ed. Yoshinobu
Hakutani and Lewis Fried. Heidelberg:
Carl Winter, pp. 136-153.
    Contends that although W began his
    literary career as a naturalist, he
    subsequently began to "oscillate
    between Marxism and humanistic Exis-
    tentialism."

72. Fanon, Frantz. Les Damnés de la
terre. Paris: François Maspero, p. 149.
    Reprint of 1961.147.

73. Farrison, W. Edward. "Much Ado About
Negro Fiction: A Review Essay." CLA
Journal, 19 (September), 90-100.
    Criticizes Roger Rosenblatt's treat-
    ment of W in Black Fiction.

74. Feuser, Willfried F. "The Men Who
Lived Underground: Richard Wright and
Ralph Ellison," in A Celebration of
Black and African Writing. Ed. Bruce
King and Kolawole Ogungbesan. Zaria and
Ibadan: Ahmadu Bello University Press
and Oxford University Press, pp. 87-101.
    Surveys W's literary career with
    emphasis on NS and O. Notes color
    symbolism in the former and intellec-
    tual exploration of "the main cur-
    rents of modern thought" in the
    latter.

75. Flanagan, John T. "Folklore," in
American Literary Scholarship: An An-
nual/1973. Ed. James Woodress. Durham,
N. C.: Duke University Press, pp. 382-
410.
    Mentions W briefly (p. 400).

76. Fleming, Robert E. "Roots of the
White Liberal Stereotype in Black Fiction." Negro American Literature Forum,
9 (Spring), 17-19.
    Discusses Mary Dalton and Jan Erlone
    in NS.

77. Foley, Martha. "Introduction," in
her 200 Years of Great American Short

Stories. Boston: Houghton Mifflin Company, pp. 1-22.
   Mentions W briefly (pp. 14, 18, 20).

78. ____. "Richard Wright (1908-1960)," in her 200 Years of Great American Short Stories. Boston: Houghton Mifflin Company, p. 598.
   Biographical-critical headnote to "Fire and Cloud."

79. Franklin, H. Bruce. "'A' Is for Afro-American: A Primer on the Study of American Literature." The Minnesota Review, No. 5 (Fall), pp. 53-64.
   Mentions W briefly (p. 55)
   Reprinted in revised form: 1978.102.

80. Franklin, Jimmie L. "Where I'm Bound: Patterns of Slavery and Freedom in Black American Autobiography. By Sidonie Smith." The Journal of American History, 62 (September), 446-447.
   Mentions W briefly.

81. Frémy, Dominique and Michèle Frémy. Quid? Tout pour tous. Paris: Editions Robert Laffont, p. 122.
   Reprint of 1963.86.

82. French, Warren. "Fiction: 1900 to the 1930s," in American Literary Scholarship: An Annual/1973. Ed. James Woodress. Durham, N. C.: Duke University Press, pp. 224-257.
   Comments on a book and six articles on W (pp. 251-252). Mentions W elsewhere (pp. 225, 226, 239).

82a. Gates, Skip [Henry Louis, Jr.]. "Ted Joans: Tri-Continental Poet." Transition, No. 48 (April/June), pp. 4-12.
   Joans mentions W briefly.

83. Gayle, Addison, Jr. "Introduction," in The Forerunners: Black Poets in America. Ed. Woodie King, Jr. Washington, D. C.: Howard University Press, pp. xv-xxix.
   Mentions and quotes from "The Literature of the Negro in the United States" (p. xv).

84. ____. "Strangers in a Strange Land." Southern Exposure, 3 (Spring-Summer), 4-7.
   Discusses W's role in black literature of the great migration.

85. ____. The Way of the New World: The Black Novel in America. Garden City, N. Y.: Anchor Press/Doubleday, pp. xi, xvi, xviii, xix, 24, 46, 57, 60, 78, 102, 127, 130, 149, 153-159, 162, 164-182, 191, 192, 197, 203, 214-215, 227, 231, 233, 255, 262, 264, 279, 288-289, 291, 302, 311.

History of the black novel arguing that the central issue has been the creation of images of black people and black life that would reflect social, racial, and cultural realities and that would point the way to amelioration. In this development the role of W has been crucial, as Gayle's many references to him attest. The extended treatment of W is in Chapter VIII, "The Black Rebel," which focuses on NS and LD. In his violent rebelliousness W is a model for black writers of the present, but his emphasis on the emotional and intuitive qualities of the black rebel should be changed to include more intellectual capacity.
   Reprinted: 1976.81.

86. Geisinger, Marion. Plays, Players, & Playwrights: An Illustrated History of the Theatre. Revised edition. New York: Hart, p. 556.
   Mentions briefly the play NS.

87. Gelfant, Blanche. "Residence Underground: Recent Fictions of the Subterranean City." The Sewanee Review, 83 (Summer), 406-438.
   Points out that "The Man Who Lived Underground" provides a paradigm for the pattern of descent to the underground in recent American fiction, a pattern present in part in NS and "The Man Who Went to Chicago." Abused because he represents the fantasies of "ordinary people," the protagonist achieves freedom only by confronting his subversive nature and rejecting the symbols of social worth. Lacking a vocabulary for his existential statement, however, he is martyred before his message, essentially a simple Christian one, is heard.

88. Gilenson, Boris. "Afro-American Literature in the Soviet Union." Negro American Literature Forum, 9 (Spring), 25, 28-29.
   Reprint of 1973.156.

89. Giovanni, Nikki. "Afterword," in A Singer in the Dawn: Reinterpretations of Paul Laurence Dunbar. Ed. Jay Martin. New York: Dodd, Mead, pp. 243-246.
   Relates a conversation Giovanni had with another poet on W's alleged desire to be white.

90. Goldman, Arnold. "A Remnant to Escape: The American Writer and the Minority Group," in American Literature Since 1900. Ed. Marcus Cunliffe. London: Barrie & Jenkins, pp. 312-341.
   Includes a discussion of W (pp. 328-332) emphasizing UTC, NC, and BB. Bigger's sense of freedom can find no

social context to sustain it. Rootlessness characterizes both the protagonist of the novel and its author.

91. Graebner, Norman A., Gilbert C.
Fite, and Philip L. White. A History of
the American People. Second edition. New
York: McGraw-Hill, p. 669.
  Mentions briefly W and NS.

91a. Graham, Maryemma. "Frank Yerby,
King of the Costume Novel." Essence, 6
(October), 70-71, 88-89, 91-92.
  Mentions W several times.

92. Gross, Seymour. "Native Son and 'The
Murders in the Rue Morgue': An Adden-
dum." Poe Studies, 8 (June), 23.
  Adduces explicit evidence as further
  proof of Poe's influence on the writing of NS. "The Murders in the Rue
  Morgue" is actually mentioned in the
  novel.

93. Gross, Theodore L. "James O. Young.
Black Writers of the Thirties." The
American Historical Review, 80 (Octo-
ber), 1058-1059.
  Mentions W briefly.

94. Gulliver, Adelaide C. "Enlisting the
Black Novelist in a Racial Struggle."
The Christian Science Monitor (27 Feb-
ruary), p. 12.
  Review of Addison Gayle, Jr.'s The
  Way of the New World mentioning W
  briefly.

95. Gurin, Patricia and Edgar Epps.
Black Consciousness, Identity, and
Achievement: A Study of Students in
Historically Black Colleges. New York:
Wiley, pp. 370, 377, 379.
  Reports that W is among the favorite
  authors of activist students.

96. Guttmann, Allen. "Integration and
'Black Nationalism' in the Plays of Lor-
raine Hansberry," in Amerikanisches
Drama und Theater im 20. Jahrhundert.
Ed. Alfred Weber and Siegfried Neuwei-
ler. Göttingen: Vanderboeck & Ruprecht,
pp. 248-260.
  Contains brief references to W.

97. Gysin, Fritz. The Grotesque in American Negro Fiction: Jean Toomer, Richard
Wright, and Ralph Ellison. The Cooper
Monographs on English and American Literature, vol. 22, ed. R. Stamm. Bern:
Francke Verlag, pp. 13, 14, 16, 18, 20,
34, 35, 36, 91-164, 276-279, 282, 327-
328.
  The section on W concentrates on NS,
  "The Man Who Lived Underground," and
  O, especially grotesque situations,
  figures, and objects in the three
  works. The section concludes with an

analysis of the structural function
of the grotesque in each of the
works. The "Conclusion" also discusses W, finding that the grotesque in
his fiction "is characterized by the
emphasis on divergence" and that it
expresses his "quest for the absolute." Gysin includes a bibliography
on W listing eighteen primary and
twenty-one secondary sources.

98. Harrison, Myrna. An Instructor's
Manual for Mirrors: An Introduction to
Literature. Ed. John R. Knott, Jr. and
Christopher R. Reaske. Second edition.
New York: Harper & Row, pp. 20-21, 35-
36, 42.
  Contains study questions on "Bright
  and Morning Star," a biographical
  sketch, and a discography.

99. Hart, Robert C. "From the Dark
Tower: Afro-American Writers 1900-1960.
By Arthur P. Davis." American Litera-
ture, 47 (May), 298-299.
  Mentions NS briefly.

100. Hatch, James V. "Theodore Ward,
Black American Playwright." Freedomways,
15 (First Quarter), 37-41.
  Mentions NS briefly.
  Reprinted: 1977.167.

101. Havlice, Patricia Pate. Index to
Literary Biography. Vol. 2. Metuchen, N.
J.: The Scarecrow Press, p. 1283.
  Refers to eight biographical sources
  for W.

102. Hill, Mildred A. "Common Folkore
Features in African and African American
Literature." Southern Folklore Quarter-
ly, 39 (June), 111-133.
  Uses "Big Boy Leaves Home" and LT as
  illustrations.

103. Hoffman, Eva. "Writing and Oppression." Commentary, 60 (September), 84-
86.
  In a generally favorable review of
  Roger Rosenblatt's Black Fiction,
  Hoffman is critical of the treatment
  of NS.

104. Howe, Irving. "Wright, Richard
1908-1960," in Contemporary Literary
Criticism. Ed. Carolyn Riley. Vol. 3.
Detroit: Gale, p. 545.
  Partial reprint of 1963.113.

105. Hudson, Theodore R. "Black Writers
of the Thirties. By James O. Young."
American Literature, 47 (May), 299-300.
  Mentions briefly TMBV.

106. Ischinger, Anne-Barbara. Der anti-
kolonialistische Roman in frankophonen
Schwarzafrika. Europäische Hochschul-

schriften, Series XIII, vol. 13. Bern: Herbert Lang, pp. 68-69, 112.
Compares BB and Ferdinand Oyono's Une Vie de boy, notes W's connection with Présence Africaine, and lists four works by W in the bibliography.

107. Jackson, Blyden. "Jean Toomer's Cane: An Issue of Genre," in The Twenties: Fiction, Poetry, Drama. Ed. Warren French. DeLand, Fla.: Everett/Edwards, pp. 318-325.
Mentions Abraham Chapman's friendship with W (p. 320) and quotes Bone on Cane, NS, and Invisible Man as "the Negro novelist's highest achievement" (p. 321).

108. _____. "Renaissance in the Twenties," in The Twenties: Fiction, Poetry, Drama. Ed. Warren French. DeLand, Fla.: Everett/Edwards, pp. 303-316.
Mentions NS briefly (p. 312).

109. _____. "Richard Wright in a Moment of Truth," in 29 Short Stories: An Introductory Anthology. New York: Knopf, pp. 382-393.
Reprint of 1971.178.

110. _____, Louis D. Rubin, Jr., Cleanth Brooks, Norman Brown, George Core, Lewis Lawson, Paschal Reeves, Walter Sullivan, Floyd Watkins, and Dan Young. "Twentieth-Century Southern Literature," in Southern Literary Study: Problems and Possibilities. Ed. Louis D. Rubin, Jr. and C. Hugh Holman. Chapel Hill: The University of North Carolina Press, pp. 133-164.
In a panel discussion Jackson mentions that "the homeland of [W's] imagination was the Delta South" (p. 150).

110a. Johnson, Albert. "The Negro in American Films: Some Recent Works," in Black Films and Film-Makers. Ed. Lindsay Patterson. New York: Dodd, Mead, pp. 153-181.
Reprint of 1965.85a.

111. Jones, Anne Hudson. "The Plight of the Modern Outsider: A Comparative Study of Dostoevsky's Crime and Punishment, Camus's L'Etranger, and Wright's The Outsider." Dissertation Abstracts International, 36 (July), 317A.
Abstracts a University of North Carolina dissertation. An anti-hero in the tradition of Raskolnikov and Meursault, Cross Damon is always fully aware he is an outsider. His quest for a personal value system is a far more graphic emblem of the position of the modern outsider than either Dostoevsky or Camus presents.

But the very futility of his quest indicates only that there is no resolution yet for the problem of attaining metaphysical freedom.

112. Justus, James H. "Fiction: The 1930s to the Present," in American Literary Scholarship: An Annual/1973. Ed. James Woodress. Durham, N. C.: Duke University Press, pp. 258-303.
Mentions W briefly (p. 271).

113. Kaname, Hiroshi. "Native Son Ron--Hiyokuatsusha no Boryoku to Naimengaika" ["Native Son: The Violence and Frustration of a Racial Victim"]. Osaka Furitsu Daigaku Eibei Bungaku Kenkyu to Kansho [University of Osaka Prefecture Studies in British and American Literature], 22 (April), 71-93.
Bigger Thomas should be considered a victim of the racial problem in the United States rather than a criminal. NS is a successful protest novel because of W's profound psychological probing of the victim. [Y. H.]

114. Kent, George E. "Maya Angelou's I Know Why the Caged Bird Sings and Black Autobiographical Tradition." Kansas Quarterly, 7 (Summer), 72-78.
Includes discussion of W's black rebel-outsider figure.

115. Kibler, James et al. "A Checklist of Scholarship on Southern Literature for 1974." Mississippi Quarterly, 28 (Spring), 219-261.
Lists twelve items on W (pp. 255-256).

116. King, Bruce and Kolawole Ogungbesan. "Introduction," in their A Celebration of Black and African Writing. Zaria and Ibadan: Ahmadu Bello University Press and Oxford University Press, pp. viii-xx.
Comments on W and NS, noting the novel's environmental determinism and Marxism (pp. xii-xiii).

117. Kinnamon, Keneth. "Black Writers of the Thirties. By James O. Young." Journal of English and Germanic Philology, 74 (January), 151-154.
Mentions TMBV and discusses Young's treatment of W's relation to Communism.

118. Klotz, Marvin and Richard Abcarian. "Questions," in their The Experience of Fiction. New York: St. Martin's Press, p. 203.
Reprint of 1973.4.

119. _____. "Richard Wright, 'The Man Who Lived Underground,'" in their Instructor's Manual to Accompany The Ex-

perience of Fiction. New York: St. Martin's Press, pp. 12-15.
Reprint of 1973.5.

120. Labovitz, Sherman. Attitudes Toward Blacks Among Jews: Historical Antecedents and Current Concerns. San Francisco: R and E Research Associates, p. 20.
Quotes from BB on black anti-Semitism.

121. Lank, David S. "Native Son." PMLA, 90 (January), 122-123.
Replies to Paul N. Siegel's "The Conclusion of Richard Wright's Native Son" by arguing that Boris Max's impersonal, rhetorical conceptualizing of Bigger's situation ignores its human actuality. Bigger, on the other hand, "accepts himself finally as a full human being."

122. Leab, Daniel J. From Sambo to Superspade: The Black Experience in Motion Pictures. Boston: Houghton Mifflin, pp. 168-169.
Includes a paragraph on NS, unfavorable in its estimate, and a still photograph from the film with a caption.

123. Lee, Brian and Mark Leaf. "American Literature: The Twentieth Century." The Year's Work in English Studies 1973. Ed. James Redmond. Vol. 54, pp. 425-465.
Contains a notice of Richard Wright: Impressions and Perspectives edited by David Ray and Robert M. Farnsworth (p. 456).

124. Lindberg, John. "'Black Aesthetic': Minority or Mainstream?" The North American Review, 260 (Winter), 48-52.
Comments on NS, BB, LD, "The Man Who Went to Chicago," and "The Man Who Lived Underground."

124a. Linton, Calvin D., ed. The Bicentennial Almanac. Nashville, Tennessee: Thomas Nelson, 1975, p. 393.
Obituary note.

125. Litz, A. Walton. "Richard Wright (1908-1960)," in his Major American Short Stories. New York: Oxford University Press, pp. 822-823.
Biographical sketch. Lists six secondary items.
Reprinted: 1980.151.

125a. Maekawa, Yuji. "A Study of Richard Wright: Flight from 'Uncle Tom.'" Nagasaki Zosen Daigaku Kenkyu Hokoku [Nagasaki Naval Architectural College Study Report], 16 (August), 112-121.
An analysis of black people's flight from "Uncle Tom" and their life after

the flight. Big Boy, Mann, and Silas are involved in a "radical conflict" as are Taylor and Sue in a "class conflict." The frequency of murder is analyzed historically and sociologically; argues that white people's deaths are caused by the white people themselves. In English. [Y. H. and T. K.]

126. Margolies, Edward. "On Black Writing." Dissent, 22 (Fall), 407-409.
Unfavorable review of Roger Rosenblatt's Black Fiction mentioning its treatment of "Big Boy Leaves Home" and NS.

127. Materassi, Mario. "La conciliazione degli opposti in 'Notes of a Native Son' di James Baldwin." Paragone, 26 (April), 3-18.
Notes Baldwin's "explicit recognition of his ideological and literary sonship" (p. 3) to W.
Reprinted: 1977.220.

128. Matheus, John F. "Prosatori Negri Americani del Novecento. By Piero Boitani." CLA Journal, 18 (March), 455-457.
Review noting that Boitani devotes forty-one pages to W.

129. Matthews, Geraldine O. and the African-American Materials Project Staff. Black American Writers, 1773-1949: A Bibliography and Union List. Boston: G. K. Hall, p. 175.
Lists three works by W.

130. McCarthy, Harold T. "Wright, Richard, 1908-1960," in Contemporary Literary Criticism. Ed. Carolyn Riley. Vol. 3. Detroit: Gale, p. 545.
Partial reprint of 1972.149.

131. Mendelson, Maurice O. "Einige Bemerkungen zur Amerikanistik in der DDR." Zeitschrift für Anglistik und Amerikanistik, 23, pp. 189-204.
Lists W as a writer who has attracted critical attention during the recent increase of interest in American literature in East Germany (p. 193).

132. Miller, James E. "American Literature," in The World Book Encyclopedia. Ed. William H. Nault. Vol. 1. Chicago: Field Enterprises, pp. 394-404b.
Mentions W briefly (pp. 397, 404a).
Reprinted: 1977.230; 1978.170; 1979.176.

133. Minakawa, Soichi. "Richard Wright no Rito" ["Richard Wright's Rift with the Party"]. Shin Nihon Bungaku [New Japanese Literature], 30 (August), 48-57.
One of the reasons for leaving the

Communist Party was W's inability to pursue his literary as well as political activities. Another more private reasons was his marriage to a white woman, which had provoked antagonism from the white members. [Y. H.]

134. Mitchell, Louis D. "Richard Wright's Artistry." The Crisis, 82 (February), 62-66.
Analyzes the style, point of view, themes, and plot development of NS, O, and BB. As stylist W was "terse, nervous, impatient, and rhetorically naturalistic."

135. Moon, Henry Lee. "Spingarn Medal," in The World Book Encyclopedia. Ed. William H. Nault. Vol. 18. Chicago: Field Enterprises, p. 617.
Reprint of 1960.201.

136. Moore, Jack B. "Richard Wright's Dream of Africa." Journal of African Studies, 2 (Summer), 231-245.
Analyzes W's ambivalent attitude toward Africa. Considers LT, NS, BP, CC, and LD.

137. Moss, Robert F. "The Arts in Black America." Saturday Review, 3 (15 November), 12-19.
Lists NS in a chronology.

138. Ndu, Pol Nnamuzikam. "The Mythology of Ancestry: Character in Black American Literature (1789-1974)." Dissertation Abstracts International, 35 (April), 6726-A.
The final chapter treats W's exile and its literary consequences.

139. Null, Gary. Black Hollywood: The Negro in Motion Pictures. Secaucus, N. J.: The Citadel Press, pp. 156-157.
Comments on the film NS and includes two photographs. "The film's subject matter made it an important movie, although poor acting and directing caused it to lose much of the urgency of the original book."

140. Obichere, Boniface I. "Afro-Americans in Africa: Recent Experiences," in Black Homeland/Black Diaspora: Cross Currents of the African Relationship. Ed. Jacob Drachler. Port Washington, N. Y.: Kennikat Press, pp. 15-39.
Mentions W briefly (p. 26).

141. Ostendorf, Bernard. "Black Poetry, Blues, and Folklore: Double Consciousness in Afro-American Oral Culture." Amerikastudien/American Studies, 20, pp. 209-259.
Study of black oral traditions in literary form citing W's comment that

oral cultures hold "the usable past" of literate cultures (p. 228).

142. Page, James A. "Wright, Richard 1908-1960," in Contemporary Literary Criticism. Ed. Carolyn Riley. Vol. 3. Detroit: Gale, p. 546.
Partial reprint of 1973.234.

142a. Patterson, Lindsay. "Introduction," in his Black Films and Film-Makers. New York: Dodd, Mead, pp. ix-xiv.
Mentions briefly the novel NS.

142b. _____. "It's Gonna Blow Whitey's Mind," in his Black Films and Film-Makers. New York: Dodd, Mead, pp. 95-100.
Reprint of 1968.177a.

143. Peden, William. The American Short Story: Continuity and Change 1940-1975. Second edition. Boston: Houghton Mifflin, pp. 13, 137, 138, 139, 140, 141-142, 143.
Reprint of 1975.144 and brief mention of W elsewhere.

144. _____. "The Black Explosion." Studies in Short Fiction, 12 (Summer), 231-241.
Contains a paragraph on W (pp. 233-234) pointing out that even though the characters are one-dimensional, "as a sad and moving testimonial to the evil of racism and its effect upon a gifted and bitterly disillusioned human being, UTC and EM constitute a disturbing and towering and permanent landmark in the history of Black-White relations, and their influence upon the younger generation of Black writers was and continues to be profound."
Reprinted: 1975.143.
Partially reprinted: 1980.198.

145. Peplow, Michael W. and Arthur P. Davis. "Chronology: 1910-1940," in their The New Negro Renaissance: An Anthology. Rinehart Editions 153. New York: Holt, Rinehart and Winston, pp. 505-516.
Lists UTC and NS.

146. _____. "The Critical Debate," in their The New Negro Renaissance: An Anthology. Rinehart Editions 153. New York: Holt, Rinehart and Winston, pp. 464-466.
Mentions NS briefly.

147. _____. "Introduction," in their The New Negro Renaissance: An Anthology. Rinehart Editions 153. New York: Holt, Rinehart and Winston, pp. xix-xxxi.
Cites the publication of NS as the end of the Renaissance (p. xxi).

148. Petesch, Donald A. "The Role of Folklore in the Modern Black Novel." Kansas Quarterly, 7 (Summer), 99-110.
Includes comments on LT, BB, NS, and LD.

149. Porter, Carolyn. "Black Writers of the Thirties. By James O. Young; Documentary Expression and Thirties America. By William Stott." The Georgia Review, 29 (Spring), 245-250.
Praises Young's treatment of W (p. 246).

150. Primeau, Ronald. "Blake's Chimney Sweeper as Afro-American Minstrel." Bulletin of the New York Public Library, 78 (Summer), 418-430.
Argues that Blake's method of confronting oppression is similar to methods used by W, Hughes, and other influential black writers.

151. Przemecka, Irena. "Search for Identity in the American Negro Novel." Kwartalnik Neofilologiczny, 22 (Spring), 185-190.
Comments on the identity theme in BB, NS, and O. Notes also the W-Baldwin controversy.

152. Pyros, John. "Richard Wright: A Black Novelist's Experience in Film." Negro American Literature Forum, 9 (Summer), 53-54.
Recounts the story of the filming of NS in the context of black films past and present. Pyros follows closely Webb's account in Richard Wright: A Biography.

153. Ray, David. "Wright's Vision. The Progressive, 39 (March), 43-44.
Favorable review of Michel Fabre's The Unfinished Quest of Richard Wright calling it the most important work on W yet to appear. It is particularly valuable for an understanding of the relation between literature and politics.

154. Reed, Ishmael. "Native Son Lives!" Literary Cavalcade, 28 (November), 10, 40.
Brief article accompanying a reprint of the play NS with photographs from the original production. Reed compares the novel NS to fugitive slave narratives and stresses the work's contemporary relevance.
Reprinted in revised form: 1978.203.

155. _____. "The Old Music." City Magazine (January).
Calls NS the best novel about the results of the Great Migration.
Reprinted: 1978.204.

156. Rees, Robert A. and Barry Menikoff. "Richard Wright, 'The Man Who Lived Underground,'" in their Instructor's Manual to Accompany The Short Story: An Introductory Anthology. Second edition. Boston: Little, Brown, p. 7.
Brief analysis of the story as "an ironic and mordant treatment of the Christian theme of rebirth."

157. _____. "Richard Wright," in their The Short Story: An Introductory Anthology. Second edition. Boston: Little, Brown, p. 126.
Reprint of 1969.206, 207.

158. Reese, Mildred L. America and Us. Philadelphia: Dorrance, p. 18.
Mentions W briefly.

159. Riley, Roberta. "'The High White Empty Building with Black Windows': Insights from the Work of Richard Wright." Illinois Schools Journal, 55 (Fall), 34-38.
Explains in general terms W's major themes, especially blindness, alienation, and role playing. The problems W identifies are still present.

160. Rivière, Jean. "French Contributions," in American Literary Scholarship: An Annual/1973. Ed. James Woodress. Durham, N. C.: Duke University Press, pp. 439-441.
Mentions NS briefly (p. 440).

161. Robinson, Herbert Spencer. "Wright, Richard," in his The Dictionary of Biography. Revised and enlarged edition. Totowa, N. J.: Rowman and Littlefield, p. 478.
Brief biographical note.

162. Rowell, Charles H. "Poetry, History and Humanism: An Interview with Margaret Walker." Black World, 25 (December), 4-17.
Walker praises W's literary qualities--"this honesty, this toughness, this power and great passion"--but deplores his lack of humanism, his black self-hatred, his excessive admiration of white writers, and his lack of admiration for black writers. She sharply criticizes Constance Webb's biography.

163. _____ et al. "Studies in Afro-American Literature: An Annual Annotated Bibliography, 1974." Obsidian, 1 (Winter), 100-127.
Lists fourteen items on W with cross-references to nine others.

164. Rubin, Louis D., Jr. "Politics and the Novel: George W. Cable and the Genteel Tradition," in his William Elliott

Shoots a Bear: Essays on the Southern Literary Imagination. Baton Rouge: Louisiana State University Press, pp. 61-81.
Mentions W briefly (p. 81).

165. Rubin, Steven J. "Contemporary American Ethnic Literature in France." The Journal of Ethnic Studies, 3 (Spring), 95-98.
Mentions recent French scholarly interest in W, particularly that of Michel Fabre.

166. Rush, Theressa Gunnels, Carol Fairbanks Myers, and Esther Spring Arata. Black American Writers Past and Present: A Biographical and Bibliographical Dictionary. Vol. 2. Metuchen, N. J.: The Scarecrow Press, pp. 786-791.
Biographical sketch of W and a classified checklist of primary and secondary sources.

167. Rushing, Andrea Benton. "Images of Black Women in Afro-American Poetry." Black World, 24 (September), 18-30.
Quotes W that "the Negro is America's metaphor."
Reprinted: 1978.216.

168. Ryan, Pat M. "African Continuities/Discontinuities in Black American Writing." Afro-American Studies: An Interdisciplinary Journal, 3, pp. 235-244.
Notes African influences in BP, CC, and WML.

168a. Satow, Toyoshi. "Some Comments on Native Son." Obirin Daigaku Eibei Bungakuhen Kiyo [Obirin Studies in English and American Literature], 15 (30 April), 183-195.
Contends that Bigger was "a typical negro" and that "even murder could seem a realistic alternative" in the situation in which he was placed. In English. [Y. H. and T. K.]

169. Savory, Jerold J. "Bigger Thomas and the Book of Job: The Epigraph to Native Son." Negro American Literature Forum, 9 (Summer), 55-56.
The numerous parallels between Job and Bigger demonstrate that the epigraph to the novel is apposite. By distinguishing between the Job of the frame story (Job 1-2, 42) and the Job of the "poem" (Job 3-31), Savory shows that the latter, like Bigger, achieves his freedom and humanity through defiance and rebellion.

170. Schenck, William Z. "Butterfield, Stephen. Black Autobiography in America." Library Journal, 100 (1 March), 495.
Mentions W briefly.

171. _____. "Smith, Sidonie. Where I'm Bound: patterns in black American autobiography." Library Journal, 100 (1 January), 59.
Mentions NS briefly.

172. Schultz, Elizabeth. "To Be Black and Blue: The Blues Genre in Black American Autobiography." Kansas Quarterly, 7 (Summer), 81-96.
Places BB in the blues tradition because it is a sensory account of life and concludes with a sense of potential rather than a clear end in view.

173. Scott, Nathan A., Jr. "Black Fiction Roger Rosenblatt; Black Autobiography Stephen Butterfield." Commonweal, 102 (6 June), 186-187.
Mentions W briefly in connection with both books.

174. Scruggs, Charles W. "The Importance of the City in Native Son." Rocky Mountain Review of Language and Literature, 29 (Summer), 73.
Abstract of a paper to be read at a scholarly meeting. Scruggs will explore "man's need for the human community and the city's failure to provide it" in NS.

175. Semel, Ann. "Richard Wright," in her Black Short Fiction: A Critical Commentary. New York: Monarch Press, pp. 43-48.
Biographical sketch and analyses of "Almos' a Man," "Bright and Morning Star," "Big Boy Leaves Home," and "The Man Who Killed a Shadow."

176. Shrodes, Caroline, Clifford Josephson, and James R. Wilson. "Richard Wright," in their Reading for Rhetoric: Applications to Writing. Third edition. New York: Macmillan, p. 638.
Biographical note to accompany an excerpt from BB.
Reprinted: 1979.233.

177. Siegel, Paul N. "Native Son." PMLA, 90 (March), 294-295.
In this rejoinder to David Lank's comments on "The Conclusion of Richard Wright's Native Son," Siegel argues that Boris Max is compassionate and sensitive toward Bigger, understanding him as an individual, not merely as the embodiment of a social problem.

178. Simms, L. Moody, Jr. "In the Shadow of Richard Wright: William Attaway." Notes on Mississippi Writers, 8 (Spring), 13-18.
Notes that W's reputation has eclipsed that of other black writers

from Mississippi.

179. Simonson, Harold P. "Richard Wright," in his Trio: A Book of Stories, Plays, and Poems. Fourth edition. New York: Harper and Row, pp. 738-739.
Biographical note.
Reprinted: 1980.229.

180. Simpson, Lewis P. "The Southern Reaction to Modernism," in Southern Literary Study: Problems and Possibilities. Chapel Hill: University of North Carolina Press, pp. 48-68.
Mentions W briefly (p. 65).
Reprinted: 1980.230.

181. Skerrett, Joseph T., Jr. "Take My Burden Up: Three Studies in Psychobiographical Criticism and Afro-American Fiction." Dissertation Abstracts International, 36 (December), 3719A.
Abstracts a Yale University dissertation discussing The Autobiography of an Ex-Coloured Man, Ellison's short fiction, and BB and NS with regard to the psychological ramifications of the act of writing.

182. Smith, Barbara. "Rich Literature." The New Republic, 172 (4 and 11 January), 28-29.
Review of Roger Rosenblatt's Black Fiction mentioning NS briefly.

183. Smith, Cynthia Janis. "Escape and Quest in the Literature of Black Americans." Dissertation Abstracts International, 36 (July), 287A.
Abstracts a Yale University dissertation noting that W is one of several writers concerned with the conflict between biblical imagery and religious experience.

183a. Smith, William Gardner. The Stone Face. Chatham, N. J.: The Chatham Bookseller, p. 135.
Reprint of 1963.171a.

184. Stadler, Quandra Prettyman. "Afterword," in her Out of Our Lives: A Selection of Contemporary Black Fiction. Washington, D. C.: Howard University Press, pp. 297-298.
Expresses a personal tribute to W and includes a quotation from BB.

185. _____. "Foreword," in her Out of Our Lives: A Selection of Contemporary Black Fiction. Washington, D. C.: Howard University Press, pp. ix-xii.
Assesses briefly W's position in the development of black short fiction.

186. Starr, Alvin J. "The Concept of

Fear in the Works of Stephen Crane and Richard Wright." Studies in Black Literature, 6 (Summer), 6-9.
Compares the innkeeper in "Big Black Good Man" to the Swede in "The Blue Hotel": both have pathological fears. Also compares "The Man Who Lived Underground" to "The Open Boat" and NS to The Red Badge of Courage.

187. _____. "The Influence of Stephen Crane, Theodore Dreiser, and James T. Farrell on the Fiction of Richard Wright." Dissertation Abstracts International, 35 (March), 6162-A.
Abstracts a Kent State University dissertation examining the influence of two Crane stories on two W stories, the indebtedness of NS to The Red Badge of Courage, the influence of An American Tragedy on NS, the influence of Studs Lonigan: A Trilogy on LT, and the impact of a speech by Farrell on W's literary development.

188. Stoller, Paul. "Black Speech in Literature," in his Black American English: Its Background and Its Usage in the Schools and in Literature. New York: Dell, pp. 191-194.
Cites W's use of Black English in the dialogue of NS and BB.

189. Suzuki, Mikio. "Bigger no Tohi no Imi--America no Musuko niokeru' ["The Meaning of Bigger's Escape in Native Son"]. Waseda Daigaku Kyoyo Shogaku Kenkyu [Waseda University General Studies], No. 49 (June), 75-90.
Bigger's escape from white society is an epitome of the struggle for black Americans in achieving freedom. Far from a fantasy, his escape signals a realistic and ultimately existentialist action. [Y. H.]

190. Targ, William. Indecent Pleasures: The Life and Colorful Times of William Targ. New York: Macmillan, pp. 66-67.
Discusses his friendship and editorial relation with W in Chicago, New York (especially), and Paris.

191. Thompson, G. R. "Poe," in American Literary Scholarship: An Annual/1973. Ed. James Woodress. Durham, N. C.: Duke University Press, pp. 32-64.
Mentions favorably two articles on W and Poe.

192. Thum, Marcella. Exploring Black America: A History and Guide. New York: Atheneum, pp. 255, 256.
Sketches W's early life and career.

193. Timko, Michael. "'Big Boy Leaves Home' Richard Wright," in his 29 Short Stories: An Introductory Anthology. New

York: Knopf, pp. 56-57.
  Biographical-critical headnote. Timko
  reprints Blyden Jackson's "Richard
  Wright in a Moment of Truth" on pp.
  382-393 and comments briefly on p.
  362.
  Reprinted: 1979.263.

194. Toppin, Edgar Allan. "Negro," in
The World Book Encyclopedia. Ed. William
H. Nault. Vol. 14. Chicago: Field Enter-
prises, pp. 106-112f.
  Reprint of 1969.230.

195. Towns, Saundra. "The New Black
Criticism." The Nation, 220 (26 April),
504-506.
  Review of Addison Gayle, Jr.'s The
  Way of the New World with a paragraph
  on NS and Gayle's treatment of it.

196. Virágos, Zsolt. A Négerség és az
Amerikai Irodalom. Budapest: Akadémiai
Kiadó, pp. 9, 58, 104, 130, 135, 136,
150, 229, 240, 280, 288-313, 314, 316,
317, 322, 329, 339, 350, 359.
  The main section on W places him in
  the protest tradition which succeeded
  the exotic primitivism of the Harlem
  Renaissance, analyzes and summarizes
  NS noting its literary naturalism and
  ideological Marxism, and discusses
  BB. Viragos compares W to Dreiser and
  Stowe. Elsewhere Viragos quotes WML,
  emphasizes W's protest, and relates
  him to Hughes, Ellison, Baldwin, and
  Cleaver.

197. Wagner, Linda Welshimer. "Poetry:
The 1930s to the Present," in American
Literary Scholarship: An Annual/1973.
Ed. James Woodress. Durham, N. C.: Duke
University Press, pp. 329-368.
  Mentions W briefly (p. 360).

198. Walker, Alice. "A Sudden Trip Home
in the Spring," in Black-Eyed Susans:
Classic Stories by and About Black
Women. Ed. Mary Helen Washington. Anchor
Books. Garden City, N. Y.: Anchor Press/
Doubleday, pp. 141-154.
  Reprint of 1971.309.

199. Waniek, Marilyn N. "The Space Where
Sex Should Be: Toward a Definition of
the Black American Literary Tradition."
Studies in Black Literature, 6 (Fall),
7-13.
  Analyzes lack of sex in NS, Invisible
  Man, and The Autobiography of an Ex-
  Coloured Man. Instead, these novels
  emphasize racial confrontation.

200. Ward, A. C. "Wright, Richard," in
his Longman Companion to Twentieth Century Literature. Second edition. London:
Longman, p. 583.
  Reprint of 1970.352.

201. Washington, Mary Helen. "Introduc-
tion," in her Black-Eyed Susans: Classic
Stories by and About Black Women. Anchor
Books. Garden City, N. Y.: Anchor Press/
Doubleday, pp. ix-xxxii.
  Mentions W briefly (p. ix).

202. White, John. "The Two-ness of Afro-
America." The London Times Literary
Supplement (18 July), p. 810.
  Mentions W and quotes from Butter-
  field's praise of BB.

203. Whittemore, Reed. William Carlos
Williams: Poet from Jersey. Boston:
Houghton Mifflin, p. 247.
  Mentions W as a contributor to New
  Masses.

204. Williams, John A. "The Crisis in
American Letters." The Black Scholar, 6
(June), 67-72.
  Mentions W (p. 68) and Bigger Thomas
  (p. 71).

205. Willingham, John R. "Minireviews."
CEA Critic, 37 (May), 39.
  Contains a notice of Houston A.
  Baker's Twentieth Century Interpreta-
  tions of Native Son.

1976

1. Abdul, Raoul. "The Negro Playwright
on Broadway," in Anthology of the Afro-
American in the Theatre: A Critical
Approach. Ed. Lindsay Patterson. Corn-
wells Heights, Pa.: The Publishers
Agency, pp. 59-63.
  Reprint of 1969.1.

2. Abrahams, Roger D. Talking Black.
Series in Sociolinguistics, ed. Roger W.
Shuy. Rowley, Mass.: Newbury House, p.
98.
  Includes LT in the bibliography.

3. Achtert, Walter S. and Eileen Mack-
esy, comps. 1974 MLA Abstracts of Arti-
cles in Scholarly Journals. Vol. 1. New
York: Modern Language Association, pp.
203-205.
  Abstracts of articles on W by Lola J.
  Amis, David P. Demarest, Jr., Mildred
  W. Everette, Robert Felgar, Jean-
  Francois Gounard, Don B. Graham,
  Seymour L. Gross, Kichung Kim, Phyl-
  lis R. Klotman, Paul N. Siegel, and
  Adrian Weiss.

4. Adelstein, Michael E. and Jean G.
Pival. The Writing Commitment. New York:
Harcourt Brace Jovanovich, pp. 115-116,
215.
  The authors quote from UTC and NS to
  illustrate stylistic points.

5. Alexander, Margaret Walker, Louis

Rubin, Blyden Jackson, T. D. Young, and Lewis Simpson. "A Native Son," in A Climate for Genius. Ed. Robert L. Phillips, Jr. Jackson: Mississippi Library Commission, pp. 67-79.

    Transcript of a panel discussion focusing on the issues of sentimentality in UTC, W's links to the South (especially to the folk art traditions), and the tension between Marxism and existentialism. Alexander recounts her contact with W and discusses the types of anger in his life and work.

6. Anon. Afro-American Studies. New Haven, Conn.: Yale University, pp. 2, 6.

    Describes the newly acquired W papers and announces the "Richard Wright Lectures" on black literature to be given each spring by a visiting scholar or artist.

7. Anon. "American Literature and Two Revolutions," in 20th Century American Literature: A Soviet View. Moscow: Progress Publishers, pp. 19-47.

    Lists W among writers of "uneven quality" whose best work was written in response to workers' problems (p. 42).

8. Anon. Bibliographic Guide to Black Studies: 1975. Boston: G. K. Hall, pp. 315-316.

    Lists three secondary items and four manuscript collections concerning W in the New York Public Library.

9. Anon. Bibliographic Guide to Black Studies: 1976. Boston: G. K. Hall, pp. 334-335.

    Lists three primary (translations) and two secondary items concerning W in the New York Public Library.

10. Anon. "Book Ends." The New York Times Book Review (4 April), p. 41.

    Includes a denunciation of the removal of BB and other books from libraries in a Long Island school district.

11. Anon. "Deux cents ans de littérature américaine." Etudes Anglaises, 29 (July-September), front cover.

    W is one of the dozen American writers whose pictures appear.

12. Anon. Dictionary Catalog of the Jesse E. Moorland Collection of Negro Life and History: First Supplement. Vol. 3. Boston: G. K. Hall, pp. 625-626.

    Reproduces thirteen catalog cards on W.

13. Anon. Dust jacket of Zoku Brakku Boi. By Richard Wright. Trans. Takao Kitamura. Tokyo: Kenkyusha.

    Contains a blurb for the Japanese translation of the work later published as AH.

14. Anon. Index Translationum 26. Paris: Unesco, pp. 494, 651.

    Lists translations of BB into Italian and LD into German.

15. Anon. "Library Notes: Richard Wright." AB Bookman's Weekly, 57 (10 May), 2659.

    Describes the W archive acquired by the Yale University Library.

16. Anon. "Native Son," in Masterplots. Ed. Frank N. Magill. Revised edition. Vol. 7. Englewood Cliffs, N. J.: Salem Press, pp. 4152-4154.

    Reprint of 1949.41.

16a. Anon. "Program," PMLA, 91 (November), 996-1057.

    Lists a paper by Barbara Smith on sexual politics in W's fiction.

17. Anon. "Richard Wright (1908-1960)." Yale Library Associates Newsletter, December, p. [2].

    Describes the W papers acquired by Yale.

18. Anon. "Union Resists Book-Banners in Long Island District." American Teacher, 60 (May), 3.

    Notes that BB was one of the books removed from school libraries and classrooms because of pressure from a "traditionalist" group.

19. Anon. "Wright, Richard," in Encyclopaedia Britannica: Micropaedia. Ed. Warren E. Preece. Vol. 10. Chicago: Encyclopaedia Britannica, p. 762.

    Biographical sketch.

20. Anon. "Wright (Richard)," in Petit Larousse illustré. Paris: Librairie Larousse, p. 1786.

    Brief biographical note.

21. Anzilotti, Rolando. "Foreign Scholarship: Italian Contributions," in American Literary Scholarship: An Annual/1974. Ed. James Woodress. Durham, N. C.: Duke University Press, pp. 447-452.

    Mentions W as treated in Loretta Valtz Manucci's I negri americani dalla Depressione al dopoguerra: Esperienze sociali e documenti letterari.

22. Arata, Esther Spring and Nicholas John Rotoli. Black American Playwrights, 1800 to the Present: A Bibliography. Metuchen, N. J.: The Scarecrow Press, pp. 213-215.

Contains forty-five items pertaining to W.

23. Areman, Zita. "Freedom, 1976." American Teacher, 60 (May), 6.
Protests the banning of books by W and others in a Long Island school district.

24. Arensberg, Liliane K. "Death as Metaphor of Self in I Know Why the Caged Bird Sings." CLA Journal, 20 (December), 273-291.
Mentions briefly BB (p. 277).

25. Ashour, Radwa M. "The Search for a Black Poetics: A Study of Afro-American Critical Writings." Dissertation Abstracts International, 36 (May), 7406-A.
Considers "Blueprint for Negro Writing" as a major effort "to write a Black literary manifesto from a Marxist perspective."

26. Baker, Houston A., Jr. "On the Criticism of Black American Literature: One View of the Black Aesthetic," in his Reading Black: Essays in the Criticism of African, Caribbean, and Black American Literature. Africana Studies and Research Center Monograph Series No. 4. Philadelphia and Ithaca, N. Y.: University of Pennsylvania Afro-American Studies Program and Cornell University Africana Studies and Research Center, pp. 48-58.
Discusses treatments of W by James O. Young (p. 52), Irving Howe (pp. 52-53), and James Emanuel (p. 55).

27. Baker, Sheridan. The Complete Stylist and Handbook. New York: Crowell, p. 158.
Includes a sentence about W and violence in an exercise on parallelism. See 1976.28.
Reprinted: 1980.37.

28. ____. Instructor's Manual: The Complete Stylist and Handbook. New York: Crowell, p. 34.
Includes an improved version of a sentence about W and violence in an exercise on parallelism. See 1976.27.
Reprinted: 1977.53.

29. Baldwin, James. The Devil Finds Work. New York: Dial Press, p. 33.
Relates his leaving church to see a matinee performance of the play NS. Praises Canada Lee's performance as Bigger.

30. ____. "James Baldwin on the Negro Actor," in Anthology of the Afro-American in the Theatre: A Critical Approach. Ed. Lindsay Patterson. Cornwells Heights, Pa.: The Publishers Agency, pp.

127-130.
Reprint of 1961.117.

31. Baron, Dennis E. "The Syntax of Perception in Richard Wright's Native Son." Language and Style, 9 (Winter), 17-28.
Analyzes syntactic patterns involving perception and cognition by Bigger to show his progress from blindness to sight. His failure to perceive directly and clearly leads to the killing of Mary, which in turn results in self-knowledge. The analysis also clarifies the relation between author, narrator, and protagonist.

32. Barrett, Virginia, Dorothy Evans, Lorraine Henry, Jennifer Jordan, and Vattel T. Rose. "An Annual Bibliography of Afro-American Literature, 1975, With Selected Bibliographies of African and Caribbean Literature." CLA Journal, 20 (September), 94-131.
Lists nine items on W (p. 107).

33. Barton, Rebecca Chalmers. Black Voices in American Fiction 1900-1930. Oakdale, N. Y.: Dowling College, p. 5.
Mentions W briefly.

34. Beards, Richard. "Gayle, Addison, Jr. The Way of the New World: The Black Novel in America; Jackson, Blyden, and Louis Rubin, Jr. Black Poetry in America: Two Essays in Historical Interpretation; Rosenblatt, Roger. Black Fiction." Journal of Modern Literature, 5, No. 4, pp. 582-584.
Comments on Rosenblatt's treatment of NS and "Big Boy Leaves Home."

35. Benston, Kimberly W. Baraka: The Renegade and the Mask. New Haven, Conn.: Yale University Press, pp. 53, 169.
Quotes W on the black writer's relation to Marxism and compares Clay in Dutchman to Bigger Thomas.

36. Benton, Mallard W., Jr. "The Dark and the Feeling: Reflections on Black American Writers and Their Works. By Clarence Major." CLA Journal, 19 (June), 577-578.
Most of this review is a refutation of Major's treatment of W.

37. Bl.[air], Wa.[lter] et al. "Literature, Western," in Encyclopaedia Britannica: Macropaedia. Ed. Warren E. Preece. Vol. 10. Chicago: Encyclopaedia Britannica, pp. 1086-1264.
Reprint of 1954.80.

38. Blake, Clarence and Donald F. Martin. Quiz Book on Black America. Boston: Houghton Mifflin, pp. 71-72.
Includes a question on W and NS.

39. Bone, Robert. "The Grotesque in American Negro Fiction: Jean Toomer, Richard Wright, and Ralph Ellison. By Fritz Gysin." American Literature, 48 (May), 251-252.
Praises Gysin's treatment of NS and "The Man Who Lived Underground."

40. Bontemps, Arna. "The Black Contribution to American Letters: Part I," in The Black American Reference Book. Ed. Mabel M. Smythe. Englewood Cliffs, N. J.: Prentice-Hall, pp. 741-766.
Reprint of 1966.23.

40a. Bracey, John H., Jr. "Black Power," in Dictionary of American History. Revised edition. Ed. Louise Bilebof Ketz. Vol. 1. New York: Scribner's, p. 316.
Mentions briefly BP.

41. Brisbane, Robert H. "Black Protest in America," in The Black American Reference Book. Ed. Mabel M. Smythe. Englewood Cliffs, N. J.: Prentice-Hall, pp. 537-579.
Mentions the influence of W on younger black novelists (p. 571).

42. Brown, Lloyd W. "Recent Studies in Black American Literature." Obsidian, 2 (Summer), 85-90.
Mentions Bigger Thomas.

43. Bryant, Jerry H. "Wright, Ellison, Baldwin--Exorcising the Demon." Phylon, 37 (June), 174-188.
Compares and contrasts NS, Invisible Man, and Go Tell It on the Mountain. Each contributed to the present black literary climate.

43a. Bryer, Jackson R., Eddy Dow, Philip R. Headings, James Nagel, Matthew O'Brien, and Joseph V. Ridgely, with the help of Joanne Giza and Donald Wharton. "American Literature," in 1974 MLA International Bibliography. Vol. I. New York: Modern Language Association, pp. 140-194.
Lists twenty-four items on W.

44. Burks, Mary Fair. "The First Black Literary Magazine in American Letters." CLA Journal, 19 (March), 318-321.
Calls Martin R. Delany's Henry Blake "the prototype of Bigger Thomas."

45. Burns, Landon C., Jr. "The Second Supplement (1976) of a Cross-Referenced Index of Short Fiction Anthologies and Author-Title Listing." Studies in Short Fiction, 13 (Spring), 113-276.
Lists two reprintings of "Big Black Good Man," six reprintings of "Big Boy Leaves Home," four reprintings of "Bright and Morning Star," two reprintings of "Fire and Cloud," two reprintings of "Long Black Song," one reprinting of "The Man Who Killed a Shadow," three reprintings of "The Man Who Lived Underground," one reprinting of "The Man Who Saw the Flood," seven reprintings of "The Man Who Was Almost a Man," and three reprintings of "The Man Who Went to Chicago."

46. C.[abau], J.[acques]. "Wright (Richard)," in La Grande Encyclopédie. Ed. Claude Dubois. Vol. 60. Paris: Librairie Larousse, pp. 12813-12814.
Biographical sketch.

47. Cargill, Oscar. "American Literature," in Collier's Encyclopedia. Ed. William D. Halsey. Vol. 2. New York: Macmillan Educational Corp., pp. 42-72.
Reprint of 1969.49.

48. Cauley, Anne O. "A Definition of Freedom in the Fiction of Richard Wright." CLA Journal, 19 (March), 327-346.
Argues that W believed that dignity is the prime element of freedom both in his writing and personal life. Analyzes in this light LT, "The Man Who Killed a Shadow," BB, NS, UTC, and "The Man Who Lived Underground." W's belief in freedom is generally hopeful in contrast to the pessimism of Cross Damon in O.

49. Cheek, Donald K. Assertive Black . . . Puzzled White. San Luis Obispo, Cal.: Impact Publishers, p. 119.
Uses a quotation from BB as an epigraph to the last chapter, "Lifting the Veil of Color."

50. Cladder, Eleonore and Willi Real. "Möglichkeiten der Lektürearbeit im Englischunterricht des 10. Hauptschuljahres: Richard Wrights Black Boy (Schulausgabe)." Englisch, II, No. 3, pp. 81-96.
Based on a simplified text of BB published by Klett (Easy Readers, Series B), this article compares this version with the original and presents a didactic analysis of the work with a detailed approach to teaching problems.

50a. Collins, Terence George. "A Psychoanalytic Introduction to Reader Response to Racial Literature." Dissertation Abstracts International, 37 (December), 3611A.
W is one of three writers given extended treatment. He subverts the "fantasy of dirt," an element of white racism.

51. Cox, James M. "Black Autobiography in America. By Stephen Butterfield." American Literature, 48 (November), 413-414.
    Mentions W briefly.

52. Coy, Juan José. "La novela actual en los Estados Unidos: notas para un entendimiento de la radicalización literaria del fenómeno dialéctico 'complicidad-inocencia,'" in La anarquía y el orden: una clave interpretativa de la literatura norteamericana. By Javier and Juan José Coy. Madrid: Ediciones José Porrúa Turanzas, pp. 65-90.
    Mentions W briefly (pp. 75, 90).

53. Daniel, Edythe, Edmund J. Farrell, Alfred H. Grommon, Olive Stafford Niles, and Robert C. Pooley. "Discussion, Word Study, The Author," in their Counterpoint in Literature. Glenview, Ill.: Scott, Foresman, p. 145.
    Reprint of 1967.79.

54. Daniel, Walter C. "Challenge Magazine: An Experiment That Failed." CLA Journal, 19 (June), 494-503.
    Analyzes Dorothy West's editorial policy and W's influence as associate editor of New Challenge and author of "Blueprint for Negro Writing."

55. Delmar, P. Jay. "Tragic Patterns in Richard Wright's Uncle Tom's Children." Negro American Literature Forum, 10 (Spring), 3-12.
    Examines each of the stories in the enlarged collection to ascertain flaws of character, elements of action, and imagery which constitute tragic patterns. Big Boy is proud and impulsive; Mann is indecisive and unable to confide in others; Sarah is too sensual; Silas is filled with hate and pride; Reverend Taylor is irresolute; Aunt Sue is unable to choose between opposed alternatives. Stressing the tragic quality of the stories, Delmar de-emphasizes the social and racial themes.

56. D'Itri, Patricia. "Richard Wright in Chicago: Three Novels That Represent a Black Spokesman's Quest for Self Identity." Midwestern Miscellany (Society for the Study of Midwestern Literature Newsletter), 4, pp. 26-33.
    Argues that "a pattern of frustrated black identity can be traced if the sequence of W's first three novels is reversed. BB explains the child's conditioning to racial tension, frustration, and stultification. NS recounts an adolescent's violent explosion out of such frustration, and LT describes the 'adjusted' black adult." In this way W uses his novels to explain the plight of his people.

57. Dixon, Melvin. "Kin of Crossroads." Obsidian, 2 (Winter), 68.
    Poem dedicated to Michel Fabre mentioning W.

58. Dommergues, Pierre. L'Alienation dans le roman américain contemporain. Paris: Union Generale d'Editions, Vol. 1, p. 113; Vol. 2, p. 162.
    Mentions W briefly.

59. Drewry, Cecilia Hodges. "Literature, Afro-American," in Dictionary of American History. Revised edition. Ed. Louise Bilebof Ketz. Vol. 4. New York: Scribner's, pp. 166-167.
    Contains a paragraph on W.

60. Du Bois, W. E. B. The Correspondence of W. E. B. Du Bois. Ed. Herbert Aptheker. Vol. 2. Amherst: University of Massachusetts Press, p. 328.
    In response to an inquiry from New Republic, Du Bois in a letter dated 23 June 1942 includes W in a list of ten recommended contributors to a proposed "Negro supplement" of the magazine.

61. Dyson, Deidra Soyini. "Annual Round-Up Black Theater in America: Chicago." Black World, 25 (April), 71-74.
    Mentions a 1975 production of The Essence of Pathos, a play by Marcus Nelson about W.

62. Eckels, Jon. "I Heard That (For All the Black Boys, Native Sons and the Outsiders, and Brother Will)." The Black Scholar, 7 (January-February), 42.
    Poem comparing W to Paul Robeson, Malcolm X, LeRoi Jones, and Muhammed Ali.

63. Eckhardt, Caroline, James F. Holahan, and David H. Stewart with the assistance of Paul Sorrentino. "The God That Failed," in their The Wiley Reader: Designs for Writing. New York: Wiley, p. 545.
    Headnote to an excerpt from W's essay.
    Reprinted: 1979.84.

64. _____. "Notes on the Authors," in their The Wiley Reader: Designs for Writing. New York: Wiley, pp. 579-581.
    Includes a brief note on W (p. 581).
    Reprinted: 1979.83.

65. Edminston, Susan and Linda D. Cirino. Literary New York: A History and Guide. Boston: Houghton Mifflin, pp. 93, 103, 220, 294, 297-298, 302, 335-336, 350, 361-362.

Notes W's residences in Brooklyn.

66. Elkins, Stanley M. Slavery: A Problem in American Institutional and Intellectual Life. Third edition. Chicago: The University of Chicago Press, pp. 132-133.
Reprint of 1959.81.

67. Ellmann, Richard and Robert O'Clair. "Richard Wright (1908-1960)," in their Modern Poems: An Introduction to Poetry. New York: Norton, p. 301.
Biographical headnote to "Between the World and Me."

68. Fabre, Michel. "The Emergence of Richard Wright by Kenneth [sic] Kinnamon." Comparative Literature Studies, 13 (March), 84-86.
Favorable review. Lacking density of biographical detail, the book contains perceptive analyses of W's early poetry, LT, and UTC. The "Epilogue" is scanty on W's later career, but generally Kinnamon's scholarship is thorough and his view of W as a representative twentieth-century man is valuable.

69. ____. "From The Unfinished Quest of Richard Wright." Yardbird Reader, 5, pp. 5-6.
Reprint of the account of W's dealings with Ebony magazine from 1973.133.

70. ____. "Tendances du roman afro-américain contemporain: vers une esthétique néo-vaudou." Etudes Anglaises, 29 (July-September), 499-509.
Cites "The Man Who Lived Underground" as a surrealistic precursor of the post-modernist mode of recent Afro-American fiction (p. 502).

71. Farrison, W. Edward. "The Waiting Years: Essays on American Negro Literature. By Blyden Jackson." CLA Journal, 20 (December), 303-305.
Gives special praise to Jackson's essay "Richard Wright in a Moment of Truth."

72. Feuser, W. F. "Afro-American Literature and Negritude." Comparative Literature, 28 (Fall), 289-308.
Comments on LD, NS, "The Man Who Lived Underground," O, and BP (pp. 299, 300-301). Discusses W's response to negritude and Africa (pp. 303-304, 305).

73. Ford, Miriam Allen de and Joan S. Jackson. Who Was When? A Dictionary of Contemporaries. Third edition. New York: H. W. Wilson, n. p.
Lists W.

74. Franklin, John Hope. "Negro," in Collier's Encyclopedia. Ed. William D. Halsey. Vol. 17. New York: Macmillan Educational Corporation, pp. 276-293.
Reprint of 1955.43.

75. Freese, Peter. "Die amerikanische Short Story der Gegenwart: Themen, Techniken und Tendenzen," in his Die amerikanische Short Story der Gegenwart. Berlin: Erich Schmidt Verlag, pp. 20-21.
Cites W's claim that "the Negro is America's metaphor" as a major point of departure for contemporary black short story writers.

76. ____. "Auswahlbibliographie," in his Die amerikanische Short Story der Gegenwart. Berlin: Erich Schmidt Verlag, p. 343.
Lists EM among postwar American short story collections.

77. Frémy, Dominique and Michèle Frémy. Quid? Tout pour tous. Paris: Editions Robert Laffont, p. 88.
Reprint of 1963.86.

78. Friedberg, Maurice. "The U.S. in the U. S. S. R.: American Literature Through the Filter of Recent Soviet Publishing and Criticism." Critical Inquiry, 2 (Spring), 519-583.
Explains the guarded assessments of W's achievement by Raisa Orlova and by the Literary Encyclopedia (p. 535, 573-574).

79. Gayle, Addison, Jr. "The Function of Black Criticism at the Present Time," in Reading Black: Essays in the Criticism of African, Caribbean, and Black American Literature. Ed. Houston A. Baker, Jr. Africana Studies and Research Center Monograph Series No. 4. Philadelphia and Ithaca, N. Y.: University of Pennsylvania Afro-American Studies Program and Cornell University Africana Studies and Research Center, pp. 37-40.
Cites W as an authority for the notion that words are weapons.

80. ____. "Notes from an Armchair Philosopher." Black Books Bulletin, 4 (Summer), 52-53.
Responding to Maria K. Mootry's review of his The Way of the New World, Gayle comments on W and offers a definition of the thesis of NS: "the American society is capable of change in relationship to black people—a thesis which no thinking Black person should any longer adhere to."

81. ____. The Way of the New World: The Black Novel in America. Anchor Books.

Garden City, N. Y.: Anchor Press/Double-
day, 412 pp.
   Reprint of 1975.85.

82. Gilenson, B. "A Socialist of the
Emotions: Upton Sinclair," in 20th Cen-
tury American Literature: A Soviet View.
Ed. Raissa Orlava. Moscow: Progress
Publishers, pp. 199-222.
   Briefly mentions W as a writer who,
   like Sinclair, moved from rebellion
   to conformity.

83. Giles, James R. Claude McKay. Boston: Twayne, pp. 24, 30, 31, 140, 144.
   Mentions W several times, including a
   contrast between W's hopelessness and
   McKay's hatred as responses to
   racism.

84. Gilliam, Dorothy Butler. Paul Robeson: All-American. Washington, D. C.:
The New Republic Book Company, pp. 101,
106.
   Notes W's appearance with Robeson at
   the Golden Gate Ballroom in 1940 and
   the recording of "King Joe" in 1942
   [sic].

85. Glenn, Robert W. Black Rhetoric: A
Guide to Afro-American Communication.
Metuchen, N. J.: The Scarecrow Press,
pp. 26, 43, 67, 113, 138.
   Lists five items by W.

86. Goldman, Robert M. and William D.
Crano. "Black Boy and Manchild in the
Promised Land: Content Analysis in the
Study of Value Change Over Time." Journal of Black Studies, 7 (December), 169-
180.
   Concentrates on Manchild in the Promised Land, comparing it to a content
   analysis of BB.

87. Goode, Stephen, ed. The American
Humanities Index for 1975 . Part 2.
Troy, N. Y.: Whitson Publishing Company,
p. 1010.
   Lists four items on W.

88. Gounard, Jean-François. "Le Carrière
mouvementée de Richard Wright." Revue
de l'Université d'Ottawa, 46, pp. 520-
543.
   Biographical-critical summary of W's
   life and career. Gounard attempts to
   convey a full sense of W, the man and
   his work.

89. Grant, William E. "Further Critical
Evaluation of the Work," in Masterplots.
Ed. Frank N. Magill. Revised editon.
Vol. 7. Englewood Cliffs, N. J.: Salem
Press, pp. 4154-4156.
   Examines the psychological, socio-
   logical, and philosophical dimen-
   sions of NS. Psychologically, Bigger

acts out of instinctive fear. Sociologically, the novel centers on the
black-white polarization in American life. Philosophically, the novel
anticipates existentialism in its
portrayal of Bigger's understanding
of the creative and vital significance of his killing of Mary Dalton.

89a. Gresham, Jewell, ed. "James Baldwin
Comes Home." Essence, 7 (June), 55, 80,
82, 85.
   Baldwin comments briefly on his quarrel with W.

90. Gross, Barry. "Art and Act: The
Example of Richard Wright." Obsidian:
Black Literature in Review, 2 (Summer),
5-19.
   Surveys black and white response to
   NS, with special emphasis on Ellison
   and Baldwin. In his own analysis,
   Gross notes that Bigger can act but
   not express himself; W can express
   himself but not act. Compares Bigger
   to Ahab and the killing of Mary to
   the pursuit of the white whale.

91. Haberly, David T. "The Literature of
an Invisible Nation." Journal of Black
Studies, 7 (December), 133-150.
   Quotes W (p. 143) and mentions Bigger
   Thomas (p. 145).

92. Hale, Thomas A. "From Afro-America
to Afro-France: The Literary Triangle
Trade." The French Review, 49 (May),
1089-1096.
   Discusses briefly W's participation
   in Présence Africaine.

93. Hamalian, Linda Bearman. "Richard
Wright's Use of Epigraphs in The Long
Dream." Black American Literature Forum,
10 (Winter), 120-123.
   Analyzes the three epigraphs in relation to the themes of the sections
   which they introduce.

94. Harris, Trudier. "Ceremonial Fagots:
Lynching and Burning Rituals in Black
Literature." Southern Humanities Review,
10 (Summer), 235-247.
   Includes discussion of the lynching
   in "Big Boy Leaves Home," noting its
   ritualistic elements.

95. Haslam, Gerald W. "Three Exotics:
Yone Noguchi, Shiesei Tsuneishi, and
Sadakichi Hartmann." CLA Journal, 19
(March), 362-373.
   Quotes two of W's haiku (p. 368).

96. Haymon, Theresa Lenora Drew. "Alienation in the Life and Works of Richard
Wright." Dissertation Abstracts International, 37 (November), 2871-A.
   Abstracts a Loyola University disser-

tation arguing that the concept of alienation, the struggle between the self and the world, is crucial to W's work. Dialogue, point of view, imagery, and action all relate to this basic human condition.

97. Himes, Chester. My Life of Absurdity: The Autobiography of Chester Himes. Vol. 2. Garden City, N. Y.: Doubleday, pp. 2, 4, 5, 7-8, 22, 23, 34, 35, 40, 53, 61, 74-75, 107, 123, 124, 144, 158, 163-164, 181, 185, 190, 195, 201-202, 214-218, 219, 220, 221, 222-223, 229, 245, 264, 265, 273, 278, 328, 357, 365.
Comments on W during the Paris years, relates his funeral, and evaluates him as an absurdist (pp. 214-218).

98. Hofstadter, Richard, William Miller, Daniel Aaron, Winthrop D. Jordan, and Leon F. Litwack. The United States. Fourth Edition. Englewood Cliffs, N. J.: Prentice-Hall, pp. 525, 526, 550, 560-561.
Reprint of 1970.181. Also mentions and quotes W on the Great Migration.

99. Howard, Daniel F. "Richard Wright 1908-1960," in his The Modern Tradition: An Anthology of Short Stories. Third edition. Boston: Little, Brown, pp. 405-406.
Reprint of 1972.100a. In this edition "The Man Who Was Almost a Man" replaces "Big Boy Leaves Home."

100. _____ and William Plummer. "Richard Wright," in their Instructor's Manual to Accompany The Modern Tradition. Third edition. Boston: Little, Brown, pp. 52-54.
Brief analyses of "The Man Who Was Almost a Man" and "The Man Who Lived Underground,"with study aids.

101. Huggins, Nathan Irvin. "Introduction," in his Voices from the Harlem Renaissance. New York: Oxford University Press, pp. 3-11.
Mentions W briefly (p. 10).

102. _____. "Reflections on the Renaissance and Art for a New Day," in his Voices from the Harlem Renaissance. New York: Oxford University Press, p. 369.
Contrasts briefly W's radicalism and toughness with the writing of the Harlem Renaissance.

103. Hughes, Langston. "Black Influences in the American Theater: Part I," in The Black American Reference Book. Ed. Mabel M. Smythe. Englewood Cliffs, N. J.: Prentice-Hall, pp. 684-704.
Reprint of 1966.79.

104. Jackson, Blyden. "The Ghetto of the Negro Novel: A Theme with Variations," in his The Waiting Years: Essays on American Negro Literature. Baton Rouge: Louisiana State University Press, pp. 179-188.
Reprint of 1971.177 with a prefatory note.

104a. _____. "The Negro's Image of His Universe as Reflected in His Fiction," in his The Waiting Years: Essays on American Negro Literature. Baton Rouge: Louisiana State University Press, pp. 92-102.
Reprint of 1960.169

104b. _____. "Richard Wright: Black Boy from America's Black Belt and Urban Ghettos," in his The Waiting Years: Essays on American Negro Literature. Baton Rouge: Louisiana State University Press, pp. 103-128.
Reprint of 1969.129.

105. _____. "Richard Wright in a Moment of Truth," in his The Waiting Years: Essays on American Negro Literature. Baton Rouge: Louisiana State University Press, pp. 129-145.
Reprint of 1971.178.

106. _____. "Singers of Daybreak: Studies in Black American Literature. By Houston A. Baker, Jr.; The Way of the New World. By Addison Gayle, Jr.; Black Fiction. By Roger Rosenblatt." American Literature, 47 (January), 652-654.
Quotes Rosenblatt mentioning briefly NS.

106a. _____. "A Survey Course in Negro Literature," in his The Waiting Years: Essays on American Negro Literature. Baton Rouge: Louisiana State University Press, pp. 198-207.
Reprint of 1974.98.

107. Jackson, Richard L. Black Writers in Latin America. Albuquerque: University of New Mexico Press, pp. 9-10, 142.
Quotes from "Blueprint for Negro Writing" and "I Tried to Be a Communist."

108. Jemie, Onwuchekwa. Langston Hughes: An Introduction to His Poetry. New York: Columbia University Press, pp. xv, xxv, 13, 97, 146.
Contains several references to W.

108a. Jones, Howard Mumford. "Literature," in Dictionary of American History. Revised editon. Ed. Louise Bilebof Ketz. Vol. 4. New York: Scribner's, 1976, pp. 160-166.
Mentions W briefly (p. 164).

109. Keady, Sylvia H. "Richard Wright's

Women Characters and Inequality." Black American Literature Forum, 10 (Winter), 124-128.

Contends that W's women characters are stereotypes. Discusses LD, NS, LT, O, and "Bright and Morning Star."

110. Kent, George E. "The 1975 Black Literary Scene: Significant Developments." Phylon, 37 (March), 100-115.

Contains a favorable notice of Addison Gayle's treatment of W in The Way of the New World (pp. 114-115).

111. K.[esteloot], L.[ilyan]. "Négritude," in La Grande Encyclopédie. Ed. Claude Dubois. Vol. 40. Paris: Librairie Larousse, pp. 8444-8448.

Mentions W briefly.

112. Kibler, James et al. "A Checklist of Scholarship on Southern Literature for 1975." Mississippi Quarterly, 29 (Spring), 269-335.

Lists sixteen items on W.

113. Kinnamon, Keneth. "Black Fiction. By Roger Rosenblatt." Journal of English and Germanic Philology, 75 (October), 619-622.

Comments on Rosenblatt's treatment of NS, especially comparisons of Bigger to literary and religious figures. Mentions "Big Boy Leaves Home."

113a. Kinugasa, Seiji. "Lawd Today as a Prelude to Native Son." Kokujin Kenkyu [Negro Studies], 48 (28 June), 9-12.

Sees LT as a stepping stone to and a prototype of NS. Based on W's own experience in the North, it is a demonstration of the perverse influences of white capitalism upon individual human nature. [Y. H. and T. K.]

114. Kitamura, Takao. "Yakusha atogaki," in Zoku Brakku Boi. By Richard Wright. Trans. Takao Kitamura. Tokyo: Kenkyusha, pp. 249-253.

Postscript to the Japanese translation of the privately printed A Hitherto Unpublished Manuscript by Richard Wright, Being a Continuation of Black Boy (published in 1977 as AH). Kitamura explains how he came into possession of the privately printed work, how he consulted with Constance Webb and others about copyright, and how Kenji Yagumo helped him with the translation. Stressing the work's importance, Kitamura expresses the hope that the original will be published and read.

115. Kobayashi, Kenji. "Richard Wright Dansho--Seiji to Bungaku Ron eno Ichi Shikaku" ["An Essay on Richard Wright: A View of Politics and Literature"]. Chiba Daigaku Kenkyu Hokoku [Chiba University Study Report], 9, pp. 209-244.

Maintains that W's work is best analyzed in terms of the relation of literature to politics. Takes issue with Irving Howe's defense of W, arguing that Howe deliberately ignores W's limitations and weaknesses as long as W's purpose to reveal racial injustice is accomplished. Also critical of Howe's attack on Baldwin's Go Tell It on the Mountain and Giovanni's Room on the grounds that Baldwin fails to portray the humanistic relationships existing among blacks. Concludes that whereas W succeeds in NS, he fails in UTC and O primarily because he has failed to evaluate the use of Communism and nihilism respectively. [Y. H.]

115a. Kusonose, Yoshiko. "Richard Wright's Black Boy, a Sequel, trans. Takeo Kitamura." Kokujin Kenkyu [Negro Studies], 48 (28 June), 12, 22.

Although the book does not largely revise W's stature or his relationship to the Communist Party, it is an impressive account of his internal struggle. [Y. H. and T. K.]

116. Larson, Charles R. The Novel in the Third World. Washington, D. C.: Inscape, pp. 90, 177.

Mentions W in relation to George Lamming.

117. LeRoy, Gaylord C. "Literary Study and Political Activism: How to Heal the Split," in Weapons of Criticism: Marxism in America and the Literary Tradition. Ed. Norman Rudich. Palo Alto, Cal.: Ramparts Press, pp. 75-104.

Mentions W briefly.

117a. Lester, Julius. All Is Well. New York: William Morrow, p. 51.

Mentions W briefly as an angry writer.

118. Lundén, Rolf. "Foreign Scholarship: Scandinavian Contributions," in American Literary Scholarship: An Annual/1974. Ed. James Woodress. Durham, N. C.: Duke University Press, pp. 455-458.

Mentions W as treated in Per Seyersted's "A Survey of Trends and Figures in Afro-American Fiction."

119. Lundquist, James. Chester Himes. Modern Literature Monographs. New York: Ungar, pp. 22, 26-28, 44, 48, 49, 50.

Contains discussions of Himes's friendship with W, his relation to the "Wright school of urban realists," and his radical political similarities to W, as well as a comparison of Bob Jones of If He Hollers Let Him Go and Bigger Thomas.

120. Maduka, Chukwudi Thomas. "Politics and the Intellectual Hero: Achebe, Abrahams, Flaubert and Wright." Dissertation Abstracts International, 37 (November), 2850A.
Examines the theme of the intellectual caught up in social change in O and novels by other writers. W thought that society was devoid of values.

120a. Maekawa, Yuji. "A Study of Richard Wright: Flight from a Protest." Nagasaki Zosen Daigaku Kenkyu Hokoku [Nagasaki Naval Architectural College Study Report], 17 (October), 87-96.
Argues that the problems posed in NS are intimately related to those of today's world: "Bigger who went over the racial wall comes to be able to connect the agony of the Negroes with the agony of a man of today." In English. [Y. H. and T. K.]

121. Mangione, Jerre. "Sterling A. Brown and the Federal Writers' Project," in Sterling A. Brown: A UMUM Tribute. Ed. Black History Museum Committee. Philadelphia: Black History Museum UMUM Publishers, pp. 14-17.
Mentions W's connection with the Writers' Project.

122. Mauro, Walter. James Baldwin. Il Castoro 119. Florence: La Nuova Italia, pp. 19-20, 25-29, 30, 31, 32-33, 41, 48, 63, 83, 96, 139, 142, 150.
Reviews W's career in relation to Baldwin's reaction to him (pp. 25-29). Mentions W frequently elsewhere.

123. Maxwell, Joan Lovell Bauerly. "Themes of Redemption in Two Major American Writers, Ralph Ellison and Richard Wright." Dissertation Abstracts International, 37 (September), 1549A.
Emphasizes the similarities between W and Ellison rather than the differences. Both are concerned with themes of individual and social redemption. Maxwell examines BB, BP, PS, and LD in the context of W's growth as a writer.

124. McBride, Rebecca Susan. "Richard Wright's Use of His Reading of Fiction: 1927-1940." Dissertation Abstracts International, 36 (June), 8062A.
Analyzes the literary influences on W's early fiction. From the beginning he was interested in writing as a craft.

125. McConnell, Frank D. "Black American Literature," in Collier's Encyclopedia.

Ed. William D. Halsey. Vol. 2. New York: Macmillan Educational Corporation, pp. 72-74.
Contains a paragraph of criticism on NS.
Reprinted: 1977.223; 1979.173.

126. McCoy, Frank Milton. Black Tomorrow. New York: Vantage Press, pp. 121, 137.
Mentions W and NS.

127. Miller, Jeanne-Marie A. "Annual Round-Up Black Theater in America: Washington, D. C." Black World, 25 (April), 83-86.
Mentions a 1975 production of the play NS.

128. Miller, Wayne C. and Fayne Nell Vowell. "Black Americans: A Guide to the Black-American Experience," in A Handbook of American Minorities. Ed. Wayne C. Miller. New York: New York University Press, pp. 3-30.
Comments on UTC and NS (p. 24).

129. _____ with Faye Nell Vowell et al. A Comprehensive Bibliography for the Study of American Minorities. Vol. 1. New York: New York University Press, pp. 243-245.
Includes a W section with primary and secondary sources, some annotated.

130. Milliken, Stephen F. Chester Himes: A Critical Appraisal. Columbia: University of Missouri Press, pp. 13, 47, 279-286.
Examines W's influence on Himes and analyzes Himes's treatment of W in The Quality of Hurt.

131. Mitchell, Loften. "The Negro Theatre and the Harlem Community," in Anthology of the Afro-American in the Theatre: A Critical Approach. Ed. Lindsay Patterson. Cornwells Heights, Pa.: The Publishers Agency, pp. 177-184.
Reprint of 1963.142.

132. Mitgang, Herbert. "Publishing: More 'Black Boy.'" The New York Times (10 December), p. C23.
Explains the circumstances of the publication of BB and announces AH.

133. Mootry, Maria K. "The Way of the New World." Black Books Bulletin, 4 (Spring), 47-48.
Review of Addison Gayle's book noting its favorable treatment of W and NS.

134. Morris, Richard B. Encyclopedia of American History. Bicentennial edition. New York: Harper & Row, pp. 662, 869.
Mentions W twice, but does not in-

clude him among the thirty-eight authors in the biographical section of "Five Hundred Notable Americans." Reprinted: 1982.103.

135. Muliarchik, A. S. "Critical Realism in the Post-War American Novel," in 20th Century American Literature: A Soviet View. Ed. Raissa Orlava. Moscow: Progress Publishers, pp. 100-120.
    Mentions W as a writer whose work succumbed to "caustic bitterness" and "spiritual apathy," particularly in O (pp. 103, 111, 113).

136. Neal, Larry. "The Black Contribution to American Letters: Part II, The Writer as Activist--1960 and After," in The Black American Reference Book. Ed. Mabel M. Smythe. Englewood Cliffs, N. J.: Prentice-Hall, pp. 767-790.
    Mentions W briefly (pp. 767, 778).

137. Newton, James E. A Curriculum Evaluation of Black Studies in Relation to Student Knowledge of Afro-American History and Culture. San Francisco: R and E Research Associates, pp. 69, 78, 79, 82, 89, 92, 93, 102.
    Includes W, NS, and Bigger Thomas in a multiple-choice test. Lists "Wright, Ellison, and Baldwin" among courses taught at colleges and universities in Illinois.

138. Niles, Olive Stafford, Edythe Daniel, Edmund J. Farrell, Alfred H. Grommon, and Robert C. Pooley. "Hunger," in their Teacher's Resource Book to Accompany Projection in Literature. Glenview, Ill.: Scott, Foresman, pp. 126-127.
    Study and teaching aids for an excerpt from BB.

139. _____. "The Kitten," in their Teacher's Resource Book to Accompany Counterpoint in Literature. Glenview, Ill.: Scott, Foresman, pp. 75-76.
    Reprint of 1967.79.

140. Olney, James. "Black Fiction. By Roger Rosenblatt." The South Atlantic Quarterly, 75 (Spring), 261-262.
    Mentions briefly NS.

141. Orlava, Raissa. "Richard Wright, Writer and Prophet, " in her 20th Century American Literature: A Soviet View. Moscow: Progress Publishers, pp. 384-410.
    After summarizing each of W's books, Orlava examines his claim that "the Negro is America's metaphor." The fate of the black man serves as an emblem of "the global fate of America," which is torn between noble aspirations and corrupt realities, a

fate also threatening the new African states. By "describing the deformities of urban capitalistic civilization," W touches universal truths.

142. Ostendorf, Bernard. "James Baldwin, 'Sonny's Blues' (1957)," in Die amerikanische Short Story der Gegenwart. Ed. Peter Freese. Berlin: Erich Schmidt Verlag, pp. 194-204.
    Claims that Baldwin's story fulfills the promise of W's "Blueprint for Negro Writing," which identifies the church and folklore as the sources of black artistic strength.

143. _____. "Ralph Ellison, 'Flying Home' (1944)," in Die amerikanische Short Story der Gegenwart. Ed. Peter Freese. Berlin: Erich Schmidt Verlag, pp. 64-76.
    Notes that Ellison's blending of pathology and transcendence in a single character contrasts with W's portrayal of total alienation in NS.

144. Peck, David. "Salvaging the Art and Literature of the 1930's: A Bibliographical Essay." The Centennial Review, 20 (Spring), 128-141.
    Contains several references to W.

145. Phillips, Robert L., Jr. "Editor's Foreword," in his A Climate for Genius. Jackson: Mississippi Library Commission, p. i.
    Refers to W as the "father of modern Afro-American literature."

146. Ploski, Harry A. and Warren Marr II. "Black Writers, Scholars and Poets," in their The Negro Almanac: A Reference Work on the Afro-American. Third edition. New York: Bellwether, pp. 711-746.
    Reprint of 1967.82.

147. Pooley, Robert C., Edythe Daniel, Edmund J. Farrell, Alfred H. Grommon, and Olive Stafford Niles. "Discussion, The Author," in their Projection in Literature. Glenview, Ill.: Scott, Foresman, p. 279.
    Reprint of 1967.83.

148. Pratt, Louis H. "James Baldwin and 'The Literary Ghetto.'" CLA Journal, 20 (December), 262-272.
    Quotes a review of Go Tell It on the Mountain mentioning W.

149. Real, Willi. "Richard Wright, 'The Man Who Lived Underground' (1944)," in Die amerikanische Short Story der Gegenwart. Ed. Peter Freese. Berlin: Erich Schmidt Verlag, pp. 54-63.
    Citing a generally lukewarm critical reaction to the novella, Real examines the early versions and traces

several of the doubling patterns. The story not only makes a social and psychological point, but also reflects the process of its own creation. Whether the self-reflexive qualities were under W's control is uncertain, but they strengthen the story.

150. Redden, Dorothy S. "Richard Wright and Native Son: Not Guilty." Black American Literature Forum, 10 (Winter), 111-116.
    Argues that instead of being an indictment of white society, NS presents a workable, rational morality as an alternative to racism. In W's view the racial issue is more moral than political.

151. Redding, Mary E. "Writers in Revolt: The Anvil Anthology. Ed. Jack Conroy and Curt Johnson." CLA Journal, 19 (March), 434-436.
    Mentions W briefly.

152. Redding, Saunders. "Afro-American Culture and the Black Aesthetic: Notes Toward a Re-Evaluation," in Reading Black: Essays in the Criticism of African, Caribbean, and Black American Literature. Ed. Houston A. Baker, Jr. African Studies and Research Center Monograph Series No. 4. Philadelphia and Ithaca, N. Y.: University of Pennsylvania Afro-American Studies Program and Cornell Africana Studies and Research Center, pp. 41-47.
    Refers to W as an example of "Negro social consciousness" and to Dan McCall's book on W.

153. Redmond, Eugene B. Drumvoices: The Mission of Afro-American Poetry: A Critical History. Garden City, N. Y.: Anchor Books, pp. 9, 10, 28, 150, 151, 153, 154, 222, 223-226, 291, 309, 313, 326, 340, 341, 342.
    In addition to many passing references to W and his influence, Redmond discusses his career and poetry (pp. 224-226) with special attention to "I Have Seen Black Hands" and "Between the World and Me."

153a. Reed, Ishmael. The Last Days of Louisiana Red. New York: Avon Books, p. 21.
    Reprint of 1974.149a.

154. _____. "You Can't Be a Literary Magazine and Hate Writers." Yardbird Reader, 5, pp. 18-20.
    Mentions W's difficulty with Johnson Publications.
    Reprinted: 1978.206.

155. Reid, Ines Smith. "Black Americans and Africa," in The Black American Reference Book. Ed. Mabel M. Smythe. Englewood Cliffs, N. J.: Prentice-Hall, pp. 648-683.
    Mentions W's support of the First International Congress of Negro Writers and Artists.

156. Richards, Stanley. "An Introductory Note," in his America on Stage: Ten Great Plays of American History. Garden City, N. Y.: Doubleday, pp. ix-xii.
    Mentions briefly the play NS.

157. _____. "Paul Green and Richard Wright," in his America on Stage: Ten Great Plays of American History. Garden City, N. Y.: Doubleday, pp. 785-788.
    Preface to the play NS quoting from Brooks Atkinson's review and providing biographical sketches of Green and W.

158. Richardson, Ben and William A. Fahey. "Richard Wright," in their Great Black Americans. Second revised edition. New York: Crowell, pp. 139-149.
    Revised reprint of 1956.278.

159. Riggio, Thomas P. "Uncle Tom Reconstructed: A Neglected Chapter in the History of a Book." American Quarterly, 28 (Spring), 56-70.
    Briefly relates W to Stowe and Thomas Dixon.
    Reprinted: 1980.208.

160. Roache, Joel. "'What Had Made Him and What He Meant': The Politics of Wholeness in 'How 'Bigger' Was Born.'" Sub-Stance, No. 15, pp. 133-145.
    Analyzes the theme and structure of the essay with attention to the interpretive implications for NS. W's view in the essay is that "the consciousness of any individual is the product of the interaction between the essential human need for self-realization and the conditions of one's historical position, conditions determined by one's class and/or caste and by the time in which one lives" (p. 141). Correcting interpretations by McCall and Margolies, Roache argues that Bigger is a revolutionary hero and that W's ideology is dialectical materialism.

161. Robinson, Wilhelmena S. "Wright, Richard," in her Historical Negro Biographies. Second edition. International Library of Negro Life and History. Cornwells Heights, Pa.: Publishers Company, pp. 265-266.
    Reprint of 1969.210.

162. Rose, Vattel T. "The Way of the New World." The Journal of Negro Education,

45 (Fall), 488-491.
    Mentions briefly NS.

163. Rosenblatt, Roger. "Black Autobiography: Life as the Death Weapon." Yale
Review, 65 (Summer), 515-527.
    Maintains that most black autobio-
    graphies constitute polemics against
    life. BB is an example. Rosenblatt
    analyzes the conclusion of BB and
    mentions also NS.
    Reprinted: 1980.210.

164. Ross, Stephen. "Roger Rosenblatt.
Black Fiction." Modern Fiction Studies,
21 (Winter), 653-655.
    Mentions briefly W's "bludgeoning
    power" (p. 653).

165. Rowell, Charles H. "Studies in
Afro-American Literature: An Annual Annotated Bibliography, 1975." Obsidian:
Black Literature in Review, 2 (Winter),
96-123.
    Lists five items about W (pp. 122-
    123) and thirteen items dealing in
    part with W.

166. _____ and Dudley Randall. "In Conversation with Dudley Randall." Obsidian: Black Literature in Review, 2
(Spring), 32-44.
    Randall mentions W briefly (p. 34).

167. Rubin, Louis D. "Out of the Past,"
in A Climate for Genius. Ed. Robert L.
Phillips, Jr. Jackson: Mississippi
Library Commission, p. 12.
    Lists W as a shaping force of the
    Southern literary renaissance.

168. Rupp, Richard H. "Subversions of
the Pastoral: The Hero in Our Time--A
Review Essay." Southern Humanities
Review, 10 (Winter), 74-80.
    Includes a review of Sam Bluefarb's
    The Escape Motif in the American
    Novel criticizing its treatment of
    NS.

169. Sadler, Jeffrey A. "Split Con-
sciousness in Richard Wright's Native
Son." The South Carolina Review, 8
(April), 11-24.
    Interprets the novel according to the
    categories of the existential psycho-
    logy of R. D. Laing. Bigger's divided
    self achieves wholeness only through
    violence and an understanding of that
    violence. Jan understands Bigger bet-
    ter than does Max, who is too ab-
    stract and political. The novel is
    more existential than Communist, more
    psychological than social.

169a. Saito, Tadatoshi. "Richard
Wright's Black Boy, a Sequel." Eigo
Seinen [The Rising Generation], 122

(August), 236-237.
    Though called a sequel, the book is a
    collection of three previously pub-
    lished writings. A rereading kindles
    one's interest in W. [Y. H. and
    T. K.]

170. Saporta, Marc. Histoire du roman
américain. Revised edition. Paris: Gallimard, pp. 358-361, 364, 365, 366, 440,
458, 463, 464, 465, 466, 504.
    Reprint of 1970.313.

171. Seymour-Smith, Martin. "Wright,
Richard," in his Who's Who in Twentieth
Century Literature. New York: Holt,
Rinehart and Winston, pp. 404-405.
    Biographical-critical sketch. Sey-
    mour-Smith admires BB and "The Man
    Who Lived Underground" but considers
    NS overrated.

172. Sherer, Ray J. "Richard Wright 'The
Man Who Lived Underground,'" in his
Twelve Short Novels. New York: Holt,
Rinehart and Winston, pp. 442-443.
    Analyzes the story as an allegory
    whose "primary purpose is to reveal
    moral and psychological truth through
    symbolic events."

172a. Shimizu, Takeo. "A View of the
Meaning of the Color White in the
Stories by Richard Wright." Kyushu Shika
Daigaku Shingaku Katei Kenkyu Kiyo [Bul-
letin of Kyushu Dental College], 7 (31
March), 19-22.
    The image of black people in BB and
    UTC symbolizes black people's long
    struggle and white people's indiffer-
    ence to it. In English. [Y. H. and
    T. K.]

173. Shreve, Darrel Rhea, Jr. "The Fact
of Blackness: Black Existentialism in
Richard Wright's Major Fiction." Dissertation Abstracts International, 37
(December), 3630A.
    Considers W's work in the context of
    black literary tradition rather than
    stressing Marxism, determinism, or
    existentialism. The focal point of
    the study is NS, but O also receives
    full treatment.

174. Singh, Amritjit. The Novels of the
Harlem Renaissance: Twelve Black Writers
1923-1933. University Park: The Pennsylvania State University Press, pp. 31,
41, 133, 134, 143, 144.
    Contains several references to W.

175. Skerrett, Joseph T., Jr. and John
A. Williams. "Novelist in Motion: Inter-
view with John A. Williams." Black
World, 25 (January), 58-67, 93-97.
    Includes comments by Williams on his
    reading of W and on his portrayal of

W as Harry Ames in The Man Who Cried
I Am.

176. Smith, Virginia W., Brian J. Benson, and Linda Brown Bragg. "An Interview with Linda Brown Bragg." CLA Journal, 20 (September), 75-87.
Mentions Benson's work on this reference guide to W.

177. Spradling, Mary Mace. "Wright, Richard Nathaniel (1908-1960)," in her In Black and White: Afro-Americans in Print. Kalamazoo: Kalamazoo Public Library, pp. 425-426.
Lists forty-five items on W.

178. Steele, Shelby. "Black Autobiography in America. By Stephen Butterfield." Western Humanities Review, 30 (Winter), 70-72.
Mentions W briefly.

179. ____. "Ralph Ellison's Blues." Journal of Black Studies, 7 (December), 151-168.
Relates Ellison's fiction to his understanding of the blues as developed in "Richard Wright's Blues." Contrasts briefly the protagonist of Invisible Man to Bigger Thomas and Cross Damon.

180. Stember, Charles Herbert. Sexual Racism: The Emotional Barrier to an Integrated Society. New York: Elsevier, p. 1.
The epigraph is a quotation from LD.

181. Stepto, Robert B. "Michael Harper's Extended Tree: John Coltrane and Sterling Brown." The Hollins Critic, 13 (June), 2-16.
Mentions Harper's poems on W (p. 11).

182. Stineback, David C. Shifting World: Social Change and Nostalgia in the American Novel. Lewisburg, Pa.: Bucknell University Press, p. 176.
Mentions briefly NS.

183. Stone, Wilfred, Nancy Huddleston Packer, and Robert Hoopes. "Introduction," in their The Short Story: An Introduction. New York: McGraw-Hill, pp. 1-23.
Comments briefly on the use of details in "The Man Who Was Almost a Man" (p. 22).

184. ____. "Richard Wright (1908-1960)," in their The Short Story: An Introduction. New York: McGraw-Hill, pp. 363-364.
Headnote to "The Man Who Was Almost a Man" reviewing W's life and career and briefly examining Dave of the story as an "existential anti-hero."

185. Talbot, William. "Every Negro in His Place: The Scene On and Off Broadway," in Anthology of the Afro-American in the Theatre: A Critical Approach. Ed. Lindsay Patterson. Cornwells Heights, Pa.: The Publishers Agency, pp. 207-209.
Reprint of 1964.121.

186. Tate, Claudia C. "Black Boy: Richard Wright's 'Tragic Sense of Life.'" Black American Literature Forum, 10 (Winter), 117-119.
Contends that BB is less a literal autobiography than W's "attempt to establish himself as a distinct and fully conscious individual." Tate places the work in the context of Miguel de Unamuno's The Tragic Sense of Life.

187. Thomas, Lorenzo. "Two Crowns of Thoth: A Study of Ishmael Reed's The Last Days of Louisiana Red." Obsidian: Black Literature in Review, 2 (Winter), 5-25.
Briefly compares Reed's Loop Garoo Kid in Yellow Back Radio Broke Down to Bigger Thomas.

188. Thomas, Walter R. "The Decade of the Twenties in Harlem," in Bubbling Brown Sugar. New York, p. [2].
In the playbill for the Media House production of the play Thomas mentions W as a participant in the Harlem Renaissance.

189. Tolliver, Johnny E. An Introduction to Richard Wright's Native Son. Mississippi Writers in Context, ed. Joseph E. Stockwell, Jr. and Robert L. Phillips. Jackson: Mississippi Library Commission, 10 pp.
Summarizes the novel noting its structure, theme, realism, and characterization. Tolliver emphasizes the representative quality of Bigger, an "Everyblackman."

190. Traylor, Eleanor E. Williams. "Wright's Mythic and Grotesque Settings: Some Critical Approaches to the Fiction of Richard Wright." Dissertation Abstracts International, 37 (September), 1558A.
Contends that W's literary practice is to objectify and then re-create imaginatively the particulars of his fiction. Traylor examines this practice in a chronological treatment of his works.

191. Trimmer, Joseph F. and Robert R. Kettler. "Authors," in their American Oblique: Writing About the American Experience. Boston: Houghton Mifflin, pp. 345-352.
Contains a very brief biographical

note on W (p. 352).

192. _____. "Discussion Questions," in their American Oblique: Writing About the American Experience. Boston: Houghton Mifflin, p. 58.
To accompany "The Ethics of Living Jim Crow."

193. _____. "Richard Wright, From 'The Ethics of Living Jim Crow,'" in their Teaching American Oblique: An Instructor's Manual. Boston: Houghton Mifflin, p. 12.
Brief analysis with emphasis on symbolic import of lawns, houses, and cinder yards; the mother's point of view; and the individual's relation to the group.

194. Turner, Darwin T. "The Negro Dramatist's Image of the Universe, 1920-1960," in Anthology of the Afro-American in the Theatre: A Critical Approach. Ed. Lindsay Patterson. Cornwells Heights, Pa.: The Publishers Agency, pp. 65-74.
Reprint of 1961.274.

195. Twombly, Robert C. "Harlem Renaissance," in Collier's Encyclopedia. Ed. William D. Halsey. Vol. 11. New York: Macmillan Educational Corporation, pp. 654-655.
Contrasts briefly W's pessimism to the optimism of the Renaissance.
Reprinted: 1977.327; 1979.268.

196. Tytell, John and Harold Jaffe. "Richard Wright," in their Affinities: A Short Story Anthology. Second edition. New York: Crowell, p. 384.
Brief biographical headnote to "Bright and Morning Star."

197. Vega, Ana Lydia. "Négritude et liberation nationale dans la littérature portoricaine." Présence Africaine, Nos. 99-100 (Third and Fourth Quarters), pp. 167-180.
Mentions the influence of W on Pedro Juan Soto's Usmail.

198. Walker, Robert H. "Protest Narratives," in his The Reform Spirit in America. New York: Putnam's, pp. 302-304.
Mentions W briefly.

199. Ward, Jerry W. "N. J. Loftis' Black Anima: A Problem in Aesthetics." Journal of Black Studies, 7 (December), 195-209.
Quotes a passage from Black Anima mentioning W.

200. Wasserman, Jerry. "Embracing the Negative: Native Son and Invisible Man." Studies in American Fiction, 4 (Spring), 93-104.

In a framework of Laing, Genet, and Sartre, Wasserman argues that Bigger achieves identity by "embracing freely and in full consciousness" (p. 94) the stereotype imposed by racist whites. By doing so he attains the only kind of freedom available to him.

201. Webb, Constance. "Introduction," in Zoku Brakku Boi [Black Boy, Second Series]. Trans. Takao Kitamura. Tokyo: Kenkyusha, pp. i-iii.
Biographical sketch translated from the privately circulated but unpublished portion of the original manuscript of BB, published in 1977 as AH.

201a. _____. "Wright, Richard Nathaniel," in Collier's Encyclopedia. Ed. William D. Halsey. Vol. 23. New York: Macmillan Educational Corporation, p. 638.
Reprint of 1969.244.

202. Wesley, Charles H. The Quest for Equality: From Civil War to Civil Rights. International Library of Afro-American Life and History. Cornwells Heights, Pa.: The Publishers Agency under the auspices of The Association for the Study of Afro-American Life and History, pp. 200, 201.
Reprint of 1969.251.

203. Wideman, John. "Frame and Dialect: The Evolution of the Black Voice in American Literature." The American Poetry Review, 5 (September-October), 34-37.
Mentions W briefly.

204. Yanagi, Kiichiro. "Richard Wright no Denenkyoku--'Big Boy Ie o Deru'" ["Richard Wright's Pastorale: 'Big Boy Leaves Home'"]. Osaka Gakuin Gaikokugo Ronshu [Osaka Gakuin University Essays on Foreign Languages], 3 (December), 75-90.
Interprets "Big Boy Leaves Home" as a typical initiation story in the tradition of Huckleberry Finn, Hemingway, and Faulkner. Big Boy revolts against white society, his "father." As if in a ritual Big Boy encounters a white man, snake, and dog; Bobo functions as a sacrifice for Big Boy. [Y. H.]

205. Zangrando, Robert L. "Sidonie Smith. Where I'm Bound: Patterns of Slavery and Freedom in Black American Autobiography; Mary Ellison, The Black Experience: American Blacks Since 1865." The American Historical Review, 81 (April), 450-451.
Mentions W briefly.

206. Zverev, A. M. "Soedinennye Shtaty

Ameriki: XIII. Literatura," in Bol'shaia Svetskiaia Entsiklopediia. Ed. A. M. Prokhorov. Vol. 24 (Bk. 1). Moscow: Sovetskaia Entsiklopedia, pp. 117-120.
    Mentions briefly W and NS.

1977

1. Abajian, James de T. Blacks in Selected Newspapers, Censuses and Other Sources: An Index to Names and Subjects. Vol. 3. Boston: G. K. Hall, p. 739.
    Contains three items pertaining to W.

2. A.[dams], P.[hoebe] L.[ou]. "American Hunger by Richard Wright." The Atlantic, 239 (June), 93-94.
    Favorable review praising W's literary artistry, especially his use of understatement.

3. Algren, Nelson. "'He Never Thanked Us for the Neckbones.'" Chicago Tribune (22 May), Sec. 7, pp. 1, 8.
    Memoir of the Algren-W relationship in Chicago in the thirties. W was a revolutionary by circumstance. He succeeded in his literary task, but his potential was never fully realized.

4. Amis, Barry. "Jacqueline Covo. The Blinking Eye: Ralph Ellison and His American, French, German and Italian Critics, 1952-1971; Blyden Jackson. The Waiting Years: Essays on American Negro Literature; Stephen F. Milliken. Chester Himes: A Critical Appraisal; Addison Gayle, Jr. The Way of the New World: The Black Novel in America." Modern Fiction Studies, 23 (Summer), 275-276.
    Mentions W briefly.

5. Anon. "American Hunger." Publishers Weekly, 211 (4 April), 82.
    Favorable review noting its treatment of W's early development as a writer and his relation to the Communist Party.

6. Anon. "American Hunger." The New Yorker, 53 (6 June), 138-139.
    Favorable review praising the work's honesty and compassion. The best part concerns W's relationship with the Communist Party.

7. Anon. "American Hunger by Richard Wright." Book-of-the-Month Club News, August, p. 9; September, p. 12; October, p. 20.
    Favorable notice of a book that together with BB is "one of the first and most eloquent accounts of a black American's journey to freedom."

8. Anon. "American Hunger. By Richard Wright." Honolulu Star-Bulletin (c. 19 July).
    Favorable review noting that W's break with the Communists resulted from his needs as a writer, not from political differences. AH "is a moving memoir of the process which led to the emergence of a major writer, not simply for blacks, or for America, but for the world."

9. Anon. "American Hunger Richard Wright." Literary Cavalcade, 30 (30 October), p. 8.
    Headnote to an excerpt from the autobiographical work.

10. Anon. "'American Hunger' to Be Published." St. Paul Dispatch (26 February), p. 24.
    Announces that Harper and Row will publish several volumes from the W papers at Yale, the first being AH.

11. Anon. "Announcing The Richard Wright Reader." 4 pp.
    Publisher's announcement with a photograph of W.

12. Anon. "Art of the Folk," in Humanities Through the Black Experience. Ed. Phyllis Rauch Klotman. Dubuque: Kendall/Hunt, pp. 43-69.
    Comments on "Big Boy Leaves Home" (p. 57).

13. Anon. Bibliographic Guide to Black Studies: 1977. Boston: G. K. Hall, p. 254.
    Lists one primary (translation) and two secondary items concerning W in the New York Public Library.

14. Anon. "Black Boy by Richard Wright." Book-of-the-Month Club News, August, p. 9; September, p. 12; October, p. 20.
    Favorable notice emphasizing the work's continuing relevance.

15. Anon. "Books Briefly: American Hunger, by Richard Wright." The Progressive, 41 (September), 44.
    Favorable notice stressing W's treatment of his relationship with the Communist Party.

16. Anon. "Current and Choice." The Washington Post (3 July), Book World Sec., p. K8.
    Contains a notice of the "poignant, bewildering" AH.

17. Anon. Dust jacket of American Hunger. New York: Harper & Row.
    Blurb and biographical sketch on front and back inside flaps. Photograph of W on back. Favorable quotation from Gwendolyn Brooks: "What a treasure! It is an event, this dis-

covery."

18. Anon. "Editor's Choice." The New York Times Book Review (3 July), p. 18.
Contains favorable notice of the "enormously moving" AH.

19. Anon. "Footprints in the Sands of Time." The Washington Post (11 December), Book World Sec., p. 9.
Contains a brief notice of AH, a "poignant, bewildering book."

20. Anon. "From the Book Shelf: American Hunger by Wright." Kenosha News (21 July), p. 7.
Very brief favorable notice.

21. Anon. "How the World Looked to Black Chicagoans in the '60s." Columbus (Ga.) Enquirer and Ledger (17 July).
Unfavorable review of AH focusing on the circumstances of its publication. Anything written by W is of interest, but the original decision to publish BB without this sequel was wise.

22. Anon. "In Perspective." First World: An International Journal of Black Thought, 1 (March-April), 31-32.
Includes an announcement that "a collection of unpublished work by the late Richard Wright is scheduled for early publication."

23. Anon. Index to Periodical Articles by and About Blacks: 1974. Boston: G. K. Hall, pp. 434-435.
Lists seven items on W.

24. _____. Index to Periodical Articles by and About Blacks: 1975. Boston: G. K. Hall, p. 527.
Lists one item on W.

25. Anon. "New Books Added at Falls Library." The Sheboygan Press (12 July), p. 9.
Lists AH.

26. Anon. "1945: Black Boy 1977: American Hunger." The New Republic, 176 (4 June), 25.
Advertisement for AH with the following quotation from Gwendolyn Brooks: "What a treasure!"

27. Anon. "People in the News." Encore, 6 (9 May), 30.
Mentions LaVar Burton's role in the television dramatization of "Almos' a Man."

28. Anon. "Published Now for the First Time, American Hunger . . . The Compelling Continuation of Richard Wright's American Classic, Black Boy." Book-of-the-Month Club News, Midsummer, p. 7.

Favorable review of AH emphasizing W's disillusionment in the North and calling the work "a courageous precursor to the books of Alex Haley, Ralph Ellison and James Baldwin."

29. Anon. "Reviews and Resources: Once Over." English Journal, 66 (November), 80-82.
Contains a notice of AH pointing out that it is a sequel to BB.

30. Anon. "Richard Wright." Book-of-the Month Club News, Midsummer, p. 7.
Favorable review-advertisement of AH, "a courageous precursor to the books of Alex Haley, Ralph Ellison and James Baldwin."

31. Anon. "Richard Wright's Hero: The Faces of a Rebel-Victim by Katherine Fishburn," in Reference Works for Language & Literature Collections. Metuchen, N. J.: The Scarecrow Press, p. 10.
Publisher's notice with quotations from Library Journal and Choice.

32. Anon. "Spingarn Medal," in The Encyclopedia Americana. Ed. Bernard S. Cayne. Vol. 25. New York: Americana Corporation, p. 506.
Mentions W briefly.
Reprinted: 1978.28.

33. Anon. "Two Generations Later, Wright's Insights 'Hold True.'" St. Petersburg Times (24 July), Sec. G., p. 3.
Favorable review of AH stressings its relevance to the present. W's aspirations to live in dignity in his native land were not fulfilled.

34. Anon. "Undercover." Rolling Stone (14 July), p. 72.
Review of AH pointing out that it offers a picture of a "strange world" in which Communists force blacks to abandon their identity in order to fit into a plan they do not control. This memoir might have weakened the appeal of BB if published as originally planned.

35. Anon. Untitled note, in Humanities Through the Black Experience. Ed. Phyllis Rauch Klotman. Dubuque: Kendall/Hunt Publishing Company, p. 57.
Brief headnote to an excerpt from "Big Boy Leaves Home" concerning the dozens.

36. Anon. "Vonnegut Joins Fight to Stop Book-Banning." The Champaign-Urbana Courier (5 January), p. 22.
Reports that one of the books banned from Long Island school libraries, BB, was restored "on a restricted

basis--a note from parents required."

37. Anon. "'What Sets Storms to Rolling in His Soul.' By Richard Wright." The New York Times (8 April), p. A27.
    Brief note to accompany an excerpt from AH.

38. Anon. "Wright, Ellen & Michel Fabre --Eds. Richard Wright Reader." Kirkus Reviews, 45 (15 November), 1257-1258.
    Favorable review describing the contents and stressing W's concern with "inner deprivation."

39. Anon. "Wright (Richard)," in Encyclopédie alphabétique Larousse. Paris: Librairie Larousse, p. 1968.
    Brief biographical note.

40. Anon. "Wright (Richard)," in Petit Larousse en couleurs. Paris: Librairie Larousse, pp. 1649-1650.
    Biographical note.

41. Anon. "Wright, Richard," in The Random House Encyclopedia. Ed. James Mitchell. New York: Random House, p. 2687.
    Biographical note.

42. Anon. "Wright, Richard," in The University Desk Encyclopedia. Ed. Herman Friedhoff and Ben Lenthall. New York: Dutton, p. 1045.
    Biographical note.

43. Anon. "Wright, Richard. American hunger." Booklist, 73 (15 May), 1390-1391.
    Favorable notice of "a poignant story of the growth of a great American writer, which also provides a timeless account of individual and collective racial awareness."

44. Anon. "Wright, Richard. American Hunger." Kirkus Reviews, 45 (15 March), 341-342.
    Favorable review noting that AH remains an impressive achievement despite the fact that many of its insights have become familiar in the years since its writing. It is particularly valuable for the glimpses it offers into W's artistic and political development prior to the publication of his first works. Reprinted: 1977.45.

45. _____. "Wright, Richard. American Hunger." Kirkus Reviews, 45 (15 May), 548.
    Reprint of 1977.44.

46. Anon. "Wright, Richard: Black Boy," in Caedmon 1952-1977. New York: Caedmon, p. 246.
    Publisher's catalog notice of the

Brock Peters recording.

47. Anon. "Wright, Richard: Native Son," in Caedmon 1952-1977. New York: Caedmon, p. 246.
    Publisher's catalog notice of the James Earl Jones recording.

48. Anon. "The Yale University Library and the Yale Afro-American Studies Program cordially invite you to attend a lecture, exhibition and reception celebrating the opening of the Richard Wright Archive in the Beinecke Rare Book and Manuscript Library, Friday, November 4, 1977."
    Printed invitation with a photograph of W. The lecture by Charles T. Davis is entitled "From Experience to Eloquence: Richard Wright's Black Boy as Art." See 1979.76.

49. Aptheker, Herbert. The Negro People in America: A Critique of Gunnar Myrdal's 'An American Dilemma'. Millwood, N. Y.: Kraus Reprint Co., pp. 30, 63, 70, 80.
    Reprint of 1946.141a.

50. Austin, Deborah M. "Addison Gayle's Theory of Fiction." Obsidian, 3 (Winter), 70-79.
    Compares Gayle's theory as expressed in The Way of the New World unfavorably to W's in "Blueprint for Negro Writing." Notes also inadequacies in Gayle's analysis of NS.

51. Avery, Evelyn Gross. "Rebels and Victims: The Fiction of Richard Wright and Bernard Malamud." Dissertation Abstracts International, 37, p. 5822A.
    Argues that both W and Malamud are "close to their heritage and write passionately of their victimized people." W's protagonists are less articulate and more forceful. Their characteristic response is violence.

52. Baker, Houston A., Jr. "A View of William Melvin Kelley's dem." Obsidian, 3 (Summer), 12-16.
    Mentions briefly SH (p. 12).

53. Baker, Sheridan and Dwight Stevenson. Problems in Exposition for the Practical Stylist. New York: Crowell, p. 83.
    Reprint of 1976.28.

54. Barksdale, Richard K. Langston Hughes: The Poet and His Critics. Chicago: American Library Association, pp. 8, 29, 40, 46, 80, 87, 100, 101.
    Contains numerous references to W, including comments on his review of The Big Sea (p. 8) and the influence of his career on Hughes (especially

pp. 80, 100).

55. Beauvoir, Simone de. Force of Circumstance. Trans. Richard Howard. 2 vols. Harper Colophon Books. New York: Harper & Row, 658 pp.
Reprint of 1965.35.

56. Beaver, Harold. "The Way of the New World: The Black Novel in America. By Addison Gayle." The Modern Language Review, 72 (April), 414-417.
Mentions W briefly.

57. Bender, Todd K., Nancy Armstrong, Sue M. Briggum, and Frank A. Knoblock. "Richard Wright," in their Instructor's Manual for Modernism in Literature. New York: Holt, Rinehart and Winston, pp. 10-11.
Contains a very brief bibliography and three discussion questions.

58. Benson, Joseph. "Wright: A Sequel to 'Black Boy.'" Greensboro Daily News (12 June), Sec. C., p. 3.
Favorable review of AH pointing out its relation to W's other autobiographical writing. Praises Fabre's afterword. W's success was achieved through intensity and work.
Reprinted: 1978.209.

59. Beppu, Keiko. "Japanese Contributions," in American Literary Scholarship: An Annual/1975. Ed. James Woodress. Durham, N. C.: Duke University Press, pp. 494-497.
Mentions W briefly in connection with a book by Masayuki Sakamoto (p. 496).

60. Berger, Morroe. Real and Imagined Worlds: The Novel and Social Science. Cambridge, Mass.: Harvard University Press, p. 244.
Cites examples from LT in a section entitled "Objectivity in the New Novel."

61. Berghahn, Marion. Images of Africa in Black American Literature. Totowa, N. J.: Rowman and Littlefield, pp. 154-167, 176, 178, 187, 190, 220.
Collects references to Africa throughout W's work to show that his attitude was ambiguous from the beginning. He did not venerate the ancestral homeland.

62. Birdoff, Harry. "Wright." The New York Times Book Review (24 July), p. 29.
The husband of W's secretary explains the author's meticulous habits of composition. W did not use the second part of his autobiographical manuscript, Birdoff explains, because it "encroached upon the first," published as BB.

63. Blair, Thomas L. Retreat to the Ghetto: The End of a Dream? New York: Hill and Wang, p. 73.
Mentions W as an intellectual precursor of the Black Power movement.

64. Blasing, Mutlu Konuk. The Art of Life: Studies in American Autobiographical Literature. Austin: University of Texas Press, p. 158.
Argues that BB is superior to W's other works because it transcends racial stereotypes and because in it Wright comes "into possession of himself as a black and as an American undergoing the archetypal American journey of self-discovery or self-creation."

65. Blum, Daniel. A Pictorial History of the American Theatre 1860-1976. Fourth edition enlarged and revised by John Willis. New York: Crown, pp. 291, 293.
Reprint of 1969.31.

66. Bontemps, Arna. "Negro in America: Contributions to American Culture," in The Encyclopedia Americana. Ed. Bernard S. Cayne. Vol. 20. New York: Americana Corporation, pp. 74-77.
Reprint of 1970.62.

67. B.[ovelle], V.[irgie] N. H. "Rosenblatt, Roger. Black fiction." Kliatt Paperback Book Guide, 11 (Winter), 23.
Mentions W briefly.

68. Boylan, Martin M. "Wright, Richard. American Hunger." Best Sellers, 37 (August), 152.
Favorable review noting that W's hunger is metaphorical in this book. "This is not a sociological study of the serious social problem facing America. Rather it is an eloquent story of one gifted black man's effort to establish himself as a writer."

69. Bracy, William. "Wright, Richard," in The Encyclopedia Americana. Ed. Bernard S. Cayne. Vol. 29. New York: Americana Corporation, p. 555.
Reprint of 1965.45.

70. Bradley, David. "Soul on Ice." Quest (July-August), pp. 80, 82.
Favorable review of AH claiming that it is more protest literature than autobiography. Bradley stresses W's fatalism.
Reprinted: 1978.209.

71. Brayton, Bradford Clark, Jr. "Richard Wright's Quest for Identity." Dissertation Abstracts International, 38 (September), 1489-A.
Abstracts a 1977 University of Minne-

sota dissertation. Rather than seeing himself as a black spokesman, W identifies with the outsider figure. First appearing in Bigger Thomas, the character type comes to dominate W's later work.

72. Breitman, George. "Books: Richard Wright's 'American Hunger.'" The Militant, 41 (5 August), International Socialist Review monthly magazine supplement, p. 22.
    Unfavorable review. Breitman corrects the notion that the work was previously unpublished. Though it has good parts, AH is a weaker work than the classic BB. Most of it concerns the author's relationship to the Communist Party, about which he is not completely candid. The main problem, however, is that "Wright did not know the difference between revolutionary Leninism and counterrevolutionary Stalinism." Reprinted: 1978.209.

73. Bruck, Peter. "Black American Short Fiction in the 20th Century: Problems of Audience, and the Evolution of Artistic Stances and Themes," in his The Black American Short Story in the 20th Century: A Collection of Critical Essays. Amsterdam: B. R. Grüner, pp. 1-19.
    Discusses UTC in the immediate context of "Blueprint for Negro Writing" and the general context of the development of a psychological treatment of the theme of racism (pp. 9-12).

74. _____. "Langston Hughes, The Blues I'm Playing (1934)," in his The Black American Short Story in the 20th Century: A Collection of Critical Essays. Amsterdam: B. R. Grüner, pp. 71-83.
    Quotes from W's review of The Big Sea (pp. 80-81).

74a. Bryer, Jackson R., Eddy Dow, Philip R. Headings, Matthew O'Brien, and Joseph V. Ridgely, with the help of Donald Wharton. "American Literature," in 1975 MLA International Bibliography. Vol. I. New York: Modern Language Association, pp. 131-186.
    Lists thirteen items on W.

74b. Bryer, Jackson R., Eddy Dow, Philip R. Headings, Matthew O'Brien, and Peter Van Egmond, with the help of Donald Wharton. "American Literature," in 1976 MLA International Bibliography. Vol. I. New York: Modern Language Association, pp. 144-214.
    Lists twenty-seven items on W.

75. Buell, Lawrence. "New Views of American Narrative: A Review-Essay." Texas Studies in Literature and Language, 19

(Summer), 234-246.
    Comments briefly on W's statement that "the Negro is America's metaphor" (p. 243).

76. Bungert, Hans. "Einleitung," in his Die amerikanische Literatur der Gegenwart: Aspekte und Tendenzen. Stuttgart: Philipp Reclam jun., pp. 7-17.
    Mentions W briefly as a forerunner of Ellison and Baldwin (p. 10).

77. Burns, Landon C. and Janet P. Alwang. "The Third (1977) Supplement to a Cross-Referenced Index of Short Fiction Anthologies and Author-Title Listings." Studies in Short Fiction, 14 (Spring), 203-232.
    Lists three stories by W in five anthologies.

78. Burt, Della. "The Legacy of the Bad Nigger." The Journal of Afro-American Issues, 5 (Spring), 111-124.
    Bigger Thomas is described as the classic example of the rebellious "bad nigger."

79. Callahan, John F. "Chaos, Complexity and Possibility: The Historical Frequencies of Ralph Waldo Ellison." Black American Literature Forum, 11 (Winter), 130-138.
    Contains a brief quotation from Ellison mentioning W (p. 130).

80. Callow, James T. and Robert J. Reilly. "Richard Wright (1908-1960)," in their Guide to American Literature from Emily Dickinson to the Present. New York: Barnes & Noble, pp. 141-143, 250-251.
    Consists of a biographical sketch, an assessment of his achievement stressing his pioneering role in stating the "mighty theme" of "the tragic dichotomy of black and white in America" that influenced much subsequent Afro-American fiction, a brief discussion of NS and BB, and a selected bibliography of primary and secondary sources.

81. Campbell, Finley C. "Prophet of the Storm: Richard Wright and the Radical Tradition." Phylon, 38 (March), 9-23.
    Analyzes W's position as one of social humanism, an ideology derived from his personal needs and experiences, communist influences, and a larger radical traditon. He became isolated, but his very isolation provided a sense of self-awareness important to his writing.

82. Campenni, Frank. "Unsatisfied Hunger." The Milwaukee Journal (3 July), Part 5, p. 5.

Favorable review of AH noting its emphasis on W's relation to the Communist Party. Honest and moving, it complements BB.
Reprinted: 1978.209

82a. C.[annon], T.[erry]. "Early Voice of Black Rebellion." New York Daily World (10 December), p. 8.
Sketch of W's literary career. "Like so many others, Wright was a victim of the Cold War, which first attempted to strip him of the Marxism that had enriched his creative gifts, and then hounded him--perhaps to death--when he began once again to be politically involved."
Reprinted: 1977.82b.

82b. ____. "Pioneer in the Literature of Black Rebellion." New York Daily World (17 December), World Magazine sec., p. M-5.
Reprint of 1977.82a with photograph of W.

82c. ____. "Was Richard Wright Assassinated?" New York Daily World (10 December), p. 8.
Speculates that W was assassinated to prevent him from renouncing his anti-Communism. Uses Ollie Harrington's recollections to support this possibility. Includes photographs of W and Harrington.

82d. Capeci, Dominic J., Jr. The Harlem Riot of 1943. Philadelphia: Temple University Press, pp. 134, 220.
Quotes W briefly on the economic causes of the riot.

83. Cargas, Harry James. "A Long-Awaited Sequel to 'Black Boy.'" St. Louis Post-Dispatch (28 August), p. 4B.
Favorable review of AH stressing the stupidity of Communists as revealed by W.

84. Cargill, Oscar. "American Literature," in Collier's Encyclopedia. Ed. William D. Halsey. Vol. 2. New York: Macmillan Educational Corporation, pp. 42-72.
Reprint of 1969.49.

85. Carter, Harriet. "Wright Autobiography Completed Belatedly." Worcester Sunday Telegram (25 September), Sec. E., p. 8.
Favorable review of AH. After summarizing briefly BB, Carter connects it to the sequel. She admires the vigorous style of AH.

86. Cassill, R. V. "Richard Wright The Man Who Was Almost a Man," in his The Norton Anthology of Short Fiction: In-structor's Handbook. New York: Norton, pp. 213-214.
Brief analysis of the story stressing the theme of initiation and the use of irony.

87. Chafe, William H. "Sex and Race: The Analogy of Social Control." The Massachusetts Review, 18 (Spring), 147-176.
Shows how W in BB develops four patterns of social control: physical intimidation, white economic control, white psychological control, and black acceptance of powerlessness.

88. Chapman, Frank E., Jr. "Pages from the Life of a Black Prisoner," in A Freedomways Reader: Afro-America in the Seventies. Ed. Ernest Kaiser. New York: International Publishers, pp. 331-347.
Reprint of 1971.68.

89. Clark, C. E. Frazer, Jr. "Richard (Nathaniel) Wright 1908-1960," in First Printings of American Authors. Ed. Matthew J. Bruccoli and C. E. Frazer Clark, Jr. Vol. 1. Detroit: Gale, pp. 427-430.
Lists W's books with brief bibliographical descriptions.

89a. Clark, Geraldine. "Afro-American Authors Represented on the ALA Notable Book List," in Handbook of Black Librarianship. Ed. E. J. Josey and Ann Allen Shockley. Littleton, Col.: Libraries Unlimited, pp. 156-160.
Lists and comments briefly on BB.

90. C.[lark], L.[uelle] M. "Richard Wright's Sequel to 'Black Boy' Published." Asheville Citizen-Times (12 June), Sec. C., p. 21.
Favorable review of AH consisting mostly of summary.

91. Clark, Sarah Brown. "Literary Expression of Resistance of Blacks in the United States from 1800 to 1940," in An Interdisciplinary Introduction to Black Studies. Ed. Clarence E. Barnes. Dubuque, Iowa: Kendall/Hunt Publishing Company, pp. 132-135.
Discusses briefly W's early career, especially in relation to Marxism.

92. Clarke, Jack A., ed. The Reader's Adviser: A Layman's Guide to Literature. 12th edition. Vol. 3. New York: Bowker, p. 667.
Lists three works by W.

93. Clayton, John J. "Richard Wright," in his The Heath Introduction to Fiction. Lexington, Mass.: Heath, p. 464.
Biographical headnote to "Bright and Morning Star."

94. Collier, Eugenia W. "The Phrase

Unbearably Repeated," in James Baldwin:
A Critical Evaluation. Ed. Therman B.
O'Daniel. Washington: Howard University
Press, pp. 38-46.
Reprint of 1964.38.

95. Collins, L. M. "The Black Boy Grows
Up: An Afro-American Saga." The Nashville Tennessean (10 July), p. 8-F.
Unfavorable review of AH. "Native Son
and Black Boy were symbolic of the
triumph of the human spirit over
demeaning adversity," but AH is weaker, seeming anachronistic and passe.

96. Collins, Terry. "American Hunger."
Minneapolis Minnesota Daily (1 August),
p. 7.
Favorable review calling W the most
important Afro-American writer. AH
adds much to one's understanding of
BB.

97. Conroy, Jack. "The Rest of 'Black
Boy.'" The Kansas City Star (15 May),
Sec. D., pp. 1-2.
Review of AH together with a memoir
of Conroy's friendship with W during
the Chicago years. Praises Fabre's
"Afterword."
Reprinted: 1977.98, 99.

98. _____. "From Richard Wright, A
Powerful Sequel." Chicago Daily News
(21-22 May), Panorama Sec., pp. 6, 10.
Reprint of 1977.97.

99. _____. "Richard Wright's Fans Have
Kept the Faith." San Francisco Sunday
Examiner and Chronicle (26 June), Scene
Sec., p. 2.
Reprint of 1977.97.

100. Cooney, John E. "Further Glimpses
of Black Reality." The Wall Street Journal (5 May), p. 20.
Favorable review of AH pointing out
the special interest of his account
of his relationship with the Communist Party.

101. Crabb, Mary Ann. "Book Shelf."
Hutchinson News (7 November), p. 5.
Favorable review of AH. W's readers
will want to peruse this sensitive
continuation of BB.

102. Crosson, Lesley. "One Black Man's
Epic Struggle." Camden Courier-Post (23
June), p. 30.
Favorable review of AH. An eloquent
indictment of racism, it is also
important for its treatment of W's
relation to the Communist Party.

103. Dahlstrom, Jo Ann Wolf and Deborah
E. Ryel. "'The Library Card' Richard
Wright," in their Promises to Keep:

Reading and Writing About Values. Englewood Cliffs, N. J.: Prentice-Hall, pp.
68-75.
Headnote and study questions to accompany reprint of Chapter XIII of
BB.

104. Dalton, Chantal B. "Teaching Black
Literature to Undergraduates: The Prob-
lem of a Sense of Perspective." Black
American Literature Forum, 11 (Fall),
102-103.
Contains a brief reference to W.

105. Daniel, Pete. Deep'n as It Come:
The 1927 Mississippi River Flood. New
York: Oxford University Press, p. 6.
Mentions "Down by the Riverside."

106. D'Epiro, Peter and Paolo Palombo.
"Hokku: Cade la neve," in their Voci
negre americane de protesta. Rome:
Trevi, p. 186.
Headnote to an Italian translation of
"In the Falling Snow."

107. Dias, Earl J. "A Black Author's
Hunger." The New Bedford Sunday Standard
Times (15 May), Sec. A, p. 6.
Favorable review of AH praising W's
crisp, lucid style and noting the
theme of loneliness. Prophetically, W
advocated social changes that have
now been effected. "American Hunger
is a powerful evocation of the black
experience in this country, undergone
by a sensitive and talented man."

108. Dickson, J. Walter. "Engaging the
'Full Person.'" The Boston Globe (c.
September).
Reprint of 1977.109.

109. _____. "Engaging the 'Full Person.'" The Houston Post (31 July), Spotlight Sec., p. 16.
Favorable review of AH noting the
emotional force of W's depiction of
racism Northern style.
Reprinted: 1977.108.

110. Dickstein, Morris. "Black Writing
and Black Nationalism: Four Generations," in his Gates of Eden: American
Culture in the Sixties. New York: Basic
Books, pp. 159-181, 287-288.
Discusses NS at length, arguing that
it is more hallucinatory and poetic
than naturalistic. Praises BB. Includes a brief bibliography of W
studies.

111. Dillard, J. L. Lexicon of Black
English. New York: The Seabury Press,
pp. xii, 14, 26, 30, 42, 85, 93, 155.
Contains several references, mainly
illustrative, to W, especially LT.
"Finding a word or expression in

Wright's works is perhaps the best possible corroboration of the hunch that it was genuinely black" (p. 155).

112. D.[orsey], D.[avid]. "On the Margin of Black Literature." Phylon, 38 (June), 219-224.
Brief references to W in a review of several books on black literature.

113. Downs, Robert B. "Introduction," in his Books That Changed the South. Chapel Hill: The University of North Carolina Press, pp. xii-xvii.
Mentions NS (p. xvii).

114. Du Bois, W. E. B. "Richard Wright Looks Back," in his Book Reviews. Ed. Herbert Aptheker. Millwood, N. Y.: KTO Press, pp. 228-229.
Reprint of 1945.883.

115. _____. "Wright, Richard. 12 Million Black Voices: A Folk History of the Negro in the United States," in his Book Reviews. Ed. Herbert Aptheker. Millwood, N. Y.: KTO Press, pp. 209-210.
Reprint of 1941.708; 1942.223.

116. Eckels, Jon. Pursuing the Pursuit-- The Black Plight in White America. Hicksville, N. Y.: Exposition Press, p. v.
Dedicated to W and other black heroes.

117. Edmondson, Locksley. "The Internationalization of Black Power: Historical and Contemporary Perspectives," in Black Separatism and Social Reality: Rhetoric and Reason. Ed. Raymond L. Hall. New York: Pergamon Press, pp. 183-194.
Comments on BP (p. 185).

118. Fabre, Michel. "Addison Gayle. Wayward Child: A Personal Odyssey." Afram Newsletter, No. 4 (December), p. 9.
Compares Gayle's autobiography to BB.

119. _____. "Afterword," in American Hunger. New York: Harper & Row, pp. 136-146.
Explains the composition and publishing history of W's two autobiographical volumes. Compares BB and AH, finding the latter to be "a more profound questioning of man's predicament in a mass consumption society whose daily practice negates its humanistic pretenses" (p. 145).

120. _____. "Concerning a Richard Wright Bibliography." CLA Journal, 21 (September), 168-169.
Apologizes for errors in the bibliography in The Unfinished Quest of Richard Wright and announces this

reference guide.

121. _____. "Fabre on His Richard Wright Bibliography." CLA Journal, 21 (September), 168.
Letter to the editor introducing 1977.120.

122. _____. "Richard Wright's Image of France." Prospects. Ed. Jack Salzman. Vol. 3. New York: Burt Franklin, pp. 315-329.
Analyzes W's ambivalent, often contradictory, but essentially favorable view of France, which he called both "an alien land" and his "sweet slum." Drawing on W's unpublished writings and on the French press, Fabre examines W's attitudes toward French racial tolerance, Paris as a cultural center, the serenity of Parisian daily life, French inefficiency, France as a vantage point from which to understand America, colonialism and assimilationism, and France as an alternative to the United States and the Soviet Union. Fabre treats more briefly France's impact on W. This essay was first delivered at the Wright Conference at the University of Iowa in 1971.

123. Felsenthal, Carol. "Heartening, Disillusioning: Communism in the Ghetto." Bremerton Sun (24 June), p. 3.
Favorable review of AH and unfavorable review of Stephen Birmingham's Certain People: America's Black Elite. Felsenthal stresses W's disillusionment with the North as a racial haven and his experience with the Communist Party.
Reprinted: 1977.124.

124. _____. "Tougher Times Recalled; Birmingham Fails in Study." Willingboro (N. J.) Burlington County Times (7 August), p. C-4.
Reprint of 1977.123.

125. Ferguson, Alfred R. "Black Men, White Cities: The Quest for Humanity by Black Protagonists in James Baldwin's Another Country and Richard Wright's The Outsider." Ball State University Forum, 18 (Spring), 51-58.
Argues that whereas Baldwin emphasizes the conflict between the city as history and Rufus Scott, W stresses the alienation of Cross Damon from all social values. Striving to achieve the existential autonomy of the self, Damon denies human relationships and experiences only horror.

126. Ferguson, Sally. "Short Stories: Wonderfully Loving Transpositions."

Humanities, 7 (April), 1-3.
Mentions the television dramatization of "Almos' a Man" sponsored by the National Endowment for the Humanities.

127. Ferris, Bill. Images of the South: Visits with Eudora Welty and Walker Evans. Southern Folklore Reports, No. 1. Memphis: Center for Southern Folklore, p. 23.
Ferris mentions W briefly in an interview with Welty.

128. Fettrow, Diane S. Diringer. "The American Experience of Richard Wright." Masters Abstracts, 15 (September), 159.
A wide range of experience and knowledge enabled W to become a racial spokesman. He traces the common experience of migration from rural South to urban South to industrialized North.

129. Fields, Perry. "American Hunger." Black Books Bulletin, 5 (Fall), 34-35.
Review emphasizing W's indictment of the failure of American democracy. W also lost faith in communism. The work alters our understanding of BB.

130. Fikes, Robert, Jr. "Blacks and Jews: An Annotated Bibliography." Black Books Bulletin, 5 (Winter), 79.
Notes W's resentment toward Jews as expressed in BB.

131. Fishburn, Katherine. Richard Wright's Hero: The Faces of a Rebel-Victim. Metuchen, N. J.: The Scarecrow Press, 225 pp.
Traces the development of Wright's fictional hero from initiate to victim to rebel to isolate. These stages correspond to the protagonists of BB and LD (Chapter II: "The Initiate and the Victim"), LT and NS (Chapter III: "The Victim and the Rebel"), O and "The Man Who Lived Underground" (Chapter IV: "The Rebel and the Isolate"). In a concluding chapter, Fishburn analyzes W's use of narrative point of view to show how he usually persuades the reader to identify with his "rebel-victims." In her literary analysis Fishburn draws heavily on Northrop Frye and Wayne Booth. In her examination of W's patterns of thought she cites extensive analogues from Camus, Sartre, Tillich, and Kierkegaard. Her psychological insights are based on the thought of Karen Horney. The evolution of W's hero is toward more universal significance, though the racial problem is never abandoned.

132. Fleissner, Robert. "How Bigger's

Name Was Born." Studies in Black Literature, 8 (Spring), 4-5.
Relates Bigger's name to Othello and compares the roles of the two characters.

133. Fontenot, Chester J. "Black Patterns." Prairie Schooner, 50 (Winter), 381-382.
Review of Roger Rosenblatt's Black Fiction mentioning briefly NS.

134. Ford, Clebert and Cynthia McPherson with Jean Bond, Max Bond, Yvette Hawkins, and Clayton Riley. A Guide to the Black Apple. New York: Louis J. Martin and Associates, p. 145.
Lists NS.

135. Ford, Nick Aaron. "The Evolution of James Baldwin as Essayist," in James Baldwin: A Critical Evaluation. Ed. Therman B. O'Daniel. Washington: Howard University Press, pp. 85-104.
Includes discussion of Baldwin's essays on W. Ford defends W against Baldwin's strictures.

136. Forsythe, Dennis. "The Dialectics of Black Separatism," in Black Separatism and Social Reality: Rhetoric and Reason. Ed. Raymond L. Hall. New York: Pergamon Press, pp. 195-207.
Quotes from BB.

137. Franklin, John Hope. "Negro," in Collier's Encyclopedia. Ed. William D. Halsey. Vol. 17. New York: Macmillan Educational Corporation, pp. 276-293.
Reprint of 1955.43.

138. Freeman, Gordon Query. "Climbing the Racial Mountain: The Folk Elements in the Works of Three Black Writers." Dissertation Abstracts International, 38 (December), 3641A-3642A.
W's use of folklore is tempered by his involvement with Communism. In general he works folklore into his proletarian fiction as a tool for survival in the face of oppression.

139. Freese, Peter. "James Baldwin 'A Talk to Teachers,'" in his Growing Up Black in America: Stories and Studies of Socialization. Texts for English and American Studies, ed. Peter Freese. Paderborn: Schöningh, p. 68.
Headnote containing a brief reference to W.

140. _____. "James Baldwin, Going to Meet the Man (1965)," in The Black American Short Story in the 20th Century: A Collection of Critical Essays. Ed. Peter Bruck. Amsterdam: B. R. Grüner, pp. 171-185.
Comments on Baldwin's relation to W

(p. 171).

141. _____. "John A. Williams, Son in the Afternoon (1962)," in The Black American Short Story in the 20th Century: A Collection of Critical Essays. Ed. Peter Bruck. Amsterdam: B. R. Grüner, pp. 141-155.
Mentions W on the sexual stereotype of the black man (p. 151).

142. Frémy, Dominique and Michèle Frémy. Quid? Tout pour tous. Paris: Editions Robert Laffont, p. 86.
Reprint of 1963.86.

143. Friedberg, Maurice. A Decade of Euphoria: Western Literature in Post-Stalin Russia, 1954-1964. Bloomington: Indiana University Press, pp. 11, 262.
Notes the posthumous "rehabilitation" of the "renegade" W. Collections of his short stories in Russian and Estonian appeared in the early sixties.

144. Galinsky, Hans. "German Contributions," in American Literary Scholarship: An Annual/1975. Ed. James Woodress. Durham, N. C.: Duke University Press, pp. 476-487.
Mentions Fritz Gysin's book on the grotesque in Toomer, W, and Ellison (p. 483).

145. Galloway, David. "William Melvin Kelley, The Poker Party (1961)," in The Black American Short Story in the 20th Century: A Collection of Critical Essays. Ed. Peter Bruck. Amsterdam: B. R. Grüner, pp. 129-140.
Mentions BB in contrast to Dancers on the Shore.

146. Galvin, Marc. "Problems of a Black in the 1930's." South Bend Tribune (29 May), Michiana Sec., p. 19.
Favorable review of AH stressing its treatment of W's relation to the Communist Party. The book is an important contribution to our understanding of race and politics in America.

147. Gayle, Addison, Jr. "Blueprint for Black Criticism." First World, 1 (January-February), 41-45.
Contains a discussion of the black response to NS. Except for Saunders Redding, Nick Aaron Ford, and some others, black opinion of W's novel "served only to demonstrate how closely allied Black criticism remained to Black middle-class aspirations and how subservient to white academic judgement."

148. Gibson, Donald B. "Individualism and Community in Black History and Fiction." Black American Literature Forum, 11 (Winter), 123-129.
Briefly examines BB, NS, O, and "The Man Who Lived Underground" in the context of the black migration from the South to the North. W is more interested in Northern individualism than in Southern community.

149. Goode, Stephen, ed. The American Humanities Index for 1976. Part 3. Troy, N. Y.: Whitson Publishing Company, p. 1736.
Lists two items on W.

150. Gounard, J.-F. "L'Avenir de James Baldwin." Europe: Revue Littéraire. Nos. 578-579 (June-July), pp. 186-197.
Contrasts W's affirmation of male virility with Baldwin's focus on homosexuality (p. 188). Both writers found themselves in positions where they could identify, but not resolve, the problems imposed by the American racial climate (p. 191).

151. Gray, Richard. The Literature of Memory: Modern Writers of the American South. Baltimore: The Johns Hopkins University Press, pp. 294, 295, 297.
Mentions W several times in a discussion of William Styron's The Confessions of Nat Turner.

152. Greene, J. Lee. "Black Literature and the American Literary Mainstream," in Minority Language and Literature: Retrospective and Perspective. Ed. Dexter Fisher. New York: Modern Language Association, pp. 20-28.
Mentions W in connection with the Adamic myth.

153. Greenlee, Bob. "A Time of Learning for Richard Wright." The New Haven Register (19 June), p. 4D.
Favorable review of AH, which Greenlee considers even better than BB. The episodes involving the Hoffmans and the spitting cook are especially effective. W prepared the way for Ellison.
Reprinted: 1978.209.

154. Grenander, M. E. "Criminal Responsibility in Native Son and Knock on Any Door." American Literature, 49 (May), 221-233.
Examines how the two novels argue that responsibility for the murders committed by their protagonists rests with society. Considering the relation of this notion to plot development, Grenader concludes that the two writers--especially W--were ahead of their time.

155. Grigorescu, Dan. Dicţionar crono-
logic literatura americană. Bucharest:
Editura stiintifică şi enciclopedică,
pp. 316, 464, 465, 491, 534, 535, 550,
560, 580, 594.
    Comments on NS, BB, O, LD, and LT.
    Quotes W on The Heart Is a Lonely
    Hunter and mentions W elsewhere.

156. Gross, Barry. "'Intellectual Over-
lordship': Blacks, Jews, and Native
Son." The Journal of Ethnic Studies, 5
(Fall), 51-59.
    Argues that black self-reliance is an
    important theme in the novel. At the
    end Bigger realizes that his black
    self-awareness is more important than
    any help Boris Max can provide.

157. Hale, Thomas A. "Pre-Roots: The
Literary Triangle Trade." Minority
Voices, 1 (Spring), 35-40.
    Contains a brief discussion of W's
    relation to Presence Africaine (pp.
    38-39).

158. [Hall, Raymond L.]. "The Leftist
Side of the Separatist/Nationalist Ques-
tion," in his Black Separatism and
Social Reality: Rhetoric and Reason. New
York: Pergamon Press, pp. 99-100.
    Mentions briefly BB.

159. Harper, Michael. "Afterword: A
Film," in his Images of Kin: New and
Selected Poems. Urbana: University of
Illinois Press, pp. 96-97.
    Reprint of 1973.167.

160. _____. "Heartblow: Messages," in
his Images of Kin: New and Selected
Poems. Urbana: University of Illinois
Press, pp. 94-95.
    Partial reprint of 1971.161.

161. _____. "The Meaning of Protest," in
his Images of Kin: New and Selected
Poems. Urbana: University of Illinois,
p. 93.
    Partial reprint of 1971.161.

162. Harrington, Michael. "Deleted Section of 'Black Boy' Released." The New
Orleans Times-Picayune (17 July), Sec.
3, p. 4.
    Reprint of 1977.164.
    Reprinted: 1978.209.

163. _____. "The Memoir of an Emerging
Writer." The Newark Sunday Star-Ledger
(26 June), Sec. 4, p. 12.
    Reprint of 1977.164.
    Reprinted: 1978.209.

164. _____. "Moving Account of Wright's
Rise." Chicago Sun-Times (29 May), Show
Sec., p. 7.
    Favorable review of AH. W was an art-
ist who had political interests, but
the work is not a tract. Rather it is
a moving story of W in the process of
becoming a major American writer.
Reprinted: 1977.162, 163; 1978.209.

165. Harrington, Ollie. "Look Homeward
Baby," in A Freedomways Reader: Afro-
America in the Seventies. Ed. Ernest
Kaiser. New York: International Publish-
ers, pp. 94-112.
    Reprint of 1973.174.

165a. _____. "The Mysterious Death of
Richard Wright." New York Daily World
(17 December), World Magazine Sec., pp.
M4-M5.
    Reviews W's early career and discus-
    ses his unwillingness to have AH
    published because of its anti-Commu-
    nism. Recalls W's complaints about
    FBI and CIA activity in Paris and
    speculates that he may have been
    assassinated.

166. Harrington, William. "Wright Has
Last Word in Biographical Fragment." The
Columbus (Ohio) Dispatch (10 July), Sec.
I, p. 6.
    Favorable review of AH emphasizing
    W's criticism of the Communist Party.
    "Wright's prose is, as always, in-
    tense, spare, quick."

167. Hatch, James V. "Theodore Ward,
Black American Playwright," in A Free-
domways Reader: Afro-America in the
Seventies. Ed. Ernest Kaiser. New York:
International Publishers, pp. 64-68.
    Reprint of 1975.100.

168. _____ and OMANii Abdullah. Black
Playwrights, 1823-1977: An Annotated
Bibliography of Plays. New York: Bowker,
pp. 250-251.
    Includes eight items on W, most of
    them unpublished.

169. Hearn, Charles R. The American
Dream in the Great Depression. Contributions in American Studies, No. 28. Westport, Conn.: Greenwood Press, pp. 126-
127.
    Discusses NS with emphasis on Bigger
    as a social outsider who is denied
    participation in the American Dream.

170. Helmreich, William B. "Afro-Ameri-
cans and Africa: Anthropological and
Sociological Investigations," in Black
Separatism and Social Reality: Rhetoric
and Reason. Ed. Raymond L. Hall. New
York: Pergamon Press, pp. 151-158.
    Mentions briefly NS.

171. Hemenway, Robert. "Phyllis Rauch
Klotman. Another Man Gone: The Black
Runner in Contemporary Afro-American

Literature." Black American Literature
Forum, 11 (Winter), 158.
      Mentions W briefly.

172. _____. Zora Neale Hurston: A Literary Biography. Urbana: University of
Illinois Press, pp. 5, 14, 220, 240,
241, 242, 244, 245, 255, 307, 333, 334,
335.
      Contains numerous mentions of W,
      including brief discussion of his
      review of Hurston's Their Eyes Were
      Watching God (pp. 240-241) and her
      review of UTC (pp. 334-335).

173. Hogan, William. "American Hunger."
San Francisco Chronicle (30 May), p. 31.
      Favorable notice pointing out that
      AH must be read with BB to have its
      full impact.

174. _____. "Richard Wright." San Francisco Chronicle (2 March), p. 43.
      Announces the publication of AH in
      May and comments on the W archive at
      Yale.

175. Howe, Irving. "Black Boy, Black
Man." The New York Times Book Review (26
June), pp. 1, 34.
      Favorable review of AH, which should
      have been published earlier. Of spe-
      cial interest is W's account of his
      relation to the Communist Party. At
      times the reader is uncertain whether
      the narrative voice is that of the
      young or the mature W, but the book
      is welcome.
      Partially reprinted: 1978.133.

176. _____ and Michael Walzer. Untitled
headnote. Dissent, 24 (Spring), 156.
      Introduces "With Black Radicals in
      Chicago," a portion of the forth-
      coming AH.

177. Isaacson, David. "Wright, Richard.
American Hunger." Library Journal, 102
(1 May), 1011.
      Favorable review. "Although not as
      emotionally powerful as Black Boy,
      this book is thematically richer
      because Wright extends his personal
      story of racial oppression in the
      South to a more considered account of
      the failure of American and Western
      culture to recognize its need for
      moral, not just political, change."

178. Iyengar, Sreenidhi. Indian Contri-
butions in American Studies, 1895-1977.
Hyderabad: The American Studies Research
Centre, p. 95.
      Lists five items on W: one by B. K.
      Mitra, one by Amritjit Singh, and
      three by Raman Singh.

179. James, C. L. R. "Laski, St. Paul

and Stalin," in his The Future in the
Present: Selected Writings. Westport,
Conn.: Lawrence Hill, pp. 95-105.
      Reprint of 1944.111.

180. _____. "The Revolutionary Answer to
the Negro Problem in the USA," in his
The Future in the Present: Selected
Writings. Westport, Conn.: Lawrence
Hill, pp. 119-127.
      Reprint of 1948.179a.

181. Jarrett, Hobart. "From a Region in
My Mind: The Essays of James Baldwin,"
in James Baldwin: A Critical Evaluation.
Ed. Therman B. O'Daniel. Washington:
Howard University Press, pp. 105-125.
      Mentions Baldwin's essays on W (p.
      107) and quotes from "Everybody's
      Protest Novel" (p. 111).

182. Jefferson, Margo. "Black Boy Grows
Up." Newsweek, 89 (30 May), 81.
      Favorable review of AH. Best read in
      conjunction with BB, it also has
      independent interest for its account
      of the conflict between W's personal
      and political needs.

182a. Jensen, Malcolm C. America in
Trial. Boston: Houghton Mifflin, pp.
254, 268.
      Includes W in a list of forty-five
      American novelists. Notes the publi-
      cation of NS in a chronology of
      "Blacks in American History."

183. Johnson, Charles. "American Hunger:
Richard Wright." American Book Review, 1
(December), 6-7.
      Highly favorable review emphasizing
      W's nature as an "archeologist of
      consciousness" who works from subjec-
      tivity outward to a "fresh encounter
      with the world."

183a. Johnson, Diane. "The Oppressor in
the Next Room." The New York Review of
Books, 24 (10 November), 6, 8.
      Mentions W briefly.

184. Johnson, Thomas A. "Search for
Dignity." The New York Times (2 July),
p. 15.
      Favorable review of AH, which reveals
      W as a young writer struggling to
      cope with a racist society. Much of
      the work's social indictment still
      holds true.

185. Jones, Gayl and Michael S. Harper.
"Gayl Jones: An Interview." The Massachusetts Review, 18 (Winter), 692-715.
      Refers to an article on W and Zora
      Neale Hurston (pp. 704-705) and com-
      ments on NS as "blues storytelling,
      blues vision" (p. 709).
      Reprinted: 1979.142.

186. Jones, Harry L. "Style, Form, and Content in the Short Fiction of James Baldwin," in James Baldwin: A Critical Evaluation. Ed. Therman B. O'Daniel. Washington: Howard University Press, pp. 143-150.
    Quotes from "Alas, Poor Richard" (p. 145).

186a. Josey, E. J. and Ann Allen Shockley. "Major Afro-American Collections," in their Handbook of Black Librarianship. Littleton, Col.: Libraries Unlimited, Inc., pp. 245-252.
    Mentions W holdings at the Carter G. Woodson Regional Library of the Chicago Public Library and at Yale.

187. Julien, Claude. "Schraufnagel, Noel: From Apology to Protest: The Black American Novel." Afram Newsletter, No. 3 (Winter), pp. 12-13.
    Review mentioning NS.

188. Kahn, Barbara. "American Hunger by Richard Wright." View Northwest (August), p. 6.
    Review contrasting the work's pessimism to the comparative optimism of BB. Notes also W's disillusionment with the Communist Party.

188a. Kaiser, Ernest. "Library Holdings on Afro-Americans," in Handbook of Black Librarianship. Ed. E. J. Josey and Ann Allen Shockley. Littleton, Col.: Libraries Unlimited, Inc., pp. 228-245.
    Mentions W holdings at the Schomburg Center, Yale, and Kent State.

189. _____. "Recent Books." Freedomways, 17 (Third Quarter), 182-191.
    Includes a rather unfavorable review of AH (p. 190) noting that other black people in W's autobiographical writings serve as foils to the author's personal development.

189a. Kanzaki, Hiroshi. "How Richard Wright Was Born." Chofu Gakuen Joshi Tanki Daigaku Kiyo [Bulletin of Chofu Gakuen Women's Junior College], 10 (September), 21-49.
    An account of W's career before and after NS, the role played by the Communist Party, and the meaning of the publication of UTC and NS. Concludes that W "has pursued the theme of the Negro's search for identity." In English. [Y. H. and T. K.]

190. Karrer, Wolfgang. "Richard Wright, Fire and Cloud (1938)," in The Black American Short Story in the 20th Century: A Collection of Critical Essays. Ed. Peter Bruck. Amsterdam: B. R. Grüner, pp. 99-110.
    Analyzes the story as proletarian

realism with special attention to language and perspective. W's combination of the elements of speech, description, and thought reinforces the thematic movement from individualism to collectivism. He develops the story's perspective by the interplay between black English and standard English.

191. Kein, Sybil. "Teaching Afro-American Literature to Undergraduates: A Humanistic Approach." Black American Literature Forum, 11 (Fall), 94-96.
    Contains a brief reference to BB (p. 95).

192. Keyssar, Helene. "Black Drama: Reflections of Class and Class Consciousness." Prospects. Ed. Jack Salzman. Vol. 3. New York: Burt Franklin, pp. 263-288.
    Includes discussion of the play NS with comparisons to A Raisin in the Sun. Keyssar stresses Bigger's lack of a place in society.

193. Kibler, James E. et al. "A Checklist of Scholarship on Southern Literature for 1976." Mississippi Quarterly, 30 (Spring), 313-377.
    Lists twelve items on W (p. 367).

194. Killens, John Oliver. "The Development of a Black Psyche: An Interview with John Oliver Killens." Black American Literature Forum, 11 (Fall), 83-89.
    Killens mentions W briefly (pp. 87, 88).

195. King, James R. "Richard Wright: His Life and Writings." Negro History Bulletin, 40 (September-October), 738-743.
    Discusses the relation between W's life in the South and his writing. Among the influences on W were family, religion, education, white values, and the Communist Party. One of the major themes deriving from these influences was a quest for individuality and identity.

196. Kinnamon, Keneth. "Isolation and Community in Richard Wright's American Hunger." Minority Voices, 1 (Fall), 104-106.
    Analyzes patterns of tension between self and society in W's account of his life in Chicago. Alienated from other blacks, W turned to the John Reed Club and the Communist Party for comradeship. Rejecting political squabbling, he used art as a means of achieving community, but he retained his radical vision.

197. _____. "Katherine Fishburn. Richard Wright's Hero: The Faces of a Rebel-Victim." Black American Literature

Forum, 11 (Winter), 157-158.
Unfavorable review complaining of problems of chronology, misreadings, and excessive reliance on secondary sources.

198. Kirkland, James W. and Paul W. Dowell. "Questions for Discussion and Writing," in their Fiction: The Narrative Art. Englewood Cliffs, N. J.: Prentice-Hall, p. 280.
Questions to accompany "Big Black Good Man" (pp. 272-280).

199. ____. "Wright, Richard," in their Fiction: The Narrative Art. Englewood Cliffs, N. J.: Prentice-Hall, p. 434.
Biographical note to introduce "Big Black Good Man."

200. Kirsch, Robert. "A Grown-Up 'Black Boy.'" Los Angeles Times (29 May), Book Sec., pp. 1, 71.
Favorable review of AH with special praise for the account of W's treatment by the Communist Party. America is now more receptive to W's social message than it was during his lifetime.

201. Kisor, Henry. "A Black Author Who Captured an Era." San Francisco Sunday Examiner and Chronicle (26 June), Scene Sec., p. 2.
Reprint of 1977.204.

202. ____. "Books." The Birmingham News (29 May), Sec. E, p. 7.
Reprint of 1977.204.

203. ____. "Out of Chicago's Past, A 'New' Richard Wright Memoir." Chicago Daily News (12-13 February), pp. 7, 9.
Announcement of forthcoming publication of AH. W is one of the most important writers of the century.

204. ____. "The Rediscovery of an American Original." Chicago Daily News (21-22 May), Panorama Sec., p. 6.
Analyzes W's status in American literature and comments on the reception of AH. Notes that other books from the unpublished material may follow. Reprinted: 1977.201, 202.

205. Klise, Thomas S. "The Odyssey of Richard Wright," in his Sound Filmstrips for Classes in Literature, Drama, and Composition. Peoria, Ill.: Thomas S. Klise Company, p. 6.
Brief estimate of W's importance. Reprinted: 1978.144.

206. Klotman, Phyllis Rauch. Another Man Gone: The Black Runner in Contemporary Afro-American Literature. National University Publications in Literary Criticism Series, ed. John E. Becker. Port Washington, N. Y.: Kennikat Press, pp. 53-64, 111-112.
Argues that BB demonstrates W's close affinity with the "rebellious slave" exemplified by Douglass and Nat Turner. W's development centers on the movement away from entrapment (in the early stories) to a heightened consciousness linked to physical escape (most clearly in O). Klotman also discusses W's role in John A. Williams's The Man Who Cried I Am. Includes revised reprints of 1972.130; 1973.197, 198.

207. L., A. D. "'American Hunger.'" Marion (Mass.) Sippican Sentinel (28 July), p. 12.
Review of AH. Although not equal to BB, it "is short and to the point."

207a. Lake, Dorothy. "Best Selling Books by Black Authors," in Handbook of Black Librarianship. Ed. E. J. Josey and Ann Allen Shockley. Littleton, Col.: Libraries Unlimited, Inc., pp. 154-155.
Lists BB.

208. Lamon, Lester C. Black Tennesseans 1900-1930. Twentieth-Century America Series, ed. Dewey W. Grantham. Knoxville: The University of Tennessee Press, p. 249.
Quotes BB on W's feelings aroused by reports of racial violence.

209. Larson, Kim. "Book Beat." Billings Gazette (28 October), Sec. D, p. 22.
Favorable review of AH mentioning the episodes of the spitting cook and the medical research laboratory.

210. Lee, Leslie. "Scene from Almos' a Man," in The American Short Story. Ed. Calvin Skaggs. New York: Dell, pp. 270-274.
Excerpt from the film script for televison.

210a. Lehman, Paul. "The Development of a Black Psyche: An Interview with John Oliver Killens." Black American Literature Forum, 11 (Fall), 83-89.
Refers briefly to WML (p. 87).

210b. Leonard, Thomas M. Day by Day: The Forties. New York: Facts on File, pp. 95, 125, 477.
Chronicles W's award of the Spingarn Medal, the selection of NS by the American Writers Congress as the best novel of 1940, and the publication of BB.

211. Libman, Valentina Abramova. Amerikanskaya literatura v russkikh perevodakh i kritike: Bibliografia, 1776-

1975. Moscow: Nauka, pp. 210-211.
Lists eleven primary and twenty-five secondary sources in Russian concerning W.

212. Lieberman, Laurence. "Derek Walcott and Michael S. Harper: The Muse of History," in his Unassigned Frequencies: American Poetry in Review, 1964-77. Urbana: University of Illinois Press, pp. 284-296.
Reprint of 1973.210.

213. Liston, Maureen. "Chester Himes, A Nigger (1937)," in The Black American Short Story in the 20th Century: A Collection of Critical Essays. Ed. Peter Bruck. Amsterdam: B. R. Grüner, pp. 85-97.
Includes discussion of Himes as a member of the "Wright School" (p. 87).

214. Loftis, N. J. "Boy at the Window Owen Dodson." The American Book Review, 1 (December), 9-10.
Mentions briefly BB.

215. Long, Robert Emmet. "Books: Richard Wright's 'American Hunger.'" The Syracuse New Times (4 September), p. 11.
Favorable review of AH stressing W's association with the Communist Party. "James Baldwin called Wright his 'spiritual father,' but he is really the kin of everyone who believes in human dignity. In him, we see a better part of ourselves."

216. Luce, Phillip Abbott. "Book Review: An American Black's Confrontation with the Communist Party." Human Events (9 July), pp. 12-13.
Favorable review of AH emphasizing its anti-Communist theme. Luce argues that Communists forty years later are similar to those W presents in this book.

217. Mackesy, Eileen M., comp. 1975 MLA Abstracts of Articles in Scholarly Journals. Vol. I. New York: Modern Language Association, p. 246.
Includes abstracts of articles on W by H. Philip Bolton, Seymour Gross, John Pyros, and Jerold J. Savory.

218. Martin, Joan M. "Teaching Afro-American Literature: The Multi-Ethnic Approach." Black American Literature Forum, 11 (Fall), 97-101.
Contains a brief reference to W (p. 97).

219. Maryknell, Herb. "'American Hunger' Takes Up Where 'Black Boy' Left Off." Evansville Press (9 June), p. 5.
Favorable review of an effective, if unoriginal, indictment of "racism, materialism and our insensitivity to our fellow man."
Reprinted: 1978.209.

220. Materassi, Mario. Il ponte sullo Harlem River: saggi e note sulla cultura e la letteratura afroamericana di oggi. Rome: Bulzoni editore, pp. 27, 35, 56, 58, 121, 140, 148, 160, 171, 189, 192, 194, 200, 256.
Mentions W briefly in the introduction and contains reprints of 1964.92; 1966.99, 100; 1968.163, 164, 165, 166; 1975.127.

221. McBride, Rebecca and David McBride. "Corrections of a Richard Wright Bibliography." CLA Journal, 20 (March), 422-423.
The authors list several errors in the bibliography and notes to Michel Fabre's The Unfinished Quest of Richard Wright.

222. McCall, Dan. "Richard Wright's American Hunger." The American Poetry Review, 6 (September-October), 40-43.
Favorable review stating that the prose is as good as that of BB, but a certain intensity is lacking. W uses "hunger" in a spiritual sense.

223. McConnell, Frank D. "Black American Literature," in Collier's Encyclopedia. Ed. William D. Halsey. Vol. 2. New York: Macmillan Educational Corporation, pp. 72-74.
Reprint of 1976.125.

223a. _____. Four Postwar American Novelists: Bellow, Mailer, Barth, and Pynchon. Chicago: The University of Chicago Press, p. 9.
Mentions Bigger Thomas.

224. McCord, Arline Sakuma and William McCord. "Urbanism, Racism and Class: Futurist Explorations in Black Separatism," in Black Separatism and Social Reality: Rhetoric and Reason. Ed. Raymond L. Hall. New York: Pergamon Press, pp. 69-78.
Mentions briefly W's feeling of alienation in Africa (p. 74).

225. McNallie, Robin. "Richard Wright's Allegory of the Cave: 'The Man Who Lived Underground.'" South Atlantic Bulletin: A Quarterly Journal Devoted to Research and Teaching in the Modern Languages and Literatures, 42 (May), 76-84.
Argues that W's model in the novella is Plato's allegory of the cave in The Republic.

226. McNally, Peter. "Painfully Honest." The Hartford Courant (9 June), p. 48.

Review of AH praising W's candor but noting that the work is fragmented. W uses anecdote, observation, and generalization to relate his apprenticeship as a writer.

227. Medler, Edward Arnold. "Howells, Wright and the Theme of Social Protest: A Comparison Using Selected Works." Dissertation Abstracts International, 37 (June), p. 7823-A.
Both Howells and W are deeply concerned with the problem of social evil. The Landlord at Lion's Head and NS present similar protagonists; A Boy's Town and BB handle the rural aspects of social experience.

228. Mendel'son, Moris Osipovich. Roman SShA segodnia. Moscow: Sovetskii pisatel', pp. 9, 29, 271-272, 299, 300.
Brief references to W and a brief discussion of Bigger Thomas (pp. 271-272).

229. Miller, James Arthur. "The Struggle for Identity in the Major Works of Richard Wright." Dissertation Abstracts International, 37 (February), 5123A-5124A.
W searched for identity in both his public and private lives. His canon constitutes a "continuum, linked by a recurring and fundamental preoccupation, stages in the development of an intellect which sought both personal and ideological solutions to the complex question of racial identity."

230. Miller, James E., Jr. "American Literature," in The World Book Encyclopedia. Ed. William H. Nault. Vol. 1. Chicago: Field Enterprises Educational Corporation, pp. 394-404d.
Reprint of 1975.132.

231. Miller, R. Baxter. "'Even After I Was Dead': The Big Sea--Paradox, Preservation, and Holistic Time." Black American Literature Forum, 11 (Summer), 39-45.
Quotes a brief mention of W by Donald C. Dickinson.

232. Millican, Arthenia Bates and Jerry W. Ward. "Legitimate Resources of the Soul." Obsidian, 3 (Spring), 14-34.
Mentions briefly BB (p. 31).

232a. Miura, Mitsuyo. "Bigger's Wandering." Junshin Kiyo [Bulletin of Junshin Junior College], 18 (20 December), 1-8.
Argues that Bigger's wandering from hatred to love prophesies W's later wandering and that Bigger's search for love is the theme of NS. [Y. H. and T. K.]

233. Mondesire, Jerome W. "After 32 Years, The Ironic Sequel to 'Black Boy.'" The Philadelphia Inquirer (12 June), Sec. H., p. 14.
Favorable review of AH summarizing its contents. Notes the different impression of the conclusion of BB gained after reading AH. Reprinted: 1978.209.

234. Monroe, Stephen A. "The Final Chapter in a Vital Odyssey." Rochester Democrat and Chronicle (15 May), Sec. G., p. 2.
Review of AH stressing W's experience with the Communist Party and his inability to make black friends. Not as good as BB, AH is important for its commentary on racism.

235. Moon, Henry Lee. "Spingarn Medal," in The World Book Encyclopedia. Ed. William H. Nault. Vol. 18. Chicago: Field Enterprises Educational Corporation, p. 619.
Reprint of 1960.201.

236. Moore, Gerian Steve. "Richard Wright's American Hunger." CLA Journal, 21 (September), 79-89.
Unfavorable review arguing that W did not really understand the black experience. Analyzes Ellison's comments on BB and compares at length AH and BB.

237. Mootry, Maria K. "Love and Death in the Black Pastoral." Obsidian, 3 (Summer), 5-11.
Considers "Big Boy Leaves Home" as an important example of the failed pastoral.

238. Moreland, Pamela. "A Personal Glimpse of Wright's Hunger.'" Pasadena Star-News (5 June), Sec. A, p. 11.
Review of AH recalling the impact of BB and stating that AH offers "a satisfying conclusion that points to the man Wright will become." W never found the eternal verities which he sought.

239. Morgan, Edward P. "In the Public Interest Commentary # 209" (5 August).
Transcript of a syndicated radio broadcast recalling Morgan's friendship with W and quoting from AH.

240. Moskowitz, Mickey. "American Hunger." School Library Journal, 24 (September), 56.
Favorable review stressing W's experience with the Communist Party. W shows a capacity for humor in AH.

241. Muliarchik, A. S. "Pisatel' i sovremennaia Amerika," in his Amerikanskaia

literatura i obshchestvenno-politiches-
kaia bor'ba. Moscow: Nauka, pp. 6-41.
Mentions W as a defender of the
Soviet Union in the thirties (p. 31).

242. _____. "Problemy mezhdunarudnoi
politiki v sovremennoi literatura SShA,"
in his Amerikanskaia literatura i ob-
shchestvenno-politicheskaia bor'ba. Moscow: Nauka, pp. 134-153.
Recalls W's disillusionment with communism (p. 137).

243. _____. "Sud'by molodezhnogo dvi-
zhenia i amerikanskii roman pervoi polo-
viny 70-kh godov," in his Amerikanskaia
literatura i obshchestvenno-politiches-
kaia bor'ba. Moscow: Nauka, pp. 79-105.
Calls W the greatest black prose
writer of the twentieth century (p.
101).

244. Murchison, William. "The Unmaking
of a Communist." New Rochelle Standard-
Star (11 June).
Favorable review of AH with quotations expressing W's reservations
about communism.

245. Myers, Carol Fairbanks. "Supplement
to 'A Bibliographical Introduction to
the American Literature of the 1930's
and the Backgrounds': Black American
Literature." Bulletin of Bibliography &
Magazine Notes, 34 (April-June), 68-72.
Lists six works by W.

245a. Nagel, James. "A Conversation in
Boston," in his American Fiction: Historical and Critical Essays. Boston:
Northeastern University Press, pp. 175-
202.
In a panel discussion Darwin Turner
mentions W briefly.

246. Nilon, Charles. "Black Literature,"
in American Literary Scholarship: An
Annual/1975. Ed. James Woodress. Durham,
N. C.: Duke University Press, pp. 417-
445.
Reviews W scholarship on pp. 426-428.
Mentions W briefly on pp. 296, 439,
483, 496.

247. O'Connell, Shaun. "Richard Wright:
An Honest Man and a Good Writer." Boston
Sunday Globe (4 September), p. A12.
Favorable review of AH. "As autobiography, 'American Hunger' is often
sketchy in particulars yet brilliant
in its capacity to draw general conclusions from experience."

248. O'Connor, Margaret Anne. "Fiction:
The 1930s to the 1950s," in American
Literary Scholarship: An Annual/1975.
Ed. James Woodress. Durham, N. C.: Duke
University Press, pp. 295-326.

Mentions W briefly in connection with
William Targ's Indecent Pleasures (p.
296).

248a. Omori, Toshikazu. "Richard
Wright's Humanism: Black Boy." Nihon
Daigaku Seisan Kogakubu Hokoku [Nihon
University Industrial Engineering Fac-
ulty Report], Series B, 10 (June), 49-
65.
An account, based on BB, of the deep
South and W's philosophical journey.
Regards the cry for regaining human-
ism as the theme of BB. [Y. H. and
T. K.]

249. Orsagh, Jacqueline E. "Baldwin's
Female Characters--A Step Forward?" in
James Baldwin: A Critical Evaluation.
Ed. Therman O'Daniel. Washington: Howard
University Press, pp. 56-68.
Contains a disparaging reference to
W's portraiture of women characters
(p. 60).

250. Ostendorf, Bernhard. "Die afro-
amerikanische Literatur nach 1945: Tendenzen und Aspekte," in Die amerikanische Literatur der Gegenwart: Aspekte
und Tendenzen. Ed. Hans Bungert. Stuttgart: Philipp Reclam jun., pp. 128-153.
Mentions W briefly (pp. 130, 132,
149).

250a. Ouchi, Giichi. "Denial and Renunciation in Richard Wright's Savage Holiday." Waseda Daigaku Kyoyo Shogaku Kenkyu [Waseda University General Studies],
56 (December), 27-43.
A historical account of the negative
criticism on SH. The novel, thriving
on a pattern of denial and renunciation, is characteristic of W's treatment and indicative of his desire to
discard the old and gain the new.
[Y. H. and T. K.]

250b. _____. "Richard Wright," in his
Amerika Kokujin Bungaku [Afro-American
Literature]. Tokyo: Hyoronsha, pp. 82-
120.
A historical and critical discussion
of W's life and work. Does not see
him as a pioneer bent on attacking
hypocrisy in a democratic society.
His anger and protest were not necessarily motivated by the race issue,
but by a universal awareness of man's
plight. The Depression that gave rise
to protest literature made the public
regard the problem of race as that of
man as a whole. W's characters--
Bigger, Cross, and Fishbelly--all
want to be Americans, but they are
not accepted as Americans because of
their skin color. As long as racial
prejudice and injustice continue to
exist in American society, Ouchi

observes, the characters will continue to be what W calls "negative Americans." [Y. H. and T. K.]

251. Øverland, Orm. "The Grotesque in American Negro Fiction: Jean Toomer, Richard Wright, and Ralph Ellison. [By] Fritz Gysin." English Studies, 58 (October), 462-465.
Unfavorable review showing Gysin's confusing terminology in his treatment of W.

252. Page, James A. "Wright, Richard," in his Selected Black American Authors: An Illustrated Bio-Bibliography. Boston: G. K. Hall, p. 304.
Includes information under the following categories: biographical-personal, career-professional writings, honors and awards, sidelights, and sources.

253. Payne, Les. "Difference Between Two Works Like Diamonds Compared with Cut Glass." Waukegan News-Sun (14 May), Sec. B, pp. 1-2.
Unfavorable review of AH complaining of thinness and fragmentation. Explains the relation of AH to BB. Reprinted: 1977.254.

254. _____. "End of Black Boy." The Houston Chronicle (22 May), p. 20.
Reprint of 1977.253.

255. Pearson, Norman Holmes. "American Literature," in The Encyclopedia Americana. Ed. Bernard S. Cayne. Vol. 1. New York: Americana Corporation, pp. 691-709.
Reprint of 1968.178.

256. Penkower, Monty Noam. The Federal Writers' Project: A Study of Government Patronage of the Arts. Urbana: University of Illinois Press, pp. 174, 177-179, 197.
Mentions "The Ethics of Living Jim Crow" and U. S. Representative Joe Starnes's attack on it. Discusses W's relation to the Project.

257. Perry, Patsy Brewington. "One Day, When I Was Lost: Baldwin's Unfulfilled Obligation," in James Baldwin: A Critical Evaluation. Ed. Therman B. O'Daniel. Washington: Howard University Press, pp. 213-227.
Notes that Baldwin makes the kind of protest in his scenario that he objected to in W's fiction.

258. Perry, Roy E. "Wright Fought for Human Dignity." The Nashville Banner (14 May), p. 5.
Favorable review of AH stressing its treatment of W's relation to the

Communist Party. Praises Michel Fabre's "Afterword."
Reprinted: 1978.209.

259. Pinckney, Darryl. "Richard Wright: The Unnatural History of a Native Son." The Village Voice (4 July), pp. 80-82.
Essay-review of AH with attention to the whole of W's career. As a black writer W was forced out of the mainstream of American literature. AH is mainly a political autobiography. Partially reprinted: 1978.192.

260. Pintarich, Paul. "For Wright, Millett, Life is a Desperate Fight." The Portland Sunday Oregonian (15 May), p. G5.
Includes a mixed review of AH. Pintarich likes the first part of the book, but finds the treatment of the Communist Party tedious. He also dislikes W's "maudlin introspection."

261. Pluto, Terry. "Wright Wrote to Right Wrongs." The Cleveland Press (4 June), Showtime Sec., p. 23.
Unfavorable review of AH complaining of sketchiness. Praises Michel Fabre's "Afterword."

261a. Polk, Noel. "New Book Traces Life of 'Black Boy' in Chicago." The Columbia (S. C.) State (14 August).
Favorable review of AH. Not "as moving as 'Black Boy,' it is still an important book by an important American writer . . . ."

262. Portelli, Alessandro. Bianchi e neri nella letteratura americana. Bari: De Donato, pp. 17, 30, 85-89, 90, 91, 92, 97-98, 142, 143, 330, 337, 338, 369.
Aruges that NS (pp. 85-89) transcends the formulas of protest and proletarian fiction because Bigger is a "victim as agressor." Comments also on "Big Boy Leaves Home" (pp. 97-98) and mentions W elsewhere.

263. Powell, Richard. "Richard Wright." The Massachusetts Review, 18 (Autumn), back cover.
An etching of W.

264. Pratt, Ilana. "Black Writer's Hope Reaches Out to Others." Joliet Herald-News (6 November), Sec. C., p. 3.
Favorable review of AH praising W's mastery of narrative and metaphor.

265. Rampersad, Arnold. "Baraka: The Renegade and the Mask by Kimberly W. Benston." The New Republic, 176 (30 April), 33-36.
Mentions W's "Blueprint for Negro Writing."

266. Rao, Vimala. "The Regionalism of Richard Wright's Native Son." Indian Journal of American Studies, 7, pp. 94-102.
    Discusses the importance of Chicago in the novel. It becomes mythic and symbolic as well as a factual setting.

267. Ravitz, Abe C. "Original Ending Is 'Black Boy' Sequel." The Sunday Cleveland Plain Dealer (15 May), Sec. 5, p. 12.
    Favorable review of AH, a gripping account of W's Chicago years.

268. Real, Willi. "Ralph Ellison, King of the Bingo Game (1944)," in The Black American Short Story in the 20th Century: A Collection of Critical Essays. Ed. Peter Bruck. Amsterdam: B. R. Grüner, pp. 111-127.
    Includes a discussion of Ellison's relation to W (p. 112).

269. ____. "Richard Wright, Native Son (1940)," in Der Roman im Englischunterricht der Sekundarstufe II. Ed. Peter Freese and Liesel Hermes. Paderborn: Schöningh, pp. 169-184.
    Describes the influence of NS, interprets the novel in terms of role behavior and prejudice, and provides some suggestions for teaching.

270. ____, ed. Racism in America. Texts for English and American Studies 4, ed. Peter Freese. Paderborn: Schöningh, 100 pp.
    Contains annotated excerpts from "The Man Who Lived Underground" and NS as well as the complete, annotated text of "The Man Who Killed a Shadow." These selections are related to passages from BB. See 1978.197.

271. Reed, Ishmael. "Black Culture and Black Consciousness Lawrence W. Levine." The American Book Review, 1 (December), 6.
    Mentions briefly that W complained that Marxists wanted to "discipline" him.

272. Reilly, John M. "Richard Wright's Curious Thriller, Savage Holiday." CLA Journal, 21 (December), 218-223.
    Analyzes the novel as an experiment with psychoanalytical fiction and with white characters. Reilly also examines the work's relation to crime literature.

273. Rogers, Rutherford D. "Report of the University Librarian July 1975-June 1976." Bulletin of Yale University, Series 73, No. 1 (15 January), 63 pp.
    Includes a description (pp. 13-14) of

the W archive, the Beinecke Rare Book and Manuscript Library's major acquisition of the year, and lists its administering committee.

274. Rose, Vattel T., Jennifer Jordan, Virginia Barrett, Dorothy Evans, Enid Bogle, Lorraine Henry, and Leota Lawrence. "An Annual Bibliography of Afro-American, African, and Caribbean Literature for the Year, 1976." CLA Journal, 21 (September), 100-157.
    Lists fourteen items about W (p. 119).

275. Rosengarten, Theodore. "Horror and Glory of a Native Son." Manchester Guardian Weekly (17 July), p. 18.
    Reprint of 1977.276.

276. ____. "Horror and Glory of a Native Son." The Washington Post (19 June), Book World Sec., p. K1.
    Favorable review of AH, a "poignant, bewildering book," stressing W's complex relations with the Communist Party. His rejection by Communists was the most bitter in a series of rejections he had experienced.
    Reprinted: 1977.275, 277, 278; 1978.209; 1982.50.

277. ____. "Horror, Glory of a 'Native Son.'" Denver Rocky Mountain News (10 July), Now Sec., p. 32.
    Reprint of 1977.276.

278. ____. "Wright's Testimony." New York Post (25 June), p. 23.
    Reprint of 1977.276.

279. Rothchild, Sylvia. "Reviews and Reflections." Boston Jewish Advocate (14 July), p. 19.
    Favorable review of AH noting its portrayal of Jews. The work has value both in a personal and a social sense.

280. Rowell, Charles H. "Studies in Afro-American Literature: An Annual Annotated Bibliography, 1976." Obsidian, 3 (Winter), 80-104.
    Lists nine items on W and crosslists nine other items.

281. Saito, Tadatoshi. "Ralph Ellison and James Baldwin in the 1950's," in American Literature in the 1950's. Tokyo: The Tokyo Chapter of the American Literature Society of Japan, pp. 32-40.
    Contrasts Ellison and Baldwin to W (pp. 32-33).

282. Sanford, John. "Richard Wright, 1908-1960: Crèche 4596, Père Lachaise," in his View from This Wilderness: American Literature as History. Santa Bar-

bara: Capra Press, pp. 179-180.
Brief meditation on W's death and cremation in relation to his life.

283. Schultz, Elizabeth. "'Free in Fact and at Last': The Image of the Black Woman in Black American Fiction," in What Manner of Woman: Essays on English and American Life and Literature. Ed. Marlene Springer. New York: New York University Press, pp. 316-344.
Refers briefly to Mrs. Thomas of NS.

284. Scruggs, Charles. "'All Dressed Up But No Place to Go': The Black Writer and His Audience During the Harlem Renaissance." American Literature, 48 (January), 543-563.
The concluding paragraph states that "Blueprint for Negro Writing" corrected the earlier view by showing that "the central concern of the black artist was not 'art' but the total culture in which his people lived."

285. _____. "The Way of the New World: The Black Novel in America. By Addison Gayle." The Arizona Quarterly, 33 (Spring), 94-96.
Review mentioning briefly W and NS.

286. Shaugnessy, Mina P. Errors and Expectations: A Guide for the Teacher of Basic Writing. New York: Oxford University Press, pp. 79, 251-255.
Includes a sample lesson plan for teaching structural analysis based on one of the catalogs in BB. Concludes that W felt safer and happier in the "world of magic" than in the "logical" America which denied him. In W's world there is "no logical connection between what you do and what happens to you."

286a. Shockley, Ann Allen. "The Best Seller List and Black Authors," in Handbook of Black Librarianship. Ed. E. J. Josey and Ann Allen Shockley. Littleton, Col.: Libraries Unlimited, Inc., pp. 153-154.
Mentions BB.

287. Silvergleid, Ina. "'Black Boy' Sequel Loses Optimism." The Champaign-Urbana Daily Illini (15 October), Spectrum Sec., p. 8.
Mixed review of AH. The work is valuable for tracing the author's life after BB, but the protracted account of his relationship with the Communist Party slows down the pace of the "novel" [sic]. W's sense of alienation is universal.

288. Skaggs, Calvin. "Introduction," in his The American Short Story. New York: Dell, pp. 11-18.

Contains a paragraph on "Almos' a Man" as an initiation story.

289. Sloan, Irving J. The Blacks in America 1492-1977: A Chronology & Fact Book. Fourth revised edition. Dobbs Ferry, N. Y.: Oceana Publications, pp. 33, 43.
Reprint of 1965.116.

290. Smidt, Kristian. An Outline History of English Literature in Britain and the United States. Stavanger: J. W. Cappelens Forlag, p. 155.
Mentions W and James T. Farrell as "tough naturalists . . . proletarians seriously at odds with society."

291. Smitherman, Geneva. Talkin and Testifyin: The Language of Black America. Boston: Houghton Mifflin, pp. 80-82, 102-103, 113-114, 121-128, 131-133, 146.
Discusses briefly aspects of language in BB, LD, and "Big Boy Leaves Home."

292. Sosna, Morton. In Search of the Silent South: Southern Liberals and the Race Issue. New York: Columbia University Press, pp. 184-185.
Mentions the reactions of David Cohn and Lillian Smith to NS.

293. Starr, Alvin. "Richard Wright and the Communist Party--The James T. Farrell Factor." CLA Journal, 21 (September), 41-50.
Analyzes W's relationship with the Communist Party in the thirties and discusses Farrell's influence, especially on "Blueprint for Negro Writing," LT, and NS. The Studs Lonigan trilogy had a strong impact on W. Both writers were successful in mixing art and propaganda.

294. Stepto, Robert B. "I Thought I Knew These People: Richard Wright & the Afro-American Literary Tradition." The Massachusetts Review, 18 (Autumn), 525-541.
Examines W's place in the tradition, giving special attention to questions of voice, audience, conception of the hero, and relation to antecedent texts such as the slave narratives, Chesnutt, and DuBois. NS and BB are emphasized. Stepto also discusses W's influence on subsequent writers and critics.
Reprinted: 1979.244.

295. _____ and Michael S. Harper. "Study and Experience: An Interview with Ralph Ellison." The Massachusetts Review, 18 (Autumn), 417-435.
Ellison comments on "Blueprint for Negro Writing" and the current interest in BB and NS.
Reprinted: 1979.247.

296. _____ and Toni Morrison. "'Intimate Things in Place': A Conversation with Toni Morrison." The Massachusetts Review, 18 (Autumn), 473-489.
    Stepto refers to Bigger as a composite portrait in asking Morrison about characterization in her novels. Reprinted: 1979.248; 1980.240.

297. Stern, Milton R. and Seymour L. Gross. "Richard Wright (1908-1960)," in their The Viking Press Portable Library American Literature Survey: The Twentieth Century. Third edition. Harmondsworth, Middlesex: Penguin Books, pp. 178-181.
    Biographical-critical headnote to "The Ethics of Living Jim Crow." Includes a bibliography.

298. Stevens, Mark. "Richard Wright: His Race Struggle Went Political." The Christian Science Monitor (12 May), p. 23.
    Mixed review of AH. An interesting sequel to BB, it fails to distinguish between racial and political oppression.

299. Stocking, Fred. "On Richard Wright and 'Almos' a Man,'" in The American Short Story. Ed. Calvin Skaggs. New York: Dell, pp. 275-281.
    Biographical sketch and brief analysis of the story stressing its psychological dimension. The theme is characteristically Wrightian: "the search for that personal freedom which enables one to discover his own identity as a human being" (p. 275).

300. Stone, Albert E. "Cato's Mirror: The Face of Violence in American Autobiography." Prospects. Ed. Jack Salzman. Vol. 3. New York: Burt Franklin, pp. 331-369.
    Mentions BB (p. 367).

301. Sugiura, Ginsaku. "The Fifties and American Fiction," in American Literature in the 1950's. Tokyo: The Tokyo Chapter of the American Literature Society of Japan, pp. 13-21.
    Contrasts NS to Invisible Man, which is "far more complex and profound" (p. 17).

301a. Suzuki, Mikio. "Another Aspect of R. Wright: The Publication of the Posthumous Lawd Today." Waseda Daigaku Kyoyo Shogaku Kenkyu [Waseda University General Studies], 55 (November), 21-39.
    LT impressively portrays a powerless black worker's remonstrance of self and humanity. The novel is indicative of Wright's talent as an artist rather than as a propagandist. [Y. H.

and T. K.]

301b. Tamiya, Masaharu. "A Study of Wright and Ellison with Special References to NS and Invisible Man." Yamanashi Eiwa Tanki Daigaku Kiyo [Bulletin of Yamanashi Eiwa Junior College], 11 (30 October), 93-112.
    The contrast in theme and treatment between the two novels reflects "the development of the American novel."

302. Tanaka, Takeshi. "Studies in English Literature, 1951-1960," in American Literature in the 1950's. Tokyo: The Tokyo Chapter of the American Literature Society of Japan, pp. 241-266.
    Lists three items on W.

303. Taylor, Clyde. "Salt Water Negars." First World, 1 (March-April), 34-36.
    Review of Chinweizu's The West and the Rest of Us mentioning W.

304. Taylor, Douglas and R. P. Powell. True Black Man's History. New York: Philosophical Library, p. 82.
    Contains a brief biographical sketch of W.

305. Thiemeyer, Joy. "Richard Wright Finishes Notes on Identity Crisis." Richmond (Va.) News-Leader (1 June), p. 9.
    Mixed review of AH. "It contains some writing both very good and very bad. When he indulges himself and quietly constructs his remarkably delicate psychological insights, he is at his best. When he attempts to be didactic he is dry and vapid." Reprinted: 1978.209.

306. Thomas, Phil. "American Hunger by Richard Wright." Gardner (Mass.) News (6 July), p. 3.
    Reprint of 1977.309.

307. _____. "American Hunger, by Richard Wright." The Gary Post-Tribune (17 July), Panorama Sec., p. H30.
    Reprint of 1977.309.

308. _____. "American Hunger. By Richard Wright." The Laredo Times (13 July), p. 17A.
    Reprint of 1977.309.

309. _____. "American Hunger. By Richard Wright." The Sheboygan Press (6 July), p. 25.
    Favorable Associated Press review mentioning W's struggle to survive, to become a writer, to cope with racism, and to come to terms with the Communist Party. Reprinted: 1977.306, 307, 308, 310, 311, 312, 313, 314, 315, 316, 317,

318, 319, 320, 321, 322.

310. _____. "American Hunger by Richard Wright." Washington (Pa.) Observer-Reporter (7 July), p. B-5.
Reprint of 1977.309.

311. _____. "'American Hunger' Detailed." Poughkeepsie Journal (10 July).
Reprint of 1977.309.

312. _____. "Black American Experience Told in Wright's New Book." The Decatur (Ala.) Daily (22 July), p. 16.
Condensed reprint of 1977.309.

313. _____. "Black Author Looks Back on Hard Road to the Top." The Bridgeport Sunday Post (11 September), p. F-4.
Reprint of 1977.309.

314. _____. "'Black Boy's' Other Half Is Published." Asheville Citizen-Times (10 July), Sec. C, p. 17.
Reprint of 1977.309.

315. _____. "Black Novelist Pens Autobiography." Hazleton Standard-Speaker (12 July), p. 3.
Reprint of 1977.309.

316. _____. "Book Worm." Nogales Herald (25 July), p. 2.
Condensed reprint of 1977.309.

317. _____. "Continuation of 'Black Boy.'" The Indianapolis Star (10 July), Sec. 8, p. 6.
Reprint of 1977.309.

318. _____. "Hunger of a Black in America." The Champaign-Urbana News-Gazette (8 July), p. 7-A.
Reprint of 1977.309.

319. _____. "New Titles: American Hunger. By Richard Wright." Bucks County (Pa.) Courier Times (10 July), Sec. C, p. 15.
Reprint of 1977.309.

320. _____. "World of Books." Fitchburg-Leominster Sentinel and Enterprise (19 July), p. 4.
Reprint of 1977.309.

321. _____. "Writer's Survival, Aspirations Detailed in 'American Hunger.'" Beckley Register Post-Herald (27 August), p. 5.
Reprint of 1977.309.

322. _____. "Writer's Survival, Aspirations Told." Vallejo Sunday Times-Herald (10 July), p. W7.
Reprint of 1977.309.

323. Toppin, Edgar Allan. "Negro," in The World Book Encyclopedia. Ed. William H. Nault. Vol. 14. Chicago: Field Enterprises Educational Corporation, pp. 106-113.
Reprint of 1969.230.

324. Trescott, Jacqueline. "Respected Scholar." The Washington Post (28 April), p. A12.
Article on Margaret Walker mentioning her friendship with W and her projected biography of him.

325. Truebent, Charles. "Rerun." Greensboro Daily News (11 December), Sec. C, p. 3.
Describes AH as an important new book by one of America's greatest writers.

325a. Turner, Darwin T. "Black Fiction: History and Myth," in American Fiction: Historical and Critical Essays. Ed. James Nagel. Boston: Northeastern University Press, pp. 109-126.
Mentions W briefly (pp. 116, 117).

326. Turner, Elvin D. "Beinecke Houses Manuscript of New Richard Wright Book." Yale Daily News (3 May), p. 8.
Explains the contents of AH and describes the W archive.

327. Twombly, Robert C. "Harlem Renaissance," in Collier's Encyclopedia. Ed. William Halsey. Vol. 11. New York: Macmillan Educational Corporation, pp 654-655.
Reprint of 1976.195.

328. Vanleer, Jay. "Book Reviews." Cleveland Call and Post (23 July), Sec. B, p. 3.
Favorable review of AH noting the conflicting accounts of reasons for its late publication. Fabre clarifies matters in his "Afterword."

329. Wagner, Jean. "Fritz Gysin.--The Grotesque in American Negro Fiction: Jean Toomer, Richard Wright and Ralph Ellison." Etudes Anglaises, 30 (July-September), 382.
Mentions the chapter on W.

330. _____. "Robert Bone.--Down Home, A History of Afro-American Short Fiction from Its Beginnings to the End of the Harlem Renaissance." Etudes Anglaises, 30 (July-September), 382-383.
Mentions Bone's pamphlet on W.

331. Walden, Daniel. "Amritjit Singh. The Novels of the Harlem Renaissance: Twelve Black Writers, 1923-1933; Margaret Perry. Silence to the Drums: A Survey of the Literature of the Harlem Renaissance; Theodore Kornweibel, Jr. No Crystal Stair: Black Life and the 'Mes-

senger,' 1917-1928." Black American Literature Forum, 11 (Fall), 118-119.
   Contains a brief reference to W.

332. Walker, Alice. "Foreword: Zora Neale Hurston--A Cautionary Tale and a Partisan View," in Zora Neale Hurston: A Literary Biography. By Robert E. Hemenway. Urbana: University of Illinois Press, pp. xi-xviii.
   Mentions studying W in a class taught by Margaret Walker at Jackson State College.

333. Walker, Kenneth. "Richard Wright Completes His Story." The Washington Star (5 June), Sec. F, p. 19.
   Favorable review of AH noting the amplified scope it provides for understanding W's development. Comments on W's relation to the Communist Party.
   Reprinted: 1978.209.

334. Walker, S. Jay. "Black Studies: Equal or Separate," in Black Separatism and Social Reality: Rhetoric and Reason. Ed. Raymond L. Hall. New York: Pergamon Press, pp. 63-68.
   Comments briefly on W, NS, and Fabre's biography.

335. Walker, Warren. "Bibliography." Studies in Short Fiction, 14 (Summer), 325.
   Notes that "Big Boy Leaves Home" is analyzed in Blyden Jackson's The Waiting Years.

336. _____. "Richard Wright," in his Twentieth-Century Short Story Explication. Third edition. Hamden, Conn.: The Shoe String Press, pp. 802-804.
   Lists sixty-six interpretations of twelve stories.

337. Ward, Jerry W. "Gatherings: Three Critical Notes." Obsidian, 3 (Summer), 58-64.
   Mentions W briefly.

338. Warner, Edwin. "Escape to Loneliness." Time, 109 (30 May), 74.
   Review of AH stressing W the outsider. His estrangement from the Communist Party increased his solitude and alienation.

339. Warnken, William P., Jr. "Dig the Nigger Up--Let's Kill Him Again. By Robert E. Chinn." Minority Voices, 1 (Fall), 108-110.
   Compares Chinn, a prison writer, to W.

340. Weatherby, W. J. Squaring Off: Mailer vs. Baldwin. New York: Mason/Charter, pp. 14, 28, 40, 131, 135.

Comments on the W-Baldwin relationship and mentions Jean Blackwell Hutson as a friend of W.

341. Webb, Constance. "Wright, Richard Nathaniel," in Collier's Encyclopedia. Ed. William D. Halsey. Vol. 23. New York: Macmillan Educational Corporation, p. 638.
   Reprint of 1969.244.

342. Weinlein, Gregg Thomas. "Book Beat: The Black Experience." Schenectady Kite (23 June), p. 10.
   Favorable review of AH, a work more humorous than BB. The narrator is now more mature, less defeatist. Weinlein praises Fabre's "Afterword."

343. Wells, Walter. Mark Twain's Sure-Fire Guide to Backgrounds in American Literature. Costa Mesa, Cal.: Educulture, Inc., pp. 95, 96, 98.
   Textbook including discussion of W and Ellison as pioneers in black literature. W is alienated but intense in his feelings about equality. Includes excerpts from BB.

344. Werner, Craig. "Gwendolyn Brooks: Tradition in Black and White." Minority Voices, 1 (Fall), 27-38.
   Refers briefly to NS and BB in order to clarify Brooks's use of the blues tradition.

345. Weyant, N. Jill. "Willard Motley's Pivotal Novel: Let No Man Write My Epitaph." Black American Literature Forum, 11 (Summer), 56-61.
   Mentions W briefly (p. 56).

346. Whitman, Alden. "Richard Wright: The Final, Perplexing Chapters of 'Black Boy.'" Chicago Tribune (22 May), Sec. 7, p. 1.
   Mixed review of AH, "essentially a sensitive vignette of Chicago life," but lacking "texture and context." Notes W's solitude and romanticism. Reprinted: 1978.209.

347. Whitman, Samuel. "Book Reviews: American Hunger." Long Beach Press-Telegram (20 May), Sec. A, p. 19.
   Favorable review noting W's calm objectivity in describing racism in America.
   Reprinted: 1978.209.

348. Williams, Jim. "Survey of Afro-American Playwrights," in A Freedomways Reader: Afro America in the Seventies. Ed. Ernest Kaiser. New York: International Publishers, pp. 69-93.
   Reprint of 1970.363.

349. Williams, Melvin G. "Black Litera-

ture Vs. Black Studies: Three Lynch-
ings." Black American Literature Forum,
11 (Fall), 104-107.
    Contains an analysis of the lynching
    scene in "Big Boy Leaves Home" empha-
    sizing literary qualities.

350. Williams, Shirley. "Bookends."
Louisville Courier-Journal and Times (27
February), Sec. D., p. 5.
    Announces AH, scheduled for publica-
    tion in May, and states that more
    books will be published from W's
    manuscripts.

351. Witt, Mary Ann. "Race and Racism in
'The Stranger' and 'Native Son.'" The
Comparatist: Journal of the Southern
Comparative Literature Association, 1
(May), 35-47.
    Compares Meursault and Bigger. Both
    are "victims of racism and colonial-
    ism." Each transcends his fate but
    still remains a tragic figure.

352. Wolff, Geoffrey. "The Lion in the
Path." New Times (27 May), pp. 57-62.
    General essay on W, Ellison, Baldwin,
    and the problems of the black writer.
    Discusses BB and AH as studies in the
    human will.

353. Wolfman, Brunetta R. "The Communist
Party Always Out of Step," in Black
Separatism and Social Reality: Rhetoric
and Reason. Ed. Raymond L. Hall. New
York: Pergamon Press, pp. 109-114.
    Comments on W's reaction to the Com-
    munist Party and quotes from The God
    That Failed.

354. Woodward, Robert H. and H. Wendell
Smith. "Richard Wright . . . 'And I
Hungered for Books,'" in their The Craft
of Prose. Fourth edition. Belmont, Cal.:
Wadsworth, p. 245.
    Headnote to an excerpt from BB.
    Reprinted: 1980.266.

355. Yardley, Jonathan. "How the World
Looked to Black Chicago in the '60s."
Columbus (Ga.) Enquirer and Ledger (17
July), Magazine Sec., p. 9.
    Unfavorable review of AH commenting
    on its puzzling history. It would
    probably have weakened BB if it had
    been published in 1945.

356. Young, Al. "My Life of Absurdity;
Chester Himes." The New York Times Book
Review (13 February), p. 24.
    Comments on Himes's ambivalent atti-
    tude toward W. They "loathed and
    loved one another."

357. Zverev, A. M. "Obshchestvennaia
bor'ba 60-kh godov i literatura SShA,"
in Amerikanskaia literatura i obshches-

tvenno-politicheskaia bor'ba. Ed. A. S.
Muliarchik. Moscow: Nauka, pp. 42-78.
    Notes the disagreement of Ellison and
    Baldwin with W's emphasis on social
    protest (p. 64).

1978

1. Abcarian, Richard and Marvin Klotz.
"Questions," in their Literature: The
Human Experience. Second edition. New
York: St. Martin's Press, p. 377.
    Reprint of 1973.1.

2. _____. "Richard Wright, The Man Who
Lived Underground," in their Instruc-
tor's Manual to Accompany Literature:
The Human Experience, Second Edition.
New York: St. Martin's Press, pp. 24-26.
    Reprint of 1973.2.

3. Andrews, William L. "From Apology to
Protest: The Black American Novel, by
Noel Schraufnagel . . . . Richard
Wright's Hero: The Faces of a Rebel-
Victim, by Katherine Fishburn." The
Mississippi Quarterly, 31 (Spring), 241-
245.
    Unfavorable review noting Schrauf-
    nagel's placement of W at the pivot
    of the development of Afro-American
    fiction. Fishburn is more sophisti-
    cated as a critic, but she relies too
    much on secondary sources and does
    not fully develop her own conclu-
    sions.

4. Anon. "Almos' a Man by Richard
Wright," in The American Short Story: A
Film Series. Chicago: Perspective Films,
p. [9].
    Advertisement with three still photo-
    graphs for the television play star-
    ring Le Var Burton.

5. Anon. "American Hunger Richard
Wright," in Literature and Language
1979. New York: Barnes & Noble/Harper &
Row, p. 36.
    Favorable notice of the paperback
    edition of "a vital, richly anecdotal
    work" scheduled for publication in
    January, 1979.

6. Anon. "American Literature, Unit 10:
Twentieth Century Fiction," in Great
People and Great Ideas for Teaching
English. Princeton, N. J.: Films for the
Humanities, p. 15.
    Publisher's advertisement for a film-
    strip mentioning W as "the most sig-
    nificant black novelist of his time."

7. Anon. "Announcing the First Omnibus
Volume from the Works of This Classic
American Writer--Richard Wright Reader."
The Black Scholar, 9 (March), 54.
    Full-page advertisment.

8. Anon. Bibliographic Guide to Black Studies: 1978. Boston: G. K. Hall, p. 181.
Lists three primary items and one secondary item concerning W in the New York Public Library.

9. Anon. "Brooks, Gwendolyn," in Current Biography Yearbook 1977. Ed. Charles Moritz. New York: The H. W. Wilson Company, pp. 83-86.
Quotes from W's recommendation of Brooks's poems to Harper.

10. Anon. Dust jacket of Richard Wright Reader. Ed. Ellen Wright and Michel Fabre. New York: Harper & Row.
Describes contents and provides biographical sketches of W (with two photographs), Ellen Wright, and Michel Fabre.

11. Anon. "Ebony Book Shelf." Ebony, 33 (April), 22.
Contains a favorable notice of Richard Wright Reader. W was a skillful writer of nonfiction as well as fiction.

12. Anon. "Elmwood Park, New Jersey." Newsletter on Intellectual Freedom, 27 (July), 97-98.
Reports the failure of an effort to have NS removed from a high school English class.

13. Anon. "Goodman Theatre." Stagebill (November), pp. 17-20, 20b-20d, 37-39.
Playbill and cast notes for the Chicago production of NS, 6 October-12 November.

14. Anon. "Green Theater Opens Today." Greensboro Daily News (29 September), Sec. B., p. 1.
Reports that the Paul Green Theater is opening with a new production of NS. Green has written a new version for the occasion.

15. Anon. "In Short." Long Island Sunday Newsday (19 March), Part II, p. 15.
Announces the revival of NS at the Perry Street Theater in New York.

16. Anon. Index to Periodical Articles by and About Blacks: 1973. Boston: G. K. Hall, p. 407.
Lists two items on W.

17. ____. Index to Periodical Articles by and About Blacks: 1976. Boston: G. K. Hall, p. 524.
Lists two items on W.

18. ____. Index to Periodical Articles by and About Blacks: 1977. Boston: G. K. Hall, p. 467.

Lists seven items on W.

19. Anon. Index Translationum 27. Paris: Unesco, pp. 195, 291, 327, 655, 713.
Lists translations of BB into Danish and French, EM into Finnish, LD into Turkish, and NS into Georgian.

20. Anon. "Meetings." American Studies Association Newsletter (March), pp. 3-4.
Announces that the Fifth Alabama Symposium on English and American Literature on the topic "The American Writer in the 1930s" invites papers on W, among others.

21. Anon. "Michael Popkin, ed. Modern Black Writers, A Library of Literary Criticism." Afram Newsletter, No. 5 (June), p. 19.
Mentions W's comments on Bontemps.

22. Anon. "Michel Fabre The Unfinished Quest of Richard Wright," in Morrow Quill Paperbacks 1979. New York: William Morrow, p. 10.
Publisher's advertisment with a blurb by Anaïs Nin.

23. Anon "Nashua, New Hampshire." Newsletter on Intellectual Freedom, 27 (May), 57.
Reports the opposition of the Concerned Parents and Taxpayers for Better Education to BB in school classes.

24. Anon. "'Native Son' Revived off Broadway." The New York Times (28 March), p. 50.
Unfavorable review of the revival of the play at the Perry Street Theater directed by Dick Garfield. Although not without power, the play does not do justice to the novel.

25. Anon. "Off-Off Broadway." The New York Village Voice (20 March), pp. 85, 88.
Announces the revival of NS at the Perry Street Theater in New York.

26. Anon. "Paperbacks: New and Noteworthy." The New York Times Book Review (11 February), p. 37.
Notice of AH pointing out that it completes BB.

26a. Anon. "Program." PMLA, 93 (November), 1110-1195.
Lists a paper by John Wideman on LT.

27. Anon. "Richard Wright Reader." Black Books Bulletin, 6 (Spring), 1.
Advertisement.

28. Anon. "Spingarn Medal," in The Encyclopedia Americana. Ed Bernard S. Cayne.

Vol. 25. Danbury, Conn.: Americana Corporation, p. 506.
Reprint of 1977.32.

29. Anon. "The Theatre Goodman." Chicago Tribune (15 October), Sec. 6, p. 6; (22 October), Sec. 6, p. 8.
Advertisement for the play NS.

30. Anon. "Traveler's Advisory." The Chronicle of Higher Education (16 October), Review Sec., p. R-2.
Announces a Chicago production of NS "that puts the 'oomph' (read violence) that Orson Wells [sic] left out in his 1941 version of the Richard Wright novel. It's playing Oct. 12 to Nov. 12."

31. Anon. "Wright (Richard)," in Dictionnaire universel des noms propres. Ed. Alain Rey and Josette Rey-Debove. Vol. 4. Paris: Dictionnaire le Robert, p. 716.
Biographical sketch.

32. Anon. "Wright, Richard," in Great Soviet Encyclopedia. Ed. A. M. Prokhorov. Vol. 21. New York: Macmillan, p. 749.
Translation of 1975.9.

33. Arata, Esther Spring with the assistance of Marlene J. Erickson, Sandra Dewitz, and Mary Linse Alexander. More Black American Playwrights: A Bibliography. Metuchen, N. J.: The Scarecrow Press, pp. 210-211.
Lists five primary and sixteen secondary sources.

34. Ashton, Thomas L. "General Introduction: The Short Novel," in his Ten Short Novels. Lexington, Mass.: Heath, pp. 1-5.
Calls W "the single most important black writer of the twentieth century" and relates "Down by the Riverside" to works by Conrad, Faulkner, and Dostoevsky.

35. ____. "Richard Wright, 'Down by the Riverside': Preface," in his Ten Short Novels. Lexington, Mass.: Heath, pp. 101-105.
Analyzes, in the context of W's career, the story as "a study of the psychology of fear." It looks forward to O.

36. Baraka, Amiri. "Introduction," in his The Motion of History and Other Plays. New York: William Morrow, pp. 11-16.
Mentions W briefly as a radical writer (p. 14).

37. Barry, Ann. "Arts and Leisure Guide." The New York Times (19 March), Sec. D, p. 36.
Announces the opening of the Dick Garfield revival of the play NS.

38. Beaver, Harold. "Time on the Cross: White Fiction and the Black Messiahs," in The Yearbook of English Studies. Ed. G. K. Hunter and C. J. Rawson. Vol. 8, pp. 40-53.
Includes a brief discussion of NS in the context of the black as messiah or as avenging zombie.

39. Beauvoir, Simone de. "Harlem in the 40s," in Black Image: European Eyewitness Accounts of Afro-American Life. Ed. Lenworth Gunther. Series in American Studies. Port Washington, N. Y.: Kennikat Press, pp. 128-134.
Partial reprint of 1952.23.

40. Benson, Joseph. "A Wright Sampler." Greensboro Daily News (5 February), Sec. C, p. 3.
Favorable review of Richard Wright Reader noting its demonstration of W's range. Praising the collection's arrangement, Benson compares it to similar collections of Hemingway and Fitzgerald.

41. Benston, Kimberly W. "Ellison, Baraka, and the Faces of Tradition." Boundary 2, 6 (Winter), 333-354.
Comments on Ellison's "Richard Wright's Blues" (pp. 341-343).

42. Bentley, Sara. "Introduction," in Minority Literature and the Urban Experience: Selected Proceedings of the 4th Annual Conference on Minority Studies. Ed. George E. Carter and James R. Parker. Vol. 6. La Crosse, Wis.: Institute for Minority Studies, University of Wisconsin--La Crosse, pp. 1-3.
Mentions W briefly.

43. Berzon, Judith R. Neither White Nor Black: The Mulatto Character in American Fiction. The Gotham Library, ed. James W. Tuttleton. New York: New York University Press, p. 52.
Quotes W briefly.

44. Bontemps, Arna. "Negro in America: Contributions to American Culture," in The Encyclopedia Americana. Ed. Bernard S. Cayne. Vol. 20. Danbury, Conn.: Americana Corporation, pp. 74-77.
Reprint of 1970.62.

45. Bracy, William. "Wright, Richard," in The Encyclopedia Americana. Ed. Bernard S. Cayne. Vol. 29. Danbury, Conn.: Americana Corporation, p. 555.
Reprint of 1965.45.

46. Bradbury, Malcolm. "Second Countries: The Expatriate Tradition in American Writing," in The Yearbook of English Studies. Ed. G. K. Hunter and C. J. Rawson. Vol. 8, pp. 15-39.
    Mentions W briefly.

47. Brady, Owen. "Wright's Lawd Today: The American Dream Festering in the Sun." CLA Journal, 22 (December), 167-172.
    Analyzes Jake Jackson's attachment to attitudes of the black bourgeoisie. Instead of the true dreams deriving from genuine emotions, he follows the false dreams of a racist, capitalist society. Brady examines structure and satire in the novel.

48. Brewton, Butler Emanuel. "Richard Wright's Thematic Treatment of Women in Uncle Tom's Children, Black Boy and Native Son." Dissertation Abstracts International, 39 (November), 2927-A.
    Abstracts a 1977 Rutgers University dissertation. Although W does not treat women as well-rounded individuals, he does treat them as important aspects of his higher thematic concerns. Black women typically contribute to the oppression of black males while white women seem more concerned with the black man's human spirit, particularly in NS.

49. Brivic, Sheldon. "Wright, Richard 1908-1960," in Contemporary Literary Criticism. Ed. Dedria Bryfonski. Vol. 9. Detroit: Gale, p. 585.
    Partial reprint of 1974.35.

50. Brown, Cecil M. "Black Literature and LeRoi Jones," in Imamu Amiri Baraka (LeRoi Jones): A Collection of Critical Essays. Ed. Kimberly Benston. Englewood Cliffs, N. J.: Prentice Hall, pp. 29-35.
    Reprint of 1970.69.

51. Brunette, Peter. "Two Wrights, One Wrong," in The Modern American Novel and the Movies. Ed. Gerald Peary and Roger Shatzkin. New York: Ungar, pp. 131-142.
    Describes and evaluates the adaptation of the novel NS to the screen. The novel itself utilized filmic techniques, but mistakes in casting (e. g., W as Bigger) and mutilation of the film by American censors seriously weakened its effect. The theme of the novel had already been softened by W and Chenal to accommodate the conservatism of the time. Brunette analyzes these changes in the film's treatment of racism, brutality, dialogue, politics, and, especially, religion. He also shows how the novel's meaning is extended by additions and camera work. But on balance the film compromises the novel's meaning.

51a. Bryer, Jackson R., Eddy Dow, Philip R. Headings, Matthew O'Brien, and Peter Van Egmond, with the help of Donald Wharton. "American Literature," in 1977 MLA International Bibliography. Vol. 1. New York: Modern Language Association, pp. 135-194.
    Lists twenty items on W.

51b. Burkey, Richard M. Ethnic & Racial Groups: The Dynamics of Dominance. Menlo Park, Cal.: Cummings Publishing Co., pp. 90, 499.
    Mentions W's subterfuge to use a white library and lists UTC in the bibliography.

52. Burns, Landon C. and Janet P. Alwang. "The Fourth (1977-1978) Supplement to a Cross-Referenced Index of Short Fiction Anthologies and Author-Title Listings." Studies in Short Fiction, 15 (Spring), 213-252.
    Lists four W stories in six anthologies.

53. Čakovsky, S. A. "Rasovyj Konflikt i Literatura SŠA XX Veka (Negritjanskaja literatura v 20-30-60-e gody)," in Literatura SŠA XX Veka: Opyt tipologičeskogo issledovanija (Avtorskaja pozicija, konflikt, geroj). Ed. Ja N. Zasursky. Moscow: Nauka, pp. 285-358.
    Includes an analysis and favorable evaluation of NS, but shows that it is less consistently Marxist than bourgeois critics suppose (pp. 302-305). Also compares NS to Invisible Man (pp. 305-306) and, briefly, to Another Country (pp. 309, 311).

54. Calloway, Earl. "Theatre Wing: Bigger Thomas Is Convincing as Character on Goodman's Stage." Chicago Defender (17 October), p. 17.
    Favorable review of the Chicago revival of the play in the version revised by Paul Green. Calloway emphasizes Bigger as a "rancorous monster" produced by society. Meshach Taylor is a good actor, but his portrayal of Bigger is not ruthless enough.

55. Campenni, Frank. "Chester Himes," in Dictionary of Literary Biography. Vol. 2: American Novelists Since World War II. Ed. Jeffrey Helterman and Richard Layman. Detroit: Gale, pp. 240-244.
    Mentions W briefly.

56. Carringer, Robert L. "The Scripts of Citizen Kane." Critical Inquiry, 5 (Winter), 369-400.
    Quotes a telegram from John Houseman stating that he is leaving for North

Carolina to confer with W and Paul Green (p. 394).

57. Cassill, R. V. "Richard Wright," in his The Norton Anthology of Short Fiction. New York: Norton, p. 1434.
   Biographical sketch.
   Reprinted: 1978.58.

58. ____. "Richard Wright," in his The Norton Anthology of Short Fiction. Shorter edition. New York: Norton, p. 713.
   Reprint of 1978.57.

58a. Caute, David. The Great Fear: The Anti-Communist Purge Under Truman and Eisenhower. New York: Simon and Schuster, p. 531.
   Mentions briefly the play NS.

59. Clark, Eleanor and Robert Penn Warren. "Interview with Eleanor Clark and Robert Penn Warren." New England Review, 1 (Autumn), 49-70.
   Clark mentions knowing W in Paris and disparages his existentialism.
   Reprinted: 1980.253.

60. Cobb, Nina Kressner. "Richard Wright: Individualism Reconsidered." CLA Journal, 21 (March), 335-354.
   Examines the search for self and identity in W's works, a quest filled with contradictions. Emphasizes BB.

61. Cohen, George. "Beyond 'Native Son' --Rediscovering Wright's Neglected Works." Chicago Tribune (15 January), Sec. 7, p. 1.
   Favorable review of Richard Wright Reader, a judicious selection.
   Reprinted: 1978.62.

62. ____. "Critics Took Dim View of Richard Wright's Work." Pasadena Star-News (22 January), p. A-11.
   Reprint of 1978.61.

63. Collier, Betty J. and Louis N. Williams. "Black Revolutionary Literature of the Sixties: The Eurocentric World View Recycled." Minority Voices, 2 (Fall), 57-66.
   Mentions W briefly (p. 60).

64. Collins, Jean. "Deep Insights Into Humanity." San Francisco Sunday Examiner and Chronicle (12 March), Entertainment Sec., p. 40.
   Favorable review of Richard Wright Reader praising W as a universal writer and thinker.

65. Conn, Annette Lois. "Richard Wright: A Marxist Approach to His Early Work." Dissertation Abstracts International, 39 (October), p. 2270-A.

Abstracts a 1978 Temple University dissertation arguing that W's work up through NS is unified by Marxist-Leninist ideology. Not only does this ideology affect W's treatment of theme; it also controls his dialectical presentation of symbols, images, character, and mood.

66. Cooke, Michael G. "Naming, Being, and Black Experience." The Yale Review, 67 (Winter), 167-186.
   Contains an analysis of NS "as the consummate story of the possibilities of being in the annihilating adverse world of the twentieth century" (p. 182).

67. Cosgrave, Mary Silva. "Outlook Tower." The Horn Book Magazine, 54 (April), 194-196.
   Contains a favorable notice of AH stressing W's relation to the Communist Party.

68. Cripps, Thomas. Black Film as Genre. Bloomington: Indiana University Press, pp. 47, 148.
   Mentions NS.

69. Dace, Letitia. "Amiri Baraka (LeRoi Jones)," in Black American Writers: Bibliographical Essays. Vol. 2. Ed. M. Thomas Inge, Maurice Duke, and Jackson R. Bryer. New York: St. Martin's Press, pp. 121-178.
   Mentions Donald B. Gibson's reference to W in the introduction to Five Black Writers.

70. Dance, Daryl. "James Baldwin," in Black American Writers: Bibliographical Essays. Vol. 2. Ed. M. Thomas Inge, Maurice Duke, and Jackson R. Bryer. New York: St. Martin's Press, pp. 73-120.
   Analyzes and evaluates writing on the W-Baldwin relationship (pp. 110-113).

71. Davis, Arthur P. "Novels of the New Black Renaissance (1960-1977): A Thematic Survey." CLA Journal, 21 (June), 457-490.
   Contains three brief mentions of W.

72. Davis, Thadious M. "Southern Literature: From Faulkner to Others." The CEA Critic, 40 (March), 14-18.
   Mentions UTC and BB (p. 17).

73. De Arman, Charles. "Bigger Thomas: The Symbolic Negro and the Discrete Human Entity." Black American Literature Forum, 12 (Summer), 61-64.
   Points out that W's protagonist combines the typical and the individual. Bigger exemplifies this combination, but finally moves toward personal identity and thus freedom.

74. [DeMott, Benjamin]. "Richard Wright," in America in Literature. Vol. 2. Ed. Alan Trachtenberg and Benjamin DeMott. New York: John Wiley, pp. 1600-1602.
    Biographical headnote to "The Ethics of Living Jim Crow."

75. Denby, Charles. (Matthew Ward). Indignant Heart: A Black Worker's Journal. Boston: South End Press, p. 178.
    Reprint of 1952.66a.

76. Deutsch, Leonard J. "Ralph Waldo Ellison," in Dictionary of Literary Biography. Vol. 2. American Novelists Since World War II. Ed. Jeffrey Helterman and Richard Layman. Detroit: Gale, pp. 136-141.
    Mentions Ellison's relation to W.

77. ____. "Second Half of Autobiography Not Compelling, Worth Reading." The Huntington Advertiser and the Herald Dispatch (29 January), Sec. D, p. 3.
    Somewhat favorable review of AH, which is more philosophical than BB. Some parts are written vividly, but W's interpolations sometimes impede the narrative. Still, AH achieves interesting insights.

78. Domini, John. "Ishmael Reed: A Conversation with John Domini." The American Poetry Review, 7 (January-February), 32-36.
    Reed notes briefly W's existential stance (p. 33).

79. Donald, Miles. The American Novel in the Twentieth Century. Newton Abbot, Devon: David & Charles, pp. 143-146.
    Appreciation of NS emphasizing the social theme.

80. Doner, Dean. "Wright, Richard," in The World Book Encyclopedia. Ed. William H. Nault. Vol. 21. Chicago: World Book--Childcraft International, p. 420.
    Reprint of 1975.60.

81. Driskell, David C. "Bibliographies in Afro-American Art." American Quarterly, 30 (Summer bibliography issue), 374-394.
    Quotes James A. Porter on the influence of W on some Afro-American artists (p. 386).

82. Duff, Gerald. "Ishmael Reed," in Dictionary of Literary Biography. Vol. 2: American Novelists Since World War II. Ed. Jeffrey Helterman and Richard Layman. Detroit: Gale, pp. 417-422.
    Mentions W briefly.

82a. Duncan, Todd. "Scene and Life Cycle in Ernest Gaines' Bloodline." Callaloo,

1 (May 1978), 85-101.
    Mentions briefly UTC and Bigger Thomas.

83. Dunning, John. "'Compact' Prose of Richard Wright Good Browsing." The Denver Post (5 March), Roundup Sec., p. 23.
    Favorable review of Richard Wright Reader, a welcome volume long overdue. It reveals that W was a good journalist as well as novelist.

84. Editorial Collective of People's College Press. "Black Culture and the Arts," in their Introduction to Afro-American Studies. Experimental Fourth Edition. Vol. 2. Chicago: People's College Press, pp. 245-262.
    Comments briefly on W as an example of the "new proletarian consciousness" (p. 258) and includes a photograph (p. 261). Reprints "Blueprint for Negro Literature" (pp. 293-299).

85. ____. "Why Afro-American Studies?" in their Introduction to Afro-American Studies. Experimental Fourth Edition. Vol. 1. Chicago: People's College Press, pp. 3-6.
    Mentions W briefly.

86. Ellis, Joyce. "American Hunger. By Richard Wright." Southern Exposure, 6 (Fall), 106, 108.
    Favorable review stressing the importance of black autobiography as genre, W's place within the tradition, and the continuing relevance of his indictment of racism.

87. Ellison, Ralph. "Wright, Richard 1908-1960," in Contemporary Literary Criticism. Ed. Dedria Bryfonski. Vol. 9. Detroit: Gale, p. 583.
    Partial reprint of 1945.890.

88. ____, Ishmael Reed, Quincy Troupe, and Steven Cannon. "The Essential Ellison (Interview)." Y'Bird Magazine, 1, No. 1, pp. 130-159.
    Ellison discusses his friendship with W in New York, mentioning their reading Miguel de Unamuno's The Tragic Sense of Life in the thirties.

89. Emmens, Carol A. Short Stories on Film. Littleton, Colo.: Libraries Unlimited, p. 311.
    Provides information on the televised version of "Almos' a Man."

90. Erhard, Thomas A. "Paul Green (1894-), " in his Nine Hundred American Plays: A Synopsis-History of American Theatre. The Theatre Student Series. New York: Richards Rosen Press, pp. 39-40.
    Contains a brief synopsis of the play NS.

91. Fabre, Michel. "Chant of Saints: A Gathering of Afro-American Literature, Art and Scholarship, edited by Michael S. Harper and Robert B. Stepto." Afram Newsletter, No. 5 (June), p. 15.
    Review mentioning Stepto's essay on W.

92. _____. "France-Etats-Unis: cent ans d'images réciproques." The French-American Review, 2 (Winter-Spring), 1-16.
    Mentions W briefly as an expatriate in Paris (p. 11).

93. _____. "Introduction," in Richard Wright Reader. Ed. Ellen Wright and Michel Fabre, notes by Michel Fabre. New York: Harper & Row, pp. vii-xxiv.
    Sketches W's present reputation, explains purpose of the present volume, and reviews at length W's literary career with emphasis on the central subject of "the interchange and conflict between the individual and society" (p. ix) in both its thematic and its stylistic manifestations. Fabre also supplies headnotes for the selections in the collection.

94. _____. "Peter Bruck, ed. The Black American Short Story in the 20th Century." Afram Newsletter, No. 6 (December), p. 11.
    Review mentioning Wolfgang Karrer's essay on W.

95. _____. "Richard Wright and the French Existentialists." MELUS, 5, No. 2, pp. 39-52.
    Arguing that W "was an existentialist long before he heard the word," Fabre analyzes his social, literary, and political contacts with Camus, Sartre, and de Beauvoir. Though the writers share concerns such as the philosophical difficulty of bridging individual and political responsibility, their actual literary influence was slight. In literary terms, the Russian and German existentialists deserve greater study for their impact on W.

96. _____. "The Richard Wright Archive: The Catalogue of an Exhibition." The Yale University Library Gazette, 53 (October), 57-78.
    General description of the W Archive at Yale and an annotated list of items displayed, divided into eight sections with introductory material for each: The Chicago Years (1927-37); Recognition in New York (1937-40); Native Son, From Novel to Film (1940-51); From "American Hunger" to Black Boy (1940-45); A Spokesman for His Race? (1941-47); Existentialist Perspectives (1942-53); Third-World

Exposure (1947-1960); Writing to the End (1954-60).

97. Fairbanks, Carol and Eugene A. Engeldinger. "Wright, Richard," in their Black American Fiction: A Bibliography. Metuchen, N. J.: The Scarecrow Press, pp. 301-316.
    Lists 368 items.

98. Farnsworth, Robert. "Emancipation from Nationalism." The Kansas City Star (15 March), p. 18A.
    Favorable review of Richard Wright Reader, an impressive contribution to American literature.

99. Ferns, John. "Caliban Without Prospero: Essays on Quebec and Black Literature. By Max Dorsinville," in The Yearbook of English Studies. Ed. G. K. Hunter and C. J. Rawson. Vol. 8, pp. 301-302.
    Mentions Bigger Thomas.

100. Fields, Raymond. "Richard Wright Reader." Black Books Bulletin, 6 (Summer), 54-55.
    Favorable review of "a most valuable reference to the extensive literary achievements of Richard Wright." The introduction is concise, the selections ample, and the chronology helpful.

101. Fishburn, Katherine. "Richard Wright: American Hunger." Modern Fiction Studies, 24 (Summer), 283-284.
    Favorable review, but Fishburn wonders why the earlier magazine publication of portions of the narrative is not documented.

102. Franklin, H. Bruce. The Victim as Criminal and Artist: Literature from the American Prison. New York: Oxford University Press, p. xix.
    Revised reprint of 1975.79.

103. Frémy, Dominique and Michèle Frémy. Quid? Tout pour tous. Paris: Editions Robert Laffont, p. 376.
    Reprint of 1963.86.

104. Fulton, Len. "Kgositsile: How You Sound." The Nation, 227 (16 December), 680-681.
    Mentions the influence of BB of Kgositsile.

105. Gaillard, Dawson and John Mosier. "Discussion of Wright's 'Long Black Song,'" in their Women and Men Together: An Anthology of Short Fiction. Boston: Houghton Mifflin, p. 244.
    Study questions.

106. _____. "Richard Wright 1908-1960,"

in their Women and Men Together: An Anthology of Short Fiction. Boston: Houghton Mifflin, pp. 223-224.
>   Photograph of W and biographical headnote to "Long Black Song."

107. _____. "Wright's 'Long Black Song,'" in their Instructor's Manual: Women and Men Together: An Anthology of Short Fiction. Boston: Houghton Mifflin, pp. 78-79.
>   Discussion questions and guide.

108. Gates, Henry Louis, Jr. "Flight to Canada. By Ishmael Reed." The Journal of Negro History, 63 (January), 78-81.
>   Mentions NS.

109. _____. "Parody of Forms." Saturday Review, 5 (4 March), 28-29.
>   Review of Ismael Reed's Shrovetide in Old New Orleans contrasting W's social realism with Reed's experimental fiction and mentioning Reed's essay on NS.

110. _____. "Soul of a Black Woman." The New York Times Book Review (19 February), pp. 13, 30-31.
>   Favorable review of Robert Hemenway's Zora Neale Hurston: A Literary Biography mentioning W's review of Their Eyes Were Watching God.

111. Gavins, Raymond. "The Ethnic Southerners. By George Brown Tindall." The Journal of Negro History, 63 (January), 82-86.
>   Review beginning with a quotation and ending with a reference to BB.

112. Gibson, Donald B. "Afro-American Fiction: Contemporary Research and Criticism, 1965-1978." American Quarterly, 30 (Summer bibliography issue), 395-409.
>   Evaluates books on W giving special praise to works by Houston A. Baker, Michel Fabre, and Keneth Kinnamon.

113. Giza, Joanne. "Ralph Ellison," in Black American Writers: Bibliographical Essays. Vol. 2. Ed. M. Thomas Inge, Maurice Duke, and Jackson R. Bryer. New York: St. Martin's Press, pp. 47-71.
>   Analyzes and evaluates writing on the W-Ellison relationship (pp. 51-52) and on comparisons of their work (pp. 61-62).

114. Glicksberg, Charles I. "Literature and Society," in Literary Taste, Culture and Mass Communication (Vol. 6 of The Sociology of Literature). Ed. Peter Davison, Rolf Meyersohn, and Edward Shils. Cambridge: Chadwyck-Healey, pp. 91-102.
>   Reprint of 1952.38.

115. Gordon, Edward J., Betty Yvonne Welch, and William Eller. "Author Biographies," in their Introduction to Literature. New edition. Lexington, Mass.: Ginn and Company, pp. 587-602.
>   Includes a biographical sketch of W.

116. _____. "Hokku Poems by Richard Wright," in their Introduction to Literature: Teacher's Handbook and Key. New edition. Lexington, Mass.: Ginn and Company, pp. 318-319.
>   Lesson plan for teaching W's poems at the seventh-grade level.

117. _____. "Reading 'Hokku Poems,'" in their Introduction to Literature. New edition. Lexington, Mass.: Ginn and Company, p. 464.
>   Brief comments on W's poems in a seventh-grade textbook.

118. Gounard, J.[ean]-F.[rançois]. "Richard Wright's 'The Man Who Lived Underground': A Literary Analysis." Journal of Black Studies, 8 (March), 381-386.
>   States that the novella "is an existentialist parable since the protagonist develops his identity through his relationships with other people." Gounard relies heavily on Michel Fabre's "Richard Wright: The Man Who Lived Underground" (1971.110).

119. Graham, Maryemma. "Aesthetic and Ideological Radicalism in the 1930's: The Fiction of Richard Wright and Langston Hughes." Dissertation Abstracts International, 38 (January), 4167-A.
>   Abstracts a 1977 Cornell dissertation arguing that W's radicalism struggled to reconcile "the concerns of personal freedom and political message," but with decreasing success. A dedicated Communist, W nevertheless lacked confidence in the black working class.

120. Gray, Valerie Bonita. Invisible Man's Literary Heritage: Benito Cereno and Moby Dick. Costerus: Essays in English and American Language and Literature. New Series. Vol. 12. Amsterdam: Rodopi, p. 136.
>   Mentions Bigger briefly.

121. Griffin, L. W. "Wright, Richard. Richard Wright Reader." Library Journal, 103 (15 January), 170.
>   Favorable notice praising the range and substance of the collection.

122. Gross, Theodore with the assistance of Michael Kramer and Marshall Wilen. "Richard Wright 'The Ethics of Living Jim Crow,'" in their Resource Manual to Accompany America in Literature Volumes

I and II. New York: Wiley, pp. 290-291.
Study questions written by Wilen.

123. Gunther, Lenworth. "Harlem in the 1940s," in his Black Image: European Eyewitness Accounts of Afro-American Life. Series in American Studies. Port Washington, N. Y.: Kennikat Press, p. 128.
Mentions W's friendship with Simone de Beauvoir.

124. Gussow, Mel. "'Native Son' Revived Off Broadway." The New York Times (28 March), p. 50.
Review of the Dick Garfield revival of the play. The production suffers from a low budget, but the acting is good. The play lacks the stature of the novel, but it has historical importance and "is still an incendiary work of theater."

125. Haight, Anne Lyon and Chandler B. Grannis. Banned Books 387 B. C. to 1978 A. D. New York: R. R. Bowker Company, p. 118.
Mentions briefly the banning of BB by the Island Trees School District of Long Island in 1975.

126. Hamalian, Leo and Frederick R. Karl. "Biographical Notes," in their The Shape of Fiction. New York: McGraw-Hill, pp. 499-513.
Includes a biographical sketch of W (p. 513).

126a. Harris, Jessica. "Sweet Memories: Old Favorites." Essence, 8 (February), 26.
Charles Harris chooses WML and Quincy Troupe chooses NS among their favorite books. A book by W is not chosen by Marie Brown, Paule Marshall, or Alice Walker.

127. Helterman, Jeffrey. "John A. Williams," in Dictionary of Literary Biography. Vol. 2: American Novelists Since World War II. Ed. Jeffrey Helterman and Richard Layman. Detroit: Gale, pp. 537-543.
Mentions The Most Native of Sons and points out that W is the prototype of Harry Ames in The Man Who Cried I Am.

128. Hicks, Jack. "A One-Man Heathen Horde." The Nation, 226 (11 March), 277-278.
Review of Ishmael Reed's Shrovetide in Old New Orleans mentioning W.

129. Hoeveler, Diane Long. "Oedipus Agonistes: Mothers and Sons in Richard Wright's Fiction." Black American Literature Forum, 12 (Summer), 65-68.
Argues that one of W's major themes

is violence, often directed toward women to an excessive degree. This theme derives from "the irreconcilable oedipal dilemmas that afflict his heroes."

130. Howe, Irving. "Introduction," in his Fiction as Experience: An Anthology. New York: Harcourt Brace Jovanovich, pp. 1-9.
Mentions W briefly as a realistic writer (p. 8).

131. _____. "Introduction," in his Fiction as Experience: An Anthology. New York: Harcourt Brace Jovanovich, p. 97.
Headnote to "Big Boy Leaves Home" commenting on W as a protest novelist and the pastoral theme in the story.

132. _____. "Questions for Writing and Discussion," in his Fiction as Experience: An Anthology. New York: Harcourt Brace Jovanovich, p. 126.
Study questions for "Big Boy Leaves Home."

133. _____. "Wright, Richard 1908-1960," in Contemporary Literary Criticism. Ed. Dedria Bryfonski. Vol. 9. Detroit: Gale, p. 585.
Partial reprint of 1977.175.

134. Hull, Gloria T. "Notes on a Marxist Interpretation of Black American Literature." Black American Literature Forum, 12 (Winter), 148-153.
Contains several references to W.

135. Jackson, Blyden. "Langston Hughes," in Black American Writers: Bibliographical Essays. Vol. 2. Ed. M. Thomas Inge, Maurice Duke, and Jackson R. Bryer. New York: St. Martin's Press, pp. 187-206.
Speaks of "the present post-Wright era in literature" (p. 186) and mentions W's review of The Big Sea (p. 205).

136. _____. "Two Mississippi Writers: Wright and Faulkner." University of Mississippi Studies in English, 15, pp. 49-59.
Argues that both race and individual temperament served to distance W from Mississippi. Nonetheless, like Faulkner's, much of W's best work, such as "Big Boy Leaves Home," draws power from its Mississippi setting. Although W did not remain a "folk Negro" like his father, he used his knowledge of the experience to create Bigger Thomas.

137. Kaiser, Ernest. "Recent Books." Freedomways, 18 (Fourth Quarter), 230-231.
Contains a review of Richard Wright

Reader objecting to Fabre's view of W as "an anti-Communist, pro-existentialist writer." Cites Ollie Harrington and Addison Gayle as sources for a more radical view of W.

138. Kazin, Alfred. New York Jew. New York: Knopf, p. 61.
Mentions briefly W's disillusion with Communism.

139. Kibler, James E. et al. "A Checklist of Scholarship on Southern Literature for 1977." The Mississippi Quarterly, 31 (Spring), 253-332.
Lists fourteen annotated items on W (pp. 319-321).

140. Kiernan, Robert F. "Carson McCullers," in Dictionary of Literary Biography. Vol. 2: American Novelists Since World War II. Ed. Jeffrey Helterman and Richard Layman. Detroit: Gale, pp. 317-325.
Mentions W briefly (p. 320).

141. Kirsch, Robert. "Posthumous Paean to a Writer." Los Angeles Times (27 February), pp. 3, 5.
Favorable review of Richard Wright Reader praising W's quality and versatility. He was one of our most important American writers.

142. Klinkowitz, Jerome. "Clarence Major's SuperFiction," in Yardbird Lives! Ed. Ishmael Reed and Al Young. New York: Grove Press, pp. 257-266.
Mentions W briefly (p. 259).

143. ____. "Early Writers: Jupiter Hammon, Phillis Wheatley, and Benjamin Banneker," in Black American Writers: Bibliographical Essays. Vol. 1. Ed. M. Thomas Inge, Maurice Duke, and Jackson R. Bryer. New York: St. Martin's Press, pp. 1-20.
Comments on W's remarks on Wheatley in his introduction to Black Metropolis.

144. Klise, Thomas S. "The Odyssey of Richard Wright," in his Sound Filmstrips for Classes in Literature, Speech, and Composition. Peoria, Ill.: Thomas S. Klise Company, p. 6.
Reprint of 1977.205.

145. La Beau, Dennis, ed. Author Biographies Master Index. Vol. 2. Detroit: Gale, p. 1161.
Lists twenty-seven biographical dictionaries containing entries on W.

146. Lee, A. Robert. "Hurts, Absurdities and Violence: The Contrary Dimensions of Chester Himes." Journal of American Studies, 12 (April), 99-114.

Includes many comments on the Himes-W relationship.

147. Lewis, David L. King: A Biography. Second edition. Urbana: University of Illinois Press, p. 266.
Reprint of 1970.245.

148. Littlejohn, David. "Wright, Richard 1908-1960," in Contemporary Literary Criticism. Ed. Dedria Bryfonski. Vol. 9. Detroit: Gale, pp. 583-585.
Partial reprint of 1966.97.

149. Lohof, Bruce A. "The Nigger as an Archetype in American Literature." Osmania Journal of English Studies, 14, No. 1, pp. 1-8.
Mentions Bigger Thomas (p. 2) and quotes from WML (p. 7).

150. Lynch, Acklyn R. "Reflections on Black Culture in the Early Forties." Black Books Bulletin, 6 (Spring), 30-37, 76-78.
Comments briefly on W (pp. 31, 37).

151. Lynch, Dennis Daley. "Visions of Chicago in Contemporary Black Literature," in Minority Literature and the Urban Experience: Selected Proceedings of the 4th Annual Conference on Minority Studies. Ed. George E. Carter and James R. Parker. Vol. 6. La Crosse, Wis.: Institute for Minority Studies, University of Wisconsin--La Crosse, pp. 25-31.
Like that of other writers (Motley, Fair, Colter), W's vision of Chicago is bleak, but his protest against the city is artfully understated. Lynch comments mainly on O.

152. Lyra, F. "American Studies in Poland." American Studies International, 16 (Spring), 28-35.
Lists W as a topic of study at the Institute of English Philology of the Marie Curie-Sktodowska University.

153. Mackey, Nathaniel. "Interview with Al Young." MELUS, 5 (Winter), 32-51.
Young pays tribute to W's representation of speech.

154. ____. "Ishmael Reed and the Black Aesthetic." CLA Journal, 21 (March), 355-366.
Quotes a passage by Reed mentioning NS.

155. Madhubuti, Haki R. "Black Writers and Critics: Developing a Critical Process Without Readers." The Black Scholar, 10 (November-December), 35-40.
Mentions W briefly.

156. Mangione, Jerre. An Ethnic at Large. New York: G. P. Putnam's Sons,

pp. 124, 263-264.
Mentions W as a member of the John Reed Club and relates a weekend stay in 1940 at Paul Corey's house in Cold-Spring-on-Hudson, New York, with W present. On an earlier occasion Mangione and W had attended the black Macbeth in Harlem. W vowed he could never marry a white woman.

157. Mapp, Edward. Directory of Blacks in the Performing Arts. Metuchen, N. J.: The Scarecrow Press, p. 404.
Entry specifying facts about W's theatrical careeer.

158. Martin, Sylvia. "Richard Wright in the Beginning." Chicago Daily News (28-29 June), Panorama Sec., p. 16.
Review of Richard Wright Reader noting the assistance given to W early in his career by Lawrence Martin, the reviewer's husband.

159. Mason, Julian. "Black Writers of the South." The Mississippi Quarterly, 31 (Spring), 169-183.
Mentions W as a black Southern writer less neglected than others.

160. Mathur, O. P. "Mulk Raj Anand's Untouchables and Richard Wright's Bigger Thomas: A Comparative Study in Social Protest and Affirmation." The Literary Half-Yearly, 19 (July), 115-128.
Compares NS with Anand's Untouchables and The Road as novels of social protest. Anand's protagonists are rebellious and alienated, like Bigger, but not violent. Anand is more hopeful than W.

161. Matthews, Fred H. "American Hunger. By Richard Wright." Queen's Quarterly, 85 (Summer), 320-321.
Favorable review stressing Wright's experience with the Communist Party and contrasting his intellectual acuity with "the hang-loose, stereotype-embracing radicals of our recent past." Matthews also relates W to the school of urban sociology of the University of Chicago.

162. McGuire, Jane. "Board Balks at Book Ban." Bergen (N. J.) Evening Record (26 April), pp. C-1, C-7.
Reports that a parent's objection to NS on a high school English reading list was overruled by the superintendent and the board of trustees.

163. McKenzie, Barbara. "Introduction," in her Fiction's Journey: 50 Stories. New York: Harcourt Brace Jovanovich, pp. 3-100.
Discusses point of view (p. 23) and mentions dialect (p. 50) in "The Man

Who Was Almost a Man."

164. ____. "Questions," in her Fiction's Journey: 50 Stories. New York: Harcourt Brace Jovanovich, pp. 197-198.
Study questions for "The Man Who Was Almost a Man."

165. Meserole, Harrison T. et al. "Articles on American Literature Appearing in Current Periodicals." American Literature, 49 (January), 685-703.
Lists one item on W (p. 702).

166. ____. "Articles on American Literature Appearing in Current Periodicals." American Literature, 50 (March), 146-157.
Lists two items on W (p. 156).

167. ____. "Articles on American Literature Appearing in Current Periodicals." American Literature, 50 (May), 318-334.
Lists one item on W (p. 333).

168. ____. "Articles on American Literature Appearing in Current Periodicals." American Literature, 50 (November), 540-551.
Lists three items on W (p. 551).

169. Miller, Adam David. "Breedlove, Peace and the Dead: Some Observations on the World of Toni Morrison." The Black Scholar, 9 (March), 47-50.
Considers W's difference from Morrison as the difference between the first and third black generations in the North.

170. Miller, James E., Jr. "American Literature," in The World Book Encyclopedia. Ed. William H. Nault. Vol. 1. Chicago: World Book--Childcraft International, pp. 394-404d.
Reprint of 1975.132.

171. Miller, Ruth and Peter J. Katopes. "The Harlem Renaissance: Arna W. Bontemps, Countee Cullen, James Weldon Johnson, Claude McKay, and Jean Toomer," in Black American Writers: Bibliographical Essays. Vol. 1. Ed. M. Thomas Inge, Maurice Duke, and Jackson R. Bryer. New York: St. Martin's Press, pp. 161-186.
Mentions W briefly (p. 180).

172. ____. "Slave Narratives," in Black American Writers: Bibliographical Essays. Vol. 1. Ed. M. Thomas Inge, Maurice Duke, and Jackson R. Bryer. New York: St. Martin's Press, pp. 21-46.
Refers to Arna Bontemps's remark that slave narratives influenced the style of W, Ellison, and Baldwin (p. 21).

173. Miller, Wayne C. "Towards a Definition of Interfacing: 'The Processes

Wherein Cultures Collide, Even Within the Shared Territory of the Text.'" MELUS, 5 (Summer), 7-14.
   Mentions W briefly (p. 10).

174. Moon, Henry Lee. "Spingarn Medal," in The World Book Encyclopedia. Ed. William H. Nault. Vol. 18. Chicago: World Book--Childcraft International, p. 619.
   Reprint of 1960.201.

175. Morozova, T L. "Tipologija Geroja," in Literatura SSA XX Veka: Opyt tipo-logiceskogo issledovanija (Avtorskaja pozicija, konflikt, geroj). Ed. Ja. N. Zasursky. Moscow: Nauka, pp. 359-560.
   Discusses NS as a novel of social protest with emphasis on the charac-terization of Bigger (pp. 485-488). Mentions W elsewhere, especially in relation to Baldwin (pp. 390, 465, 466, 493, 496, 500).

176. Morris, Willie. James Jones: A Friendship. Garden City, N. Y.: Double-day & Company, p. 95.
   Mentions W as an expatriate in Paris.

177. Morris, Wright. "Richard Wright: Real and Imagined Black Voices," in his Earthly Delights, Unearthly Adornments: American Writers as Image-Makers. New York: Harper & Row, pp. 147-154.
   Argues that W's style derives from his reading and his sense of per-sonal outrage, not from reliance on dialect or folk roots. He found naturalism congenial because his own experience confirmed the precepts of Darwin and Marx. His best work is BB because it is his most personal. His fiction, especially O, is less suc-cessful.

178. Moss, Robert F. "Caged Misery." Saturday Review, 5 (21 January), 45-47.
   Favorable review of AH and Richard Wright Reader. After surveying brief-ly Wright's major works, Moss praises AH as honest and penetrating. Partially reprinted: 1980.179.

179. Mwenifumbo, Tone. "Richard Wright: Revolutionary or Cynic?" Africa, No. 82 (June), pp. 107, 109.
   Summary of W's biography concluding that he was essentially a cynic because he had no real hope that his revolutionary ideas could ever be implemented. Nevertheless, he is in-dispensable to emerging Africa.

180. Naremore, James. The Magic World of Orson Welles. New York: Oxford Univer-sity Press, p. 141.

Quotes Welles's comments on BB.

181. Newman, Dorothy K., Nancy J. Ami-dei, Barbara L. Carter, Dawn Day, Wil-liam J. Kruvant, and Jack S. Russell. Protest, Politics, and Prosperity: Black Americans and White Institutions, 1940-75. New York: Pantheon, p. 47.
   Mentions W's employment by WPA.

182. [Newman, Katherine]. "MELUS News and Notes." MELUS, 5 (Summer), 66-69.
   Mentions John M. Reilly's essay on W in Black American Writers: Biblio-graphical Essays.

183. Nicholson, C. E. "Black Fiction. By Roger Rosenblatt," in The Yearbook of English Studies. Ed. G. K. Hunter and C. J. Rawson. Vol. 8, pp. 302-303.
   Praises Rosenblatt's analysis of Big-ger Thomas.

184. Nilon, Charles. "Black Literature," in American Literary Scholarship: An Annual/1976. Ed. J. Albert Robbins. Durham, N. C.: Duke University Press, pp. 369-399.
   Describes and evaluates several items on W.

184a. Ogata, Susumu. "Richard Wright's Black English." Otemon Gakuin Daigaku Bungakubu Kiyo [Bulletin of Otemon Ga-kuin University School of Literature], 12 (30 December 1978), 131-150.
   A study of the phonological and syn-tactical characteristics of black English in UTC and BB. Cites such anomalies as "col" (for "cold"), "yuh gits," and "I ain't got nothing"; concludes that there is little dif-ference between standard English and black English.

185. Oleneva, Valentina I. Sotsialnye motivy v Amerikanskoi novelistike. Kiev: "Nauka Dumka," pp. 2, 6, 16, 20, 50, 52-53, 79, 80-89, 90, 92-93.
   Study of the recent American short story in its social context, espe-cially the work of W, Flannery O'Con-nor, Langston Hughes, Joyce Carol Oates, and James Baldwin. The main section on W (pp. 80-89) comments on "Bright and Morning Star," "The Man Who Killed a Shadow," "Man of All Work," "Man, God Ain't Like That," "The Man Who Lived Underground," "Big Boy Leaves Home," "Long Black Song," and "The Man Who Saw the Flood." Men-tions W and his influence elsewhere.

186. Otten, Kurt. "Der Protestroman Richard Wrights," in Black Literature: Zur afrikanischen und afroamerikanischen Literatur. Ed. Eckhard Breitinger. Munich: Fink, pp. 317-344.

Argues that NS and LD, W's "adolescent novels," help to resolve the
tensions he recorded in BB. The focus
moves away from a Dreiserian emphasis
on victimization to a Dostoevskian
explanation of metaphysics. LD follows up Bigger's struggle for self-
knowledge and gives hope of cultural
self-acceptance for American blacks.

187. Payne, James Robert. "Richard
Wright. American Hunger." World Literature Today, 52 (Winter), 111.
    Favorable review praising the treat-
ment of W's relation to the Communist
Party. AH is less artistically coherent than BB, but still "extremely
interesting."

188. Pearson, Norman Holmes. "American
Literature," in The Encyclopedia Americana. Ed. Bernard S. Cayne. Vol. 1.
Danbury, Conn.: Americana Corporation,
pp. 691-709.
    Reprint of 1968.178.

189. Peters, Erskine. "American Hunger.
By Richard Wright." CLA Journal, 21
(March), 443-445.
    Favorable review. The work is stylis-
tically more mature than BB and seems
to fit better into W's pattern of
development. Seemingly more pessimistic than BB, it is actually more
hopeful.

190. Petesch, Donald A. "Rosenblatt,
Roger. Black Fiction." Studies in American Fiction, 6 (Spring), 120-121.
    Discusses briefly Rosenblatt's treat-
ment of NS.

191. Pickering, James H. Instructor's
Manual Fiction 100. Second edition. New
York: Macmillan, p. 105.
    Lists four items on W.

192. Pinckney, Darryl. "Wright, Richard
1908-1960," in Contemporary Literary
Criticism. Ed. Dedria Bryfonski. Vol. 9.
Detroit: Gale, pp. 585-586.
    Partial reprint of 1977.259.

193. Popkin, Michael, ed. Modern Black
Writers. A Library of Literary Criticism
series, ed. Leonard S. Klein. New York:
Ungar, pp. 456-470.
    Includes critical excerpts on W by
Zora Neale Hurston, Sterling A.
Brown, Melvin B. Tolson, Alain Locke,
Alfred Kazin, Ralph Ellison, Sinclair
Lewis, Senator Bilbo, Jean-Paul
Sartre, Arna Bontemps, James Baldwin,
Gilbert Highet, Ben Burns, Peter
Abrahams, Langston Hughes, John A.
Williams, Eldridge Cleaver, Constance
Webb, Edward Margolies, Dan McCall,
Margaret Walker Alexander, and Michel

Fabre.

194. Pratt, Louis H. James Baldwin.
Boston: Twayne, pp. 22, 126-127, 130.
    Mentions W, noting that "Everybody's
Protest Novel," in which Baldwin
attacks W, is self-serving. Quotes
Addison Gayle on Eldridge Cleaver's
comparison of W and Baldwin.

195. Przemecka, Irena. The Work of Robert Penn Warren and the Main Trends in
American Literature. Krakow: Nakladem
Uniwersytetu Jagiellonskiego, pp. 62-65.
    Discusses BB, NS, O, W's relation to
communism and existentialism, and
Baldwin's quarrel with W in a chapter
entitled "The Question of Identity."

196. Rayson, Ann. "George Schuyler:
Paradox Among 'Assimilationist' Writers." Black American Literature Forum,
12 (Fall), 102-106.
    Mentions W briefly.

197. Real, Willi. Teacher's Book. Paderborn: Schöningh, 224 pp.
    Interpretations and suggestions for
teaching to accompany Racism in America. See 1977.270.

198. Reed, Ishmael. "An American
Romance," in his Shrovetide in Old New
Orleans. Garden City, N. Y.: Doubleday,
pp. 50-52.
    Article on the Patricia Hearst case
with comparison to Bigger Thomas and
Mary Dalton.

199. _____. "The Before Columbus Foundation." Y'Bird Reader, 1, pp. 7-8.
    Mentions NS as a work "socially com-
mitted yet of a high artistic order."

200. _____. "Bird Lives!" in his Shrovetide in Old New Orleans. Garden City, N.
Y.: Doubleday, pp. 105-109.
    Reprint of 1973.250.

201. _____. "Chester Himes: Writer," in
his Shrovetide in Old New Orleans. Garden City, N. Y.: Doubleday, pp. 77-99.
    Reprint of 1972.168.

202. _____. Mumbo Jumbo. New York: Avon
Books, p. 239.
    Reprint of 1972.168a.

203. _____. "Native Son Lives!" in his
Shrovetide in Old New Orleans. Garden
City, N. Y.: Doubleday, pp. 44-49.
    Revised and expanded reprint of
1975.154.

204. _____. "The Old Music," in his
Shrovetide in Old New Orleans. Garden
City, N. Y.: Doubleday, pp. 64-66.
    Reprint of 1975.155.

205. _____. "Shrovetide in Old New
Orleans," in his Shrovetide in Old New
Orleans. Garden City: N. Y.: Doubleday,
pp. 9-33.
   Compares briefly the Patricia Hearst-
   Cinque case to NS.

206. _____. "You Can't Be a Literary
Magazine and Hate Writers," in his
Shrovetide in Old New Orleans. Garden
City, N. Y.: Doubleday, pp. 246-248.
   Reprint of 1976.154.

207. Reilly, John M. "Criticism of Ethnic Literature: Seeing the Whole Story."
MELUS, 5 (Spring), 2-13.
   Maintains that W provides the classic
   example of a writer whose work has
   been simplified by "naive" reading
   which forces it into an ethnic mold.
   In fact, W's "mediating" strategies
   change greatly from UTC to "The Man
   Who Lived Underground." The revisions
   of "The Man Who Lived Underground"
   reveal Wright's dedication to new
   "freedom of invention" in ethnic
   literature which later came to frui-
   tion in the work of Amiri Baraka,
   Ishmael Reed, and others.

208. _____. "Richard Wright," in Black
American Writers: Bibliographical Essays. Vol. 2. Ed. M. Thomas Inge, Maurice Duke, and Jackson R. Bryer. New
York: St. Martin's Press, pp. 1-46.
   Analysis and evaluation of the most
   essential materials for the study of
   W, including sections on bibliography, editions, manuscripts and
   letters, biography, and criticism.
   The last is divided into the following categories: books, pamphlets,
   parts of books, articles on W's
   career and literary influence, articles on his exile, and studies of the
   individual works. The essay concludes
   with a section on the prospects for
   future Wright criticism. Reilly does
   not consider reviews in detail, but
   he does discuss some foreign scholarship, especially German and Japanese.
   His general preference throughout the
   essay is for work which takes into
   account social, historical, and ideological elements in W as well as
   esthetic values.

209. _____, ed. Richard Wright: The
Critical Reception. New York: Burt
Franklin, xli + 400 pp.
   Collection of American reviews of
   W's published books with checklists
   of uncollected reviews. The long
   introduction traces W's reputation as
   developed by his reviewers, who identified the concerns that subsequent
   critics must address: "to examine his
   perception of human personality in a

social environment, define his style,
and judge the validity of his conception of the prophetic experience
of outsiders" (p. xl). The body of
the book contains reprints--some
abridged--of the following: 1938.1,
2, 38, 111, 123, 132, 135, 138, 163,
164, 165, 169, 176, 179, 181, 182,
197, 198, 201, 209, 213, 219, 221,
222, 223, 224, 225, 231, 234, 241,
244, 255, 256, 259, 260, 278, 286,
288; 1939.94; 1940.22, 265, 396, 572,
590, 592, 608, 614, 617, 620, 625,
644, 661, 694, 727, 729, 744, 769,
771, 784, 794, 842, 858, 865, 873,
916, 918, 919, 921, 939, 991;
1941.680, 702, 759, 846, 863, 912,
970, 982, 996; 1942.292, 311, 313;
1945.1, 6, 303, 310, 568, 671, 737,
770, 799, 801, 802, 823, 845, 860,
862, 883, 885, 901, 909, 913, 914,
916, 919, 922, 930, 933, 935, 945,
948, 957, 959, 976, 980, 982, 987,
990, 997, 999, 1019, 1020, 1034,
1038, 1042, 1068, 1080, 1100, 1103,
1117, 1120, 1132, 1136, 1139, 1153,
1155, 1163, 1165, 1167, 1172, 1176,
1180, 1196; 1953.3, 7, 10, 26, 41,
70, 91, 93, 100, 115, 119, 129, 140,
146, 150, 151, 155, 181, 186, 193,
197, 202, 204, 207, 208, 209, 210,
219, 220, 223, 236, 240, 248, 253;
1954.38, 73, 75, 76, 77, 89, 91, 92,
94, 95, 113, 118, 121, 126, 127, 130,
139, 149, 150, 155, 159, 160, 162,
163, 167, 170, 171, 181; 1955.39, 81,
82, 85, 87; 1956.18, 96, 115, 146,
235, 306, 307, 311, 333, 334;
1957.48, 52, 95, 124, 154, 155, 159,
169, 177, 186, 189, 204, 205, 207,
210, 215, 219, 225, 233, 234, 260,
263, 266, 270, 280, 281, 282, 284,
296, 302, 323, 328, 346; 1958.58, 76,
81, 109, 121, 123, 135, 146, 154,
177, 210, 215, 217, 226, 249;
1959.61, 119, 121, 140; 1961.129,
149, 160, 178, 197, 232, 240, 242,
270; 1963.24, 88, 91, 96, 105;
1964.56; 1977.58, 70, 72, 82, 97,
153, 162, 163, 164, 219, 233, 258,
276, 305, 333, 346, 347.

210. _____. "Richard Wright's Discovery
of the Third World." Minority Voices, 2
(Fall), 47-53.
   Argues that W's late works focusing
   on "foreign" cultures, while not
   masterpieces, demonstrate his struggle to discover a form capable of
   expressing the insights of his expatriate years. BP is of great significance because it marks the height of
   W's faith in technology and the
   beginning of his commitment to national liberation. This commitment
   allows W to transcend his difficulties regarding the definition of
   class and brings him close to Fanon's

conception of cultural politics.

211. ____. "The Utopian Impulse in Early Afro-American Fiction." Alternative Futures, 1 (Fall), 59-71.
Cites NS as an example (p. 63).

212. Roberts, Edgar V. Thinking and Writing About Literature. Starpath Series. Englewood Cliffs, N. J.: Prentice-Hall, p. 269.
Mentions W briefly.

213. Rodman, Selden. "The Freethinker." National Review, 30 (3 February), 164-165.
Favorable review of AH emphasizing its anti-Communist theme. W's integrity could not be reconciled to the Party's conformism.

214. Rubin, Steven J. "The Early Short Fiction of Richard Wright Reconsidered." Studies in Short Fiction, 15 (Fall), 405-410.
Argues that although W's early stories were filled with violence and protest, they contained the seeds of his later, more mature fiction. In them he "developed such themes as the possibility of freedom, man's isolation and alienation, the inherent irrationality of modern American society, and the nature and form of personal rebellion within that society."

215. Rushing, Andrea Benton. "An Annotated Bibliography of Images of Black Women in Black Literature." CLA Journal, 21 (March), 435-442.
Mentions an essay by Saundra Towns treating W.

216. ____. "Images of Black Women in Afro-American Poetry," in The Afro-American Woman: Struggles and Images. Ed. Sharon Harley and Rosalyn Terborg-Penn. National University Publications Series in American Studies. Port Washington, N. Y.: Kennikat Press, pp. 74-84.
Reprint of 1975.167.

217. Salzman, Jack and Leo Zanderer. "The Authors," in their Social Poetry of the 1930s: A Selection. New York: Burt Franklin, pp. 321-331.
Includes a biographical sketch of W (p. 331).

218. Sander, Reinhard W. "Black Literature and the American Dream: Richard Wrigth's [sic] Lawd Today." Nsukka Studies in African Literature, 1, No. 1, pp. 91-107.
Placing LT in the context of black and white fiction about the American

dream, Sander shows that the protagonist of W's novel first embraces the dream (Part I), becomes ambivalent toward it (Part II), and finally rejects it (Part III). For whites only, the American dream becomes for blacks the American nightmare.

219. Sarotte, Georges-Michel. Like a Brother, Like a Lover. Trans. Richard Miller. Garden City, N. Y.: Anchor Press/Doubleday, p. 97.
Quotes Cleaver on Baldwin's attitude toward W.

220. Sayre, Robert F. "Autobiography and the Making of America." The Iowa Review, 9 (Spring), 1-19.
Mentions the theme of "education-as-freedom" (p. 17) in W's autobiography.

221. Schultz, Elizabeth. "The Heirs of Ralph Ellison: Patterns of Individualism in the Contemporary Afro-American Novel." CLA Journal, 22 (December), 101-122.
Refers, for purposes of comparison, to Baldwin's relation to W (p. 122).

222. Scruggs, Charles W. "The Importance of the City in Native Son." Ariel, 9 (July), 37-47.
Maintains that the "real theme" of NS is "man's need for human community," a theme which W develops through three conflicting visions of the city, which does not satisfy the need. Bigger presents the city as meaningless, Buckley as destructive, and Max as a dream of the future. Only by rejecting Max's vision, grounded in European and Puritan traditions, does Bigger prove himself a "true Native Son."

223. Seidel, Alison P. Literary Criticism and Authors' Biographies: An Annotated Index. Metuchen, N. J.: Scarecrow Press, p. 196.
Lists four items on W.

224. Shange, Ntozake. "The Suspect Is Black & in His Early 20's," in her Nappy Edges. New York: St. Martin's Press, pp. 118-120.
Poem comparing Patricia Hearst to Mary Dalton and commenting on Bigger and Bessie.

225. Shenton, James P., Judith R. Benson, and Robert E Jakoubek. These United States. Boston: Houghton Mifflin, p. 511.
Mentions briefly W and NS.

226. Shimizu, Takeo. "America Kokujin Sakka Richard Wright Ron--Gaisho Taiken

o Sozai toshite" ["On Richard Wright, An American Negro Writer, On the Basis of His Injury"]. Waseda Daigaku Eibungaku [Waseda University English Literature], 48 (March), 106-115.

Claims that W's work can be interpreted in terms of the injury he had received in American society. The earliest injury came from his sexual relations with his Aunt Laura; another was derived from an Oedipus complex he felt toward his parents. His mother was his only protection and the other women in his life contributed to his injury. For W, the white race was represented by his mother and so was the black race. Consequently, his marriage to the two white women might have been responsible for the relative failure of his later work. [Y. H.]

227. ____. "Uncle Tom no Kodomotachi--Hairetsu no Gui" ["Uncle Tom's Children: Rationale for Its Order"]. Eigo Seinen [The Rising Generation], 124 (September), 244-248.

The order of the five stories in the collection instead of following the order of W's writing is in accord with a history of black people in the United States. It also coincides with a history of man described in the Bible: Adam and Eve, as they clothed themselves, were taken out of the Garden of Eden by God just as blacks were chased out of Africa and set on a journey to the unknown and hostile world. [Y. H.]

227a. Shoji, Mitsuko. "Richard Wright Study in Japan, 1940-1960." Nihon Joshi Daigaku Eibeibungaku Kenkyu [Japan Women's University Studies in English and American Literature], 13 (March), 73-80.

A survey of W criticism in Japan with a list of fifty-seven items.

228. Silberman, Charles E. Criminal Violence, Criminal Justice. New York: Random House, p. 152.

Quotes from TMBV.

229. Simama, Jabari Onaje. "Black Writers Experience Communism: An Interdisciplinary Study of Imaginative Writers, Their Critics, and the CPUSA." Dissertation Abstracts International, 39 (October), 2377A-2378A.

Abstracts a 1978 Emory University dissertation treating W.

230. Simson, Renate Maria. "Black Literature Course: 1972 vs. 1977." Obsidian, 4 (Winter), 114-118.

Survey of black literature courses in colleges and universities in the state of New York indicating that W was taught more than any other author, "but his popularity declined considerably between 1972 and 1977" (p. 115). In 1972 W was ranked first in literary merit and Ellison second; in 1977 these positions were reversed.

231. Singh, Amritjit. "Self-Definition as a Moral Concern in the Twentieth-Century Afro-American Novel." Indian Journal of American Studies, 8 (July), 23-38.

Comments briefly on NS as a turning point in black fiction away from light, middle-class protagonists and Christian morality.

232. Sitkoff, Harvard. A New Deal for Blacks: The Emergence of Civil Rights as a National Issue. Vol. 1: The Depression Decade. New York: Oxford University Press, pp. 72, 160, 206, 210, 212-215.

In addition to brief mention of W, Sitkoff reviews his career (pp. 212-215) with emphasis on NS as a protest novel. Quotes from Irving Howe, Dorothy Canfield Fisher, and W.

233. Skerrett, Joseph T., Jr. "Ralph Ellison and the Example of Richard Wright." Studies in Short Fiction, 15 (Spring), 145-153.

Analyzes Ellison's early stories to show that he gradually found his own voice through testing and rejecting W's approaches. W encouraged Ellison to emphasize the craft of writing, but was anxious that Ellison not be imitative. Ellison's first attempt at a novel, "Slick's Gonna Learn," suffers from too heavy a reliance on W's example and on the specific influence of LT.

234. Sojka, Gregory S. "The American Short Story Into Film." Studies in Short Fiction, 15 (Spring), 203-204.

Mentions the adaptation of "Almos' a Man" by Leslie Lee.

235. Sollors, Werner. Amiri Baraka/LeRoi Jones: The Quest for a "Populist Modernism." New York: Columbia University Press, pp. 1, 78, 127, 129, 135, 162, 179, 187, 249.

Brief references to W.

236. Standley, Fred L. "James Baldwin," in Dictionary of Literary Biography. Vol. 2: American Novelists Since World War II. Ed. Jeffrey Helterman and Richard Layman. Detroit: Gale, pp. 15-22.

Mentions W's early support of Baldwin.

237. Stanford, Barbara Dodds and Karima

Amin. Black Literature for High School Students. Urbana, Ill.: National Council of Teachers of English, pp. 6, 14, 32, 40-41, 42, 50-52, 54, 57, 94, 95, 117, 126, 143, 167, 168, 174, 191, 192, 196, 198, 203-204, 213, 239, 240.

Biographical-critical sketch of W (pp. 50-52) and a lesson plan for "The Ethics of Living Jim Crow" (pp. 203-204). Contains numerous other references to W.

238. Stone, Albert E. "After Black Boy and Dusk of Dawn: Patterns in Recent Black Autobiography." Phylon, 39 (March), 18-34.

Views BB as the pivotal black autobiography.

239. Stoneman, E. Donnell. "'Native Son' Inaugurates UNC's Paul Green Theater." Greensboro Daily News (30 September), Sec. A, p. 14.

Review praising the excellent performance of Gordon T. Cureton as Bigger. Toward the end the production lacks emotion, however.

240. _____. "Paul Green, The Man Whose Dramas Grace World's Stage." Greensboro Daily News (24 September), Sec. C, pp. 1, 5.

Interview with Green on the opening of a new production of NS at the University of North Carolina at Charlotte on 30 September. He has changed the original ending. Ellen Wright will attend the production.

241. Syse, Glenna. "Meshach Taylor a Powerful 'Native Son.'" Chicago Sun-Times (14 October), p. 31.

Favorable review of the Chicago revival of the play stressing its social indictment and its effective use of melodrama. Praises the acting and the production, but faults Max's courtroom speech as propaganda, not drama.

242. _____. "Meshach Taylor: Native Son Reaching for Theater Stardom." Chicago Sun-Times (11 October), p. 82.

Article on the actor playing Bigger in the Chicago revival of NS.

243. Tate, Claudia C. "Marion Berghahn. Images of Africa in Black American Literature." Black American Literature Forum, 12 (Fall), 112-113.

Objects to Berghahn's notion that the attitude toward Africa of Jake in LT represents W's own view.

244. Thomson, Phillip, ed. An Index to Book Reviews in the Humanities. Vol. 18. Williamston, Mich.: Phillip Thomson, p. 419.

Lists four reviews of AH.

245. Toppin, Edgar Allan. "Black Americans," in The World Book Encyclopedia. Ed. William H. Nault. Vol. 2. Chicago: World Book--Childcraft International, pp. 306-306m.

Reprint of 1969.230.

246. Triche, Charles W. and Diane Samson Triche, eds. The American Humanities Index for 1977. Part 2. Troy, N. Y.: Whitson Publishing Company, p. 1213.

Lists five items on W.

247. Turner, Darwin T. "Introductory Remarks About the Black Literary Tradition in the United States of America." Black American Literature Forum, 12 (Winter), 140-147.

Reprint of 1978.248.

248. _____. "Introductory Remarks About the Black Literary Tradition in the United States of America," in Ethnic Literatures Since 1776: The Many Voices of America Part 1. Ed. Wolodmyr T. Zyla and Wendell M. Aycock. Proceedings of the Comparative Literature Symposium, Texas Tech University. Vol. 9. Lubbock: Texas Tech Press, pp. 71-86.

Contains several references to W. Reprinted: 1978.247.

248a. Verzea, Ileana. "Tradiţie şi modernitate in romanul american de culoare." Revista de istorie şi teorie literară, 27, No. 2, pp. 239-245.

Article in Romanian including discussion of NS as a work of social protest, but noting that some critics detect existential elements. Compares the novel to An American Tragedy.

249. Vopat, James B. "Beyond Sociology? Urban Experience in the Novels of James Baldwin," in Minority Literature and the Urban Experience: Selected Proceedings of the 4th Annual Conference on Minority Studies. Ed. George E. Carter and James R. Parker. Vol. 6. La Crosse, Wis.: Institute for Minority Studies, University of Wisconsin--La Crosse, pp. 51-58.

Mentions briefly NS (p. 51).

250. Wadud, Ali. "'Native Son,' The Play, Back After 36 Years." New York Amsterdam News (25 March), p. D-6.

Discusses the original production, reports a recent interview with Paul Green, and notes that the revival directed by Richard Garfield opened on 21 March at the Perry Street Theatre in New York. Garfield did some rewriting to alter "the white liberal view" of Green.

251. Waghmare, Janasdan M. "Richard

Wright: Eak Petlele Akash," in his Amer-
ican Negro: Sahitya Anni Sanskruti.
Bombay: Lokvangamaya Griha, pp. 77-115.
Chapter in a book in Marathi on Afro-
American literature and culture.
Waghmare surveys W's life and works
with emphasis on the American years.
Stresses the social and racial dimen-
sions of W's career with special
attention to NS.

252. Wald, Alan M. James T. Farrell: The
Revolutionary Socialist Years. New York:
New York University Press, pp. 79, 123,
146, 161.
Contains several brief references to
W.

253. Ward, Jerry W. "Richard Wright's
Hunger." Virginia Quarterly Review,
54 (Winter), 148-153.
Review of AH pointing out that although it has value as a literary
artifact, its publication comes thirty-two years too late to give it an
impact on the contemporary sensibility. Where BB draws on the power of
black folklore and myth, AH is important because of what it tells us of
W's individual growth.

254. Weixlmann, Joe. "Michael Popkin,
comp. and ed. Modern Black Writers: A
Library of Literary Criticism." Black
American Literature Forum, 12 (Fall),
113-114.
Mentions W briefly.

255. Werksman, Mark. "Novelist Toni Morrison Writes About Black Culture and
Identity." Yale Daily News (3 April), p.
5.
Notes that Song of Solomon is the
first main selection of the Book-of-
the-Month Club by a black author
since W.

256. Wideman, John. "Native Son." The
New York Times Book Review (5 March),
pp. 11, 32.
Favorable review of Richard Wright
Reader. Fabre has made good selections, but more of the inaccessible
material might have been included. W
is still a fascinating writer.
Partially reprinted: 1980.258.

257. ____. "Publish and Still Perish:
The Dilemma of Black Educators on White
Campuses." Black Enterprise, 9 (Septem-
ber), 44-45, 47, 49.
Mentions a photograph of W, Senghor,
Césaire, and William T. Fontaine.

258. Williams, Sherley Anne. "Anonymous
in America." Boundary 2, 6 (Winter),
435-441.
Review of two books on Amiri Baraka

mentioning W briefly.

259. ____. "Foreword," in Their Eyes
Were Watching God. By Zora Neale Hurston. Illini Books 686-0. Urbana: University of Illinois Press, pp. v-xv.
Mentions W briefly (p. vii).

260. Williamson, Marilyn L. "Reviewing
Graduate Programs: Have You Looked at
the JIL Lately?" ADE Bulletin, No. 56
(February), pp. 5-8.
States that NS should be read by
undergraduates and scrutinized by
scholars.

261. Wright, Ellen and Michel Fabre,
eds. Richard Wright Reader. New York:
Harper & Row, 886 pp.
Contains the complete TMBV, three
essays, three printed letters, a
review, twenty-seven poems (mostly
haikus), four stories, and excerpts
from BB, BP, PS, LT, NS, O, SH, and
LD. Fabre supplies an introduction,
headnotes, chronology, and bibliography.

261a. Wynes, Charles E. "Albery Allson
Whitman--The 'Black Mocking Bird' (?)
Poet." Illinois Quarterly, 41 (Fall),
38-47.
Quotes W on Whitman.

262. Yellin, Jean Fagan. "Towards a
Definition of Interfacing: 'Bread-and-
Butter Comparative Literature.'" MELUS,
5 (Summer), 4-6.
Mentions NS briefly.

263. Youdelman, Jeffrey. "Limiting Students: Remedial Writing and the Death of
Open Admissions." College English, 39
(January), 562-572.
Quotes from "The Psychological Reactions of Oppressed People" to clarify
a pattern of behavior of urban college students.

264. Young, Al. "Introduction," in Yard-
bird Lives! Ed. Ishmael Reed and Al
Young. New York: Grove Press, pp. 17-22.
Mentions W briefly.

265. Zasursky, Ja. N. "Vvedenie," in his
Literatura SSA XX Veka: Opyt tipologičeskogo issledovanija (Avtorskaja pozicija, konflikt, geroj). Moscow: Nauka,
pp. 3-11.
Mentions W as one of the four major
twentieth-century American writers on
the important theme of racial conflict. The others are Baldwin, Faulkner, and Sinclair Lewis.

1979

1. Alexander, Margaret Walker. "Zora

Neale Hurston: A Literary Biography. By
Robert E. Hemenway." American Litera-
ture, 50 (January), 661-663.
 Attributes "a profound influence" by
 Hurston on W.

2. Algren, Nelson. "Motley: He Was an
'Invisible Man' Among Black Writers."
Chicago Tribune (25 February), Sec. 7,
p. 1.
 Review of The Diaries of Willard
 Motley comparing him unfavorably to
 W. Quotes from a letter by W commenting on the black response to NS: "I
 really think Negroes are to blame for
 the reaction to 'Native Son.' So few
 of them have ever tried to tell the
 truth about how they feel. They are
 shamed, scared, and want to save
 their pride. In writing that book I
 threw shame, fear, and pride out the
 window."

3. Anon. "American Hunger." PMLA, 94
(March), 367.
 Half-page advertisement with blurbs
 by Irving Howe and Gwendolyn Brooks.

4. Anon. "American Hunger. Richard
Wright," in Harper Torchbooks 1979. New
York: Harper & Row, p. 20.
 Notice of the paperback edition in
 the publisher's catalog.

5. Anon. "An Audio Visual History of
American Literature," in Audio Visual
Teaching Materials. Pleasantville, N.
Y.: Educational Audio Visual Inc., p.
24.
 Catalog advertisement listing W as
 one of the authors treated.

6. Anon. "L'Auteur: Richard Wright."
Lire, No. 49 (September), p. 79.
 Biographical note to an excerpt from
 the French translation of AH.

7. Anon. Bibliographic Guide to Black
Studies: 1979. Boston: G. K. Hall, p.
217.
 Lists two primary and two secondary
 items concerning W in the New York
 Public Liberary.

8. Anon. "Bibliographie." La Quinzaine
littéraire, No. 304 (16/30 June), pp.
29-30.
 Contains a brief notice of the French
 translation of AH.

9. Anon. "The Black American Short Story
in the 20th Century: A Collection of
Critical Essays. Edited by Peter Bruck."
American Literature, 50 (January), 691-
692.
 Brief notice listing an essay on W.

10. Anon. "Black Authors," in 1979 Lis-

tening Library. Old Greenwich, Conn.:
Listening Library, pp. 10, 48.
 Advertisement listing a color film-
 strip on W.

10a. Anon. "Earthly Delights, Unearthly
Adornments. By Wright Morris." Business
Week, No. 2576 (12 March), p. 11.
 Mentions W briefly.

11. Anon. "Foster, Frances Smith. Witnessing Slavery: The Development of
Ante-Bellum Slave Narratives." Choice,
16 (December), 1307.
 Notice mentioning W.

12. Anon. "The Harlem Renaissance and
Beyond," in Audio Visual Teaching Mater-
ials. Pleasantville, N. Y.: Educational
Audio Visual Inc., p. 34.
 Catalog advertisement listing W as
 one of the authors treated.

13. Anon. Index to Periodical Articles
by and About Blacks: 1978. Boston: G. K.
Hall, p. 352.
 Lits four items on W.

14. Anon. Index Translationum 28. Paris:
Unesco, pp. 604, 664.
 Lists translations of BB into Swedish
 and NS into Turkish.

15. Anon. "James Baldwin (b. 1924),"
in The Short Story: 25 Masterpieces.
New York: St. Martin's Press, pp.
413-414.
 Mentions W briefly.

16. Anon. "Michel Fabre The Unfinished
Quest of Richard Wright," in Morrow
Quill Paperbacks. New York: William
Morrow, p. 10.
 Publisher's advertisement for the
 paperback edition.

17. Anon. "Paperbacks: New and Noteworthy." The New York Times Book Review
(11 February), p. 37.
 Contains a brief notice of AH.

17a. Anon. "Program." PMLA, 94 (November), 1060-1145.
 Lists a paper on W by Steven Rubin.

18. Anon. "Ralph Ellison (b. 1914)," in
The Short Story: 25 Masterpieces. New
York: St. Martin's Press, p. 416.
 Mentions W briefly.

19. Anon. "Rebels and Victims: The Fiction of Richard Wright and Bernard Malamud. Evelyn Gross Avery," in A Multidisciplinary Catalog of Ethnic Studies.
Port Washington, N. Y.: Kennikat Press,
p. 2.
 Publisher's notice.
 Reprinted: 1979.20.

20. _____. "Rebels and Victims: The Fiction of Richard Wright and Bernard Malamud. Evelyn Gross Avery," in American Literature in the Twentieth Century. Port Washington, N. Y.: Kennikat Press, p. 2.
     Reprint of 1979.19.

21. Anon. "Richard Wright (1908-1960)," in Magill's Bibliography of Literary Criticism. Ed. Frank N. Magill. Vol. 4. Englewood Cliffs, N. J.: Salem Press, pp. 2356-2360.
     Lists sixty-nine secondary sources on BB, "Bright and Morning Star," "Long Black Song," NS, and O.

22. Anon. "Richard Wright Une faim d'égalité." La Brussels Libre Belgique (14-15 August), p. 15.
     Favorable review of the French translation of AH. Instead of following capitalism or communism, W follows the dictates of his genius.

23. Anon. "Richard Wright Une faim d'égalité." Lire, No. 49 (September), p. 72.
     Headnote to an excerpt from the French translation of AH. Praises W's poignance, realism, and humor.

24. Anon. "Social Poetry of the 30's." PMLA, 94 (May), 517.
     Publisher's advertisement mentioning W.

25. Anon. "Sound Filmstrips About Fifty Great Novels," in 1979 Listening Library. Old Greenwich, Conn.: Listening Library, p. 11.
     Advertisement listing a filmstrip on NS.

26. Anon. "Thèses inscrites en 1979 dans la formation 3ème C." Afram Newsletter, No. 8 (December), p. 2.
     Lists "L'Afrique dans l'oeuvre de Richard Wright" by Colette Messe and "Images de la femme dans les romans de Wright, Ellison, et Himes" by Marie-Claire Ogandaga, both directed by Michel Fabre.

27. Anon. "The Twentieth Century American Novel," in 1979 Listening Library. Old Greenwich, Conn.: Listening Library, p. 10.
     Advertisement listing a cassette lecture on NS and O.

28. Anon. "Wright, Richard," in Meyers Enzyklopädisches Lexikon. Ed. Michael Wegner. Vol. 25. Mannheim: Bibliographisches Institut, pp. 515-516.
     Biographical note with bibliography.

29. Anon. "Wright, Richard," in 1979 Listening Library. Old Greenwich, Conn.: Listening Library, pp. 10, 47.
     Advertisement for recording by James Earl Jones of an abridged version of NS.

30. Auguste, Yves L. "Littérature noire des États-Unis et d'Haiti: la couleur: appat o barrière." Présence Africaine, No. 112 (Fourth Quarter), 113-120.
     Comments briefly on the black male-white female situation in "Big Boy Leaves Home" and NS (p. 117).

31. Avery, Evelyn Gross. Rebels and Victims: The Fiction of Richard Wright and Bernard Malamud. National University Publications Literary Criticism Series, ed. John E. Becker. Port Washington, N. Y.: Kennikat Press, 116 pp.
     Like the fiction of Bernard Malamud, W's work deals with characters in situations in which "impotency is enforced." Unlike the Jewish tradition, however, the black tradition represented by W rejects passivity. W's victims are either minor characters or else they evolve into rebels who seek affirmation through action. Partially reprinted: 1980.35.

32. Baker, Houston A., Jr. "A Psychodrama." First World, 2, No. 3, pp. 47-49.
     Review of Morris Dickstein's Gates of Eden: American Culture in the Sixties mentioning its treatment of W.

33. Baldwin, Richard E. "Charles W. Chesnutt," in The Critical Temper: A Survey of Modern Criticism on English and American Literature from the Beginnings to the Twentieth Century. Ed. Martin Tucker. A Library of Literary Criticism, Vol. 4: Supplement. New York: Ungar, pp. 482-483.
     Partial reprint of 1971.35.

34. Baraka, Imamu Amiri. "A Reply to Saunders Reddings' [sic] 'The Black Revolution in American Studies.'" American Studies International, 17 (Summer), 15-24.
     Calls W "the voice of the 30s" and "the most important fiction writer in Afro-American literature" (p. 23).

35. _____. "The Revolutionary Tradition in Afro-American Literature," in his Selected Plays and Prose of Amiri Baraka/LeRoi Jones. New York: William Morrow, pp. 242-251.
     Overview of Afro-American literature citing W as a Marxist-influenced writer whose "individualism and idealism finally sabotaged him." The defining characteristic of the fifties was a "reevaluation" of W led by Ellison and Baldwin.

36. _____. "War/Philly Blues/Deeper Bop," in his Selected Plays and Prose of Amiri Baraka/LeRoi Jones. New York: William Morrow, pp. 228-241.
Mentions W, along with Paul Robeson, as a "left-oriented" black artist. Cites the play NS as a major expression of "black national oppression" and "the illness of the entire society" (p. 238).

37. _____ and VéVé Clark. "Restaging Langston Hughes' Scottsboro [sic] Limited: An Interview with Amiri Baraka." The Black Scholar, 10 (July/August), 62-69.
Baraka mentions the W papers at Yale and speaks of corresponding with Ellen Wright about making a screenplay of UTC.

37a. Barth, John. Letters. New York: Putnam, p. 721.
Mentions briefly BB.

38. Bell, Pearl K. "Roth & Baldwin: Coming Home." Commentary, 68 (December), 72-75.
Contains a review of Just Above My Head mentioning Baldwin's rejection of W's protest fiction and Cleaver's support of W.

39. Beppu, Keiko. "Japanese Contributions," in American Literary Scholarship: An Annual/1977. Ed. James Woodress. Durham, N. C.: Duke University Press, pp. 499-504.
Mentions W briefly (p. 501).

40. Berthoff, Warner. A Literature Without Qualities: American Writing Since 1945. Quantum Books. Berkeley: University of California Press, pp. 15, 61-62, 160, 183-184.
Mentions NS and BB as classics comparable to works by Eliot, Faulkner, Hemingway, Stevens, and O'Neill. Comments on the theme of paranoia in W and Ellison.

41. Bigsby, C. W. E. "The Divided Mind of James Baldwin." Journal of American Studies, 13 (December), 325-342.
Comments on Baldwin's misinterpretation of NS, which Bigsby considers important not for its protest, but for "its conviction that individual action and the individual mind are not socially determined or socially bound" (p. 337).

42. Boitani, Piero. "Introduction to Prosatori Negri Americani del Novecento." Trans. Patrick Brancaccio. Colby Library Quarterly, 15 (December), 210-223.
Partial translation of 1973.66.

43. Bond, Jean Carey. "Two Views of Black Macho and the Myth of the Superwoman." Freedomways, 19 (First Quarter), 13-21.
Refers to comments on W in this book by Michele Wallace.

44. Boni, Silvia. "La donna nera e la sua poesia," in Saggi sulla cultura afro-americana. Ed. Alessandro Portelli. Rome: Bulzoni editore, p. 230.
Mentions W briefly.

45. Breitinger, Eckhard. "Bibliographie," in his Black Literature. Kritische Information 73. Munich: Wilhelm Fink Verlag, pp. 345-365.
Lists thirteen secondary items on W.

46. _____. "Einleitung: Zum Rahmen einer afrikanischen und afroamerikanischen Literatur," in his Black Literature. Kritische Information 73. Munich: Wilhelm Fink Verlag, pp. 12-58.
Mentions W (pp. 22, 49, 50) and quotes from his preface to George Lamming's In the Castle of My Skin (p. 28).

47. Brenni, Vito Joseph. The Bibliographic Control of American Literature 1920-1975. Metuchen, N. J.: The Scarecrow Press, pp. 79, 188.
Mentions briefly the Fabre-Margolies bibliography of W.

48. Brièrre, Annie. "Lectures américaines: le choix d'Annie Brièrre." France-USA, No. 223 (October-December), pp. 2, 7.
Contains a notice of the French translation of AH. Praises the style, but considers the work less moving than BB.

49. _____. "Richard Wright: 'Une Faim d'égalité.'" La Paris Croix (10 September), p. 8.
Review of the French translation of AH commenting on the style, mentioning W's break with the Communist Party, and comparing the sequel unfavorably to BB.

50. Brooks, Cleanth and Robert Penn Warren. "Discussion," in Understanding Fiction. Third edition. Englewood Cliffs, N. J.: Prentice-Hall, pp. 220-221.
Comments and study questions to accompany "The Man Who Was Almost a Man."

51. _____. Instructor's Manual Understanding Fiction. Englewood Cliffs, N. J.: Prentice-Hall, pp. 39-40.
Interprets "The Man Who Was Almost a Man" and provides answers to the

study questions in 1979.50.

52. Brown, Sterling A. "A Son's Return: 'Oh, Didn't He Ramble,'" in Chant of Saints: A Gathering of Afro-American Literature, Art and Scholarship. Ed. Michael S. Harper and Robert B. Stepto. Urbana: University of Illinois Press, pp. 3-22.
    Refers to the theme of hunger in BB (p. 18) and expresses admiration for W (p. 20).

53. Bruck, Peter. "James Baldwin geb. 1924," in Der moderne Roman des amerikanischen Negers: Richard Wright, Ralph Ellison, James Baldwin. Ed. Rolf Franzbecker. Darmstadt: Wissenschaftliche Buchgesellschaff, pp. 83, 84.
    Contains a brief summary of Baldwin's attempt to "free himself" from W and the tradition of the protest novel.

54. Bryer, Jackson R. "Richard Wright (1908-1960)," in Southern Writers: A Biographical Dictionary. Ed. Robert Bain, Joseph M. Flora, and Louis D. Rubin, Jr. Baton Rouge: Louisiana State University Press, pp. 508-510.
    Biographical sketch emphasizing the American years.

55. Burns, Landon C. and Janet P. Alwang. "The Fifth (1978-1979) Supplement to a Cross-Referenced Index of Short Fiction Anthologies and Author-Title Listings." Studies in Short Fiction, 16 (Spring), v-vi, 93-170.
    Lists four W stories in seven anthologies.

56. Bus, Heiner. "Afro-Amerikanische Autobiographien von Frederick Douglass bis Eldridge Cleaver: Dokumente der Suche nach personlicher, sozialer und literarischer Identität," in Black Literature. Ed. Eckhard Breitinger. Kritische Information 73. Munich: Wilhelm Fink Verlag, pp. 255-294.
    Mentions W as a father figure for James Baldwin (p. 268).

57. Callahan, John. "The Testifying Voice in Michael Harper's Images of Kin." Black American Literature Forum, 13 (Fall), 89-92.
    Mentions Harper's poems on W (p. 90).

58. Cargill, Oscar. "American Literature," in Collier's Encyclopedia. Ed. Louis Shores. Vol. 2. New York: Macmillan Educational Corporation, pp. 42-72.
    Reprint of 1969.49.

59. Carlsen, G. Robert, Anthony Tovatt, and Patricia O. Tovatt. "Biographical Notes," in their Insights: Themes in Literature. Third edition. New York: McGraw-Hill, pp. 490-493.
    Reprint of 1973.81.

60. _____. "The Fight," in their Teacher's Resource Guide for Third Edition Insights: Themes in Literature. New York: McGraw-Hill, p. 134.
    Reprint of 1973.82.

61. _____. "He Passed the Test, Implications, Techniques," in their Insights: Themes in Literature. Third edition. New York: McGraw-Hill, p. 510.
    Reprint of 1973.83.

62. _____. "Hokku Poems," in their Teacher's Resource Guide for Third Edition Insights: Themes in Literature. New York: McGraw-Hill, p. 118.
    Reprint of 1973.84.

63. Charpentreau, Jacques. "Richard Wright, Une faim d'égalité. L'Officiel des Comités d'Enterprise et Services Sociaux, No. 218 (November), p. 58.
    Notice of the French translation of AH. Charpentreau calls BB a world-renowned classic.

64. Chisholm, Shirley. "White Racism and Black Americans," in Words in Action: A Rhetoric Reader. Ed. Martin Steinman, Jr. New York: Harcourt Brace Jovanovich, pp. 86-93.
    Reprint of 1972.50.

65. Clark, Beverly Lyon. "Bigger Thomas' Name." North Dakota Quarterly, 47 (Winter), 80.
    Brief note stressing the manner in which Bigger's name plays on a variety of stereotypes.

66. Clemons, Walter. "Black Feminism." Newsweek, 93 (5 February), 78.
    Review of Michele Wallace's Black Macho and the Myth of the Superwoman mentioning W briefly.

67. Cobb, Nina Kressner. "Richard Wright: Exile and Existentialism." Phylon, 40 (December), 362-374.
    Traces W's relationship with Sartre and argues that their affinity had a political rather than a philosophical base. Rather than showing the influence of existentialism, O clearly refutes the precept that existence precedes essence. Cross Damon's fate is predetermined by the fact that he is an intellectual and a black man.

68. Coles, Robert Arnold. "The Later Nonfiction of Richard Wright." Dissertation Abstracts International, 40 (October), 2059A-2060A.
    Abstracts a State University of New York at Buffalo Ph.D. dissertation

correcting the critical neglect of O and W's nonfiction of the fifties. As an Afro-American writer, W should not be judged by Euro-American standards.

69. Conroy, Jack. "Days of 'The Anvil,'" in The Jack Conroy Reader. Ed. Jack Salzman and David Ray. American Cultural Heritage Series 2, ed. Jack Salzman. New York: Burt Franklin, pp. 145-150.
    Mentions W briefly (p. 148).

70. ____. "Home to Moberly," in The Jack Conroy Reader. Ed. Jack Salzman and David Ray. American Cultural Heritage Series 2, ed. Jack Salzman. New York: Burt Franklin, pp. 135-144.
    Mentions W as "perhaps the most significant writer introduced by The Anvil" (p. 139).

71. ____. "Memories of Arna Bontemps-- Friend and Collaborator," in The Jack Conroy Reader. Ed. Jack Salzman and David Ray. American Cultural Heritage Series 2, ed. Jack Salzman. New York: Burt Franklin, pp. 281-290.
    Reprint of 1974.47.

72. Corey, Stephen. "The Avengers in Light in August and Native Son." CLA Journal, 23 (December), 200-212.
    In NS, W solves the problem of balancing universal and personal meanings by creating a malevolent individual embodying social forces. Like Faulkner's Percy Grimm, Buckley has the power to carry out society's symbolic wishes and kill Bigger Thomas. The ostensible symbols of justice cannot withstand the onslaught of Buckley, who uses them ironically to effect Bigger's destruction.

73. Courlander, Harold. "Roots of the Case Against Alex Haley." Chicago Sunday Sun-Times (29 April), Sec. 2, pp. 1-4.
    Mentions W as a black writer who has brought honor to his people (p. 2).

74. Dance, Daryl C. "Black Eve or Madonna? A Study of the Antithetical Views of the Mother in Black American Literature," in Sturdy Black Bridges: Visions of Black Women in Literature. Ed. Roseann P. Bell, Bettye J. Parker, and Beverly Guy-Sheftall. Garden City, N. Y.: Anchor Press/Doubleday, pp. 123-132.
    Cites the passage from "The Ethics of Living Jim Crow" in which W's mother reprimands him for fighting white boys.

75. Dandridge, Rita B. "Male Critics/ Black Women's Novels." CLA Journal, 23 (September), 1-11.
    Mentions W briefly (pp. 1, 2).

76. Davis, Charles T. "From Experience to Eloquence: Richard Wright's Black Boy as Art," in Chant of Saints: A Gathering of Afro-American Literature, Art, and Scholarship. Ed. Michael S. Harper and Robert B. Stepto. Urbana: University of Illinois Press, pp. 425-439.
    After examining the relation of BB to AH and noting the critical reception of the former, Davis analyzes W's shaping of his Southern experience into autobiographical art by means of fictional principles. Omitting by design the support actually provided by some members of his family, by teachers, by friends, and even by a white family, W depicts himself in isolation, without even the compensation of sex. Through three narrative voices--objective, lyrical, and didactic--he shows also the growth of his artistic impulse, especially the qualities of detachment and curiosity that made his physical survival so precarious until he fled the South. Neither the whole factual truth nor the perfectly ordered design of fiction, BB is nevertheless the supreme example of W's art. Reprinted: 1982.36.

77. Delmar, P. Jay. "The Mask as Theme and Structure: Charles W. Chesnutt's 'The Sheriff's Children' and 'The Passing of Grandison.'" American Literature, 51 (November), 364-375.
    Contains a footnote reference to 1976.55 (p. 368).

77a. DeVeaux, Alexis. "Paule Marshall: In Celebration of Our Triumph." Essence, 10 (May), 70-71, 96, 98, 123-124, 126, 131, 133, 135.
    Marshall states that she "was also influenced by Richard Wright, to a lesser degree" than by Thomas Mann.

78. Diedrich, Maria. "Fritz Gysin: The Grotesque in American Negro Fiction. Jean Toomer, Richard Wright, and Ralph Ellison." Archiv für das Studium der neueren Sprachen und Literaturen, 216 (Second Half), 434-436.
    Comments on Gysin's treatment of W.

79. ____. Kommunismus im afroamerikanischen Roman. Amerikastudien: Eine Schriftenreihe, vol. 53, ed. Hans Galinsky, Gerhard Hoffmann, and Günter Moltmann. Stuttgart: J. B. Metzlersche Verbuchshandlung, pp. 1, 2, 49, 63, 101, 103, 124, 125, 127, 139, 140, 145, 146, 151, 152, 153, 154, 156, 157, 158, 170, 173-291, 297, 298, 299,, 301, 303, 305, 306, 309, 311, 316, 326, 332, 339, 344, 345, 346, 347, 348, 384, 391, 395, 396, 397, 398, 399, 400, 401, 402.
    Includes an extensive biographical-

critical account of W's attitude toward communism. Ambivalent toward the Communist Party from the start, he turned to it because the romantic cultural nationalism of the Harlem renaissance offered no viable alternative. The pessimism of LT, the agrarianism of UTC, and the mixed existentialism and naturalism of NS anticipate the open break with communism in O and W's third-world writings.

80. Dietz, Karl Wilhelm. Ralph Ellisons Roman Invisible Man: Ein Beitrag zu seiner Rezeptionsgeschichte und Interpretation mit besonderer Berucksichtigung der Figuren-, Raum- und Zeitgestaltung. Mainzer Studien zur Amerikanistik, vol. 12, ed. Hans Galinsky. Frankfurt am Main: Peter Lang, pp. 17, 18, 22, 31, 32, 33, 34-35, 37, 40, 41, 44-45, 46, 52, 53, 60, 212, 229, 232, 233, 239, 240, 241, 242, 243, 250, 251, 254, 259, 262, 267, 290, 291, 296, 300, 304, 307, 308, 310, 313, 314, 316, 317, 320, 321.
    Mentions W frequently in connection with the reception of Ellison's work, somewhat less frequently in connection with Ellison's own literary opinions.

81. Dixon, Melvin. "Rivers Remembering Their Source: Comparative Studies in Black Literary History--Langston Hughes, Jacques Roumain, and Negritude," in Afro-American Literature: The Reconstruction of Instruction. Ed. Dexter Fisher and Robert B. Stepto. New York: Modern Language Association, pp. 25-43.
    Comments on W's statement that "I see both worlds from another, and third, point of view" (pp. 27-28).

82. Doner, Dean. "Wright, Richard," in The World Book Encyclopedia. Ed. William H. Nault. Vol. 21. Chicago: World Book-Childcraft International, p. 420.
    Reprint of 1975.60.

82a. Dow, Eddy, Douglas Fricke, Philip R. Headings, Matthew O'Brien, and Joan Stockard. "American Literature," in 1978 MLA International Bibliography. Vol. 1. New York: Modern Language Association, pp. 161-228.
    Lists twenty-six items on W.

83. Eckhardt, Caroline D. and David H. Stewart. "Author Notes," in their The Wiley Reader: Designs for Writing. Brief edition. New York: Wiley, pp. 317-319.
    Reprint of 1976.63.

84. _____. "The God That Failed," in their The Wiley Reader: Designs for Writing. Brief edition. New York: Wiley,

p. 270.
    Reprint of 1976.62.

85. Eddleman, Floyd Eugene. American Drama Criticism: Interpretations, 1890-1977. Second edition. Hamden, Conn.: The Shoe String Press, pp. 128-129, 424.
    Lists fourteen items on the play NS and two on Daddy Goodness. See 1967.80a.

86. Ellison, Ralph, Robert B. Stepto, and Michael S. Harper. "Study & Experience: An Interview with Ralph Ellison," in Chant of Saints: A Gathering of Afro-American Literature, Art, and Scholarship. Ed. Michael S. Harper and Robert B. Stepto. Urbana: University of Illinois Press, pp. 451-469.
    Ellison mentions W's relation to Farrell, discusses his own friendship with W, comments on "Blueprint for Negro Writing" and BB, and explains the current vogue of W.

87. Emblen, D. L. "Richard Wright, 'The Library Card,'" in his Instructor's Manual to Accompany A Writer's Reader. Boston: Little, Brown, pp. 130-131.
    Answers the study questions following a reprinting of Chapter XIII of BB.

88. Emerson, O. B. and Marion C. Michael. Southern Literary Culture: A Bibliography of Masters' and Doctors' Theses. Revised and enlarged edition. University: The University of Alabama Press, pp. 195-196.
    Lists five doctoral dissertations and fifteen master's theses on W.

89. Ensslen, Klaus. "Peter Bruck, ed. The Black American Short Story in the 20th Century: A Collection of Critical Essays." Amerikastudien, 24, No. 1, pp. 178-179.
    Mentions W briefly.

90. Erickson, Peter. "'Cast Out Alone/To Heal/And Re-Create Ourselves': Family-Based Identity in the Work of Alice Walker." CLA Journal, 23 (September), 71-94.
    Discusses Walker's use of W in the short story entitled "A Sudden Trip Home in the Spring" (pp. 82, 84).

91. Fabre, Geneviève E. "Afro-American Drama, 1850-1975," in Afro-American Poetry and Drama, 1760-1975: A Guide to Information Sources. Ed. William P. French, Michel J. Fabre, Amritjit Singh, and Geneviève E. Fabre. American Literature, English Literature, and World Literatures in English Information Guide Series, vol. 17, ed. Theodore Grieder. Detroit: Gale, pp. 257, 273, 336-337.
    Lists NS and four unpublished plays,

as well as six secondary sources.

92. Fabre, M.[ichel]. "Edward Mapp. Dir-ectory of Blacks in the Performing Arts." AFRAM Newsletter, No. 7 (March), p. 34.
Review noting that the W entry is correct in all particulars.

93. _____. "Marion Berghahn. Images of Africa in Black American Literature." AFRAM Newsletter, No. 8 (December), p. 16.
Mentions W briefly.

94. _____. "Michel Terrier. Le Roman Américain. 1914-1945." AFRAM Newsletter, No. 8 (December), p. 17.
Mentions favorably Terrier's treat-ment of W, especially NS.

95. _____. "Peter Freese. Growing Up in Black America; Willi Real. Racism in America." AFRAM Newsletter, No. 7 (March), p. 34.
Review of two textbooks noting the importance of W in the second.

96. Farrell, Edmund J., Ruth S. Cohen, L. Jane Christensen, and H. Keith Wright. "Discussion," in their Purpose in Literature. Glenview, Ill.: Scott, Foresman, p. 156.
To accompany a passage from BB.

97. _____. "'Hunger' Richard Wright," in their Teacher's Manual for Purpose in Literature. Glenview, Ill.: Scott, Foresman, pp. 44-45.
Study and discussion aids.

98. _____. "Richard Wright," in their Purpose in Literature. Glenview, Ill.: Scott, Foresman, p. 156.
Biographical sketch.

99. Ferruggia, Gabriella. "Il Black Theatre Movement negli anni '60," in Saggi sulla cultura afro-americana. Ed. Alessandro Portelli. Rome: Bulzoni edi-tore, pp. 279-304.
Quotes from The God That Failed on W's experience with the Federal Thea-tre (p. 283) and mentions the play NS (p. 285).

100. Fiedler, Leslie A. The Inadvertent Epic: From Uncle Tom's Cabin to Roots. New York: Touchstone Books, pp. 29, 71.
Mentions W briefly as a writer who rejected classic literary representa-tion of blacks and who failed to attract the mass audience of Roots.

101. Fisher, Dexter and Robert B. Stepto. "Rethinking the Afro-American Literature Survey Course," in their Afro-American Literature: The Recon-struction of Instruction. New York: Modern Language Association, pp. 234-243.
Suggests ways of treating NS as well as other works.

102. _____. "Rethinking the Interdiscip-linary Course Embracing Afro-American Literature," in their Afro-American Lit-erature: The Reconstruction of Instruc-tion. New York: Modern Language Associa-tion, pp. 250-255.
Mentions W and NS.

103. Fontenot, Chester J., Jr. "Black Fiction: Apollo or Dionysus?" Twentieth Century Literature, 25 (Spring), 73-84.
Includes a discussion of NS (pp. 78-80) stressing Bigger's self-realiza-tion through rejecting the linear conception of history and creating through violence his "own private dystopia." To achieve manhood "he must accept responsibility for his own actions as conscious choices and not simply as the products of pre-ordained history."

104. _____. Frantz Fanon: Language as the God Gone Astray in the Flesh. Uni-versity of Nebraska Studies, new series no. 60. Lincoln: The University of Neb-raska, pp. 24, 27-28.
Discusses NS as a story of the con-flict between white and black cul-tures. "Bigger's plight symbolizes that of the black person caught be-tween the tension to see the language and values of the dominant society as a means to liberation and enlighten-ment, and to see them as a way of manipulating white society." Thus W's novel provides a gloss on Fanon's ideas.

105. Foster, Frances Smith. Witnessing Slavery: The Development of Ante-bellum Slave Narratives. Contributions in Afro-American and African Studies, No. 46. Westport, Conn.: Greenwood Press, pp. x, 153.
Mentions W briefly.

106. Franzbecker, Rolf. "Einleitung: Der moderne Roman des amerikanischen Negers und das kritische Dilemma," in his Der moderne Roman des amerikanischen Negers: Richard Wright, Ralph Ellison, James Baldwin. Darmstadt: Wissenschaftliche Buchgesellschaft, pp. 1-9.
Survey of criticism of black fiction mentioning W frequently. Cites NS as a work which presents special prob-lems for white critics (pp. 4-5).

107. _____. "Ralph Ellison (geb. 1914)," in his Der moderne Romane des amerikan-ischen Negers: Richard Wright, Ralph

Ellison, James Baldwin. Darmstadt: Wissenschaftliche Buchgesellschaft, pp. 53, 54, 55, 67, 68, 74.

Summarizes the debate over W's influence on Ellison, stressing their shared interest in existentialism and the absurd.

108. Frémy, Dominique and Michèle Frémy. Quid: Tout pour tous. Paris: Editions Robert Laffont, p. 262.
Reprint of 1963.109.

109. Gates, Henry-Louis, Jr. "Preface to Blackness: Text and Pretext," in Afro-American Literature: The Reconstruction of Instruction. Ed. Dexter Fisher and Robert B. Stepto. New York: Modern Language Association, pp. 44-69.
Quotes W on the Harlem Renaissance (p. 55) and refers to NS (p. 68).

110. Géniès, Bernard. "La Suite de 'Black Boy.'" La Quinzaine littéraire, No. 309 (16-30 September), pp. 8-9.
Favorable review of the French translation of AH, which seems closer to O than to BB. Géniès emphasizes W's relation to the Communist Party and his efforts to learn to write.

111. Gilenson, B. "'Vtoroe rozhdenie' Richarda Raita." Voprosy Literatury, No. 6, pp. 278-290.
Discusses W's "second birth"--the renewed interest in his work during the sixties and seventies. After reviewing W's life and career, Gilenson notes his relation to recent black militance and then evaluates the scholarly work on the author of Webb, Margolies, the Iowa Conference, Hyman, Brignano, Gysin, Kinnamon, and Fabre. The last two are the most satisfactory critics of W because they recognize the importance of Communism and humanism in his world view.
Translated: 1980.109.

112. Goode, Stephen, ed. The American Humanities Index for 1978. Troy, N. Y.: Whitson Publishing Company, p. 374.
Lists five items on W.

113. Gounard, J. F. and Beverley Roberts Gounard. "Richard Wright's Savage Holiday: Use or Abuse of Psychoanalysis?" CLA Journal, 22 (June), 344-349.
Argues that Erskine Fowler's reaction to his guilt in SH follows a classic Freudian pattern, demonstrating that W is "faithful to psychoanalysis" (p. 348). This patterning harms the novel artistically, however, because W seems to have substituted the pattern for a true knowledge of how his characters would react to their situation.

114. Graves, Neil. "Richard Wright's Unheard Melodies: The Songs of Uncle Tom's Children." Phylon, 40 (September), 278-290.
Argues that W uses spirituals not as a form of secret communication between black characters, but as a way to convey information to his readers. Rather than making direct propagandistic statements through lyrics, however, W employs them in subtle ways to comment, frequently ironically, on the narratives. Ultimately the songs must be seen as the most important unifying technique in the book.

115. Greene, J. Lee. "Black American Fiction: A Bibliography. Compiled by Carol Fairbanks and Eugene Engeldinger; The Afro-American Novel 1965-1975: A Descriptive Bibliography of Primary and Secondary Material. Edited by Helen Ruth Houston; Black American Writers: Bibliographical Essays. Edited by M. Thomas Inge, Maurice Duke, and Jackson R. Bryer; James Weldon Johnson and Arna Wendell Bontemps: A Reference Guide. Compiled and edited by Robert E. Fleming." The Mississippi Quarterly, 32 (Fall), 678-685.
Refers to this reference guide to W as an example of important bibliographical work still to be done.

116. Guerin, Wilfred L., Earle G. Labor, Lee Morgan, and John R. Willingham. A Handbook of Critical Approaches to Literature. Second edition. New York: Harper & Row, p. 275.
Comments briefly on James G. Kennedy's "The Content and Form of Native Son" in a section on Marxist criticism.

117. Guy-Sheftall, Beverly. "The Women of Bronzeville," in Sturdy Black Bridges: Visions of Black Women in Literature. Ed. Roseann P. Bell, Bettye J. Parker, and Beverly Guy-Sheftall. Garden City, N. Y.: Anchor Press/Doubleday, pp. 157-170.
Includes brief comparison of Gwendolyn Brooks and W.

118. Hafsia, Jelila. "La Plume en liberté: Une faim d'egalité." La Tunis Presse de Tunisie (26 September), p. 3.
Review of the French translation of AH in the context of W's career. W attempts to explain blacks and whites to each other in all the psychological and social irrationality of their behavior.

119. Hakutani, Yoshinobu. "Native Son

and An American Tragedy: Two Different
Interpretations of Crime and Guilt." The
Centennial Review, 23 (Spring), 208-226.
Summarizes parallels between NS and
An American Tragedy. Dreiser's hero
is a type while W's is an individual.
W's novel draws its meaning from the
result of the crime; Dreiser's from
the cause. W's language mirrors Big-
ger's developing consciousness.
Reprinted: 1982.66.

120. Hall, Donald and D. L. Emblen.
"Considerations," in their A Writer's
Reader. Second edition. Boston: Little,
Brown, pp. 491-492.
Study questions to accompany Chapter
XIII of BB.

121. _____. "Richard Wright, 'The
Library Card,'" in their A Writer's
Reader. Second edition. Boston: Little,
Brown, p. 483.
Headnote to a reprinting of Chapter
XIII of BB.

122. Hammond, Karla and Calvin Forbes.
"Karla Hammond Talks with Calvin
Forbes." Obsidian, 5 (Winter), 118-138.
Forbes mentions briefly W's interest
in Dostoevsky.

123. Harris, Trudier. "The Barbershop in
Black Literature." Black American Literature Forum, 13 (Fall), 112-118.
Discusses Jake Jackson in LT, who
finds in the barbershop fulfillment
denied him elsewhere.

124. Hedin, Raymond. "Teaching Literature in Prisons." College English, 41
(November), 280-285.
Reports success in teaching NS to a
highly responsive inmate audience.

125. Heigl, Otto, Dieter Herms, Wolfgang
Schneider, and Bianca Witzel. Von James
Baldwin zum Free Southern Theater: Posi-
tionen schwarzamerikanischer Dramatik im
soziokulturellen Kontext der USA. Bremen: Übersee-Museum Bremen, pp. 83, 107,
131, 134.
Mentions W's influence on Cleaver,
Bullins, and others.

125a. Hemenway, Robert. "Are You a
Flying Lark or a Setting Dove?" in Afro-
American Literature: The Reconstruction
of Instruction. Ed. Dexter Fisher and
Robert B. Stepto. New York: Modern Lan-
guage Association, pp. 122-152.
Mentions briefly Bigger's desire to
fly an airplane (p. 141).

126. Hoffman, Daniel. "Preface," in his
Harvard Guide to Contemporary American
Writing. Cambridge, Mass.: Harvard Uni-
versity Press, pp. [vii-ix].

Lists W, Faulkner, Steinbeck, Hemingway, and Dos Passos as the "important
fiction writers" in 1945.

127. H.[olab]-A.[belman], R.[obin] S.
"Wright, Richard. American hunger."
Kliatt Young Adult Paperback Book Guide,
13 (April), 35.
Favorable notice.

128. Holdt, Marvin. "James E. Emanuel:
Black Man Abroad." Black American Literature Forum, 13 (Fall), 79-85.
Claims Emanuel's poem "At Bay" is
"somehow reminiscent of the manhunt
for Bigger Thomas in Native Son."

128a. Holland, Laurence B. "American
Literature Revisited." The Yale Review,
69 (December), 279-285.
Contains a review of Wright Morris's
Earthly Delights, Unearthly Adorn-
ments praising its treatment of W.

129. Holman, C. Hugh. Windows on the
World: Essays on American Social Fiction. Knoxville: The University of Tennessee Press, pp. 160-161.
Comments that despite W's residence
elsewhere, "being southern and black
. . . proved to be one of the most
effective subjects of his work."

130. Homberger, Eric. "Proletarian Literature and the John Reed Clubs 1929-
1935." Journal of American Studies, 13
(August), 221-244.
Mentions W briefly (p. 233).

131. Houseman, John. Front and Center.
New York: Simon and Schuster, pp. 16,
130, 155.
Mentions his relation to W and W's
friendship with Jack Berry.

132. Howard, Daniel F. "Richard Wright
1908-1960," in his The Modern Tradition:
An Anthology of Short Stories. Fourth
edition. Boston: Little, Brown, pp. 373-
374.
Reprint of 1972.100a.

133. _____ and John Ribar. "Richard
Wright," in their Instructor's Manual to
Accompany The Modern Tradition: An
Anthology of Short Stories. Boston:
Little, Brown, pp. 53-55.
Contains comments on "Big Boy Leaves
Home" and "The Man Who Lived Under-
ground," notes and queries on them,
and suggestions for further reading.

134. Howe, Irving. "Richard Wright: A
Word of Farewell," in his Celebrations
and Attacks: Thirty Years of Literary
and Cultural Commentary. New York: Horizon Press, pp. 89-92.
Reprint of 1961.178.

135. Huggins, Nathan Irvin. "Amiri Baraka/LeRoi Jones: The Quest for a Populist Modernism by Werner Sollors." The New Republic, 180 (21 April), 32-36.
Mentions briefly Michel Fabre's biography of W (p. 33).

135a. Ikegami, Hideo, Minoru Suda, Hiroshi Tanaka, and Kenji Ito. "Wright and Uncle Tom's Children," "Wright's Native Son," "Wright's Autobiography," and "Wright and The Outsider." Amerika Kokujin no Kaiho to Bungaku [The Liberation and Literature of Black Americans]. Tokyo: Shinnihon Shuppansha, pp. 92-95, 95-99, 128-131, 131-138.
A symposium: (1) NS subtly reflects the black liberation movement in the 1930s. (2) W's work shows that the movement in the initial stage directs its rage not against whites but against obsequious blacks. (3) The movement at times rejects the notion of black solidarity. (4) Alienation and individualism, however, do not guarantee freedom. [Y. H. and T. K.]

136. Ischinger, Anne-Barbara. "Stromungen in der Literaturgeschichte des frankophonen Schwarzafrika," in Black Literature. Ed. Eckhard Breitinger. Kritische Information 73. Munich: Wilhelm Fink Verlag, pp. 193-213.
Mentions W's influence on Ferdinand Oyono (p. 202).

137. Jackson, Blyden. "Wright, Richard," in The Encyclopedia of Southern History. Ed. David C. Roller and Robert W. Twyman. Baton Rouge: Louisiana State University Press, pp. 1363-1364.
Biographical sketch with a bibliographical note.

138. Jarrett, David and Mary Jarrett. "American Literature: The Twentieth Century," in The Year's Work in English Studies. Ed. James Redmond. Vol. 58, 1977. London: John Murray, pp. 449-479.
Mentions W briefly (pp. 450, 465, 474).

139. Jefferson, Margo. "There's a Heaven Somewhere." The Nation, 229 (3 November), 437-438.
Review of James Baldwin's Just Above My Head mentioning W and Bigger Thomas.

140. Jenkinson, Edward B. Censors in the Classroom: The Mind Benders. Carbondale and Edwardsville: Southern Illinois University Press, pp. xvi, 19, 29, 59, 60-61, 62, 85.
Discusses school censorship cases involving NS and, especially, BB.

141. Johnson, Abby Arthur and Ronald Maberry Johnson. Propaganda and Aesthetics: The Literary Politics of Afro-American Magazines in the Twentieth Century. Amherst: The University of Massachusetts Press, pp. 70, 98, 100, 102, 105-107, 110, 112-113, 115, 116-119, 124, 130, 136, 147-149, 170, 175-176, 192, 198-199, 203, 220, 223-224.
Mentions treatment of W in little magazines by such critics as Sterling Brown, Alain Locke, Countee Cullen, and Larry Neal. Discusses W's involvement with New Challenge (pp. 116-119) and other magazines.

142. Jones, Gayl and Michael S. Harper. "Gayl Jones: An Interview," in Chant of Saints: A Gathering of Afro-American Literature, Art, and Scholarship. Ed. Michael S. Harper and Robert B. Stepto. Urbana: University of Illinois Press, pp. 352-375.
Reprint of 1977.185.

143. Jung, Udo O. H. "Die Dichtung Jean Toomers und die Negerrenaissance," in Black Literature. Ed. Eckhard Breitinger. Kritische Information 73. Munich: Wilhelm Fink Verlag, pp. 295-316.
Mentions W briefly (p. 298).

144. Kaiser, Ernest. "Recent Books." Freedomways, 19 (First Quarter), 54-64.
Mentions W in connection with Black American Fiction: A Bibliography by Carol Fairbanks and Eugene A. Engeldinger (p. 60) and Black American Writers edited by M. Thomas Inge, Maurice Duke, and Jackson R. Bryer.

145. _____. "Recent Books." Freedomways, 19 (Second Quarter), 118-128.
Mentions "casebooks on Ralph Ellison and Richard Wright" (p. 121).

146. Kellner, Bruce. "Chester Himes," in his "Keep A-Inchin' Along": Selected Writings of Carl Van Vechten About Black Arts and Letters. Contributions in Afro-American and African Studies, No. 45. Westport, Conn.: Greenwood Press, pp. 186-187.
Notes that Van Vechten met Himes through W.

147. _____. "Correspondence," in his "Keep A-Inchin' Along": Selected Writings of Carl Van Vechten About Black Arts and Letters. Contributions in Afro-American and African Studies, No. 45. Westport, Conn.: Greenwood Press, pp. 247-248.
Mentions briefly correspondence between Van Vechten and W.

148. Kibler, James E. et al. "A Checklist of Scholarship on Southern Literature for 1978." The Mississippi Quarter-

ly, 32 (Spring), 305-389.
Lists and annotates briefly twenty-
one items on W.

149. Kilpatrick, Thomas L. and Patsy-
Rose Hoshiko. Illinois! Illinois!: An
Annotated Bibliography of Fiction.
Metuchen, N. J.: The Scarecrow Press,
pp. 476-477, 570.
Contains synopses of LT, NS, and O.

150. Kinnamon, Keneth. "'Big Boy Leaves
Home,'" in 38 Short Stories: An Intro-
ductory Anthology. Ed. Michael Timko.
Second edition. New York: Knopf, pp.
671-676.
Partial reprint of 1972.123.

151. _____. "Ellison, Ralph (Waldo)," in
Great Writers of the English Language:
Novelists and Prose Writers. Ed. James
Vinson. New York: St. Martin's Press,
pp. 374-376.
Notes Ellison's indebtedness to W.
Reprinted: 1980.138.

152. Klinkowitz, Jerome. "Introduction,"
in his The Diaries of Willard Motley.
Ames: The Iowa State University Press,
pp. xv-xx.
Mentions W (p. xv).

153. _____. "Notes on a Novel-in-Prog-
ress: Clarence Major's Emergency Exit."
Black American Literature Forum, 13
(Summer), 46-50.
Quotes a reference to W from Major's
novel (pp. 48, 49).

154. Klise, Thomas S. "The Odyssey of
Richard Wright," in his Sound Filmstrips
for Classes in Literature, Speech and
Composition. Peoria: Thomas S. Klise, p.
6.
Reprint of 1977.205.

154a. Klotman, Phyllis Rauch. Frame by
Frame--A Black Filmography. Bloomington:
Indiana University Press, p. 371.
Includes an annotated entry on NS.

155. Kom, Ambroise. "'In the Castle of
My Skin' on George Lamming et les Cara¶-
bes coloniales." Présence Africaine, No.
112 (Fourth Quarter), pp. 137-153.
Mentions briefly BB (p. 151).

156. Lawall, Sarah N. "Richard Wright,"
in The Norton Anthology of World Masterpieces. Fourth edition. Ed. Maynard
Mack, Bernard M. W. Knox, John C. Mc-
Gailliard, P. M. Pasinetti, Howard E.
Hugo, Rene Wellek, Kenneth Douglas, and
Sarah Lawall. New York: Norton, Vol. 2,
pp. 1285-1287, 1307-1308.
Critical essay on W's career (pp.
1285-1287), a sketch of his life, and
a bibliography of primary and secon-

dary sources. Lawall stresses the
universality of W's central theme:
the struggle to maintain or develop a
sense of individual identity in a
hostile or indifferent society.

157. Lawson, Carol. "News of the Theater: Miller's 'Paradise' Broadway
Bound." The New York Times (10 October),
p. C20.
Mentions the Washington closing of
the musical version of Daddy Goodness.

158. _____. "News of the Theater: Singer
Play Due on Broadway." The New York
Times (3 October), p. C22.
Announces the postponement of the New
York opening of the musical version
of Daddy Goodness.

159. Leary, Lewis with John Auchard.
Articles on American Literature, 1968-
1975. Durham, N. C.: Duke University
Press, pp. 561-565.
Lists 146 articles on W.

160. Lester, Julius. "Brothers and Sisters." The Nation, 228 (17 February),
181-182.
Review of Michele Wallace's Black
Macho and the Myth of the Superwoman
criticizing its treatment of W.

161. Lynn, Conrad. There Is a Fountain:
The Autobiography of a Civil Rights
Lawyer. Westport, Conn.: Lawrence Hill,
pp. 196-197.
Mentions briefly W and Ellen Wright.

162. Mack, Maynard, Bernard M. W. Knox,
John C. McGalliard, P. M. Pasinetti,
Howard E. Hugo, Rene Wellek, Kenneth
Douglas, and Sarah Lawall. "Preface to
the Fourth Edition," in their The Norton
Anthology of World Masterpieces. Fourth
edition. New York: Norton, vol. 1, pp.
xiii-xv; vol. 2, pp. xiii-xv.
Mentions the inclusion of W in the
fourth edition.

163. Mackey, Nathaniel. "To Define an
Ultimate Dimness: Deconstruction in
Clarence Major's Poems." Black American
Literature Forum, 13 (Summer), 61-68.
Quotes Major on W (p. 67).

164. Madden, David. "Brief Notes on the
Authors: For Further Reading," in
Studies in the Short Story. Ed. Virgil
Scott and David Madden. Fifth edition.
New York: Holt, Rinehart and Winston,
pp. 552-556.
Includes a brief note on W (p. 556).

165. Major, Clarence. Emergency Exit.
Madison, Wis.: Fiction Collective, pp.
4, 47, 126.

Contains several brief allusions to W and Bigger Thomas.

166. _____. "Foreword," in The Diaries of Willard Motley. Ed. Jerome Klinkowitz. Ames: The Iowa State University Press, pp. vii-x.
   Makes several references to W.

167. Margolies, Edward and David Bakish. "Checklist of Novels," in their Afro-American Fiction, 1853-1976: A Guide to Information Sources. American Literature, English Literature, and World Literatures in English Information Guide Series, ed. Theodore Grieder, vol. 25. Detroit: Gale, pp. 1-47.
   Lists W's novels (p. 45).

168. _____. "Introduction," in their Afro-American Fiction, 1853-1976: A Guide to Information Sources. American Literature, English Literature, and World Literatures in English Information Guide Series, ed. Theodore Grieder, vol. 25. Detroit: Gale, pp. xi-xv.
   Contains a paragraph on W (pp. xiii-xiv).

169. _____. "Richard Wright (1908-60)," in their Afro-American Fiction, 1853-1976: A Guide to Information Sources. American Literature, English Literature, and World Literatures in English Information Guide Series, ed. Theodore Grieder, vol. 25. Detroit: Gale, pp. 63-68.
   Annotated bibliography of thirty-six secondary sources, with cross references to five others.

170. _____. "Short Story Collections," in their Afro-American Fiction, 1853-1976: A Guide to Information Sources. American Literature, English Literature, and World Literatures in English Information Guide Series, ed. Theodore Grieder, vol. 25. Detroit: Gale, pp. 49-56.
   Lists UTC and EM (p. 55).

171. Marshall, Sara. "About the Authors," in her America in Literature: The South. New York: Scribner's, pp. 237-242.
   Contains a biographical sketch of W (p. 242).

172. Martin, Judith. "'Daddy Goodness': Good, But Still Not Good Enough." The Washington Post (21 September), Weekend Sec., p. 11.
   Mixed review of the musical version praising the conception and some of the numbers, but criticizing lack of plot and excessive length.

173. McConnell, Frank D. "Black American Literature," in Collier's Encyclopedia.

Ed. Louis Shores. Vol. 2. New York: Macmillan Educational Corporation, pp. 72-74.
   Reprint of 1976.125.

174. Meserole, Harrison T. et al. "Articles on American Literature Appearing in Current Periodicals." American Literature, 51 (November), 445-462.
   Lists eight items on W, four of them briefly annotated.

175. Michael, Marion C. "Southern Literature in Academe." The Mississippi Quarterly, 32 (Winter), 3-11.
   Notes that forty-nine theses or dissertations have been written on W since 1948.

175a. Mickelson, Anne Z. Reaching Out: Sensitivity and Order in Recent American Fiction by Women. Metuchen, N. J.: The Scarecrow Press, pp. 138, 150, 177.
   Contrasts W to Toni Morrison in their attitudes toward the black past, compares Bigger Thomas to the character Guitar in Song of Solomon, and notes W's social protest.

176. Miller, James E., Jr. "American Literature," in The World Book Encyclopedia. Ed. William H. Nault. Vol. 1. Chicago: World Book--Childcraft International, pp. 394-404d.
   Reprint of 1975.132.

177. _____, Carlota Cardenas de Dwyer, Robert Hayden, Russell J. Hogan, Kerry M. Wood. "Discussion, Extension, Richard Wright 1908-1960," in their United States in Literature. Glenview, Ill.: Scott, Foresman, p. 419.
   Study aids to accompany "The Man Who Saw the Flood" and a biographical sketch of W.

178. Miller, R. Baxter. "Book Review: M. Thomas Inge, Maurice Duke, and Jackson R. Bryer, eds. Black American Writers: Bibliographical Essays." Black American Literature Forum, 13 (Fall), 119-120.
   Mentions John Reilly's essay on W and Joanne Giza's comments on the W-Ellison relationship in her essay on the latter.

179. Moon, Henry Lee. "Spingarn Medal," in The World Book Encyclopedia. Ed. William H. Nault. Vol. 18. Chicago: World Book--Childcraft International, pp. 619-620.
   Reprint of 1960.201.

180. Moulton, Elizabeth. "Remembering George Davis." The Virginia Quarterly Review, 55 (Spring), 284-295.
   Mentions a party W attended given by Davis, the editor of Mademoiselle.

181. Newman, Katharine. "A Reading List of Ethnic Books in Print." MELUS, 4 (Supplement), 1-24.
Lists six books by W.

182. Newman, Richard and R. Glenn Wright. Index to Birthplaces of American Authors. Boston: G. K. Hall, pp. 135, 183.
Lists W's birthplace as "near Natchez."

183. Nilon, Charles. "Black Literature," in American Literary Scholarship: An Annual/1977. Ed. James Woodress. Durham, N. C.: Duke University Press, pp. 405-431.
Discusses eight articles and a book on W (pp. 410-414) and mentions W elsewhere (pp. 426, 427, 429, 430).

184. O'Connor, Margaret Anne. "Fiction: The 1930s to the 1950s," in American Literary Scholarship: An Annual/1977. Ed. James Woodress. Durham, N. C.: Duke University Press, pp. 273-302.
Mentions briefly W and NS (pp. 279, 288).

185. Olney, James. "The Value of Auto-biography for Comparative Studies: African vs. Western Autobiography." Comparative Civilizations Review, 2 (Spring), 52-64.
Contrasts Camara Laye's L'Enfant noir and W's BB as examples of African "autophylography," emphasizing the communal self, and Western "autoauto-graphy," emphasizing the individual self.

186. O'Meally, Robert G. "Invisible Man: 'Black and Blue.'" Minority Voices, 3 (Fall), 21-35.
Mentions W briefly (p. 21).
Reprinted in revised form: 1980.165.

187. _____. "Riffs and Rituals: Folklore in the Work of Ralph Ellison," in Afro-American Literature: The Reconstruction of Instruction. Ed. Dexter Fisher and Robert B. Stepto. New York: Modern Language Association, pp. 153-169.
Discusses Ellison's admiring evaluation of W's work in the forties (pp. 158-159).

188. Osborne, Charles. "A Small House in Brooklyn." New York, 12 (19 November), 52-53.
Mentions briefly W's residence at 7 Middagh Street.
Reprinted: 1979.189.

189. _____. W. H. Auden: The Life of a Poet. New York: Harcourt Brace Jovanovich, pp. 196-198.
Reprint of 1979.188.

190. Otten, Kurt. "Der Protestroman Richard Wrights," in Black Literature. Ed. Eckhard Breitinger. Kritische Information 73. Munich: Wilhelm Fink Verlag, pp. 317-344.
Emphasizes W's protest novels focusing on the struggle of black people for self-understanding. Resembling Dostoevsky more than Dreiser, he focuses on characters struggling to find their place in the metaphysical scheme. The existentialism of Kierkegaard and Heidegger provides the basic vocabulary of their search.

191. Ouchi, Giichi. "'The Outsider' nit-suite" ["'The Outsider' by Richard Wright"]. Waseda Daigaku Kyoyo Shogaku Kenkyu [Waseda University General Studies], Nos. 58-60 (March), 39-54.
Although O was received without much enthusiasm, Ouchi feels it aptly delineates modern man's struggle with the dilemma of politics and morality. Cross Damon's life ends in complete estrangement from the human world, a tragedy that stems from his desire to see the inside of himself from outside. [Y. H.]

192. Ousby, Ian. A Reader's Guide to Fifty American Novels. London: Heinemann, p. 278.
Brief mention of NS as a "seminal book."

193. Pac, Robert. "Une Faim d'égalité ou le combat des blacks boys." Droit et Liberté (December), p. 24.
Favorable review of the French translations of AH and Chester Himes's Black on Black. "Both works constitute a passionate condemnation of social injustice, racism, and spiritual oppression."

194. Paredes, Raymond A. "Editor's Column: Oppression and American Ethnic Literature: An Introduction." MELUS, 6 (Spring), 1-5.
Brief mention of W as a writer discussed in the issue.

195. Payne, Les. "Bookshelf." Black Enterprise, 9 (February), 108.
Review of AH and John Howard Griffin's Black Like Me praising the former and criticizing the latter. Payne sketches the career of W, "one of the authentic writers focusing a true image of the black experience."

196. Peavy, Charles D. "Richard Wright," in his Afro-American Literature and Culture Since World War II: A Guide to Information Sources. American Studies Information Guide Series, ed. Donald Koster. Detroit: Gale, pp. 252-257.

Annotated bibliography of twelve primary sources and thirty-one secondary sources. W is also mentioned elsewhere in the volume.

197. Perrin, Noel. "James Gould Cozzens." The New York Times Book Review (12 August), p. 30.
Letter to the editor reporting that Perrin's students in a twentieth-century American novel course at Dartmouth College considered NS "truest to our century" among the novels read. See 1979.224.

198. Piccinato, Stefania. "La letteratura afro-americana in Italia--1900-1975--Bibliografia," in Saggi sulla cultura afro-americana. Ed. Alessandro Portelli. Rome: Bulzoni editore, pp. 337-390.
Mentions W, BB, and NS in the introductory note. Lists two Italian interviews with W, thirteen Italian translations of W's works, five anthologies containing selections by W, and ninety-nine secondary items.

199. ____. "Negro Renaissance e New Negro Movement: il nuovo intellettuale afro-americano," in Saggi sulla cultura afro-americana. Ed. Alessandro Portelli. Rome: Bulzoni editore, pp. 125-144.
Quotes W's statement that "the Negro is America's metaphor" (p. 129) and quotes Abraham Chapman mentioning W (p. 142).

200. ____. Testo e contesto della poesia di Langston Hughes. Rome: Bulzoni editore, pp. 24, 36, 67, 69-70.
Discusses "Blueprint for Negro Writing" in relation to Hughes's "To Negro Writers," a speech at the first American Writers Congress (pp. 69-70). Mentions W briefly elsewhere.

201. Pinckney, Darryl E. "Black Women and the Myths of Macho." The Village Voice (2 April), pp. 85-87.
Review of Michele Wallace's Black Macho and the Myth of the Superwoman mentioning briefly its discussion of W.

202. Plumpp, Sterling D. "For Richard Wright." Obsidian, 5 (Winter), 84-85.
Poem paying tribute to W's racial protest and rebelliousness.

203. ____. "I Hear the Shuffle of the People's Feet." Obsidian, 5 (Winter), 75-82.
Poem alluding to Bigger Thomas: "i am a bigger bad trigger greedy / no name boy prowling chitown" (p. 79).

204. Polk, Noel. "Mississippi Writers in

Context." Notes on Mississippi Writers, 11 (Winter), 95-96.
Lists pamphlets published by the Mississippi Library Commission, including Roy Hudson's Richard Wright and Johnny E. Tolliver's An Introduction to Richard Wright's "Native Son".

205. ____ and James R. Scafidel. "Bibliography," in their An Anthology of Mississippi Writers. Jackson: University Press of Mississippi, pp. 527-547.
Lists nineteen primary and four secondary items.

206. ____. "Richard Wright (1908-1960)," in their An Anthology of Mississippi Writers. Jackson: University Press of Mississippi, pp. 258-259.
Biographical headnote to "The Man Who Was Almost a Man."

207. Pryse, Marjorie. The Mark and the Knowledge: Social Stigma in Classic American Fiction. Columbus: Ohio State University Press for Miami University, pp. 152-153, 155, 167.
Mentions W while discussing Ellison.

208. Pujols, Carmen. "The Omission." Freedomways, 19 (Second Quarter), 100-102.
Obituary of the actor and radical Lou Gilbert mentioning his friendship with W.

209. Quarles, Benjamin. "Negro," in Collier's Encyclopedia. Ed. Louis Shores. Vol. 17. New York: Macmillan Educational Corporation, pp. 276-293.
Mentions W briefly (p. 289).

210. Rampersad, Arnold. "W. E. B. Du Bois as a Man of Literature." American Literature, 51 (March), 50-68.
Points out that the early fiction of Du Bois anticipates the theme of rebellion of NS.

211. Real, Willi. "Richard Wright (1908-1960)," in Der moderne Roman des Amerikanischen Negers: Richard Wright, Ralph Ellison, James Baldwin. Ed. Rolf Franzbecker. Darmstadt: Wissenschaftliche Buchgesellschaft, pp. 11-47.
This overview of the critical response to W's novels stresses the unresolved questions which resist various approaches. W's reputation rests on the intensity of NS. Real discusses at length the significance of Bigger, the development of the plot, and the aesthetic difficulties of the work.

212. Reilly, John M. "The Reconstruction of Genre as Entry Into Conscious His-

tory." Black American Literature Forum, 13 (Spring), 3-6.
Includes analysis of the narrative voice in TMBV and the "parodic adaptation of the mode of the hard-boiled mystery story" in O. The former is important in moving toward a black collective historical awareness and the latter in pointing out the dangers of extreme individualism.

213. ____. "Wright, Richard (Nathaniel)," in Great Writers of the English Language: Novelists and Prose Writers. Ed. James Vinson. New York: St. Martin's Press, pp. 1328-1330.
Provides biographical facts, a list of twenty-two primary and nine secondary sources, and a sketch of W's career emphasizing "the realist protesting racial oppression, the typifier of the experience of entry into modern history, and the author who makes his themes seem inevitable by the power of artistic craft."
Reprinted: 1980.207.

214. Riegelhaupt, Barbara. "Banned: The Classroom Censors Return." The Champaign-Urbana Morning Courier (7 January), p. 34.
Reports that BB is one of the books banned in the Anaheim Unified School District.

215. Rive, Richard. "Writing and the New Society." Contrast, 12, No. 3, pp. 60-67.
Compares the biographical and literary careers of W and Peter Abrahams in order to refute James Baldwin's attacks on protest writing. W's protest must be seen in the context of liberal writing. Its purpose was to improve the position of blacks. In this respect W's contribution cannot be denied.

216. Roditi, Edouard. Untitled excerpt, in Die zarte Pflanze Demokratie: Amerikanische Re-education in Deutschland im Spiegel ausgewählter politischer und literarischer zeitschriften (1945-1949). By Hans Borchers and Klaus W. Vowe. Tübingen: Gunter Narr Verlag, p. 147.
Partial reprint of 1948.228a.

217. Rohrberger, Mary. "Richard Wright," in her Story to Anti-Story. Boston: Houghton Mifflin, p. 466.
Biographical headnote to "The Man Who Killed a Shadow."

218. ____. "Study Questions," in her Story to Anti-Story. Boston: Houghton Mifflin, p. 475.
To accompany "The Man Who Killed a Shadow."

219. Romano, John. "James Baldwin Writing and Talking." The New York Times Book Review (23 September), pp. 3, 33.
Mentions W briefly.

220. Rouse, John. "The Politics of Composition." College English, 41 (September), 1-12.
Comments on Mina Shaughnessy's analysis of a passage from BB, noting how she ignores the emotive qualities of the work while analyzing structural features (pp. 9-11).

221. Rubin, Louis D., Jr. "Richard Wright," in his The Literary South. New York: John Wiley, pp. 561-562.
Biographical-critical sketch.

222. ____. "Trouble on the Land: Southern Literature and the Great Depression." Studies in American Literature, No. 16, pp. 1-27.
Mentions briefly W and UTC (pp. 2, 4).
Reprinted: 1979.223.

223. ____. "Trouble on the Land: Southern Literature and the Great Depression." The Canadian Review of American Studies, 10 (Fall), 153-174.
Reprint of 1979.222.

224. Sale, Roger. "James Gould Cozzens." The New York Times Book Review (12 August), p. 30.
Letter to the editor reporting that Sale's students at the University of Washington disliked NS. Calling the novel "primitive" and "crude," Sale expresses his preference for Zora Neale Hurston's Their Eyes Were Watching God. See 1979.197.

225. Salzman, Jack and David Ray. "Introduction," in their The Jack Conroy Reader. American Cultural Heritage Series 2, ed. Jack Salzman. New York: Burt Franklin, pp. ix-xv.
Mentions W briefly.

226. Saracino, Maria Antonietta. "Alla riscoperta delle origini: momenti del dialogo tra le letterature africana ed afro-americana," in Saggi sulla cultura afro-americana. Ed. Alessandro Portelli. Rome: Bulzoni editore, pp. 85-105.
Mentions and quotes from W (pp. 86, 95).

227. Scharine, Richard G. "Ed Bullins Was Steve Benson (But Who Is He Now?)." Black American Literature Forum, 13 (Fall), 103-106, 108-109.
Compares Bullins to the exiled W "severed from his roots and his hate" (p. 109).

228. Schiff, Ellen. "To Be Young, Gifted and Oppressed: The Plight of the Ethnic Artist." MELUS, 6 (Spring), 73-80.
Discusses BB and Chaim Potok's My Name Is Asher Lev as books typifying the plight of the ethnic artist. The artist preserves himself only by accepting the scorn of his own oppressed people. Yet his ability to maintain contact with his community makes him part of a special group of "disciplined drop-outs" such as Gide, Swann, and Paul Morel.

228a. Schoener, Allon, ed. Harlem on My Mind: Cultural Capital of Black America 1900-1978. New York: Dell, p. 163.
Reprint of 1968.195.

229. Scholes, Robert. Fabulation and Metafiction. Urbana: University of Illinois Press, p. 194.
Refers to Maxwell Kasavubu, a character in Ishmael Reed's The Last Days of Louisiana Red who is writing a book on NS.

230. Schultz, Elizabeth A. "The Insistence Upon Community in the Contemporary Afro-American Novel." College English, 41 (October), 170-184.
Contrasts W's theme of alienation to the theme of community in recent black novels.

231. Scott, Nathan A., Jr. "Black Literature," in Harvard Guide to Contemporary American Writing. Ed. Daniel Hoffman. Cambridge, Mass.: Harvard University Press, pp. 287-341.
Discusses NS and, briefly, O as strident works of protest which dehumanize the black protagonists (pp. 289-291). Comments also on W's relation to subsequent black literature (pp. 291-292, 323) and mentions favorably BB (p. 335).

232. Shands, Annette Oliver. "A Dramatic Transformation of Richard Wright's Autobiography." Dissertation Abstracts International, 40 (September), 1153-A.
Abstracts a New York University Ph.D. dissertation analyzing the process of dramatizing BB.

232a. Shimizu, Takeo. "A Study of the Thematic Links Among the Five Short Stories in Uncle Tom's Children." Kyushu Shika Daigaku Shingaku Katei Kiyo [Bulletin of Kyushu Dental College], 10 (28 February), 25-33.
Defines the themes of the stories in UTC, respectively, as "the great earth, woman, and home"; "persona, shadow, and mania"; "the solidarity of black people"; and "symbolism of the woods." [Y. H. and T. K.]

233. Shrodes, Caroline, Clifford A. Josephson, and James R. Wilson. "Biographical Notes," in their Reading for Rhetoric: Applications to Writing. Fourth edition. New York: Macmillan, pp. 535-543.
Reprint of 1975.176.

234. ____. "Purpose and Structure, Diction and Tone, Applications to Writing," in their Reading for Rhetoric: Applications to Writing. Fourth edition. New York: Macmillan, pp. 324-326.
To accompany an excerpt from BB.

235. Siegel, Paul N. "Richard Wright's 'Native Son': The Black Nationalist Revolution in America," in his Revolution and the 20th-Century Novel. New York: Monad Press, pp. 90-104.
Expanded and revised reprint of 1974.158. Siegel also mentions W elsewhere in this volume (pp. 7, 110, 129).

236. S.[ion], G.[eorges]. "Richard Wright: 'Une faim d'égalité.'" Le Brussels Soir (21 November), p. 20.
Favorable notice of the French translation of AH. A continuation of BB, "it is dramatic and often very beautiful."

237. Skerrett, Joseph T., Jr. "Richard Wright, Writing and Identity." Callaloo, 2 (October), 84-94.
Argues that W's writing involves a therapeutic release of the psychosocial burdens enforced by his awareness of "the white death" in his early environment. Rather than succumb to one of the forms of "psychic numbing" prevalent in the black community, W reacted with guilt and aggression. Writing reduced but did not remove the distrust he felt towards his family and society.

238. Solotaroff, Theodore. "The Integration of Bigger Thomas," in his The Red Hot Vacuum & Other Pieces on the Writing of the Sixties. Boston: Nonpareil Books, pp. 122-132.
Reprint of 1964.117.

239. ____. "Irving Howe and the Socialist Imagination," in his The Red Hot Vacuum & Other Pieces on the Writing of the Sixties. Boston: Nonpareil Books, pp. 133-141.
Reprint of 1964.118.

240. Southgate, Robert L. Black Plots and Black Characters: A Handbook for Afro-American Literature. Syracuse: Gaylord Professional Publications, pp. 142-144, 197, 266, 314, 368-369.
Contains a plot summary of SH; notes

on Bigger Thomas, Mary Dalton, and W; and a bibliography of W listing fourteen primary and eleven secondary sources.

241. Stein, Judith. "Black, Red . . . and Sometimes Green." Reviews in American History, 7 (June), 246-255.
    Review of AH and Harry Haywood's Black Bolshevik in the context of the historiography of race and communism. "Although Wright gives us a classical portrait of the dilemmas of Communist intellectuals, his discussion of the intellectuals is thin and self-serving" (p. 251).

242. Stein, Rita. A Literary Tour Guide to the United States: South and Southwest. Americans-Discover-America Series. New York: William Morrow, p. 86.
    Mentions W's Mississippi roots.

243. Stepto, Robert B. From Behind the Veil: A Study of Afro-American Narrative. Urbana: University of Illinois Press, pp. x, xii, 24, 44, 116, 124, 128-162, 163, 175, 176, 179, 182.
    A chapter on Black Boy argues that the work fuses elements of the narrative of immersion and the dominant narrative of ascent. The book focuses on "Wright's persona's sustained effort to gain control of the text of his environment" (p. 134). Stepto discusses W's use of motifs from slave narratives, his use of catalogs, and his differences with Ellison relating to the "barrenness of black life."

244. _____. "I Thought I Knew These People: Richard Wright and the Afro-American Literary Tradition," in Chant of Saints: A Gathering of Afro-American Literature, Art, and Scholarship. Ed. Michael S. Harper and Robert B. Stepto. Urbana: University of Illinois Press, pp. 195-211.
    Reprint of 1977.294.

245. _____. "Preface," in Chant of Saints: A Gathering of Afro-American Literature, Art, and Scholarship. Ed. Michael S. Harper and Robert B. Stepto. Urbana: University of Illinois Press, pp. xiii-xviii.
    Quotes W on the making of anthologies and mentions essays on W in the present anthology.

246. _____. "Teaching Afro-American Literature: Survey or Tradition: The Reconstruction," in Afro-American Literature: The Reconstruction of Instruction. Ed. Dexter Fisher and Robert B. Stepto. New York: Modern Language Association, pp. 8-24.

Mentions W briefly (p. 9).

247. _____ and Michael S. Harper. "Study & Experience: An Interview with Ralph Ellison," in their Chant of Saints: A Gathering of Afro-American Literature, Art, and Scholarship. Urbana: University of Illinois Press, pp. 451-469.
    Reprint of 1977.295.

248. _____ and Toni Morrison. "'Intimate Things in Place': A Conversation with Toni Morrison," in Chant of Saints: A Gathering of Afro-American Literature, Art, and Scholarship. Ed. Michael S. Harper and Robert B. Stepto. Urbana: University of Illinois Press, pp. 213-229.
    Reprint of 1977.296.

249. Stern, Adele. "About the Authors," in her America in Literature: The City. New York: Scribner's, pp. 231-242.
    Contains a biographical sketch of W (p. 242).

250. Stineman, Esther. "Wallace, Michele. Black Macho and the Myth of the Superwoman." Library Journal, 104 (1 March), 616.
    Review mentioning W briefly.

251. Stone, Albert E. "Autobiography and the Childhood of the American Artist: The Example of Louis Sullivan," in American Character and Culture in a Changing World: Some Twentieth-Century Perspectives. Ed. John A. Hague. Contributions in American Studies, No.42. Westport, Conn.: Greenwood Press, pp. 293-322.
    Mentions W briefly.

252. _____. "Visions and Versions of Childhood," in American Character and Culture in a Changing World: Some Twentieth-Century Perspectives. Ed. John A. Hague. Contributions in American Studies, No. 42. Westport, Conn.: Greenwood Press, pp. 275-277.
    Mentions W briefly.

253. Suzuki, Mikio. "Kogi Shosetsu no Genten: Richard Wright no Uncle Tom's Children" ["The Origin of the Protest Novel: Richard Wright's Uncle Tom's Children"]. Waseda Daigaku Kyoyo Shogaku Kenkyu [Waseda University General Studies], Nos. 58-60 (March), pp. 55-78.
    Comments on W's realistic portrayal of the black struggle in fighting segregation. Without these efforts W's most celebrated book, NS, would not have been contemplated or written. [Y. H.]

254. Szymanski, Ronald. "About the Authors," in his America in Literature: The Midwest. New York: Scribner's, pp.

221-232.
   Contains a biographical sketch of W.

255. Tanaka, Hiroshi. "Sanju Nendai no Kokujin Sakka--Hughes to Wright no Baai" ["The Thirties and Black Writers: The Case of Hughes and Wright"]. Minshu Bungaku [Democratic Literature], No. 161 (April), pp. 138-144.
   Refers to the writing of the thirties which was devoted to discussion of social structure and criticism of capitalism in particular. The same voice is heard in Langston Hughes's poetry, in which his criticism of injustice is raised to a universal level. Likewise, W's attack on American society is aimed not ony at the white world but also at the black masses, especially black women. [Y. H.]

256. Tate, Claudia C. "On White Critics and Black Aestheticians." CLA Journal, 22 (June), 383-389.
   Compares BB and A Portrait of the Artist as a Young Man. Like Joyce, W expresses "universal truths about the growth of human consciousness." True critical objectivity, which white critics lack, absolves W of charges of parochialism and poor craftsmanship.

257. Taylor, Clyde. "Scoping the Seventies: Black Writing in a Comatose Decade." Obsidian, 5 (Winter), 41-47.
   Mentions W briefly.

258. Terrier, Michel. Le Roman américain 1914-1945. Le Monde anglophone series, ed. Paul Bacquet. Paris: Presses Universitaires de France, pp. 19, 20, 27, 34, 35, 113-124.
   Surveys W's life and literary career (pp. 113-118) and analyzes NS (pp. 119-124). Basically Marxist and naturalistic, NS also develops existentialist themes.

258a. Terry, Esther. "Wright's Native Son: The Burden It Bears." Five College Contributions in Black Studies, No. 2, pp. 3-26.
   Unfavorable evaluation of the novel. W undervalues Afro-American culture and overvalues Communism.

259. Thomas, Lorenzo. "By the Numbers: Response to Questionnaire frm Jerry W. Ward in Callaloo 4." Callaloo, 2 (October), 103-104.
   Mentions W briefly.

260. Thomson, Phillip, ed. An Index to Book Reviews in the Humanities. Vol. 19. Williamston, Mich.: Phillip Thomson, p. 401.
   Lists one review of Richard Wright Reader.

261. Tiedt, Iris M. Exploring Books with Children. Boston: Houghton Mifflin, p. 441.
   Lists John A. Williams's The Most Native of Sons.

262. Timko, Michael. "Preface," in his 38 Short Stories: An Introductory Anthology. Second edition. New York: Knopf, pp. ix-x.
   Mentions favorably "Big Boy Leaves Home" and Keneth Kinnamon's analysis.

263. _____. "Richard Wright Big Boy Leaves Home," in his 38 Short Stories: An Introductory Anthology. Second edition. New York: Knopf, p. 124.
   Reprint of 1975.193.

264. Toll, William. The Resurgence of Race: Black Social Theory from Reconstruction to the Pan-African Conferences. Philadelphia: Temple University Press, pp. vii, 62, 174.
   Quotes briefly from AH and WML.

265. Toppin, Edgar Allan. "Black Americans," in The World Book Encyclopedia. Ed. William H. Nault. Vol. 2. Chicago: World Book--Childcraft International, pp. 306-306m.
   Reprint of 1969.230.

266. Traylor, Eleanor. "I Hear Music in the Air: James Baldwin's 'Just Above My Head.'" First World, 2, No. 3, pp. 40-43.
   Favorable review with a favorable mention of W.

267. Turner, Darwin T. "Richard Wright's Hero: The Faces of a Rebel-Victim. By Katherine Fishburn." American Literature, 50 (January), 667.
   Unfavorable review criticizing Fishburn's rearrangement of chronology and her identification of Fred Daniels as W's "ultimate concept of a hero."

268. Twombly, Robert C. "Harlem Renaissance," in Collier's Encyclopedia. Ed. Louis Shores. Vol. 11. New York: Macmillan Educational Corporation, pp. 654-655.
   Reprint of 1976.195.

269. Van Vechten, Carl. "A Belated Introduction," in his "Keep A-Inchin' Along": Selected Writings of Carl Van Vechten About Black Arts and Letters. Ed. Bruce Kellner. Contributions in Afro-American and African Studies, No. 45. Westport, Conn.: Greenwood Press,

pp. 79-81.
Reprint of 1951.240.

270. _____. "The James Weldon Johnson Memorial Collection of Negro Arts and Letters," in his "Keep A-Inchin' Along": Selected Writings of Carl Van Vechten About Black Arts and Letters. Ed. Bruce Kellner. Contributions in Afro-American and African Studies, No. 45. Westport, Conn.: Greenwood Press, pp. 124-133.
Reprint of 1942.327 and 1944.152.

271. Wages, Jack D. and William L. Andrews. "Southern Literary Culture: 1969-1975." The Mississippi Quarterly, 32 (Winter), 13-215.
Lists thirty-one theses and dissertations on W with cross references to fifty-three others.

272. Walker, Robert H. "Patterns in Recent American Literature," in American Character and Culture in a Changing World: Some Twentieth-Century Perspectives. Ed. John A. Hague. Contributions in American Studies, No. 42. Westport, Conn.: Greenwood Press, pp. 65-80.
Mentions W briefly.

273. Wallace, Michele. Black Macho and the Myth of the Superwoman. New York: The Dial Press, pp. 55-57, 73.
Discusses NS as "the starting point of the black writer's love affair with Black Macho." Wallace agrees with Baldwin's view of Bigger.

274. Ward, Jerry Washington, Jr. "Richard Wright and His American Critics, 1936-1960." Dissertation Abstracts International, 40 (December), 3305-A.
Abstracts a University of Virginia Ph.D. dissertation emphasizing "the incorporation of social change in the language of criticism." Ward considers the American reception of all of W's books except the play NS and SH.

275. Washington, Mary Helen. "Introduction: Zora Neale Hurston: A Woman Half in Shadow," in I Love Myself When I am Laughing . . . And Then Again When I Am Looking Mean and Impressive: A Zora Neale Hurston Reader. Ed. Alice Walker. Old Westbury, N. Y.: The Feminist Press, pp. 7-25.
Contrasts Hurston and W (pp. 17-18).

276. Wearing, J. P. American and British Theatrical Biography: A Directory. Metuchen, N. J.: The Scarecrow Press, p. 998.
Refers to 1966.8.

277. Webb, Constance. "Wright, Richard Nathaniel," in Collier's Encyclopedia. Ed. Louis Shores. Vol. 23. New York: Macmillan Educational Corporation, p. 638.
Reprint of 1969.244.

278. Weever, Jacqueline de. "The Inverted World of Toni Morrison's The Bluest Eye and Sula." CLA Journal, 22 (June), 402-414.
Mentions NS briefly (pp. 402, 413).

279. Werner, Craig. "The Economic Evolution of James Baldwin." CLA Journal, 23 (September), 12-31.
Includes a brief mention of Baldwin's feud with Wright (p. 13).

280. Wexelblatt, Robert. "The Unintelligible Hero." Denver Quarterly, 14 (Fall), 49-65.
Includes discussion of the protagonist of "The Man Who Lived Underground" as an example of "the hero who is intelligible to himself but cannot make himself understood by anyone else, because he is unable to or must not" (p. 57).

281. Williams, Melvin G. "Bringing Readers to Their Senses: Imagery in Richard Wright's Uncle Tom's Children." Black American Literature Forum, 13 (Spring), 18-20.
Argues that the function of imagery in UTC is not symbolic or metaphorical. Instead, W uses sense imagery to make his readers experience vicariously the suffering of his protagonists. Williams analyzes the imagery of "Big Boy Leaves Home," showing that sight and sound dominate but the other senses also appear. Through imagery W reinforces emotionally the intellectual message of the book.

282. Young, T. D. "Mississippi: A Personal View of Its Past and a Hope for Its Future," in A Sense of Place. Edited by Peggy W. Prenshaw and Jesse O. McKee. Jackson: University Press of Mississippi, p. 50.
Lists W with Faulkner and Welty as an important Mississippi writer.

283. Zverev, A. M. Modernizm v literature SSA: Formirovanie Evoljucija Krizis. Moscow: Nauka, pp. 180-182, 183-184.
Discusses W's existentialism, especially in "The Man Who Lived Underground." Like other American existentialists, W distorted social reality less than European existentialits did in developing philosophical ideas.

1980

1. Abcarian, Richard and Marvin Klotz. "Questions," in their Literature: The

Human Experience. Shorter edition. New York: St. Martin's Press, p. 216.
Reprint of 1973.4.

2. _____. "Richard Wright, 'The Man Who Lived Underground,'" in their Instructor's Manual to Accompany Literature: The Human Experience. Shorter edition. New York: St. Martin's Press, pp. 18-20.
Reprint of 1973.5.

3. A[dams], P[hoebe]-L[ou]. "Richard Wright: Ordeal of a Native Son by Addison Gayle." The Atlantic, 246 (August), 84.
Brief review ascribing the interest of the first part of the book to paraphrase of W's autobiographical writings. The information derived from United States Government sources is ambiguous and unreliable.

4. Adams, Russell L. "An Analysis of the 'Roots' Phenomenon in the Context of American Racial Conservatism." Présence Africaine, No. 116 (Fourth Quarter), pp. 125-140.
Mentions W briefly (p. 139).

5. Adande, Alexandre Sènou. "Paul Hazoumé: Ecrivain et chercheur." Présence Africaine, No. 114 (Second Quarter), pp. 197-203.
Mentions W briefly (p. 199).

6. Ahrends, Günter. Die amerikanische Kurzgeschichte: Theorie und Entwicklung. Sprache und Literatur 107. Stuttgart: Verlag W. Kohlhammer, pp. 19, 183-186, 189, 202.
Comments on W's short stories in their literary and ideological context. Analyzes briefly "Almos' a Man" as an initiation story with comparisons to Hemingway's "The Killers."

7. Algren, Nelson. "The Liberating Vision of Richard Wright." Chicago Tribune (8 June), Sec. 7, pp. 1, 11.
Favorable review of Addison Gayle's Richard Wright: Ordeal of a Native Son, which Algren prefers to the biographies by Webb and Fabre. Algren discusses W's racial hardships, his struggle against white racists and black bourgeoisie, his experience with Communism, and his persecution by the United States Government. "Richard Wright was not a writer of the highest order. He possessed passion, insight, clarity, simplicity, and imagination. But he was utterly without humor."

8. Allen, Michael. "Writing Away from Fear: Mina Shaughnessy and the Uses of Authority." College English, 41 (April), 857-867.

Discusses student writing about NS at Rust College in Mississippi.

9. Altenbernd, Lynn. "James Baldwin 1924-   ," in Introduction to Literature: Stories. Ed. Lynn Altenbernd and Leslie L. Lewis. Third edition. New York: Macmillan, p. 603.
Mentions W briefly.

10. Andrews, W. D. E. "Theater of Black Reality: The Blues Drama of Ed Bullins." Southwest Review, 65 (Spring), 178-190.
Mentions briefly W and NS.

11. Andrzejczak, Krzysztof. "Poczatki literatury murzyńskiej w Stanach Zjednoczonych." Acta Universitatis Lodziensis, Seria I, 66, pp. 191-217.
Points out the influence of the slave narrative on W and others (p. 212). Mentions W briefly elsewhere.

12. Anon. "Avery, Evelyn Gross. Rebels and victims: the fiction of Richard Wright and Bernard Malamud." Booklist, 76 (1 February), 749-750.
Favorable notice.

13. Anon. "Avery, Evelyn Gross. Rebels and victims: the fiction of Richard Wright and Bernard Malamud." Choice, 16 (February), 1578.
Favorable notice.

14. Anon. "Baldwin, James," in Novels and Novelists: A Guide to the World of Fiction. Ed. Martin Seymour-Smith. New York: St. Martin's Press, p. 94.
Mentions W briefly.

15. Anon. "Black Studies: Just a Fad or Here to Stay?" U. S. News & World Report, 88 (28 January), 64.
Mentions W briefly.

16. Anon. Dust jacket of Black Fiction: New Studies in the Afro-American Novel Since 1945. Ed. A. Robert Lee. London: Vision Press.
Inside front flap emphasizes the pivotal importance of NS.

17. Anon. Dust jacket of Richard Wright: Ordeal of a Native Son. By Addison Gayle: Garden City, N. Y.: Anchor Press/ Doubleday.
Blurb on inside flaps stressing Gayle's use of FBI files.

18. Anon. "Ebony Book Shelf." Ebony, 36 (November), 30.
Bibliography of thirty-four important books by or about blacks published since 1945 including BB.

19. Anon. "Un Faim d'égalité par Richard Wright." Lire, No. 53 (January), p. 15.

Favorable notice of the French translation of AH, designated by the magazine as one of the year's twenty best books.

20. Anon. Filmstrip Collection for Students and Teachers of English. Princeton, N. J.: Films for the Humanities, p. 13.
Mentions W and NS.

21. Anon. "Gayle, Addison. Richard Wright: ordeal of a native son." Booklist, 76 (15 June), 1482.
Favorable notice. "Gayle is not a restrained writer, nor carefully neutral, but warm and often lyrical in the cause of a man he much admires."

22. Anon. "Gayle, Addison. Richard Wright: ordeal of a native son." Choice, 18 (December), 528.
Mixed review praising Gayle's use of new sources but preferring the earlier biographies of Webb and Fabre.

23. Anon. "Gayle, Addison. Richard Wright: Ordeal of a Native Son." Kirkus Reviews, 48 (15 April), 552-553.
Unfavorable review complaining that the work is "muddled" and inconclusive.

24. Anon. Index Translationum 29. Paris: Unesco, pp. 199, 334, 467, 511.
Lists translations of BB into Danish (2) and Finnish, NS into Italian, and AH into Japanese.

25. Anon. "A Mississippi 'Jubilee' for Margaret Walker Alexander." Ebony, 35 (September), 146-148, 150-151.
Mentions her work in progress on W.

26. Anon. 1980 Summer Seminars for College Teachers. Washington, D. C.: National Endowment for the Humanities, p. 2.
Announces courses treating W by Jules Chametzky ("Immigrant and Ethnic Literature") and Michael G. Cooke ("Modern Fiction: Portraits in Black and White").

27. Anon. "Program." PMLA, 95 (November), 983-1056.
Announces a convention session on "Richard Wright's Novels: A Revaluation." The panelists are Yoshinobu Hakutani, Keneth Kinnamon, Fred L. Standley, and John A. Williams.

28. Anon. "Richard Wright Black Boy/ American Hunger (2 Vols.)." Book-of-the-Month Club Book Dividend Catalogue (Spring), p. 10.
Brief notice.

29. Anon. "Richard Wright: Ordeal of a Native Son. Addison Gayle, Jr." Publish-ers Weekly, 217 (13 June), 62.
Favorable review emphasizing W's harassment by the American government.

30. Anon. "SCMLA." S. S. S. L.: The Newsletter of the Society for the Study of Southern Literature, 12 (November), 1-2.
Mentions a paper by William E. Tanner on "The Metaphor of the Underground Man in Richard Wright's The Outsider."

31. Anon. "Stepto, Robert B. From behind the veil: a study of Afro-American narrative." Choice, 17 (July-August), 675.
Review praising Stepto's treatment of W.

32. Anon. "Varieties of Afro-American Culture," in Popular Culture Association Tenth Annual Meeting, American Culture Association Second Annual Meeting. Bowling Green, Ohio: Bowling Green State University, p. 52.
Lists a paper by Ross J. Pudaloff on "Native Son--The Novel in Popular Culture."

33. Anon. "Wright, Richard," in Novels and Novelists: A Guide to the World of Fiction. Ed. Martin Seymour-Smith. New York: St. Martin's Press, p. 239.
Biographical note with photograph.

34. Arnez, Nancy L. "Black Poetry: A Necessary Ingredient for Survival and Liberation." Journal of Black Studies, 11 (September), 3-22.
Quotes Conrad Kent Rivers on W (p. 10).

35. Avery, Evelyn Gross. "Evelyn Gross Avery," in Contemporary Literary Criticism. Ed. Debra Bryfonski and Laurie Lanzen Harris. Vol. 14. Detroit: Gale, pp. 597-599.
Excerpt from 1979.31.

36. Baker, Houston A., Jr. The Journey Back: Issues in Black Literature and Criticism. Chicago: The University of Chicago Press, pp. 51, 53, 56, 57, 58, 59, 60, 62-68, 71, 72, 75, 81, 106, 118, 137, 153, 158.
The chapter on "Black Historical Consciousness in the Fifties" discusses W's "rational secularism" (pp. 62-68). W maintains a "firm discipleship to the West" which leads to a "tolerance for neocolonialism." SH and LD, however, indicate his awareness of the continuing power of past bondage.

37. Baker, Sheridan. The Complete Stylist and Handbook. Second edition. New York: Harper & Row, pp. 147, 158.

Quotes a long sentence from <u>NS</u> to illustrate the effective use of a series of participial phrases. Page 158 reprints 1976.27.

38. Balmir, Guy-Claude. "Ecrivains et folklores nègres du Nouveau Monde." <u>Présence</u> <u>Africaine</u>, No. 110 (Second Quarter), pp. 49-85.
Mentions W briefly (p. 59).

39. Baraka, Amiri. "Afro-American Literature & Class Struggle." <u>Black</u> <u>American</u> <u>Literature</u> <u>Forum</u>, 14 (Spring), 5-14.
Discusses W's work and importance, giving special praise to <u>UTC</u>, <u>BB</u>, and <u>AH</u> (p. 7).

40. _____. "Confessions of a Former Anti-Semite." <u>The</u> <u>Village</u> <u>Voice</u>, 25 (17-23 December), pp. 1, 19-20, 22-23.
Mentions reading at age twelve <u>BB</u>. It made a deep impression.

41. Baylor, Robert and James Moore. "Biographical Author Index," in their <u>People and Ideas: A Rhetoric Reader</u>. New York: McGraw-Hill, pp. 391-397.
Contains a biographical sketch of W (p. 397) with a favorable comment by Mark Schorer.

42. _____. Instructor's <u>Manual</u> to Accompany <u>People and Ideas: A Rhetoric Reader</u>. New York: McGraw-Hill, pp. 3, 4, 6, 8, 33.
Suggests pedagogical uses for an excerpt from <u>BB</u>.

43. _____. "Rhetoric, Style and Content," in their <u>People and Ideas: A Rhetoric Reader</u>. New York: McGraw-Hill, pp. 36-37.
Comments on "The Library Card," an excerpt from <u>BB</u>.

44. _____. "Suggestions for Writing," in their <u>People and Ideas: A Rhetoric Reader</u>. New York: McGraw-Hill, p. 37.
To accompany "The Library Card," an excerpt from <u>BB</u>.

45. Bennett, James R. "American Literature and the Acquisitive Society, Background and Criticism: A Second Bibliography, Part II." <u>Bulletin of Bibliography</u>, 37 (April-June), 53-71, 79.
Contains eleven annotated items on W.

46. Berry, Jay R., Jr., and Frank E. Moorer. "Addison Gayle, <u>Richard Wright: Ordeal of a Native Son</u>." <u>MLN</u>, 95 (December), 1455-1456.
Unfavorable review complaining of mistakes, misreading, and an unscholarly style.

47. Bigsby, C. W. E. "Judgement Day Is Coming! The Apocalyptic Dream in Recent Afro-American Fiction," in <u>Black Fiction: New Studies in the Afro-American Novel Since 1945</u>. Ed. A. Robert Lee. Vision Critical Studies, ed. Anne Smith. London: Vision Press, pp. 149-172.
Mentions W several times and quotes him once (pp. 151-152).

48. _____. "Richard Wright and His Blueprint for Negro Writing." <u>PN</u> <u>Review</u>, 19, pp. 53-55.
Examines W's essay in relation to Afro-American literary tradition before and after its appearance, to Communist ideology, and to literary modernism.

49. _____. The <u>Second</u> <u>Black</u> <u>Renaissance: Essays in Black Literature</u>. Contributions in Afro-American and African Studies, No. 50, ed. Hollis R. Lynch. Westport, Conn.: Greenwood Press, pp. 3-4, 9, 10, 12, 18-21, 22, 23, 26, 27, 28, 29, 30-32, 35, 37, 39-40, 43, 45, 47, 48, 54-84, 89, 93, 95, 100, 101, 115, 117, 120, 122, 126, 135, 136, 156, 162, 165, 166, 174, 177, 210, 214, 223, 230, 267, 269, 287, 302.
Identifies W as the primary source of black writing in the fifties, sixties, and seventies. His belief that finding an "adequate definition of selfhood" would provide the "clue to group identity" led him from Marxism, existentialism, and an interest in Africa to a "visionary transcendentalism." Chapter 2, "The Self and Society: Richard Wright's Dilemma," examines the changes in W's use of the Negro as metaphor, concentrating on "The Man Who Lived Underground," <u>NS</u>, <u>O</u>, and <u>LD</u>.

50. Blake, Susan L. "Frances Smith Foster. <u>Witnessing Slavery: The Development of Ante-bellum Slave Narratives</u>; Robert B. Stepto. <u>From Behind the Veil: A Study of Afro-American Narrative</u>." <u>Black American Literature Forum</u>, 14 (Winter), 160-163.
Notes briefly Stepto's treatment of <u>BB</u>.

51. Blicksilver, Edith. "Striking Out." <u>Callaloo</u>, 3 (February-October), 237-238.
Favorable review of Evelyn Gross Avery's <u>Rebels and Victims: The Fiction of Richard Wright and Bernard Malamud</u>.

52. Bontemps, Arna and Langston Hughes. <u>Arna Bontemps--Langston Hughes Letters 1925-1967</u>. Ed. Charles H. Nichols. New York: Dodd, Mead, pp. 24, 37, 43, 45, 47, 56, 62, 74, 80, 84, 87, 93, 94, 125, 144, 146, 155, 158, 160, 168, 179, 205, 207, 240, 260-261, 288, 302, 303, 308,

384, 402, 404, 406, 408, 413, 476, 484, 485.

Bontemps mentions W in one letter from 1936, one from 1939, two from 1940, five from 1941, one from 1942, two from 1943, three from 1944, one from 1946, one from 1949, one from 1959, one from 1960, three from 1961, and one from 1967. Hughes mentions W in two letters from 1939, one from 1941, one from 1943, one from 1944, one from 1945, one from 1946, one from 1948, one from 1952, two from 1953, one from 1960, and one from 1966. Topics mentioned include works in progress, publishing matters, critical reception, social occasions, family matters, travel plans, etc.

53. Brinkmeyer, Bob. "Wright and Crews: Southern Childhoods." Southern Exposure, 8 (Fall), 120-123.

Compares the unhappy childhoods of the two writers as revealed in BB, AH, and Harry Crews's A Childhood: The Biography of a Place.

54. Bronner, Edwin. The Encyclopedia of the American Theatre 1900-1975. San Diego: A. S. Barnes, pp. 278-279, 330.

Contains entries for LD and NS.

55. Broughton, Panthea Reid. "Faulkner," in American Literary Scholarship: An Annual/1978. Ed. J. Albert Robbins. Durham, N. C.: Duke University Press, pp. 127-151.

Mentions Blyden Jackson's essay on W and Faulkner (p. 132).

56. Brown, Jerry Elijah. "The Literary South, ed. Louis D. Rubin, Jr." The Mississippi Quarterly, 33 (Spring), 160-166.

Mentions Rubin's inclusion of W in the anthology (p. 165).

57. Brownfield, Allan C. "Outdated Gomorrahs." Chronicles of Culture, 4 (March-April), 21-22.

Review of James Baldwin's Just Above My Head mentioning W briefly.

58. Bruck, Peter. "Black Innocent Eyes: William Melvin Kelley's 'The Only Man on Liberty Street' als Ausgangstext für eine Unterrichtssequenz zur afro-amerikanischen Kruzgeschichte." Arbeiten aus Anglistik und Amerikanistik, 5, pp. 255-269.

Quotes W on the reception of UTC (p. 256).

59. Brünig, Eberhard. "US-amerikanische Literatur in der DDR seit 1965." Zeitschrift für Anglistik und Amerikanistik, 28, pp. 293-319.

Discusses briefly W's place as the first black writer to attract widespread attention from East German readers.

60. Bryfonski, Dedria and Laurie Lanzen Harris. "Wright, Richard 1908-1960," in their Contemporary Literary Criticism. Vol. 14. Detroit: Gale, p. 595.

Headnote to excerpts from June Jordan, William Peden, Robert F. Moss, John Wideman, and Evelyn Gross Avery (pp. 595-599).

61. Burns, Landon C. and Janet P. Alwang. "The Sixth (1979) Supplement to a Cross-Referenced Index of Short Fiction Anthologies and Author-Title Listings." Studies in Short Fiction, 17 (Spring), 193-245.

Lists five W stories in five anthologies.

62. Burt, Della Ann. "The Widening Arc and the Closed Circle: A Study of Problematic Novel Endings." Dissertation Abstracts International, 40 (January), 4011A.

Abstracts a 1979 Indiana University dissertation including NS among seven novels treated.

63. Butcher, Philip. "Propaganda & Aesthetics: The Literary Politics of Afro-American Magazines in the Twentieth Century. By Abby Arthur Johnson and Ronald Maberry Johnson." American Literature, 52 (March), 144-145.

Mentions W briefly.

64. Butler, Robert J. "Patterns of Movement in Ellison's Invisible Man." American Studies, 21 (Spring), 5-21.

Comments on the motif of movement in NS and UTC.

65. Caldeira, Maria Isabel. "'All coloured people sing': Do Estereotipo a Identidade." Revista Critica de Ciencias Sociales, Nos. 4/5 (October), pp. 157-184.

Comments on W as a protest writer (p. 179).

66. Case, Frederick Ivor. "Addison Gayle, Richard Wright: Ordeal of a Native Son." Journal and Bulletin of the Canadian Alliance of Black Educators, 1, No. 4, 48-54.

Mixed review. Too derivative from Fabre and BB and containing factual errors, the work is valuable for its documentation of government persecution of W. A resident of France in the fifties, Case emphasizes the white racism there that W ignores.

67. Christian, Barbara. Black Women Novelists: The Development of a Tradition

1892-1976. Contributions in Afro-American and African Studies, No. 52, ed. Hollis R. Lynch. Westport, Conn.: Greenwood Press, pp. 62-63, 64, 67, 248.
Discusses W's literary goals and achievements, especially in his review of Hurston's Their Eyes Were Watching God, in "Blueprint for Negro Writing," and in NS. Compares W to Ann Petry in The Street and to Paule Marshall in The Chosen Place, The Timeless People.

68. Clark, S. L., Eddy Dow, Douglas Fricke, Philip R. Headings, Dennis C. Landis, David Manuszak, Matthew O'Brien, and Joan Stockard. "American Literature," in 1979 MLA International Bibliography. Vol. 1. New York: Modern Language Association, pp. 173-241.
Lists twenty-three items on W.

69. Clarke, Graham. "Beyond Realism: Recent Black Fiction and the Language of 'The Real Thing,'" in Black Fiction: New Studies in the Afro-American Novel Since 1945. Ed. A. Robert Lee. Vision Critical Studies, ed. Anne Smith. London: Vision Press, pp. 204-221.
Uses Wrightian realism, constrained by the thesis of social determinism even while developing "the energy of its vision, the often ferocious violence of its language" (p. 205), as a point of departure for a discussion of Julian Mayfield, Ronald Fair, Cyrus Colter, Robert Dean Pharr, and Hal Bennett.
Reprinted: 1982.27.

70. Conroy, Jack. "Social Poetry of the 1930s edited by Jack Salzman and Leo Zanderer." New Letters, 46 (Winter), 121-123.
Mentions W briefly.

71. Couturier, Maurice. "Foreign Scholarship: French Contributions," in American Literary Scholarship: An Annual/ 1978. Ed. J. Albert Robbins. Durham, N. C.: Duke University Press, pp. 439-445.
Comments on Fabre's work on W.

72. Cowley, Malcolm. The Dream of the Golden Mountains: Remembering the 1930s. New York: Viking, pp. 141-143, 145.
Recounts W's association with the John Reed Club and Left Front.

73. Cudjoe, Selwyn R. Resistance and Caribbean Literature. Athens, Ohio: Ohio University Press, pp. 99-100, 129.
Comments on Bigger's transition from "thing" to "person."

74. Deck, Alice Anita. "I Am Because We Are: Four Versions of the Common Voice

in African and Afro-American Autobiography." Dissertation Abstracts International, 41 (December), 2591A-2592A.
Abstracts a 1980 State University of New York at Binghamton dissertation containing a chapter on BB focusing on W's "role within an Afro-American extended family network."

75. Delmar, P. Jay. "Charles W. Chesnutt's 'The Web of Circumstance' and Richard Wright's 'Long Black Song': The Tragedy of Property." Studies in Short Fiction, 17 (Spring), 178-179.
Argues that Chesnutt and W, diverse in many ways, agree that economic success without political power will not achieve justice for black people. Chesnutt has no solution in mind, but W endorses Marxist unity to resolve the dilemma.

76. _____. "Elements of Tragedy in Charles W. Chesnutt's The Conjure Woman." CLA Journal, 23 (June), 451-459.
Contains a footnote reference to 1976.55.

77. _____. "Robert B. Stepto. From Behind the Veil / A Study of Afro-American Narrative." American Literary Realism 1870-1910, 13 (Spring), 156-158.
Mentions W briefly.

78. Dickey, Ed. "Gayle, Addison, Jr. Richard Wright: Ordeal of a Native Son." Best Sellers, 40 (September), 214.
Favorable review of "a scholarly and readable biography."

79. Dobie, Ann B. and Andrew J. Hirt. "An Analysis of 'Holding My Life in My Mind,'" in their Comprehension and Composition: An Introduction to the Essay. New York: Macmillan, pp. 66-67.
Elementary rhetorical analysis of a passage from BB.

80. Donelson, Kenneth L. and Alleen Pace Nilsen. Literature for Today's Young Adults. Glenview, Ill.: Scott, Foresman, pp. 161, 416.
Comments briefly on NS and BB, mentioning censorship of the latter.

81. Edwards, Harry. The Struggle That Must Be: An Autobiography. New York: Macmillan, p. 147.
Mentions reading BB.

82. El'Zabar, Kai. "Nappy Edges Ntozake Shange." Black Books Bulletin, 6 (Spring), 75-76.
Quotes Shange's poem on NS.

83. Evans, James Henry, Jr. "The Problem of Religious Language in the Fiction of Richard Wright." Dissertation Abstracts

International, 41 (September), 1100A-1101A.
   Abstracts a 1980 Union Theological Seminary dissertation considering its topic "as a literary query and as a theological challenge."

84. Fabre, Michel. "Fantasies and Style in Richard Wright's Fiction." New Letters, 46 (Spring), 55-81.
   Argues that certain patterns of key words used by W in his conversations with Frederic Wertham reveal the existence of a system of connotations specific to W. This system in turn provides an underlying structure in many of W's works. The crucial elements of the system include fires and fluffy white clothes. The result is a tonality connecting voyeurism, sexual and racial prohibitions, and women as both objects of desire and "authors of disapproval."

85. _____. "Introduction," in his Regards sur la littérature noire américaine. Paris: Publications du Conseil Scientifique de la Sorbonne Nouvelle, pp. 3-5.
   Mentions W briefly.

86. [_____]. "Jerome Klintowitz [sic], ed., The Diaries of Willard Motley." AFRAM Newsletter, No. 11 (November), p. 11.
   Notes that Motley wrote Knock on Any Door before reading NS.

87. _____. "'The Man Who Killed a Shadow': A Study in Compulsion," in his Regards sur la littérature noire américaine. Paris: Publications du Conseil Scientifique de la Sorbonne Nouvelle, pp. 45-64.
   Compares the short story to its factual source, a murder in 1944. Changing the details to develop the theme of black pathology induced by white racism, W also introduces in his story a compulsive fear of female sexuality.

88. [_____]. "Melvin Tolson. A Gallery of Harlem Portraits, edited with an afterword by Robert Farnsworth." AFRAM Newsletter, No. 10 (April), p. 21.
   Mentions Farnsworth as co-editor of a book on W.

89. [_____]. "Robert Stepto. From Behind the Veil. A Study of Afro-American Narrative." AFRAM Newsletter, No. 11 (November), p. 6.
   Notes that Stepto treats BB.

90. _____. "Wright, Richard Nathaniel," in Dictionary of American Biography. Supplement Six: 1956-1960. Ed. John A.

Garraty. New York: Scribner's, pp. 715-717.
   Biographical essay.

91. _____ et al. "Réactions françaises à la littérature noire des Etats-Unis," in his Regards sur la littérature noire américaine. Paris: Publications du Conseil Scientifique de la Sorbonne Nouvelle, pp. 203-240.
   Reports results of questionnaires sent to French writers and students in 1973 and 1974. W was best known among the students. See 1973.125 for a partial translation of this report.

92. Farnsworth, Robert M. "Rebels and Victims: The Fiction of Richard Wright and Bernard Malamud. By Evelyn Gross Avery." American Studies, 21 (Spring), 104.
   Unfavorable review questioning Avery's acceptance of W's representation of Afro-American experience.

93. Feeney, Joseph J., S. J. "Black Childhood as Ironic: A Nursery Rhyme Transformed in Jessie Fauset's Novel Plum Bun." Minority Voices, 4 (Fall), 65-69.
   Mentions NS as a work of "pure naturalism" and quotes from "How 'Bigger' Was Born" (p. 65).

94. Felgar, Robert. Richard Wright. Boston: Twayne Publishers, 189 pp.
   Presents W as the father of contemporary black fiction and of the "Black Renaissance" of the sixties. His primary theme is that oppression dehumanizes both victim and victimizer. Ultimately, W finds the "meaning of life in meaningless suffering." UTC, NS, and BB will maintain W's status in spite of weaknesses in other works. The seven chapters are "An American Son's Life," "His Apprenticeship" (LT and UTC), "His Fulfillment" (NS), "An Exile's Fiction," "An Exile's Nonfiction," "Eight Men," and "Conclusion." The "Selected Bibliography" contains thirty-four primary sources and forty-nine annotated secondary sources.

95. Feuser, Willfried F. "Black Literature, par Eckhard Breitinger." Présence Africaine, No. 116 (Fourth Quarter), pp. 229-234.
   Mentions W briefly.

96. Fleming, Robert E. "Jerome Klinkowitz, ed. The Diaries of Willard Motley." Black American Literature Forum, 14 (Summer), 84-85.
   Mentions W briefly.

97. Foley, Barbara. "History, Fiction, and the Ground Between: The Uses of the Documentary Mode in Black Literature." PMLA, 95 (May), 389-403.
In addition to mentioning BB and noting that W appears in fictional guise in The Man Who Cried I Am, Foley discusses briefly "The Ethics of Living Jim Crow" and "How 'Bigger' Was Born" as validating prefaces to UTC and NS used by W to place his fictions in the context of historical reality (p. 394).

98. Foley, Martha. The Story of Story Magazine. Ed. Jay Neugeboren. New York: Norton, pp. 68-69, 141, 209.
Reports an account by W of Sylvia Beach's dislike of Gertrude Stein, who "had been a Nazi collaborator" according to W. Foley also mentions W as a socially conscious writer and as a friend of Simone de Beauvoir.

99. Fontenot, Chester J., Jr. "Richard Wright's Native Son: The Novel and the Film." Urbana: mimeographed flyer.
Announces a symposium at the University of Illinois on 13-14 October 1980 with a showing of the film and papers by George Kent and Keneth Kinnamon.

100. Foreman, Ellen. "The Negro Ensemble Company: A Transcendent Vision," in The Theater of Black Americans: A Collection of Critical Essays. Vol. 2: The Participators: Audiences and Critics. Ed. Errol Hill. Englewood Cliffs, N. J.: Prentice-Hall, pp. 72-84.
Lists Daddy Goodness (p. 82).

101. Forrest, Leon. "Milestones in Black History: A Basic Reading List." Chicago Tribune (3 February), Sec 7, p. 3.
Lists and comments briefly on BB and NS.

102. French, Warren. "Introduction," in 20th-Century American Literature. Great Writers Student Library, Vol. 13, ed. James Vinson. New York: St. Martin's Press, pp. 1-20.
Contains a brief paragraph on W's early career (p. 9) and mentions his exile (p. 11).

103. Gallup, Donald. "Carl Van Vechten, 17 June 1880: 17 June 1980. A Centennary Exhibition of Some of His Gifts to Yale." The Yale University Library Gazette, 55 (October), 53-94.
Includes a description of and quotation from one of W's letters to Van Vechten commenting on Gertrude Stein.

104. Gates, Henry Louis, Jr. "Michael S. Harper and Robert B. Stepto, ed. Chant of Saints: A Gathering of Afro-American Literature, Art, and Scholarship." Black American Literature Forum, 14 (Fall), 126-128.
Favorable review including a paragraph on W and Ellison as forefathers of opposed black literary traditions.

105. _____. "Negroes Old, Negroes New: On Afro-American Modernism." ADE Bulletin, No. 64 (May), pp. 34-36.
In a review of Chant of Saints, Gates distinguishes sharply divergent traditions in black fiction initiated by W (social realism) and Ellison (symbolism). "Wright's literary heirs dictated the shape of the black arts movement in the sixties; Ellison's emerged as important individual writers during the seventies" (p. 35).

106. Gayle, Addison, Jr. Richard Wright: Ordeal of a Native Son. Garden City, N. Y.: Anchor Press/Doubleday, 342 pp.
Employing information released under the Freedom of Information Acts, this biography argues that the key to understanding W's later years lies in State Department harassment. W's alienation, which underlies all his later work, was increased by the fact that he was also isolated from progressive political forces. Ultimately W should be seen as a humanist rather than as a subversive.

107. _____. "Wright, Richard," in Academic American Encyclopedia. Ed. Sal J. Foderaro. Vol. 20. Princeton, N. J.: Aretê Publishing Company, pp. 290-291.
Biographical sketch with photograph.

108. Gibbons, Reginald. "Afro-American Texts . . . and Contradictions." The Michigan Quarterly Review, 19 (Summer), 430-433.
Review of Chant of Saints with comments on Robert B. Stepto's essay on W.

109. Gilenson, B. "Die 'zweite Geburt' von Richard Wright." Kunst und Literatur, 28, pp. 95-103.
German translation of 1979.111.

110. Goode, Stephen, ed. The American Humanities Index for 1979. Troy, N. Y.: Whitson Publishing Company, p. 409.
Lists two items on W.

111. Goodman, Burton. "About the Author," in his Random House Spotlight on Literature Collection 3. New York: Random House, p. 39.
Brief biographical sketch of W to accompany an excerpt from BB.

112. _____. "Focus on the Story," in his

Random House Spotlight on Literature Collection 3. New York: Random House, pp. 40-41.
    Study questions on an excerpt from BB.

113. _____. Teachers Guide Random House Spotlight on Literature Collections 1-6. New York: Random House, p. 34.
    Includes brief commentary and study aids for an excerpt from BB.

114. Greene, J. Lee. "The Pain and the Beauty: The South, the Black Writer, and Conventions of the Picaresque," in The American South: Portrait of a Culture. Ed. Louis D. Rubin, Jr. Baton Rouge: Louisiana State University Press, pp. 264-288.
    Comments on BB and NS.

115. Gross, Theodore L. "Ann Petry: The Novelist as Social Critic," in Black Fiction: New Studies in the Afro-American Novel Since 1945. Ed. A. Robert Lee. Vision Critical Studies, ed. Anne Smith. London: Vision Press, pp. 41-53.
    Relates Petry to W (pp. 41, 47, 52).

116. Gwynne, James B. "Richard Wright: Ordeal of a Native Son. By Addison Gayle." America, 144 (3 January), 24-25.
    Favorable review emphasizing the issue of harassment by the United States Government. Claims that W "was to cling to the tenets . . . of Communism" even after leaving the Party.

117. H., W. B. "Stepto, Robert B. From behind the veil: a study of Afro-American narrative." Booklist, 76 (15 March), 1024.
    Mentions briefly BB.

118. Hakutani, Yoshinobu. Young Dreiser: A Critical Study. Rutherford-Madison-Teaneck, N. J.: Fairleigh Dickinson University Press, p. 19.
    Mentions W briefly.

119. Hansen, Klaus P. "Yoshinobu Hakutani and Lewis Fried, ed., American Literary Naturalism: A Reassessment." Amerikastudien, 25 (Spring), 215-217.
    Mentions briefly Michel Fabre's "Richard Wright: Beyond Naturalism?"

120. Harding, Vincent. The Other American Revolution. Los Angeles and Atlanta: Center for Afro-American Studies and Institute of the Black World, p. 119.
    Comments on W's attraction to Communism and quotes from "I Have Seen Black Hands."

121. Harris, Jeanette. "Tragic Vision: 'A Stone of Hope.'" CLA Journal, 24 (December), 184-189.

Cites the play NS as an example of pessimism in black drama.

122. Harris, William J. "Chant of Saints Edited by Michael S. Harper and Robert B. Stepto." The American Book Review, 2 (July-August), 5.
    Review including criticism of Stepto's essay on W.

123. Hart, John E. Albert Halper. Boston: Twayne Publishers, p. 125.
    Mentions the inclusion of W in Halper's anthology This Is Chicago.

124. Hill, Errol. "Chronology of Important Events," in his The Theater of Black Americans: A Collection of Critical Essays. Vol. 2: The Participators: Audiences and Critics. Englewood Cliffs, N. J.: Prentice-Hall, pp. 153-156.
    Lists the play NS.

125. Hodgins, Francis. "Frederick Douglass 1817?-1895," in Adventures in American Literature. Heritage edition. Ed. Francis E. Hodgins and Kenneth Silverman. New York: Harcourt Brace Jovanovich, p. 303.
    Mentions W briefly.

126. Holman, C. Hugh. "The Southern Provincial in Metropolis," in The American South: Portrait of a Culture. Ed. Louis D. Rubin, Jr. Baton Rouge: Louisiana State University Press, pp. 254-263.
    Mentions W briefly.

127. Holt, Thomas C. "Afro-Americans," in Harvard Encyclopedia of American Ethnic Groups. Ed. Stephen Thernstrom, Ann Orlov, and Oscar Handlin. Cambridge: Harvard University Press, pp. 5-23.
    Mentions briefly W and NS.

128. Hurst, Catherine Daniels. "A Survey of the Criticism of Richard Wright's Fiction." Dissertation Abstracts International, 41 (August), 672A-673A.
    Abstracts a University of Alabama dissertation categorizing academic criticism according to sociological, political, existential, and aesthetic perspectives.

129. Iwamoto, Iwao and Masayuki Sakamoto, eds. A Compact History of American Literature. Tokyo: Aratake Shuppan, pp. 221-222.
    Contains a paragraph on W noting his importance as a literary pioneer and mentioning NS and BB. The text is in Japanese.

130. Jackson, Blyden. "From Behind the Veil: A Study of Afro-American Narrative. By Robert B. Stepto." American

Literature, 52 (November), 489-491.
 Review mentioning W briefly.

131. Johnson, Charles. "Philosophy and Black Fiction." Obsidian, 6 (Spring, Summer), 55-61.
 Mentions O, "The Man Who Lived Underground," LT, and AH.

132. Jordan, June. "June Jordan," in Contemporary Literary Criticism. Ed. Dedria Bryfonski and Laurie Lanzen Harris. Vol. 14. Detroit: Gale, p. 595.
 Partial reprint of 1974.102.

133. Joyce, Joyce Ann. "Richard Wright's The Long Dream: An Aesthetic Extension of Native Son." Dissertation Abstracts International, 40 (January), 4038A.
 Abstracts a University of Georgia dissertation comparing the two novels with respect to setting, structure, point of view, and style. Finds LD to be more realistic than NS.

134. Karcher, Carolyn L. Shadow Over the Promised Land: Slavery, Race, and Violence in Melville's America. Baton Rouge: Louisiana State University Press, p. 51.
 Mentions W briefly.

135. Kazin, Alfred. "Writers Who Made Chicago a Heartland." Chicago Tribune (8 June), Sec. 7, pp. 1, 12.
 Mentions W briefly.

136. Kennedy, Randall. "An American Dissident." The New York Times Book Review (3 August), pp. 10, 27.
 Mixed review of Addison Gayle's Richard Wright: Ordeal of a Native Son. With new information from government files about its persecution of W, the work is "impressive in its array of new facts," but factual inaccuracies and florid prose make it "disappointing in the crudity of its composition."

137. King, Richard H. A Southern Renaissance: The Cultural Awakening of the American South, 1930-1955. New York: Oxford University Press, pp. 8, 178, 186.
 Mentions W briefly.

138. Kinnamon, Keneth. "Ellison, Ralph (Waldo)," in 20th-Century American Literature. Great Writers Student Library, Vol. 13, ed. James Vinson. New York: St. Martin's Press, pp. 192-194.
 Reprint of 1979.151.

139. ____. "Johnson, Abby Arthur, and Ronald Maberry Johnson, Propaganda and Aesthetics: The Literary Politics of Afro-American Magazines in the Twentieth

Century." Journalism Quarterly, 57 (Summer), 352.
 Mentions W briefly.

140. Kirby, John B. Black Americans in the Roosevelt Era: Liberalism and Race. Twentieth-Century America Series, ed. Dewey W. Grantham. Knoxville: The University of Tennessee Press, pp. 67, 153.
 Mentions Lillian Smith's interest in W and comments on AH.

141. Kirszner, Laurie G. and Stephen R. Mandell. "Comprehension, Purpose and Audience, Style and Structure, Writing Workshop," in their Patterns for College Writing: A Rhetorical Reader and Guide. New York: St. Martin's Press, pp. 117-118.
 Study aids for "The Ethics of Living Jim Crow."

142. ____. "The Ethics of Living Jim Crow Richard Wright," in their Instructor's Manual to Accompany Patterns for College Writing: A Rhetorical Reader and Guide. New York: St. Martin's Press, pp. 20-21.
 Comments and answers on the study aids of 1980.141.

143. ____. "The Ethics of Living Jim Crow Richard Wright," in their Patterns for College Writing: A Rhetorical Reader and Guide. New York: St. Martin's Press, p. 116.
 Brief headnote.

144. Klinkowitz, Jerome. The Practice of Fiction in America: Writers from Hawthorne to the Present. Ames: The Iowa State University Press, pp. 7, 72, 78, 79, 80.
 Mentions W while discussing Willard Motley.

145. Lawlor, William. "The Politics of Rouse." College English, 42 (October), 195-199.
 Mentions BB as discussed by John Rouse and Mina Shaughnessy. See 1977.286 and 1980.211.

146. Lee, A. Robert. "Introduction," in his Black Fiction: New Studies in the Afro-American Novel Since 1945. Vision Critical Studies, ed. Anne Smith. London: Vision Press, pp. 7-9.
 Emphasizes W's pivotal position in ending the "classic" and beginning the "modern" phase of Afro-American fiction.

147. ____. "Making New: Styles of Innovation in the Contemporary Black American Novel," in his Black Fiction: New Studies in the Afro-American Novel Since 1945. Vision Critical Studies, ed. Anne

Smith. London: Vision Press, pp. 222-250.
> Mentions W briefly (pp. 223, 224, 226).

148. Lee, Dorothy H. "Denial of Time and the Failure of Moral Choice: Camus's The Stranger, Faulkner's Old Man, Wright's The Man Who Lived Underground." CLA Journal, 23 (March), 364-371.
> Points out that Fred Sanders, like the heroes of Camus and Faulkner, attempts to withdraw from an absurd society by "denying the continuum of time." His decision to return reflects moral awareness, but it is doomed.

149. Levin, Harry. "A Literary Enormity: Sartre on Flaubert," in his Memories of the Moderns. New York: New Directions, pp. 135-144.
> Reprint of 1972.137a.

150. Litz, A. Walton. "A National Art Form," in his Major American Short Stories. Revised edition. New York: Oxford University Press, pp. 357-375.
> Comments on W and "The Man Who Was Almost a Man" (pp. 373, 374).

151. ____. "Richard Wright (1908-1960)," in his Major American Short Stories. Revised edition. New York: Oxford University Press, p. 830.
> Reprint of 1975.125 with two additional secondary items.

152. Longest, George C. et al. "A Checklist of Scholarship on Southern Literature for 1979." The Mississippi Quarterly, 33 (Spring), 167-287.
> Lists and annotates eighteen items on W.

153. Madden, David. "Brief Notes on the Authors: For Further Reading," in Studies in the Short Story. Ed. Virgil Scott and David Madden. Fifth edition. New York: Holt, Rinehart and Winston, pp. 552-556.
> Contains a note on W (p. 556).

154. ____. "Richard Wright" 'The Man Who Was Almost a Man,'" in Instructor's Manual for Studies in the Short Story. Ed. Virgil Scott and David Madden. Fifth edition. New York: Holt, Rinehart and Winston, pp. 87-88.
> Analysis of the story followed by "Questions for Discussion and Writing" and a brief bibliography. Madden emphasizes the protagonist's childishness and comments on dialogue.

155. Maduka, Chidi T. "Personal Identity & the Revolutionary Intellectual: Richard Wright's Cross Damon." Kiabara, 3,

No. 1, 159-175.
> Analyzes O as an examination of Nietzschean and Sartrean ideas on the individual as ethically autonomous and self-realizing. Cross is correct in rejecting both communism and capitalism, but his quest for freedom is finally too egocentric.

156. Mandel, Barrett J. "Full of Life Now," in Autobiography: Essays Theoretical and Critical. Ed. James Olney. Princeton, N. J.: Princeton University Press, pp. 49-72.
> Notes that BB provides an example of "how memories of the past are nothing but themselves--not useful as insights into past experience" (pp. 51-52).

157. Materassi, Mario. "Afro-Americana letteratura," in Dizionario della letteratura mondiale del 900. Ed. Francesco Licinio Galati. Vol. I. Rome: Edizioni Paoline, pp. 35-36.
> Mentions W and his influence on Baldwin.

158. ____. "Wright, Richard," in Dizionario della letteratura mondiale del 900. Ed. Francesco Licinio Galati. Vol. 3. Rome: Edizioni Paoline, pp. 3271-3272.
> Biographical sketch emphasizing W's intellectual development and his influence on Afro-American culture. Includes a primary and secondary bibliography with Italian translations.

158a. Mauri i Soldevila, Ferran. "Wright, Richard," in Gran Enciclopedia Catalana. Barcelona: Enciclopedia Catalana, p. 690.
> Biographical sketch.

159. McConnell, Frank. "Ishmael Reed's Fiction: Da Hoodoo Is Put on America," in Black Fiction: New Studies in the Afro-American Novel Since 1945. Ed. A. Robert Lee. Vision Critical Studies, ed. Anne Smith. London: Vision Press, pp. 136-148.
> Mentions W briefly (pp. 136, 138).

160. McDowell, Deborah E. "New Directions for Black Feminist Criticism." Black American Literature Forum, 14 (Winter), 153-159.
> Mentions briefly "The Man Who Lived Underground."

161. McDowell, Margaret B. Carson McCullers. Boston: Twayne Publishers, pp. 21, 40.
> Mentions W's residence in February House in Brooklyn and his approval of The Heart Is a Lonely Hunter.

162. McMichael, George. "James Baldwin 1924-," in his Anthology of American Literature. Second edition. Vol. 2. New York: Macmillan, p. 1718.
Reprint of 1974.125.

163. _____. "Ralph Ellison 1914-," in his Anthology of American Literature. Second edition. Vol. 2. New York: Macmillan, pp. 1474-1475.
Reprint of 1974.126.

164. _____. "Richard Wright 1908-1960," in his Anthology of American Literature. Second edition. Vol. 2. New York: Macmillan, pp. 1465-1466.
Reprint of 1974.128.

165. McQuade, Donald and Robert Atwan. "Classics," in their Popular Writing in America: The Interaction of Style and Audience. Second edition. New York: Oxford University Press, pp. 473-477.
Mentions W briefly (p. 476).

166. _____. "Richard Wright / Black Boy," in their Popular Writing in America: The Interaction of Style and Audience. Second edition. New York: Oxford University Press, p. 554.
Reprint of 1974.129.

167. Mebane, Mary E. "Black Folk of the American South: Two Portraits," in The American South: Portrait of a Culture. Ed. Louis D. Rubin, Jr. Baton Rouge: Louisiana State University Press, pp. 86-100.
Includes discussion of the problem of stasis and change in UTC and LD.

168. Mellard, James M. The Exploded Form: The Modernist Novel in America. Urbana: University of Illinois Press, p. 17.
Mentions briefly NS as a naturalistic novel.

169. Meltzer, Milton. "Gayle, Addison, Jr. Richard Wright: ordeal of a native son." Library Journal, 105 (1 June), 1309.
Favorable notice emphasizing the work's political element.

170. Meserole, Harrison T. et al. "Articles on American Literature Appearing in Current Periodicals." American Literature, 51 (January), 596-607.
Lists one item on W.

171. _____. "Articles on American Literature Appearing in Current Periodicals." American Literature, 52 (November), 521-539.
Lists one item on W.

172. Meyn, Rolf. Die 'Rote Dekade': Studien zur literaturkritik und Romanliteratur der dreissiger Jahre in den USA. Hamburg: Hamburger Buchangentur, pp. 45, 62, 73, 75, 130, 156, 158, 236, 275, 325, 340, 349, 350-351, 366, 402, 405.
Mentions W frequently and discusses NS (pp. 350-351), emphasizing the roles of Bigger and Boris Max.

173. Miller, Morton A. "My First Lesson in How to Live as a Negro," in his Reading and Writing Short Essays. New York: Random House, p. 118.
Very brief headnote to an excerpt from "The Ethics of Living Jim Crow."

174. _____. "Questions About 'Personal Experience,' Questions on Diction and Writing Techniques," in his Reading and Writing Short Essays. New York: Random House, pp. 120-121.
To accompany an excerpt from "The Ethics of Living Jim Crow."

175. Miller, R. Baxter. "Window on the Night: Etymology of the Cultural Imagination." Obsidian: Black Literature in Review, 6 (Winter), 68-81.
Mentions W briefly.

176. Mitchell, Solace. "From Slogans to Tropes." The London Times Literary Supplement, No. 4,027 (30 May), p. 626.
Mentions briefly W and WML.

177. Moore, Geoffrey. "Americana letteratura: Romanzo racconto," in Dizionario della letteratura mondiale del 900. Ed. Francesco Licinio Galati. Vol. 1. Rome: Edizioni Paoline, pp. 75-80.
Mentions W briefly (p. 80).

178. Morano, Alberto Pignatti. "Neoafricana letteratura," in Dizionario della letteratura mondiale del 900. Ed. Francesco Licinio Galati. Vol. 2. Rome: Edizioni Paoline, pp. 2077-2080.
Mentions W briefly (p. 2078).

179. Moss, Robert F. "Robert F. Moss," in Contemporary Literary Criticism. Ed. Dedria Bryfonski and Laurie Lanzen Harris. Vol. 14. Detroit: Gale, p. 596.
Excerpt from 1978.178.

180. Motley, Willard. "Preface," in The Practice of Fiction in America: Writers from Hawthorne to the Present. By Jerome Klinkowitz. Ames: The Iowa State University Press, pp. 75-79.
In a preface to the long novel published in a much revised and shortened version as Knock on Any Door, Motley mentions Bigger Thomas.

181. Munro, C. Lynn. "Robert L. Southgate. Black Plots and Characters: A

Handbook for Afro-American Literature." Black American Literature Forum, 14 (Winter), 167-168.
>Mentions W briefly.

182. Neal, Larry. "Into Nationalism, Out of Parochialism," in The Theater of Black Americans: A Collection of Critical Essays. Vol. 2: The Participators: Audiences and Critics. Ed. Errol Hill. Englewood Cliffs, N. J.: Prentice-Hall, pp. 95-102.
>Reprint of 1972.155.

183. Neugeboren, Jay. "Afterword," in The Story of Story Magazine. By Martha Foley. Ed. Jay Neugeboren. New York: Norton, pp. 242-274.
>Mentions W as a Story magazine "find" (pp. 257, 265).

184. _____. "Introduction," in The Story of Story Magazine. By Martha Foley. Ed. Jay Neugeboren. New York: Norton, pp. 7-24.
>Mentions W briefly (pp. 8, 10, 21, 23).

185. Nichols, Charles H. "Chronological Table of Afro-American Affairs," in his Arna Bontemps--Langston Hughes Letters 1925-1967. New York: Dodd, Mead, pp. 495-497.
>Lists UTC, NS, and TMBV.

186. _____. "Epilogue: The Summing Up," in his Arna Bontemps--Langston Hughes Letters 1925-1967. New York: Dodd, Mead, pp. 489-492.
>Mentions W briefly.

187. _____. "Prologue," in his Arna Bontemps--Langston Hughes Letters 1925-1967. New York: Dodd, Mead, pp. 1-13.
>Mentions W briefly (p. 13).

188. Nin, Anaïs. The Diary of Anaïs Nin 1966-1974. Ed. Gunther Stuhlmann. New York: Harcourt Brace Jovanovich, p. 57.
>Mentions correspondence with Michel Fabre concerning W.

189. Nkashama, P. Ngandu. "La Poesie et le reveil de l'homme noir, par Bernard Fonlon." Présence Africaine, No. 114 (Second Quarter), pp. 213-217.
>Mentions briefly BP.

190. Nordell, Roderick. "The Travail of Richard Wright." The Christian Science Monitor (11 August), pp. B1, B7.
>Review of Addison Gayle's Richard Wright: Ordeal of a Native Son. Nordell is defensive about the American racial record.

191. Ogunyemi, Chikwenye Okonjo. "Richard Wright and Africa." The International Fiction Review, 7, No. 1, 1-5.
>Explains reasons for lack of understanding and appreciation of W by African readers. Discusses BP, LT, NS, and O.

192. Oliver, Lawrence J., Jr. "Images of Africa in Black American Literature. By Marion Berghahn." Minority Voices, 4 (Spring), 81-83.
>Mentions W briefly.

193. Olney, James. "Some Versions of Memory / Some Versions of Bios: The Ontology of Autobiography," in his Autobiography: Essays Theoretical and Critical. Princeton, N. J.: Princeton University Press, pp. 236-267.
>Includes an analysis of BB (pp. 243-248). W is "the autobiographer of memory--a creative memory that shapes and reshapes the historic past in the image of the present, making that past as necessary to the present as this present is the inevitable outcome of that past" (p. 243). The recurring pattern of BB is fear, violence, flight, elements that also characterize NS.

194. Olsen, Paul Victor. "The Message of Horror: Violence in the Works of Richard Wright." Dissertation Abstracts International, 40 (March-April), 5058A.
>Abstracts a University of Georgia dissertation arguing that W uses physical violence throughout his work to suggest the deeper social and spiritual horror of black life in a racist society. Ultimately he destroys his characters in order "to destroy the old world symbolically and replace it with his vision of a new one."

195. O'Meally, Robert G. The Craft of Ralph Ellison. Cambridge: Harvard University Press, pp. 1, 4, 11, 30, 32, 38, 41, 44-49, 54, 57, 60, 77, 78, 106, 163-165.
>Discusses Ellison's criticism concerning W. Stressing Ellison's belief that W oversimplifies experience by using Marxist formulas, O'Meally concludes that Ellison in fact oversimplifies W's practice.

196. _____. "Richard Wright: Ordeal of a Native Son by Addison Gayle." The New Republic, 183 (26 July), 39-40.
>Unfavorable review. Recognizing Gayle's contribution of new material from government files, O'Meally criticizes his Freudian interpretations, "his blurrings of biographical fact and fictional creation," his criticism, and his prose style.

197. Parlato, Salvatore J., Jr. Films ex Libris: Literature in 16mm and Video. Jefferson, N. C.: McFarland & Company, p. 215.
Contains a note on the television dramatization of "Almos' a Man."

198. Peden, William. "Wright, Richard 1908-1960," in Contemporary Literary Criticism. Ed. Dedria Bryfonski and Laurie Lanzen Harris. Vol. 14. Detroit: Gale, p. 596.
Partial reprint of 1975.144.

199. Peebles, Joan B. "Literature, Folklore," in her Black Studies II: A Dissertation Bibliography. Ann Arbor, Mich.: University Microfilms International, pp. 46-50.
Lists twenty-three doctoral dissertations and master's theses on W.

200. Pinckney, Darryl. "A Kind of Paranoia." The Village Voice (29 October, pp. 47-48.
Review of Addison Gayle's Richard Wright: Ordeal of a Native Son. Research on government persecution of W is fresh and revealing, but otherwise Gayle relies too much on Fabre, Webb, BB, and AH.

200a. _____. "A Very Mixed Bag." The Nation, 230 (21 June), 760-763.
Mentions briefly W and BB.

201. Pinsker, Sanford. "Evelyn Gross Avery. Rebels and Victims: The Fiction of Richard Wright and Bernard Malamud." Black American Literature Forum, 14 (Fall), 130-131.
Unfavorable review arguing that "neither Richard Wright not Bernard Malamud is well-served by thematic comparisons." Avery's reductive treatment of W overemphasizes black rage and violence.

202. P.[ownall], D.[avid], B.[ernard] K.[neiger], W.[arren] G. F.[rench], W. J. L., E. P. G., G. C., W.[illiam] F.[reedman], K. M. W., V. E., R. A. K.[ing, Jr.], G.[eorge] K.[linger], A. S. W., H. S. "Wright, Richard," in Articles on Twentieth Century Literature: An Annotated Bibliography 1954 to 1970. Ed. David E. Pownall. Vol. 7. New York: Kraus, Thomson, pp. 4807-4817.
Includes forty-eight items.

203. Prampolini, Gaetano. "Americana letteratura: Critica," in Dizionario della letteratura mondiale del 900. Ed. Francesco Licinio Galati. Vol I. Rome: Edizione Paoline, pp. 95-99.
Mentions W briefly as a Southern writer (p. 95).

204. _____. "Americana letteratura: La narrativa dopo il 1945," in Dizionario della letteratura mondiale del 900. Ed. Francesco Licinio Galati. Vol 1. Rome: Edizione Paoline, pp. 80-88.
Mentions W briefly (p. 85).

205. Ramsey, Priscilla R. "Blind Eyes, Blind Quests in Richard Wright's Native Son." CLA Journal, 24 (September), 48-60.
Points out that both white and black characters in NS are blind to each other and to Bigger. Only when he is alone with Bessie does Bigger share clarity of vision with another. By committing murder, however, he attains a vantage point which allows him to see both sides, though it does not give him consolation or joy.

206. Ray, David. "On New Letters Books." New Letters, 46 (Spring), 3.
Mentions briefly Richard Wright: Impressions and Perspectives.

207. Reilly, John M. "Wright, Richard (Nathaniel)," in 20th-Century American Literature. Great Writers Student Library, Vol. 13, ed. James Vinson. New York: St. Martin's Press, pp. 646-649.
Reprint of 1979.213.

207a. Ren Tuo. "Ming Liang de Chenxin" ["Bright and Morning Star"]. Contemporary Foreign Literature, No. 1, p. 93.
Biographical headnote on W.

208. Riggio, Thomas P. "Uncle Tom Reconstructed: A Neglected Chapter in the History of a Book," in Critical Essays on Harriet Beecher Stowe. Ed. Elizabeth Ammons. Boston: G. K. Hall, pp. 139-151.
Reprint of 1976.159.

209. Rodnon, Stewart. "Abby Arthur Johnson and Ronald Maberry Johnson. Propaganda and Aesthetics: The Literary Politics of Afro-American Magazines in the Twentieth Century." Black American Literature Forum, 14 (Fall), 128-130.
Favorable review mentioning the importance of W in the thirties and after.

210. Rosenblatt, Roger. "Black Autobiography: Life as the Death Weapon," in Autobiography: Essays Theoretical and Critical. Ed. James Olney. Princeton, N. J.: Princeton University Press, pp. 169-180.
Reprint of 1976.163.

211. Rouse, John. "Feeling Our Way Along." College English, 41 (April), 868-875.
Describes the content of BB (p. 872), which Mina Shaughnessy ignores in

Errors and Expectations to concentrate on form.

212. Rushing, Andrea Benton. "Jumping at the Sun." Callaloo, 3 (February-October), 228-230.
    Mentions briefly June Jordan's article on W and Hurston.

213. Russell, Mariann. Melvin B. Tolson's Harlem Gallery: A Literary Analysis. Columbia: University of Missouri Press, pp. 8, 25-26, 33, 34-35, 38, 42, 104, 111.
    Mentions W several times and discusses his work with New Challenge, especially "Blueprint for Negro Writing," and his radicalism.

214. S., E. A. "From Behind the Veil: A Study of Afro-American Narrative. By Robert B. Stepto." American Studies, 21 (Spring), 106-107.
    Review mentioning briefly BB.

215. Saito, Tadatoshi. "Americateki Tagenshugi to America Kokujin--Ralph Ellison to James Baldwin no Sakuhinwo Chushinni" ["American Multiplicity and American Blacks--Focused on the Works of Ralph Ellison and James Baldwin"]. The American Review, 14, pp. 24-38.
    Although W in NS successfully protested the deprivation of human rights for black people, his stance resulted in a failure to establish the rights and led to his own exile in France. To Baldwin, on the other hand, "the Negro problem" in American society, caused by over three hundred years' interracial coexistence, is not a shame, but a great contribution to the advancement of society for mankind. Likewise, Invisible Man is considered a masterpiece, for Ellison succeeds in restoring black identity in a "separate but equal" multiracial society. [Y. H.]

216. Salzman, Jack. "Fiction: The 1930s to the 1950s," in American Literary Scholarship: An Annual/1978. Ed. J. Albert Robbins. Durham, N. C.: Duke University Press, pp. 247-282.
    Mentions W briefly (p. 256).

217. Sane, Ibrahima and James Baldwin. "James Baldwin repond à Ibrahima Sane (Interview, Novembre 1979)." AFRAM Newsletter, No. 10 (April), pp. 3-5.
    Sane mentions W's presence at the First Congress of Black Writers and Artists.

218. Sayre, Robert F. "Autobiography and the Making of America," in Autobiography: Essays Theoretical and Critical. Ed. James Olney. Princeton, N. J.:

Princeton University Press, pp. 146-168.
    Cites W as a black writer whose autobiography (BB) follows the archetypal pattern set by Douglass's Narrative (p. 166).

219. Schlereth, Thomas J. Artifacts and the American Past. Nashville: American Association for State and Local History, p. 165.
    Mentions W briefly.

220. Schultz, Elizabeth. "African and Afro-American Roots in Contemporary Afro-American Literature: The Difficult Search for Family Origins." Studies in American Fiction, 8 (Autumn), 127-145.
    Uses as a point of departure W's sense of black rootlessness in BB and NS.

221. Schwartz, Lawrence H. Marxism and Culture: The CPUSA and Aesthetics in the 1930s. National University Publications Literary Criticism Series, ed. John E. Becker. Port Washington, N. Y.: Kennikat Press, pp. 51, 64, 89, 90, 127.
    Brief mentions of W.

222. Seydor, Paul. Peckinpah: The Western Films. Urbana: University of Illinois Press, p. 120.
    Mentions Norman Mailer's possible indebtedness to W for an "apparent belief in the creative and redemptive possibilities of violent action."

223. Seymour-Smith, Martin. "Origins and Development of the Novel," in his Novels and Novelists: A Guide to the World of Fiction. New York: St. Martin's Press, pp. 9-50.
    Mentions briefly W and NS.

224. Shapiro, Adrian M., Jackson R. Bryer, and Kathleen Field. Carson McCullers: A Descriptive Listing and Annotated Bibliography of Criticism. New York: Garland, pp. 134, 149, 188.
    Lists two items about W and McCullers and one item by W.

225. Shaw, Harry B. Gwendolyn Brooks. Boston: Twayne Publishers, p. 26.
    Mentions favorably Brooks's review of LT.

226. Shimizu, Takeo. "Uncle Tom's Children Eternal Recurrence." Kyushu American Literature, 21, pp. 33-41.
    Analyzes the five stories "from the viewpoint of depth psychology," finding Freudian as well as Biblical implications. Emphasizes connections and continuities in the stories.

227. Sievert, William A. "Notes on Arts:

American Short Stories on PBS." Books & Arts, 1 (25 January), 35.
　　Announces another presentation of the telecast of the dramatic version of "Almos' a Man" on 31 March 1980.

228. Silver, Linda R. "Adult Novels for Young Teens." School Library Journal, 26 (August), 44.
　　Includes a brief comment on NS.

229. Simonson, Harold P. "Biographical Notes," in his Trio: A Book of Stories, Plays, and Poems. Fifth edition. New York: Harper & Row, pp. 745-759.
　　Reprint of 1975.179.

230. Simpson, Lewis P. "Slavery and Modernism," in his The Brazen Face of History: Studies in the Literary Consciousness in America. Baton Rouge: Louisiana State University Press, pp. 67-83.
　　Reprint of 1975.180.

231. Sisney, Mary Frances. "Black Fiction, To Discriminate or Not to Discriminate: A Comparative and Rhetorical Study of Native Son,, Invisible Man, The Man Who Cried I Am, Intruder in the Dust, and The Confessions of Nat Turner." Dissertation Abstracts International, 40 (January), 4045A.
　　Abstracts a University of Southern California dissertation concluding that "there is little or no difference between black and white fiction."

232. Skerrett, Joseph T., Jr. "I Love Myself When I Am Laughing: A Zora Neale Hurston Reader. Ed. Alice Walker." MELUS, 7 (Fall), 90-91.
　　Mentions W briefly.

233. _____. "The Wright Interpretation: Ralph Ellison & the Anxiety of Influence." The Massachusetts Review, 21 (Spring), 196-212.
　　After tracing Ellison's personal contact with W, Skerrett argues that Invisible Man "completes" BB by asserting the value as well as the limitations of Afro-American culture. An example of Harold Bloom's theory of influence, the Ellison-W tension is resolved only when Ellison excludes W from his literary ancestry.

234. Sollors, Werner. "Carol Fairbanks and Eugene A. Engeldinger (eds.), Black American Fiction: A Bibliography. Peter Bruck (ed.), The Black American Short Story in the 20th Century: A Collection of Critical Essays." Journal of American Studies, 14 (April), 170-173.
　　Contains brief references to W.

235. _____. "Literature and Ethnicity," in Harvard Encyclopedia of American Ethnic Groups. Ed. Stephen Thernstrom, Ann Orlov, and Oscar Handlin. Cambridge: Harvard University Press, pp. 647-665.
　　Notes Christ symbolism in "Bright and Morning Star" and NS (p. 653).

236. Somer, John and Barbara Eck Cooper. American & British Literature: 1945-1975: An Annotated Bibliography of Contemporary Scholarship. Lawrence: The Regents Press of Kansas, pp. 6, 17, 27, 28, 31, 34, 35, 40, 45, 46, 48, 58, 70, 73, 117-118, 120, 122, 128, 129, 130, 133, 136, 143, 146, 156, 159, 167, 180.
　　Lists secondary works treating W.

237. Spradling, Mary Mace, ed. In Black and White: A Guide to Magazine Articles, Newspaper Articles, and Books Concerning More Than 15,000 Black Individuals and Groups. Third edition. Vol. 2. Detroit: Gale, pp. 1079-1080.
　　Lists fifty-eight secondary sources on W.

238. Standley, Fred L. and Nancy V. Standley. James Baldwin: A Reference Guide. Boston: G. K. Hall, pp. 16, 18, 29, 31, 33, 34, 55, 58, 65, 71, 79, 83, 84, 90, 93, 104, 111, 117, 119, 123, 127, 128, 131, 133, 137, 139, 141, 154, 155-157, 160, 163, 164, 165, 166, 167, 168, 169, 178, 179, 183, 189, 195, 196, 200, 201, 205, 206, 210, 215, 216, 220, 224, 228, 231, 234, 239, 241, 246-247, 253, 254, 258, 260, 262.
　　References to W, many concerning his relation to Baldwin.

239. Stepto, Robert B. "Literacy and Hibernation: Ralph Ellison's Invisible Man." The Carleton Miscellany, 18 (Winter), 112-141.
　　Includes a discussion of portraiture in the novel as compared to that in BB (pp. 123-127).

240. _____ and Toni Morrison. "'Intimate Things in Place': A Conversation with Toni Morrison," in The Third Woman: Minority Women Writers in the United States. Ed. Dexter Fisher. Boston: Houghton Mifflin, pp. 167-182.
　　Reprint of 1977.296.

241. Stuewe, Paul. "Richard Wright: Ordeal of a Native Son, Addison Gayle." Quill & Quire, 46 (October), 41.
　　Mixed review praising the material on government persecution of W, but noting that it overshadows other aspects of his life and career.

242. Sylvander, Carolyn Wedin. James Baldwin. New York: Ungar, pp. 6-8, 25,

40, 44, 144, 145.
    Mentions Baldwin's relation to W in
    his life and writing.

243. Thomson, Phillip, ed. An Index to
Book Reviews in the Humanities. Vol. 20.
Williamston, Mich.: Phillip Thomson, p.
396.
    Lists two reviews of AH.

244. Tidwell, John Edgar. "Afro-American
Literature Reinterpreted." Callaloo, 3
(February-October), 233-236.
    Mentions W.

245. Turner, Darwin T. "Black Literature," in American Literary Scholarship:
An Annual/1978. Ed. J. Albert Robbins.
Durham, N. C.: Duke University Press,
pp. 381-411.
    Reviews W scholarship for the year.

246. ____. "The Harlem Renaissance: One
Facet of an Unturned Kaleidoscope," in
Toward a New American Literary History:
Essays in Honor of Arlin Turner. Ed.
Louis J. Budd, Edwin H. Cady, and Carl
L. Anderson. Durham, N. C.: Duke Univer-
sity Press, pp. 195-210.
    Mentions W briefly.

247. Vassilowitch, John, Jr. "Richard
Wright's Clintonville: An Ironic Comment
on the 'Talented Tenth.'" Notes on Mississippi Writers, 12 (Winter), 63-66.
    Argues that in LD W is reacting
    against the view of W. E. B. Du Bois
    that a "talented tenth" would elevate
    the black masses.

248. Walker, Ian. "Black Nightmare: The
Fiction of Richard Wright," in Black
Fiction: New Studies in the Afro-Ameri-
can Novel Since 1945. Ed. A. Robert Lee.
Vision Critical Studies, ed. Anne Smith.
London: Vision Press, pp. 11-28.
    Arguing that W was more a writer of
    psychological nightmare than natural-
    istic social and political emphasis,
    Walker reviews his career, discussing
    UTC, LT, NS, O, "The Man Who Lived
    Underground," SH, and LD.

249. Walker, Margaret. "On Being Female,
Black, and Free," in The Writer on Her
Work. Ed. Janet Sternburg. New York:
Norton, pp. 95-106.
    Mentions working on the Writers'
    Project as a graduate of Northwestern
    making $85 per month while W as
    supervisor was making $125 per month.

250. Walker, Warren S. "Bibliography."
Studies in Short Fiction, 17 (Summer),
365-395.
    Lists one item on W.

251. ____. Twentieth-Century Short

Story Explication. Third edition. Supplement I. Hamden, Conn.: The Shoe
String Press, p. 225.
    Lists twelve items.

252. Waniek, Marilyn Nelson. "The Schi-
zoid Implied Authors of Two Jewish-
American Novels." MELUS, 7 (Spring), 21-
39.
    Contains a brief mention of NS as a
    work frequently treated from a sim-
    plistic critical perspective (p. 37).

253. Warren, Robert Penn. Robert Penn
Warren Talking: Interviews 1950-1978.
Ed. Floyd C. Watkins and John T. Hiers.
New York: Random House, pp. 260-277.
    Reprint of 1978.59.

254. Washington, Mary Helen. "Frenchy
Hodges," in her Midnight Birds: Stories
by Contemporary Black Women Writers.
Anchor Books. Garden City, N. Y.: Anchor
Press/Doubleday, pp. 95-96.
    Compares briefly the protagonist of a
    story by Hodges to Bigger, Black Boy,
    Bobo, and Big Boy.

255. Wasserstrom, William. "James Bald-
win: Stepping Out on the Promise," in
Black Fiction: New Studies in the Afro-
American Novel Since 1945. Ed. A. Robert
Lee. Vision Critical Studies, ed. Anne
Smith. London: Vision Press, pp. 74-96.
    Discusses Cleaver's disparagement of
    Baldwin and praise of W (pp. 82-83),
    and mentions W elsewhere.

256. Weixlmann, Joe. "Book Reviews."
Black American Literature Forum, 14
(Spring), 44-48.
    Mentions W briefly (p. 45).

257. ____. "Richard Wright: The Critical Reception, ed. with intro. John M.
Reilly; Rebels and Victims: The Fiction
of Richard Wright and Bernard Malamud,
by Evelyn Gross Avery." The Mississippi
Quarterly, 33 (Fall), 507-513.
    Review praising Reilly for providing
    an informative guide to W's American
    reputation. The work by Avery, how-
    ever, is marred by an oversimplified
    thesis and critical misreadings.

258. Wideman, John. "John Wideman," in
Contemporary Literary Criticism. Ed.
Dedria Bryfonski and Laurie Lanzen Harris. Vol. 14. Detroit: Gale, pp. 596-
597.
    Excerpt from 1978.256.

259. Widmer, Kingsley. Edges of Extrem-
ity: Some Problems of Literary Modernism. The University of Tulsa Monograph
Series, No. 17. Tulsa: The University of
Tulsa, pp. vii, 62-68.
    Revised partial reprint of 1960.268.

260. Williams, Sherley Anne. "Sherley Anne Williams," in Midnight Birds: Stories By Contemporary Black Women Writers. Ed. Mary Helen Washington. Anchor Books. Garden City, N. Y.: Anchor Press/Doubleday, pp. 195-198.
    Mentions reading W.

261. W[illiamson], C[hilton]. "Random Notes." National Review, 32 (11 July), 850.
    Contains a brief notice of Addison Gayle's Richard Wright: Ordeal of a Native Son.

262. Wilson, Judith. "Chant of Saints: A Gathering of Afro-American Literature, Art, and Scholarship. Edited by Michael S. Harper and Robert B. Stepto." Essence, 10 (March), 18-20.
    Mentions W briefly.

263. ____. "Richard Wright: Ordeal of a Native Son. By Addison Gayle." Essence, 11 (December), 19.
    Rather unfavorable notice.

264. Witt, Mary Ann Frese, Charlotte Vestal Brown, Roberta Ann Dunbar, Frank Tirro, and Ronald G. Witt. "Art and Literature in the Industrial World: Realism," in their The Humanities: Cultural Roots and Continuities. Vol. 2. Lexington, Mass.: D. C. Heath, pp. 191-203.
    Mentions W as a naturalist (p. 203).

265. ____. "Protest Tradition and the Blues Tradition: James Baldwin," in their The Humanities: Cultural Roots and Continuities. Vol. 2. Lexington, Mass.: D. C. Heath, pp. 327-328.
    Contains a paragraph on NS.

266. Woodward, Robert H. "Richard Wright '. . . and I Hungered for Books,'" in his The Craft of Prose. Fifth edition. Belmont, Cal.: Wadsworth, p. 297.
    Reprint of 1977.354.

267. ____. "Vocabulary, Questions for Study and Discussion," in his The Craft of Prose. Fifth edition. Belmont, Cal.: Wadsworth, pp. 305-306.
    Study aids for a selection from BB.

268. Wright, John. "Chimed Chants from Dark and Dutiful Dyelis: A Review Essay." The Carleton Miscellany, 18 (Winter), 215-230.
    Mentions BB and "The Man Who Lived Underground."

269. ____. "Dedicated Dreamer, Consecrated Acts: Shadowing Ellison." The Carleton Miscellany, 18 (Winter), 142-199.
    Includes discussion of the interest of Ellison and W in Miguel de Una-

muno's The Tragic Sense of Life (pp. 157-158) and Ellison's early relation to W (pp. 170-173).

270. Wydeven, Joseph J. "Wright Morris. Earthly Delights, Unearthly Adornments: American Writers as Image-Makers." Modern Fiction Studies, 26 (Summer), 348-349.
    Mentions W briefly.

271. Young, Thomas Daniel. "Religion, the Bible Belt, and the Modern South," in The American South: Portrait of a Culture. Ed. Louis D. Rubin, Jr. Baton Rouge: Louisiana State University Press, pp. 110-117.
    Cites an incident from BB to exemplify Southern evangelical religion.

1981

1. Adams, Jimmie R. "Jack Conroy and the Disinherited." Dissertation Abstracts International, 42 (September), 1147A.
    Mentions Conroy's role in W's early career.

2. Agosta, Lucien L. "Millenial Embrace: The Artistry of Conclusion in Richard Wright's 'Fire and Cloud.'" Studies in Short Fiction, 18 (Spring), 121-129.
    Argues that the conclusion of the story is artistically satisfactory, not contrived. Location imagery of church parlor, basement, and Bible Room prepares for the ending. Likewise, the inseparable connections of black and white in the South touched on in the preceding three stories make the final scene of "Fire and Cloud" an appropriate conclusion for the collection UTC as well.

3. Anderson, Jervis. "That Was New York: Harlem IV--Hard Times and Beyond." The New Yorker, 57 (20 July), 42-44, 47-50, 53-54, 58-77.
    Discusses W's residence in Harlem, the publication of UTC and NS, and his tutelage of Ellison.
    Reprinted: 1982.1.

4. Andrews, William L. "The Journey Back: Issues in Black Literature and Criticism. By Houston A. Baker, Jr." American Literature, 53 (March), 140-142.
    Mentions briefly W and WML.

5. Anon. "Black Novelists and the Southern Literary Tradition, by Ladell Payne." Ebony, 36 (July), 22.
    Mentions W briefly.

6. Anon. "1980-1981 Annual Review." Journal of Modern Literature, 8, No. 3/4, pp. 337-684.

Lists ten items on W.

7. Anon. "Program." PMLA, 96 (November), 1009-1106.

Announces a convention session on "Richard Wright's Nonfiction: A Reassessment." The panelists are Arthur O. Lewis, Yoshinobu Hakutani, Edward Margolies, and Charles H. Nilon.

8. Anon. "The Second Black Renaissance, by C. W. E. Bigsby." Ebony, 35 (October), 30.

Mentions W briefly.

9. Anon. "Wright, Richard," in Encyclopedia of Black America. Ed. W. Augustus Low and Virgil A. Clift. New York: McGraw-Hill, p. 869.

Biographical sketch.

10. Aycock, Wendell. "The American Short Story Into Film, Once Again." Studies in Short Fiction, 18 (Summer), 324-326.

Mentions briefly "Almos' a Man."

11. Baker, Houston A., Jr. "Generational Shifts and the Recent Criticism of Afro-American Literature." Black American Literature Forum, 15 (Spring), 3-21.

Discusses "The Literature of the Negro in the United States" as the leading example of "the poetics of integrationism."

12. _____. "Introduction," in English Literature: Opening Up the Canon. Selected Papers from the English Institute, 1979. Ed. Leslie A. Fiedler and Houston A. Baker, Jr. Baltimore: The Johns Hopkins University Press, pp. ix-xiii.

Comments on BB and CC in relation to English as a literary and Third World language.

13. Baldwin, James. "Atlanta: The Evidence of Things Not Seen." Playboy, 28 (December), 140-142, 308, 310, 312, 314, 316.

Cites W's comment on Poe and horror in American life (p. 142).

14. Baraka, Amiri. "Black Literature and the Afro-American Nation: The Urban Voice," in Literature and the Urban Experience. Ed. Michael C. Jaye and Ann Chalmers Watts. New Brunswick, N. J.: Rutgers University Press, pp. 139-159.

Comments on BB and AH as expressive of black feelings about the South and the North, notes W's break with the Communist Party, and praises UTC.

15. Barksdale, Richard K. "Black Autobiography and the Comic Vision." Black American Literature Forum, 15 (Spring), 22-27.

Mentions briefly BB (p. 22).

16. _____. "The Journey Back: Issues in Black Literature and Criticism. By Houston A. Baker, Jr." English Language Notes, 19 (December), 167-169.

Praises Baker's treatment of W.

17. Barthold, Bonnie J. Black Time: Fiction of Africa, the Caribbean, and the United States. New Haven: Yale University Press, pp. 6, 7, 34-35, 36, 44, 56, 62-69, 75, 78, 79-82, 94-95, 103, 104, 116, 120, 122, 131, 135, 159.

Analyzes the role of time in NS, finding Bigger in rebellion against white linear time in an effort to affirm his own inner temporal rhythms. But he is cut off from "the time of Western history and of the traditional African cycle." Barthold also comments on narrative point of view in relation to the reader's intimacy with W's fictional protagonist in NS, "Down by the Riverside," and "Big Boy Leaves Home." Includes comparisons of NS to Chinua Achebe's Things Fall Apart.

18. Baxandall, Lee. "Richard Wright Is Our Companion." The Minnesota Review, No. 17 (Fall), pp. 153-155.

Favorable review of Addison Gayle's Richard Wright: Ordeal of a Native Son from a Marxist point of view.

19. Bell, Bernard W. "Black Literary Biography: Theory and Practice." CLA Journal, 25 (December), 141-161.

Contains a critique of Michel Fabre's The Unfinished Quest of Richard Wright (pp. 152-156). Notes Fabre's emphasis on the psychology of his subject, but complains that the "external reality" of his life is not adequately presented.

20. Benedict, Stewart. "New York & Environs," in his The Literary Guide to the United States. New York: Facts on File, pp. 1-50.

Mentions W briefly (p. 35).

21. Blake, Susan L. "Houston A. Baker, Jr. The Journey Back: Issues in Black Literature and Criticism; A. Robert Lee, ed. Black Fiction: New Studies in the Afro-American Novel Since 1945." Modern Fiction Studies, 26 (Winter), 673-675.

Mentions W briefly.

22. Bowers, Neal. "Ten Years of New Letters: A Critical Appraisal." New Letters, 48 (Fall), 105-113.

Discusses the special W issue (p. 107).

23. Brasch, Walter M. Black English and the Mass Media. Amherst: University of Massachusetts Press, pp. xiv, 232-234, 237.
Describes W's style in LT, quoting a long passage from pp. 84-85. Mentions UTC, NS, and BB.

24. Brauneck, Manfred, ed. Weltliteratur im 20. Jahrhundert. Vol. 4. Reinbeck bei Hamburg: Rowohlt Taschenbuch Verlag, p. 1382.
Brief biographical entry identifying BB and NS as W's major works.

25. Brennan, Timothy. "Ellison and Ellison: The Solipsism of Invisible Man." CLA Journal, 25 (December), 162-181.
Mentions W briefly.

26. Brewton, Butler. "The South and Border States," in The Literary Guide to the United States. Ed. Stewart Benedict. New York: Facts on File, pp. 129-158.
Comments on W's indictment of racism in BB (pp. 150-151).

27. Brooks-Shedd, Virgia. "The Second Black Renaissance: Essays in Black Literature. By C. W. E. Bigsby." The Journal of Negro History, 66 (Summer), 158-159.
Mentions W briefly.

28. Brown, Cecil. "Brown's Ten." The Black Scholar, 12 (March-April), 82.
Lists AH among the ten best books of the seventies.

29. Bryant, Jerry H. "The Violence of Native Son." The Southern Review, 17 (April), 303-319.
Analyzes violence in the novel in relation to racial protest and historical trends, to existentialist ideas, and to the need for human community. Includes comparison of NS to The Day of the Locust, The Young Manhood of Studs Lonigan, Nausea, The Flies, and The Stranger.

30. Bryer, Jackson R. "Richard Wright (1908-1960)," in A Bibliographical Guide to Midwestern Literature. Ed. Gerald Nemanic. Iowa City: University of Iowa Press, pp. 360-362.
After an explanatory paragraph on W scholarship, Bryer lists fifteen primary and fifty-six secondary sources.

31. Burns, Landon C. and Janet P. Alwang. "The Seventh (1980) Supplement to a Cross-Referenced Index of Short Fiction Anthologies and Author-Title Listings." Studies in Short Fiction, 18 (Spring), 203-237.
Lists two anthologies containing "The Man Who Was Almost a Man."

31a. Cadot, Michel. "Avant-propos." Revue du Littérature Comparée, 55 (July-December), 269-270.
Mentions briefly Horst-Jürgen Gerigk's article on Dostoevsky, Dreiser, and W.

32. Carson, Clayborne. In Struggle: SNCC and the Black Awakening of the 1960s. Cambridge, Mass.: Harvard University Press, p. 209.
Mentions briefly W's use of the phrase "black power."

33. Ciner, Elizabeth June. "The Problem of Freedom in Richard Wright's Fiction." Dissertation Abstracts International, 41 (May), 4711A-4712A.
Abstracts a 1980 University of Washington dissertation. Lacking freedom in America, blacks can achieve it through mastery of language, but "only at the moment of their deaths." W's basic view of the matter is pessimistic.

34. Clark, S. L., Eddy Dow, Wilson F. Engel, III, Philip R. Headings, Dennis C. Landis, David Manuszak, Matthew O'Brien, and Joan Stockard. "American Literature," in 1980 MLA International Bibliography. Vol. I. New York: Modern Language Association, pp. 188-268.
Lists twenty-four items on W.

35. Clubbe, John. "Autobiography: Essays Theoretical and Critical. Edited by James Olney; Approaches to Victorian Autobiography. Edited by George P. Landow." Journal of English and Germanic Philology, 80 (July), 435-439.
Mentions Olney's essay on BB.

36. Daniel, Walter C. "Richard Wright: Priests and Potency," in his Images of the Preacher in Afro-American Literature. Washington: University Press of America, pp. 147-179.
Argues that the starkly contrasting images of black preachers in "Fire and Cloud" and NS represent "an essence of Wright's social vision." Moving away from the early work's "celebration of the community-conscious, pragmatic leader," NS condemns Reverend Hammond, who is capable only of condemning communism without offering Bigger an alternative.

37. Dathorne, O. R. Dark Ancestor: The Literature of the Black Man in the Caribbean. Baton Rouge: Louisiana State University Press, pp. 256, 261-262.
Comments on and quotes from BP.

38. Davis, Thadious M. "Southern Writers: Notes Toward a Definition of

Terms." The Southern Quarterly, 19 (Winter), 10-16.
Mentions W briefly.

39. Elshtain, Jean Bethke. "Forgetting Who Are 'The People.'" The Nation, 232 (2 May), 543-548.
Mentions W and AH in a review of five books on questions of race, equality, and inequality.

40. Emerson, O. B. "Wright, Richard: 1908-1960," in Lives of Mississippi Authors, 1817-1967. Ed. James B. Lloyd. Jackson: University Press of Mississippi, pp. 481-484.
Biographical sketch with a list of W's books.

41. [Fabre, Michel]. "Black Fiction, New Studies in the Afro-American Novel since 1945; edited by A. R. Lee." Afram Newsletter, No. 14 (November), p. 48.
Mentions W briefly.

42. ____. "En bref et en vrac . . ." Afram Newsletter, No. 14 (November), pp. 5-9.
Mentions briefly a review of Addison Gayle'sbiography of W.

43. ____. "Lillie P. Howard. Zora Neale Hurston." Afram Newsletter, No. 14 (November), pp. 52-53.
Mentions W briefly.

44. ____. "Robert Felgar. Richard Wright." Afram Newsletter, No. 14 (November), pp. 51-52.
Unfavorable review.

45. Fiedler, Leslie. "Mythicizing the City," in Literature and the Urban Experience. Ed. Michael C. Jaye and Ann Chalmers Watts. New Brunswick, N. J.: Rutgers University Press, pp. 113-121.
Mentions W briefly (p. 116).

46. Flowers, Sandra Hollin. "Colored Girls: Textbook for the Eighties." Black American Literature Forum, 15 (Summer), 51-54.
Mentions NS briefly.

47. Foley, Barbara. "The Documentary Mode in Black Literature." PMLA, 96 (January), 106-107.
Mentions W briefly in a rejoinder to David Leverenz's letter.

48. Fontenot, Chester J., Jr. "Angelic Dance or Tug of War? The Humanistic Implications of Cultural Formalism," in Black American Literature and Humanism. Ed. R. Baxter Miller. Lexington: The University Press of Kentucky, pp. 33-49.
Applies a critical theory derived from Eliseo Vivas to NS (pp. 39-40).

49. ____. "The Journey Back: Issues in Black Literature and Criticism. By Houston A. Baker, Jr." Journal of English and Germanic Philology, 80 (July), 466-468.
Mentions Baker's treatment of NS.

50. ____. "Robert G. O'Meally, The Craft of Ralph Ellison." Black American Literature Forum, 15 (Summer), 79-80.
Mentions W briefly.

51. Fuller, Chet. I Hear Them Calling My Name: A Journey Through the New South. Boston: Houghton Mifflin, p. 194.
Mentions briefly W's "straight-edged prose."

52. Fuller, Hoyt. "Richard Wright: Ordeal of a Native Son. Addison Gayle." The Black Collegian, 11 (February/March), 32, 37, 38.
Favorable review emphasizing government surveillance and intimidation of W during his expatriation.

52a. Galinsky, Hans. "Foreign Scholarship: German Contributions," in American Literary Scholarship: An Annual/1979. Ed. James Woodress. Durham, N. C.: Duke University Press, pp. 481-511.
Comments on two books and one article treating W.

53. Gates, Henry Louis, Jr. "A. Robert Lee, ed. Black Fiction: New Studies in the Afro-American Novel Since 1945." Black American Literature Forum, 15 (Spring), 36-39.
Discusses W's portrayal of his heroic self in contrast to the defeated black masses, contrasting him to Zora Neale Hurston.

54. ____. "Introduction: Criticism in de Jungle." Black American Literature Forum, 15 (Winter), 123-127.
Mentions W briefly.

55. ____. "Michael S. Harper, ed. The Collected Poems of Sterling A. Brown: The National Poetry Series." Black American Literature Forum, 15 (Spring), 39-42.
Review claiming that W's naturalism came out of Brown's realism.

56. Gayle, Addison, Jr. "Introduction," in The Forerunners: Black Poets in America. Ed. Woodie King, Jr. Washington: Howard University Press, pp. xv-xxix.
Comments on and quotes from "The Literature of the Negro in the United States."

57. Gelfant, Blanche H. "Mingling and Sharing in American Literature: Teaching Ethnic Fiction." College English, 43

(December), 763-772.
Mentions briefly <u>NS</u>.

58. Gerigk, Horst-Jürgen. "Culpabilité et liberté: Dostoevskij, Dreiser et Richard Wright." <u>Revue de Litérature Comparée</u>, 55 (July-December), 358-376.
Compares <u>The Brothers Karamazov</u>, <u>An American Tragedy</u>, and <u>Native Son</u>, all of which turn on a judicial error condemning the protagonist for a crime he did not commit. In Dostoevsky human freedom and moral agency are affirmed through acceptance of guilt, but this affirmation is not available to the social victims Clyde Griffiths and Bigger Thomas. Bigger achieves freedom by rejecting the injustice of white racism and affirming his revolutionary identity.

59. Gibson, Donald B. "Richard Wright: The Politics of a Lone Marxian," in his <u>The Politics of Literary Expression: A Study of Major Black Writers</u>. Westport, Conn.: Greenwood Press, pp. 21-57.
Uses W as the touchstone for a general thesis concerning the need for socially (as opposed to formally) based approaches to the criticism of black literature. Within the social framework established in "Blueprint for Negro Writing," W becomes "increasingly personal and subjective" throughout his career. Includes discussion of each of W's published novels and major short stories.

60. Gullason, Thomas A. "The Story of Story Magazine, by Martha Foley." <u>Studies in Short Fiction</u>, 18 (Winter), 97-99.
Mentions W briefly.

61. Hakutani, Yoshinobu. "Richard Wright in Japan: An Annotated Checklist of Criticism." <u>Resources for American Literary Study</u>, 11 (Autumn), 241-256.
Lists and copiously annotates fifty-seven items dating from 1954 to 1979. Hakutani's introduction (pp. 241-243) traces the main outlines of Japanese response to W.

62. Hall, Donald, ed. <u>The Oxford Book of American Literary Anecdotes</u>. New York: Oxford University Press, pp. 305, 312-315.
Quotes anecdotes from Fabre and Webb about borrowing library books in Memphis and going through customs in Texas on his way back from Mexico.

63. Hamamoto, Takeo. "Giichi Ouchi and Mikio Suzuki, <u>The World of Richard Wright</u>." <u>Eigo Seinen</u> [<u>The Rising Generation</u>], 127 (July), 269.
An unfavorable review. Claims that

the book is marred by many errors. [Y. H. and T. K.]

64. Harper, Michael S. "My Poetic Technique and the Humanization of the American Audience," in <u>Black American Literature and Humanism</u>. Ed. R. Baxter Miller. Lexington: The University Press of Kentucky, pp. 27-32.
"Richard Wright I remember most clearly because he was talked about in Brooklyn when I was a kid" (p. 29).

65. Healy, J. J. "Literature, Removal and the Theme of Invisibility in America: A Complex Fate Revisited." <u>Dalhousie Review</u>, 61 (Spring), 127-142.
Mentions W briefly (p. 133).

66. Hedin, Raymond. "Muffled Voices: The American Slave Narrative." <u>Clio</u>, 10 (Winter), 129-142.
Mentions W briefly (pp. 133, 142).

67. Hendrick, George. "An Anthology of Mississippi Writers. ed. Noel E. Polk and James R. Scafidel." <u>Studies in Short Fiction</u>, 18 (Winter), 96-97.
Mentions W briefly.

68. Jackson, Blyden. "<u>The Second Black Renaissance</u>. By C. W. E. Bigsby." <u>American Literature</u>, 53 (November), 526-527.
Mentions briefly <u>NS</u>.

69. Jaye, Michael C. and Ann Chalmers Watts. "Introduction," in their <u>Literature and the Urban Experience</u>. New Brunswick, N. J.: Rutgers University Press, pp. ix-xv.
Mentions W briefly (p. xiii).

70. Jordan, June. "Notes Toward a Black Balancing of Love and Hatred," in her <u>Civil Wars</u>. Boston: Beacon Press, pp. 84-89.
Reprint of 1974.102 with headnote.

71. _____. "Where Is the Love?" in her <u>Civil Wars</u>. Boston: Beacon Press, pp. 140-146.
Mentions W briefly.

72. Joyce, Joyce A. "Semantic Development of the Word Black: A History from Indo-European to the Present." <u>Journal of Black Studies</u>, 11 (March), 307-312.
Includes comment on W's use of unfavorable connotations of the word.

73. Kazin, Alfred. "New York from Melville to Mailer." <u>Partisan Review</u>, 48, No. 2, pp. 85-95.
Mentions briefly <u>NS</u> (p. 93).
Reprinted: 1981.74.

74. _____. "New York from Melville to

Mailer," in *Literature and the Urban Experience*. Ed. Michael C. Jaye and Ann Chalmers Watts. New Brunswick, N. J.: Rutgers University Press, pp. 81-92.
Reprint of 1981.73.

75. Kilson, Martin. "Politics and Identity Among Black Intellectuals." *Dissent*, 28 (Summer), 339-349.
Analyzes W as an exemplary "marginal man," balancing freedom and commitment. Includes consideration of *TMBV*, *LT*, and *BP*.

76. Klein, Marcus. "Black Boy and Native Son," in his *Foreigners: The Making of American Literature 1900-1940*. Chicago: The University of Chicago Press, pp. 270-287, 321-322.
Analyzes W's relation to leftist politics, which nurtured his talent and provided an audience. As spokesman, however, W showed how little blacks were understood by whites who professed good will. Klein comments on *BB*, *AH*, *UTC* (especially "Big Boy Leaves Home"), and *NS*.

77. Kiuchi, Toru. "Richard Wright's *Black Boy* and *American Hunger*." *Kokujin Kenkyu [Negro Studies]*, 51 (28 June), 11-14.
Traces W's spiritual development in *BB* and *AH*. [Y. H. and T. K.]

78. Kumasi, Kandi Baba. "The Critical Reputation of Richard Wright's 'Native Son,' (1940-1975)." *Dissertation Abstracts International*, 42 (August), 704A.
Abstracts a 1980 University of Detroit dissertation tracing the American response to the novel and showing that political considerations conditioned critical attitudes until the mid-sixties, when aesthetic values became paramount.

79. Lautermilch, Steven. "A Check List of Explication (1979)." *The Explicator*, 39 (Winter), 2-56.
Lists one item on W.

80. Lenz, Günter H. "Southern Exposure: The Urban Experience and the Re-Construction of Black Folk Culture and Community in the Works of Richard Wright and Zora Neale Hurston." *New York Folklore*, 7 (Summer), 3-39.
Considers W as a writer effecting the transition from the Harlem Renaissance to postwar black literature by focusing on urban experience. Treats *BB*, *LT*, "Blueprint for Negro Writing," *NS*, and *TMBV*.

81. Leverenz, David. "The Documentary Mode in Black Literature." *PMLA*, 96

(January), 105-106.
Letter to the editor responding to Barbara Foley's 1980 article and mentioning favorably *UTC*.

82. Lewis, David Levering. *When Harlem Was in Vogue*. New York: Knopf, pp. 292, 304.
Mentions W briefly.

83. Lewis, R. W. B. "Warren's Long Visit to American Literature." *The Yale Review*, 70 (July), 568-591.
Comments on Robert Penn Warren's preference for *BB* over *NS*.

83a. Lin Zhi-he. "Chabodou Shi Nanzihan" ["The Man Who Was Almost a Man"]. *Anhui Literature*, No. 8, p. 57.
Headnote explaining that publication of W's story is intended "to promote the cultural exchange between the East and the West."

84. Longest, George C., et al. "Bibliography: A Checklist of Scholarship on Southern Literature for 1980." *The Mississippi Quarterly*, 34 (Spring), 153-277.
Lists eight annotated items on W with cross-references to sixteen others.

84a. Lyra, F. "Foreign Scholarship: East European Contributions," in *American Literary Scholarship: An Annual/1979*. Ed. James Woodress. Durham, N. C.: Duke University Press, pp. 459-472.
Comments on one book and two articles treating W.

85. Markowitz, Norman. "William Faulkner's 'Tragic Legend': Southern History and *Absalom, Absalom!*" *The Minnesota Review*, No. 17 (Fall), pp. 104-117.
Mentions W briefly (p. 105).

86. McCluskey, John, Jr. "'Aim High and Go Straight': The Grandmother Figure in the Short Fiction of Rudolph Fisher." *Black American Literature Forum*, 15 (Summer), 55-59.
Mentions W briefly.

87. McDowell, Edwin. "Behind the Best Sellers: Toni Morrison." *The New York Times Book Review* (5 July), p. 18.
Mentions briefly *NS* as a selection of the Book-of-the-Month Club.

88. McHenry, Susan. "'. . . The Jumping Into It.'" *The Nation*, 232 (11 April), 437-438.
Review of June Jordan's *Civil Wars* comparing her view of words as weapons to W's.

89. Miller, R. Baxter. "Charles H. Nichols, ed. *Arna Bontemps--Langston*

Hughes Letters, 1925-1967." Black American Literature Forum, 15 (Fall), 113-116.
Mentions W briefly.

90. _____. "The 'Etched Flame' of Margaret Walker: Biblical and Literary Re-Creation in Southern History." Tennessee Studies in Literature, 26, pp. 157-172.
Mentions W briefly.

91. _____. "Harry B. Shaw. Gwendolyn Brooks." Black American Literature Forum, 15 (Fall), 116-118.
Mentions briefly Bigger Thomas.

92. _____. "Introduction," in his Black American Literature and Humanism. Lexington: The University Press of Kentucky, pp. 1-7.
Mentions Howard Mumford Jones's unfavorable assessment of NS (p. 4).

93. Morgan, Gordon D. America Without Ethnicity. Port Washington, N. Y.: Kennikat Press, p. 70.
Mentions briefly NS.

94. Morrison, Toni. "City Limits, Village Values: Concepts of the Neighborhood in Black Fiction," in Literature and the Urban Experience. Ed. Michael C. Jaye and Ann Chalmers Watts. New Brunswick, N. J.: Rutgers University Press, pp. 35-43.
Mentions W briefly (p. 37).

95. Muirhead, Pamela Buchanan. "The Picaresque in Six Afro-American Novels." Dissertation Abstracts International, 42 (December), 2678A.
NS is one of six.

96. Naison, Mark. "Communism and Harlem Intellectuals in the Popular Front: Anti-Fascism and the Politics of Black Culture." The Journal of Ethnic Studies, 9 (Spring), 1-25.
Discusses W's ambiguous attitude toward the Communist Party, citing evidence from an interview with Abner Berry (p. 13). The Party's attitude toward W was divided, James Ford showing hostility and Ben Davis and V. J. Jerome protecting him.

97. Nelson, Randy F. The Almanac of American Letters. Los Altos, Cal.: William Kaufmann, pp. 243, 290.
Mentions W's role in the film NS and his departure from 7 Middagh Street in Brooklyn in 1940 "because the black superintendent refuse[d] to fire the furnace for another black man."

98. Newman, Richard. Black Index: Afro-Americana in Selected Periodicals 1907-

1949. Critical Studies on Black Life and Culture, Vol. 4, ed. Charles T. Davis and Henry Louis Gates. New York: Garland, p. 265.
Lists one item on W.

99. Noah, Timothy. "Censors Left and Right." The New Republic, 184 (28 February), 12-14.
Mentions BB as an object of censorship.

100. Olney, James. "From Behind the Veil: A Study of Afro-American Narrative. By Robert B. Stepto." The South Atlantic Quarterly, 80 (Autumn), 483-484.
Review mentioning Stepto's treatment of BB.

101. O'Meally, Robert. "Ralph Ellison," in American Writers: A Collection of Literary Biographies. Supplement II, Part 1. Ed. A. Walton Litz. New York: Scribner's, pp. 221-252.
Discusses Ellison's friendship with W.

102. _____. "Ralph Ellison's Invisible Novel." The New Republic, 184 (17 January), 26-29.
Mentions W briefly.

103. Ouchi, Giichi and Mikio Suzuki. Richard Wright no Sekai [The World of Richard Wright]. Tokyo: Hyoronsha, 210 pp.
A book-length introduction. The biographical section deals with W's life in Mississippi, Chicago, New York, and Paris. The critical section, dealing with each of the eight books of fiction, provides a publication history, plot summary, and critical reception. Defines W's work as the literature of fear: NS focuses on the tragic plight of an individual, Bigger Thomas, who tries to transcend his fear through understanding, as do W in BB, Cross Damon, and Fishbelly Tucker. Interprets UTC in terms of W's involvement in the Communist Party. Evaluates O as an existentialist novel. Does not consider SH an anomaly in W's fictional canon, but an experimental work designed to demonstrate an individual's fear, unintentional crime, escape, attack, and arrest. Regards LD as a failure, a work that betrays W's unfamiliarity with both American reality and French existentialism. Explains that LT is pure naturalism and that W is basically a humanist. [Y. H. and T. K.]

104. Payne, James Robert. "Robert B. Stepto. From Behind the Veil: A Study of

Afro-American Narrative." World Literature Today, 55 (Winter), 109.
    Mentions BB briefly.

105. Payne, Ladell. "A Clear Case:
Richard Wright, 1908-1960," in Black
Novelists and the Southern Literary
Tradition. Athens: University of Georgia
Press, pp. 54-79.
    Presents W as a Southern writer. BB
    is indebted to Look Homeward, Angel.
    NS reflects the Southern Gothic trad-
    ition, especially Faulkner.

106. Perry, John Oliver. "The Survival
of Black Literature and Its Criticism."
The Georgia Review, 35 (Spring), 170-
177.
    Essay-review of four books including
    comments on Stepto on W in Chant of
    Saints and From Behind the Veil.

107. Pinckney, Darryl. "Opinions and
Poems." The New York Times Book Review
(9 August), pp. 8, 26.
    Review of June Jordan's Civil Wars
    and Passion mentioning W briefly.

107a. _____. "Phantom." The New York
Review of Books, 28 (5 March), pp. 34-
36.
    Review of The Wayward and the Seek-
    ing: A Collection of Writings by Jean
    Toomer mentioning NS briefly.

108. Pizer, Donald. "The Dream of the
Golden Mountains: Remembering the 1930s.
By Malcolm Cowley." American Literature,
53 (March), 155-156.
    Mentions W briefly.

109. Pori-Pitts, Aaron Ibn. "Ten Books I
Recently Read Plus Others." The Black
Scholar, 12 (March-April), 86.
    Includes Michel Fabre's The Unfin-
    ished Quest of Richard Wright.

110. Porter, Horace Anthony. "James
Baldwin and the Problem of Vocation."
Dissertation Abstracts International, 42
(December), 2679A.
    Emphasizes Baldwin's relationship
    with W.

111. _____. "Propaganda and Aesthetics:
The Literary Politics of Afro-American
Magazines in the Twentieth Century. By
Abby Arthur Johnson and Ronald Maberry
Johnson." The Journal of Negro History,
66 (Spring), 41-42.
    Review mentioning W briefly.

112. _____. "Spreading the Word." The
American Scholar, 50 (Spring), 281-
286.
    Review of Arna Bontemps--Langston
    Hughes Letters, 1925-1967 mentioning
    briefly the W-Baldwin quarrel.

113. Porter, Roger J. "Autobiography:
Essays Theoretical and Critical. Ed.
James Olney." English Language Notes, 18
(March), 233-236.
    Mentions W briefly.

114. Primeau, Ronald. "Black Literature," in A Bibliographical Guide to
Midwestern Literature. Ed. Gerald Nemanic. Iowa City: University of Iowa
Press, pp. 99-105.
    Quotes BB to show "the beginning of a
    ... midwestern black literature."

115. Rampersad, Arnold. "The Universal
and the Particular in Afro-American
Poetry." CLA Journal, 25 (September), 1-
17.
    Quotes briefly from "Blueprint for
    Negro Writing."

116. Raphael, Frederic and Kenneth
McLeish. The List of Books. New York:
Harmony Books, p. 66.
    Lists NS with favorable comment.

116a. Reilly, John M. "Black
Literature," in American Literary
Scholarship: An Annual/1979. Ed. James
Woodress. Durham, N. C.: Duke University
Press, pp. 393-427.
    Comments on two books and nine
    articles on W.

117. Rosenblatt, Roger. "The Great Black
and White Secret." Time, 117 (16 March),
93-94.
    Cites BB to illustrate the dehumani-
    zation of blacks.

118. Rubin, Steven J. "Ethnic Autobiography: A Comparative Approach." Journal
of Ethnic Studies, 9 (Spring), 75-79.
    Contrasts BB and In Search, the auto-
    biography of Meyer Levin. The former
    is belligerent and rebellious; the
    latter is confessional and accommoda-
    tionist. These differences are repre-
    sentative of the two ethnic groups.

119. _____. "Richard Wright and Albert
Camus: The Literature of Revolt." International Fiction Review, 8 (Winter), 12-
16.
    Notes similarities between NS and The
    Stranger with respect to alienation
    and metaphysics. Whereas Camus's pro-
    tagonist acts out of his comprehen-
    sion of the chaotic universe, Bigger
    responds "unthinkingly to the under-
    lying contradictions of American
    society."

120. Rushing, Andrea B. "An Annotated
Bibliography of Images of Black Women in
Black Literature." CLA Journal, 25
(December), 234-262.
    Contains an entry on Sylvia H.

Keady's "Richard Wright's Women Characters and Inequality" and mentions W elsewhere.

121. Sazawa, Masahiro. "Native Son: Denial and Acceptance," in his Ima Eibei Bungaku o Do Yomu ka [How to Read English and American Literature Now]. Tokyo: Sanyusha, pp. 347-362.
    Like Dostoevski, W does not equate the denial of one's existence with the denial of one's liberation. Reversing Bigger's denial with his acceptance is W's original theme. [Y. H. and T. K.]

122. Schraufnagel, Noel. "Literature: The Novel," in Encyclopedia of Black America. Ed. W. Augustus Low and Virgil A. Clift. New York: McGraw-Hill, pp. 523-530.
    Treatment of W emphasizes NS.

123. Sims, L. Moody, Jr. "Attaway, William Alexander: 1911-   ," in Lives of Mississippi Authors, 1817-1967. Ed. James B. Lloyd. Jackson: University Press of Mississippi, pp. 14-16.
    Mentions W briefly.

124. Stern, Frederick C. "Native Son as Play: A Reconsideration Based on a Revival." MELUS, 8 (Spring), 55-61.
    Arguing that the central meaning of NS is the liberating effect of violence, Stern shows the artistic inconsistency of Max's "proletarian ideology." This problem has affected dramatic versions. The 1978 Goodman Theatre production was also generally successful, but failed to overcome the Bigger-Max problem.

125. Strouse, Jean. "Toni Morrison's Black Magic." Newsweek, 97 (30 March), 52-57.
    Mentions briefly NS (p. 54).

126. Taylor, Clyde. "The Ordeal of Richard Wright." The Black Collegian, 11 (April/May), 162-163.
    Favorable review of Addison Gayle's Richard Wright: Ordeal of a Native Son. Taylor emphasizes United States government harassment of W.

127. Taylor, Gordon O. "Voices from the Veil: Black American Autobiography." The Georgia Review, 35 (Summer), 341-361.
    Considers BB and AH in relation to The Souls of Black Folk, The Autobiography of an Ex-Coloured Man, Notes of a Native Son, and The Autobiography of Malcolm X. Emphasizes W's autobiographical writing as a means of self-realization which is also racially representative.

128. Tolson, Melvin B. "I Am Thankful for the Great Depression--II." New Letters, 47 (Summer), 109-113.
    Reprint of 1939.111c.

129. Trippett, Frank. "The Growing Battle of the Books." Time, 117 (19 January), 85-86.
    Mentions censorship of BB.

129a. Vanderbilt, Kermit. "19th-Century Literature," in American Literary Scholarship: An Annual/1979. Ed. James Woodress. Durham, N. C.: Duke University Press, pp. 197-221.
    Mentions briefly UTC (p. 206).

130. Vassilowitch, John, Jr. "'Erskine Fowler': A Key Freudian Pun in Savage Holiday." English Language Notes, 18 (March), 206-208.
    Argues that "phonologically, the name 'Erskine Fowler' is almost identical to 'her skin--foul her (or 'fouler'). This curious pun signals, in oxymoronic fashion, the paradoxical 'love-hate-mother' complex which afflicts that character."

131. Vickery, John B. "American Literature: The Twentieth Century." The Year's Work in English Studies, 60, pp. 433-459.
    Review of scholarship for 1979 mentioning an essay by Chester Fontenot treating NS.

132. _____. "American Literature to 1900." The Year's Work in English Studies, 60, pp. 411-432.
    Review of scholarship for 1979 commenting on Yoshinobu Hakutani's essay on NS and An American Tragedy.

133. Wald, Alan. "Remembering the Answers." The Nation, 233 (26 December), 708-711.
    Mentions briefly AH.

134. Walker, Warren S. "Bibliography," Studies in Short Fiction, 18 (Summer), 345-381.
    Lists two items on W.

135. Werner, Craig. "From Behind the Veil: A Study of Afro-American Narrative. By Robert B. Stepto." Journal of English and Germanic Philology, 80 (April), 286-288.
    Comments on the implications of Stepto's decision to treat BB rather than NS.

136. Winslow, Henry F., Sr. "Richard Wright: Ordeal of a Native Son. By Addison Gayle." The Crisis, 88 (January/February), 47-49.
    Mixed review of Gayle's book along

with qualified praise of Fabre's biography and criticism of most other W scholarship as timid and evasive. Asks for more emphasis on LD.

137. Yarborough, Richard. "Addison Gayle. Richard Wright: Ordeal of a Native Son." Black American Literature Forum, 15 (Spring), 31-33.
Mixed review noting Gayle's work with declassified documents regarding harrassment of W by government agencies. The biography has several scholarly defects, however.

138. _____. "The Crisis in Afro-American Letters." College English, 43 (December), 773-778.
Notes that paperback editions of several of W's books are out of print.

1982

1. Anderson, Jervis. This Was Harlem: A Cultural Portrait, 1900-1950. New York: Farrar Straus Giroux, pp. 281-284.
Reprint of 1981.3

2. Andrews, Clarence A. Chicago in Story: A Literary History. Iowa City, Iowa: Midwest Heritage Publishing Company, pp. 229, 261, 264, 279-280, 283, 284, 293, 306, 310, 311.
Discusses briefly NS (the novel and the play), O, and LT.

3. Andrews, William L. "Black Novelists and the Southern Literary Tradition. By Ladell Payne." American Literature, 54 (March), 137-138.
Mentions briefly BB.

4. Anon. "B. R. Grüner Publishing Co." Afram Newsletter, No. 16 (December), p. 49.
Advertisement for The Afro-American Novel Since 1960 mentioning W briefly.

5. Anon. "Brief Mention." American Literature, 54 (October), 469-487.
Lists Richard Wright: A Primary Bibliography by Charles T. Davis and Michel Fabre.

6. Anon. "Ebony Book Shelf." Ebony, 37 (January), 22.
Quotes from TMBV.

7. _____. "Ebony Book Shelf." Ebony, 37 (February), 20.
Brief bibliography for Black History Month listing NS as one of the five novels included.

8. Anon. Index Translationum 31. Paris:

Unesco, pp. 123, 224, 486, 820, 968, 1002.
Lists translations of BB into German, French,, and Russian; AH into Danish and Swedish; and O into Serbo-Croatian.

9. Anon. "The literary magazines that first published thhese great writers are going out of business." The Nation, 235 (24-31 July), 78.
Advertisement listing W as one of fourteen such writers.

10. Anon. "1981-1982 Annual Review." Journal of Modern Literature, 9 (December), 317-589.
Lists eleven items on W.

11. Anon. "Program." PMLA, 97 (November), 1010-1105.
Announces a convention session on "Richard Wright's Short Fiction: A Reassessment," with panelists Arthur O. Lewis, Houston A. Baker, Jr., Yoshinobu Hakutani, F. Jefferson Hendricks, and Virginia Whatley Smith.

12. Anon. "The Schomburg Center." Ebony, 37 (September), 62-63, 66.
Mentions the library's "original manuscript of Richard Wright's Native Son."

13. Ashmore, Harry S. Hearts and Minds: The Anatomy of Racism from Roosevelt to Reagan. New York: McGraw-Hill, pp. 94-95.
Mentions W briefly.

14. Baker, Houston A., Jr. "Racial Wisdom and Richard Wright's Native Son," in Critical Essays on Richard Wright. Ed. Yoshinobu Hakutani. Boston: G. K. Hall, pp. 66-81.
Reprint of 1972.26.

15. Baldwin, James. "Many Thousands Gone," in Critical Essays on Richard Wright. Ed. Yoshinobu Hakutani. Boston: G. K. Hall, pp. 107-119.
Reprint of 1951.129.

16. Barnette, William Joseph. "Redeemed Time: The Sacramental Vision and Implicit Covenant in the Major Fiction of Richard Wright." Dissertation Abstracts International, 42 (March), 3997A.
Abstracts a 1981 University of Tennessee dissertation making a religious interpretation of W's fiction and autobiography.

17. Benston, Kimberly W. "'I Yam What I Am': Naming and Unnaming in Afro-American Literature." Black American Literature Forum, 16 (Spring), 3-11.
Includes discussion of names in BB.

18. Berry, Mary Frances and John W. Blassingame. Long Memory: The Black Experience in America. New York: Oxford University Press, pp. 86, 225, 364-365, 419.
Quotes from BB on the black mother as emasculator, mentions W's Marxism, comments on protest in UTC and NS, and notes W's call for black power.

19. Blount, Roy, Jr. "What Authors Do." The New York Times Book Review (17 October), pp. 11, 38-39.
Mentions W briefly.

20. Bogardus, Ralph F. and Fred Hobson. "Introduction," in their Literature at the Barricades: The American Writer in the 1930s. University, Alabama: The University of Alabama Press, pp. 1-9.
Mentions briefly Jack Moore on W.

21. Bradley, David. "Where People Lived, Loved and Made Art." The New York Times Book Review (9 May), pp. 7, 16-17.
Review of Jervis Anderson's This Was Harlem mentioning W and NS.

21a. Breshnahan, Roger J. "A Bibliographical Guide to Midwestern Literature. Edited by Gerald C. Nemanic." Resources for American Literary Scholarship, 12 (Spring), 111-116.
Mentions W briefly.

22. Bryant, Earle V. "The Sexualization of Racism in Richard Wright's 'The Man Who Killed a Shadow.'" Black American Literature Forum, 16 (Fall), 119-121.
Analyzes psychosexual racism in the story, drawing on Hernton, Dollard, Poussaint, and Michele Wallace.

23. Budd, Louis. "Other Books of Interest." The South Atlantic Quarterly, 81 (Summer), 358.
Review of Ladell Payne's Black Novelists and the Southern Literary Tradition mentioning W briefly.

24. Burns, Landon C. and Elizabeth Buckmaster. "The Eighth (1981) Supplement to a Cross-Referenced Index of Short Fiction Anthologies and Author-Title Listings." Studies in Short Fiction, 19 (Spring), 189-219.
Lists anthologies containing "Big Boy Leaves Home" and "The Ethics of Living Jim Crow."

25. Byerman, Keith. "Barbara Christian. Black Women Novelists: The Development of a Tradition, 1892-1976; Robert G. O'Meally. The Craft of Ralph Ellison; Ladell Payne. Black Novelists and the Southern Literary Tradition." Modern Fiction Studies, 28 (Summer), 303-306.
Mentions W briefly.

26. ____. "Stepto, Robert B. From Behind the Veil: A Study of Afro-American Narrative." Studies in the Novel, 14 (Summer), 214-216.
Mentions W briefly.

26a. Chenétier, Marc. "Foreign Scholarship: French Contributions," in American Literary Scholarship: An Annual/1980. Ed. J. Albert Robbins, Durham, N. C.: Duke University Press, pp. 513-525.
Mentions an article by Michel Fabre.

27. Clarke, Graham. "Beyond Realism: Recent Black Fiction and the Language of 'The Real Thing.'" Black American Literature Forum, 16 (Spring), 43-48.
Revised version of 1980.69.

28. Cobb, Nina Kressner. "Richard Wright and the Third World," in Critical Essays on Richard Wright. Ed. Yoshinobu Hakutani. Boston: G. K. Hall, pp. 228-239.
Discusses BP, CC, WML, and PS. W wanted the Third World to abandon race, religion, and tradition and to emulate the secular, rational, industrial West. W's ideas derived from his personal experience.

29. Collier, Eugenia. "Dimensions of Alienation in Two Black American and Caribbean Novels." Phylon, 43 (Spring), 46-56.
Quotes from O (p. 50).

30. Conant, Oliver. "The Hunger and the Journey: Communism in the Thirties." Book Forum, 6, No. 2, pp. 248-256.
Comparison of AH and Lionel Trilling's The Middle of the Journey. Different in background and temperament, W and Trilling conclude that communism stifles individualism and maturity, but both understand its appeal.

31. Cooley, John R. Savages and Naturals: Black Portraits by White Writers in Modern American Literature. Newark: University of Delaware Press, pp. 40-86.
Comments briefly on NS.

32. Davis, Charles T. "The American Scholar, the Black Arts, and/or Black Power," in his Black Is the Color of the Cosmos: Essays on Afro-American Literature and Culture, 1942-1981. Ed. Henry Louis Gates, Jr. New York: Garland, pp. 29-47.
Praises W's artistic integrity in NS prevailing over political motives.

33. ____. "Black Is the Color of the Cosmos," in his Black Is the Color of the Cosmos: Essays on Afro-American Literature and Culture, 1942-1981. Ed.

Henry Louis Gates, Jr. New York: Garland, pp. 3-28.
Reprint of 1970.99.

34. _____. "Black Leadership as a Cultural Phenomenon: The Harlem Renaissance," in his Black Is the Color of the Cosmos: Essays on Afro-American Literature and Culture, 1942-1981. Ed. Henry Louis Gates, Jr. New York: Garland, pp. 63-79.
  Comments on W as a black leader, especially in his analysis of African issues in BP and WML.

35. _____. "Black Literature and the Critic," in his Black Is the Color of the Cosmos: Essays on Afro-American Literature and Culture, 1942-1981. Ed. Henry Louis Gates, Jr. New York: Garland, pp. 49-62.
  Mentions W briefly (p. 60).

36. _____. "From Experience to Eloquence: Richard Wright's Black Boy as Art," in his Black Is the Color of the Cosmos: Essays on Afro-American Literature and Culture, 1942-1981. Ed. Henry Louis Gates, Jr. New York: Garland, pp. 281-298.
  Reprint of 1979.76.

37. _____. "The Mixed Heritage of the Modern Black Novel: Ralph Ellison and Friends," in his Black Is the Color of the Cosmos: Essays on Afro-American Literature and Culture, 1942-1981. Ed. Henry Louis Gates, Jr. New York: Garland, pp. 313-325.
  Considers the personal relations of Ellison, W, and Baldwin as well as the literary connections between Invisible Man, O, and Go Tell It on the Mountain. All three novels extend the tradition of Afro-American fiction beyond naturalism.

38. _____. "Richard Wright: The Artist as Public Figure," in his Black Is the Color of the Cosmos: Essays on Afro-American Literature and Culture, 1942-1981. Ed. Henry Louis Gates, Jr. New York: Garland, pp. 271-280.
  Traces W's political development from Communism to sociological liberalism to non-Communist international leftism to advocacy of African-Asian nationalism. Against this background Davis assesses O, LD, UTC, and BB.

39. _____. "The Slave Narrative: First Major Art Form in an Emerging Black Tradition," in his Black Is the Color of the Cosmos: Essays on Afro-American Literature and Culture, 1942-1981. Ed. Henry Louis Gates, Jr. New York: Garland, pp. 83-119.
  Mentions W briefly.

40. _____ and Michel Fabre. Richard Wright: A Primary Bibliography. Boston: G. K. Hall, 232 pp.
  Comprehensive, chronologically arranged list of W's published and unpublished works with appendices on translations and "Material by Others Related to Wright's Published Works." All editions are listed, including reprints and extracts. For published works, drafts and variant versions are included. Locations are given for all unpublished material, including call numbers for the W archive at Yale. The only important omission is W's correspondence. "The objective of the volume is to enable a scholar to reconstruct the genesis of each work and to trace its textual history."

41. Dietze, Rudolf F. Ralph Ellison: The Genesis of an Artist. Erlanger Beiträge zur Sprach- und Kuntswissenschaft, Band 70. Nürnberg: Verlag Hans Carl, pp. 15-16, 27-42, 45-46, 49-50, 135, 137-138, 176, 179-180, 181, 182, 188.
  Treats in detail W's relation to Ellison, including extended comparison of "The Man Who Lived Underground" and Invisible Man. Similarities exist, but Dietze considers the differences much more important. W's nihilistic existentialism is derived from European sources; Ellison's humanistic existentialism is native Afro-American.

42. Echevarria, Evelio. "Revolution and the Novel." Contemporary Literature, 23 (Winter), 123-125.
  Mentions NS briefly.

43. Ellison, Ralph. "Richard Wright's Blues," in Critical Essays on Richard wright. Ed. Yoshinobu Hakutani. Boston: G. K. Hall, pp. 201-212.
  Reprint of 1945.890.

44. Ensslen, Klaus. Einfuhrung in die schwarzamerikanische Literatur. Stuttgart: Verlag W. Kohlhammer, pp. 10, 13, 87, 95, 119, 124-138, 147-150, 153, 159, 171, 178, 194, 204-205, 216.
  Argues that W's work marks the closest approach of Afro-American literature to left-wing commitment. Traces W's gradual movement from the folk-based expression of UTC to the extreme emphasis on individual consciousness in BB.

45. Evans, Charles J. "Richard Wright's Depiction of the Black Experience: A Study in Stereotypes." Dissertation Abstracts International, 42 (June), 5121A.
  Abstracts a 1982 Loyola University dissertation arguing that W's fiction

perpetuates stereotypes of black life "in works that are lacking in verisimilitude, with implausible action, defective plots, one-dimensional characters and superficial thoughts."

46. [Fabre, Michel]. "Craig Werner Hansen [sic]. Paradoxical Resolutions: American Fiction since James Joyce." Afram Newsletter, No. 16 (December), p. 23.
Favorable review mentioning W.

47. ____. "Edward Margolies. Which Way Did He Go?" Afram Newsletter, No. 15 (June), p. 48.
Mentions briefly The Art of Richard Wright.

48. ____. "En bref et en vrac." Afram Newsletter, No. 15 (June), pp. 5-10.
Includes brief reviews of Charles Davis and Michel Fabre's Richard Wright: A Primary Bibliography and Yoshinobu Hakutani's Critical Essays on Richard Wright.

49. ____. "The Poetry of Richard Wright," in Critical Essays on Richard Wright. Ed. Yoshinobu Hakutani. Boston: G. K. Hall, pp. 252-272.
Reprint of 1970.124.

50. ____. "Richard Wright," in Dictionary of Literary Biography Documentary Series: An Illustrated Chronicle. Vol. 2. Ed. Margaret A. Van Antwerp. Detroit: Gale, pp. 397-460.
Consists of a brief bibliography followed by photographs and documents of various kinds: letters by W; reviews of his books; dust jackets and advertisements; portions of typed or written drafts; articles by W and interviews with him; and brief excerpts from some of his published and unpublished works. Fabre provides headnotes for many of the items. Contains reprints of 1938.165; 1940.919; 1941.680; 1945.451, 997; 1950.134; 1953.150; 1954.89; 1956.307; 1957.204, 207; 1959.140; 1960.85; 1961.178; 1963.105; 1977.276.

51. ____. "Richard Wright, French Existentialism, and The Outsider," in Critical Essays on Richard Wright. Ed. Yoshinobu Hakutani. Boston: G. K. Hall, pp. 182-198.
Traces the personal, literary, and philosophical influence of Camus, Sartre, and de Beauvoir on W's novel. Sartre's Les Chemins de la liberte, Camus's "The Human Crisis," and de Beauvoir's "Literature and Metaphysics" and "Freedom and Liberation" all have similarities to O, but the differences are more revealing.

52. ____. "Rudolf Dietze. Ralph Ellison: The Genesis of an Artist." Afram Newsletter, No. 15 (June), pp. 53-54.
Review criticizing Dietze's treatment of the W-Ellison relationship.

53. ____. "Wright, Richard," in Dictionary of American Negro Biography. Ed. Rayford W. Logan and Michael R. Winston. New York: Norton, pp. 671-673.
Biographical essay praising O.

53a. Farnsworth, Robert M. "Introduction," in his Caviar and Cabbages: Selected Columns by Melvin B. Tolson from the Washington Tribune, 1937-1944. Columbia: University of Missouri Press, pp. 1-25.
Mentions W briefly (p. 13).

54. Fleischmann, Fritz. "Introduction," in his American Novelists Revisited: Essays in Feminist Criticism. Boston: G. K. Hall, pp. 1-5.
Mentions W briefly.

55. Foster, Mamie Marie Booth. "Southern Black Writers Look Into the South." Dissertation Abstracts International, 42 (February), 3600A.
No author is mentioned by name, but W is presumably included.

56. Gaines, David Jeffrey. "The Sun Also Sets: American Writers in Paris After the Second World War." Dissertation Abstracts International, 42 (January), 3157A.
Mentions W.

57. Galinsky, Hans. "The Give-and-Take of an American Section: Literary Interrelations Between the American South and Germany in the Early Post-War Period (1945-1950)," in Die amerikanische Literatur in der Weltliteratur. Ed. Claus Uhlig and Volker Bischoff. Berlin: Erich Schmidt Verlag, pp. 363-391.
Mentions W briefly as a novelist influenced by Kafka (pp. 373, 382).

58. Gallagher, Brian. "Explorations of Black Identity from The New Negro to Invisible Man." Perspectives on Contemporary Literature, 8, pp. 1-9.
Includes a paragraph on NS emphasizing Bigger's alienation from black culture and impotence toward white culture.

59. Gates, Henry Louis, Jr. "Charles T. Davis and the Critical Imperative in Afro-American Literature," in Black Is the Color of the Cosmos: Essays on Afro-American Literature and Culture, 1942-1981. By Charles T. Davis. Ed. Henry Louis Gates, Jr. New York: Garland, pp. xiii-xxxv.

Includes discussion of Davis's view of W as craftsman and survival figure in Afro-American literary modernism.

60. Georgakas, Dan. "The Screen Playwright as Author: An Interview with Budd Schulberg." Cineaste, 11 (Winter), 6-15, 39.
Mentions W's relation to the Communist Party.

61. Gibson, Donald B. "Richard Wright: Aspects of His Afro-American Literary Relations," in Critical Essays on Richard Wright. Ed. Yoshinobu Hakutani. Boston: G. K. Hall, pp. 82-90.
Compares W to Chesnutt and Dunbar, finding the chief differences to be W's emphasis on black power, his literary and philosophical naturalism, his Marxism, and his rebellious personality. Considers most of W's fiction, stressing UTC and NS.

62. Göbel, Walter. "Schreckbild Stadt: Chicago im naturalistischen Roman." Zeitschrift für Literaturwissenschaft und Linguistik, 12, No. 48 (special issue on "Die Stadt und Literatur," ed. Wolfgang Haubrichs), 88-102.
Contains brief discussion of NS in relation to literature of the lower classes in Chicago. Compares Bigger with Studs Lonigan and emphasizes the power of the environment.

63. Gresson, Aaron David, III. The Dialectics of Betrayal: Sacrifice, Violation, and the Oppressed. Norwood, N. J.: Ablex, pp. 26, 42n, 74n.
Mentions W briefly.

64. Hakutani, Yoshinobu, ed. Critical Essays on Richard Wright. Boston: G. K. Hall, 305 pp.
Consists of 1982.14, 15, 28, 43, 49, 51, 61, 65, 66, 72, 77, 83, 84, 90, 96, 106, 107, 118, 130, 136.

65. _____. "Introduction," in his Critical Essays on Richard Wright. Boston: G. K. Hall, pp. 1-35.
Survey of W's literary reception, including both reviews and subsequent criticism. The categories are "General Commentaries," "Criticism of Fiction," "Criticism of Nonfiction," and "Commentaries on Poetry." Hakutani ends by noting bibliographical scholarship and calling for more work on the poetry and the later books.

66. _____. "Native Son and An American Tragedy: Two Different Interpretations of Crime and Guilt," in his Critical Essays on Richard Wright. Boston: G. K. Hall, pp. 167-181.
Reprint of 1979.119.

67. Harper, Michael S. "Don't They Speak Jazz?" Triquarterly, No. 55 (Fall), pp. 177-180.
Mentions reading W while young.

68. Harris, Trudier. "An Anomaly in Southern Territory," in her From Mammies to Militants: Domestics in Black American Literature. Philadelphia: Temple University Press, pp. 71-86.
Analysis of "Man of All Work" in its sociological, historical, and psychological context. Emphasizes the theme of sexual exploitation, but notes other sociological implications. W is also mentioned on pp. 18, 20, 25, 26, 31, 64-65.

69. Hedin, Raymond. "The Structuring of Emotion in Black American Fiction." Novel, 16 (Fall), 35-54.
Includes discussion of Bigger's anger in relation to the structure of NS.

70. _____. "White Teacher / Black Literature." The CEA Critic, 44 (March), 27-31.
Mentions NS briefly.

70a. Henderson, Stephen E. "The Blues as Black Poetry." Callaloo, 5 (October), 22-30.
Mentions W briefly.

71. Hoagland, Edward. "They Loved New York." The New York Times Book Review (21 November), pp. 3, 28-29.
Review of the reissue of The WPA Guide to New York City commenting on W's section on Harlem.

72. Howe, Irving. "Black Boys and Native Sons," in Critical Essays on Richard Wright. Ed. Yoshinobu Hakutani. Boston: G. K. Hall, pp. 39-47.
Reprint of 1963.113.

73. _____. A Margin of Hope: An Intellectual Autobiography. San Diego: Harcourt Brace Jovanovich, p. 240.
Includes a paragraph on Howe's relationship with W, whom he met in 1959. Emphasizes W's low morale: "rootless in Paris," unwilling to return to America, resentful of Baldwin's attack, interested in but critical of African nationalism.

74. Huffman, James R. "A Psychological Critique of American Culture." The American Journal of Psychoanalysis, 42 (Spring), 27-37.
Includes comments on NS and Bigger from a Horneyan perspective.

75. Hunter, Kathryn. "Possessions and Dispossessions: Objects in Afro-American Novels." The CEA Critic, 44 (March), 32-

40.
Uses NS, among other works, to show that unlike their white counterparts, "black novelists, whatever their style or story, have conveyed their values by other means than the character's identification with or quest for objects."

76. Ilacqua, Alma A. "Paul Green--In Memoriam: A Bibliography and Profile." The Southern Quarterly, 20 (Spring), 76-87.
Mentions briefly the play NS.

77. Jackson, Blyden. "Richard Wright: Black Boy from America's Black Belt and Urban Ghettos," in Critical Essays on Richard Wright. Ed. Yoshinobu Hakutani. Boston: G. K. Hall, pp. 48-65.
Reprint of 1969.129.

78. Joyce, Joyce Ann. "Style and Meaning in Richard Wright's Native Son." Black American Literature Forum, 16 (Fall), 112-115.
Examines previously neglected aspects of W's style in the novel: alliteration, syntactic rhythms and patterns, and symbolic import of the words black and white.

79. Kanashiki, Noriko. "Native Son: My Notes," in Suzuki Yokio Sensei Koki Kinen Ronbunshu: Phoenix o Motomete [Essays in Honor of Professor Yukio Suzuki's Seventieth Birthday: In Search of Phoenix]. Tokyo: Nanundo, pp. 339-357.
Discusses the murders of Mary and Bessie, as well as the symbolism of whiteness and blindness. Sees W as Bigger's prototype and argues that W should have remained in America. [Y. H. and T. K.]

80. Kato, Tsunehiko. "Black Boy: Richard Wright's Southern Experience and Character Formation." Kochi Joshi Daigaku Kiyo [Bulletin of Kochi Women's University], 30 (25 March), 25-36.
The hostile environment in the deep South played a large role in the formation of W's character, but his powerful self-will led to his becoming a writer. [Y. H. and T. K.]

81. _____. "Richard Wright and Communism: The Problem of Conversion." Gaikoku Bungaku Kenkyu [Studies in Foreign Literature], 56 (20 December), 105-137.
Examines the problems in W's conversion from Communism in the light of the leftist literary movement in the 1930s. Summarizes his activities as a Party member and the circumstances under which he left the Party, and suggests a reevaluation of W's experience in the 1930s. [Y. H. and T. K.]

82. Kemp, Yakini Belinda. "From Mammies to Militants: Domestics in Black American Literature. By Trudier Harris." CLA Journal, 26 (December), 262-264.
Review commenting on Harris's treatment of "Man of All Work."

83. Kinnamon, Keneth. "Native Son: The Personal, Social, and Political Background," in Critical Essays on Richard Wright. Ed. Yoshinobu Hakutani. Boston: G. K. Hall, pp. 120-127.
Reprint of 1969.144.

84. _____. "Richard Wright: Proletarian Poet," in Critical Essays on Richard Wright. Ed. Yoshinobu Hakutani. Boston: G. K. Hall, pp. 243-251.
Reprint of 1969.147.

85. Kiuchi, Toru. "Nature in Richard Wright's Haiku." Waseda Review, 21 (18 February), 64-73.
A comparative study of W's published haiku with those haiku (included in R. H. Blyth's four-volume Haiku) which seem to have influenced them. [Y. H. and T. K.]

86. _____. "Richard Wright's Naming of Bigger Thomas," in Suzuki Yukio Sensei Koki Kinen Ronbunshu: Phoenix o Motomete [Essays in Honor of Professor Yukio Suzuki's Seventieth Birthday: In Search of Phoenix]. Tokyo: Nanundo, pp. 371-383.
A study of W's motives for naming Bigger Thomas: the connotations of the word big in the South, a comparison of Bigger Thomas with Big Boy, the derivation of Thomas from Uncle Tom, the use of homophones in nigger and bigger. [Y. H. and T. K.]

87. _____. "Richard Wright's Native Son and Alan Paton's Cry, the Beloved Country." Waseda Daigaku Eibungaku [Waseda University English Literature], 56 (25 January), 71-79.
A comparative study of an Afro-American novel and a South African novel. Focuses on the themes of accidental murder, fear, and racial rebellion. [Y. H. and T. K.]

88. Kutzinski, Vera M. "The Distant Closeness of Dancing Doubles: Sterling Brown and William Carlos Williams." Black American Literature Forum, 16 (Spring), 19-25.
Mentions W briefly.

89. Lautermilch, Steven et al. "A Check List of Explication (1980)." The Explicator, 40 (Winter), 10-64.
Lists two items on W.

90. Leary, Lewis. "Lawd Today: Notes on Richard Wright's First/Last Novel," in Critical Essays on Richard Wright. Ed. Yoshinobu Hakutani. Boston: G. K. Hall, pp. 159-166.
Reprint of 1972.136.

91. Light, James F. "Foreigners: The Making of American Literature 1900-1940. By Marcus Klein." American Literature, 54 (May), 308-310.
Mentions W briefly.

92. List, Robert N. Daedalus in Harlem: The Joyce-Ellison Connection. Washington: University Press of America, pp. 4, 6, 9, 10, 12-16, 22, 24-25, 37, 41, 42-44, 63, 65, 76-79, 82, 84, 158, 167-168, 177, 178-181, 183-186, 200, 221, 269-271, 273-274, 287-289, 291, 292, 295-296, 304, 305-307.
Extensive treatment of W in relation to Ellison and Joyce, including such topics as common traits of oppressed peoples, the W-Ellison friendship, W's knowledge of Irish suffering, religion and imperialism, the "pathology of family life," masking, "the devaluation of fatherhood," the unconscious, and rites of passage. Contains many extended quotations from most of W's books.

93. Longest, George C. "Bibliography: A Checklist of Scholarship on Southern Literature for 1981." The Mississippi Quarterly, 35 (Spring), 138-239.
Lists nine annotated items on W with cross references to thirteen others.

94. Lottman, Herbert R. The Left Bank: Writers, Artists, and Politics from the Popular Front to the Cold War. Boston: Houghton Miffflin, pp. xiv, 245-246, 280.
Describes briefly W's life in Paris and his involvement with Rassemblement Démocratique Révolutionnaire.

95. Magistrale, Anthony Samuel. "The Quest for Identity in Modern Southern Fiction: Faulkner, Wright, O'Connor, Warren." Dissertation Abstracts International, 42 (March), 4001A-4002A.
Abstracts a 1981 University of Pittsburgh dissertation. W and Faulkner emphasize that the destructive legacy of slavery hinders the quest for identity.

96. Margolies, Edward. "The Short Stories: Uncle Tom's Children; Eight Men," in Critical Essays on Richard Wright. Ed. Yoshinobu Hakutani. Boston: G. K. Hall, ppp. 128-150.
Partial reprint of 1969.167.

97. _____. Which Way Did He Go? New

York: Holmes & Meier, p. 61.
Notes that some of Chester Himes's early stories "were of the racial protest variety in the Richard Wright vein."

98. Meserole, Harrison T. et al. "Articles on American Literature Appearing in Current Periodicals." American Literature, 53 (January), 763-775.
Lists two items on W (p. 775).

99. Miller, Eugene E. "Richard Wright and Gertrude Stein." Black American Literature Forum, 16 (Fall), 107-112.
Traces W's interest in Stein expressed and reflected in AH, "Tarbaby's Dawn," "Memories of My Grandmother," his review of Wars I Have Seen, and his correspondence. Stein stimulated his interest in language, surrealism, and the folk imagination.

100. _____. "Yoshinobu Hakutani, ed. Critical Essays on Richard Wright." Black American Literature Forum, 16 (Fall), 122-123.
Favorable review noting conflicting points of view. Praises especially essays by Fred Standley and John Reilly, approving the latter's emphasis on W's imagination.

101. Miller, James E., Jr. "Foreigners: The Making of American Literature, 1900-1940. By Marcus Klein." Western Humanities Review, 36 (Autumn), 283-285.
Review mentioning W briefly.

102. Moore, Jack B. "The View from the Broom Closet of the Regency Hyatt: Richard Wright as a Southern Writer," in Literature at the Barricades: The American Writer in the 1930's. Ed. Ralph F. Bogardus and Fred Hobson. Tuscaloosa: University of Alabama Press, pp. 126-143.
Argues that W's fiction of the thirties is doubly important for its Southern and Marxist perspectives. Unlike Southern white writers W does not emphasize locale and genealogy, but he does stress white oppression, the immediate family, food, a moment of crisis in a rural environment, and religion. The analysis focuses on the stories in UTC (except "Long Black Song").

103. Morris, Richard B., ed. Encyclopedia of American History. Sixth edition. New York: Harper & Row, pp. 662, 869.
Reprint of 1976.134.

104. Moses, Wilson Jeremiah. Black Messiahs and Uncle Toms: Social and Literary Manipulations of a Religious Myth.

University Park: The Pennsylvania State University Press, pp. 144, 270.
Calls W. E. B. Du Bois's Dark Princess a precursor of The Outsider. Lists two items by W.

105. Munro, C. Lynn. "Donald B. Gibson. The Politics of Literary Expression: A Study of Major Black Writers." Black American Literature Forum, 16 (Summer), 80.
Review praising the treatment of W.

106. Nagel, James. "Critical Essays on American Literature," in Critical Essays on Richard Wright. Ed. Yoshinobu Hakutani. Boston: G. K. Hall, p. v.
Prefatory note.

107. _____. "Images of 'Vision' in Native Son," in Critical Essays on Richard Wright. Ed. Yoshinobu Hakutani. Boston: G. K. Hall, pp. 151-158.
Reprint of 1969.180.

108. Naylor, Carolyn A. "Cross-Gender Significance of the Journey Motif in Selected Afro-American Fiction." Colby Library Quarterly, 18 (March), 26-38.
Compares Their Eyes Were Watching God, Song of Solomon, "The Man Who Lived Underground," and Invisible Man, finding that the female protagonists of the first two achieve humanistic self-knowledge, but that the male protagonists of W and Ellison do not because they think in terms of "power and invincibility."

109. Nesteby, James R. Black Images in American Films, 1896-1954: The Interplay Between Civil Rights and Film Culture. Lanham, Maryland: University Press of America, pp. 112, 259-260.
Comments on UTC, NS, and O.

110. Nishiyama, Emi. "The Inner World of Richard Wright: Two Autobiographies." Nihon Fukushi Daigaku Kenkyo Kiyo [Bulletin of Japan University of Social Welfare], 52 (30 June), 105-176.
Traces W's search for identity in BB and AH, noting his changing attitude toward white and black people. [Y. H. and T. K.]

111. Nocera, Joseph. "The Big Book-Banning Brawl." The New Republic, 187 (13 September), 20, 22-25.
Mentions the banning of BB by a Long Island school district in 1975.

112. Olney, James. "Bonnie J. Barthold. Black Time: Fiction of Africa, the Caribbean, and the United States; O. R. Dathorne. Dark Ancestor: The Literature of the Black Man in the Caribbean." The Minnesota Review, No. 19 (Fall), pp.

132-136.
Review criticizing Barthold's treatment of NS.

113. Pickering, James H. Instructor's Manual Fiction 100 Third Edition. New York: Macmillan, pp. 7, 14, 26, 44, 129, 130.
Mentions W and "The Man Who Was Almost a Man." Lists four critical works.

114. Reed, Ishmael. "Complaint." The New York Review of Books (21 October), p. 52.
Letter to the editors mentioning briefly LD.

114a. Reilly, John M. "Black Literature," in American Literary Scholarship: An Annual/1980. Ed. J. Albert Robbins. Durham, N. C.: Duke University Press, pp. 437-468.
Comments on two books and nine articles treating W.

115. _____. "Black Novelists and the Southern Literary Tradition, by Ladell Payne." The Mississippi Quarterly, 35 (Fall), 449-453.
Review commenting on Payne's treatment of W.

116. _____. "Charles T. Davis and Michel Fabre. Richard Wright: A Primary Bibliography." Black American Literature Forum, 16 (Fall), 123-124.
Favorable review describing the contents and their utility for scholars wishing to go beyond NS and BB. Notes the omission of the correspondence.

117. _____. "Richard Wright Preaches the Nation: 12 Million Black Voices." Black American Literature Forum, 16 (Fall), 116-118.
Describes the background of TMBV in W's own migration and in nationalism in Marxist and sociological thought. These are developed stylistically as a simulated sermon affirming black national consciousness.

118. _____. "The Self-Creation of the Intellectual: American Hunger and Black Power," in Critical Essays on Richard Wright. Ed. Yoshinobu Hakutani. Boston: G. K. Hall, pp. 213-227.
Departing from fact and chronology, AH is constructed "to explain or to justify the identity of the isolated persona," whose posture is rationalistic. Detached rationalism is also characteristic of BP.

119. Rowell, Charles H. "An Interview with Gayl Jones." Callaloo, 5 (October), 32-53.

Rowell mentions W briefly.

120. Scruggs, Charles S. "The Nature of Desire in Toni Morrison's Song of Solomon." Arizona Quarterly, 38 (Winter), 311-335.
    Rates Morrison's novel with Invisible Man and NS.

121. _____. "The Politics of Literary Expression: A Study of Major Black Writers. By Donald B. Gibson." Arizona Quarterly, 38 (Summer), 171-176.
    Review commenting briefly on Gibson's treatment of W.

122. Shimizu, Takeo. "Richard Wright's Novels: The Fear of 'Great Mother,'" in Suzuki Yukio Sensei Koki Kinen Ronbunshu: Phoenix o Motomete [Essays in Honor of Professor Yukio Suzuki's Seventieth Birthday: In Search of Phoenix]. Tokyo: Nanundo, pp. 357-369.
    An application of Jungian psychology. Interprets W's fiction in terms of the loss of father and the overwhelming presence of mother. [Y. H. and T. K.]

123. Silet, Charles L. P. "The American Caravan: An Author Index." Bulletin of Bibliography, 39 (June), 63-68.
    Mentions and lists W.

124. Sims, Rudine. Shadow and Substance: Afro-American Experience in Contemporary Children's Fiction. Urbana, Ill.: National Council of Teachers of English, pp. 6-7.
    Applies comments by W in "Blueprint for Negro Writing" to children's fiction.

125. Simson, Rennie. "White Teacher / Black Literature: A Brief Response to Raymond Hedin." The CEA Critic, 45 (November), 35-36.
    Mentions W briefly.

126. Singal, Daniel Joseph. The War Within: From Victorian to Modernist Thought in the South, 1919-1945. Chapel Hill: The University of North Carolina Press, pp. 296, 326, 413.
    Comments briefly on NS and quotes from Boris Max's courtroom speech.

127. Singleton, Gregory Holmes. "Birth, Rebirth, and the 'New Negro' of the 1920s." Phylon, 43 (Spring), 29-45.
    Mentions W briefly (p. 43).

128. Smith, Valerie A. "Naming One's Own Experience." The Sewanee Review, 90 (April-June), xxxvii-xxxix.
    Mentions W briefly.

129. Spillers, Hortense J. "Formalism Comes to Harlem." Black American Literature Forum, 16 (Summer), 58-63.
    Mentions briefly Bigger Thomas and "The Man Who Lived Underground."

130. Standley, Fred L. "'. . . Farther and Farther Apart': Richard Wright and James Baldwin," in Critical Essays on Richard Wright. Ed. Yoshinobu Hakutani. Boston: G. K. Hall, pp. 91-103.
    Standley's intentions are "(1) to present a chronology of the activities and events pertaining to their relationship, (2) to specify and summarize the principal interpretations that have been thus far advanced about that relationship, and (3) to indicate the fundamental points of disagreement." The latter concern "the perceived nature of the relationship, the question of the betrayal of friendship, the definition of the term protest literature, and the interpretation of the character of Bigger Thomas in Native Son."

131. Starr, Al. "A 'Blue Hotel' for a 'Big Black Good Man.'" American Notes & Queries, 21 (September/October), 19-21.
    Argues the influence of Crane's story of W's, which "is in many ways a mirror image." Starr notes parallels in plot, style, and the theme of paranoia.

132. Stone, Albert E. "Two Recreate One: The Act of Collaboration in Recent Black Autobiography," in his Autobiographical Occasions and Original Acts: Versions of American Identity from Henry Adams to Nate Shaw. Philadelphia: University of Pennsylvania Press, pp. 227-266.
    Reprint of 1982.133.

133. _____. "Two Recreate One: The Act of Collaboration in Recent Black Autobiography." R. E. A. L.: The Yearbook of Research in English and American Literature. Vol. 1. Ed. Herbert Grabes, Hans-Jürgen Diller, and Hans Bungert. Berlin: Walter de Gruyter, pp. 227-266.
    Uses BB and W. E. B. Du Bois's Dusk of Dawn as points of departure. Reprinted: 1982.132.

134. Tamada, Yoshiyuki. "Theme and Point of View in Richard Wright's 'The Man Who Lived Underground': In Reference to Its Publication Details." Kokujin Kenkyu [Negro Studies], 52 (28 June), 1-4.
    Reads the story as a social criticism and sees the "protest against violence" as its theme. Its point of view transcends that of NS, as well as that of racial problems. [Y. H. and T. K.]

135. Tate, Claudia. "Christian Existen-

tialism in Richard Wright's <u>The Outsider</u>." <u>CLA Journal</u>, 25 (June), 371-395.
    Detailed analysis of the Kierkegaardian influence on the novel. The concepts of "dread" and "despair" are especially crucial to the theme and structure of <u>O</u>, as well as to the psychological development of Cross Damon. An atheist, W was nevertheless inclined, even before he began to read Kierkegaard, to create protagonists who fall "into the Christian existential tradition."

136. Tener, Robert. "The Where, the When, the What: A Study of Richard Wright's Haiku," in <u>Critical Essays on Richard Wright</u>. Ed. Yoshinobu Hakutani. Boston: G. K. Hall, pp. 273-298.
    Analyzes W's published haiku in the full context of an historical explanation of the Japanese form. His attraction to haiku derives from his lifelong affinity to the natural order.

136a. Tolson, Melvin B. "The Biggest Event of 1938 in Black America, March 19, 1938," in his <u>Caviar and Cabbage: Selected Columns by Melvin B. Tolson from the Washington Tribune, 1937-1944</u>. Ed. Robert Farnsworth. Columbia: University of Missouri Press, pp. 198-200.
    Reprint of 1938.283.

136b. _____. "Fighting Preachers in the District of Columbia, April 12, 1941," in his <u>Caviar and Cabbage: Selected Columns by Melvin B. Tolson from the Washington Tribune, 1937-1944</u>. Ed. Robert Farnsworth. Columbia: University of Missouri Press, pp. 52-54.
    Reprint of 1941.997a.

136c. _____. "I Am Thankful for the Great Depression, October 7, 1939," in his <u>Caviar and Cabbage: Selected Columns by Melvin B. Tolson from the Washington Tribune, 1937-1944</u>. Ed. Robert Farnsworth. Columbia: University of Missouri Press, pp. 84-87.
    Reprint of 1939.111c.

136d. _____. "The Negro and Radicalism, August 12, 1939," in his <u>Caviar and Cabbage: Selected Columns by Melvin B. Tolson from the Washington Tribune, 1937-1944</u>. Ed. Robert Farnsworth. Columbia: University of Missouri Press, pp. 37-40.
    Reprint of 1939.111e.

136e. _____. "Richard Wright, the Negro Emancipator: His Tribute to the Washington Tribune, April 6, 1940," in his <u>Caviar and Cabbage: Selected Columns by Melvin B. Tolson from the Washington Tribune, 1937-1944</u>. Ed. Robert Farns-

worth. Columbia: University of Missouri Press, pp. 218-220.
    Praises W's work, emphasizing his racial relevance. <u>NS</u> "is not only a work of art; it is a work of education . . . . It is as radical as truth itself."

137. Velie, Alan R. <u>Four American Indian Literary Masters</u>. Norman: University of Oklahoma Press, p. 8.
    Quotes from Baldwin's comparison of W to Harriet Beecher Stowe.

138. Walker, Alice. "Embracing the Dark and the Light." <u>Essence</u>, 13 (July), 67, 114, 117-118, 121.
    Mentions W briefly.

139. Walker, Warren S. "Bibliography." <u>Studies in Short Fiction</u>, 19 (Summer), 297-327.
    Lists one item on W.

140. Ward, Jerry W., Jr. "All in Whose Family?" <u>Callaloo</u>, 5 (February-May), 208-212.
    Mentions W briefly.

141. _____. "A Black and Crucial Enterprise: An Interview with Houston A. Baker, Jr." <u>Black American Literature Forum</u>, 16 (Summer), 51-58.
    Ward mentions W briefly (p. 56).

142. _____. "Black Intellectuals." <u>Dissent</u>, 29 (Winter), 126.
    Letter to the editor chiding Martin Kilson for taking his biographical information on W from Constance Webb rather than Michel Fabre. See 1981.75.

143. _____. "Escape from Trublem: The Fiction of Gayl Jones." <u>Callaloo</u>, 5 (October), 95-104.
    Mentions W briefly.

144. Watts, Emily Stipes. <u>The Businessman in American Literature</u>. Athens: The University of Georgia Press, pp. 80, 92.
    Mentions W briefly.

145. Watts, Jerry G. "The Case of a Black Conservative." <u>Dissent</u>, 29 (Summer), 301-313.
    Mentions W briefly.

146. Weixlmann, Joe. <u>American Short-Fiction Criticism and Scholarship, 1959-1977: A Checklist</u>. Chicago and Athens, Ohio: Swallow Press and Ohio University Press, pp. 613-616.
    Lists 126 items on W.

147. Werner, Craig Hansen. "The Dangers of Domination: Joyce, Faulkner, Wright," in his <u>Paradoxical Resolutions: American</u>

Fiction since James Joyce. Urbana: University of Illinois Press, pp. 9-32.

Traces W's use of Joyce in LT, UTC, and NS, moving from close imitation to full and subtle imaginative assimilation. LT is modeled on Ulysses, and UTC is structurally similar to Dubliners. Less obviously Joycean, NS develops Bigger's expanding "awareness of the symbolic significance of his naturalistic fate" in a way analogous to the psychological progression of Stephen Dedalus. Werner also relates W's work to the conflicting American traditions of realism and romanticism. W is mentioned elsewhere in the book, especially in relation to James Baldwin (pp. 64, 65, 66).

148. Williams, Sherley Anne. "Papa Dick and Sister-Woman: Reflections on Women in the Fiction of Richard Wright," in American Novelists Revisited: Essays in Feminist Criticism. Ed. Fritz Fleischmann. Boston: G. K. Hall, pp. 394-415.

Examines W's treatment of women in both his fiction and autobiographical writing. Lulu Mann of "Down by the Riverside" in her silent suffering is representative of W's black women, but the strong matriarch also appears. Usually minor characters, black women serve to point up the heroic rebellion of the black male protagonist. Aunt Sue of "Bright and Morning Star," however, is a complex, fully realized character. Other works treated are "Long Black Song," AH, O, LD, BB, and NS. Black women readers may honor W's overall achievement, but they must reject his "racist misogyny" and "male narcissism."

149. Winslow, Henry F., Sr. "The Whole World in His Hands: A Pictorial Biography of Paul Robeson, by Susan Robeson." The Crisis, 89 (October), 49-50.

Mentions W briefly.

150. Wright, John S. "King of the Bingo Game." Callaloo, 5 (February-May), 199-203.

Mentions W briefly.

151. Yow, John. "Foreigners: The Making of American Literature, 1900-1940. By Marcus Klein." The Georgia Review, 36 (Summer), 461-463.

Review mentioning W briefly.

152. Zender, Karl F. "Faulkner," in American Literary Scholarship: An Annual/1980. Ed. J. Albert Robbins. Durham, N. C.: Duke University Press, pp. 143-172.

Mentions briefly an article treating "The Man Who Lived Underground" (p. 166).

Index

References are to year and item number, not to page number. In entries for W's books (and the play <u>Native Son</u>), an asterisk preceding the item number indicates special importance.

Antonini, Giacomo, 1963.45
La Antwerp Métropole, 1951.234
Anudsen, Kristin, 1969.22
The Anvil, 1934.5; 1936.9; 1971.74; 1972.66; 1973.97, 98; 1976.151; 1979.69, 70
The Anxious Years: America in the Nineteen Thirties: A Collection of Contemporary
   Writings, 1963.81
Anzilotti, Rolando, 1976.21
Apartment in Athens, 1945.316
Aperçus de littérature américaine, 1946.177
Apilado, Ruth, 1945.748, 749
Apollo, 1979.103
Apollo Theater, 1941.142, 248, 342
Appel, Benjamin, 1971.25; 1973.48, 49
Appel, David, 1945.24, 750, 751, 752, 753, 926; 1946.139
Appleby, John, 1938.154
Approaches to Victorian Autobiography, 1981.35
An Approach to Literature, 1975.30, 31
L'approdo letterario, 1963.92
"Apropos Prepossessions," 1955.6
Apter, David E., 1954.73
Aptheker, Herbert, 1940.368, 542; 1946.140, 141, 141a, 142, 173; 1948.182; 1956.100,
   101, 115; 1965.30; 1966.45; 1971.26; 1974.21, 22; 1976.60; 1977.49, 114, 115
Aqui Está, 1949.86, 99
Arabs, 1972.153
Araki, Hiroyuki, 1956.102
Arata, Esther Spring, 1975.166; 1976.22; 1978.33
L'Arbalète, 1944.139; 1945.1074
Arban, Dominique, 1952.17
Arbeiten aus Anglistik und Amerikanistik, 1980.58
Arbeitskreis Berliner Volksbibliothekäre, 1957.318
Arbor, 1952.70
L'Arche, 1947.151
Archer, Leonard B., Jr., 1955.23; 1958.73
Les Archives Internationales, 1949.57
Areman, Zita, 1976.23
Arensberg, Liliane K., 1976.24
"Are We Solving America's Race Problem?" 1945.614, 632, 667, 768
Argentina, 1945.828; 1949.49; 1950.5, 43, 50, 73, 74, 78, 79, 177, 178, 241, 246;
   1951.56, 106, 107, 161, 193, 209; 1961.137
Argentinisches Tageblatt, 1956.181
The Argonaut, 1938.107; 1940.516; 1941.180, 282; 1945.1199, 1200; 1946.111, 286
Argosy, 1951.177
L'Argus des Industries du Livre, 1946.112
Ariel, 1978.222
Aries, Philippe, 1947.137
Aristarcho, Guido, 1952.18
Aristotle, 1938.111; 1940.991
The Arizona Quarterly, 1952.38; 1963.155; 1969.250; 1971.313; 1973.268; 1982.120,
   121
Arkansas, 1958.32
Armfield, Eugene, 1937.12
Arms, George, 1954.74
Armstrong, Alicia, 1950.104; 1952.19
Armstrong, Jerry, 1958.74
Armstrong, Louis, 1948.192
Armstrong, Nancy, 1977.57
Arna Bontemps-Langston Hughes Letters 1925-1967, 1980.52, 185, 186, 187; 1981.89,
   112
Arnavon, Cyrille, 1953.73
Arndt, Clinton, 1970.46
Arnez, Nancy L., 1969.23; 1972.21; 1980.34
Arnof, Dorothy S., 1969.66
Arnold, Aerol, 1941.634
Arnold, Paula, 1962.32
Aron, Raymond, 1950.105, 106

A Bibliography of Negro History and Culture for Young Readers, 1968.132
A Bibliography of Neo-African Literature from Africa, America, and the Caribbean, 1965.84
"Bibliotaph," 1941.544, 545
La Bibliothèque idèale de poche, 1966.81
Bicek, Bruno, 1942.24
The Bicentennial Almanac, 1975.124a
Bielefeld Freie Presse, 1956.182; 1962.16
Bierce, Ambrose, 1937.28; 1938.135, 138
Bierstadt, Robert, 1945.724
"Big Black Good Man," 1958.59, 153, 175, 218; 1961.178, 197, 222, 243, 280; 1962.53, 107; 1963.72, 129; 1969.96a; 1971.155; 1972.175; 1973.163, 164; 1974.142; 1975.186; 1976.45; 1977.198, 199; 1979.134; 1982.50, 131
"Big Boy Leaves Home," 1936.7, 10, 11, 12, 13, 14, 15; 1937.10, 17, 19, 26, 27, 28, 34, 38, 122, 123, 155, 157, 181, 182, 212, 219, 226, 232, 249, 254, 280, 289; 1939.91, 99; 1940.664, 785; 1944.139; 1945.1074; 1947.171; 1948.43; 1950.12; 1964.86; 1965.83; 1969.106, 245, 247; 1970.199, 200, 203, 205, 256, 257, 307; 1971.142, 178, 183, 203, 237, 267; 1972.46b, 73, 79a, 100a, 103, 105, 197; 1973.50, 266; 1974.115, 153; 1975.39, 102, 109, 126, 175, 193; 1976.34, 45, 94, 99, 105, 113, 204; 1977.12, 35, 237, 262, 291, 335, 349; 1978.131, 132, 136, 185; 1979.30, 132, 150, 262, 263, 281; 1981.17, 76; 1982.24
Big City Stories by Modern American Writers, 1971.64c, 64d
Bigiaretti, Libero, 1947.148
Big Mat, 1941.1020
Bigsby, C. W. E., 1967.14; 1968.45; 1969.4, 25a, 29, 71, 81, 90, 93, 111, 117, 139, 199, 224, 231, 242, 253; 1970.58; 1971.5, 34a, 42, 127, 128, 150, 157, 192, 255, 278, 299, 304, 316, 319; 1974.27; 1979.40; 1980.47, 48, 49; 1981.8, 27, 68
The Big Sea, 1968.168; 1977.54, 74, 231
Big White Fog, 1941.937, 941
Bikhalji-Merin, Oto, 1959.29
Bilbo, Theodore G., 1945.15, 17, 277, 773, 880; 1971.43; 1973.59, 60; 1978.193
Bildungsarbeit, 1966.62
Billings Gazette, 1977.209
Billingsley, Ronald G., 1975.23, 24
Billy, André, 1951.159, 192
Binderup, Hortense, 1957.142
Binghamton Press, 1959.63
The Binghamton Sunday Press, 1954.84
A Bio-Bibliography of Langston Hughes 1902-1967, 1967.27; 1972.59
The Biographical Encyclopaedia & Who's Who of the American Theatre, 1966.8
A Biographical History of Blacks in America Since 1528, 1971.297
Biotani, Piero, 1975.128
Birbaumer, Alfred, 1962.39
Bird, William, 1946.153, 154
Birdoff, Harry, 1971.44; 1973.61, 62; 1977.62
Birkins, R. Parker, 1945.774
Birmingham, 1964.67
Birmingham, Stephen, 1977.123, 124
Birmingham Age-Herald, 1940.943
The Birmingham News, 1940.23, 576, 687, 690, 715, 790, 963, 964; 1953.187; 1954.117; 1956.194; 1957.216, 218; 1977.202
Birmingham News-Age-Herald, 1938.176
The Birmingham Post, 1940.575, 610, 691, 763
Birmingham Public Library, 1940.199, 317, 430, 575, 576, 610, 687, 690, 691, 715, 763, 790, 927, 963, 964
The Birth of a Nation, 1940.750
"The Birth of Bigger Thomas," 1940.333
Bischoff, Volker, 1982.57
Bisol, Gaetano, 1965.38
Bitker, Marjorie M., 1963.52
Bitossi, Sergio, 1950.110
The Bitter Years: The Thirties in Literature, 1969.32, 33, 34
Bittner, Markus, 1958.82
Bixler, Paul, 1953.90, 121; 1954.78; 1956.116
Biyidi, Alexandre, 1954.79
Bizet, Georges, 1959.117
Black, Paul, 1941.226

Black Fiction, 1974.153; 1975.10, 22b, 57, 73, 103, 126, 173, 182; 1976.34, 106, 113, 140, 164; 1977.67, 133; 1978.183, 190
Black Fiction: New Studies in the Afro-American Novel Since 1945, 1980.16, 47, 69, 115, 146, 147, 159, 248, 255; 1981.21, 41, 53
Black Film as Genre, 1978.68
Black Films and Film-Makers, 1975.110a, 142a, 142b
Black Fire: An Anthology of Afro-American Writing, 1968.124, 171, 172; 1969.125, 181, 184
Blackford, Frank, 1958.83
Black Hands on a White Face: A Timepiece of Experiences in a Black and White America, 1971.63, 64
The Black Hero, 1970.270
The Black Hero Teaching Guide, 1970.79
Black History: A Reappraisal, 1969.67, 69
Black Hollywood: The Negro in Motion Pictures, 1975.139
Black Homeland/Black Diaspora: Cross-Currents of the African Relationship, 1975.21, 62, 63, 140
Black Hope, 1942.233, 277
"Black Hunger," 1944.120
Black Identity: A Thematic Reader, 1970.221
Black Image: Education Copes with Color, 1972.46
Black Image: European Eyewitness Accounts of Afro-American Life, 1978.39, 123
Black Image on the American Stage: A Bibliography of Plays and Musicals 1770-1970, 1970.169
Black Images in American Films, 1896-1954: The Interplay Between Civil Rights and Film Culture, 1982.109
Black Index: Afro-Americana in Selected Periodicals 1907-1949, 1981.98
Black Insights: Significant Literature by Black Americans--1760 to the Present, 1971.56, 71, 93, 117, 118, 119, 120, 121, 122, 186
Black Is the Color of the Cosmos: Essays on Afro-American Literature and Culture, 1942-1981, 1982.32, 33, 34, 35, 36, 37, 38, 39, 59
Black Leadership in American History, 1971.217
Black Like Me, 1979.195
Black Literature, 1979.45, 46, 56, 136, 143, 190; 1980.95
Black Literature: An Anthology of Outstanding Black Writers, 1972.204, 205
Black Literature: Zur afrikanischen und afroamerikanischen Literatur, 1978.186
Black Literature for High School Students, 1978.237
Black Literature in America, 1971.29, 31, 32, 114a
Black Literature in America: A Casebook, 1970.90, 113, 150, 186, 189, 191, 207, 249, 323
Black Macho and the Myth of the Superwoman, 1979.43, 66, 160, 201, 250, 273
Black Magic, 1969.134
Blackman, Peter, 1946.155
The Black Man and the Promise of America, 1970.47
The Black Man in White America, 1944.151
Black Man's Burden, 1965.89
Black Masks: Negro Characters in Modern Southern Fiction, 1969.228; 1970.232a
Black Metropolis, 1945.311, 323, 340, 377, 443a, 612, 781, 808, 817, 1037, 1047, 1079, 1082, 1111, 1118, 1124, 1187, 1198; 1946.31, 56, 140, 171, 173, 239, 243, 263, 264, 275, 279; 1947.198; 1951.148; 1962.50, 51, 53, 71, 76; 1965.107; 1970.19; 1975.22; 1978.143
The Black Migration: The Journey to Urban America, 1972.91a
Blackmur, R. P., 1951.181; 1952.24; 1956.203; 1963.110
Black Muslims, 1968.161; 1969.171
Blackness and the Adventure of Western Culture, 1972.111, 113, 114, 115, 116, 117; 1973.144
The Black Novelist, 1970.50, 60, 63, 89, 118, 126a, 171, 172, 173, 174, 175, 176, 177, 315, 325, 364
Black Novelists and the Southern Literary Tradition, 1981.5, 105; 1982.3, 23, 25
Black Odysseus, 1960.215
Black Odyssey: The Story of the Negro in America, 1948.214; 1950.193
Black on Black: Commentaries by Negro Americans, 1968.1; 1969.17; 1970.11
Black on Black (Himes), 1979.193
Black on White: A Critical Survey of Writing by American Negroes, 1966.97, 135; 1967.56; 1968.182; 1969.156; 1970.249
Black Orpheus: A Journal of African and Afro-American Literature, 1957.4, 229; 1958.101

Black Studies: Threat-or-Challenge?, 1973.150
Black Studies II: A Dissertation Bibliography, 1980.199
Black Tennesseans 1900-1930, 1977.208
Black Theater, U. S. A.: Forty-Five Plays by Black Americans 1847-1974, 1974.89
Black Theatre, 1968.37; 1971.62
Black Time: Fiction of Africa, the Caribbean, and the United States, 1981.17;
    1982.112
Black Tomorrow, 1976.126
Black Virgin, 1957.138; 1960.113
Black Voices: An Anthology of Afro-American Literature, 1968.39, 40, 53, 60, 62,
    63, 64, 74, 84, 130, 140, 183, 204
Black Voices in American Fiction 1900-1930, 1976.33
Black Women Novelists: The Development of a Tradition, 1892-1976, 1980.67; 1982.25
Black World, 1970.69, 87, 94, 145, 213, 259, 272, 290, 336; 1971.149, 195; 1972.28,
    65, 78, 83, 98, 112, 168, 190, 203; 1973.54; 1974.57, 102; 1975.23, 42, 69,
    162, 167; 1976.61, 127, 175
The Black Writer in Africa and the Americas, 1973.93, 100, 122, 216
Black Writers in French: A Literary History of Negritude, 1974.104
Black Writers in Latin America, 1976.107
Black Writers of America: A Comprehensive Anthology, 1972.29a, 31, 52, 71, 122,
    124, 125, 126, 127, 128
Black Writers of the Thirties, 1973.312; 1974.76, 107; 1975.70, 93, 105, 117,
    149
Blagojević, Borislav, 1959.26
Blair, Thomas L., 1977.63
Blair, Walker, 1954.80; 1959.59
Blair, Walter, 1956.117; 1957.143; 1958.84; 1960.119; 1962.40; 1963.53; 1965.39;
    1968.46; 1970.59; 1973.63; 1976.37
Blake, Christopher, 1946.156
Blake, Clarence, 1976.38
Blake, Henry, 1976.44
Blake, Mrs., 1965.18
Blake, Nelson Manfred, 1969.30, 126
Blake, Pamella, 1965.40
Blake, Susan L., 1980.50; 1981.21
Blake, William, 1969.138; 1975.150
Blake or the Huts of America, 1976.44
Blalock, John V., 1945.613, 775
Blanch, Antonio, S. J., 1968.47
Bland, Alden, 1958.85; 1965.42; 1973.68, 148, 256
Blanke man, luister!, 1963.163
Blanket Boy, 1953.123
Blanzat, Jean, 1947.149, 150; 1949.85; 1951.133
Blas, Alvaro, 1949.86
Blasing, Motlu Konuk, 1977.64
Blassingame, John W., 1971.188, 291, 302; 1974.28; 1982.18
Blast, 1934.5
Blaustein, Albert, 1957.166, 252
Blaustein, Phillis, 1957.166, 252
Blicksilver, Edith, 1980.51
The Blinking Eye: Ralph Waldo Ellison and His American, French, German, and Italian
    Critics, 1952-1971, 1974.51; 1977.4
Blitzstein, Marc, 1941.746
Bloch-Michel, Jean, 1963.48
Blodgett, Phil, 1945.776
Bloodline, 1978.82a
Blood on the Forge, 1941.1020; 1974.60
Bloom, Harold, 1980.233
Bloomfield, Morton W., 1970.307
Bloomingdale's, 1945.333
The Bloomington (Ill.) Sunday Pantagraph, 1940.279
Blount, Roy, Jr., 1982.19
Bluefarb, Sam, 1972.33; 1975.25; 1976.168
"The Blue Hotel," 1961.197; 1975.186; 1982.131
The Blue Pencil, 1940.142
"Blueprint for Negro Literature," 1971.317; 1976.142; 1978.84
"Blueprint for Negro Writing," 1937.22; 1938.216; 1939.111a; 1944.144; 1947.178;
    1956.145; 1966.32, 64, 65, 110; 1967.25, 78; 1968.4, 69, 171; 1969.181, 183;

Bosquet, Marie-Louise, 1949.88
Bosschère, Guy de, 1960.121, 122; 1963.60
Boston, 1941.343, 364, 547, 1027; 1945.344, 499; 1965.78
Boston Chronicle, 1940.709; 1945.945; 1955.87
The Boston Daily Globe, 1941.787; 1944.106; 1945.30, 31, 32, 33, 34, 35, 36, 37,
   38, 39, 40, 41, 42, 43, 44, 45, 46, 47, 48
Boston Evening Globe, 1945.31, 32, 33, 34, 35, 36, 37, 38, 39, 40, 41, 42, 43,
   44, 45, 46, 47, 48, 49, 987
Boston Evening Transcript, 1938.285; 1940.3, 10, 306, 601, 602, 603, 604, 605,
   606, 744; 1941.762a
The Boston Globe, 1977.108
The Boston Guardian, 1953.25
The Boston Herald, 1938.287; 1940.13, 560, 656; 1941.649, 764; 1945.743, 864,
   1033; 1946.113, 228; 1953.145; 1956.262; 1957.287
Boston Jewish Advocate, 1977.279
Boston Public Library, 1945.1065
The Boston Sunday Globe, 1940.29, 30, 31, 32, 65, 66; 1953.245; 1956.269; 1957.327;
   1958.79; 1963.80; 1966.20; 1977.247
Boston Sunday Herald, 1954.151; 1958.147
Boston Sunday Post, 1944.14; 1945.1062
Boston Traveller, 1946.255; 1961.124; 1963.152
Botkin, B. A., 1945.784
Bouma, Donald H., 1955.27
Boundary 2, 1978.41, 258
Bourdeaux Courrier Français du Sud-Ouest, 1946.37
Le Bourges Berry Républicain, 1947.35, 40
Bourke-White, Margaret, 1938.110; 1941.361, 758, 759; 1963.153
Bourne, Randolph, 1941.100
Bourne, St. Clair, 1940.562, 563
Bourne Award, 1941.100
Bourneuf, Philip, 1943.57
Bourniquel, Camille, 1964.32a; 1969.43
Boutell, Clip, 1944.57, 58, 59, 60; 1945.785, 786, 787, 788, 789, 790, 791, 792,
   793; 1946.157; 1947.153, 154
Bovelle, Virgie N. H., 1977.67
Bowen, John, 1965.44
Bower, Helen, 1938.160; 1941.650; 1944.61; 1945.794, 795
Bower, Warren, 1941.964
Bowers, Neal, 1981.22
Bowles, Patrick, 1953.92
Bowling, G. E., (Mrs.), 1952.26
Bowman, Barc, 1954.82; 1957.146, 147
Bowman, Betty, 1945.796
Bowman, Len, 1946.157a
Bowman, Sylvia E., 1962.98; 1964.111; 1971.194; 1975.53
Boy at the Window, 1973.117; 1977.214
Boyd, G. N., 1973.69
Boyd, L. A., 1973.69
The Boyds of Black River, 1953.156
Boylan, Martin M., 1977.68
Boyle, Kay, 1959.118
Boyle, Sarah Patton, 1953.93
Bozman, E. F., 1959.50
Bracey, John H., Jr., 1971.50; 1976.40a
Bracy, William, 1965.45; 1968.49; 1970.65; 1977.69; 1978.45
Bradbury, John M., 1963.61
Bradbury, Malcolm, 1971.51, 52; 1978.46
Bradford, Ben, 1942.206
Bradford, David H., 1941.651; 1945.797
Bradford, Roark, 1938.164; 1947.8; 1960.207
Bradley, David, 1977.70; 1982.21
Bradley, Hugh, 1938.161
Bradley, Preston, 1940.235, 564
Bradley, Sculley, 1956.118; 1974.142
Bradley, Van Allen, 1953.94, 95, 96; 1954.83; 1955.28; 1958.89, 90; 1959.63
Bradshaw, Barbara, 1969.77, 78, 79, 80
Brady, Owen, 1978.47
Braem, Helmut M., 1960.123, 124; 1961.126, 127, 128; 1966.27

Brooks, Charlotte, 1967.18; 1968.213
Brooks, Cleanth, 1973.73; 1975.30, 31, 110; 1979.50, 51
Brooks, Ernest, 1941.504
Brooks, Gwendolyn, 1948.221, 222; 1949.42, 53; 1963.62, 145; 1971.196; 1972.35,
    115; 1973.7, 155; 1975.32; 1977.17, 26, 344; 1978.9; 1979.3, 117; 1980.225;
    1981.91
Brooks, Mary Ellen, 1972.36
Brooks, Richard, 1945.345
Brooks, Samuel I., 1940.571
Brooks, Samuel L., 1941.660
Brooks, Thomas R., 1974.36
Brooks, Van Wyck, 1941.493; 1944.102; 1952.27; 1953.99; 1955.31; 1963.78
Brooks-Shedd, Virginia, 1981.27
Brossard, Chandler, 1955.86
Brothers and Sisters: Modern Stories by Black Americans, 1970.12; 1975.2
The Brothers Karamazov, 1981.58
Broughton, Panthea Reid, 1980.55
Brousch, Michael, 1941.661
Browder, Earl, 1940.269, 518, 700; 1941.111, 112, 225, 241, 360, 440, 540; 1942.175
Brown, Adger, 1966.29
Brown, Cecil M., 1968.51, 52; 1970.69, 70; 1971.96; 1972.62; 1978.50; 1981.28
Brown, Charlotte, 1940.7
Brown, Charlotte Vestal, 1980.264, 265
Brown, Claude, 1971.117; 1976.86
Brown, Deming B., 1948.202; 1954.85; 1962.42; 1971.147
Brown, Dorothy, 1940.733; 1941.771; 1953.161, 162; 1954.128, 129; 1955.52; 1956.214,
    215; 1957.230, 231; 1958.170, 171
Brown, Earl, 1945.807; 1948.133
Brown, Francis J., 1952.51a
Brown, Frank London, 1961.126, 127, 221, 286; 1965.42; 1973.148
Brown, Glenora W., 1954.85
Brown, Ina Corinne, 1961.138; 1962.49; 1963.73; 1964.42
Brown, Ivor, 1942.209
Brown, Jack E., 1950.116
Brown, Jerry Elijah, 1980.56
Brown, Joe C., 1968.145, 146; 1971.64a
Brown, John, 1954.86
Brown, John L., 1946.162
Brown, John Mason, 1941.662, 663, 664, 665, 666, 790, 902
Brown, John S., 1947.156
Brown, Lester, 1945.808
Brown, Linda Weaver, 1973.74
Brown, Lloyd L., 1951.138; 1952.28; 1953.100; 1958.85; 1970.71; 1973.256; 1974.35,
    36, 166
Brown, Lloyd W., 1970.72, 73; 1972.37; 1973.93, 100, 122, 216; 1974.37, 38, 177;
    1976.42
Brown, Marie, 1978.126a
Brown, Norman, 1975.110
Brown, Rap, 1970.156
Brown, Richard Maxwell, 1975.33
Brown, Roscoe C., Jr., 1967.82; 1972.37a
Brown, Ross, 1943.22
Brown, Sterling A., 1937.16, 17, 18, 164, 165; 1938.164, 165; 1939.60; 1940.572;
    1941.538, 667, 668, 669; 1942.210; 1951.139; 1955.32; 1956.152; 1960.207; 1965.65;
    1966.30; 1967.19; 1968.53, 100; 1969.44, 45; 1970.74, 75, 134; 1971.56, 56a,
    57; 1976.121, 181; 1978.193; 1979.52, 141; 1981.55; 1982.50, 88
Brown, Thelma, 1940.654
Brown Americans: The Story of a Tenth of a Nation, 1943.34
Brown Daily Herald, 1957.291
Browne, Jack A., 1959.67
Brownfield, Allan C., 1980.57
Brown Girl, Brownstones, 1975.22a
Browning, Alice C., 1944.62, 63; 1945.809, 810, 811, 812; 1946.163, 164, 165
Browning, D. C., 1962.43
Broyard, Anatole, 1974.39
Bruccoli, Matthew J., 1969.201, 232, 234, 235, 236, 240, 241; 1970.50, 60, 63,
    89, 118, 171, 172, 173, 174, 175, 176, 177, 315, 326, 339, 340, 341, 342, 343,
    346, 347, 364; 1971.46, 95, 153; 1977.89

Bruchac, Joseph, 1971.58, 59
Bruck, Peter, 1975.34; 1977.73, 74, 140, 141, 145, 190, 213, 268; 1978.94; 1979.9,
    53, 89; 1980.58, 234; 1982.4
Bruegel, Pete, 1939.61
Brulé, Claude, 1965.46
Brunette, Peter, 1978.51
Brüning, Eberhard, 1975.35; 1980.59
La Brussels Cité, 1951.43
Brussels Dernière Heure, 1950.107
Le Brussels Drapeau Rouge, 1965.57
La Brussels Lanterne, 1947.143
La Brussels Libre Belgique, 1979.22
De Brussels Linie, 1962.11
Brussels L'Occident, 1946.146
Le Brussels Peuple, 1950.226
Le Brussels Phare, 1946.114
Le Brussels Soir, 1950.40; 1979.236
Bryan, A. P., 1941.670
Bryant, Earle V., 1982.22
Bryant, Jerry H., 1971.60; 1972.38; 1973.75; 1976.43; 1981.29
Bryer, Jackson R., 1960.126; 1966.128; 1968.54; 1969.46, 47; 1972.39, 40; 1973.76;
    1974.39a; 1975.35a; 1976.43a; 1977.74a, 74b; 1978.51a, 69, 70, 113, 135, 143,
    171, 172, 208; 1979.54, 115, 144, 178; 1980.224; 1981.30
Bryfonski, Dedria, 1978.49, 87, 133, 148, 192; 1980.35, 60, 132, 179, 198, 224,
    258
Bubbling Brown Sugar, 1976.188
Bucaille, Victor, 1958.91
Buchalter, Helen, 1940.573, 574
Buchanan-Brown, J., 1973.204, 205, 290, 291
Buchanzeiger, 1958.132; 1961.158; 1962.61
Das Bücherblatt, 1957.305; 1959.80; 1961.140
Bücherei und Bildung, 1953.120; 1954.100; 1958.131; 1959.60; 1961.157; 1962.62
Büchereiwesen, 1962.32
Büchereiwesen in Holstein, 1962.1, 30
Die Bücherkommentare, 1958.222; 1960.209; 1961.221, 222; 1966.19
Bücherschau, 1958.70
Bücherschiff, 1958.53; 1959.33; 1962.5, 17, 19; 1965.9; 1966.15
Buch und Volk, 1960.168; 1961.272
Buck, Pearl, 1940.289; 1942.68
Buckley, 1969.148; 1972.135; 1974.69; 1978.222; 1979.72
Buckley, Marylou, 1947.228
Buckmaster, Elizabeth, 1982.24
Buckmaster, Henrietta, 1941.352, 956, 958; 1963.63
Bucks County (Pa.) Courier Times, 1977.319
Budd, Louis J., 1971.61; 1975.36; 1980.246; 1982.23
Budinová, H., 1948.178, 238
Budry, Paul, 1947.157
Buell, Lawrence, 1977.75
Buenos Aires, 1941.753; 1945.376, 488, 621, 745, 1164, 1168; 1949.3, 17, 22, 23,
    25, 34, 35, 37, 38, 42, 55, 59, 61, 63, 72, 73, 89, 94, 108; 1950.61, 70, 240;
    1951.56, 75, 90, 91, 108, 195; 1956.318
Buenos Aires Clarín, 1949.35, 59; 1951.106; 1956.271
Buenos Aires Crítica, 1949.36, 72
La Buenos Aires Epoca, 1949.17, 70; 1951.172
Buenos Aires France-Journal, 1949.94
La Buenos Aires France Nouvelle, 1946.40
Buenos Aires Herald, 1949.42, 49; 1950.131; 1951.55
Buenos Aires Laborista, 1949.23; 1951.209
Buenos Aires Leoplan, 1950.172
Buenos Aires Líder, 1949.64
El Buenos Aires Mundo, 1951.189
La Buenos Aires Nación, 1940.823; 1951.103
La Buenos Aires Prensa, 1949.37, 38
El Buenos Aires Pueblo, 1951.193
Le Buenos Aires Quotidien 1949.58
La Buenos Aires Razón, 1949.25; 1951.13
The Buenos Aires Standard, 1949.63; 1950.85; 1951.67
Buenzod, Emmanuel, 1948.140

Cacciaguerra, Perla, 1964.101a, 101b
Cadot. Michel, 1981.31a
Cady, Edwin H., 1980.246
Cady, Ernest, 1945.835, 836
Cady, Priscilla, 1955.34
Caedmon, 1971.23
Caedmon 1952-1977, 1977.46, 47
Café Monaco, 1973.174; 1977.174
Cafe Society, 1942.276
Café Tournon, 1958.138; 1965.98; 1970.308
Cahen, Jacques-Fernand, 1950.120
Cahiers Critiques du Communisme, 1951.208
Cahiers des Langues Modernes, 1946.269
Cahiers du Monde Nouveau, 1948.14; 1950.14, 188
Cahill, Susan, 1971.64c, 64d
Cahill, Tom, 1971.64c, 64d
Caillet, Gérard, 1948.142; 1951.142
Cain, 1961.261
Cain, Eugene, 1970.79
Cain, James M., 1947.260
Čakovsky, S. A., 1978.53
Calais Nord-Littoral, 1947.62
Caldeira, Maria Isabel, 1980.65
Caldwell, Erskine, 1938.110, 165; 1940.618, 773, 782, 807, 810, 823, 930, 1005;
   1941.506, 596, 753, 758, 759, 894; 1945.771, 779, 951; 1947.8, 194; 1948.134,
   140, 154, 163, 197, 247; 1949.122; 1960.132; 1961.275a; 1963.153; 1972.185;
   1982.50
Il calendario del popolo, 1961.208
The Calgary Herald, 1941.868; 1953.241; 1955.35; 1965.108
Caliban, 1945.349; 1956.255; 1973.118; 1974.60; 1978.99
Caliban, Tucker, 1964.94a
Caliban Without Prospero: Essay on Quebec and Black Literature, 1974.60; 1978.99
California, 1956.116
California English Journal, 1965.97
California Voice, 1938.153
Caliver, Ambrose, 1947.163, 164; 1951.143, 144; 1954.87, 88; 1957.157, 158; 1959.69
The Call, 1945.982; 1950.232
Callahan, John F., 1977.79; 1979.57
Callaloo, 1978.82a; 1979.237, 259; 1980.51, 212, 244; 1982.70a, 119, 140, 143,
   150
Callaway, H. L., 1953.106
Callow, James T., 1977.80
Calloway, Earl, 1978.54
Calmer, Alan, 1935.5, 9; 1938.53, 169, 180, 210; 1939.2
Calmes, Dallas L., 1947.164a
Calta, Louis, 1950.121
Calverton, V. F., 1940.588, 589
Calvin, Bernice, 1941.678
Calvin, Dolores, 1941.678
The Calvin Forum, 1955.27
Camden Courier-Post, 1977.102
Cameron, Kate, 1951.145
Cameron, May, 1938.170, 171; 1939.63; 1940.590
Campbell, Arthur, 1956.276
Campbell, Finley C., 1977.81
Campbell, Mary, 1968.58
Campbell, Ouida, 1940.591
Campbell, Richard, 1943.36, 46; 1968.57
Campbell (Cal.) Press, 1945.1015
Campenni, Frank, 1977.82; 1978.55
Camp Unity, 1938.101
Camus, Albert, 1948.49, 58; 1949.52, 151; 1953.92, 177; 1954.112; 1958.136, 137;
   1959.111, 112, 136a; 1960.159; 1967.54a; 1969.214; 1971.65, 107; 1973.79, 80,
   129, 130; 1975.58, 111; 1977.131, 351; 1978.95; 1980.148; 1981.29, 119; 1982.51
Canada, 1973.112
The Canadian Forum, 1940.1005; 1950.125
The Canadian Review of American Studies, 1979.223
The Canadian Tribune, 1940.983

Carter, Luther, 1957.160
Carter, Michael, 1940.595; 1944.74, 75; 1945.841, 842
Carter, Tom, 1975.40a
Carter G. Woodson Regional Library, 1977.186a
Cartey, Wilfrid G. O., 1969.52
Cartier-Bresson, Henri, 1956.124
Cartosio, Bruno, 1969.53
Cartwright, Marguerite, 1953.107, 108, 109
Carver, George Washington, 1947.293a
Cary, Joyce, 1940.278; 1954.89, 90; 1955.6; 1956.28; 1962.45, 60; 1982.50
Casablanca Maroc-Presse, 1950.23
Casablanca Paris, 1950.18
Le Casablanca Petit Marocain, 1947.240; 1948.197
La Casablanca Vigie Marocaine, 1951.39, 154
Un Cas de viol, 1972.65
Case, Frederick Ivor, 1980.66
The Case for African Freedom and Other Writings on Africa, 1962.45, 60
Caselli, Ron, 1975.41
Casey, Catherine, 1949.88
Casey, Joe, 1939.75
Cash, Earl A., 1973.90
Casmier, Adam A., 1972.46a, 46b
Cassell's Encyclopaedia of Literature, 1953.106
Cassell's Encyclopaedia of World Literature, 1973.204, 290, 291
La Casserole, 1950.186
Cassidy, T. E., 1952.30
Cassill, R. V., 1977.86; 1978.57, 58
Casson, R. Habenicht, 1938.174
The Castle, 1947.236
Casto, John W., 1940.596
Castrence, Pura Santillán, 1940.597
Castro, Américo, 1958.126; 1959.84
Castro, Ramiro Alberto, 1949.89
Catastrophe and Imagination: An Interpretation of the Recent English and American
    Novel, 1957.268
The Catholic Citizen-Herald, 1942.13
Catholic Interracialist, 1955.82
The Catholic Messenger, 1946.275, 284
The Catholic Mirror, 1945.1167
The Catholic News, 1942.12, 14, 17, 45, 101a, 152, 171, 199
Catholics and Catholicism, 1940.961, 962; 1941.795; 1942.12, 13, 14, 17, 18, 31,
    37, 43, 45, 66, 70, 76, 95, 101a, 119, 120, 127, 152, 171, 184, 199, 200, 240,
    354; 1945.998, 999, 1031, 1153; 1956.308; 1957.141, 146, 164, 189, 191, 205,
    215, 219, 243, 255, 266, 270, 273, 284, 302, 306, 319, 333, 345; 1958.86, 102,
    103, 104, 105, 106, 115, 117, 179, 205, 270; 1959.15, 23, 75, 84, 93, 105, 106,
    108, 113, 116, 127, 128; 1960.219, 243; 1962.68; 1971.271; 1973.269, 270
Catholic Theater Movement, 1942.12, 45, 119, 184, 240
The Catholic Worker, 1945.894
The Catholic World, 1940.794; 1941.1058; 1942.268; 1945.1031; 1953.156; 1958.3
Cau, Jean, 1948.65
Cauley, Anne O., 1976.48
Caute, David, 1964.35; 1978.58a
Cavalcade, 1946.115
Cavalcade: Negro American Writing from 1760 to the Present, 1971.7, 57, 82, 83,
    84, 85, 92, 187, 256a, 270
Cavalcade of the American Negro, 1940.239
Cavalcade of the American Novel, 1952.66
Cavallaro, Carmen, 1951.37
Cavanaugh, William C., 1974.41a
Caviar and Cabbage: Selected Columns By Melvin B. Tolson from the Washington Tribune,
    1937-1944, 1982.53a, 136a, 136b, 136c, 136d, 136e
Cayne, Bernard S., 1967.43, 89; 1977.32, 66, 69, 255; 1978.28, 44, 45, 188
Cayton, Horace R., 1940.19, 598, 848; 1941.321, 341, 428, 680, 681, 851; 1942.43,
    196, 216; 1943.31; 1944.76; 1945.311, 323, 340, 355, 443a, 590a, 612, 781, 808,
    817, 843, 844, 845, 846, 1037, 1047, 1079, 1111, 1118, 1124, 1187, 1198; 1946.31,
    56, 140, 141, 142, 170, 171, 172, 173, 174, 239, 243, 263, 264, 275, 279; 1947.166a,
    198; 1948.143; 1950.56; 1951.148; 1953.110; 1960.130; 1962.50, 53, 71, 76, 78;
    1965.48; 1966.25, 32, 33, 76, 125; 1968.59; 1970.19, 64, 80, 81, 82, 180, 296,

Claude-Max, M. C., 1946.77
Claude McKay, 1976.83
Claudia, 1941.121, 123, 155, 220, 231, 334, 487; 1942.41
Clay, 1976.35
Clay, Eugene, 1935.6; 1947.288
Clay, George, 1956.133
Clayton, Ed, 1959.71
Clayton, John J., 1977.93
Clayton, Robert, 1942.217
The Clearwater Sun, 1956.268; 1957.285
Cleaver, Eldridge, 1966.37, 38; 1967.23, 47; 1968.5, 52, 65, 66, 67, 111, 155;
   1969.56a, 57, 63, 169; 1970.5, 70, 88, 89, 90, 250; 1971.70, 71, 87, 147, 307;
   1972.52; 1973.103, 113, 114; 1974.46, 69, 117; 1975.196; 1977.70; 1978.193,
   194, 219; 1979.38, 56, 125; 1980.255
Clefs pour l'Amérique, 1947.265
Clements, Clyde C., Jr., 1970.91
Clemons, Walter, 1979.66
Cleveland, 1941.1027; 1945.477
Cleveland Call and Post, 1945.590; 1977.328
Cleveland Eagle, 1938.247
The Cleveland Gazette, 1941.168, 169, 170, 171, 172; 1945.329
The Cleveland News, 1940.953; 1942.222; 1945.313, 521; 1946.214; 1947.46, 189,
   285, 286, 303; 1953.196; 1954.153
Cleveland Plain Dealer, 1940.866; 1945.293, 465, 1105; 1951.113; 1953.139; 1956.208;
   1958.29; 1963.130, 131; 1966.122
Cleveland Press, 1940.833; 1945.5; 1953.31; 1956.294; 1957.292; 1958.219; 1961.236,
   275; 1977.261
Clift, Virgil A., 1981.9
A Climate for Genius, 1976.5, 145, 167
Climats, 1947.202, 272; 1948.184
Clintonville, 1961.165; 1980.247
Clio, 1981.66
Clouard, Henri, 1950.124
Clough, Ben C., 1944.79
Clubbe, John, 1981.35
Clubbs, Abram A., 1940.607
Club Maintenant, 1946.100; 1948.26, 27
Club St.-Germain-des-Prés, 1948.44
Coates, Robert M., 1936.10
Cobb, Humphrey, 1940.627
Cobb, Nina Kressner, 1975.50; 1978.60; 1982.28
Coblentz, Stanton A., 1945.851
Coburn, Oliver, 1968.133
Cockey, Sarah F., 1957.163
Cocteau, Jean, 1971.72; 1973.95, 96
Coffman, Lillian, 1954.93
Cohan, George M., 1942.13, 14
Cohen, George, 1978.61, 62
Cohen, Octavus Roy, 1945.951
Cohen, P., 1972.177
Cohen, Ruth S., 1979.96, 97, 98
Cohn, Adrian A., 1970.56
Cohn, David L., 1940.379, 608, 612, 696, 697, 713, 854, 914, 926, 940, 996; 1971.72a,
   237a; 1977.292
Cohn, Herbert, 1941.687
Coin, 1973.117
Coindreau, Maurice-Edgard, 1946.177
Coit, Betty Brooks, 1945.852
Colby Library Quarterly, 1979.42; 1982.108
Colcarton, 1944.115
Cold-Spring-on-Hudson, New York, 1978.156
Cole, Charles W., 1970.65a
Cole, Joseph H., 1940.917
Coleman, Robert, 1941.688, 1025; 1960.135, 136
Coleman, William R., 1950.125
Coles, L. F., 1941.689
Coles, Robert, 1971.73, 73a
Coles, Robert Arnold, 1979.68

Flight to Canada, 1978.108
Flight to the West, 1941.837
Flora, Joseph M., 1979.54
Flowers, Paul, 1945.901; 1953.124; 1965.63
Flowers, Sandra Hollin, 1981.46
The Flowers of Friendship: Letters Written to Gertrude Stein, 1953.132, 238, 239,
    249
Floyd, Mrs. T. M., 1940.654
"Flying Home," 1976.143
Focus, 1959.49; 1969.68
Focus: Themes in Literature, 1969.50, 51
Focus/Midwest, 1963.70
Foderaro, Sal J., 1980.107
Foerster, Norman, 1970.126
Fogarty, Robert S., 1963.83
Fohlen, C., 1971.116a
Foi et Vie, 1950.238
Foley, Barbara, 1980.97; 1981.47, 81
Foley, Martha, 1938.13, 253; 1941.250; 1946.145; 1947.217; 1948.159; 1949.101;
    1958.59, 175, 209; 1965.20, 31, 64, 79; 1968.141; 1969.61; 1975.77, 78; 1980.98,
    183, 184; 1981.60
Folket i Bild, 1956.200a; 1959.135a
The Folk Roots of Contemporary Afro-American Poetry, 1974.24
Foner, Philip S., 1972.70
Fonlon, Bernard, 1980.189
Fontaine, André, 1950.147
Fontaine, Pierre, 1947.188; 1948.164
Fontaine, William T., 1959.82; 1967.41; 1978.257
Fontellio-Nanton, H. I., 1953.125
Fontemara, 1949.85
Fontenot, Chester J., 1977.133; 1979.103, 104; 1980.99; 1981.48, 49, 50, 131
Fonzi, Bruno, 1947.25; 1959.143
Foote, Bird, 1970.130
Foote, Robert O., 1945.902
"Footnote on Filth," 1938.203
Forbes, Calvin, 1979.122
La Force des choses, 1963.51
Force of Circumstance, 1965.35; 1977.55
Force Ouvrière, 1947.268; 1950.150
For Colored Girls Who Have Considered Suicide When the Rainbow Is Enuff, 1981.46
Ford, Clebert, 1977.134
Ford, Guy Stanton, 1957.7, 46, 113; 1958.6, 36, 68
Ford, James W., 1938.48, 151, 199, 243; 1939.15, 49; 1940.269, 518, 700; 1941.360,
    723; 1942.230; 1944.89; 1981.96
Ford, Miriam Allen de, 1976.73
Ford, Nick Aaron, 1941.538, 724, 725; 1949.20, 103; 1950.148; 1953.126; 1954.103,
    104; 1958.121, 122, 123, 124; 1961.149; 1962.57; 1964.56, 57; 1969.86; 1970.131;
    1971.56a, 71, 93, 117, 118, 119, 120, 121, 122, 186; 1973.149, 150; 1977.135,
    147
Ford's Theater, 1942.61, 180
Foree, James J., 1953.127, 128
Foreign Affairs, 1950.36, 245; 1956.21, 282; 1957.299
Foreigners: The Making of American Literature 1900-1940, 1981.76; 1982.91, 101,
    151
Foreign Literature, 1957.311
Foreman, Ellen, 1980.100
Foreman, Paul B., 1967.99
"Forerunner and Ambassador," 1977.54, 74; 1978.135
The Forerunners: Black Poets in America, 1975.83; 1981.56
Forever Amber, 1946.153, 154
Forgotten Pages of American Literature, 1970.114, 161, 163, 164, 165, 166, 167,
    168
For Malcolm: Poems on the Life and Death of Malcolm X, 1967.55
Formes et Couleurs, 1946.277
"For My People," 1970.220
Forrest, Alma, 1941.251
Forrest, Leon, 1971.14, 123; 1980.101
Förster, I., 1966.55

Friday, 1940.357, 539; 1941.424
Fried, Erich, 1966.4, 6, 40
Fried, Lewis, 1975.71; 1980.119
Friedberg, Maurice, 1976.78; 1977.143
Friede, Donald, 1940.656a
Die Friedens Rundschau, 1957.69
Friedhoff, Herman, 1977.42
Friedland, Jacques, 1948.165
Friedman, Emanuel, 1973.255
Friedman, Saul, 1966.60, 61
Friedrich, Patterson McLean, 1945.906
Friese Koerier, 1957.32; 1960.195
"Frightened Children of Frightened Parents," 1945.590a; 1950.56
Frihet, 1956.70
Frings, Ketti, 1959.28, 41, 98, 139, 145; 1960.7, 9, 11, 12, 15, 16, 30, 32, 33,
    34, 42, 45, 46, 48, 49, 52, 86, 90, 91, 95, 102, 110, 111, 115, 131, 135, 136,
    137, 139, 152, 153, 157, 176, 177, 186, 188, 189, 193, 196, 203, 205, 237, 251,
    260, 262, 263, 264, 265, 266, 270; 1961.117; 1962.36; 1964.121; 1966.79; 1969.24,
    227; 1976.30, 103, 185
Frisch, Morton J., 1968.99
Frisé, Adolf, 1958.126; 1959.84; 1960.150, 151; 1961.150
From a Black Perspective: Contemporary Black Essays, 1970.230
From Apology to Protest: The Black American Novel, 1973.266; 1977.187; 1978.3
From Behind the Veil: A Study of Afro-American Narrative, 1979.243; 1980.31, 50,
    77, 89, 117, 130, 214; 1981.100, 104, 106, 135
"From Experience to Eloquence: Richard Wright's Black Boy as Art," 1977.48
From LeRoi Jones To Amiri Baraka: The Literary Works, 1973.186
From Mammies to Militants: Domestics in Black American Literature, 1982.68, 82
From Plantation to Ghetto: An Interpretive History of American Negroes, 1966.103
From Sambo to Superspade: The Black Experience in Motion Pictures, 1975.122
From Self to Society, 1919-1941, 1972.56
From Slavery to Freedom: A History of American Negroes, 1947.190; 1956.158
From Slavery to Freedom: A History of Negro Americans, 1967.42; 1974.73
From the Ashes: Voices of Watts, 1967.92; 1969.217
From the Dark Tower: Afro-American Writers 1900 to 1960, 1974.52; 1975.5, 18,
    99
From the Mountain, 1972.185
From the Roots, 1970.193, 194, 195, 196, 197, 198, 200, 201, 202, 203, 204
Front and Center, 1979.131
Frye, Northrup, 1977.131
F.-T., 1948.162
Ft. Lauderdale News, 1957.147
Fujii, Motoharu, 1972.76b
Fujikura, Koichiro, 1973.195a
Fujita, Takemasa, 1969.91a
Fulks, Bryan, 1969.92
Fuller, Chet, 1981.51
Fuller, Edmund, 1949.6, 43; 1953.129; 1956.162; 1958.127; 1963.87
Fuller, Hoyt W., 1953.130, 131; 1961.151, 152; 1964.59; 1965.68; 1967.46; 1968.102,
    103, 104, 105; 1969.93, 94, 95; 1971.128, 129, 130; 1972.77, 78, 79, 98; 1981.52
Fuller, John G., 1965.69
Fuller, Ruth Wolfe, 1961.124
Fullerton, Garry, 1956.163
Fullinwider, S. P., 1969.96; 1974.76
Fulton, Len, 1978.104
Funaroff, Ben, 1938.245
Funk, Charles Earle, 1939.88; 1941.892; 1942.212; 1946.259
Funke, Lewis, 1960.152, 153
Furfey, Paul Hanly, 1945.907
The Furious Passage of James Baldwin, 1966.46; 1968.79
Furman, A. L., 1946.29, 283
Furnas, J. C., 1956.164
Fürst, Ludwig, 1961.153
Furukawa, Hiromi, 1969.96a, 97; 1970.139b; 1973.151b
Fussell, Edwin, 1970.140, 286
The Future in the Present: Selected Writings, 1977.179, 180
Fyfe, Christopher, 1962.60
Fyfe, Hamilton, 1946.200

Green, Ralph Waldo, 1940.754
Green, Rita, 1971.154
Green Bay Press-Gazette, 1940.805; 1945.572
Greene, Beatrice, 1940.188
Greene, Graham, 1947.223, 236; 1956.122
Greene, J. Lee, 1977.152; 1979.115; 1980.114
Greenlee, Bob, 1977.153
Greenlee, Sam, 1969.114
Green Pastures, 1941.852, 936; 1942.13, 14
Greensboro Daily News, 1938.265, 876; 1941.538, 757, 947; 1954.159; 1957.275;
  1973.55; 1977.58, 325; 1978.14, 40, 239, 240
Greensburg (Pa.) Tribune-Review, 1961.11
Greenspan, Charlotte, 1971.155
Greenville, Mississippi, 1952.42
The Greenville (N.C.) Daily Reflector, 1956.239; 1958.1
Greenwall, June, 1941.747
Greenway, John, 1953.142
Greenwich Press, 1938.129; 1940.11, 165; 1941.569
Greenwich Village, 1945.673, 787, 791, 792, 1178; 1946.218; 1947.122; 1949.132
Gregg, Charles, 1953.143
Gregory, Claude, 1971.116a
Gregory, Horace, 1938.7
Greiff, John B., 1957.194; 1958.141
Grenander, M. E., 1977.154
Grene, Marjorie, 1961.184
Grennard, Elliott, 1942.246
Gresham, Jewell, 1976.89a
Gresson, Aaron David, III, 1982.63
Grevenius, Herbert, 1945.925
Grey, 1951.172
Grieder, Theodore, 1979.91, 167, 168, 169, 170
Griffin, John Howard, 1979.195
Griffin, L. W., 1978.121
Griffin, Tom F., 1940.687
Griffith, Albert J., 1957.195
Griffith, D. W., 1940.743, 750
Griffith, Paul, 1945.789
Griffiths, Clyde, 1940.729; 1955.49; 1960.210; 1972.92; 1979.119; 1981.58; 1982.66
Griggs, Sutton, 1974.156, 167
Grigorescu, Dan, 1977.155
Grigor'ev, V., 1938.211
Grigson, Geoffrey, 1963.23
Grillparzer, Franz, 1961.153
Grimes, Alan, 1956.173
Grimm, Percy, 1979.72
Grippe-Soleil, 1946.209
Grodzins, Morton, 1956.174, 329
Groh, George W., 1972.91a
Grommon, Alfred H., 1967.79, 83; 1976.53, 138, 139, 147
Gromo, Mario, 1951.173, 174
Gromyko, Andrei, 1944.24
Gross, Barry, 1976.90; 1977.156
Gross, Ben, 1941.748
Gross, Bernard, 1970.16a, 43a
Gross, R. H., 1940.308
Gross, Robert A., 1969.115
Gross, Seymour L., 1966.18, 21, 47, 64, 65, 66; 1967.56, 67; 1968.182; 1969.52;
  1974.85; 1975.92; 1976.3; 1977.217, 297
Gross, Theodore L., 1964.63; 1968.83, 86, 119, 120; 1969.116, 117, 233; 1970.129;
  1971.156, 157, 158; 1975.93; 1978.122; 1980.115
Der grosse Brockhaus, 1957.105
Das grosse Duden-Lexikon, 1968.29
Der grosse Herder, 1956.88
Der grosse Knaur, 1968.30
Das grosse Nymphenburger Volkslexikon, 1964.20
Grosse Pointe, Michigan, 1966.60, 61
Grosset & Dunlap, 1942.10, 191
Grossman, Sid, 1941.749

H., B. K., 1940.689
H., E., 1956.179, 180, 181, 182, 183, 184, 185, 186, 187, 188, 189, 190; 1957.197,
    198, 199, 200; 1961.166
H., E. N., 1963.98
H., Ed., 1950.162
H., H., 1952.39; 1960.160
H., H. H., 1938.212
H., H. J., 1954.108
H., H. W., 1962.66
H., J., 1966.67; 1974.87
H., J.-J., 1947.208
H., M., 1951.177
H., R. F., 1941.751; 1945.931; 1950.163; 1957.201
H., R. O., 1956.191
H., W., 1960.161
H., W. B., 1980.117
Haagsch Dagblad, 1957.90
Haagsche Courant, 1947.107
Haagsche Post, 1947.107
Haas, Joseph, 1969.119; 1970.154
Haas, Robert Bartlett, 1964.65; 1973.154
Haas, Rudolf, 1973.162; 1974.87a
Haas, Victor P., 1967.52
Haas, Willy, 1956.192
Habe, Hans, 1950.41, 238
Haberly, David T., 1976.91
Hach, Clarence W., 1970.155, 283, 284
Hackett, Alice Payne, 1941.752; 1945.932; 1953.144; 1954.109; 1956.193; 1964.66
Hackett, Walter, 1957.202
Haddon, Bruce, 1944.96; 1945.933
Haden, Allen, 1941.753
Hafner, Richard P., Jr., 1954.110
Hafsia, Jelila, 1979.118
Hagelberg, Günter, 1967.53
Hagen Hessische Nachrichten, 1956.316
Haginome, Hiromichi, 1955.49
Hagnauer, Roger, 1973.160
Hagopian, John V., 1963.99; 1969.120; 1971.160
Hague, John A., 1979.251, 252, 272
Hahn, K. J., 1957.203
Haight, Anne Lyon, 1978.125
Haiku, 1962.40a; 1964.78; 1966.73, 85, 102; 1967.28; 1969.76, 77, 78, 170; 1970.124,
    167, 233, 234; 1973.70, 84, 121, 151b; 1974.41a, 42, 132; 1976.95; 1977.106;
    1982.49, 85, 136
Haiku, 1982.85
Hairston, Loyle, 1963.100
Haislip, Bryan, 1959.89
Haiti, 1950.5, 48, 63, 67, 68, 155, 156, 157, 158, 159, 160, 161, 184, 200; 1959.120;
    1961.134; 1972.151; 1973.228
Haiti Journal, 1950.63, 200
Hajek, Friederike, 1972.92
Hakel, Hermann, 1962.67
Hakutani, Yoshinobu, 1954.184; 1955.49; 1956.102, 200, 304; 1957.224, 310, 311;
    1958.155, 239, 246; 1959.95, 104, 118; 1960.210, 211, 213, 236, 241, 249, 252,
    253; 1961.223, 224; 1964.77, 95; 1971.247; 1972.90, 129, 179, 197; 1973.159,
    280; 1974.132, 141, 171; 1975.133; 1976.115, 204; 1978.226, 227; 1979.119, 191,
    253, 255; 1980.27, 118, 119; 1981.7, 61, 132; 1982.11, 14, 15, 28, 43, 48, 49,
    51, 61, 64, 65, 66, 72, 77, 83, 84, 90, 96, 100, 106, 118, 130, 136
Halcrow, J. M., 1970.156
Hale, T. L., 1956.194
Hale, Thomas A., 1976.92; 1977.157
Haley, Alex, 1965.128; 1966.150; 1977.28, 30, 157; 1979.73; 1980.4
Half a Hundred Tales, 1945.434, 443, 610, 938, 1083, 1109, 1110, 1189
Hall, Cameron P., 1945.934
Hall, Clara, 1940.199, 690, 691
Hall, Donald, 1979.120, 121; 1981.62
Hall, Florencia, 1941.754
Hall, Juanita, 1951.37

Haywood, Harry, 1979.241
Hayworth, Rita, 1940.836; 1948.17
Hazard, Eloise Perry, 1952.43
Hazleton News, 1940.840
Hazleton Standard-Sentinel, 1940.896
Hazleton Standard-Speaker, 1977.315
Hazoumé, Paul, 1980.5
Headings, Philip R., 1964.111; 1966.128; 1968.54; 1969.47; 1972.40; 1973.76; 1974.39a;
   1975.35a; 1976.43a; 1977.74a, 74b; 1978.51a; 1979.82a; 1980.68; 1981.34
Headlines and Pictures, 1945.335, 674; 1946.58
Healy, J. J., 1981.65
Heard, Nathan, 1974.177
Hearings Before the Committee on Un-American Activities, House of Representatives,
   Eighty-Fourth Congress, First Session, 1955.62
Hearings Before the Committee on Un-American Activities, Ninetieth Congress, Second
   Session, 1968.188
Hearn, Charles R., 1977.169
Hearst, Patricia, 1978.198, 205, 224
Hearst, William Randolph, 1941.159, 161, 215, 223, 228, 363, 365, 390, 602, 603,
   604, 624, 845, 900, 1025
The Heart Is a Lonely Hunter, 1966.48; 1969.89, 149; 1973.106; 1977.155; 1980.161
Hearts and Minds: The Anatomy of Racism from Roosevelt to Reagan, 1982.13
Heath, Gordon, 1945.583
Heathcliff, 1940.823
The Heath Introduction to Literature, 1977.93
Heaton, Joan, 1972.49
Hedin, Raymond, 1979.124; 1981.66; 1982.69, 70, 125
Heermance, J. Noel, 1964.70
Heer, wat een Dag, 1967.3
Heidegger, Martin, 1948.221, 222; 1979.190
Heidelberg Rhein-Neckar-Zeitung, 1960.3
Heidenheimer Zeitung, 1957.23; 1961.64
Heidnisches Spanien, 1958.24, 25, 48, 49, 50, 54, 61, 62, 77, 102, 103, 104, 105,
   106, 117, 126, 128, 145, 149, 150, 151, 156, 157, 179, 183, 184, 222, 223, 242,
   269, 270; 1959.10, 11, 14, 15, 16, 17, 23, 24, 25, 33, 35, 40, 44, 52, 54, 57,
   58, 60, 64, 75, 76, 77, 80, 84, 92, 93, 105, 106, 108, 113, 116, 123, 127, 128,
   129, 133, 135, 138, 144; 1960.26, 94, 168, 239, 243; 1961.87, 227; 1962.54
Heigl, Otto, 1979.125
Heil, Piet, 1962.68
Heimat und Welt, 1962.20
Heipen, J. J. van, 1958.148
Heise, H.-J., 1962.69
Helbig, Karl, 1961.172
Held, Robert, 1958.149
Helfling, Dorothy, 1940.714
Helgesen, Hjalmar, 1956.89
Heller, Arno, 1972.95
Hellman, Lillian, 1941.29, 107, 117, 118, 119, 123, 125, 160, 217, 220, 236, 242,
   411, 446, 447, 581, 635, 762, 780, 831, 891, 905, 1012, 1037, 1038, 1040; 1942.149,
   160, 190, 261; 1944.104; 1972.6
Hellström-Kennedy, Marika, 1956.200a
Helmreich, William B., 1977.170
Helsinki Hufvudstadsbladet, 1949.127
Helterman, Jeffrey, 1978.55, 76, 82, 127, 140, 236
Helwig, Werner, 1958.150; 1959.92
Helyar, Thelma, 1963.103
Hemenway, Robert, 1970.50, 60, 63, 89, 118, 126a, 171, 172, 173, 174, 175, 176,
   177, 315, 325, 364; 1977.171, 172, 332; 1978.110; 1979.1, 125a
Hemingway, Ernest, 1938.186, 197, 288; 1939.44, 45; 1940.723, 746, 860, 974; 1941.493;
   1944.3, 64; 1946.153, 154, 256; 1947.142, 208; 1948.149, 219, 227; 1953.248;
   1956.314; 1957.332, 333; 1958.270; 1961.66; 1962.48, 67, 105; 1963.64; 1969.106;
   1973.132; 1974.44; 1976.204; 1978.40; 1979.40, 126; 1980.6
Henderson, David, 1969.123
Henderson, Ernie, 1941.189, 190
Henderson, Mae Gwendolyn, 1972.37a
Henderson, Rudy, 1941.193
Henderson, Sam H., 1970.302
Henderson, Stephen E., 1969.59, 124; 1972.96, 107, 172; 1973.179; 1982.70a

Just Above My Head, 1979.38, 139, 266; 1980.57
Justice, 1940.933
Justice Denied: The Black Man in White America, 1970.83, 84
Justus, James H., 1970.211a; 1971.191; 1972.105a; 1974.103; 1975.112

K., 1961.187
K., G., 1951.187
K., J. S., 1946.221
K., R., 1957.235, 236
K., V. E., 1948.181
Kabnis, 1971.116
Kaempffert, Waldemar, 1944.113
Kafka, Franz, 1940.823; 1947.8, 236, 248; 1948.76, 96; 1958.231; 1972.146; 1973.100a;
    1982.57
Kahin, George McT., 1956.97, 169, 208, 260, 336
Kahle, Roger, 1970.212
Kahn, Barbara, 1977.188
Kaichoon, 1957.224
Kaiser, Ernest, 1948.182; 1962.76; 1963.122, 123; 1964.81; 1967.67; 1969.136,
    137; 1970.213, 214; 1971.189, 249; 1972.106; 1977.88, 165, 167, 188a, 189, 348;
    1978.137; 1979.144, 145
Kakonis, Thomas E., 1969.138
Kala-Lobé, Iwiye, 1961.188
Kallen, Horace M., 1966.91
Kalmucks, 1956.319
Kamarck, Edward L., 1968.138
Kaminsky, Marc, 1971.190
Kanagawa Kenritsu Gaigo Tanki Daigaku Kiyo, 1972.179
Kaname, Hiroshi, 1973.191a; 1975.113
Kanapa, Jean, 1947.218; 1948.54, 87, 183; 1955.78
Kanapa, M., 1948.17
Kanashiki, Noriko, 1982.79
Kanashiki, Tsutomu, 1972.154
Kane, Harnett T., 1947.46, 54
Kann, Red, 1951.188
Kansas, 1969.189, 197
Kansas Authors Club, 1938.49
Kansas City, Missouri, 1945.472, 473, 477, 541, 542, 543, 544, 545, 546, 547,
    548, 549
The Kansas City Call, 1938.104, 142, 188; 1940.387, 628; 1941.363, 624
The Kansas City Star, 1940.346, 347, 348, 349, 350, 351, 352, 353, 354, 355, 853;
    1945.377, 456, 541, 542, 543, 544, 545, 546, 547, 548, 549, 550, 551, 552, 553,
    554, 555, 556, 557, 558, 559, 560, 561, 562, 563, 564, 565, 566, 567, 1088;
    1963.162; 1973.36, 241; 1977.97; 1978.98
Kansas English, 1969.91, 197
Kansas Quarterly, 1975.26, 37a, 114, 148, 172
Kantor, MacKinlay, 1945.975
Kanzaki, Hiroshi, 1977.189a
Kaplan, Sidney, 1969.204
Kapustka, Bruce, 1940.745, 746
The Kapustkan, 1940.745, 746
Karas, Edith, 1973.223
Karcher, Carolyn L., 1980.134
Karger, George, 1945.282, 630
Karim, 1948.156, 179
Karl, Frederick R., 1971.191; 1973.163, 164; 1978.126
Károly, Ákos, 1972.19
Karowski, Adam, 1972.18
Karrer, Wolfgang, 1973.192; 1977.190; 1978.94; 1982.4
Kasavubu, Maxwell, 1974.149a; 1976.153a; 1979.229
Kasseler Post, 1956.180
Kasunose, Yoshiko, 1974.103a
Kato, Tsunehiko, 1982.80, 81
Katopes, Peter J., 1978.171, 172
Kattan, Naim, 1966.92
Katterjohn, Elsie, 1969.68
Katz, 1945.456
Katz, Joseph, 1969.201, 232, 234, 235, 236, 240, 241; 1970.50, 60, 63, 89, 118,

171, 172, 173, 174, 175, 176, 177, 315, 326, 339, 340, 341, 342, 343, 346, 347, 364; 1971.46, 95, 153
Katz, Sidney M., 1946.223
Katz, William Loren, 1971.191a
Katzenschlager, Hans, 1962.77
Kauffman, George, 1939.89
Kauffmann, Stanley, 1967.68
Kaufman, Bob, 1965.87; 1972.107
Kaufman, Kenneth C., 1940.747
Kaufman, Wallace, 1969.209
Kaufmann, Herbert, 1956.222, 223
Kaukosen, Väinö, 1971.308
Kawabe, Koichi, 1970.214a
Kaye, Danny, 1941.163; 1958.85; 1973.68, 256
Kaye, Philip B., 1965.42; 1974.177
Kazin, Alfred, 1942.254; 1944.114; 1951.180; 1956.203, 224; 1961.118, 182, 189; 1963.110, 113, 114; 1969.139; 1971.192; 1972.27; 1973.192a; 1975.104; 1978.138, 193; 1980.135; 1981.73, 74; 1982.72
Keady, Sylvia H., 1976.109; 1981.120
Kearns, Edward, 1971.193; 1973.6, 256
Kearns, Francis E., 1970.117, 215, 216, 217, 218, 219, 220, 221, 222, 223
Keating, L. Clark, 1971.49
Keene Evening Sentinel, 1944.9
"Keep A-Inchin' Along": Selected Writings of Carl Van Vechten About Black Arts and Letters, 1979.146, 269, 270
Kees, Weldon, 1937.27
Kein, Sybil, 1977.191
Keith, Allen, 1938.228
Keller, Allen, 1941.776
Kelley, William Melvin, 1964.94a; 1966.45; 1967.27b; 1968.4, 156; 1972.130; 1973.197; 1977.52, 145; 1980.58
Kellner, Bruce, 1968.139; 1979.146, 147, 269, 270
Kelly, Ernece B., 1972.108, 109
Kelly, J. Livert, 1941.133
Kelly, James, 1958.175
Kelly, Mary, 1970.224
Kelly, Paul, 1937.28
Kemp, Yakini Belinda, 1982.82
Kempton, Murray, 1964.82
Kendricks, Ralph, 1970.225, 226
Kennedy, Ellen Conroy, 1974.104
Kennedy, Gerald, 1959.103
Kennedy, James G., 1972.53, 110; 1974.1; 1979.116
Kennedy, John F., 1960.27; 1961.19; 1963.40
Kennedy, Mark, 1953.5
Kennedy, Randall, 1980.136
Kennedy, Raymond, 1945.976
Kennedy, Robert, 1968.43; 1969.158
Kenny, Howard N., 1961.190
Kenny, Vincent S., 1971.194
Kenosha News, 1977.20
Kent, George E., 1967.69; 1968.140; 1969.140, 141; 1970.227; 1971.195, 196; 1972.27, 111, 112, 113, 114, 115, 116, 117; 1973.144; 1975.114; 1976.110; 1980.99
Kent, Rockwell, 1941.467
Kent Cleaner, 1942.310
Kentera, George, 1958.176
Kent State University, 1975.187; 1977.188a
Kenya, 1956.25; 1959.1; 1960.2; 1963.1
Kenyatta, Jomo, 1963.1
The Kenyon Review, 1951.170; 1961.260; 1966.63
Keown, Don, 1963.124
Keraly, Charlotte, 1947.219
Kerkblad, 1957.91
Kerk en Missie, 1958.133
Kermesse héroïque, 1951.45
Kerr, Walter, 1960.176, 177
Kerr, Wilfred H., 1945.977
Kessel, Patrick, 1960.178

Literature and Morality, 1947.184
Literature and Religion: A Study in Conflict, 1960.159
Literature and the Urban Experience, 1981.14, 45, 69, 74, 94
Literature at the Barricades: The American Writer in the 1930s, 1982.20, 102
Literature V, 1970.234, 235
Literature V: Teacher's Guide, 1970.233
Literature for Adolescents: Teaching Poems, Stories, Novels, and Plays, 1975.65
Literature for Today's Young Adults, 1980.80
Literature in the Modern World, 1954.81a
The Literature of America, 1971.267
The Literature of Memory: Modern Writers of the American South, 1977.151
The Literature of the American People, 1951.249
"The Literature of the Negro," 1933.1
"The Literature of the Negro in the United States," 1945.522, 620; 1948.223, 231;
    1949.117; 1951.15, 83, 84, 137, 158, 221; 1957.93, 260, 265, 323; 1958.121,
    214, 238; 1959.76, 79; 1962.100; 1964.8; 1967.54; 1968.62, 166; 1969.137; 1970.367;
    1971.298; 1972.193; 1973.179; 1975.83; 1978.261a; 1981.11, 56
The Literature of the South, 1952.13, 22; 1968.218
A Literature Without Qualities: American Writing Since 1945, 1979.40
Literaturlexikon 20. Jahrhundert, 1971.305
Literaturnaia gazeta, 1940.2
Literaturnyi kritik, 1938.157
Litt, Iris, 1947.228
Littell, Robert, 1940.771
Le Littéraire, 1946.100, 106, 209
Litterair Paspoort, 1947.211; 1953.222, 237; 1956.296; 1959.130; 1961.255, 277;
    1963.164
La Littérature, 1970.16a, 43a
La Littérature américaine, 1950.120
Littérature de notre temps: Ecrivains americains, 1972.41, 61, 68, 137b, 142a,
    176a
Littérature du vingtième siècle, 1955.70; 1961.248
Littérature noire américaine, 1949.117
Les Littératures d'expression française: Négritude africaine, negritude caraibe,
    1973.131, 193
Little, Stuart W., 1960.188, 189
"The Little Black Boy," 1969.138
Littlejohn, David, 1966.97, 135; 1967.56; 1968.182; 1969.75, 160; 1970.249; 1978.148
Little Rock, 1957.24; 1959.110
Little Rock Arkansas Gazette, 1953.50; 1956.140; 1957.217
Litwack, Leon F., 1976.98
Litz, A. Walton, 1975.125; 1980.150, 151; 1981.101
Lives of Mississippi Authors, 1981.40, 123
Living American Literature, 1947.301
The Living Torch, 1940.719
Le Livre, 1948.247
Livres, 1964.35a
Llellewyn, Richard, 1940.635; 1941.493
Llorens, David, 1968.155; 1969.161; 1973.175
Lloyd, James B., 1981.123
Lobenthal, Martin, 1940.772
Lochard, Metz T. P., 1945.1000
Locke, Alain, 1937.29, 30; 1938.232; 1939.1, 13, 91, 92, 93; 1940.773; 1941.796,
    797, 798; 1942.269, 270, 271; 1943.47; 1947.229; 1948.129, 190; 1949.125; 1950.174;
    1952.49, 50, 51; 1953.174; 1954.31, 138; 1958.187; 1960.190; 1968.126; 1971.215;
    1978.193; 1979.141; 1982.58
Locke, Louis, 1954.74
Locke, W. R., 1957.255
Lockhart, Jack, 1940.774
Lockridge, Richard, 1941.799, 800
Lockwood, Lee, 1970.250
Lodi Times, 1938.269
Loetscher, Hugo, 1959.113
Loewel, Pierre, 1947.230; 1950.175
Loewen, James W., 1974.45
Loftis, N. J., 1973.211; 1976.199; 1977.214
Logan, Floyd, 1961.199
Logan, Rayford Whittingham, 1940.775; 1945.1149; 1952.51a; 1955.32, 55; 1957.184;

Lubis, Mochtar, 1956.237; 1960.257
Lucas, Curtis, 1958.85; 1965.42; 1973.68, 256; 1974.177
Luccock, Halford E., 1941.802
Luce, Phillip Abbott, 1962.82; 1977.216
Ludington, Charles Townsend, Jr., 1970.251
Ludington, Tracy, 1945.1003
Ludwig, Richard M., 1959.114; 1963.71, 89, 172, 177; 1972.187; 1973.212; 1974.52,
77, 88, 165, 169
Lukas, Paul, 1941.29, 832
Lund, 1956.66
Lund, Helen, 1947.228
Lundén, Rolf, 1976.118
Lundquist, James, 1976.119
Lunds Dagblad, 1956.66
Lunger, Phil, 1956.238; 1957.257
Il lungo sogno, 1962.9, 14
Lunin, D., 1940.778
Luskin, Michael M., 1956.239
Lyman, Helen H., 1961.202
Lynch, Acklyn R., 1978.150
Lynch, Dennis Daley, 1978.151
Lynch, Hollis R., 1973.213; 1980.49, 67
The Lynchburg Daily Advance, 1938.122
Lynd, Helen Merrell, 1945.1124
Lynd, Robert S., 1945.1124
Lynd, Stoughton, 1963.135
Lynn, Conrad, 1979.161
Lynn, Kenneth S., 1969.162, 163, 164; 1971.216; 1973.214
Lyon Libre, 1946.120; 1947.252
Le Lyon Progrès, 1947.5; 1951.76
Lyons, Eugene, 1941.803
Lyons, Leonard, 1938.233; 1940.779; 1941.804, 805, 806, 807, 808, 809, 810, 811,
812, 813, 814, 815, 816, 817, 818, 819, 820, 821, 822, 823, 824, 825; 1942.273,
274, 275, 276, 277, 278; 1943.48, 49; 1944.118, 119, 120, 121; 1945.1004; 1946.228,
229, 230, 231, 232; 1947.233, 234; 1949.126; 1955.60; 1956.240; 1960.192
Lyons, Thomas T., 1971.217
Le Lyons Journal du Soir, 1951.40
Lyra, F., 1978.152; 1981.84a
Lytell, 1942.76
Lytle, Andrew, 1958.188
Lytle, Charlotte, 1961.202a

M., A., 1951.193
M., A. M. W., 1942.279
M., A. S., 1940.780
M., B., 1957.258
M., E., 1962.83
M., F., 1961.203; 1962.84
M., G. E., 1938.234
M., H., 1942.280; 1948.191; 1962.85
M., I., 1956.241
M., J., 1941.826
M., J. S., 1949.127
M., M. H., 1946.233
M., S., 1961.204
M., T., 1961.205
M., T. B., 1958.189
M., W., 1952.52
M., W. E. J., 1942.280a
Maas, Willard, 1941.826a
Maasbode, 1947.107
McAleer, John J., 1968.167; 1974.121
Macbeth, 1940.534; 1943.14; 1966.31; 1978.156
McBride, David, 1977.221
McBride, Rebecca Susan, 1976.124; 1977.221
McC., R., 1940.787
McCabe, Bernard J., 1971.172
McCaffrey, John, 1945.451, 728; 1982.50

Marden, Charles F., 1968.159
A Margin of Hope: An Intellectual Autobiography, 1982.73
Margolies, Edward L. 1965.59; 1966.98; 1968.94, 160, 211, 217; 1969.10, 18, 19,
    22, 54, 58, 76, 90, 118, 120, 128, 131, 136, 153, 154, 167, 168, 169, 177, 189,
    225, 237, 243, 250, 252; 1970.190, 253, 254, 255, 256, 257, 262, 335, 359; 1971.112,
    313; 1972.144a; 1973.133, 137, 216; 1974.118; 1975.126, 160; 1976.68; 1978.193;
    1979.47, 111, 167, 168, 169, 170; 1980.109; 1981.7; 1982.47, 96, 97
Margolies, Joseph A., 1945.623, 1008
Margolin, Leo, 1941.842
Margot, 1951.198
Marguth, George, 1956.243
Maria-Nègre, 1948.65
Mariano, Louis, 1940.982
Mar'ianov, M., 1938.240; 1939.46
Marie Curie-Sktodowska University, 1978.152
Marietta, 1950.177
Marinette Eagle-Star, 1945.464
Marion, George, Jr., 1942.151
The Marion Star, 1940.372
Mariott, Charles, 1940.783
Marja, A., 1960.194, 195
The Mark and the Knowledge: Social Stigma in Classic American Fiction, 1979.207
Marker, Chris, 1948.193
Markmann, Charles Lam, 1967.37; 1968.95
Markowitz, Norman, 1981.85
Marks, Robert, 1965.99
Mark Twain's Sure-Fire Guide to Backgrounds in American Literature, 1977.343
Marqués, Claudio, 1956.244
The Marquette Daily Mining Journal, 1940.541
Marquis, Albert Nelson, 1942.194
Marquis, Riley F., Jr., 1961.10
Marr, Warren, III, 1976.146
La Marseillaise, 1947.291
Marseilles Dernière Heure, 1948.17, 59
Marseilles Midi-Soir, 1946.39; 1948.134
Marsh, Fred T., 1938.241
Marsh, Robert C., 1957.263
Marshall, Carol, 1969.170
Marshall, Illinois, 1957.128
Marshall, John, 1954.140
Marshall, Margaret, 1940.261, 784; 1946.278; 1960.207
Marshall, Paule, 1966.45; 1967.27b; 1975.22a; 1978.126a; 1979.77a; 1980.67
Marshall, Russell, 1937.4
Marshall, Sara, 1979.171
Marshall, Stanley, 1950.178
Marshall, Thurgood, 1965.56
Martellotti, Guido, 1955.21
Martens, Johannes Skancke, 1948.194; 1950.179; 1953.177; 1954.141; 1956.245, 246
Martin, Donald F., 1976.38
Martin, Fletcher, 1954.142, 143; 1956.247
Martin, Gertrude Scott, 1945.1009, 1010, 1011, 1012, 1013; 1953.178, 179, 180
Martin, Helen, 1941.368
Martin, Herbert W., 1973.217
Martin, Jay, 1970.259a; 1975.68
Martin, Joan, 1977.218
Martin, Judith, 1979.172
Martin, Katherine Anne, 1972.145
Martin, Kenneth K., 1965.100
Martin, Lawrence, 1938.242; 1940.564, 785; 1978.158
Martin, Linton, 1942.287
Martin, Lowell A., 1960.190, 197
Martin, Mildred, 1951.199
Martin, Ralph G., 1946.236
Martin, Ron, 1963.139
Martin, S. Rudolph, Jr., 1974.119
Martin, Suzanne, 1945.1014
Martin, Sylvia, 1978.158
Martin Eden, 1953.135; 1957.283

1949.116; 1951.217; 1966.42, 96; 1967.41; 1968.201; 1969.109; 1970.73, 228;
   1972.27, 88, 92, 135; 1974.112, 158, 171; 1975.121, 177; 1976.169; 1977.156;
   1978.222, 241; 1979.235; 1980.172; 1981.124; 1982.50, 126
Maxwell, Allen, 1938.244; 1940.786
Maxwell, Joan Lovell Bauerly, 1976.123
May, John Allan, 1954.145
May, John R., S. J., 1970.261; 1972.147, 148
Mayberry, George, 1945.1018
May Day Committee, 1941.467
Mayer, Milton, 1945.1019; 1950.181
Mayfield, Julian, 1958.220; 1963.140; 1973.218; 1980.69; 1982.27
Maynard, René, 1947.240; 1948.197, 198
Mayoux, Jean-Jacques, 1952.54
Mays, Benjamin, 1968.123
Maywood, Illinois, 1942.216
Mazía, Floreal, 1946.108; 1959.38
Me., 1958.203, 204
Meacham, William Shands, 1941.846; 1942.290; 1954.147
"The Meaning of Bigger Thomas," 1940.917
The Meanings of Literature, 1973.228, 229
Mears, Bessie, 1940.743, 907; 1950.172; 1961.275a; 1965.87; 1971.310; 1972.107;
   1973.37, 38, 41, 42, 287, 295, 296; 1974.69, 171; 1978.224; 1980.205; 1982.79
Mears, Clara, 1941.349, 907
Mebane, Mary E., 1974.130; 1980.167
Medborgarhuset, 1957.61
Medler, Edward Arnold, 1977.227
Meeker, Oden, 1954.124
Megret, Christian, 1948.200, 201
Meier, August, 1959.115; 1965.90; 1966.103, 104; 1969.45; 1971.13, 200
Meiji Daigaku Eibei Bungaku, 1956.304; 1958.246; 1972.76b
Meiji University English and American Literature, 1956.304; 1958.246; 1972.76b
Meine, Franklin J., 1953.63, 171
Melanctha, 1946.257, 285; 1957.326; 1959.66; 1968.28
Mélèze, Josette, 1963.141
Mellard, James M., 1971.222; 1980.168
Meller, Sidney, 1940.439, 795
Meltzer, Milton, 1939.97; 1941.847; 1958.161; 1966.104; 1967.72, 73; 1968.168;
   1970.263; 1971.47, 69; 1980.169
MELUS, 1978.95, 153, 173, 182, 207, 262; 1979.181, 194, 228; 1980.232, 252; 1981.124
Melville, Herman, 1961.217; 1963.121; 1969.133; 1970.207, 208, 209, 210; 1971.187;
   1976.90; 1978.120; 1980.134; 1981.73, 74
Melvin B. Tolson's Harlem Gallery: A Literary Analysis, 1980.213
"Memories of My Grandmother," 1982.99
Memories of the Moderns, 1980.149
Memphis, 1940.883; 1942.226, 336; 1945.630; 1948.199; 1960.236; 1969.190; 1971.314;
   1973.304, 305; 1981.62
Memphis Commercial Appeal, 1938.286; 1940.28, 233, 723, 774; 1941.731; 1944.122;
   1945.469, 901; 1952.13, 42; 1953.124, 182; 1954.136; 1957.67, 183; 1958.75;
   1965.63; 1966.9
Memphis Down in Dixie, 1948.199
Memphis Hebrew Watchman, 1938.255
Memphis Press-Scimitar, 1940.213, 297, 845
Memphis Public Library, 1963.58; 1964.31; 1974.32
Menck, Clara, 1960.199
Mencken, H. L., 1938.62, 170; 1945.788, 790, 1087; 1960.236; 1962.94; 1964.25,
   99a; 1973.132
Mendelson, Moris Osipovich, 1941.848; 1948.202, 249; 1964.94; 1965.71; 1975.131;
   1977.228
Mendez, Edith, 1938.245
Menikoff, Barry, 1969.206, 207; 1975.156, 157
Menmur, Ruth, 1973.223
Das Menschenrecht, 1959.24
Menta, Narciso Ibañez, 1945.385, 488, 1168
The Merchant of Venice, 1948.238
Mercure de France, 1947.60; 1948.42; 1954.176; 1956.323, 324; 1965.17
Mercury Theatre, 1941.405, 693; 1974.81
Mercury Theatre, 1941.747
Meredith, J. Mercer, 1941.849

1976.56
The Midwest Journal, 1956.138
Migrants, Sharecroppers, Mountaineers, 1971.73
Milan, 1948.114; 1957.106
Milan Corriere della sera, 1951.93
Milan Corriere d'informazione, 1951.137
Milano sera, 1951.140
Milenković, Dragi, 1959.29
Miliander, Sven, 1945.1175
The Militant, 1945.962; 1977.72
The Militant Black Writer in Africa and the United States, 1969.59, 124
Miller, Adam David, 1978.169
Miller, Albert H., 1957.271
Miller, Arthur, 1979.157
Miller, Bill, 1961.211
Miller, Carrie G., 1940.798, 799
Miller, Elizabeth W., 1966.105; 1970.265
Miller, Eugene E., 1972.151; 1974.1; 1982.99, 100
Miller, Henry, 1947.129, 227; 1948.17, 149, 209; 1962.63; 1971.224; 1973.221, 222
Miller, James A., 1977.229
Miller, James E., 1967.73a; 1975.132; 1977.230; 1978.170; 1979.176, 177; 1982.101
Miller, Jeanne-Marie A., 1976.127
Miller, Marie, 1945.590
Miller, Maud M., 1951.204
Miller, Merle, 1950.182, 183
Miller, Morton A., 1980.173, 174
Miller, R. Baxter, 1977.231; 1979.178; 1980.175; 1981.48, 64, 89, 90, 91, 92
Miller, Richard, 1978.219
Miller, Ruby King, 1940.800
Miller, Ruth, 1971.3, 6, 34, 48, 70, 91, 225, 226, 227, 228, 229, 230, 231, 300, 301; 1978.171, 172
Miller, Wayne Charles, 1972.152; 1976.128, 129; 1978.173
Miller, William, 1959.96; 1967.58; 1970.181; 1972.99a; 1976.98
Millett, Kate, 1977.260
Millgate, Michael, 1968.97
Millican, Arthenia Bates, 1977.232
Milliken, Stephen F., 1976.130; 1977.4
Mills, Moylan Chew, 1974.131
Milner, Ronald, 1967.74; 1970.266; 1973.223
Milwaukee, 1942.13, 46, 47, 124; 1945.103, 105, 107, 108, 109, 110, 111, 113, 115, 116, 117, 118, 119, 127, 128, 129, 130, 133, 134, 135, 136, 137
Milwaukee Evening Post, 1940.413
Milwaukee Journal, 1940.641; 1945.1188, 1189; 1946.187; 1950.15; 1953.137; 1957.189; 1958.264; 1961.136; 1963.52; 1969.216; 1977.82
Mimo Club, 1941.285
Mims, A. Grace, 1967.75
Minakawa, Soichi, 1964.95; 1974.132; 1975.133
Minchero, Vilasaró Angel, 1957.272
The Mind and Mood of Black America: 20th Century Thought, 1969.96
The Mind of the Negro: An Intellectual History of Afro-Americans, 1961.271; 1970.334
Mine Boy, 1946.193; 1954.124
Miner, Ward L., 1955.78
Minne, P., 1948.203
Minneapolis, 1942.46, 94, 125, 128; 1945.472, 473, 474
Minneapolis Minnesota Daily, 1977.96
Minneapolis Morning Tribune, 1942.73, 267, 289
The Minneapolis Star, 1952.63; 1954.91
Minneapolis Star-Journal, 1940.616; 1942.74, 319
Minneapolis Sunday Tribune, 1945.422, 423, 424, 425, 426, 427, 428, 429, 430, 431, 432, 433, 895; 1953.218; 1961.220
Minneapolis Sunday Tribune and Star Journal, 1942.9, 75
Minneapolis Tribune, 1945.1132
The Minnesota Review, 1975.79; 1981.18, 85; 1982.112
Minor, Delores, 1971.232
Minor, Marcia, 1938.246
Minor, Robert, 1944.125, 136, 138
Minorities in American Society, 1968.159

The Most Native of Sons, 1969.8, 95; 1970.17, 20, 22, 26, 27, 30, 31, 41, 42,
    43, 130, 263, 277, 287, 304, 306, 319, 365; 1971.10, 11, 170, 171, 184, 189,
    319; 1972.201; 1978.127; 1979.261
Mother, 1938.53, 289; 1939.99
Mother AME Zion Church, 1940.7
The Motion of History and Other Plays, 1978.36
Motley, Mary Penick, 1957.277
Motley, Willard, 1947.166a; 1948.3, 190; 1952.49; 1954.103; 1958.92; 1965.54a;
    1974.177; 1977.154, 345; 1979.2; 1978.151; 1979.152, 166; 1980.86, 144, 180
Moton, R. M., 1940.200
Mott, Frank Luther, 1947.244, 303; 1949.95
Mottram, Eric, 1971.51, 52
Moulin, Charles, 1940.802
Moulin d'Andé, 1957.56
Moulton, Elizabeth, 1979.180
Mount Vernon, Iowa, 1945.523, 579, 598, 1192
Mount Vernon Hawkeye-Record and Lisbon Herald, 1945.31
Mourey, Richard, 1954.150
Moussin, René, 1950.186
Mphahlele, Ezekiel, 1961.213; 1962.89; 1963.146; 1971.238; 1973.232; 1974.136
MT, 1956.136
Mt. Zion Baptist Church, 1941.320
Mufti of Jerusalem, 1956.341
Muhammed Speaks, 1971.14, 123
Muir, Edwin, 1940.803
Muirhead, Pamela Buchanan, 1981.95
Mulatto, 1940.966
Mulder, Arnold, 1940.804, 805
Mules and Men, 1970.344
Mulholland, John Field, 1942.291, 292
Muliarchik, A. S., 1976.135; 1977.241, 242, 243, 357
Mullaney, Bernard J., 1940.806
A Multidisciplinary Catalog of Ethnic Studies, 1979.19
Mumbo Jumbo, 1972.168a; 1978.202
Münchner Merkur, 1957.62; 1961.286
The Muncie Morning Star, 1940.899
The Muncie Sunday Star, 1940.421
El mundo negro, 1970.240
Mungin, Joe, 1942.252
Muni, Paul, 1941.856, 986
Munich Deutsche Woche, 1959.35; 1961.166
Die Munich Neue Zeitung, 1946.63
Munich Süddeutsche Zeitung, 1957.325; 1958.150; 1961.150
Munn, L. S., 1953.190
Munro, C. Lynn, 1971.147, 239; 1973.207, 226; 1980.181; 1982.105
Munro, Ian, 1971.238
Munro, John M., 1972.153
Munson, Gorham, 1936.11
Muntu, 1958.169; 1961.184
Munz, Charles Curtis, 1938.287; 1941.863
Muray, Jean, 1947.245
Murchison, William, 1977.244
Murchland, Bernard, 1968.55
Murciaux, Christian, 1947.20
"The Murders in the Rue Morgue," 1972.163; 1975.92
Murdock, Henry T., 1960.203
Murmures 5, 1958.265
Murphey, Robert W., 1961.54
Murphy, Beatrice M., 1938.249; 1940.807, 808, 809, 810, 811, 812, 813; 1941.864;
    1945.1042
Murphy, Carl, 1945.1043
Murphy, Gertrude B., 1945.1044
Murphy, William S., 1963.147
Murray, Albert, 1966.106; 1968.170; 1970.269; 1971.201a; 1973.227
Murray, Alma, 1970.270, 271; 1971.240
Murray, Chalmers S., 1942.252
Murray, David, 1972.137
Murray, Don, 1954.151

Murray, Florence, 1942.293; 1944.126; 1947.246
Murray, Jacques, 1948.209
Musaraigne, 1951.207
Musard, François, 1950.187
Muse, Clarence, 1941.865, 866
Le Musée Vivant, 1948.66; 1949.113
Musgrave, Marian E., 1971.241
Music Corporation of America, 1941.580, 918
The Muslim Sunrise, 1956.24
Mwenifumbo, Tone, 1978.179
My Black Me, 1974.49
Myers, Carol Fairbanks, 1975.166; 1977.245
Myers, J. S., 1940.814; 1941.867
Myers, John A., Jr., 1969.170
Myers, Miles, 1973.228, 229
My Fair Ladies, 1941.1006
My Life of Absurdity: The Autobiography of Chester Himes, 1976.97; 1977.356
My Name Is Asher Lev, 1979.228
My Native Land, 1940.765
Myrdal, Gunnar, 1944.127; 1945.855, 937, 943; 1946.56, 141, 141a, 142, 260; 1948.182;
    1956.99, 136, 251, 252; 1960.155; 1962.90; 1964.98; 1969.179; 1977.49
My Sister Eileen, 1941.120, 121, 216, 447
The Myth of Southern History: Historical Consciousness in Twentieth-Century Southern
    Literature, 1970.97a

N., 1961.214; 1966.107
N., G., 1947.247
N., J. K., 1961.215
N., M., 1950.188; 1951.208
N., R. J., 1941.868
Nadeau, Maurice, 1946.244; 1947.248; 1948.210, 211; 1950.189; 1958.205; 1960.204,
    205
Nagano, 1956.157
Nagasaki Gaikokugo Tanki Daigaku, 1970.214a
Nagasaki Junior College for Foreign Studies Treatises, 1970.214a
Nagasaki Naval Architectural College Study Report, 1975.125a; 1976.120a
Nagasaki Zosen Daigaku Kenkyu Hokoku, 1975.125a; 1976.120a
Nagase, Hiroshi, 1972.154
Nagel, James, 1969.180; 1975.35a; 1976.43a; 1977.245a, 325a; 1982.106, 107
Naguère, Jean, 1958.206
Naison, Mark, 1981.96
Nakao, Kiyoaki, 1955.13a
The Naked I: Fictions for the Seventies, 1971.191
"The Name and the Nature of American Negro Literature: An Interpretive Study in
    Genre and Ideas," 1965.107
The Napa Register, 1961.170
Il Naples mattino, 1966.101
Nappy Edges, 1978.224; 1980.82
Narasimhaiah, C. D., 1972.153, 165, 200
Naremore, James, 1978.180
Narizhory, Grigory, 1941.345, 869
Narodni osvobozeni, 1948.178
Narrative of the Life of Frederick Douglass, An American Slave, 1980.218
Nashua, New Hampshire, 1978.23
Nashville, Tennessee, 1968.59; 1971.147
Nashville Banner, 1938.254; 1942.294; 1944.39; 1953.163; 1977.258
Nashville Defender, 1940.629; 1941.603
The Nashville Tennessean, 1945.613, 979; 1954.94; 1956.163; 1957.261; 1963.161;
    1977.95
Nasser, Gamal Abdel, 1958.124
Natchez, Mississippi, 1945.354, 489, 490, 827, 847; 1947.46, 54, 271a; 1954.184;
    1957.178; 1959.140; 1960.236; 1979.182
Nathan, George Jean, 1941.870; 1943.51
Nathan, Paul S., 1949.133
Nathaniel West: The Art of His Life, 1970.259a
The Nation, 1938.109, 164, 204; 1940.227, 621, 784, 942; 1941.784, 863; 1944.142;
    1945.284, 1037, 1172; 1950.191; 1953.41; 1954.89; 1956.333; 1957.319; 1958.146;
    1959.88; 1960.19, 207; 1961.3; 1964.54, 80, 90; 1971.60; 1973.75; 1975.195;

*332; 1943.1, 2, 3, 4, 5, 7, 9, 10, 11, 12, 14, 16, 35, 36, 46, 50, *51, 54,
57; 1944.15, 32, 33, 35, 46, 48, 104, 105, 118, 152; 1945.321, 338, 344, 348,
349, *376, 385, 460, 488, 532, *619, 621, 622, *771, *772, *777, 828, *915,
*925, *1045, 1051, *1154, *1162, *1164, *1168, *1175; 1946.32, 206, 220, 241;
1947.156, 170, *216, 232, 296; 1948.*20, 21, 33, *36, *57, 74, 99, 100, *161,
166, *178, *181, 189, 213, 214, *238; 1949.8, *109, 112, 129; 1950.108, 110,
155, 156, 157, 158, 159, 160, 161, 178, 234; 1951.58, 139, 176, 190, 195, 205,
212, 242, 252; 1952.3; 1953.*130, 131, 141, 154; 1954.44; 1955.*77; 1957.152,
161; 1959.142; 1960.138, 142; 1961.201, 274; 1963.*109, 142; 1964.*110; 1965.73,
*77, 120, 122a; 1966.7, 77, 79; 1967.19, 49a, 51, *76, 80a; 1968.*78, 106, 204,
205; 1969.1, *2, 31, 174, 175, *231, 238; 1970.*66, 169, 231, 338, 343, 363;
1971.27, 28, 44, 119, 139, 147, *173, *194, 299, 300; 1972.6, 13, 14, 100, 171a,
206; 1973.78, *133, 183, 184, 199; 1974.2, 37, 47, 62, *81, 89; 1975.28, 86,
154; 1976.1, 22, 29, 103, 127, 131, 156, *157, 194; 1977.65, *192, 348; 1978.*13,
14, 15, *24, 25, 29, 30, 33, 37, *54, 90, *124, 157, 203, *239, *240, *241,
242, *250; 1979.36, 71, 85, 91, 270, 274; 1980.10, 54, *106, 121, 124; 1981.*124;
1982.2, 76
"Native Son, From Novel to Stage Play," 1941.461
Native Son: The Playbill, 1941.335
Native Son Inc., 1941.917
Native Son Notes, 1971.8
Native Sons: A Critical Study of Twentieth-Century Negro American Authors, 1968.160;
   1969.120, 168, 237, 250
A Native Sons Reader, 1970.253, 254, 256, 257
The Native's Return, 1940.189
Naturalism, 1938.170; 1940.919; 1941.872, 979; 1942.254, 259; 1944.114; 1945.588;
   1947.203; 1952.59; 1953.174a, 204, 217a, 255; 1955.31; 1956.224; 1957.256, 268,
   283, 310; 1958.85, 233; 1960.132; 1963.75, 177; 1964.85, 99a, 112; 1965.42,
   77, 107; 1966.15; 1968.110, 117; 1969.4, 70, 109, 122a, 247; 1970.5, 99; 1971.5,
   142a, 165, 175, 259, 267; 1972.27, 60, 145, 199; 1973.66, 100a, 281; 1974.169;
   1975.36, 71, 196; 1977.110, 290; 1978.177; 1979.79, 258; 1980.93, 119, 168,
   248, 264; 1981.55, 103; 1982.61, 62
Natural Man, 1941.47
The Nature of Prejudice, 1954.3; 1958.2; 1972.55
Nault, William H., 1969.230; 1975.60, 132, 135, 194; 1977.230, 235, 323; 1978.80,
   170, 174, 245; 1979.82, 176, 179, 265
Nausea, 1981.29
Naville, Pierre, 1948.212
Naylor, Carolyn A., 1982.108
La nazione, 1968.166
Nazis, 1941.362, 536; 1942.15, 21; 1943.17; 1945.677; 1980.98
Nazi-Soviet Pact, 1940.717; 1951.211
NCTE Task Force on Racism and Bias in the Teaching of English, 1972.109
N. D. R. Rundfunkhaus, 1956.299
Ndu, Pol Nnamuzikam, 1975.138
Neal, Lawrence P., 1965.103; 1966.108, 109, 110; 1967.78; 1968.4, 124, 171, 172;
   1969.125, 181, 182, 183, 184; 1970.272; 1972.155; 1974.137; 1976.136; 1979.141;
   1980.182
Neander-Nilsson, S., 1945.1045
Needham, Wilbur, 1940.815
La Nef, 1947.30, 31; 1948.10, 63, 83, 104; 1957.24
Negerjongen, 1953.19
A Négerség és az Amerikai Irodalom, 1975.196
Negri, Alfred, 1963.148
I negri americani dalla depressione al dopoguerra, 1974.117; 1976.21
El negrito, 1950.28, 54
Négritude, 1960.4, 158; 1961.213, 223; 1962.64; 1964.115; 1965.112; 1966.43, 80;
   1970.106; 1971.6, 7; 1973.131, 193; 1974.97; 1976.72, 111, 197
The Negro, 1945.284, 285, 728; 1967.87
The Negro Almanac, 1967.82; 1976.146
Negro American Heritage, 1968.147
Negro American Literature Forum, 1967.12, 17; 1968.43, 72, 113, 126, 203, 205;
   1969.112, 188, 190; 1970.91, 122, 127, 128, 129, 264, 268; 1971.98, 214, 232;
   1972.135, 156; 1973.71, 104, 148, 152, 263, 307; 1974.4, 37, 56, 69; 1975.22a,
   76, 88, 152, 169
"The Negro and Literature Today," 1938.101
The Negro and the Communist Party, 1951.222; 1952.25; 1971.254
The Negro as Playwright, 1954.44

Pelswick, Rose, 1951.219
Pen-Club, 1946.92
Pendexter, Faunce, 1966.115
The Penguin Companion to American Literature, 1971.51, 52
Penkower, Monty Noam, 1977.256
Pensacola News-Journal, 1956.11; 1970.26
Il pensiero nazionale, 1964.93
People and Ideas: A Rhetoric Reader, 1980.41, 43, 44
Peoples Church, 1940.235, 564
People's Daily World, 1939.61, 68; 1940.455, 579, 580, 581, 582, 672; 1941.78,
    79, 351, 675; 1942.23
People's Meeting, 1941.746
The People's Voice, 1942.11, 310; 1945.1036
People's World, 1941.256, 641, 653, 885
Peoria, Illinois, 1945.109, 110, 111, 112, 113, 114, 115, 116, 119, 125, 126,
    129, 130, 131, 132, 133, 136; 1946.19
Peoria Journal Star, 1961.190
Peplow, Michael W., 1975.145, 146, 147
Pepys, Samuel, 1940.3; 1947.3
Pequeño Larousse ilustrado, 1964.23
Performance, 1972.155
The Perilous Journey, 1973.189
Perkins, Eugene, 1970.290; 1974.132
Perkins, George, 1974.142
Perlman, Anne, 1946.254
Perosa, Sergio, 1968.179
Perrin, Noel, 1979.197
Perry, Al, 1958.212
Perry, Edward G., 1943.54
Perry, John Oliver, 1981.106
Perry, Margaret, 1977.331
Perry, Patsy Brewington, 1977.257
Perry, Roy E., 1977.258
Perry Street Theater, 1978.15, 24, 25, 250
Personals, 1963.59
Perspectives, 1966.67
Perspectives on Contemporary Literature, 1982.58
Perspectives USA, 1953.77
Perth Amboy Evening News, 1940.216
Peterkin, Julia, 1938.164; 1947.8; 1960.207
Peters, Brock, 1970.48, 247; 1971.23; 1977.46
Peters, Erskine, 1978.189
Peters, Marjorie, 1945.1073
Peters, Paul, 1935.9
Peters, Richard, 1940.833
Petersen, Hans, 1960.216
Peterson, Ed, 1940.834, 835; 1941.879, 880; 1942.298
Petesch, Donald A., 1975.148; 1978.190
Petit, Henri, 1950.198
Petitjean, A., 1950.199
Petit Larousse en couleurs, 1977.40
Petit Larousse illustré, 1974.18; 1976.20
Le Petit Matin, 1958.206
Petree, Nellie, 1956.268; 1957.285
Petrina, Tony, 1949.77
Petry, Ann, 1946.3, 55, 167, 185, 238, 255, 281; 1947.287, 297; 1948.4, 194, 235;
    1949.62, 127; 1950.236; 1958.85; 1965.42; 1972.122; 1973.68, 256; 1974.60, 177;
    1980.67, 115
Pettey, Tom, 1940.836
Pettigrew, Thomas F., 1964.101
Peyre, Henri, 1947.256
Peyrol, Pierre, 1948.220
Der Pfälzer, 1957.29
Pharr, Robert Dean, 1980.69; 1982.27
Philadelphia, 1942.51, 52, 53, 78, 160; 1945.236, 237, 238, 239, 240, 241, 242,
    243, 244, 245, 246, 247, 248, 249, 250, 251, 252, 253, 254, 255, 256, 257, 258,
    259, 260, 261, 262, 263, 264, 265, 266, 267, 351, 491, 492, 529, 539; 1960.261
Philadelphia Daily News, 1961.51

Puissance noire, 1954.50; 1955.15, 16, 18, 38, 50, 65, 71; 1956.54, 122, 127,
 150, 178, 229, 323; 1957.2; 1958.26, 216; 1968.21
Pujols, Carmen, 1979.208
Pulitzer Prize, 1938.241; 1939.68, 69; 1940.8, 366, 628, 629, 630, 1003; 1941.159,
 161, 177, 178, 179, 182, 209, 223, 226, 329, 438, 549, 791, 838, 893, 1015;
 1946.54, 65
Pulse, 1945.16, 804, 871, 896, 904, 907, 1042, 1081, 1097, 1161
Purcell, Malcolm, Jr., 1938.259
Purdue University, 1961.171
Purgerson, Mattie, 1940.240
Puritanism, 1953.211; 1956.69; 1966.117; 1978.222
Purpose in Literature, 1979.96, 98
Purser, John Thibaut, 1975.30, 31
Pursuing the Pursuit--The Black Plight in White America, 1977.116
La Putain respectueuse, 1948.228; 1951.27, 46, 77
Putnam, Samuel, 1941.894; 1943.55; 1944.136; 1964.15
Putnam's, 1964.15
Pütz, Manfred, 1973.240
Putzel, Henry, Jr., 1945.1081
Pyle, Ernie, 1944.39; 1945.421, 576, 805
Pynchon, Thomas, 1973.192a
Pyros, John, 1975.152; 1977.217

Quade, A., 1941.39
Quality, 1946.274
The Quality of Hurt: The Autobiography of Chester Himes, 1972.97, 182a; 1976.130
Qualls, Youra, 1945.1082
Quantic, Diane Dufva, 1969.197
Quarante contre un, 1947.152, 176, 207
Quarles, Benjamin, 1964.105; 1969.198; 1979.209
The Quarterly Review, 1942.307
The Quarterly Review of Higher Education Among Negroes, 1938.250; 1941.667, 725;
 1945.1030
Quarterly Review of Literature, 1944.64
Quartet: A Book of Stories, Plays, Poems, and Critical Essays, 1973.274
Quartiere, 1968.164
Quebec, Quebec, 1945.10, 18, 450, 577, 578; 1971.321; 1974.60
Quebec Chronicle-Telegraph, 1945.10, 577
Que día Señor, 1964.13; 1966.5
Queen, Ellery, 1945.926
Queensboro Theater, 1944.32, 33, 46, 48
Queen's Quarterly, 1978.161
Die Quelle, 1956.63; 1958.51; 1960.67; 1962.18
Quelques, 1948.45
Queneau, 1946.220
Quercus, P. E. G., 1940.851
Quest, 1977.70
Qu'est-ce que la littérature?, 1948.242
The Quest for Equality: From Civil War to Civil Rights, 1969.251; 1976.202
Quest for Meaning: Modern Short Stories, 1975.39
Quests Surd and Absurd: Essays in American Literature, 1967.73a
Quick, 1949.60
Quid? Encyclopedie annuelle, 1963.86
Quid? Tout pour tous, 1964.58; 1965.66; 1966.58; 1967.44; 1968.101; 1969.88; 1970.138;
 1971.126; 1972.76; 1973.151; 1974.74; 1975.81; 1976.77; 1977.142; 1978.103;
 1979.108
Quigly, Isabel, 1954.156
Quill & Quire, 1980.241
Quillen, Robert, 1940.852
Quinn, Anthony, 1959.98, 139
Quinn, Arthur Hobson, 1951.249; 1967.86
Quinn, Kerker, 1936.13a; 1940.852a; 1942.307a, 307b, 307c; 1943.55a, 55b, 55c;
 1944.136a; 1945.1082a; 1946.259a; 1947.259a, 259b, 259c; 1948.226a; 1950.205a;
 1951.219a; 1952.60a; 1953.205a, 205b; 1954.156a, 156b, 156c; 1955.66a, 66b;
 1956.271a, 271b, 271c; 1957.293a, 293b; 1958.219a
Quinn, Susan A., 1944.137; 1945.1083, 1084, 1085, 1086, 1087; 1946.260
Quintet, 1961.38a, 38b
La Quinzaine littéraire, 1971.308a; 1979.8, 110

1982.114
Reed, John, 1939.35; 1959.118; 1961.2; 1967.66; 1968.200; 1975.35; 1978.156; 1979.130;
    1980.72
Reed, Kenneth T., 1970.298; 1972.137
Reed, W. A., Jr., 1963.161
Reed College Bulletin, 1946.171
Reely, Mary Katharine, 1945.1095
Rees, Robert A., 1969.206, 207; 1975.156, 157
Reese, Mildred L., 1975.158
Reeve, Agnes M., 1938.260
Reeves, Edward, 1960.226
Reeves, Paschal, 1969.208; 1970.299; 1971.258; 1972.170; 1973.230, 253; 1974.140,
    151; 1975.110
Reference Library of Black America, 1971.249
Reference Works for Language & Literature Collections, 1977.31
Reflections on Segregation, Desegregation, Power and Morals, 1967.41
Reflets du Luxembourg, 1965.3
Réflexions sur question juive, 1946.266
Réforme, 1955.72
The Reform Spirit in America, 1976.198
Regards sur la littérature noire américaine, 1980.85, 87, 91
Der Regensburger, 1961.74
The Regina Leader-Post, 1955.20
Regional Perspectives: An Examination of America's Literary Heritage, 1973.151b
Rehder, Jessie, 1945.417, 1096; 1969.209
Reid, Inez Smith, 1976.155
Reid, Ira De A., 1945.1097
Reifenrath, J. W., 1959.127
Reilly, John Marsden, 1966.126, 127; 1968.16, 184; 1970.61, 71, 151, 185, 192,
    243, 279, 300, 301, 310; 1971.259, 260, 261; 1972.171; 1973.6, 254; 1977.212;
    1978.182, 207, 208, 209, 210, 211; 1979.178, 212, 213; 1980.207, 257; 1981.116a;
    1982.100, 114a, 115, 116, 117, 118
Reilly, Robert J., 1977.80
Reims Concorde, 1947.169
Reinhold, Kurt von, 1957.298
Reitz, Helmuth, 1959.128
Religion in Contemporary Fiction: Criticism from 1945 to the Present, 1973.69
Religion in Life, 1958.158
The Reluctant African, 1960.191
Relyea, Harold C., 1968.185
Remini, Robert V., 1975.43, 44
Ren, Tuo, 1980.207a
Renaissance in the South: A Critical History of the Literature, 1920-1960, 1963.61
Renascence, 1970.261; 1971.159
Renaud, P.-A., 1958.227
Reninger, H. Willard, 1974.113
Rennert, Leo, 1958.228
Rennes Ouest-France, 1948.120
Renshaw, Charles C., 1945.1098
The Reporter, 1949.131; 1954.38; 1956.124; 1960.193, 207; 1961.116; 1964.134
Report from Part One, 1972.35
Report on Africa, 1954.124
The Republic, 1977.225
Republika, 1951.129a
La République de Toulon, 1965.10
Research Studies (Washington State University), 1969.122
Resistance, 1953.251
Resistance and Caribbean Literature, 1980.73
Resource Manual to Accompany America in Literature Volumes I and II, 1978.122
Resources for Literary Study, 1971.260; 1981.61; 1982.21a
The Respectful Prostitute, 1947.201, 202; 1966.113
"Rest for the Weary," 1934.5; 1935.6
The Resurgence of Race: Black Social Theory from Reconstruction to the Pan-African
    Conferences, 1979.264
The Retail Bookseller, 1941.548, 555; 1942.295; 1944.18, 50, 51; 1945.86, 87,
    88, 89, 90, 91, 92, 93, 141, 299, 343, 345, 383, 442, 444, 569, 668; 1946.5,
    30, 105; 1953.14, 37, 38, 46; 1954.20, 22, 29, 33; 1956.20, 53, 99; 1957.15,
    27, 54, 57, 83
Rétif, André, 1956.276; 1960.227

127, 128, 129, 130, 135, 136, 137, 138, 140, 141, 142, 143, 146, 147, 153, 154,
166, 167, 169, 170, 171, 172, 173, 183, 184, 208, 209, 221, 222, 236, 237, 242,
243, 244, 245, 258, 259, 260, 261, 269, 270, 277, 278, 282, 283, 295, 296, 299,
300, 304, 305; 1974.14, 114, 174, 178; 1975.123; 1980.88, 206
Richard Wright: Ordeal of a Native Son, 1980.3, 7, 17, 21, 22, 23, 29, 46, 66,
78, 106, 116, 136, 169, 190, 196, 200, 241, 261; 1981.18, 42, 52, 126, 136,
137
Richard Wright: The Critical Reception, 1978.209; 1980.257
"Richard Wright: The Major Themes, Ideas, and Attitudes in His Works," 1966.28,
1967.16
"Richard Wright: The Man Who Lived Underground," 1978.118
Richard Wright and His Influence, 1971.9, 79, 80, 239, 322
Richard Wright (Bakish), 1973.15, 16, 19, 50, 126; 1974.173
Richard Wright (Bone), 1969.36, 127; 1970.214, 359; 1971.313; 1973.126; 1977.330
"Richard Wright et la condition noire américaine," 1962.38
Richard Wright (Felgar), 1980.94; 1981.44
Richard Wright (Hudson), 1979.204
"Richard Wright in a Moment of Truth," 1975.193; 1976.71
"Richard Wright in Retreat," 1948.182
"Richard Wright Lectures," 1976.6
"Richard Wright (1908-1960): A Bibliography," 1979.47
Richard Wright no Sekai, 1981.103
"Richard Wright ou l'universe n'est pas noir," 1947.53
Richard Wright Reader, 1977.11, 38; 1978.7, 10, 11, 27, 40, 61, 64, 83, 93, 98,
100, 121, 137, 141, 158, 178, 256, 261; 1979.260
Richard Wright (Rickels), 1970.302
"Richard Wright's Blues," 1970.162, 227; 1971.208; 1972.116; 1973.120; 1976.179;
1978.41
Richard Wright's Fiction: The Critical Response 1940-1971, 1971.147
Richard Wright's Hero: The Faces of a Rebel-Victim, 1977.31, 131, 197; 1978.3;
1979.267
Richard Wright's Native Son, 1972.158; 1973.120
Richard Wright's Native Son: A Critical Handbook, 1970.2, 3, 4, 5; 1971.21; 1972.137;
1973.126
"Richard Wright's Nonfiction: A Reassessment," 1981.7
"Richard Wright's Short Fiction: A Reassessment," 1982.11
Richeimer, Mary Jane, 1970.283, 284
Richmond, California, 1965.24, 25
The Richmond Hill High School Domino, 1941.716
The Richmond News Leader, 1953.232; 1954.149; 1957.328; 1977.305
Richmond Times-Dispatch, 1940.619; 1941.656, 657, 658; 1944.72, 137; 1945.613,
1016, 1083, 1084, 1085, 1086, 1087; 1946.2, 237, 260, 265; 1953.93; 1954.171;
1957.346, 347; 1958.255
Richter, Conrad, 1940.843
Richter, F. K., 1945.669, 1100
Rickels, Milton, 1970.302
Rickels, Patricia, 1970.302
Ricksecker, Robert S., 1954.164, 164a; 1955.67
Rickshaw Boy, 1945.848
Riddell, Hugh J., 1940.863
Ridenour, Ronald, 1970.303
Rideout, Walter B., 1956.280; 1960.229, 230, 231; 1967.89; 1973.255
Rider, Ione, 1945.1101
Ridgely, Joseph V., 1964.111; 1966.128; 1968.54; 1969.47; 1972.40; 1973.76; 1974.39a;
1975.35a; 1976.43a; 1977.74a
Riecke, Charlotte, 1962.95
Riegelhaupt, Barbara, 1979.214
Riesman, David, 1953.211; 1955.68
Rigdon, Walter, 1966.8
Riggio, Thomas P., 1976.159; 1980.208
Right On: A List of Books by and About the American Negro, 1973.43
Rights and Reviews, 1967.49
Rikkyo Daigaku Eibei Bungaku, 1973.225
Rikkyo Daigaku Kenkyu Hokoku, 1961.275a
The Rikkyo Review, 1973.225
Rikkyo University Study Report, 1961.275a
Riley, Carolyn, 1973.50, 68, 256; 1975.29, 104, 130, 142
Riley, Clayton, 1968.186; 1977.134

Rubin, Louis D., Jr., 1961.249; 1965.113a; 1969.46; 1973.52a; 1975.110, 164; 1976.5,
   34, 167; 1979.54, 221, 222, 223; 1980.56, 114, 126, 167, 271
Rubin, Steven Joel, 1969.214; 1975.165; 1978.214; 1979.17a; 1981.118, 119
Rubinstein, Annette T., 1968.190
Rudich, Norman, 1976.117
Rudolf, Ernst, 1957.304
Rudwick, Elliott M., 1966.103; 1971.13, 200
La Rue cases-nègres, 1950.71, 72
Der Ruf, 1959.34
Rufus, 1965.42, 43; 1966.21; 1970.60; 1974.29
Rugoff, Milton, 1940.261, 635, 873; 1953.219
Ruin, Olaf, 1956.288
Ruitenbeck, Hendrick M., 1964.129
Rumley, Larry, 1958.236
Runes, Richard N., 1973.53
Run-Through, 1971.173; 1972.100
Rupp, Richard H., 1976.168
R. U. R., 1942.155
Rush, Theressa Gunnels, 1975.166
Rushing, Andrea Benton, 1975.167; 1978.215, 216; 1980.212; 1981.120
Russell, Bertrand, 1950.215, 216
Russell, Caro Green, 1938.265; 1940.874, 875, 876, 877; 1941.946, 947, 948, 950,
   951, 952
Russell, Jack S., 1978.181
Russell, Mariann, 1980.213
Russell, Oland D., 1956.289, 290, 291, 292, 293, 294
Russian Studies in American Literature, 1969.159
Rust College, 1980.8
Rutgers University, 1978.48
Ruth, Babe, 1940.749
Ruth, Kent, 1953.220
Rutherford, William A., 1951.227
Rutland Daily Herald, 1955.23
Rutland Herald, 1958.73
Ryan, Pat, 1975.168
Ryan, Stephen P., 1961.250
Ryel, Deborah E., 1977.103
Ryskind, Morrie, 1941.120, 154, 156, 231, 487; 1942.41
Rywell, Martin, 1974.7, 9, 10, 11, 13, 19

S., 1961.251
S., B. H., 1956.295
S., B. K., 1944.140
S., C., 1947.268; 1957.305; 1961.252
S., D. J., 1951.228
S., Dr., 1958.237
S., E., 1949.77; 1961.253
S., E. A., 1948.237; 1980.214
S., E. J., 1941.953
S., G., 1947.269
S., G. M., 1938.266
S., H., 1947.270
S., H., 1980.202
S., H. L., 1946.265
S., H. M., 1957.306
S., J., 1953.221
S., J.-P., 1950.217
S., M. H., 1962.97
S., N., 1940.878
S., R., 1957.307
S., S., 1957.308
S., W. L., 1961.254
Saal, Rollene W., 1969.215
Saarbrücker Zeitung, 1960.99, 221; 1961.179, 228
Saarländisches Rundfunk, 1962.87
Sabbath, Lawrence, 1957.309
Sablonière, Margrit de, 1953.222; 1954.62, 165; 1956.296; 1958.238; 1959.130;
   1960.235; 1961.255; 1963.163, 164, 165; 1965.114

Staley, Thomas F., 1968.195a; 1969.219
Stalin, Joseph, 1940.190, 648, 732; 1944.111, 112; 1948.93; 1956.178; 1961.205; 1970.187; 1977.179
Stalinism, 1946.31; 1950.199; 1977.72
Stamford Advocate, 1938.30
Stamm, R., 1975.97
Stammler, Heinrich, 1950.228a
Stampa sera, 1951.131
Stanard, Hugh, 1945.1149
Stander, Lionel, 1941.207, 210, 219, 243, 244
Standley, Fred L., 1970.329; 1978.236; 1980.27, 238; 1982.100, 130
Standley, Nancy V., 1980.238
Standpoints on African Literature: A Critical Anthology, 1973.232
Der Standpunkt, 1957.96
Stane, Frédéric, 1946.270
Stanford, Barbara Dodds, 1971.282, 283, 284, 285, 286, 303; 1978.237
Stanford, Don, 1941.979
Stanford, Theodore, 1941.980
Stang, Nic., 1956.89
Stanley, Lee, 1940.936
Stanton, Robert, 1969.226
The Star, 1954.169; 1960.50
Starke, Catherine Juanita, 1971.287
Starkey, Marion L., 1957.327
Starnes, Joe, 1938.156, 203; 1939.75; 1977.256
Starr, Alvin J., 1975.186, 187; 1977.293; 1982.131
Starr, Ernest, 1941.980a
The Stars and Stripes Magazine, 1945.1157
Startsev, A., 1940.937; 1941.64, 506
The State and the Columbia (S. C.) Record, 1966.29
State Department, 1946.248; 1956.169; 1980.106
The State of the Union, 1970.291
State Publishing House, 1938.172
State University of New York at Binghamton, 1980.74
State University of New York at Buffalo, 1979.68
Stauffer, Donald B., 1966.128; 1968.54; 1969.47; 1972.40
Stauffer, William H., 1958.255
Ste. Petronille, 1945.10
Steele, A. T., 1956.311
Steele, Margaret, 1940.938
Steele, Oliver, 1953.232
Steele, Shelby, 1976.178, 179
Stegner, Wallace, 1940.939; 1946.131
Stein, Allen F., 1971.288, 289
Stein, Gertrude, 1940.291; 1945.730, 815, 1010, 1150; 1946.69, 220, 257, 285; 1953.132, 230, 238, 239, 249; 1959.56, 66; 1960.238; 1963.178; 1964.65; 1968.28; 1970.99; 1971.64a; 1973.132, 154; 1980.98, 103; 1982.99
Stein, Judith, 1979.241
Stein, Rita, 1979.242
Steinbarger, Helen T., 1941.981
Steinbeck, John, 1938.19, 135, 138, 185, 197, 244, 277; 1940.4, 215, 272, 277, 291, 300, 301, 335, 366, 372, 395, 398, 447, 529, 534, 540, 541, 544, 573, 574, 593, 609, 611, 614, 618, 627, 635, 640, 642, 644, 646, 661, 662, 663, 671, 674, 678, 679, 720, 753, 759, 764, 782, 788, 796, 803, 807, 810, 819, 820, 833, 838, 840, 842, 853, 860, 923, 938, 960, 966, 974, 983, 984, 986, 987, 999, 1005; 1941.506, 679, 894, 896; 1942.144; 1944.3, 97; 1945.1060, 1061; 1946.156, 256; 1947.145, 211, 227; 1948.36, 134, 154, 188, 219, 227, 246; 1952.24; 1953.153; 1955.46, 49; 1957.283; 1958.249; 1959.112a; 1961.275a; 1963.162; 1969.90, 159a; 1972.27; 1973.256; 1979.126
Steinberg, S. H., 1953.106; 1973.204, 205, 290, 291
Steinberg, Steve, 1961.266
Steinem, Gloria, 1964.120
Steinman, Martin, Jr., 1979.64
Steinway Hall, 1938.42
Stember, Charles Herbert, 1976.180
Sten, Hemming, 1956.148
Stephen, S., 1947.282, 283
Stephens, Martha, 1971.290; 1973.6, 256

Stephenson, Mary Ellen, 1957.328
Stephenson, Wendell Holmes, 1967.98
Stepto, Robert B., 1976.181; 1977.294, 295, 296; 1978.91; 1979.52, 76, 81, 86,
   101, 102, 109, 125a, 142, 187, 243, 244, 245, 246, 247, 248; 1980.31, 50, 77,
   89, 104, 108, 117, 122, 130, 214, 239, 240, 262; 1981.100, 104, 135; 1982.26
Sterling, Dorothy, 1968.197
Sterling A. Brown: A UMUM Tribute, 1976.121
Sterling Bulletin, 1940.714
Stern, Adele, 1979.249
Stern, Frederick C., 1981.124
Stern, Malcolm E., 1970.283, 284
Stern, Milton, 1977.297
Stern, Philip Van Doren, 1944.146; 1945.1151
Stern, Richard G., 1961.143, 267; 1964.53; 1968.84
Sternburg, Janet, 1980.249
Stevens, Mark, 1977.298
Stevens, Mrs. Arthur K., 1940.940
Stevens, Walalce, 1979.40
Stevenson, David L., 1952.64; 1953.233; 1955.79; 1956.312; 1957.329; 1958.256;
   1960.244; 1963.174
Stevenson, Dwight, 1977.53
Stewart, David H., 1976.63, 64; 1979.83, 84
Stewart, Donald Ogden, 1940.941; 1941.568
Stewart, Ollie, 1957.330; 1960.245, 246; 1961.268
Stewart, Paul, 1941.368, 396, 423, 806, 818, 821, 841
Stewart's, 1945.616
Steyrer Zeitung, 1956.68; 1962.46
Stil, André, 1960.247
Stimmen der Zeit, 1950.192; 1959.58
Stimpson, Catherine R., 1970.330; 1971.291
Stineback, David C., 1976.182
Stineman, Esther, 1979.250
Stockard, Joan, 1979.82a; 1980.68; 1981.34
Stockholm, 1956.4, 64, 136
Stockholm Afton Tidningen, 1945.771
Stockholm Dagens Nyheter, 1945.915; 1956.62, 261
Stockholm Dagstidningen, 1956.313
Stockholm Expressen, 1945.1154; 1947.247; 1956.148
Stockholm Morgon Tidningen Social Demokraten, 1945.772
Stockholms Tidningen, 1945.925; 1956.4, 45
Stockholm Svenska Dagbladet, 1956.112
Stocking, Fred, 1977.299
Stockwell, Joseph E., 1976.189
Stokely Speaks: Black Power Back to Pan-Africanism, 1971.66
Stokley, Wilma D., 1953.234
Stoller, Paul, 1975.188
Stone, Albert, 1977.300; 1978.238; 1979.251, 252; 1982.132, 133
Stone, Edward, 1966.135b
Stone, I. F., 1940.942
Stone, Wilfred, 1976.183, 184
The Stone Face, 1963.171a; 1964.116a; 1975.183a
Stoneman, E. Donnell, 1978.239, 240
Stopsky, Fred H., 1971.217a
Storia dei negri degli Stati Uniti, 1963.93
Stories of the American Experience, 1973.200, 201, 202
Störig, Hans Joachim, 1968.30
Story, 1938.3, 12, 18, 19, 23, 39, 62, 63, 74, 80, 118, 119, 120, 139, 143, 163,
   168, 183, 184, 193, 195, 218, 265; 1939.90; 1940.345, 397, 424, 432, 578; 1941.250,
   747; 1980.98, 183, 184; 1981.60
The Story of Story Magazine, 1980.98, 183, 184; 1981.60
Story of the Negro, 1948.137; 1955.26; 1958.88; 1964.32; 1969.42
Story to Anti-Story, 1979.217, 218
Stott, William, 1974.149
Stover, Carl F., 1957.331
Stowe, Harriet Beecher, 1938.159, 194, 208, 211, 240, 289; 1939.99, 110; 1940.2,
   4, 745, 986, 998; 1941.53, 553, 707, 873, 929; 1945.914, 924, 1062; 1949.79;
   1950.204; 1953.77; 1955.25; 1957.318; 1958.144; 1959.133; 1960.199; 1962.83;
   1972.29a; 1975.196; 1976.159; 1980.208; 1982.137

Tindall, William York, 1947.293
Tinkle, Lon, 1961.273
Tirro, Frank, 1980.264, 265
Tirsdag, 1952.32
Tischler, Nancy M., 1968.203; 1969.228, 229; 1970.232a, 335
Titus, Joseph, 1946.272
Tjader, Marguerite, 1946.273
Tobacco Road, 1941.753; 1945.771; 1947.194; 1961.275a
To Be a Black Woman: Portraits in Fact and Fiction, 1970.355, 356, 360
Tobias, Rowena Wilson, 1938.282; 1940.972
Todd, John E., 1968.54; 1969.47
Together, 1959.103
Tohoku Daigaku Kyoyobu Kiyo, 1965.107a
Toklas, Alice B., 1963.178
Toledo Blade, 1940.556, 557; 1963.158
Toledo Sunday Blade, 1953.86; 1954.59; 1956.34
Toledo Sunday Times, 1945.606
Toledo Times, 1941.959
Toliver, Clarence, 1940.973
Toll, William, 1979.264
Toller, Ernst, 1961.173
Tolliver, Johnny E., 1976.189; 1979.204
Tolson, Melvin B., 1938.283; 1939.111a, 111b, 111c, 111d, 111e; 1940.973a, 973b,
    973c, 974; 1941.997a, 997b, 997c; 1943.57a; 1966.142; 1972.203; 1978.193; 1980.88,
    213; 1981.128; 1982.53a, 136a, 136b, 136c, 136d, 136e
Tolstoy, Leo, 1940.394, 788; 1946.146; 1947.248
Tomms, Sonia, 1945.857, 986, 1166, 1184
Tomorrow, 1945.669, 898, 1013; 1946.145; 1948.133
Toms, Coons, Mulattoes, Mammies, and Bucks: An Interpretive History of Blacks
    in American Films, 1973.65
"To Negro Writers," 1979.200
Tonnar, Bernard A., 1945.1167
Tooill, Kenneth D., 1938.284; 1940.975; 1941.998
Toomer, Jean, 1938.165, 232; 1940.638; 1953.174; 1958.85; 1963.121; 1965.42; 1966.24;
    1969.38, 133; 1970.63, 207, 208, 209, 210; 1971.48, 116, 187, 215; 1973.256;
    1974.53; 1975.97, 107; 1976.39; 1977.144, 251, 329; 1978.171; 1979.78, 143;
    1981.107a; 1982.50
Toppin, Edgar Allan, 1969.230; 1971.297; 1975.194; 1978.245; 1979.265
Tops, 1938.134
"To Richard Wright," 1961.246; 1962.95b, 95c; 1963.162b; 1972.173
Toronto, 1942.48, 49, 88
Toronto Daily Star, 1953.9; 1954.9; 1956.23; 1957.81
The Toronto Globe and Mail, 1950.132; 1953.152
The Toronto Telegram, 1950.128
Toro y Gisbert, Miguel de, 1964.23
Torrassa, A. E., 1945.1168
Torrey, Volta, 1943.58
Torsdag, 1956.79
Tortilla Flat, 1948.246
To Serve the Devil, 1971.180
Tougaloo College Alumni, 1940.240
Touhey, Eleanor, 1945.1169
Toulon La République Varoise, 1948.83; 1949.14
La Toulouse Dépêche du Midi, 1949.101; 1951.196
Toulouse Victoire, 1947.38
Tours La Nouvelle République du Centre-Ouest, 1948.18; 1949.31
Tours Le Courrier de la Loire, 1948.185
Tourtellot, Arthur Bernon, 1938.285
Tovatt, Anthony, 1969.50, 51; 1973.81, 82, 83, 84, 85, 86, 87, 88; 1979.59, 60,
    61, 62
Tovatt, Patricia O., 1969.50, 51; 1979.59, 60, 61, 62
Tove, Shirley Ruth, 1954.174
Toward a New American Literary History: Essays in Honor of Arlin Turner, 1980.246
Toward a New Earth: Apocalypse in the American Novel, 1972.148
Toward the Morning, 1954.30
Toward the New America, 1970.56, 57
Townend, Marion, 1940.976; 1944.149; 1945.1170; 1946.274
Town Hall Lecture Division Annual Announcement Fifty-First Season 1945-1946, 1945.666

257, 258, 259, 261, 272, 278, 279, 281, 283, 284, 286, 288, 289; 1962.1, 3,
4, 5, 7, 8, 9, 10, 11, 12, 13, 14, 16, 17, 18, 19, 20, 21, 22, 23, 24, 25, 30,
31, 32, 33, 39, 46, 47, 48, 53, 54, 56, 61, 62, 65, 66, 67, 68, 69, 70, 75,
77, 78, 80, 83, 84, 85, 87, 92, 93, 94, 95, 97, 100, 105, 106; 1963.11, 18,
19, 27, 45, 60, 72, 141, 154, 165a; 1964.6, 7, 8, 13, 89, 92; 1965.2, 3, 4,
5, 6, 10, 11, 14, 17, 21, 27, 41, 46, 47, 57, 67, 92, 94, 95, 101, 104, 113,
123; 1966.4, 6, 10, 11, 12, 13, 15, 16, 19, 27, 31, 40, 41, 50, 52, 55, 56,
62, 67, 78, 82, 90, 95, 107, 116, 119, 120, 121, 131, 132, 134, 144, 147; 1967.3,
53; 1968.10, 11, 13, 14, 16, 20, 21, 23, 112; 1969.16, 43, 61, 152, 159, 237,
238; 1970.24, 106a, 142, 188; 1971.102, 104, 105, 108, 109, 224, 248, 307; 1972.11,
61, 138, 188a; 1973.18, 25, 125, 156, 162, 221, 222, 265, 266, 288; 1974.16,
132; 1975.6; 1976.13, 14, 114; 1977.106, 143; 1978.19, 32; 1979.6, 8, 14, 22,
23, 48, 49, 63, 118, 193, 198; 1980.19, 24, 158; 1982.8
Transport Workers Union, 1941.362
Traylor, Eleanor E. Williams, 1976.190; 1979.266
A Treasury of Short Stories, 1947.220a; 1948.95
"The Treatment of the Negro Woman as a Major Character in American Novels 1900-1950,"
   1955.53
Trédant, Paul, 1950.234
The Trees, 1940.843
Trenton (N. J.) Evening Times, 1953.76
Trenton Sunday Times Advertiser, 1940.378; 1945.727; 1953.94; 1956.327; 1958.42;
   1963.32, 179
Trescott, Jacqueline, 1977.324
Treworgy, Mildred L., 1967.99
Tribune and Register, 1940.453
Tribune de Genève, 1950.95
Tribune des Nations, 1940.802; 1946.78
Triche, Charles W., 1978.246
Triche, Diane Samson, 1978.246
Tri-Cities (Davenport, Moline, and Rock Island), 1945.110, 114, 115, 116, 117,
   119, 120, 121, 122, 136, 137, 138, 139, 140; 1946.14, 15, 16, 17, 18, 20, 21
Trierer Landeszeitung, 1958.104
Der Trier Sonntag, 1957.344
Trigg, W. S., 1947.293a
Trilling, Lionel, 1945.1172; 1982.30
Trimmer, Joseph F., 1976.191, 192, 193
Trinidad, 1950.48, 61, 67, 88
Trio: A Book of Stories, Plays, and Poems, 1975.179; 1980.229
Tripp, Thomas Alfred, 1944.150
Trippett, Frank, 1981.129
Tri-Quarterly, 1965.43; 1982.67
Troppa morte, troppa vita: viaggi e pensieri intorno agli USA, 1969.194
Trotsky, Leon, 1940.732; 1949.148; 1952.66a; 1956.178; 1978.75
Trotskyism, 1944.84; 1952.66a; 1978.75
Trouble in July, 1940.823, 930; 1941.506, 596; 1948.140, 163; 1972.185
Troupe, Quincy, 1978.88, 126a
The Troy Observer-Budget, 1942.24
True, 1946.70, 157a; 1947.43a, 164a, 248a, 271a, 293a, 300b
Truebent, Charles, 1977.325
True Black Man's History, 1977.304
True Detective, 1971.108
Truman, Harry, 1949.148
Trumbull Park, 1961.221
Truth, Sojourner, 1944.139; 1947.101
Tsuneishi, Shiesei, 1976.95
Tuck, James L., 1947.294
Tuck, William A., 1940.977
Tucker, Fishbelly, 1958.15, 200, 201, 210, 249, 260, 264; 1959.125; 1960.6, 8,
   18, 31, 77, 78, 79, 114, 121, 178, 181, 184, 185, 200, 203, 213, 216, 233, 259,
   269; 1961.76, 93, 106, 123, 153, 155, 163, 164, 166, 204, 224, 230, 256, 261,
   279, 281; 1965.116a; 1968.13; 1971.281; 1973.18, 240, 251, 265, 277, 278; 1974.141;
   1977.250b; 1981.103
Tucker, Martin, 1964.123; 1967.99a; 1979.33
Tucker, Tyree, 1958.79, 173, 210, 213; 1960.121, 122, 139, 177, 184, 185, 193,
   203, 208, 216; 1961.153, 155, 279, 281; 1971.281; 1973.18, 240, 277, 278
Tucker family, 1960.177
The Tucson Arizona Daily Star, 1940.612; 1954.152

About the Compiler

KENETH KINNAMON is Ethel Pumphrey Stephens Professor of English and Chairman of the English Department at the University of Arkansas, Fayetteville.